# HANDBOOK OF CHILD AND ADOLESCENT DRUG AND SUBSTANCE ABUSE

Pharmacological, Developmental, and Clinical Considerations

LOUIS A. PAGLIARO

ANN MARIE PAGLIARO

Professors Emeriti
University of Alberta
Substance Abusology and Clinical Pharmacology Research Group

**WILEY**
John Wiley & Sons, Inc.

Copyright © 2012 by John Wiley & Sons, Inc. All rights reserved.

Published by John Wiley & Sons, Inc., Hoboken, New Jersey.

Published simultaneously in Canada.

For general information on our other products and services please contact our Customer Care Department within the United States at (800) 762-2974, outside the United States at (317) 572-3993 or fax (317) 572-4002.

Wiley publishes in a variety of print and electronic formats and by print-on-demand. Some material included with standard print versions of this book may not be included in e-books or in print-on-demand. If this book refers to media such as a CD or DVD that is not included in the version you purchased, you may download this material at http://booksupport.wiley.com. For more information about Wiley products, visit www.wiley.com.

*Library of Congress Cataloging-in-Publication Data:*

Pagliaro, Louis A.
  Handbook of child and adolescent drug and substance abuse: pharmacological, developmental, and clinical considerations / Louis A. Pagliaro and Ann Marie Pagliaro.
    p. ; cm.
  Includes bibliographical references and index.
  ISBN 978-0-470-63906-1 (cloth : alk. paper)
  ISBN 978-1-118-11793-4 (ebk)
  ISBN 978-1-118-11795-8 (ebk)
  ISBN 978-1-118-11794-1 (ebk)
  ISBN 978-1-118-10105-6 (obk)
    1. Drug and substance abuse—North America.   2. Children—Drug and substance use—North America.
  3. Adolescents—Drug and substance use—North America.   I. Pagliaro, Ann Marie.   II. Title.
    [DNLM: 1. Substance-Related Disorders—North America.   2. Adolescent—North America.   3. Child—North America.   4. Pharmaceutical Preparations—North America. WM 270]
  RJ506.D78P34 2012
  618.92'860097—dc22

                                                                                    2011010982

Printed in the United States of America

10 9 8 7 6 5 4 3 2 1

To all North American children and adolescents. It is our fervent hope that this text will help to bring about a greater awareness and a deeper understanding of the nature and extent of your exposure to and use of the drugs and substances of abuse. We trust that this awareness and understanding will help to stem the growing tide and assuage your associated pain and suffering.

LAP/AMP

# Contents

# Preface

Children and adolescents throughout North America, regardless of age, culture, education, ethnicity, gender, race, religion, sexual orientation, or socioeconomic status, may be exposed to and may actively use the various drugs and substances of abuse (see Figure P.1, Table P.1)[1] in a variety of ways that adversely affect their health, safety, and well-being (see Figure P. 2). Their exposure to and use of these drugs and substances of abuse also may adversely affect the health, safety, and well-being of their families, including siblings, and that of their friends and schoolmates and the larger communities, including the schools and neighborhoods, of which they are a part.[2] Consequently, all those who work to promote the optimal growth and development of children and adolescents—child and adolescent psychiatrists and psychologists; community health, mental health, and school nurses; family physicians; family therapists; home health-care workers; juvenile justice workers; midwives; pediatric nurse practitioners; pediatricians; pharmacists; school counselors; school psychologists; and social workers—require an unbiased and specialized reference source that presents current research, across the lifespan, concerning the prevalence and characteristics of child and adolescent exposure to and use of the drugs and substances of abuse in North America.

These health and social care professionals also require a reference text that provides up-to-date clinical pharmacological informa-

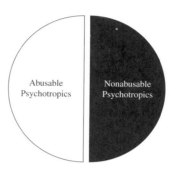

**Figure P.1    The Drugs and Substances of Abuse:** *The Abusable Psychotropics*[a]

[a]The term "psychotropics" refers to all exogenous substances (i.e., chemicals, including plant products, drugs, and xenobiotics) that: (1) elicit a direct effect on the central nervous system resulting in changes in cognition, learning, memory, behavior, perception, or affect; and (2) are used specifically for these major effects. The psychotropics can be further divided into either abusable or nonabusable psychotropics. The regular, long-term use of the abusable psychotropics is generally associated with the development of physical and/or psychological dependence characterized by (a) the need to use more and more of the drug or substance of abuse in order to achieve desired psychotropic actions (i.e., because of the development of tolerance) and (b) a withdrawal syndrome that occurs with the abrupt discontinuation of its regular, long-term use and that is terminated immediately when use is resumed. The nonabusable psychotropics—anticonvulsants, antidepressants, antiparkinsonians, and antipsychotics (see Table P.1)—while also used for their major psychotropic actions, have not been consistently associated with physical or psychological dependence and thus are not considered in this reference text. The proposed classification presented here has been found to be both accurate and parsimonious. However, because the term "abusable psychotropics" may be awkward for many readers, we consistently use the more common phrase "drugs and substances of abuse" to denote this major class of chemicals, drugs, and xenobiotics.

---

[1]See related discussion in Chapter 1, *The Psychodepressants*, Chapter 2, *The Psychostimulants*, and Chapter 3, *The Psychodelics*, for specific detailed information regarding these drugs and substances of abuse and their use by North American children and adolescents.

[2]We now find ourselves in the midst of "reaping the whirlwind" because of the woeful inattention over the past three decades by society, in general, and the North American governments, in particular, to the serious nature and growing extent of problems associated with the use of the drugs and substances of abuse by children and adolescents. This situation will be examined in depth in the chapters of this text.

**TABLE P.1    The Abusable and Nonabusable Psychotropics**

| *Abusable* Psychotropics[a] | *Nonabusable* Psychotropics |
|---|---|
| PSYCHODEPRESSANTS<br>   *Opiate Analgesics* (e.g., codeine, heroin, meperidine [Demerol®], morphine [MS Contin®]) | ANTICONVULSANTS[b] (e.g., carbamazepine [Tegretol®], phenytoin [Dilantin®], primidone [Mysoline®], valproic acid [Depakene®]) |
|    *Sedative-Hypnotics* (barbiturates, benzodiazepines, Z-drugs, miscellaneous sedative-hypnotics (e.g., alcohol [beer, wine, distilled liquor]; gamma-hydroxybutyrate [GHB]) | ANTIDEPRESSANTS<br>   *Monoamine Oxidase Inhibitors* (e.g., moclobemide [Manerix®], phenelzine [Nardil®], tranylcypromine [Parnate®])<br><br>   *Selective Serotonin Reuptake Inhibitors* (e.g., Fluoxetine [Prozac®], paroxetine [Paxil®], sertraline [Zoloft®]) |
|    *Volatile Solvents and Inhalants* (e.g., gasoline, glue) |    *Tricyclic Antidepressants* (e.g., amitriptyline [Elavil®], desipramine [Norpramin®], imipramine [Tofranil®], nortriptyline [Aventyl®]) |
| PSYCHOSTIMULANTS (e.g., amphetamines, caffeine, cocaine, nicotine [tobacco]) |    *Miscellaneous Antidepressants* (e.g., amoxapine [Ascendin®], bupropion [Wellbutrin®], maprotiline [Ludiomil®]) |
| PSYCHODELICS (e.g., cannabis [i.e., marijuana, hashish, hash oil], lysergic acid diethylamide [LSD], mescaline [peyote], phencyclidine [PCP], methylenedioxymethamphetamine [MDMA]) | ANTIPARKINSONIANS (e.g., amantadine [Symmetrel®], levodopa [Dopar®], selegiline [Eldepryl®], trihexyphenidyl [Artane®])<br><br>ANTIPSYCHOTICS (e.g., chlorpromazine [Thorazine®], clozapine [Clozaril®], haloperidol [Haldol®], olanzapine [Zyprexa®], risperidone [Risperdal®]) |

[a] See Chapters 1, *The Psychodepressants*, 2, *The Psychostimulants*, and 3, *The Psychodelics* for a comprehensive listing and discussion of the abusable psychotropics.
[b] Some abusable psychotropics (e.g., barbiturates, benozdiazepines) are clinically used as anticonvulsants. However, these listed anticonvulsants are not used as abusable psychotropics.

tion about these drugs and substances of abuse and state-of-the-art clinical strategies that focus on: (1) identifying children and adolescents, a priori, who are at risk for using the drugs and substances of abuse; (2) assessing actual or potential harmful patterns of using the drugs and substances of abuse with attention to the personal and social consequences of such use; (3) providing effective treatment for children and adolescents when an active drug or substance use disorder is encountered; and (4) monitoring the efficacy of prevention and treatment approaches that have been implemented.

It is fairly axiomatic that an understanding of the nature and extent of child and adolescent exposure to and use of the drugs and substances of abuse is vital for optimal professional practice among all health and social care providers who have an interest in, and/or provide direct care to, North American children and adolescents. However, a few specific examples are offered to help to support this assertion. For example, this understanding will help to alert:

- *Juvenile justice workers* to patterns of criminal and violent behavior that are associated with the use of particular drugs and substances of abuse, such as the use of gamma-hydroxybutyrate (GHB) and flunitrazepam (Roofies) for the perpetration of date-rape, particularly in the context of parties and raves, or the use of alcohol, amphetamines, cocaine, or phencyclidine (PCP) that can contribute to, or exacerbate, the perpetration of physical assault, including homicide.

- *Nurses* to the accidental injuries and other health consequences, including death, that may be associated with the use of the various drugs and substances of abuse by children and adolescents, such as burns related to the use of the volatile solvent, gasoline, and sudden-sniffing-death associated with the use of the volatile inhalant, glue. It also will alert them, for example, to the need for the prevention of infections (e.g., hepatitis C, human immunodeficiency virus) associated with sharing contaminated intravenous

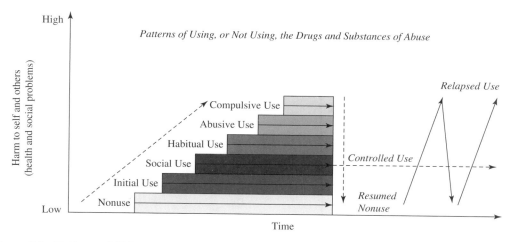

**Figure P.2    Patterns of Using the Drugs and Substances of Abuse and Associated Harm**

needles and syringes or having unprotected sex with multiple partners—as occurs in the context of sex-for-drug exchanges.

- *Pharmacists* to actual and possible problems such as significant drug interactions, polypharmacy, and illicit patterns of use (e.g., an adolescent selling his legitimate prescription for mixed amphetamines [Adderall®], which he received for the management of his attention-deficit/hyperactivity disorder [A-D/HD], at school to criminal youth gang members; a child who has Type 1 diabetes mellitus [insulin dependent] giving, selling, or trading her injection supplies [i.e., insulin needles and syringes] to siblings, friends, or parents to be used for the injection of their drugs and substances of abuse).

- *Physicians* to rule out the use of drugs and substances of abuse by children and adolescents when formulating diagnoses (e.g., clinical depression; learning disorders; unexplained injuries) and when clinically monitoring therapeutic response (e.g., lack of therapeutic improvement). It also alerts them to the possibility of patients faking signs and symptoms to obtain prescriptions for desired drugs and substances of abuse (e.g., amphetamines; opiate analgesics) and to focus more carefully on the prevention of associated pathology (e.g., teratogenesis, such as the fetal alcohol syndrome [FAS][3] among offspring of adolescent girls who drink alcohol while pregnant).

- *Psychologists* to the need to consider the use of drugs and substances of abuse by children and adolescents as a possible explanation for problem behavior (e.g., amotivational syndrome associated with cannabis use). It also will alert them to consider other mental disorders (e.g., anxiety disorders, major depressive disorder, and psychotic disorders, including cannabis-induced psychosis) that may occur with, or be masked by, the use of various drugs and substances of abuse.

- *Social workers* to investigate high-risk drug or substance of abuse related problems in the home (e.g., child or parental physical, psychological, or sexual abuse; use as a marijuana grow-op or mom-and-pop meth lab) and community (e.g., increased presence and development of criminal youth gangs). It also alerts them to needed action

---

[3] Fetal alcohol syndrome also is commonly referred to in the published literature as the fetal alcohol spectrum disorder (FASD). For additional discussion, see Chapter 5, *Exposure to the Drugs and Substances of Abuse from Conception Through Childhood.*

to decrease associated potential harm to children and adolescents, their families, and their communities.

- *School psychologists* and *teachers* to the effects of child or adolescent use of the drugs and substances of abuse on classroom performance (e.g., inattention; poor learning outcomes; memory impairment) and troublesome schoolyard behavior (e.g., bullying). It also alerts them to recognize that selling drugs and substances of abuse, and related crime and violence, do not stop at the schoolyard fence or even at the school's main entrance.

Unfortunately, a true understanding of the nature of the use of the drugs and substances of abuse and the characteristics and extent of their use by children and adolescents is not easily gained by those who require this information and would benefit from it. There are many reasons for this situation, including:

1. An overwhelming majority of the published research findings and conclusions reported over the last decade in textbooks and journal articles, as well as over the Internet, provide very little direct attention and insight.[4]

2. Potentially valuable research often presents only equivocal or mixed results in terms of the incidence and consequences.[5]

3. Available published research findings and conclusions do not address children and adolescents in a major way and rarely separate children and adolescents from adults, either in research designs or in conclusions and recommendations.[6]

4. Authors often demonstrate a significantly biased perspective in their conclusions and recommendations. For example, some writers go to extremes in their attempts to inaccurately minimize, or trivialize, the harm associated with using various drugs and substances of abuse,[7] perhaps, in order to rationalize their own use of these drugs and substances of abuse or to help further the social agenda for the decriminalization/legalization of all drugs and substances of abuse (i.e., these biased views are most often ensconced in a libertarian or secular progressive perspective that those authors are attempting to advance). Other writers may exaggerate associated harm, perhaps to rationalize harsh legal penalties and consequences associated with possession and use of the various drugs and substances of abuse. This latter viewpoint is often laden with moral underpinnings (i.e., that the use of a drug or substance of abuse is not only illegal but immoral—a view

---

[4] Some of these limitations in research design, methods, and dissemination of results are understandable because of the difficulty inherent in obtaining data from children and adolescents. As minors who are identified as a vulnerable population group, children and adolescents require their own consent (and/or assent) to participate in research studies as well as that of their parents or legal guardians and schools or school districts if the research is being conducted in school. In addition, the nature of the very behavior being studied (i.e., use of the drugs and substances of abuse) is generally illegal and, therefore, makes it more difficult to obtain accurate reports of behavior from participants who may fear being arrested or having their parent(s) informed about their illegal behavior.

[5] In addition, these published research studies often conclude with the phrase: "more (or additional) research is necessary." Therefore, the use of potentially helpful findings is limited because of the need for study replication or extension into more specific population groups (e.g., boys versus girls, tweens versus teens). In addition, the phrase is rarely followed with specific recommendations for replicating the study or for research questions aimed at extending the reported findings.

[6] In these studies, the population sample, while often including adolescents, is generally age neutral when results are presented (i.e., the subjects may be identified solely as, for example, Americans of Hispanic descent or as 16 years of age and older).

[7] Such authors may use, for example, the accurate but deliberately misleading argument that the harm associated with the use of marijuana in North America would be, in comparison, significantly less than that associated with the use of alcohol (see related discussion in Chapters 1, *The Psychodepressants*, and 3, *The Psychedelics*).

most often ensconced in a conservative perspective).[8]

Consequently, health and social care providers desperately require, but do not currently have, ready access to an objective, and subjectively explicit and truthful, reference—a scholarly reference that presents a deep depth and wide breadth of understanding coincident with a timely analysis and synthesis of the available research conclusions and recommendations regarding the status, trends, and individual pharmacology of the drugs and substances of abuse used by children and adolescents throughout North America. This text fills that void for required knowledge (i.e., current and accurate data and informed, reflective interpretation). Thus, this text assists readers to understand the use of the drugs and substances of abuse by children and adolescents in a current and unbiased context that reflects a comprehensive interpretation of the published research and related available information—complete with referenced documentation.

Since we began work on our first textbook, *Problems in Pediatric Drug Therapy,* which was initially published by Drug Intelligence in 1979, the particular needs of readers and our approach to preparing professional texts for publication have changed dramatically. For example, at that time there was no such thing as a personal computer (PC) or the Internet. The primary challenge for clinicians—our intended audience—was obtaining relevant published research findings that could be appropriately applied in their respective areas

of clinical practice. This challenge motivated us in the early 1970s to begin work on our first clinical pharmacology text. At that time, we physically had to go through printed volumes of the *Index Medicus, by hand,* in order to find needed published journal article citations and, then, literally, go into the medical library stacks (i.e., the storage area for bound copies of published journals from the mid-1800s to date) in order to compile the data for the users of our texts. One difficulty was obtaining some of the most recent journal articles (i.e., those articles that were published over the last year or two) that were often waiting to be bound and added to the stacks. Journals that were waiting to be bound could not be borrowed, or checked out, or removed from the library. Thus, articles had to be read in the circulation area of the library and notes taken on index cards—copy machines had just been invented and were not widely available (1 or 2 per library), and the cost of Xeroxing an article seemed to be, for us at that time, a very high 25 cents per page. Thus, the primary challenge then was to find and access the rather limited amount of published data available (and often well and deeply hidden in the stacks of university medical libraries).

The challenge for us and our readers today has changed from too little available data to too much available data. So, too, has our approach to the preparation of clinical pharmacology and other texts, particularly those focusing solely on the drugs and substances of abuse, changed. We no longer have to physically go into the stacks in order to retrieve relevant

---

[8] On this point, it should be made explicit that we tend to view the use of the various drugs and substances of abuse as being neither good nor bad, neither moral nor immoral. As scientists rooted in several views of science (e.g., positivism, postpositivism, postmodernism) and as expert clinicians, our focus instead is on evaluating the results of these sciences based on their inherent assumptions, research methods, and claims to fact (i.e., their theories and inherent *truth*). Most important, as subscribers to the scientist-clinician model, we are concerned with the contribution of a study or research program in regard to its ability to further knowledge and understanding that will lead to valuable outcomes for children and adolescents in regard to their use of the drugs and substances of abuse. Thus, we are concerned with the result of the interaction of the use of a particular drug or substance of abuse by a particular child or adolescent in a particular context (e.g., the use of an opiate analgesic, such as morphine, for a child hospitalized with a broken leg to relieve his pain versus the use of morphine by a homeless adolescent girl that results in her death due to an overdosage). Thus, for us, it is not the use of a particular drug or substance of abuse by a particular child or adolescent that is good or bad. Rather, it is the result or outcome of the use of the drug or substance of abuse by a particular child or adolescent in a particular context that is *good* or *bad*.

data; most journal abstracts and articles can be accessed through numerous Internet sites where they can be read online or printed out immediately at minimal cost. In fact, prepublication copies of relevant research, reviews, and opinions are often available. Having turned in our electric typewriters long ago, we now can write, revise, store, manipulate, and send for immediate access drafts and final copies of texts with a click of a mouse. Thus, as noted, the challenge today is not so much the search for relevant available data of importance for the development of our ideas and texts but, instead, its compilation, sorting, analysis, interpretation, reflection, synthesis, and assimilation into what is most valid and reliable, or true, and most useful for clinical application (i.e., best practices) from a virtual mountain of data—some relevant, much not; some accurate, much not—before it is shared with the reader.

In addition to being of benefit to health and social care professionals, this text also should be of benefit to students who are assimilating knowledge in their respective fields of professional study. Last, but not least, we trust that it also may be of benefit to health and social policy makers (e.g., government officials, such as the Surgeon General; politicians, such as mayors and governors; public health administrators, such as the members of boards of public health or healthcare authorities; and social administrators, such as school principals

and public school board members) who must increasingly address both the direct and indirect healthcare and social consequences and costs[9] associated with the use of the various drugs and substances of abuse by children and adolescents and then appropriately deal with the related adverse impact on all levels and for all segments of North American society.[10]

In an effort to meet the identified informational needs of these health and social care professionals, students, and policy makers, this text presents the authors' distillation and reflective interpretation of the current published clinical literature and available demographic statistical reports addressing the use of the drugs and substances of abuse among children and adolescents in North America. Historical and other relevant published literature (e.g., formalized theories, personal stories and experiences, citations from general review articles, significant textbooks, and helpful related Web sites) also have been used.[11]

These data have been obtained from a variety of computerized (e.g., PubMed®) and non-computerized database sources utilizing available internet search engines (e.g., BING®; Google®) in order to more accurately reflect the diverse scientific findings, theoretical orientations, and clinically relevant views that exist in the study of why children and adolescents use the drugs and substances of abuse in various ways.[12]

The text is divided into three parts. Part I, *Extent of Use and Pharmacological*

---

[9]These costs are: (1) *biological* (e.g., physical injuries to body systems, such as cirrhosis of the liver related to chronic alcohol use, which is being identified at younger ages, or lung cancer related to tobacco smoking which usually begins during adolescence); (2) *psychological* (e.g., emotional distress and mental disorders, such as amphetamine-related psychosis or cannabis-related memory impairment); and (3) *sociological* (e.g., child neglect and family violence related to the use of the drugs and substances abuse, particularly alcohol, cocaine, or methamphetamine, by parents or caregivers).

[10]For example, in regard to learning and school achievement (see Chapter 6, *Effects of the Drugs and Substances of Abuse on Learning and Memory During Childhood Adolescence*).

[11]It is important to note that this reflective interpretation of the available published data has been performed by the authors in the combined context of over 70 years of academic experience and clinical practice in the fields of pharmacology and psychology specifically dealing with clinical issues related to the use of the drugs and substances of abuse. The authors used this method of analysis and synthesis of these published data (i.e., data produced from the three contemporary views of science—positivism, postpositivism, and postmodernism—that dominate knowledge and its production at the present time) to help to ensure, for the reader, the data's proper evaluation and the best approximation of truth (i.e., in an earnest attempt to eliminate, or at least minimize, any potential biases).

[12]Hand searches of the available databases were completed to complement the computer searches of relevant databases and to validate and extend the conclusions proffered by the original sources and their suggested leads.

*Considerations,* contains three chapters: Chapter 1, *The Psychodepressants*; Chapter 2, *The Psychostimulants*; and Chapter 3, *The Psychodelics.* Each of these three chapters presents and discusses the general pharmacology of its respective major class of the drugs and substances of abuse—their mechanisms of action, associated toxicities, and signs and symptoms of overdosage. Particular attention also is given to the prevalence and characteristics of their current use among North American children and adolescents.

Part II, *Developmental Considerations,* presents three chapters that consider the use of the drugs and substances of abuse by children and adolescents[13] from a developmental perspective. Chapter 4, *Explaining Child and Adolescent Use of the Drugs and Substances of Abuse,* presents contemporary theoretical explanations of why children and adolescents use alcohol and other drugs and substances of abuse. Although the preponderance of theorizing has been directed at explaining why children and adolescents drink alcohol and smoke tobacco cigarettes, theories attempting to explain cannabis, cocaine, methylenedioxymethamphetamine (MDMA, ecstasy), and opiate analgesic use, also are included. Major biological (e.g., genetic, neuropharmacological), psychological (e.g., learning, personality), and sociological (e.g., deviance, family systems, sociocultural) theories are addressed. The *eclectic* (interdisciplinary) and *pluralistic* (intradisciplinary) theories also are addressed.

Chapter 5, *Exposure to the Drugs and Substances of Abuse from Conception Through Childhood,* presents and offers detailed information about the potential teratogenic and fetotoxic effects of the drugs and substances of abuse on the developing embryo/fetus and neonate. Chapter 5 also presents a comprehensive overview of the drugs and substances of abuse that are excreted in breast milk and the potential risks to neonates and young infants who are breast-feeding. Also presented in this chapter are the effects of exposing infants, children, and adolescents to passive smoke by parents or primary caregivers who smoke cannabis (marijuana), tobacco cigarettes, cigars, or pipe tobacco, or other drugs and substances of abuse (e.g., crack cocaine) in their presence. Unintentional childhood poisonings involving the drugs and substances of abuse also are addressed in this chapter.

Chapter 6, *Effects of the Drugs and Substances of Abuse on Learning and Memory During Childhood and Adolescence,* presents and discusses the specific drugs and substances of abuse that can enhance learning and memory (e.g., nicotine [tobacco]) or impair it (e.g., cannabis). A cognitive input-output learning and memory model, which was originally developed by the authors over 30 years ago, is further developed and discussed using specific drugs and substances of abuse as examples in order to facilitate the readers' understanding of how the use of the specific drugs and substances of abuse by children and adolescents directly affects their learning and memory. In addition, various related disorders (e.g., A-D/HD) are briefly presented and discussed, particularly those that are caused by, or are associated with, the use of the drugs and substances of abuse and significantly affect learning or memory, or both.

Part III, *Clinical Considerations,* concludes the text with three chapters. Chapter 7,

---

[13] The term "adolescence" is currently widely defined as the second decade of life and thus includes people who are 10 years of age to 20 years of age. Accordingly, "childhood" is defined as the first decade of life and thus includes people who are 1 year of age to 10 years of age. However, in regard to developmental abilities and the characteristic patterns of using the drugs and substances of abuse, we also, where necessary and appropriate, use the conventional divisions, including: "neonate," covering the first 30 days of life; "infant," covering the first year of life; "toddler," covering 1 to 3 years of age; "preschooler," covering 3 to 5 years of age; "child," covering 5 to 12 years of age; "preadolescent," 12 to 13 years of age; "adolescent," 13 to 18 years of age; and "young adult," 19 to 25 years of age. In addition, in order to avoid any additional confusion when presenting research findings, we provide, whenever possible, the specified age ranges for participants in research studies that are cited and also include the reported primary and secondary school grade levels.

*Detecting Adolescent Use of the Drugs and Substances of Abuse: Selected Quick-Screen Psychometric Tests*, presents, describes, and discusses several psychometric tests that can be used for detecting the use of specific drugs and substances of abuse by adolescents. Attention is given to the selection and clinical use of these psychometric tests and to their utility and limitations, including their general use, scoring, and associated statistics, such as their measures of sensitivity, specificity, validity, and reliability.

Chapter 8, *Dual Diagnosis Among Adolescents*, presents an overview of the substance use disorders (SUDs) that may occur concomitantly among adolescents with other mental disorders (OMDs), including anxiety disorders, depressive mood disorders, and psychotic disorders. Also discussed is the relationship between SUDs and sexual or gender identity disorders. The prevalence of these disorders among adolescents and related factors are discussed with emphasis on the importance of accurate diagnosis and the inter-relationship of these co-occurring mental disorders.

Chapter 9, *Preventing and Treating Child and Adolescent Use of the Drugs and Substances of Abuse,* focuses on specific strategies and programs aimed at preventing the initial use of the drugs and substances of abuse by children and adolescents and treating various levels, or patterns, of use once use has been initiated in order to prevent associated harm. Age-specific primary, secondary, and tertiary prevention strategies, including relapse prevention, are identified and discussed. School-based programs; family therapy; social skills training; Alcoholics Anonymous; therapeutic communities; and short-term residential programs, including age-specific treatment programs, also are discussed. In addition, attention is given to the role that pharmacotherapy plays in treating and managing adolescent SUDs, including: (1) substance-assisted abstinence and substitution (e.g., nicotine [Nicorette®, Nicotrol® for tobacco

cessation programs]); (2) antidotes for specific acute overdosage (e.g., naloxone [Narcan®] for opiate analgesic overdosage); (3) treatment of withdrawal syndromes, particularly those associated with the use of the various benzodiazepines (e.g., diazepam [Valium®] to prevent or manage sedative-hypnotic withdrawal syndromes); and (4) abstinence maintenance (e.g., methadone [Dolophine®] for opiate analgesic dependence).

Chapter 9 also presents the Meta-Interactive Model of Child and Adolescent Use of Drugs and Substances of Abuse. This multivariate, interactive model was specifically developed by the authors to facilitate a better understanding among readers of the many interacting variables that have been related to, or have been identified as influencing, the use of drugs and substances of abuse by children and adolescents. Comprised of four major variable dimensions, particular attention is given to the child or adolescent dimension and its inter-action with the other three dimensions—the drug or substance of abuse dimension, societal dimension, and time dimension—in order that these interactions can be more fully and properly understood in an actual clinical context.

The backmatter consists of the appendix, which lists abbreviations used in the text, and the reference list, which is a comprehensive, alphabetized listing of all of the published references and other data sources cited in this text. These references are prepared in the standardized format of the American Psychological Association (APA) and listed in alphabetical order by the surname of the primary author. A comprehensive subject index follows. This cross-referenced subject index was carefully constructed by the authors in order to facilitate rapid and accurate retrieval of needed information.

By reading the information presented in this text, health and social care professionals, students, and policy makers alike should better understand the current, unique nature and extent of the exposure to, and use of, the various drugs and substances of abuse by children and adolescents in North America and the associated direct impact on their health, safety, and well-being as well as on that that of their families and their communities. By understanding the extent of child and adolescent exposure to and use of the drugs and substances of abuse, and the associated pharmacological, developmental, and clinical aspects of this exposure and use, health and social care professionals, students, and policy makers should be better able to develop and provide appropriate and effective prevention and treatment services for children and adolescents.

It is our fervent hope that, by using the information presented in this text and working together with children and adolescents and their families and communities,

optimal health, safety, and well-being may be achieved for the countless children and adolescents in North America who, in various ways and to various degrees, have been, are, or will be adversely affected by the exposure to and use of the various drugs and substances of abuse.

Louis A. Pagliaro
Ann Marie Pagliaro
2012

*Common sense in an uncommon degree,*
*Which has been derived experientially*
*over time,*
*Is called wisdom…*

—*Sun Tzu/Pagliaro*

# *Acknowledgments*

We wish to acknowledge and express our sincerest gratitude to John Wiley & Sons for our long and positive working relationship that began in the early 1990s. We also would like to express our sincere appreciation to all of the employees at Wiley for their diligent and professional work on this text. Particularly, we would like to acknowledge: Marquita Flemming, the senior editor for this text; her excellent editorial assistants, Fiona Brown and Sherry Wasserman; and Leigh Camp, the production editor for this text. Thank you again to all the staff at John Wiley who worked so hard on this text.

We also wish to acknowledge and express our sincerest thanks to all of the readers of our various texts. For over 30 years, they have been our "silent," but essential, partners in our efforts to reduce the incidence of drug and substance abuse in North America and to effectively treat as many patients as possible who are suffering as a result of these disorders. We are confident that you, our readers, will find this text to be the quintessential text on child and adolescent drug and substance abuse in your library and, as such, it will provide you with valuable data and tools to assist you in your professional efforts on behalf of affected children and adolescents and their families.

PART I

*Extent of Use and*
*Pharmacological Considerations*

# CHAPTER 1

# *The Psychodepressants*

## INTRODUCTION

The first major group of the drugs and substances of abuse that is discussed in this reference text is the psychodepressants. (See Figure 1.1.) These drugs and substances of abuse can be divided into three major subgroups: (1) opiate analgesics, (2) sedative-hypnotics, and (3) volatile solvents and inhalants. (See Table 1.1.) This chapter presents an overview of each major subgroup of the psychodepressants with attention to the prevalence and characteristics of their use among children and adolescents across North America. It also presents an overview of their general pharmacology—their proposed mechanisms of psychodepressant action and common toxicities, including their propensity for physical and psychological dependence and for overdosage.

Before beginning this overview, it is important to note that much of the information presented in this chapter in regard to demographics and use statistics, as well as that presented in Chapter 2, *The Psychostimulants*, and Chapter 3, *The Psychodelics*, is based on government-supported or sponsored national surveys. While generally constructed to be valid and reliable measurement instruments, these surveys suffer from some noted limitations that may affect the generalizability of their related findings and also bias readers toward trends of use that are significantly lower than they actually are. As such, they may detrimentally influence decisions regarding the need for prevention and treatment programs aimed

specifically at children and adolescents. These noted limitations include nonrepresentative, nonstratified sampling flaws that rely very heavily—and in some cases exclusively—on: (1) data obtained from convenience samples of children and adolescents who are attending school and ignore other groups of children and adolescents; and (2) methodological flaws, such as sampling and collecting data solely by telephone contact surveys.

Even when the survey methods are inclusive in terms of sampling techniques, they may suffer from other inherent limitations that require explicit identification and discussion. For example, limitations in sampling methods are relatively common as most surveys generally do not include data from children and adolescents who are usually identified as being at particular high risk for using the drugs and substances of abuse. These children and adolescents include

1. Homeless, runaways, or those living on the streets

2. Absent or truant students or school drop-outs who are not in attendance at the school when the survey is administered

3. Those incarcerated in youth correctional facilities

4. Those living in homes that do not have a land-line telephone[1]

5. Those living on American Indian/Canadian Aboriginal reservations and reserves, respectively

---

[1] The absence of a land-line home telephone is particularly high among low-income households, particularly those below the poverty level and those that are transient, or otherwise mobile—groups that are not mutually exclusive. For example, American Indian and Aboriginal children of the United States and Canada, respectively, who are living on reservations and reserves have a significantly higher incidence of absenteeism and school drop-out rates in comparison to the other children and adolescents usually sampled for national surveys (Sarche & Spicer, 2008).

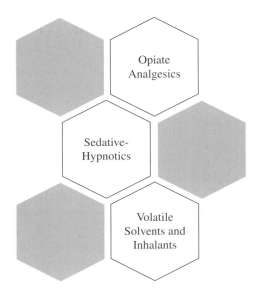

**Figure 1.1 The Psychodepressants**

Thus, the findings of the national surveys and reports generally tend to underestimate the use of the drugs and substances of abuse by North American children and adolescents. In order to address this limitation of these widely cited national government-supported and sponsored surveys and reports, we have included, whenever possible, the findings of studies and reports that specifically address the generally higher-risk subpopulations of children and adolescents that the large, national surveys often miss or neglect.

## OPIATE ANALGESICS

The opiate analgesics comprise a group of natural (e.g., morphine; codeine), semisynthetic (e.g., heroin; hydrocodone [Lortab®]; oxycodone [OxyContin®]), and synthetic (e.g., meperidine [Demerol®]; pentazocine [Talwin®]) derivatives of the opium resin that is obtained from the plant *Papaver somniferum*—the "poppy that causes sleep." One to three weeks after flowering, the opium resin is harvested from the unripe seed pod and dried.[2] Classified as an herb, *Papaver somniferum* is indigenous to southeastern Europe and western Asia where it has been widely cultivated for millennia. It also has been introduced to other countries throughout the world by travelers and immigrants. However, climatic conditions similar to those of southeastern Europe and western Asia are required for its successful cultivation.

## Prevalence and Characteristics of Opiate Analgesic Use Among North American Children and Adolescents

During the 1990s, the use of prescription opiate analgesics (e.g., hydrocodone [Hycodan®]) rapidly increased among adolescents. In fact, the use of hydrocodone became epidemic in California, where it also was commonly used by movie stars and other celebrities. Traditionally, youth were thought to be at low risk for opiate analgesic use. However, it was during this time that changes in the availability of opiate analgesics and their methods of use (i.e., intranasal insufflation, or snorting) significantly increased their popularity among high school students, particularly in the United States (Pagliaro & Pagliaro, 2009). Today, hydrocodone actively competes with the other opiate analgesics[3] for first place.

For example, over 10% of U.S. high school seniors who were surveyed between 2002 and 2006 reported nonmedical use of an opiate analgesic. The majority of these

---

[2] The dried resin of the opium poppy contains opium and the isoquinoline alkaloids codeine, morphine, noscapine, papaverine, and thebaine. Semisynthetic opiate analgesics are derived from natural products (e.g., heroin is chemically derived from morphine, and hydrocodone [Lortab®] and oxycodone [OxyContin®] are derived from codeine and thebaine). Other opiate analgesics, such as meperidine (Demerol®) and pentazocine (Talwin®), are totally chemically synthesized.

[3] Other prescription opiate analgesics that also are commonly used by children and adolescents, listed in descending order of use, are oxycodone (OxyContin®), methadone (Dolophine®), and fentanyl (Duragesic®) (C. P. O'Brien, 2008; Pagliaro & Pagliaro, 2009).

TABLE 1.1   The Psychodepressants

| Subclassification, Category, and Generic Name | Brand/Trade Names®ª | Common Street Namesᵇ |
|---|---|---|

*Opiate Analgesics:* Used for dreams (pipe dreams); euphoria; pain relief; prevention/self-management of the opiate analgesic withdrawal syndrome; warm rush; and a sleepy state (on the nod)

**PURE AGONISTS, NATURAL**

| | | |
|---|---|---|
| Opium | | Poppy |
| Codeineᶜ | Codeine Contin®, Ratio-Codeine® | Codies, cough syrup, school boy, T3 |
| Morphine | M.O.S.®, MS Contin® | Drug store, good ole M, hospital heroin, morph, MS |

**PURE AGONISTS, SYNTHETIC/SEMISYNTHETIC**

| | | |
|---|---|---|
| Fentanyl | Actiq®, Duragesic® | Fen, murder 8, perc-O-pop |
| Heroin | | Black tar, brown, capital H, charley, horse, junk, shit |
| Hydrocodoneᵈ | Dicodid®, Hycodan® | Hyke, tuss, vikes |
| Hydromorphone | Dilaudid® | Delaud, dillies, hillbilly heroin |
| Levorphanol | Levo-Dromoran® | |
| Meperidine | Demerol® | Dems, mep |
| Methadone | Dolophine® | Adolph, dollies, done, wafer |
| Oxycodone | OxyContin® | Cotton, oxycotton, poor man's heroin, percs |
| Oxymorphone | Numorphan® | |
| Propoxypheneᵉ | Darvon® | Footballs, yellows |

**MIXED AGONIST/ANTAGONISTS, SYNTHETIS**

| | | |
|---|---|---|
| Buprenorphine | Buprenex® | Tems |
| Butorphanol | Stadol® | |
| Nalbuphine | Nubain® | Nubian |
| Pentazocine | Talwin® | Big T, Ts |

*Sedative-Hypnotics:* Used for an alcohol-like disinhibitory euphoria or high; anxiety/stress reduction; prevention/self-management of the related alcohol, barbiturate, benzodiazepine, or miscellaneous sedative-hypnotic withdrawal syndromes; relaxation; tranquility. Also, particularly some of the benzodiazepines and miscellaneous sedative-hypnotics, are purposely administered to others without their knowledge in the context of perpetration of a drug facilitated crime (e.g., robbery; sexual assault, including date-rape)

**BARBITURATES**

| | | |
|---|---|---|
| Amobarbital | Amytal® | |
| Butalbitalᶠ | | |
| Butabarbital | Butisol® | |
| Pentobarbital | Nembutal® | Abbots, nembs, yellows |
| Phenobarbital | Luminal® | Pheno, sleepers |
| Secobarbital | Seconal® | Lillys, pinks, reds |
| Thiopental | Pentothal® | |

**BENZODIAZEPINES**

| | | |
|---|---|---|
| Alprazolam | Xanax® | Coffins, footballs, xannies |
| Bromazepam | Lectopam® | |
| Chlordiazepoxide | Librium® | Libs, libbies |
| Clonazepam | Clonopin®, Rivotril® | Clo, klonnies |
| Clorazepate | Tranxene® | |
| Diazepam | Valium® | Blues, mother's little helper, Vs |

*(Continued)*

**TABLE 1.1   The Psychodepressants (Continued)**

| Subclassification, Category and Generic Name | Brand/Trade Names[®a] | Common Street Names[b] |
|---|---|---|
| Estazolam | ProSom® | |
| Flunitrazepam[g] | Rohypnol® | Forget-me pill, La Roche, Mexican Valium, papas, roofies |
| Flurazepam | Dalmane® | |
| Lorazepam | Ativan® | Zzz |
| Midazolam | Versed® | |
| Nitrazepam | Mogadon® | Dons, moggies |
| Oxazepam | Serax® | |
| Temazepam | Restoril® | Green devils, temmies |
| Triazolam | Halcion® | Halcyon, halcyon daze |
| **Z-Drugs** | | |
| Eszopiclone | Lunesta® | |
| Zaleplon | Starnoc®, Sonata® | |
| Zopiclone | Imovane® | |
| Zopidem | Ambien®, Lunata® | Nappien, tic-tacs |
| **Miscellaneous Sedative-Hypnotics** | | |
| Alcohol[h] | Beers, wines, and distilled spirits are available by various brand names | Booze, drink, brew, liquid courage, moonshine, suds, vino |
| Chloral Hydrate | Noctec®[i] | Chlorals, green frogs, mickeys |
| Gamma-hydroxybutyrate | Xyrem® | Easy lay, Georgia home boy, GHB, grievous bodily harm |
| Paraldehyde | Paral®[i] | |

*Volatile Solvents and Inhalants[j]:* Used for alcohol-like disinhibitory euphoria or high

| **Volatile Solvents** | | |
|---|---|---|
| Acetone | | Sniff |
| Benzene | | |
| Butane | | Gas |
| Gasoline | | Gas, petro, petrol |
| Glue | | Gluey |
| Methanol | | |
| Toluene | | |
| Trichloroethane | | |
| Trichloroethylene | | |
| **Inhalants** | | |
| Chloroform | | |
| Ether | | |
| Nitrous Oxide | | Hippie crack, laughing gas, nitrous, whippets |
| Propane | | |

[a]Examples of common brand/trade names are provided, when available.

[b]Partial list. Examples of three to five of the most common street names are provided, when available. See Pagliaro and Pagliaro (2009) for a comprehensive listing of the drugs and substances of abuse and their common street names.

[c]Usually available as one of the ingredients in a multi-ingredient product (e.g., Empirin® #4; Tylenol® #4).

[d]Usually available as one of the ingredients in a multi-ingredient product (e.g., Lortab®, Vicodin®).

[e]In December 2010, the FDA removed propoxyphene from licit production and use within the United States. This action followed a similar move in Europe and was in response to related risk for developing potentially serious, or even fatal, cardiac dysrhythmias associated with propoxyphene use (Gandey, 2010).

[f]Butalbital is available only in combination products (e.g., Fiorinal®).

[g]Although not legally produced in North America, flunitrazepam is widely available worldwide under the brand/trade name Rohypnol® It is commonly known and used as a date-rape drug.

[h]Available as beers, wines, and distilled spirits.

[i]Usually available by generic name.

[j]Partial list.

students reported using opiate analgesics to: (1) "feel good and get high," (2) "see what it's like," and (3) "have a good time with friends" (Anderson, 2009). A series of national studies surveyed adolescent use of the drugs and substances of abuse in the United States from 2002 through 2010. These studies found a similar incidence of approximately 13% for reported use of opiate analgesics "other than heroin" (e.g., hydrocodone [e.g., Vicodin®, a combination product] and oxycodone [OxyContin®]) (Johnston, O'Malley, Bachman et al., 2008, 2010b).[4] In regard to these same prescription opiate analgesics, the national study of U.S. adolescents conducted by the Partnership for a Drug-Free America (2006) found that: (1) a majority of adolescents (i.e., 62%) reported that opiate analgesics are easily obtained from parents' medicine cabinets; (2) almost a third of adolescents (32%) reported that opiate analgesics are readily available and easily purchased over the Internet; and (3) a significant percentage of adolescents (i.e., 37%) reported having friends who used opiate analgesics.

The largest group of opiate analgesic users among children and adolescents is street users—children and adolescents who are homeless, or runaways, and living on the street. Heroin is the primary drug of choice. Currently, approximately 40% of the heroin that reaches North America comes from the opium grown in Afghanistan, Burma, Iran, and Pakistan. Most of the opium is processed into heroin in these countries, with the remainder being processed in Italy, primarily in Sicily. Since the early 1990s, the bulk of the remaining heroin that reaches the streets of the United States (about 40%) comes from opium that is grown in the western hemisphere, primarily from the countries of Colombia and Mexico. Mexico alone supplies a significant and increasing proportion of heroin (about 30%) to the United States, primarily in the form of black tar heroin.

In their survey, Johnston, O'Malley, Bachman, et al. (2008) found that 1% of high school students reported having used heroin within the previous 12 months. The incidence of heroin use varies with fluctuations in availability and with continental descent or ethnicity. In this study and most others, North American adolescents of Hispanic descent report a significantly higher incidence of heroin use than do adolescents of other continental descents or ethnicities. For example, over 5% of high school students who were sampled in Arizona and New Mexico in 2007 reported having used heroin (M. P. O'Brien, 2008).[5] Approximately 1.5% of Americans 18 years of age or older reported having used heroin at least once in their lifetime (Heroin Use USA, 2010).[6] It is interesting to note that most adults who are regular, long-term heroin users report that they began their heroin use during late adolescence (i.e., around 16 years of age) (Pagliaro, Pagliaro, Thauberger, et al., 1993; Pagliaro & Pagliaro, *Clinical Patient Data Files*). In comparison, the Partnership for a Drug-Free America (2006), in its nationwide survey of over 7,000 adolescents, found that 5% of their sample reported having tried heroin and 16% reported having a close friend who had used heroin. An apparently related finding is that, since 1999, fewer

---

[4] In addition, approximately one-third of sampled high school students reported that it was either fairly easy or very easy to obtain these opiate analgesics.

[5] The reasons for the apparent significantly higher incidence of heroin use among North American adolescents of Hispanic descent, when compared to other adolescents, appears to be primarily related to the availability of, and preference for, black tar heroin from Mexico and multigenerational membership in Hispanic criminal youth gangs that are heavily involved in drug trafficking and related activities (Pagliaro & Pagliaro, 2009; Pagliaro & Pagliaro, *Clinical Patient Data Files*).

[6] This percentage is significantly higher (i.e., approximately 2.5%) for high school students (M. P. O'Brien, 2008). Similarly, M. P. O'Brien (2008), in an analysis of data from the Community Epidemiology Work Group of the National Institute of Drug Abuse, found that 2.3% of U.S. high school students reported lifetime heroin use. Johnston, O'Malley, Bachman, et al. (2010b) report similar percentages. However, their reported data are a little more difficult to quantify precisely because, although they present the reported lifetime prevalence of heroin use among 8th-, 10th-, and 12th-grade students, they present it as two sets of data—with a needle and without a needle; the composite statistic is 1.6%, 1.7%, and 2.5%, respectively. However, they do not report how many students may have used both methods of heroin use.

and fewer adolescents report that they view heroin as a dangerously addictive drug.

Currently, opium and heroin production is at an all-time high. Transshipped from Asian and Colombian sources to North America for distribution at specified geographical locations, heroin is readily available in both higher concentrations and higher purity than it was during the last 4 decades.[7] Its distribution and commerce in the United States and Canada is largely controlled by ethnically defined criminal gangs.[8] Much of the actual distribution and street-level sale of this heroin is accomplished by criminal youth gangs, whose members are both more desperate and desirous of the money to be made and less likely, if arrested, to serve any significant jail time because of their ages (Pagliaro & Pagliaro, *Clinical Patient Data Files*). The ready availability of this high-grade heroin, at relatively low prices, has contributed significantly to an increase in intranasal use (i.e., snorting), particularly among adolescents living in suburban areas.[9]

While the norm for the 1950s, 1960s, 1970s, and 1980s was the intravenous injection of heroin, only approximately 40% of heroin users in North America, men and women alike, now intravenously inject heroin (Pagliaro & Pagliaro, 2009). A re-emerging trend from the 1970s is the more casual, nonintravenous, nondaily, social use of heroin. In the 1970s, this pattern of use was often referred to as chipping (Hanson, 1985). Chipping is a technique in which heroin, rather than being intravenously injected, or mainlined, is subcutaneously injected. However, these more casual heroin users now generally completely avoid needles and syringes by either chasing the dragon (i.e., orally inhaling heroin vapor through a glass tube, or rolled currency, that is held in the mouth) or snorting (i.e., intranasally insufflating the heroin in its powder form). They also may use intranasal instillation, or instill what is known on the street as heroin nose drops[10] into the nostrils in much the same way as they would common nose drops.

Most adolescent heroin users who do not initially inject heroin intravenously but continue to use it usually begin intravenous injection by the time they are young adults. This change in method of use is generally related to both the desired actions associated with heroin use and economics. For example, while desired psychodepressant actions can be achieved with intranasal use, this requires the use of heroin that is higher in purity and concentration and, consequently, more expensive than heroin that can be intravenously injected. Both the desired psychodepressant actions of heroin and a very pleasant rush[11] can be achieved with the intravenous injection of lower-quality, and less expensive, heroin.

---

[7] The average concentration of injectable forms of heroin, at street level, is approximately 27% in comparison to approximately 7% during the 1980s. The purity of street-level Colombian heroin typically ranges from 25% to 80% pure, while Mexican black tar heroin typically ranges from 14% to 60% pure with the highest purity found in cities along the U.S.–Mexican border (e.g., El Paso, Texas) (Pagliaro & Pagliaro, 2009).

[8] For example, the importation and distribution of heroin in Vancouver, Canada, is controlled mostly by Chinese gangs; a significant amount of the retail-level heroin distribution and sales along the northeastern coast is controlled by Dominican gangs, based primarily in New York City; most of the importation and distribution of heroin from Mexico into the southwestern United States is controlled by Mexican gangs (e.g., Sinaloan Cowboys); much of the smuggling of heroin into the United States from southeastern Asia is by Nigerian gangs, based primarily in Chicago; and much of the distribution of Asian heroin that is transshipped through the Port of Los Angeles is controlled by Thai gangs (*Drug trafficking in*, n.d.; National Drug Intelligence Center, 2001; Pagliaro & Pagliaro, 2009).

[9] However, given the observed cyclic trends reported in regard to the use of the drugs and substances of abuse over the past decades, the primary method of use among inner-city adolescents, particularly those living in the northeastern United States, is beginning to shift from snorting (i.e., intranasally insufflating) to mainlining (i.e., intravenously injecting).

[10] Some heroin users dissolve their high-purity, white powdered heroin, usually from Asian or Colombian sources, to make an aqueous solution of heroin nose drops for intranasal instillation.

[11] The rush associated with the intravenous injection of heroin is actually related to a rapid release of histamine in the body that is not directly related to heroin's psychotropic actions. An overwhelming majority of heroin users report that the rush is a very pleasant and highly anticipated experience (Pagliaro & Pagliaro, *Clinical Patient Data Files*).

## General Pharmacology

This section discusses the general pharmacology of the opiate analgesics—their apparent mechanisms of psychodepressant action; common toxicities, including their propensity for physical and psychological dependence; and overdosage.

### Proposed Mechanism of Psychodepressant Action

The various opiate analgesics primarily achieve their unique and desired psychodepressant actions by acting at specific receptor sites in the brain and the spinal cord. Five major groups of opiate, or endorphin, receptors have been identified: delta, epsilon, kappa, mu, and sigma. Pure opiate analgesic agonists (see Table 1.1) act at the delta, mu, and kappa receptors. These receptors are found in the highest concentrations in the brain stem; cortex; limbic system, including the hypothalamus; midbrain; spinal cord; and thalamus (see Figure 1.2). Acting at the delta receptors, they primarily mediate spinal analgesia. Acting at the mu receptors, specifically the mu 1 and mu 2 receptors, they primarily mediate, respectively, analgesia and various physiologic functions, including: slowing gastrointestinal (GI) motility; causing pupil constriction, or miosis; and depressing respiratory function. The mu 2 receptors also mediate feelings of euphoria and dysphoria and the development of physical dependence (i.e., the development of tolerance to the opiate analgesic agonists and the characteristic opiate analgesic withdrawal syndrome that occurs when they are abruptly discontinued). Kappa receptors mediate analgesia, other than that mediated by the mu 1 receptors; dysphoria; miosis; and respiratory depression. Mixed opiate analgesic agonists/antagonists (e.g., butorphanol [Stadol®], nalbuphine [Nubain®], pentazocine [Talwin®]) appear to act primarily at the kappa receptors. The nausea and vomiting associated with the opiate analgesics are related primarily to their stimulation of the chemoreceptor trigger zone in the medulla oblongata of the brain stem.

### Common Toxicities

Several significant toxicities, or adverse effects, have been associated with the use of the opiate analgesics—directly related to their pharmacologic actions and indirectly related to their methods of use. *Direct* toxicities, which can be acute or chronic, affect most body systems, including the cardiovascular, central nervous, GI, and respiratory systems. (See Table 1.2.) *Indirect* toxicities have been associated particularly with both the intranasal and intravenous use of the opiate analgesics.

**Intranasal Use** Intranasal use of the opiate analgesics, which became increasingly prevalent during the 1990s, has been associated with several adverse effects, including: (1) erosion of the lateral nasal walls, nasopharynx, and soft palate; (2) fungal invasion of the nasal surfaces and rhinosinusitis; (3) infections involving the nasal surfaces with associated mucopurulent exudates; and (4) nasal septal perforation. In addition, severe, life-threatening asthma attacks have been associated with intranasal sniffing (snorting) of heroin by people who have preexisting asthma.[12]

**Intravenous Use** The adverse effects associated with the intravenous use of the opiate analgesics are often serious, including:

- Human immunodeficiency virus (HIV) infection and acquired immune deficiency syndrome (AIDS)
- Abscesses and infections at injection sites
- Cardiovascular abnormalities, including scarred and collapsed veins
- Respiratory abnormalities, including talc granulomas
- Hepatitis
- Tetanus

---

[12] For several decades, virtually identical toxicities have been commonly associated with the intranasal use of cocaine. (See Chapter 2, *The Psychostimulants*, for additional related discussion.)

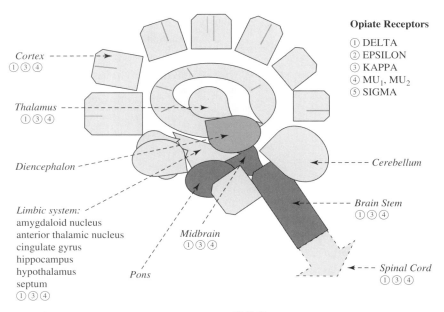

**Opiate Receptors**

① DELTA
② EPSILON
③ KAPPA
④ MU₁, MU₂
⑤ SIGMA

*Cortex*
① ③ ④

*Thalamus*
① ③ ④

*Diencephalon*

*Limbic system:*
amygdaloid nucleus
anterior thalamic nucleus
cingulate gyrus
hippocampus
hypothalamus
septum
① ③ ④

*Midbrain*
① ③ ④

*Pons*

*Cerebellum*

*Brain Stem*
① ③ ④

*Spinal Cord*
① ③ ④

**Pure Opiate Analgesic Agonists:** primarily act at ① ③ ④
**Mixed Agonist/Antagonists:** primarily act at ③

**Figure 1.2    Opiate Analgesic Receptors and Sites**

(See Table 1.3). These adverse effects and their associated complications are not caused by the opiate analgesics themselves; rather, they are caused by the adulterants used to cut the opiate analgesics for illicit use, nonsterile or shared needles and syringes, and improper injection techniques. It is important to note that if opiate analgesics were ingested, or even smoked or snorted, most of these adverse effects and more serious complications, including those that are life-threatening, would not occur.

### Physical and Psychological Dependence

The development of both physical and psychological dependence has been associated with the long-term, regular use of the opiate analgesics. Thus, the abrupt discontinuation of this pattern of use will result in the opiate analgesic withdrawal syndrome. This syndrome also may occur among regular, long-term users of opiate analgesic agonists (e.g., those users who are physically dependent on heroin or morphine) when an opiate analgesic antagonist (e.g., naloxone [Narcan®]) or a mixed opiate analgesic agonist/antagonist (e.g., pentazocine

[Talwin®]) is used. The signs and symptoms of the acute opiate analgesic withdrawal syndrome are listed in Table 1.4. Although this withdrawal syndrome is not usually fatal, generally it should be medically managed with appropriate pharmacotherapy and monitoring, particularly when children and adolescents are involved. For children and adolescents who are undergoing detoxification for physical dependence on opiate analgesics, the gradual discontinuation of the opiate analgesic will help to prevent, or minimize, these signs and symptoms. Unfortunately, following detoxification and treatment, relapse commonly occurs.

### Overdosage

Opiate analgesic overdosage requires emergency medical support, particularly for the management of the respiratory depression that is characteristically associated with overdosages involving this subclass of the psychodepressants. Attention also must be given to increasing opiate analgesic elimination. Naloxone (Narcan®), a pure opiate analgesic

TABLE 1.2   Signs and Symptoms of Acute and Chronic Opiate Analgesic Toxicity

| Body System | Signs and Symptoms | |
| --- | --- | --- |
| | Acute | Chronic |
| Central nervous | Cognitive impairment; fainting (syncope); headache | Physical dependence and psychological dependence |
| Cardiovascular | Bradycardia; cardiac arrest; circulatory depression; dilation of superficial blood vessels with resultant warming of the skin (flushing); orthostatic, or postural, hypotension; sedation; shock; with intravenous injection, local pain or phlebitis at injection site (also see Table 1.3) | Anemia |
| Cutaneous | Diaphoresis, or excessive perspiration; pruritus; with subcutaneous injection, pain at injection site | |
| Gastrointestinal | Constipation; nausea; vomiting | Constipation |
| Genitourinary | Impotence (boys); reduced sexual desire; urinary retention | Menstrual irregularities (girls); reduced sexual desire |
| Muscular-skeletal | With intramuscular injection, pain at injection site | |
| Ophthalmic | Miosis; urticaria | |
| Respiratory | Laryngospasm; respiratory arrest; respiratory depression | |

antagonist, is the specific antidote for the respiratory depression associated with overdosages involving opiate analgesic agonists and mixed opiate analgesic agonist/antagonists. However, it must be administered cautiously to children and adolescents who may be physically dependent on opiate analgesics because the usual dosage of the antagonist may precipitate the opiate analgesic withdrawal syndrome.[13] Common signs and symptoms of opiate analgesic overdosage are listed in Table 1.5.

It is important to note that many cases of opiate analgesic overdosage also involve other drugs and substances of abuse. For example, psychostimulants (see Chapter 2, *The Psychostimulants*), such as cocaine and methamphetamine, are concomitantly used, particularly with heroin (i.e., speedball). However, more common, and deadly, is the concomitant use of other psychodepressants, such as alcohol and the benzodiazepines (see "Sedative-Hypnotics" section for additional related discussion). These psychodepressants potentiate the respiratory depression associated with opiate analgesic overdosage and, consequently, significantly increase the risk for fatal overdosage (Pagliaro & Pagliaro, 2009; Sporer, 1999). Note, too, that the respiratory depression associated with the concomitant use of the nonopiate psychodepressants is not reversible by the administration of naloxone [Narcan®]).

## SEDATIVE-HYPNOTICS

The second major subgroup of the psychodepressants, the sedative-hypnotics, is comprised of drugs and substances of abuse from four general pharmacological classes: (1) barbiturates; (2) benzodiazepines; (3) Z-drugs; and (4) miscellaneous sedative-hypnotics, including alcohol. (See Table 1.1.) Of these four pharmacologic classes, children and adolescents are most likely to use, or be exposed to, alcohol, followed by the

---

[13] The severity of the withdrawal syndrome depends on the severity of physical dependence (i.e., the characteristics of regular, long-term use in regard to the amount of the opiate analgesic used and the frequency of its use) and the dose of the antagonist administered. If the opiate analgesic antagonist is required for the medical management of serious respiratory depression for children or adolescents who are physically dependent on opiate analgesics, lower dosages and cautious dosage titration, together with careful monitoring, are recommended.

TABLE 1.3   Indirect Toxicities Associated With the Intravenous Injection of the Drugs and Substances of Abuse

| Indirect Toxicity |
| --- |
| Abscess |
| Aerobic gram-positive *cocci* infection |
| Anerobic infection |
| Aneurysm |
| Bacteremia |
| Cellulitis |
| CNS Infection |
| Cutaneous venous ulcer[a] |
| Endocarditis |
| Gangrene[b] |
| Hepatitis B |
| Hepatitis C[c] |
| HIV infection |
| Hyperpigmentation and scarring of skin tissue at injection site(s) (i.e., *needle tracks*, *railroad tracks*) |
| Myonecrosis |
| Myositis |
| Necrotizing fasciitis |
| Phlebitis |
| Polymicrobial infection |
| Pyomyositis |
| Sepsis |
| Skin and other soft-tissue infection |
| Tetanus |
| Thrombophlebitis |
| Thrombosis |
| Venous insufficiency, chronic |
| Venous sclerosis |
| Wound botulism |

[a] Often is a long-term, chronic condition. When affecting the lower extremities, it can be debilitating.

[b] Often requires removal of the infected body tissue or, depending on the extent of the infection, amputation of the fingers, hand, toes, or foot.

[c] Often a precursor to cirrhosis of the liver or cancer of the liver (i.e., hepatocellular carcinoma), either of which may be fatal or require liver transplantation. The most common cause of hepatitis C in North America is the sharing of contaminated needles and syringes.

Notes: These toxicities are identified as indirect toxicities because they are not directly associated with the specific pharmacological actions of the specific psychodepressant drug or substance of abuse itself but rather with the general method of administration: intravenous injection.

Commonly used anatomic sites for intravenous injection of the various drugs and substances of abuse, in decreasing order of use, include the antecubital fossa, forearm, hand, foot, leg, breast, groin, and neck (Pagliaro & Pagliaro, *Clinical Patient Data Files*).

TABLE 1.3   (Continued)

Adulterants (e.g., quinine) and small, unfiltered particles (e.g., powder, talc, and other components of the drug or substance of abuse being injected) significantly contribute to these harmful effects. In addition, unsterile injection equipment, poor methods of injection, and poor hygiene contribute as well.

M. P. O'Brien (2008), reporting for the Community Epidemiology Work Group of the NIDA, found that 2% of U.S. high school students reported lifetime use of illegal injection drugs. As a cross-check of this finding, we note that Johnston, O'Malley, Bachman, et al. (2010b), in their in-school 2010 survey of adolescent use of the drugs and substances of abuse, found that approximately 1% of 8th-grade students, 10th-grade students, and 12th-grade students reported a lifetime prevalence of using a needle to self-administer heroin.

benzodiazepines. The barbiturates, Z-drugs, and the other miscellaneous sedative-hypnotics are least likely to be used by children and adolescents.[14] Thus, they are not specifically discussed in this chapter. However, one miscellaneous sedative-hypnotic, gamma-hydroxybutyrate (GHB), is used primarily by adolescents and young adults and thus is included in this section. We begin with an overview of the use of alcohol by children and adolescents and then turn our attention to the benzodiazepines and, finally, to GHB.

## Alcohol

Alcohol is one of the most widely used drugs and substances of abuse. It is used throughout the world for its dose-dependent disinhibition euphoria, or high, and to decrease social and sexual inhibitions (i.e., to achieve a sense of well-being; to relax; and to relieve anxiety, tension, and stress). It also is used by regular, long-term alcohol users to prevent or manage the alcohol withdrawal syndrome, and it is administered to victims for the perpetration of such drug-facilitated crimes as robbery and sexual assault, including date rape.

[14] Children and adolescents occasionally encounter these sedative-hypnotics when "pharming"—gathering any prescription drugs available in the family medicine cabinet or on a parent's dresser or bedside table and taking them to a friend's house, where, along with everyone else who is participating, they dump them in a bowl, spread them on a table, or pile them on the floor, for general selection and use by all.

**TABLE 1.4  Opiate Analgesic Withdrawal Syndrome: Common Signs and Symptoms**

| Body System | Signs and Symptoms |
|---|---|
| Central nervous | Anxiety, dysphoria, insomnia, irritability, restlessness, sensitivity to pain, yawning |
| Cardiovascular | Hypertension, tachycardia |
| Cutaneous | Chills and shivering, piloerection (goose flesh), sweating (excessive) |
| Gastrointestinal | Abdominal cramps and pain, anorexia, diarrhea, nausea |
| Musculoskeletal | Backache and other body aches, tremors, weakness |
| Respiratory | Hyperventilation, rhinitis, rhinorrhea, sneezing |
| Thermoregulatory | Fever, unexplained |

In spite of its desirable psychotropic actions (as noted earlier) and certain other qualities (e.g., pleasant taste; quenching of thirst) the general use of alcohol has been associated with more harm than all of the other drugs and substances of abuse combined (Pagliaro & Pagliaro, 2009).[15] Alcohol-related harm includes: (1) direct physical harm (e.g., fetal alcohol syndrome/fetal alcohol spectrum disorder—see Chapter 5, *Exposure to the Drugs and Substances of Abuse From Conception Through Childhood*); (2) mental harm (e.g., depression; suicide [see also related discussion in Chapter 8, *Dual Diagnosis Among Adolescents*]); and (3) social harm (e.g., increased incidence of child abuse; decreased academic achievement; domestic violence; motor vehicle crashes; and violent crime, including homicide) (e.g., Involvement by young, 2002; Levy, Miller, & Cox, 1999; Miller, Levy, Spicer, et al., 2006; Pagliaro & Pagliaro, 2002, 2009; Sheppard, Snowden, Baker, et al., 2008; Sindelar, Barnett, & Spirito, 2004; Spirito, Rasile, Vinnick, et al., 1997).

## Prevalence and Characteristics of Alcohol Use Among North American Children and Adolescents

The personal use of alcohol (and other drugs and substances of abuse) by children and adolescents, as well as adults, is characterized by nine well-defined patterns, or levels, of use from nonuse to resumed nonuse and relapsed use. (See Figure 1.3.) The initial use of alcohol during childhood may occur in association with religious ceremonies (i.e., Holy Communion) or as a result of curiosity (e.g., when a child wants to "see what it's like to taste a sip of beer"—often provided by a parent). The most common form of personal use is social use, which involves the use of alcohol in a wide range of social situations. In North America and other parts of the world, alcohol is socially ingested in the form of beers, wines, and distilled spirits (i.e., whiskey, vodka, liqueurs). Alcohol use is highly variable among individuals and societies and is significantly affected by a variety of factors, including age, race (i.e., genetic predisposition to tolerance or lack thereof [i.e., sensitivity, Asian flush]), cultural and religious customs, personal preferences, and availability and cost.

**Trends**  Alcohol use, other than a sip or a taste, increases with age throughout late childhood (i.e., from around 8 years of age) and adolescence (i.e., to around 20 years of age) (Pagliaro & Pagliaro, 2009). As noted by Donovan (2007) in a review of children's alcohol use in the United States, more than 6% of 9-year-old children reported having consumed more than a few sips of alcohol. This observation also is supported by Eaton, Kann, Kinchen, et al. (2010), who found, in their analysis of data from the Youth Risk Behavior Surveillance System for 2009, that, nationwide, 21.1% of U.S. students in grades 9 through

---

[15] In the United States, alcohol consumption has been cited as the third leading cause of preventable death (Centers for Disease Control and Prevention, 2004b; McGinnis & Foege, 1993). See related discussion throughout this text for specific examples and reference citations.

**TABLE 1.5   Opiate Analgesic Overdosage: Common Signs and Symptoms**

| Body System | Signs and Symptoms |
|---|---|
| Central nervous | Diminished or absent reflexes; stupor or coma; however, convulsions may occur with meperidine (Demerol®) or propoxyphene (Darvon®) |
| Cardiovascular | Hypertension; shock |
| Cutaneous | Chills and shivering; piloerection (goose flesh); sweating (excessive) |
| Gastrointestinal | Constipation |
| Musculoskeletal | Backache and other body aches, tremors, weakness |
| Ophthalmic | Miosis; however, mydriasis may occur with extreme hypoxia or with meperidine (Demerol®) overdosage |
| Respiratory | Decreased or absent respirations with cyanosis; pulmonary edema |
| Thermoregulatory | Subnormal body temperature |

12 reported having drunk alcohol (other than a few sips) for the first time before they were 13 years of age (range 11.5% to 29.4 % across state surveys)—an age range reported by most adults as the time they first consumed their non-sip alcoholic drink (*Alcohol Use USA*, 2010).

The Partnership for a Drug-Free America and the Metlife Foundation (2010), in their 2009 study of over 3,000 adolescents in grades 9 through 12, found that 39% of their adolescent participants reported having drunk alcohol during the past month. Another study, the National Institute on Drug Abuse (NIDA)–sponsored Monitoring the Future survey for 2009, found that 14.9% of 8th-grade students, 30.4% of 10th-grade students, and 43.5% of 12th-grade students reported past month use of alcohol (Adolescent cigarette smoking, 2010). These data have been relatively constant

over the past several years in regard to alcohol use with a very slight downward trend. However, in comparison to data for the early 1990s, each grade level currently sampled reports an approximately 10% overall decrease in alcohol use during the previous month (Johnston, O'Malley, Bachman, et al., 2010b).

In Canada, average reported age of initial use of alcohol is 16 years of age (Health Canada, 2010b)—an initial age of use noted to be significantly higher than that reported for the United States. Although the legal age for drinking in Canada varies from province to province (i.e., from 18 years of age to 21 years of age), the minimal legal drinking age across the entire United States (i.e., in all 50 states) is 21 years of age. As such, all alcohol use by children and adolescents in the United States (i.e., all underage drinking) is illicit (Substance Abuse and Mental Health Services Administration, 2010). Once alcohol consumption begins, it generally continues throughout a user's lifetime—except for users who discontinue alcohol use, primarily for religious or health reasons.

Currently, most studies indicate that approximately 80% of North Americans regularly consume alcoholic beverages.[16] For example, M. P. O'Brien (2008), in an analysis of data from the Community Epidemiology Work Group of the NIDA, found that 75% of U.S. high school students reported lifetime use of alcohol—the highest reported lifetime use rate for any of the drugs or substances of abuse selected for analysis. Similarly, Eaton, Kann, Kinchen, et al. (2010), in their analysis of data from the Youth Risk Behavior Surveillance System for 2009, found that more than 72% of U.S. students in grades 9 through 12 reported alcohol use with a range of approximately 40% to 80% across state surveys. Over 25% of these students reported having consumed alcohol on more than 100 days during the past

---

[16] Of the 20% of North Americans who do not consume alcohol, approximately half do not consume alcohol for religious reasons (e.g., Church of Jesus Christ of Latter-day Saints [Mormons], Muslims, Seventh-day Adventists), and the remaining half do not consume alcohol for medical reasons. Included in the latter group are people who are recovering from alcoholism and who subscribe to the principles of Alcoholics Anonymous or other similar 12-step programs (e.g., see Chapter 9, *Preventing and Treating Child and Adolescent Use of the Drugs and Substances of Abuse*).

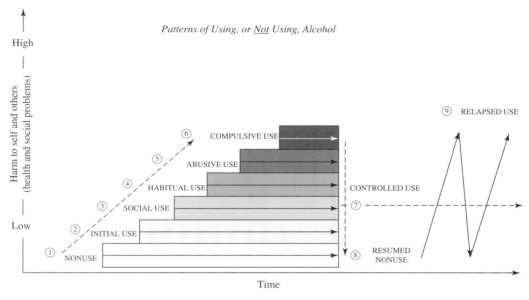

**Figure 1.3    Patterns of Alcohol Use and Increasing Harm**

year (*Alcohol Use USA*, 2010). Interestingly, Eaton, Kann, Kinchen, et al. (2010) also found that 4.5% of U.S. students nationwide in grades 9 through 12 had drunk at least one alcoholic beverage while on school property during the previous 30 days (range, 2.7% to 8.0% across state surveys).[17] In addition, Johnston, O'Malley, Bachman, et al. (2010b), in their 2010 in-school survey, *Monitoring the Future*, found that 16.3% of 8th-grade students, 36.9% of 10th-grade students, and 54.1% of 12th-grade students reported a lifetime prevalence of having been drunk.

**Binge Drinking**    Binge drinking (i.e., traditionally defined for adolescent boys and young men as consuming five or more alcoholic drinks on a single occasion and for adolescent girls and young women as consuming four or more alcoholic drinks on a single occasion) is highly correlated with acute impairment and significant adverse health consequences (Pagliaro & Pagliaro, 2009; Wechsler, Davenport, Dowdall,

et al., 1994).[18] However, more recently, Donovan (2009), using a modified version of the Widmark equation to calculate blood alcohol concentrations (BACs) for boys and girls, suggested a significant revision to the binge-drinking criteria.

Specifically based on his calculated estimates of differences between children and adults in total body water and alcohol elimination rates, Donovan (2009) recommends that binge drinking be defined as:

- Three or more drinks per drinking occasion for children and adolescents 9 to 13 years of age
- Three or more drinks for adolescent girls 14 to 17 years of age
- Four or more drinks for adolescent boys 14 and 15 years of age
- Five or more drinks for adolescent boys 16 and 17 years of age

While we would agree that the number of drinks needed to define binge drinking should be lowered for children and adolescents, we

---

[17] The incidence was reportedly highest (i.e., 7.9%) for boys of Hispanic descent.

[18] The defined pattern of alcohol consumption for binge drinking is generally equivalent for both adolescent boys and girls to the amount of alcohol consumption necessary to achieve a blood alcohol concentration (BAC) of 0.08 gram% (i.e., 80 mg%)— the legal level of alcohol intoxication in the United States (National Institute on Alcohol Abuse and Alcoholism, 2004).

would caution that there are, as yet, no empirical data to support Donovan's recommendations, and genetic differences in body weight and alcohol metabolism and elimination may vary significantly among North American children and adolescents.

For example, alcohol is predominantly water soluble. As such, doses of alcohol based on body weight will yield a significantly higher BAC among obese children and adolescents when compared to children and adolescents who are of normal body weight for their height and age. In addition, for postpubescent adolescents, on average, girls have significantly more body fat than do boys. Thus, we would expect a significant amount of variance in regard to binge-drinking definitions and criteria for children and adolescents.

Johnston, O'Malley, Bachman, et al. (2008), in their national study of adolescent drug use in the United States during 2007, found that approximately 20% of 10th- and 12th-grade students surveyed reported binge drinking (i.e., consuming five or more drinks in a row) during the 2 weeks prior to the survey. In addition, more than 41% of 10th-grade students and more than 55% of 12th-grade students, reported a lifetime prevalence of having been drunk. Even though they are underage drinkers, 90% of 12th-grade students reported that alcohol was either fairly easy or very easy to obtain.

Grucza, Norberg, and Bierut (2009) analyzed available data from the National Survey on Drug Use and Health (i.e., a pooled sample of more than 500,000 adolescent and young adult subjects) in regard to binge drinking among adolescents and young adults in the United States. Overall, from 1979 to 2006, they found that the incidence of binge drinking decreased significantly for boys (i.e., by approximately 15%) but increased significantly for girls (i.e., by approximately 50%). Their findings for adolescents for 2006, classified according to gender and age cohorts, are displayed in Table 1.6. As noted in the table, the incidence of binge drinking among adolescents: (1) increases with increasing age; (2) is significantly higher among boys, although

**TABLE 1.6   Binge Drinking: Incidence for Boys and Girls in the United States, 2006**

| Gender | Age (years) | Binge Drinkers (%) |
|--------|-------------|--------------------|
| Girls  | 12–14       | 3.5                |
|        | 15–17       | 15.1               |
|        | 18–20       | 30.1               |
| Boys   | 12–14       | 2.7                |
|        | 15–17       | 18.1               |
|        | 18–20       | 41.0               |

Source: Grucza, Norberg, & Bierut, 2009.

girls are gaining parity; and (3) there appears to be an interaction effect between age and gender in regard to the incidence of binge drinking (i.e., for adolescents 12 to 14 years of age, girls have a significantly higher incidence of binge drinking than do boys; for adolescents 15 to 17 years of age, the incidence of binge drinking is essentially the same; and for adolescents 18 to 20 years of age, boys have a significantly higher incidence of binge drinking). Similarly, Miller, Naimi, Brewer, et al. (2007), in a study of approximately 14,000 high school students, found that 27.5% of boys and 23.5% of girls had engaged in binge drinking during the 30 days preceding their survey.

Although the results indicate a higher incidence of binge drinking among boys, this finding may be due to the definitional use of five or more drinks in a row on 1 or more of the 30 days preceding the survey to measure binge drinking—instead of the standard measurement of binge drinking for girls as 4 or more drinks (see earlier discussion in this section). Using the same definitional and measurement criteria as Miller, Naimi, Brewer, et al. (2007), Eaton, Kann, Kinchen, et al. (2010), in their analysis of the data from the Youth Risk Surveillance System for 2009, found that 24.2% of U.S. students in grades 9 through 12 reported binge drinking (range across state surveys, 11.5% to 30.7%). Among U.S. high school students, who reported current alcohol use, binge drinking was reported by an alarming 60.9% (Centers for Disease Control and Prevention, 2010d).

Among the adolescents who binge drink, it has been noted that approximately:

- 60% drink with others
- 40% drink to get high
- 30% drink when bored

McKinnon, O'Rourke, Thompson, et al. (2004) examined the rates of binge drinking among high school students in grades 9 through 12 who were sampled from 16 U.S. high schools along the United States–Mexico border. The majority of students who participated in the study were of Hispanic descent. Of these students, 45% reported binge drinking, 19% reported high-risk driving behaviors (e.g., drinking and driving), and 46% reported riding with a driver who had been drinking. These percentages were found to be significantly higher than U.S. national averages and highly correlated with reported alcohol-related problems and lower academic grades. Equally significant and disturbing, the students who participated in the study reported even higher rates of binge drinking (i.e., odds ratio [OR] = 6.44), risky driving (OR = 5.39), and riding with a driver who had been drinking (OR = 5.39) "when visiting Mexico."

Per-capita binge drinking episodes have increased significantly over the past two decades and appear to continue to increase across North America, particularly among young adults (Courtney & Polich, 2009; Grucza, Norberg, & Bierut, 2009; Pagliaro & Pagliaro, 2009).[19] Grucza, Norberg, and Bierut (2009), in their study of binge drinking, found the highest rates among young adults 21 to 23 years of age (i.e., 58.5% for young men and 38.6% for young women). It has long been noted that binge drinking is significantly higher among lesbian and bisexual adolescents and young women than among those who are not lesbian or bisexual (Drabble, Midanik, &

Trocki, 2005; Hughes & Wilsnack, 1997; Hyde, Comfort, McManus, et al., 2009). (Also see related discussion in Chapter 8, *Dual Diagnosis Among Adolescents*, in the "Sexual or Gender Identity Disorders" section.)

### Alcohol and Caffeinated Energy Drinks

Since the beginning of the new millennium, older adolescents and young adults have been increasingly drinking energy drinks—nonalcoholic drinks that are highly laden with caffeine (see related discussion in Chapter 2, *The Psychostimulants,* "Caffeine" section). These energy drinks, including Red Bull®, RevItUp®, and Rock Star®, often are used by adolescents and young adults in an attempt to enable them to drink more alcohol during a drinking episode without becoming drunk (Kaminer, 2010). For example, Malinauskas, Aeby, Overton, et al. (2007) found that over 50% of U.S. college students reported regularly consuming energy drinks and almost half of these adolescents and young adults reported commonly consuming three or more energy drinks, together with alcohol, while partying.[20] Miller (2008), in a similar study of North American undergraduate college students, found that the association between energy drink consumption and related problem behaviors (e.g., aggression, insomnia) was particularly significant for students of European descent but not for those of African descent. Use statistics and related behaviors for senior high school students are expected to be very similar to the data reported for undergraduate college students (Pagliaro & Pagliaro, *Clinical Patient Data Files*).

As noted, many adolescents and young adults generally assume that the psychostimulant actions of caffeine can ameliorate the psychodepressant actions of alcohol and, consequently, enable them to consume as much alcohol as they like. However, it is important

---

[19]Among college students of European American descent, the rate of binge drinking has been significantly correlated with the use of volatile solvents and inhalants during adolescence (Bennett, Walters, Miller, et al., 2000).

[20]Interestingly, Oteri, Salvo, Caputi, et al. (2007) reported similar findings for a large sample of medical students in Italy.

to note that the cognitive and psychomotor impairment associated with increasing BACs (see Table 1.7) are not significantly reduced by the caffeine consumed in energy drinks (Ferreira, de Mello, Pompéia, et al., 2006; Ferreira, de Mello, Rossi, et al., 2004)—even though the adolescent's or young adult's self-perception of his or her alcohol intoxication is significantly reduced (Marczinski & Fillmore, 2006). As we have noted previously in other venues, what is achieved is a wide-awake drunk. Instead of falling asleep or passing out with a BAC of 0.25 to 0.30, the adolescent or young adult remains awake and, consequently, is able to engage in hazardous behavior (e.g., drunk driving, physical assault) that may result in increased personal and social harm (see related discussion in "Common Toxicities" section, below; also see Table 1.8). Adolescents and young adults also use energy drinks to help them to stay awake to study (e.g., cram for a final examination; finish a term paper). (Also see related discussion in Chapter 2, *The Psychostimulants.*)

### General Pharmacology

This section considers the proposed mechanism of alcohol's psychodepressant action and its common toxicities, including the development of physical and psychological dependence and the occurrence of the alcohol withdrawal syndrome when regular, long-term alcohol use is abruptly discontinued.

**Proposed Mechanism of Psychodepressant Action**    The exact mechanism of action by which alcohol exerts psychodepression has not been determined. It appears to act by modifying the membrane environment of the gamma-aminobutyric acid (GABA) receptor complex (see Figure 1.4). Thus, the affinity for both endogenous GABA and other exogenous sedative-hypnotics, such as the barbiturates and benzodiazepines, is significantly increased

(i.e., GABAergic inhibition is enhanced). Acute alcohol consumption significantly decreases overall brain glucose metabolism, which may also result in psychodepressant effects, including those that adversely affect learning and memory among children and adolescents. (See Chapter 6, *Effects of the Drugs and Substances of Abuse on Learning and Memory During Childhood and Adolescence.*) The pharmacologic effects, both physical and psychological, of alcohol use are well correlated with BACs (Pagliaro & Pagliaro, 2009). (See Table 1.7.)

**Common Toxicities**    Among the acute and chronic physical and psychological toxicities associated with alcohol use (see Table 1.8), the use of alcohol among adolescent girls and young adult women of reproductive age has been associated with the leading cause of mental retardation in North America, the fetal alcohol syndrome/fetal alcohol spectrum disorder (FAS/FASD) among their offspring. In addition, approximately 1 in 5 North Americans report significant harm associated with their use of alcohol at least 1 time during their lives (Pagliaro & Pagliaro, 2009), with adolescents and young adults, including college and university students, experiencing significant alcohol-related injuries and sometimes death.[21] Also of concern is the occurrence of physical and psychological dependence and its associated sequelae, including the development of alcoholism and Wernicke-Korsakoff Syndrome, a condition that remains relatively rare among adolescents and young adults but appears to be increasing.

*Fetal Alcohol Syndrome/Fetal Alcohol Spectrum Disorder.*    In North America, FAS/FASD is the third most commonly known cause of mental retardation and is the most common preventable cause of mental deficiency. Although suspected for centuries, FAS/FASD was fully described only during

---

[21] Alcohol-related injuries result in over 2 million hospitalizations of adolescents in the United States annually and 3,400 deaths (Miller, Levy, Spicer, et al., 2006).

**TABLE 1.7    Blood Alcohol Concentration (BAC) and Associated Physical and Psychological Effects**

| BAC grams %, or grams per 100 ml | *Associated Effects* | |
| --- | --- | --- |
| | Physical | Psychological |
| 0.01–0.03 | Generally normal appearance | Generally normal behavior |
| 0.03–0.06 | Mild impairment of coordination and ability to perform fine motor tasks<br>Feeling relaxed<br>Sense of warmth | Mild euphoria with decreased inhibitions and increased sociability and talkativeness<br>Mild decrease in alertness and concentration |
| 0.06–0.08 | Increasing loss of coordination with slight loss of balance<br>Slight loss of speaking ability | Mild impairment of reasoning and memory<br>Intensification of emotions<br>Increased disinhibition euphoria with apparent stimulant effect on behavior and extroversion<br>Lowered interest in sex |
| 0.08–0.11 | Mild impairment of hearing, speech, and vision | Mild impairment of both judgment and self-control with an increased probability or incidence of accidents |
| 0.10–0.15 | Continued loss of coordination<br>Marked impairment of balance<br>Slowed reaction time<br>Slightly slurred speech | Increased emotional instability<br>Euphoria is increasingly replaced with dysphoria<br>Significant impairment of judgment and ability to make good decisions<br>Probability or incidence of accidents is increased 10-fold |
| 0.15–0.20 | Significant drowsiness<br>Slurred speech<br>Significantly prolonged reaction times<br>Significant visual impairment with blurred vision, reduced glare recovery, and decreased peripheral vision | Significant impairment of perception<br>Further deterioration of judgment<br>Gross intoxication<br>Probability or incidence of accidents is increased by up to 30-fold |
| 0.20–0.30 | Severe motor and speech impairment with an appearance of a sloppy drunk<br>May require assistance to stand upright or to walk<br>Impaired gag reflex with risk of choking on food or own vomit<br>Risk of serious injury related to falls, walking into traffic, being attacked or robbed (i.e., being rolled) | Significant mental confusion—may be dazed or disoriented<br>Loss of normal understanding<br>Significant pain tolerance (feeling no pain)<br>Memory loss and alcoholic blackouts<br>May become stuporous, or achieve a state of near-unconsciousness |
| 0.30–0.35 | Total loss of motor control<br>Reflexes are significantly depressed or absent<br>Incontinence, or loss of voluntary bladder control<br>Heart rate is significantly slowed<br>Respiratory rate is significantly slowed | Level of consciousness diminishes to a state of stupor, a complete lack of mental alertness or a condition of significantly impaired ability to respond to external environmental stimuli<br>Level of consciousness diminishes to coma, or an extremely deep stupor—a condition in which the person cannot be aroused by external environmental stimuli (e.g., talking to the person, calling the person by name, or gently shaking the person in an effort to arouse him or her)<br>Total lack of response to painful stimuli, such as pinching the skin or pricking the skin with a pin or needle (i.e., level of surgical anesthesia) |
| 0.35–0.40+ | Impaired circulation of the blood throughout the body<br>Death, usually due to respiratory arrest | Severe CNS depression<br>Unconsciousness |

*(Continued)*

**TABLE 1.7    Blood Alcohol Concentration (BAC) and Associated Physical and Psychological Effects (Continued)**

Notes: The BACs listed and their associated effects are meant to provide a general guideline. Variability from one drinker to another does occur and can be significant, particularly in the context of acquired tolerance.

Because of a paucity of relevant available data for children and adolescents, this table was constructed from adult data. Given the known pharmacokinetics of alcohol, the extrapolation of these data to adolescents is expected to be quite valid and reliable. However, the data in this table should *not* be applied directly to children.

0.1 grams % = 100 mg %

the late 1970s. The condition is caused by the consumption of alcohol by adolescent girls and women during pregnancy. Although the ingestion of up to 2 drinks per day by pregnant adolescent girls and women generally has been considered to be safe to the fetus, the safe amount of alcohol ingested during pregnancy has not been well documented and may be highly variable. Controversy regarding the incidence of FAS continues. However, because of the serious nature and irreversibility of the related sequelae, we recommend that adolescent girls and women of reproductive age completely avoid the consumption of alcohol during pregnancy (Pagliaro & Pagliaro, 2000, 2002, 2009).

Since 1977, published data have accumulated implicating high maternal alcohol consumption during pregnancy with FAS. Alcohol ingestion during the first trimester is most likely to cause fetal malformations resulting in physical birth defects. Alcohol ingestion later during pregnancy is most likely to adversely affect fetal nutrition with resultant decrements in head circumference, body length, and body weight. However, maternal alcohol use throughout gestation can adversely affect central nervous system (CNS) development and related neurocognitive processes (i.e., result in mental birth defects) among offspring.

Current available data suggest that neuronal apoptosis,[22] induced by maternal alcohol consumption during pregnancy, may be the underlying pathophysiologic basis for the development of the FAS/FASD and its associated neurobehavioral impairments (Olney, Wozniak, Jevtovic-Todorovic, et al., 2002). In this case, the third trimester of pregnancy, which correlates with the beginning of the brain growth spurt period (i.e., period of high synaptogenesis that commences in the sixth month of fetal development), would appear to be the time of maximal vulnerability for the development of the FAS/FASD-related neurobehavioral disorders (Ikonomidou, Bittigau, Koch, et al., 2001). The incidence of FAS/FASD in North America remains at a significantly high level and, unfortunately, actually is increasing among some subpopulations, such as Native Americans (Eustace, Kang, & Coombs, 2003; Pagliaro & Pagliaro, 2009). (Also see related discussion in Chapter 5, *Exposure to the Drugs and Substances of Abuse From Conception Through Childhood.*)

***Alcohol-Related Injury and Death: College Drinking***    Annually, across college campuses in North America, it is estimated that there are 1,400 student deaths, 500,000 unintentional injuries, and 600,000 physical assaults (including rape) directly related to alcohol consumption (Hingson, Heeren, Winter, et al., 2005; Hingson, Heeren, Zakocs, et al., 2002; Hingson, Zha, & Weitzman, 2009).[23] In addition, over 30% of four-year college students sampled in the United States report problems specifically related to their alcohol use (e.g., alcohol-related academic problems;

---

[22] Neuronal apoptosis is the process in which brain cells disintegrate into particles that are consumed (i.e., phagocytosed) by other cells (e.g., leukocytes, macrophages). Thus, brain growth and development is prevented, inhibited, or slowed.

[23] College students are more likely to engage in problematic drinking behaviors than are same-age cohorts who do not attend college (O'Malley & Johnston, 2002).

**TABLE 1.8   Alcohol Use Among Children and Adolescents:** *Acute (A)* **and** *Chronic (C)* **Toxicities**

Absenteeism from school or work (*A*) (*C*)

Accidents, general (e.g., drowning, falls) (*A*) (*C*)

Abusive and aggressive behavior, physical and psychological (*A*) (*C*)

Alcoholic blackouts (*A*) (*C*)

Alcoholic ketoacidosis *(A) (C)*

Alcoholism (*C*)

Alcohol withdrawal syndrome (*C*)

Amnesia (*A*) (*C*)

Anemia (*C*)

Boyfriend or girlfriend abuse, physical and psychological (*A*) (*C*)

Cardiac dysrhythmias (*C*)

Cardiovascular heart disease (*C*)

Child abuse, physical and psychological (*A*) (*C*)

Cognitive dysfunction (*A*) (*C*)

Coma *(A) (C)*

Criminal behavior *(A) (C)*

Date-rape (facilitation of perpetration) *(A)*

Decreased immune response *(C)*

Decreased social inhibitions *(A)*

Diabetes mellitus *(C)*

Dual diagnosis *(C)*

Dysfunctional parenting *(A) (C)*

Dysmenorrhea, or severe pain associated with menstruation (C)

Eye movements, diminished (*A*)

Fetal alcohol syndrome/fetal alcohol spectrum disorder among offspring of adolescents and young women of reproductive age who drink during pregnancy (*A*) (*C*)

Gastritis (*A*) (*C*)

Guilt (*A*) (*C*)

Hallucinations (*A*)

Hangover (*A*)

Homicide, increased involvement—both as perpetrator or victim (*A*)

Hypertension (*C*)

Hypertriglyceridemia (*C*)

Hypoglycemia (*A*) (*C*)

Hypokalemia *(A)*

Hypothermia, or a decrease in body temperature *(A)*

Korsakoff's psychosis (C)[a]

Malnutrition (e.g., thiamine deficiency) (*C*)

Memory dysfunction (*A*) (*C*)

Mental depression (*A*) (*C*)

Motor vehicle crashes, increased (*A*)

Neuropathy *(C)*

Neurotoxicity (*A*) (*C*)

Peripheral neuropathy (*C*)

Peripheral vasodilation (flush) (*A*)

Physical dependence (*C*)

Psychological dependence (*C*)

Psychomotor impairment (*A*)

Psychosis (*A*)

Respiratory depression (*A*)

Risk taking, increased (*A*)

Schoolwork/academic performance, decreased (*A*) (*C*)

Self-neglect (*A*) (*C*)

Sexual abuse/assault (facilitation of perpetration by decreasing social inhibitions) (*A*)

Sexual activity, increased (*A*)

Sexual dysfunction (males) (*A*)

Sexual inhibitions, decreased (*A*)

Sexually transmitted diseases, increased (*A*)

*(Continued)*

**TABLE 1.8    Alcohol Use Among Children and Adolescents:** *Acute (A)* **and** *Chronic (C)* **Toxicities (Continued)**

Short-term memory, impaired (*A*)
Sick days, increased (*C*)
Slurred speech (*A*)
Social problems (e.g., absence from school or work; arguments with family members; delinquency) (*A*) (*C*)
Strained or impaired relationship with parent(s)/primary care giver(s) (*A*) (*C*)
Suicide, increased (attempted or completed suicide) (*A*) (*C*)
Victimization (e.g., physical assault, sexual assault) (*A*) (*C*)
Violent behavior, including homicide, physical assault, and rape (*A*)
Vomiting *(A)*
Wernicke's encephalopathy *(C)*[b]
Work productivity, decreased (*A*) (*C*)

[a] Korsakoff's psychosis is an extremely rare occurrence among adolescents and young adults. However, some few cases have been identified among older adolescents who are homeless and have a long history (i.e., several years) of heavy drinking (Pagliaro & Pagliaro, *Clinical Patient Data Files*).
[b] Wernicke's encephalopathy is an extremely rare occurrence among adolescents and young adults. However, some few cases have been identified among older adolescents who are living on the streets and have long histories (i.e., several years) of heavy drinking and associated malnourishment (Pagliaro & Pagliaro, *Clinical Patient Data Files*).

drinking in hazardous situations, such as drinking and driving[24] (Knight, Wechsler, Kuo, et al., 2002). (See Figure 1.5.) Student risk for excessive alcohol use is highest at U.S. colleges and universities (1) at which fraternities and sororities play a dominant social role, (2) where athletic events and campus sports are held in particularly high esteem, and (3) that are located in the Northeast (Presley, Meilman, & Leichliter, 2002).[25] The toxicities associated with alcohol use are specifically related to its pattern of use. (See Figure 1.3.)

***Physical and Psychological Dependence***
Alcohol has a high abuse potential for both physical and psychological dependence. The former is characterized by the development of tolerance, which is commonly identified among chronic alcoholics, and a classic alcohol withdrawal syndrome that occurs when regular, long-term alcohol use is abruptly discontinued. Tolerance—the need to drink more and more alcohol to achieve

desired psychodepressant actions (i.e., a disinhibition euphoria, relief of tension)—and the desire to avoid the alcohol withdrawal syndrome work in unison along with the development of psychological dependence—a craving for alcohol characterized by continued use despite harmful effects to self and others with the recognition by alcoholic adolescents or young adults that they "just can't help" themselves. The extent to which physical and psychological dependence develop, and their associated physical, psychological, and social consequences occur, is directly related to the specific patterns in which alcohol is consumed. (See Figure 1.3.)

Although infrequent use in small amounts (e.g., 1 or 2 drinks on holidays and special occasions) generally has been associated with little or no harmful effects among children and adolescents, both physical dependence and psychological dependence, in the form of increasingly serious forms of alcoholism, have been noted when moderate to large

[24] Even at lower BACs, drinking and driving have been demonstrated to be particularly hazardous for inexperienced drivers, including adolescents, 16 to 18 years of age (*Alcohol implicated*, 2010; Car crashes, 2007) (see Figure 1.5). Drinking and driving, particularly by inexperienced drivers, contributes significantly to automobile crashes, which is the leading cause of death for North American adolescents and young adults (Centers for Disease Control and Prevention, 2010c; Female auto crash, 2007; Pagliaro & Pagliaro, 2009). This statistic may not be too surprising given that, annually, over 30 million Americans admit to driving while drunk, and the highest percentage is in the 16- to 25-year-old age group (Hendrick, 2010).

[25] The correlates of underage drinking on college campuses by students who are younger than 21 years of age include, in decreasing order: (1) drinking beer; (2) residing in a fraternity or sorority; (3) having easy access to alcohol; and (4) being able to obtain alcohol at lower prices (Wechsler, Kuo, Lee, et al., 2000).

**GABA$_A$ Receptor Complex**

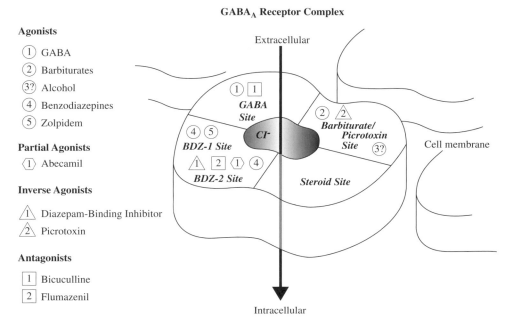

**Agonists**

① GABA
② Barbiturates
③? Alcohol
④ Benzodiazepines
⑤ Zolpidem

**Partial Agonists**

⟨1⟩ Abecamil

**Inverse Agonists**

⟨1⟩ Diazepam-Binding Inhibitor
⟨2⟩ Picrotoxin

**Antagonists**

1 Bicuculline
2 Flumazenil

**Figure 1.4   Stylized Model of the GABA$_A$ Receptor Complex**

Reproduced with permission from: L. A. Pagliaro & A. M. Pagliaro (1998), Chapter 2, The Psychotropics (p. 51). In L. A. Pagliaro & A. M. Pagliaro, *The pharmacologic basis of psychotherapeutics: An Introduction for psychologists.* Washington, DC: Brunner/Mazel.

amount of alcohol are regularly ingested over prolonged periods of time (i.e., months). As noted by the American Academy of Pediatrics (2001):

> Addiction to alcohol is underdiagnosed in adolescents. . . . Alcoholism should be suspected in young people who are often intoxicated or experience withdrawal symptoms from chronic or recurrent alcohol use; those who tolerate large quantities of alcohol; those who attempt unsuccessfully to cut down or stop alcohol use; those who experience blackouts attributable to drinking; or those who continue drinking despite adverse social, educational, occupational, physical, or psychological consequences or alcohol-related injuries. (p. 186)

*Alcoholism*   The term "alcoholism" may be defined as the use of alcohol that results in increasing harm to the user as measured by related changes in physical and mental health, school/work productivity, family relationships, and social life. The development of alcoholism has several specific characteristics, including

notions that it is: (1) progressive, in that it becomes more serious with time; (2) chronic, in that it is continuous; and (3) insidious, in that there is a general inability on the user's part to recognize, without outside assistance, that her or his use of alcohol is resulting in significant personal and social harm. As mentioned, the incidence of alcoholism is approximately 15% of the entire North American adult population (Pagliaro & Pagliaro, 2009).

Although complex in nature and more specifically identified as consisting of several alcoholisms, or like FAS/FASD as a spectrum disorder, the clinical entity of alcoholism has been characterized by various specific behaviors, including:

- Drinking alone
- Sneaking drinks
- Gulping down drinks
- Developing increased tolerance to alcohol
- Experiencing personality changes
- Inability to account for specific periods of time (i.e., alcoholic blackouts)

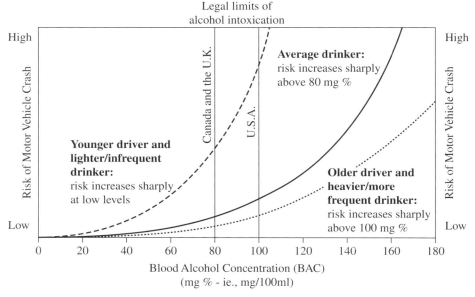

**Figure 1.5    Age and Alcohol-Related Risk for Motor Vehicle Crashes**
Reproduced with permission from: A. M. Pagliaro & L. A. Pagliaro (1996), Chapter 8, Substance-related accidents and violence: Children and adolescents as victims (p. 187). In, *Substance use among children and adolescents: Its nature, extent, and effects from conception to adulthood.* New York, NY: John Wiley & Sons.

Among North Americans 18 years of age or older, approximately one-third will develop an alcohol use disorder (AUD) sometime during their lifetime (Hasin, Stinson, Ogburn, et al., 2007).[26] Although adequate and reliable data regarding the incidence of alcoholism or AUD among North American adolescents is not currently available, case reports, clinical experience, and drug and substance abuse treatment center records provide evidence that it is a serious and growing problem (Pagliaro & Pagliaro, *Clinical Patient Data Files*).

*Alcohol Withdrawal Syndrome*    As tolerance develops for many of the physiological and psychological effects of alcohol, regular, long-term drinkers will increasingly use larger and larger amounts of alcohol in an effort to achieve these desired effects. They also may drink more frequently or throughout the day in an effort to prevent the occurrence of the signs and symptoms of the alcohol withdrawal syndrome. This withdrawal syndrome, which commences upon the abrupt discontinuation of heavy, prolonged alcohol consumption, is characterized by anxiety, craving for alcohol, hallucinations, insomnia, irritability, psychomotor agitation, restlessness, tremulousness, and a variety of other associated physiological effects (e.g., diaphoresis, fever, mydriasis) (Bayard, McIntyre, Hill, et al., 2004).

When particularly acute or severe, this group of signs and symptoms has been generally identified as the syndrome of delirium tremens (DTs), historically referred to as alcoholic delirium and colloquially as rum fits. This form of the alcohol withdrawal syndrome is characterized by various classic signs and symptoms, including: agitation (severe), confusion, delirium, diarrhea, disorientation, fever, grand mal seizures, hallucinations

---

[26] For adolescent boys and adults of American Indian descent, the reported incidence is significantly higher (i.e., approximately 42%).

(often bizarre and extremely frightening), hypertension, hyperthermia, mydriasis, nausea, sweating (profuse), and tachycardia. The signs and symptoms appear to be moderated, at least in part, by a decrease in GABA-ergic inhibitory function and an increase in glutamatergic excitatory function (Malcolm, 2003).[27] Cardiovascular collapse may occur if DTs is left untreated, and may be fatal. Medical management of DTs generally involves hospitalization in order to provide cautious administration of long-acting benzodiazepines,[28] careful monitoring of body systems, and appropriate supportive care.

*Wernicke-Korsakoff Syndrome* Wernicke-Korsakoff syndrome is a major syndrome associated with the regular, long-term heavy drinking of alcohol. This syndrome, comprised of Wernicke's encephalopathy and Korsakoff's psychosis, is not directly caused by alcohol itself but by a vitamin B1, or thiamine, deficiency. This vitamin deficiency occurs as a result of inadequate nutrition—a condition that commonly occurs among people who have severe alcoholism. Severe alcoholism can be displayed by people of all socioeconomic and cultural backgrounds. However, it is particularly prevalent among people who live on the street or in hostels that are provided by social agencies and charities, such as the Salvation Army. This nutritional deficiency results in acute Wernicke's encephalopathy and, if treatment is delayed, the chronic syndrome of Korsakoff's psychosis.

Korsakoff's psychosis is characterized by increasing memory impairment as severe brain damage occurs. Because the syndrome is characterized by confusion, defective muscular coordination, disorientation, double vision, hallucinations, hypotension, memory failure, and muscular spasticity (i.e., many of the common signs and symptoms associated with acute

alcohol intoxication), it is often confused with acute alcohol intoxication—particularly by law enforcement officers. The treatment for this condition involves thiamine replacement, the establishment of proper nutrition, and supportive care. However, even with appropriate treatment, the prognosis for this condition is poor. Unfortunately, only 20% of people diagnosed as having Korsakoff's psychosis are cured, 30% have little to moderate improvement, and 50% demonstrate no improvement.

### Benzodiazepines

The benzodiazepine molecule was synthesized in the late 1950s. Over the following 50 years, more than 2,000 different benzodiazepine derivatives were developed. Touted as being the safest sedative-hypnotics available for clinical use because of their high therapeutic index, the benzodiazepines became the most widely prescribed, and abused, sedative-hypnotics in the world, including North America. Although the benzodiazepines continue to be widely used by adults for their desired anxiolytic and hypnotic actions, their therapeutic use has now been increasingly replaced in North America with the more recently developed sedative-hypnotics, the Z-drugs. (See Table 1.1, "Sedative-Hypnotics" section.)

*Prevalence and Characteristics of Benzodiazepine Use Among North American Children and Adolescents*

Children and adolescents generally use the benzodiazepines to: (1) achieve an alcohol-like disinhibitory euphoria, or high; (2) reduce anxiety and stress (e.g., family, school, or job-related stress); or (3) sleep better (i.e., cope with the anxiety or insomnia related to their everyday problems, including parental expectations and household rules, schoolwork demands,

---

[27] This explanation is consistent with the observed clinical efficacy of the benzodiazepines (e.g., chlordiazepoxide [Librium®], diazepam [Valium®]) in managing the signs and symptoms of the alcohol withdrawal syndrome.

[28] The benzodiazepines (e.g., chlordiazepoxide [Librium®]) are the drugs of choice for the medical management of DTs as well as for milder forms of alcohol withdrawal (Pagliaro & Pagliaro, 2000, 2009).

job requirements, financial needs, and dating and sexual issues).[29] Children and adolescents also may use benzodiazepines in an effort to prevent, or self-manage, the benzodiazepine withdrawal syndrome. Increasingly, some children and adolescents use benzodiazepines (e.g., flunitrazepam [Rohypnol®, roofies]) to facilitate robberies and sexual assaults (i.e., date-rape).[30]

Children and adolescents generally obtain benzodiazepines by: (1) pharming—stealing prescription benzodiazepines from their parent(s) or other family members and then sharing them with other children or adolescents or trading them for more desired drugs and substances of abuse (See earlier discussion); (2) buying them from illicit dealers, including older siblings and schoolmates; and (3) obtaining them by purchase over the Internet. As noted by Johnston, O'Malley, Bachman, et al. (2008) in their national study of adolescent drug use in the United States for 2007, 20% of the high school students surveyed reported that the benzodiazepines were either fairly easy or very easy to obtain.

Although the overall use of the benzodiazepines by children and adolescents has decreased significantly from the highs of the 1970s and 1980s, it is still significant, as indicated by reports of drug-related admissions from both addiction treatment centers and hospital emergency departments across the United States (Forrester, 2006a; M. P. O'Brien, 2008). The benzodiazepines, particularly alprazolam

(Xanax®), clonazepam (Rivotril®), diazepam (Valium®), and lorazepam (Ativan®), account for the majority of these reports. In addition, a significant number of children and adolescents who seek assistance from addiction counselors for cocaine or opiate analgesic dependence (actually, up to one-third) also have issues with benzodiazepine dependence (Pagliaro & Pagliaro, *Clinical Patient Data Files*.

The most popular benzodiazepines used by U.S. high school students are alprazolam (Xanax®) and diazepam (Valium®). Johnston, O'Malley, Bachman, et al. (2008) found that approximately 6% of U.S. high school students reported personal benzodiazepine use within the previous 12 months. In comparison, available Canadian data for benzodiazepine use for 2009 indicated that 4% of youth 15 to 24 years of age used them during the previous year (Health Canada, 2010b).

### General Pharmacology

This section considers the proposed mechanism of action of the benzodiazepines and their common toxicities, including their potential for physical and psychological dependence and overdosage.

**Proposed Mechanism of Psychodepressant Action** The benzodiazepines cause dose-related CNS depression ranging from mild impairment of cognitive and psychomotor functions to hypnosis. They appear to act at

[29] See, for example, Chapter 8, *Dual Diagnosis Among Adolescents*, for related discussion of alcohol and other sedative-hypnotic use by adolescents in the context of the combination of substance use disorders and other mental disorders.

[30] Flunitrazepam (Rohypnol®, forget-me drug, La Roche, roofies) is a widely used date-rape drug. (See Table 1.1.) Although not legally available in North America, it is available by prescription in over 70 countries in Europe and Latin America, where it is used to treat anxiety and insomnia and as a preoperative adjunct to anesthesia (Anglin, Spears, & Hutson, 1997; Pagliaro & Pagliaro, 2009). The majority of this pharmaceutically produced drug is smuggled into the United States from Mexico.

In their national in-school survey of adolescent use of the drugs and substances of abuse, Johnston, O'Malley, Bachman, et al. (2010b) found that 0.9% of 8th-grade students and 1.4% of 10th-grade students reported lifetime prevalence of flunitrazepam use. The highest incidence of use, often in combination with beer and cannabis, is found among adolescent boys and young men of European or Hispanic descent. Among this latter group, use primarily occurs in bars, nightclubs, and raves. Of concern is the increasing use of flunitrazepam by sexually active adolescent girls and young women, who use it in combination with alcohol and other drugs and substances of abuse, particularly psychodelics (e.g., 3,4-methylenedioxymethamphetamine [MDMA]), in order to decrease inhibitions and enhance sexual experiences (Pagliaro & Pagliaro, 2009). A significant number of these adolescent girls and young women have reportedly been physically or sexually assaulted while under the influence of flunitrazepam.

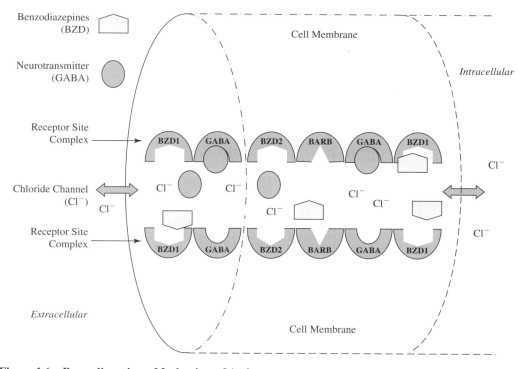

**Figure 1.6   Benzodiazepines: Mechanism of Action**
Reproduced with permission from: L. A. Pagliaro & A. M. Pagliaro (2009), *Pagliaros' Comprehensive Guide to Drugs and Substances of Abuse* (2nd ed.) (p. 40). Washington DC: American Pharmacists Association.

the benzodiazepine receptors (types 1 and 2). These receptors are found at several sites in the CNS, particularly in the cerebral cortex and the limbic system. The benzodiazepine receptors are found primarily in conjunction with the GABA$_A$ receptor. Thus, it appears that the benzodiazepines elicit their pharmacologic actions by potentiating the actions of GABA, a major inhibitory neurotransmitter, within the CNS. A simplified, stylized representation of the principal sites and mechanisms of action of the benzodiazepines is shown in Figure 1.6.

**Common Toxicities**   Although relatively safe to use, the benzodiazepines have been associated with various adverse cognitive effects. (See, for example, the discussion of their adverse effects on memory in Chapter 6, *Effects of the Drugs and Substances of Abuse on Learning and Memory During Childhood and Adolescence*.) Their potential for physical

and psychological dependence, including the development of tolerance and a benzodiazepine withdrawal syndrome upon the abrupt discontinuation of regular, long-term use, have now been well documented. The benzodiazepines also have been associated with overdosage fatalities, particularly when used with alcohol (Pagliaro & Pagliaro, 2009).

**Physical and Psychological Dependence**
In regard to abuse potential, the benzodiazepines have a low to moderate potential for physical dependence and a moderate to high potential for psychological dependence. It has been long recognized that psychological dependence could develop with the regular, long-term use of benzodiazepines—at both lower and higher dosages. Available data now indicate that the regular, long-term use of benzodiazepines, even within therapeutic dosage ranges, can lead to true physical dependence in a significant minority of users (Pagliaro & Pagliaro, 2009).

In addition, benzodiazepine users, including children and adolescents, who have a past personal or family history of alcoholism appear to be at increased risk for developing physical dependence, including the development of tolerance and a withdrawal syndrome that occurs with the discontinuation of use.

*Tolerance*   Tolerance to the actions of the benzodiazepines develops within 4 months of initial, daily use regardless of the dosage range (i.e., low or high) or if medically prescribed or not. However, the rate of tolerance development varies from person to person and from benzodiazepine to benzodiazepine. Generally, tolerance develops more quickly to the hypnotic effects of the benzodiazepines than to their anxiolytic effects.

Some general indicators of benzodiazepine dependence include: (1) regular use of a benzodiazepine extending over 30 days; (2) expressed craving or a desire for the benzodiazepine; (3) a need to increase the dosage of the benzodiazepine in order to achieve, or maintain, the desired effect(s); and (4) the appearance of the characteristic signs and symptoms of the benzodiazepine withdrawal syndrome when the use of the benzodiazepine is abruptly discontinued for any reason (e.g., inability to renew a prescription; lack of funds to buy more of the drug; inability to obtain the drug from others by begging, stealing, or trading). (Also see the "Benzodiazepine Withdrawal Syndrome" section for additional related discussion.)

*Benzodiazepine Withdrawal Syndrome*   The characteristic signs and symptoms of what is now identified as the benzodiazepine withdrawal syndrome have been widely documented in regard to the abrupt discontinuation of regular, long-term benzodiazepine use (e.g., Bateson, 2002).[31] Usually mild to moderate in intensity, these signs and symptoms include anxiety (rebound), convulsions, dysphoria (generally mild), insomnia, irritability, muscle cramps, nervousness, shaking, sweating, tension, and tremors. These characteristic signs and symptoms, which are essentially the opposite of the desired effects of the benzodiazepines, are more likely to occur with: (1) short-acting benzodiazepines (e.g., alprazolam [Xanax®], lorazepam [Ativan®], triazolam [Halcion®]); (2) higher dosages of the benzodiazepine; (3) regular, daily use of the benzodiazepine for 4 months or longer; and (4) the abrupt discontinuation of the benzodiazepine after regular, daily use.[32]

Signs and symptoms of the benzodiazepine withdrawal syndrome have included life-threatening seizures at dosages within the recommended range for some benzodiazepines (e.g., alprazolam [Xanax®]). Children and adolescents who have a history of epilepsy or other seizure disorders are at particular risk for seizures related to benzodiazepine withdrawal. The severity and duration of the withdrawal syndrome appear to be related primarily to the dosage and duration of benzodiazepine pharmacotherapy or regular personal use.

Generally, the benzodiazepine withdrawal syndrome can be avoided, or at least minimized, by gradually decreasing the dosage. It is often handled cold turkey (without medical care or prescribed pharmacotherapy) but can be managed with the substitution of an equivalent dose of a long-acting benzodiazepine (e.g., diazepam [Valium®]) that is gradually reduced over a period of 2 to 3 weeks.

---

[31] Interestingly, the signs and symptoms of the benzodiazepine withdrawal syndrome also have been noted with the discontinuation of concurrent pharmacotherapy that inhibits the cytochrome P450 isoenzymes responsible for the metabolism of the benzodiazepines (Ninan, 2001) (e.g., the antifungals itraconazole [Sporanox®] and ketoconazole [Nizoral®]; the antisecretory proton pump inhibitor omeprazole [Losec®, Prilosec®]) (Pagliaro & Pagliaro, 1998).

[32] Short-acting benzodiazepines are more likely to produce insomnia when abruptly discontinued than are long-acting benzodiazepines and may contribute to their continued use. Long-acting benzodiazepines are less likely to produce insomnia when they are discontinued, probably because of their longer half-lives of elimination, which may provide an automatic tapering-off effect when use is abruptly discontinued.

**Overdosage** Signs and symptoms of benzodiazepine overdosage include coma, confusion, diminished reflexes, incoordination, and somnolence. Respiratory arrest is more common with short-acting benzodiazepines (e.g., alprazolam [Xanax®], midazolam [Versed®], and triazolam [Halcion®]). Benzodiazepine overdosage is usually not fatal, because the benzodiazepines possess a high $LD_{50}$ (i.e., the median lethal dose, or the dose that would be expected to cause death in 50% of an exposed population). However, fatalities commonly occur when overdosages involve the use of benzodiazepines in combination with alcohol or opiate analgesics. Benzodiazepine overdosage requires emergency medical support of body systems, with attention to increasing benzodiazepine elimination. The benzodiazepine receptor antagonist flumazenil (Anexate®, Romazicon®) may be required.

### Gamma-Hydroxybutyrate

Gamma-hydroxybutryrate (GHB) occurs naturally in the human body as both a precursor and a metabolite of GABA. It was first chemically synthesized in 1960 in France as an anesthetic. However, the use of GHB was associated with insufficient analgesia and seizure activity, particularly tonic-clonic movements of the face or limbs (Vickers, 1969). During the 1980s, GHB gained popularity as a nutritional supplement (i.e., a growth hormone stimulator) among body builders, and its availability and sales greatly increased in health food stores and over the Internet. During this time, GHB also became widely known as a date-rape drug (see later discussion in this section).

In 2000, the use of GHB was made illegal across the United States with the passage of the federal Hillory J. Farias and Samantha Reid Date-Rape Drug Prohibition Act (H.R. 2130).

However, its chemical precursor, gamma-buty-rolactone (GBL; blue nitro, gamma G), which can be easily converted to GHB, continued to be widely available over the Internet.[33] In late 2002, the use of GBL decreased when the United States Drug Enforcement Agency arrested over 100 dealers in 84 cities in the United States and Canada. Despite these efforts, GHB use remains high, and is expected to increase, with diversions of the recently approved prescription product from its legitimate clinical use as adjunctive pharmacotherapy for the symptomatic management of narcolepsy. When legally used in this context, GHB generally is referred to by its generic name, sodium oxybate, or brand/trade name, Xyrem®.

GHB is often illicitly used in combination with other drugs and substances of abuse (see "Overdosage" section) to enhance their actions or diminish their associated toxicities. For example, GHB may be used with 3,4-methyl enedioxymethamphetamine (MDMA, ecstasy) because it reportedly attenuates the unpleasant effects (e.g., anxiety, tachycardia) associated with MDMA use.

### *Prevalence and Characteristics of GHB Use Among North American Adolescents*

The primary users of GHB are adolescents and young adults who use the drug to relieve anxiety or to achieve alcohol-like disinhibitory euphoria, or high, without the hangover associated with alcohol use. Other major desired actions or reasons for use include: (1) arousal of sexual desire and increased sociability, along with decreased sexual inhibitions, particularly among bisexual and gay adolescent boys and young men; (2) as a nutritional supplement for body builders; and (3) the prevention or self-management of the alcohol and opiate analgesic withdrawal syndromes. In addition,

---

[33] Simple-to-follow recipes for the conversion of GBL to GHB are widely available over the Internet. In fact, some sites even offer kits complete with instructions and the requisite chemicals. Also illicit and available over the Internet is 1,4-butanediol (BD, thunder nectar, weight belt cleaner), which is converted (metabolized) in the body by the enzymes alcohol dehydrogenase and aldehyde dehydrogenase to GHB.

GHB continues to be administered to others without their knowledge in the context of perpetrating drug-facilitated crimes (e.g., robbery and sexual assault, including date-rape) (Lee & Levounis, 2008; Pagliaro & Pagliaro, 2009).

GHB is available as an oral solution by its generic name. Illicit powders and oral solutions also are produced in, imported into, and distributed across North America. Prior to ingestion, these illicit powders and solutions may be added to a container of bottled water at a rave or mixed into an alcoholic beverage at a circuit party (i.e., a gay dance/sex event party) or dance club. They also may be secretly mixed into another person's drink at a bar or mixed into a punch bowl at a social gathering (e.g., frat house party, postgame celebration).[34]

The typical user is a young man in his early 20s of European descent. Use predominantly occurs in the social context of all-night parties, dance clubs, music festivals, and raves. Increasingly, sexually active adolescent boys and girls and young adult men and women deliberately use GHB to enhance their sexual experiences. In this context, GHB is often used in combination with alcohol and other drugs and substances of abuse, particularly the psychodelics. (See Chapter 3, *The Psychodelics*.) Another population group that is associated with extremely high GHB use is bisexual and gay adolescent boys and men, regardless of continental descent. In fact, GHB is one of the five main club drugs (i.e., cocaine, GHB, ketamine, methamphetamine, and MDMA [ecstasy]) commonly used socially by this population group at circuit parties.

In their national survey of more than 7,000 students in the 7th through 12th grades, the Partnership for a Drug-Free America (2006) found that 4% of their participants reported use of GHB. Hopfer, Mendelson, Van Leeuwen, et al. (2006), in their study of youth in treatment for substance abuse, found that 7% reported GHB use.

### General Pharmacology

GHB is a naturally occurring, or endogenous, precursor and metabolite of the major inhibitory neurotransmitter gamma-hydroxybutyric acid (GABA). It is found in several body tissues but has been studied most intensively in the CNS. Consequently, it has been used therapeutically as an adjunct to general anesthesia, for the treatment of alcohol and opiate analgesic dependence (in Europe) (Caputo & Bernardi, 2010; Leone, Vigna-Taglianti, Avanzi, et al., 2010), and to treat cataplexy associated with narcolepsy (Fuller, Hornfeldt, Kelloway, et al., 2004; Galloway, Frederick, Staggers, et al., 1997). In order to prevent the diversion of medical GHB to illicit markets for distribution and sale, several precautions were undertaken by the Food and Drug Administration, including the use of a different generic and brand/trade name (i.e., sodium oxybate [Xyrem®]) and the development of a restricted drug distribution system (i.e., the Xyrem® Success Program).

The use of GHB as a date-rape drug became increasingly common in North America during the 1980s and 1990s, when it was found to facilitate sexual assault while reducing the likelihood that a perpetrator would be charged, arrested, and convicted of aggravated sexual assault as a direct result of the drug's pharmacologic characteristics and actions. In this regard, GHB was the perfect drug—it is odorless, colorless, and easily dissolved in alcohol (Pagliaro & Pagliaro, 2009; Stillwell, 2002). It also is capable of causing muscle relaxation, profound sedation, social disinhibition (with associated increased sexual desire), and anterograde amnesia. Thus, along with public concern about the frequency and seriousness of GHB-facilitated date-rapes, another major concern was the difficulty associated with achieving successful prosecutions of perpetrators because of: (1) its relatively short half-life of elimination (i.e., approximately 30 minutes);

---

[34] GHB is available as a powder or as a liquid solution. The solution has a distinctly salty or soapy taste that is masked most often by chilling it in the refrigerator or mixing it in an alcoholic beverage.

(2) the lack of readily available specific assays for detecting GHB in victims; (3) the difficulty of differentiating levels of endogenous GHB from exogenous, or illicitly administered, GHB; and (4) its pharmacologic actions, including anterograde amnesia (Borgen, Okerholm, Lai, et al., 2004; Carter, Koek, & France, 2009; Ferrara, Zotti, Tedeschi, et al., 1992; Scharf, Lai, Branigan, et al., 1998; Slaughter, 2000).

**Proposed Mechanism of Sedative-Hypnotic Action**  The exact mechanism of GHB's psychodepressant action has not been determined. However, four contributory mechanisms have been empirically confirmed:

1. GHB binds to its own endogenous receptors in the CNS that are found predominantly in the basal ganglia and hippocampus.
2. GHB appears to enhance the inhibitory actions that are modulated by the $GABA_B$ receptors.
3. GHB acts both presynaptically and postsynaptically to modulate the activity of other neurotransmitters in the CNS (e.g., the firing of dopaminergic neurons).
4. GHB presynaptically inhibits the release of dopamine into the synaptic cleft, resulting in an accumulation of dopamine in the presynaptic neuron (Pagliaro & Pagliaro, 2009).

Thus, it has been demonstrated that GHB is both a weak agonist of the $GABA_B$ receptor and a potent agonist of the excitatory GHB receptor with a biphasic effect on dopamine (i.e., initially dopamine release is inhibited, but at higher GHB concentrations, it is stimulated). Exogenously administered GHB also elicits its effects indirectly by means of its conversion to GABA (Carter, Koek, & France, 2009; Sewell & Petrakis, 2011).

**Common Toxicities**  The use of GHB has been associated with several acute and chronic toxicities. Acute toxicities include: amnesia (anterograde); apnea; ataxia; bradycardia;

cognitive impairment; coma (i.e., deep sleep, usually of short duration, from which the child or adolescent is difficult to arouse); confusion; diarrhea; dizziness; drowsiness; enuresis; headache; heartburn; hypersalivation; hypotension (particularly orthostatic); hypotonia; loss of consciousness; myoclonic seizures; nausea; psychomotor impairment; respiratory depression (with higher dosages); sleep (deep); slurred speech; sweating; vomiting; and weakness. Chronic toxicities include menstrual irregularities, physical and psychological dependence, somnambulism, and tinnitus (Garrison & Mueller; 1998; O'Connell, Kaye, & Plosay, 2000; Pagliaro & Pagliaro, 2009).

**Physical and Psychological Dependence: GHB Withdrawal Syndrome**  A specific GHB withdrawal syndrome has been identified and described. Characteristic signs and symptoms include: agitation (severe), anxiety, autonomic excitation or instability, delirium (prolonged), diaphoresis, dizziness, dysphagia, hallucinations (auditory and visual), hypertension, insomnia, muscle aches, nystagmus, psychosis, rhabdomyolysis, seizures, tachycardia, and tremor (Rosenberg, Deerfield, & Baruch, 2003; Stijnenbosch, Zuketto, Beijaert, et al., 2010; van Noorden, Kamal, de Jong, et al., 2010; Wojtowicz, Yarema, & Wax, 2008; Zepf, Holtmann, Duketis, et al., 2009). As with other drugs and substances of abuse, the signs and symptoms of the GHB withdrawal syndrome vary in expression and intensity, according to the level of regular, long-term use prior to abrupt discontinuation.

The most severe forms of the GHB withdrawal syndrome occur among regular, long-term users who use GHB every 1 to 3 hours around the clock. Among these users, the GHB withdrawal syndrome may begin within 1 hour of the last use of GHB and last up to 15 days (Dyer, Roth, & Hyma, 2001; Perez, Chu, & Bania, 2006). This withdrawal syndrome may be potentially life threatening. It also is often quite resistant to pharmacotherapeutic management with the benzodiazepines, such as diazepam (Valium®) or lorazepam (Ativan®), and significantly higher than usual dosages are often required (Rosenberg, Deerfield, & Baruch, 2003; Stijnenbosch, Zuketto, Beijaert, et al., 2010; Tarabar & Nelson, 2004; van Noorden, van Dongen, Zitman, et al., 2009). The cases of GHB withdrawal that are refractory to benzodiazepine pharmacotherapy may respond to other sedative-hypnotic pharmacotherapy, such as barbiturate (e.g., phenobarbital [Luminal®]) or chloral hydrate (Noctec®) pharmacotherapy (McDonough, Kennedy, Glasper, et al., 2004). Along with medical support and monitoring, physical restraint may be required (Dyer, Roth, & Hyma, 2001).

**Overdosage**    GHB overdosage may be fatal. However, fatalities are relatively rare (i.e., less than 200 fatalities have been reported to date) and are usually associated with polyuse of the drugs and substances of abuse, particularly other psychodepressants, including alcohol and other sedative hypnotics and the opiate analgesics (Knudsen, Jonsson, & Abrahamsson, 2010).[35] Alcohol, heroin, and MDMA (ecstasy) are the other drugs and substances of abuse that are most often involved in GHB overdosage. GHB users who overdose usually present to the emergency department in an unconscious state, often in a coma. Other presenting signs and symptoms of overdosage may include agitation, apnea, blurred vision, bradycardia, confusion, delirium, headache, hypothermia, loss of bladder and bowel control, muscle weakness, myoclonic seizures, nausea, psychomotor impairment, respiratory impairment, sweating, and vomiting. Generally, with proper recognition and care—in particular, with attention to cardiac and respiratory support, including aspiration precautions—complete recovery, without sequelae, can be expected within 6 to 8 hours. There is no known antidote (Carter, Pardi, Gorsline, et al., 2009; Mason & Kerns, 2002; Pagliaro & Pagliaro, 2009).

## VOLATILE SOLVENTS AND INHALANTS

The volatile solvents are a diverse group of chemical compounds that are liquid at room temperature and readily evaporate when exposed to air. Virtually any marketed product that contains a volatile organic solvent is capable of being used for its major psychodepressant action that produces a desirable, alcohol-like disinhibitory euphoria, or high. The volatile inhalants are primarily anesthetic gases (e.g., nitrous oxide or laughing gas) but also include propane and other gases, all of which are inhaled in much the same way as volatile solvents. These psychodepressants (see Table 1.1) are generally easy to use, and the large surface area of the lungs assures both their rapid absorption into the circulatory system and rapid onset of action.

The major volatile solvents include:

- Acetone, found in nail polish remover, model (e.g., airplane, car) glue, permanent markers, and rubber cements
- Benzene, found in cleaning fluids, gasoline, rubber cements, and tire tube repair kits
- Butane, found in cigarette lighters, cooking fuel gas, hair spray, spray paint, and some air fresheners and deodorants
- Chlorinated hydrocarbons (e.g., toluene), found in airplane glues, correction fluids, degreasers, gasoline, lacquer thinners, nail polish, plastic cements, shoe polish, and spray paints)
- Fluorinated hydrocarbons (e.g., freons), found in aerosols, air conditioning units, refrigerants, and propellants #11 and #12
- Gasoline
- Paint thinner
- Trichloroethylene and trichloroethane, which are also chlorinated hydrocarbons,

---

[35] This incidence is notably higher among adults in some other countries, such as Sweden, and is expected to increase initially among adults primarily as the prescription form of GHB (i.e., sodium oxybate, Xyrem®) increasingly is diverted for personal use (Zvosec, Smith, & Hall, 2009).

found in degreasers, dry cleaner formulations, Liquid Paper® or other correction fluid, refrigerants, spot removers, and PVC cement.

- Xylene, used in chemical production and manufacturing[36]

The volatile gases include several gases that are used for their psychodepressants actions, including nitrous oxide and propane.[37] Nitrous oxide, once commonly used as an anesthetic in dentistry, is still used as a short-acting anesthetic for some dental procedures. Propane is commonly used as a motor vehicle and cooking fuel. It also is used for home heating.

## Prevalence and Characteristics of Volatile Solvent and Inhalant Use Among North American Children and Adolescents

Over 25 million North Americans have abused volatile solvents or inhalants at least once in their lives (Pagliaro & Pagliaro, 2009; Volkow, 2009). Currently, largely due to easy accessibility and relatively low cost, the number of new volatile solvent and inhalant users in the United States appears to be increasing (Brouette & Anton, 2001; Pagliaro & Pagliaro, 2009; Pagliaro & Pagliaro, *Clinical Patient Data Files*) with over 1 million new users being recorded annually from across all of North America (Spiller, 2004).[38] Among adolescents, these psychodepressants are now the fifth most commonly used drugs and substances of abuse after alcohol, caffeine, cannabis (marijuana), and nicotine (tobacco) (Pagliaro & Pagliaro, 2009).

### Trends

The reported lifetime prevalence of volatile solvent and inhalant use peaked at approximately 20% in the mid-1990s among North American adolescents 10 to 20 years of age (U.S. Department of Health and Human Services, 2001). Since that time, use has remained relatively constant at approximately 15% (Anderson & Loomis, 2003; Crocetti, 2008; Intelligence brief, 2001; Lorenc, 2003; Muilenburg & Johnson, 2006; J. F. Williams & Storck, 2007). For example, in its national survey of over 7,000 adolescents, the Partnership for a Drug-Free America (2006) found, in regard to inhalant use, that 20% of respondents reported lifetime use, 12% reported past-year use, and 7% reported past-month use (i.e., use during the previous 30 days).

Johnston, O'Malley, Bachman, et al. (2008), in their national study of adolescent drug use, found in 2007 that the use of inhalants within the previous year was reported by 8.3% of 8th-grade students, 6.6% of 10th-grade students, and 5% of 12th-grade students. More recently, in an analysis of the data for the Community Epidemiology Work Group of the NIDA, M. P. O'Brien (2008) found that 13.3% of U.S. high school students reported lifetime inhalant use. In their 2010 in-school survey of adolescent use of the drugs and substances of abuse, Johnston, O'Malley, Bachman, et al. (2010b) found that 14.5% of 8th-grade students, 12% of 10th-grade students, and 9% of 12th-grade students reported a lifetime prevalence of inhalant use. These reported percentages of inhalant use across grade levels are interesting because they decrease with increasing grade level—a pattern of use that is exactly the opposite of what is observed for virtually all of the other drugs and substances of

---

[36] This is only a partial list of commonly used volatile solvents. Literally hundreds of other volatile solvents can be, and have been, used for their psychodepressant actions. Between 1993 and 2008, U.S. poison control centers dealt with exposures to over 3,400 different volatile solvent and inhalant products (Marsolek, White, & Litovitz, 2010).

[37] Propane is used in some products (e.g., certain hair sprays and spray paints) as an aerosol propellant.

[38] Widespread use of the volatile solvents and inhalants among children and adolescents also is increasing worldwide, in both developed and developing countries, particularly among girls (e.g., Basu, Jhirwal, Singh, et al., 2004; Medina-Mora & Real, 2008).

abuse, which conversely increase with increasing grade level, at least through adolescence.

### Attraction to Use

Children and adolescents primarily use the volatile solvents and inhalants to get high. Although some adults,[39] including those who are homeless or have mental disorders (e.g., schizophrenia), sometimes use volatile solvents as their major drug of choice, children and adolescents currently comprise the largest group of users (Marsolek, White, & Litovitz, 2010; Pagliaro & Pagliaro, 2009; Spiller, 2004).

Virtually all of these children and adolescents are introduced to the volatile solvents and inhalants by their siblings, classmates, or friends. Among these children and adolescents, volatile solvent and inhalant use typically is a shared group experience. As such, peer pressure plays a significant role in regard to which volatile solvents and inhalants are used, where they are used, and their frequency of use. In their state-wide interviews of adolescents who were in youth services residential care, Perron and Howard (2008) found that those who had friends or siblings who used volatile solvents and inhalants were significantly more likely to associate little or no risk with volatile solvent and inhalant use and indicate intentions for future volatile solvent and inhalant use.

Although volatile solvent use has been reported for both boys and girls[40] as young as 4 or 5 years of age, young adolescent boys[41] are the major users. These boys usually are from low socioeconomic backgrounds and are often members of families that are experiencing severe financial problems, parental alcoholism, and other significant family discord.[42] Reports of lifetime use of the volatile solvents and inhalants also are extremely high among samples of youth involved with the juvenile justice system (Barclay, 2009; Howard, Balster, Cottler, et al., 2008; Howard & Perron, 2009).

The overwhelming majority of youth who have used the volatile solvents and inhalants can be categorized as experimental users. Few become regular, long-term users. Of the wide variety of volatile solvents and inhalants currently available in North America, the most abused products are correction fluid, gasoline, glue, lighter fluid, nitrous oxide, paint thinner, shoe polish, and spray paint (Pagliaro & Pagliaro, 2009; Wu, 2005). Some of the common signs and symptoms associated with the use of volatile solvents and inhalants for the achievement of their psychodepressant effects are presented in Table 1.9.

### Common Methods of Use

The volatile solvents are not deliberately ingested orally in order to get high.[43] Generally they are poured onto a rag, or into a balloon or plastic bag, that is then held up to the face, where the fumes are inhaled through the mouth or sniffed through the nostrils. Other common

---

[39] For example, volatile solvents and inhalants may be used by refrigeration and air conditioning repair technicians, who selectively use freon, and anesthetists, who selectively use nitrous oxide.

[40] Over the 1990s, published studies (e.g., McGarvey, Clavet, Mason, et al., 1999; Neumark, Delva, & Anthony, 1998) increasingly found no differences between boys and girls in regard to the use of the volatile solvents.

[41] Excluding North American adolescents of African or Asian descent, among whom volatile solvent and inhalant use has always been low.

[42] For example, use traditionally has been very high among preadolescents and adolescents of Aboriginal descent, including First Nations peoples and Inuits in Canada and American Indians and Alaskan Natives in the United States (Pagliaro & Pagliaro, 2009). Although the United States observed a significant decline in volatile solvent use among American Indian youth during the 1990s (Beauvais, Wayman, Jumper-Thurman, et al., 2002), Saylor, Fair, Deike-Sims, et al. (2007) found, in their study of preadolescent students, that 11.5% of 5th-, 6th, and 7th-grade students of Alaskan Native descent reported lifetime use of inhalants. In addition, since 2000, several Indian reserves in Canada reported volatile solvent use affecting over 50% of their youth (Dell, 2005; D. O'Brien, 2005; Pagliaro & Pagliaro, *Clinical Patient Data Files*).

[43] Volatile solvents may be accidentally ingested in poisoning cases, which may be fatal, particularly for young children. (See related discussion of unintentional childhood poisoning with the drugs and substances of abuse in Chapter 5, *Exposure to the Drugs and Substances of Abuse From Conception Through Childhood.*)

**TABLE 1.9    Volatile Solvents and Inhalants: Common Signs and Symptoms of Use**

| | |
|---|---|
| Anxiety | Inattentiveness |
| Anorexia | Incoordination |
| Apathy | Insomnia |
| Appearance of drunkenness | Irritability |
| Ataxia | Light-headedness |
| Belligerence | Memory impairment or loss |
| Burns | Muscle weakness |
| Cache (i.e., "stash") of solvents or inhalants in unusual location (e.g., bedroom, school locker) | Nausea |
| | Nystagmus |
| Chest pain | Paint stains on clothes or face |
| Chemical odor on breath or clothes | Perioral pyodermas |
| Cognitive impairment | Pneumonitis |
| Contact dermatitis, or inflammation of the skin by direct contact with the solvent or inhalant that may result in a rash or blistering of the skin and redness, swelling, and itching | Poor grooming and hygiene |
| | Rapid mood change |
| | Rash around the mouth or nose |
| Coughing | Red-colored nose |
| Dazed appearance | Rhinitis |
| Depression | Rhinorrhea |
| Diplopia | Runny or watery eyes |
| Disorientation | Slurred speech |
| Dizziness | Sneezing |
| Drowsiness | Sores around the mouth or nose |
| Drunken appearance | Spray paint speckles around the mouth or nose |
| Dypsnea | Strong chemical odor on the breath |
| Empty solvent or spray paint containers in unusual location (e.g., bedroom, school locker) | Strong chemical odor from clothing |
| | Sudden decrease in academic performance |
| Epistaxis, unexplained | Sudden decrease in school attendance |
| Encephalopathy (i.e., any brain dysfunction) | Thirst, unusual or persistent |
| Euphoria | Tinnitus |
| Excitability | Tremor |
| Falling asleep in class (often after recess) | Volatile solvent-soaked clothes or rags (e.g., in closet or school locker) |
| Fatigue | |
| Forgetfulness | Vomiting |
| Headache | Weight loss |
| Impaired judgment | Wheezing |

Note: These signs and symptoms, when uncharacteristic or cannot be explained by other causes for a child or adolescent, may be indicative of volatile solvent or inhalant use. However, they are not exclusive to their use and are thus not pathognomonic. However, the more signs and symptoms that a child or adolescent has, the more likely he or she is to be using volatile solvents or inhalants. Note also that, in addition to the individual differences that may be observed among children and adolescents in regard to these signs and symptoms, significant variability also occurs in relation to the specific volatile solvent or inhalant used and the dosage or amount used.

methods of use include spraying an aerosol product directly into the mouth or nose, placing a solvent-soaked rag in the mouth and inhaling the fumes as the rag is held in the mouth, and removing the lid of a solvent container and directly inhaling the fumes from the container. The use of volatile solvents and inhalants for their psychodepressant actions is variously referred to by users as airblasting, bagging, gasing, glading, huffing, oiling, painting, penny cleaning, sacking, sniffing, spraying, or Texas shoe-shining. Users, alone or in small groups, also simply may go into a small enclosed space (e.g., bathroom, car, or closet), spray several cans of computer duster spray, cooking spray, hair spray, or spray deodorant into the air, and then breathe in the fumes. They often warm the container by holding it in their hands or over an external heat source, such as the stove or radiator of a car. Warming the container significantly increases the volatility and amount of the solvent inhaled, which intensifies the resultant high (Pagliaro & Pagliaro, 2009).

## Association with Mental Disorders

Volatile solvent and inhalant use by children and adolescents often has been identified as presaging problematic behavior and the diagnosis of several mental disorders among older adolescents and young adults. For example, heroin use in young adulthood (Storr, Westergaard, & Anthony, 2005; Wu & Howard, 2007), problematic patterns of alcohol use in college students (Bennett, Walters, Miller, et al., 2000), and injection drug use among adolescents (Wu & Howard, 2007) have all been noted to follow significant histories of childhood or early-adolescent volatile solvent and inhalant use.

In regard to the nature of the relationships between volatile solvent and inhalant use and the problematic use of other drugs and substances of abuse among children and adolescents, we tend to agree with the observation made by Wu, Pilowsky, and Schlenger (2004) that, "Adolescents with an inhalant use disorder may represent a subgroup of highly troubled youths with multiple vulnerabilities" (p. 1206).

Other clinicians and researchers (e.g., Perron & Howard, 2009; Sakai, Hall, Mikulich-Gilbertson, et al., 2004) have shared similar observations. Thus, the use of volatile solvents and inhalants may precede the development of other substance use disorders and other mental disorders (OMDs). However, it does not appear to cause them. Some intervening variables(s), or cofactor(s), that may be genetically or environmentally controlled appear to be instrumental in this regard. For example, FAS/FASD or severe childhood physical or sexual abuse may, in some cases, be the factor primarily responsible for both the use of volatile solvents and inhalants and the related OMDs that are later diagnosed. (See related discussion in Chapter 8, *Dual Diagnosis Among Adolescents.*)

This view appears to account largely for the commonly observed related behavior of children and adolescents who live on reservations and reserves in the United States and Canada. As previously noted, Aboriginal peoples of North America (i.e., Alaska Natives, First Nations Peoples, American Indians, Inuits)—particularly children and adolescents—have the highest combined rate of volatile solvent and inhalant use of all groups in North America (Pagliaro & Pagliaro, 2009; Pagliaro & Pagliaro, *Clinical Patient Data Files*; Siqueira & Crandall, 2006). These children and adolescents also have extremely high rates of FAS/FASD (see Chapter 5, *Exposure to the Drugs and Substances of Abuse From Conception Through Childhood*), and the highest rates of: physical abuse (7%) (D. K. Bohn, 2003; Libby, Orton, Novins, et al., 2004); sexual abuse (4% to 5% overall, and much higher for girls than boys) (Duran, Malcoe, Skipper, et al., 2004; Koss, Yuan, Dightman, et al., 2003; Libby, Orton, Novins, et al., 2004); and extreme poverty, including food insecurity (Brenneman, Rhoades, & Chilton, 2006; Sarche & Spicer, 2008; Singleton, Holve, Groom, et al., 2009; Willows, Veugelers, Raine, et al., 2009). Consequently, they also suffer more than their fair share of "pains, disappointments, and impossible tasks" (Freud, 1930/1989). As identified in a study of adolescent volatile solvent and inhalant users, they used these drugs and substances of abuse as a means of mental escape (Siegel, Alvaro, Patel, et al., 2009, p. 597).

Novins and colleagues (e.g., Novins, Beals, & Mitchell, 2001; O'Connell, Novins, Beals, et al., 2007) have characterized the use of other drugs and substances of abuse as progressing from the use of volatile solvents or inhalants (i.e., serving as gateway drugs) by American Indians as consonant with stage theory. While we agree, it is probably worthwhile to state the obvious: that is, the reasons that children begin using volatile solvents and inhalants, as opposed to other drugs and substances of abuse, include that they are readily available at home or in school and are easy to use, as illustrated by the example of a 5-year-old sniffing glue rather than snorting cocaine.

## General Pharmacology

The various volatile solvents are used to rapidly achieve a short-lived disinhibition euphoria that is similar to that achieved with acute alcohol intoxication. Volatile solvents have no generally approved medical use and, thus, little is known about their actual human pharmacology because they were never intended for personal use by humans.[44] From what is known, they appear to demonstrate similar pharmacologic actions and desired and undesired effects and toxicities. These actions are generally associated with their concentration, method of use, and frequency of use. Once inhaled into the lungs, the volatile solvents and inhalants are readily absorbed into the bloodstream and rapidly reach their psychotropic site of action—the brain. The effects of the volatile solvents and inhalants occur within minutes of inhalation and, depending on the solvent or inhalant used, its concentration, and its method of use, last from 10 to 60 minutes—the perfect time frame for a child to get high at school during lunch or recess and return to class without his or her use of the volatile solvent or inhalant being readily detected by the teacher.

### Proposed Mechanism of Psychodepressant Action

The volatile solvents and inhalants depress the CNS through a variety of mechanisms that have not been fully elucidated. The result of use is a rapid and short-lived disinhibition euphoria that is very similar to acute alcohol intoxication. As previously noted, the volatile solvents have no generally approved medical use, and little is known about their actual human pharmacology because they were never intended for human personal use involving inhalation. However, most of the inhalant gases were developed for use during surgical procedures as anesthetics. Thus, there is more information about their therapeutic use and toxicities in humans.

### Common Toxicities

The human data that are available are predominantly based on case studies and reports of either accidental or deliberate overdosage. Still, even in these cases, it is extremely difficult to identify the exact cause or mechanism associated with the observed toxicity for three reasons:

1. Products (e.g., cleaning products; glues) are often reformulated as new or improved products, which increases the likelihood of changes being made to their ingredients and concentrations.

2. The nature of the case reports, which are based largely on interviews of children and adolescents, including, in many cases, friends of the deceased who have been engaged in the same activity.

3. The nature of the volatile solvent or inhalant, as noted above in regard to its proposed mechanism of psychodepressant action.

For example, in relation to the third reason listed, a pregnant adolescent girl may huff gasoline and subsequently give birth to a baby with FAS/FASD-characteristic physical features. Consequently, because these features also have been associated with toluene, which is found in gasoline, they may be identified as being the result of toluene embryopathy. (See Chapter 5, *Exposure to the Drugs and Substances of Abuse From Conception Through Childhood.*) However, gasoline typically contains more than 150 different chemicals, including benzene, ethyl benzene, MTBE, toluene, and other chemicals that may vary with the source of the crude petroleum base, the manufacturer,

---

[44] No controlled studies on the use of volatile solvents by humans have been conducted, and none is expected to be conducted in the future. The major reason for the lack of research in this area is the difficulty in designing ethical research studies that do not pose a high risk to subjects. The data that are available include: published retrospective studies obtained from emergency room medical histories and progress notes; published medical case histories that report observed toxicities, related sequelae, and treatment; reports and statistics on overdose deaths; and published qualitative studies and anecdotal reports obtained from volatile solvent and inhalant users who may also share this information over various Internet sites.

the production process, and even the time of year. Therefore, while ascribing the noted effects to toluene may be correct, it is at best only speculative. In addition, it is highly likely that the pregnant adolescent also consumed alcohol during her pregnancy.

Marsolek, White, and Litoritz (2010) analyzed data from the National Poison Data System of 35,453 cases involving volatile solvents and inhalants reported to U.S. poison control centers from 1993 to 2008. Gasoline, paint, and propellants were the volatile solvents and inhalants most frequently involved, but air fresheners, butane, and propane had the highest associated fatality rates. In terms of lethality, Spiller (2004), using national data from the Toxic Exposure Surveillance System, found that air fresheners, butane, gasoline, and propane were responsible for the majority of deaths. Although the use of volatile solvents and inhalants for their psychodepressant actions is generally reported as occurring roughly equally among boys and girls, 75% of the poison system cases involved boys. This finding suggests, as noted by Marsolek, White, and Litoritz (2010), "that boys may pursue riskier usage behaviors" (p. 906).

The toxicity of the solvents and inhalants are difficult to categorize because of their diverse nature. However, in general, they typically are directly irritating to the respiratory system upon inhalation, the GI system when orally ingested (e.g., in the context of accidental poisoning or deliberate suicide attempts), and the cutaneous system when, for example, they are inadvertently spilled or splashed on the face, or in the eyes, or otherwise come into contact with the hands, legs, or other parts of the body. In addition, as noted by their classification as psychodepressants, they can directly cause varying degrees of CNS depression, ranging from drowsiness or mild sedation to profound sedation. They also can cause dose-dependent respiratory depression that can, in the worst-case scenario, be fatal (Pagliaro & Pagliaro, 2009).

**Acute Toxicities**   The signs and symptoms of acute toxicity that have been associated with

the use of the volatile solvents include anorexia; fatigue; slowed, unclear thinking; and thirst. The volatile solvents primarily adversely affect the central and peripheral nervous systems. Most volatile solvents seem to cause a rapid depression of the CNS resulting in an alcohol-like disinhibition euphoria. Concomitantly, there is drowsiness and gross motor and fine motor incoordination that result in impaired ambulation and slurred speech. Amnesia also can occur, and hallucinations occasionally have been reported. The extent of these toxic effects depends on the volatile solvent or inhalant used, the amount used, and the acute duration of use. If the user is otherwise healthy, the toxicities associated with the acute use of volatile solvents are generally temporary and reversible. However, acute toxicity can be fatal, as described in the following sections.

*Fatalities*   Fatalities associated with child and adolescent use of the volatile solvents and inhalants for the purpose of getting high was first reported in 1970 (Bass, 1970). Two fatalities attributed to butane and propane abuse serve to emphasize the potential for death. As shared by Siegel and Wason (1990):

> An 11-year-old boy collapsed in a movie theater bathroom. A butane cigarette lighter fuel container and a plastic bag were found next to him. He also had several bottles of typewriter correction fluid in his pocket. Cardiopulmonary resuscitation was instituted; efforts proved unsuccessful and he was pronounced dead shortly thereafter. Post mortem examination showed no evidence of organic disease or anatomic cause of death. Toxicologic analysis confirmed the presence of butane in the patient's blood and lung tissue.
>
> A 15-year-old boy was found unconscious in a backyard. Three companions related that the four teenagers had taken a 20-gallon propane tank from the family gas grill, placed some of the gas in a plastic bag and were inhaling it in order to get high. They also engaged in "torch breathing" whereby they purposefully exhaled the propane gas and ignited it. The subject collapsed soon after inhaling the gas; fumes,

ignited by a match, resulted in a flash fire. The patient did not sustain any burns. He could not be resuscitated and died en route to the hospital. Post mortem examination in this case, too, failed to reveal an organic cause of death. Propane was detected in the blood and lung tissues. (p. 1638)

In North America, approximately 200 deaths occur annually in relation to the use of the volatile solvents and inhalants. Related deaths have been reported among children as young as 8 years of age (Maxwell, 2001). These volatile solvent and inhalant-related deaths have been attributed to severe damage to internal body organs, as well as accidental injury, asphyxiation or suffocation, and sudden sniffing death (see the following sections for further discussion).

*Accidental Injury*  Death by accidental injury typically results from falls and other events that may be associated with the poor judgment and impulsive behavior that occurs during intoxication with a volatile solvent or inhalant. Death by accidental injury also may be due to fires associated with the use of these flammable substances or to head injuries sustained when losing consciousness or passing out. (Also see the next section, "Asphyxiation.")

*Asphyxiation*  Asphyxiation, or suffocation, has been associated directly with the method of volatile solvent and inhalant use as well as the pharmacology of volatile solvents and inhalants as psychodepressants. Quite often, a plastic bag is placed over the nose and mouth or the entire head to contain the fumes of the volatile solvent and, thus, increase the amount inhaled. This method of use creates the risk of death as a result of fainting, or losing consciousness, and suffocating as a result of the plastic bag being left in place over the

nose and mouth. Death in these cases also is associated with the amount of the volatile solvent or inhalant used. For example, any of the volatile solvents, when used in sufficient quantities, can depress the CNS and cause respiratory arrest. In addition, the inhalation of butane may induce severe laryngeal edema and laryngospasm resulting in death. The inhalation of propane and other volatile inhalants directly displaces oxygen from the surrounding atmosphere that can induce asphyxia and resultant death. In some cases, death has been a deliberate outcome of a suicide attempt (Gross & Klys, 2002). However, in other cases, it has been the undesired consequence of deliberately using propane to induce hypoxia in order to obtain associated autoerotic stimulation (Jackowski, Römhild, Aebi, et al., 2005; Musshoff, Padosch, Kroener, et al., 2006; Sauvageau & Racette, 2006).

*Sudden Sniffing Death*  Sudden sniffing death may occur among children and adolescents who use the volatile solvents and inhalants as a result of heart failure or severe respiratory depression. For example, the use of halogenated (e.g., fluorinated) hydrocarbons (e.g., freon), in particular, has been associated with fatal cardiac dysrhythmias.[45] As well, any volatile solvent or inhalant can cause paralysis of the respiratory centers if a large enough dose is absorbed into the bloodstream. In most cases, however, sudden sniffing death occurs when a child or adolescent has been engaged in some type of strenuous activity (e.g., running) or has experienced sudden unexpected stress (e.g., being unexpectedly discovered by a parent or teacher) immediately after heavy use of the solvent or inhalant. Both strenuous activity and unexpected stress cause the sudden release of epinephrine in the body. It is believed that volatile solvents and inhalants increase the

---

[45]The use of nonhalogenated hydrocarbons, including butane, isobutane, and propane, also has been associated with fatal cardiac dysrhythmias (Edwards & Wenstone, 2000; Girard, Le Tacon, Maria, et al., 2008; Sugie, Sasaki, Hashimoto, et al., 2004; Williams & Cole, 1998). Some researchers (e.g., El Menyar, 2006; El-Menyar, El-Tawil, & Al Suwaidi, 2005) have suggested that these heart attacks may be a result of volatile solvent or inhalant-induced coronary artery spasm.

heart's sensitivity to the stimulant actions of epinephrine and thus contribute to the heart attack (i.e., myocardial infarction) experienced by the child or adolescent (Pagliaro & Pagliaro, 2009).[46]

**Chronic Toxicities**   Regular, long-term use of the volatile solvents (e.g., gasoline) and inhalants can result in gradual and progressive polyneuropathy, including optic neuropathy and peripheral neuropathy. In addition, cerebellar ataxia, encephalopathy, and Parkinsonism may occur, depending on the solvent or inhalant used (Burns, Shneker, & Juel, 2001; Williams & Storck, 2007).[47]

Toluene (methylbenzene) is one of the most common compounds found in volatile solvents, particularly glues, and its use causes a central neuropathy characterized by encephalopathy with ataxia, behavioral changes (e.g., self-mutilation), convulsions, and hallucinations. Regular, long-term use of toluene has been associated with the deterioration of the CNS characterized by neuropsychiatric disorders (e.g., dementia), persistent cerebellar ataxia, and peripheral neurotoxicity (Filley, Halliday, & Kleinschmidt-DeMasters, 2004). Although reflexes are normal, profound muscle weakness and rhabdomyolysis have been reported. The profound weakness may be related to electrolyte imbalance, particularly hypokalemia (Baskerville, Tichenor, & Rosen, 2001). Renal toxicity with severe

electrolyte imbalances has been reported among adults, as have renal calculi. These toxicities are thought to be due to increased renal excretion of hippurate, a metabolite of toluene. Other effects have been reported, such as abdominal pain, nausea, and vomiting, including hematemesis.

Although many of the volatile solvents and inhalants are associated with significant morbidity and mortality, currently they are used widely by North American children and adolescents, primarily because of their: 1) desired actions; 2) universal availability; and 3) low cost.

### Physical and Psychological Dependence

The use of toluene as a means to achieve desired psychodepressant actions has been associated with both physical and psychological dependence. However, the abuse potential for the majority of the other volatile solvents and inhalants has not been well characterized and is still not completely understood. It now appears that tolerance to the desired actions of the volatile solvents generally occurs with regular, long-term use. In addition, several signs and symptoms, including anxiety, depression, dizziness, insomnia, irritability, and tremors, are commonly observed among users when regular, long-term volatile solvent use is abruptly discontinued. However, it has not been established whether these signs and symptoms are

---

[46] The majority of reported cases of sudden sniffing death over the past two decades, which involved children and adolescents deliberately abusing the volatile solvents and inhalants (primarily, butane), have originated primarily in Europe and the Middle East.

[47] As previously noted, volatile solvents are usually available to the public not as pure single chemicals but as mixtures containing two or more ingredients in a commercial product. A variety of additives are added to improve performance, stability, or production of these products. Often a second minor ingredient that does not cause the high is more dangerous to the health of the user than the major high-producing ingredient. In addition, the various ingredients sometimes can work together, causing serious toxicity or death, even though, when used individually, toxicity would not result.

Manufacturers frequently change the ingredients of their volatile solvent products or their concentrations (e.g., labels that read *new, improved, reformulated, extra strength*) so that a product that was safe and nontoxic previously may subsequently, due to a change in formulation or concentration, cause serious toxicity or death. For example, during the early 1970s, seven young men used a popular lacquer thinner that they had safely used many times previously. However, the product was reformulated to decrease production costs during an oil embargo. The result was death for one of the men as a result of respiratory failure; permanent respiratory paralysis for two of the men; and severe muscle and nerve damage for four of the men, who subsequently required the use of wheelchairs. From this tragic example, it is apparent that the potential for serious toxicity accompanies the use of all volatile solvents—even those that have been used previously and were believed to be safe.

physical or psychological in origin (Pagliaro & Pagliaro, 2009).

### Overdosage

Relatively few overdosages have been associated with the use of the volatile solvents and inhalants other than those occurring as a result of accidental poisonings among infants and toddlers. (See related discussion in the earlier "Acute Toxicities" section under "Fatalities" and "Accidental Injury.")

## CHAPTER SUMMARY

This chapter presented an overview of the prevalence and characteristics of North American child and adolescent use of the psychodepressants—the opiate analgesics, particularly heroin and oxycodone (OxyContin®); the sedative-hypnotics, particularly alcohol, the benzodiazepines, and GHB; and the volatile solvents and inhalants, particularly air fresheners, butane, gasoline, and propane, which have been associated with the highest rates of death among North American children and adolescents. The general pharmacology of these drugs and substances of abuse also was presented with attention to their proposed mechanisms of action and related common acute and chronic toxicities, including physical and psychological dependence, and overdosage.

Changing trends in the use of these drugs and substances of abuse, including their methods of use, also were presented. For example, the intravenous use of opiate analgesics generally has been replaced with intranasal insufflation (i.e., snorting) and pulmonary inhalation (i.e., smoking). Other trends include the "pharming" of prescription sedative-hypnotics and the troubling illicit use of GHB in the perpetration of date-rape and other serious crimes. Binge drinking among adolescents and young adults, particularly college students, has increased significantly along with the more recent trend of drinking large amounts of alcohol with the concomitant drinking of caffeinated energy drinks in an attempt to prevent or slow the occurrence of drunkenness. Also troubling is the increased use of alcohol by adolescent girls and young adult women while pregnant, regardless of the potential risk of FAS/FASD. While volatile solvents and inhalants are generally used experimentally by children and adolescent boys, they continue to be related to several fatalities each year related to internal body organ damage, accidental injury, asphyxiation, and sudden sniffing death. Aboriginal peoples of North America, particularly children and adolescents, continue to have the highest combined rate of volatile solvent and inhalant use.

This chapter also identified the potential limitations of government-supported and sponsored national surveys and other studies that may be biased and restricted in the generalizability of their findings and subsequent reporting of lower levels of child and adolescent use of the drugs and substances of abuse. These limitations may occur because of methodological and sampling flaws, such as the neglect of groups of children and adolescents at particularly high risk—including those without land-line phones, those who are school drop-outs, and those who are homeless runaways, living on the streets. Regardless, the various psychodepressants continue to be readily available, and, often mediated by peer influences and other related factors, children and adolescents continue to commonly use these drugs and substances of abuse for their psychodepressant actions and effects.

# *The Psychostimulants*

## INTRODUCTION

The psychostimulants comprise a major class of natural and synthetic drugs and substances of abuse. (See Table 2.1.) As their name implies, they excite the central nervous system (CNS), resulting in varying degrees of euphoria and other desired effects, such as increased wakefulness, vigilance, and relief from hunger and fatigue. This chapter describes the prevalence and characteristics of the use of the psychostimulants by North American children and adolescents. It also considers the general pharmacology of these drugs and substances of abuse—their proposed mechanisms of action and common toxicities, including their potential for physical and psychological dependence. Particular attention is given to the four subclasses of psychostimulants (see Figure 2.1) that are particularly used by North American children and adolescents: amphetamines, caffeine, cocaine, and nicotine.

## AMPHETAMINES

Over the last decade, children and adolescents have been increasingly attracted to the use of the amphetamines—variously known as amps, bennies, bombers, cartwheels, crank, crystal, dexies, ice, pep pills, speed, truck drivers, uppers, wake-ups, and West Coasts—including those that are primarily prescribed for the medical management of attention-deficit/hyperactivity disorder (A-D/HD). These latter amphetamines include the mixed amphetamines (Adderall®—also known as addies or tic-tacs; lisdexamfetamine (Vyvanse®, LDX),[1] a more recently developed amphetamine that is beginning to be more widely used to treat A-D/HD (Blick & Keating, 2007; Popovic, Bhattacharya, & Sivaswamy, 2009); and methylphenidate (Ritalin®, Rs, the smart drug), a psychostimulant that is very closely related to the amphetamines and that has been extensively used for decades to treat A-D/HD. In this context, some adolescents who have A-D/HD use their own prescription psychostimulants to get high or, more commonly, adolescents who do not have A-D/HD buy or steal the prescription psychostimulants for their own use from children and adolescents for whom they were prescribed—their classmates and younger siblings (Pagliaro & Pagliaro, 2009; Wilens, Adler, Adams, et al., 2008).

During the 1980s, the use of the amphetamines was largely replaced by the use of cocaine among adolescents and young adults. (See the "Cocaine" section in this chapter.) However, by the mid-1990s, there was a renewed interest in the use of the amphetamines, particularly methamphetamine, as a less expensive alternative to cocaine. This interest was fostered by the increased availability of both the powdered form of methamphetamine[2] and

---

[1] Lisdexamfetamine is actually an inactive prodrug that is metabolically converted to dextroamphetamine.

[2] The powder form of methamphetamine (crank, speed, Tina) is generally of lower purity than the crystalline form (i.e., 60% to 70% versus 90% to 100% purity). In addition, it is less coarse, or sharp, than the crystalline form, even when the crystalline form is ground. Thus, the powdered form, being less irritating to the nasal passages, is the preferred form for intranasal insufflation, or snorting. The powdered form of methamphetamine also can be orally ingested and, following dissolution, may be intravenously injected. Although the powdered form can be smoked, this method of use is less popular because the pyrolysis of the methamphetamine combined with the impurities and adulterants found in the powdered form decreases the amount of drug that is vaporized and delivered to the pulmonary system for absorption.

TABLE 2.1   Psychostimulants

| Subclassification/Generic Name | Brand/Trade Names [®] | Common Street Names[a] |
|---|---|---|
| *Amphetamines* | | |
| Amphetamine[b] | | Ace; amp; copilot |
| Benzphetamine | Didrex® | |
| Dextroamphetamine | Dexedrine® | Dex; dexies |
| Lisdexamfetamine | Vyvanse® | LDX |
| Mephentermine | Wyamine® | |
| Methamphetamine* | Desoxyn® | Crank; crystal meth; glass; hillbilly crack; ice; jib; meth; stove top; Tina; West Coast |
| Mixed Amphetamines[c] * | Adderall® | Addies; blueberries; oranges; tic-tacs |
| *Miscellaneous Psychostimulants* | | |
| Armodafinil | Nuvigil® | |
| Atomoxetine | Strattera® | |
| Betel Cutch | | Betel quid; betel nut; paan; quid |
| Caffeine* | | Caffy; java; joe |
| Cathinone | | Abyssinian tea; cat; kat; khat; quat |
| Cocaine* | | Blow; C; coke; crack; flake; lady; nose candy; powder; snow; toot |
| Diethylpropion | Tenuate® | |
| Ephedrine* | | Brigham tea; desert tea; Mormon tea; squaw tea |
| Ibogaine | | Bocca; boga; iboga |
| Mazindol | Sanorex® | |
| Mephedrone | | Bath salts; drone; MCAT; meow; meph; miaow |
| Methcathinone | | Cat; ephedrone; kitty; star; wannabe-speed |
| Methylphenidate* | Concerta®; Ritalin® | Jif; mph; rs; the smart drug |
| Modafinil[d] | Alertec®; Provigil® | |
| Nicotine* | | Baccy; butts; cancer stick; cig; coffin nails; lung darts; plug; smokes |
| Pemoline | Cylert® | |
| Phendimetrazine | Anorex-SR®; Bontril®; Prelu-2® | Diet pills; green and yellows |
| Phentermine | Fastin®; Ionamin®; Obenix® | |
| Prolintane[e] | | Katovit |
| Sibutramine | Meridia® | |

[a] Partial list. Examples of the most common street names are provided, when available. See  Pagliaro and Pagliaro (2009) for a comprehensive listing of the drugs and substances of abuse and their common street names.

[b] Amphetamine, in its salt forms (i.e., amphetamine aspartate and amphetamine sulfate) is legally available only in North America in the combination, mixed amphetamines product, Adderall®.

[c] This product contains the amphetamine salt forms amphetamine aspartate and amphetamine sulfate. It also contains dextroamphetamine.

[d] Johnston, O'Malley, Bachman, et al. (2010b), in their 2010 in-school survey of adolescent drug and substance use, found that 1.3% of 12th-grade students reported the use of modafinil (Alertec®, Provigil®) during the previous year.

[e] Prolintane is a sympathomimetic amine with pharmacological properties very similar to the amphetamines.

*Note: The psychostimulants that are most commonly used by children and adolescents are indicated by an asterisk.

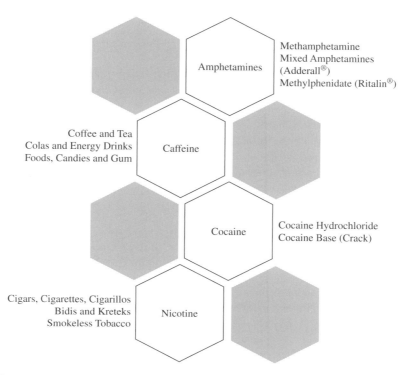

**Figure 2.1   Psychostimulants Commonly Used by Children and Adolescents**

the crystalline form.[3] The use of the crystalline, or smokable, form had its North American origin in Hawaii from where it quickly spread to California (hence the street name West Coast) and, subsequently, across North America (Gonzales, Mooney, & Rawson, 2010; Pagliaro & Pagliaro, 2009). The use of methamphetamine has become prevalent across both urban and rural areas in the midwestern and southern states (hence the street name hillbilly crack) (Hauer, 2010; Sexton, Carlson, Leukefeld, et al., 2006).

During the first decade of the 21st century, bisexual and gay adolescent boys and young men—regardless of continental descent or human immunodeficiency virus (HIV) status—were identified as having the highest percentage of methamphetamine use in North American (Hurt, Torrone, Green, et al., 2010; Kelly, Parsons, & Wells, 2006; Mimiaga, Reisner, Fontaine, et al., 2010; Parsons, Halkitis, & Bimbi, 2006).[4] Another troubling trend that developed during the latter part of the decade was the increased use of methamphetamine particularly by adolescent girls, 16 to 17 years of age (Wu, Schlenger, & Galvin, 2006). However, as the second decade of the 21st century began, these trends appeared to be already changing. The next section presents an overview of the prevalence and characteristics

---

[3] The crystalline form of methamphetamine (crystal, crystal meth, glass, ice) is the purest form of the drug with available purity generally exceeding 90%. This form of methamphetamine is preferentially used by pulmonary inhalation (i.e., smoked)—heating it in a glass pipe and inhaling the vaporized methamphetamine. The crystalline form is not intranasally insufflated because it cannot be ground finely enough—when ground, the resultant powder often contains small, sharp crystals that can irritate or actually damage (i.e., cut), the mucosa of the nasal passages.

[4] The typical North American methamphetamine user was identified as young male of European descent (M. P. O'Brien, 2008; Pagliaro & Pagliaro, 2009).

of the use of the amphetamines and related psychostimulants by North American children and adolescents with particular attention to both continuing and new trends of use. (Also see Chapter 5, *Exposure to the Drugs and Substances of Abuse From Conception Through Childhood*, for related discussion.)

A decade ago, over 2% of North Americans reported methamphetamine use (Anglin, Burke, Perrochet, et al., 2000). During this time, methamphetamine, which quickly became widely available, was obtained from illicit methamphetamine laboratories. These "meth labs" ranged from well-organized, highly efficient laboratories that were capable of producing 50 kg (110 lbs) of methamphetamine per week, to university laboratories and the kitchens and bathrooms of small apartments where amounts of less than 30 g (1 oz) per week were produced.[5] A significant percentage of the illegal methamphetamine production and sale in North America was handled by drug-trafficking organizations and various formal criminal gangs (e.g., Asian street gangs and organized crime syndicates; outlaw motorcycle gangs, such as the Hell's Angels; and the Mexican mafia). Although relatively easy to produce, the improper order of the mixing of ingredients or the lack of quality control during the preparation of the methamphetamine can result in the formation of toxic by-products.[6]

The use of methamphetamine, primarily in its crystalline form—crystal meth, glass, or ice—soared between 2005 to 2010, as a result of its ready availability, relatively low cost, and ability to rapidly achieve high blood concentrations (and desired psychostimulant effects) without intravenous injection (M. P. O'Brien, 2008).[7] "Crystal meth," smoked in much the same way as crack cocaine, also produces a longer duration of desired psychostimulant effects than does crack cocaine (i.e., 4–8 hours versus 15–60 minutes). As such, it quickly became the "poor man's cocaine."

### Prevalence and Characteristics of the Use of the Amphetamines among North American Children and Adolescents

In their review and analysis of the data available from the 2002 National Survey on Drug Use and Health for adolescents and young adults 16 to 23 years of age, Wu, Schlenger, and Galvin (2006) found that 4.9% of participants reported lifetime use of methamphetamine and 1.8% reported use within the past year. They also found that the highest past-year use for methamphetamine correlated best with participants who were: girls rather than boys; 16 to 17 years old rather than older participants; and of multiple continental descent rather than single continental descent. In another study, Lampinen, McGhee, and Martin (2006) found a significantly increased odds ratio for previous-year use of methamphetamine among high school girls who identified themselves as bisexual or lesbian.[8]

---

[5] Laboratories capable of producing 10 pounds (4.5 kg) or more of methamphetamine per day are generally referred to as super labs. Most of these super labs are now located in southern California and along the border separating Mexico and the southwestern states. They generally are operated by various Mexican drug-trafficking organizations, including the Mexican mafia (Pagliaro & Pagliaro, 2009; United Press International, 2010). Because North American production and distribution of the major constituent ingredients (i.e., ephedrine and pseudoephedrine) used in the production of methamphetamine are under Drug Enforcement Administration regulation, currently the majority of these chemicals are produced in China and India and subsequently sold to drug producers in Mexico (Booth & O'Connor, 2010).

[6] Sometimes formulas are printed in reference texts (e.g., drug manufacturers' catalogs) or on the Internet in incorrect order. Serious toxicities have resulted from following such recipes. For example, when methamphetamine is produced improperly, mercury, a toxic heavy metal associated with brain damage, is a common contaminant.

[7] Similar to cocaine, lysergic acid diethylamide (LSD), and various other drugs and substances of abuse, there are various routes of administration for methamphetamine, including rectal insertion (Gupta, Bailey, & Lovato, 2009), particularly by bisexual and gay adolescent boys and young men.

[8] Adolescent girls, regardless of sexual orientation, are more likely to smoke methamphetamine than inject it intravenously (Pagliaro & Pagliaro, *Clinical Patient Data Files*).

In their national review of adolescent drug use in the United States for 2007, Johnston, O'Malley, Bachman, et al. (2008) found that approximately 8% of all 12th graders in their survey reported having used amphetamines during the year prior to the survey with the highest rates of use being reported by adolescent boys of Hispanic descent. In terms of availability, half of these 12th graders reported that the amphetamines were either fairly easy or very easy to obtain. In comparison, lifetime amphetamine use was reported by 6.2% of Canadian adolescents and young adults, 15 to 24 years of age, who participated in the study (Health Canada, 2010b). M. P. O'Brien (2008), referencing data obtained for the Community Epidemiology Work Group (CEWG) of the National Institute on Drug Abuse (NIDA), found that 4.4% of U.S. high school students reported lifetime use of methamphetamine. In a study that involved the analysis of data from the Youth Risk Behavior Surveillance System for 2009, Eaton, Kann, Kinchen, et al. (2010) found similar results for methamphetamine use. Nationally, 4.1% of U.S. high school students reported previous use of methamphetamine on at least one occasion (ranging from 2.3% to 7.9% across state surveys). The highest rate of use (5.9%) was reported by 12th-grade adolescent boys of Hispanic descent. In comparison, in a study of Canadian adolescents and young adults 15 to 24 years of age, 1.8% reported lifetime use of methamphetamine (Health Canada, 2010b). In a study of youth in treatment for drug and substance abuse who were younger than 18 years of age, Hopfer, Mendelson, Van Leeuwen, et al. (2006) found that 30.2% reported having used methamphetamine.

Several studies and reports (e.g., Beauvais, Jumper-Thurman, & Burnside, 2008; Mullins, 2010) have noted that adolescents of American Indian descent, particularly those who have dropped out of school, have higher rates of methamphetamine use than do their non–American Indian cohorts. Rates of methamphetamine use are particularly high among Alaskan Natives. Rates also are high among American Indian youth living on reservations in the southwestern states of the United States where methamphetamine-related commerce often flourishes, including the operation of "meth labs" (Mullins, 2010; Pagliaro & Pagliaro, *Clinical Patient Data Files*).

However, by 2010, methamphetamine use was slowly beginning to be replaced with cocaine—the "rich man's drug" (see "Cocaine" section, "Prevalence and Characteristics of Use," later in this chapter). For example, Johnston, O'Malley, Bachman, et al. (2010b) reported that, between 2009 and 2010, lifetime prevalence of methamphetamine use declined among 10th-grade students, from 2.8% to 2.5%, and among 12th-grade students, from 2.4% to 2.3%. In addition, they found that the use of crystal meth, or ice, declined among 12th-grade students, from 2.1% to 1.8%, over the same time period. It may seem ironic or surprising to some readers that the same attributes that made methamphetamine so popular—its widespread availability, cheaper price, and longer duration of action in comparison to cocaine—are now contributing to its decline in popularity as it increasingly becomes pejoratively known as the "poor man's cocaine" (Pagliaro & Pagliaro, *Clinical Patient Data Files*).

### General Pharmacology

The amphetamines produce potent actions on both the central and peripheral nervous systems. Centrally, their actions are very similar to the endogenous catecholamine neurotransmitters dopamine, epinephrine, norepinephrine, and serotonin. As sympathomimetics,[9] the amphetamines are chemically related to ephedrine, the active ingredient of

---

[9] The sympathomimetics are drugs that mimic the actions of the sympathetic nervous system. The sympathetic nervous system is involved with the homeostatic regulation of heart rate, force of cardiac contraction, vasomotor tone, blood pressure, bronchial airway tone, and carbohydrate and fatty acid metabolism during periods of physical activity or psychological stress.

*(continued)*

the herb ephedra. Compared with ephedrine and other catecholamines, the amphetamines produce greater CNS stimulation (e.g., enhanced alertness, increased psychomotor activity, and suppressed feelings of drowsiness or fatigue). These actions have made the amphetamines attractive as performance enhancers to a variety of people, including aircraft pilots, athletes, college and university students, entertainers, long-haul truck drivers, soldiers, and surgeons.

### Proposed Mechanism of Psychostimulant Action

The amphetamines are indirect-acting psychostimulants. As such, they stimulate the release of the biogenic amines (i.e., dopamine, norepinephrine, and serotonin) from the presynaptic nerve terminal storage vesicles, particularly those that are located in the midbrain. They also inhibit the reuptake of the biogenic amines, primarily by blocking the dopamine transporter and the monoamine transporter-2. A simplified, stylized representation of the principal sites and mechanisms of the psychostimulant action of the amphetamines is shown in Figure 2.2. These actions result in CNS stimulation and other expected pharmacologic effects, including anorexia, bronchodilation, contraction of the urinary bladder sphincter, elevated mood, hypertension, mydriasis, tachycardia, and increased wakefulness. (Also see the next section, "Common Toxicities.")

### Common Toxicities

The use of the amphetamines has been associated with several undesired, harmful effects, or toxicities. These effects can be either acute or chronic and can range from mild (e.g., anxiety) to severe (e.g., psychosis). Amphetamine overdosage may be fatal, particularly among children. The frequen    cy and severity of the undesired or toxic effects associated with the amphetamines are generally related to:

- The amount used (e.g., 40 mg versus 1000 mg)
- The method of use (e.g., oral ingestion versus intravenous injection)
- The frequency of use (e.g., twice a week versus every hour)
- The period of use (e.g., several days versus several years)
- The specific characteristics of the user (e.g., a new, or novice, user versus a regular, long-term user)[10]

Amphetamine-related toxicities can be conveniently divided into acute toxicities and chronic toxicities (Pagliaro & Pagliaro, 2009).

**Acute Toxicities**   Acute toxicities generally begin within 20 to 60 minutes after amphetamine oral ingestion or within 30 to 60 seconds after intravenous injection or pulmonary inhalation. Acute psychological toxicities may include: aggressiveness,[11] agitation, anxiety, confusion, delirium, euphoric grandiosity,

---

[9](*continued*)

These responses usually are controlled by the hormones epinephrine (adrenaline) and norepinephrine (noradrenaline) that circulate in the bloodstream and act at $\alpha$, $\beta_1$, and $\beta_2$ receptors. Agonist action at $\alpha$-receptors is associated with decreased gut motility, diaphoresis, glycogenolysis, mydriasis, piloerection, urinary retention, and vasoconstriction. Agonist action at $\beta_1$ receptors is associated with decreased gut motility and secretions, increased heart rate, lipolysis, and renin release. Agonist action at $\beta_2$ receptors is associated with bronchodilation, fine skeletal muscle tremor, glycogenolysis, mast cell stabilization, and vasodilation of blood vessels supplying the skeletal  muscles.

[10] In addition, the pattern and mechanism of methamphetamine-related neurotoxicity is suggested to be similar to the neurotoxicity related to HIV infection (Yamamoto, Moszczynska, & Gudelsky, 2010). HIV infection consequently augments methamphetamine-related neurotoxicity. This augmentation becomes particularly significant in the context of the significant use of methamphetamine by bisexual and gay adolescent boys and young adult men—regardless of HIV status. (See earlier discussion.)

[11] This aggressiveness has been noted to result in violent confrontations, particularly involving, for example, users not sharing their drugs equally or stealing them from one another (Sexton, Carlson, Leukefeld, et al., 2009).

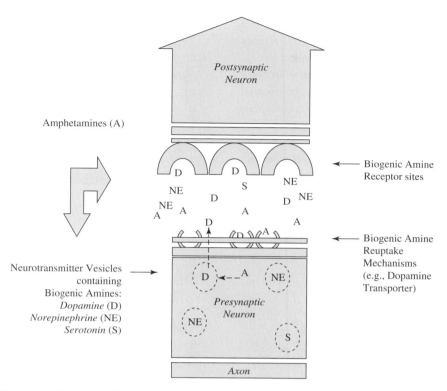

Amphetamines (A)

Postsynaptic
Neuron

Biogenic Amine
Receptor sites

D          D          NE
              S
     NE         D   NE
NE          D
A     A          A
    D                A
              A

Biogenic Amine
Reuptake
Mechanisms
(e.g., Dopamine
Transporter)

Neurotransmitter Vesicles
containing
Biogenic Amines:
*Dopamine* (D)
*Norepinephrine* (NE)
*Serotonin* (S)

D  ◄ - - A       NE

Presynaptic
Neuron

NE

S

Axon

**Figure 2.2   Amphetamines: Mechanism of Psychostimulant Action**
Reproduced with permission from: L. A. Pagliaro & A. M. Pagliaro (2009), *Pagliaros' Comprehensive Guide to Drugs and Substances of Abuse* (2nd ed.) (p. 25). Washington DC: American Pharmacists Association.

hallucinations, hostility, hyperactivity, hyper-vigilance (hyperalertness), impaired judgment, insomnia, irritability, loquacity (i.e., talkative-ness) extending to pressured speech (i.e., loud and uncontrollable talking), panic attacks, and restlessness. Other, more serious psychological toxicities (e.g., psychosis) may occur within 24 hours following amphetamine use (also see later discussion of Amphetamine Psychosis in the next section).

Acute physical toxicities associated with amphetamine use are more likely to occur among novice and occasional users than among regular, long-term users who also are likely to be high-dosage users. These toxicities include: bruxism, cardiac dysrhythmias, chest pain, coma, convulsions, cramps, diaphoresis, dizziness, dysuria, headache, heart palpitations, hypertension, hyperthermia, hyperpyrexia, rhabdomyolysis, tachycardia, tremor, urinary retention, vomiting, and weight loss. However,

the most severe, and potentially fatal, toxicities are hypertensive crisis, which is characterized by a drastic increase in blood pressure, and hyperpyrexic crisis, which is characterized by a sustained elevated body temperature exceed-ing 106°F (41°C). Both of these conditions require emergency treatment, including medi-cal support and monitoring of body systems.

Several acute toxicities also have been directly related to the method of amphet-amine use, particularly the intravenous injec-tion of amphetamines with increasing dosages and frequency. This pattern of use can be divided into two phases, an early phase and a late phase (also referred to as phase 1 and phase 2, respectively). During the early phase, users may inject 20 to 40 mg in order to obtain a flash or rush. The rush is character-ized by marked euphoria (a sense of increased physical energy, mental capacity, and self-confidence) and heightened sexual orgasm.

During the late phase, primarily as a result of the development of tolerance, users may inject increasingly higher dosages of amphetamine more frequently in an effort to achieve the same desired psychostimulant actions that they experienced during the early phase. Users commonly continue to inject the drug every 2 to 3 hours, around the clock, for several days.[12] During this time, they usually remain awake, eating very little, if at all. This pattern of use is referred to as a "run."

After several days, the run typically ends, when: (1) amphetamine supplies are depleted (e.g., the total available supply is used); (2) users are unable to obtain additional amphetamine because funds are exhausted; or (3) users become so disorganized, or paranoid, that they are unable to continue their amphetamine use. At this time, they usually fall into a deep but restless sleep that lasts for 12 to 18 hours or more. Upon awakening, they are typically anergic (i.e., feeling tired and weak), depressed, and hungry (Pagliaro & Pagliaro, *Clinical Patient Data Files*).

**Chronic Toxicities**    The regular, long-term oral ingestion of 50 mg or more per day of the amphetamines can produce a range of chronic toxicities, including neurotoxicity.[13, 14] As the amount, or dosage, of the amphetamine is increased, abdominal pain (severe), anorexia, blurred vision, chest pain, constipation, diarrhea, dizziness, emotional lability, headache, nausea, palpitations, tremor, and urinary retention may be experienced. In addition, the use of higher dosages of methamphetamine has been associated with cardiomyopathy and related medical complications (e.g., heart failure) in several case reports (e.g., Hong, Matsuyama, & Nur, 1991; Wijetunga, Seto, Lindsay, et al., 2003; Yeo, Wijetunga, Ito, et al., 2007). The related risk appears to be significantly higher for methamphetamine users who have heart disease and other related risk factors (e.g., diabetes mellitus, hypertension, obesity) (Mau, Asao, Efird, et al., 2009).[15] Further increases in dosage may be associated with other chronic toxicities, including automatic jerking movements and compulsive, stereotypic repetitive behaviors (i.e., punding) that may culminate in toxic amphetamine psychosis (see next section for further discussion).

---

[12] In notably extreme cases of amphetamine intoxication that have come to our attention, up to 1 gram of amphetamine has been intravenously injected on an hourly basis (Pagliaro & Pagliaro, *Clinical Patient Data Files*).

[13] Neurotoxicity has long been associated with methamphetamine-induced damage to dopaminergic neurons and reduced dopamine transporter density in the brain (Quinton & Yamamoto, 2006). Data currently indicate that regular, long-term high-dosage methamphetamine use selectively damages the nigrostriatal dopamine projection of the brain, resulting in permanent Parkinsonian-like effects (e.g., pill-rolling tremor, shuffling gait) (Pagliaro & Pagliaro, 2009). In many cases, the onset of these effects may be delayed for up to three decades. In any event, the damage caused by regular, long-term high-dose methamphetamine use increases the overall risk for developing full-blown Parkinson's disease by up to 800% (Cruickshank & Dyer, 2009). In addition, this damage does not appear to be either reversible or treatable.

Another form of methamphetamine-induced neurotoxicity that has been observed among adolescents is impaired executive functioning (i.e., complex cognitive functioning, such as problem solving) (King, Alicata, Cloak, et al., 2010). Short periods of abstinence from methamphetamine use (e.g., 1 month of nonuse) do not produce significant gains in cognitive performance (Simon, Dean, Cordova, et al., 2010). However, longer periods of abstinence may result in improved performance (i.e., partial, if not complete, neurocognitive recovery of executive functions) (King, Alicata, Cloak, et al., 2010).

[14] Meth mouth, for example, a characteristic toxicity associated with methamphetamine use, is typified by a distinctive pattern of dental caries and tooth loss (Curtis, 2006; Klasser & Epstein, 2005). The caries, usually involving the front teeth, are generally multiple and typically occur on the smooth surfaces of the dentition (Heng, Badner, & Schlop, 2008). In addition, methamphetamine-induced bruxism, which is associated with the general use of methamphetamine, contributes to broken or loose teeth (V. Shetty, Mooney, Zigler, et al., 2010).

[15] In fact, Native Hawaiians are the most frequently reported population group to experience methamphetamine-related heart failure (Mau, Asao, Efird, et al., 2009). This increased incidence is most likely because: (1) the use of methamphetamine is endemic in Hawaii (Freese, Obert, Dickow, et al., 2000; Kim & Jackson, 2008; Winslow, Voorhees, & Pehl, 2007) (also see earlier discussion); and (2) Native Hawaiians are identified as being at high risk for the related factors of diabetes mellitus, hypertension, and obesity (Aluli, Reyes, Brady, et al., 2010; Diabetes mellitus and heart disease, 1994).

Chronic toxicities associated with the intravenous use of the amphetamines[16] become prominent during phase 2, particularly:

- Grinding of the teeth (i.e., bruxism associated with spasm of the jaw muscles) that usually occurs during sleep
- Touching and picking at the arms and face, usually related to the delusional sensation of something (e.g., bugs) crawling under the skin (i.e., formication)
- Paranoia
- Preoccupation with thinking processes and philosophical concerns about meaning
- Compulsive, purposeless, stereotypic repetitive behavior (punding; e.g., a need to take apart mechanical devices and to put them back together—or at least attempt to do so)
- Amphetamine psychosis, which is discussed below

**Amphetamine Psychosis**  Amphetamine psychosis, which is similar to paranoid schizophrenia in terms of observed behavior, is the major psychological toxicity that is usually associated with the regular, long-term use of amphetamines over several weeks or months. However, amphetamine psychosis also may occur within 2 days following the ingestion of a single large dose of amphetamine by a sensitive user. Once users have experienced an episode of amphetamine psychosis, they are at increased risk for its recurrence. This increased sensitivity to amphetamine psychosis is thought to be associated with a lowering of the threshold for this effect. In fact, amphetamine psychosis may recur in some users following the single oral ingestion of as little as 75 mg of amphetamine (Pagliaro & Pagliaro, *Clinical Patient Data Files*).

Efforts have been made to differentiate the clinical similarities and differences between amphetamine psychosis and schizophrenia. Although both conditions may display delusional thinking, depression, flattening of affect, and hallucinations, they differ in the etiology of the presenting thought disorder and its duration. In addition, aggressive and violent behavior is relatively more common during an amphetamine run, when users can be found peering out of windows from behind curtains for the enemy or, perhaps, a narc (i.e., drug enforcement officer) while holding a loaded handgun or rifle. This behavior has been well documented and has been recognized for some time in medical, psychological, and legal contexts of practice (Pagliaro & Pagliaro, *Clinical Patient Data Files*).

Mild forms of psychotic-like behavior associated with amphetamine use (e.g., acute agitation; mild paranoia) generally can be medically managed by "talking a person down" and by administering a sedative-hypnotic (i.e., diazepam [Valium®]). However, acute or severe forms of psychosis usually require medical management with both a sedative-hypnotic (i.e., diazepam [Valium®]) and an antipsychotic (e.g., chlorpromazine [Largactil®, Thorazine®]; haloperidol [Haldol®]), which promptly reverse many of the signs and symptoms of the psychosis (Buxton & Dove, 2008). Untreated, amphetamine psychosis generally resolves within 2 to 14 days.

**Fatal Amphetamine Toxicities**  Although relatively uncommon, the use of amphetamines can result in death—both directly and indirectly. For example, amphetamine use has been directly related to the occurrence of myocardial infarctions (Kaye, McKetin, Duflou, et al., 2007), cerebral vascular accidents, and overdosage deaths. However, these

---

[16] The intravenous use of methamphetamine has contributed significantly to the continuing spread of HIV infection and acquired immune deficiency syndrome (AIDS) particularly among bisexual and gay adolescents and young men (Garofalo, Mustanski, McKirnan, et al., 2007). This increased spread of disease has been related to two primary mechanisms: sharing contaminated needles and syringes; and increasing risky sexual behavior, including unprotected sex with anonymous partners. These risky behaviors are generally observed in the context of clubbing and partying (i.e., attendance at gay club parties and participation in local and distant gay circuit parties), during which methamphetamine is commonly used (Pagliaro & Pagliaro, 2009; Parsons, Kelly, & Weiser, 2007). Also see Chapter 1, The *Psychodepressants*, Table 1.2, for related discussion.

fatal toxicities rarely occur among tolerant, generally healthy users. The use of amphetamines also has been indirectly related to: fatal hepatitis and HIV infections contracted by the use of contaminated needles and syringes; fatal injuries occurring during psychotic episodes and homicidal rages; and the injection of an amphetamine dose that was adulterated, or contaminated (Pagliaro & Pagliaro, *Clinical Patient Data Files*). (Also see the "Overdosage" section.)

### *Physical and Psychological Dependence*

Most current drug and substance abuse experts agree that the amphetamines are capable of causing both physical and psychological dependence (Anglin, Burke, Perrochet, et al., 2000; Pagliaro & Pagliaro, 2002, 2009).[17] The physical and psychological dependence associated with the use of the amphetamines, particularly methamphetamine, has contributed to over 1 million North Americans, across the life span, seeking assistance from psychiatrists and psychologists as well as other health and social care professionals, particularly in the western states (i.e., Arizona, California, Hawaii, New Mexico, and Texas) (M. P. O'Brien, 2008).

**Tolerance to Amphetamines**   Regular, long-term use of the amphetamines results in a tolerance to their desired psychostimulant actions and other related actions, particularly those that are centrally mediated, including cardiovascular effects and hyperthermia. Thus, users often increase their dosages to several grams per day in an effort to achieve desired psychostimulant actions and associated euphoria (Pagliaro & Pagliaro, *Clinical Patient Data Files*). However, tolerance to other chronic toxicities, such as amphetamine psychosis, does not generally occur. Thus, the continuation of regular, long-term use of the amphetamines, particularly high-dosage use, will inevitably, eventually result in amphetamine psychosis.

**Amphetamine Withdrawal Syndrome** A true amphetamine withdrawal syndrome (i.e., one that can be relieved by additional use of the amphetamine) has not been documented for any of the amphetamines. However, the abrupt discontinuation of regular, long-term high-dosage methamphetamine use may result in anxiety, apathy, cognitive impairment, depressed mood (which may be severe), drug craving (often quite intense), fatigue, increased appetite, and sleep disturbances (e.g., excessive sleep).[18] Phase 1 of the methamphetamine withdrawal syndrome is largely resolved within 1 week of the discontinuation of methamphetamine use. Phase 2, which is characterized by similar but significantly less severe signs and symptoms, may follow and last 2 additional weeks (McGregor, Srisurapanont, Jittiwutikarn, et al., 2005). There is no specific pharmacotherapy for the management of the methamphetamine or other amphetamine withdrawal syndrome (Shoptaw, Kao, Heinzerling, et al., 2009). Medical management remains symptomatic (Pagliaro & Pagliaro, 2009).

### *Overdosage*

Overdosages involving the amphetamines are common because, for example, it is difficult for users to know the purity of an illicit street supply that they are intravenously injecting. It also is difficult for users to judge how much methamphetamine they are inhaling, particularly when they are already intoxicated or high. Although the fatalities associated with amphetamine overdosage among older adolescents and young adults are uncommon, children are much more susceptible. Consequently, the

---

[17] However, it should be noted that the American Psychiatric Association, in the revised 5th edition of the DSM, deleted the diagnosis, "amphetamine dependence," which is now generally subsumed under "amphetamine-use disorder." (Also see earlier discussion of the DSM in this text.)

[18] In reference to these signs and symptoms, the American Psychiatric Association (2000) and other groups use the terms, "amphetamine withdrawal" or "amphetamine-type stimulant withdrawal syndrome."

reported acute lethal dosage ($LD_{50}$) is approximately 5 mg/kg body weight for children as compared to approximately 20 mg/kg for older adolescents and young adults.

Fatalities associated with amphetamine overdosage among novice users are usually preceded by hyperpyrexia, hypovolemic shock, and seizures. The treatment of amphetamine overdosage involves supportive medical treatment to maintain vital body organ functions and pharmacotherapy to manage troublesome symptoms. Both chlorpromazine (Largactil®, Thorazine®), a phenothiazine antipsychotic tranquilizer, and olanzapine (Zyprexa®), an atypical antipsychotic, effectively antagonize many of the toxic effects associated with the amphetamines. The benzodiazepine sedative-hypnotic/anticonvulsant diazepam (Valium®) (see Chapter 1, *The Psychodepressants*) is generally effective for managing associated seizures. Ammonium chloride may be used to acidify the urine in order to increase the renal excretion of amphetamines.

For poisonings associated with the oral ingestion of the amphetamines, slurries of activated charcoal can be administered in order to prevent the further absorption of the drug from the stomach. Emetics should not be used to induce vomiting because of the associated risk for precipitating seizures and the potential for the aspiration of vomitus.

## CAFFEINE

Caffeine (1,3,7-trimethylxanthine) is found in more than 60 plants. However, the major natural sources of the caffeine that is consumed in North America are the beans of two species of coffee,[19] *Coffea arabica* and *Coffea robusta*; the leaves of one species of tea, *Thea sinensis*; and the beans of *Theobroma cacoa*, from which cocoa is obtained and chocolate is made. Caffeine also is ingested in the form of caffeine-containing foods and beverages, including carbonated soft drinks and energy drinks.[20] These beverages contain considerable amounts of caffeine because they are made with the caffeine-containing extracts of the nuts of the *Cola acuminata* (i.e., guru nuts, which are chewed by indigenous peoples of the Sudan) and because additional caffeine is added during their production. (See Table 2.2 for the caffeine content of common selected foods and beverages.)

### Prevalence and Characteristics of Caffeine Use Among North American Children and Adolescents

Caffeine, as the principal psychoactive ingredient in coffee, tea, chocolate, and cola beverages, generally is identified as the most widely consumed drug or substance of abuse in the entire world (Chawla & Suleman, 2008; Nawrot, Jordan, Eastwood, et al., 2003; Pagliaro & Pagliaro, 2009). Over 90% of North American adolescents and adults use caffeine, as evidenced by the universal inclusion of the coffee break into the social structure of the normal working day. Although all children and adolescents do not use caffeine, many do, and often to extremes. For example, as found by Calamaro, Mason, and Ratcliffe (2009) in their study of 100 middle and high school students 12 to 18 years of age attending a suburban pediatric primary care office, daily caffeine intake ranged from 0 mg to 1,458 mg with a median of 144 mg and a mean of 215 mg per day. In comparison, American adults consume approximately 250 mg of caffeine per day with coffee contributing, on average, 65%; tea contributing 12%; caffeinated soft drinks contributing 16%; and chocolate contributing most of the remaining 7% (Frary, Johnson, & Wang, 2005; Pagliaro & Pagliaro, 2009).

---

[19] Coffee beans typically contain between 1.1% and 1.4 % caffeine, depending on the specific type and variety.

[20] Caffeine replaced the cocaine that was part of the original formulation of one of the earliest and most popular soft drink beverages, Coca-Cola® (see the "Cocaine" section for further discussion). These and other beverages were called soft drinks because they did not contain alcohol, or other "hard liquor."

**TABLE 2.2   Average Caffeine Content of Selected Beverages, Foods, and Other Products Commonly Used by Children and Adolescents**

| Beverages, Foods, and Other Products | Caffeine Content[a] |
|---|---|
| **Beverages** | |
| Ammo® | 171 mg per 1 oz |
| AMP® energy drink | 75 mg per 8.4 oz |
| Chocolate milk | 1 to 2 mg per oz |
| Coffee, decaffeinated[b] | 3 to 12 mg per 8 oz |
| Coffee, Dunkin Donuts® regular brewed | 206 mg per 16 oz |
| Coffee, Einstein Bros.® espresso | 75 mg per 1 oz |
| Coffee, Einstein Bros.® regular brewed | 300 mg per 16 oz |
| Coffee, espresso | 30 to 90 mg per 1 oz |
| Coffee, instant | 60 to 100 mg per 8 oz |
| Coffee, regular brewed | 80 to 200 mg per 8 oz |
| Coffee, Starbucks® brewed | 320 mg per 16 oz, *grande* cup |
| Coffee, Starbucks® brewed house blend | 260 mg per 16 oz |
| Coffee, Starbucks® espresso | 75 mg per 1 oz |
| Coffee, Starbucks® espresso decaffeinated | 4 mg per 1 oz |
| Cola drinks | 30 to 50 mg per 12 oz[c] |
| Enviga® energy drink | 100 mg per 12 oz |
| Fanta® soda | 0 mg per 12 oz |
| Frappuccino, Starbucks® | 115 mg per 9.5 oz |
| Fresca® | 0 mg per 12 oz |
| Fuel Cell® | 180 mg per 2 oz |
| Full Throttle® energy drink | 144 mg per 16 oz |
| Hot cocoa | 3 to 13 mg per 8 oz |
| Jolt® | 71.2 mg per 12 oz |
| Latte (vanilla), Starbucks® | 150 mg per 16 oz |
| Monster® energy drink | 160 mg per 16 oz |
| Morning Spark® energy drink | 200 mg per ready-mix packet |
| Mountain Dew MDX® | 71 mg per 12 oz |
| Mug Root Beer® | 0 mg per 12 oz |
| No Name® (formerly, Cocaine®) | 280 mg per 8.4 oz |
| NOS® energy drink[d] | 125 mg per 16 oz |
| NOS Powershot® | 125 mg per 2 oz |
| Powershot® | 100 mg per 1 oz |
| Red Bull® energy drink | 80 mg per 8.3 oz |
| Rip It® energy drink | 100mg per 8 oz |
| Rock Star® energy drink[e] | 160 mg per 16 oz |
| SoBe Adrenaline Rush® energy drink | 79 mg per 8.3 oz |
| SoBe Essential Energy® energy drink | 48 mg per 8 oz |
| SoBe No Fear® energy drink | 174 mg per 16 oz |
| Spike Shooter® energy drink | 300 mg per 8.4 oz |
| Sprite® soda | 0 mg per 12 oz |
| Tea, Arizona® black iced | 32 mg per 16 oz |
| Tea, Arizona® green iced | 15 mg per 16 oz |
| Tea, black brewed | 40 to 120 mg per 8 oz |
| Tea, black decaffeinated | 2 to 10 mg per 8 oz |
| Tea, green | 30 to 60 mg per 8 oz |
| Tea, herbal | 0 mg per 8 oz |
| Tea, iced | 70 mg per 12 oz |
| Tea, iced Lipton® Brisk Lemon | 7 mg per 12 oz |
| Tea, iced Nestea® | 26 mg per 12 oz |
| Tea, Snapple® flavored | 42 mg per 16 oz |
| Tea, Snapple® plain unsweetened | 18 mg per 16 oz |

**TABLE 2.2    Average Caffeine Content of Selected Beverages, Foods, and Other Products Commonly Used by Children and Adolescents (Continued)**

| Beverages, Foods, and Other Products | Caffeine Content[a] |
| --- | --- |
| Vault® soft drink | 71 mg per 12 oz |
| Water Joe® bottled water | 60 mg per 16.9 oz |
| Whoop Ass® energy drink | 50 mg per 8.3 oz |
| 7-Up® | 0 mg per 12 oz |
| **Foods** | |
| Bakers® Chocolate | 26 mg per 1 oz |
| Ben & Jerry's Coffee Buzz® Ice Cream | 72 mg per 8 oz |
| Ben & Jerry's Coffee-Flavored Ice Cream | 68 mg per 8 oz |
| Ben & Jerry's Coffee Heath Bar Crunch® | 84 mg per 8 oz |
| Butterfinger Buzz® candy bar | 80 mg per bar |
| Buzz Bites Chocolate Chews® | 100 mg per 1 piece, or chew |
| Chocolate candy bar (dark) | 19 mg per 1 oz |
| Chocolate candy bar (milk) | 7 mg per 1 oz |
| Chocolate (dark, semi-sweet) | 20 mg per 1 oz |
| Chocolate-flavored syrup | 4 mg per 1 oz |
| Dannon® Coffee Yogurt | 36 mg per 6-oz tube |
| Häagen-Dazs® Coffee Frozen Yogurt | 58 mg per 8 oz |
| Häagen-Dazs® Coffee Ice Cream | 58 mg per 8 oz |
| Hershey's Chocolate Kisses® | 1 mg per piece, or *kiss*® |
| Hershey's® cocoa powder | 66 mg per 1 oz |
| Hershey's Special Dark® chocolate bar | 31 mg per bar (1.45 oz) |
| Hershey's® unsweetened baking chocolate | 30 mg per 1 oz |
| Morning Spark Oatmeal® cereal | 80 mg per individual serving packet |
| NRG Phoenix Fury® potato chips | 350 mg per 3.5 oz bag |
| Perky Jerky® | 150 mg per 1 oz |
| Raging Bull® candy | 80 mg per 1 piece |
| Snickers Charged® candy bar | 60 mg per 1.83 oz bar |
| Starbucks® Coffee Ice Cream | 60 mg per 8 oz |
| **Other Products** | |
| AMP® energy gum | 40 mg per 1 piece |
| Black Black® gum | 5 mg per 1 piece |
| Blitz® energy gum | 55 mg per 1 piece |
| Foosh® mints | 100 mg per 1 mint |
| Go Fast!® energy gum | 100 mg per 1 piece |
| Jolt® gum | 33 mg per 1 piece |
| Revive® mints | 85 mg per 1 mint |
| Rock Star® energy gum | 40 mg per 1 piece |
| Stay Alert® gum | 100 mg per 1 piece |
| Think® gum | 10 mg per 1 piece |

Note: Nutritional supplements are not included in this list because they are not primarily used to achieve psychotropic effects (e.g., to achieve feelings of euphoria or to get high). Generally, they are primarily used for body building, to improve physical physique, and to increase athletic performance (i.e., they are used as an ergogenic aid). However, readers are reminded that adolescents and young adults, in particular, are among the largest group of users of caffeine-containing nutritional supplements. The use of these multi-ingredient products, which, in addition to caffeine, often contain a variety of vitamins, minerals, proteins, and ephedrine, can contribute significantly to the user's total daily caffeine consumption and consequently to the occurrence of caffeine toxicity.

For comparison, these are some common nonprescription products that contain caffeine: Anacin®, extra strength, 32 mg per tablet; Excedrin®, extra strength, 65 mg per tablet; No-Doz®, maximum strength, 200 mg per tablet; and Vivarin®, 200 mg per tablet.

[a]The average amount of caffeine content is listed with the typical beverage serving size.

*(Continued)*

**TABLE 2.2    Average Caffeine Content of Selected Beverages, Foods, and Other Products Commonly Used by Children and Adolescents (Continued)**

[b]When coffee beans are decaffeinated by the typical Swiss water process, approximately 98% of the natural caffeine is removed.
[c]The FDA limit for the amount of caffeine added to cola drinks is 71 mg per 12 oz.
[d]NOS® products are advertised as being able to provide the same boost to the user's performance as nitrous oxide gives to motor vehicle performance.
[e]Rock Star® + Vodka contains 30 mg of caffeine and 6.9% alcohol per 16 oz. Generally across North America, distillers are forbidden by law to add caffeine directly to alcoholic beverages. However, when the source of the caffeine is a natural product, such as guarana or yerbe mate—as is the case for Rock Star® + Vodka—then it is permitted. (For further related discussion, also see Chapter 1, *The Psychodepressants*, "Alcohol" section.)

Source: Pagliaro & Pagliaro, 2009; product Web sites.

Consumption patterns in Canada are very similar to those reported for the United States except for the reversal of order of tea and caffeinated soft drinks, primarily due to the higher consumption of tea by Canadian adults and to the significantly lower reported rate of regular consumption of caffeinated soft drinks by Canadian children (i.e., 36%) compared to American children (i.e., 56%) (Knight, Knight, & Mitchell, 2006). Based on data from Nawrot, Jordan, Eastwood, et al. (2003), the Canadian government currently recommends that children consume a maximum amount of 2.5 mg/kg body weight per day of caffeine (Health Canada, 2010a). This recommendation converts to approximately: 45 mg/day for children 4 to 6 years of age; 62.5 mg/day for children 7 to 9 years of age; and 85 mg/day for children and adolescents 10 to 12 years of age. It is also recommended that adolescents follow the same maximum amount of 2.5 mg/kg body weight per day of caffeine.

It should not be surprising that 92% of North Americans 18 years of age and older consume caffeine products on a daily basis for reasons ranging from "it gives you a feeling of well-being" and "makes you relax," to it "helps you think" and "keeps you going."[21, 22] Since the end of World War II, children and adolescents have been the fastest-growing group of caffeine users in North America (Harnack, Stang, & Story, 1999).

In addition, caffeine use steadily increases from birth through adolescence as socially controlled consumption patterns change from milk-based products (e.g., milk, hot chocolate) to caffeine-containing products (e.g., caffeinated soft drinks, coffee). The average amount of caffeine consumed by a sample of junior high school students in the United States was found to be approximately 65 mg per day (range 0–800 mg/day). Boys, on average, consumed significantly more caffeine per day than did girls (Pollak & Bright, 2003). Caffeine-containing soft drinks are the major source of caffeine for children and young adolescents while coffee becomes the major source for older adolescents (Frary, Johnson, & Wang, 2005; Pagliaro & Pagliaro, 2009).

Since the beginning of the new millennium, a significantly increasing source of caffeine for older adolescents and young adults in North American has been energy drinks, primarily, and related food products. These energizing drinks and food products are differentiated from other drinks and food products in two major ways: (1) their relatively high caffeine contents (see Table 2.2); and (2) their advertising campaigns, which target adolescents

---

[21] The energizing effects of caffeine are related to its direct pharmacologic action, whereas other effects (e.g., relaxation, decreased irritability, avoidance of headache) are related primarily to the prevention of the signs and symptoms associated with the caffeine withdrawal syndrome.

[22] The approximately 8 percent of North American adults who avoid the use of caffeine generally deliberately do so because of: (1) religious concerns (e.g., Seventh-day Adventist doctrine condemns the use of caffeine and other drugs and substances of abuse); or (2) health concerns (e.g., caffeine use stimulates gastric acid secretion, which, consequently, causes acid indigestion or gastritis with associated pain and discomfort. It also is medically contraindicated in the management of peptic ulcer disease).

with promises of relief from fatigue and improved physical, sexual, and athletic performance (Oddy & O'Sullivan, 2009; Pagliaro & Pagliaro, 2009). The sale and use of energy drinks increased over 500% from 2002 to 2006 (Reissig, Strain, & Griffiths, 2009).

Many older adolescents and young adults know that caffeine, being a psychostimulant, can attenuate the effects of alcohol, a psychodepressant. Consequently, they believe the urban myth that the use of energy drinks can allow them to "drink all the alcohol they want without getting drunk" or otherwise experiencing the usual, undesired alcohol-related effects (e.g., drowsiness, sexual dysfunction) (O'Brien, McCoy, Rhodes, et al., 2008; Pagliaro & Pagliaro, *Clinical Patient Data Files*). (See Chapter 1, *The Psychodepressants*, "Alcohol" section, for further related discussion.)

**General Pharmacology**

Caffeine, a methylxanthine, is a potent psychostimulant. The cerebral cortex of the brain is the most sensitive part of the CNS to the actions of caffeine and is affected first, followed next by the brain stem, or medulla. The spinal cord is the last part of the CNS that is affected, but only with the ingestion of extremely large amounts of caffeine. Initially, the use of caffeine produces wakefulness with increased mental alertness and a faster and clearer flow of thoughts. The actions on the cerebral cortex may be observed after the ingestion of as little as 100 to 200 mg, or 1 to 2 cups of coffee (Pollak & Bright, 2003). Restlessness also occurs because the cerebral cortex is affected by smaller amounts of caffeine than are necessary to excite the brain stem (Brice & Smith, 2002). These psychostimulant

actions may result in sustained intellectual effort without disrupting coordinated intellectual or psychomotor performance.[23]

The effects of caffeine on the cardiovascular system result in increased cardiac contractility and output. Caffeine also causes dilation of the coronary arteries. This action increases oxygenated blood supply to the myocardium and, thus, increases work capacity. By increasing cardiac performance, caffeine also exerts a diuretic effect.[24] Caffeine also produces increased blood pressure and increased heart rate. It decreases blood flow to the brain by constricting the cerebral blood vessels. This action is thought to provide relief for hypertensive headaches and certain types of migraine headaches, conditions for which caffeine has been used medically. (Also see the "Caffeine Withdrawal Syndrome" section for further related discussion.)[25]

In regard to the respiratory system, caffeine stimulates the respiratory center in the medulla, particularly during pathophysiologic states (e.g., during the respiratory depression associated with opiate analgesic overdosage). It appears to increase the sensitivity of the respiratory center in the medulla to the stimulant actions of carbon dioxide, thereby increasing respiratory minute volume at any given value of alveolar partial pressure of carbon dioxide. Caffeine also affects the smooth muscles of the respiratory tract, producing mild bronchodilation.

The use of caffeine has long been thought to produce energy and endurance. For example, in Tibet, the distance between villages traditionally was accounted for in terms of the number of cups of tea necessary to sustain the person while completing the trip. The

---

[23] In usual amounts (100–500 mg), caffeine potently stimulates the cerebral cortex, promoting wakefulness and improving psychomotor performance. (For further related discussion, see Chapter 6, *Effects of the Drugs and Substances of Abuse on Learning and Memory During Childhood and Adolescence*.)

[24] The increased urinary excretion of sodium (i.e., the natriuretic effect) caused by caffeine appears to work by reducing the reabsorption of sodium in both the proximal and distal renal tubules (Shirley, Walter, & Noormohamed, 2002). In addition, caffeine also increases the renal excretion of calcium and other minerals.

[25] In addition to caffeine, coffee, particularly unfiltered coffee, contains other chemicals, such as cafestol and kahweol, that contribute to raising cholesterol levels among coffee drinkers (Higdon & Frei, 2006).

exact mechanism for these actions remains to be elucidated. However, several possible mechanisms have been proposed to explain the ergogenic effects associated with the use of caffeine (i.e., the ability of caffeine to increase work output), including its ability to: (1) decrease the use of glycogen in muscles and increase the availability of free fatty acids for muscle metabolism; and (2) increase epinephrine concentrations in plasma.

Caffeine inhibits an enzyme that ordinarily breaks down cyclic adenosine monophosphate (cyclic AMP) to its inactive end product. The resultant increase in cyclic AMP leads to increased glucose production within cells. This increased intracellular glucose production makes more energy available to allow higher rates of cellular activity.[26] Thus, the use of caffeine can enable athletes to train at greater power output and run races with increased speed (Davis & Green, 2009; Graham, 2001). It also has been suggested that the CNS-mediated hypoanalgesic effects of caffeine can dampen pain perception and, consequently, allow a more sustainable and forceful muscle contraction (Davis & Green, 2009). The resultant benefits can be noted for submaximal endurance activities, such as swimming and team sports (e.g., hockey, soccer), even at moderate caffeine dosages (e.g., 3 mg or more per kg body weight) (Astorino & Roberson, 2010; Burke, 2008; Hogervorst, Bandelow, Schmitt, et al., 2008; Keisler & Armsey, 2006). Consequently, many adolescents use caffeine—in the form of candy, coffee, energy drinks, and nutritional supplements—to augment their bodybuilding and sports performance (Alves & Lima, 2009; Bramstedt, 2007; Dascombe, Karunaratna, Cartoon, et al., 2010; Dorsch & Bell, 2005; Pagliaro & Pagliaro, 2009).

### Proposed Mechanism of Psychostimulant Action

On a cellular level, caffeine appears to elicit most of its psychostimulant actions within the CNS by competitively binding with adenosine receptors. (See Figure 2.3.) These receptors are found in many body organs but particularly within the brain. In the CNS, adenosine functions as an inhibitory neurotransmitter (Chawla & Suleman, 2008; Nehlig, Daval, & Debry, 1992). Adenosine binds to its receptor sites and, consequently, inhibits: (1) the firing of neurons; (2) synaptic transmission; and (3) the release of neurotransmitters, particularly dopamine. Caffeine does not have its own specific receptors. However, because it is structurally similar to the adenosine molecule, it can bind to some of the adenosine receptor subtypes and act as an adenosine antagonist. Thus, caffeine indirectly causes CNS stimulation by competitively binding to selected adenosine receptor subtypes, specifically A1 and A2a, and, consequently, blocking adenosine's inhibitory actions[27] (Pagliaro & Pagliaro, 2009).

### Common Toxicities

In usual dietary amounts, caffeine is generally well tolerated by children and adolescents as well as adults (Castellanos & Rapoport, 2002; Health Canada, 2010a). The toxicities associated with the use of caffeine primarily are extensions of its pharmacologic actions. We expect that caffeine toxicity will increase significantly among adolescents and young adults during the next decade because of their increasing deliberate use of caffeine-containing candies, energy drinks, foods, ice creams, and nutritional products. (See Table 2.2.)

---

[26] Although the exact mechanism has not yet been determined, regular, long-term coffee consumption has been reported to decrease the risk for developing type 2 diabetes mellitus (Greenberg, Owen, & Geliebter, 2010; Ranheim & Halvorsen, 2005; Salazar-Martinez, Willett, Ascherio, et al., 2004; van Dam, 2008; van Dam & Hu, 2005; van Dam, Willett, Manson, et al., 2006).

[27] For example, in the absence of caffeine, one of adenosine's inhibitory actions is to help promote sleep (Porkka-Heiskanen, 1999, 2011).

Various *Adenosine* Receptors:
*A1, A2a, A2b, & A23*

**Figure 2.3    Caffeine: Mechanism of Psychostimulant Action**

**Acute Caffeine Toxicity** Generally, acute caffeine toxicity (i.e., caffeinism) occurs when large amounts of caffeine are ingested over a short time frame. For example, drinking 12 or more cups of coffee (1.5 g caffeine) through the night to study for a final examination can cause intense psychostimulation with resultant signs and symptoms, including agitation, anxiety, cardiac dysrhythmias, heart palpitations, hyperventilation, tachycardia, and tremors. The spinal cord becomes stimulated only after 20 to 50 cups of coffee (i.e., 2–5 g caffeine) have been consumed and can cause increased stimulation of the spinal reflexes. Convulsions and death may occur with the consumption of 100 cups of coffee (i.e., over 10 g caffeine). However, because such massive amounts of coffee are required, the occurrence of fatalities solely from ingesting common caffeine beverages (i.e., the ingestion of regular coffee,

tea, or caffeinated cola drinks) and other products is highly unlikely. Caffeine intoxication is usually medically diagnosed when at least 5 of these effects are noted: acid indigestion, or dyspepsia; diuresis; excitement; flushed face; muscle twitching; nervousness; periods of inexhaustibility; psychomotor agitation; rambling thought or speech; restlessness; and tachycardia.

Another common, and clinically interesting, sign and symptom of caffeine toxicity is excessive daytime sleepiness, a condition associated with the regular, long-term, high-dose consumption of caffeine. This condition, which includes falling asleep during classes at school, also has been identified as an undesired effect associated with the caffeine withdrawal syndrome (see the section with that title). As older adolescents and young adults increasingly use high-potency sources of caffeine (see Table 2.2) as a means to remain awake late into the night in order to play video games or to party with friends, they are increasingly experiencing payback, particularly in the form of excessive daytime sleepiness (Bryant Ludden & Wolfson, 2010; Calamaro, Mason, & Ratcliffe, 2009; Malinauskas, Aeby, Overton, et al., 2007).

**Chronic Caffeine Toxicity**   The regular, long-term use of caffeine has been reportedly associated with various cancers and other effects, including teratogenesis when used during pregnancy. These toxicities are discussed in the next sections.

*Cancer*   The consumption of coffee reportedly has been associated with the development of various cancers, including breast, colon, ovarian, and pancreatic cancers (Slattery, West, Robison, et al., 1990). However, the role of caffeine in the development of these cancers has not been clearly substantiated—that is, it has not been determined whether other substances found in coffee, or other related cofactors (e.g., age, gender, years of drinking coffee, continental descent) may have been responsible for these reported research results. At this time, the available research does not support a causal relationship between caffeine consumption, in the form of coffee or tea, and breast, colon, ovarian, pancreatic, or rectal cancers (Michaud, Giovannucci, Willett, et al., 2001; Michels, Holmberg, Bergkvist, et al., 2002; Tavani, Gallus, Dal Maso, et al., 2001; Tavani & La Vecchia, 2004). In fact, some studies have suggested a protective relationship between caffeine and cancer. For example, van Dam (2008) reported that frequent coffee consumption had a protective effect in regard to liver cancer.

*Teratogenesis*   Caffeine has been associated with teratogenesis among certain animal species. However, its use in a number of

caffeinated beverages by women during pregnancy has not provided evidence to support a significant risk for human teratogenic or fetotoxic effects (Christian & Brent, 2001). There have been no reported cases of major morphological abnormalities associated with maternal caffeine use during pregnancy. In addition, the only apparent teratogenic effect associated with maternal caffeine use during pregnancy is a reduced birth weight when mothers consumed three or more cups of coffee a day (Bracken, Triche, Belanger, et al., 2003; Nawrot, Jordan, Eastwood, et al., 2003; Pagliaro & Pagliaro, 2002) (i.e., that the consumption of up to 300 mg per day of caffeine is generally considered to be safe for adolescent girls and young women who are pregnant [Health Canada, 2010a; Higdon & Frei, 2006]). For cautionary reasons, some studies and guidelines have suggested limiting caffeine use during pregnancy to approximately two cups of coffee per day (i.e., $\leq$ 200 mg per day) in order to reduce any associated risk, however small, for miscarriage or low birth weight among neonates (Food Standards Agency, 2008; Rubin, 2008).[28] See Table 2.2 for caffeine content of selected common foods and beverages. (For further related discussion, also see Chapter 5, *Exposure to the Drugs and Substances of Abuse From Conception Through Childhood*.)

### *Physical and Psychological Dependence*

Although doubted by some authors (e.g., Dews, O'Brien, & Bergman, 2002; Satel, 2006), the overwhelming consensus, based on all available published data, is that caffeine can cause both physical and psychological dependence (Pagliaro & Pagliaro, 2009). In regard to the former, both tolerance and a caffeine withdrawal syndrome also have been associated with regular, long-term caffeine consumption among children and adolescents (Bernstein, Carroll, Dean, et al., 1998; Bernstein, Carroll,

---

[28] The Canadian government recommends that pregnant adolescents and women limit their caffeine consumption to 300 mg, or less, per day (Health Canada, 2010a).

Thuras, et al., 2002). In their review of related survey data, Griffiths and Chausmer (2000) found that 9% to 30% of caffeine consumers met the criteria from the *Diagnostic and Statistical Manual of Mental Disorders, Fourth Edition* (*DSM-IV-TR*) (American Psychiatric Association, 2000) for caffeine dependence.[29]

**Tolerance**  The regular, long-term ingestion of small amounts of caffeine has been associated with the development of a low level of tolerance, particularly to its psychostimulant actions (e.g., insomnia, jitters*)* (Evans & Griffiths, 1992; Watson, Deary, & Kerr, 2002). A higher level of tolerance may develop with the regular, long-term use of larger amounts of caffeine.

**Caffeine Withdrawal Syndrome**  The regular, long-term ingestion of moderate amounts of caffeine (e.g., approximately three to five cups of caffeinated coffee daily)[30] may result in a caffeine withdrawal syndrome upon the abrupt discontinuation of caffeine use (Evans & Griffiths, 1999; Sigmon, Herning, Better, et al., 2009). This withdrawal syndrome is characterized by anxiety, decreased alertness, depressed mood, drowsiness, dysphoria, fatigue, headaches,[31] impaired concentration, irritability, lassitude, nausea, and weakness (Dews, O'Brien, & Bergman, 2002; Juliano & Griffiths, 2004; Ozsungur, Brenner, & El-Sohemy, 2009). These characteristics generally begin within 12 to 24 hours of last use, peak between 24 and 48 hours after onset, and last for up to 1 week

(Juliano & Griffiths, 2004). The caffeine withdrawal syndrome is promptly relieved by the ingestion of caffeine (Pagliaro & Pagliaro, 2009), even among children (Heatherley, Hancock, & Rogers, 2006). Not surprisingly, therefore, several authors (e.g., Griffiths & Chausmer, 2000) have suggested that attempting to avoid the caffeine withdrawal syndrome is a major contributor to continued caffeine use and increasing dependence.

## COCAINE

Cocaine, both in powder form (i.e., cocaine hydrochloride) for intranasal insufflation or intravenous injection and cocaine base (i.e., crack or freebase cocaine) for smoking, continues to be widely available in North America. This section discusses the prevalence and characteristics of cocaine use by North American children and adolescents. It also presents the general pharmacology of cocaine, including its proposed mechanism of action and common toxicities with attention to its potential for psychological dependence.

### Prevalence and Characteristics of Cocaine Use Among North American Children and Adolescents

It is estimated that approximately 40 million North Americans 12 years of age and older (approximately 15% of North Americans) have used cocaine at least once in their lifetimes—an estimated number that generally is maintained

---

[29] The American Psychiatric Association (2011) has generally recommended that the use of the word, "dependence," be limited to physical dependence in the DSM-V and not be used as a diagnostic category for any of the drugs or substances of abuse. We have chosen to continue to use the terms physical dependence and psychological dependence for this text because they are the more familiar terms used and because the DSM-V is not the sole reference source for all readers. As presented in the Preface, we use the term "patterns of use" to more clearly differentiate the development of these two types of dependence, with psychological dependence being denoted by the pattern of habitual use and physical dependence, as traditionally defined, being denoted by the development of abusive use and compulsive use.

[30] For many children and adolescents, even those who do not drink coffee, it is relatively easy to reach the daily maximal amount of caffeine consumption. (See Table 2.2.)

[31] The exact etiology of the withdrawal headache is unclear, but it most likely involves reflex dilation of the cerebral blood vessels, particularly the basilar arteries and the posterior cerebral arteries (Couturier, Laman, van Duijn, et al., 1997; Griffiths & Chausmer, 2000).

with approximately 1 million new users initiating cocaine use annually (Office of National Drug Control Policy, 2010). It also has been estimated that 5.3 million North Americans (i.e., 1.6%) 12 years of age and older, including an estimated 2 million parents, have used cocaine in the previous year (NIDA, 2009).[32] In addition, club-going adolescents and young adults (16 to 30 years of age)—who are usually polyusers of the drugs and substances of abuse—reportedly have one of the highest rates of cocaine use (Kelly & Parsons, 2008; Parsons, Grov, & Kelly, 2009). Other adolescents and young adults also use various combinations of cocaine and other drugs and substances of abuse,[33] including alcohol (Pagliaro & Pagliaro, 2009).

In their national survey of 50,000 high school students across the United States in 2007, Johnston, O'Malley, Bachman, et al. (2008) found that approximately 6% of 10th- and 12th-grade students reported using cocaine (either as cocaine hydrochloride or crack cocaine; see the section titled "General Pharmacology") within the year prior to the survey. Approximately 50% of these students also reported that it was fairly easy or very easy to obtain cocaine. Although the availability of cocaine remained high for the 2008, 2009, and 2010 surveys, Johnston, O'Malley, Bachman, et al. (2010b) found a decline in reported cocaine use to approximately 4% among 10th- and 12th-grade students for the year prior to the surveys.

M. P. O'Brien (2008), reporting on data from the CEWG of the NIDA, found that 7.2% of U.S. high school students reported lifetime use of cocaine. In another study, Eaton, Kann, Kinchen, et al. (2010), reporting on data obtained from the *Youth Risk Behavior Surveillance System* in the United States for 2009, found that 2.8% of high school students had used cocaine at least once during the 30 days preceding the survey (range 1.7% to 5.6% across state surveys). Twelfth-grade adolescent boys of Hispanic descent had the highest reported rate of use (i.e., 4.9%). In comparison, 6.2% of Canadian adolescents and young adults 15 to 24 years of age reported lifetime use of cocaine (Health Canada, 2010b).

## General Pharmacology

Cocaine is an alkaloid extracted from the leaves of two varieties of the coca plant, *Erythroxylon coca,* which is indigenous to the eastern slopes of the Andes Mountains of South America. The coca leaves from these plants contain typically, by weight, about 1% cocaine. The cocaine is generally produced for distribution and sale in two forms, cocaine base and cocaine hydrochloride. Each of these forms has its own pharmacologic characteristics and patterns of use.

### Cocaine Base

Cocaine base, the natural form that is extracted from the coca leaves, is only slightly soluble in water (i.e., 1 g in 1300 ml). However, it dissolves readily in ethanol (i.e., 1 g in 7 ml), ether (i.e., 1 g in 4 ml), and chloroform (i.e., 1 g in 0.5 ml).[34] The melting point of cocaine base is significantly lower than that for cocaine hydrochloride (i.e., 208.4°F [98°C] versus 383°F [195°C]). Thus, when heated, cocaine base vaporizes much more readily and is involved

---

[32] Delaney-Black, Chiodo, Hannigan, et al. (2010) suggest that the relatively early onset of adolescent cocaine use by 14 years of age is related to mother's use of cocaine during pregnancy and mother's (or primary caregiver's) use of cocaine postnatally. (Also see Chapter 5, *Exposure to the Drugs and Substances of Abuse From Conception Through Childhood.*)

[33] For example, the combined use of cocaine and heroin is referred to as a Belushi, dynamite, H & C, murder one, or speedball. This combination added to a tobacco cigarette results in a flamethrower. The combined use of cocaine, heroin, and LSD is referred to as a Frisco special or a Frisco speedball.

[34] Cocaine base, in the form of crude coca paste, is commercially extracted from cocaine leaves by using an organic solvent because of its low solubility in water. Over a dozen different solvents have been used in this process, depending on their availability and cost. These solvents include acetone, butane, diesel fuel, gasoline, kerosene, and methanol (Pagliaro & Pagliaro, 2009).

in less pyrolysis.[35] Accordingly, inhaling the vaporized cocaine base (i.e., smoking crack cocaine or freebase cocaine) can achieve cocaine blood concentrations that are equal to those achieved by intravenously injecting cocaine hydrochloride. In addition, with pulmonary inhalation, or smoking, because of the mechanisms inherent in pulmonary absorption, the onset of action is actually more rapid than with intravenous injection, and it produces a subjectively more intense desired action. For these and other reasons (e.g., convenience; lower cost; avoidance of intravenous injection and associated risk for infections, such as HIV infection, or other harmful effects), users often prefer the pulmonary inhalation of cocaine to any other method of use.

### Cocaine Hydrochloride

The hydrochloride salt form of cocaine readily dissolves in water (i.e., 1 g in 0.5 ml). Thus, it is more easily used for selected medical and dental purposes, such as local anesthesia for the eye or mouth, respectively. It also is the form of cocaine that is generally used by intranasal insufflation because it is readily absorbed from the mucous membranes lining the nasal cavity. In addition, because of its high solubility in water, cocaine hydrochloride is the form that is used for intravenous injection.

### Proposed Mechanism of Psychostimulant Action

After absorption into the systemic circulation, cocaine is found in virtually all areas of the brain. However, it appears to preferentially accumulate in the caudate nucleus, the nucleus accumbens, and the ventral tegmental areas. Cocaine decreases the dopamine transporter mediated clearance of dopamine from the synaptic cleft by blocking its reuptake into the presynaptic cells. It also appears to block the reuptake of other monoamines, including serotonin and norepinephrine. Consequently, it increases the amount of neurotransmitters present in the synaptic cleft. A simplified representation of the proposed principal site and mechanism of cocaine's action is shown in Figure 2.4.

The ability of cocaine to increase neurotransmitter activity in the brain causes several effects that contribute to its continued use. These effects include:

- An intense euphoria
- Feelings of increased energy and competence
- Heightened sociability and sexual desire
- Decreased feelings of fatigue and hunger
- Indifference to pain and discomfort

Over 20 years ago, Dackis and Gold (1990) suggested that the action of cocaine could be divided into three phases. This theory has remained a popular and useful theory for explaining the observed actions and effects of cocaine. During Phase I, cocaine stimulates the CNS, beginning with the cortex, by decreasing the reuptake of neurotransmitters (e.g., dopamine and serotonin). Mild stimulation and euphoria are usually experienced. As the amount of cocaine that is used is increased by smoking, injecting, or snorting more lines, Phase II, the excitation phase, begins. During Phase II, more pronounced CNS stimulation occurs with various associated signs and symptoms (e.g., anxiety, hypertension, mydriasis, rapid speaking, tremors, tachycardia, vomiting). As cocaine use is continued, Phase II is followed by Phase III, a phase of depression of the cortical areas of the CNS[36] that may progress to medullary depression and associated respiratory failure. This phase results from the depletion of the

---

[35] Pyrolysis is a chemical reaction moderated by heat (i.e., higher temperatures). The major product of the pyrolysis of crack cocaine is methylecgonidine. The amount of methylecgonidine produced is variable, generally ranging from 1% to 5%, and depends on the rate of air flow through the crack pipe and its temperature (Pagliaro & Pagliaro, 2009).

[36] This cocaine-induced depression of the CNS is directly related to the depletion of neurotransmitters caused by the continued use of cocaine and the related changes in dopamine transporters and receptors that are associated with cocaine withdrawal.

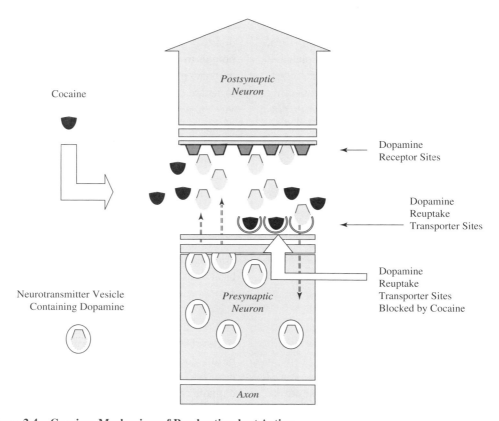

**Figure 2.4    Cocaine: Mechanism of Psychostimulant Action**
Reproduced with permission from L. A. Pagliaro & A. M. Pagliaro (2009), *Pagliaros' comprehensive guide to drugs and substances of abuse (2nd ed.)* (p. 95). Washington DC: American Pharmacists Association.

neurotransmitters in the CNS. (See Figure 2.4.) Phase III spontaneously resolves, but not until after the neurotransmitters, as noted in the "Physical and Psychological Dependence" section, which concludes the "Cocaine" section, have had sufficient time to be naturally replenished (Pagliaro & Pagliaro, 2009).

### Common Toxicities

The use of cocaine has been commonly associated with several acute and chronic toxicities that are directly related to its specific pharmacologic actions on various body systems. It has also been implicated with the development of teratogenesis when used by adolescent girls and young women during pregnancy (see Chapter 5, *Exposure to the Drugs and Substances of Abuse From Conception Through Childhood*) and other toxicities that have been

specifically related to its methods of use and adulteration prior to sale. These common toxicities are presented and discussed in the next sections.

**Toxicities Related to the Direct Action of Cocaine**    The use of cocaine has been associated with several acute toxicities, including: agitation, anxiety, apathy, cerebral vascular accidents, difficulty concentrating, headache, hyperpyrexia, hypertension, insomnia, irritability, loss of sexual desire, memory impairment, mydriasis, myocardial infarction, panic attacks, seizures, suicide attempts, tachycardia, and tremors. Regular, continued, or long-term use has been associated with the development of additional toxicities, including depression, paranoia, and cocaine psychosis.

Cocaine psychosis is virtually indistinguishable from amphetamine psychosis, although it is usually of shorter duration. (See "Amphetamines" section in this chapter.) It also shares with amphetamine psychosis its similarity to paranoid schizophrenia. Both cocaine and amphetamine psychosis often are characterized by hypervigilance and paranoia and have been associated with an increased incidence of aggressive and violent behavior, including homicide (Pagliaro & Pagliaro, *Clinical Patient Data Files*).

**Toxicities Associated with Method of Cocaine Use**    Several toxicities have been associated with three common methods of cocaine use[37]: (1) intranasal insufflation, or snorting; (2) pulmonary inhalation, or smoking; and (3) intravenous injection, or mainlining. These toxicities are highlighted here.

*Intranasal Insufflation, or Snorting*    Intranasal insufflation of cocaine hydrochloride is associated with both minor irritation and severe injury to the nasal mucous membranes and the related underlying structures. Although less serious effects may occur, such as congestion (i.e., rhinitis) and eczema in and around the nostrils, more serious effects, such as nasal erosion and perforation of the nasal septum, also may occur, particularly with regular, long-term use (Vilela, Langford, McCullagh, et al., 2002). The minor irritation and more serious injury are caused by the direct action of cocaine (i.e., vasoconstriction) on the surrounding skin and mucous membranes and by the direct irritation of the hydrochloride salt form of cocaine, which, when it comes into contact with nasal secretions, forms a dilute but irritating solution of hydrochloric acid. The occurrence of these local effects, together with the relatively small surface area of the nasal mucosa that restricts absorption rates to begin with, have helped to increase the popularity of the pulmonary inhalation, or smoking, of cocaine in its freebase, or crack, form—currently the most popular method of cocaine use in North America. Unfortunately, smoking is associated with its own toxicities, particularly pulmonary toxicities.

*Pulmonary Inhalation, or Smoking*    The toxicities associated with smoking cocaine result in both irritation and damage to the lungs, including pulmonary infiltrates and pneumonia. Acute exacerbation of asthma and bronchitis also may occur among users who already have these chronic medical conditions (i.e., chronic obstructive pulmonary diseases) (Ali, Krugar, & Houghton, 2002; Gatof & Albert, 2002).[38] In addition, the regular, long-term smoking of crack cocaine has been associated with alveolar and microvascular lung damage at the microscopic level—a condition that has been commonly referred to as "crack lung."

*Intravenous Injection, or Mainlining*    The intravenous injection of cocaine has been related to a number of toxic effects. These effects include the development of local infections and abscesses at the sites of injection and the development of phlebitis when injected veins become irritated and inflamed as a response to being pierced with a needle and injected with an irritating solution of cocaine. Intravenous injection of cocaine also is associated with the development of thrombosis, which may be fatal. These toxicities are not directly related to the action of cocaine but rather to its chemistry (e.g., alkaline or basic pH, adulteration) and method of use—intravenous injection.

---

[37] Other less common methods of cocaine use (e.g., "balling," or intravaginal insertion) that may be used by older adolescents and young adults are not discussed here.

[38] These effects are very similar to those associated with smoking other drugs and substances of abuse (e.g., tobacco smoking, marijuana smoking).

Related to the method of use (i.e., piercing the protective skin barrier, causing injury to the epidermis and dermis as the needle is inserted through the skin in order to pierce the vein below), these effects may commonly occur with the intravenous use of any of the various drugs and substances of abuse. (Also see Chapter 1, *The Psychodepressants*, Table 1.2.)

It is important to note that the intravenous injection of cocaine was a *major* contributing factor to the spread of the HIV infection during the late 1980s and 1990s (Pagliaro & Pagliaro, 2000; Pagliaro, Pagliaro, Thauberger, et al., 1993). *Coke burns*, which are associated with the repeated inadvertent subcutaneous injection of cocaine by intravenous cocaine users who *miss the vein*, are caused in much the same way as the intranasal irritation and damage that occurs with *snorting* of cocaine (see previous discussion). These burns are related to the formation of dilute hydrochloric acid when the cocaine interacts with the subcutaneous body fluids.

**Toxicities Associated with Adulterants**
Adulterants (e.g., arsenic; lactose, or milk sugar; quinine) are often used to "cut" various drugs and substances of abuse prior to selling in order to increase dealer profits. The adulterants that are used have been associated with several unique toxicities that can be more serious than those directly associated with cocaine use or other drugs and substances of abuse (see, for example, the related discussions of opiate analgesics and volatile solvents and inhalants in Chapter 1, *The Psychodepressants*). Unfortunately, the potential risk for unique and unexpected toxicities can occur whenever any illicitly manufactured drug or substance of abuse is prepared, sold, bought, and used.

For example, during 2008–2009, a specific adulterant, levamisole, was found in approximately two-thirds of all cocaine samples that were seized and analyzed by the U.S. government.[39] It has a stimulant action and may have been added to the illicit cocaine product to boost its effects. More likely, it was used to cut the cocaine in order to increase its weight and, consequently, the related profits of the distributor/seller. The use of the adulterated cocaine was associated with several toxic effects, including a flu-like syndrome, loss of the senses of smell and taste, leukopenia, and stomatitis. Levamisole also can cause agranulocytosis. Over 30 cases of agranulocytosis, some fatal, were associated with using the adulterated cocaine in 2008 and 2009 (Brackney, Baumbach, Ewers, et al., 2009; Zhu, LeGatt, & Turner, 2009).

According to the National Drug Abuse Warning Network, cocaine is involved in most of the admissions related to illegal drug and substance abuse reported by emergency departments across the United States. Approximately 0.5% of all emergency room admissions, on an annual basis, involve the use of cocaine (Office of National Drug Control Policy, 2010).

**Potentially Fatal Toxicities**   Four major potentially fatal toxicities associated with the use of cocaine can occur regardless of a user's age or the method of use: (1) cardiotoxicity, (2) CNS hemorrhage, (3) hyperpyrexia, and (4) seizures. Other potentially fatal toxicities include those that are associated with the contamination or adulteration of street supplies of cocaine prior to their distribution, sale, and use (see earlier discussion in this section, *Toxicities Associated with Adulterants*) and those that are related to the concomitant use of other drugs and substances of abuse, particularly alcohol and heroin (Bernstein, Bucciarelli, Piper, et al., 2007; Molina & Hardgrove, 2011; Pagliaro & Pagliaro, 2009).

---

[39] Levamisole, a veterinary deworming agent (i.e., anthelminthic) also has been experimentally used in the treatment of some types of human cancers.

*Cardiotoxicity* Cocaine's actions on the cardiovascular system have been associated with an increase in both heart rate and blood pressure. These actions, in turn, may lead to increased risk for aortic ruptures, dysrhythmias, end-stage renal disease, heart failure, myocardial infarction[40], stroke[41], and sudden death (Lippi, Plebani, & Cervellin, 2010; Maraj, Figueredo, & Lynn Morris, 2010; Norris, Thornhill-Joynes, Robinson, et al., 2001; Pagliaro, 2002). These severe, and possibly fatal, cardiotoxicities occur, in large part, as a result of the decrease in blood pH that is associated with cocaine use. The acidemia causes scarring and disruption of the heart's electrical conduction system with prolongation of the QRS complex and QTc duration on the electrocardiogram (Wang, 1999).

Although relatively rare, deaths among young, apparently healthy athletes (Basavarajaiah, Shah, & Sharma, 2007; Bauman, Grawe, Winecoff, et al., 1994; Maron, 2003; Richman & Nashed, 1999) have occurred that have been directly related to the cardiotoxic effects of cocaine. Predominantly covered in the popular lay press, most often these deaths are due to cardiovascular collapse or respiratory failure. However, sudden cardiac death related to cocaine use has been associated with up to 500 deaths annually in North America involving children and adolescents (Berger, Utech, Hazinski, 2004). Several researchers (e.g., Bauman & DiDomenico, 2002; Karch, 2005; Pagliaro & Pagliaro, *Clinical Patient Data Files*) have suggested that congenital long QT syndrome, whether fully or partially expressed, is a significant underlying risk factor for the development of this cocaine-induced toxicity (i.e., ventricular tachycardia).

*CNS Hemorrhage* CNS hemorrhage (i.e., cerebrovascular accident, stroke) results from the combined effects of the vasoconstriction and increased cardiac output associated with cocaine use.[42] CNS hemorrhage occurs more often among users who have cerebral aneurysms. Although it is estimated that approximately 1 in 20 people have a cerebral aneurysm, most people who use cocaine are unaware of this risk. In addition, risk of a CNS hemorrhage increases with age, irrespective of previous length of time of cocaine use.

*Hyperpyrexia* Cocaine-induced hyperpyrexia, a body temperature exceeding 104°F (41°C), is usually caused by the combined effects of an excessively stimulated body metabolism and vasoconstriction, which significantly impairs the ability of the body to cool itself. A body temperature of this magnitude, causing convulsions and coma, may be fatal in up to 20% of cases. In nonfatal cases, irreversible brain damage may occur. Hyperpyrexia also is an associated sign observed in both cocaine-induced fatal excited delirium and cocaine-induced rhabdomyolysis.

*Seizures* Seizures, which may terminate in cardiovascular collapse, can be caused by a number of cocaine effects, including: (1) hyperactivity of the CNS; (2) increased body temperature; and (3) lack of sufficient oxygen in the CNS. On a molecular level, it has been proposed that the convulsions associated with cocaine use are mediated by means of interaction with $GABA_A$ receptors and N-methyl-D-aspartate (NMDA) receptors (Lason, 2001).

### Physical and Psychological Dependence

Over the last two decades, the general consensus has been that there is no true physical

---

[40] Chest pain is the cardinal symptom of cocaine-induced myocardial infarction, particularly for young men because other commonly used diagnostic indicators (e.g., electrocardiogram and serial cardiac markers) are not as accurate for this age group (Lippi, Plebani, & Cervellin, 2010; Maraj, Figueredo, & Lynn Morris, 2010; Phillips, Luk, Soor, et al., 2009).

[41] Particularly hemorrhagic or ischemic strokes (Westover, McBride, & Haley, 2007).

[42] The related neurological damage (i.e., sequelae of a cocaine-induced minor stroke) may be expressed as an increased incidence of cognitive deficits (e.g., forgetfulness; slowed thinking). (Also see related discussion in Chapter 6, *Effects of the Drugs and Substances of Abuse on Learning and Memory During Childhood and Adolescence*.)

dependence associated with the regular, long-term use of cocaine as defined by the development of tolerance with continued use and the occurrence of a withdrawal syndrome that is immediately relieved by the resumed use of the drug or substance of abuse—in this case, cocaine. Similar to the amphetamines, cocaine does not fit the classic definition of physical dependence because once the neurotransmitters are depleted, even if all the cocaine in the world was used, it would not relieve the undesired effects. The endogenous neurotransmitters that have been depleted in association with cocaine use must be replenished before the use of cocaine can again achieve its desired effects.

The abrupt discontinuation of cocaine after regular, long-term use may result in several undesired effects, including: anxiety, apathy, depression, dysphoria, fatigue (extreme), headaches, irritability, mental depression, muscle cramps, psychomotor fatigue, sleep disturbances (e.g., insomnia), and vivid unpleasant dreams.[43] These signs and symptoms may begin within a few hours of discontinuing cocaine use and generally resolve within 24 hours (Walsh, Stoops, Moody, et al., 2009). However, as previously noted, they cannot be relieved by the resumed use of cocaine. Thus, the classic definitional criteria for a true cocaine withdrawal syndrome are not met (i.e., the development of tolerance and, upon abrupt discontinuation of use, signs and symptoms of withdrawal that can be relieved by the resumed use of the drug or substance of abuse). These signs and symptoms have been ascribed to severe psychological dependence produced by the use of cocaine (i.e., craving). However, they are not viewed as being indicative of a true cocaine withdrawal syndrome according to the classic definition and are more commonly referred to, in the drug culture vernacular, as the "cocaine blues."

The underlying cellular mechanism involved in cocaine withdrawal appears to be related to a decrease in mesolimbic dopamine activity (Hu, 2007; Kuhar & Pilotte, 1996). Dopamine modulates neuronal activity in the prefrontal cortex and is necessary for optimal cognitive functioning (Nogueira, Kalivas, & Lavin, 2006). The decrease in dopamine activity associated with cocaine withdrawal is related to associated anhedonia and relapse (Kuhar & Pilotte, 1996; Walsh, Stoops, Moody, et al., 2009).

It has been estimated that of 100 people who try cocaine, 30 will become abusers and 10 of these 30 individuals will become compulsive users.[44] (See Figure P.2 in the Preface of this text.) Thus, for a significant number of cocaine users, the cocaine high becomes the only—or, at least, primary—reason for living (i.e., cocaine use is preferred to personal likes, desires, or needs including family, food, friends, recreation, sex, or career). This pattern of cocaine use has resulted in significant adverse social consequences[45] for the cocaine user (be she or he a child, adolescent, or adult) and her or his family, friends, and community.

## NICOTINE

Nicotine is a naturally occurring liquid alkaloid found in the leaves of two New World tobacco plants, *Nicotiana rustica* and *Nicotiana tabacum*. *Nicotiana rustica* appears to be of North American origin, while *Nicotiana tabacum* appears to be of South American origin. The leaves of the tobacco plant are dried, or cured, using various procedures. They are then chopped into tobacco for smoking. Nicotine is

---

[43] Most of these signs and symptoms appear to be particularly severe among cocaine users who have a dual diagnosis of a cocaine use disorder and a major depressive disorder (Helmus, Downey, Wang, et al., 2001; Shaffer & Eber, 2002). (See Chapter 8, *Dual Diagnosis Among Adolescents*, for further related discussion.)

[44] Of the 10 cocaine users who become compulsive users, 7 or 8 will likely have a family history of alcoholism (Pagliaro & Pagliaro, *Clinical Patient Data Files*). This observation suggests a possible genetic predisposition to cocaine dependence.

[45] These consequences include, for example, divorce, embezzlement, exchanging sex for drugs, HIV infection, homicide, incarceration, job loss, loss of child custody, and suicide (Pagliaro & Pagliaro, *Clinical Patient Drug Files*).

available in many tobacco products, including chewing tobacco, tobacco cigarettes and cigars, pipe tobacco, and tobacco snuff. Tobacco smoking, which is the most convenient and economical method of use, is an efficient means for achieving desired blood concentrations of nicotine and corresponding effects. As such, tobacco smoking remains the most popular method of use. The tobacco usually contains from 1% to 2% nicotine—the psychostimulant that produces such desired actions as increased alertness and attentional performance, memory improvement, relaxation, and weight loss (i.e., associated with appetite suppression). However, it is nicotine's high potential for both physical and psychological dependence that helps to ensure that those who begin to smoke tobacco continue to do so.

## Prevalence and Characteristics of Nicotine Use Among North America Children and Adolescents

Worldwide, there are currently over 1 billion tobacco smokers, and use is increasing (World Health Organization, 2010). The use of nicotine in the form of smoking tobacco in cigarettes, cigarillos, cigars, and pipes continues to be widespread throughout North America and is actually increasing among certain population groups, particularly adolescent girls,[46] despite the wide publicity of its association with lung and oral cancers as well as teratogenic and other harmful effects (Pagliaro, 2002; Pagliaro & Pagliaro, 2009; Satcher, 2001). The use of smokeless tobacco products (e.g., chewing tobacco, snuff) is, likewise, prevalent and, with the more widespread availability of newer dissolvable forms of tobacco products (see Table 2.5 for a listing

of available products and comments regarding their use), is expected to increase significantly among children and adolescents over the coming decades (Pagliaro & Pagliaro, *Clinical Patient Data Files*; Sapundzhiev & Werner, 2003).[47]

Tobacco smokers cannot be defined as preferentially belonging to any single ethnic, racial, or social group. They currently include approximately one-fourth of the adult population of North America, most of whom (i.e., 80%) began to smoke tobacco on a regular basis before they were 18 years of age (DiFranza, Savageau, Fletcher, et al., 2007; Marshall, Schooley, Ryan, et al., 2006). In fact, most users begin to smoke tobacco before they are 14 years old, and it is estimated that every day of the year more than 4,000 North American children and adolescents begin to smoke tobacco, with 1,000 becoming daily smokers (U.S. Food and Drug Administration, 2010a). Youth who have attentional disorders (e.g., A-D/HD) or mood disorders (e.g., major depressive disorder) are more likely to smoke tobacco, possibly as an unconscious effort to self-medicate these disorders. (Also see Chapter 8, *Dual Diagnosis among Adolescents,* for further related discussion.)

### Trends

**Tobacco Cigarette Smoking and Use of Smokeless Tobacco Products**   Although currently plateauing, lifetime prevalence of tobacco cigarette smoking among adolescents has demonstrated a significant and dramatic decrease over the past 40 years. As reported by Johnston, O'Malley, Bachman, et al. (2010b) in their in-school survey of adolescent use of the drugs and substances of abuse, lifetime prevalence of tobacco cigarette smoking by

---

[46] An interesting finding by Jaszyna-Gasior, Schroeder, Thorner, et al. (2009) is the significant correlation between age at menarche and onset of daily tobacco smoking among adolescent girls. Early age of menarche appears to be a risk factor for tobacco smoking and for the use of other drugs and substances of abuse. However, it remains unclear as to whether smoking among adolescent girls is more likely related to hormonal factors, alone, or to hormonal and other factors, including attempts to maintain or lose body weight or to appear older and more mature.

[47] Interestingly, when North American tobacco use is observed from a historical perspective, previous significant changes in patterns of use are noted. For example, in 1900, chewing tobacco accounted for 50% of tobacco use in North America, and from 1900 to 2000, tobacco use, in the form of cigarettes, increased from 2% to 80% (Hammond, 2009).

12th-grade students was approximately 75% during the mid- to late 1970s and has been in the low 40% range as the first decade of the 21st century ended (e.g., 42.2% in their 2010 survey).

Rates of tobacco use increase in a roughly linear fashion throughout adolescence. As reported by Marshall, Schooley, Ryan, et al. (2006) in their analysis of data from the *National Surveillance of Tobacco Use by U.S. Youth,* current use of any tobacco product increases from 13.3% for middle school students to 28.2% for high school students. Likewise, current tobacco cigarette smoking, the most prevalent form of tobacco use among U.S. youth, increases from 9.8% of middle school students to 22.5% of high school students. Cigar smoking, the second most prevalent form of tobacco use among U.S. youth, also increases from 6% for middle school students to 11.6% for high school students.

Johnston, O'Malley, Bachman, et al. (2008), in their NIDA-sponsored national survey of adolescent use of the drugs and substances of abuse, found that: 1) approximately 20% of 12th-grade students reported smoking cigarettes in the past 30 days (12.3% were daily users); and 2) approximately 6% of 12th-grade students (i.e., 11.9% of boys and 1.2% of girls) reported using smokeless tobacco during the same time period (2.8% were daily users—5.6% of boys and 0.2% of girls). These data for smokeless tobacco use display significant gender effects.[48] However, Rodu and Cole (2010), in their analysis of data from the 2003, 2005, and 2007 *National Survey on Drug Use and Health,* found that smokeless tobacco use among adolescent boys did not serve as a gateway to cigarette smoking among young men.

Eaton, Kann, Kinchen, et al. (2010), reporting for the Centers for Disease Control on an analysis of data obtained from the *Youth Risk Behavior Surveillance System,* found that, nationwide, 26.0% of U.S. students in grades 9 through 12 reported current tobacco use. The prevalence ranged from a low of 10.7% to a high of 33.5% across state surveys (median 25.3%). The highest rate of use (i.e., 40.4%) was among high school senior boys of European descent (see Table 2.3). In their study of over 3,000 adolescents in the 9th through 12th grades, the Partnership for a Drug-Free America and the Metlife Foundation (2010) found that 25% of their participants reported smoking tobacco cigarettes during the past month.

**Polyuse of Tobacco, or Dual Tobacco Use**    The polyuse of tobacco, or dual tobacco use, refers to the concurrent use of both smoking tobacco and smokeless tobacco products. Dual tobacco use has increased significantly in North America since the beginning of the new millennium. Dual tobacco users are significantly more likely to be:

- Adolescent boys or young adult men
- Susceptible to peer influence
- Nicotine dependent
- Exposed to tobacco advertising
- Of European descent[49]
- Living in the rural, rather than urban, midwestern, southern, or western United States
- Users of smokeless forms of tobacco in places where smoking is prohibited (e.g., churches; restaurants; schools) (Bombard, Rock, Pederson, et al., 2008; Centers for Disease Control and Prevention, 2008b; Lutfiyya, Shah, Johnson, et al., 2008; McClave-Regan & Berkowitz, 2010; Pagliaro & Pagliaro, *Clinical Patient Data Files*; Timberlake & Huh, 2009)

Bombard, Rock, Pederson, et al. (2008), using data from the 2002 and 2004 National Youth

---

[48] In their study of tobacco use, Remafedi, Jurek, and Oakes (2008) found that adolescents and young adults (13 to 24 years of age) who were bisexual, gay, lesbian, or transgendered were significantly less likely to use smokeless tobacco products than were other adolescents and young adults.

[49] North American adolescents of American Indian or Alaskan Native descent living on reservations and those in grades 6 through 12 reportedly have the highest rate of dual tobacco use (i.e., 33%) (Wolsko, Mohatt, Lardon, et al., 2009; Yu, 2010).

TABLE 2.3    Common Forms of Tobacco Used by US High School Students

| Common Form of Tobacco | Average Percentage of Nationwide Use (range across state surveys) | Highest Percentage of Use (specific high school group) |
|---|---|---|
| Cigarettes | 19.5%[a] | 28.1% |
| | (range 8.5%–26.1%) | (senior boys of European descent) |
| Cigars | 14.0 %[b] | 26.8% |
| | (range 6.8%–18.1%) | (senior boys of European descent) |
| Smokeless tobacco | 8.9%[c] | 20.1% |
| (e.g., chewing tobacco; dip; snuff; snus) | (range 4.9%–6.2%) | (senior boys of European descent) |
| Any form of tobacco use | 25.3% | 40.4% |
| | (range 10.7%–33.5%) | (senior boys of European descent) |

[a] Johnston, O'Malley, Bachman, et al. (2010b), in their 2010 in-school survey of adolescent use of the drugs and substances of abuse, found that 42.2% of their 12th-grade student participants reported lifetime prevalence of cigarette use and that 19.2% reported smoking a cigarette within the previous 30 days (i.e., month).

[b] Johnston, O'Malley, & Bachman (2010b), in their 2010 in-school survey of adolescent use of the drugs and substances of abuse, found that 23.1% of their 12th-grade student participants reported smoking small cigars within the previous year.

[c] Johnston, O'Malley, Bachman, et al. (2010b), in their 2010 in-school survey of adolescent use of the drugs and substances of abuse, found that 17.6% of the 12th- grade student participants reported lifetime prevalence of smokeless tobacco use and that 8.5% reported using smokeless tobacco within the previous 30 days (i.e., month). When considered alone, 15.7% of adolescent boys reported smokeless tobacco use within the previous 30 days (i.e., month).

Source: Eaton, Kann, Kinchen, et al., 2010.

Tobacco Surveys, found that: (1) overall, 6.9% of participants reported polytobacco use; (2) among adolescent boys who were current cigarette smokers, 62% used other tobacco products; and (3) among adolescent girls who were current cigarette smokers, 30.9% used other tobacco products.

**Influence of Ethnicity and Continental Descent** Data from all the major published studies indicate that North American adolescents of African descent have lower rates of all forms of tobacco use than adolescents of either European or Hispanic descent (e.g., Eaton, Kann, Kinchen, et al., 2010; Johnston, O'Malley, Bachman, et al., 2010b; Kelder, Prokhorov, Barroso, et al., 2003). In addition, adolescents of African descent, who do smoke tobacco, preferentially select and use menthol-flavored cigarettes (e.g., Kool®, Newport®, Salem®)[50] significantly more so than

do adolescents of other continental descents (Allen & Unger, 2007; Johnston, O'Malley, Bachman, et al., 2008; Unger, Allen, Leonard, et al., 2010).[51]

Interestingly, Muilenburg and Legge (2008) noted a significant interaction effect in their study of adolescent smoking behavior at six urban secondary schools. Their findings supported previous findings that North American adolescents of African descent had lower rates of tobacco use than adolescents of other continental descents and also had a preference for smoking menthol cigarettes. However, they also found that adolescents of African descent, who did smoke, smoked more cigarettes per day than did adolescents of other continental descents. Also interesting in this context is the finding of Robles, Singh-Franco, and Ghin (2008) who, in their study of smoking-cessation pharmacotherapy in nonwhite U.S. populations, found that North Americans of

[50] Menthol is the only tobacco additive actively promoted in advertisements by the tobacco industry in North America (Ahijevych & Garrett, 2004; Kreslake, Wayne, & Connolly, 2008).

[51] Conversely, in the National Youth Tobacco Survey, adolescents of American Indian or Alaska Native descent were found to have significantly higher rates of all forms of tobacco use than did all other adolescents, including those of European or Hispanic descent (Yu, 2010). They also were found to be significantly more likely to actively engage in polyuse of tobacco (i.e., use both smoking tobacco and smokeless tobacco) (Wolsko, Mohatt, Lardon, et al., 2009; Yu, 2010).

African descent who smoked mentholated cigarettes were significantly less likely to achieve desired smoking cessation outcomes than those who smoked nonmentholated cigarettes.

The preferential selection of menthol-flavored cigarettes by North American adolescents of African descent has been ascribed to: (1) a reduction in the harshness and irritating effects that are commonly associated with tobacco smoking (i.e., the menthol produces a cooling and mild local anesthetic effect); and (2) a developed taste, or liking, for the menthol-flavored tobacco smoke (Ahijevych & Garrett, 2004; Hersey, Ng, Nonnemaker, et al., 2006; Kreslake, Wayne, & Connolly, 2008). We would also add another factor: (3) *social persuasion*. For most of the past 100 years, the application of principles of social psychology has been an integral component in the successful marketing of tobacco products (Pagliaro & Pagliaro, 2004). The significant presence of flashy billboards with advertisements for Newport® cigarettes in neighborhoods where there is a higher percentage of North Americans of African descent, as well as advertisements in popular ethnic magazines that are available and sold in stores in these communities, certainly has had a significant effect on exposed adolescents in relation to their choices as to which tobacco product to use initially.[52]

In addition, several studies of adolescents of African or Hispanic descent (e.g., Brook, Pahl, & Ning, 2006; Fagan, Brook, Rubenstone, et al., 2009) have found that the smoking behavior of parents and peers significantly influences their decision to smoke or not to smoke tobacco cigarettes. Brook, Zhang, Finch, et al. (2010), in their analysis of their past research and current related work, found that such factors as family conflict and weak ethnic identity were related to antisocial behavior, which, in turn, was related to associating with peers who smoked, which,

in turn, was related to decisions to initiate or continue smoking.

**Tobacco Cigarillo Smoking**   Another tobacco smoking trend observed among adolescents that has significantly increased over the past 10 years, particularly among adolescent boys, is the use of cigarillos. With such popular brand names as Black & Mild®, Cheroots®, and Prime Time®, these tobacco products appear to have been designed intentionally for this market. In addition, they are particularly attractive to youth because they are: (1) small in size and are easier to handle and smoke than larger cigars; (2) commonly sold in corner convenience stores individually or in "kiddy packs"—packages containing three to eight cigarillos; (3) less expensive than typical packages of 20 cigarettes; and (4) flavored—with such flavors as cherry, chocolate, grape, piña colada, rum, strawberry, and vanilla.

Cigarillos typically contain 5 to 12 times more nicotine than regular cigarettes. In addition, when smoked, they deliver significantly higher concentrations of hydrogen cyanide and cancer-causing nitrosamines. Although cigarette smoking has either declined significantly or remained stable across all jurisdictions and among all age groups in North America over the past decade, the use of cigars has increased by up to 50% and the use of cigarillos has increased by up to 150%, particularly among adolescents and young adults (Pagliaro & Pagliaro, 2009).

**Bidis and Kretek Smoking**   In addition to tobacco cigarettes and cigarillos, North America adolescents also are smoking bidis and kreteks. While patterns in the use of these East Indian and Indonesian cigarettes has waxed and waned over the last few years, their use is expected to continue—albeit at relatively low levels.

---

[52] This observed effect tends to snowball with generational effects as these youth age, mature, and continue to smoke, providing themselves as role models for smoking as national sports stars, entertainers, and public leaders for new generations of youth (Allen & Unger, 2007; Pagliaro & Pagliaro, *Clinical Patient Data Files*).

*Bidis* Bidis are hand-rolled, unfiltered cigarettes imported from India primarily for purchase and use by immigrants who are now living in North America. The tobacco in bidi cigarettes contains 25% to 50% more nicotine per gram than does the tobacco in conventional North American cigarettes (Malson, Sims, Murty, et al., 2001). In addition, bidi cigarettes are available in a wide variety of candy-like flavors (e.g., chocolate, clove, dewberry) that appeal, in particular, to children and adolescents (Stanfill, Brown, Yan, et al., 2006). Although the additional flavoring appears to contribute to the use of these and other non-traditional alternative tobacco products by North American youth, other factors may also contribute to their use. As noted by Soldz and Dorsey (2005, p. 549), adolescents in grades 7 through 12 most frequently endorsed the statements that these products "smell good" and "are something different to try."

The use of bidis by North American adolescents increased during the 1990s (Soldz, Huyser, & Dorsey, 2003), reaching a peak of 9.2% among 12th-grade students in 2000. Since that time, use among all North American adolescents has steadily decreased, and annual use is now less than 1% (Honstok, O'Malley, Bachman, et al., 2008; Pagliaro & Pagliaro, 2009). (Also see the next discussion of Kreteks.)

*Kreteks* Many North American adolescents and young adults, along with recent immigrants from Indonesia, are smoking kreteks (i.e., the primary form of cigarettes used in Indonesia). Kreteks contain a blend of tobacco, cloves, and other flavoring ingredients and have a significantly higher tar and nicotine content (i.e., approximately 50% higher) than do typical North American tobacco cigarettes (Guidotti, 1989; Pagliaro & Pagliaro, 2009). However, it is the addition of dried clove bud (i.e., 15% to

40% by weight) that truly distinguishes these cigarettes from others (Polzin, Stanfill, Brown, et al., 2007). Kretek use in the United States reached levels similar to bidis use in 2001 (i.e., 10.1% of 12th-grade students) but has decreased significantly in recent years and is now well below 1% (Johnston, O'Malley, Bachman, et al., 2008). The primary reason for this significant drop in the use of kreteks was related to the passage of law HR1256 by the U.S. Congress in 2009. (Also see related following discussion in the next section.) This law banned the sale of kreteks and any other candy-flavored cigarettes in the United States. However, they continue to be available in Canada and Mexico and through purchase over the Internet.[53] In addition, as a way around the law, kretek cigars/cigarillos are available for sale in the United States.

### Recommendations for Decreasing Tobacco Sales to Minors

The possession and use of tobacco products is legal for adults across North America, where they can be found in a wide variety of retail outlets, including corner grocery and convenience stores, gas stations, and most drugstores. Thus, these products, unlike illicit smokable drugs and substances of abuse (e.g., cannabis; see related discussion in Chapter 3, *The Psychodelics*), are commonly seen and are generally availability to children and adolescents by various means (e.g., an opened carton in the parents' bedroom; common easy purchase without proof of age).[54] In addition, these products are available in self-service vending machines and by e-mail or courier delivery through Internet purchases locally, nationally, and internationally.

Several community-based antismoking groups, along with several researchers (e.g., Chriqui, Ribisl, Wallace, et al., 2008; DiFranza, Savageau, & Fletcher, 2009), have recommended

---

[53] Djarum Black® is a very popular brand of kreteks that is internationally available.

[54] In an analysis of data from the Virginia Youth Tobacco Survey of current tobacco users, Kaestle (2009) found that girls were significantly more likely to receive free cigarettes, particularly from older adults (and, we would add, older boyfriends [Pagliaro & Pagliaro, *Clinical Patient Data Files*]).

that legislative regulatory changes be made to significantly reduce the access to and the sale of tobacco products to children and adolescents. These changes include: (1) increasing the associated state excise tax to encourage merchants to raise the cost of a package of cigarettes;[55] (2) requiring merchants, at the point of sale, to prominently display a conspicuous sign that clearly states that the sale of tobacco to minors is illegal and that proof of age is required for tobacco purchase; and (3) more aggressively enforce enacted existing laws that forbid the sale of tobacco products to minors. To date, these recommendations generally have not been fully or aggressively implemented. In fact, merchants continue to ignore many of the existing laws aimed at preventing the sale of tobacco cigarettes and other tobacco products to children and adolescents, and local police departments generally do not enforce them (Centers for Disease Control and Prevention, 1996; DiFranza & Brown, 1992; DiFranza, Savageau, & Aisquith, 1996; Stead & Lancaster, 2005a). (Also see additional related discussion in Chapter 9, *Preventing and Treating Child and Adolescent Use of the Drugs and Substances of Abuse*.)

In recent years, the Food and Drug Administration (FDA) has taken more proactive steps to reduce tobacco smoking by children and adolescents. For example, on September 22, 2009, a ban on cigarettes containing certain characterizing flavors went into effect.[56] As designated by the ban:

A cigarette, or any of its component parts (including the tobacco, filter, or paper), shall not contain, as a constituent (including a smoke constituent) or additive, an artificial or natural flavor (other than tobacco or menthol) or an herb or spice, including strawberry, grape, orange, clove, cinnamon, pineapple, vanilla, coconut, licorice, cocoa, chocolate, cherry, or coffee, that is a characterizing flavor of the tobacco product or tobacco smoke. (U.S. Food and Drug Administration, 2009b, p. 1)

On June 22, 2010, the FDA issued a new rule, Regulations Restricting the Sale and Distribution of Cigarettes and Smokeless Tobacco to Protect Children and Adolescents. This rule included requirements related to the sale and distribution of tobacco products as well as their labeling, advertising, and promotion, in the United States (Department of Health and Human Services, 2010). (See Table 2.4; also see Chapter 9, *Preventing and Treating Child and Adolescent Use of the Drugs and Substances of Abuse*, for related discussion concerning strategies for reducing child and adolescent tobacco use.)

Finally, in November 2010, the multibillion-dollar tobacco industry was put under the control of the FDA, and on June 21, 2011, the FDA unveiled nine new warning labels that must be placed prominently on cigarette packages (Johnson, 2011; Reuters, 2011). As noted by the Secretary of Health and Human Services, Kathleen Sebelius, "We hope it [the new warning labels] will prevent our children and future generations from picking up this addictive and deadly habit" (Sebelius, 2011, p. 1). The nine new warning labels, each of which is accompanied

---

[55] This particular initiative has been widely and well implemented across North America, with the average price of a package of commercial cigarettes rising significantly over the past decades. However, it appears that, given the relative lack of concerted action in regard to the sale of tobacco cigarettes from corner convenience stores to minors and a similar lack of action in regard to illegal and untaxed sales of tobacco cigarettes that originate from American Indian reservations and Aboriginal reserves across North America, the primary effect of this initiative has been to increase tax revenue rather than to decrease adolescent use of tobacco cigarettes and other tobacco products.

Nevertheless, several researchers (e.g., DiFranza, Savageau, & Fletcher, 2009; Roeseler & Burns, 2010) have identified that the strategy of increasing excise taxes on tobacco products, when consistently used in the context of a comprehensive strategy, can significantly contribute to deceasing tobacco sales to children and adolescents and, consequently, their use of these products.

[56] This ban, as noted, is specific to cigarettes. Therefore, it does not apply to the flavoring agents that are routinely added to the newer and increasingly popular dissolvable tobacco products (e.g., Camel Orbs®, Stonewall®; see later related section, "Smokeless Tobacco").

**Table 2.4   FDA 2010 Regulations Restricting Tobacco Products**

**Requirements Relating to Sale, Distribution, and Marketing of Tobacco Cigarettes and Smokeless Tobacco Products**

**Requirements Relating to Sale and Distribution**

- Prohibits the sale of cigarettes and smokeless tobacco to anyone younger than 18 years of age
- Prohibits the sale of packages of cigarettes that contain fewer than 20 cigarettes
- Prohibits the sale of cigarettes and smokeless tobacco products in vending machines, self-service displays, and other impersonal means of sale, except in limited, specified situations
- Prohibits the use of free samples of cigarettes for promoting sales and limits the distribution of smokeless tobacco products

**Requirements Relating to Marketing**

- Prohibits the use of tobacco brand name sponsorship of any athletic, musical, or other cultural or social event, and any team or other entry in these events
- Prohibits gifts or other items in exchange for buying cigarettes or smokeless tobacco products
- Requires that audio advertisements use only words and not music or sound effects that may be associated with the use of tobacco cigarettes or other tobacco products including smokeless tobacco products
- Prohibits the sale or distribution of ball caps, tee shirts, and other products that display tobacco brands or logos

Source: U.S. Food and Drug Administration, 2010b.

by an appropriate graphic image, read as follows:

- Warning: Cigarettes are addictive.
- Warning: Cigarette smoke can harm your children.
- Warning: Cigarettes cause fatal lung disease.
- Warning: Cigarettes cause cancer.
- Warning: Cigarettes cause strokes and heart disease.
- Warning: Smoking during pregnancy can harm your baby.
- Warning: Smoking can kill you.
- Warning: Tobacco smoke causes fatal lung disease in nonsmokers.
- Warning: Quitting smoking now greatly reduces serious risks to your health.

## General Pharmacology

Nicotine stimulates the CNS at all levels, including the cerebral cortex, where its action causes increased cognitive activity. (For further related discussion, see Chapter 6, *Effects of Drugs and Substances of Abuse on Learning and Memory During Childhood and Adolescence*). Tobacco smoking typically produces an increase in hand tremor and an alerting pattern on the electroencephalogram. However, at the same time, there is a decreased tone in some skeletal muscles (e.g., anterior thigh muscle, or quadriceps femoris) and a decrease in deep-tendon reflexes. These effects may involve stimulation of the Renshaw cells in the spinal cord. Its action on motor neurons may be associated with the feelings of relaxation that are generally reported with tobacco smoking.

### Proposed Mechanism of Psychostimulant Action

The pharmacologic action of nicotine is dose-dependent. Lower doses stimulate autonomic ganglia, whereas higher doses block autonomic ganglia (Heeschen, Weis, Aicher, et al., 2002; Kimura, Ushiyama, Fujii, et al. 2003; Shytle, Silver, Lukas, et al., 2002). The action of nicotine on autonomic ganglia also varies according to the degree of tolerance that a user has developed to nicotine. (Also see the section "Physical and Psychological Dependence.")

The smoking of one or two tobacco cigarettes after a few hours of abstinence produces a significant rise in the plasma concentration of several hormones and neurotransmitters. For example, nicotine stimulates neurons in specific areas of the brain (e.g., ventral tegmental area) to release dopamine and further stimulate the release of glutamate. In turn, glutamate triggers additional dopamine release in the limbic system producing euphoria, or a pleasurable sensation (Zickler, 2003). Nicotine also has cardiovascular actions. These actions result in tachycardia and vasoconstriction, consequently resulting in an increase in blood pressure.

Pharmacologically, nicotine appears to exert its psychostimulant actions secondarily to a direct stimulation of nicotinic acetylcholine receptors (nAChRs).[57] Several distinct subtypes of nicotinic receptors are widely distributed in the CNS.[58] (See Figure 2.5.) Nicotinic receptors, which are ligand-gated ion channels, are structurally diverse and have many roles. The activation of these channels causes a rapid increase in cellular permeability to sodium ($Na^+$) and potassium ($K^+$) ions, with resultant depolarization and excitation.

Nicotinic receptors in the CNS are composed of two subunits, alpha ($\alpha$) and beta ($\beta$), which are found in discrete regions of the brain.[59] The specific actions of the nicotinic receptors in the CNS are still largely undetermined. However, nicotinic receptors in autonomic ganglia affect depolarization and firing of postganglionic neurons. Nicotinic receptors in the adrenal medulla affect the secretion of catecholamines, which results in the opening of the cation channel in nAChRs (Araki, Suemaru, & Gomita, 2002). The $alpha_4$ and $beta_2$ receptor subunits appear to contribute to the euphoria associated with nicotine use. In addition, nicotine acetylcholine receptors, specifically subunits $\alpha_3$, $\alpha_5$, and $\beta_3$,

appear to be responsible for determining a user's risk for developing nicotine dependence—as well as its severity (Whitten, 2009).

Because responses to nicotine use are thought to be genetically influenced, research in this area eventually should help to explain the variations observed among nicotine users in regard to their patterns of use and their development of physical and psychological dependence (also see "Physical and Psychological Dependence" later in this section). It also would help to explain the variations in the physical and psychological withdrawal observed among users when they quit, or attempt to cease, their regular, long-term use of nicotine (e.g., some users are able to quit nicotine use successfully without relapsing, or returning to resumed use, while others are unable to quit even after many tries—regardless of the method used [e.g., cold turkey, use of nicotine replacement products, various types of counseling]). As noted by Whitten (2009, p. 1):

> Individuals inherit different forms of half a dozen genes that dictate the features of the brain receptor to which nicotine binds.

### Common Toxicities

The common toxicities associated with the use of nicotine, either chewed, dissolved, smoked, or snorted, are related to its direct actions on the CNS and other body systems, particularly the cardiovascular, gastrointestinal (GI), and respiratory systems. These toxicities can be acute (i.e., sudden and severe) or chronic

---

[57] Acetylcholine is one of several major chemical neurotransmitters in the body. Although it acts predominantly at neuromuscular junctions in the parasympathetic division of the autonomic nervous system, it also acts in the cholinergic portion of the sympathetic nervous system. In addition, acetylcholine acts at some synapses in the brain, where it influences arousal, attention, memory, and mood.

[58] Nicotinic acetylcholine receptors have been identified in various other body organ systems, including lymphocytes and nasal mucosa. It is thought that the nAChRs in lymphocytes may play a role in the regulation of immune function (Kawashima & Fujii, 2003; Kimura, Ushiyama, Fujii, et al., 2003). The nAChRs found in nasal mucosa may be involved in producing the nasal reactions (e.g., sensitivity) to tobacco smoke and to nicotine intranasal spray products that occur among some people (Keiger, Case, Kendal-Reed, et al., 2003).

[59] Nine different alpha ($\alpha$) and three different beta ($\beta$) subunits have been identified in the nervous systems of vertebrates. By convention, these subunits are labeled $\alpha_{2-10}$ ($\alpha_2$, $\alpha_3$, $\alpha_4$, $\alpha_5$, $\alpha_6$, $\alpha_7$, $\alpha_8$, $\alpha_9$, $\alpha_{10}$) and $\beta_{2-4}$ ($\beta_2$, $\beta_3$, $\beta_4$). This number of subunits allows for the possibility of many combinations of subtypes of nAChRs. These subtypes are defined by their constituent subunits (e.g., $\alpha_4\beta_2$ subtype, $\beta_7$ subtype [Kellar, Davila-Garcia, & Xiao, 1999]).

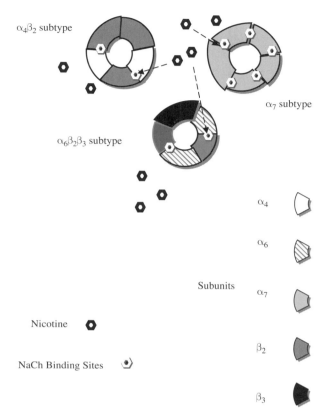

α4β2 subtype

α7 subtype

α6β2β3 subtype

α4

α6

Subunits    α7

Nicotine ⬡

β2

NaCh Binding Sites

β3

**Figure 2.5    Nicotine: Mechanism of Psychostimulant Action**

(i.e., long-lasting and recurring). For example, unintentional, acute nicotine poisoning, particularly involving infants, toddlers, and young children, can be fatal (see Chapter 5, *Exposure to the Drugs and Substances of Abuse From Conception Through Childhood*). In another example, regular, long-term cigarette smoking is the leading preventable cause of disease and death in the United States, accounting for over 440,000 deaths among adults annually (Johnston, O'Malley, Bachman, et al., 2008; Marshall, Schooley, Ryan, et al., 2006). However, in regard to the former, death is caused by the direct action of nicotine. In regard to the latter, it is due to

the method of nicotine use (i.e., smoking). This section discusses the acute and chronic toxicities associated directly with the pharmacological actions of nicotine in the body and those that are associated with its methods of use.

**Toxicities Directly Related to the Actions of Nicotine**    The toxicities related to the direct actions of nicotine usually are acute and associated with the stimulation of the cortex of the brain. These toxicities include diarrhea, dizziness, fluid retention, GI cramps, headache, hypertension, irritability, tachycardia, tremors, and vomiting.[60, 61] Seizures

[60] Many smokers report that when they initially began to smoke tobacco cigarettes, smoking their very first few cigarettes was generally an unpleasant experience that induced nausea, dizziness, vomiting, and headache. These effects reportedly disappeared with continued smoking but could recur if the amount of smoking was suddenly and significantly increased (Pagliaro & Pagliaro, *Clinical Patient Data Files*).

[61] These same signs and symptoms of nicotine toxicity have been observed and related to percutaneous absorption of nicotine among farm workers who hand-harvest or otherwise handle fresh, wet tobacco leaves. It is commonly referred to in the tobacco industry as "green tobacco sickness" (Rao, Quandt, & Arcury, 2002).

can occur if large amounts of nicotine are intentionally used. Seizures also can occur in cases of unintentional poisoning (e.g., when a toddler or pet finds and chews a discarded nicotine patch or ingests a nicotine-containing insecticide).

The acutely fatal dose of nicotine for an adolescent is probably about 60 mg of the base. Signs and symptoms of acute nicotine poisoning include: abdominal pain, agitation, cold sweat, confusion, diarrhea, dizziness, disturbed hearing and vision, headache, hypotension, lethargy, light-headedness, nausea, pallor, profuse sweating, salivation (excessive), tearing or watery eyes, vomiting, and a weak, irregular pulse. Death, which may be preceded by seizures, usually is due to the nicotine-induced respiratory arrest caused by both central paralysis and peripheral blockade of the respiratory muscles. When unintentional nicotine poisoning is suspected, it should be considered a medical emergency, particularly when infants, toddlers, and young children are involved. (Also see related discussion of nicotine in Chapter 5, *Exposure to Drugs and Substances of Abuse From Conception Through Childhood*).

**Indirect Toxicities Related to Tobacco Smoke and Smokeless Tobacco**  Several chronic toxicities have been associated with nicotine use.[62] However, these toxicities are *indirectly* caused by nicotine. In fact, they actually are due to a combination of the nicotine, ammonia, carbon monoxide, tars, and over 4,000 other chemicals that are found in tobacco smoke (World Health Organization, 2009). The toxicities associated with exposure to these chemicals and gases are usually related to regular, long-term tobacco smoking or to long-term exposure to tobacco smoke (i.e., environmental smoke or passive exposure to side-stream, or secondhand, smoke) (U.S. Department of Health and Human Services, 2006). (Also see Chapter 5, *Exposure to Drugs and Substances of Abuse From Conception Through Childhood*.) Several chronic toxicities also have been directly related to the regular, long-term use of smokeless tobacco. These toxicities are discussed in this section.

*Tobacco Smoke*  Tobacco smoke has been associated with an increased occurrence of several cancers and cardiovascular diseases. In fact, tobacco smoke is the largest single preventable cause of illness and disease in North America and the largest single cause of premature deaths worldwide. It is currently estimated that tobacco smoke is responsible for, or contributes in a significant way to, over 1,500 deaths *every day* in North America. Tobacco use is the leading cause of preventable death in the world and is estimated to kill more than 5 million people each year worldwide (Hatsukami, Stead, & Gupta, 2008; Warner & Mackay, 2006).[63] These deaths have been associated with several medical conditions directly related to tobacco smoking, including various cancers and cardiovascular diseases. The effects of environmental exposure of infants and children to tobacco smoke, as well as the exposure of their mothers during pregnancy, particularly in regard to teratogenic effects, also is of increasing concern. For over three decades, we have consistently noted that nicotine, in the form of tobacco smoke, is unique among all of the other drugs and substances of abuse in that it has *no* safe level of use. The

---

[62] The toxicities generally would not occur if the smokable and nonsmokable products were irregularly used over short periods of time. In this regard, it is the nicotine in these products, because of its propensity to cause physical and psychological dependence—the development of tolerance, and a nicotine withdrawal syndrome that occurs when nicotine use is abruptly discontinued—that increases and reinforces the regular, long-term use that contributes to these toxicities.

[63] In North America, these preventable and unnecessary deaths annually add up to over 500,000 deaths with approximately 50,000 resulting from passive exposure to secondhand smoke. (Also see related discussion in Chapter 5, *Exposure to the Drugs and Substances of Abuse From Conception Through Childhood*.)

therapeutic index for tobacco smoke is zero. As noted by the World Health Organization (2009, p. 14):

> There is no safe level of exposure to tobacco smoke. All people should be protected from such exposure.

*Cancers* In 1964, the U.S. Surgeon General's report, *Smoking and Health* (U.S. Department of Health, Education and Welfare, 1964) stimulated the beginning of a drastic change in attitudes toward tobacco smoking in North America. The report was highly contested by large tobacco companies that sought to defend themselves against the thousands of lawsuits being brought against them related to the cancer-causing effects of tobacco smoking. Great efforts to refute the claims of the report also were put forward by many physicians and scientists who continued to smoke tobacco themselves in their offices, clinics, and hospitals.[64] However, over the ensuing decades, as more and more data were accumulated by researchers and released by tobacco companies, it became clearly established and demonstrated that the use of tobacco, which contains over 50 identified cancer-causing chemicals, or carcinogens (Kuper, Adami, & Boffetta, 2002), causes approximately 500,000 deaths annually in North America (Cokkinides, Bandi, McMahon, et al., 2009). Approximately half of these deaths are due to cancer; the remaining half are due to nonmalignant cardiovascular and respiratory disorders (Thun, Henley, & Calle, 2002).

Tobacco smoking has been clearly and directly associated with an increased risk for various cancers, including cancer of the breast, cervix of the uterus, esophagus, head, kidney, larynx, liver, lung, neck, mouth and oropharynx, pancreas, stomach, and urinary bladder (Johnson, 2001; Kuper, Boffetta, &

Adami, 2002; Nagata, Mizoue, Tanaka, et al., 2006; Shetty & Brown, 2009; Tanaka, Tsuji, Wakai, et al., 2006; Thun, Henley, & Calle, 2002). Today risk for tobacco-associated mortality is the same for women as it is for men (Pagliaro & Pagliaro, 2009). The reason for this statistic includes a "600-percent increase since 1950 in women's death rates for lung cancer, a disease primarily caused by cigarette smoking" (Satcher, 2001, p. 368).

In North America, deaths associated with lung cancer have a particular high incidence among men of African descent. A number of studies and reports (e.g., Benowitz, Herrera, & Jacob, 2004) have suggested a relationship between the regular, long-term smoking of menthol cigarettes and the development of lung cancer. (See earlier discussion of menthol cigarettes.) Although several large epidemiological studies examined this proposed relationship, no evidence was found in its support. Other research directions also were taken, and it is now thought that the high incidence of lung cancer among North American men of African descent is primarily genetically determined (Werley, Coggins, & Lee, 2007).

*Cardiovascular Diseases* Over 70 years ago, the association between tobacco smoking and cardiovascular disease (i.e., coronary heart disease) had been well recognized by English, Willius, and Berkson (1940). Currently, it is generally estimated that tobacco smoking is associated with a 2- to 4-fold increased risk for coronary heart disease among regular, long-term tobacco smokers—both men and women.

*Environmental Smoke Exposure: Effects on Mothers During Pregnancy, Infants, and Children* The maternal use of nicotine during pregnancy and its relationship to teratogenesis has not been well documented. However, cigarette smoking has been related

---

[64]This opposition was most likely due, in large part, to the psychological construct that Leon Festinger (1957) referred to as "cognitive dissonance" (i.e., resistance to rejecting existing beliefs and practices when confronted with new contradictory evidence).

to increased rates of spontaneous abortion, stillbirth, and neonatal death. Neonates of mothers who smoke tobacco during pregnancy have a lower birth weight (Pagliaro & Pagliaro, 2002). They also are twice as likely to die during early infancy of the sudden infant death syndrome (SIDS). In this context, SIDS is thought to be related to the infant's exposure to tobacco smoke from mothers, fathers, and other household members and caregivers. Nicotine, and its principal metabolite, cotinine, can achieve higher concentrations in maternal milk than in maternal plasma. Thus, even neonates and infants whose mothers avoid smoking tobacco in their presence may be placed at increased risk during breastfeeding (O'Mara & Nahata, 2002). (For further related discussion, see Chapter 5, *Exposure to Drugs and Substances of Abuse From Conception Through Childhood*.)

***Smokeless Tobacco***   Some individuals who use nicotine for its desired psychostimulant actions have turned to smokeless forms of tobacco in an effort to decrease their risks for both cardiovascular and respiratory diseases, including lung cancer. Several types of smokeless tobacco products, including dissolvable tobacco products, are currently available for use in North America.[65] (See Table 2.5.) Smokeless forms of tobacco are generally much safer to use in relation to their cardiovascular and pulmonary toxicities, including lung cancer (Accortt, Waterbor, Beall, et al., 2002). However, they are not completely safe. In fact, they have been implicated in several gum and mouth disorders (e.g., irritation) and oral cancer (i.e., the incidence among users is more than 4 times higher than among nontobacco-using controls). Interestingly, moist snuff (i.e., wet or spit snuff) and chewing tobacco generally have been found to be significantly less toxic, in this regard, than dry snuff (Rodu & Cole, 2002).

Smokeless tobacco products contain potent human carcinogens (i.e., tobacco-specific nitrosamines; Richter, Hodge, Stanfill, et al., 2008). Swedish snus, because of its unique method of preparation (see Table 2.5), is a low-nitrosamine form of smokeless tobacco. Consequently, in comparison to tobacco cigarette smoking, the use of Swedish snus has been associated with a 90% lower relative risk for heart disease, lung cancer, and oral cancer (Levy, Mumford, Cummings, et al., 2004). However, its regular, long-term use has been linked to a doubling of the risk for pancreatic cancer (i.e., approximately 1 in 1,000) when compared to nonusers of tobacco products (Fesinmeyer, 2006; Use of Swedish "snus," 2007).

In regard to the nicotine replacement products (e.g., Nicoderm®), they work simply by providing nicotine in dosage formulations (e.g., chewing gum, nasal spray, skin patch or transdermal delivery system) that are associated with significantly fewer undesired, or harmful, effects and toxicities than is tobacco smoking. (Also see "Tobacco Smoke" section and related discussion in Chapter 9, *Preventing and Treating Child and Adolescent Use of the Drugs and Substances of Abuse*.)

One additional form of smokeless tobacco is the e-cigarette, or electronic cigarette. The e-cigarette, introduced during the early 2000s, is a small, hand-held device that resembles the size and shape of a conventional cigarette. It houses a disposable cartridge of nicotine solution, which, when electrically heated within the cigarette, produces a vapor that is inhaled by the user. The behaviors associated with using an e-cigarette (e.g., holding the e-cigarette between the first two fingers of the dominant hand; inhaling the vapor after positioning the device between the lips) are very similar to smoking a conventional

---

[65] Although several researchers (e.g., Carpenter & Gray, 2010) have suggested that smokeless tobacco, particularly the more recently available dissolvable forms, can be used to facilitate tobacco smoking cessation, this use is neither approved by the FDA nor endorsed by the smokeless tobacco manufacturers.

**TABLE 2.5 Commonly Available Forms of Smokeless Tobacco**

| Name (Synonyms) Brand® Names | Description | Method of Use | Comments |
|---|---|---|---|
| *Conventional Smokeless Tobacco Products* | | | |
| **Chew** (chewing tobacco) Copenhagen®, Red Man®, Skoal® | Long strands of cured, whole leaf tobacco | Placed between the cheek and the gum or the teeth, and chewed for oral transmucosal absorption | Traditional method used by American Indians Requires spitting Available as: *Loose-leaf tobacco* packaged in aluminum-lined pouches. *Plug tobacco*, which is sweetened with molasses, pressed into sheets, and cut into plugs that are wrapped with fine tobacco. Users must bite or cut off individual servings from the plug. *Tobacco bits* that consist of flavored, sweetened tobacco leaf that has been rolled and cut into bits or individual mint-size servings. Typically, loosely packaged in tins. *Tobacco twists*, dried, cured tobacco leaves that are spun and rolled into rope-like strands and then twisted into a knot. |
| **Dip** (dipping or spit tobacco) Copenhagen Straight®, Skoal Long Cut Mint® | Chopped moist tobacco that has undergone a fermentation process | Placed under the upper lip, or between the lower lip and gums, for oral transmucosal absorption over 45–60 minutes | Causes excessive salivation Requires spitting Often flavored with cherry, licorice, mint, or wintergreen and sweetened with molasses |
| **Snuff** (nasal snuff; dry snuff; dry snus) McChrystal's Apricot Snuff®, Poschl Lowen-Prise® | Dry, powdered tobacco | Intranasally insufflated (snuffed or snorted) into the nostrils for intranasal absorption | Does not require spitting Available in a variety of aromas, such as aniseed, apricot, clove, and menthol |
| **Snus**, American (American snuff) Camel Snus®, Marlboro Snus® | Moist, powdered, fire-cured tobacco | Placed under the upper lip for oral transmucosal absorption | Does not require spitting Low moisture content Low pH Available in unit-dose pouches |
| **Snus**, Swedish (Scandinavian snuff) General® | Moist, powdered, air-dried tobacco (steam pasteurized) | Placed under the upper lip for oral transmuscosal absorption over extended periods of time | Does not require spitting High moisture content (greater than 50%) Better absorption than American Snus Swedish Snus is prepared by heating the tobacco and adjunct ingredients (e.g., aromas, salt, sodium carbonate, and water) with steam (i.e., it is not smoke cured or fermented) Available as: Loose tobacco that is pinched into a spherical shape with the fingertips prior to placement. Portioned tobacco that is prepackaged in small unit-dose teabag-like sachets for use. |
| *Recently Developed Dissolvable Smokeless Tobacco Products* | | | |
| **Film Strips** Camel Strips® | Thin film of very finely powdered tobacco, similar in form to Listerine PocketPaks® breath-freshening strips | Placed on the tongue and allowed to dissolve over 2–3 minutes for oral transmucosal absorption | Contains 0.6 mg nicotine per strip Packaged in child-resistant dispensers |

*(Continued)*

TABLE 2.5    Commonly Available Forms of Smokeless Tobacco (Continued)

| Name (Synonyms) Brand® Names | Description | Method of Use | Comments |
|---|---|---|---|
| Lozenges Ariva®, Stonewall® | Powdered, flue-cured Virginia tobacco that has been compressed into lozenges | Dissolved in the mouth over 10–30 minutes for oral transmucosal aborption | Ariva® contains 1.5 mg nicotine per lozenge Stonewall® contains 4 mg nicotine per lozenge Available in java, natural, and wintergreen flavors Packaged in child-resistant dispensers |
| Pellets Camel Orbs® | Flavored tobacco powder mixed with various pharmaceutical adjuncts (e.g., disintegration aids, fillers, preservatives) and compressed into a pellet | Dissolved in the mouth over 10–15 minutes for oral transmucosal absorption | Contains 1 mg nicotine per pellet Available in mellow and fresh flavors Packaged in child-resistant dispensers |
| Twisted Sticks Camel Sticks® | Thinly twisted stick of tobacco, similar in form to a toothpick | Inserted between the upper lip and gum and allowed to dissolve over 20–30 minutes for oral transmucosal absorption | Contains 3.1 mg nicotine per stick Available in fresh flavor Packaged in child-resistant dispensers |

Source: Modified from brand manufacturers' Web sites.

cigarette.[66] However, because there is no pyrolysis of tobacco leaves and cigarette paper, there is no exposure to any additional chemicals, additives, and products of pyrolysis, including various carcinogens (see earlier related discussion).

In 2010, the FDA lost several court cases during which it attempted to regulate the e-cigarette as a drug-delivery device (Kirshner, 2011). As long as they are not marketed as aids to stop smoking, e-cigarettes are regulated simply as other tobacco products (Associated Press, 2011).

*Physical and Psychological Dependence*
During the 1970s and 1980s, the regular,

long-term use of nicotine was found to cause both physical and psychological dependence. A decade later, Collins (1990) summarized the 20th Report of the Surgeon General on the health consequences of smoking, which was titled *Nicotine Addiction*. This summary, a 500-page comprehensive review of over 1,000 published studies, concluded that: (1) the use of tobacco products was associated with the development of physical dependence; (2) nicotine was the substance identified as causing the physical dependence in these products; and (3) the process of becoming physically dependent on nicotine[67] was similar to that observed for heroin and cocaine (p. 84).

---

[66] Reported research on the e-cigarette (e.g., Bullen, McRobbie, Thornley, et al., 2010; Trtchounian, Williams, & Talbot, 2010) has suggested that e-cigarettes primarily require significantly stronger vacuums to inhale the aerosolized nicotine (i.e., suction, "drag" or "pull") than do conventional cigarettes for inhaling tobacco smoke. Consequently, the e-cigarette may produce a nicotine pharmacokinetic profile that is more similar to that of the nicotine replacement inhaler (e.g., Nicorette® inhaler) than to a conventional cigarette.

[67] Most hard science, or positivist, researchers in this field of study (e.g., Vetulani, 2001) agree that the development of physical dependence to nicotine is mediated by the release of brain dopamine. Subsequently the dopamine interacts at neural reward centers located primarily in the limbic structures of the brain. However, other positivist researchers have suggested that the nicotine-mediated release of other neurotransmitters and neuromodulators (e.g., Domino, 2002; Kenny & Markou, 2001), up-regulation of nAChRs following prolonged exposure to nicotine (Buisson & Bertrand, 2002), or nicotine-induced alteration in nAChR synaptic plasticity (Dani & De Biasi, 2001; Dani, Ji, & Zhou, 2001), also plays a major role in the development of physical dependence on nicotine.

In addition, because the use of smokeless tobacco products can result in the same blood concentrations of nicotine as smoked tobacco products, the physical dependence observed from the use of smokeless products is the same. Since this time, it has been generally agreed that nicotine is the major component of tobacco smoke that is responsible for the observed physical dependence (Benowitz, 1999; Dani & De Biasi, 2001; Pagliaro & Pagliaro, 2009).

Most of the earlier studies and related findings concerning nicotine dependence were conducted using adult samples. More recently, many of these studies have been replicated using adolescent samples (e.g., Caraballo, Novak, & Asman, 2009; Lessov-Schlaggar, Hops, Brigham, et al., 2008). In addition, it also has been found that infrequent smoking (i.e., as little as 1 cigarette per month), specifically among adolescents, may be associated with the signs and symptoms of nicotine withdrawal, particularly a strong desire to smoke (Doubeni, Reed, & DiFranza, 2010; Rose, Dierker, & Donny, 2010). Physical dependence also has been demonstrated among recent-onset adolescent smokers (Rose & Dierker, 2010).

**Tolerance**  The regular, long-term use of nicotine can result in the development of tolerance as occurs with many other drugs and substances of abuse (e.g., opiate analgesics; see Chapter 1, *The Psychodepressants*). Thus, as people smoke tobacco cigarettes, over time, they need to increase the number of cigarettes they smoke, change the brand of cigarettes that they smoke to stronger brands (i.e., brands that contain more nicotine per gram of cut tobacco leaf), or change the smoking techniques that they use (e.g., increase the number of puffs per cigarette; inhale the tobacco smoke more deeply and hold it in the lungs for a longer period of time). These changes are made in order to introduce additional nicotine to the systemic circulation and, consequently, to achieve once again the desired effects associated with smoking tobacco.

Tolerance to the actions of nicotine has been well established in humans. Although tolerance develops to most of the undesired effects of nicotine (e.g., dizziness, nausea, vomiting), it does not develop in regard to all of the effects. For example, following 1 or 2 cigarettes, most regular, long-term smokers still exhibit an increase in blood pressure, pulse rate, and hand tremor (Perkins, Gerlach, Broge, et al., 2001). Smokers appear to metabolize nicotine more rapidly than do nonsmokers. However, it is more likely that the development of tolerance is due primarily to pharmacodynamic changes rather than to pharmacokinetic changes. There also are conflicting reports on the duration of tolerance. Some aspects of tolerance may wax and wane rapidly. For example, the first cigarette of the day generally produces a much greater cardiovascular and subjective response than do those that follow throughout the day.

**Nicotine Withdrawal Syndrome**  A large amount of research has accumulated that provides evidence to support the occurrence of a nicotine withdrawal syndrome among users following their abrupt discontinuation of regular, long-term use of tobacco products (Pagliaro & Pagliaro, 2009). The nicotine withdrawal syndrome (as defined by *DSM* criteria) is characterized by various signs and symptoms that vary in intensity during the course of withdrawal and can be seen as long as 14 days after the use of tobacco products is discontinued. These signs and symptoms include: anxiety; bradycardia; craving for tobacco;[68] dysphoria; difficulty concentrating; fatigue; headache; hostility; hunger, or an increased appetite; insomnia; irritability; restlessness; and weight gain (usually as a result of an increased appetite) (American Psychiatric Association, 2000). These signs

---

[68] Craving for tobacco is the symptom of withdrawal that is most commonly reported by adolescents (Colby, Tiffany, Shiffman, et al., 2000).

and symptoms reportedly are similar for both adolescent girls and boys. However, when compared to adolescent boys, adolescent girls report significantly stronger craving for nicotine during withdrawal (Dickmann, Mooney, Allen, et al., 2009). In addition, as noted by Weinberger, Desai, and Mckee (2010), the signs and symptoms of nicotine withdrawal are reportedly more intense for those with another concurrent substance use disorder or other mental disorder. (Also see Chapter 8, *Dual Diagnosis Among Adolescents*).[69] Colby, Tiffany, Shiffman, et al. (2000), in their meta-analysis of adolescent tobacco smokers, found that, across studies, two-thirds or more of adolescent smokers reported experiencing signs and symptoms of withdrawal during their attempts to stop or reduce their smoking.

These signs and symptoms of the nicotine withdrawal syndrome can be related specifically to nicotine blood concentrations.[70] For example, adolescents and young adults who are physically dependent on the nicotine they receive from smoking tobacco cigarettes will need to smoke right away in the morning when they wake up because of nicotine's relatively short half-life of elimination (i.e., approximately 2 hours). At home, if they find that they have no cigarettes left in the house and are unable to obtain a smoke from a parent or a sibling, they will go out on a rainy night to buy a pack of cigarettes. At school, they will head for the nearest smoking area at recess,[71] even if off school grounds, and they will take a coffee break as soon as they can at work—to have a smoke.[72] These adolescents and young

adults smoke primarily to forestall the signs and symptoms of nicotine withdrawal.

Among those who are trying to kick the habit, the signs and symptoms of withdrawal, including craving, more often than not lead quickly to relapse for most smokers (Allen, Bade, Hatsukami, et al., 2008; Colby, Tiffany, Shiffman, et al., 2000). Many, if not most, smokers who successfully kick the habit must endure the common uncomfortable signs and symptoms associated with the nicotine withdrawal syndrome—signs and symptoms that can be immediately relieved by resuming smoking. For many smokers, the signs and symptoms of the nicotine withdrawal syndrome can be managed more comfortably and effectively with the help of nicotine replacement therapy (Henningfield, Shiffman, Ferguson, et al., 2009). (Also see Chapter 9, *Preventing and Treating Child and Adolescent Use of the Drugs and Substances of Abuse.*)

A related area that requires more study is the investigation of individual differences associated with the experience of nicotine withdrawal among adolescents and young adults who use nicotine. For many years, variation in individual experience has been largely ignored. The lack of attention to this important area of addictions study may be due to the acceptance of the general assumption that a regular, long-term tobacco smoker becomes physically dependent on tobacco. However, this assumption may be as incorrect as is the assumption that a regular, long-term drinker is physically dependent on alcohol. It may be that some tobacco smokers[73] can use nicotine regularly over a long period of time,

---

[69] Perhaps not surprisingly, these adolescents and young adults are more likely to experience relapse.

[70] Consequently, tobacco smokers who metabolize nicotine more quickly than others (i.e., are faster metabolizers of nicotine) report more frequent and heightened signs and symptoms of nicotine withdrawal. Therefore, they also are more likely to smoke another cigarette to relieve these signs and symptoms (i.e., self-medicate) and consequently have a relatively more difficult time quitting smoking.

[71] Nationally, 5.1% of high school students smoked cigarettes on at least 1 day during the month preceding their survey (range 2.4% to 9.4% across state surveys) (Eaton, Kann, Kinchen, et al., 2010).

[72] One in 7 high school students in the United States (i.e., 14%; range 4.5% to 26.1% across state surveys) who smoke tobacco have purchased their own cigarettes from local convenience stores or gas stations (Eaton, Kann, Kinchen, et al., 2010).

[73] Most likely largely due to genetically determined factors. For example, see the related discussion in the "Proposed Mechanism of Psychostimulant Action" section.

regardless of method of use, without developing physical dependence on nicotine (Pagliaro & Pagliaro, *Clinical Patient Data Files*; Saito & Murakami, 1998). In addition, because these tobacco users often use other drugs and substances of abuse (e.g., alcohol, caffeine), the synergistic actions and effects associated with the polyuse of the drugs and substances of abuse may also play a significant role in the occurrence of and individual experience with the nicotine withdrawal syndrome.

Rubinstein, Benowitz, Auerback, et al. (2009) examined the number of cigarettes smoked per day by light-smoking adolescents (range 1 to 5 cigarettes per day) and the variance in the signs and symptoms of nicotine withdrawal that were experienced upon the abrupt discontinuation of smoking. Adolescents who were very light smokers (i.e., those who smoked 1 to 3 cigarettes per day) reported a decrease in signs and symptoms by 12 hours following smoking cessation and a decrease in withdrawal scores at 24 hours. Conversely, adolescents who were light smokers (i.e., those who smoked 4 to 5 cigarettes per day) reported an increase in symptoms at 12 hours and an increase in withdrawal scores at 24 hours.

Perhaps the greatest contribution of this line of research and the associated findings is the stimulation of new research questions aimed at better understanding the signs and symptoms of nicotine withdrawal among different levels of smokers upon the cessation of smoking. These questions may include: (1) Is there a difference in the severity of the signs and symptoms of withdrawal as experienced by different levels of smokers? (2) Is there a relationship between the withdrawal experienced by different levels of smokers and the risk for relapse? and (3) Is there a difference in beneficial response to relapse prevention, including nicotine replacement pharmacotherapy, among different levels of smokers? The answers to these questions appear to be in large part genetically mediated.

In this regard, Lerman, Jepson, Wileyto, et al. (2010), in a placebo-controlled study of the efficacy of extended-duration (i.e., 6-month)

transdermal nicotine replacement pharmacotherapy, found that significantly better results were obtained among smokers who phenotypically were reduced metabolizers of nicotine. To date, the most promising research has involved the dopamine (i.e., D2 and D4) receptor genes (i.e., DRD2 and DRD4). Although findings are still preliminary and, as such, are nongeneralizable, specific functional polymorphisms (e.g., variable number of tandem repeats and transitional changes at specific positions) appear to be specifically involved in withdrawal symptoms, response to nicotine replacement pharmacotherapy, and relapse (e.g., Breitling, Twardella, Hoffmann, et al., 2010; David, Munafo, Murphy, et al., 2008; McGeary, 2009). (Also see the related discussion in Chapter 9, *Preventing and Treating Child and Adolescent Use of the Drugs and Substances of Abuse*.)

## CHAPTER SUMMARY

This chapter provided an overview of the major psychostimulants that are currently used by North America children, adolescents, and young adults—the amphetamines, caffeine, cocaine, and nicotine. Particular attention was given to the prevalence and characteristics of the use of these drugs and substances of abuse and their general pharmacology, including their mechanism of action and common toxicities that are often extensions of their known pharmacologic actions. As one of the three major subclasses of the drugs and substances of abuse, the psychostimulants are unique in that they are most often used in an attempt to enhance performance—study for longer hours, party through the night, run farther and faster. In addition, their regular, long-term use may be associated with both physical and psychological dependence.

Selected psychostimulants, including the mixed amphetamines (Adderall®) and methylphenidate (Ritalin®) are used extensively in North America for the medical management of A-D/HD. Children and adolescents with A-D/HD may sell or trade their prescription drug for money, clothes, or other drugs and substances of abuse. More commonly, children and adolescents who do not have A-D/HD buy, or steal, these psychostimulants from children and adolescents for whom they were prescribed for their own personal use.

Although cocaine was popular during the 1980s, its use was largely replaced by methamphetamine, both in powdered and crystalline forms, during the 1990s. The crystalline form gained popularity among adolescents and young adults across the United States because of its increased availability, relatively low cost, and smokability. By the beginning of the first decade of the 21st century, bisexual and gay adolescent boys and young men became the group that had the highest reported percentage of methamphetamine use in North America. By the end of the decade, methamphetamine was increasingly used by adolescent girls, including those who identified themselves as bisexual or lesbian. High rates of use also were found for adolescent boys of Hispanic descent, school drop-outs, and adolescents of American Indian descent, particularly those who lived on reservations and reserves where methamphetamine-related commerce flourishes. As the second decade began, methamphetamine use declined as cocaine once again regained popularity.

Many children, adolescents, and young adults have used cocaine, usually by either snorting cocaine hydrochloride or smoking crack cocaine. Several older adolescents and young adults also intravenously inject cocaine hydrochloride, which remains a high-risk behavior for HIV infection. Club-going adolescents have one of the highest rates of cocaine use and also commonly use cocaine with other drugs and substances of abuse.

While children and young adolescents, particularly boys, used caffeine-containing soft drinks as their major source of caffeine, older adolescents and young adults used coffee as their major source. In addition, over the last two decades, older adolescents and young adults have increasingly used highly caffeinated energy drinks, foods, and other products, including gums and mints, to prevent fatigue and to enhance athletic performance and sexual experiences. They also used energy drinks so that they could drink "all the alcohol they wanted without getting drunk." As this trend continues, the incidence of caffeine toxicity is expected to increase significantly.

While the use of many of the psychostimulants is increasing among children and adolescents, the use of nicotine, in the form of tobacco smoking, has decreased significantly over the past 40 years, with North American children and adolescents of African descent having the lowest reported rates of use. However, children who do smoke are smoking at younger and younger ages despite warnings of cancer and other risks. In addition, they are being increasingly attracted to smokeless tobacco products that appear to be marketed just for them, particularly the more recently developed dissolvable forms of tobacco that, in essence, "just melt in their mouths."

These dissolvable tobacco products are sold in youth-friendly packaging (e.g., packaging similar to the Tic-Tac® breath mint), tooth pick-like twists of tobacco to hold in the mouth, and film strips to melt on the tongue—similar to Listerine® PocketPaks). While attention has been given to restricting marketing approaches for tobacco cigarettes, the legal restrictions were not applied to the newer dissolvable tobacco products. The success of these marketing strategies has resulted in a new category of child and adolescent smokers: "dual tobacco users," or polyusers—which is becoming increasingly common among North American adolescents of European descent. In addition, high numbers of dual tobacco users can be found among American Indian and Alaskan Native children and adolescents, particularly those living on reservations.

# CHAPTER 3

# *The Psychodelics*

## INTRODUCTION

The third major subgroup of the drugs and substances of abuse is the psychodelics. (See Figure 3.1.) The term "psychedelics" (i.e., mind-manifesting) was first used for this group of drugs and substances of abuse by Osmond (1957). It was used as a term by other authors to differentiate the psychodelics from the hallucinogens. As explained by Cohen (1967), the term "hallucinogens" was generally used to denote the drugs and substances of abuse that produce a temporary madness, whereas the term "psychedelics" was used to denote the drugs and substances that induce variable states of self-transcendence and mystical unity.

Various other terms have been used that most often reflect either the specific professional stance of the person proposing the term or the identified action of this major group of the drugs and substances of abuse. For example, these terms include: psychotogens (inducers of psychosis), psychotomimetics (mimickers of psychosis), schizophrenomimetics (mimickers of schizophrenia), mysticomimetics (mimickers of mystic states), and psychotomystics (a term combining psychoto- and mysticomimetics—mimickers of psychosis and mystic states).

Reflecting the vivid sensory experiences associated with the use of many of these drugs and substances of abuse, other terms, such as "phantasticants," also have been used. In addition, with the synthesis of 3,4-methylene-dioxymethamphetamine (MDMA, ecstasy) and other related drugs and substances of abuse, the terms "empathogens" (drugs and substances of abuse that generate, or promote, feelings of empathy toward others) and "entactogens" (hug drugs) have been used to reflect their action in regard to promoting feelings of closeness and love or their ability to increase feelings of belonging.

A more precise, but less commonly used, term is "illusinogens," which reflects the visual phenomena (i.e., illusions or misperceptions) that are often associated with the use of the psychodelics. For the purpose of this chapter, and in keeping with the other terms used to denote the other two major groups of the drugs and substances of abuse discussed in this text (i.e., psychodepressants and psychostimulants), the term "psychodelics" is used here and throughout this text.

The psychodelics include three subgroups (see Figure 3.2):

1. Amphetamine-like psychodelics—the phenethylamines—including mescaline (peyote), MDMA (ecstasy) and other related psychodelics
2. Lysergic acid diethylamide (LSD) and other LSD-like psychodelics—the indoles, tryptamines, and indoles/tryptamines
3. Miscellaneous psychodelics—primarily cannabis in its various forms (i.e., hashish, hashish oil, marijuana), phencyclidine (PCP), and other related psychodelics (see Table 3.1)[1]

---

[1] Several commonly available natural substances can produce hallucinations and other psychodelic actions (e.g., jimsonweed contains belladonna alkaloids that can produce hallucinations). The use of these substances is relatively uncommon among North American children and adolescents. Thus, they are not discussed in this chapter.

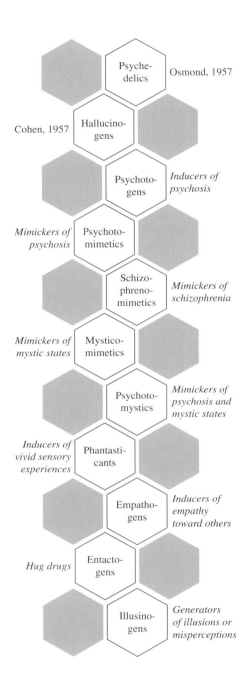

**Figure 3.1   Various Terms Used to Denote the Psychodelics**

The pharmacologic characteristic that separates the psychodelics from the other drugs and substances of abuse is the ability to alter perception, thought, and feelings from a normal state to a dreamlike state during which users may feel like passive observers who often are unable to identify the boundaries of one physical object from another or to differentiate self from the environment. During this state, the occurrence of illusions and hallucinations is common. For these reasons, the natural forms of several of the psychodelics have been used worldwide over the millennia as a component of magico-religious ceremonies and shamanistic beliefs and healing practices.

While the various psychodelics display similar psychotropic actions, they may differ in regard to their mechanisms of action, intensity of their desired actions, potency (i.e., dose required to achieve a desired response)[2], pharmacodynamics (e.g., receptor site activity), pharmacokinetics (i.e., processes of absorption, distribution, metabolism and excretion from the human body), and common toxicities. They also may vary in relation to their prevalence and characteristics of use among North American children and adolescents. More important, although capable of producing psychological dependence (i.e., habituation), the psychodelics, generally have not been associated with producing physical dependence (i.e., addiction).[3]

Although many of the psychodelics, such as LSD and cannabis, have remained popular over the last four decades of the 20th century, as the new millennium began, other psychodelics, particularly MDMA (ecstasy), began to receive increased attention by both adolescents and young adults, particularly those involved with the clubbing and rave scenes (Golub, Johnson, Sifaneck, et al., 2001; Gross, Barrett, Shestowsky, et al., 2002).

---

[2] For example, the order of potency substantiated by human reports is that LSD is approximately 10 times as potent as psilocybin and 100 times as potent as mescaline.

[3] See the related discussion of both cannabis and MDMA as noted exceptions to this general assertion.

# AMPHETAMINE-LIKE PSYCHODELICS—THE PHENETHYLAMINES

The phenethylamines (see Figure 3.2 and Table 3.1) comprise a subgroup of psychodelics that possess a chemical structure that resembles the neurotransmitter norepinephrine (noradrenaline). This subgroup of psychodelics generally exhibits LSD-like effects. However, as doses are increased, they exhibit greater amphetamine-like effects. Mescaline (peyote) is the natural prototype for this subgroup of psychodelics. Although methylenedioxyamphetamine (MDA) traditionally was designated as the synthetic prototype for this subgroup of psychodelics, MDMA has now become the designated synthetic prototype because of its popularity and widespread use, which is related to its ability to produce effects generally similar to those of LSD, but without the associated hallucinations and illusions. Much of the increased interest in and use of the synthetic phenethylamines over the years has been due to the original work of Alexander (Sasha) Shulgin, who, for the last four decades of the 20th century, synthesized, experimented with (including self-experimentation), and popularized their use (e.g., Shulgin, 1964, 1966, 1973, 1975, 1979, 1981, 1986). MDMA, now the most widely used psychodelic of this subgroup, is discussed in the next section.

## MDMA

Methylenedioxymethamphetamine (MDMA) has a relatively recent history (Eiserman, Diamond, & Schensul, 2005; Pagliaro & Pagliaro, 2009; Schensul, Diamon, Disch, et al., 2005). After a slow start in the 1970s, its use virtually exploded worldwide, particularly in response to two relatively recent trends: clubbing and raving.[4]

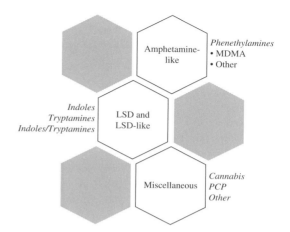

**Figure 3.2    The Psychodelics**

This section presents an overview of the prevalence and characteristics of MDMA use among North American adolescents and young adults and its general pharmacology with attention to its mechanism of action and common toxicities, including its associated potential for physical and psychological dependence.

### Prevalence and Characteristics of MDMA Use Among North American Children and Adolescents

The worldwide use of MDMA increased from approximately 10,000 doses in all of 1976 to more than 30,000 doses per month in 1980. By 1985, MDMA had gained widespread acclaim as the perfect safe drug. In July 1985, the United States Drug Enforcement Agency classified MDMA as a controlled substance and banned its legal use. In spite of its illegal status, the use of MDMA, particularly at dance clubs, music festivals, raves, and underground nightclubs, or acid houses, increased exponentially during the 1990s (Drug trafficking, 2010; Gross, Barrett, Shestowsky, et al., 2002; Klein & Kramer, 2004; Koesters, Rogers, & Rajasingham, 2002; Pentney, 2001; Smith,

---

[4]As described by the Centers for Disease Control and Prevention (2010a):

A rave is an all-night dance party with electronic music. When raves first emerged in the late 1980s, they were underground parties usually held at abandoned warehouses and outdoor sites. Since then, raves have become organized commercial events staged by promoters at established venues, often with high ticket prices and elaborate laser light effects. (p. 1)

TABLE 3.1    The Psychodelics

| Subclassification, Generic Name[a] | Common Street Names[b] |
| --- | --- |
| *Amphetamine-like Psychodelics—Phenethylamines* | |
| 4-Bromo-2,5-dimethoxyphenethylamine | 2-CB, bromo, nexus |
| 2,5-Dimethoxy-4-methylamphetamine | DOM, STP |
| Mescaline | Buttons, cactus, peyote |
| 3,4-Methylenedioxyamphetamine | Adam, love drug, MDA |
| 3,4-Methylenedioxyethylamphetamine | Eve, MDE, MDEA |
| 3,4-Methylenedioxymethamphetamine | Dancing shoes, ecstasy, MDMA, XTC |
| N-Methyl-1-(3,4-methylenedioxyphenyl)-2-butanamine | Eden, fido-dido, MBDB |
| 4-Methylthioamphetamine | 4-MTA, flatliners, golden eagle |
| Nutmeg | Magic, muskatbaum, *noz moscada* |
| Paramethoxyamphetamine | Death, Mitsubishi, PMA |
| 3,4,5-Trimethoxyamphetamine | Mescalamphetamine, TMA |
| *LSD and LSD-like Psychodelics* | |
| **INDOLES** | |
| *Amanita muscaria* | Flesh of the gods, fly agaric, soma |
| Harmala alkaloids | Yage, yaje |
| Lysergic acid amide | Blue stars, LSA, morning glory |
| Lysergic acid diethylamide | Acid, LSD, twenty-five |
| **TRYPTAMINES**[c,d] | |
| Alpha-ethyltryptamine[e] | Alpha-ET, ET, love pearls |
| N,N-Diethyltryptamine | DET |
| N,N-Dipropyltryptamine | DIPT |
| 5-Hydroxy-N,N-dimethyltryptamine[f] | Bufo, 5-0H-DMT, toad |
| 5-Methoxy-N,N-dimethyltryptamine | 5-MeO-DMT |
| **INDOLES/TRYPTAMINES** | |
| Alpha-methyltryptamine | 3-IT, AMT, spirals |
| N,N-Dimethyltryptamine | 45-minute trip, businessman's lunch, DMT |
| 5-Methoxy-N,N-diisopropyltryptamine | Foxy, foxy methoxy, 5-MeO-DIPT |
| Psilocin | Magic mushrooms, pizza toppings, shrooms |
| Psilocybin | Fungus, sacred mushrooms, smurfhats |
| *Miscellaneous Psychodelics* | |
| Cannabis | Ganja, grass, pot, weed |
| Ibogaine[g] | Bocca, iboga, lebuga |
| Ketamine | Cat, K, Special K, vitamin K |
| Phencyclidine | Angel dust, PCP, peace pill |
| Piperazine derivatives | A2, fly, nemesis |
| *Salvia divinorum*[h] | Big Sal, diviner's mint, ska Maria pastora |

[a]There are no brand/trade names for the psychodelics, other than those for the therapeutically approved and available cannabinoids: dronabinol (Marinol®) in the United States and nabilone (Cesamet®) in Canada.

[b]Partial list. Examples of the most common street names are provided, when available. See Pagliaro and Pagliaro (2009) for a comprehensive listing of the drugs and substances of abuse and their common street names.

[c]Virtually all of the tryptamines are classified as LSD-like psychodelics because of their observed psychotropic actions. However, they also are classified as tryptamines in this taxonomy because each has the amino acid tryptamine as its core chemical structure.

[d]Psilocybin (i.e., O-phosphoryl-4-hydroxy-N,N-ethyltryptamine) and psilocin (i.e., 4-hydroxy-N,N-dimethyltryptamine) also can be added to this taxonomy.

[e]Alpha-ethyltryptamine is not currently widely used and available data are extremely limited.

[f]Also known as bufotenine. There is some question as to its psychodelic action, but the lack of psychodelic activity in human subjects may be simply due to its poor ability to cross the blood-brain barrier.

(*Continued*)

TABLE 3.1 (Continued)

Larive, & Romanelli, 2002; Strote, Lee, & Wechsler, 2002).

The last decade witnessed continued widespread use of MDMA in North America, particularly among middle-class adolescents and young adults (Parsons, Grov, & Kelly, 2009). These adolescents and young adults had little difficulty obtaining MDMA from supplies that were primarily produced in western Europe—particularly Belgium, Luxembourg, and the Netherlands—and imported—often through Canada or Mexico—for distribution and sale across the United States (Drug trafficking, 2010). As found by the Partnership for a Drug-Free America (2006) in its 2005 national survey of 7,216 adolescents in the 7th through 12th grades, 8% of respondents reported lifetime use of MDMA; 6% reported past-year use of MDMA; and 4% reported past-month use of MDMA. In their 2007 national survey of adolescents in the 8th, 10th, and 12th grades, Johnston, O'Malley, Bachman, et al. (2008) found that MDMA use within the previous month (i.e., 30 days prior to the survey) was reported by: 0.6% of 8th graders, 1.2% of 10th graders, and 1.6% of 12th graders. MDMA use within the previous 12 months was reported by: 1.5% of 8th graders, 3.5% of 10th graders; and 4.5% of 12th graders. Lifetime prevalence of use was reported by 2.3% of 8th graders; 5.4% of 10th graders; and 6.5% of 12th graders. By 2010, these numbers had increased to 3.3%, 6.4%, and 7.3%, respectively (Johnston, O'Malley, Bachman, et al., 2010b). In addition, 40% of the high school seniors reported that MDMA was either fairly easy or very easy to obtain. In comparison, reported rates of MDMA use for Canada in 2010 were significantly lower (i.e., 0.9%) than those reported for the United States (Health Canada, 2010b).

Wu, Schlenger, and Galvin (2006), in their review of data from the National Survey on Drug Use and Health (NSDUH), found that among 16-year-old to 23-year-old noninstitutionalized, household Americans who participated in the survey, 13.6% reported lifetime prevalence of MDMA use and 6% reported past-year use. M. P. O'Brien (2008), reporting on data for the Community Epidemiology Work Group (CEWG) of the National Institute on Drug Abuse (NIDA), found that the use of MDMA has now crossed over from the club and rave scenes to the street scene, with increasing numbers of North American adolescents of African descent both using MDMA and seeking treatment for its use. She also found that, across the United States, 5.8% of high school students reported lifetime use of MDMA.

Several factors highly correlate with the use of MDMA among adolescents (see: Martins & Alexandre, 2008; Martins, Storr, Alexandre, et al., 2009; Singer, Linares, Ntiri, et al., 2004; Wu, Schlenger, & Galvin, 2006; P. Wu, Liu, & Fan, 2010). These factors include:

- A high-sensation-seeking personality
- History of physical abuse during childhood
- Initiation of the use of drugs and substances of abuse during childhood
- Low academic achievement
- Multiple ethnicity or continental descent
- Parental use of the drugs and substances of abuse
- Peer use of the drugs and substances of abuse
- Polyuse of the drugs and substances of abuse

In addition, the use of MDMA has been found to be highest among adolescents who are: (1) homeless or runaways living on the streets; (2) bisexual, gay, or lesbian; and

(3) currently in a treatment program aimed at discontinuing their use of the various drugs and substances of abuse (Hopfer, Mendelson, Van Leeuwen, et al., 2006; Parsons, Kelly, & Wells, 2006; Ramo, Grov, Delucchi, et al., 2010; Van Leeuwen, Hopfer, Hooks, et al., 2004). Although it is too early to say whether a long-term trend has developed, the Partnership for a Drug-Free America and the Metlife Foundation (2010) found that, in their survey of over 3,000 adolescents in grades 9 to 12, MDMA use increased significantly from 2008 to 2009 and, for 2009, MDMA use was the highest it had been in over a decade (i.e., 6% of participants reported past-month use, 10% reported past-year use, and 13% reported lifetime use).

**Bisexual, Gay, and Lesbian Adolescents and Young Adults** Bisexual, gay, and lesbian adolescents and young adults, including those who are college and university students (e.g., medical students), reportedly use significant amounts of MDMA (Horowitz, Galanter, Dermatis, et al., 2008; Parsons, Kelly, & Wells, 2006). In fact, bisexual, gay, and lesbian college and university students are twice as likely as their heterosexual cohorts to have used MDMA in the past year (Boyd, McCabe, & d'Arcy, 2003). In addition, several studies (e.g., Eiserman, Diamond, & Schensul, 2005; Ramo, Grov, Delucchi, et al., 2010) have reported significant correlations between MDMA use and a recent history of unprotected anal intercourse among bisexual and gay adolescent boys and young men. It also has been reported that, particularly during circuit party weekends, MDMA use by bisexual and gay adolescent boys and young men has been highly correlated with unprotected sex with multiple partners as well as with partners who knowingly are positive with the human immunodeficiency virus (HIV) (e.g., Klitzman, Pope, & Hudson, 2000; Pagliaro & Pagliaro, *Clinical Patient Data Files*; Waldo, McFarland, Katz, et al., 2000).

MDMA use by bisexual and lesbian adolescent girls and young women is significantly greater than that reported for heterosexual adolescent girls and young women (McCabe, Boyd, Hughes, et al., 2003; Parsons, Kelly, & Wells, 2006). This difference also was found to be more pronounced during adolescence (i.e., 12 to 17 years of age) than during young adulthood (i.e., 18 to 23 years of age) by Corliss, Rosario, Wypij, et al. (2010) in their study of U.S. adolescents and young adults.

*General Pharmacology*

Chemically, MDMA is related to the amphetamines and mescaline (peyote). It also is related to MDA, but not as closely. MDMA is derived from methamphetamine, nutmeg, or sassafras (safrole) and was originally synthesized as an appetite suppressant in 1914 by Merck and Company. However, there was little interest in MDMA for the next 60 years, when it was rediscovered and popularized by the hippies of the counterculture movement.

Commonly known on the street as ecstasy, or E, MDMA is used by adolescents and young adults primarily to achieve feelings of euphoria and to decrease inhibitions—most often in order to enhance sexual experiences. It also produces psychostimulation and mild hallucinations that last from 4 to 8 hours—without the anxiety, dissociation, perceptual distortion, and other effects that are commonly associated with the use of most other psychodelics. These pharmacologic actions have made MDMA particularly appealing to adolescents and young adults (Pagliaro & Pagliaro, 2009; Piper, 2007).

**Proposed Mechanism of Psychodelic Action** The feelings of elation, emotional closeness, and sensory pleasure that are associated with MDMA use are thought to be caused by the release of neurotransmitters, primarily serotonin (5-hydroxytryptamine [5HT]), and the prevention of their reuptake. This mechanism of action involves the interaction of MDMA with 5-HT transporters (also known as serotonin transporters [SERTS]) as substrates.

**Common Toxicities**  The use of MDMA has been associated with several common acute toxicities, including: agitation, bruxism, cardiac dysrhythmias, diaphoresis (profuse), hepatitis (drug-induced), hyperkinesia, hypertension, impulsive behavior, mental confusion, mydriasis, seizures, tachycardia, and urinary retention (Pagliaro & Pagliaro, 2009; Smith, Larive, & Romanelli, 2002). In addition, the regular, long-term use of MDMA has been associated with several chronic toxicities, including: insomnia, neurogenic bladder, soreness of the jaw muscles related to jaw clenching or grinding of the teeth, and weight loss.

Regular, long-term use of MDMA also has been associated with more serious neurotoxicities including those that that affect attention and memory, particularly verbal memory[5] (Parrott, 2006; Piper, 2007). The use of MDMA has been directly associated with the loss of serotonergic axons in the corpus striatum and other higher brain regions. Adolescents and young adults may be at particular risk for these MDMA-related neurotoxicities (Montoya, Sorrentino, Lukas, et al., 2002). Of increasing concern is the observation that some of this neurotoxicity does not appear to abate, even after several years following the discontinuation of MDMA use, and, therefore, may be permanent (Gouzoulis-Mayfrank & Daumann, 2006, 2009; Pagliaro & Pagliaro, 2009). (Also see Chapter 6, *Effects of the Drugs and Substances of Abuse on Learning and Memory During Childhood and Adolescence.*)

**Physical and Psychological Dependence**
Although neither physical nor psychological dependence is generally associated with the use of most of the other psychodelics (e.g., LSD), the regular, long-term use of MDMA has been increasingly associated with both physical and psychological dependence (Leung & Cottler, 2008; Wu, Ringwalt, Weiss, et al., 2009). Acute and chronic tolerance have been noted in relation to the use of MDMA (Parrott, 2006). In addition, an MDMA withdrawal syndrome also has been identified. The withdrawal syndrome generally occurs 3 to 5 days following the abrupt discontinuation of MDMA use and is characterized by feelings of dysphoria.

**Overdosage**  Over 300 MDMA-overdosage fatalities have been reported over the past decade in North America (Centers for Disease Control and Prevention, 2010a; Pagliaro & Pagliaro, 2009). The vast majority of these fatalities have involved adolescent boys and men, 15 to 40 years of age, usually of European descent (Gill, Hayes, deSouza, et al., 2002). In many of these cases, uncharacteristic behavior and vomiting were observed initially and were followed by seizures, disorientation or coma, and death. Death usually was associated with acute renal failure, cardiac dysrhythmias, cerebrovascular accidents, disseminated intravascular coagulation, hyperthermia, hyponatremic encephalopathy, and rhabdomyolysis (Pagliaro & Pagliaro, 2009; Patel, Belson, Longwater, et al., 2005).

However, a clear picture as to the cause and sequelae of MDMA overdosage is difficult to obtain because the overwhelming majority of MDMA users (i.e., 80% to 90%) are known to be polyusers of the drugs and substances of abuse (see earlier discussion) who commonly report the concomitant use of alcohol, LSD, and other drugs and substances of abuse. It also has been suggested that what has been identified as MDMA overdosage may, in many cases, actually be the serotonin syndrome, which may occur as a result of the interaction of MDMA with a selective serotonin reuptake inhibitor

---

[5]Memory and other neurological impairment associated with regular, long-term MDMA use is not experienced by all users (Gouzoulis-Mayfrank & Dauman, 2006; Gouzoulis-Mayfrank, Fischermann, Rezk, et al., 2005). The reason for this apparent variation in response to MDMA is currently unknown. However, it is most likely associated with the: (1) concomitant use of other neurotoxic drugs and substances of abuse (e.g., alcohol, methamphetamine); (2) dosage of MDMA used; and (3) user's genetic predisposition.

(e.g., fluoxetine [Prozac®]) or other interacting drug that was used (Dinse, 1997; Pilgrim, Gerostamoulos, & Drummer, 2010; Schifano, 2004). In addition, many of the signs and symptoms of fatal MDMA overdosage (e.g., hyponatremic encephalopathy) can be related to several other risk factors, including the concurrent oral ingestion of an excessive amount of beer or water. In any case, because of the serious and potentially fatal consequences of MDMA overdosage, it should always be treated as a medical emergency. There is no known antidote.

MDMA also has been associated with a number of overdosages worldwide (e.g., England, Germany, Spain, Taiwan, and the United States), which are actually unintentional poisonings involving infants and toddlers, usually 2 years of age or younger. Although reports of these poisonings are relatively few in number (Chang, Lai, Kong, et al., 2005; Duffy & Swart, 2006; Eifinger, Roth, Kroner, et al., 2008; Fang & Lai, 2006; Feldman & Mazor, 2007; Melian, Burillo-Putze, Campo, et al., 2004), they exceed the total number of unintentional poisonings reported for all of the other psychodelics combined. (For further related discussion, see Chapter 5, *Exposure to the Drugs and Substances of Abuse From Conception Through Childhood.*)

## LSD AND LSD-LIKE PSYCHODELICS—THE INDOLES, TRYPTAMINES, AND INDOLES/ TRYPTAMINES

The LSD and LSD-like psychodelics (see Figure 3.2 and Table 3.1) comprise a subgroup of psychodelics that possesses a chemical structure that resembles the neurotransmitter serotonin (i.e., 5-hydroxytryptamine [5-HT]). LSD is the prototype drug for this subgroup of psychodelics, which also includes:

- The harmala alkaloids, which are found in the South American vine *Banisteriopsis caapi* (i.e., ayahuasca or yajé), and other plant species

- Lysergic acid amide (LSA), a naturally occurring substance found in morning glory seeds
- N,N-dimethyltryptamine (DMT), a naturally occurring substance found in the *Piptadina peregrina* plant
- Psilocin and psilocybin, naturally occurring substances found in psilocybe and conocybe mushrooms
- Other psychodelic tryptamines

Of these drugs and substances of abuse, LSD is the most commonly used among North American adolescents and young adults. Thus, it is discussed in the next section.

## LSD

LSD, a substance of abuse that was probably used by many of their grandparents, or great-grandparents, during the 1960s and 1970s, continues to attract new generations of adolescents. This section presents an overview of the prevalence and characteristics of LSD use and its general pharmacology, including its mechanism of action and common toxicities.

### Prevalence and Characteristics of LSD Use Among North American Children and Adolescents

Partnership for a Drug-Free America (2006) found that 6% of adolescents in grades 7 through 12 who participated in their national survey reported having ever tried LSD. This finding was 50% lower than the 12% that was reported for their 2000 survey and followed the decline in adolescent LSD use that was observed through 2004—at which time the use of LSD appeared to stabilize at 6%.

In their 2007 nationwide survey of 50,000 8th, 10th, and 12th graders, Johnston, O'Malley, Bachman, et al. (2008) found that 1.1% of 8th graders, 1.9% of 10th graders, and 2.1% of 12th graders (range 1.1%– 2%) reported LSD use within the 12 months prior to the survey. They also found that 0.5% of

8th graders, 0.7% of 10th graders, and 0.6 % of 12th graders reported using LSD within the previous month (i.e., 30 days prior to the survey). Their 2010 survey (i.e., Johnston, O'Malley, Bachman, et al., 2010b) found essentially the same level of reported LSD use—0.6%, 0.7%, and 0.8%, respectively. While reported lifetime use increased slightly among respondents from 8th grade through 12th grade over the past several years, recent use reportedly remained low (i.e., less than 1%) and relatively unchanged. Wu, Schlenger, and Galvin (2006), in their review of data from the National Survey on Drug Use and Health (NSDUH), found that among their participants of 16-year-old to 23-year-old, noninstitutionalized, household Americans, 13.2% reported lifetime prevalence of LSD use and 2.3% reported use within the past year.

### General Pharmacology

LSD is considered to be the most widely used indole psychodelic in North America. First synthesized in 1938 by Albert Hofmann (1979), a large amount of data have accumulated during the ensuing 75 years in regard to its general pharmacology, including its proposed mechanism of action and the common toxicities associated with its use.

**Proposed Mechanism of Psychodelic Action** LSD is a semisynthetic derivative of ergot alkaloid that produces profound psychodelic actions for which it has been used for almost three-quarters of a century. The exact mechanism of its psychodelic action remains largely unknown (Passie, Halpern, Stichtenoth, et al., 2008). However, its action appears to involve interaction with the serotonin 5-HT(2A) receptors (Gonzalez-Maeso & Sealfon, 2009), particularly those expressed on neocortical pyramidal cells (Nichols, 2004).

**Common Toxicities** At lower doses, the common toxicities, which can be both physical and psychological, generally last from 6 to 12 hours. The intensity of these

toxicities is directly related to the amount of LSD used.

**Physical Toxicities** The physical toxicities associated with the use of LSD include blurred vision, diaphoresis, heart palpitations, incoordination, mydriasis, and tachycardia. Although the use of LSD has been associated with a number of deaths, it has a high $LD_{50}$. Thus, it is relatively safe to use and, in actuality, has not been directly associated with overdosage fatalities. However, LSD has been indirectly related to a number of accidental deaths and suicides that occurred while users were under its influence (e.g., running across a street in terror of an illusionary figure and being fatally struck by an automobile; believing that he or she could fly like a bird and, subsequently, fatally jumping from the roof of a building).

In regard to teratogenesis, no data have been published that demonstrate a clear link between LSD use and congenital malformations, including chromosomal damage, among the offspring of mothers who used LSD prior to or during pregnancy. (For additional related discussion, see Chapter 5, *Exposure to the Drugs and Substances of Abuse From Conception Through Childhood.*)

**Psychological Toxicities** The psychological toxicities associated with LSD use include: anxiety; difficulty locating the source of a sound; distortions of body image; fear of fragmentation, or disintegration, of the self; mood swings from happiness to sadness; perceptual changes (e.g., macropsia, micropsia); prolonged visual afterimages; synesthesias (i.e., hearing colors, seeing sounds); temporal disintegration (i.e., the perception of time passing extremely slowly); visual illusions; and vivid thoughts and memories. While troublesome, these psychological toxicities are generally short-lived. However, other, more serious psychological toxicities have been associated with the use of LSD including depression; severe panic reactions, or bad trips; and paranoia, or prolonged psychosis, particularly among people who have a pre-disposition for these toxicities (Abraham & Aldridge, 1993).

These common and more serious psychological toxicities have been classified into several substance-induced disorders according to *Diagnostic and Statistical Manual* taxonomy (American Psychiatric Association, 2000, 2011):

1. Anxiety disorders, characterized by anxiety or panic, which may occur either during LSD intoxication or following its use

2. Hallucinogen-persisting perception disorder, the transient recurrence of perceptual disturbances (i.e., flashbacks) that occur sometimes days, months, or even years after LSD was last used and cause clinically or socially significant stress or impairment

3. Mood disorders, characterized by depression and possible suicide, which may occur either during LSD intoxication or following its use with effects persisting for more than 24 hours

4. Psychotic disorders, which may occur during intoxication with LSD and resolve within hours of use or progress to a long-term schizophreniform disorder

Sedative-hypnotics (e.g., diazepam [Valium®]) may be required to relieve associated anxiety. Flashbacks typically involve visual hallucinations but also may involve other sensory hallucinations (e.g., olfactory, tactile) that can last for minutes to hours. Flashbacks may be triggered by any type of environmental stimuli, but are commonly associated with the frequent use of LSD and the people, places, and things related to the first time that LSD was used.[6]

Flashbacks also have been related to mental or physical stress (Pagliaro & Pagliaro, *Clinical Patient Data Files*). Flashbacks should be treated in the same way as LSD psychosis (see brief discussion in this section). Virtually all flashbacks have the potential to be unpleasant because they are unplanned and unexpected. Although they are encountered more commonly when LSD has been used several times, flashbacks also can occur following the initial use of LSD.[7]

LSD-induced psychosis, which is similar to amphetamine-induced psychosis (see Chapter 2 *The Psychostimulants*, "Amphetamines" section), is more likely to occur with repeated use. The psychosis generally resolves on its own with the discontinuation of LSD use or, if necessary, responds well to appropriate antipsychotic pharmacotherapy. However, the psychosis may last for several days or several months, even with treatment. Less severe bad trips are usually temporary and last for approximately 24 hours. They generally can be managed successfully in a familiar environment by providing reassurance and other psychological support. Antipsychotic pharmacotherapy (e.g., chlorpromazine [Thorazine®]), which antagonizes most of the pharmacological actions of LSD, usually is not required (Blaho, Merigian, Winbery, et al., 1997).

**Physical and Psychological Dependence**
There is no available evidence, anecdotal or otherwise, that supports the occurrence of a withdrawal syndrome when regular, long-term LSD use is abruptly discontinued. However, tolerance to the psychological effects of LSD may be seen after 3 to 4 days of daily use. The extent of tolerance to LSD can be significant—in the same order of magnitude as that observed with alcohol or other sedative-hypnotics

---

[6]We have suggested, for example, that flashbacks, like the experience of déjà vu, may be related to olfactory memory (Pagliaro, 1991).

[7]More recently, particularly with the generally lower dosages of LSD that are being used (i.e., approximately half the dosage used during the 1960s and 1970s), the incidence of flashbacks has been reduced to the point that they are becoming relatively uncommon events.

and phencyclidine (PCP). Lower tolerance develops to the cardiovascular effects of LSD. Reverse tolerance, or increased sensitivity to the actions of LSD, has been reported by some users (Pagliaro & Pagliaro, *Clinical Patient Data Files*) but is considered to be rare. In addition, cross-tolerance has been reported to occur among LSD, MDMA, mescaline, and psilocybin—suggesting a common molecular mechanism of action. Usually, when not used for 3 to 4 days, sensitivity to the effects of LSD rapidly returns (Pagliaro & Pagliaro, *Clinical Patient Data Files*).

## MISCELLANEOUS PSYCHODELICS

The miscellaneous psychodelics (see Figure 3.2 and Table 3.1) comprise a subgroup of the psychodelics that is chemically diverse and includes cannabis, ketamine, phencyclidine (PCP), piperazine derivatives, and *Salvia divinorum*. Among adolescents and young adults, the most widely known and used member of this subgroup is cannabis, followed by PCP. These two psychodelics are discussed in the next sections, beginning with cannabis.

### Cannabis

Several species of cannabis exist, including *Cannabis lativa* and *Cannabis sativa* (i.e., Indian hemp). *Cannabis sativa* is the principal variety from which marijuana, hashish, and hashish oil are prepared. Within the species of *Cannabis sativa*, there are several varieties, including *Cannabis sativa indica*, *Cannabis sativa ruderalis*, and *Cannabis sativa sativa.* These varieties differ significantly in regard to their concentration of delta-9-tetrahydrocannabinol (THC), the major active psychodelic ingredient of cannabis (see "General Pharmacology" section), with the *indica* varieties having the greatest concentrations.[8]

The highest concentration of THC is found in the bracts, or small leaves, at the base of the cannabis flowers, and their resin. The next highest concentration is found in the flowering tops and then, in decreasing order, the upper leaves, large stems, and seeds, with the roots having the lowest concentration. The female plants tend to have a much higher THC concentration than do the male plants. This explains the advertisements and sales of tools (e.g., ultraviolet lights) in drug-paraphernalia stores (i.e., head shops, hemp stores) and drug culture magazines (e.g., *High Times*) to detect plant sex. The desire for higher THC concentrations also accounts for the popularity of *sinsemilla*—unfertilized female cannabis plants that are cultivated specifically for their higher THC concentration. The cultivation of *sinsemilla* is generally accomplished by planting only female seeds or by destroying the male plants before pollen is produced and the female plants are fertilized. These procedures allow the unfertilized female plants to flower more abundantly and to produce more THC-containing resin.

Cannabis is produced worldwide, as illustrated by the names given to the many varieties that are distributed and sold across North America. These names include: Amsterdam, BC bud, Cambodian red, Hawaiian buds, Indian hash, Jamaican ganja, Lebanese hash, Moroccan kif, New Mexico sinse, Panama gold, Thai sticks, and Ukrainian ditchweed. In addition to worldwide production, distribution, and sale, a number of states (i.e., Alabama, California, Florida, Hawaii, Kentucky, North Carolina, Oregon, Tennessee, Washington, West Virginia, Wisconsin) and provinces (i.e., British Columbia) produce cannabis to the extent that it is the state's or province's most significant cash crop with combined annual revenues reaching the tens of billions of dollars (Drug trafficking, n.d.; Pagliaro & Pagliaro, 2009).

---

[8] Some botanical taxonomies classify *indica*, *ruderalis*, and *sativa* as belonging to different species of cannabis.

As noted by Gettman (2006, p. 4):

---

The domestic marijuana crop is: larger than cotton in Alabama; larger than grapes, vegetables, and hay combined in California; larger than peanuts in Georgia; and larger than tobacco in both South Carolina and North Carolina.

---

However, approximately 50% of the cannabis that is more currently used in the United States is smuggled into the country, primarily from Mexico.[9]

### Marijuana, Hashish, and Hash Oil

Marijuana (grass, pot, weed) is the dried plant form of cannabis.[10] It is prepared for smoking by methods that are similar to the methods used for preparing tobacco leaves for smoking. However, fewer steps and less time is generally required in regard to curing and drying. Marijuana is generally grayish green to greenish brown in color and contains the lowest concentration of THC (in comparison to hashish or hashish oil). Hashish is prepared from the dried resin and compressed flowers of the cannabis plant and is generally light brown to black in color. Prepared and distributed for use in compressed blocks or cubes, it has a relatively high concentration of THC. Hashish oil is prepared from hashish by the means of extraction with an organic solvent, often isopropyl alcohol. It is then filtered and concentrated. Hashish oil contains the highest concentration of THC

and ranges in color from clear to almost black. Food coloring often is added for color enhancement.

The concentration of THC can generally range from: 1% to 10% for marijuana cigarettes (i.e., doobie, joint, reefer);[11] 15% to 25% for hashish; and up to 60% for hashish oil. These concentrations vary depending on the specific part of the plant (e.g., buds, leaves, stems) from which the marijuana was prepared and the quality and source of the cannabis—the country or region of origin (e.g., British Columbia, Canada; Hawaii, U.S.; Mexico) and cultivation techniques (e.g., hydroponic cultivation). Today, the average high-potency joint contains approximately 150 mg THC.[12] However, the amount of THC that reaches the lungs and is absorbed into the bloodstream is variable and depends on: (1) the amount of THC in the cannabis smoked; (2) the smoking technique used, including the rate, depth, and length of inhalation before exhaling (i.e., the drag); and (3) the amount of THC that is destroyed by pyrolysis.

### Prevalence and Characteristics of Cannabis Use Among North American Children and Adolescents

Cannabis is the most commonly used illicit drug or substance of abuse in North America (Fischer, Rehm, & Hall, 2009; Pagliaro & Pagliaro, 2009). As with many of the drugs and substances of abuse, the available statistics for reported cannabis use by the age of the user indicate two distinct patterns or trends: (1) use increases from late childhood (i.e., 8–10 years

---

[9] Over the past decade, increasing amounts of high-potency marijuana (i.e., 15% to 25% THC) have been entering the United States from Canada, produced predominantly from indoor growing operations (i.e., grow ops) in the province of British Columbia (i.e., BC bud) (Drug trafficking, n.d.).

[10] Kif (kaif, keef, kief), an Arabic word meaning "well-being" or "pleasure," was originally the name given to a powder that was made from the dried flowers of the female cannabis plant. Indigenous to the Rif Mountain area of northern Morocco, it was usually mixed with tobacco (1 part to 2 parts) prior to smoking (Nahas, Zeidenberg, & Lefebure, 1975). Although the use of kif in North America has been reported over the years, its use is relatively uncommon (Pagliaro & Pagliaro, Clinical Patient Data Files). The term is now more commonly used to denote marijuana or hashish that is from Morocco.

[11] Also the same for blunts (i.e., marijuana that is rolled in a cigar wrap).

[12] For comparative purposes, it is important to note that during the 1960s and early 1970s (i.e., during the counter-culture revolution generally associated with "hippies"), a joint of average potency contained only approximately 10 mg THC.

of age)[13] through adolescence (i.e., 10–20 years of age); and (2) use decreases from late adolescence and early adulthood (15–25 years of age) through middle adulthood (i.e., 25–50 years of age). For example, the reported rate of cannabis use among Canadians was over 4 times higher (i.e., 33%) among adolescents and young adults 15 to 24 years of age in comparison to older adults 25 years of age and older (i.e., 7%) (Health Canada, 2010b).

Eaton, Kann, Kinchen, et al. (2010), in their analysis of the results obtained from the Youth Risk Behavior Surveillance System for 2009, found that, nationwide in the United States, 36.8% of high school students (grades 9–12) reported using marijuana at least once (range 20.6% to 44.5% across state surveys). Overall, use was higher for boys (39.6%) than for girls (34.3%) with the highest percentage reported for boys of African descent (44.3%). They also found that the use of cannabis increased steadily among high school students from 9th grade (26.4%) to 12th grade (45.6%). In regard to current use, Eaton, Kann, Kinchen, et al. (2010) found that 1 in 5 students (i.e., 20.8%) reported cannabis use on one or more occasions during the 30 days prior to the survey (range 10.0% to 28.0% across state surveys). Data from the 2005 study of 7,216 adolescents nationwide revealed similar results (Partnership for a Drug-Free America, 2006). For students in the 7th through 12th grades: 37% reported lifetime use, 28% reported past-year use, and 16% reported past month use (i.e., use during the past 30 days). M. P. O'Brien (2008), reporting for the Community Epidemiology Work Group (CEWG) of the NIDA, also found similar results with 38.1% of U.S. high school students reporting lifetime marijuana use.

Johnston, O'Malley, Bachman et al. (2008), in their survey of 50,000 students in the 8th, 10th, and 12th grades, nationwide, found that, although availability of cannabis was reported as being high (i.e., 37% of 8th graders, 69% of 10th graders, and 84% of 12th graders reported that cannabis was either fairly easy or very easy to obtain), reported use was significantly lower in comparison to data for the 1970s, 1980s, and 1990s. Use of marijuana/hashish in the year prior to the survey was reported by 10.3 % of 8th graders, 24.6% of 10th graders, and 31.7% of 12th graders. Use of marijuana/hashish during the month (30 days) prior to the survey was reported by 5.7% of 8th graders, 14.2% of 10th graders, and 18.8 % of 12th graders. However, after several consecutive years of decline, reported use increased in the 2009 survey with 6.5% of 8th graders, 15.9% of 10th graders, and 20.6% of 12th graders reporting past month use of marijuana (Adolescent cigarette smoking, 2010).

Data from the 2010 cohort sample demonstrated a continued increase in marijuana smoking, with 8% of 8th graders, 16.7% of 10th graders, and 21.4% of 12th graders reporting past-month use of marijuana (Johnston, O'Malley, Bachman, et al., 2010b). In addition, the number of daily marijuana smokers increased to 1 in 16 high school seniors—the highest reported rate since the 1970s, when it was reported as 1 in 11 high school seniors (Cassels, 2010b).

Health Canada (2010b) conducted telephone interviews with a sample of over 13,000 participants across all ten provinces as part of the Canadian Alcohol and Drug Use Monitoring Survey (CADUMS). Data revealed that for participants who were 15 to 24 years of age: (1) 42.4% had used cannabis at some time over their lifetimes; (2) 10.6% had used cannabis within the previous year; and (3) the average age for initiating cannabis use was 15.6 years of age.

Given the current prevailing social/political climate regarding the decriminalization of marijuana and general efforts aimed

---

[13] Preteen marijuana users are reportedly more likely to: (1) be of Hispanic descent, (2) be of lower socioeconomic status, and (3) have parents who have less than a high school education (Broughton, 2010).

at securing legislation in support of the use of medical marijuana across North America, it is not surprising that these changes in public attitudes are reflected in adolescent attitudes toward marijuana use. For example, the Partnership for a Drug-Free America and the Metlife Foundation (2010) found that measures of favorability toward marijuana use by both self and peers were significantly increased among adolescents. Also not surprising is their finding that marijuana use among adolescents in grades 9 to 12 has increased significantly, with 25% of their study participants reporting past-month use; 38% reporting past-year use; and 44% reporting lifetime use of marijuana (i.e., marijuana use increased in a manner commensurable with the increasingly favorable attitudes toward marijuana use).[14]

This increased trend in adolescent marijuana use also has been reported by several other researchers. For example, Johnston, O'Malley, Bachman, et al. (2010b) found that, in their 2010 in-school survey of adolescent use of the drugs and substances of abuse, 43.8% of 12th graders reported a lifetime prevalence of marijuana use. These observed increases in adolescent marijuana use are also consonant with research studies (e.g., Researchers find, 2007) that report a "desire to fit in with friends" and a "desire to have peers approve of their use of marijuana" as contributing factors to initial and continued marijuana use among adolescents.

### General Pharmacology

Over 400 different chemicals have been identified in cannabis smoke, including ammonia, benzpyrene, carbon monoxide, cresols, hydrogen cyanide, nitric oxide, phenols, and tars.[15] These chemicals include approximately 60 different cannabinoids (i.e., chemicals that are found naturally only in cannabis plants). Of these, the principal active cannabinoid, in terms of psychodelic actions, is THC.

A variety of clearly defined dose-related effects, from euphoria to toxic psychosis, have been associated with THC. Lower doses may produce decreased intraocular pressure, drowsiness, euphoria, hypertension, increased appetite, memory impairment, reddened eyes, relaxation, tachycardia, and temporal disintegration. Moderate doses may produce anxiety, decreased muscle strength and motor performance, decreased visual acuity, and paranoia. Higher doses may produce confused thinking, delusions, hallucinations, and toxic psychosis. They also may produce synesthesia:

---

the interchanging of the senses ... the hashish eater knows what it is ... to smell colors, to see sounds, and, much more frequently, to see feelings. (Ludlow, 1857, p. 72)

---

**Proposed Mechanism of Psychodelic Action**    The mechanism by which cannabis exerts its psychodelic and other actions is not yet fully understood. However, important strides have been made over the last 15 years in this regard. Undoubtedly, the greatest advancement has been the identification of the endocannabinoid system—the endogenous system of cannabinoid receptors and agonists, or ligands (Breivogel & Childers, 1998).[16] Overall, the endocannabinoid system

---

[14] We, too, have noted the same effects in our own clinical practice and research (e.g., "What's wrong with using marijuana when it's practically legal in California?"; "I know someone who takes medical marijuana"; "If it's so bad [i.e., illegal], why is it used by doctors to help so many people?") (Pagliaro & Pagliaro, *Clinical Patient Data Files*).

[15] Several of these chemicals are known human carcinogens (e.g., benzpyrene, cresols, phenols, and tars).

[16] Anandamide (N-arachidonoyl ethanolamine) and arachidonoylglycerol have been identified as the major endogenous agonists, or ligands, of the endocannabinoid receptors. These endogenous chemicals have been demonstrated to elicit several of the pharmacologic actions associated with the use of THC (Maccarrone & Finazzi-Agro, 2002; Martin, Mechoulam, & Razdan, 1999).

appears to function primarily as a neuromodulator of the central nervous system (CNS) by affecting the release of several identified neurotransmitters, including acetylcholine, dopamine, endorphins, gamma-aminobutyric acid (GABA), glutamate, noradrenaline, and serotonin (López-Moreno, Gonzalez-Cuevas, Moreno, et al., 2008; Moreira & Lutz, 2008). Two major cannabinoid G-protein coupled receptor subtypes appear to exist, Subtype 1 (i.e., CB1 receptors) and Subtype 2 (i.e., CB2 receptors) (Pertwee, 2000).

CB1 receptors are primarily present on central and peripheral neurons, predominantly within the CNS (Pertwee, 2000). These receptors appear to mediate the: (1) inhibition of adenylate cyclase and various calcium channels; (2) stimulation of potassium channels; and (3) activation of mitogen-activated protein kinase (Ameri, 1999). The endocannabinoid activity of these receptors suggests a role in the modulation of neurotransmitter release and action (e.g., increasing dopaminergic neuronal activity in the ventral tegmental area-mesolimbic pathway) (Di Marzo, Melck, Bisogno, et al., 1998).

CB2 receptors are present primarily on immune cells, predominantly outside of the CNS (Klein, Lane, Newton, et al., 2000). These receptors appear to mediate the activation of mitogen-activated protein kinase and the inhibition of adenylate cyclase (Ameri, 1999). The endocannabinoid activity of these receptors (e.g., enhancement of the physiologic response to cytokines) suggests a role in immunosuppression and anti-inflammatory action (Nocerino, Amato, & Izzo, 2000).

**Methods of Use**  Generally, cannabis is used by two common methods: oral ingestion and pulmonary inhalation (i.e., smoking, vaporizing). During the 19th century, cannabis was commonly eaten as candy bon-bons or baked in foods, such as cookies and brownies, and eaten.[17] This method of use continued through the 1960s and 1970s—often using a classic hashish fudge recipe by Alice B. Toklas (1954). The more recent legalization of medicinal marijuana in several states and provinces (see Table 3.2) has resulted in the development of a wide variety of edible marijuana products (e.g., brownies, butters, cakes, caramels, chocolates, granola bars, and lollipops)[18] that can be purchased at marijuana dispensaries as an alternative to smoking or vaporizing the marijuana that also is sold at these dispensaries. However, in order to produce equivalent actions, the oral dose of cannabis must be approximately 5 times higher than the dose that is smoked because absorption from the lungs is much greater than that from the gastrointestinal tract (i.e., oral bioavailability is approximately 10%).[19] Thus, smoking, or toking, is the most common method of use for all three forms of cannabis. In fact, cannabis users usually roll the cannabis into a cigarette (i.e., a reefer or joint) or sometimes smoke it from a water pipe (bong or hookah).

With pulmonary inhalation, the THC in cannabis smoke is readily absorbed, along with other chemicals and constituents—including carcinogens—into the lungs. Increasingly, because of the associated cancer risk (see "Common Toxicities" section), many users vaporize their cannabis in order to avoid burning it and the cigarette paper used to roll it into joints for smoking. Vaporizing the cannabis involves using a commercial vaporizer (e.g., Volcano® forced-air vaporizer) to heat

---

[17] Marijuana beer, a beverage brewed using the cannabis plant, has not gained much acceptance because of its notably poor taste.

[18] Concern regarding the attraction of these products and their use by children and adolescents has been voiced by public health departments and other groups (e.g., San Francisco Health Department, 2010).

[19] Although hashish oil may be injected, this method of use is relatively rare because of the severe pain and inflammation that occurs at the site of injection associated with injecting oils. Therefore, it is more often orally ingested, smoked, or vaporized.

**TABLE 3.2    Medical Marijuana: Eligible Medical Conditions for the Legal Prescription of Marijuana in California**

Acquired immune deficiency syndrome (AIDS)

Anorexia

Arthritis

Cachexia

Cancer pain

Chronic pain

Glaucoma

Migraine headaches

Nausea (severe)

Persistent muscle spasms (e.g., as related to multiple sclerosis)

Seizures (e.g., epilepsy)

Any other chronic or persistent medical sign or symptom that either: (1) limits the ability to conduct a major life activity as defined in the *Americans With Disabilities Act* of 1990, Public Law 101-3336; or (2) if not alleviated, may cause serious harm to the patient's safety or physical or mental health.[a]

[a]For example, medical marijuana has been prescribed for children and adolescents for the treatment of attention-deficit/hyperactivity disorder (Ellison, 2009).

Note: People who have a wide range of mental and physical disorders are allowed, with a medical prescription, to legally purchase, possess, and use varying prescribed amounts of marijuana. Marijuana also can be grown for personal use. However, it is more commonly purchased from specialized marijuana dispensaries. Currently, these states have some form of active, voter-approved medical marijuana program: Alaska, Arizona, California, Colorado, Delaware, District of Columbia, Hawaii, Maine, Maryland, Michigan, Montana, Nevada, New Jersey, New Mexico, Oregon, Rhode Island, Vermont, and Washington (McCullough, 2010; NORML, 2011). In Canadian provinces, the medical use, by prescription, of a pharmaceutical-grade synthetic cannabinoid (i.e., nabilone [Cesamet®]) has been available since 1976 (Pagliaro & Pagliaro, 2009). In addition, Health Canada has implemented a national policy to screen applications and to grant, where deemed appropriate, access to medical marijuana use for people "who are suffering from grave and debilitating illnesses" (Health Canada, 2011, p. 1).

the cannabis. The required temperature is lower than that needed for smoking, and thus the cannabis (or the cigarette paper) is not burned. The result is the evaporation of the THC into a gas that, when inhaled, delivers up to 95% of THC with significantly less carbon monoxide and other toxins (e.g., tars found in marijuana smoke). Although not as effective in THC delivery or in preventing cancer risk, cannabis users also may use a traditional conical pipe, small-bowl pipe, or water pipe—also referred to as a chillim, galyan, hookah, nargile, or shisha—to smoke the cannabis.

**Common Toxicities** Acute cannabis use can be identified by several signs and symptoms, primarily the characteristic pungent odor of the cannabis smoke in the air and on clothing and the red, bloodshot eyes of the user. Whether the user becomes intoxicated or not, common toxicities that are associated with the use of cannabis can

be readily divided into those associated with short-term use and long-term use. (See Table 3.3.)

Surprisingly, given the 10,000 years of cannabis use among various human populations (Pagliaro & Pagliaro, 2004; Pagliaro & Pagliaro, 2009), the toxicities associated with its use have not yet been fully evaluated (Pope, Gruber, Hudson, et al., 2001). However, it appears that fatal overdosages are relatively rare. In fact, during the last two centuries, the general medical consensus has been that the occasional use of cannabis is not particularly harmful to healthy adult users and that the intermittent use of low-potency cannabis is not generally associated with obvious signs and symptoms of toxicity (Addiction Research Foundation/World Health Organization, 1981).

However, it is important to note that during the 1970s, 1980s, and 1990s, the potency of cannabis increased 5-fold, from an average of 2% to 10% THC content

**TABLE 3.3   Cannabis: Acute and Chronic Toxicities**

*Acute Toxicities*

- Academic achievement, decreased
- Anxiety
- Appetite, increased
- Blood pressure, increased (hypertension)
- Cognitive impairment (i.e., impaired executive functioning)
- Confusion
- Delusions
- Depersonalization
- Drowsiness
- Hallucinations
- Memory impairment, particularly short-term memory
- Panic reaction
- Paranoia
- Psychomotor impairment (with related motor vehicle crashes)
- Psychotic disorders
- Pulmonary irritation (e.g., coughs; colds)
- Reddened eyes
- Synesthesia
- Short-term memory impairment
- Tachycardia
- Temporal disintegration
- Toxic delirium
- Visual acuity, decreased

*Chronic Toxicities*

- Academic achievement, decreased
- Amotivational syndrome[a]
- Cannabis withdrawal syndrome, relatively mild
- Depression
- Developmental or maturational delay or arrest
- Immunosuppression[b]
- Physical dependence (relatively mild)
- Psychological dependence
- Psychotic disorders
- Pulmonary irritation (e.g., cough and colds) with the eventual development of related chronic obstructive pulmonary disease (e.g., asthma; bronchitis)[c]

[a]This syndrome has been generally recognized since the 1970s. However, supporting evidence is largely anecdotal and is derived from uncontrolled studies. Currently, several researchers question the validity of this syndrome and suggest that what actually is observed is simply the expected behavior associated with chronic, long-term *intoxication* among cannabis users (Johns, 2001).

[b]Appears to be modulated by interaction with the CB2 receptor (see "Proposed Mechanism of Psychodelic Action" section).

[c]Although not listed because of a paucity of available reliable published data, lung cancer would be an expected chronic toxicity associated with regular, long-term cannabis smoking. This toxic effect would be expected because of the presence of known human carcinogens in cannabis smoke in concentrations significantly higher than those found in tobacco cigarette smoke (Ashton, 2001; Pagliaro, 1983) and the method of smoking cannabis (i.e., inhaling the cannabis smoke deeply into the lungs and holding it in the lungs as long as possible. This smoking technique is thought to maximize the contact of the smoke with the alveoli and hence increase the amount of THC absorbed by the capillaries for distribution through the circulatory system). Reportedly, vaporization of the smoke decreases or eliminates this risk. (See earlier discussion.)

Note: The intensity and clinical significance of these toxicities depend, to a significant degree, on the amount of THC absorbed, the environmental setting or circumstances of use, and the physical, mental, and social characteristics of the user.

(Harrison, Backenheimer, & Inciardi, 1995). This increase in potency occurred as users preferentially changed from *Cannabis (sativa) sativa* to *Cannabis (sativa) indica* and as *sinsemilla* varieties were increasingly selectively cultivated (see earlier discussion). Consequently, several toxicities now have been associated with the regular, long-term use of cannabis. These toxicities include cognitive impairment, decreased sperm count and motility, depression, disruption of normal ovulation, impairment of the human immune response, interference with prenatal development, male breast enlargement (i.e., gynecomastia), and psychosis.[20] In addition, because the endocannabinoid system appears to be involved in brain development—cell proliferation and differentiation—several authors (e.g., Cannabis damages, 2009; Long-term cannabis, 2008; Schneider, 2008; Trezza, Cuomo, & Vanderschuren, 2008) have expressed concerns that there is significant risk for cannabis toxicity during periods of high neuronal plasticity (e.g., late adolescence) and, consequently, its associated adverse effects on executive functioning, including problem solving and other higher cognitive functions. We, too, share this concern.

Although these and other toxicities have been documented in the published literature, there also have been erroneous reports and rather wild speculations regarding toxicities associated with cannabis use.[21] In fact, relatively few serious toxicities have been directly associated with cannabis use. However, the available evidence from controlled clinical studies, and common sense, point to the following toxicities that may be directly linked to the regular, long-term use of cannabis:

- The amotivational syndrome
- Motor vehicle and other crashes, including airplane, all-terrain vehicle, boat, snowmobile, and train crashes (Beirness & Porath-Waller, 2009; Cannabis almost doubles, 2005; Hall, 2009; Kalant, 2004; Kurzthaler, Hummer, Miller, et al., 1999; Pagliaro & Pagliaro, 2003; Pagliaro, 1995b; Pagliaro & Pagliaro, *Clinical Patient Data Files*)[22]
- Physical and psychological dependence on cannabis (Fischer, Rehm, & Hall, 2009; Pagliaro & Pagliaro, 2009) (see later discussion in *Physical and Psychological Dependence* section)
- Pulmonary toxicity (i.e., lung damage and pulmonary disease [chronic obstructive pulmonary disease {COPD}] and lung cancer (Fischer, Rehm, & Hall, 2009; Pagliaro, 1983; Pagliaro & Pagliaro, 2009; Pagliaro & Pagliaro, *Clinical Patient Data Files*)
- Toxicities associated with maternal use during pregnancy and lactation (Pagliaro, 2002; Pagliaro & Pagliaro, 1996; Pagliaro, 1995b).

The people who have the greatest risk for these major toxicities associated with cannabis use are:

- Preadolescents as well as young adolescents, who are at particular risk for developing

---

[20] Better current understanding of cannabis pharmacology (see "Proposed Mechanism of Psychodelic Action" section) provides possible mechanistic explanations for many of these observed undesired and toxic effects. For example, the undesired effects involving immune response are likely mediated by interactions involving THC, or other cannabinoids, with the CB2 receptor. The depression and psychosis are likely mediated by effects of the endocannabinoid system on the neurotransmitters dopamine and serotonin. (Also see discussion "Cannabis and Schizophrenia" in Chapter 8, *Dual Diagnosis Among Adolescents*).

[21] These "erroneous" harmful and toxic effects can be found published in the lay press and scientific journals and textbooks from the 1930s through the 1990s. (Also see Pagliaro and Pagliaro [2004, 2009] for additional related discussion.)

[22] These crashes are directly related to the recognized acute adverse effects associated with cannabis use, including cognitive impairment, psychomotor impairment, temporal disintegration, and decreased visual acuity.

amotivational syndrome and poor coping abilities[23, 24]

- Drivers who use cannabis and alcohol, because the deleterious effects on driving ability are compounded
- People who are regular, long-term users, particularly of high-potency cannabis
- People 65 years of age and older who have associated cardiovascular conditions, because cannabis can affect blood pressure and cardiac function and, consequently, place these people at particular risk for the exacerbation of these conditions (e.g., chest pain among patients with angina pectoris and precipitation of a myocardial infarction among predisposed people [Sidney, 2002])[25]
- People, including those who are 65 years of age and older, who have pulmonary disease, because cannabis smoking can irritate and damage lung tissue and further compromise lung function (Taylor, Fergusson, Milne, et al., 2002)[26]
- People who have mental disorders, because of the potential for the aggravation of these disorders (See the related discussion of cannabis-induced psychosis in Chapter 8, *Dual Diagnosis Among Adolescents*.)
- Offspring of adolescent girls and women who used cannabis during pregnancy or when breast-feeding

Children and adolescents are at particular risk for the toxicities discussed next and their associated effects.

***Amotivational Syndrome***   The amotivational syndrome, or burnout, has been identified among children and adolescents who regularly smoke large amounts of cannabis over prolonged periods of time. Generally, after several months to years of using cannabis to mellow out or to forget their problems, these youth tend to lose interest in their external environments and the challenges of life associated with growing up. They typically become content to spend hours of potentially productive time each day alone, doing little else than listening to and watching their favorite music videos while they smoke cannabis. Whether the use of cannabis actually causes the amotivational syndrome, or whether it merely brings out a latent personality characteristic of the user, has not yet been clearly determined.[27]

***Motor Vehicle Crashes***   While a consensus among cannabis researchers generally has been reached concerning the direct relationship between increased acute cannabis intoxication and decreased driving performance, some researchers have continued to argue the contrary. For example, "While smoking marijuana does impair driving ability, it does not share alcohol's effect on judgment. Drivers on marijuana remain aware of their impairment,

---

[23] For example, if the response to commonly encountered challenges faced as part of growing-up, such as: failing a history test; having acne; being chosen last for a sports team; not having a date for a school dance; is simply to become intoxicated with cannabis, then the child or adolescent has missed a valuable opportunity to learn how to deal with common problems that do occur during childhood and adolescence. In addition, these missed opportunities generally leave the child or adolescent *ill-equipped* to grow from and effectively deal with relatively bigger and more serious problems that may be encountered as they get older, such as: death of a loved one; marriage; raising children; marital difficulties; divorce; or job loss. Thus, while children and adolescents who regularly use cannabis to cope with *life's problems* can be expected to progress chronologically in years, they are not expected to progress psychologically into healthy adulthood, in terms of coping abilities.

[24] In addition, initiation of cannabis use before 13 years of age has been associated with a higher incidence of: (1) posttraumatic stress disorder (PTSD); (2) substance use disorders (SUDs); and (3) suicide attempts (Broughton, 2010) (Also see related discussion in Chapter 8, *Dual Diagnosis Among Adolescents*).

[25] Some data suggest that this risk also may extend to children and adolescents who have preexisting cardiovascular defects (e.g., congenital heart defects) or diseases that would increase their risk for acute cardiovascular death (Bachs & Morland, 2001).

[26] This risk also may be extended to children and adolescents with COPDs (e.g., asthma, bronchitis) or cystic fibrosis.

[27] Another alternate explanation is that this syndrome is nothing more than the observation of chronic cannabis intoxication among some users.

prompting them to slow down and drive more cautiously to compensate" (Smiley, 1999, p. 1). For another example: "Although cannabis use was associated with increased risks for traffic accidents among members of this birth cohort, these increased risks appear to reflect the characteristics of the young people who use cannabis rather than the effects of cannabis use on driver performance" (Fergusson & Horwood, 2001, p. 703). We disagree and instead posit that the risk-associated characteristics that often are found among adolescents, combined with being a new or relatively inexperienced driver, significantly increase the deleterious effects of cannabis use on driving performance in a manner similar to that observed with alcohol use. (See related discussion in Chapter 1, *The Psychodepressants*.)

In North America, it has been widely documented that:

- Motor-vehicle crashes are one of the leading causes of death among adolescents and young adults
- Approximately 25% of adolescents and young adults are current users of cannabis[28]
- Approximately 25% of current cannabis users drive while under the influence of cannabis (Beirness & Beasley, 2010; Grunbaum, Kann, Kinchen, et al., 2002; Pagliaro & Pagliaro, *Clinical Patient Data Files*; Walsh & Mann, 1999)

We believe that it is socially irresponsible to disregard the significance of cannabis use in relation to motor vehicle crashes by simply stating that the statistics are not as bad as those related to alcohol use. The fact is that drivers who are under the influence of cannabis cannot drive as well as they can when they are not under the influence of cannabis. The driving impairment, which is directly related to the acute toxicities associated with cannabis use, becomes increasingly severe in direct relation to increasingly high cannabis dosages (i.e., using larger amounts of cannabis or using cannabis that is more potent in terms of relative THC concentration) (Ramaekers, Berghaus, van Laar, et al., 2004; Sewell, Poling, & Sofuoglu, 2009).[29]

---

The sister-in-law of the woman who killed herself and seven others when she hit another car head-on while driving the wrong way on the Taconic State Parkway in July told investigators that the woman smoked marijuana regularly and was a heavy drinker, according to a lawyer for the family of two of the victims.

A toxicology report indicated that [the woman] had a blood-alcohol level of 0.19, more than twice the legal limit, and a significant level of tetrahydrocannabinol, the active ingredient in marijuana. (O'Connnor & Schweber, 2009, p. 1)

---

Although this case may have involved an autocide, the seriousness of impaired driving caused by cannabis use cannot be overemphasized. People who use cannabis should not smoke and drive.[30]

---

[28] This is a conservative estimate. See earlier related discussion in the section, "Prevalence and Characteristics of Cannabis Use Among North American Children and Adolescents."

[29] In addition, when cannabis is used in combination with alcohol (a fairly common practice, particularly among older adolescents and young adults), the research is abundantly clear that the degree of driving impairment is significantly greater than that caused by the use of either cannabis or alcohol alone (Brault, Dussault, Bouchard, et al., 2004; Crowley & Courtney, 2003; Ramaekers, Berghaus, van Laar, et al., 2004; Sewell, Poling, & Sofuoglu, 2009).

[30] To illustrate the lack of awareness commonly observed among the general public in regard to the deleterious effects of cannabis use on motor vehicle driving performance, we would like to share two anecdotal cases that we recently observed. In the first case, a middle-age woman whose driver's license had been revoked because of an impaired driving conviction requested that her adolescent daughter—a daily user of marijuana—be her designated driver. In another case, an elderly man was in the waiting room of his ophthalmologist's office with his daughter who was his designated driver because his eyes were being dilated as part of his examination. After a while, the man's daughter told him that she needed to go out for a smoke and

(*continued*)

***Pulmonary Toxicity*** Pulmonary toxicity has been observed among heavy cannabis users and is related primarily to the components (e.g., ammonia, hydrogen cyanide, nitric oxide, and tars) in cannabis smoke other than THC (Marijuana smoke, 2007; Pagliaro, 1983). Therefore, the severity of these effects depends more on the amount of cannabis smoked, the smoking techniques employed by the user, and the combustion properties of the material used to smoke the cannabis rather than on its actual THC content (Impact on lungs, 2007; Marijuana smokers, 2008; Pagliaro & Pagliaro, 2009).[31] Asthma, bronchitis, bullous lung disease, chronic cough, irritation of the respiratory tract, and sore throat have been commonly associated with the regular, long-term smoking of cannabis in North America since the 1970s (Marijuana smokers, 2008; Pagliaro, 1983, 1988). In addition, it has long been recognized that cannabis smoke has the potential, like tobacco smoke, to induce hepatic microsomal isoenzymes. In this regard, regular, long-term cannabis users generally eliminate THC more rapidly (half-life of elimination, approximately 28 hours) than nonusers (half-life of elimination, approximately 57 hours).

***Toxicities Associated with Maternal Use During Pregnancy and Lactation*** Although THC crosses the placenta, studies of infrequent or moderate cannabis use during pregnancy have not been significantly associated with teratogenic effects. However, some studies (e.g., Fried & Smith, 2001; Richardson, Ryan, Willford, et al., 2002) suggest that higher-order cognitive functioning among children, such as attentional processes and visual analysis/hypothesis testing, is negatively correlated with in utero exposure to cannabis. We also note concerns regarding possible long-term negative effects of in utero exposure on subsequent memory processes (e.g., encoding and retrieval mechanisms) (Pagliaro & Pagliaro, 2009). THC also is excreted into breast milk and expected effects (e.g., drowsiness) can be observed among breast-fed neonates and infants.

Thus, it is a cause for concern that cannabis use has become the primary reason for seeking inpatient treatment for drug and substance abuse among pregnant adolescent girls. In 2007, 45.9% of the admissions of pregnant adolescent girls for inpatient treatment of drug and substance use disorders across the entire United States were primarily related to cannabis use (Substance Abuse and Mental Health Services Administration, 2010). This statistic reflects a significant change from the statistics reported in 1992, when admissions of pregnant adolescent girls for inpatient treatment of drug and substance use disorders were primarily related to alcohol use—with marijuana use accounting for only 19.3% of the admissions at that time.

Adolescent girls and young women who are pregnant or who are breast-feeding should

---

[30](*continued*)

stretch because of her back pain. When another elderly patient shared that he had recently lost a son to lung cancer and that perhaps she should stop smoking, her father quickly clarified that it was okay. His daughter was not going out to smoke a tobacco cigarette but was going out to smoke her medical marijuana, which she used to manage her chronic back pain.

[31] Over 400 chemicals (primarily formed by means of pyrolysis) can be found in marijuana smoke, including many of the chemicals that are found in tobacco smoke. When marijuana is smoked, it yields more tar than does tobacco when smoked. In addition, the tar from marijuana smoke has higher concentrations of certain carcinogens (e.g., benzpyrene) than are found in the tar from tobacco smoke. Thus, it is probable that marijuana smoking will produce more lung cancer when compared to tobacco smoking, which currently is the leading cause of lung cancer. Based on the chemical constituents found in the pyrolysis products of marijuana smoke versus the pyrolysis products of tobacco smoke, and the comparative differences in smoking techniques for marijuana versus tobacco (i.e., smoking the entire joint and inhaling the marijuana smoke more deeply into the lungs where it is held in the lower respiratory tract for a longer period of time), we have, for several decades (e.g., Pagliaro, 1983; Pagliaro & Pagliaro, 1996, 2004, 2009), estimated that smoking 1 joint of marijuana exposes users to as much irritation and associated damage to the respiratory system, along with subsequent risk for lung cancer, as smoking 1 package (i.e., 20) filter-tipped tobacco cigarettes.

not smoke, or otherwise use, cannabis because of the potential risks to offspring (O'Mara & Nahata, 2002; Pagliaro & Pagliaro, 1996; Pagliaro & Pagliaro, 2002). (For further related discussion, see Chapter 5, *Exposure to the Drugs and Substances of Abuse From Conception Through Childhood.*) Cannabis use by young mothers of infants and young children may also negatively affect their parenting.

**Physical and Psychological Dependence**
The question as to whether the regular, long-term use of cannabis results in physical dependence has been extensively argued over the last century. The general consensus is that it does.[32] Currently, the regular, long-term, high-dosage use of cannabis is clearly recognized as being associated with the development of physical dependence (Khalsa, Genser, Francis, et al., 2002; Maldonado & Rodriguez de Fonseca, 2002; Pagliaro & Pagliaro, 2009). In North America, the increase in the average potency of cannabis since the 1960s (as noted earlier) has been tremendous (i.e., a 5- to 10-fold increase in THC concentration), and this increase appears to have significantly increased the probability for developing physical dependence or, likely, the recognition of the clinical significance of the cannabis withdrawal syndrome.

A cannabis withdrawal syndrome has long been noted in relation to the discontinuation of regular, long-term cannabis use—even among adolescents (e.g., Duffy & Milin, 1996). The physical neurobiological basis of the signs and symptoms associated with this withdrawal syndrome has been established by: (1) the identification and characterization of the endocannabinoid system (see earlier discussion in the "Proposed Mechanism of Psychodelic

Action" section); and (2) the demonstration of the precipitation of the signs and symptoms associated with this syndrome when a cannabinoid receptor (i.e., CB1) antagonist is administered to an active cannabis user (Budney & Hughes, 2006; Cooper & Haney, 2009).

The usual signs and symptoms of the cannabis withdrawal syndrome include anorexia, anxiety, craving for cannabis, depression, insomnia, irritability, nervousness, restlessness, rebound increase in rapid eye movement sleep, and weight loss (Cornelius, Chung, Martin, et al., 2008; Haney, 2005; Hasin, Keyes, Alderson, et al., 2008). Chills, hypersomnia, hyperthermia, tremor, and weakness also may occur. These signs and symptoms, which are relatively mild, begin within several hours after cannabis was last used and peak on day 1 (Pagliaro & Pagliaro, 2009; Preuss, Watzke, Zimmermann, et al., 2010). The withdrawal syndrome can last for up to 5 days.

The overwhelming majority of cannabis-using adolescents who have been studied report experiencing the characteristic signs and symptoms of the cannabis withdrawal syndrome. However, the reported severity of the signs and symptoms varies widely and appears to be predicated on several identified factors, including: (1) amount and potency of the cannabis used and its duration of use; (2) genetic characteristics, or predisposition, of the user; (3) concurrent use of other drugs and substances of abuse; and (4) presence of a dual diagnosis (e.g., a substance use disorder with a major depressive or a psychotic disorder) (Arendt, Rosenberg, Foldager, et al., 2007; Preuss, Watzke, Zimmermann, et al., 2010; Vandrey, Budney, Kamon, et al., 2005). (Also see Chapter 8, *Dual Diagnosis Among Adolescents.*)

---

[32] For example, since its fourth edition in 1994, the *Diagnostic and Statistical Manual of Mental Disorders (DSM)* (American Psychiatric Association, 2000) listed cannabis dependence in its taxonomy based largely on noted tolerance and a well-recognized withdrawal syndrome. However, until the last decade of the 20th century, it was generally thought that only psychological dependence, not physical dependence, was likely to develop with the regular, long-term use of cannabis. As noted elsewhere in this text, the American Psychiatric Association (2011), for the 5th edition of the DSM, has decided to discontinue the use of the term "dependence" in regard to the diagnosis of drug and substance use disorders—including cannabis dependence.

## Phencyclidine

Phencyclidine (PCP), known as angel dust, hog, and many other street names, was originally synthesized in 1958. It was developed for use in veterinary medicine as an animal tranquilizer. It also was used as an anesthetic for people who were undergoing various surgical procedures. When a low to moderate dose of PCP (Sernylan®) was intravenously administered according to recommended dosing schedules, it was physically well tolerated during surgery and produced few undesired physical effects (e.g., excessive changes in blood pressure, depth and rate of respirations, or heart rate) during surgery. However, during the immediate recovery period following surgery, several troublesome psychological effects were observed among patients, including agitation, hallucinations, and violent behavior. As a result, PCP was withdrawn from medical use and was replaced with a derivative—the dissociative anesthetic, ketamine[33] (Bradford Baldridge & Bessen, 1990). However, PCP had already gained popularity among many groups of users (e.g., members of outlaw motorcycle gangs). No longer able to obtain legal pharmaceutical-grade PCP for their use, these users soon found that PCP could be illegally produced and sold on the street in various forms for intravenous injection, intranasal insufflation, oral ingestion, or pulmonary inhalation (e.g., smoking a "dipped" Nat Sherman® cigarette).

The Hell's Angels motorcycle gang was extremely successful in producing tremendous profits in relation to the production, distribution, and sale of PCP across the United States during the early 1970s. It was during this time, and as a result of their marketing campaign, that PCP received its most popular street names (i.e., angel dust and hog)—names that continue to be used today.

### Prevalence and Characteristics of PCP Use Among North American Children and Adolescents

Currently in the United States, it is estimated that approximately 1 in 20 young adults, 18 to 25 years of age, has used PCP during the previous year. However, this estimate may be low because accurate data regarding the actual use of PCP by adolescents and young adults is relatively difficult to obtain for several reasons, including: (1) adolescents and young adults who use PCP often cannot be reached in a survey of high school seniors (i.e., often they are high school drop-outs); (2) the use of the PCP does not often result in emergency room visits for which data usually would be available; and (3) PCP is not always detected in blood or urine screening tests for drugs and substances of abuse because, for economic reasons, it is not often included in the general drug screen.

Contributing to PCP's ability to fly under the radar is its changing pattern of use over the last decade, including: 1) its use in combination with other drugs and substances of abuse, particularly marijuana; and 2) its use in lower dosages (Pagliaro & Pagliaro, *Clinical Patient Data Files*; Pagliaro & Pagliaro, 2009). However, Johnston, O'Malley, Bachman, et al. (2008), in their 2007 national survey of secondary school students in the United States,

---

[33] Ketamine (Ketalar®) and other dissociative anesthetics allow sensory impulses to reach the brain but cause them to be interpreted in a distorted manner. As the dosage increases, analgesia progresses to anesthesia and then coma. The eyes remain open. Ketamine, referred to on the street as cat, K, or Special K, is currently commonly used, as are other drugs and substances of abuse, in the context of clubbing and attendance at dance parties and raves (Pagliaro & Pagliaro, 2009). A smaller group of North American ketamine users inject ketamine intramuscularly rather than intravenously. This smaller group of users are almost exclusively older adolescent boys and young adult men (16 to 25 years of age), predominantly of European descent, who are homeless and live on the streets. They also commonly share their gear or rigs—their needles and syringes (Lankenau, Bloom, & Shin, 2010; Lankenau & Clatts, 2004; Lankenau & Sanders, 2007; Lankenau, Sanders, Bloom, et al., 2007), which increases their risk for exposure to viral infections, such as hepatitis B and C and HIV.

found that 2.1% of 12th graders reported having ever used PCP and 0.5% reported use within the previous 30 days. Since 2008, the reported lifetime prevalence of PCP use among 12th-grade students has remained relatively constant at approximately 1.8% (Johnston, O'Malley, Bachman, et al., 2010b). Of the 12th graders who participated in the 2007 survey, 21% reported that PCP was either fairly easy or very easy to obtain. In addition, more recent data suggest increasing use of PCP among young adults of Hispanic descent living in the large metropolitan areas of Houston, Texas, and Los Angeles, California (Drug trafficking, n.d).

**Fry, Illy, or Wet** Since the beginning of the new millennium, a liquid mixture containing PCP and formaldehyde or embalming fluid[34] has been used increasingly by North American adolescents, particularly those of Hispanic descent, with boys outnumbering girls 2 or 3 to 1 (e.g., D'Onofrio, McCausland, Tarabar, et al., 2006; Peters, Tortolero, Addy, et al., 2003; Singer, Clair, Schensul, et al., 2005). Known on the street as AMP, clickems, frios, fry, illy, Sherm sticks, or wet, cannabis joints or tobacco cigarettes are simply dipped into the mixture of PCP with formaldehyde or embalming fluid, briefly allowed to dry, and then smoked (Pagliaro & Pagliaro, 2009). Fry usually is smoked in a small group of 3 to 5 adolescents and frequently is accompanied with drinking beer or fortified wine that is often referred to as Cisco.

Signs and symptoms associated with the use of fry are virtually identical to those associated with PCP alone and include aggressive or violent behavior (intermittent), ataxia, blurred vision, delusions, depression, dry mouth, edema, hallucinations, headache, memory impairment, and vomiting (Elwood, 1998). The signs and symptoms usually subside within

24 to 36 hours after the fry was last used. However, benzodiazepine and antipsychotic pharmacotherapy may be required to ameliorate or terminate prolonged or problematic signs and symptoms (Modesto-Lowe & Petry, 2001). (Also see related discussion in the "General Pharmacology" section.)

*General Pharmacology*

This section provides a brief overview of PCP's proposed mechanism of action and associated common toxicities, including dose-dependent toxicities and propensity for physical and psychological dependence. Attention also is given to other relatively serious toxicities associated with its use, including: (1) aggressive and violent behavior, or bad trips; (2) PCP psychosis; and (3) the less commonly occurring delusional and mood disorders. The signs and symptoms of overdosage and the indirect causes of associated fatalities also are presented.

**Proposed Mechanism of Psychodelic Action** PCP is generally used at lower dosages to achieve a buzz, or an alcohol-like disinhibitory euphoria and elevated mood. It also may be used to relieve pain and to promote relaxation. In addition, PCP often is used to achieve such psychodelic actions as distortions in the perception of time, space, and body image and feelings of unreality. The exact mechanism by which PCP exerts these actions has not been determined. However, noncompetitive antagonism of the N-methyl-D-aspartate (NMDA) receptor channel complexes located in the cortex and limbic regions of the brain has been postulated as a primary contributory mechanism. The antagonism is thought to block the action of the excitatory amino acids aspartate and glutamate (Morris, Cochran, & Pratt, 2005). PCP also inhibits GABA and increases dopamine concentrations by both increasing the synthesis of dopamine

---

[34] Typically, embalming fluid is comprised of a mixture of formaldehyde (5% to 29%), ethanol (9% to 56%), methanol, and various other solvents (Elwood, 1998).

and inhibiting its presynaptic reuptake. In addition, PCP possesses significant anticholinergic activity. The acute effects of PCP begin within 5 minutes after pulmonary inhalation, or within 1 hour after oral ingestion, and can last for up to 24 hours.

**Common Toxicities**  Two decades ago, Carroll (1990) summarized published retrospective studies that examined the effects of PCP and identified two different categories of effects: (1) subjective effects that appear to vary dramatically in relation to personality type, or predisposition, of the user; and (2) secondary effects that appear to vary dramatically during different episodes of PCP use by the same user. Lower dosages of PCP, along with desired effects, were associated with cognitive impairment in most cases. Higher dosages were associated with severe psychological impairment—a "wasted" psychological state—characterized by anxiety, confusion, disorientation, fear of death, illusions, irritability, obsession with trivial matters, panic, paranoia, and restlessness.

Other surveys of PCP users have found that the effects of PCP generally are regarded as being pleasant only about half of the time; the other half of the time, they are generally aversive or negatively experienced. However, as reported by many regular, long-term users of PCP, it is the unpredictable action of the drug that is one of its attractions (Pagliaro & Pagliaro, *Clinical Patient Data Files*) (Also see related discussion in the later following section, "Bad Trips"). It also has been suggested that users who experience a positive subjective experience are more likely to develop a pattern of regular, long-term use than those who initially experience dysphoria, or other unpleasant effects.

Several common toxicities that appear to be dose-related have been associated with the use of PCP. Lower dosages of PCP generally are associated with: amnesia; ataxia; decreased sensitivity to pain; dry mouth; edema; impaired judgment; muscle rigidity; polydipsia with polyuria; rapid mood swings; and speech disturbances. Higher dosages generally are associated with: abnormal breathing; a facial expression characterized by a blank stare; bradycardia; coma; compulsive and repetitive movements; convulsions; hallucinations; hypotension; incoherent speech; and vomiting. Aggressive and violent behavior; agitation; belligerence; memory impairment; nystagmus, both vertical and horizontal; paranoia; and PCP psychosis have been associated with both lower and higher dosages of PCP (Pagliaro & Pagliaro, 2009; Peters, Kelder, Meshack, et al., 2005).

Brief overviews of several of the troublesome psychological toxicities associated with PCP use are presented next: amnesia, aggressive and violent behavior, bad trips, delusional and mood disorders, and PCP psychosis. The General Pharmacology section concludes with a discussion of toxicities involving exposures to PCP during fetal development (i.e., teratogensis) or breast-feeding during infancy, and child exposures to PCP in various contexts (see the "Contexts of Fetal, Infant, and Child Exposure" section); physical and psychological dependence; and overdosage. We begin with amnesia.

*Amnesia*  Amnesia often begins immediately after PCP has been ingested or smoked and lasts until its effects begin to wear off.[35] During this period of time, users may behave uncharacteristically in ways that, while not generally harmful, are later identified by the users as being "stupid" (e.g., removing their clothing and running around naked). At the other extreme, they may perform brutal and violent acts resulting in death. Usually users "blackout" and later

---

[35]This anterograde amnesia is similar to that associated with the use of alcohol or the benzodiazepine group of sedative-hypnotics. (See related discussion in Chapter 1, *The Psychodepressants.*)

report no conscious memory of the events that occurred during the episode (Pagliaro & Pagliaro, 2009). Although injurious and embarrassing acts may occur while high on PCP, its amnestic effects probably contribute to its continued use (i.e., the potentially aversive behaviors are not remembered by the user and thus do not serve as a deterrent to future use). In addition, the PCP-induced memory impairment has resulted in the use of the amnesia defense in some criminal trials to establish diminished capacity (Berman & Coccaro, 1998; Fauman & Fauman, 1982; Siegel, 1978). (Also see the next section, "Aggressive and Violent Behavior.")

*Aggressive and Violent Behavior*    One of the most troublesome toxicities associated with the regular, long-term use of PCP is its tendency to precipitate, or aggravate, aggressive and violent behavior—behavior that is often bizarre, sudden, and unexpected. Three contexts of aggressive and violent behavior have been observed: (1) toxic organic brain disorders (i.e., psychosis); (2) primitive sadistic criminal behaviors (e.g., brutal murders, extreme self-mutilation); and (3) bad trips (see "Bad Trips" section, following).

While the disinhibition caused by PCP may explain uncharacteristic behavior, the aggressive and violent behavior associated with PCP use is most likely related to underlying, or latent, psychological characteristics of the user (e.g., anger, depression, fear, hostility). The superhuman strength that has been observed among PCP users during these episodes probably is due to the analgesic and dissociative anesthetic effects of the drug. Because PCP decreases or eliminates pain, users are able to perform violent and aggressive acts with what appears to be superhuman strength that they would otherwise not be able to perform because of the associated injury to body tissues and resultant pain. As such, users do not become superhuman; they only think or feel that they have become superhuman.

*Bad Trips*    The bad trips associated with PCP use occur suddenly and unexpectedly among users and are characterized by sudden and severe acts of violence against themselves and others. Generally users who experience a bad trip have previously used PCP with the achievement of expected desirable effects (e.g., alcohol-like euphoria). Often these users have had no previous history of violent or aggressive behavior. For these reasons, it has been suggested that the bad trips may be due to the contamination of street supplies of PCP with formaldehyde or other impurities that could cause these effects (Marceaux, Dilks, & Hixson, 2008). (Also see earlier related discussion in the "Fry, Illy, or Wet" section.)

The unpredictable toxicities associated with PCP actually have contributed to its street folklore and to its increased popularity of use among certain groups of users. For example, North American adolescent boys and young men of Hispanic descent, particularly those who are involved in criminal youth gangs (Pagliaro & Pagliaro, *Clinical Patient Data Files*), are attracted to PCP and other drugs and substances of abuse that have unpredictable, and possibly horrific, consequences associated with their use. For these young people, the use of PCP is seen as a sign of being *macho,* or brave. As such, the use of PCP is their "red badge of courage." Mixing PCP with embalming fluid, or merely saying that the PCP has been mixed with embalming fluid, further increases the mystique and the machismo associated with the use of PCP among these adolescent boys and young men.

*Delusional and Mood Disorders*    PCP-induced delusional disorder may emerge up to 1 week following a PCP overdosage and is characterized by:

• Mild cognitive impairment
• Ritualistic stereotypic behavior
• Dysphoria
• Rambling, garbled, and incoherent speech
• A disheveled or an eccentric appearance

The mood disorder may present within 1 or 2 weeks following PCP use and is characterized by a prominent and persistently depressed, elevated, or expansive mood with feelings of anxiety, irritability, somatization, panic attacks, hallucinations, and delusions. Although these two mental disorders are relatively uncommon, they may be long lasting and have been associated with suicide.

*PCP Psychosis*    Although available data do not provide strong evidence implicating the regular, long-term PCP use with major body organ (e.g., cardiac, hepatic, renal) or cellular damage, they do provide evidence for the occurrence of several toxicities, including a PCP psychosis— a psychosis that is similar to amphetamine psychosis (Murray, 2002). PCP psychosis can occur after a single use of PCP, whether the user has a prior positive history of mental illness or not. However, it is more likely to occur among users who have previously used PCP or who have a genetic predisposition, or family history, of schizophrenia. The psychosis may last for several days or months, even with medical treatment. It also may spontaneously recur, even when lower dosages of PCP are used. Other psychological toxicities have been associated with PCP use and can be quite severe, including bad trips and delusional and mood disorders (see previous 2 sections for further discussion).

**Contexts of Fetal, Infant, and Child Exposure**    The maternal use of PCP during pregnancy has been implicated with neonatal dysmorphogenesis, characterized by distorted facial features, low birth weight, and small head circumference. However, this reported teratogenic effect has been deemed to be generally clinically insignificant and poorly documented. The long-term effects of prenatal PCP exposure on the later development of infants and children, including effects on learning, have been raised but remain inconclusive (Bradford Baldridge & Bessen, 1990; Pagliaro & Pagliaro, 1996; Pagliaro & Pagliaro, 2009). (For further related discussion, see Chapter 5, *Exposure*

*to the Drugs and Substances of Abuse From Conception Through Childhood.*)

Young children who are exposed to PCP by means of, for example, passive or environmental smoke exposure or the accidental ingestion of the butts of PCP-adulterated cigarettes (e.g., fry) (also see Chapter 5, *Exposure to the Drugs and Substances of the Abuse From Conception Through Childhood*) usually display alterations in neurological signs and consciousness (e.g., coma, seizures, stupor) rather than aggressive psychotic behavior. As noted by Bradford Baldridge and Bessen (1990), the most common clinical findings among PCP-exposed children younger than 5 years of age are ataxia, lethargy or more severe depression of consciousness, nystagmus, and staring episodes. Miosis is more commonly observed among children than among adults (Mvula, Miller, & Ragan, 1999).

**Physical and Psychological Dependence** In response to the epidemic use of PCP reported during the late 1960s and 1970s, a considerable amount of research was undertaken in an effort to identify its abuse potential and addiction liability. Although the long-term, regular use of PCP has not been associated with the development of physical dependence, it has been associated with the development of various degrees of psychological dependence. Tolerance, a need to increase the amount of PCP used in order to achieve initial desired pharmacologic actions, appears to occur, but a definite physical withdrawal syndrome has not been identified. The development of cross-tolerance between PCP and other drugs and substances of abuse has not been reported.

**Overdosage**    The signs and symptoms of PCP overdosage, which may be fatal (Baldridge & Bessen, 1990; McCarron, Schulze, Thompson, et al., 1981), include coma, hyperthermia, rhabdomyolysis, and seizures. Similar to LSD overdosage, the associated fatalities are often indirectly caused and are related to accidental injuries, drownings, and other physical trauma. Overdosage fatalities may also involve homicides and suicides (Burns, Lerner, Corrado, et al., 1975; Garey, 1979). Most PCP overdosage victims who present to the emergency department require only observation and supportive care (D'Onofrio, McCausland, Tarabar, et al., 2006). There is no known antidote. If necessary, benzodiazepine (e.g., diazepam [Valium®]) pharmacotherapy may be used to manage associated anxiety and fear. An antipsychotic without high anticholinergic actions (e.g., haloperidol [Haldol®] or risperidone [Risperdal®]) may be of benefit for the management of behavioral toxicities associated with PCP.

## CHAPTER SUMMARY

This chapter presented an overview of the third major subclass of the drugs and substances of abuse, the psychodelics—the phenethylamines, or amphetamine-like psychodelics; the indoles, tryptamines, and indoles-tryptamines, LSD and LSD-like psychodelics; and the miscellaneous psychodelics. Of these psychodelics, the ones that are primarily used by children and adolescents in North America are cannabis, LSD, MDMA, and PCP. Each of these psychodelics was discussed with attention to their prevalence and characteristics of use and general pharmacology—their proposed mechanisms of action and common toxicities.

As a unique group of drugs and substances of abuse, the psychodelics have been used since well before the earliest human records began. Some of the unique characteristics and features shared by the psychodelics include their use to: (1) deliberately and significantly alter consciousness in the absence of an aversive environment

(e.g., severe physical pain); (2) practice magico-religious ceremonies (e.g., shamanistic use; healing); and (3) achieve a mystic state to either facilitate communication with God or to become a god (i.e., all-powerful, all-knowing being) in lieu of established, formalized religions.[36]

Patterns of use do vary from generation to generation, and today's children and adolescents may report different reasons for their use, including using a particular psychodelic to enhance sexual encounters and performance, such as the use of MDMA at raves, circuit parties, and when clubbing. They also may display different methods of use, such as vaporizing marijuana rather than smoking it.

The use of the various psychodelics has cyclically increased and decreased in North America during the last five decades primarily as a result of availability, prevailing social norms, and the presence of new generations of users. Today, the psychodelics are the only major group of the drugs and substances of abuse for which virtually all use is legally prohibited in North America. Theoretical and clinical research involving the psychodelics[37] has been almost totally legally banned because of political concerns, primarily those associated with the personal use or abuse of the psychodelics, which, as noted in this chapter, are generally associated with less harm than the use of either the psychodepressants or the psychostimulants. (For additional related discussion, see Chapters 1, *The Psychodepressants*, and 2, *The Psychostimulants*.) As their patterns of use once again increase, researchers must judiciously disentangle the social and political restraints placed on the study of the psychodelics in order that a better understanding of their use and effects can be obtained.

---

[36] In this regard, as established measures of religiosity continue to decrease among North American children and adolescents, we would expect, along with other theorists and researchers (e.g., Miller, Davies, & Greenwald, 2000; Newport, 2009a, b; Saad, 2008; Smith, Faris, Lundquist Denton, et al., 2003), that the use of the psychodelics will correspondingly increase over the next several decades in North America.

[37] While reliance on positive empiricism as a basis for scientific investigation of the drugs and substances of abuse is foundational for the production of claims to pharmacological facts, it is sometimes surprising that the basic pharmacology of the psychodelics, including their synthesis and identified actions and toxicities, often involved the non–hard science methods of human self-experimentation, synthesis of personal subjective accounts of experience, and accidental trial-and-error approaches as the main forms of study (e.g., Cohen, 1967; Hofmann, 1979; Shulgin, 1964, 1986). The fruitfulness of these methods, however, cannot be denied.

PART II

# Developmental Considerations

# CHAPTER 4

# Explaining Child and Adolescent Use of the Drugs and Substances of Abuse

## INTRODUCTION

The use of the drugs and substances of abuse by North American children and adolescents—traditionally considered by many North Americans to be a rite of passage to adulthood—has increased significantly over the last five decades, an increase that continues into the second decade of the new millennium. During this time, girls have increasingly gained parity with boys in regard to the use of many of the drugs and substances of abuse and actually have overtaken them in regard to tobacco smoking. The diversity of the drugs and substances of abuse that are available and are being used also has greatly increased as old favorites (alcohol, cannabis, glue, lysergic acid diethylamide [LSD]) have been joined by relatively more recently developed drugs and substances of abuse (e.g., 3,4-methylenedioxymethamphetamine [MDMA, ecstasy], methamphetamine) and novel ways of using them (e.g., vaporization of cannabis and crack or meth pipe smoking). Other drugs and substances of abuse popular in other countries around the world (e.g., bidis and Kreteks from Southeast Asia) are now becoming more familiar and more widely available to North American children and adolescents. (Also see Chapter 1, *The Psychodepressants,* Chapter 2, *The Psychostimulants,* and Chapter 3, *The Psychodelics.*)

The involvement of children and adolescents, both girls and boys, in criminal youth gangs has increased both their use of the drugs and substances of abuse and their roles as foot soldiers for organized crime syndicates and outlaw motorcycle gangs, where they are involved in the production, distribution, and sale of cocaine, marijuana, methamphetamine, black tar heroin, and other drugs and substances of abuse. Invariably, these trends have been accompanied by significant concern among parents, teachers, communities, health and social care providers, researchers, and governmental policy makers. However, the question as to why children and adolescents use, or do not use, the drugs and substances of abuse remains largely unanswered.

It should be noted that concern about child and adolescent use of the drugs and substances of abuse is not new. For example, the use of marijuana by children and adolescents during the 1920s—the Prohibition Era—was cause for alarm in many states and provinces, as was the use of heroin during the 1950s in New York City and other major North American cities. The use of LSD and magic mushrooms by the flower children in the Haight-Ashbury district of San Francisco and other areas across the United States during the 1960s and 1970s occasioned much public outcry, as did alcohol, nicotine, and cocaine use by North American youth during the 1980s. The 1990s was characterized by worries about the increasing use of crack cocaine and polyuse of the drugs and substances of abuse, including prescription drugs (e.g., OxyContin®; Ritalin®) by girls and boys from all socioeconomic levels living in both rural and urban regions of North America. More recently, concern has been directed at the relationship between the use of the drugs and substances of abuse at

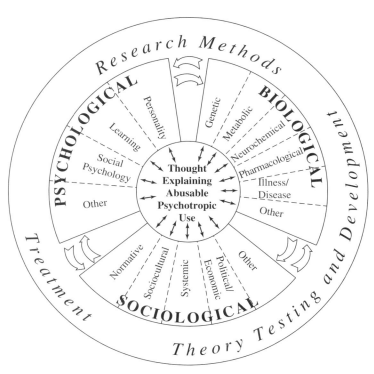

**Figure 4.1    Major Sciences and Theoretical Orientations: Pluralistic Combinations of Theory Development**

popular dance clubs and raves that may be attended by hundreds or thousands of adolescents and young adults. The increasingly rising incidence of violent youth crime over the past three decades continues to be troublesome. In fact, by the end of the 1990s, homicide became the leading cause of death in North America for young adolescent boys of African descent while suicide became the leading cause of death for young adolescent boys of European descent (Heninger & Hanzlick, 2008; Hu & Baker, 2008; Karch, Dahlberg, & Patel, 2010; Miniño, 2010; Shepherd & Ferslew, 2009).

In response to these serious concerns, parents, teachers, health and social care professionals, and government stakeholders who are involved with various aspects of childhood and adolescent education and healthcare increasingly have sought to understand why children and adolescents use the various

drugs and substances of abuse, so that such use can be more effectively prevented or, at least, controlled or minimized. Over the last century, more than 100 theories[1] were published to explain why children and adolescents use, or do not use, the drugs and substances of abuse (Pagliaro & Pagliaro, 1996). Although providing fruitful directions for research and treatment, none of these theories, or claims to fact, has achieved lawful status nor has any achieved wide acceptance for preferential use across the biological, psychological, and sociological sciences and their respective disciplinary fields of study—or theoretical orientations—from which they were produced, or extended: (1) individually (i.e., from one science and a single theoretical orientation, as illustrated by the *theory of adolescent psychological individuation*); (2) pluralistically (i.e., from one science and two or more theoretical orientations, as illustrated

---

[1] Over the same time period, over 300 published theories were identified that addressed the use of the drugs and substances of abuse by adults (Pagliaro & Pagliaro, 1996).

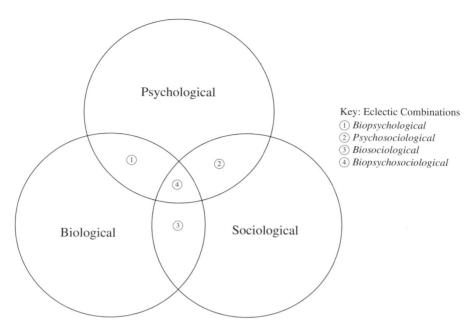

**Figure 4.2    Major Sciences: Eclectic Combinations of Theoretical Development**

by the *theory of drug subcultures* [*drug subculture theory*] (Figure 4.1); or (3) eclectically (i.e., from one or more sciences and two or more theoretical orientations, as illustrated by the *biological theory of sensation seeking and optimal catecholamine system activity theory* [Figure 4.2]). See Figure 4.1 and Figure 4.2. Although fruitful, sometimes beautiful, and often practical, these theories have yet to explain definitively why children and adolescents use, or do not use, the drugs and substances of abuse. In addition, over the last 50 years, many of these potentially valuable explanations have been lost or forgotten as new directions in theory production have increasingly taken the lead.

This chapter highlights 40 theories published between 1960 and 2011. These theories, or claims to fact, represent biological, psychological, and sociological attempts to answer the question of why children and adolescents use, or do not use, the drugs and substances of abuse. As such, they provide a glimpse into the ever-changing research world of the major sciences over the last 50 years—their scientific aims, research

methods, and contributions to promoting a better understanding of why children and adolescents use the drugs and substances of abuse. It is hoped that the attention given to these theories will: (1) provide readers with a better understanding of the varied explanations that have been advanced by the major disciplines of study; (2) encourage increased formal choice, testing, and use of these published theories; and (3) put into perspective the work that has been done, with a view to the need for further research aimed at preventing child and adolescent use of the drugs and substances of abuse.

## BIOLOGICAL THEORIES

Since the 1960s, several biological theories were advanced in an effort to explain child and adolescent use of the drugs and substances of abuse. Using longitudinal human studies, several of these theories sought to identify the natural history associated with the use of alcohol and the other drugs and substances of abuse. More recently, new research techniques have led to increased attention to the roles of neurobiology and neurochemistry in explaining child and adolescent developmental vulnerability in regard to using the drugs and substances of abuse.

## Neurobiology of Human Behavior: Personality Traits and Temperment Theories

Several eclectic theories related child and adolescent use of the drugs and substances of abuse to the biological correction of hormonal, neurotransmitter, and other biological systems. Presented in chronological order, these theories include the: *chronobiological control theory; somatosensory affectional deprivation (SAD) theory of drug and alcohol use; biological theory of sensation seeking and optimal catecholamine system activity theory;* and *four-circuit neurobehavioral model of addiction: loss of control and compulsive drug use.*

### Chronobiological Control Theory

Hochhauser (1978a, b, c, 1980), extending animal studies, considered the role of chronobiological rhythms in the use of the drugs and substances of abuse, including alcohol (and other sedative-hypnotics) and heroin, by adolescents (and adults, including elderly adults) in his *chronobiological control theory.* An eclectic theory, the theory was an extension of biological (metabolic and neurochemical) and psychological theories. According to Hochhauser (1978c):

The adolescent differs in many ways from the older drug user. . . . The period of adolescence is characterized by significant internal changes: hormonal changes, brain maturation, cognitive development, etc. As a potential consequence of these changes, it may be that the adolescent responds uniquely to drugs consumed during these critical periods. . . . Such internal changes will significantly affect the adolescent's response to the environment, both in terms of behavioral

events (the development of helpless behaviors) and chemical events (the use of drugs as agents of control). (pp. 67–68)

Assuming that drugs and substances of abuse may be used as agents of control:

(1) Drug use may present an initial attempt to achieve some degree of internal control over perceptions of helplessness. . . [and] may be a relatively quick and effective means of obtaining such control, especially when other control measures are unavailable; (2) If a drug is used for control and is found effective, then its use will probably escalate, as the individual may develop a relatively predictable and controllable method of coping; (3) Dependency may develop if there are no other effective coping mechanisms available; (4) Depending upon the addictive liability of the drug, addiction may occur with continued use, as the physiological consequences of the drug (e.g., withdrawal symptoms) may eventually establish control over the user. . . . Addicts may seek treatment, since they are no longer using the drug for control; rather, they are being controlled by the drug. (Hochhauser, 1980, p. 267)

Thus, according to Hochhauser (1978c):

Chronobiology may affect the development and maintenance of alcohol and drug abuse problems, insofar as an individual's response to a particular chemical substance will be a function of several chronobiological variables: time of day, light-dark cycles, sleep-wake patterns, and other intrinsic biochemical rhythms.

Consequently, an accurate analysis of alcohol and drug abuse problems requires not only an understanding of the psychopharmacological properties of the particular drugs involved, but a corresponding awareness of the drug user's unique responsivity to that drug, insofar as such responses may be rhythmically determined. Such an analysis is necessary to account for individual variations in the acquisition and continuation of alcohol and drug problems, since not only will the biological rhythm determine, in part, the effect of a given drug, but a drug may well affect the biological rhythm itself. (p. 855)

Both animal and human behavior varies as a function of chronobiological rhythms. As such, the effects of a drug or substance of abuse may be particularly sensitive to changes in rhythms. If the use of a drug or substance of abuse is viewed as a possible form of self-medication (i.e., an agent of control or "regulating device"), then it is conceivable that some use of the drugs or substances of abuse represents an attempt, on the part of the user, to artificially induce certain rhythmic patterns where none had existed. It is likewise conceivable that use be directed at reestablishing such patterns when they have been lost. Rather than studying only retrospective patterns of the use of the drugs and substances of abuse (e.g., what drug or substance of abuse was used and how often it was used in the past), the research focuses on: (1) when a given drug or substance of abuse is used; and (2) its long-term chronobiological patterns of use. For example, heroin users may use heroin in an attempt to maintain some rhythm in their physiological and psychological functioning. Death from a heroin or other drug overdosage, according to this theory, may be due in part to when the drug or substance of abuse was used. If it was used at a time of maximal susceptibility within the chronobiological rhythm, the effect may be quite different than if it was used during a time of minimal susceptibility (i.e., the individual may have survived). As such, drugs and substances of abuse may be used as agents of control to permit users to exert some degree of internal control over their perceptions of helplessness.

### Somatosensory Affectional Deprivation (SAD) Theory of Drug and Alcohol Use

As explained by Prescott (1980), the *SAD theory of drug and alcohol use* was proposed and developed during the 1960s and 1970s as "a developmental psychobiological theory to account for the common ground of the many and diverse theories of substance abuse" (p. 286). The basic assumptions of the theory are that: (1) the neurobiology of human behavior is inseparable from, as well as largely shaped by, culture (i.e., the shaping process of culture upon the developing brain is accomplished through various sensory modalities and through the sensory processes of deprivation and stimulation); and (2) certain sensory modalities and processes (i.e., the emotional senses of touch, movement, and smell) are more important than others in accounting for emotional/social behaviors (e.g., violence) and substance abuse.

Relating research reflecting the neurobiology of animal (e.g., primates) and human (primitive peoples throughout the world) behavior (e.g., touching, holding, and carrying of infants by their mothers) that is strongly influenced by sensory processes of stimulation and deprivation, Prescott identified that the transformation of these processes into perceptual experiences by encoding and decoding are strongly influenced by social, physical, and cultural environments during the formative periods of brain development (i.e., the formulation of affectional bonds). The theorist also believed that the brain endorphin systems may be one of the most important neurobiological systems mediating the development of affectional bonds, including sexual affectional bonds. As argued by Prescott, it is not the deprivation of cognitive senses (i.e., visual auditory senses) during the formative periods of brain development that account for, and predict, emotional affective social behavior, such as the use of drugs and substances of abuse and abusive social behaviors in general (i.e., violence and destructive, exploitive behaviors toward self and others); it is the deprivation of emotional senses (i.e., touch, smell, and movement).

Accordingly, the use of drugs and substances abuse that primarily alter our emotional/affective state must be understood within the context of our emotional senses, and those, such as the hallucinogens (i.e., psychodelics) that primarily alter the cognitive state must be understood within the context of the visual/auditory senses. Three basic groups of substance abusers are proposed: (1) pleasure seekers (users of heroin, marijuana), (2) pleasure avoiders (e.g., users of alcohol, depressants), and (3) altered states of consciousness seekers (users of hallucinogens [psychodelics]). As summarized by Prescott (1980):

> The social-emotional dysfunctioning of the individual in society, in whatever form it may be expressed, is not only an intrinsic aspect of neurobiological functioning of the individual but also of the social-psychological forces of culture that shape the individuality of neurobiological functioning through the formative developmental processes of sensory stimulation and deprivation, and through a culture of chemical and physical environments that influence fetal, neonatal, and postnatal development. Maternal habits of chemical ingestion, e.g., alcohol, drugs, food/spice preferences, or exposure to certain chemical environments during gestation, may well *imprint* upon the developing fetus certain *sensitivities* and predispositions for use or avoidance of those chemical agents during postnatal life with all the implications that this has for behavior. (p. 296)

As such, prevention and treatment programs cannot be based solely on molecular biological strategies aimed at the reconstruction of the individual but also must be aimed at the reconstruction of society and culture—shaping a safe, beneficent physical environment of human relationships that are nurturing, caring, and affectionate.

### Biological Theory of Sensation Seeking and Optimal Catecholamine System Activity Theory

Zuckerman, Kolin, Price, et al. (1964) proposed the sensation-seeking scale that was designed to quantify the construct of optimal stimulation level. Interest in the study of sensation came from studies on sensory deprivation (Zubek, 1969) and the attempt to define personality traits that could predict reactions

to the experimental situation of reduced and restricted stimulation. As the trait was originally construed, it represented an attempt to operationalize and quantify the constructs of optimal levels of stimulation and arousal (Zuckerman, 1969) in the form of a personality questionnaire (Zuckerman, Kolin, Price, et al., 1964). The use of the scale assumed that: (1) individuals differ in a reliable fashion in their optimal levels of stimulation or arousal; and (2) individual differences in optimal levels of stimulation or arousal are basic personality dimensions that were not adequately measured by then-existing tests.

Extending an earlier theory, Zuckerman (1983a, b, c) advanced the *biological theory of sensation seeking* incorporating biological constructs of neurochemistry and personality with psychological constructs of social psychology. The theory addresses the use of psychodepressants (i.e., the sedative-hypnotics, alcohol, and barbiturates), psychostimulants (i.e., amphetamine and cocaine), and psychodelics (i.e., LSD and marijuana) with attention to their patterns of initial use and polyuse. The main focus of the theory is the sensation seeker. As such, the theory is built around the major assumption that a personality trait, which is rooted in biological structure and function, plays a major role in the "reckless willingness" to initiate the use of, and continue to use, the drugs and substances of abuse (Zuckerman, 1983b, p. 202).

Central to this extended theory are four hypotheses:

1. Intense or varied sensations are sought because they affect the release of catecholamines in the reward, or pleasure, circuits of the limbic system (i.e., arousal has been relegated to a secondary role in this theory.)

2. Biological traits that underlie sensation seeking are the functional levels of the catecholamine neurotransmitters as influenced by their production and disposal and the enzymes (e.g., monoamine

oxidase [MAO]) that regulate these processes.

3. Sensations seekers are attracted to psychostimulants.
4. Other drugs and substances of abuse are sought because of their direct or indirect effects on neurotransmitter systems.

As further explained by Zuckerman, psychostimulants are sought by sensation seekers for the same reasons that exciting stimulation and activities (e.g., mogul skiing; sky diving) are sought—both increase the turnover of the neurotransmitters of the reward systems in the central nervous system (CNS). Other drugs and substances of abuse are sought because of their effects, directly or indirectly, on neurotransmitter systems. For example, LSD produces a rise in dopamine but a fall in norepinephrine. It also appears to be an agonist for tryptamine and serotonin. There also is evidence that alcohol increases the synthesis and turnover of all MAO systems, including norepinephrine and dopamine, although it may block receptor systems for norepinephrine.

Noting that Segal, Huba, and Singer (1980) had found little support for two common explanations—anxiety reduction and peer influence—for adolescent use of the drugs and substances of abuse, Zuckerman (1979) decided to further explore specific reasons for their use. "Curiosity" was the reason given by 86% of marijuana users, a reason also frequently given by opiate analgesic users. "To get kicks" or "to get high"—terms used to describe the euphoric arousal produced by the drug or substance of abuse—were cited by between 25% and 38% of the users, respectively. Getting "pep" or "energy" was a reason for using drugs and substances of abuse that typically produced energizing effects,

particularly the psychostimulants. However, of all the various reasons given for using the drugs and substances of abuse, the most frequent reason was "to experience something new and different." This finding led Zuckerman to the identification of the trait of sensation seeking—a trait he defined as "the need for varied, novel, and complex sensations and experiences and the willingness to take physical and social risks for the sake of such experience" (p. 10).[2]

By 1983, the proposition that sensation seeking was a motive for the initial use of the drugs and substances of abuse was formally advanced by Zuckerman:

> Theories of drug abuse typically offer social or intrapsychic causes for the initial experimentation with drugs and physiological conditioning causes for maintenance of the addiction. In this paper a proposition will be presented: a personality trait that is rooted in biological structure and functions plays a major role in the reckless willingness to try drugs. (1983b, p. 202)

The theory was extended by Tonkin (1987) as the risky behavior paradigm—sensation seeking may influence the feedback loop by modifying motivational state or by affecting the perceptual skills that depend on the level of arousal.

Zuckerman's biological approach to human traits necessarily required a comparative approach—a model for comparative study of the biological bases of personality. The theorist developed and presented such a model in 1984. The model related mood, behavioral activity and sociability, and clinical states to the actions of the central catecholamine neurotransmitters and to the neuroregulators and other transmitters that act in opposite ways on behavior or that stabilize activity in the arousal systems. For example, as explained by Zuckerman (1987), as a marker for alcoholism, low MAO levels

---

[2]These adolescent users of the drugs and substances of abuse would be the same adolescents who consciously and deliberately ignore posted warnings restricting the use of hazardous ski areas and, preferentially, snowboard in areas designated as "out of bounds."

may indicate a disposition toward an impulsive, extroverted, sensation-seeking temperament—a risk factor for other drug abuse as well:

> Sensation seekers seek intense and novel external stimulation and use catecholamine-releasing drugs like amphetamine and cocaine in order to activate these systems. In an unstimulated state (producing boredom), high sensation seekers may be below an optimal level of activity in catecholaminergic systems. Low MAO levels may allow these monoamine systems to fluctuate within wide limits. Thus, a period of intense excitement could be followed by a depletion of catecholamines leading to further attempts to stimulate the system.
>
> How does this apply to alcohol use?. . . According to my new *Optimal Catecholamine System Activity (CSA) Theory*, moderate levels of CSAs are optimal and associated with rewarding or pleasurable effects, while very low or high levels are associated with dysphoria. Actually, such a theory is compatible with the effects of increasing doses of alcohol which show mild euphoria and disinhibition at lower doses and increased anxiety and depression at higher doses or after more prolonged drinking. The alcoholic seems to follow the maxim "if a little is good a lot is better." Unfortunately, the central nervous system follows the maxim "moderation and homeostasis in all systems." (Zuckerman, 1987, p. 298)

### Four-Circuit Neurobehavioral Model of Addiction: Loss of Control and Compulsive Drug Use

Several technologies, including brain imaging studies (e.g., positron emission tomography [PET] and functional magnetic resonance imaging [fMRI]), are being increasingly recognized for their important contributions to identifying the effects of various drugs and substances of abuse on neurochemical mechanisms and functional changes in the brains of drug-addicted subjects. A theory recognizing these contributions is the *four-circuit neurobehavioral model of addiction: loss of control and compulsive drug use*. Proposed by Volkow, Fowler, and Wang (2003), this biopsychological learning model integrates biological factors (i.e., protein expression,[3] including gene polymorphisms, and neuronal circuits) and environmental factors (i.e., social factors) to explain the loss of control and compulsive drug use that characterize addictive behavior in humans. The model was developed from preclinical findings from their own imaging program in drug addiction integrated with the analysis of the "rich literature" available in regard to imaging the brains of "drug addicts" (e.g., Volker, Chang, Wang, et al., 2001; Volkow, Fowler, & Wang, 2002; Voklow, Rosen, & Farde, 1997; Volkow, Wang, Fowler, et al., 1997, 1999, 2000).

The model is based on eight assumptions:

1. In drug addiction, the value of the drug and drug-related stimuli is enhanced at the expense of other reinforcers (i.e., the drugs of abuse are considered to be much *stronger* reinforcers than natural reinforcers, such as food or sex).

2. The saliency value of the drug of abuse and its associated cues is enhanced in the reward and motivation/drive circuits but that of other reinforcers is markedly decreased. (The enhanced saliency value of the drug of abuse is initiated partly by the much higher intrinsic reward properties of the drugs of abuse, including: (a) increases in dopamine induced by

---

[3] PET images show the effects of regular long-term use of drugs and substances of abuse on various proteins involved in dopamine neurotransmission and on brain function as assessed by brain glucose metabolism. Some effects are common to many drugs and substances of abuse, such as a decrease in dopamine D2 receptors in striatal neurons and decreased metabolic activity in the orbitofrontal cortex with methamphetamine use that is possibly a result of neurotoxicity to dopamine terminals and the decrease in brain monoamine oxidase B, the enzyme involved in dopamine metabolism, in cigarette smokers (Volkow, Fowler, & Wang, 2003, p. 3).

drugs and substances of abuse in the nucleus accumbens that are 3- to 5-fold higher than those of natural reinforcers; and (b) the lack of habituation of drugs and substances of abuse as compared with that of natural reinforcers.)

3. The high reward value of drugs and substances of abuse leads to a resetting of reward thresholds, which then result in decreased sensitivity to the reinforcing properties of naturally occurring stimuli.

4. Through conditioned learning and a lack of competition by other reinforcers, acquisition of the drug or substance of abuse becomes the main motivational drive for the individual.

5. The decrease in the number of dopamine D2 receptors, coupled with the decrease in dopamine cell activity, in the drug or substance abuser would result in a decreased sensitivity of reward circuits to stimulation by natural reinforcers and lead to decreased interest in ordinary environmental stimuli, possibly predisposing subjects for seeking drug stimulation as a means to temporarily activate these reward circuits.

6. During addiction, the value of the drug or substance of abuse as a reinforcer is so much greater than that of any natural reinforcer that the latter can no longer compete as a viable alternative choice, and the enhanced saliency value of the drug or substance of abuse becomes fixed.

7. Exposure to the drug or substance of abuse, or to related stimuli in the withdrawal state, reactivates the orbitofrontal cortex and results in compulsive intake of the drug or substance of abuse.

8. Disruption of the prefrontal cortex could lead to loss of self-directed/willed behavior in favor of automatic sensory-driven behavior that is exacerbated during intoxication with a drug or substance of abuse from the loss of inhibitory control that the prefrontal cortex exerts over the amygdala.

As such, the theorists advanced two hypotheses:

1. During intoxication, the qualitative difference in activity in the dopamine-regulated reward circuit (greater and longer-lasting activation compared with the activation by nondrug stimuli) produces a corresponding overactivation of the motivational drive and memory circuits, which deactivate and remove the control exerted by the frontal cortex. Without the inhibitory control, a positive feedback loop is set forth that results in compulsive drug or substance use. Because the interactions between the circuits are bidirectional, the activation of the network during intoxication serves to further strengthen the salience value of the drug or substance of abuse.

2. Decreased sensitivity of reward circuits to natural reinforcers, decreased activation of control circuits, or an increase in sensitivity of memory, learning, or motivation circuits to drug-related stimuli could make an individual more vulnerable to addiction.

As described by the theorists:

In this model, during exposure to the drug or drug-related cues, the memory of the expected reward results in overactivation of the reward and motivation circuits while decreasing the activity in the cognitive control circuit. This contributes to an inability to inhibit the drive to seek and consume the drug and results in compulsive drug intake. (Volkow, Fowler, & Wang, 2002, p. 355)

As they explained, whereas acute use of the drugs and substances of abuse results in increased dopamine neurotransmission, chronic use results in marked decreases in dopamine activity, which persists after detoxification, and is associated with dysregulation of frontal brain regions. PET and MRI studies also have identified the brain areas and circuits involved in various states of the addiction process associated with the drug or substance of abuse (i.e., intoxication, withdrawal, and craving) and have linked the activity in these neural circuits to behavior. Acute intoxication results in a complex and dynamic pattern of activation and deactivation that includes regions neuroanatomically connected with the dopamine system and known to be involved in reward, memory, motivation/drive, and control.

The model comprises a network of four circuits that are involved in drug abuse and addiction, each with a specific concept of importance to the theory: (1) reward (salience), located in the nucleus accumbens and ventral pallidum; (2) motivation/drive (internal state), located in the orbitofrontal cortex and the subcallosal cortex; (3) memory and learning (learned associations), located in the amygdala and hippocampus; and (4) control (conflict resolution), located in the prefrontal cortex and the anterior cingulate gyrus. The four circuits work together and change with experience. During addiction, the enhanced value of the drug or substance of abuse in the reward, motivation, and memory circuits overcomes the inhibitory control exerted by the prefrontal cortex, thereby favoring a positive feedback loop initiated by the use of the drug and perpetuated by the enhanced activation of motivation/drive and memory circuits.

According to the theorists, the pattern of activity in the circuit network influences how a person makes choices among behavioral alternatives. These choices are influenced systematically by the reward, memory, motivation, and control circuits. The response to a stimulus is affected by its momentary salience (i.e., expected reward), which is processed in part by dopamine neurons projecting into the nucleus accumbens in a hierarchical matrix where the saliency value of stimuli changes as a function of the context and the previous experience of the individual. If the individual has been exposed to the stimulus previously, its saliency value is affected by memory, processed in part by the amygdala and hippocampus. Memories are stored as associations between the stimulus and the positive (pleasant) or negative (aversive) experience it elicited and facilitated by dopamine activation. The value of the stimulus is weighted against that of other alternative stimuli and changes as a function of the internal needs of the individual, which are processed in part by the orbitofrontal cortex.

For example, the saliency value of food is increased by hunger but decreased by satiety. The stronger the saliency value of the stimulus, which is in part conveyed by the prediction of reward from previously memorized experiences, the greater the activation of the motivational circuit and the stronger the drive to procure it. The cognitive decision to act to procure the stimulus is processed in part by the prefrontal cortex and the anterior cingulate gyrus.

Addiction is initiated by the qualitatively different and larger reward value of the drug or substance of abuse, which triggers a series of adaptations in the reward, motivation/drive, memory, and control circuits of the brain. These changes result in an enhanced and permanent saliency value for the drug or substance of abuse and in the loss of inhibitory control, favoring the emergence of compulsive use. The model suggests treatment strategies that include both pharmacological approaches and behavioral therapy. For example, treatment might include: (1) pharmacotherapeutic approaches aimed at decreasing the rewarding value of the drug or substance of abuse, such as those that interfere with its reinforcing effects or approaches that make the effects unpleasant (e.g., the classic use of disulfiram [Antabuse®] for the management of alcoholism); (2) pharmacotherapeutic and behavioral approaches to increase the value of nondrug reinforcers, such as increasing sensitivity to natural reinforcers and establishing alternative reinforcing behaviors; (3) behavioral approaches to weaken learned responses, such as those aimed at extinguishing the learned positive associations with cues associated with the drug or substance of abuse; and (4) cognitive therapy aimed at strengthening frontal control.

## Natural History Theories

The four natural history theories that were selected for presentation here—genesis of male alcoholism, natural history of drug use, natural history of alcoholism, and natural history of drug use from adolescence to the mid-30s—are eclectic in nature and emphasize age, environmental, and other factors important to the development of the use of alcohol and other drugs and substances of abuse.

### Genesis of Male Alcoholism

McCord and McCord (1960) proposed a theory, the *genesis of male alcoholism*, that purported to explain the development of male alcoholism using the results of their longitudinal study that was undertaken between 1935 and 1945. In the study, 255 male subjects and their families were repeatedly observed. An additional group of 255 subjects were interviewed and less extensively studied. On average, the subjects were 9 years of age when initial contact was made. All of the boys were subjects in the Cambridge-Somerville project and were selected for reasons other than their potential for becoming alcoholic (i.e., half were selected because of their potential for becoming delinquents and half were selected because of their normal behavior). The subjects differed from a random American sample because all were male and all came from urban areas. The sample also overrepresented social deviants and Roman Catholic immigrants of lower socioeconomic levels—subjects identified as having certain advantages for the study of alcoholism (p. 20).

The physiological, psychological (e.g., intelligence and personality), familial, and social backgrounds of all of the subjects were obtained, over an average of 5 years, using a series of interviews and assessments conducted by the physicians, psychologists, and psychiatrists and categorized by the staff of the Cambridge-Somerville project. "These observations were detailed, extensive, and considered to be relatively free from preconceived biases" by McCord and McCord (1960) because they were recorded in "raw" form by a number of different observers representing a variety of theoretical traditions (pp. 20–21). In addition, the observers had no knowledge of the adult lives of the boys nor did they have knowledge as to the research questions being asked. As emphasized by McCord and McCord:

> These raw observations were then rated into discrete, largely behaviorally defined categories. *The raters had no knowledge about which of their subjects were alcoholic and which were nonalcoholic.* Rigid definitions of the categories and repeated tests of inter-rater agreement resulted in a relatively high degree of reliability and, presumably, the elimination of "the halo effect" in rating. (p. 21)

In order to make sense of their data, McCord and McCord completed an extensive review of the literature on published theories of alcoholism. In 1957, their analysis of these data led to a set of hypotheses concerning its genesis.

According to the theorists, the development of adult alcoholism was influenced by pressures placed on a boy's personality structure during childhood, including: (1) being exposed to intense parental conflict; (2) having a neural disorder, especially in combination with exposure to intense family conflict; (3) being reared in a family characterized by incest or illegitimacy; and (4) having a weakly Catholic mother. As explained by McCord and McCord (1960), "By creating anxiety or by offering outlets for anxiety, these influences tended to promote alcoholism or retard it" (p. 53).

### Natural History of Drug Use

Robins and her colleagues proposed the *natural history of drug use*, an eclectic biological (personality) and sociological (sociocultural) theory reflective of a decade of study and research (e.g., Robins, 1966, 1973, 1974, 1977, 1978a, b;

Robins, Davis, & Wish, 1977; Robins, Helzer, & Davis, 1975; Robins, Hesselbrock, Wish, et al., 1978).[4] They also considered opiate addiction and polyuse of the drugs and substances of abuse among North American youth of African descent (Robins & Murphy, 1967) and Vietnam War veterans (Robins, Davis, & Wish, 1977). Particular attention was given to the use of the: psychodepressants (e.g., opiate analgesics [i.e., heroin]; sedative-hypnotics); psychostimulants (e.g., amphetamines; cocaine); and the psychodelics by children and adolescents. The theory came about as an attempt to fashion a natural history of the use of the drugs and substances of abuse by summarizing what was known about the circumstances of their use (i.e., initiation of use; which groups were most vulnerable; motivations for use; methods of use; and to what extent dosages tend to increase). The theorists recognized the limitations of their studies in regard to their task of attempting to construct a natural history of substance use, noting that their focus would describe only a particular historical phase of the drug epidemics and would be relative to time and culture. The researchers' attention was focused on the extent to which "the natural history of drug abuse suggests that it is a disorder for which those with antisocial personalities are particularly at risk" (Robins, 1980, p. 216). As further described by Robins:

> The behavior of drug abusers prior to the onset of drugs resembles that of mild delinquents. They tend to be sexually active at a very young age; they tend to have committed a number of minor socially disapproved acts, such as getting into fights, truancy, getting drunk at a young age, and smoking early. Few have held full-time jobs at the time they take up drug abuse. If they delay drug use until they enter college, those in the humanities or social sciences seem more vulnerable than those in the hard sciences and mathematics. The belief system of those vulnerable to drug use has clearly been nonconformist. They are generally areligious, not greatly attached

to home, and generally tolerant of deviance in others. They do not, for instance, voice strong disapproval of shoplifting or truancy.

> The characteristics we have described not only tell us which children who have not yet used drugs are particularly liable to become drug users, but they also predict the timing of use—those with these characteristics tend to use at a younger age than those without them—and the frequency of use—those who have these characteristics tend to use more heavily than children without these characteristics even when both use drugs. . . . The present picture is a confusing one. . . . The most reasonable position at the present time seems to be that drug abuse can be part of antisocial personality, but that most drug abusers probably do not have that syndrome, since the typical drug abuser is so different in terms of IQ, social class, history of elementary school problems, and very early termination. . . . It is exposure to drugs itself that may be harmful, in addition to any underlying effects of the predisposition of the drug user. . . . I am afraid that the implications of these findings are that we must continue to rely on supply control as a chief preventive measure, until we can provide some other explanation for the adverse outcomes of those who become frequent users of illicit drugs. (pp. 219, 224)

### Natural History of Alcoholism

Vaillant's (1983a, b, c, 1992) theory, the *natural history of alcoholism*, emphasized the illness/disease conceptualization of alcoholism with attention to college sophomores and Boston schoolboys. Focus was on patterns of initial to compulsive use, resumed nonuse, and relapsed use. Based on the general assumptions inherent in illness/disease theories and medical practice, seven questions were posited for longitudinal study:

1. Is alcoholism a symptom or a disease?
2. Does alcoholism get progressively worse?
3. Before they begin to abuse alcohol, are alcoholics different from nonalcoholics?

---

[4]This theory was later modified by Sadava (1984), as the *generalized tendency toward psychoactive drug use*.

4. Rather than being counterproductive, is abstinence a necessary goal of treatment for alcoholism?

5. Is a return to safe social drinking possible for alcoholics?

6. Does treatment alter the natural history of alcoholism?

7. Is Alcoholics Anonymous helpful in the treatment of alcoholism?

A prospective longitudinal study involving 204 upper middle-class, elite college men and 456 less-privileged inner-city boys of high school age as subjects was conducted over 40 years (1940–1980). A clinical sample of 100 alcohol-dependent men and women admitted for detoxification also was selected and followed for 8 years. Data that were collected included alcohol use data and life data. As noted by Vaillant (1983a), the development of the theory actually began during the late 1930s in that his sample included the sample obtained by Sheldon and Eleanor Glueck at the Harvard Law School for their study of juvenile delinquency (the Core City sample). Vaillant obtained a control (the college sample) by using the sample taken by Clark Heath and Arlie Bock at Harvard University Health Services, who were associated with the Grant Study of Adult Development.

In 1972, the two research groups came together, under the auspices of the Harvard Medical School, as the Study of Adult Development. The research groups, of which Vaillant was a member, attempted to contrast medical and social models for alcoholism in an effort to see whether they are congruent. The researchers concluded that alcoholism is a continuum of negative consequences, one end of which can best be viewed as a disease. Vaillant (1983a) recognized that the answer to the question "Why do people use alcohol?" required formal study so that the rational treatment of alcoholism could be provided. Information should come from "meticulously conducted, long-term prospective studies—studies in which subjects were selected for study before they developed problems with alcohol and then followed for many years." In this regard, cross-sectional studies would not be able to adequately "capture the genesis of alcoholism" (p. 2).

Vaillant (1992) reported the results of his multivariate analyses of data from a 33-year prospective study of the 456 nondelinquent controls from the Gluecks' delinquency study, concluding that "both environment and genes may make important and quite different contributions to alcoholism":

> The data suggested that presence or absence of South European ethnicity (perhaps as a result of attitudes toward alcohol use and abuse) and the number of alcoholic relatives (perhaps more due to heredity rather than environment) accounted for most of the variance in adult alcoholism explained by childhood variables. Premorbid antisocial behavior also added significantly to the risk of alcoholism. However, an unstable family environment was a more important predictor of whether an individual loses control of alcohol at an early age and/or has multiple symptoms, than whether he has many alcoholic relatives. (p. 71)

(Also see "Sociological Theories" section, "Family Systems Theories.")

### Natural History of Drug Use from Adolescence to the Mid-30s

As part of the National Household Survey on Drug Abuse, Kandel and her colleagues (e.g., Chen & Kandel, 1995) studied the natural history of drug use from adolescence to adulthood for the period 1977 to 1994, using data from seven successive surveys for successive age groups of participants 12 years of age to 35 years of age. The researchers found, in their 19-year follow-up of a representative population cohort, as did Raveis and Kandel (1987), that the major period of risk for initiating the use of cigarettes, alcohol, and marijuana is mostly over by 20 years of age. They also found what appears to be a maturation trend for the use of marijuana and alcohol but not for the use of cigarettes.

Not only does the prevalence of high-frequency use decline in adulthood, but for most drugs and substances of abuse other than cigarettes, the quantities consumed during the periods of heavy use decline as well. These findings raised several questions for their theory, the *natural history of drug use from adolescence to the mid-30s*, including: "Why does use, whether light or heavy, decline in the middle 20s?" As concluded by the theorists:

> Adolescents and young adults are most vulnerable to new experiences, new ideas, and new fads. For many youths, the use of drugs may represent a way of participating in the youth culture, while for a subgroup, drug use may represent a form of self-medication. With increasing age, two parallel processes may converge to lead to a reduction in the use of illicit drugs. The assumption of adult roles, especially family roles such as getting married or becoming a parent, may be associated with greater conformity and a decreased motivation to use illicit drugs. Furthermore, increased access to the medical system may lead those who used drugs as self-medication to seek out prescribed psychoactive drugs instead; the finding that the use of prescribed psychoactive drugs is the last stage in the sequence of drug involvement lends support to this interpretation. Thus, different drugs may serve similar functions at different stages of the life span.
>
> It seems clear, however, that most drug-related intervention programs, whether focused on prevention or on treatment, must target adolescents and young adults in their early to mid-20s. By the mid-30s, most drug use is a behavior of the past. (Raveis and Kandel, 1987, p. 47)

(Also see "Psychological Theories" section, "Ego-Self Theory of Substance Dependence: The Self-Medication Hypothesis.")

## Neurobiology and Pathophysiology of Addiction

This section highlights three theories produced over the last decade that reflect changing research directions aimed at better understanding brain neurobiology and pathophysiology as related to child and adolescent use of the drugs and substances of abuse. These theories, named accordingly for convenience, are the: *pathological learning model of addiction*; *theory of pathophysiological pathways of stress-related addiction*; and *theory of brain emotional systems and addiction*.

### Pathological Learning Model of Addiction

Summarizing the converging neurobiological evidence produced from animal models, Hyman (2005) advanced the *pathological learning model of addiction* that conceptualized addiction as a disease of learning and memory:

> Evidence at the molecular, cellular, systems, behavioral, and computational levels of analysis is converging to suggest the view that addiction represents a pathological usurpation of the neural mechanisms of learning and memory that under normal circumstances serve to shape survival behaviors related to the pursuit of rewards and the cues that predict them. (p. 1414)

As explained by Hyman (2005), the rewarding properties of many addictive drugs depend on their ability to increase dopamine in synapses made by midbrain ventral tegmental area neurons on the nucleus accumbens, which occupies the ventral striatum, especially within the nucleus accumbens shell region. Ventral tegmental area dopamine projections to other forebrain areas, such as the prefrontal cortex and amygdala, also play a critical role in shaping drug-taking behaviors. Other drugs and substances of abuse, such as the opiates, cause dopamine release. Opiates may act directly in the nucleus accumbens to produce reward, and norepinephrine may play a role in the rewarding effects of opiates as well. The dopamine hypothesis, which has been generally embraced over the last several decades, conceptualizes dopamine as a hedonistic signal, and addiction is understood largely in hedonistic terms with dependence and withdrawal seen as the key driver of compulsive use of the drugs and substances of abuse. Hyman, rejecting the dopamine hypothesis, argued that what is known about addiction is best represented by the view that it is a pathological usurpation of the mechanisms of reward-related learning and memory.

### Theory of Pathophysiological Pathways of Stress-related Addiction

Recognizing that stress is a well-known risk factor in the development of addiction and relapse vulnerability, Sinha (2008) proposed *the pathophysiological pathways of stress-related addiction theory.* This theory is supported by population-based and epidemiological studies that have identified specific stressors and individual-level variables as predictive of abusive and compulsive use of the drugs and substances of abuse. As emphasized by Sinha (2008), the deleterious effects of early life stress, child maltreatment and abuse, and various traumatic mental and physical disorders can cause alterations in the: corticotropin-releasing factor (CRF) and hypothalamic-pituitary-adrenal (HPA) axis; the extrahypothalamic CRF; the autonomic arousal system; and the central noradrenergic system. These alterations also affect the corticostriatal-limbic motivational, learning, and adaptation systems that include mesolimbic dopamine, glutamate, and gamma-aminobutyric acid pathways underlying the pathophysiology associated with stress-related risk of addiction. While further research and theoretical development are required, the *theory of pathophysiological pathways of stress-related addiction* offers promise for the increased understanding of child and adolescent use of the drugs and substances of abuse.

### Theory of Brain Emotional Systems and Addiction

The *theory of brain emotional systems and addiction* was proposed by Koob (2008, 2009),

who argued that the emotional systems of the brain that mediate arousal and stress systems in the amygdala, are important for understanding the development of addiction, including the negative emotional state that occurs when the use of a drug or substance of abuse is abruptly discontinued. These systems are comprised of the CRF and the norepinephrine found in extrahypothalamic systems in the extended amygdala, including the central nucleus of the amygdala, the bed nucleus of the striae terminalis, and the transition area in the shell of the nucleus accumbens.

It appears that these two brain stress systems contribute to the development and maintenance of addiction. As emphasized by the theorist, understanding the role of the stress and anti-stress systems of the brain in the development and maintenance of addiction provides insight into the neurobiology of addiction and the organization and function of the basic brain emotional circuitry that guides motivated behavior. It also offers a new focus for the prevention and treatment of addiction.

### Future Directions

Many theoretical advances have been made within the biological perspective, over the last 40 years, in an effort to explain why children and adolescents use the drugs and substances of abuse. While many theorists emphasized the importance of "nature and nurture," more recent attention, with the help of more advanced research technologies, has been given to the role of neurobiological factors, such as those associated with stressful events during childhood, genomic and neuro-molecular mechanisms of actions of the drugs and substances of abuse (e.g., endogenous opioid and other systems, mesocorticolimbic dopamine systems), and the neurocircuitry associated with the various patterns of using the drugs and substances of abuse.

In regard to these advances, Koob & Simon (2009) identified four questions that still remain in regard to understanding why children and adolescents use the drugs and substances of abuse:

1. What neurobiological processes (i.e., molecular, cellular, or systemic) convey vulnerability to the transition from the initial use of a drug or substance of abuse to the more harmful patterns of abusive or compulsive use?

2. What neurobiological processes make a child or adolescent more vulnerable to patterns of relapsed use?

3. How do genetic and environmental factors relate to the neurobiological processes that place children and adolescents at risk for, or protect them from, developing harmful patterns of using the drugs and substances of abuse, particularly abusive, compulsive, and relapsed use?

4. What treatment measures best assist brain recovery from patterns of abusive and compulsive use and prevent the development of relapsed use (e.g., cognitive-behavioral therapies, pharmacotherapies)?

Finally, during the last decade, increased attention has been given to the significance of adolescence as a period of brain growth and maturation between childhood and adulthood, and further theoretical attention and development is expected in this direction. As described by Guerri and Pascual (2010):

> Plastic and dynamic processes drive adolescent brain development, creating flexibility that allows the brain to define itself, specialize, and sharpen its functions for specific demands. Maturing connections enable increased communication among brain regions, allowing greater integration and complexity. Compelling evidence has shown that the developing brain is vulnerable to the damaging effects of ethanol . . . alcohol exposure during the critical adolescent developmental stages could disrupt the brain plasticity and maturation processes, resulting in behavioral and cognitive deficits. . . . Early exposure to alcohol sensitizes the neurocircuitry of addiction, and affects chromatin remodeling, events that could induce abnormal plasticity in reward-related learning processes that contribute to adolescents' vulnerability to drug addiction. (p. 15)

## PSYCHOLOGICAL THEORIES

The psychological theories included in this section are developed from personality, learning, and social psychological theories that have been proposed since 1960 to explain child and adolescent use of the drugs and substances of abuse. Interestingly, many of these theories are eclectic, as they were also developed by using, or extending, biological and sociological theories. (See Figures 4.1 and 4.2.)

### Personality Theories

The personality theories selected for presentation in this section are eclectic ones. For example, we begin with the classic *disruptive environment theory*, a biopsychological, or psychophysiological, theory. This theory is followed by the *existential theory of drug dependence; ego-self theory of substance dependence: the self-medication hypothesis; theory of adolescent psychological individuation; right-brain model of substance abuse; theory of object relations and compulsive drug use;* and *initiatory model of drug use.* The section concludes with the *theory of emerging adulthood (extended).*

### *Disruptive Environment Theory*

> "H" is for Heaven; "H" is for Hell, and "H" is for Heroin. In the life of the addict, these three meanings of "H" seem inextricably intertwined. (Chein, Gerard, Lee, et al., 1964, p. 3)

Chein, Gerard, Lee, et al. (1964) advanced the now-classic *disruptive environment theory*, a psychophysiological theory, to explain the Road to H as traveled by adolescent boys and girls and young adult men and women (16 to 20 years of age) living in the urban areas of New York City (the Bronx, Brooklyn, and Manhattan). The theorists originally put forward two major hypotheses in order to "help put the manifold characteristics of the addict in clear perspective": (1) opiate analgesic addiction is an extension of, or develops out of, a long-lasting, severe personality disturbance and maladjustment; and (2) opiate analgesic addiction is adaptive, functional, and dynamic (Chein, Gerard, Lee, et al. 1964, p. 194). However, they subsequently advanced a third hypothesis because, among the adolescents they studied, the opiate analgesic addiction often occurred in a context in which neither the personality structure nor the maladjustment was considered sufficient to account for the behavior. Thus:

> Assuming that other conditions are favorable, the probability of addiction is greater if the adolescent experiences changes in his situation in connection with his use of opiates, a change that can be described as adaptive, functional, or ego-syntonic and which he describes in terms which tell us that he regards the use of opiates worthwhile despite, or perhaps especially because of, the inconveniences and difficulties of being an addict in our society. (Chein, Gerard, Lee, et al., 1964, pp. 227–228)

The theorists conceptualized these changes as forces that operated at four levels within the adolescent, the level of: (1) conscious experience; (2) certain defenses; (3) unconscious process; and (4) psychophysiological reaction.

At the first level, the conscious experience level, certain common adaptive aspects of opiate analgesic use are known to the users—symptom relief, social facilitation, and the experienced high. Symptom relief is considered the most remarkable by the users. Overt symptoms of anxiety, obsessive thinking, and early delusional formations are modified or eliminated. Prior to their initiation of opiate analgesic use, many adolescents reported feeling tense and restless. Following the use of the

opiate analgesic, they reported feeling comfortable, relaxed, and peaceful—the symptom relief phenomenon that had been previously formally reported by Lindesmith (1947) and Wikler (1953). (Also see in this section the ego-self theory of substance dependence [self-medication hypothesis].)

The intoxication experience—the high—is another consciously experienced phenomenon. Regular users and addicts appreciated and enjoyed this experience, whereas only a minority of experimental normal subjects did so. According to the theorists, the high is not, in any true sense, a euphoria—a feeling of stimulation, happiness, or excitement (Chein, Gerard, Lee, et al., 1964). Rather, it is an enjoyment of negatives: (1) awareness that tension and distress is markedly reduced; (2) contact with reality diminishes; and (3) ideational and fantasy activity are decreased, often blotting out disquieting and disturbing fantasy life that is characteristic of the unintoxicated (i.e., "straight," drug-free) state.

At the second level, the level of certain defenses, the addiction to opiate analgesics is integrated into the psychological defenses of the adolescent addict. The general function of a psychic defense is to avoid anxiety and may be accomplished by a subtle reordering of experience—an alteration in the perception or in the manifestations of inner impulses or outer events (e.g., denial, projection, and reaction formation). Whereas the first-level phenomena are mainly expressions of the capacity of opiate analgesics to inhibit, or blunt, the perception of inner anxiety and outer strain, at the second level, the opiate analgesic itself is a *diffuse pharmacological defense*. The general structure of this integration is a mixture of projection, rationalization, and denial: "Not I, but the drug in me does these things. I am not responsible; it is the monkey on my back" (Chein, Gerard, Lee, et al., 1964, p. 234). As further explained by the theorists:

> The wishes and impulses expressed through this auxiliary ego are highly individualized. In the

course of the addiction, the unspeakable is spoken and that which should never be done is done. This does not occur in diffuse, *patternless*, or random misbehavior, but with remarkable precision of aim and aptness to the life situations and the relationships with important people in the lives of the addicts. They do not, of course, recognize the intentions of their behavior, however obvious these intentions may be to us. It requires months of work before a patient can accept the integration of this behavior with ideas or feelings he fears to perceive or communicate. Although there is no limit to the variety of such integrations, there are a few general classes which occur frequently.

In the course of the addiction, the addict may begin to express hostility toward parental figures—whom he regards as emasculating or controlling—through theft from the parental home, overt anger (becoming evil and nasty), or through the spiteful, wasteful, or destructive use of parental furnishing, money, decorations, or clothing. Even his general delinquency and the use of narcotics may contain a strong component vector aimed at his parents. By becoming an addict, he can disappoint or frustrate those parents whose hopes or ambitions for their son were of the highest. Similarly, he may use his addiction for the expression of passive-dependent wishes, e.g., by giving up or avoiding employment; begging for money and gifts; soliciting loans without attempt to repay them; and withdrawing from activities, interests, and relationships outside his parental home. (Chein, Gerard, Lee, et al., 1964, pp. 234–235)

At the third level, the level of unconscious process, the role of unconscious symbolism in addiction becomes foremost. As clarified by the theorists:

Dreams, neurotic symptoms, wit, and the psychopathology of everyday life are enriched or burdened by their unconscious meanings. Similarly, many aspects of the addiction experience and process are linked with and emotionally colored by wishes, drives, and bodily experiments pertinent to the addict's early development and relationships. With exceptions, these tend to be communicated or expressed symbolically in the dreams and in the artwork of the patients and in their responses to projective test material. . . . Dreams have the manifest content of a needle, fat, long, sticking into my body; being snowed under a mound of heroin; drinking heroin or being attacked by a monster with a huge syringe. . . . Exceptions . . . are patients who tell quite directly that the syringe and needle. . . are like a breast; when he is *high*, he feels that he is together with his mother, long ago, warm, comfortable, happy, at peace; when he injects the opiate solution, he mixes the solution with his blood [in the syringe] and bounces the blood-opiate mixture back and forth from syringe to vein, and, as he does this, he has fantasies about intercourse. (Chein, Gerard, Lee, et al., 1964, pp. 235–236)

(Also see Pagliaro, Pagliaro, Thauberger, et al., 1993.)

As further explained by the theorists, adolescents who directly associate their addiction experiences with oral concepts have the most clinically evident ego disturbances:

They suffer from anxiety verging on panic or are overtly psychotic. They are least able to repress or otherwise defend themselves against the perception of such ideas and images, and they are thus able to directly verbalize what may only be inferred from the symbolic communication of the others. (Chein, Gerard, Lee, et al., 1964, p. 236)

As emphasized by the theorists, adolescent boys do not become opiate analgesic addicts simply because they have unconscious oral fantasies and cravings for breasts, sustenance, or warmth. Rather, as they become addicts, "the techniques and circumstances of drug use lend themselves as vehicles of expression for these factors of their unconscious mental processes." Although these unconscious symbolizations are less likely to be the major motivations for becoming an addict—being secondary to "the forces of conscious experience, especially the high, or the forces of integration of the addiction in the psychic defenses" (Chein, Gerard, Lee, et al., 1964, p. 236)—they are important contributions to the appetite for opiate analgesic use "in the same sense that spices, with their volatile oils and esters, may contribute to the appetite for otherwise prosaic foods." As the addiction progresses and the adolescent becomes increasingly involved with the addiction and correspondingly less involved in any attempt to deal with the world and current relationships, "ever-larger portions of this psychic life are given over to this primitive level of gratification."

The fourth and final level is the level of psychophysiological reaction. This level addresses the concepts of craving, dependence, and tolerance as developed by the theorists. Craving—identified as a pathological phenomenon—demands recurrent states of liking, wanting, and seeking an entity. As such, craving differs from normal wanting, liking, and seeking in several ways. For the theorists, craving implies an: (1) abnormal intensity of desire; (2) abnormal intensity of the reaction to an inability to fulfill the desire (e.g., instead of using legitimate means to fulfill the desire, there are "intense emotional reactions of anger, rage, sulking, withdrawal, sullen resentment, or action aimed at getting that which is desired without regard to the consequence"); and (3) abnormal limitations in the "modifiability" of the desire (e.g., giving it up or accepting a substitute) as a result of experiences that emphasize the costs or the consequences associated with its fulfillment (Chein, Gerard, Lee, et al., 1964, p. 237).

Dependence—the need for opiate analgesics to maintain normal physiological functioning—variably occurs with regular, long-term use and is seen by the theorists as an unconscious process. Rather than being associated with psychological needs or motives, dependence is associated with a biological process that requires the maintenance of a certain level of opiate analgesics for the continuation of normal daily function. As such, "the biological dependence on the opiates can be a force in the addiction process; without the opiate, the person becomes physically ill" (Chein, Gerard, Lee, et al., 1964, p. 247).

Accordingly, when opiates analgesics are used regularly, they become essential elements of the psychological processes of the CNS. Consequently, the abstinence syndrome, a conscious process, is influenced and modified by psychological factors. "In the novice addict, the intensity of this self-limiting illness is far from unbearable, hardly justifying the illicit use of opiates for the relief of symptoms, particularly because each evasion of the acute abstinence syndrome intensifies the ultimate experience of the abstinence syndrome." To adolescents who are addicted to opiate analgesics or those who are in the process of becoming addicted, "even this relatively minor distress is intolerable"; their "inability to act in terms of long-range goals precludes consideration of the inevitable consequences of permitting the degree of dependence to build up" (Chein, Gerard, Lee, et al., 1964, p. 247). For experienced addicts, who depend on four or more injections of heroin a day to prevent the abstinence syndrome, "abrupt withdrawal is an unquestionably severe physiological disturbance, the intensity of which is affected by the setting in which the distress is experienced (e.g., alone or in the care of hospital staff)."

Chein, Gerard, Lee, et al. (1964) argued that tolerance involved the body's adaptation to the effects of the opiate analgesic. More specifically, "tolerance is developed to the subtle emotional effects of the opiate which the addict craves. . . . He can 'keep normal' but 'can't get high.' . . . He is 'tranquilized' so long as he can avoid withdrawal symptoms, but gets 'no kicks,' and cannot 'go on the nod'" (p. 249). If his "life situation is particularly difficult at this point in his addiction, he will not be satisfied with keeping normal; he will strive to get high again by increasing his dosage either in frequency or in quantity." He has reached a point in a cycle of addiction at which "he cannot do more than keep normal either for economic reasons . . . or because he has become negatively adapted to the subtle emotional effects of the drugs." This type of opiate analgesic addict usually undergoes a few weeks of detoxification in an effort to "recapture the most valued experience of being *high* at a far lower level of dosage." "Such patterns (postponement of drug taking to enhance the effects, seeking a 'free period,' and discontent with dosage levels sufficient to merely ward off the abstinence syndrome) . . . may well provide diagnostic criteria of craving" (pp. 249–250).

As summarized by the theorists:

> Insofar as psychophysiological factors play a role in addiction, the primary force in initiating and intensifying a cycle of addiction is craving. Dependence is a sustaining force, both physiologically and psychologically—relevant, but clearly secondary. Tolerance is a psychophysiological phenomenon which forces either increasing dosage or a free period, i.e., a period of abstinence to recapture certain of the satisfactions of opiate intoxication. Dependence is, of course, also relevant in the noncraving types of addiction, but is again secondary in importance to the major role in affecting the likelihood of getting into trouble. The development of tolerance is relatively unimportant in the involvement–without-craving type of addiction; in the noncraving, noninvolvement type, it plays a role in those searching for "kicks." (Chein, Gerard, Lee, et al., 1964, p. 250).

### Existential Theory of Drug Dependence

Greaves (1974, 1980) addressed the use of drugs and substances of abuse among adolescents (as well as adults) in his *existential theory of drug dependence*. Assuming Weil's (1972) assertion that the desire to periodically alter consciousness is an innate, normal drive analogous to hunger or sex, Greaves (1980, p. 26) hypothesized that:

1. Alternative states serve an adaptive purpose for the organism.
2. It is natural to pursue such states.
3. Children, because of their relative lack of rational enculturation, more readily enter some of these states.

4. People use the drugs and substances of abuse to restore themselves to a state of being from which they are able to access both usual and alternate states.
5. Drugs and substances of abuse, as a form of automedication, or self-medication, are used in an attempt to rectify an abnormal state of personality that forms the cornerstone of all drug dependency.
6. If people could access altered states to a more normal degree—in the ways people with normal personalities do—they might use drugs and substances of abuse, but they would not abuse them or become dependent on them.

As summarized by Greaves (1980):

> Persons who become drug dependent are those who are markedly lacking in pleasurable sensory awareness, who have lost the childlike ability to create natural euphoria through active play, including recreational sex, and who, upon experimentation with drugs, tend to employ these agents in large quantities as a passive means of euphoria, or at least as a means of removing some of the pain and anxiety attending a humorless, dysphoric life style. (p. 27)

An outspoken critic of treatment programs based on "asceticism, privation, and harsh behavioral treatment," Greaves (1980) argued for programs more commensurate with his theory and its underpinnings:

> Instead of conceiving of drugs as the enemy and seeing drug abstinence as a great struggle against the enemy, to be hopefully brought about through great striving and strictly regimented behavior, we need to adopt a human growth and need-fulfillment model. We need to help persons to become the agents of their pleasure, not the passive recipients. We need to provide body-sensory awareness programs, meditation, expressive art therapy, psychotherapy. We need to turn our clients on to music, dancing, fishing, camping, boating, photography,

and sex. . . . We need to help clients to realize that not only is it all right to pursue actively a wide range of pleasurable experiences, but how to. (p. 28)

(See, for example, "The Alternatives Model", in Chapter 9, *Preventing and Treating Child and Adolescent Use of the Drugs and Substances of Abuse*, for related discussion.)

### Ego-Self Theory of Substance Dependence: The Self-Medication Hypothesis

According to Khantzian (1980), becoming and remaining addicted to drugs and substances of abuse is related to severe and significant psychopathology, particularly severe impairments and disturbances in the ego and the sense of self that involve difficulties with drive, affect defense, self-care, dependency, and need satisfaction. During his early work with opiate addicts, including the repeated life histories that he obtained from them, he found that many used heroin and other opiate analgesics to effectively deal with their dysphoric feelings (e.g., anger, rage, restlessness). This finding became even more apparent when the aggressiveness and restlessness he observed among addicts in treatment subsided when they were given methadone. From these observations, he began "to suspect that heroin addicts might be using opiates specifically as an antiaggression drug" (p. 30). This preliminary hypothesis was published as "A Preliminary Dynamic Formulation of the Psychopharmacologic Action of Methadone" in 1972. Subsequently, Khantzian (1974) formulated the hypothesis that problems with aggression predisposed certain individuals to opiate dependence and were also central to its maintenance.

In 1985, Khantzian elaborated the *self-medication hypothesis of addictive disorders* by emphasizing problems with heroin and cocaine dependence based on his theoretical observations and study of narcotic and cocaine addicts. According to Khantzian, the specific psychotropic effects of these drugs: (1) interact with psychiatric disturbances and painful affective states and (2) make their use compelling in susceptible individuals. "The drug an individual comes to rely on is not a random choice" (p. 1261). In regard to cocaine, Khantzian proposed that certain individuals use cocaine to augment a hyperactive, restless lifestyle and an exaggerated need for self-sufficiency. He proposed a number of factors that may predispose an individual to become and remain dependent on cocaine: (1) preexisting chronic depression; (2) cocaine abstinence depression; (3) hyperactive, restless syndrome or "attention deficit disorder"; and (4) cyclothymic or bipolar illness.

Other case studies provided evidence to suggest that cocaine addicts might be medicating themselves for mood disorders and behavioral disturbances, including attention-deficit/hyperactivity disorder (A-D/HD). Khantzian's successful methylphenidate (Ritalin®) treatment of several patients who had A-D/HD provided further evidence to support a self-medication hypothesis of drug dependency. While unable to conclude precisely what disorder(s) cocaine addicts are self-medicating, "all of the patients experienced a relief of dysphoria and improved self-esteem on cocaine; they also experienced improved attention leading to improved interpersonal relations, more purposeful, focused activity, and improved capacity for work" (1985, p. 1236)

Although recognizing that there were other determinants of addiction, Khantzian (1985) believed that a self-medication motive is one of the "more compelling reasons" for explaining the "overuse" of, and dependence on, the drugs and substances of abuse:

Clinical findings based on psychoanalytic formulations have been consistent with and complemented by diagnostic and treatment studies that support this perspective, which, I believe will enable researchers and clinicians to further understand and treat addictive behavior. Rather than simply seeking escape, euphoria, or self-destruction, addicts are attempting to medicate themselves for a range of psychiatric problems and painful emotional states. Although most such efforts at self-treatment are eventually doomed, given the hazards and complications of long-term, unstable drug use patterns, addicts discover that the short-term effects of their drugs of choice help them to cope with distressful subjective states and an external reality otherwise experienced as unmanageable or overwhelming. I believe that the perspective provided by the self-medication hypothesis has enabled me and others to understand better the nature of compulsive drug use and that it has provided a useful rationale in considering treatment alternatives. (p. 1263)

The self-medication of anxiety disorders with alcohol and drugs was studied by Robinson, Sareen, Cox, et al. (2009) using a nationally representative sample (National Epidemiologic Survey on Alcohol and Related Conditions, $n = 43,093$). Expanding on previous self-medication findings, the researchers examined the prevalence and comorbidity of self-medication for anxiety disorder, panic disorder, social phobia, specific phobia, and generalized anxiety disorder. The researchers found that prevalence rates ranged from 3.3% for self-medication for both alcohol and drugs for specific phobia and panic disorder without agoraphobia to 18.3% for self-medication with alcohol for generalized anxiety disorder. Multiple logistic regression analyses determined that self-mediation with alcohol was associated with increased likelihood of any mood or personality disorder diagnosis, while self-medication with both alcohol and drugs further increases these associations over and above self-medication with alcohol alone. Findings were noted to remain significant after adjusting for sociodemographic and substance use disorder variables.

Other evidence supporting the self-medication hypothesis comes from Stewart, Sherry, Comeau, et al. (2011), who hypothesized that Aboriginal adolescents with higher levels of hopelessness are more susceptible to depressive symptoms, which in turn predispose them to drinking to cope, which places them at greater risk for excessive drinking. Participants in their study were 551 Aboriginal adolescent drinkers, 52% boys, with a mean age 15.9 years, from 10 Canadian schools. Structural

equation modeling demonstrated the excellent fit of a model linking hopelessness to excessive drinking indirectly via depressive symptoms and drinking to cope. The results of the research survey led the theorists to suggest that both depressive symptoms and drinking to cope should be intervention targets that can be used to prevent or decrease excessive drinking among Aboriginal youth who are high in measures of hopelessness.

Finally, Mason, Hitchings, and Spoth (2009) studied the transition from middle to late adolescence with attention to the risk for emotional, behavioral, and social problems. Their theoretically hypothesized longitudinal study, funded by the National Institute on Drug Abuse, examined the interrelationships of adolescent negative affect, substance use, and peer deviance. Participants were 429 students in the 6th grade, of whom 222 were girls, residing in the midwestern United States. Recruited in 1993, multiwave youth and parent questionnaire data were collected during in-home visits and analyzed using structural equation modeling. After the baseline assessment, follow-up data were collected five times:

1. At approximately 9 months, when participants were 12 years of age
2. At 21 months, when they were 13 years of age
3. At 33 months, when they were 14 years of age
4. At 51 months, when they were 16 years of age
5. At 75 months, when they were 18 years of age

The conceptual framework guiding this study consisted of several theoretically hypothesized longitudinal links among their study variables: negative affect, substance use, and peer deviance during the transition from middle to late adolescence. Three compatible theoretical orientations were selected from which to develop testable hypotheses, including the self-medication hypothesis proposed by Khantzian (1985).

Controlling for prior substance use, results showed that, at 16 years of age, negative affect was a positive statistical predictor of substance use at 18 years of age . . . As reported by the researchers, this finding is consistent with the self-medication hypothesis proposed by Khantzian (1985), which suggests that some individuals may turn to substance use to escape from or cope with their symptoms of negative affect. Rather than being isolated problems, there is evidence that adolescent negative affect, substance use, and peer deviance are interrelated. Consistent with the self-medication hypothesis, negative affect predicated increased use of the drugs and substances of abuse over time.

Mason, Hitchings, and Spoth (2009) identified that the major strengths of the study included its theory-guided approach, prospective longitudinal design, and structural equation modeling analyses. Limitations included the restricted generalizability of results in regard to race, ethnicity, and rural settings. Nevertheless, the authors believed that "this study provided a stringent test of theoretical expectations regarding longitudinal relations among negative affect, substance use, and peer deviance, and findings enhance our understanding of the development of these problems among teens in late adolescence" (p. 10).

As noted by Khantzian (2004), in his review of *Trauma and Substance Abuse: Causes, consequences, and treatment of comorbid disorders* (Ouimette & Brown, 2003):

> A major portion of my career has been spent developing an etiological model for substance use disorders based on clinical experience and a psychodynamic perspective. This effort has culminated in the development and articulation of the self-medication hypothesis. The main implication of the self-medication hypothesis is that in the majority of cases suffering leads to substance use disorders and not the other way around—a debate or controversy that is not inconsequential. It is impressive and validating how much the empirical data amassed in this volume complement and affirm the role of self-medication as a major mediating factor between

PTSD [posttraumatic stress disorder] and substance use disorders. (p. 588)

(Also see discussion in Chapter 8, *Dual Diagnosis Among Adolescents*).

### Theory of Adolescent Psychological Individuation

One of the few theories extending Jungian psychoanalytic theory was that proposed by Spotts and Shontz (1982, 1985), the *theory of adolescent psychological individuation and substance abuse*. The theory addressed the use of opiate analgesics, sedative-hypnotics (barbiturates), amphetamines, and cocaine. The theory was produced by using the representative case method (see Spotts & Shontz, 1980b)—a method embraced and developed by the theorists that required an "intensive, holistic study of persons, who are not sampled from a population, but are deliberately sought out because they epitomize a condition of theoretical or practical interest, or present an extraordinarily clear opportunity to critically examine hypotheses about an important human state or problem" (Spotts & Shontz, 1985, p. 119).

As explained by the theorists, generalization proceeds from individuals who are studied as whole people to other individuals who are studied as whole people, not from individuals to group means; thus, findings take into account the "complexity and uniqueness of personal psychological structures." The method was also considered to be "a powerful and cost efficient way to conduct 'clinical studies of individuals.'" Although the method does not primarily describe populations or test specific hypotheses, it generates findings that may be particularly useful to practitioners who deal with people on an individual basis. The theorists also note that sequential selection of people permits participants to be combined into groups that may be described by summary statistics and quantitative comparisons among groups (Spotts & Shontz, 1985, p. 119).

In 1974, Spotts and Shontz began a series of studies sponsored by the National Institute on Drug Abuse of people who were identified as heavy, chronic users of cocaine (Spotts & Shontz, 1980b). As described by Spotts and Shontz (1985), this research involved an interlocking series of intensive, multidimensional studies of people who reportedly were heavy chronic users of a variety of different drugs and substances of abuse—amphetamines, barbiturates, cocaine, and opiate analgesics. "Nonusers" also were studied. The research program was continued for 8 years. The theoretical inferences that were drawn from the study led to the development of the theory of adolescent substance abuse.

The theory of adolescent substance abuse purported that the predisposition to commitment to heavy, chronic use of a specific drug or substance of abuse, or class of drugs and substances of abuse, originates early in life developing from failures, delays, blockages, or only partial successes in meeting challenges and crises of normal individuation. According to the theory, people who become committed to heavy, chronic use of specific drugs and substances of abuse do so because the drugs and substances of abuse induce a distinctive ego state that allows temporary escape from currently experienced problems or creates the illusion that these problems have been solved. Using concepts proposed by other theorists, the theory was expanded to include ideas about the overall structure and the process of individual psychological life. As claimed by Spotts and Shontz (1980b), their ideas were not limited to adolescent drug users but, in fact, they could be applied to "all human beings," particularly those living in "Western cultures" (p. 67).

According to the theorists, their research program led them to conclude that there was an aspect of human existence that quickly becomes apparent when an individual, rather than a group, is studied: the potential for *numinous* (i.e., spiritual) experience. Numinous factors are not obvious

among substance users when substances are used to produce some form of transcendent experience or are incorporated into quasi-religious rituals. However, it is believed that numinous factors operate overtly or covertly in everyone's life, give human existence a mythic quality, and lie behind the search for meaning and the occasional feelings of being driven or possessed by life-shaping forces over which personal control is impossible (Spotts & Shontz, 1980b).

A fundamental postulate of the theory is that:

> There exists within each individual a counterpart of the Ego, which is called the Self. As the Ego perceptually and motorically relates to external reality, the Self intuitively and creatively relates to the realities of inner life. The *person* is both the battle ground upon which Ego and Self struggle for supremacy and the integrated structure within which the two may function harmoniously, at least from time to time. (Spotts & Shontz, 1980b, p. 68)

Accordingly, the ego must develop through encounters with the outer world, while the self must develop through encounters with the world of dreams, myth, and revelation. Intertwined, both must grow and develop if normal psychological individuation is to occur. Thus, successful personal growth runs a spiraling course that carries the person on a generally ascending path, back and forth between these two "realities." This process is depicted in a diagrammatic representation provided by the theorists: the spiral of individuation as related to the core problems of heavy, chronic drug abusers (Shontz & Spotts, 1986). Adolescent substance abusers are described as having difficulty "'putting away childish things,' letting go of past behaviors, and accepting the new ones of the future." As such, "adolescent substance abuse is anchored in the individuation process (particularly the Second Individuation Crisis [see Stages of Psychological Individuation in Spotts & Shontz, 1985, p. 123]) and is rooted in the failures, conflicts, and dysfunctional relationships with parental figures which make it impossible for individuation to proceed in a normal manner" (Spotts & Shontz, 1985, p. 131).

### *Right-Brain Model of Adolescent (and Adult) Substance Abuse*

The *right-brain model* was proposed by Mace (1992) to explain adolescent (and adult) use of alcohol and other drugs and substances of abuse. The developmental theories of Erikson, Piaget, and Kohlberg were combined with the psychoanalytic personality theories of Freud and Jung and with family systems theory. Lateral specialization theory (i.e., split brain theory) also contributed to the development of this theory. In regard to the latter, Mace argued that mental health required people to be truly in touch with their *nondominant needs*, or *right*-hemispheric needs. In addition, in order for mental health professionals to better communicate with their clients' nondominant needs, they needed to be in touch with their own nondominant needs.

Mace (1992) advanced two hypotheses: (1) alcohol and other drugs and substances of abuse are used by adolescents (and adults) to relieve stress from *left*-brain tasks and to access right-brain activities; and (2) accessing right-brain activities[5] satisfies developmental stage needs that are carried over from early childhood into adolescence and subsequently into adulthood—belonging needs (oral), self-control needs (anal), and power-seeking needs (phallic). As explained by Mace, all adolescents and adults are not driven by the same developmental needs. Thus, those who experiment with the use of alcohol and other drugs and substances of abuse may do so in an attempt to satisfy different developmental needs.

Six assumptions were advanced by Mace (1992) for the development of his theory:

1. The built-in conflict between the left and right hemispheres produces many incompatible needs and conflicting self-concepts that make possible the changes that underlie personal growth and without which there would be no internal mechanisms for change.

2. The left and right hemispheres develop independently and have their own stages of development that are displayed in adults as either left or right dominance.

3. Early childhood education generally focuses on the rigid programming and development of the left brain, while little attention is given to the right brain and its development.

4. The lack of right-brain development may lead to the tendency for some people to get stuck in the left hemisphere.

5. People who become stuck in the left hemisphere may find that they are unable to obtain relief from the stress associated with being stuck there or may be unable to access right-hemisphere activities except by temporarily deadening the left hemisphere by using alcohol and other drugs and substances of abuse.

6. When the left hemisphere regains control after the right hemisphere has been accessed by the use of alcohol or other drugs and substances of abuse, anger, self-reproach, and partial amnesia occur as a means for these adolescents and adults to deal with the associated low self-esteem and self-hatred they may experience as a result of their use of alcohol and other drugs and substances of abuse.

An important aspect of the theory is the ability of the right- and left-brain hemispheres to split. The right hemisphere splits into

---

[5] The right brain often is characterized as being responsible for feelings, intuitive insights, artistic expression, personal relationships, and having fun. The left brain, which is considered the dominant hemisphere (at least for the male gender), is responsible for verbal expression, mathematics, cause-and-effect reasoning, and dealing analytically with one thing at a time (Mace, 1992).

two personality types: a good guy and a bad guy. The latter has the problem of addiction, expresses all the anger associated with using alcohol and other drugs and substances of abuse, and has all the fun. In fact, sometimes the right hemisphere is identified as being the more mentally healthy hemisphere because the repressed, bad-guy part is more honest in regard to the inner self and the person's world. The amnesia can be viewed as a symptom of vertical repression or split personality that helps adolescents and adults, particularly those who have above-average intelligence, to deal with severe conflict. Mental health professionals can help these people by putting them in touch with the healthy part of the right hemisphere by awakening their buried dreams—the wishes people have, what they want to do, and what they want to be—that have been repressed and, consequently, if appropriate, encouraging them to seek these dreams.

The left hemisphere also splits into two parts—an extraordinarily righteous part and a super sense of self part. The righteous part listens to and behaves in accordance with the wishes of significant others. It thrives on outbreaks from the right hemisphere's buried bad part fueled by repression from the left hemisphere's righteous part, as they complement one another. The super sense of self part of the left hemisphere listens to the advice of others but questions that advice and makes decisions that may or may not coincide with it. It is for this reason that family members and mental health professionals frequently are unsuccessful when they try to use rational arguments to convince their family members or patients, respectively, to moderate their use of alcohol or other drugs and substances of abuse.

Various integrative techniques can be used by mental health and other professionals to help adolescents and adults bridge the conflicting needs of the two hemispheres. Mental health and other professionals also can help adolescents and adults find alternative ways to satisfy the needs of their nondominant right hemisphere without resorting to the use of alcohol or other drugs and substances of abuse. Not only is the right hemisphere immune to advice from its own dominant left hemisphere, but it also is immune to any rational interventions that may be offered by a family member, counselor, or other therapist. Thus, in order to be effective, mental health professionals need to achieve rapport with the nondominant right hemisphere of the adolescent or adult and legitimize the inner needs that have been carried over from childhood. According to Mace (1992), family members also need to be taught to use integrative techniques. For example, parents should understand that an adolescent family member may simply want their respect, honesty, or praise; if given by the parents, it could do much to prevent the adolescent's use of alcohol or other drugs and substances of abuse.

### Theory of Object Relations and Adolescent (and Adult) Compulsive Drug Use

Volkan (1994) proposed the *theory of object relations and adolescent (and adult) compulsive drug use* addressing the compulsive use of psychodepressants (opiate analgesics), psychostimulants (amphetamines), and psychodelics (LSD). Based on assumptions inherent in Freudian psychoanalytic theory (Fairbairn, 1952) and modern object relations theory (Kernberg, 1967, 1975), the theorist proposed that: (1) adolescents (and adults) who have satisfactory object relations will not feel the need to use the drugs and substances of abuse compulsively, including those that are highly addictive; (2) adolescents (and adults) who have poor object relations, weak ego formation, narcissistic disturbances, and introjective depression are likely to begin to use the drugs and substances of abuse as reactivated transitional objects, continue to use them, and, finally, use them compulsively; and (3) adolescents (and adults) who use drugs and substances of abuse compulsively eventually may increase ego destruction, schizoid pathology, or risk for suicide.

As explained by Volkan (1994), adolescents (and adults) use the drugs and substances of abuse to achieve a regressive experience of a primary good object because of: (1) a deficit in early object relations; and (2) the internalization of harsh and frustrating parental objects. The experience induced by the drug or substance of abuse—a primary good object—masks the harsh, introjected (bad) objects and their associated dysphoric feelings of self-criticism and worthlessness. As the actions of the drug or substance of abuse wear off, the dysphoric feelings of the bad objects return all the stronger for being repressed. In this way, the bad objects and the dysphoria they produce are linked to the drug and substance of abuse. If more of the drug or substance of abuse can be obtained, the dysphoria can be controlled, and the cycle is complete as the user searches for, obtains, and, again, uses the drug or substance of abuse. This internalization of bad object representations allows users to be controlled while the influence of the drug or substance of abuse is repressed. However, because the bad object representations carry tremendous aggressive energy, they may surface and overpower the ego.[6]

According to Volkan, the overpowering of the ego is the reason why drug users report feeling a loss of control when they are under the influence of a drug or substance of abuse. This feeling alternates with a feeling of being in control when the effects of the drug or substance of abuse wears off. This cycle of control is seen as important to the theory. If the cycle is not maintained, control over internalized bad object representations become more difficult to maintain. This situation is characteristic of recovering drug users. As noted by Volkan (1994), drug users who abstain from using drugs or substances of abuse can become intensely depressed, hostile, rageful, or suicidal. The use of the drug or substance of abuse serves to control their bad object representations, and, when *not* used, the bad object representations may threaten to surface.

In regard to treatment from an object relations understanding of the use of drugs and substances of abuse, the task of the therapist would be one of maintaining a supportive neutral presence while helping the drug user to reestablish healthy object relations dynamics. The successful treatment of adolescents (and adults) who use drugs and substances of abuse compulsively requires engendering a transference relationship with a possible role model. "Only when this relationship is established is there a chance to release or integrate the bad internalized object representations, that is, heal the split between the good and bad object representations" (Volkan, 1994, p. 116). As emphasized by Volkan:

> Programs such as the twelve-step or co-dependency groups which include elements designed to bond drug abusers to a positive environment and role models may work for this reason. . . . Although . . . some severely pathological patients may not tolerate the self-help approach, many patients will derive benefit from this type of supportive, contained environment. Also . . . self-help groups like AA (Alcoholics Anonymous), NA (Narcotics Anonymous) or CA (Cocaine Anonymous) force compulsive drug users to face the defensive denial and narcissism associated with their drug problem. Both the admission of addiction and the storytelling of drug experiences by patients in self-help groups may play a valuable psychodynamic role in overcoming these defenses. Nevertheless, without the insight engendered in psychoanalytic therapy, the success of the self-help approach alone may be transitory. Without the support of an external agency (e.g., supportive therapist or self-help group), the drug user will likely fall back into his old habits. Because the addict has relied on an external, reactivated transitional object for support, he does not necessarily have the motivation to internalize this support. This internalization comes about through introspective psychoanalytic work which requires some ability

---

[6] Fairbairn (1952) characterized this situation as an experience of *being possessed*, a characterization also noted by Wurmser (1994) as an experience of *being demonically possessed*.

to tolerate painful affect. . . . Of course, this is why psychotherapeutic treatment with compulsive drug users is reported to be extremely difficult. . . . For this reason, it is perhaps best to do introspective work in combination with psychotherapies or self-help modalities which provide some external support. Although there is no good evidence which delineates the effectiveness of different types of drug treatment programs, this type of multimodal approach may have the best chance of success. (1994, pp. 116–117)

(Also see related discussion of multimodal therapeutic approaches in Chapter 9, *Preventing and Treating Child and Adolescent Use of the Drugs and Substances of Abuse*.)

### Initiatory Model of Drug Abuse

Zoja (1989) proposed the *initiatory model of drug abuse*, a Jungian psychoanthropologic theory that addressed substance use in general with a focus on adolescent and adult "drug addicts." Inherent in the theory are the basic assumptions that:

1. The disappearance of *initiation* (initiation rituals) is one of the principal differences between the ancient and modern worlds.

2. Death and regeneration are the keys to every process of initiation, or rebirth. (In primitive societies, the relationship between initiation and death is so close that many initiatory processes are analogous to death rites.)

3. Modern western society lacks meaningful initiation and death rituals. (Death and initiation have been repressed and belong to the same area of repression).

4. Death and initiation are archetypically related terms.

5. When family affections, ideals, and values are dead, life experiences worthy of that name are sought, even those that are purely subjective experiences shared by a restricted few.

6. Through the world of drugs, the themes of death and initiation are continually

activated and reactivated (e.g., heavy drug users typically experience a sensation of death during periods of abstinence that are relieved only by the reuse of the drug or substance of abuse—a phenomenon that probably contributes to the exaggerated importance given to "physical addiction.")

7. There is an unconscious link between drug use and the theme of death and renewal.

8. Drug use is an attempt to create a form of self-initiation.

9. Drug addiction is the response to a natural universal need for initiation or, more generally, for rebirth (i.e., an unconscious need for death experiences is inherent among drug addicts, and less overtly in society as a whole, and requires an archetypal perspective in order to be understood).

Several related hypotheses are advanced:

1. People in modern western society use drugs (or turn to membership in terrorist and other groups, such as criminal youth gangs) in order to meet a latent need for initiation.

2. Individual drug users are prone to group phenomena (i.e., the ways group members acquire and use drugs have a practical and ritual function that enables them to unconsciously recall the ancient rites of entrance though which initiates are elevated into a more prestigious group or social class).

3. A personified archetypal reality known as the negative hero is present in drug addiction.

4. The archetypal need to transcend one's present state at any cost, even when it entails the use of physically harmful substances, is especially strong in those who find themselves in a state of meaninglessness, lacking both a sense of identity and a precise societal role.

5. Drug addiction is not an escape from society but a desperate attempt to occupy a place in it.

6. Drug addicts have an unconscious need for death.

7. The consumerism of the modern western world leads people to the initiatory process that begins with renewal and ends with the death experience.

From this theoretical perspective, Zoja argues that the treatment for drug addicts is more difficult than for other types of patients. The values and aims of medicine are different from those of analysis. In the case of drug addiction, medicine will seek to overcome a state of intoxication, and its goal will be to repair battered organs. Depth psychology strives to resolve certain contradictions and unconscious psychic sufferings. The use of a toxic substance is for medicine an evil in itself, while for depth psychologists, its represents a symptom that may become chronic and that may exist independently of its cause—a psychic disturbance whose nature, development, and essences are hard to verify. A second element affecting the therapy of drug addicts is linked to the question of motivation. Whereas organic medical treatment can be performed on an unwilling and uncooperative person, by definition, analytic theory can be conducted only with deep personal motivation on the part of the patient. From this perspective, one encounters problems in "forcing" drug addicts to undergo treatment.[7]

### Theory of Emerging Adulthood, Extended

Arnett (1998, 2000, 2004) proposed the *theory of emerging adulthood* to conceptualize the developmental characteristics of adolescents and young adults 18 to 25 years of age. The theory was extended by Arnett (2005) to explain the high rates of using the drugs and substances that are particularly noted in this age group. The original theory was developed to address the dramatic, worldwide changes that have been observed in industrialized societies regarding the transition of their adolescents to adulthood. Occurring over the last 50 years, changes appear to be related to the extension of the education and training of youth into the mid- and later-second decade of life with the delaying of marriage and parenthood. The delay in these traditional adult roles, along with their related obligations and restrictions, has enabled "unprecedented freedom from social control" for these emerging adults and the need for the development of a separate period of the life course, emerging adulthood. As explained by Arnett (2005):

> It has been proposed that emerging adulthood is characterized by five main features: it is the age of identity explorations, especially in love and work; it is the age of instability; it is the most self-focused age of life; it is the age of feeling in-between, in transition, neither adolescent nor adult; and it is the age of possibilities, when hopes flourish, when people have an unparalleled opportunity to transform their lives.
>
> Elsewhere it has been explained in detail how these features distinguish emerging adulthood from the adolescence that precedes it or the young adulthood that follows it. . . . Here, the features are applied specifically to drug use in order to explain the high rates of drug use during this age period. For each of the features, hypotheses are offered that present opportunities for empirical investigation. Some of these hypotheses have been addressed in existing studies, some have not been tested at all, but all of them are intended to represent promising directions for further research. (p. 239)

These hypotheses are generally related to other theoretical perspectives, including the self-medication, sensation-seeking, and social control theories explaining the use of the drugs

---

[7] As occurs, for example, when adolescents (and adults) involved with harmful use of the drugs and substances of abuse: (1) receive a judicial sentence for treatment rather than a sentence of incarceration for drug-related offenses; or (2) are the subject of a well-meaning intervention to force or are cajoled into participating in a drug treatment program. Perhaps this theory helps to explain the high failure rates (i.e., high recidivism) associated with forcing adolescents to undergo treatment.

and substances of abuse. For example, in comparison to adolescence, during age-of-identity explorations, identity-related explorations in love not only occur but require that emerging adults seriously consider the kind of person they wish to form a long-term partnership with. As such, this feature demands emerging adults to obtain a more serious understanding of who they really are and what qualities they desire in a lifelong romantic partner. The type of work they do and the type they want to do for the long term also becomes more serious and identity focused. In regard to the drugs and substances of abuse, persons of this age may want to (1) experience the various states of consciousness that they induce (e.g., hypothesis 3, sensation seeking, will be found to be higher in emerging adults than in either adolescents or young adults); or (2) relieve their identity confusion (e.g., hypothesis 1, identity explorations in emerging adults, will predict the use of drugs and substances of abuse, especially in the absence of commitment).

During the age of instability, arguably the most unstable period of the life course according to Arnett (2005), emerging adults make frequent changes in their lives in terms of love partners, jobs, education (including dropping in and out of college or changing majors), and moving residences, a particularly common form of instability in this age group. Hypothesis 4, for example, reflects this feature: Instability will increase substance use in emerging adulthood, mediated by mood disruptions (e.g., anxiety; sadness) that will also motivate the use of the drugs and substances of abuse as self-medication. In fact, there is a sharp increase in serious psychopathology in emerging adulthood, including major depressive disorders.

The features associated with the self-focused age, which is probably the most self-focused period of life, are not related to being egocentric or selfish. Rather, emerging adults are seen as being freer than people during other age periods in regard to making decisions independently, without being required to

obtain permission or consent from others (e.g., parents, spouse). "They decide independently everything from what groceries to buy to what job to seek . . . where to live, how to manage money, what kind of education or training to pursue, whom to date or live with or break up with, and so on" (Arnett, 2005, p. 243).

For emerging adults who are self-focused, forms of social networks and relationships that act as a means of social control for other age periods are likely to be less effective or may be more transient and unstable. Emerging adults also spend much of other leisure time alone, although friendship groups become much stronger. However, as found for adolescents, emerging adults who are attracted to using the drugs and substances of abuse are more likely to establish friendships or join friendship groups that encourage rather than discourage their use. For example, as identified in hypothesis 8: Within groups of emerging adults, those who report higher self-focus and lower social control will have the highest rates of using the drugs and substances of abuse. Hypothesis 9 also identifies that:

> emerging adults who use drugs and substances of abuse, and/or who are similar in other characteristics that place them at risk for using the drugs and substances of abuse, will tend to select each other as friends and, following the formulation of their friendship, will increase their use of the drugs and substances of abuse as they provide each other with a social context for using them. (p. 243)

For the age of feeling in between, emerging adults are characterized by the theorist as "neither adolescent nor fully adult, on the way to adulthood but not there yet." Rather than traditional markers designating adulthood (e.g., marriage, parenthood), "more intangible, psychological, gradual qualities such as accepting responsibility for one's self and making independent decisions, along with the more tangible, but still gradual criterion of financial independence" are the markers (Arnett, 2005,

p. 245). These features are important in regard to the use of the drugs and substances of abuse by emerging adults. As noted in hypothesis 10, emerging adults who feel that they have not yet reached adulthood will be more likely to use the drugs and substances of abuse than those who feel they have reached adulthood. Further, hypothesis 11 identifies that emerging adults who use drugs and substances of abuse will view their behavior as acceptable until they grow into adulthood, at which time they will give it up.

The theory concludes by stating that the age of possibilities, a time when emerging adults have the opportunity to make dramatic changes in their lives and hopes are high, also is characterized as having features of optimistic bias (e.g., believing that potential negative consequences of behavior, including those associated with the use of the drugs and substances of abuse—such as being involved in a fatal motor vehicle accident while driving under the influence of alcohol—will likely not happen to them).

## Learning Theories

Behaviorism, cognitivism, and neobehaviorism (social learning theory) contributed to several theories that attempted to explain the use of the drugs and substances of abuse by children and adolescents, particularly during the 1970s and 1980s.[8] Two more recently developed theories, the *life process program theory of natural recovery* and the *cognitive-behavioral theory of adolescent chemical dependency*, are presented here.

### Life Process Program Theory of Natural Recovery

Peele, Brodsky, and Arnold (1991) advanced the *life process program (LPP) theory of natural recovery*, a cognitively based learning theory. The use—controlled use, slips, and relapse—of alcohol and other drugs and substances of

abuse by children and adolescents (and adults) are addressed along with other destructive habits (e.g., codependence, excessive exercise, gambling, love and sex, overeating, and shopping). The major focus of the theory is self-help and, in regard to children and adolescents, the role of parents in instilling healthful rather than addictive habits in their offspring.

The LPP theory proposes five assumptions:

1. Belonging to a supportive social group—a group that has prosocial values and does not support addictive excesses—makes it unlikely that a person will be addicted.

2. Having a job and a family provides most people with a structure in life and a sense of value—conversely, addictions result when people's lives are unstructured and made to seem worthwhile by activities that harm them or those close to them, detract from their environments and relationships, and deepen their feelings of self-doubt.

3. Addictive activities, although a part of essential human experiences, subvert and substitute for genuine satisfactions.

4. The *addictive cycle* is the self-feeding reliance on feelings that the addiction makes harder to get in any other way (e.g., anxieties are masked by substance use and, thus, are not dealt with constructively) and, as the substance is used more and more for this purpose, health is undermined.

5. Addiction is not an accident but a consequence of the confluence of forces in people's lives, of their needs, and available ways of satisfying these needs.

The LPP offers an alternative therapeutic approach for the treatment of addictions to the drugs and substances of abuse and addictions to other destructive habits. Rejecting the *disease theory* because of its lack of therapeutic success and its basic assumptions, the theorists

---

[8] For more information regarding these theories, readers are referred to the previous edition of this text (i.e., Pagliaro & Pagliaro, 1996).

provide a nondisease self-help or therapist-assisted approach that emphasizes the natural processes of recovery—a process that includes building on individual strengths and developing and using community strengths. Rather than lifelong, treatment is finite. People are seen as evolving beings who require individualized, client-centered treatment. The development of coping abilities is seen as essential to the process of becoming nonaddicted. In this regard, the goal of treatment is personal efficacy, which is developed through motivation, identification of personal values, and development of life skills and life involvements, including those inherent in family, work, and community (Peele, Brodsky, & Arnold, 1991).

The LPP is proposed as a successful therapy for people who have destructive habits. The goal of the LPP is to change these habits. The focus of treatment is not the past but the current situation—current rewards, satisfactions, and obstacles—and the treatment is aimed at helping people mobilize their assets. Thus, instead of focusing on past failures and weaknesses, as is done with psychoanalytic therapy, the LPP draws on the personal strengths and resources that are available to the addicted person. The LPP also differs from behavioral techniques that shape behavior through contrived rewards and punishments in that it seeks rewards and punishments to encourage new behavior in the natural structure of the person's life. In essence, the LPP is a values-based approach. Values are believed to be most crucial in orienting or reorienting a person's life. Developing and living by a set of values, expanding connections to the world, and aiming for and accomplishing worthwhile goals are key factors in the LPP. As described by Peele, Brodsky, and Arnold (1991):

> The Life Process Program presents a recipe for change through toning down overblown and frightening rhetoric about addictions and by instead appealing to the strength, intelligence, and instinct for self-preservation in every person. Addiction *is* a problem, and for some people, a very serious problem. But you can best

address that problem by reminding yourself of everything about you that is normal and healthy and by applying those strengths to your weakest areas of functioning.

> Similarly, if your child [or adolescent] is abusing drugs, you rightly worry about the potentially serious consequences of that behavior. But these immediate concerns do not obviate the need to address the values, relationships, and activities that constitute the young person's life. Whether it is you or a loved one who must cope with an addiction, don't discount your own resourcefulness. . . . The Life Process Program we recommend . . . does not focus exclusively or even primarily on addiction itself. You will certainly need to work on your addiction specifically, but the most crucial work you need to do is on the direction of your overall life, of which an addiction is just one expression. (pp. 167–168)

### Cognitive-Behavioral Theory of Adolescent Chemical Dependency

Ross (1994) proposed the *cognitive-behavioral theory of adolescent chemical dependency* integrating biological (illness/disease theory) and psychological (learning theory: neobehaviorism) orientations with the spiritual component inherent in AA. Abusive use and compulsive use patterns were addressed in regard to the use of the drugs and substances of abuse by adolescent girls and boys. Ross also stated that the theories and techniques could be applied to adult substances abusers as well to other forms of addiction and to oppositional defiant and conduct disorders. According to Ross (1994):

> Whether the practitioner considers chemical dependency a disease or a behavior disorder, or attributes its cause to genetic factors, environmental, family, and cultural influences, or underlying personality conflicts, clinical evidence clearly suggest that a faulty cognitive structure, or "self-defeating self-talk," is a critical element in the assessment and treatment of adolescents suffering from the use and abuse of mind-altering substances. (p. 7)

Thus, Ross advanced several hypotheses and a conceptual model that considered the emerging personality and cognitive structure of the chemically dependent adolescent. Defining chemical dependency as "a disease of attitudes leading to the use and abuse of mind-altering substances" (e.g., alcohol, cocaine, and marijuana) that culminates in "physical deterioration of the body, emotional instability, and spritual bankruptcy," he advocates that essential assessment and treatment be guided by his theory (Ross, p. 10).

Using Rokeach's (1970) definition of "attitude" (i.e., a relatively enduring organization of beliefs around an object or situation predisposing a person to respond in some preferential manner), Ross (1994) identified two types of attitudes that contribute to the development of a chemically dependent personality: (1) a priori attitude (i.e., an enduring organization of beliefs around a perception or images of the environment that helps people to make sense of their external experiences); and (2) a posteriori attitude (i.e., an enduring organization of beliefs around automatically mediated physiological responses, or emotions, that help people to make sense of their internal experiences). These two types of attitudes produce automatic emotional and behavioral responses that eventually result in the formation of distinct personality structures. According to Ross, adolescent chemical use, abuse, and dependency occur when a distinct set of a priori beliefs about the environment results in a multitude of self-defeating emotional responses. These responses activate a distinct set of a posteriori beliefs that, in turn, activate a distinct set of self-defeating behavioral responses.

Critical factors in the adolescent's environment (e.g., family, peer culture, media, and readily available drugs and substances of abuse) influence a priori beliefs. These beliefs, and associated subsequent feelings, create a distinct mind-set conducive to chemical use, abuse, and, when left unchallenged, habitual chemical use. Over time, the behavior of chemical use reinforces a set of a posteriori beliefs.

According to these beliefs, the use of drugs or substances of abuse is a way to seek stimulation, gain self and peer acceptance, and avoid or escape responsibility. With repeated use of the drugs and substances of abuse, the adolescent eventually develops an erroneous obsessive thinking pattern—what was once "a way" eventually becomes "the only way" to seek stimulation, gain self and peer acceptance, and avoid or escape responsibility. As use continues, the adolescent's life becomes increasingly unmanageable as a sense of powerlessness, or loss of control intensifies, fueled by the erroneous obsession. The adolescent also finds that he or she is faced with behavioral consequences, including the: (1) violation of well-learned ethical, value, and legal standards; (2) deterioration of cognitive, affective, and behavioral functioning; and (3) emergence of more pronounced psychological defenses.

As the addictive personality develops, an added set of a priori beliefs emerge that concern the fear of discovery and possible punishment. This additional internal dialogue significantly increases the adolescent's anxiety level and creates an increased demand for emotional relief. The obsession becomes greater as the temporary emotional relief provided by the use of the drug or substance of abuse reinforces the erroneous a posteriori belief that the only way to find relief from unpleasant feelings is to, once again, use the drug or substance of abuse to get high. As the addictive process continues to repeat itself, a distinct personality pattern and cognitive structure emerge that ultimately maintains a cauldron of emotional pain and self-defeating behavior patterns that culminate in physical deterioration of the body, emotional instability, and spiritual bankruptcy.

Recognizing the value his theory presents for treatment, Ross (1994) provides a multimodal approach to assessment that includes: screening for the use of the drugs and substances of abuse; a signs and symptoms checklist; psychosocial assessment and family interviews; parental evaluation; teenage drug or substance abuser interviews; medical examination; psychological and psychiatric evaluation; and clinical observations. Three dimensions that can be used to formulate a diagnosis of an adolescent who abuses the drugs and substances of abuse also are provided and explained. The theorist offers: (1) treatment options and environments (e.g., treatment climate, staffing patterns, and supportive services); (2) four distinct plateaus of recovery (i.e., admitting, submitting, committing, and transmitting); and (3) 30 useful treatment strategies for helping adolescents develop healthier cognitive structures.

The development of healthier cognitive structures is thought to enable adolescents to reach the four plateaus and involves teaching them how to: (1) be more aware and honest with themselves; (2) more effectively manage their feelings; (3) change self-defeating emotions and behavior; and (4) identify self-defeating self-talk, change it, and keep it from recurring. Codependency among parents and other family members also is addressed with treatment strategies and methods for developing more effective communication and interaction patterns. The attributes (i.e., character strengths, confidentiality, timing and tack, listenership, objectivity and discernment, empathy and understanding, honesty, genuine interest and love, and patience and perseverance) and the requisite skills (e.g., basic one-on-one and group cognitive-behavioral substance abuse counseling skills, including a working knowledge of the steps and principles of AA and knowledge of developmental, family system, and other theories, especially gestalt, reality, and actualizing therapies) of an effective substance abuse counselor are outlined. As emphasized by Ross (1994), successful diagnosis and treatment involve helping adolescents who abuse the drugs and substances of abuse to identify and change the a priori and a posteriori attitudes that constitute a self-defeating personality and cognitive structure that keep them in a state of intoxication and emotional and behavioral turmoil.

## Psychosocial Theories

Two theories combining aspects of psychological and sociological theories are presented: the *predictive model of adolescent use of the drugs and substances of abuse* and the *four-factor model of adolescent drug involvement (psychosocial model of adolescent drug involvement)*.

### Predictive Model of Adolescent Use of the Drugs and Substances of Abuse

Mercer and Kohn (1980) produced the *predictive model of adolescent use of the drugs and substances of abuse* to explain the use of the drugs and substances of abuse by adolescents with attention to the constructs of authoritarianism, child-rearing practices, and drug use attitudes. More a personality and social psychological theory than purely a sociological theory, this model gives attention to polyuse of alcohol, tobacco, and marijuana by adolescents. The theorists hypothesized that parental child-rearing practices produce within children a personality that shapes their attitudes toward the use of drugs and substances of abuse that, in turn, affect their use of alcohol, tobacco, and marijuana. As a predictive model of adolescent use of the drugs and substances of abuse, the model was found to be more successful for predicting illicit rather than licit drug use, with "love" on the part of the mother and "positive control" on the part of the father the most salient dimensions in regard to positive parental child-rearing practices.

### Four-Factor Model of Adolescent Drug Involvement (Psychosocial Model of Adolescent Drug Involvement)

McDonald and Towberman (1993) developed the *four-factor model of adolescent drug involvement*. The theorists argued that their model was needed because, "no one model has been developed that fully explains the cause of substance abuse." In fact, "present theories are bound by reductionist interpretation from different disciplines," with "psychological theories tend[ing] to focus on the individual rather than on environmental and cultural contributors to individual behavior," and "sociological theories tend[ing] to focus on external factors, which has the effect of ignoring individual differences" (p. 925). In order to address these limitations, they presented a four-factor model based on a larger, multiyear psychosocial study of emergent adolescent drug involvement. McDonald and Towberman's study considered both environmental and intrapsychic forces as they interact on the individual. The study tracked students from grade 5 through grade 9. The cross-sectional findings were derived from analysis of sample data collected when the subjects were in grades 7 and 8. As described by the theorists:

> In accordance with the theory that internal and external forces affect youths' decisions to experiment with or continue the use of substances, fourteen psychosocial measures were selected as independent variables. . . . Before submission for multiple regression analysis, the explanatory variables were factor analyzed to reduce multicollinearity and to produce a more efficient model of factors underlying drug involvement. . . . Analysis of the fourteen variables produced the four-factor model. (McDonald & Towberman, 1993, pp. 931–932)

The results of their study of the antecedents of adolescent drug use were identified as being important in several ways: (1) the psychosocial focus expanded the view of drug use causation, which, according to the theorists, generally was limited to either psychological or sociological theories; (2) causation was viewed in terms of both external and internal factors; and (3) interdisciplinary research cooperation was supported. Summarizing their work, McDonald and Towberman (1993) note:

> The explanatory potency of the four-factor model is a notable contribution to adolescent drug use research. The significant amount of variance in drug experimentation and the magnitude of drug use that is explained in this model may serve as a building block for further study.

> The fact that both internalized values and external influences were important in explaining adolescent drug use is not surprising. It is somewhat surprising, however, that the internality of self-concept was not significantly associated with either drug experimentation or frequency of drug use. This finding is in contrast with others linking self-concept and adolescent drug use. Given the relatively young age or maturity level of the study sample, individuation may not have been developed to a point consistent with an integrated self-identity. It may be that self-concept factors may emerge as significant predictors of adolescent drug use in the later adolescent years. (p. 935)

The results of this work emphasize the importance of children: (1) bonding with parents, peers, and other people who have drug-resistant attitudes; and (2) connecting with, and achieving in, school.

## SOCIOLOGICAL THEORIES

This section presents selected examples of sociological theories published over the last 50 years that attempt to explain why children and adolescents use the drugs and substances of abuse. These theories reflect the major subdisciplinary orientations of sociology, including anthropology, criminology and deviance, economics, integrative models, sociocultural/acculturation, systemic (family), and other orientations. (See Figure 4.2.) While theories, particularly those that are eclectic or pluralistic, do not always fit into these categories, they have been used to help organize the discussion presented. We begin with criminology and deviance.

### Criminology and Deviance

Three theories are presented in this section: the *theory of drug subcultures;* the *theoretical framework of developmental stages in adolescent drug involvement: the gateway hypothesis*; and the *deviance theory: an explanatory model.*

### Theory of Drug Subcultures (Drug Subculture Theory)

In an effort to explain alcohol and marijuana use (and later, heroin and polydrug use) among adolescents and young adults 11 to 25 years of age, Johnson (1973) advanced the *theory of drug subcultures (drug subculture theory)*. As explained by Johnson (1980):

> Drug-subculture theory is designed to explain group behavior. Individual behavior is defined as a function of following the subculture's values, conduct norms, roles, argot. The greater a person's commitment to a drug-using group and to subcultural values, conduct norms, roles, rituals, and argot, the greater the predictability of behavior of that individual. (p. 117)

In order to better study the youthful use of the drugs and substances of abuse, the anthropologic concept of subculture was approached as emerging from, being maintained by, and changing over time through a complex process of interaction involving many persons and groups that may not be directly connected (Johnson, 1980). The theory, specifically focusing on illicit drug and substance use, emerged from middle-range theories in criminology and deviant behavior. Attention also was given to the fundamental sociological concepts of values, norms, and roles. Johnson identified the theory as a distinctly sociological one that did not attempt to incorporate biological (including pharmacological) or psychological orientations and insights about the use of the drugs and substances of abuse. However, he noted that it could overlap with these disciplinary orientations in regard to some points.

Johnson (1980) used the term "drug subculture" to refer to values, conduct norms, roles and role performance, and highly valued argot and rituals associated with the nonmedical use of the drugs. As he emphasized, "[V]alues and conduct norms governing the medical use of drugs; the use of drugs for dieting and sleeping; the consumption of cigarettes, coffee, and tea, and the social use of alcohol," were excluded because they were "*not* socially defined as *drugs* by law, social custom, or most illicit drug users" (p. 113).

The values, conduct norms, performance roles, argot, and rituals were identified as being important for understanding a drug subculture. As explained by Johnson (1980), the most important value for a drug subculture is the intention, or desire, to get high from the nonmedical use of drugs and substances of abuse. The most important conduct norm is whether a member has intentionally used, or wishes to use, a particular drug or substance of abuse to get high. And, in regard to roles and role performance, there are three central roles in drug subcultures: seller, buyer, and user—the performance of which is usually covert, or hidden, because of possible exposure to arrest and incarceration. Thus, drugs and rituals also have a specific argot (e.g., "smack" for "heroin"; "rig" for "hypodermic syringe"; "mainlining" for "intravenous injection").

The American middle-class culture, or parent culture, defines what adults expect adolescents and young adults to do (e.g., avoid alcohol, tobacco, and nonmedical drug use) or not to do (e.g., use alcohol, tobacco, and nonmedical drugs). These norms become internalized and continue to influence youth and young adults following their departure from their homes. The peer culture, or youth culture, governs youthful behavior and friendship groups and their norms of conduct—loyalty; maintenance of group association; social interaction in the group in locations where adult controls are absent (e.g., college dorms; fraternity, or frat houses); and competition for status and prestige that leads to new forms of behavior. Youth generally experience the peer culture as it is mediated through a peer group. While there are many types of subcultures (e.g., athletic, homosexual, political), the participation of youth in a delinquent subcultures (e.g., criminal youth gangs) emerges from conduct norms and values that influence behaviors that promote criminal acts. The competition for status in these subcultures, which is usually concealed from adults, leads to the development of their own morality norms, standards, and rewards. These nonconventional behaviors are adopted, while parent culture conduct norms, or expectations for conventional behavior, are denigrated or denied.

When the drug subculture was originally presented by Johnson in 1973, two different subcultures were identified: a white subculture and a black subculture. As explained by Johnson (1980), members of both subcultures began with marijuana use, but the former used hallucinogens and "pills" while the latter disproportionately used cocaine and heroin. Although the use of all drugs and substances of abuse has expanded greatly since that time, four varieties of subcultures within the broader drug subculture were identified: (1) the alcohol-abuse subculture; (2) the cannabis subculture; (3) the multiple-drug-use subculture; and (4) the heroin injection subculture. These subcultures are strongly related (see Kandel's *gateway hypothesis* in the next section). As emphasized by Johnson, the drug-subculture theory provides a conceptual framework for analyzing why and how youth become differentially involved in using the drugs and substances of abuse.

In order to illustrate these subcultures and the differences in their conduct norms for governing the central activities of the group and its participants, or members, Johnson (1980) provides four specific examples, emphasizing that while these norms may shift over time, they generally include: (1) experimentation conduct norms that expect members to consume the focal drug(s); (2) maintenance conduct norms that expect members to enjoy the use of the drug(s) and to repeat the use of the drug(s) while increasing both the frequency of use and the amount used to that which is common among group members; (3) reciprocity conduct norms that expect members to provide other members a portion of their drugs for free or at low cost, with the knowledge that the obligation is reciprocal for future occasions; and (4) distribution conduct norms that

expect members to buy the relevant drug(s), to understand the informal and illegal distribution system, and to engage in drug selling on a systematic basis. As illustrated by Johnson's description of the alcohol abuse subculture:

> Alcohol is a powerful psychoactive substance that is widely and legally available in America. . . . Moreover, alcohol is widely used in the conventional middle-class culture as a beverage and as an agent for promoting social interaction and relaxation. Experimentation with alcohol is the rule rather than the exception. The alcohol-abuse subculture, however, has maintenance norms that stress the use of alcohol to get high, smashed, ripped, and to promote inebriating consumption. Reciprocity conduct norms include the pooling of money to buy alcohol, the obligation to buy drinks for others at some time in the immediate future, and bottle passing in drinking groups. Distribution norms include purchasing liquor when younger than the legal drinking age, or selling it to the under-age drinker. For the most part, however, this subculture's conduct norms governing distribution are not well developed because alcohol can be easily and legally obtained; during prohibition, however, illicit distribution conduct norms quickly develop. (1980, p. 116)

### Theoretical Framework of Developmental Stages in Adolescent Drug Involvement: The Gateway Hypothesis

Recognizing that the use of drugs and substances of abuse by children and adolescents followed well-defined stages and sequences in patterns of use as demonstrated by several cohort and longitudinal studies, Kandel (1980a) emphasized that: (1) the position on a particular point in the sequence does not indicate that the child or adolescent would necessarily progress to the use of other drugs higher up in the sequence; and (2) the use of a drug or substance of abuse that is lower in the sequence is a necessary but not a sufficient condition for a child or adolescent to progress to a higher stage indicating involvement with more serious drugs and substances of abuse. From her secondary Guttman scale analysis of data from a cross-section of New York State adolescents ($n = 8,206$) in public high schools, Kandel identified at least four distinct developmental stages of adolescent involvement in using the drugs and substances of abuse: (1) beer or wine; (2) cigarettes or hard liquor; (3) marijuana; and (4) other illicit drugs (see Kandel, 1975; Kandel & Faust, 1975). As described by Kandel (1980a):

> The legal drugs are necessary intermediates between nonuse and marijuana. For example, whereas 27 percent of high school students who had smoked marijuana and had drunk hard liquor progressed to marijuana within the five-month followup period, only two percent of those who had not used any legal substances did so. Marijuana, in turn, was a crucial step on the way to other illicit drugs. While 26 percent of marijuana users progressed to LSD, amphetamines, or heroin, only one percent of nonusers of any drug and four percent of legal users did so. This sequence was found in each of the four years in high school and in the year following graduation. The same steps were followed in regression as in progression in patterns of use within the followup interval. . . . In the absence of other contradictory evidence, the longitudinal analyses of patterns of drug behavior over time that we have conducted and the inferential data provided by other investigators constitute to date strong evidence for the existence of stages in drug use. (pp. 121, 123–124)

The *gateway theory* has been tested by several researchers (e.g., Fergusson, Boden, & Horwood, 2006; Ginzler, Cochran, Domenech-Rodriguez, et al., 2003; Golub & Johnson, 1994; Hall & Lynskey, 2005), including Kandel and her colleagues (e.g., Kandel, Davies, Karus, et al., 1986; Kandel, Yamaguchi, & Chen, 1992; Kandel, Yamaguchi, & Klein, 2006). More recently, Degenhardt, Chiu, Conway, et al. (2009) investigated violations of the gateway hypothesis using a representative sample of the U.S. adult population from the National Comorbidity Survey Replication. Three

violations were examined: (1) cannabis use before alcohol and tobacco; (2) other illicit drug use before alcohol and tobacco; and (3) other illicit drug use before cannabis. As concluded by the researchers:

> Drug use and initiation are clearly nested within a social normative context, yet neither adherence to nor deviation from this order signals highly elevated risks for drug problems in and of themselves although some violations are predictive by pre-existing mental disorders that seem to be more powerful risk factors for subsequent substance dependence. Although a gateway violation might be a marker of such risk factors, their associations with gateway violations are relatively modest. In targeting intervention efforts, if it would probably be more productive to screen directly for these factors (i.e., internalizing disorder, early-onset substances use) than to screen for gateway violations. (p. 4)

The researchers concluded that drug use initiation follows a strong normative pattern, deviations from which are strongly predictive of later problems. By contrast, adolescents who have already developed mental health problems are at risk for deviations from the normative sequence of the initiation of drugs and substances of abuse and for the development of dependence. (See related discussion in Chapter 8, *Dual Diagnosis Among Adolescents*.)

### Deviance Theory: An Explanatory Model

Elliott, Huizinga, and Ageton (1985) advanced *the deviance theory: An explanatory model* extending traditional strain, social control, and social learning theories in an effort to account for the relationship between delinquency and the use of the drugs and substances of abuse. The individual level was the focus for explaining how adolescents become involved in delinquent acts, including the use of the drugs and substance of abuse. (The dependent variable in this causal model is the variation in individual rates of offending.) The extension of the explanatory model to the use of the drugs and substances of abuse was justified by these two assumptions: (1) the use of illicit drugs and substances of abuse may be considered a specific form of delinquent behavior in that their possession involves the violation of criminal statutes and carries the risk of formal legal sanction; and (2) there is considerable empirical evidence that the use of alcohol and marijuana, the most generally used substances of abuse, is a part of a general deviance syndrome that involves a wide range of minor criminal acts and other forms of norm-violating behavior (as noted by Donovan & Jessor, 1984; Elliott & Ageton, 1976; Huizinga & Elliott, 1981; Jessor, Carman, & Grossman, 1968; Jessor & Jessor, 1977a; Kandel, 1980a, b; Kandel, Kessler, & Margulies, 1978a, b; Robins & Murphy, 1967).

A major contribution of Elliott, Huizinga, and Ageton's (1985) explanatory model is the support it has given, through research findings, to the critical role that adolescent friends play in the production of delinquent behavior. Adolescents involved with prosocial friends have a low risk for delinquency, whereas adolescents involved with delinquent friends have a high risk. Unfortunately, although strong bonds to the family and/or school help to diminish the prodelinquent influences of delinquent friends, they do not totally protect adolescents from these influences.

## Family Systems Theories

By the 1970s, attention was focused increasingly on the role of the family in childhood and adolescent use of the drugs and substances of abuse. Several theorists turned their attention to explaining alcohol use and alcoholism using a family systems approach, including Steinglass and his colleagues (e.g., Steinglass, Weiner & Mendelson, 1971a, b), who advanced the *family systems model of alcoholism*, which was later extended as the *interactional model of alcoholism in families* (Steinglass, Davis, & Berenson, 1977) and the simulated *drinking gang experimental model* (Steinglass, 1975).

Other family theorists included Stanton and his colleagues (Stanton, 1977, 1978a, b, c;

Stanton, Todd, Heard, et al., 1978), who addressed heroin use in their *theory of addiction as a family phenomenon*. Later work with Coleman (Stanton & Coleman, 1980) continued the focus on family with the *familial interpersonal system model of addict suicide* (*addict as savior model*), which, reflecting Menninger's (1938) concepts, also addressed families that included heroin addicts and approaches to treatment. Coleman (1980, 1985) and her colleagues (Coleman & Davis, 1978; Coleman & Stanton, 1978a, b) advanced the *incomplete mourning theory*, which addressed the relationship among adolescents who used the drugs and substances of abuse and their family members.

This section presents three theories, including the *incomplete mourning theory*, the *circumplex model of marriage and family systems*, and the *structural family systems theory*.

### Incomplete Mourning Theory

According to Coleman (1980), the use of the drugs and substances of abuse by a family member occurs when an unusual number of traumatic or premature deaths, separations, or losses are experienced within critical or transitional stages of a family's development cycle that are not effectively resolved or mourned by the family. Homeostatic family processes and interlocking transactional patterns of family behavior encourage the use of the drugs and substances of abuse by family members as a means for coping with the overwhelming stress associated with the experience of loss. The use of the drugs and substances of abuse also serves to "keep the using member helpless and dependent on the family"—a process that "unifies and sustains" the family's intactness. However, within the family's complex set of interpersonal relationships is "an overall sense of helplessness, despair, and a lack of purpose or meaning in life" (pp. 83–84).

Early support for the *incomplete mourning theory* can be found in a pilot study that reported an unusually high prevalence of premature, or untimely, deaths among recovering heroin addicts and their families. Additional clinical evidence for the significance of death and death-related issues in addict families was also found in work with siblings of recovering addicts (Coleman, 1978, 1979a, b). A sense of faith, or religiosity, was seen as a major interface between death and the family's adaptive behavior. Thus, it was proposed that a sense of faith either alleviated or exacerbated the sorrow, rage, and guilt that accompany or follow the loss of a loved one (Coleman, 1980).

Clinical findings were supported by statistical evidence that the incidence of death differed significantly across groups, with addicts having a more distinct orientation to death, being more suicidal, and having more premature and bizarre death experiences. It was also noted that during childhood, they had more family separations and developed a unique pattern of continuously separating from, and returning to, their families. In addition, they were found to be less likely to have a clearly defined purpose in life. The incomplete mourning theory also was consistent with systematic research that supported the hypothesis that the use of the drugs and substances of abuse was due to unpredictable, unexpected experiences of death and loss and to structural or functional imbalances in the family. As such, what was needed in order to understand the phenomenon was not a linear, causal model but a "new epistemology" or "cybernetic model" that viewed family relationship patterns and feedback systems as essential to the observed "addictive symptoms" (Coleman, 1980, 1985).

### Circumplex Model of Marriage and Family Systems

Olson and colleagues proposed the *circumplex model of marriage and family systems* (Olson, 1980, 1986; Olson, Russell, & Sprenkle, 1979, 1980; Olson, Sprenkle, & Russell, 1979). The theory reflects a sociological family systems orientation (Olson, Russell, & Sprenkle, 1979, 1980, 1983; Olson, Sprenkle, & Russell, 1979) and addresses general use of the drugs and substances of abuse by adolescents and their

families with attention to these family constructs: adaptability (rigid, structured, flexible, or chaotic), boundaries, coalitions, cohesion (disengaged, separated, connected, or enmeshed), decision making, emotional bonding, members, power structure (assertiveness, control, or discipline), mutual interests, negotiation styles, relationship rules, role relationships, sharing of friends, sharing of recreation, space, stress (developmental or situational), and time.

Of these constructs, two are particularly relevant to understanding marital and family functioning: adaptability and cohesion. Family adaptability is defined as the ability of a marital or family system to change its power structure, role relationships, and relationship rules in response to situational and developmental stress. Family cohesion is defined as the emotional bonding that the family members have toward one another and ranges from disengaged (very low) to separated (low to moderate) to connected (moderate to high) to enmeshed (very high) (Olson, Russell, & Sprenkle, 1983).

The theory was formalized in an unpublished manuscript and tested by Smart, Chibucos, and Didier (1990) and other theorists, who explored the relationship between levels of drug and alcohol use and adolescents' perceptions of family functioning and other individual risk factors. In addition to testing the *circumplex model*, Smart, Adlaf, Porterfield, et al. (1990) showed that their findings could be useful for developing strategies that would decrease or prevent the use of drugs and substances by adolescents. Several researchers have identified an association between extreme family closeness or distance and high levels of adolescent alcohol and drug use and have shown that extreme closeness precipitates drug use, especially alcohol use (e.g., Brook, Lukoff, & Whiteman, 1980). Less clear evidence exists in the literature regarding the relevance of adaptability. For example, Hendin, Pollinger, Ulman, et al. (1981), among others, suggested that levels of alcohol and drug use are higher in rigidly structured, tightly controlled families that allow little deviation or independence (families expected to be low on adaptability). Other theorists concluded that, when comparing families that had members with problematic patterns of alcohol and drug use to those that did not, the latter displayed greater flexibility and adaptability (e.g., Brook, Lukoff, & Whiteman, 1980; Brook, Nomura, & Cohen, 1989a, b; Brook, Whiteman, & Gordon, 1985; Brook, Whiteman, Gordon, et al., 1986).[9]

Smart, Adlaf, Porterfield, et al. (1990) reported clear support for the hypothesis that extreme family functioning is related to a greater risk for adolescent use of the drugs and substances of abuse than are balanced or mid-range functioning. Although adolescents from extreme-functioning families consistently used more alcohol and other psychodepressants, nicotine (tobacco) and other psychostimulants, and marijuana and other psychodelics, it also was found that, except for alcohol, most of the adolescents in their sample did not use the drugs and substances of abuse.

Within extreme-functioning families, the presence or absence of a drinking problem within the family serves generally to increase or decrease the level of risk for using alcohol or other drugs and substances of abuse. Smart, Adlaf, Porterfield, et al.'s (1990) findings were identified as consistent with the view that family variables are important determinants of adolescent use of the drugs and substances of abuse. Other research has substantiated that variables conceptually similar to cohesion (e.g., Barnes, 1984; Barnes & Weite, 1986) and adaptibility (e.g., Pandina & Schuele, 1983) are related to adolescent use of the drugs and substances of abuse.

In regard to other family-related variables, the presence of a drinking problem in the family was found to differentiate adolescent users from nonusers in extreme families.[10] Additional research (e.g., Kandel & Andrews, 1987) suggested the importance of a combination of parental modeling and parental attitudes toward their children.

Family structure proved to be a less important discriminator for adolescent use of the drugs and substances of abuse among extreme-functioning families. Among adolescents from extreme-functioning families who currently used alcohol, there were no differences associated with family structure. However, adolescents from extreme-functioning single-parent families were more likely to have previously used alcohol than those from extreme-functioning families with two parents (both biological or biological and stepparent) present. There are many potential explanations for these results.

For example, perhaps adolescents from single-parent families have more opportunity to experiment with alcohol than do adolescents who live in families with two parents. Richardson, Dwyer, McGuigan, et al. (1989) reported that 8th-grade children who cared for themselves for 11 or more hours a week were at twice the risk for using drugs and substances of abuse as those who did not care for themselves. As concluded by Smart, Adlaf, Porterfield, et al. (1990), adolescents who perceive their families as being extremely high or low on cohesion and adaptability appear to be vulnerable to the use of drugs and substances of abuse as early as 9th grade.

### Structural Family Systems Theory and Hispanic Child and Adolescent Use of the Drugs and Substances of Abuse

Szapocznik, Kurtines, Santisteban, et al. (1990) extended the *structural family systems theory*, as proposed by Minuchin (1974), to the development of a program aimed at the general use of the drugs and substances of abuse by North

---

[9] As noted by Smart, Adlaf, and Porterfield et al. (1990), this ability to adapt flexibly to stress, particularly to stressors from outside the family and over which the family members have little control, may lead to fewer problems related to alcohol and drug use in regard to those stressors.

[10] Although it could not be assumed that the family member with the problem was a parent, previous research has noted the importance of parental modeling on adolescent use of the drugs and substances of abuse (Jessor & Jessor, 1975, 1977a, b).

American children and adolescents of Hispanic descent. Attention also was given to their families. The program, which had been under way since 1970, emphasized the importance of culturally appropriate intervention strategies, including brief strategic and one-person family therapy. As described by Szapoczik, Kurtines, Santisteban, et al. (1990):

> Our program of research . . . provided a solid foundation from which to pursue new advances in the field. For example, the Structural Family System Rating (SFSR) Scale enabled us to evaluate the effectiveness of structural family therapy in a way that is immensely relevant to structural family theory and therapy. . . . Our refinement of structural family theory strategies and goals in the form of brief strategic family therapy (BSFT), in turn, enabled us to understand how to modify these strategies to achieve the same goals without having [the] entire family in therapy, thus making one-person family therapy possible. Our success in bringing about change in family interactions by working primarily through one person became the foundation of our breakthrough in engaging resistant families in treatment. Our findings that changes in family functioning are not necessary for reduction in symptoms has challenged our most basic postulate regarding the relationship between family interaction and symptom change. Although it appears that family therapy "works," our findings raise more questions than they answer about the mechanisms through which family therapy brings about change. (p. 702)

## Role Strain Theory

This section presents one example of *role strain theory* in the explanation of child and adolescent use of the drugs and substances of abuse.

### Role Strain Theory

Winick (1973, 1974a, b, c) advanced the *role strain theory*, a social psychological/sociological theory of the genesis of drug dependence. The theory addressed psychodepressant (i.e., opiate analgesics, sedative-hypnotic), psychostimulant (i.e., amphetamine), and psychodelic use (nonuse, to compulsive use, resumed nonuse, and relapsed use) among adolescents (and adults, including musicians, nurses, and physicians). As defined by Winick (1980) in regard to his theoretical work: "a *role* is a set of expectations and behaviors associated with a specific position in a social system; a *role strain* is a felt difficulty in meeting the obligations of a role; and *role deprivation* is the reaction to the termination of a significant role relationship" (p. 226). Winick hypothesized that: (1) all points of taking on new roles or all points of being tested for adequacy in a role are likely to be related to role strain and, thus, to a greater incidence of drug dependence in a group; (2) incompatible demands within one role, such as between two roles in the role set, are likely to lead to a greater incidence of drug dependence; and (3) the amount of role strain is a function of various factors, so that the larger the volume of properties of a role set, the greater the potential for strain. The theory views relapse as reflecting the adolescent's (or adult's) inability to sustain the role of nonuser.[11]

The theory suggests that the tendency for drug dependence in a population or subgroup will cease when: (1) access to the drugs or substances of abuse declines; (2) negative attitudes to the use of drugs and substances of abuse become salient; and (3) role strain and/or deprivation are less prevalent. If all three of these

---

[11] An earlier formulation of the theory argued that drug-dependent people mature out of the use of drugs and substances of abuse when there is a lessening of the role pressures that had led to the beginning of the regular use of a drug or substance of abuse (Winick, 1962a). The process of maturing out is slow and, typically, involves a stop-start pattern of using a drug or substance of abuse until the person feels comfortable with the role of nonuser. This way of ceasing the use of a drug or substance of abuse was the most frequent, and probably remains the most prevalent, form of terminating the regular use of a drug or substance of abuse. In the original study that led to the formulation of the maturing-out theory, based on a national sample, the mean age of maturing out was 35 years of age (Winick, 1962a). The narrow clustering of age (around 35 years of age) at maturing out in different samples at different times suggested, according to the theorist, that there are underlying regularities in the process.

trends are operative, as opposed to only one or two of the trends, the rate of drug dependence will have a more rapid decline (Winick, 1980).

In order to directly test the predictive ability of the theory, Winick (1974a) developed a role inventory for adolescents, which was administered to 1,311 high school juniors in New York City. As Winick (1980) noted, "There is good reason to expect that the adolescent years will be heavily complicated because of the ambiguity of the status of adolescents in our society, who have lost the role of children but are not yet able to assume an adult role" (p. 227). In a large-scale study of the life cycle of addiction (Winick, 1964), it was concluded that "its genesis was concentrated during the years of late adolescence and early adulthood because of the role strain stemming from decisions about sex, adult responsibility, social relationships, family situations, school, and work, as well as from role deprivation resulting from the loss of familiar patterns of behavior" (Winick, 1980, p. 228).[12] Reflecting the later emphasis of Zoja (1989) on the importance of initiation and ritual[13], Winick (1980), citing his earlier work (Winick, 1968), explained:

> Americans have increasingly been deprived of significant role-related ritual experiences that help in the achievement of an emotional state that could bridge the gap between old and new.

The role-related ritual helped to give meaning to the conclusion of one phase of the life cycle and the commencement of another, providing a sense of community and publicly affirming the subject's social and personal identity and the move from one age and status group to another. As modern American rites of passage have become more subdued, people have had a lesser role identity and less opportunity to develop a sense of self. Insufficiently graded sequences of role positions through which people move may be dysfunctional and could be related to the onset of drug dependence. (p. 229)

## Social Control Theory

One of the most important concepts put forward in regard to understanding the use of drugs and substances of abuse was inherent in the *social control theory*, which was developed during the 1970s by Harding and Zinberg and their colleagues.[14] As explained by Harding and Zinberg, the evidence presented from their theoretical efforts supports the recommendation that theories attempting to explain the use of the drugs and substances of abuse must address drug, set, and setting and that research attention must be given to understanding "how the specific characteristics of the drug and the personality of the user interact and are modified by the social setting and its controls" (Zinberg, 1980, p. 244).

---

[12] According to Winick (1980), many other existing theories of drug dependence among young people can be constructively interpreted in terms of the theory of role strain/deprivation, access, and attitudes, including Finestone (1957; Chicago heroin addicts), Cloward and Ohlin (1960; delinquents), Chein, Gerard, Lee, et al. (1964; New York City addicts), and Jessor and Jessor (1973, 1978; Colorado marijuana users). The theory also can explain the high incidence of drug dependence in a variety of groups: American Indians (see Spindler, 1952), soldiers in Vietnam (see Robins, 1973), college students (see Groves, 1974; Marra, 1967; McKenzie, 1969; Suchman, 1968; Winick, 1973), jazz musicians (see Winick, 1959–1960, 1961b, 1962b), physicians (see Winick, 1961a), and nurses (see Winick, 1974a). The theory has been used successfully to clarify the reason for the increase in drug dependence in the three countries that experienced the most thoroughly documented post–World War II epidemics: Japan, Switzerland, and Sweden.

[13] Interestingly, we have noted a similar observation among adolescents of Aboriginal descent (i.e., First Nations and Inuit Peoples of Canada). Specifically, adolescent girls and boys who are actively involved in traditional ceremonies and rituals (e.g., becoming the bundle holder for the family or clan; participating in traditional cleansing [e.g., smudging or sweat lodge], dancing, drumming, pipe smoking, and womanhood or manhood ceremonies) have fewer, and less severe, problems related to using drugs and substances of abuse than those who are not actively involved in these ceremonies and rituals. We also have seen "bicultural" children and adolescents, living on or off the reserves, thrive as they practice the beliefs, values, and traditions of the dominant Canadian society and those of their Bands and Tribes. (Pagliaro & Pagliaro, *Clinical Patient Data Files*)

[14] See Harding, Zinberg, Stelmack, et al., 1980; Zinberg & Harding, 1979; Zinberg, Harding, Stelmack, et al., 1978; Zinberg, Harding, & Winkeller, 1977; and Zinberg, Jacobson, & Harding, 1975.

### Social Control Theory: Drug, Set, and Setting

Zinberg and Harding (1979) proposed the *social control theory*, which addressed illicit use of the drugs and substances of abuse by adolescents (and adults). Focusing on controlled use, the theorists argued that "the decision to use an intoxicant [i.e., a drug or substance of abuse], the effects it has on the user, and the ongoing psychological and social implications of that use depend not only on the pharmaceutical properties of the intoxicant [the drug] and the attitudes and personality of the user [the set], but also on the physical and social setting in which such use takes place [the setting]" (Zinberg, 1980, p. 236). Attention is given to the precise ways in which the setting influences the use of a drug or substance of abuse—either acting in a positive way to help to strengthen control of use or in a negative way to weaken control. The focus of the theory is on the mechanisms of control (natural processes of social learning) developed within the social setting and the internalization of social sanctions (informal and formal norms defining whether and how a particular drug or substance of abuse should be used, such as "Don't drink and drive") and rituals (stylized, prescribed behavior patterns that surround the use of a drug or substance of abuse, such as "Let's have a drink") and how these mechanisms become active in controlling use.

> Centuries of experience with intoxicants point clearly to social control, not prohibition, as the only humane and reasonably successful means for managing their use. Social control means that a society permits the use of intoxicants under various legal restraints and develops various customs, rituals, and social sanctions which define acceptable use. The elements which comprise social control are often unarticulated and nonspecific, thus allowing for regional, ethnic, and class diversity. From early childhood individuals learn both consciously and unconsciously about the acceptable use of intoxicants. Support for use and reinforcement against abuse continue throughout adult life, as use is normalized with

other life activities. . . . Despite the lack of larger cultural support for controlled illicit drug use and other obstacles, users are able to develop and maintain moderate, long-term, nonabusive, i.e., controlled, drug using patterns . . . primarily supported by the development of social drug-using situations in which sanctions and rituals permit use while condemning abuse. (Zinberg, Jacobson, & Harding, 1975, pp. 165–166)

## Interactive Models

This section presents examples of six theories: the *interactive models of nonmedical drug use (multiple model theory)*; *problem behavior theory: a field theory of problem drinking*; *orthogonal cultural identification theory*; *family interactional theory of adolescent drug use*; *integrative family therapy model*; and *biopsychosocial model of adolescent susceptibility to a substance abuse disorder*.

### Interactive Models of Nonmedical Drug Use (Multiple Model Theory)

The *interactive models of nonmedical drug use,* or *multiple model theory*, proposed by Gorsuch and Butler (1976a, b), emphasized multiple pathways to the use of the drugs and substances of abuse and multiple stages of drug involvement: initial use, continual use, and addiction. The theory assumes that initial use of the drugs and substances of abuse, and the development of continual use and addiction, probably have different causes. Three independent models—(1) the nonsocialized drug users model, (2) the prodrug socialization model, and (3) the iatrogenic model—are proposed. For example, the prodrug socialization model assumes that there are prodrug socializing agents in the child's or adolescent's immediate environment that provide easy access to the drugs and substances of abuse and both the opportunity and models for their use. In contrast, the iatrogenic model explains the primary motivation for initial use of the drugs and substances of abuse as physical pain or mental anguish that leads the child or adolescent to self-prescribe the drug or substance of abuse.[15] In the former, the drug or substance of abuse is used when life is going well; in the latter, when life is going poorly. (See earlier discussion of the *ego-self theory of drug dependence* [*self-medication hypothesis*].)

### Problem Behavior Theory: A Field Theory of Problem Drinking

Jessor and Jessor (1977a, b) advanced the *problem behavior theory*, which was derived from the differential opportunity perspective (Cloward & Ohlin, 1960), field theory (Lewin, 1951; Yinger, 1965), anomie formulations (Merton, 1957), and social learning theory (Rotter, 1954; Rotter, Chance, & Phares, 1972) to explain alcohol and marijuana use as well as other deviant behavior among adolescents. The theory revised and extended the earlier work of Jessor, Graves, Hanson, et al. (1968) and Jessor, Collins, and Jessor (1972) in the Tri-Ethnic Project.

The Tri-Ethnic Project, as summarized by Sadava (1987), studied adolescents of Anglo-American, Ute Indian, and Hispano-American backgrounds living in a small town in Colorado. Jessor, Graves, Hanson, et al. (1968) sought to explain both intergroup differences and intragroup individual differences in deviant behavior within one integrated theoretical framework. Differences in ethnic group rates of problem drinking and other deviant behaviors were explained in terms of a set of group characteristics, a *sociocultural* system. Differences between individual adolescents in problem drinking, other than their group membership, were explained in terms of a set of relevant individual characteristics, a *personality* system. Finally, linkages between characteristics of groups and of individuals were explained

through relevant characteristics and practices of parents, a *socialization* system (the process by which a sociocultural system is transmitted to the adolescent and becomes incorporated within the individual as a personality system). Thus, by a set of logical linkages, person and environment were combined to form a *field theory of problem drinking*.[16] In contrast to subsequent theoretical work (i.e., Jessor, 1985), the environment is conceived and measured as external to the perception of the person.[17] Jessor and Jessor (1977b) describe their theory and its development:

> The study reported in this book is the second phase of a long-term program of research on problem behavior. Like the earlier study [i.e., Jessor, Carman, & Grossman, 1968] from which it grew, it has taken nearly a decade. . . . Initiated toward the end of the 1960s in the midst of the turmoil that marked that period of American history, the research focused on problem behavior in youth—on drug use, sexual activity, drinking and the problem use of alcohol, activism and protest, and deviant behavior generally. Our aim was to see whether a contribution could be made to understanding what was happening among young people by applying the theoretical perspectives developed in our earlier work. That perspective—problem-behavior theory—is from the intersection of the fields of social psychology, developmental psychology, and the psychology of personality. . . . The approach to theory testing involved a longitudinal design, a method that enabled us to follow the lives of young people over a significant portion of their adolescent years. It made possible to plot trajectories of change over time in personality, the social environment, and behavior and to use the theory to forecast important transitions—beginning to drink, starting to use marijuana, becoming a nonvirgin. Thus, in addition to learning more about the areas of behavior that occasioned the study,

---

[15] The term, "iatrogenic", is used to denote conditions or disorders (e.g., substance use disorders) that are the result of the direct actions of a physician or other prescriber—albeit usually inadvertent or unintentional.

[16] As noted by Sadava (1987), extending several theories and a broad literature in developmental psychology, while the concepts and variables were not novel and their individual relationships to problem drinking and deviant behavior were already well established, their integration into a coherent multidisciplinary theory represented a new and significant contribution.

[17] The theory also was later extended by Sadava (1984), Orford (1985), and Tonkin (1987).

it became possible to see them as an integral part of psychosocial growth and development. (pp. xiii–xiv)

Among their results, the theorists conclude:

In relation to the personality system as a whole, the adolescent who is less likely to engage in problem behavior is one who values academic achievement and expects to do well academically, who is not concerned much with independence, who treats society as unproblematic rather than as deserving of criticism and reshaping, who maintains a religious involvement and is more uncompromising about transgressions, and who finds little that is positive in problem behavior relative to the negative consequences of engaging in it. The adolescent who is more likely to engage in problem behavior shows an opposite personality pattern—a concern with personal autonomy, a relative lack of interest in the goals of conventional institutions (such as school and church), a jaundiced view of the larger society, and a more tolerant attitude about transgression.

The most salient finding about the perceived environment system is the powerful contributions it made to the explanation of variation in problem behavior. . . . Within the distal structure of perceived environment, the variables that indicate whether a youth is parent oriented or peer oriented are the most significant. In the proximal structure, the variables referring to peer models and support for problem behavior are most important. Together they suggest the character of a problem-prone environment; adolescents who are likely to engage in problem behavior perceive less compatibility between the expectations that their parents and their friends hold for them, they acknowledge greater influence of friends relative to parents, they perceive greater support for problem behavior among their friends, and they have more friends who provide models for engaging in problem behavior. (Jessor & Jessor, 1977b, p. 237)

### *Orthogonal Cultural Identification Theory*

Oetting and Beauvais (1990–1991), also concerned with the use of drugs and substances of abuse among North American children and

adolescents of Hispanic, as well as American Indian, descent, presented the *orthogonal cultural identification theory*. The theory, they claimed, had several advantages as a model of cultural adaptation over previously proposed sociological models or theories (e.g., alienation; bicultural or transcultural; dominant majority; multidimensional; and transitional models). As argued by Oetting and Beauvais:

Identification with any culture is essentially independent of identification with any other culture. Instead of two cultures being placed at opposite ends of a single dimension or single line, cultural identification dimensions are at right angles to each other. At the origin of the angles is lack of identification with any culture, cultural anomie or cultural alienation. The change from the previous models may appear to be minor, but differences are profound. All of the other models placed limits on what patterns of cultural identification and on what adaptations to change are possible. The orthogonal identification model indicates that any pattern, any combination of cultural identification, can exist and that any movement or change is possible. There can be highly bicultural people, unicultural identification, high identification with one culture and medium identification with another [culture], or even low identification with either culture. (pp. 661–662)

However, in regard to the general results obtained from their research program that focused on the relationship between cultural identification and adolescent use of the drugs and substances of abuse, Oetting and Beauvais (1990–1991) report:

While higher cultural identification seems to be consistently associated with greater personal and social resources, the links to drug use are inconsistent and seem to depend on many other intervening factors. There is no one simple relationship nor is there even one pattern of results that is consistent across groups. . . . It is apparent that if we are to truly understand how cultural identification and drug use are connected, we will have to carefully assess all of the intermeshing links, covering process (the general levels and patterns of identification with the cultures involved), content (covering cultural content including gender roles), peer relationships (links to peers and their behaviors), and environmental factors (such as isolation, epidemiology and access to drugs). (p. 677)

## Family Interactional Theory of Adolescent Drug Use

Brook and her colleagues (Brook, Brook, Scovell Gordon, et al., 1990) proposed the *family interactional theory of adolescent drug use*, an eclectic model for explaining adolescent drug use. The use of marijuana was selected as the paradigm from which the use of other drugs and substances of abuse could be understood. The two-component developmental model emphasized three themes: (1) the extension of developmental perspectives on drug use; (2) the elucidation of family influences leading to drug use, particularly parental influences; and (3) the exploration of factors that increase or mitigate the adolescent vulnerability to drug use. The first component deals with adolescent pathways to drug use, while the second incorporates childhood factors. As described by the theorists:

> Our theoretical model is drawn from a number of conceptual orientations, such as social learning theory, attachment theory, psychoanalytic theory, and deviant behavior proneness. In our framework, which is psychobiologically based, we stress psychological issues while recognizing that growth and development occur on the basis of a biological, species-specific anlage [i.e., foundation of subsequent development]. Such mechanisms as introjection and identification are emphasized because they affect parent-child attachment. Learning is important in the transgenerational passage of values and behavior. The child's attitudes and behavior not only reflect the parent-child interaction but also are influenced by the shaping power of peer group affiliations and influences. This later process is particularly powerful if the peer group sanctions deviant behavior. The consequences of

adolescent marijuana use thus ensue from both earlier and current parent-child relationships and from current peer interactions. . . . The parental peer socialization systems in which children develop interact with and influence each other uniquely. (Brook, Brook, Scovell Gordon, et al., 1990, pp. 119–120).

The model was tested in two studies: (1) a cross-sectional study of 649 college students and their fathers; and (2) a longitudinal study of 429 children and their mothers. The subjects were given self-administered questionnaires containing scales measuring the personality, family, and peer variables relevant to the model. The results of each study supported the proposed model, with some differences between parental influences. The theorists noted that individual protective factors (e.g., adolescent conventionality and parent-child attachment) could offset risk factors (e.g., peer drug use) and enhance other protective factors, resulting in less adolescent marijuana use. As noted by Brook, Brook, Scovell Gordon, et al. (1990), the result of their studies has implications for prevention and treatment, future research, and public policy.

## Integrative Family Therapy Model

The *integrative family therapy model* was developed by Natakusumah, Irwanto, Piercy, et al. (1992), extending the work of Olson, Sprenkle, and Russell, et al. (1979). Natakusumah, Irwanto, Piercy, et al. (1992) examined the family dimensions of cohesion and adaptability and the relationship of these constructs to substance use severity among American and Indonesian families of adolescent substance users. They were specifically concerned with studying the perceived levels of cohesion and adaptability of the individual members of these families, the manner and extent to which they differed from one another, and the extent to which their adaptability and cohesion were related to substance use severity. The third version of the Family Adaptability and Cohesion Evaluation Scale (FACES III) was used as a cross-cultural measure of family functioning. As described by Natakusumah, Irwanto, Piercy, et al. (1992):

> The development of the various versions of FACES is theoretically based on the *Circumplex Model of Family Functioning* developed by Olson, Sprenkle, Russell, et al. (1979). . . . This model postulated three important dimensions of family functioning: cohesion (the emotional bonding among family members), adaptability (flexibility of family structure, role relationships, and family rules), and communications (how family members relate to each other). FACES III measures the dimensions of cohesion and adaptability. (p. 391)

Inherent in the model is the assumption that it is optimal for a family to have a balance of cohesion between the extremes of enmeshment and disengagement and a balance of adaptability between the extremes of rigidity and chaos. However, the validity of this curvilinear hypothesis, as well as its cross-cultural consistency in regard to nuclear versus extended families, has been questioned by several researchers, including those who argue for a linear relationship for cohesion and adaptability—that is, the greater the cohesion and adaptability displayed by a family, the better is its functioning. Thus, Natakusumah, Irwanto, Piercy, et al. (1992) also sought to test its generalizability with culture as the independent variable.

The American adolescents who used drugs and substances of abuse were much more likely to see their families as disengaged (60% versus 5%), while Indonesians were more likely to see their families as either balanced (separated or connected) or enmeshed. These findings suggest some possible interventions within the two cultures. The *integrative family therapy model* that Natakusumah, Irwanto, Piercy, et al. (1992) developed for substance-abusing American adolescents strongly emphasized getting parents involved with their children again. In this regard, an attempt is made to decrease family disengagement by putting

parents back in charge of their adolescent children. More culturally appropriate goals should take precedence with Indonesian adolescent substance abusers, such as involving extended family members in treatment (p. 406). In addition, while 17% of the Indonesian adolescents saw their families as being enmeshed (i.e., the extreme end of cohesion), the theorists were hesitant to consider this finding as necessarily dysfunctional within the culture. "In a close-knit family system, as in Indonesia, family enmeshment may indeed be a positive characteristic that prevents adolescents from using drugs" (p. 406).

Adaptability was not found to predict the severity of substances use for Indonesian or American adolescents. However, cohesion had predictive power in both samples, although to a lesser extent in the American sample. The finding that family cohesion was related to substance use severity in these samples supports the link between close family relationships and substance use patterns among adolescents.

### Biopsychosocial Model of Adolescent Susceptibility to a Substance Abuse Disorder

The *biopsychosocial model of adolescent susceptibility to a substance abuse disorder* was proposed by Muisener (1994). The model presents five possible levels of causal interacting factors that increase an adolescent's susceptibility to developing a substance abuse disorder:

1. Biological factors—genetic, neurological, and idiosyncratic physiological factors.
2. Adolescent psychological developmental factors.
3. Interpersonal relationship factors—family functioning and peer factors.
4. Community factors—schools, churches, criminal justice systems, prevention services and programs.
5. Societal factors—government policies and media.

Of these factors, the adolescent psychological development factors and interpersonal relationship factors are seen as the most important.

According to Muisener (1994), as the toxic agent—the drug or substance of abuse—penetrates all five factor levels, what is manifested is the adolescent substance abuse disorder. The interaction of the drug or substance of abuse with the adolescent's biological, psychological, and social systems can culminate in an addiction process—a process that simultaneously infiltrates every aspect of the young person's life. As further explained by Muisener, the addiction process unfolds across three stages—initiation, escalation, and maintenance—and is composed of three dynamics: (1) compulsion—the driving urge to obtain, use, and continue to use drugs and substances of abuse (i.e., the central addiction dynamic); (2) relapse, which involves four stages—immediate determinants stage, crossroads stage, breaking of abstinence stage, and abstinence violation coping stage; and (3) denial—the systems and processes that most immediately and directly diminish the awareness of the use of the drugs and substances of abuse and their adverse effects. Together, these three addiction dynamics can be understood as having biopsychosocial expressions as symbolized in this metaphor:

> The growing teenager is represented by an apple tree in an orchard. This tree is in the season of blossoming and is on the threshold of bearing fruit. A fire, like the toxic agent drugs, becomes a predator of the maturing tree. The origin of this fire—whether matches, or heat friction, or some random synergy of elements—cannot be easily determined. How this sprouting tree resists or succumbs to the fire is, in part, reflective of its overall combustibility—analogous to the adolescent's intrapsychic structure. Depending on this young tree's overall combustibility, it may be able to withstand the fire or be susceptible to severe burns. The endogenous constitution of the wood of the tree—similar to the biological factors of addiction—may, in part, contribute to the flourishing of the fire. The cluster of other trees surrounding the apple tree is similar to the teenager's interpersonal environment of family and peers. By fueling the fire, this cluster of surrounding trees may enable the fire to continue much in the way that family and peers can enable an adolescent's continued substance abuse. Larger environmental elements, within and beyond the orchard—climate and weather conditions—can encourage or impede the burning of the tree just as community and society factors can enable the teenagers continued chemical abuse. The addiction dynamics of compulsion, relapse, and denial also resemble some dynamics of this fire. Compulsion is akin to the driving symbiosis between the burning fire and the apple tree, relapse is analogous to smoldering roots of the tree that can reignite a later fire, and denial is similar to the smoke that billows from the fire, engulfing the tree so as to obscure awareness of the extent of the fire. The interplay of all of these factors will determine if the apple tree experiences only minor charring, much like a substance use problem, or suffers extensive fire damage, similar to a substance abuse disorder. (pp. 56–57)

According to the theorist, few adolescents progress to serious patterns of use. However, those who do usually require external intervention in order to regress to a less serious pattern of use or discontinue use all together. Adolescents rarely experience spontaneous remission or practice self-prescribed abstinence for any length of time. Thus, Muisener, for these reasons and because he rejects the arguments of maturing out, natural recovery, or growing out of harmful patterns of use, proposed an extension of his biopsychosocial model for recovery-oriented treatment of adolescent substance abuse. This model considers multiple and interacting systems that may require treatment and the multiple and interacting interventions that can be used. As emphasized by Muisener (1994), the possible factors that contribute to adolescent substance abuse can become "a part of the solution" (p. 99).

Muisener's recovery-oriented treatment embraces a hybrid combination of treatment approaches that integrate biomedical and mental health approaches with those offered by AA and other 12-step self-help programs—for example, Al-Anon for family members, including teens of alcoholics; Alateen for teens with alcoholic parents; and Family Anonymous. Muisener (1994) provides the Adolescent Chemical Use Problem Index as a tool to assist in identifying an adolescent's substance use problem so that his or her difficulties can be dealt with effectively. The model also provides guidelines for promoting recovery among vulnerable adolescents (e.g., adolescents who have a dual diagnosis [see Chapter 8, *Dual Diagnosis Among Adolescents*] or who have been victims of physical or sexual abuse) for whom treatment seeks to "bring awareness, growth and developmental insight" so that they may "thrive in recovery" (p. 198).

### Economic Theory: Advertising

Over the last decade, theoretical focus on the availability of alcohol and tobacco cigarettes has received increased attention, as did the relationship of media influences on their initial use by children and adolescents. We begin with alcohol advertising.

### *Alcohol Advertising*

A related theoretical direction is that of advertising. Recognizing that exposure to alcohol advertisements appears to have little influence on drinking among middle adolescents, Collins, Ellickson, McCaffrey, et al. (2007) sought to determine whether early adolescents were more vulnerable to alcohol marketing. Two in-school surveys were completed with 1,786 South Dakota 6th-grade students.

As noted by the researchers, "This is the youngest sample that has been studied longitudinally." In addition, as described by Collins, Ellickson, McCaffrey, et al. (2007):

We also look at a wider variety of advertising than any previous study. Guided by the general framework of the Elaboration Likelihood Model of persuasion, we allowed for advertising influences through both high-attention information-processing and more automatic, minimally attentive processes. (p. 2)

The researchers found that exposure to alcohol advertisements in magazines, beer advertisements on television, in-store beer displays and beer concessions, radio-listening time, and owning beer promotional items during 6th grade was strongly predictive of drinking during 7th grade and grade 7 intentions to drink. The researchers also found that youth in the 75th percentile of alcohol marketing exposure had a predicted probability of drinking that was 50% higher than that for youth in the 25th percentile. Thus, while the limitations of their research was acknowledged, it was recommended that policy makers consider restricting marketing practices that could contribute to early adolescent drinking.

Anderson, de Bruijn, Angus, et al. (2009) assessed the impact of alcohol advertising and media exposure on future alcohol use among adolescents using a systematic review of longitudinal studies, published between 1990 and September 2008, that were identified using MEDLINE, Cochrane Library, Sociological Abstracts, and PsycLIT databases. For inclusion, studies were required to assess participants' exposure to: (1) commercial communications and media; and (2) alcohol drinking behavior at both baseline and at follow-up. The researchers also were interested in studies that included receptivity of attitudes to alcohol advertising, or brand awareness, and individual drinking behavior. Participants were adolescents, 18 years of age or younger. Thirteen longitudinal studies were identified that followed up a total of over 38,000 youth who met the inclusion criteria. The researchers concluded that alcohol advertising and promotion (e.g., giveaways and items bearing alcohol industry logos) increases the likelihood that adolescents will initiate alcohol use and that they will to drink more if they already are alcohol drinkers.

### Tobacco Advertising

The extent to which tobacco marketing and tobacco use in films contributed to the use of tobacco by children was approached by Wellman, Sugarman, DiFranza, et al. (2006) in their meta-analysis of published studies obtained from systematic searches of Medline, PsychInfo, and other databases as well as unpublished studies solicited from selected researchers. Of 401 citations initially identified, 51 met the inclusion criteria for participants younger than 18 years of age. Main exposures (i.e., tobacco advertising, promotions, samples, and pro-tobacco depictions in films, television, and videos) were categorized as low or high engagement based on the degree of psychological involvement required. Outcomes were categorized as cognitive (attitudes or intentions) or behavioral (initiation, tobacco use status, or progression of use). The researchers found that exposure to pro-tobacco marketing and media increases the odds of youth holding positive attitudes toward tobacco use and more than doubles the odds of initiating tobacco use. Highly engaging marketing and media are more effective in promoting use (Wellman, Sugarman, DiFranza, et al., 2006). The strength of their results led them to conclude that pro-tobacco marketing and media encourage tobacco use among youth, and, thus, "a ban on all tobacco products is warranted to protect children" (p. 1285).

## Contemporary Sociological Themes in Theoretical Development

Contemporary theoretical work in sociology includes the increased use and testing of previously published theories and preliminary research leading to new theory development.

For example, theoretical development in sociology has turned to defending itself from accusations of theoretical indifference in regard to the study of child and adolescent use of the drugs and substances of abuse and the need for defining related terms and phrases (e.g., the problem of addiction) within the social context (e.g., Adrian, 2003).

From the anthropological perspective, Bruehl, Lende, Schwartz, et al. (2006) contributed to the qualitative understanding of craving with the results of their study, which used in-depth interviews of 82 active methamphetamine users from the metropolitan Atlanta, Georgia, area. Using grounded theory and the constant comparative method to analyze their data, they found that the narrative responses corresponded with three types of craving: cue, drug, and withdrawal-induced craving—as leading to methamphetamine use, individually or together with the same context or situation. Participants in the study also described being able to overcome craving through personalized methods of control.

Acculturation theory also received attention in a study by De La Rosa (2002), who reviewed the published literature examining acculturation among Latino adolescents in regard to traditional European American cultural values and its effect on their use of drugs and substances of abuse—particular their mental well-being. The paper also examined the limitations of the published research and proposed the development of acculturation scales that focus on measuring the role that predominant Latino and American attitudes, values, and norms play in the development of various patterns of using the drugs and substances of abuse among Latino adolescents. A conceptual framework is proposed to account for the impact of acculturation-related stress and the mitigating factors affecting such stress on the use of the drugs and substances of abuse by Latino adolescents. As emphasized by De La Rosa, "understanding the effects of acculturation-related stress and accompanying mitigating factors could begin to explain the increasing high rates of substance use reported for Latino adolescents" (p. 1).

In an earlier use of acculturation theory, Epstein, Botvin, and Diaz (2001) examined the relationship between linguistic acculturation and the use of alcohol, marijuana, and tobacco smoking among Hispanic 6th and 7th graders in 22 New York City middle schools (mean age 13 years). At baseline assessment and at one-year follow-up, children who spoke English with their parents were found to smoke marijuana more frequently than those who spoke Spanish with their parents. At a 1-year follow-up, students who spoke English with their parents and bilingual students who spoke English and Spanish with their parents had increased levels of polyuse of the drugs and substances of abuse than those who only spoke Spanish with their parents.

As part of a larger study aimed at understanding the link between acculturation and the use of drugs and substances of abuse by Hispanic/Latino adolescents, Wagner, Ritt-Olson, Soto, et al. (2008) conducted focus groups with adolescents ($n$ = 16; 68% girls; mean age, 14 years) and their mothers ($n$ = 18; mean age, 42 years). Adolescents and their mothers agreed on some areas, such as pride in ethnic identity. However, they disagreed on others, such as ideas of freedom and independence. Interestingly, they did not endorse the association between acculturation and substance use that had been reported in quantitative studies.

Finally, Unger, Ritt-Olson,Wagner, et al. (2009), studying 1,683 Hispanic students in the 9th and 10th grades living in southern California, evaluated the hypothesis advanced by acculturation theory, which predicts that conflicting cultural preferences between adolescents and their parents increases the adolescents' risk for developing behavior problems, including the use of the drugs and substances of abuse. Increases in parent-child Hispanic acculturation discrepancy—the difference between the adolescents' own cultural orientations and their perceived parental cultural orientations, with adolescents perceiving that their parents wanted them to be more Hispanic oriented than they actually were—for sampled 9th and 10th grade students were associated with an increased risk for using the drugs and substances of abuse. These findings led the researchers to suggest that family-based interventions for acculturating Hispanic families may be of benefit for decreasing the likelihood of the use of drugs and substances of abuse by Hispanic adolescents (i.e., a group of North Americans who often have significantly elevated rates of using the drugs and substances of abuse). (See related discussion in Chapter 1, *The Psychodepressants;* Chapter 2, *The Psychostimulants*; and Chapter 3, *The Psychodelics.*)

## CHAPTER SUMMARY

This chapter has highlighted many of the theories that have been advanced since the 1960s to explain child and adolescent use of the drugs and substances of abuse. These theories have been developed by researchers, educators, and clinicians from the three major disciplines of biology, psychology, and sociology. As claims to fact, these theories reflect the basic assumptions and research methods embraced by these disciplines.

While theories have been produced individually as well as produced or extended pluralistically and eclectically, no single theory currently available, or group of theories from a single scientific discipline, has been able to completely explain or account for why some children and adolescents use the drugs and substances of abuse while others do not. However, each of the presented theories accounts for at least some of the observed behavior—even if from diametrically opposing, and often conflicting, theoretical perspectives. What is becoming clear, after more than a century of related theory development, is that, in the end, most likely several theories—produced individually or produced and extended plural-istically and eclectically—will be needed to explain why children and adolescents use, or do not use, the various drugs and substances of abuse. Although reflecting decidedly different reasons for use, they will surely depend on: (1) the drug or substance of abuse involved; (2) the characteristics of the users; and (3) the context of use.

My worthy friend, all theories are gray,
And green alone Life's golden tree.
—Johann Wolfgang von Goethe
*1749–1832*

# CHAPTER 5

# *Exposure to the Drugs and Substances of Abuse From Conception Through Childhood*

## INTRODUCTION

This chapter discusses exposure to the drugs and substances of abuse from conception through childhood. We begin at the beginning, with embryonic and fetal exposure associated with the maternal use[1] of the drugs and substances of abuse during pregnancy—the prevalence of which is increasingly observed among adolescent girls and young women of reproductive age. The exposure of neonates and infants to the drugs and substances of abuse by mothers who are breast-feeding is then considered with attention to human studies only.[2] To assist readers, a comprehensive table is presented that identifies average concentrations of the drugs and substances of abuse that are excreted in human breast milk, expected effects on maternal breast-feeding (e.g., reduced milk production), and the related negative effects that may be observed among

breast-fed neonates and infants (e.g., decreased milk consumption).

The exposure of infants and children to passive, or secondhand, smoke[3] is then discussed. For this form of exposure, the major vectors are mothers, fathers, or others living in the family household;[4] babysitters; day-care workers; and teachers who smoke various drugs and substances of abuse in the presence of the infant or child, including: cocaine base (crack); methamphetamine (crystal meth, ice); tobacco (nicotine) cigarettes; or opiate analgesics, including black tar heroin and prescription opiate analgesics, such as oxycodone (OxyContin®).

Finally, this chapter concludes with a brief overview and discussion of unintentional childhood poisonings. In regard to this form of exposure, specific focus is given to unintentional poisonings that involve each of the three classes of the drugs and substances of abuse:

---

[1] We have deliberately selected the more general term "use" rather than other terms that denote increasingly harmful patterns of use (e.g., abusive use, compulsive use) because relatively little data are available that specifically correlate patterns of using the drugs and substances of abuse with teratogenesis or fetotoxicity. In this regard, it also is important to recognize that for some drugs and substances of abuse that are used during pregnancy—even patterns of use that are not harmful for the mother (e.g., an occasional drink of alcohol in a social context)—may result in devastating effects for the developing embryo, fetus, neonate, and infant. (See related discussion later in this chapter.) Similar rationale applies for mothers who use the drugs and substances of abuse and breast-feed their neonates and infants.

[2] Although published data are available regarding the prevalence and characteristics of these potentially harmful effects involving mothers across the reproductive age span (i.e., from menarche to menopause), specific data involving pregnant adolescent girls (10 to 20 years of age) and those who are breast-feeding are relatively scant. However, these data are included whenever possible.

[3] Smoke, by definition, is simply a gas, or mixture of gases (e.g., in the case of air, primarily oxygen, nitrogen, and carbon dioxide) in which common pollutants, or particulate matter (e.g., in regard to the air we breathe, allergens, dust, and pollen) are suspended. Active products of drugs and substances of abuse are also released into smoke together with the products formed by pyrolysis.

[4] For a detailed overview of the exposure of infants and children to the drugs and substances of abuse by older siblings and peers, see Chapters 1, *The Psychodepressants*, 2, *The Psychostimulants,* and 3, *The Psychodelics*.

the psychodepressants; the psychostimulants; and the psychodelics.

## EMBRYONIC AND FETAL EXPOSURE DURING PREGNANCY: TERATOGENESIS AND FETOTOXICITY

Maternal use of the drugs and substances of abuse, both those that are obtained illicitly and those that are obtained by prescription—an increasing area of concern—are considered in regard to their effects on the developing embryo and fetus. Particular attention is given to the potential of these drugs and substances of abuse for teratogenesis[5] and fetotoxicity[6] when used by mothers during pregnancy. It is estimated that teratogenesis occurs among 2% to 3% of all live births (Centers for Disease Control and Prevention [CDC], 2006) and that their associated effects, which can be acute and self-limiting, or chronic and irreversible, account for 20% of all deaths that occur during the first 5 years of life (Pagliaro & Pagliaro, 1996, 2002).The majority of teratogenic effects are due to unknown causes. However, for *known* causes, genetic aberrations (e.g., having an extra copy of chromosome 13, 18, or 21) are most often implicated (Brent, 2004). Although drugs, including the drugs and substances of abuse, account for only 1% to 2% of all teratogenic effects (Pagliaro & Pagliaro, 2002), their consideration is extremely important because the associated effects are largely preventable and often irreversible.

The use of the drugs and substances of abuse by adolescent girls and young women increased significantly over the last decade (Substance Abuse and Mental Health Services Administration, 2010; Wang, 2010), as did the rate of pregnancy. The reported live birth rate for 15- to 19-year-old adolescent girls is 42 per 1,000 population, which resulted in 435,436 live births for this age cohort in the United States in 2006 (CDC, 2009). In addition, the data for 2006, which was based on 100% of all birth certificates registered in the United States, indicated that the birth rate for adolescent girls increased significantly (i.e., 4%) in that year (following a 14-year decline from 1991 to 2005) and that this increase occurred across the entire country (Martin, Hamilton, Sutton, et al., 2009).

Although all adolescent girls and young women do not become pregnant, nor do they all use the drugs and substances of abuse, many do become pregnant and many do use the various drugs and substances of abuse. Of increasing concern to obstetricians, pediatricians, pediatric nurse practitioners, psychologists, social workers, and other health and social care professionals is the fact that increasing numbers of adolescent girls and young women who become pregnant also use the drugs and substances of abuse during their pregnancy. Although affecting North American adolescent girls of all continental descents, particular concern has been noted in regard to adolescent girls of American Indian and Canadian Aboriginal descent (Barlow, Mullany, Neault, et al., 2010). These adolescent girls have higher pregnancy rates than do their cohorts of other continental descents. They also comprise a higher percentage of children and adolescents that have significantly higher

---

[5]The word "teratogen" is derived from the Greek words *terato*, meaning "monster," and *genesis*, meaning "origin" or "beginning." While originally concerned with severe physical defects or malformations (e.g., hypospadias, phocomelia, spina bifida), the term is now used for any physical or mental abnormalities that may occur during embryonic or fetal development. Some of these abnormalities, although developed in utero, may not be fully displayed until later childhood (e.g., behavioral and learning deficits associated with the fetal alcohol syndrome/fetal alcohol spectrum disorder—see later discussion in this chapter; also see Chapter 6, *Effects of the Drugs and Substances of Abuse on Learning and Memory During Childhood and Adolescence*).

[6]"Fetotoxicity," or fetal toxicity, is defined as any adverse drug reaction that may be displayed by the fetus/neonate as a consequence of maternal use of the drugs and substances of abuse.

rates of using the drugs and substances of abuse (e.g., alcohol, cannabis, cocaine, and methamphetamine) (Beauvais, Jumper-Thurman, & Burnside, 2008; Pagliaro & Pagliaro, 2009).

As noted over two decades ago in a survey conducted for the National Association for Perinatal Addiction Research and Education:

> Eleven percent of all American babies are born with evidence of drug exposure. We know that we are seeing just the first few months and years in the lives of an entire generation of children who are maimed and deformed physically, emotionally, and mentally by the drug addictions of their mothers. We will be mourning for decades if not generations the waste of human and financial resources that these children represent. (Gore, 1991, p. 99)

Although some drugs and substances of abuse, including alcohol and the barbiturates, have been strongly implicated in producing teratogenic effects, health and social care providers need to recognize that others have not been strongly implicated. For example, both cannabis and lysergic acid diethylamide (LSD) have been incorrectly identified as being particularly harmful teratogens, when, in fact, very little credible, supportive evidence has been accumulated in this regard. It also is important to recognize that the use of drugs and substances of abuse by pregnant adolescent girls and young women of reproductive age, even those drugs and substances of abuse that are known teratogens (e.g., alcohol), does not always result in human teratogenesis—generally because of the absence of requisite cofactors. (See the section "Factors Affecting Teratogenic Risk of the Drugs and Substances of Abuse" later in this chapter for related discussion.)

This section provides an overview and summary of the current published studies that have positively implicated, or that have failed to implicate, the drugs and substances of abuse as teratogens when they are used during pregnancy. Although related animal studies are more widely available than are human studies, attention is given solely to human data. This exclusive focus on human data is deliberate because of the inherent difficulties associated with extrapolating research findings from animal studies to humans. These difficulties include determining the physiologic and genetic differences in teratogenic susceptibility between various animal species and humans and establishing comparable

- Doses.
- Stages of pregnancy.
- Environmental conditions.
- Ages.
- Levels of maternal health (Hemminki & Vineis, 1985; Hoyme, 1990; Nau, 1986; Pagliaro & Pagliaro, 2002, 2009).

A classic example of the difficulties associated with the extrapolation of the results of animal studies to humans is the thalidomide tragedy. When thalidomide, a sedative-hypnotic, was tested using several pregnant rodent species, no teratogenic effects were noted. However, when thalidomide was prescribed to women to treat their anxiety and insomnia during the first trimester of pregnancy, devastating teratogenic effects (i.e., phocomelia, or major limb reduction) were produced among offspring (Knapp & Lenz, 1963; Lenz, 1962; McBride, 1961; Mellin & Katzenstein, 1962).[7]

---

[7] Although thalidomide was withdrawn from North American and European markets because of its associated severe teratogenic effects, it continued to be used in many other parts of the world, including Africa and South America (Teixeira, Hojyo, Arenas, et al., 1994). Amid some degree of controversy, it was reapproved for use in North America in 1998 for the treatment of several medical disorders, including leprosy and multiple myeloma (Glasmacher, Hahn, Hoffmann, et al., 2006; Rajkumar, 2004).

TABLE 5.1   FDA Pregnancy Codes

| Code | Level of Risk | Supportive Evidence |
|---|---|---|
| A | Controlled studies show no risk | Adequate, well-controlled studies in pregnant women have failed to demonstrate a risk to the fetus in any trimester of pregnancy. |
| B | No evidence of risk in humans | Adequate, well-controlled studies in pregnant women have not shown increased risk of fetal abnormalities despite adverse findings in animals, or, in the absence of adequate human studies, animal studies show no fetal risk. The chance of fetal harm is remote, but remains a possibility. |
| C | Risk cannot be ruled out | Adequate, well-controlled human studies are lacking, and animal studies have shown a risk to the fetus or are lacking as well. There is a chance of fetal harm if the drug is administered during pregnancy, but the potential benefits may outweigh the potential risk. |
| D | Positive evidence of risk | Studies in humans or investigational or postmarketing data have demonstrated fetal risk. Nevertheless, potential benefits from the use of the drug may outweigh the potential risk. For example, the drug may be acceptable if needed in a life-threatening situation or with serious disease for which safer drugs cannot be used or are ineffective. |
| X | Contraindicated in pregnancy | Studies in animals or humans or investigational or postmarketing reports have demonstrated positive evidence of fetal abnormalities or risk that clearly outweigh any possible benefit to the patient. |

Source: L. A. Pagliaro & A. M. Pagliaro (Eds.). (2002). Chapter 2, Drugs and human teratogens and fetotoxins (p. 97). In *Problems in Pediatric Drug Therapy* (4th ed.). Washington, DC: American Pharmaceutical Association.

## Prevalence of Drug and Substance Use During Pregnancy

As noted by Schwarz, Postlethwaite, Hung, et al. (2007): "In the United States, women of reproductive age [including adolescents] receive 11.7 million prescriptions for potentially teratogenic class *D* or *X* medications each year" (p. 370)[8]. (See Table 5.1.)

Similarly, in their retrospective study of over 1 million prescriptions filled in California for adolescent girls and women between 15 and 44 years of age, Schwarz, Postlethwaite, Hung, et al. (2007) found that 1 out of 6 received a prescription for a Food and Drug Administration (FDA) pregnancy category *D* or *X* drug. Of these prescriptions, many were for drugs and substance of abuses, including:

- The barbiturates (i.e., henobarbital [Luminal®] secobarbital [Seconal®])

- The benzodiazepines (i.e., diazepam [Valium®], Estazolam [ProSom®], Oxazepam [Serax®], Temazepam Restoril®], Triazolam [Halcion®])
- The miscellaneous sedative-hypnotic meprobamate (Equanil®)

As noted by Keegan, Parva, Finnegan, et al. (2010): "Substance abuse in pregnancy has increased over the past three decades in the United States, resulting in approximately 225,000 infants yearly with prenatal exposure to illicit substances" (p. 175).

The extent of drug and substance use by adolescent girls and women who are pregnant appears to be determined primarily by such factors as age, race, and socioeconomic status (Cornelius, Richardson, Day, et al., 1994; Jorgensen, 1992; Wheeler, 1993).[9] However, it also has been associated with the mother's experience of physical and sexual abuse during

---

[8] Table 5.1 presents the five categories developed and used by the Food and Drug Administration to categorize and classify teratogenic risk for drugs that are available by prescription in the United States, including several of the drugs of abuse.

[9] Other factors also may play a significant role. For example, among a large statewide sample of both pregnant and nonpregnant women from Alabama, positive urine screens for illicit drugs and substances of abuse varied according to obstetrical history. These data indicated a linear increase in the percentage of positive urines in direct correlation with the number of reported abortions and premature births (Pegues, Engelgau, & Woernle, 1994).

childhood (Pagliaro & Pagliaro, 2009). (Also see related discussion in Chapter 8, *Dual Diagnosis Among Adolescents*.)

The Mental Health Administration (2006) estimated that approximately 47% of pregnant women in the United States use the drugs and substances of abuse, including cannabis, cocaine, heroin, methamphetamine, and methylenedioxymethamphetamine (MDMA, ecstasy).[10] Unfortunately, a reliable estimate of the exact nature and extent of drug and substance use among pregnant adolescent girls and young women of reproductive age is not available. There are many reasons for this paucity of data, including the fact that many drugs and substances of abuse are obtained illegally, stolen from a parent's supply, bought from a dealer at school, or supplied by a boyfriend or girlfriend. Thus, their use is often carefully hidden and deliberately underreported.[11]

## Factors Affecting Teratogenic Risk

In order to better identify and confirm the teratogenic risk associated with the maternal use of a particular drug or substance of abuse during pregnancy, attention also must be given to possible relevant cofactors. These cofactors include:

- Maternal factors
- Placental factors
- Fetal factors
- Environmental factors

- Drug or substance of abuse factors (Pagliaro & Pagliaro, 1996, 2002)

(See Figure 5.1.)

### *Maternal Factors*

Maternal factors include the mother's age and overall health and well-being at the time of conception and throughout the normal progression of pregnancy and uncomplicated delivery. Thus, these factors include the stage of pregnancy and the presence or absence of concomitant medical disorders (e.g., epilepsy; gestational diabetes; human immunodeficiency virus (HIV) and other infections; preeclampsia; thyroid disorders) and psychological disorders (e.g., major depressive disorder; schizophrenia). They also include the mother's use of the various drugs or substances of abuse and the: (1) associated pattern of use (e.g., social use, abusive use); (2) specific characteristics of use (e.g., amount used, frequency of use, method of use); and (3) related teratogenic risk. (See "Drug or Substance of Abuse Factors.")[12]

### *Placental Factors*

Placental factors include the:

- Size and thickness of the placenta
- Placental blood flow
- Ability of the placenta to metabolize the drug and substance of abuse to an inactive, active, or teratogenic metabolite

---

[10] As noted by Zimmerman (1991), "the addictive properties of psychoactive drugs lead individuals to increase usage, both frequency and dose, which lead to varying degrees of toxicity to themselves and, if pregnant, their offspring" (p. 541).

[11] Maternal use of the drugs and substances of abuse raises a potential plethora of legal and ethical issues (Fasouliotis & Schenker, 2000; Flagler, Baylis, & Rodgers, 1997; Mahowald, 1992; Mohaupt & Sharma, 1998). As noted by Garcia (1993), "Some policies have pitted mothers against their fetuses and children ... new paradigms [are required] to minimize conflict and to achieve just and therapeutic balances between the rights and needs of those involved" (p. 1311). McCormack (1999) reviewed the appellate process and Canadian constitutional law related to a prototypical case that involved a young Aboriginal woman who was pregnant and ordered by the court to remain in a drug treatment program at a health center until the baby was born (p. 77). As noted by Harris and Paltrow (2003) in their review of related cases involving U.S. criminal law: "Women were generally charged with 1 of 3 types of crimes: (1) child endangerment/abuse; (2) illegal drug delivery to a minor; or (3) fetal murder/manslaughter" (p. 1697). We will not attempt to address, let alone resolve, these issues here. However, our focus remains, as it has been throughout our professional lives, on optimizing the health and well-being of both pregnant women and their developing fetuses and neonates. In addition, it has been found that adolescents who use drugs and substances of abuse while pregnant are significantly more likely to neglect, physically abuse, or sexually abuse their newborns and infants.

[12] Polyuse of the drugs and substances of abuse is relatively common and include such combinations of use as alcohol and cannabis, cocaine and oxycodone, caffeine (coffee) and nicotine (tobacco cigarettes), and LSD and MDMA.

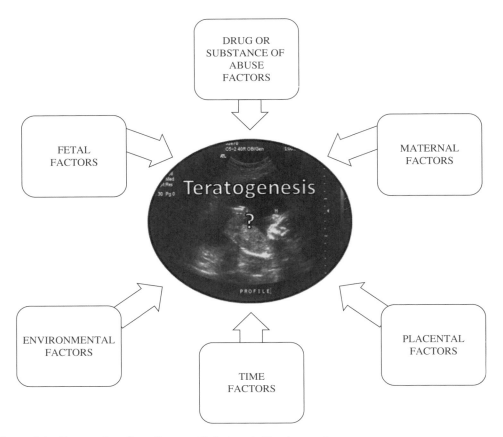

**Figure 5.1   Factors that Contribute as Cofactors to Teratogenesis**

- Placental age
- Placental endocrine function
- Ability of the placenta to transport nutrients, and the drugs and substances of abuse, from the maternal circulation to the fetal circulation (Goodman, James, & Harbison, 1982; Pagliaro & Pagliaro, 2002; Sastry, 1991)

### Fetal Factors

Fetal factors include:

- Fetal age, or the state of fetal development
- Maturity of the fetal hepatic metabolic enzyme systems
- Amount of blood flow through the fetal liver
- Fetal blood pH
- Fetal genetic predisposition
- Concomitant fetal exposure to other potential teratogens (Pagliaro & Pagliaro, 2002)

### Environmental Factors

Environmental factors include factors that may promote or adversely affect fetal development. Factors that promote maternal health and fetal development include:

- Availability of nutritional sources of dairy products, meats, poultry, and vegetables
- Clean drinking water
- Warmth and shelter
- Safety from physical injury or other harm
- Appropriate prenatal care

Factors that may adversely affect maternal health and fetal development include:

- Inadequate nutrition
- Ingestion of food additives (e.g., aspartame, nitrates)
- Contact with pesticides (e.g., chlordane)

- Poor air and water quality, including pollutants
- Exposure to radiation and other toxins (e.g., mercury, organic solvents)
- Unsafe and violent living conditions
- Lack of prenatal care

### Drug or Substance of Abuse Factors

The drug or substance of abuse factors include:

- Purity
- Availability and cost
- Basic physical chemistry (e.g., degree of ionization, lipid solubility, molecular weight)
- Pharmacokinetics (i.e., the amount absorbed into the maternal circulation, or concentration in blood, plasma, or serum; distribution throughout the body [e.g., intracellular, extracellular, and other body water compartments]; metabolism and excretion; and concentration that is free or non–protein bound at the placenta)
- Pharmacology (i.e., the expected pharmacological effects as a psychodepressant, psychostimulant, or psychodelic) and associated adverse effects and toxicities, including teratogenic potential

See Figure 5.2 for an illustration of the effect of the size, ionization, and protein binding of drugs and substances of abuse and their corresponding ability to cross the placenta from the maternal circulation to the fetal circulation (Pagliaro & Pagliaro, 2002).

### Time Factors

Of the five factors identified as being involved in producing a teratogenic effect, an often overlooked factor is time. As a factor, time is particularly important because of the concept of organogenesis (Figure 5.3, Table 5.2) (Pagliaro & Pagliaro, 2002). In this regard, there is a critical period of greatest teratogenic susceptibility. Although this critical period of susceptibility varies slightly among different organ systems, teratogenic effects associated with the production of physical malformations generally occur during the first trimester, or first 3 months of pregnancy. It is anxiomatic but important to note that physical teratogenic effects will not occur if exposure to a known teratogen happens after organogenesis is complete. For example, the maternal use of diazepam (Valium®) during pregnancy has been implicated in cleft palate anomaly. (See later discussion in this chapter.) However, this teratogenic effect would not occur if maternal use of diazepam occurred after the fusion of the fetal palate. Thus, when evaluating the teratogenic potential of a particular drug or substance of abuse, it is essential to identify: (1) if the drug or substance of abuse, or one in the same class, is a known teratogen (i.e., has been implicated in producing human teratogenic effects); (2) the stage of embryo and fetal development at which time the exposure to the drug or substance of abuse occurred; and (3) if exposure to the drug or substance of abuse was within the critical period of greatest teratogenic susceptibility.

## Teratogenic Potential of the Drugs and Substances of Abuse

The teratogenic potential of the various drugs and substances of abuse are presented and discussed in the next sections. The use of any drug or substance of abuse during pregnancy always involves some degree of risk to the developing embryo or fetus. Therefore, regardless of how safe a drug or substance of abuse appears to be, or is reported to be, it should not be used during pregnancy unless it is clearly indicated and only when the benefits of its use outweigh its potential risks for harm to both the mother and the developing embryo or fetus. Adolescent girls and young women who are pregnant or who are considering becoming pregnant should limit their use of all drugs and substances of abuse—whether they are licit or illicit, prescription or nonprescription. If the use of a particular drug

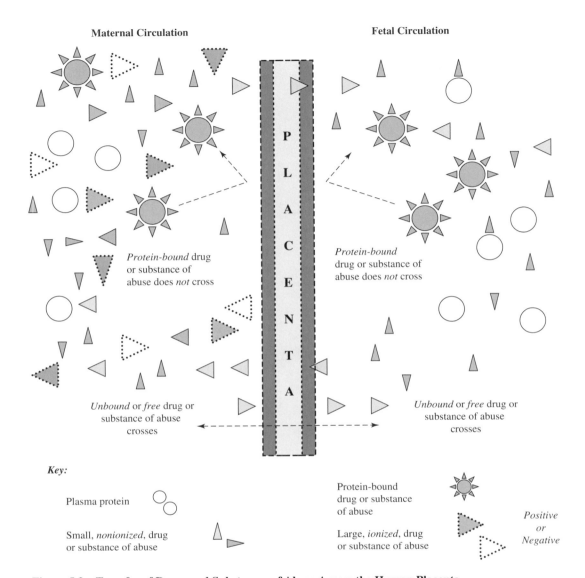

**Figure 5.2   Transfer of Drugs and Substances of Abuse Across the Human Placenta**
Note: Both the concentration of plasma protein and the protein-binding capacity may be significantly different between mother and fetus.

or substance of abuse has been discontinued, focus should turn to preventing resumed use, or relapse. Adolescent girls and women who abusively or compulsively use a drug or substance of abuse should, following medically supervised withdrawal, be referred to treatment programs aimed at promoting resumed nonuse of the drug or substance of abuse and preventing relapse.

The next section, organized according to major pharmacological classification (i.e., psychodepressants, psychostimulants, and psychodelics—see Chapter 1, *The Psychodepressants*; Chapter 2,

*The Psychostimulants*; and Chapter 3, *The Psychodelics*), discusses the teratogenic potential of the various drugs and substances of abuse. When a history of the maternal use of the drugs and substances of abuse is unknown, unclear, or questionable, confirmation by means of neonatal screening may be appropriate as described at the conclusion of this section. (Also see Table 5.3.)

### Psychodepressants

The psychodepressants include alcohol and other sedative-hypnotics, opiate analgesics,

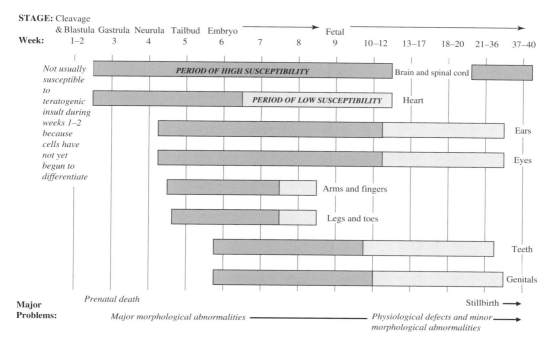

**Figure 5.3    Gestational Teratogenic Susceptibility**
Note: Average time from fertilization to parturition is 38 weeks.
Modified from: A. M. Pagliaro & L. A. Pagliaro, 2000; L. A. Pagliaro & A. M. Pagliaro, 1979, 1995).

and volatile solvents and inhalants. Of particular note is the fact that, of all the drugs and substances of abuse, the psychodepressants, when used by pregnant adolescent girls and young women, are associated with the highest incidence of teratogenesis and the most clinically significant teratogenic effects.

**Alcohol and other Sedative-Hypnotics**    In addition to alcohol, the sedative-hypnotics include the barbiturates, benzodiazepines, Z-drugs, and the miscellaneous sedative-hypnotics, such as the date-rape drug gamma-hydroxybuturate (GHB); meprobamate (Equanil®); and the knock-out drops, chloral hydrate (Noctec®). Of all of the drugs and substances of abuse used by adolescent girls and young women, data accumulated over the last 50 years support a particularly strong and significant teratogenic risk for alcohol. Thus, a much more comprehensive discussion of alcohol is included in this section because of its high risk as the most common and significant

teratogen responsible for causing diverse birth defects and neurological injury, which result in serious long-term effects—both physical and mental—for neonates, infants, children, and adolescents.

*Alcohol*    Alcohol (ethanol, ethyl alcohol) is a known human teratogen. As such, it has the potential to adversely affect the physical and neurological development of all embryos and fetuses of mothers who drink alcohol during their pregnancies (Chiriboga, 2003; Goodlett, Horn, & Zhou, 2005; Pagliaro & Pagliaro, 1996, 2002). In fact, the fetal alcohol syndrome (FAS) or fetal alcohol spectrum disorder (FASD) (see later discussion) is well recognized as the leading preventable cause of mental retardation and associated neurobehavioral and developmental abnormalities worldwide (Banakar, Kudlur, & George, 2009; Pagliaro & Pagliaro, 2009). Once ingested and absorbed into the maternal bloodstream, alcohol readily crosses the placental barrier into the amniotic fluid and fetal

TABLE 5.2    Human Gestational Development

| Time After Fertilization | Developmental Stage | Daily Developmental Activity |
| --- | --- | --- |
| 1st month (Days 1–28) | *Cleavage stage (Days 1–3)* | Day 1: Fertilization and first cell division occur. Day 2: 2 cells appear and then 4 cells. Day 3: Morula (16 cells) forms. |
| | *Blastula stage (Days 4–6)* | Day 4: Early blastocyst (58 cells) forms. Day 5: Free blastocyst (107 cells) forms. Day 6: Attachment occurs. |
| | *Gastrula stage (Days 7–13)* | Day 7: Implantation occurs. Day 8: Bilaminar disc forms. Day 9: External embryonic mesoderm forms. Day 10: Primary yolk sac forms. Days 11–13 : Secondary yolk sac lined by endoderm forms; primitive streak begins. |
| | *Primitive streak stage (Days 14–19)* | Days 14–17: Primitive streak becomes half length. Day 18: Intra-embryonic mesoderm forms. Day 19: Primitive streak is completed. |
| | *Neurula stage (Days 20–28)* | Day 20: Presomite neurula forms; yolk sac becomes visible; neural plate and neural groove form. Days 21–22: Neural folds form; heart tube forms; intra-embryonic vessels start to form; head fold encloses foregut; cloacal membrane tail fold encloses hindgut; occipital somites (1–4) form; embryonic epidermis forms. Day 23: Tail fold progresses. Days 24–26: Cervical somites (5–12) form; rhombencephalic folds close; neural tube starts to form. Day  27: Thoracic somites (13–20) form; thalamus starts to form; urachus starts to form; otic disc and vesicle start to form; optic vesicle starts to form; oral membranes start to form; heart tubes fuse and loop; laryngo-tracheal groove forms; pharyngeal pouches form; hepatic diverticulum forms; primary brain vesicles form; nephrogenic cord forms; nephric ducts form. Day 28: Thoracic somites (21–24) form; tongue primordia develop; Rathke's pouch (anterior pituitary gland) forms; thyroid rudiment forms; heart begins to beat; neural tube closes; crown-rump length 4–5 mm. |
| 2nd month (Days 29–56) | *Tailbud stage (Days 29–35)* | Day 29: Lumbar somites (25–27) form; appendicular ridges appear. Day 30: Lumbar somites (28–29) form; visceral arches become well separated. Day 31: Sacral somites (30–32) form; limb buds start to form; optic cup appears; otic cup appears; pancreatic diverticula form; midbrain flexure forms; spinal nerve roots form. Day 32: Sacral somites (33–34) form. Day 33: Caudal somites (35–36) form. Day 34: Caudal somite (37) forms; greater curvature of stomach appears. Day 35: Caudal somites (38–44) form. |
| | *Embryo stage (Days 36–56)* | Days 36–39: Somite formation ends; tailbud regresses; aortico-pulmonary septation occurs; cardiac muscle begins to form; hemopoiesis begins in liver; dental laminae form; primitive nasal septum forms; pontine flexure forms; nerve plexus forms; cerebellum begins to form; intramembraneous ossification begins; chondrification begins; Mullerian ducts begin to form; urethral plate begins to form; secondary bronchi begin to form. Day 40: Hand plate appears; umbilical hernia begins to form. Days 41–42: 3rd and 4th visceral arches become covered by operculum; cervical flexure of head onto chest appears; pentadactyl rudiment appears. Days 43–44: Cervical sinus closes. Days 45–47: Urorectal septum appears; median processes of maxillaries begin to form; premaxilarly processes start to form; sex differentiation begins. Day 48: Premordial germ cells become visible. |

TABLE 5.2   (Continued)

| Time After Fertilization | Developmental Stage | Daily Developmental Activity |
|---|---|---|
| | | Day 49: Testes begin to form in males. Days 50–51: Facial clefts begin to close. Days 52–53: Phalanges and first links appear; fingers and toes become visible. Days 54–56: Origin of submandibular, parotid, and sublingual glands begin to develop; external ear begins to form; large umbilical hernia becomes visible; smooth muscle begins to develop; Mullerian ducts fuse to form utero-vaginal rudiment in females; primary follicles begin to develop in females; embryo assumes recognizable human appearance; crown-rump length ~24–34 mm; weight ~1 gram. |
| 3rd month (Weeks 9–12) | *Fetal stage (9–38 weeks)* | Week 9: Finger- and toenail formation begins; testes begin to descend in males; crown-rump length ~41 mm. Week 10: Eyelids become fused; permanent tooth buds form; bones ossify; distinctive external genitalia appear; hematopoiesis begins in bone marrow; periderm plug forms in nostrils; periderm plug forms in ears; Islets of Langerhans form; epidermis formation becomes complete; thyroid gland formation becomes complete; lung formation becomes complete; gallbladder secretes bile; brain formation becomes essentially complete to that of the neonate. Week 11: Respiratory movement begins. Week 12: Crown-rump length ~50–70 mm, weight ~15–20 grams. |
| 4th month (Weeks 13–16) | | Week 13: Gender becomes recognizable. Weeks 14–15: Skeleton becomes visible on X-ray; vernix becomes visible; myelination occurs; mesenteries become well-formed; metanephros (permanent kidney) formation becomes complete to that of the neonate; heart formation nears completion; hematopoiesis begins in spleen; Sylvian fissure in the brain becomes visible. Week 16: Cerebral parenchymal layering observed; meconium begins to collect in bowel; crown-rump length ~155 mm; weight ~165 grams. |
| 5th month (Weeks 17–20) | | Lanugo appears on body; hair forms on head; fetal movements begin to be detected by mother; crown-rump length ~185–210 mm; weight ~200–310 grams. |
| 6th month (Weeks 21–24) | | Fetal outline becomes palpable; dentine and enamel begin to form; eyebrows and lashes become well defined; pulmonary alveoli form; skin appears red and wrinkled; usually nonviable if born; crown-rump length ~220–240 mm; weight ~635–720 grams. |
| 7th month (Weeks 25–28) | | Cornification of epidermis surface layer occurs; eyelids open; periderm plugs in nostrils disappear; periderm plugs in ears disappear; testes approach scrotum in males; ovaries shift from dorsal to more caudal location within pelvis in females; brain sulcus formation observed in various locations including the central sulcus and occipital lobe; viable if born (good chance of survival with proper care); crown-rump length ~345 mm; weight ~1350 grams. |
| 8th month (Weeks 29–32) | | Calcium storage begins; deep sulcation observed in the entire cerebral cortex; fat becomes deposited subcutaneously; viable if born (good chance of survival with proper care); crown-rump length ~395 mm; weight ~1800 grams. |
| 9th month (Weeks 33–36) | | Sulcation of the brain complete; brain ventricles reduce in size; body rounds out; skin wrinkles smooth out; dull redness of skin fades; calcium storage continues; iron storage begins; viable if born; crown-rump length ~445 mm; weight ~2400 grams. |
| 10th month (Weeks 37–40) *Average time from fertilization to parturition: 38 weeks* | | Body becomes plump; labia majora come in contact in females; nails extend to tips of fingers and toes; skin loses lanugo coat; vernix caseosa becomes deposited on skin surface; testes usually appear in the scrotum in males; upper limbs become slightly longer than lower limbs; crown-rump length at term (~38 weeks) ~470 mm; weight ~3400 grams. |

Modified from Pagliaro & Pagliaro, 2002.

TABLE 5.3    Criteria for Neonatal Urine Testing Following Delivery

**Criteria for Adolescent Mother, Neonate, and Others Present at Birth**

**Adolescent mother**

- Displays signs and symptoms of intoxication or withdrawal
- Displays abusive or otherwise disruptive behavior

Has a history of:

- No, or inadequate, prenatal care (e.g., prenatal care is infrequent, fewer than 5 visits, or initiated after 28 weeks)
- Undocumented prenatal care, or prenatal care obtained in clinics accessed in areas characterized by a high incidence of drug and substance use
- Alcohol, cocaine, heroin, marijuana, methamphetamine; or other drug and substance use anytime during the antepartum period or any physical evidence suggesting drug or substance use (e.g., needle marks; nicotine stains on fingertips or teeth; hepatitis; HIV infection; missing front teeth; nasal septum erosion; clothes smelling of volatile solvents or inhalants) or other behavior (e.g., signs and symptoms of overexcitement or hyperstimulation, drowsiness or oversedation, hallucinations)
- Previous birth of an infant maternally exposed to drugs and substances of abuse
- Enrolment or participation in a drug or substance of abuse treatment program
- Residing with a husband, boyfriend, or other family members who use drugs and substances of abuse
- Prostitution
- Sexually transmitted diseases, including HIV infection
- Multiple abortions or stillbirths, placenta abruptia, placenta previa, precipitous delivery, premature rupture of the membranes, or premature births
- Poor maternal weight gain during pregnancy

**Neonate[a]**

Neonate displays:
- Abnormal neurobehavioral activity: high-pitched cry; hyperreflexia; irritability; extreme drowsiness
- Common signs of the expected pharmacological effects of specific drugs and substances of abuse or a particular neonatal withdrawal syndrome
- Microcephaly
- Prematurity
- Observable teratogenic effects associated with drugs and substances of abuse commonly used by adolescent girls (e.g., displays craniofacial characteristics of FAS/FASD, see Figure 5.4)
- Small for gestational age (SGA)

**Father of neonate, grandparent, or other family member of friend present prior to delivery, at birth, or postpartum**

- Displays signs and symptoms of intoxication or withdrawal
- Displays abusive or otherwise disruptive behavior

[a] Usually several of the listed criteria are present among neonates born to mothers who use drugs and substances of abuse during pregnancy.

Note: These criteria may be used to assist health and social care providers to determine the need to test a neonate's urine for drugs or substances of abuse that may have been used by his or her mother toward the end of the third trimester or prior to her hospital admission for delivery.

Modified from Bays, 1992; Pagliaro & Pagliaro, 2002.

circulation. There it can be found in significant concentrations, even after the maternal ingestion of just a single, moderate dose or amount of alcohol. Alcohol is eliminated from the amniotic fluid and fetal circulation at a rate that is only one-half that of its elimination from the maternal circulation. Thus, following its total elimination from the maternal circulation, it remains for a prolonged period in the amniotic fluid and fetal circulation.

Many adolescent girls and young women drink quantities of alcohol that are known to be potentially harmful to their unborn babies (CDC, 2004a; Cornelius, Richardson, Day, et al.,

1994; Substance abuse, 1994). It is estimated that approximately 1 out of every 3 or 4 fetuses are exposed to the harmful effects of alcohol by mothers who drink during pregnancy (Pagliaro & Pagliaro, 1996, 2002).[13] Among pregnant adolescent girls admitted for the treatment of a substance use disorder (SUD) in the United States during 2007, 20.3% reported alcohol as their primary drug and substance of abuse (Substance Abuse and Mental Health Services Administration, 2010). In addition, it has been reported that: (1) more than 50% of adolescent girls and young women who did not use birth control and thus could become pregnant drank alcohol; (2) more than 12% of these adolescent girls and young women engaged in binge drinking; and (3) of these adolescent girls and young women known to be pregnant, 10% drank alcohol and approximately 2% engaged in binge drinking (CDC, 2010d). For adolescent girls or young women who either smoked tobacco or who were 18 to 24 years of age, these percentages were significantly higher (Tsai, Floyd, Green, et al., 2007).

*Fetal Alcohol Syndrome (FAS)*    The harmful effects associated with the maternal ingestion of alcohol during pregnancy have been long recognized[14] (i.e., Pagliaro & Pagliaro, 1995). However, its specific teratogenic effects on physical and mental development were not formally identified as comprising FAS until the early 1970s (Jones & Smith, 1973, 1975; Lemoine, Harousseau, Borteyru, et al., 1968). Subsequently, these specific developmental characteristics have been identified and have been used to diagnose FAS among neonates, infants, and children. (See Table 5.4.) These characteristics include, in particular, certain craniofacial features. (See Figure 5.4.) Although

the characteristic features of FAS vary among affected neonates, infants, and children and can present difficulties in clinical diagnosis (Little, Snell, & Rosenfeld, 1990), their consistent clinical application has been found to be generally reliable in identifying or diagnosing the syndrome (Abel, Martier, Kruger, et al., 1993).

In addition to the use of these characteristic features, the Fetal Alcohol Study Group of the Research Society on Alcoholism established a consensus case definition for FAS (Pagliaro & Pagliaro, 1996, 2002) that includes three major criteria:

1. Prenatal and/or postnatal growth retardation (i.e., weight and/or length or height below the 10th percentile when corrected for gestational age)
2. Central nervous system (CNS) involvement, including neurological abnormality, developmental delay, behavioral dysfunction or deficit, intellectual impairment and/or structural abnormality (e.g., microcephaly [head circumference below 3rd percentile] or brain malformation found on neuroimaging studies or autopsy)
3. Characteristic facial features qualitatively described as including short palpebral fissures, an elongated midface, a long and flattened philtrum, a thin upper lip, and a flattened maxilla. (See Figure 5.4.)

Currently, many clinicians use the 4-digit diagnostic criteria developed by Astley (2004) (see Table 5.5). These criteria assist in making the diagnosis of fetal alcohol spectrum disorder (FASD) more valid and reliable (also see the discussion of FASD in this chapter).

---

[13] This statistic is similar to that reported in several other countries. For example, it is generally agreed that FAS, a totally preventable condition, is currently the leading cause of mental retardation and neurobehavioral deficits in North America (Pagliaro & Pagliaro, 1996, 2002). This statistic also is true for several other countries. For example, Lamy and Thibaut (2010), in their review of French data, found that FAS is the major cause of mental retardation in France.

[14] For example, references to harmful effects associated with the use of alcohol by women who are pregnant can be found throughout recorded history, including the Old Testament of the Bible (i.e., the book of Judges 14:4).

TABLE 5.4  Prevalence of Abnormalities Associated with FAS

| Category | Abnormality | Incidence (Approximate Percentage of Occurrence) |
|---|---|---|
| Growth | Prenatal growth deficiency (i.e., SGA; height and weight ≤ 10th percentile) | 100 |
| | Postnatal growth deficiency (i.e., SGA; height and weight ≤ 10th percentile)[a] | 100 |
| Development | Developmental delay | 100 |
| | Fine-motor dysfunction | 80 |
| Craniofacies (facial features) | Short palpebral fissures (i.e., ≤ 3rd percentile) | 100 |
| | Microcephaly | 91 |
| | Maxillary hypoplasia | 64 |
| | Epicanthal folds | 36 |
| | Micrognathia | 27 |
| | Cleft palate | 18 |
| Body organ anomalies | Capillary hemangiomata | 36 |
| | Cardiac anomalies | 70 |
| | External genitalia anomalies | 36 |
| Limb anomalies | Altered palmar crease pattern | 73 |
| | Joint anomalies | 73 |

[a] May not persist and, in many cases, corrects toward normal as the infant matures through childhood.
Source: Original list from Jones & Smith, 1973; Hanson, Jones, & Smith, 1976) has been expanded by several other authors (e.g., Pagliaro & Pagliaro, 1996; Rosett, 1980; Sokol & Clarren, 1989) to account for additional features (e.g., asymmetrical or low-set ears; flat, smooth, or absent philtrum; hypoplastic, flat midface; short, up-turned nose; and thin vermilion of the upper lip) commonly identified by other researchers (e.g., Astley & Clarren, 1996, 2000; Clarren & Smith, 1978; Haddad & Messer, 1994; May, Gossage, Smith, et al., 2010).

Appropriate caution, knowledge, and clinical skills still must be used to differentiate FAS/FASD from other syndromes (e.g., Brachman-de Lange syndrome, fetal anticonvulsant [i.e., phenytoin; valproate] syndrome, maternal phenylketonuria-induced fetal effects, toluene embryopathy [also see the related discussion later in this chapter], and William's syndrome) that have overlapping diagnostic features.

The incidence of FAS/FASD in North America varies among cultural, ethnic, racial, and socioeconomic groups (Spagnolo, 1993), likely because of genetic polymorphisms (Warren & Li, 2005) or epigenic mechanisms (Haycock, 2009), with the highest incidence generally reported among North Americans of African or American Indian descent. (See Table 5.6.) The incidence of FAS/FASD appears to increase directly in relation to the magnitude of alcohol use by adolescent girls and women during pregnancy (Eliason & Williams, 1990;

May, McCloskey, & Gossage, 2000). However, its actual incidence is difficult to specify for a number of reasons, including: (1) unreliability of self-reports of maternal drinking (i.e., consistently biased underreporting); (2) qualitative and quasi-experimental research designs (e.g., case report, retrospective studies, convenience sampling) that do not provide population statistics; and (3) possible confusion, or overlap, with published fetal alcohol effects (FAE) and FASD research findings (Remkes, 1993; Wallace, 1991).

Even with these limitations in mind, it is distressing to note that several researchers have estimated the incidence of FAS/FASD as having significantly increased in the racially and socioculturally diverse population of the United States over the past several decades (e.g., from 0.5 to 2 cases per 1,000 live births during the 1980s and 1990s [May & Gossage, 2001][15] to 2 to 7 cases per 1,000 live births

[15] The CDC (1997) calculated lower estimates of FAS during this time period (i.e., 0.2 to 1.0 per 1,000 live births).

**Eyes**
 1. ptosis (drooping lid)
 2. strabismus (squint)
 3. shortened palpebral fissure
    (opening between eyelids)
 4. epicanthal fold

**Ears**
 5. smaller or larger than normal,
    malformed, or low-set

**Nose**
 6. low nasal bridge
 7. short with high or
    upturned nasal tip

**Mouth**
 8. philtrum (groove in upper lip):
    underdeveloped or absent
 9. micrognathia (small jaw) or
    retrognathia (posteriorly
    displaced jaw)
 10. teeth: absent enamel,
    malformed, or maloccluded
 11. wide mouth
 12. thin vemilion border of
    upper lip

**Head**
 13. microcephaly (small head size)
 14. abnormally shaped cranium
 15. midface hypoplasia (broad, flat face)
 16. marrow receding forehead

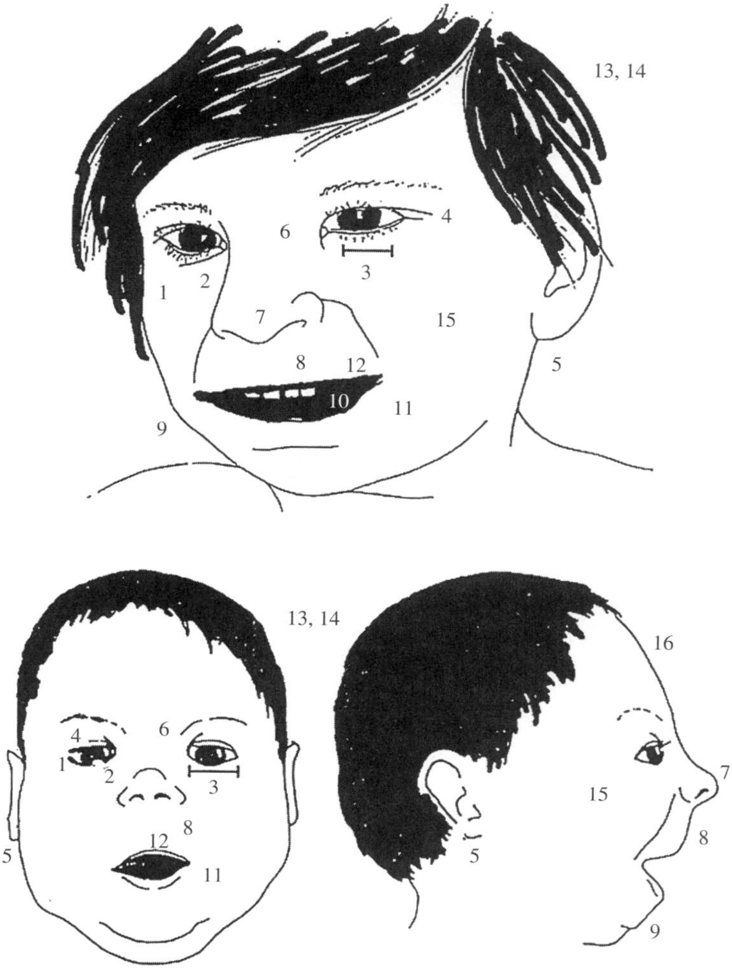

**Figure 5.4    Craniofacial characteristics of FAS/FASD[16]**

Reproduced with permission from: A. M. Pagliaro & L. A. Pagliaro (1996), Chapter 3, Prenatal exposure to substances of abuse (p. 111). In, *Substance use among children and adolescents: Its nature, extent, and effects from conception to adulthood*. New York, NY: John Wiley & Sons.

during the 2000s [May, Gossage, Kalberg, et al., 2009]).

*Fetal Alcohol Effects and Other Related Disorders*    "Fetal alcohol effects" is a term that is used to identify neonates, infants, and children who exhibit fewer of the characteristics deemed necessary, by definition or convention, to establish a diagnosis

of FAS (Caruso & Bensel, 1993; Ginsberg, Blacker, Abel, et al., 1991; Smitherman, 1994). Other diagnostic labels and definitions also have been suggested in this regard in the published clinical literature, including alcohol-related birth defects (ARBD) and alcohol-related neurodevelopmental disorder (ARND) (Harris, Os-born, Weinberg, et al., 1993; Jacobson, Jacobson, Sokol, et al.,

---

[16] Source: Pagliaro & Pagliaro, 2000.

TABLE 5.5   Four-Digit Diagnostic Code for FASD

| Rank | Growth Deficiency | FAS Facial Phenotype | CNS Damage or Dysfunction | Gestational Exposure to Alcohol |
|---|---|---|---|---|
| 4 | **Significant** Height and weight below 3rd percentile | **Severe** All 3 features: 1. Palpebral fissure length 2 or more standard deviations below mean 2. Thin lip: Rank 4 or 5 3. Smooth philtrum: Rank 4 or 5 | **Definite** Evidence of structural or neurological involvement | **High risk** Confirmed exposure to high levels |
| 3 | **Moderate** Height and weight below 10th percentile | **Moderate** Generally 2 of the 3 FAS features | **Probable** Significant dysfunction across 3 or more domains | **Some risk** Confirmed exposure although level of exposure is unknown or less than that for Rank 4 |
| 2 | **Mild** Height and weight at or above 10th percentile | **Mild** Generally 1 of the 3 FAS features | **Possible** Evidence of dysfunction, but less than that for Rank 3 | **Unknown** Exposure not confirmed as present or absent |
| 1 | **None** Height and weight at or above 10th percentile | **Absent** None of the 3 FAS features | **Unlikely** No structural, neurological, or functional evidence of impairment | **No risk** Confirmed absence of exposure from conception to birth |

Source: Astley, 2004, as modified by Chudley, Conry, Cook, et al., 2005.

1993; Sampson, Streissguth, Bookstein, et al., 1997; Sokol & Clarren, 1989; Stratton, Howe, & Battaglia, 1996). We have, for several decades, strongly discouraged the use of these diagnostic labels and definitions, arguing that neonates, infants, and children who display fewer or more specifically clustered classic characteristics of FAS simply have less or more severe forms of FAS and not a different syndrome (e.g., Pagliaro & Pagliaro, 1987, 1995, 1996).

We continue to argue that this approach for diagnosing FAS:

- More accurately reflects the anticipated normal distribution of FAS among affected neonates, infants, and children in the general population and its subpopulation groups
- More completely indicates the extent of FAS in the general population
- More fully represents the nature and characteristics of FAS

- More clearly identifies that even low to moderate drinking during pregnancy places exposed embryos and fetuses at significant risk for FAS
- Better identifies the relationship among possible cofactors in the development of FAS and its severity (see Figure 5.1)
- Increasingly encourages the development of more rational and comprehensive prevention strategies and treatment programs aimed at promoting the optimal development of neonates, infants, and children who are affected by maternal alcohol use.

To this end, we have been very pleased with the currently more common use of the diagnostic nomenclature "fetal alcohol spectrum disorder (FASD)," which is more reflective of the variability in the type and severity of neurobehavioral deficits induced by maternal alcohol use during pregnancy (Goodlett, Horn, & Zhou, 2005).

TABLE 5.6   Reported Incidence of FAS

| Country (Ethnic or Racial Group) | Incidence per 1,000 Live Births | Reference Source |
|---|---|---|
| Canada (Aboriginal Peoples) | 190 | Robinson, Conry, & Conry, 1987 |
| | 100 | Square, 1997 |
| | 25–46 | Asante & Nelms-Matzke, 1985 |
| USA (Alaska Natives) | 3–5 | Egeland, Perham-Hester, Gessner, et al., 1998 |
| USA (American Indians) | 5–30 | May, 1991 |
| | 10 | May, Hymbaugh, Aase, et al., 1983 |
| | 4–8 | Duimstra, Johnson, Kutsch, et al., 1993 |
| | 3 | Chavez, Cordero, & Becerra, 1988 |
| USA (mixed) | 1.3 | Bertucci & Krafchik, 1994 |
| | 2–7 | May, Gossage, Kalberg, et al., 2009 |
| | 2 | Abel, 1995 |
| | 1 | Rosett, Weiner, Lee, et al., 1983 |
| | 0.5–2 | May & Gossage, 2001 |
| | 0.3 | Shoemaker, 1993 |
| Europe (mixed) | 2–3 | Hill, Hegemier, & Tennyson, 1989 |
| Western World (mixed) | 1–2 | Clarren & Smith, 1978 |
| | 0.3–0.6 | Abel & Sokol, 1991 |
| Worldwide (mixed) | 2 | Abel & Sokol, 1987 |

*Long-Term Sequelae of FAS/FASD*   The physical and psychological developmental deficits that are generally associated with FAS/FASD do not end in infancy but persist into childhood, adolescence, and throughout adulthood (Pagliaro & Pagliaro, 2009; Smitherman, 1994; Spohr, Willms, & Steinhausen, 1993, 2007). Unfortunately, even with early identification and intervention, "The growth and neurological disabilities associated with alcohol consumption in pregnancy persist even when the child grows up in a good home" (Karp, Qazi, Hittleman, et al., 1993, p. 101). For example, behavioral problems, including a higher incidence of attention-deficit/hyperactivity disorder (A-D/HD), conduct disorder, and externalizing behavior (e.g., acting out, aggressiveness, delinquency, hostility) (Bada, Das, Bauer, et al., 2007; Pagliaro & Pagliaro, 2002; Sood, Delaney-Black, Covington, et al., 2001) are not easily managed with pharmacological and/or psychological intervention. (Also see Chapter 8, *Dual Diagnosis Among Adolescents*, for further related discussion.) While the lifelong effects of FAS/FASD require increased attention, greater focus on prevention of the disorder and its treatment is

required. In this regard, we have long concurred with Streissguth, Randels, and Smith (1992) that, for infants and children affected with FAS/FASD and their parents and caregivers, realistic expectations for performance during childhood and adolescence is much more likely to result in: (1) the availability of more appropriate educational and health care services; (2) less frustration; and (3) improved behavioral outcomes during later adolescence and adulthood.

*Screening*   The diagnosis of FAS/FASD is particularly challenging because it must involve confirmation of maternal alcohol use, and, as previously noted, approximately 40% of mothers who drink during their pregnancies deny doing so. Thus, significant research efforts have been directed at finding a valid and reliable biological marker that can confirm prenatal alcohol exposure among neonates. Fatty acid ethyl esters (FAEE), which are products of nonoxidative fetal alcohol metabolism, have proven to be a satisfactory biological marker (Klein, Karaskov, & Korent, 1999). In addition, neonatal meconium (see later discussion in the section "Screening for Prenatal Exposure to the Drugs and Substances of Abuse") has been shown to be the best biological sample to use when testing for FAEE (Chan, Klein, Karaskov, et al., 2004). The presence of meconium-derived FAEEs, including ethyl arachidonate, ethyl linoleate, ethyl linolenate, ethyl oleate, ethyl palmitoleate, ethyl palmitate, and ethyl stearate, typically are confirmed by gas chromatography/mass spectrometry (GC/MS) analysis (Gareri, Lynn, Handley, et al., 2008). More recent efforts have been directed at measuring FAEEs in samples of neonatal hair (Caprara, Klein, & Koren, 2006). In addition, the practicality of performing this analysis with hair samples obtained from mothers of at-risk children has been explored (Kulaga, Pragst, Fulga, et al., 2009).

*Recommendations*    Alcohol is a known human teratogen that can cause significant, lifelong deficits in relation to physical growth, cognitive functioning, psychomotor skills, and psychological health. Although some authors (e.g., Knupfer, 1991; Koren, 1991; Walpole, Zubrick, Pontre, et al., 1991) disagree, we concur with the recommendation made by the National Institute of Child Health and Human Development, the American Academy of Pediatrics, and the U.S. Surgeon General (American Academy of Pediatrics, Committee on Substance Abuse, and Committee on Children with Disabilities, 1993; Schydlower & Perrin, 1993), and others (e.g., Caruso & Bensel, 1993; Olson, 1994; Olson, Sampson, Barr, et al., 1992; Streissguth, Barr, Sampson, et al., 1994) that adolescent girls who are pregnant as well as those who are sexually active and do not want to become pregnant, even if they use safer sexual practices, including the use of condoms and more effective methods of birth

control (e.g., oral contraceptives; subcutaneously or intravaginally/cervical placed contraceptives), totally abstain from alcohol use (CDC, 2004a; Pagliaro & Pagliaro, 2002, 2009). This recommendation is based on the observations that no safe level of alcohol use has been demonstrated and that there is no known cure for FAS/FASD (i.e., it is irreversible and lifelong).

As noted by Karp, Qazi, Hittleman, et al. (1993) and many others (e.g., Spohr, Willms, & Steinhausen, 2007), FAS/FASD is not a treatable disease in the literal sense.[17] In this regard, it is essential that prevention and treatment programs be developed to assist adolescent girls and young women to understand the relationship between alcohol use and pregnancy and to abstain from alcohol use, particularly if sexually active or when pregnant. In addition, increased attention must be given to adolescent girls and young women who are developing problematic patterns of alcohol use, particularly those who abuse or use alcohol compulsively or frequently engage in binge drinking, for whom abstinence may be difficult to achieve or maintain (i.e., relapse prevention). See Table 5.7 for a list of risk factors that are associated with maternal alcohol use during pregnancy and consequently giving birth to a baby with FAS/FASD.

***Barbiturates***    The barbiturates that are discussed in this section include mephobarbital (Mebaral®), pentobarbital (Nembutal®), phenobarbital (Luminal®), and secobarbital (Seconal®). Although the use of the barbiturates has decreased dramatically over the past four decades as a result of the synthesis and clinical use of the benzodiazepines, they are still generally available, particularly by

---

[17]However, although FAS as a teratogenic effect is lifelong and incurable, it is treatable, and important advances have been made in this regard (Bertrand, 2009). As noted by Chudley, Conry, Cook, et al. (2005), infants, children, and adolescents who have been diagnosed with FAS/FASD have an opportunity to achieve optimal clinical outcomes with the help of specialized core teams of experts in the disorder, including: (1) nurses and social workers with expertise in case management and coordination of core team member activities; (2) physicians specially trained in diagnosis and medical management of FAS/FASD; (3) clinical infant, child, and adolescent psychologists; (4) occupational therapists; and (5) speech language pathologists. These core team members, along with parents and caregivers, child care workers, family therapists, and teachers, can help infants, children, and adolescents who are diagnosed with FAS/FASD achieve optimal personal outcomes.

**TABLE 5.7    Risk Factors Associated with Significant Maternal Alcohol Use During Pregnancy**

- Alcohol use by spouse or others living in the household
- Childhood physical or sexual abuse
- Low educational achievement
- Low socioeconomic status
- American Indian descent[a]
- Parental alcoholism
- Previously giving birth to a neonate with FAS/FASD
- Unmarried status
- Use of other drug of substance of abuse (e.g., cannabis, cocaine, nicotine [if of Aboriginal or Native American Indian descent, nonceremonial use of tobacco])

[a]This published statistic may be a statistical artifact because virtually all pregnant adolescent girls of Aboriginal or American Indian descent meet one or more of the other listed risk factors.

Internet purchases. In addition, they may be used for the medical management of seizure disorders among adolescent girls and young women who are unresponsive, or refractory, to other anticonvulsant pharmacotherapy.

The use of the barbiturates during pregnancy has been generally associated with a number of teratogenic effects. However, possible covariables, particularly maternal epilepsy, have not as yet been completely rejected or ruled out as the principal or major cofactor for teratogenic risk. Regular long-term barbiturate use during pregnancy or the maternal use of high dosages near term may result in neonatal respiratory depression and the neonatal barbiturate withdrawal syndrome (Pagliaro & Pagliaro, 1999). The barbiturates (i.e., pentobarbital, phenobarbital, secobarbital) are categorized by the FDA as pregnancy category *D* drugs. (See Table 5.1.)

*Benzodiazepines*    The benzodiazepines that are most commonly used by adolescent girls and young women include alprazolam (Xanax®), diazepam (Valium®), flunitrazepam (Rohypnol®), lorazepam (Ativan®), and triazolam (Halcion®) (Forrester, 2006a, b; Pagliaro & Pagliaro, 2009; Peters, Meshack, Kelder, et al., 2007; Wu, Schlenger, & Galvin, 2006). Although the use of the benzodiazepines during

pregnancy has been generally associated, overall, with a low teratogenic risk (Pagliaro & Pagliaro, 2000, 2009), their use during pregnancy has been associated with various degrees of teratogenesis, particularly cleft lip and palate (Laegreid, Olegard, Conradi, et al., 1990; Safra & Oakley, 1975; Saxen & Saxen, 1975). However, these associations may be confounded by the concurrent use of alcohol and other drugs and substances of abuse (Bergman, Rosa, Baum, et al., 1992; DuPont & Saylor, 1992).

The use of the benzodiazepines by adolescent girls and young women near term may result in expected pharmacological effects among their neonates, including lethargy, poor muscle tone, and respiratory depression. Fortunately, these effects are fully reversible with proper recognition and care (Chesley, Lumpkin, Schatzki, et al., 1991; Pagliaro & Pagliaro, 2009; Sanchis, Rosique, & Catala, 1991).

The benzodiazepines (i.e., chlordiazepoxide [Librium®], clonazepam [Rivotril®], clorazepate [Tranxene®], diazepam [Valium®], lorazepam [Ativan®], midazolam [Versed®], and oxazepam [Serax®]) are generally categorized by the FDA as pregnancy category *D* drugs. However, some benzodiazepines (e.g., estazolam [ProSom®], flurazepam [Dalmane®], temazepam [Restoril®], and triazolam [Halcion®]) have been categorized by the FDA, primarily based on animal data, as pregnancy category *X* drugs. (See Table 5.1.)

*Meprobamate*    Meprobamate (Equanil®, Miltown®) is classified as a miscellaneous sedative-hypnotic. It is seldom used by adolescents in North America. Meprobamate crosses the placenta, and its use by adolescent girls and young women during the first trimester of pregnancy generally has been associated with an increased risk for congenital malformations. However, a large prospective study of meprobamate use for the treatment of anxiety disorders during pregnancy, as well as a retrospective review of attempted suicide by pregnant women who used meprobamate as their means of attempted suicide by overdosage, failed to confirm any associated risk for teratogenisis or fetotoxicity (Belafsky, Breslow, Hirsch, et al., 1969; Timmermann, 2008). Meprobamate is categorized by the FDA as a pregnancy category *D* drug. (See Table 5.1.)

**Opiate Analgesics** Among pregnant adolescent girls 13 to 19 years of age who were admitted for the treatment of a SUD in the United States during 2007, 3.1% reported heroin as their primary drug or substance of abuse (Substance Abuse and Mental Health Services Administration, 2010).

Teratogenesis has been associated with the maternal use of several of the opiate analgesics during pregnancy. However, a comprehensive review of available data provides only weak support for teratogenic effects involving codeine, heroin, meperidine (Demerol®), methadone (Dolophine®), morphine (MS Contin®), and pentazocine (Talwin®). In regard to opiate analgesic use by pregnant adolescent girls and young women during the first trimester of pregnancy, the FDA generally categorizes the opiate analgesics (i.e., meperidine [Demerol®], methadone [Dolophine®], and oxycodone [OxyContin®]) as pregnancy category *B* drugs, *no evidence of risk in humans*. (See Table 5.1.) Although major morphological abnormalities among offspring have not been associated with the use of the opiate analgesics during pregnancy, concern has been raised regarding visual impairment, or ocular morbidity, among neonates exposed in utero to the opiate analgesics. The ocular mobidity identified among children whose

mothers regularly used opiate analgesics during pregnancy includes

- Defective neonatal visual evoked potentials
- Delayed visual maturity
- Nystagmus
- Refractory errors
- Reduced acuity (Hamilton, McGlone, MacKinnon, et al, 2010; McGlone, Mactier, Hamilton, et al., 2008; McGlone, Mactier, & Weaver, 2009; Nischal, 2010)

Other potential long-term effects of maternal embryo/fetal exposure to the opiate analgesics during pregnancy have not yet been clearly identified.

***Neonatal Opiate Analgesic Dependence*** The regular, long-term use of higher dosages of any one of the opiate analgesics by adolescent girls and women during pregnancy may result in fetal opiate analgesic dependence and, upon delivery, CNS and respiratory depression with decreased Apgar scores.[18] (See Table 5.8.) Following delivery, the neonate may display signs and symptoms of the neonatal opiate analgesic withdrawal syndrome, with diarrhea, irritability, sneezing, tremors, and vomiting (Pagliaro & Pagliaro, 2002) (see next section).

Opiate dependency programs (e.g., methadone maintenance programs) are generally recommended for adolescent girls and women who are pregnant and physically dependent on opiate analgesics, particularly heroin.[19] Fetuses of mothers enrolled in methadone maintenance programs during pregnancy may display expected pharmacological responses

---

[18] An Apgar score is calculated using the scoring system devised by Virginia Apgar to determine the physical condition of a neonate at 1 and 5 minutes following birth. The final score provides an evaluation of the stability, improvement, or the need for continued monitoring or intensive neonatal pediatric support (i.e., medical and nursing management in a neonatal intensive care unit).

[19] Opiate dependency programs have been shown to provide positive benefits for adolescent girls and women during pregnancy, including improved fetal health, associated with: (1) changing the route of opiate analgesic use from intravenous injection to oral ingestion and thus decreasing their risk for infection (e.g., hepatitis, HIV) as well as other benefits (e.g., establishing more stable opiate analgesic blood levels; reducing episodes of opiate analgesic withdrawal that occur when they are unable to "score"); (2) reduced involvement in prostitution or the sex trade because of reduced need for money to obtain opiate analgesics; and (3) enrollment in prenatal health programs where they can learn and practice better prenatal health behaviors (e.g., nutrition, rest) while receiving helpful counseling and other prenatal social support.

**TABLE 5.8   Neonatal Apgar Scoring**

| Acronym[a] | Sign | Scoring[b] | | |
|---|---|---|---|---|
| | | 0 | 1 | 2 |
| *Appearance* | Color of skin[c] | Blue, pale | Body, pink; extremities blue | Completely pink |
| *Pulse* | Heart rate | Absent | Slow, less than 100 beats per minute | 100 beats per minute or higher |
| *Grimace* | Response to stimuli, reflex irritability | Absent (no response) | Grimace | Cough or sneeze (or actively pulls away) |
| *Activity* | Muscle tone | Absent (limp) | Some flexion, or bending, in the extremities | Active motion (movement of limbs: arms and legs resist extension; well flexed) |
| *Respiration* | Respirations | Absent | Slow, irregular (gasping, weak) | Good (strong crying) |

[a]"Apgar" serves as a mnemonic memory aid for neonatal assessment.
[b]The maximal Apgar score is 10. Scores of 7 to 10 are considered good to excellent. Scores of 4 to 6 are considered fair. Scores below 4 are considered poor.
[c]Skin color generally is not a valid or reliable criterion measure for assessing newborns of non-European descent.
Modified from Apgar, 1953.

as a result of their prenatal exposure to methadone, including reduced motor activity and slowed fetal heart rate (Jansson, Dipietro, & Elko, 2005). Following delivery, they require careful monitoring for the signs and symptoms of the neonatal methadone withdrawal syndrome. (See the next section, "Neonatal Opiate Analgesic Withdrawal Syndrome.") Follow-up treatment programs for mothers and their infants should be encouraged, as should further research, particularly that exploring the effects of maternal opiate analgesic use during pregnancy and its long-term effects on offspring throughout infancy, childhood, and adolescence.

Alternatively, the use of buprenorphine (Buprenex®), a synthetic mixed opiate analgesic agonist/antagonist (see Chapter 1, *The Psychodepressants*), has been recommended for the medical management of opiate analgesic dependence during pregnancy. For example, Jones, Kaltenbach, Heil, et al. (2010) conducted a study funded by the National Institute on Drug Abuse comparing methadone versus buprenorphine use among 175 pregnant women who were opiate analgesic dependent. In comparison to the methadone-treated group, the buprenorphine-treated group had: (1) a significantly reduced

requirement for morphine (i.e., 1.1 mg versus 1.4 mg); (2) a significantly shorter hospital stay (i.e., 10.0 days versus 17.5 days); and (3) a significantly shorter duration of treatment for the opiate analgesic withdrawal syndrome among neonates (i.e., 4.1 days versus 9.9 days).

***Neonatal Opiate Analgesic Withdrawal Syndrome***   The neonatal opiate analgesic withdrawal syndrome occurs most frequently among neonates who have been exposed in utero by mothers who regularly used methadone during pregnancy. This syndrome, characterized, in severe cases, by convulsions that require medical management and support of the neonate's body systems, has encouraged detoxification of mothers during pregnancy. However, methadone detoxification during the first and third trimesters of pregnancy has been associated with an increased incidence of spontaneous abortions and fetal distress, respectively.

Thus, whenever possible adolescent girls and young women who use methadone, including those who are enrolled in methadone maintenance or opiate dependency programs, should first undergo opiate analgesic detoxification before becoming pregnant. When this is not possible, methadone detoxification should be attempted between the 14th and 28th weeks of gestation with a slow tapering of the mother's methadone dosage. Intrauterine growth may be retarded, but it appears to be related primarily to such confounding variables as poor maternal nutrition and concurrent alcohol and nicotine use during pregnancy (Pagliaro & Pagliaro, 2002).

**Volatile Solvents and Inhalants**  Despite finding repeated periodic calls for "more research" in published reviews of the reproductive toxicology of the volatile solvents and inhalants (e.g., Bukowski, 2001; Hannigan & Bowen, 2010), an analysis of the published literature to date found fewer than 12 studies or reports that were exclusively concerned with the potential teratogenic effects associated with the use of the volatile solvents and inhalants during pregnancy. Most of these studies and reports were published prior to 1995 and almost all deal only, or primarily, with toluene (i.e., methylbenzene), a volatile solvent found in many commonly available household products, including glues and spray paints.

*Toluene*  Hersh, Podruch, Rogers, et al. (1985) first described the occurrence of toluene embryopathy in three children that was associated with maternal toluene use during pregnancy. This report was augmented with two additional cases in 1989 (Hersh, 1989). The reported embryopathy was supported by Arnold, Kirby, Langendoerfer, et al. (1994) and Pearson, Hoyme, Seaver, et al. (1994) as well as Wilkins-Haug and Gabow (1991), who reported data on 30 pregnancies among 10 women with chronic glue- and paint-sniffing abuse. Arnold, Kirby, Langendoerfer, et al. (1994) reviewed the case records of 35 deliveries with antenatal exposure to toluene. Data from these last two studies provided support for the occurrence of these teratogenic effects as being associated with maternal volatile solvent and inhalant use during pregnancy:

- Preterm delivery
- Neonatal electrolyte disturbances (i.e., hypobicarbonatemia, hypokalemia)

- Minor craniofacial anomalies (e.g., short palpebral fissures; flat, wide nasal bridge; deficient philtrum; microcephaly; and micrognathia)
- Intrauterine growth retardation (e.g., low birth weight)
- Postnatal growth retardation

Behavioral problems (i.e., A-D/HD) also were described during later childhood. The associated teratogenic features are extremely similar to those associated with FAS/FASD. (See the previous discussion in the "Alcohol" section.)

This similarity of these features may be due to the pharmacological similarity of alcohol and the volatile solvents and inhalants. It also is possible that these mothers concomitantly used alcohol with the toluene (Wilkins-Haug, 1997). Pearson, Hoyme, Seaver, et al. (1994) proposed a "common mechanism of craniofacial teratogenesis [for toluene and alcohol], namely a deficiency of craniofacial neuroepithelium and mesodermal components due to increased embryonic cell death" (p. 211). Wilkins-Haug (1997) suggested that toluene-induced maternal renal tubular acidosis and resultant hypokalemia may have a contributory role in the production of the associated teratogenic effects. Supporting this view are data from two cases reported by Lindemann (1991) of neonatal "renal tubular dysfunction and metabolic acidosis" related to maternal sniffing of a toluene-containing product (p. 882).

### Psychostimulants

Several of the psychostimulants, including caffeine, cocaine, methamphetamine, and nicotine (tobacco), have been associated with possible teratogenic risk when used by North American adolescent girls during pregnancy. However, research results are mixed in this regard. These data are discussed in the next sections.

**Caffeine**  Caffeine, in the form of coffee, tea, and other beverages (e.g., caffeinated soft drinks, energy boost drinks) probably is consumed to a greater extent by pregnant adolescent girls and young women than any other drug or substance of abuse, including alcohol. Although research has not been as prolific as that for alcohol, some studies have associated caffeine consumption with birth defects (Jacobson, Goldman, & Syme, 1981; Rossenberg, Mitchell, Shapiro, et al., 1982). For example, the consumption of 8 or more cups of coffee per day was related to fetal limb defects in 3 case reports, and a significant correlation between increased caffeine consumption during pregnancy and fetal loss was reported (Infante-Rivard, Fernandez, Gauthier, et al., 1993). In another example, Schmidt, Romitti, Burns, et al. (2009), in a retrospective analysis of the available data from the National Birth Defects Prevention Study, found a positive association between maternal caffeine consumption during pregnancy and neural tube defects. Specifically, caffeine consumption was associated with an increased odds ratio (i.e., OR = 1.4) for infants with spina bifida.

However, most recent studies have shown that the only teratogenic effect clearly associated with maternal caffeine use during pregnancy appears to be low birth weight (Olsen, Overvad, & Frische, 1991; Pagliaro & Pagliaro, 2002, 2009). Low birth weight is associated with the consumption of 3 or more cups of coffee (i.e., 300 mg or more caffeine) per day and appears to be most significant among adolescent girls and women who smoke (i.e., as a likely cofactor). Several studies conducted within the past decade have examined other specific teratogenic effects associated with maternal caffeine consumption—cardiovascular malformations (Browne, Bell, Drushel, et al., 2007), orofacial clefts (i.e., cleft lip and/or cleft palate) (Collier, Browne, Rasmussen, et al., 2009; Johansen, Wilcox, Lie, et al., 2009)—and found no evidence to support a significant risk.

Although these studies generally support the relative safe use of caffeine during pregnancy (Browne, Hoyt, Feldkamp, et al., 2011; Christian & Brent, 2001), adolescent girls and young women who are pregnant should be encouraged to minimize their caffeine consumption, particularly if they smoke tobacco cigarettes. Tobacco smoking, which is significantly correlated with coffee consumption and which is also related to decreased neonatal birth weight, is an obvious confounding factor in the interpretation of data supporting the possible teratogenic risk of the use of caffeine during pregnancy. (Also see the "Nicotine (Tobacco Smoking)" section.)

## Cocaine

Cocaine's $pK_{[a]}$ [acid ion dissociation constant] is alkaline. Thus the drug would tend to accumulate in the ionized form on the side of a membrane where protons abound. Because fetal pH is normally lower than maternal, and is even lower during asphyxia episodes, cocaine can accumulate in the fetus. Therefore, at equilibrium fetal tissue levels may exceed maternal concentrations. Demethylation, a hepatic enzyme activity, may also be developmentally reduced, resulting in prolonged fetal exposure. (Scanlon, 1991, pp. 89–90)

Cocaine use by pregnant North American adolescent girls and young women, particularly those of African descent who live in inner cities, increased significantly during the last three decades (Frank, Jacobs, Beeghly, et al., 2002; Lester, Bagner, Liu, et al., 2009; Martinez, Larrabee, & Monga, 1996). In fact, among inner cities across the United States, cocaine is now the most commonly used illicit drug and substance of abuse after marijuana. Overall estimates of cocaine use among all pregnant women in the United States are approximately 1% (Finch, Vega, & Kolody, 2001; Mathias, 1995). Specific data for pregnant adolescent girls are not available but are expected to be significantly higher. Among pregnant adolescent girls 13 to 19 years of age who were admitted for the treatment of a

SUD in the United States during 2007, 6.8% reported cocaine as their primary drug or substance of abuse (Substance Abuse and Mental Health Services Administration, 2010).

Regardless of the method of use (i.e., intravenously injecting or intranasally insufflating cocaine hydrochloride or smoking cocaine base, or crack), cocaine use has been associated with a number of teratogenic effects, including

- Intrauterine death, including spontaneous abortions
- Intrauterine growth retardation and low birth weight (i.e., less than 5.5 pounds [2,500 grams])
- Preterm delivery
- Neonatal seizures, tachycardia, and hypoxemia
- A variety of fetal physical anomalies, particularly affecting the ocular and urogenital systems, and limb reduction defects (Bandstra & Burkett, 1991; Bateman & Chiriboga, 2000; Brouhard, 1994; Calhoun & Watson, 1991; Chasnoff, 1992; Chavez, Mulinare, & Cordero, 1989; Frank, Jacobs, Beeghly, et al., 2002; Hannig & Phillips, 1991; Hume, Gingras, Martin, et al., 1994; Keegan, Parva, Finnegan, et al., 2010; Nucci & Brancato, 1994; Offidani, Pomini, Caruso, et al., 1995; Plessinger & Woods, 1991; Scanlon, 1991; Sheinbaum & Badell, 1992; Stafford, Rosen, Zaider, et al., 1994; van den Anker & Sauer, 1992; Zimmerman, 1991).

Autopsies of fetuses exposed to cocaine in utero often reveal cerebral hemorrhages (Gieron-Korthals, Helal & Martinez, 1994; Kapur, Cheng, & Shephard, 1991), presumably due to a rapid and significant increase in systemic and cerebral blood pressure and hyperthermia (Jones, 1991). However, some researchers have attributed these effects to confounding factors associated with maternal cocaine use (e.g., poor nutrition, inadequate prenatal care) (Church, 1993; Gingras, Weese-Mayer, Hume, et al., 1992; Hutchings, 1993;

Koren, 1993; Neuspiel, 1992; Racine, Joyce, & Anderson, 1993; Snodgrass, 1994). (See Table 5.9 for a list of obstetrical complications that have been associated with cocaine use during pregnancy.)

There also appears to be a significantly higher incidence of behavioral and learning disorders (e.g., A-D/HD; delays in receptive and expressive language skills; externalizing behavior; oppositional defiant disorder [ODD]) among preschool and school-age children exposed to cocaine in utero (Ackerman, Riggins, & Black, 2010; Bada, Das, Bauer et al., 2007; Cone-Wesson, 2005; Jones, 1991; Linares, Singer, Kirchner, et al., 2006; Morrow, Vogel, Anthony, et al., 2004; Pagliaro & Pagliaro, 1992; Richardson, Goldschmidt, Leech, et al., 2010; Rivers & Hedrick, 1992; Van Dyke & Fox, 1990), particularly when exposure occurred during the first trimester (Richardson, Goldschmidt, & Willford, 2002). In addition, several researchers (e.g., Bennett, Bendersky, & Lewis, 2008; Singer, Minnes, Short, et al., 2004) have found small but significant deficits in several IQ subscales (i.e., arithmetic skills, general knowledge, visual-spatial skills), which may display a gender interaction effect with cocaine-exposed boys being more susceptible.

TABLE 5.9    Maternal Cocaine Use and Obstetrical Complications

Abortion
Abruptio placentae
Breech presentation
Chorioamnionitis (inflammation of fetal membranes)
Eclampsia
Gestational diabetes
Intrauterine fetal death
Intrauterine growth retardation (IGR)
Placental insufficiency
Postpartum hemorrhage
Preeclampsia
Preterm labor
Premature rupture of the membranes (i.e., at term, but before the onset of labor.)
Septic thrombophlebitis

Sources: Dinsmoor, Irons, & Christmas, 1994; Lesar, 1992; Martinez, Larrabee, & Monga, 1996; Refuerzo, Sokol, Blackwell, et al., 2002; Witlin & Sibai, 2001.

(Also see Chapter 6, *Effects of the Drugs and Substances of Abuse on Learning and Memory During Childhood and Adolescence,* for additional related discussion.)

However, noting the absence of the often-predicted deluge of "crack babies" from reports and editorials published during the early 1980s, some authors (e.g., Beattie, 2005; Chavkin, 2001) have outright dismissed any and all adverse fetal effects associated with maternal use of cocaine during pregnancy. We would disagree. Rather than characterizing the teratogenic effects associated with the maternal use of cocaine during pregnancy as nonexistent, the effects should, at least, be characterized as being inconclusive because of the difficulties associated with interpreting and evaluating related data.

These difficulties can be grouped into four categories.

1. The retrospective case report methodology that is generally used has several inherent limitations, including the possible inaccuracy of reported information. These limitations make definitive conclusions highly speculative (Dow-Edwards, 1993; Frank & Zuckerman, 1993; Hume, Gingras, Martin et al., 1994; Konkol, 1994; Neuspiel, 1993; Slutsker, 1992; Spear, 1993). Fortunately, research studies published over the last 5 years have increasingly used study designs that have significantly improved the validity and reliability of findings and better support presented conclusions. For example, prenatal cocaine exposure now often is measured by methods other than solely self-reports of maternal use and includes such quantitative methods as meconium analysis and structured interviews. (Also see the later related discussion in the "Screening for Prenatal Exposure to the Drugs and Substances of Abuse" section of this chapter.)

2. Pregnant adolescent girls and young women who use cocaine also commonly use alcohol, a known teratogen, to come down from a cocaine high. This additional risk factor, along with similar risk factors (e.g., poor prenatal care; tobacco smoking), further confound the interpretation of data (Frank, Augustyn, Knight, et al., 2001; Rizk, Atterbury, & Groome, 1996; Snodgrass, 1994).

3. Residual amounts of the organic solvents (e.g., benzene) that are used in the extraction of cocaine from *Erythroxylon coca* leaves are commonly found in samples of cocaine sold on the street.

4. Several replicative studies have failed to substantiate previous findings relating cocaine use during pregnancy to teratogenic effects. For example, Bauer, Langer, Shankaran et al. (2005), using a large randomized prospective study, failed to support previously published physical teratogenic effects except for intrauterine growth retardation (IGR). As noted by Chae and Covington (2009): "[W]ell-designed human studies are needed to elucidate the effects of prenatal cocaine exposure on older human children" (p. 318).

In summary, a general consensus seems to be that the use of high dosages of cocaine, whether cocaine hydrochloride or cocaine base (i.e., crack cocaine), probably has a significant but low potential for teratogenesis (Bandstra, Morrow, Mansoor, et al., 2010; Coles, 1993; Koren, Gladstone, Robeson et al., 1992; Martin, Khoury, Cordero et al., 1992; Martin & Khoury, 1992). In addition, when used by mothers near term, the neonate may experience CNS excitation with associated signs and symptoms, including:

- High-pitched cry
- Hyperalertness
- Insomnia
- Irritability
- Poor feeding response (Bauer, Langer, Shankaran, et al., 2005; Pagliaro & Pagliaro, 2002, 2009).

What remains to be resolved are the potential subtle but significant effects of prenatal cocaine exposure on subsequent learning, memory, and higher levels of cognitive ability (i.e., executive functioning) among children and adolescents (Salisbury, Ponder, Padbury, et al., 2009).

**Methamphetamine**   The use of methamphetamine (Desoxyn®)—crank, crystal, ice, meth, or speed—received increased interest among adolescent girls and young women during the last two decades. Prescribed primarily in the past as an oral anorexiant for weight management, it is most commonly illicitly used for its psychostimulant effects. In regard to methamphetamine use during pregnancy, Della Grotta, Lagasse, Arria, et al. (2010) found that:

1. Methamphetamine use generally decreased over each of the succeeding trimesters of pregnancy (i.e., first trimester, 84.3%; second trimester, 56.0%; and third trimester, 42.4%).
2. The frequency of methamphetamine use correspondingly decreased (i.e., first trimester, 3.1 days/week; second trimester, 2.4 days/week; third trimester, 1.5 days/week).
3. As methamphetamine use decreased, the use of other drugs and substances of abuse, particularly alcohol, increased.
4. Approximately one-third of mothers maintained consistently high levels of methamphetamine use throughout their entire pregnancies.

Among pregnant adolescent girls 13 to 19 years of age who were admitted for treatment of a SUD in the United States during 2007, 18.8% reported methamphetamine as their primary drug or substance of abuse (Substance Abuse and Mental Health Services Administration, 2010). Cox, Posner, Kourtis, et al. (2008), in their analysis of data obtained from the Nationwide Inpatient Sample, found that hospitalizations for amphetamine abuse among pregnant women: (1) more than doubled from 1998 to 2004; (2) were more likely to involve adolescent girls and young women under 24 years of age; and (3) occurred primarily in the western states. The researchers also reported that amphetamine use during pregnancy was significantly more likely to result in maternal physical complications (e.g., hypertension) than fetal physical complications.

Although data are contradictory regarding the teratogenic potential of methamphetamine use during pregnancy, it would appear that there is moderate risk. Various case reports have suggested that the maternal use of methamphetamine during the first trimester is associated with abnormal brain development, biliary atresia, cleft lip and palate, and congenital heart disease. In addition, maternal use of methamphetamine during the third trimester has been associated with prematurity among neonates who may be small for their gestational age and, even at full term, may have low birth weight and a smaller than normal head circumference (i.e., IGR) (Smith, LaGasse, Derauf, et al., 2006), which may be due simply to the anorexic effects associated with methamphetamine use among mothers (Salisbury, Ponder, Padbury, et al., 2009). Preterm delivery, low Apgar scores, and a higher incidence of neonatal mortality also have been reported (e.g., Good, Solt, Acuna, et al., 2010). These effects also could be related to both the lifestyle of pregnant adolescents who use methamphetamine or to their use of additional drugs and substances of abuse. Although some prospective studies have found no increase in fetal malformations, it appears prudent to advise adolescent girls not to use methamphetamine during pregnancy (Pagliaro & Pagliaro, 1996, 2000, 2002, 2009), particularly because of possible long-term neurotoxicity associated with its direct damage to dopamine receptors in the striatal and limbic structures of the brain (Chang, Alicata, Ernst, et al., 2007; Sowell, Leow, Bookheimer, et al., 2010).

**Nicotine (Tobacco Smoking)**   For adolescent girls and women who are pregnant, the rate of tobacco use appears to be approximately 25% to 35% (e.g., Arria, Derauf, Lagasse, et al., 2006; CDC, 2002; Hofhuis, de Jongste, & Merkus, 2003). Although these percentages vary among different ethnic groups, geographic regions, and races (Pagliaro & Pagliaro, 2002), they are reflective of the estimated 20% to 30% of pregnant women throughout the world who use tobacco (Lamy & Thibaut, 2010).

Nicotine, available to pregnant adolescent girls and young women from several sources (e.g., tobacco cigarettes and other forms of smoking tobacco, secondhand smoke, smokeless tobacco products, and nicotine replacement pharmacotherapy products), readily crosses the placenta into fetal tissues, where it becomes concentrated (Pagliaro & Pagliaro, 2009; Rogers, 2009). Unfortunately, tobacco smoking during pregnancy is associated with teratogenesis. There is a direct, inverse relationship between the number of cigarettes smoked per day by an adolescent or woman who is pregnant and the corresponding birth weight of her neonate. Neonates, who are born to mothers who smoked tobacco during pregnancy, weighed an average of 200 grams (range 100 to 400 grams) less than neonates who were born to mothers who did not smoke tobacco during pregnancy. They also had a shorter body length and a smaller head circumference at birth (i.e., IGR) (Hofhuis, de Jongste, & Merkus, 2003; Nash & Persaud, 1988; Wigle, Arbuckle, Turner, et al., 2008).

The IGR appears to be related to decreased maternal nutrient consumption (i.e., nicotine is an anorexiant)[20] with consequently fewer nutrients being delivered to the fetus and to early morphological changes to the placenta resulting in reduced oxygen diffusion and reduced amino acid transport (Bush, Mayhew, Abramovich, et al., 2000a, b; Lambers & Clark, 1996; Sastry, 1991). Fortunately, a period of accelerated growth occurs during the first year of life, and generally no differences in body weight or length are observed among fetally exposed toddlers at 1 year of age. Mothers who cease smoking during the first trimester of pregnancy generally deliver neonates of normal size and weight (Pagliaro & Pagliaro, 2002).

Mothers who continue to smoke tobacco during pregnancy have higher rates of obstetric and perinatal complications, including:

- Abruption placente
- Ectopic pregnancy
- Placenta previa
- Increased perinatal mortality
- Preterm birth[21]
- Spontaneous abortion (DiFranza & Lew, 1995; Gupton, Thompson, Arnason, et al., 1995; Hofhuis, de Jongste, & Merkus, 2003).

Preeclampsia, a complication of pregnancy that is characterized by maternal edema, hypertension, and proteinuria, is the leading cause of maternal and fetal morbidity and death. Its incidence is higher among adolescent mothers but, interestingly, is reduced among those who smoke tobacco products. However, the incidence of preeclampsia is increased among pregnant adolescent girls and young women who use smokeless tobacco (e.g., snuff, snus). Thus, it has been suggested that it is not the nicotine but rather the combustion products in tobacco smoke that may actually provide protection against preeclampsia (England, Levine, Mills, et al., 2003; Wikstrom, Stephansson, & Cnattingius, 2010).

The risk of the sudden infant death syndrome (SIDS) is estimated to be several times higher for infants born to mothers who smoked

---

[20] Although adolescent girls and young women often smoke tobacco cigarettes to decrease or maintain their body weight, they also smoke cigarettes when pregnant in order to "not gain so much weight" and "to have a *smaller* baby," so that their labor and delivery will be "easier" (Pagliaro & Pagliaro, *Clinical Patient Data Files*).

[21] A higher incidence of preterm birth also has been correlated with the use of smokeless tobacco products (e.g., snuff, snus) during pregnancy (England, Levine, Mills, et al., 2003; Wikstrom, Cnattingius, Galanti; et al., 2010).

tobacco during pregnancy than for infants whose mothers did not and may account for over 2,000 SIDS deaths annually (DiFranza & Lew, 1995; Dybing & Sanner, 1999; Mitchell, Ford, Stewart, et al., 1993). Mitchell and Milerad (2006) have estimated that approximately one-third of all SIDS deaths could have been prevented if the respective mothers had not smoked tobacco while pregnant. Some authors (e.g., Dezateux & Stocks, 1997; Stick, Burton, Gurrin, et al., 1996) have suggested that the reduced lung function (e.g., reduced forced expiratory volume) noted among neonates and children whose mothers smoked during pregnancy may be a major contributing cofactor for SIDS among infants who are otherwise susceptible to SIDS (i.e., either genetically susceptible or susceptible because of other related factors, such as sleeping position).[22] Other authors (e.g., Fregosi & Pilarski, 2008) suggest that prenatal nicotine exposure modifies the nicotinic acetylcholine receptor (nAChR), thereby impairing respiratory function.

In addition, several studies (e.g., Carter, Paterson, Gao, et al., 2008; Cornelius, Goldschmidt, De Genna, et al., 2007; Cornelius, Leech, Goldschmidt, et al., 2009; Eskenazi & Castorina, 1999; Langley, Holmans, Van den Bree, et al., 2007; Milberger, Biederman, Faraone, et al., 1996; Wakschlag & Hans, 2002; Wakschlag, Pickett, Cook, et al., 2002; Weitzman, Gortmaker, & Sobol, 1992) have found a significantly higher incidence of severe behavioral problems (e.g., A-D/HD, antisocial behavior, conduct disorder) among children—particularly boys—whose mothers smoked half a pack of cigarettes or more per day during pregnancy. Boys who have the dopamine transporter (DAT1) gene appear to be at even greater risk (Becker, El-Faddagh, Schmidt, et al., 2008; Neuman, Lobos, Reich,

et al., 2007). Stone, La Gasse, Lester, et al., (2010), as part of a prospective longitudinal study of maternal lifestyle, examined the association between prenatal maternal use of a drug or substance of abuse (i.e., alcohol, cannabis, cocaine, nicotine, or opiate analgesic) and maternal report of sleep problems among their children. Only prenatal nicotine exposure was positively correlated with persistent sleep problems among their children. However, as with other drugs and substances of abuse, the teratogenic effects of heavy tobacco smoking are confounded by the concurrent use of alcohol. (See the "Alcohol" section for additional discussion.)

Finally, several studies (e.g., Al Mamum, O'Callaghan, Alati, et al., 2006; Buka, Shenassa, & Niaura, 2003; Cornelius, Leech, Goldschmidt, et al., 2000; Kandel, Wu, & Davies, 1994) have found that maternal smoking during pregnancy is associated with a significantly increased incidence of tobacco smoking among offspring when assessed during their late adolescence or early adulthood. However, a definitive association cannot be confirmed because of several confounding factors—including the entire "nature versus nurture" argument. Based on the available data, and as a precaution, pregnant adolescent girls should be advised not to smoke during pregnancy. Nicotine is categorized by the FDA as a pregnancy category *D* drug. (See Table 5.1.)

### Psychodelics

The psychodelics comprise a variety of drugs and substances of abuse that are generally used for their *hallucinatory* and *consciousness-expanding effects*. (See Chapter 3, *The Psychodelics*.) A review of the published literature associating the psychodelics with

---

[22] In this regard, several researchers (e.g., Early exposure, 2008; Pattenden, Antova, Neuberger, et al., 2006) have noted a significant association between maternal tobacco use and childhood asthma. However, a major confounding variable is that adolescent mothers who smoked during pregnancy are likely to continue to smoke after delivery. In this latter situation, they will invariably expose their newborn, infant, or child to secondhand tobacco smoke that may cause asthma (EPA, 2003). (See the related discussion of secondhand smoke exposure later in this chapter.)

teratogenic effects resulted in both positive and negative results, depending on the particular drug or substance of abuse. In this regard, no studies were found that linked teratogenic effects with the maternal use of psilocybin (magic mushrooms) or peyote during pregnancy. However, several publications were found that linked teratogenic effects with: LSD; tetrahydrocannabinol (THC), the major active ingredient in cannabis; and phencylidine (PCP). For example, Fried and Watkinson (1990) noted that, at "48 months [of age], significantly lower scores in verbal and memory domains [among children] were associated with maternal marijuana use" (p. 49). However, the use of LSD, THC, and PCP during pregnancy has not been clearly and consistently associated with major physical or developmental teratogenic effects (Pagliaro & Pagliaro, 2002; Tabor, Smith-Wallace, & Yonekura, 1990). Published studies and reports (i.e., case histories) generally have reported minor or subjective teratogenic effects. For example, agitation, diarrhea, sleep problems, and vomiting have been variably reported in association with maternal PCP use (e.g., Chasnoff, Burns, Hatcher, et al., 1983; Strauss, Modaniou, & Bosu, 1981; Wachsman, Schuetz, Chan, et al., 1989). Given the widespread use of the psychodelics, particularly by adolescent girls,[23] and the relative paucity of reported teratogenic effects, the potential for teratogenesis among offspring of mothers who use the psychodelics during pregnancy, if it does exist, appears to be very low (Pagliaro & Pagliaro, 2002, 2009).

## Screening for Prenatal Exposure to the Drugs and Substances of Abuse

Increasingly, neonates are screened for prenatal exposure to the drugs and substances of abuse. Samples for testing can be obtained from: (1) umbilical cord blood or tissue; (2) neonatal hair; (3) neonatal meconium;[24] and (4) neonatal urine (usually first-voided urine). Following collection, these samples are subjected to analysis by class-specific enzyme immunoassay methods. Positive results generally are confirmed by further analysis with GC/MS or LC/MS (Gareri, Klein, & Koren, 2006; Montgomery, Plate, Alder, et al., 2006; Wingert, Feldman, Kim, et al., 1994). Testing and analysis has been performed for the maternal use of alcohol, amphetamines, benzodiazepines, cannabis, cocaine, codeine, methadone, morphine, nicotine, and phencyclidine (Marin, Keith, Merrell, et al., 2009; Moore, Negrusz, & Lewis, 1998; Wingert, Feldman, Kim, et al., 1994).

Screening for prenatal exposure to the drugs and substances of abuse is most often used to confirm a positive history of maternal use of the drugs and substances of abuse during pregnancy or to confirm a dubious maternal history of use (e.g., when a frightened young adolescent mother who has been living on the street denies drinking or using other drugs and substances of abuse while pregnant). It also may be used during the postpartum period when clinical data (e.g., maternal or infant blood concentrations; maternal or neonatal signs and symptoms; neonatal meconium analysis) or the maternal

---

[23] Among pregnant adolescents 13 to 19 years of age who were admitted for the treatment of a SUD in the United States during 2007, 45.9% reported cannabis as their primary drug or substance of abuse (Substance Abuse and Mental Health Services Administration, 2010).

[24] Meconium, the first fecal material excreted by the neonate, is an excellent depository for identifying the various drugs and substances of abuse to which the fetus may have been exposed. It literally contains a life history of prenatal metabolism. However, the use of meconium for identifying fetal exposure to the drugs and substances of abuse also has some limitations. For example, laboratory analysis of the meconium is generally more difficult and time consuming than is the analysis of neonatal hair and umbilical cord tissue. Also, the meconium, in some cases, can be passed in utero and therefore unable to be tested. In other cases, it can be passed several days following birth and, thus, delay test analysis and results (Montgomery, Plate, Alder, et al., 2006).

history of previous use of the drugs and substances of abuse during pregnancy suggest use during pregnancy (Pagliaro & Pagliaro, *Clinical Patient Data Files*). For example, Lester, El Sohly, Wright, et al. (2001), in a study involving the analysis of meconium samples obtained from over 8,500 neonates, found that 38% of the cases in which the mother denied use of drugs and substances of abuse proved positive for maternal use of the drugs and substances of abuse.

The screening of mothers and neonates for use or exposure to the drugs and substances of abuse, respectively, raises several ethical and legal questions, including: What is the reason for screening? Which mothers and neonates require screening, and under what circumstances? Should all mothers and neonates be screened universally? Is separate consent required from legal parents or guardians prior to the screening of neonates? And whose rights take precedence—the rights of the mother or the rights of the neonate? As noted by Marcellus (2007), positive screens have the potential to harm the mother by labeling her as a bad mother with the potential of also involving child welfare services, which may find her to be unfit to care for her baby and remove the baby from her care, placing him or her in foster care. However, some researchers (e.g., Lester, El Sohly, Wright, et al., 2001), as noted, have found mothers often to be untruthful in regard to self-reporting use of the drugs and substances of abuse, thus, preventing the delivery of needed services to both mother and infant.

Other clinicians and researchers (e.g., Ellsworth, Stevens, & D'Angio, 2010; Kunins, Bellin, Chazotte, et al., 2007) have expressed concern that larger numbers of North American neonates born to mothers of African descent are postnatally screened for exposure to the drugs and substances of abuse than are neonates of mothers of other continental descents, suggesting racism. Still other clinicians and researchers (e.g., Anachebe, 2006; Lu &

Halfon, 2003) have noted that North American neonates of African descent have the poorest birth outcomes when compared to cohorts of neonates of other continental descents. They also have a higher incidence of infant mortality, which suggests a greater need for screening in consideration of increasing the welfare and best interests of the neonate. The issue of neonatal screening continues to be debated, and few of the questions asked have been answered satisfactorily. Although further discussion of this issue goes beyond the scope of this text, readers are encouraged to delve more deeply into these ethical issues with particular attention to what is best for both neonates and their mothers.

## EXPOSURE DURING BREAST-FEEDING

The use of drugs and substances of abuse by adolescent girls and young women who are breast-feeding can cause expected psychotropic effects among breast-fed neonates and infants if both a significant concentration of the drug or substance of abuse is excreted in the breast milk and a nursing neonate or infant consumes a sufficient amount of the breast milk. Depending on the abuse potential of a particular drug or substance of abuse, it also may cause physical dependence, when mothers are regular, long-term users; and a withdrawal syndrome, when either breast-feeding or a mother's regular, long-term use is discontinued abruptly. In addition to these expected effects, of increasing concern are the possible effects that neonatal and infant exposure to the drugs and substances of abuse through breast milk may have on neurocognitive development that may not be fully observed until later childhood (e.g., academic problems when the child begins school).

Over half of all new mothers in North America, including adolescent girls and young women, breast-feed their neonates and infants

(Pierre, Emans, Obeidallah, et al., 1999; Spear, 2006).[25] Breast milk generally is considered to be the best form of nutrition for neonates and infants and, early on, provides essential immunity to several diseases and conditions. For example, breast-fed neonates and infants experience a lower incidence of diarrhea, inflammatory bowel disease, meningitis, otitis media, and pneumonia than do infants who are not breast-fed (Moretti, 2009). Breast-feeding also is considered an important part of maternal-infant bonding and healthy psychological development over the first year of life that can have long-reaching effects. However, mothers who use the various drugs and substances of abuse—all of which can be excreted in breast milk—may not practice healthy eating habits or be as psychologically healthy as mothers who do not use the drugs and substances of abuse.

Depending on their level of drug and substance use, these mothers may: (1) neglect their neonate or infant in regard to regular feeding, basic care, and other developmental needs, including the prevention of accidents and injuries (Donohue, 2004); (2) live in abusive relationships that may endanger their neonate or infant, directly or indirectly; or (3) expose their neonate or infant to serious infectious diseases directly related to their use of the drugs and substances of abuse, including HIV infection (Figure 5.5), and other sexually transmitted diseases and infections (e.g., hepatitis) (Pagliaro & Pagliaro, 2000).[26] This section identifies and describes the drugs and substances of abuse that generally should not be used by adolescent girls and young women who are breast-feeding.

## Drugs and Substances of Abuse Excreted in Breast Milk

In order to cross the blood-brain barrier and elicit their primary psychodepressant, psychostimulant, or psychodelic effects, the drug or substance of abuse must be lipid, or fat, soluble. The lipid solubility of a drug or substance of abuse also ensures that it will be excreted in breast milk in significant amounts. In fact, for some drugs and substances of abuse (e.g., nicotine/tobacco smoke), concentrations in breast milk can be higher than those in maternal serum. (See Table 5.10.) Other related variables that may significantly influence the transfer of a particular drug or substance of abuse into breast milk and, consequently, the concentration it achieves include degree of ionization and molecular weight, or size of the drug or substance of abuse molecule. In this regard, as a general rule, nonionized forms of a drug or substance of abuse, as well as those with a lower molecular weight, achieve higher concentrations in breast milk. As identified in

---

[25]This number can range from 20% to 60%, depending on custom and attitudes toward breast-feeding in various reporting jurisdictions. For example, in North America, low-income levels or low socioeconomic status (SES) have been associated with lower rates of breast-feeding (Baisch, Fox, & Goldberg, 1989) while higher income levels or higher SES have been associated with higher rates of breast-feeding (Heck, Braveman, Cubbin, et al., 2006). Higher rates of breast-feeding have also been found among recent groups of immigrants (Merewood, Brooks, Bauchner, et al., 2006; Singh, Kogan, & Dee, 2007), particularly adolescent girls and young women of Hispanic descent (Heck, Braveman, Cubbin, et al., 2006). Other variables—embarrassment with public exposure of breasts during breast-feeding, fear of pain or discomfort associated with breast-feeding, and history of sexual abuse as a child—tend to significantly reduce the reported incidence of breast-feeding (Bowman, 2007; Hannon, Willis, Bishop-Townsend, et al., 2000). In addition, lower rates of breast-feeding have been reported among mothers of preterm infants when compared to mothers of full term infants (Merewood, Brooks, Bauchner, et al., 2006).

[26]Several decades ago, Newell (1991) noted in a European Collaborative Study that mothers with established infection can transmit HIV infection through breast milk. Also reported was a 2-fold increase in risk of HIV infection among breast-fed infants and young children. Other authors (e.g., Black, 1996; Dunn, Newell, Ades, et al., 1992; Kennedy, Fortney, Bonhomme, et al., 1990) have confirmed the risk for HIV transmission from mothers to their offspring by breast-feeding. Therefore, because intravenous drug use is a major route of transmission of HIV to adolescent girls and young women, adolescent girls and young women, who are, or previously were, intravenous drug users generally should be advised to refrain from breast-feeding their neonates and infants until they are confirmed to be HIV-negative. (See earlier discussion in Chapter 1, *The Psychodepressants,* regarding intravenous drug use and risk of HIV infection.)

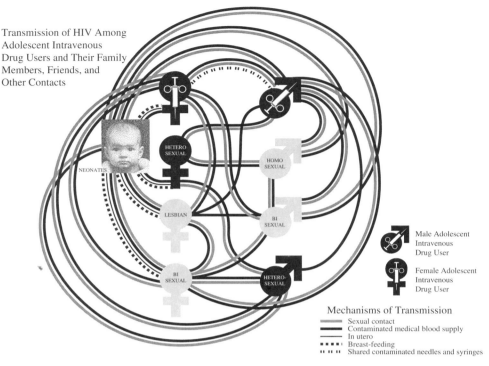

**Figure 5.5   Major Lines of HIV Transmission Among Infants, Children, Adolescents, and Others**
Reproduced with permission from: A. M. Pagliaro & L. A. Pagliaro (1996), Chapter 6, Dual diagnosis among adolescents (p. 162). In, *Substance use among children and adolescents: Its nature, extent, and effects from conception to adulthood.* New York, NY: John Wiley & Sons.

Table 5.10, the regular, long-term moderate to high maternal use of the drugs or substances of abuse that have potential for moderate to high abuse places breast-fed neonates and infants at risk for their direct expected pharmacological effects, including physical dependence.

The effects experienced by the nursing neonate or infant will be related to three major factors: (1) concentration of the drug or substance of abuse excreted in breast milk; (2) amount of milk consumed; and (3) rate at which the drug or substance of abuse is metabolized by the neonate or infant. For most of the drugs and substances of abuse, metabolism is significantly reduced due to the immature development of the hepatic microsomal enzyme systems in neonates and infants younger than 3 months of age and, particularly so, in premature neonates and infants. Although we have taken these listed variables into account when constructing

Table 5.10, it should be noted that, in general, related studies and reports concerning the excretion of the drugs and substances of abuse in breast milk have these limitations: (1) small sample sizes; (2) use of quasi-experimental designs, including case reports; (3) failure to document timing of maternal drug use in relation to timing of breast-feeding or collection of breast-milk samples; and (4) failure to document whether breast-milk samples were foremilk or hindmilk samples.

### Recommendations

When mothers require psychodepressant pharmacotherapy (e.g., opiate analgesic) for acute, short-term use (e.g., a few days for the medical management of a badly sprained ankle), these guidelines are recommended: (1) the lowest effective dose should be prescribed; (2) the prescribed drug or substance of abuse should be taken as long before breast-feeding as possible (e.g., shortly after breast-feeding) in order to avoid any adverse effects on breast-feeding (see Table 5.10); and (3) the breast-fed neonate or infant should be carefully monitored for any untoward effects (e.g., oversedation or respiratory depression related to the opiate analgesic). When mothers require regular, long-term psychodepressant pharmacotherapy (e.g., benzodiazepines) for the medical management of epilepsy or other seizure disorder, it is recommended that breast-feeding be discontinued indefinitely, or until the pharmacotherapy is no longer needed (Pagliaro & Pagliaro, 1999, 2000). For mothers who use various drugs and substances of abuse, particularly those who have active alcohol use disorders or substance use disorders, it is recommended that breast-feeding be discontinued. In addition, appropriate treatment and referral services should be provided for these mothers and their neonates and infants, as needed.

## EXPOSURE TO SECONDHAND SMOKE

Neonates, infants, and children may be exposed on a daily basis to chemicals and pollutants in the air they breathe, the water that they drink, and the foods that they eat. They also may be exposed to various drugs and substances of abuse that may be used by their mothers, fathers, siblings, babysitters or nannies, or other household members and visitors to the home, including extended family members and friends. Pulmonary inhalation is the primary method of exposure of young infants and children to these drugs and substances of abuse—they directly inhale a smoker's exhaled smoke or simply breathe the air in a room that has become laden with the smoke from a burning tobacco cigarette, marijuana joint, crack pipe, or meth pipe.

The smoking of these drugs and substances of abuse by parents and others in the presence of neonates, infants, and children places them at significant risk for harmful effects.

The testing of scalp hair samples from infants and children can reveal environmental smoke exposure[27] to several drugs and substances of abuse, including cannabis (i.e., THC), cocaine (i.e., crack cocaine and its inactive metabolite, benzoylecgonine), methamphetamine (i.e., crystal, ice, speed); and nicotine/tobacco (along with nicotine's inactive metabolite, cotinine) (Florescu, Ferrence, Einarson, et al., 2007; Klein & Koren, 1999; Lewis, Moore, Morrissey, et al., 1997). Positive results can help guide therapeutic intervention and help to formulate recommendations for the prevention of continued, long-term exposure. They also can be used to help support cases involving child protection services in regard to the removal of infants and young children from dangerous home situations and unhealthy living environments.

The level of harm associated with the environmental exposure to cannabis, methamphetamine, tobacco, or other smoke is related directly to the concentration of the drug or substance of abuse that is inhaled by the neonate, infant, or child and to the length of time that he or she is exposed. For example, a mother could smoke a joint in the backyard while watching her toddler play in his playpen for 10 minutes, could smoke a crack cocaine pipe for 3 minutes while her preschooler watches TV on the floor in a small apartment living room, on could smoke a tobacco cigarette while driving to the store, a 20-minute trip, with her infant daughter strapped into an infant car seat behind her with the car windows tightly rolled up on a cold winter day.

The type of smoke, its concentration in the air, and the length of time that an infant, child, or adolescent is exposed to the smoke are the primary factors involved in determining the

---

[27] Previously, environmental smoke exposure to the drugs and substances of abuse was referred to as *involuntary smoking*, *passive smoking*, or *side-stream smoking*.

**TABLE 5.10 Drugs and Substances of Abuse Excreted in Human Breast Milk**

| Drug or Substance of Abuse | Average Concentration in Breast Milk[a] | Expected Effects on Breast-Feeding and Behavior of Breast-Fed Neonates and Infants |
|---|---|---|
| **Alcohol** (ethanol) (e.g., beer, wine, distilled liquor) | 0.5–1 mg/ml | • *Low to moderate* maternal use of alcohol is *not* generally significant.<br>• *High* maternal use of alcohol may affect oxytocin and prolactin (the hormones predominantly involved in milk production and excretion) and consequently:<br>  • reduce milk production by approximately 20%<br>  • inhibit milk ejection<br>  • decrease neonatal milk consumption because of effect on taste<br>  • adversely affect the *quantity* and *quality* of various constituents of breast milk resulting in diminished available nutrients for breast-fed neonates and infants.<br>• Of maternally consumed alcohol, 2% or less is generally transferred to breast milk.<br>• Following maternal consumption, alcohol concentrations in breast milk generally peak in 30–60 minutes. |
| **Alfentanil** *See Opiate Analgesics* | | |
| **Alprazolam** *See Benzodiazepines* | | |
| **Amphetamines** (e.g., amphetamine, dextroamphetamine [Dexedrine®]; methamphetamine) | 50 to 200 µg/ml | • Maternal amphetamine use may produce expected psychostimulant effects among breast-fed neonates and infants. However, no significant adverse effects have been reported for breast-fed neonates and infants. |
| **Barbiturates** (e.g., pentobarbital [Nembutal®]; phenobarbital; [Luminal®]; secobarbital [Seconal®]) | There is significant interpatient variability, and actual concentrations also vary in regard to specific barbiturate used and its dose: Phenobarbital: 5–10 µg/ml | • May cause drowsiness, hypotonia, lethargy, and poor feeding among breast-fed neonates and infants.<br>• Regular, long-term maternal use of high doses may result in physical dependence among breast-fed neonates and infants who may display the barbiturate withdrawal syndrome when either breast feeding or maternal use is discontinued abruptly.<br>• Phenobarbital in breast milk actually may prevent the occurrence of the neonatal barbiturate withdrawal syndrome among neonates born physically dependent on barbiturates. |

**Benzodiazepines**
(e.g., alprazolam [Xanax®]; clonazepam [Rivotril®]; clorazepate [Tranxene®]; diazepam [Valium®]; lorazepam [Ativan®]; midazolam; oxazepam [Serax®]; quazepam [Doral®]; temazepam [Restoril®])

Varies in regard to the specific benzodiazepine used and its dose:
Alprazolam: 3.7 ng/ml
Clonazepam: 12 ng/ml;
Clorazepate: 7.5 to 15 ng/ml (as nordiazepam)
Diazepam: 80 ng/ml[b]
Lorazepam: 10 ng/ml
Midazolam: 12 ng/ml[c]
Oxazepam: 20 µg/ml
Quazepam: 100 ng/ml
Temazepam: 27 ng/ml

- Generally excreted in amounts that are sufficient to cause sedation among breast-fed neonates and infants. However, effects are less significant for lorazepam (Ativan®) and oxazepam (Serax®), which do *not* have active metabolites.
- Benzodiazepines and their metabolites can accumulate among breast-fed neonates because of their immature hepatic metabolizing enzyme systems, particularly during the first week of life.
- High maternal use may result in the development of benzodiazepine physical dependence among neonates who are breast-feeding. The neonatal benzodiazepine withdrawal syndrome, characterized by crying and irritability, also may occur with the abrupt discontinuation of either breast feeding or the mother's use of benzodiazepines.

**Buprenophine**
*See Opiate Analgesics*

**Butorphanol**
*See Opiate Analgesics*

**Caffeine** (e.g., caffeinated soft drinks; coffee; energy drinks; tea)

2.5 µg/ml (range: 1–9 µg/ml)

- Low maternal use is not significant because caffeine is excreted in relatively small amounts in breast milk.
- Effects may be more significant among neonates and premature infants because of their immature hepatic metabolizing systems that may result in a corresponding increase in the elimination half-life of caffeine.
- High maternal use (i.e., more than 5 cups of coffee daily) may cause insomnia, irritability, jitteriness, restlessness, or trembling among neonates and infants with effects being more significant among neonates who are premature.
- Maternal consumption of 3 or more caffeinated beverages (e.g., cup of regular coffee, can of Coca-Cola Classic®) per day may significantly *decrease* the iron concentration of breast milk.

**Cannabis** (THC) (e.g., marijuana; hashish; hashish oil)

200 ng/ml

- THC, the active ingredient of cannabis, is highly lipophilic, and breast milk is high in fat. Thus, breast milk concentrations of THC can be up to 8 times higher than maternal blood concentrations.
- THC may cause drowsiness among breast-fed neonates and infants. However, because of the paucity of reported data, other potential effects on neonates and infants, other than THC-related red-eyes, are unknown. Most available studies report no significant differences between breast-fed neonates whose mothers smoked marijuana and those whose mothers did not. The American Academy of Pediatrics has contraindicated the use of cannabis by mothers who are breast-feeding. We concur with this recommendation, not only because of the available empirical data on maternal marijuana use and breast-feeding, but also because of the available empirical data on the effects of secondhand smoke. (See previous related discussion.)

*(Continued)*

TABLE 5.10  Drugs and Substances of Abuse Excreted in Human Breast Milk (Continued)

| Drug or Substance of Abuse | Average Concentration in Breast Milk[a] | Expected Effects on Breast-Feeding and Behavior of Breast-Fed Neonates and Infants |
|---|---|---|
| Carisoprodol (Soma®, Vanadom®) | 1 µg/ml (as carisoprodol) 11 µg/ml (as meprobamate, see note) | • NOTE: Carisoprodol is metabolized to its active metabolite, meprobamate. Thus, the associated concentration of meprobamate in breast milk is of clinical relevance. Also see meprobamate entry in this table.<br>• May cause drowsiness or lethargy among breast-fed neonates and infants whose mothers use higher doses of carisoprodol. |
| Chloral Hydrate (Noctec®) | 10 µg/ml (i.e., greater than or equal to 50% of maternal blood concentration) 20 µg/ml (trichloroethanol, see note) | • NOTE: Chloral hydrate and its active metabolite (trichloroethanol) are excreted in significant concentrations in breast milk and may be detectable for up to 24 hours following maternal ingestion.<br>• May cause drowsiness or sedation among breast-fed neonates and infants, particularly 1 to 3 hours after maternal ingestion when its concentration in breast milk is at its peak. |
| Clonazepam See *Benzodiazepines* | | |
| Clorazepate See *Benzodiazepines* | | |
| Cocaine (Crack)[d] | The analysis of breast-milk samples obtained from mothers who were using cocaine tested positive for both cocaine and its major metabolite, benzoylecgonine. Further analysis of the breast milk from 1 mother found: cocaine, 12.1 µg/ml benzoylecgonine, 119 ng/ml norcocaine, 119 ng/ml | • Cocaine is detectable in breast milk for up to 36 hours after maternal use.<br>• May cause dilated pupils and CNS excitation (e.g., irritability, tremors, or seizures) among neonates and infants whose mothers use high doses of cocaine.<br>• Effects may be more significant among premature neonates in particular because they are unable to metabolize cocaine as readily as older infants due to their immature hepatic metabolizing systems.<br>• The American Academy of Pediatrics contraindicates the use of cocaine by mothers who are breast-feeding. We concur with this recommendation not only based on the available empirical data on maternal use of cocaine and breast-feeding but also based on the available empirical data on the effects of secondhand smoke related to the maternal use of cocaine base (i.e., crack or freebase). (See previous related discussion.) |
| Codeine See *Opiate Analgesics* | | |
| Coffee See *Caffeine* | | |
| Dextroamphetamine See *Amphetamines* | | |
| Diazepam See *Benzodiazepines* | | |

| Drug | | |
|---|---|---|
| Ethanol<br>See *Alcohol* | | |
| Fentanyl<br>See *Opiate Analgesics* | | |
| Hashish<br>See *Cannabis* | | |
| Hashish Oil<br>See *Cannabis* | | |
| Heroin<br>See *Opiate Analgesics* | | |
| Hydrocodone<br>See *Opiate Analgesics* | | |
| Hydromorphone<br>See *Opiate Analgesics* | | |
| Lorazepam<br>See *Benzodiazepines* | | |
| Marijuana<br>See *Cannabis* | | |
| Meperidine<br>See *Opiate Analgesics* | | |
| Meprobamate (Equanil®, Miltown®) | Concentrations may be 2–4 times maternal blood concentrations. (Also see *Carisoprodol* entry in this table.) | • Seldom used today in the U.S. and Canada but available in Mexico and through Internet sellers.<br>• Neonates and infants may display drowsiness and lethargy.<br>• Regular, long-term maternal use of large doses may result in meprobamate physical dependence among nursing neonates and infants. A meprobamate withdrawal syndrome may occur among breast-fed neonates and infants when breast-feeding or maternal meprobamate use is discontinued abruptly. |
| Methadone<br>See *Opiate Analgesics* | | |
| Methamphetamine<br>See *Amphetamines* | | |
| Midazolam<br>See *Benzodiazepines* | | |

207

(Continued)

**TABLE 5.10   Drugs and Substances of Abuse Excreted in Human Breast Milk (Continued)**

| Drug or Substance of Abuse | Average Concentration in Breast Milk[a] | Expected Effects on Breast-Feeding and Behavior of Breast-Fed Neonates and Infants |
|---|---|---|
| Morphine *See Opiate Analgesics* | | |
| Nalbuphine *See Opiate Analgesics* | | |
| Nicotine (e.g., tobacco cigarettes, cigars, cigarillos; nicotine pipe tobacco; nicotine replacement products, such as Nicoderm®, Nicorette®, and Nicotrol®) | 50–200 ng/ml | • Nicotine and its *inactive* metabolite, cotinine, are excreted in breast milk in concentrations that are up to 3 times higher than maternal blood or serum concentrations. Nicotine breast milk concentrations vary in regard to low, moderate, or heavy maternal use.<br>• Maternal nicotine use may reduce breast-milk production by up to 20%.<br>• Breast-fed neonates and infants may display CNS excitation (e.g., increased heart rate, restlessness). Diarrhea and vomiting also may occur.<br>• A neonatal nicotine withdrawal syndrome may occur when breast feeding or maternal use of nicotine is discontinued abruptly.<br>• Adolescent girls who smoke tobacco cigarettes or use nicotine replacement products should not breast-feed. |
| Opiate Analgesics (e.g., alfentanil [Alfenta®]; buprenorphine [Buprenex®]; butorphanol [Stadol®]; codeine; fentanyl [Duragesic®]; heroin; hydrocodone [Hycodan®]; hydromorphone [Dilaudid®]; meperidine [Demerol®]; methadone; morphine; nalbuphine [Nubain®]; oxycodone [OxyContin®]; propoxyphene [Darvon®]) | Breast-milk concentrations greater than 100% of maternal serum concentrations may be achieved depending on the specific opiate analgesic used:<br>Alfentanil: 1 ng/ml<br>Buprenorphine: 0.5–15 ng/ml (depending on dosage)<br>Butorphanol: 4 ng/ml<br>Codeine: 150–350 ng/ml<br>Fentanyl: 0.15 ng/ml<br>Hydrocodone: 5–125 ng/ml<br>Hydromorphone: 1 ng/ml<br>Meperidine: 200 ng/ml (range 130 to 500 ng/ml)<br>Methadone: 100 ng/ml (range: 50–230 ng/ml)<br>Morphine: 10–50 ng/ml<br>Nalbuphine: 5–100 ng/ml<br>Oxycodone: 100 ng/ml (range 5–230 ng/ml)<br>Propoxyphene 20–210 ng/ml (for *active* metabolite, norpropoxyphene, 50–600 ng/ml) | • All may cause bradycardia, drowsiness, lethargy, sedation, and respiratory depression (e.g., apnea) among neonates and infants, depending primarily on maternal dosage.<br>• Codeine (methylmorphine) has several active metabolites, including morphine, which generally is excreted in low concentrations in breast milk. Rapid metabolism of codeine by mothers who are breast-feeding, as well as their nursing infants, is determined primarily by genotypic expression of the cytochrome P450–2D6 isoenzyme and can result in elevated, potentially fatal, levels of morphine in the infant. Adolescent mothers and infants of African or Asian descent are at greater risk of metabolizing codeine rapidly. This rapid metabolism may occur even with relatively low maternal dosing of codeine (e.g., 2 Tylenol #3® tablets twice daily—a dosage often administered for the management of pain associated with episiotomy and cesarean section). If nursing mothers cannot be genotyped, breast-feeding should be suspended or the nursing neonate or infant should be closely monitored for signs and symptoms of opiate analgesic toxicity, including excessive drowsiness, lethargy, and poor feeding.<br>• For those neonates who develop opiate analgesic dependence in utero, methadone present in breast milk may prevent or reduce the severity of the associated neonatal opiate analgesic withdrawal syndrome.<br>• General consensus regarding breast-feeding by mothers enrolled in a methadone maintenance program is that it is *safe*, posing minimal risk to the nursing neonate or infant.<br>• A neonatal opiate analgesic withdrawal syndrome may occur when either breast-feeding or maternal opiate use is discontinued abruptly. This syndrome is particularly significant for neonates and infants whose mothers use heroin. |

| | | |
|---|---|---|
| Oxazepam<br>*See Benzodiazepines* | | |
| Oxycodone<br>*See Opiate Analgesics* | | |
| Pentobarbital<br>*See Barbiturates* | | |
| Phencyclidine (PCP) | Breast milk sampled from mothers using phencyclidine tests positive for the drug | • Breast-fed neonates of mothers who use PCP may display behavioral problems, coma, irritability, or lethargy.<br>• Although not yet documented, a cause for concern is the potential for long-term neurocognitive impairment related to phencylidine's antagonism of N-methyl-D-aspartate (NMDA) receptors. |
| Phenobarbital<br>*See Barbiturates* | | |
| Propoxyphene<br>*See Opiate Analgesics* | | |
| Quazepam<br>*See Benzodiazepines* | | |
| Secobarbital<br>*See Barbiturates* | | |
| Tea<br>*See Caffeine* | | |
| Temazepam<br>*See Benzodiazepines* | | |
| Tobacco<br>*See Nicotine* | | |
| Zaleplon<br>*See Z-Drugs* | | |
| Zolpidem<br>*See Z-Drugs* | | |
| Zopiclone<br>*See Z-Drugs* | | |

*(Continued)*

TABLE 5.10   Drugs and Substances of Abuse Excreted in Human Breast Milk (Continued)

| Drug or Substance of Abuse | Average Concentration in Breast Milk[a] | Expected Effects on Breast-Feeding and Behavior of Breast-Fed Neonates and Infants |
|---|---|---|
| Z-Drugs (e.g., miscellaneous sedative-hypnotics: zaleplon [Sonata®]; zolpidem [Ambien®]; zopiclone [Imovane®]) | Zopiclone: 34 ng/ml (range, 23 to 57 ng/ml) | The maternal *milk-to-plasma ratio* for both zaleplon and zopiclone is approximately 0.5. |

[a] Neonates who are exclusively fed breast milk consume, on average, approximately 150 ml breast milk per kg body weight per day.

The composition of colostrum (i.e., breast fluid excreted prior to actual milk production that begins prior to delivery and peaks during the first few days following delivery) is significantly different from breast milk. Colostrum, known as first milk or foremilk, is higher in protein content but lower in fat (lipid) content than breast milk. It also contains higher concentrations of immune factors, particularly the immunoglobulins (e.g., IgA, IgG, IgM). Colostrum is helpful in aiding the elimination of the neonate's first stool, or meconium, and in providing antibodies against viral and bacterial infections. However, because it has a different composition than breast milk, transfer of the drugs and substances of abuse into this fluid from maternal serum may be significantly different from that for breast milk. Thus, data from studies reporting concentration of drugs and substances of abuse in colostrum have not been included in this table.

[b] Also, nordiazepam (desmethyldiazepam), an active metabolite of diazepam: 50 ng/ml.

[c] Use of a single preanesthetic dose of midazolam during delivery results in negligible concentrations in breast milk. Consequently, use of midazolam in this therapeutic context does not require the interruption of breast-feeding.

[d] A related exposure to cocaine was reported for a neonate admitted to the emergency department with hypertension, tachycardia, and status epilepticus. His mother had applied cocaine powder to her nipples prior to breast-feeding to relieve associated pain.

New mothers who use cocaine are less likely to initiate breast-feeding with their newborns than are new mothers who do not use cocaine.

[e] When a single dose of fentanyl is administered as an adjunct to anesthesia, negligible breast milk concentrations are obtained. Consequently, use of fentanyl in this therapeutic context does not require interruption of breast-feeding.

Sources: Abdel-Latif, Pinner, Clews, et al., 2006; American Academy of Pediatrics, Committee on Drugs, 2001; Anderson, Sauberan, Lane, et al., 2007; Bartu, Dusci, & Ilett, 2010; Bowes, 1980; Chaney, Franke, & Wadlington, 1988; Cohen, 2009; Dahlstrom, Ebersjo, & Lundell, 2008; Darwish, Martin, Cevallos, et al., 1999; Dryden, Young, Hepburn, et al., 2009; Dyer, 2007; Edwards, Rudy, Wermeling, et al., 2003; FDA Public Health Advisory, 2007; Findlay, DeAngelis, Kearney, et al., 1981; Garry, Rigourd, Amirouche, et al., 2009; Glatstein, Garcia-Bournissen, Finkelstein, et al., 2008; Grimm, Pauly, Poschl, et al., 2005; Heil & Subramanian, 1998; Ilett, Hale, Page-Sharp, et al., 2003; Ilett, Paech, Page-Sharp, et al., 2008; Jacqz-Aigrain, Serreau, Boissinot, et al., 2007; Jansson, Choo, Harrow, et al., 2007; Jansson, Velez, & Harrow, 2004; Kaufman, Petrucha, Pitts, et al., 1983; Kohen, 2005; Kozer & Koren, 2001; Lindemalm, Nydert, Svensson, et al., 2009; Llewellyn & Stowe, 1998; Madadi, Koren, Cairns, et al., 2007; Madadi, Ross, Hayden, et al., 2009; Matheson, Sande, & Gaillot, 1990; McCarthy & Posey, 2000; Mennella, 2001; Meny, Naumburg, Alger, et al., 1993; Moretti, 2009; Nitsun, Szokol, Saleh, et al., 2006; Nordeng, Zahlsen, & Spigset, 2001; O'Mara, & Nahata, 2002; Pagliaro & Pagliaro, 2009; Perez-Reyes & Wall, 1982; Philipp, Merewood, & O'Brien, 2003; Rigourd, Amirouche, Tasseau, et al., 2008; Willmann, Edginton, Coboeken, et al., 2009; Winecker, Goldberger, Tebbett, et al., 2001; Wojnar-Horton, Kristensen, Yapp, et al., 1997.

rate and amount of the drug or substance of abuse absorbed into the bloodstream and its related effects and the extent of respiratory toxicity and direct pulmonary damage (e.g., asthma, bronchitis, cancer, respiratory tract infections) that may develop. Of increasing concern is the fact that neonates, infants, children, and adolescents also can be exposed to the fumes of various drugs and substances of abuse, such as methamphetamine, that are being cooked up in the kitchen while they are sleeping in a stroller, eating dinner, or playing on the floor.

The drugs and substances of abuse that are commonly smoked by adolescent mothers include:

- Cannabis
- Cocaine base (crack)
- Nicotine (tobacco)
- Methamphetamine
- Various opiate analgesics, particularly heroin

The exposure of neonates, infants, and children to these drugs and substances of abuse by secondhand smoke and their related effects are discussed in the next sections.

## Cannabis

Adolescent girls commonly smoke *cannabis* in its various forms, particularly marijuana, which is both generally affordable and widely available. While all adolescent girls do not expose their infants and children (or those of others) to their marijuana smoke, some do. In addition, even those who do not smoke may expose their infants and children as well as themselves if their boyfriends (or other friends) smoke marijuana in their presence. Neonates, infants, children, and adolescents also are commonly subjected to exposure to a variety of volatile toxic chemicals that may be used to grow marijuana hydroponically or to produce hashish in a home-based grow-op.

## Cocaine

Since the early 1990s, numerous case studies and reports have been published concerning infants and children who have tested positive for cocaine following exposure to secondhand smoke associated with crack cocaine use by their older siblings and adult caregivers (Bateman & Heagarty, 1989; Heidemann & Goetting, 1990; Randall, 1992). Many of the infants and children exposed to the smoke from cocaine base (crack, freebase) have displayed expected psychostimulant effects, including agitation, irritability, and seizures. They also have displayed adverse smoke-related pulmonary effects, including irritation to upper and lower airway structures—characterized by coughing and the development of asthma—and other associated respiratory conditions (Lustbader, Mayes, McGee, et al., 1998). The passive exposure to secondhand crack cocaine smoke also has been implicated in several cases of cocaine poisoning that have resulted in infant death (Mirchandani, Mirchandani, Hellman, et al., 1991). Not surprisingly, Garcia-Bournissen, Nesterenko, Karaskov, et al. (2009) found a significant correlation between the presence of cocaine in the hair samples of adult primary caregivers and the hair samples of their infants.

## Methamphetamine

Home-based methamphetamine production sites in house trailers (mobile homes), apartment kitchens and bathrooms, and single-home basements and garages are increasingly being used by mom-and-pop producers and suppliers of both powdered and crystalline methamphetamine, where they expose their children to chemicals and fumes related to methamphetamine production and use (Swetlow, 2003). When tested, up to 50% of the children who are exposed to the fumes released when the meth is cooked up have demonstrated positive urine analysis for methamphetamine (Grant, Bell, Stewart, et al., 2010). The principal routes of exposure for these children are breathing in the vapors that are formed during the production process and inhaling the residual smoke that is exhaled as their parent smokes the crystal meth or ice just produced or purchased (Pagliaro & Pagliaro, *Clinical Patient Data Files*).

The production and sale of powdered methamphetamine offers other concerns that are associated with one of its principal methods of use: intravenous injection. While mom-and-pop methamphetamine production sites expose infants and children to generally extremely filthy and unsanitary conditions, those that produce and sell powdered methamphetamine commonly are found strewn with used needles and syringes, or the discarded works of users, who cannot wait to inject the meth they just purchased[28] (Pagliaro & Pagliaro, *Clinical Patient Data Files*). Many infants and young children living in these conditions have been found with needle puncture marks over their arms, hands, legs, and feet that have been associated with hepatitis, HIV, and other infections (Swetlow, 2003).

### Nicotine (Tobacco Smoke)

The incidence of exposure among children in the United States to secondhand tobacco smoke[29] is significant (Marshall, Schooley, Ryan, et al., 2006) and has been related to significant morbidity and mortality (Gehrman & Hovell, 2003; Mbulo, 2008; Vargas, Brenner, Clark, et al., 2007). For example, Klerman (2004) estimated that more than 20 million children in the United States (i.e., approximately one-third of all children in the nation) are exposed to secondhand tobacco smoke and that 10% of these children are exposed at home, primarily from parents, on a regular basis. The Environmental Protection Agency (2003, p.1) presented similar findings based on a national survey:

> "Almost 3 million children (11%) aged 6 and under, were reported to be exposed to environmental tobacco smoke … on a regular basis [i.e., 4 or more days per week] in their home."

The incidence of SIDS[30] is significantly higher, by several-fold, among infants whose parent(s) or primary caregiver(s) smoke tobacco (Anderson & Cook, 1997; Blackburn, Bonas, Spencer, et al., 2004; Hofhuis, de Jongste, & Merkus, 2003; Mitchell, Ford, Stewart, et al., 1993; U.S. Department of Health and Human Services, 2006). Several theories, supported by both clinical observation and quantitative research studies, have been advanced to help to explain this incidence and to identify infants who may be at particular risk. For example, Horne, Ferens, Watts, et al. (2002) found that maternal smoking significantly elevated the arousal threshold from quiet sleep for young infants at a high-risk age for SIDS (i.e., 2 to 3 months of age) when they were placed in their cribs on their abdomens (prone position) to go to sleep as opposed to being placed on their backs (supine position). It was found that spontaneous arousals occurred less frequently among infants whose mothers smoked regardless of sleep position.

Adgent (2006) argued that nicotine binds to the infant's nAChRs, which, consequently, stimulate a cholinergic response that adversely affects the infant's natural hypoxia response and contributes to the occurrence of SIDS. It should be noted that the tobacco industry reportedly has engaged in a deliberate attempt to influence professional authors and researchers to mitigate their findings in regard to the significance of the relationship between secondhand smoke exposure and SIDS (Tong, England, & Glantz, 2005).

---

[28] Another source of these used needles and syringes is often the mom-and-pop producers of the methamphetamine—the parents of the young children (Pagliaro & Pagliaro, *Clinical Patient Data Files*).

[29] "Secondhand tobacco smoke" also has been referred to as side-stream tobacco smoke or environmental tobacco smoke.

[30] Also see the related discussion in the earlier sections, "Teratogenic Potential of the Drugs and Substances of Abuse," "Psychostimulants," and "Nicotine (Tobacco Smoking)."

The risk for

- Allergies (Early exposure, 2008)
- Chronic obstructive pulmonary disease (COPD), including asthma and bronchitis (Dybing & Sanner, 1999; EPA, 2003; Gerald, Gerald, Gibson, et al., 2009; Hofhuis, de Jongste, & Merkus, 2003)
- Otitis media (CDC, 2008a; Dybing & Sanner, 1999)
- Respiratory infections (Gilliland, Berhane, Islam, et al., 2003; Klerman, 2004)

also is significantly increased among neonates, infants, children, and adolescents who are exposed to tobacco smoke by their primary caregivers (U.S. Department of Health and Human Services, 2006).

In addition to pulmonary effects, several studies (e.g., Bada, Das, Bauer, et al., 2007; Chiriboga, 2003; Cornelius, Ryan, Day, et al., 2001; Fagnano, Conn, & Halterman, 2008) have reported an increased incidence of externalizing and other behavior problems, such as A-D/HD, particularly among children whose mothers smoked tobacco cigarettes—even after controlling for maternal tobacco smoking during pregnancy (see the "Prenatal Exposure: Teratogenesis and Fetotoxicity" section of this chapter for additional discussion).

## Heroin and Other Opiate Analgesics

Opium smoking (e.g., chasing the dragon) has been practiced for thousands of years. However, over the last 50 years, smoking black tar heroin from Mexico has increased steadily in North America. In addition, over the last 20 years, a variety of different prescription opiate analgesics have been smoked in a similar manner by crushing the prescription tablets into a fine powder, heating the resultant powder until it vaporizes, and then smoking the vapor trail. Similarly, some users cut, empty, and vaporize the contents of transdermal fentanyl delivery system, or skin patch (Duragesic®) and inhale, or smoke, the vaporized fentanyl.

Although related published data are unavailable, it would be expected that the vaporized drug or substance of abuse, in this case opiate analgesics, offers less risk for exposed neonates, infants, children, and adolescents as compared to more traditional methods of use (e.g., smoking an opium pipe). However, if they are exposed to high concentrations of opium vapor, or if they are frequently exposed to low concentrations, children more than likely will display expected psychodepressant effects (e.g., be on the nod). In addition, as occurs with any form of smoke[31] inhalation, regular, long-term exposure to the smoke may result in expected pulmonary toxicities, including pulmonary irritation and damage to both the upper and lower airways.

## EXPOSURE BY UNINTENTIONAL CHILDHOOD POISONINGS

This section presents a brief overview and discussion of unintentional childhood poisonings that have involved the drugs and substances of abuse.[32] Deliberate ingestion of the

---

[31] Smoke is simply a gas or a mixture of gases (e.g., carbon dioxide, carbon monoxide, and oxygen) that also contains particulate matter (i.e., solids, including the waste by-products of pyrolysis), thus making it visible to the naked eye (e.g., a puff of smoke, a cloud of smoke). It is the particulate matter in smoke that both makes the gas visible to the naked eye and causes most of the associated pulmonary irritation or damage.

[32] The CDC (2010, p. 1) defines "unintentional poisoning" as taking or giving a substance *without* intentionally meaning to cause harm. In comparison, an "intentional poisoning" is meant to cause harm to oneself or others (e.g., ingesting an overdose of sleeping pills as a suicide attempt; poisoning a parent in order to get an inheritance).

Thus, according to the definition, the unintentional overdosage of an adolescent in the context of experimenting with a couple of new and popular drugs and substances of abuse would be considered an unintentional poisoning, as would the ingestion of a drug or substance of abuse by a toddler who found some capsules or tablets on the floor and ate them. For this chapter, we are focusing only on the latter. The former, overdosages, are specifically considered and discussed in relation to their general pharmacology in Chapter 1, *The Psychodepressants*, Chapter 2, *The Psychostimulants*, and Chapter 3, *The Psychodelics*.

drugs or substances of abuse by children in the context of a suicide attempt are extremely rare and are not discussed. Likewise, deliberate poisoning of infants and children by their siblings or parents (or other primary caregivers) with the use of the drugs and substances of abuse (e.g., Couper, Chopra, & Pierre-Louis, 2005; Pagliaro & Pagliaro, *Clinical Patient Data Files*; Perez, Scribano, & Perry, 2004; Sidlo, Valuch, Ocko, et al., 2009) is not discussed, including those that are associated with Munchausen by proxy (Associated Press, 2009; Pagliaro & Pagliaro, *Clinical Patient Data Files*; Sanders & Bursch, 2002; Stirling, 2007). Not surprisingly, unintentional childhood poisonings have involved each of the three major classes of the drugs and substances of abuse: the psychodepressants, the psychostimulants, and the psychodelics. However, before reviewing and analyzing the research that has been published on these unintentional poisonings, it seems reasonable to comment on what has not been published.

Comprehensive computerized searches, using the major search engines and specialized Web sites (e.g, Bing, Google, PubMed), were completed in order to identify published research on childhood poisonings over the past three decades in North America. Excluding nicotine, these searches revealed only a few dozen related professional or scholarly articles and research studies that implicated the drugs and substances of abuse, and these were primarily case reports. The reasons for this paucity of published research could include the fact that unintentional poisoning is extremely rare. For example, perhaps parents and caregivers who use the various drugs and substances of abuse take extra precautions not to use them in front of their children and to ensure that they do not have inadvertent access to them. However, it seems incongruous, and highly unlikely, that users,

particularly when they are high on their drugs or substances of abuse, would be taking special precautions to protect their children from unintentional exposure. Thus, a more likely and plausible explanation is that the majority of related unintentional exposures go unreported—primarily to avoid confiscation of the parent's (legal guardian's) or caregiver's stash and possible legal prosecution.

In this regard, health and social care providers are encouraged to follow serious cases of parent or caregiver use of the drugs and substances of abuse carefully and to remain vigilant in regard to the safety and well-being of affected infants and children. When such cases do occur, health and social care professionals also are encouraged to publish their case histories and research in order to increase attention to the incidence and context of unintentional childhood poisonings involving the drugs and substances of abuse and thus contribute to both prevention and treatment.

Over the past three decades, several relatively consistent patterns and statistics associated with unintentional childhood poisonings have been repeatedly observed and reported in the available published literature. For example, the majority of reported cases of unintentional childhood poisonings in North America involve: (1) cleaning supplies; (2) cosmetics; (3) prescription and nonprescription drugs, including the drugs and substances of abuse; and (4) personal care products. Of all of the poisoning cases reported, more than 80% are unintentional,[33] more than 90% occur in the home or place of residence, and more than 50% involve children younger than 6 years of age. In addition, approximately 80% involve oral ingestion; approximately 90% result in little or no significant toxicity; and boys and girls are equally involved. On a positive note, the number of reported deaths involving young children decreased significantly during this

---

[33] Intentional poisonings are more likely to occur among adolescents, often in the context of a suicide attempt, and account for 90% of reported poisoning deaths in this age group.

time period[34] (e.g., American Association of Poison Control Centers, 2011; CDC, 2010; Klein-Schwartz & Oderda, 2002; National Capital Poison Center, 2011).

## Psychodepressants Involved in Unintentional Childhood Poisonings

This section presents an overview and analysis of the limited available published research studies and case histories that involve alcohol and other sedative-hypnotics, the opiate analgesics, and the volatile solvents and inhalants in unintentional childhood poisonings.

### *Alcohol and Other Sedative-Hypnotics*

Massey and Shulman (2006), in their analysis of data from the American Association of Poison Control Centers (AAPCC), found that alcohol poisoning associated with the ingestion of alcohol-containing mouthwashes by children was significant, even after the requirement for child-resistant packaging was enacted. Shulman and Wells (1997) found that a child weighing 33 pounds (15 kg) who ingests 7.2 oz Listerine® mouthwash (containing 26.9% alcohol) has ingested a potentially lethal amount of alcohol.

### *Opiate Analgesics*

Published data derived from the formal study of reported cases of opiate analgesic poisonings among children in North America is extremely limited. In fact, Bailey, Campagna, and Dart (2008) referred to this situation as an unrecognized toll. In their single review of data from U.S. poison centers for January 2003 to June 2006, they found 9,240 cases of unintentional poisoning among children younger

than 6 years of age that involved the opiate analgesics. Among these poisoning cases:

Buprenorphine (Subutex®)[35] accounted for 176 cases
Fentanyl (Actiq®) for 123 cases
Hydrocodone (Hycodan®) for 6,003 cases
Hydromorphone (Dilaudid®) for 68 cases
Methadone (Dolophine®) for 415 cases
Morphine (MS Contin®) for 419 cases
Oxycodone (OxyContin®) for 2,036 cases

The median age of the children who were involved in these poisonings was 2 years of age (range neonate to 5.5 years of age). Boys and girls were equally involved, and 92% of the poisonings occurred in the child's home. Virtually all of the opiate analgesics that were involved in these cases had been prescribed for an adult residing in the child's home, and virtually all of the poisonings (i.e., more than 99%) were unintentional. Out of the total 9,240 cases, only 8 were fatal—2 involving hydrocodone, 2 involving methadone, and 4 involving oxycodone.

The most commonly observed signs and symptoms of opiate analgesic poisoning among children include: miosis, respiratory depression, and somnolence. (Also see related discussion in Chapter 1, *The Psychodepressants*.) Although deaths related to opiate analgesic poisoning among North American children are relatively rare (i.e., fewer than 1 in 1,000, as found in the Bailey, Campagna, and Dart [2008] study), the potentially lethal amount of an opiate analgesic for a 22-pound (10-kg) toddler has been estimated to be only 1 or 2 tablets for several of the commonly available opiate analgesics (e.g., codeine, 60–120 mg; hydrocodone, 60 mg; methadone, 40 mg; and morphine, 200 mg). Standard, and apparently efficacious,

---

[34] This decrease in reported childhood poisonings has been related to several factors, including: (1) use of child-resistant product packaging, such as child-resistant closures on both prescription and nonprescription drugs; (2) increased public awareness of ways to prevent childhood poisonings; (3) development and implementation of poison prevention projects (e.g., prescription drug roundup); (4) establishment of regional poison control centers; and (5) improved medical management of childhood poisoning cases.

[35] The brand or trade names listed are not meant to imply the involvement of a particular brand or trade name in the reported unintentional poisoning. They are included simply as examples for the specific generic drug reportedly involved.

emergency treatment for cases of childhood poisoning involving the opiate analgesics for the last 40 years has included: (1) supportive medical care (e.g., maintaining a patent airway; providing respiratory assistance, if required) and monitoring; and (2) the use of the opiate-analgesic antagonist, naloxone (Narcan®) (e.g., Pagliaro & Pagliaro, 2009; Tenenbein, 1984).

Of all of the various opiate analgesics (see Chapter 1, *The Psychodepressants*) that are used throughout North America, methadone was the only one that was consistently implicated in unintentional childhood poisonings, including several fatalities, in the research published over the last 30 years (e.g., Aronow, Paul, & Woolley, 1972; Blatman, 1974; Glatstein, Finkelstein, & Scolnik, 2009; Klupp, Risser, Stichenwirth, et al., 2000). Typically, the overwhelming majority of these cases involved infants or children younger than 2 years of age and parents or caregivers who were enrolled in methadone maintenance programs. A minority of cases involved mothers who deliberately administered methadone to their infants or young children to sedate them (Kintz, Villain, Dumestre-Toulet, et al., 2005). Unfortunately, both of the children involved died of methadone overdosage.[36] (Also see Chapter 1, *The Psychodepressants*.)

### Volatile Solvents and Inhalants

Although unintentional childhood poisonings involving the volatile solvents and inhalants account for up to 10% of all reported cases, it is virtually impossible to identify the characteristics and context of these poisonings based on the limited data available in the published studies. For example, in a hypothetical case of the unintentional poisoning of a toddler with gasoline, was the gasoline container used during a huffing party by an older brother and some friends and subsequently left where the toddler had access to it, or was it simply left

open by an older brother on the backyard patio after he refilled the gasoline lawn mower?

Similarly, for a case of unintentional poisoning of a 5-year-old girl with glue, were the tubes of glue simply left behind in her 10-year-old brother's bedroom after he and his friends got high by inhaling fumes from some of the glue that they had squeezed into a paper bag and heated over the bedroom's radiant wall heater, or did she find the glue in her 16-year-old sister's bedroom along with a variety of scrapbooking and crafting supplies? Unfortunately, published data regarding the context of unintentional childhood poisonings involving the volatile solvents and inhalants as drugs and substances of abuse are not generally provided. Consequently, we cannot determine their relationship to actual patterns of using the drugs and substances of abuse. (Also see "Volatile Solvents and Inhalants" section in Chapter 1, *The Psychodepressants*.)

### Psychostimulants Involved in Unintentional Childhood Poisonings

The psychostimulants implicated in the published research on unintentional childhood poisonings include cocaine, methamphetamine, and nicotine. Each of these psychostimulants is discussed in relation to its involvement in cases of unintentional poisoning.

### Cocaine

Although several case studies and reports (e.g., Kharasch, Glotzer, Vinci, et al., 1991; Rosenberg, Meert, Knazik, et al., 1991) have implicated cocaine in suspected incidents of childhood poisoning, they generally did not identify the nature or route of the exposure (e.g., breast-feeding, secondhand smoke, or intentional administration). Only one case report (i.e., Havlik & Nolte, 2000) clearly

---

[36] In our clinical practice, several somewhat similar cases—fortunately, not fatal—were drawn to our attention in which mothers or grandmothers of Afghani or Ukrainian descent reported making a slurry of opium poppy pods, or seeds—available directly from their gardens or pantries (i.e., to make traditional poppy-seed breads and cakes, etc.)—that was often heated on the stove, cooled, and administered with a spoon, or a *sachet* that could be sucked like an infant pacifier, in order either to sedate fussy infants and young children or to help to relieve teething pain (Pagliaro & Pagliaro, *Clinical Patient Data Files*).

documented the nature of the cocaine exposure. In this case, the parents, who were regular users of crack cocaine, initially claimed that their 10-month old daughter had ingested rat poison. It was later determined that the infant's 2-year-old brother was eating crack cocaine and feeding it to his baby sister, who subsequently died from the oral ingestion of the cocaine. Based on our clinical experience, including discussions with many crack-addicted parents, this case is probably "just the tip of the iceberg" (Pagliaro & Pagliaro, *Clinical Patient Data Files*). The unintentional poisoning of children by ingesting cocaine generally results in cases that are self-limiting and nonfatal, as occurred in the previous reported case study in regard to the 2-year-old brother. Thus, many cases are left unreported and undocumented because medical assistance is not sought, the parents never report the nonfatal, unintentional poisoning, and, consequently, the case is never documented in annual poisoning statistics reports for infants and children or other published research literature.

Standard emergency medical treatment of unintentional poisonings that are associated with the oral ingestion of cocaine has included administration of a slurry of activated charcoal,[37] supportive care (e.g., management of associated agitation or seizures), and monitoring. Generally, vomiting is not induced because of the concern for precipitation of an associated seizure.

### Methamphetamine

As the abuse of methamphetamine increased, particularly during the 1990s, so, too, did the reported incidents of unintentional childhood poisonings (Kolecki, 1998). The presenting signs and symptoms of methamphetamine poisoning among infants and children primarily include agitation, crying, irritability, tachycardia, and vomiting. In addition, both the blood pressure and rectal temperature are slightly elevated. Although rhabdomyolysis can occur, no deaths have been reported (Kolecki, 1998; Matteucci, Auten, Crowley, et al., 2007). The treatment of infants and children in poisoning cases includes supportive medical care and pharmacotherapy with a benzodiazepine (e.g., diazepam [Valium®] or an antipsychotic tranquilizer (e.g., haloperidol [Haldol®]) (Ruha & Yarema, 2006).

Children also have been unintentionally poisoned by their direct contact with the caustic chemicals (e.g., sulfuric acid found in drain cleaner) that are used for the home-based illicit production of methamphetamine (Farst, Duncan, Moss, et al., 2007; Pagliaro & Pagliaro, *Clinical Patient Data Files*)— ingestion of these chemicals has resulted in death (Burge, Hunsaker, & Davis, 2009). (Also see Chapter 2, *The Psychostimulants*.)

### Nicotine (Tobacco Cigarettes and Other Products)

Drug and poison information centers commonly receive calls from concerned parents or other caregivers regarding the oral ingestion of tobacco products by an infant or toddler, particularly involving cigarettes or cigarette butts (Pagliaro & Pagliaro, *Clinical Patient Data Files*). Almost 14,000 ingestions of tobacco products by children younger than 6 years of age were reported to the AAPCC during 2006 through 2008 (Connolly, Richter, Aleguas, et al., 2010). Although this number of ingestions is higher than that for any other drug or substance of abuse, it is significantly lower than the number of ingestions reported during the 1990s. For example, during 1994 alone, the AAPCC received almost 8,000 reports involving the ingestion of tobacco products by children younger than 6 years of age (Litovitz, Felberg, Soloway, et al., 1995).

---

[37]Activated charcoal (Actidose-Aqua,® Charcodote Pediatric®) has been extensively used in the past as part of the standard medical management of a variety of oral childhood poisonings. The use of this so-called universal antidote has been questioned, particularly over the last decade (e.g., American Academy of Clinical Toxicology, 1999; Chyka, Seger, Krenzelok, et al., 2005; Lapus, 2007). Its continued use also has its supporters (e.g., Olson, 2010) for patients who have a patent airway, or are intubated, and do not have an intestinal obstruction. However, multiple sequential doses of activated charcoal, followed by the routine use of a cathartic, are no longer generally recommended.

Unintentional childhood poisonings have involved virtually every dosage form of nicotine available, including tobacco cigarettes and cigarette butts (CDC, 1997; Sisselman, Mofenson, & Caraccio, 1996); nicotine chewing gum (Smolinske, Spoerke, Spiller, et al., 1988); nicotine transdermal delivery systems, or patches (Woolf, Burkhart, Caraccio, et al., 1997); and smokeless tobacco (Connolly, Richter, Aleguas, et al., 2010). Following oral ingestion, children may display one or more of these signs and symptoms: abdominal pain, agitation, diarrhea, dizziness, hypotension, irregular pulse, nausea, vomiting, and weakness. Signs and symptoms generally are evident within 30 minutes after ingestion and usually resolve, uneventfully, without sequelae within 1 hour (Smolinske, Spoerke, Spiller, et al., 1988; Woolf, Burkhart, Caraccio, et al., 1997).

A major factor contributing to the relatively low toxicity associated with the oral ingestion of tobacco cigarettes and nicotine products by infants and young children is the pharmacokinetics of nicotine. Nicotine, when orally ingested, is generally slowly and incompletely absorbed (i.e., oral bioavailability is approximately 33%). In addition, when ingested orally, any nicotine that is absorbed readily undergoes extensive first-pass hepatic metabolism (Pagliaro & Pagliaro, 2009). (Also see related discussion in the "Nicotine" section of Chapter 2, *The Psychostimulants.*)

## Psychodelics Involved in Unintentional Childhood Poisonings

In the published research and case studies reviewed and analyzed, two psychodelics were implicated in unintentional childhood poisonings, cannabis and methylenedioxymethamphetamine (MDMA, ecstasy).

### Cannabis

The unintentional ingestion of cannabis by infants and young children generally follows a clinical course that is self-limiting and benign. However, it can progress to coma in a significant but small number of cases (Appelboam & Oades, 2006;

Boros, Parsons, Zoanetti, et al., 1996; Macnab, Anderson, & Susak, 1989). Hashish, because of its higher THC concentration, is often a source of cannabis poisoning (Pagliaro & Pagliaro, *Clinical Patient Data Files*; Spadari, Glaizal, Tichadou, et al., 2009). Unintentional childhood poisoning also has been reported from exposure to more unusual sources (e.g., cannabis cookies) (Boros, Parsons, Zoanetti, et al., 1996). Related signs and symptoms of unintentional cannabis poisoning among infants and children, most of which occur within the infant's or child's own home, include conjunctival hyperemia, drowsiness, hypotonia, lid lag, mydriasis (moderate), presence of granules or chopped cannabis leaf material in the mouth, and tachycardia. In addition, unexplained coma in a previously well infant or young child may be indicative of unintentional cannabis poisoning.

### Methylenedioxymethamphetamine

A review of published research and case studies over the last three decades implicated methylenedioxymethamphetamine (MDMA, ecstasy) in unintentional childhood poisonings, particularly during the last two decades (e.g., Cooper & Egleston, 1997). Presenting signs and symptoms of unintentional MDMA poisoning among infants and children include agitation, hypertension, hyperthermia, mydriasis, seizures, tachycardia, and tachypnea (Duffy & Swart, 2006; Melian, Burillo-Putze, Campo, et al., 2004). In addition, unexplained convulsions accompanied by fever in a previously well infant or young child may be indicative of unintentional MDMA poisoning (Chang, Lai, Kong, et al., 2005; Cooper & Egleston, 1997; Eifinger, Roth, Kroner, et al., 2008). (Also see Chapter 3, *The Psychodelics.*)

Standard emergency medical treatment of infants and children who have been unintentionally poisoned by the ingestion of MDMA has included: (1) the administration of a slurry of activated charcoal; (2) supportive care, including the management of associated hyperthermia with rapid cooling measures and the management of associated seizures with diazepam (Valium®); and (3) careful monitoring of clinical response.

## CHAPTER SUMMARY

Infants and children often are exposed to the drugs and substances of abuse before they themselves begin to use them. The earliest exposure occurs prenatally and is related to a mother's use of drugs and substances of abuse during pregnancy. Postnatal exposure may occur during breast-feeding, as many drugs and substances of abuse are transferred into breast milk. Throughout infancy and childhood, exposure may also occur by their inhalation of secondhand smoke produced by parents or primary caregivers, older siblings, or other family members who smoke cannabis, cocaine, heroin, methamphetamine, or tobacco cigarettes or other tobacco products.

This chapter has presented an overview of the prenatal and postnatal exposure of neonates, children, and adolescents to the drugs and substances of abuse and associated untoward effects. These effects include teratogenesis (when used at critical times of development) and fetotoxicity associated with the use of the drugs and substances of abuse during pregnancy. Although all of the drugs and substances of abuse have not been implicated in teratogenic effects when used by mothers who are pregnant, alcohol and several of the other sedative-hypnotics and the volatile inhalant toluene have been strongly implicated. These drugs and substances of abuse should not be used by adolescent girls who are pregnant. In fact, in order to minimize the risk for and incidence of drug and substance abuse–related teratogenic effects among offspring, all of the drugs and substances of abuse should be recognized as having the potential to cause teratogenic effects under certain conditions. Thus, as a precaution, adolescent girls who are pregnant, or who are thinking about becoming pregnant, should be encouraged whenever possible to abstain from or to minimize their use of the various drugs and substances of abuse. It also is important for them to understand that the maternal use of the drugs and substances of abuse during pregnancy, and especially near term, may cause expected pharmacological effects and toxicities among neonates. Fortunately, whereas some teratogenic effects (e.g., FAS/FASD) are lifelong, associated withdrawal syndromes and other pharmacologically related effects are generally reversible with appropriate recognition and treatment.

Although not as widely researched as the teratogens, clinical experience and the available data suggest that the maternal exposure of breast-fed neonates and infants to the drugs and substances of abuse is significant. Formalized research is required to assess the prevalence and characteristics of this concern as is research to help mothers cease, reduce, or adjust their patterns of breast-feeding when they are unable to discontinue their use of a drug or substance of abuse. An increased awareness and greater recognition of the course of exposure also is needed both: to decrease the incidence of exposure of neonates, infants, and children; and to recognize and deal effectively with the consequences of maternal drug and substance use when related behavior is observed among exposed neonates and infants.

Attention also was given to the postnatal exposure of infants, children, and adolescents to secondhand smoke as related to cocaine base (i.e., crack), methamphetamine (i.e., ice, meth), and the opiate analgesics, particularly fentanyl (Duragesic®), heroin (e.g., black tar heroin), and oxycodone (OxyContin®), in the home and other settings by their mothers and fathers, other primary caregivers, and other siblings or adults who may be living in the households or who may visit on a regular basis. Finally, a review and analysis of the limited published research reporting the involvement of the drugs and substances of abuse in unintentional childhood poisonings over the last 30 years was presented with attention to the involvement of alcohol and other sedative-hypnotics, cannabis, cocaine, methadone, methamphetamine, MDMA (ecstasy), and nicotine.

## CHAPTER 6

# Effects of the Drugs and Substances of Abuse on Learning and Memory During Childhood and Adolescence

## INTRODUCTION

While a few of the drugs and substances of abuse have been associated with certain positive effects on the processes of learning and memory, the use of most of the drugs and substances of abuse by children and adolescents has been clearly and consistently associated with several negative effects, particularly those affecting school attendance, academic performance, educational aspirations, and rates of completing high school (Franklin, 1992; Friedman, Bransfield, & Kreisher, 1994; Hawkins, Lishner, Catalano, et al., 1985; Pagliaro & Pagliaro, 1996, 2009; Paulson, Coombs, & Richardson, 1990). For example, both cannabis and methylenedioxymethamphetamine (MDMA, ecstasy) use by children and adolescents consistently has been associated with low academic achievement (Cox, Zhang, Johnson, et al., 2007; Jeynes, 2002; Lynskey & Hall, 2000; Martins & Alexandre, 2008; C. E. Sanders, Field, & Diego, 2001).

These reported negative effects are not spurious associations. In fact, they appear to be related directly to the pharmacological actions of the drugs and substances of abuse on specific areas of the brain, particularly those that are responsible for the core processes of learning: attention, motivation, perception, and cognitive processing and for the various processes of memory. This chapter presents an overview of both the positive and negative

effects that the drugs and substances of abuse have on these learning and memory processes. Attention also is given to the mediating factors, or underlying cofactors, that contribute to these effects, including the role of parents and teachers, medical/neurological disorders (e.g., fetal alcohol syndrome/fetal alcohol spectrum disorder [FAS/FASD]), and mental disorders (e.g., conduct disorder [CD]; major depressive disorder [MDD]). The relationship of these cofactors to child and adolescent use of the drugs and substances of abuse and their combined effects on learning and memory are discussed in the related sections of this chapter.

Another increasingly recognized cofactor that may adversely affect core learning and memory processes among children and adolescents is their prenatal exposure to various drugs and substances of abuse by their mothers. For example, a child born with FAS/FASD as a result of his or her mother's use of alcohol during pregnancy may have significant learning problems, often observed during infancy and early childhood as behavioral problems, such as not listening, not paying attention, not following directions, and not behaving as expected. Unfortunately, the extent of the learning problems may not be fully identified (e.g., as A-D/HD or lowered IQ score) until he or she enters school. Other examples of the effects of parental use of the drugs and substances of abuse on childhood learning is related to a child's regular, long-term exposure to secondhand tobacco smoke by parents[1] or other caregivers (e.g., babysitters, day-care workers) who smoke cigarettes. This common method of exposure may significantly increase absenteeism from school as a consequence of associated respiratory irritation and infections, particularly if the child has asthma (Gilliland, Berhane, Islam, et al., 2003). (See Chapter 5, *Exposure to the Drugs and Substances of Abuse From Conception Through Childhood*, for other examples and further related discussion.)

The effects of parental drug and substance use on child-rearing and other parenting functions that involve teaching and learning processes also are receiving increased attention. For example, in their study of maternal-infant dyads, Johnson, Morrow, Accornero, et al. (2002) found that, for mothers who reported cocaine use, both prenatally and postnatally, significant decrements in parent-child teaching interactions occurred. These decrements included diminished child persistence, greater maternal intrusiveness and hostility, lower maternal confidence, and poorer quality of instruction.

In addition, the regular, long-term use of cocaine, heroin, methamphetamine, and other drugs and substances of abuse by parents often leads to the disruption of the emotional and social development of children and adolescents because of the parents' inability to provide adequate and consistent parenting, a stable home environment, emotional support, and protection from mental or physical abuse (Smith, 1993). (Also see Chapter 8, *Dual Diagnosis Among Adolescents,* for related discussion of both

physical and sexual abuse, and family-based therapies.) Conversely, good parenting encourages: (1) the setting of high academic goals (e.g., completing high school) and achievement (e.g., obtaining good grades); (2) consistent, regular school attendance; and (3) completing homework (e.g., as a requisite to being allowed to watch television, drive the family car, or play video games) and other related academic school assignments (e.g., science fair projects; Pagliaro & Pagliaro, *Clinical Patient Data Files*).

The effects of the drugs and substances of abuse on learning and memory are of interest to all who are involved, directly or indirectly, in the education and care of children and adolescents.[2] Interest also exists, for both clinicians (e.g., school psychologists, psychiatrists) and teachers, in distinguishing between true learning disorders and those elicited by the infrequent, short-term or regular, long-term use of the drugs and substances of abuse. As noted over two decades ago by Fox and Forbing (1991):

> The effects of substance abuse have produced a population of students who exhibit behaviors similar to the behaviors of many youth with learning problems. . . . To differentiate between behavior resulting from a learning handicapped condition and that resulting from [drug or] substance use, trained diagnosticians need to evaluate both the potential causes and the context in which these behaviors are exhibited. (p. 24)

It appears that, in the 20-plus years that have elapsed since Fox and Forbing made this

---

[1] It is recognized that North American children and adolescents may live in two-parent families (biological or nonbiological parent[s]), single-parent families, blended families, and foster care families. They also may be primarily cared for by grandparents and other extended family members, such as grandparents, aunts and uncles, or older siblings. Thus, the term "parent" is used in this chapter, and throughout this text, to denote the person who is the primary caregiver and guardian of the child.

[2] Although several theoretical orientations concerning learning have been developed over the last century (e.g., behaviorism [e.g., Pavlov, 1927; Skinner, 1931; Watson, 1913]; humanism (e.g., Rogers, 1969); neobehaviorism [e.g., cognitive social learning theory (Bandura, 1977), this chapter is based on a cognitive approach to and understanding of learning and memory, as proposed by Ausubel (1968), Piaget and Inhelder (1969), and other theorists who look beyond observable behavior to explain brain-based learning and memory—where memory works to promote learning—with attention to changes at the micro levels, the neuronal synapses.

observation, the only thing that has changed is that the referenced population is significantly larger today.

Although a great deal of research has been accrued over the past decades in regard to increasing our understanding of the process of learning, this observation still rings true:

> Unequivocal causal relations between a change in cell structure or function and learning still remain to be demonstrated ... [and] terms encountered in this field, such as memory, learning, perception, attention, and cognition, need to be recognized as essentially abstract constructs used to name phenomena that can be observed only by behavioral experiments. (Cooper, Bloom, & Roth, 1978/1991, p. 428)

The term, "learning," has been defined in many ways, and these definitions generally reflect a diversity of theoretical orientations that may, or may not, be commensurable (e.g., cognitive social learning theory and Gestalt theory). For the purpose of this chapter, the next definition—a definition that we developed, as academics, over the past four decades—is used:

> "Learning" is a change in mental associations due to experience. As such, it is the acquisition of new information due to sensory input that, in order to be confirmed, or validated, must be accompanied by a change in a related observable, or *measurable*, behavior. Typically, this behavior takes the form of the results obtained from oral, written, or psychomotor testing—and, in order to perform such tests, must involve the process of memory.

Obviously, learning and memory are complex processes. The many metavariables affecting these processes at the macro level, including the various drugs and substances of abuse, are identified in Figure 6.1.

As noted in Figure 6.1, the use of the drugs and substances of abuse by children and adolescents can directly affect their learning and memory processes. These processes also can be indirectly affected when the drugs and substances of abuse are used by their teachers,

particularly during the school day to deal with the stresses of teaching (e.g., the new, young teacher who tokes up with cannabis between classes in order to relax; the teacher of 20 years with all the signs and symptoms of alcoholism, who drinks lunch from a Thermos® to just get through another day).

As further illustrated in this figure, the nature and extent of the effects of the use of drugs or substances of abuse on children and adolescents may be significantly mitigated by the other variables, such as IQ. For example, if the IQ of a child or adolescent is 90, and if he or she uses a drug or substance of abuse (e.g., takes several tokes from a joint of cannabis at lunchtime with a couple of friends) that results in the equivalent of a temporary 10-point reduction in IQ, then the use of the drug or substance of abuse would be expected to have a significant adverse effect on his or her subsequent learning and memory during the remainder of the school day. However, if the child or adolescent has an IQ of 140, the same 10-point reduction associated with using the drug or substance of abuse would be expected to have a minimal adverse effect on subsequent learning and memory during the remainder of the school day.

Mechanistically, the drugs and substances of abuse (i.e., the psychodepressants, psychostimulants, and psychodelics) affect learning and memory in significant ways based on their major psychotropic effects: psychodepression, psychostimulation, and psychodelic alteration of sensory perception, respectively. As previously noted, the exact neuronal mechanisms by which the drugs and substances of abuse affect these processes remain unclear. However, a significant amount of human data have accumulated in regard to the effects of the drugs and substances of abuse on the four specific core processes that are directly associated with learning: (1) attention; (2) motivation; (3) perception; and (4) cognitive processing. Each of these processes, along with the processes of memory (also see the "Memory" section), is necessary for optimal learning to occur, as illustrated by the cognitive input-output model of learning and memory.

**Child or Adolescent Learner:**

*Demographic and social variables*

Age
Continental descent
Culture, ethnicity
Gender
Parent(s)
  ▪ Attitude toward drug use
  ▪ Attitude toward education
  ▪ Use of drugs & substances of abuse
  ▪ Education
  ▪ IQ
  ▪ Socioeconomic status
Race
Socioeconomic status

*Learning variables*
Core processes of learning:
  ▪ Attention
  ▪ Motivation
  ▪ Perception
  ▪ Cognitive processing
Education
Genetics (IQ)
Memory
Other

*Drug and substance of abuse variables*
  ▪ Class/Type (Psychodepressant, Psychostimulant, Psychodelic)
  ▪ Patterns of use
  ▪ Pharmacology
  ▪ Pharmacokinetics

**Time**

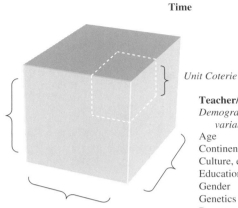

*Unit Coterie*

**Teacher/Instructor:**
*Demographic and social variables*
Age
Continental descent
Culture, ethnicity
Education
Gender
Genetics (IQ)
Race
Socioeconomic status

*Teaching Preparation/Experience*
  ▪ Attention
  ▪ Motivation
  ▪ Perception
  ▪ Cognitive processing
  ▪ Memory
  ▪ Other

*Drug and substance of abuse variables*
  ▪ Class/Type (Psychodepressant, Psychostimulant, Psychodelic)
  ▪ Patterns of use
  ▪ Pharmacology
  ▪ Pharmacokinetics

**Instructional Context:**
Primary School
Middle School
High School
Other

Availability of drugs and substances of abuse

Tolerance of family, community, and school for, or acceptance of, the use of drugs and substances of abuse by children and adolescents

**Figure 6.1    Meta-Variables Affecting Learning at the Macro Level: A Multivariate-Interactive Model**
The unit coterie reflects the interactive outcome of all relevant variables for each dimension in regard to an individual child's or adolescent's learning and memory. While a unit coterie reflects a specific child or adolescent, a collection of unit coteries reflects a specifically defined group of children and adolescents (e.g., 5th-grade students; boys; North American adolescents of Hispanic descent).

## COGNITIVE INPUT-OUTPUT MODEL OF LEARNING AND MEMORY

The cognitive input-output model of learning and memory was initially developed over 30 years ago by the authors to parsimoniously explain the relationship between learning and memory. Over the years, it has been further developed and applied as a useful heuristic model, particularly for understanding the effects of the drugs and substances of abuse on the core processes of learning and memory. As illustrated in Figure 6.2, sensory input data, or environmental stimuli, are mediated by the five sensory organs involved in hearing, sight,

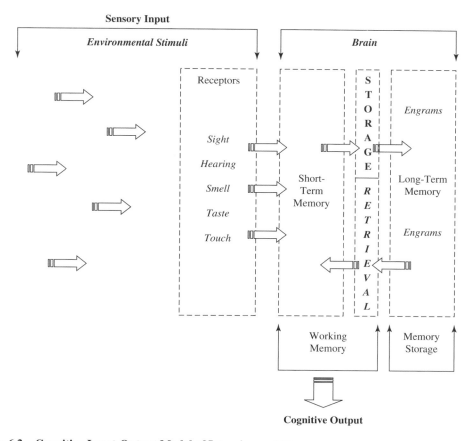

**Figure 6.2    Cognitive Input-Output Model of Learning and Memory**

smell, taste, and touch.[3] Once the sensory input has been received by a sensory organ (e.g., the eyes) and transmitted to the brain (generally by the peripheral nervous system, including the cranial nerves), it undergoes initial processing and temporary storage in short-term memory. As originally proposed by Miller (1956) and currently still widely accepted, short-term memory generally is capable of holding only

5 to 9 (i.e., 7 ± 2) chunks of information, such as digits, people's faces, or words. Once stored, the processed sensory information usually is lost or forgotten in approximately 20 seconds, unless it is subsequently transferred, or encoded, into long-term memory.

The encoding process is facilitated by the use of rehearsal strategies (e.g., repeating to oneself a new telephone number as it

---

[3]Consequently, functional deficits in these sense organs may have significant adverse effects on learning. Thus, whenever students are referred to us for psychoeducational assessments in regard to poor classroom performance, we routinely request visual and auditory testing to rule out problems with vision or hearing. For example, a student may not complete an assignment simply because he or she cannot clearly see what the teacher wrote on the chalkboard (or the small print in the textbook). Another student may persistently ask the teacher to "repeat the question," simply because he or she cannot hear what the teacher is saying. These learning problems are related to visual and hearing impairment rather than, for example, A-D/HD, low IQ (e.g., in association with FAS/FASD), or oppositional defiant disorder—common conditions associated with students not completing assignments, not promptly responding to questions, or otherwise not participating in classroom activities (Pagliaro & Pagliaro, *Clinical Patient Data Files*).

is inserted into one's cell phone directory). The encoding process also incorporates cues, such as visual cues obtained from the use of visualization techniques that help to facilitate later retrieval. Data are stored as a pattern of connections between groups of neurons in the brain known as engrams. Stored engrams are retrieved from long-term memory using specific strategies, including the use of mnemonics and other memory aids.

In the absence of pathology, long-term memory has virtually unlimited capacity for the storage of: (1) declarative information (i.e., facts); (2) procedural information (i.e., how to do things, such as play the piano or ride a bike); (3) episodic information (i.e., memories of specific events that have been experienced in one's life); and (4) metacognitive information (i.e., how to learn, which involves simultaneous use of multiple core processes, including the use of effortful and noneffortful processing).

## REQUISITES FOR OPTIMAL LEARNING: *THE CORE PROCESSES*

Each of the three major classes of the drugs and substances of abuse—the psychodepressants, the psychostimulants, and the psychodelics—has been studied in relation to its ability to affect the four core processes of learning: (1) attention; (2) motivation; (3) perception; and (4) cognitive processing. In addition, various mental disorders, including anxiety disorders, A-D/HD (also see the "A-D/HD" section), major depressive disorder (also see the "MDD" section), pain disorders, and substance use disorders (SUDs) may affect these processes. (Also see the related discussion of these mental disorders in Chapter 8, *Dual Diagnosis Among Adolescents*.) This section discusses both the positive and

negative effects of the drugs and substances of abuse on learning, including drugs that may be prescribed for the medical or psychological management of selected mental or neurological disorders commonly identified among children and adolescents (e.g., psychostimulant pharmacotherapy, such as methylphenidate [Ritalin®], for the symptomatic management of A-D/HD).

## Attention

"Attention" may be defined as the process of preferentially responding to a stimulus or range of stimuli. As such, attention is integral to learning. Even if learners are motivated to learn, have intact senses that are functioning properly, and have adequate intelligence, they cannot optimally learn without paying adequate attention to what is being taught. Whereas the drugs and substances of abuse are generally thought to decrease attention, which commonly occurs with the psychodepressants (i.e., opiate analgesics, sedative-hypnotics, and volatile solvents and inhalants), the psychostimulants (at optimal, generally lower dosages) actually can increase attention and associated learning and memory.

### *Positive Effects on Attention*

The psychostimulants—the amphetamines, caffeine, cocaine, and nicotine—are often used, in addition to their other actions,[4] to achieve increased alertness, vigilance, or wakefulness; feelings of decreased fatigue; euphoria; intense exhilaration; a heightened sense of well-being; and a rapid flow of ideas (Pagliaro & Pagliaro, 2009). (Also see Chapter 2, *The Psychostimulants*.)

Perhaps surprisingly, by itself, caffeine—the legal drug of choice for staying up all night to cram for exams—has not been associated consistently with positive effects on attention or other aspects of learning. However, a

---

[4]The psychostimulants (e.g., in the form of amphetamine-based diet pills or nicotine in tobacco cigarettes) also have been used, particularly by adolescent girls, to suppress their appetites and feelings of hunger in order to achieve or maintain a desired body weight. (See related discussion in Chapter 2, *The Psychostimulants*.)

few studies (e.g., Bernstein, Carroll, Crosby, et al., 1994; Brice & Smith, 2002) have demonstrated an increase in attention, or alertness, and corresponding improved performance on a cognitive vigilance test. In addition, the use of caffeine may slightly attenuate the learning and memory decrements associated with sedative-hypnotic (e.g., alcohol) use (Loke, Hinrichs, & Ghoneim, 1985; Rush, Higgins, Bickel, et al., 1993), presumably by attenuating the sedative-hypnotic–induced psychodepression. Since their synthesis, the amphetamines and methylphenidate (Ritalin®) have been used illicitly by college and university students to stay awake to complete term papers that are due the next morning or to cram for midterm and final examinations. As noted by Sussman, Pentz, Spruijt-Metz, et al. (2006), these so-called study drugs are "being misused annually by approximately 4% of older teens" (p. 15) in the United States.

As a psychostimulant, nicotine can moderately increase attention and hence facilitate learning (Graham, 1988; Kelemen & Fulton, 2008; Levin, 2002). Thus, when adolescents who are dependent on nicotine are allowed to smoke prior to engaging in an academic task, such as taking a test, their attention, as well as their associated academic performance and learning, is significantly increased in comparison to allowing them to smoke after the completion of the academic task. In fact, nicotine is the only psychostimulant that consistently, at normal dosages (i.e., those usually achieved by smoking a cigarette) facilitates learning and memory among regular users (e.g., regular, long-term tobacco smokers; Pagliaro & Pagliaro, 1996, 2004, 2009). This observation does not mean that we encourage smoking. However, it does help to explain the generally increased work performance and productivity commonly noted among students and teachers, as well as others who smoke tobacco, following

a smoke break. In a placebo-controlled study of 28 current tobacco smokers, Myers, Taylor, Moolchan, et al. (2008) found that overnight smoking deprivation resulted in impaired cognitive test performance; and nicotine, which was administered by nasal spray, improved cognitive test performance, including an arithmetic test, in a dose-related manner.

### Negative Effects on Attention

Generally, the psychodepressants (i.e., alcohol and other sedative-hypnotics, opiate analgesics, and volatile solvents and inhalants) decrease attention to sensory input.[5] As noted by Rush, Higgins, Bickel, et al. (1993), the benzodiazepines "dose-dependently disrupted learning and psychomotor performance and increased subject ratings of sedation" (p. 1218). In addition, it has been reported that cannabis use can adversely affect selective attention (Solowij, Michie, & Fox, 1991) as well as the core process of attention (Lundqvist, 2005; Solowij & Michie, 2007). (See the "Cannabis" section in Chapter 3, *The Psychodelics*, for related discussion.)

Interestingly, prenatal exposure to the psychostimulant cocaine has been associated with deficits in various attentional processes among infants, preschoolers, and school-age children. For example, Singer, Arendt, Minnes, et al. (2000) reported differences in arousal-modulated attention among infants; Heffelfinger, Craft, White, et al. (2002) reported visual attention deficits among preschool children; and Savage, Brodsky, Malmud, et al. (2005) reported attention problems among school-age children. Several mechanisms, have been proposed to explain these observed attentional deficits associated with the prenatal exposure to cocaine, including functional alterations in monoaminergically regulated arousal systems (Mayes, 2002). (Also see related discussion of cocaine in Chapter 5, *Exposure*

---

[5] In addition, it has been suggested that heavy drinking of alcohol by adolescents can adversely affect the development of the frontal lobes, resulting in decreased performance in regard to both tasks of attention and executive functioning (e.g., decision making) (Heavy alcohol use, 2010).

*to the Drugs and Substances of Abuse From Conception Through Childhood.*)

In addition, the excess use of psychostimulants by adolescents, including the use of highly caffeinated energy drinks (see Chapter 2, *The Psychostimulants*), which often are used to stay awake late at night to play video games or to party, may result in decreased attention the next day in school. In severe cases, signs and symptoms similar to those associated with sleep apnea may occur, such as adolescents suddenly falling asleep at their desks during afternoon classes (Anderson, Storfer-Isser, Taylor, et al., 2009; Pagliaro & Pagliaro, *Clinical Patient Data Files*). (Also see the "A-D/HD" section for a discussion of the effects, both positive and negative, that psychostimulant pharmacotherapy may have on attention.)

## Motivation

"Motivation" can be defined simply as the core process that is intrinsically responsible for an orientation toward the attainment of a specific goal. Consequently, effortful cognitive processing (i.e., working on an arithmetic assignment) and explicit memory (i.e., memory tasks, such as those measured by free recall and recognition tests that require conscious retrieval of stored information from long-term memory) will be significantly impaired when motivation is low. Thus, children and adolescents who are not sufficiently motivated (i.e., have low motivation) in regard to a particular learning goal will not be able to optimally achieve that goal, even if all of the other core processes of learning (i.e., attention, perception, cognitive processing) and other related variables (e.g., sufficient intelligence, capable teacher, and an optimal learning environment)

are present. In this context, it should be noted that cognitive processing has been defined as being either effortful, or active; or noneffortful, or automatic.[6] Effortful processing, unlike noneffortful processing (or at least to a significantly greater extent), requires both attention and motivation on the part of the learner.

### Negative Effects on Motivation: Amotivational Syndrome

Motivation can be adversely affected by the use of virtually any of the drugs and substances of abuse. However, on the basis of available research data, the barbiturates and cannabis are particularly troublesome in this regard, as demonstrated by their association with the amotivational syndrome. The amotivational syndrome, which is characterized by apathy and a profound deficit in normal interactions with family, friends, schoolmates, teachers, coworkers, and supervisors, originally was associated during the 1950s and 1960s with the regular, long-term heavy use of the barbiturates (e.g., pentobarbital [Nembutal®], secobarabital [Seconal®]). However, over the past 40 years, as the use of the barbiturates significantly diminished, the amotivational syndrome has been associated more often with the regular, long-term heavy use of cannabis in its various forms—marijuana, hashish, and hashish oil (Andrews, 1972; Baumrind & Moselle, 1985; Tunving, 1987).[7] (Also see Chapter 3, *The Psychodelics*, for further discussion of the amotivational syndrome in the context of childhood and adolescent cannabis use.) Lack of motivation also may help to account, at least partially, for the positive correlation between "teenage drug usage and school dropout" (Eggert, Seyl, & Nicholas, 1990, p. 773).

---

[6] This division of cognitive processing is also referred to as conscious processing and unconscious processing, respectively.

[7] Several authors (e.g., Barnwell, Earleywine, & Wilcox, 2006) doubt the existence of the amotivational syndrome and posit that related symptomatology may be due rather to effects on subjective well-being associated with either the direct effects of cannabis use or the context of its use, including the general health and mental status of the user. In this regard, Musty and Kaback (1995) suggested that the behavior described as the amotivational syndrome in heavy marijuana users was actually related to depression in these cannabis users.

For example, in their 25-year longitudinal birth cohort study of 1265 children, Fergusson, Horwood, and Beautrais (2003) found that "increasing cannabis use was associated with increasing risks of leaving school without qualifications, failure to enter university, and failure to obtain a university degree" (p. 1681). Lynskey and Hall (2000), in their analysis of cross-sectional studies that examined the relationship between cannabis use and educational attainment among youth, noted: "significant associations between cannabis use and a range of measures of educational performance including lower grade point average, less satisfaction with school, negative attitudes to school, increased rates of school absenteeism, and poor school performance" (p. 1621). However, they go on to note that the relationship may not be causal, but may rather reflect "common risk factors," including: a delinquent lifestyle, association with drug using peers, and disregard for social norms. (Also see related discussion in the "Memory" section, "Cannabis: Disrupted Short-Term Memory Encoding into Long-Term Memory.")

## Perception

The optimal perception of sensory information or input (see Figure 6.2) depends on the proper functioning of the five senses of hearing, sight, smell, taste, and touch. If a child's or adolescent's perception of sensory input is reduced or distorted—to any degree (e.g., because of associated brain injury, hearing loss, vision loss)—so, too, by definition, will his or her optimal learning be reduced or distorted. While the psychodepressants and psychostimulants may cause some related effects on perception,[8] it is the psychodelics (e.g., cannabis [marijuana, hashish, hashish oil] ], lysergic acid diethylamide [LSD], mescaline [peyote], phencyclidine [PCP]) that have the intrinsic ability, at usual pharmacological dosages, to distort sensory perception, sometimes intensely. In fact, the psychodelics are classified as such specifically because of their ability to disrupt the interpretation of sensory stimuli sent to the brain. Consider, for example, the classic children's book *Alice's Adventures in Wonderland* (Carroll, 1866) and the perceptual distortions that Alice experienced during her adventures. The perceptual distortions may also include misinterpretations, illusions, or hallucinations.[9]

In terms of the cognitive input-output model (Figure 6.2), the psychodelics primarily affect the process of encoding adversely. Thus, it is not so much that learning and memory do not occur—rather, they occur incorrectly (i.e., factually correct learning does not occur, and the incorrect learning is stored in memory). If the interpretation of sensory data is distorted, so, too, by definition, is the encoding of this information (i.e., what is stored for later retrieval and use in long-term memory). A well-known example of the distortion of sensory information is the intrinsic ability of the psychodelics to cause synesthesia— "color is heard" and "sound is seen" while time appears to be slowed to "watching the grass grow." Other common causes of severe distortion of sensory information involve acute

---

[8] Several of the psychostimulants, including the amphetamines and cocaine, can cause perceptual distortion, as can several of the psychodepressants, including alcohol and some opiate analgesics (e.g., meperidine [Demerol®]). These perceptual distortions usually occur only with large or toxic dosages of the psychodepressants or psychostimulants. (See related discussion in Chapter 1, *The Psychodepressants*, and Chapter 2, *The Psychostimulants*.)

[9] Misinterpretations of stimuli involve the incorrect interpretation of sensory input (e.g., sudden lifting of the arm of a teacher to scratch her head is interpreted by a nearby student as an imminent threatening gesture prefatory to being struck). Illusions involve the perceptual distortion of existing patterns of stimuli (e.g., a straight pencil placed in a glass of water appears to bend at the waterline). Hallucinations involve false perceptions that are not merely distortions of reality but the generation by the mind of the individual of a different perceptual reality (e.g., seeing and talking to a large, pink, rabbit friend named Harvey). Although primarily involving the sense of vision, the various perceptual distortions may involve any of the five senses. They also can involve mixing the stimuli obtained from the senses, or synesthesia (e.g., seeing sound, hearing color).

psychostimulant intoxication with the amphetamines or cocaine and acute, severe psychodepressant intoxication with alcohol. Both of these types of intoxication may result in the misinterpretation of stimuli characterized by severe signs and symptoms of psychosis, including delusions and hallucinations.

## Cognitive Processing

In the context of learning, "cognitive processing" refers to what occurs in the black box (i.e., the brain) between the sensory input of data and the output of new mental associations (i.e., learning) that can be measured and verified by various behavioral demonstrations. (See Figure 6.2.) While it is commonly recognized and agreed that cognitive processing involves the recording (encoding), analysis/synthesis, and interpretation of sensory input data, the actual exact molecular, neurochemical, or neuronal mechanism(s) involved are still in debate, as illustrated by the many theories that have been posited before and after Hebb's (1949) 60-year-old theory of perceptual learning that implicated reverberatory neuronal circuits, or synaptic plasticity, within the central nervous system (CNS). Virtually all of the drugs and substances of abuse can impair cognitive processing—an assertion supported by the research on reduced global cerebral metabolic rate and state-dependent learning (see related discussion in the following sections).

Although these are the two most predominantly studied areas of neurocognition related to the use of the drugs and substances of abuse in humans, there is still much that remains unknown. Thus, for several drugs and substances of abuse (e.g., cocaine, MDMA), regular, long-term use has been associated with deficits that remain tentatively mechanistically related to such variables as altered brain perfusion and neurotoxicity (Fox, Parrott, & Turner, 2001; Nnadi, Mimiko, McCurtis, et al., 2005; Pagliaro & Pagliaro, 2009; Salisbury, Ponder, Padbury, et al., 2009). (Also see the

related discussion in the "Memory" section.) Methamphetamine-related neurotoxicity has been characterized by both impaired executive functioning (e.g., decreased problem-solving ability) and increased risk for Parkinsonism (King, Alicata, Cloak, et al., 2010; Simon, Dean, Cordova, et al., 2010). (Also see Chapter 2, *The Psychostimulants*, for further related discussion.) Suggested mechanisms for explaining these effects have included loss of dopaminergic and serotonergic neurons due to mitochondrial dysfunction, neuroinflammation, and oxidative stress (Quinton & Yamamoto, 2006; Yamamoto, Moszczynske, & Gudelsky, 2010). In addition, several of the psychodelics (e.g., LSD) appear to adversely affect neurocognition through their effects on serotonin (i.e., 5-HT-[2A]) receptors. These receptors purportedly play a significant role in the entire process of cognition, including working memory (Nichols, 2004).

### *Reduced Global Cerebral Metabolic Rate*

The use of a psychodepressant (e.g., alcohol, sedative-hypnotics, opiate analgesics, or volatile solvents and inhalants) initially, reduces the global cerebral metabolic rate (GCMR) with an associated slowing of cognitive processing. As higher dosages of a psychodepressant are used, there is a disruption of cognitive processing. Consider, for example, the acute progressive decrease in the rate and ability of cognitive processing commonly observed among young college students as they become increasingly drunk (i.e., as they increasingly consume alcoholic beverages over the continuum from sobriety to severe drunkenness; Pagliaro & Pagliaro, 1995). This slowing of GCMR and its associated disruption in cognitive processing also can be demonstrated when the barbiturates (e.g., phenobarbital [Luminal®]), or the benzodiazepines (e.g., clonazepam [Rivotril®]) are medically used for the symptomatic management of seizure disorders (e.g., epilepsy) among children and adolescents (Anderson, 2010; Corbett, Trimble, & Nichol, 1985; Leiderman, Balish, & Bromfield,

1991; Pagliaro & Pagliaro, 1999; Trimble & Thompson, 1983).[10]

### *State-Dependent Learning*

As first formally noted several decades ago by Feldman and Quenzer (1984):

> Tasks learned in the presence of a psychotropic drug may subsequently be performed better in the drugged state. Conversely, learning acquired in the nondrug state may be more available in the nondrugged state. This phenomenon has been called *state dependent learning* and demonstrates the inability to transfer learning from a drugged to a nondrugged condition. An example of this is the alcoholic who during a binge hides his supply of liquor for later consumption but is unable to find it while he is sober (in the nondrugged state). Once he has returned to the alcoholic state, he can readily locate his cache. (p. 22)

Although state-dependent learning in humans was originally demonstrated by observation and studies involving the use of alcohol, it has been known for some time that other drugs and substances of abuse, including amobarbital (Amytal®), amphetamine, cannabis, diazepam (Valium®), methylphenidate (Ritalin®), and triazolam (Halcion®) also can produce state-dependent learning (e.g., Craig, 1985; Reus, Weingartner, & Post, 1979; Weingartner, Putnam, George, et al., 1995).[11]

It is important to note that these drugs and substances of abuse can potentially cause negative effects on learning regardless if they are used illicitly by children and adolescents or if they are prescribed for them by physicians for the medical management of various chronic disorders. For example, methylphenidate (Ritalin®), which can produce state-dependent learning, is widely and routinely used for the chronic medical management of A-D/HD among children and adolescents. As such, the potential exists (although it has not yet been adequately studied in a controlled, systematic manner) that a child or adolescent who complies with his or her methylphenidate pharmacotherapy will, at a later time when the methylphenidate pharmacotherapy is discontinued, be unable to transfer a significant amount of the learning that he or she acquired in the "drugged state." (Also see the "A-D/HD" section for further related discussion.)

## MEMORY

In the context of learning, "memory" can be defined simply as the ability to store and retrieve mental associations. (See Figure 6.2.) As is readily apparent in the figure, memory is integral to both the optimal active processes of learning and the ability of the learner to demonstrate that learning actually has occurred (i.e., while memory is not requisite for learning to occur, without memory, learning can never be demonstrated, or confirmed). The use of various drugs and substances of abuse—including the psychodepressants, particularly alcohol, the benzodiazepines, and GHB; the psychostimulants, particularly cocaine and methamphetamine; and the psychodelics, particularly cannabis and MDMA (ecstasy)—can adversely affect memory in a number of ways. The ways by which these drugs and substances of abuse affect memory, both directly and indirectly, are discussed, in alphabetical order, in the next sections.

---

[10]The use of these sedative-hypnotics slows the GCMR and, consequently, also effectively raises the seizure threshold (Pagliaro & Pagliaro, 1999, 2009).

[11]Results from similar studies have not always been consistent in this regard (e.g., Becker-Mattes, Mattes, Abikoff, et al., 1985; Stephens, Pelham, & Skinner, 1984). The major confounding variables are: (1) the individual study designs (e.g., the use of different doses or comparing different time frames of use for the drug or substance of abuse under investigation); and (2) the dependent variable chosen to measure state-dependent learning, *memory* (e.g., even if memory truly was subject to the effects of state-dependent learning, all forms of memory may not exhibit similar effects).

## Alcohol: Related Forms of Anterograde and Retrograde Amnesia

Alcohol is a known human neurotoxin. As such, it can adversely affect the development of the CNS from conception through adolescence (Pagliaro & Pagliaro, 1995, 2002, 2009; also see the "FAS/FASD" section later in this chapter, and Chapter 5, *Exposure to the Drugs and Substances of Abuse From Conception Through Childhood*). The use of alcohol throughout adolescence and adulthood has been long associated with specific detrimental effects on episodic memory and spatial working memory (Hartley, Elsabagh, & File, 2004; Weissenborn & Duka, 2003). Several factors have been implicated in the development of these effects, including the: (1) frequency of alcohol use (e.g., drinking on a birthday or holiday versus drinking every Friday at the end of the school week); (2) dosage or amount of alcohol used (e.g., 2 drinks versus 8 drinks per drinking occasion); and (3) duration of alcohol use (a heavy drinking episode once a year versus heavy weekly drinking for several years). Although several protective factors (e.g., overall general good health, high IQ) may mitigate or obfuscate the expression of the neurotoxic effects associated with alcohol use, two major types of effects on memory have been commonly recognized: anterograde amnesia and retrograde amnesia.

Anterograde amnesia (e.g., alcoholic blackouts) may occur as a direct result of acute alcohol intoxication, and generally may last for the period of intoxication (Pagliaro & Pagliaro, 1995 ). (See Chapter 1, *The Psychodepressants*, "Alcohol" section.) Consider, for example, the significant number of adolescents who drink alcohol until they are literally falling down drunk and, upon awakening at home in their beds, cannot remember what they did the night before or how they got home safely (Pagliaro & Pagliaro, *Clinical Patient Data Files*).

A chronic pattern of alcohol intoxication, which usually is associated with the accumulation of multiple episodes of anterograde amnesia, may result in significant retrograde amnesia, as seen with the Wernicke-Korsakoff syndrome (Kopelman, 1991; Parkin, Dunn, Lee, et al., 1993). Although this syndrome predominantly occurs among older adults who drink heavily over their lifetimes and have chronic alcoholism, it is reportedly occurring more often among older adolescents and young adults who are chronic heavy drinkers (e.g., Brown, McColm, Aindow, et al., 2009; Parkin, Dunn, Lee, et al., 1993). Although still considered rare, we have encountered several older adolescents and young adults who have been diagnosed with Wernicke-Korsakoff syndrome (Pagliaro & Pagliaro, *Clinical Patient Data Files*).[12] These adolescents and young adults typically present with both impaired short-term memory and significant retrograde amnesia. In these cases, the impairment in short-term memory is directly related to alcohol use and is believed to be due, at least in part, to a 20% decrease in the rate of brain metabolism (McCann, 1992). In regard to the Wernicke-Korsakoff syndrome, the retrograde amnesia actually is caused indirectly by alcohol—use due primarily to brain changes associated with chronic thiamine (vitamin $B_1$) deficiency that usually accompanies chronic alcoholism and resultant  poor nutrition. (Also see Chapter 1, *The Psychodepressants*, for further related discussion of alcohol use and its associated toxic effects.)

Heffernan and colleagues (e.g., Heffernan, 2008; Heffernan, Clark, Bartholomew, et al., 2010) have found that both reported excessive drinking, as well as, binge drinking by adolescents and young adults leads to impairments in prospective memory (i.e., both the short-term and long-term memory involved in the "cognitive ability of remembering to carry out

---

[12] Typically, these youth, who also may suffer from mental disorders (e.g., MDD, PTSD, SUD), have spent many homeless years living in poverty on the streets of major cities where they have endured chronic hunger, physical assaults, and police arrests for drunkenness and vagrancy (Pagliaro & Pagliaro, *Clinical Patient Data Files*).

an intended action at some future point in time" [p. 36]—such as studying for a classroom examination or submitting a term paper on the due date).

## Benzodiazepines: Explicit Memory Impairment and Antrograde Amnesia

The benzodiazepines (e.g., triazolam [Halcion®]) have been studied more than any other drug or substance of abuse in regard to their effects on memory. This large amount of research attention is related to their extensive therapeutic use, primarily as anxiolytics and sedative-hypnotics, and their troublesome effects on memory, particularly among older adults (Pagliaro & Pagliaro, 1983, 1992). The memory impairment associated with the benzodiazepines is similar to, but not identical with, that observed with alcohol. In this regard, the benzodiazepines appear to: (1) impair explicit memory, which involves contextual and associative information related to conscious recollection (Danion, Peretti, Grange, et al., 1992; Ghoneim, Block, Ping, et al., 1993; Mallick, Kirby, Martin, et al., 1993; Mintzer & Griffiths, 1999; Polster, McCarthy, O'Sullivan, et al., 1993; Vidailhet, Danion, Kauffmann-Muller, et al., 1994); and (2) cause anterograde amnesia, which affects long-term visual and verbal episodic memory storage (Barbee, 1993; Roehrs, Merlotti, Zorick, et al., 1994; Unrug-Neervoort, van Luijtelaar, & Coenen, 1992).

Although contradictory studies can be found in the published literature, it appears that explicit memory, which does not require conscious awareness, and both semantic memory and short-term memory are not significantly

and consistently affected by benzodiazepine use (Brown, Brown, & Bowes, 1983; Curran, Gardiner, Java, et al., 1993; Ghoneim, Hinrichs, & Mewaldt, 1984; Knopman, 1991; Mallick, Kirby, Martin, et al.,1993; Polster, McCarthy, O'Sullivan, et al., 1993; Weingartner, Hommer, Lister, et al., 1992).[13]

### Acute Adverse Effects on Memory

The acute adverse effects of the benzodiazepines on memory[14] appear to be mediated through the gamma-aminobutyric acid (GABA) receptor complex, which contains the benzodiazepine receptor binding sites (Barbee, 1993; Izquierdo & Medina, 1991). (See related discussion in Chapter 1, *The Psychodepressants.*) This hypothesis is supported by studies that have demonstrated that both the sedative and the memory effects of the benzodiazepines can be reversed by the administration of the benzodiazepine antagonist flumazenil (Anexate®), which blocks the benzodiazepine receptors (Ghoneim, Block, Ping, et al., 1993). Consonant with this hypothesis are supportive research findings that the effects of the benzodiazepines on memory are dose-related and directly associated with the degree of psychodepression that is achieved (Barbee, 1993; Hindmarch, Sherwood, & Kerr, 1993; Roehrs, Merlotti, Zorick, et al., 1994).

### Chronic Adverse Effects on Memory

In relation to the regular, long-term use of the benzodiazepines, it appears that tolerance to the memory effects never fully develops (Gorenstein, Bernik, & Pompeia, 1994) and that the cognitive deficits, including observable effects on learning and memory, may persist following the withdrawal from

---

[13] Of course, dosage is a significant factor in this context. (Also see the earlier related discussion in the "Attention" section.)

[14] The labeling of these benzodiazepine effects as *adverse* or *negative* is appropriate within the learning-focused context of this chapter. So, too, is the labeling of the amnestic effects of the benzodiazepines (e.g., flunitrazepam [Rohypnol®, roofies] and GHB) when used for the perpetration of date-rape. (See the related discussion in Chapter 1, *The Psychodepressants.*) However, in other contexts (e.g., use of the benzodiazepines as an anesthetic or as an adjunct to anesthesia), the same effects on memory are generally, and properly, labeled as *positive* and *therapeutically desired*.

regular, long-term benzodiazepine use (Tata, Rollings, Collins, et al., 1994). This area of research has obvious potential significance in regard to adolescent learning and memory, particularly for adolescents who may have initiated their regular, long-term benzodiazepine use during childhood, either medically (e.g., as pharmacotherapy for a seizure disorder) or personally (e.g., as experimental or social use with peers).

## Cannabis: Disrupted Short-Term Memory Encoding into Long-Term Memory

The use of cannabis in its various forms can impair memory (Hanson & Luciana, 2010; Heavy alcohol use, 2010); Millsaps, Azrin, & Mittenberg, 1994; Nestor, Roberts, Garavan, et al., 2008.), presumably by adversely affecting the encoding of short-term memory into long-term memory (Lundqvist, 2005; Solowij & Battisti, 2008). The effects of cannabis on memory have been clearly and widely documented (e.g., Di Forti, Morrison, Butt, et al., 2007; Pagliaro, 1983, 1987; Pagliaro & Pagliaro, 2004). Thus, even articles in magazines favoring cannabis legalization and use, such as *High Times*, have long accepted and published this fact: "Clearly, cannabis acts ... on memory by way of the receptors in the limbic system's hippocampus, which 'gates' information during memory consolidation" (Gettman, 1995, p. 29).

The negative effects of cannabis use on human cognition appear to be dose-related depending on the quality, amount, and frequency of cannabis use (i.e., related to the amount of THC absorbed into the bloodstream). These effects are most pronounced among daily, long-term heavy cannabis users (Block & Ghoneim, 1993; Indlekofer, Piechatzek,

Daamen, et al., 2009).[15] Published research findings indicate that these effects are mediated through the action of the endogenous cannabinoid, or endocannabinoid, system (Pagliaro & Pagliaro, 2009; Solowij & Michie, 2007). This system putatively affects memory by mediating the flow of information in the brain by means of the effects of its endogenous ligands (i.e., anandamide [N-arachidonoyl ethanolamine] and 2-arachidonoyl-glycerol) on the cannabinoid CB1 receptors (Chevaleyre, Takahashi, & Castillo, 2006; Howlett, Breivogel, Childers, et al., 2004; Piomelli, 2003).

Although some studies (e.g., Solowij, Stephens, Roffman, et al., 2002) have suggested that cannabis-induced cognitive impairment is long-term and possibly permanent, the cannabis-induced adverse effects on memory primarily appear to be acute and self-limiting (i.e., they occur when the child or adolescent is actively using cannabis). Pope, Gruber, Hudson, et al. (2002) demonstrated that even heavy cannabis users, "who had smoked cannabis at least 5000 times in their lives" (p. 41S) and who had previously demonstrated cannabis-induced cognitive impairment, could—following a one-month period of supervised abstinence—return to normal cognitive test performance (i.e., the cannabis-induced cognitive deficits are reversible). However, a return to "sobriety" does not ameliorate the cumulative effects of previous cannabis-induced cognitive impairment (see related discussion in the earlier section, "Motivation," "Negative Effects on Motivation: Amotivational Syndrome.")

In addition, cannabis users are usually polydrug and substance of abuse users, as noted in several studies and reports (e.g., de Sola Llopis, Miguelez-Pan, Pena-Casanova, et al., 2008; Gouzoulis-Mayfrank, Daumann, Tuchtenhagen, et al., 2000; Hanson & Luciana,

---

[15] The current definition of "heavy use" has changed significantly based on the 10-fold increase in the THC concentration of the cannabis generally available during the last two decades compared to that which was generally available during the 1960s and 1970s.

2010; Hoshi, Mullins, Boundy, et al., 2007; Indlekofer, Piechatzek, Daamen, et al., 2009; Pagliaro & Pagliaro, *Clinical Patient Data Files*). As such, they are at particular risk for the additive, or synergistic, negative effects associated with the concurrent use of cannabis and other drugs or substances of abuse (e.g., alcohol, MDMA [ecstasy]) that also adversely affect memory (e.g., visual memory), as suggested by Laws and Kokkalis (2007). (Also see Chapters 3, *The Psychodelics*, and Chapter 8, *Dual Diagnosis Among Adolescents*, for additional related discussion.)

## Cocaine: Residual Memory Impairment

The published research findings on cocaine use and its effects on human memory are less extensive than those for some of the other drugs and substances of abuse. However, several studies (e.g., Berry, van Gorp, Herzberg, et al., 1993; Gillen, Kranzler, Bauer, et al., 1998; Manschreck, Schneyer, Weisstein, et al., 1990; Mittenberg & Motta, 1993) have found significant residual memory impairment among former cocaine-using subjects who, at the time of testing, had been abstinent from cocaine for varying periods of time, ranging from 1 week to 3 months. Several diverse mechanisms (e.g., elevation of cortisol activity, constriction of cerebral blood vessels) have been suggested for these negative effects of cocaine on memory (Cromie, 1998; Fox, Jackson, & Sinha, 2009). However, none of the mechanisms has yet been substantiated. A major confounding variable is, of course, the concurrent use of other drugs and substances of abuse, particularly alcohol, by regular, long-term cocaine users (Nnadi, Mimiko, McCurtis,

et al., 2005; Pagliaro & Pagliaro, 2009). (Also see Chapter 2, *The Psychostimulants*, for additional related discussion.)

## Gamma-Hydroxybutyrate: Anterograde Amnesia, Episodic Memory, and Working Memory

Gamma-hydroxybutyrate (Xyrem®), a miscellaneous sedative-hypnotic (see Chapter 1, *The Psychodepressants*), can produce lasting anterograde amnesia—an effect that significantly contributes to its use as a date-rape drug (Pagliaro & Pagliaro, 2009; Schwartz, Milteer, & LeBeau, 2000; Varela, Nogue, Oros, et al, 2004). In addition, the use of GHB can adversely affect the encoding of episodic memory (i.e., as measured by the number of words recalled in a free recall test) as well as working memory (Carter, Griffiths, & Mintzer, 2009; Carter, Richards, Mintzer, et al., 2006).

## Methamphetamine: Effects on Verbal Memory

Methamphetamine, as well as other amphetamines, appears to be clearly neurotoxic, causing damage to both the dopaminergic and serotonergic neurotransmitter systems (Gouzoulis-Mayfrank & Daumann, 2009; Pagliaro & Pagliaro, 2009). However, the degree of neurotoxicity depends on such variables as the: (1) specific amphetamine used; (2) dosage or amount used; (3) timing of use in regard to brain development (e.g., periods of rapid brain growth and development, such as occurs from around the 20th week of pregnancy and postnatally through the 2nd year of life);[16] and (4) concurrent use of other

---

[16]Adolescence is another period of significant brain growth and development as well as maturation. During this period, there is an overproduction of gray matter (i.e., neuron cell bodies), particularly in the frontal lobes just prior to puberty, around 11 years of age (Giedd, Blumenthal, Jeffries, et al., 1999), and in the temporal lobes during midadolescence, around 16 to 17 years of age (Giedd, 2004). The development of executive functioning, which can take until early adulthood for completion, appears to be dependent on the maturation of the prefrontal cortex and limbic system (i.e., the completion of the myelination and interconnections of the gray matter in the frontal lobes) (Sowell, Thompson, Holmes, et al., 1999).

*(continued)*

neurotoxins that can act as cofactors, including other drugs and substances of abuse.[17]

In this regard, methamphetamine use, as well as prenatal exposure, has been associated with physical damage to specific brain structures, particularly the striatum (e.g., reduced striatal volume) (Berman, O'Neill, Fears, et al., 2008; Chang, Alicata, Ernst, et al., 2007). Associated effects on learning and memory include deficits, or impaired performance, in verbal memory (Chang, Smith, LoPresti, et al., 2004; Lu, Johnson, O'Hare, et al., 2009). (Also see Chapter 5, *Exposure to the Drugs and Substances of Abuse From Conception Through Childhood.*)

## Methylenedioxymethamphetamine: Disrupted Episodic Memory, Short-Term Memory, Verbal Memory, and Working Memory

The regular, long-term use of MDMA (ecstasy) has been associated with memory impairment mediated by decreased serotonin activity (i.e., serotonergic neurotoxicity, including depletion of serotonin and loss of serotonin axons, particularly in the hippocampus, the temporal lobes, and the frontal lobe) (Gouzoulis-Mayfrank & Daumann, 2009; Quednow, Jessen, Kuhn, et al., 2006). Residual neurotoxicity (e.g., memory impairment) appears to persist long after the use of MDMA has been discontinued (Gouzoulis-Mayfrank & Daumann, 2006; Morgan, 1999). The associated memory impairment appears to involve several types of memory, including episodic, long-term, short-term, spatial, verbal, and working memory (Fox, Parrott, & Turner, 2001; Laws & Kokkalis, 2007; McCann, Mertl, Eligulashvili, et al., 1999; Morgan, 1999; Nulsen, Fox, & Hammond, 2010; Parrott, 2006; Parrott, Lees, Garnham, et al., 1998; Piper, 2007; Quednow, Jessen, Kuhn, et al., 2006).

The degree of memory impairment, as demonstrated for verbal memory, appears to be related directly to the complexity (difficulty) of the memory task (i.e., the more complex or difficult the task, the more significant the associated memory impairment; Brown, McKone, & Ward, 2010). This observation may be reflective, at least in part, of the adverse effect that the regular, long-term use of MDMA also has on executive functioning (Fox, Parrott, & Turner, 2001; Murphy, Wareing, Fisk, et al., 2009; Parrott, 2006).

In addition, because most MDMA users also use cannabis, several studies have examined the concurrent use of these two drugs and substances of abuse. Findings indicate that additive, or synergistic, adverse effects on both attention and memory appear to occur (de Sola Llopis, Miguelez-Pan, Pena-Casanova, et al., 2008; Gouzoulis-Mayfrank, Daumann, Tuchtenhagen, et al., 2000; Indlekofer, Piechatzek, Daamen, et al., 2009; Roberts, Nestor, & Garavan, 2009). This apparent synergistic effect of MDMA and cannabis, when used concurrently, may well account for some reports (e.g., Hanson & Luciana, 2010) that have found that the use of MDMA alone does not appear to significantly impair cognitive function. (Also see earlier remarks concerning the complexity of the memory tasks.)

---

[16] *(continued)*

The limbic system consists of a collection of neural structures that includes the amygdala, cingulate gyrus, and hippocampus. It regulates emotional experience, memory, and motivational learning. The maturation of connections between the prefrontal cortex, basal ganglia, and cerebellum during adolescence also appears to be crucial for the development of higher cognitive, or executive, functions (Schepis, Adinoff, & Rao, 2008).

[17] For example, in a large study of the demographic and psychosocial characteristics of women who used methamphetamine while pregnant, Derauf, LaGasse, Smith, et al. (2007) found that nearly 50% also used alcohol. (See earlier discussion in this chapter concerning alcohol for additional related discussion of memory impairment.)

# EFFECTS OF NEUROLOGICAL AND MENTAL DISORDERS ON LEARNING AND MEMORY: ATTENTION-DEFICIT/ HYPERACTIVITY DISORDER; FETAL ALCOHOL SYNDROME/ FETAL ALCOHOL SPECTRUM DISORDER; AND MAJOR DEPRESSIVE DISORDER

In addition to their respective relationship to SUDs and substance-related disorders (e.g., alcohol abuse, cannabis dependence), the drugs and substances of abuse are related to three other disorders that have particular relevance in regard to learning and memory: (1) attention-deficit hyperactivity disorder; (2) fetal alcohol syndrome/fetal alcohol spectrum disorder; and (3) major depressive disorder, which are discussed in the next sections. (Also see related discussion in Chapter 8, *Dual Diagnosis Among Adolescents.*)

## Attention-Deficit/Hyperactivity Disorder

Reportedly, A-D/HD is the most prevalent psychological disorder of childhood and adolescence in North America with a diagnostic incidence of approximately 8% (Dopheide & Pliszka, 2009; Mayes, Bagwell, & Erkulwater, 2008). Although initially thought of solely as a childhood disorder, it is now widely recognized that when A-D/HD is identified during childhood, approximately 80% of affected children will be expected to have the associated signs and symptoms persist into adolescence and adulthood (Staller & Faraone, 2006). Generally, the incidence of A-D/HD is estimated to range from 6% to 9% among school-age children. In this age group, it is approximately 5 to 10 times

higher among boys than girls,[18] with reported estimates of prevalence as high as 10% for boys.

A-D/HD is not simply a random group of rambunctious children whose behavior happens to irritate parents and teachers. It is a distinct genetic, behavioral syndrome that is expressed in children and may be a lifelong problem resulting in antisocial personality and alcoholism in adult men and in a hysteric-histrionic personality in adult woman (Comings, 1990, p. 87).

Although the etiology of A-D/HD is currently unknown, many different factors have been implicated, including diet, genetics, and social factors (National Institutes of Health, 2000). On a molecular level, dysregulation of the dopaminergic, noradrenergic, and nicotinic neurotransmitter systems has been suggested as being central to the development of A-D/HD (Manos, Tom-Revzon, Bukstein, et al., 2007). The authors' clinical experience, as well as the published literature, also suggests a strong positive association between A-D/HD and FAS/FASD (Brown, Coles, Smith, et al., 1991; Driscoll, Streissguth, & Riley, 1990; Nanson & Hiscock, 1990; Spohr & Steinhausen, 1984; Streissguth, Barr, Sampson, et al., 1994). In addition, children and adolescents with A-D/HD have been found to be significantly more likely than their matched cohorts without A-D/HD to illicitly use drugs and substances of abuse (Bukstein, 2008; Dopheide & Pliszka, 2009; Kollins, 2008; Pagliaro & Pagliaro, 1996). (Also see Chapter 8, *Dual Diagnosis Among Adolescents,* for additional related discussion.)

Children and adolescents who have been medically prescribed methylphenidate (Ritalin®) or other psychostimulants (e.g., mixed amphetamines [Adderall®]) for the management of A-D/HD are commonly approached

---

[18] Several clinicians and researchers (e.g., Rucklidge, 2008; Staller & Faraone, 2006) have suggested that A-D/HD is underestimated among girls because of societal biases, including gender-related biases of parents and teachers, and presentation of signs and symptoms (i.e., girls are as likely as boys to present with inattention, but without associated hyperactivity [i.e., as attention deficit disorder {ADD}]).

by peers and older children and adolescents to give, sell, or trade their psychostimulants (Pagliaro & Pagliaro, 2004, 2009; Pagliaro & Pagliaro, *Clinical Patient Data Files*; Wilens, Adler, Adams, et al., 2008). Feeling pressured or bullied, they often comply. (See Chapter 2, *The Psychostimulants*, for additional related discussion.)

Children and adolescents with A-D/HD invariably have learning disorders (Golden, 1991; Pagliaro & Pagliaro, 1996; Shaywitz & Shaywitz, 1991)—a relationship that is both complex and controversial (Biederman, Newcorn, & Sprich, 1991). For example: Is A-D/HD the cause of learning disorders, or are learning disorders the cause of A-D/HD? Do learning disorders and A-D/HD co-occur in an unrelated manner, or are they otherwise related? Regardless of the answers to these questions, the specific behaviors associated with A-D/HD, which appear to contribute to learning disorders, are self-evident and can be readily identified. Table 6.1 lists the common signs and symptoms of A-D/HD. Obviously, from a perusal of this list, it is apparent that problems with attention are at the core of the associated learning problems. (See earlier discussion in the "Attention" section.)

These learning problems translate into long-term adverse academic outcomes for children and adolescents who have A-D/HD (Merrell & Tymms, 2001; Pagliaro & Pagliaro, *Clinical Patient Data Files*). For example, Barbaresi, Katusic, Colligan, et al. (2007), in a controlled retrospective study of over 1,000 children and adolescents (including 370 with A-D/HD), found that, when compared to children and ado-

**Table 6.1    Attention-Deficit/Hyperactivity Disorder: Common Signs and Symptoms[a]**

| Grouping | Signs and Symptoms |
| --- | --- |
| Inattention | Often fails to give close attention to details or makes careless mistakes in schoolwork, work, or other activities. |
| | Often has difficulty sustaining attention in tasks or play activities. |
| | Often does not seem to listen when spoken to directly. |
| | Often does not follow through on instructions and fails to finish schoolwork, chores, or duties in the workplace (not due to oppositional behavior or failure to understand instructions). |
| | Often has difficulty organizing tasks and activities. |
| | Often avoids, dislikes, or is reluctant to engage in tasks that require sustained mental effort (such as schoolwork or homework). |
| | Often loses things necessary for tasks or activities (e.g., toys, school assignments, pencils, books, or tools). |
| | Often is easily distracted by extraneous stimuli. |
| | Often is forgetful in daily activities. |
| Hyperactivity | Often fidgets with hands or feet or squirms in seat. |
| | Often leaves seat in classroom or in other situations in which remaining seated is expected. |
| | Often runs about or climbs excessively in situations where it is inappropriate (among adolescents, may be limited to subjective feelings of restlessness). |
| | Often has difficulty playing or engaging in quiet leisure activities. |
| | Often is *on the go* or often acts as if *driven by a motor.* |
| | Often talks excessively. |
| Impulsivity | Often blurts out answers before questions have been completed. |
| | Often has difficulty awaiting turn. |
| | Often interrupts or intrudes on others (e.g., butts into conversations or games). |

[a]According to criteria from the *Diagnostic and Statistical Manual of Mental Disorders* (American Psychiatric Association, 2000), the signs and symptoms of A-D/HD have been divided into three groups: inattention, hyperactivity, and impulsivity.

lescents who did not have A-D/HD, the children and adolescents with A-D/HD: (1) had significantly lower reading achievement at 13 years of age; (2) were absent from grammar school or high school significantly more often; (3) were 3 times more likely to be retained a grade (i.e., held back or failed a grade); and (4) were twice as likely to drop out of school before completing high school.

Learning among children and adolescents who have A-D/HD also can be affected by the adverse effects associated with the pharmacotherapy that is commonly prescribed for its treatment and management—the psychostimulants (Allen & Drabman, 1991; Pagliaro, 1994; Swanson, Cantwell, Lerner, et al., 1991). These adverse effects are discussed in the next section in regard to methylphenidate (Ritalin®), one of the most widely used drugs for the treatment and management of A-D/HD in North America.

Although the use of psychostimulant pharmacotherapy generally has resulted in observed improvement in classroom manageability, many questions have been raised consistently, for some time now, concerning its potentially negative effect(s) on learning. For example, over 20 years ago, Handen, Breaux, Gosling, et al. (1990) found that "gains in measures of attention were not associated with improvement in learning, as measured by a paired associate learning task" (p. 922). Even more recently published studies (e.g., Scheffler, Brown, Fulton, et al., 2009) have demonstrated only moderate improvements, at best, in regard to standardized mathematic and reading test scores among children and adolescents with A-D/HD who receive psychostimulant pharmacotherapy.

Figure 6.3 clearly illustrates how psychostimulant pharmacotherapy can either improve or harm cognitive performance as a function of dosage and therapeutic goal. Note that as the dosage of the psychostimulant is increased beyond optimal for cognitive performance (i.e., in an effort to achieve optimal social per-

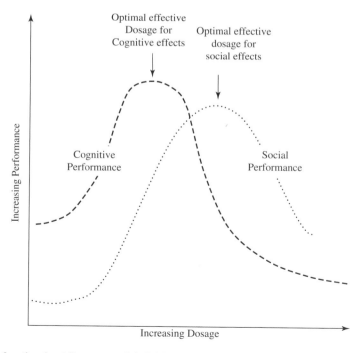

**Figure 6.3   Psychostimulant Dosage and A-D/HD: Corresponding Cognitive and Social Performance Among Children and Adolescents**
Source: Modified from Swanson, Cantwell, Lerner, et al., 1991.

formance, or control of unwanted, negative behavior), cognitive performance begins to decline—usually well before optimal social performance is achieved. Unfortunately for many children and adolescents in regard to learning, the endpoint for pharmacotherapy is most commonly the achievement of optimal social performance, or control.

### Methylphenidate

Methylphenidate (Concerta®; Ritalin®) has been used for almost 50 years for the symptomatic management of A-D/HD (Pagliaro & Pagliaro, 2004). A review of the published literature indicates that methylphenidate's reported effects on learning and memory have been mixed and must be evaluated individually. The factors that appear to be related to an increased incidence of learning and memory impairment in this clinical context include: (1) the use of higher-than-optimal therapeutic doses of methylphenidate (as illustrated in Figure 6.3); and (2) the use of methylphenidate for children who do not fully meet the diagnostic criteria for A-D/HD (Pagliaro & Pagliaro, 1996; Swanson, Cantwell, Lerner, et al., 1991).

For several decades now, we have, both in print and in clinical practice, lamented and criticized the seemingly pro forma diagnosis of A-D/HD, particularly among boys, based solely on the signs and symptoms reported by parents, usually mothers, and teachers—without ever actually observing the child's behavior firsthand (e.g., by a visit to the classroom).[19, 20] A significant number of cases of A-D/HD continue to be misdiagnosed, resulting in the overdiagnosis of this condition among children and adolescents.

For example, in their population-based birth cohort study, Barbaresi, Katusic, Colligan, et al. (2002) found that: when less stringent diagnostic criteria were used, "the highest estimate of the cumulative incidence [of A-D/HD] at age 19 years (i.e., 16%)" was obtained; and when the most stringent diagnostic criteria were used, "the lowest estimate of the cumulative incidence [of A-D/HD] at age 19 years (i.e., 7.4%)" was obtained (p. 217). Even in cases where A-D/HD is diagnosed appropriately, it is frequently treated inappropriately. In this regard, there is a significant overreliance on the use of psychostimulant pharmacotherapy, particularly for those adolescents with a dual diagnosis of A-D/HD and a SUD (see Chapter 8, *Dual Diagnosis Among Adolescents*) and a general neglect of: (1) appropriate cognitive-behavioral therapies; (2) nonpsychostimulant pharmacotherapy, such as the use of the selective norepinephrine reuptake inhibitor atomoxetine (Strattera®); and (3) the use of selected dietary supplements (Bukstein, 2008; Kollins, 2008; Pagliaro & Pagliaro, 2009; Rucklidge, 2008; Schubiner, 2005).

The prescription and use of methylphenidate for children and adolescents must be given special attention and should never be treated pro forma (Kollins, 2008; Pagliaro, 1994; Pagliaro & Pagliaro, 2009) because of the potential cognitive impairment associated with its inappropriate use for children and adolescents who do not fully meet the criteria for A-D/HD and other potential physical and psychological adverse effects (e.g., anorexia; dyskinesia; insomnia; seizures; sudden death; tics). In addition, even in clinical situations where A-D/HD is diagnosed correctly and methylphenidate is prescribed appropriately

---

[19] Given that this process, although sound, is generally impractical for most clinicians (i.e., pediatricians) who diagnose A-D/HD, we have suggested that they either: (1) collaborate with a school psychologist who can observe a child or adolescent in the usual classroom and general school environment; or (2) carefully and appropriately use valid and reliable psychometric tests, generally administered by parents or teachers, to collect data that are used to assist in the formation of a tentative diagnosis of A-D/HD (e.g., Barkley Home Situations Questionnaire®; Barkley School Situations Questionnaire®; Conners Teachers and Parents Rating Scales®; Parent Completed Child Behavior Checklist®).

[20] Several European studies have presented similar findings and concerns. For example, in a Spanish study, Moran Sanchez, Navarro-Mateu, Robles Sanchez, et al. (2008) found that "the presumptive diagnosis [of A-D/HD] in primary care behaved [only] as a screening test" (p. 29).

to achieve optimal learning outcomes, the confounding effects associated with its use and the risk for state-dependent learning (see "Cognitive Processing" section, "State-Dependent Learning" for related discussion) requires careful consideration. The old adage, which seems so apropos in many clinical contexts, readily comes to mind in this situation: There is no such thing as a "free lunch."

## Fetal Alcohol Syndrome/Fetal Alcohol Spectrum Disorder

Alcohol is a known human teratogen capable of causing CNS dysfunction, growth retardation, characteristic facies, and associated morphological abnormalities in the developing fetus (Pagliaro & Pagliaro, 1995). Commonly known as the fetal alcohol syndrome (FAS) or fetal alcohol spectrum disorder (FASD), most of the effects, which are present at birth, persist through childhood and adolescence and into adulthood. (See Chapter 5, *Exposure to the Drugs and Substances of Abuse From Conception Through Childhood*, for a comprehensive discussion.) Perhaps the most serious and enduring consequences of FAS/FASD are varying degrees of mental retardation[21] and a high incidence of A-D/HD (Pagliaro & Pagliaro, 1987, 1996; Streissguth, Barr, Sampson, et al., 1994). Specific cognitive-processing-related learning deficits also have been associated with the FAS/FASD among school-age children and may affect

approximately 1% of these children (Koren, Fantus, & Nulman, 2010).[22]

These deficits include:

- Deficits for sequential processing, or short-term memory and encoding (i.e., working memory; Attention, 1994; Becker, Warr-Leeper, & Leeper, 1990; Coles, Brown, Smith, et al., 1991; Green, Mihic, Nikkel, et al., 2009; Kodituwakku, 2009; Pagliaro, 1992; Rasmussen, 2005)
- Deficits in memory strategies and verbal memory/verbal executive functioning (Kaemingk, Mulvaney, & Halverson, 2003; Manji, Pei, Loomes, et al., 2009; Mattson & Roebuck, 2002; Rasmussen & Bisanz, 2009; Rasmussen, Pei, Manji, et al., 2009; Riley & McGee, 2005; Willford, Richardson, Leech, et al., 2004)
- Deficits in spatial learning/memory/organization and arithmetic skills (Streissguth, Barr, Sampson, et al., 1994; Streissguth, Bookstein, Sampson, et al., 1989)

As noted by Streissguth, Barr, and Sampson (1990), these deficits are not restricted to the offspring of mothers who drank heavily throughout their entire pregnancies:

Learning problems were associated with the alcohol "binge" pattern of five or more drinks on at least one occasion. This study shows that alcohol use patterns within the social drinking range can have long lasting effects on IQ

---

[21] In regard to mental retardation associated with FAS/FASD, not as a *DSM* or *ICD* diagnosis but as a concept or process, we have argued since the 1970s that just because you can't see it, doesn't mean it doesn't exist (or hasn't occurred). For example, if the specific amount of alcohol consumed by a pregnant adolescent girl was sufficient to cause FAS/FASD with an associated decrement, or loss, in this specific case of 10 IQ points and the resultant child is subsequently tested and found to have an IQ score of 120 (i.e., a score at the high end of the normal range), it does not mean that the loss of IQ points did not occur, but rather that, if not for the mother's alcohol consumption during pregnancy, her child would have had an IQ of 130 (i.e., 120 IQ points measured in addition to 10 points lost due to the effects of maternal alcohol use during pregnancy). This concept became self-evident to us when we were involved in assessing specific population groups with a high incidence of FAS/FASD and noted that not only was true mental retardation present (i.e., that met defined, preexisting diagnostic criteria) but that the entire IQ curve for the population had been shifted to the left (i.e., possessed the same variance but a lower central tendency [i.e., *mean, median, mode*]) (Pagliaro & Pagliaro, *Clinical Patient Data Files*).

[22] The incidence among students in North America of Aboriginal and American Indian descent may be as much as 5 times greater (Sarche & Spicer, 2008). See related discussion of FAS/FASD in Chapter 5, *Exposure to the Drugs and Substances of Abuse From Conception Through Childhood*.

and learning problems in young school aged children. (p. 662)

## Major Depressive Disorder

In addition to the accepted cognitive model of depression proposed by Beck (1967), several other theoretical approaches "emphasize information processing concepts as being at the core of depressive symptomatology" (Ingram & Holle, 1992, p. 187). In this regard, it has been noted that active cognitive processing (such as that which occurs during problem solving), as well as memory (e.g., explicit memory), is severely impaired among people experiencing major depression (Austin, Ross, & Murray, et al., 1992; Colombel, 2007; Query & Megran, 1984; Smith, Tracy, & Murray, 1993). Depression may also have a significant negative effect on two other core processes—attention and motivation. (See "Attention" and "Motivation" sections earlier in this chapter for related discussion of these processes.)

The negative effects of depression on memory may be associated with, or be more pronounced in relation to, specific types or contexts of memory, such as: implicit memory (Norman & Turner, 1993), positive memories (Moffitt, Singer, Nelligan, et al., 1994), and positively valenced words (Denny & Hunt, 1992). (Also see Chapter 8, *Dual Diagnosis Among Adolescents*, for further related discussion of MDD.)

## CHAPTER SUMMARY

This chapter briefly reviewed the concepts of learning and memory. Related definitions and the cognitive input-output model of learning and memory were presented and discussed. In addition, the core processes of optimal learning—attention, motivation, perception, and cognitive processing—and the various types of memory were presented and discussed. Particular attention was given to the significant effects associated with the drugs and substances of abuse on these processes, including the varied effects on memory, particularly of the psychodepressants (i.e., alcohol, the benzodiazepines, and GHB), the psychostimulants (i.e., cocaine and methamphetamine), and the psychodelics (i.e., cannabis and MDMA).

The use of the drugs and substances of abuse by children and adolescents, including their use when medically prescribed for the symptomatic management of A-D/HD, FAS/FASD, and MDD, can have significant adverse effects on the core processes of learning and memory. These neurological and mental disorders also can have their own direct negative effects on learning and memory. Psychiatrists and psychologists, as well as teachers and others, must be aware of the nature and extent of these effects. They also need to differentiate, for therapeutic reasons, between behavior resulting from organically (e.g., genetically or pathologically) based learning disorders and those that result from the use of the various drugs and substances of abuse (e.g., alcohol, cannabis).

In addition, as noted at the beginning of this chapter, the use of the drugs and substances of abuse by children and adolescents has been clearly and consistently associated with negative effects on attendance at school, academic performance, educational aspirations, and rates of completing high school. As recognized by Scheier and Botvin (1995) over two decades ago, echoing similar earlier observations by others (e.g., Cohen, 1981; Hollister, 1986): "Early drug use may impede acquisition of critical thinking skills and hinder the learning of important cognitive strategies required for successful transition to adulthood" (p. 379).[23]

---

[23] In a developmental context, this observation is particularly relevant, as well as a cause for concern, because the major developmental goal of adolescence is to prepare children for their transition to adulthood.

PART III

*Clinical Considerations*

# CHAPTER 7

# *Detecting Adolescent Use of the Drugs and Substances of Abuse*

## *Selected Quick-Screen Psychometric Tests*

## INTRODUCTION

The use of the drugs and substances of abuse among North American children and adolescents is significant and has reached alarming proportions. (For an overview of the prevalence and characteristics of psychodepressant, psychostimulant, and psychodelic use among children and adolescents, see Chapters, 1, 2, and 3, respectively). However, only a small proportion of pediatricians and adolescent family physicians include the standard assessment of alcohol use disorders (AUDs) or other drug and substance use disorders (SUDs) during annual physical examinations or other office visits (Aspy, Mold, Thompson, et al., 2008; Habis, Tall, Smith, et al., 2007; Marcell, Halpern-Felsher, Coriell, et al., 2002; Mersy, 2003; National Center on Addictions and Substance Abuse, 2000; C. P. O'Brien, 2008). This lack of attention to screening for AUDs and SUDs also is true for other health and social care professionals who are involved in the promotion of adolescent health and well-being. Thus, many AUDs and SUDs are unidentified and remain untreated until their associated personal and social problems escalate. (See Table 7.1.)

As noted in Table 7.1, adolescents, as well as other people who have active issues or problems associated with their use of the drugs and substances of abuse, often deliberately conceal this information from their health care providers. For example, Delaney-Black, Chiodo, Hannigan, et al. (2010), in their longitudinal cohort study of over 400 high-risk, urban North American adolescents of African descent, found that, "teen specimens (hair) were 52 times more likely to identify cocaine use compared with self-report" (p. 887). In addition, none of the adolescent participants admitted to using opiate analgesics—even though assured that their responses would remain confidential. However, approximately 7% tested positive on laboratory analysis for opiate analgesic use.

It has long been established that delayed treatment or intervention can result in increasingly harmful consequences that are largely preventable (Buchsbaum, 1994; Gallant & Head-Dunham, 1991). Selected quick-screen psychometric tests offer health and other social care professionals accurate, efficient, and economical means for identifying adolescents for immediate and necessary intervention (Eberhard, Nordström, Höglund, et al., 2009), including referral to other appropriate health and social care professionals (Searight, 2009), as needed. (See Figure 7.1.) Indeed, as we and others (e.g., Crome, Bloor, & Thom, 2006) have long noted, drug and substance use disorders—particularly when left unidentified or undiagnosed—also can exacerbate or predispose, mask, or otherwise interfere with the diagnosis and management of other mental and physical disorders. (See Chapter 8, *Dual Diagnosis Among Adolescents*, for related discussion.)

In an effort to help pediatricians, psychologists, psychiatrists, and other health and social care professionals in their efforts

**TABLE 7.1    Alcohol Use Disorders (AUDs) and Substance Use Disorders (SUDs): Missed Diagnoses**

| Percentage of Physician Respondents | Physicians' Behaviors in Managing AUDs and SUDs |
|---|---|
| 94% (primary care physicians) | Fail to diagnose alcohol abuse when presented with early signs and symptoms in an adult patient. |
| 58% (physicians) | Fail to discuss the use of drugs and substances of abuse with their patients because they believe their patients lie about it.[a] |
| 41% (pediatricians) | Fail to diagnose illicit use of the drugs and substances of abuse when presented with a classic description of a drug-abusing teenage patient. |
| 35% (physicians) | Fail to treat a patient who abuses the drugs and substances of abuse because of time constraints. |
| 30% (physicians) | Identify that they are prepared to diagnose drug abuse. |
| 20% (physicians) | Identify that they are prepared to diagnose alcoholism. |
| 17% (physicians) | Identify that they are prepared to diagnose illicit use of the drugs and substances of abuse. |
| 11% (physicians) | Fail to treat a patient who abuses the drugs and substances of abuse because they are concerned that they will not be reimbursed for the time necessary to screen and treat the patient. |

| Percentage of Patient Respondents[b] | Patients' Reports of Physician Behaviors in Managing AUDs and SUDs |
|---|---|
| 75% | Say their primary care physician was not involved in their decision to seek treatment for AUDs or SUDs. |
| 54% | Say their primary care physician did nothing about their addiction. |

[a] 58% of patients agree that they lie about their substance abuse.
[b] The typical patient had a substance use problem for 10 years before receiving treatment.
Modified from: The National Center, 2000; Center for Health Justice, 2005.

to ensure accurate and timely diagnosis and management of AUDs and SUDs, several approaches to screening, brief intervention, and referral to treatment have been developed and implemented (Babor, McRee, Kassebaum, et al., 2007; Levy, Vaughan, & Knight, 2002; Madras, Compton, Ăvula, et al., 2009; Searight, 2009). This chapter presents an overview of the quick-screen psychometric tests that have been found to be particularly effective for detecting AUDs and SUDs among adolescents. It should be noted, and kept in mind, that a positive screening test result does not, in and of itself, establish a related diagnosis of an AUD or SUD. While indicative of a related diagnosis, the actual diagnosis of an AUD or SUD for a specific adolescent must be confirmed by an additional focused clinical assessment, including a detailed history of his or her use of the drugs and substances of abuse by the primary clinician responsible for planning and delivering his or her treatment, including any referrals to specific adolescent treatment programs. (See Chapter 9, *Preventing and Treating Child and Adolescent Use of the*

*Drugs and Substances of Abuse*, for an overview of selected approaches for children and adolescents who are diagnosed with these disorders.)

## IMPORTANCE OF SCREENING

Since the 1980s, the early identification of the harmful use of the drugs and substances of abuse has been recommended for adolescents (e.g., Babor, McRee, Kassebaum, et al., 2007; Hays & Spickard, 1987). However, screening adolescents for alcoholism and other harmful effects of the regular, long-term use of the drugs and substances of abuse is now just becoming widely recognized as a necessary part of routine clinical or office practice (e.g., Madras, Compton, Avula, et al., 2009; Winters & Kaminer, 2008). For example, prenatal screening for problem drinking among pregnant adolescents is now becoming routine (Burns, Gray, & Smith, 2010). In this regard, some professional groups, such as the U.S. Preventive Services Task Force (USPSTF),

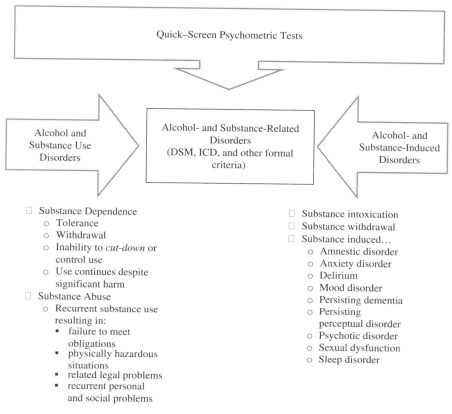

**Figure 7.1   Diagnosing Alcohol and Substance Use Disorders**

claiming that available data to support screening are lacking, have refrained from recommending the screening of adolescents for the use of alcohol and other drugs and substances of abuse (USPSTF, 2004), particularly as part of well-child care (i.e., in the absence of a related presenting complaint or positive past history) (Stagg Elliott, 2007).

We could not disagree more with this stance and, instead, wholeheartedly support the diametrically opposed recommendations of several professional organizations, including the American Academy of Child and Adolescent Psychiatry, American Academy of Pediatrics, American Medical Association (AMA), American Society of Addictions Medicine, Canadian Task Force on Preventive Health Care, and others that do recommend the routine screening of children and adolescents for drug and substance use disorders (e.g., Committee on Substance Abuse, 2010; Kulig, 2005; Schweer, 2009; Winters & Kaminer, 2008). Since 2006, the U.S. Centers for Medicare and Medicaid Services, under the Department of Health and Human Services, have devised and approved codes for health and social care providers to receive reimbursement for screening these disorders. In 2007, the AMA released an associated set of Current Procedural Terminology codes to further assist in this regard (Late, 2007).[1]

At the time of writing this text, we recommend that, minimally, seven groups of adolescents be screened for AUDs and SUDs

---

[1] Correspondingly in child and adolescent healthcare settings, there is an increasing call for the screening of parents for drug and substance use disorders (e.g., Wilson, Harris, Sherritt, et al., 2008.)

because of the associated high incidence of the use of the drugs and substances of abuse among these groups of adolescents and the significant potential and opportunity for preventing associated harm once problem use has been identified:

1. Adolescents who are being assessed, or who are already being treated, for any mental disorder, including any specific learning disorder (See Chapters 6, *Effects of the Drugs and Substances of Abuse on Learning and Memory During Childhood and Adolescence*, and 8, *Dual Diagnosis Among Adolescents*.)

2. Adolescents who are in the process of being committed, or have already been committed, to youth detention or correctional facilities

3. Adolescent girls who may become pregnant, or who are pregnant, because of the serious and lifelong teratogenic effects and related sequelae associated with the maternal use of alcohol and the fetal alcohol syndrome/fetal alcohol spectrum disorder (FAS/FASD; See Chapter 5, *Exposure to the Drugs and Substances of Abuse From Conception Through Childhood*).

4. Adolescents who are being assessed, or are being treated for, a sexually transmitted disease

5. Adolescents who are accessing emergency department services[2] for acute injuries associated with motor vehicle crashes, violent assaults, including rape, or acute mental disorders (e.g., psychosis)

6. Adolescents who are suicidal or who have attempted suicide

7. Adolescents who are homeless and living on the streets

However, many clinicians have argued that screening adolescents for the use of drugs and substances of abuse, particularly when performed as a part of an annual physical examination or as part of a routine office visit, is both time consuming and an inefficient use of valuable clinical resources. (See Table 7.2.) Other clinicians have argued that screening adolescents for their use of the drugs and substances of abuse can result in both missed diagnoses and misdiagnoses. (See the next section, "Type 1 and Type 2 Diagnostic Errors.") Thus, in order for screening to be more highly valued by clinicians, it is essential that it can be performed quickly and that it can produce an accurate diagnosis. In order to meet these needs, several quick-screen psychometric tests have been developed for use in clinical practice settings, both institutional and office settings. These tests are capable of being quickly administered (i.e., efficient) and providing high levels of accuracy in regard to detecting the use of the drugs and substances of abuse and their associated disorders (Bradley, 1992). These quick-screen psychometric tests are presented and discussed in this chapter, with particular attention to their application, associated statistical strength, efficacy, and practicality in regard to diagnosing AUDs and SUDs among adolescents. (See Figure 7.2.)

## TYPE 1 AND TYPE 2 DIAGNOSTIC ERRORS

The accurate diagnosis of SUDs is the cornerstone for designing and implementing appropriate treatment plans for achieving optimal therapeutic outcomes. In this regard, the best-designed treatment program in the world would have essentially no effect if an individual was diagnosed with a SUD that, in actuality, he or she did not have. Likewise, the best-designed

---

[2] Alcohol-related injuries (e.g., injuries related to falling down when drunk; injuries due to motor vehicle crashes associated with drinking and driving) have been estimated to result in over 20,000 emergency department visits in the United States *daily* (Emergency Nurses Association, 2004). In addition, the significance of the relationship between alcohol use and nonfatal injuries has been documented in several countries by the World Health Organization (Borges, Cherpitel, Orozco, et al., 2006).

**TABLE 7.2   Major Constraints Affecting Appropriate Use of Quick-Screen Psychometric Tests Among Adolescents**

**Personal and Professional Constraints**

Beliefs regarding professional role and responsibilities that do not include testing for harmful use of the drugs and
  substances of abuse, their treatment, or patient referral

Negative attitudes toward adolescents and/or adolescents who use the drugs and substances of abuse

Inadequate training/education or confidence in delivering optimal adolescent care in regard to the use of the drugs and
  substances of abuse

  Poor interpersonal skills (e.g., uncomfortable with test administration procedures)

  Poor social skills (e.g., uncomfortable discussing AUDs and SUDs with adolescents and their parents or legal guardians)

  Poor technical skills (e.g., unable to answer related questions from adolescent test-taker)

  Unable to effectively administer structured interviews

  Unfamiliarity with administering quick-screen psychometric tests

  Unable to discuss positive results with adolescent test-taker and parents or legal guardians

**Environmental Constraints**

Lack of time (i.e., already overbooked and overburdened)

Difficulties scheduling and conducting necessary follow-up appointments

Lack of space

Limited resources, including staff turnover of those who would administer quick-screen psychometric tests

Inflexible electronic medical records

Lack of ready access to standardized validated Quick-Screen Psychometric Tests

Modified from: Aspy, Mold, Thompson, et al., 2008; Crome, Bloor, & Thom, 2006; Habis, Tall, Smith, et al., 2007; Searight, 2009; Stagg Elliot, 2007.

treatment program in the world for an individual with an actual SUD would have essentially no effect if his or her SUD was not diagnosed. These two types of misdiagnosis are commonly conceptualized as Type 1 and Type 2 diagnostic errors (see Figure 7.3).[3] Type 1 diagnostic error represents the false positive diagnosis of an individual with a SUD when he or she does not, in fact, have a SUD. Type 2 diagnostic error represents the false negative diagnosis of an individual (i.e., failure to detect a SUD when, in fact, he or she does have a SUD).

Unfortunately, in clinical practice, psychiatrists, psychologists, and other health and social care professionals often are faced with Type 1 and Type 2 diagnostic errors. This situation occurs because the science guiding the understanding and treatment of SUDs (i.e., addiction-

ology) is not as precise a science as would be desired. It suffers from many limitations and also from the nature of human error—as hard as clinicians strive to minimize error, they are not always as successful as they strive to be. Fortunately, selection criteria can be determined and set to adjust the probability of the occurrence of either Type 1 or Type 2 diagnostic errors. In general, when using standardized psychometric tests to screen for possible SUDs among adolescents, test scores can be cut off at various levels in order to provide better statistical discrimination and fewer false positives, or Type 1 diagnostic errors.

For example, increasing the cut-off score, or criterion value, reduces the number of false positive results (i.e., reduces Type 1 diagnostic error). However, it also increases the number of false negative results (i.e., increases Type 2

---

[3] The statistics discussed in this chapter are population statistics. That is, they are meant to represent the true state of affairs in a population (e.g., all adolescents with SUDs). The population is sampled to test various related assumptions or premises. Depending on the precision of the sampling procedures (e.g., random or convenience sampling) and research design (e.g., experimental or quasi-experimental) used, the statistical results can be generalized to the population under study (e.g., all of the adolescents with SUDs). However, these statistics may not be always applicable to the individual adolescent whom a psychiatrist, psychologist, or other health or social care professional may be screening (e.g., he or she may be the exception to the rule because, in this statistical context, he or she is an outlier in the population. That is, he or she is one of the members of the population that resides at one extreme, or the other, of the normal distribution population curve—the normal, or bell-shaped, Gaussian curve). Therefore, when establishing a diagnosis of a SUD, health and social care providers must recognize the statistical limitations of these psychometric screening tests. With this in mind, the results should be interpreted with clinical caution and should be used in conjunction with other data sources (e.g., clinical interview).

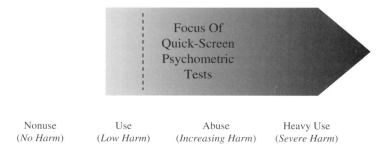

| Nonuse | Use | Abuse | Heavy Use |
| *(No Harm)* | *(Low Harm)* | *(Increasing Harm)* | *(Severe Harm)* |

**Figure 7.2    Focus of Quick-Screen Psychometric Tests**

diagnostic error). Correctly diagnosing a SUD (i.e., minimizing Type 1 and Type 2 diagnostic errors) involves careful clinical assessment with both subjective (e.g., data obtained from structured interviews, such as a medical or patient history or assessment instrument, and clinical observation) and objective data (e.g., laboratory[4] and psychometric test results) along with professional clinical judgment and analysis, including the determination of potential diagnoses (i.e., multiple working hypotheses) and, subsequently, ruling out these diagnoses until the final diagnosis is determined.

In an effort to prevent or decrease diagnostic errors and also to increase and expedite the delivery of needed clinical services, several psychometric tests have been developed.[5] The goal of these tests is to quickly and accurately screen adolescents for SUDs so that further assessment and diagnosis can be completed (i.e., in an effort to provide optimal therapy as soon as possible and to reduce the unnecessary expenditure of human and other resources). Several brief, or quickly administered, psychometric screening tests have been commonly used to assess adolescents (and adults) for possible SUDs, including alcoholism. Prior to discussing the specific quick-screen psychometric tests, basic test statistics—test specificity, sensitivity, validity, and reliability—are reviewed briefly.

---

[4] Laboratory tests (i.e., biological markers), such as those that are used to help to detect alcoholism (e.g., elevated bilirubin, gamma-glutamyl transpeptidase [GGT; GGTP; GTP], mean corpuscular volume [MVC], and carbohydrate-deficient transferrin [CDT]) generally have excellent reliability, but their validity is problematic (Bianchi, Ivaldi, Raspagni, et al., 2010; Golka & Wiese, 2004; Leigh & Skinner, 1988; Rosman & Lieber, 1990; Salaspuro, 1999). (See "Test Validity" "and "Test Reliability" sections for further discussion.) For example, the GGT may be elevated by alcoholic liver disease, anticonvulsant pharmacotherapy (e.g., phenytoin [Dilantin®]), congestive heart failure, nonalcoholic liver disease, or various carcinomas—potentially resulting in many false positive results for alcoholism.

Laboratory tests also can be used to detect the actual physical presence of drugs and substances of abuse, including their concentrations and active or inactive metabolites. However, the accuracy of these tests, including their validity and reliability as well as their sensitivity (see related discussion of these concepts later in the following section, "Basic Test Statistics"), depend on the method of analysis, such as the instruments used (e.g., immune-assay versus GC/MS) and the drug or substance of abuse being detected (e.g., cocaine, which has a mean half-life of elimination of 1.25 hours, can be detected for less than 12 hours following last use, versus tetrahydrocannabinol, which has a mean half-life of elimination of 3.5 days, can be detected for over 2 weeks following last use or exposure) (Pagliaro & Pagliaro, 2009).

[5] These psychometric screening tests also are generally referred to in the clinical literature as psychometric instruments, psychometric questionnaires, or psychometric tools. However, in this chapter we generally use the term "quick-screen psychometric tests." Although we may use the term that is used in the title of a particular screening test (e.g., Maternal Substance Use Screening Questionnaire or Michigan Alcoholism Screening Test) when discussing the test, we generally prefer "quick-screen psychometric test" because each test selected for discussion in this chapter was developed to expediently, and accurately, measure, or detect, patterns of behavior denoting problem use of the drugs and substances of abuse. In this regard, basic statistical procedures were used to help to ensure that each test, which often comprises a list of questions, expediently measures, by means of an objective score that was set a priori, the construct of concern every time it is administered to a member of the particular population for which it was designed. As such, these quick-screen psychometric tests strive to provide desired levels of statistical robustness in test specificity, sensitivity, validity, and reliability that help to ensure both accuracy and expediency in clinical diagnosis.

Adolescent's Actual Condition

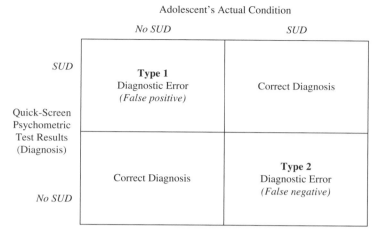

*No SUD*                    *SUD*

*SUD*

| | Type 1<br>Diagnostic Error<br>*(False positive)* | Correct Diagnosis |

Quick-Screen
Psychometric
Test Results
(Diagnosis)

| | Correct Diagnosis | Type 2<br>Diagnostic Error<br>*(False negative)* |

*No SUD*

**Figure 7.3    Type 1 and Type 2 Diagnostic Errors**

## BASIC TEST STATISTICS

For optimal selection and use of quick-screen psychometric tests, attention must be given to three basic test statistics: (1) specificity and sensitivity and negative and positive predictive values; (2) test validity; and (3) test reliability. These and other related test statistics are reviewed in this section. In this regard, attention also is given to both the person administering the test, the tester, and the adolescent who is completing the test, the test-taker, in regard to their roles in assuring accurate testing outcomes.

### Test Specificity and Sensitivity, and Positive and Negative Predictive Values

Two closely related test statistics are test specificity and test sensitivity. "Test specificity" is the term used to identify the probability that a subject who does not have a SUD is correctly identified by a quick-screen psychometric test as not having the SUD. For example, if the selected psychometric test detects only a total of 5 out of 10 people who actually do not have the disorder, how specific is the test, or what is its specificity? In this case, its specificity would be 50%. (See Table 7.3 for all related calculation formulae.) Conversely, "sensitivity"

is the probability that a subject who actually has a SUD is correctly detected by a selected quick-screen psychometric test. For example, if the selected psychometric test only detects a SUD in a total of 7 out of 10 people who actually have the disorder, how sensitive is it? In this case, its sensitivity would be 70%. While these test statistics are closely related, we generally recommend preferentially using the sensitivity test statistic when selecting quick-screen psychometric tests for clinical use so as to err on the inclusive side of detecting AUDs or SUDs.

Two other related test statistics are positive predictive value and negative predictive value. "Positive predictive value" is the probability that a subject who actually has a SUD will be detected by the selected quick-screen psychometric test as having the disorder. For example, if the psychometric test detected that all 10 subjects in a sample were positive for the SUD being screened for and only 2 subjects actually had the SUD, then the positive predictive value would be 20%. (See Table 7.3 for all related calculation formulae.) Similarly, negative predictive value is the probability that a subject who actually does not have a SUD will be detected by the selected quick-screen psychometric test as not having the disorder.

**TABLE 7.3**   Quick-Screen Psychometric Test Criterion Variables: Efficacy; Positive Predictive Value; Negative Predictive Value; Specificity, and Sensitivity

| Quick-Screen Psychometric Test Results | Actual Condition of Adolescent | | Quick-Screen Psychometric Test Totals |
|---|---|---|---|
| | *Positive* | *Negative* | |
| *Positive* | a[a] | b[b] | a + b |
| *Negative* | c[c] | d[d] | c + d |
| | | | |
| Totals | a + c | b + d | a + b + c + d |

| |  |
|---|---|
| where $efficacy = \dfrac{a+d}{a+b+c+d}$ = overall percentage of correctly *categorized* subjects | Equation 1 |
| where $positive\ predictive\ value = \dfrac{a}{a+b}$ = probability that a subject with a *positive* screening score has the SUD[e] | Equation 2 |
| where $negative\ predictive\ value = \dfrac{d}{c+d}$ = probability that a subject with a *negative* screening score does *not* have the SUD[f] | Equation 3 |
| where $specificity = \dfrac{d}{b+d}$ = probability that a subject who actually does *not* have the SUD is correctly detected as *not* having it | Equation 4 |
| where $sensitivity = \dfrac{a}{a+c}$ = probability that a subject who actually has the SUD is correctly detected as having it | Equation 5 |
| where the *false positive rate* $= \dfrac{b}{b+d}$ = 1 minus the specificity of the test[g] | Equation 6 |
| where the *false negative rate* $= \dfrac{c}{a+c}$ = 1 minus the sensitivity of the test[h] | Equation 7 |

[a] n for true positives.
[b] n for false positives.
[c] n for false negatives.
[d] n for true negatives.
[e] This value may be influenced by the characteristics of the sample population. Thus, if the attribute being screened for is common (e.g., screening is done in a clinical population), then a positive test will be more likely to detect drug or substance use (i.e., high positive predictive value). Conversely, a negative test will be less likely to detect the absence of drug or substance use (i.e., low negative predictive value).
[f] This value may be influenced by the characteristics of the sample population. Thus, if the attribute being screened for is rare (e.g., screening is done in the general population), then a negative test will be more likely to detect no drug or substance use (i.e., high negative predictive value). Conversely, a positive test will be less likely to detect drug or substance use (i.e., low positive predictive value).
[g] Also see Figure 7.3.
[h] Also see Figure 7.3.

## Test Validity

The "validity" of a psychometric screening test is simply a test statistic that indicates whether the test measures what it purports to measure.[6] For example, validity is an indicator that an IQ test actually measures IQ or that an alcoholism screening test detects alcoholism. In this context, validity is determined by both empirical evidence and theoretical support. Validity, as a construct, is extremely important to psychometric tests because it provides evidence that the test actually measures what it purports to measure. There are several types of related validity, including content, construct, convergent, divergent, concurrent, criterion-related,

---

[6] Most often, when tests do not measure what they purport to measure, it is because of poor design, particularly related to the inadvertent incorporation of bias. An excellent general review of this topic that goes beyond the purview of this chapter and text was prepared by Choi and Pak (2005) for the Centers of Disease Control and Prevention.

face, and predictive validity.[7] These types of validity are defined and briefly reviewed with particular attention to their use and value in regard to selecting quick-screen psychometric tests for detecting AUDs and SUDs.

## Content Validity

"Content validity" refers to how well the items that are included in a psychometric test measure the entire domain that the test purports to measure. As such, it is a measure of the comprehensiveness of a test. For example, if a test includes items that relate to only one type of adolescent alcoholism, then the other types of alcoholism would be missed. In this regard, it is important to ask: If the test purports to measure adolescent alcoholism, does it measure *all* aspects of this disorder, including, for example, binge drinking or early-onset versus late-onset alcoholism? Thus, a test with high content validity would include as many measures of constructs, or factors, of the domain as possible while excluding other constructs, or factors, that are not related to the domain of interest.

Content validity is commonly validated by agreement (i.e., kappa scores—see "The Tester" section) among experts in the domain of interest. Content validity often is conceptualized as being subsumed within the concept of construct validity, which is validated by the statistical procedure of confirmatory factor analysis. Content validity is generally considered to be a requisite first step in determining test validity. (Also see "Construct Validity.")

## Construct Validity

"Construct validity" refers to the extent to which a test actually measures what it intended to measure—a quick-screen psychometric test that purports to measure, or detect, harmful alcohol use, measures, or detects, harmful alcohol use. Two statistics generally are used to demonstrate construct validity: (1) convergent validity; and (2) divergent validity. Both of these statistics can be thought of in practical terms as measures of Type 1 and Type 2 error as applied to a specific construct. (See earlier discussion of "Type 1 and Type 2 Diagnostic Errors.")

## Convergent Validity

Convergent validity is essentially the same as concurrent validity. (See discussion that follows.)

## Divergent, or Discriminant, Validity

Divergent, or discriminant, validity is used primarily to help to establish construct validity. It is used to establish, for example, that a quick-screen psychometric test does not measure what it is not supposed to measure (i.e., divergent validity is the flip side of convergent validity). Thus, as a measure of divergent validity, we would expect that a quick-screen psychometric test for detecting an AUD would not have a high correlation with a test that detects being a devout Muslim (i.e., it would be incongruent to be both a devout Muslim and a heavy drinker of alcohol).

## Concurrent Validity

Concurrent validity is simply a measure of a test's similarity in results when compared to similar tests—generally with similar subjects, at

---

[7] The different types of validity are not mutually exclusive and are presented here to assist readers to identify the similarities and differences of the terms used for this statistic by various authors in the published related clinical and research literature. Indeed, they can be conceptualized as all representing a particular aspect of the larger construct of validity by providing statistical information about, for example, test content, response process, internal structure, relationship to other constructs or test items, and the consequences of testing (i.e., the application of test results) (American Educational Research Association, 1999; Campbell & Fiske, 1959; Cronbach & Meehl, 1955; Kendall & Jablensky, 2003; Messick, 1995).

the same point in time. It is commonly measured or validated by using Spearman's rank correlation coefficient (Spearman's *rho*).[8] Convergent validity measures how similar, or convergent, a test is to other theoretically similar tests. (Also see "Construct Validity.") For example, we would expect that one quick-screen psychometric test that detects AUDs would correlate well with a different quick-screen psychometric test that detects AUDs. For all practical purposes, concurrent validity is considered to be one and the same as convergent validity.

### Criterion-Related Validity

Criterion-related validity is a measure of the extent to which the results of a quick-screen psychometric test agree with an independent indicator (i.e., most often a benchmark or "gold standard") for detecting a particular AUD or SUD—for example, finding agreement between a quick-screen psychometric test and a clinical interview or other established criteria (e.g., *Diagnostic and Statistical Manual of Mental Disorders* [*DSM*] or *International Classification of Diseases* [*ICD*] criteria) when detecting harmful drinking. Criterion-related validity is most often measured statistically by the correlation between the test (i.e., predictor) and the criterion (e.g., DSM criterion-based diagnosis of cocaine-use disorder). This correlation generally is referred to as the criterion-related validity coefficient. Concurrent validity can be considered to be a type of criterion-related validity.

### Face Validity

Face validity is simply an indicator that the items on a quick-screen psychometric test appear appropriate. For example, if a screening test claims that it measures cannabis use, it should include items that reflect a wide range of typical cannabis use behaviors (e.g., How often do you use marijuana? Have you ever used

hashish or hashish oil?). Face validity and content validity generally are closely related but are not always statistically equivalent. In this case, content validity is considered to be the more important statistic. For example, the MacAndrew Alcoholism Scale, a successful psychometric test for diagnosing alcoholism among adults, does not appear to have good face validity. However, it does include many questions that have good content validity. Thus, face validity generally is considered to be a good starting point in the development of quick-screen psychometric tests. However, it should be kept in mind that, because face validity is readily apparent, even to the test-taker, it makes faking good or faking bad (malingering) easier to accomplish.

### Predictive Validity

Predictive validity is concerned with a test's ability to predict a future outcome (e.g., future harm associated with regular, long-term heavy drinking). Most quick-screen psychometric tests for detecting AUDs and SUDs are concerned with detecting *current* behavior. Thus, concurrent predictive validity would be the more useful statistic (i.e., in terms of clinical performance) for measuring a test's ability to detect current outcomes. Predictive validity can be considered to be a type of criterion-related validity.

## Test Reliability

In terms of quick-screen psychometric tests, reliability is simply an indicator that the test consistently provides the same results. Statistical synonyms for reliability in this context are consistency, repeatability, replicability, reproducibility, and stability. Reliability allows for both comparison and generalization with reliability estimates obtained from various researchers. However, it should be noted that some significant degree of variance can be

---

[8] Spearman's *rho* is a nonparametric statistic that is commonly used to determine the relationship between different rankings (as provided by different tests) on the same set of items (e.g., test-taker characteristics or responses to related questions). It is essentially the equivalent of the Pearson correlation coefficient (i.e., *r*), which is the statistic used for parametric data. Spearman rho values range from +1, perfect positive correlation, to 0, absolutely no correlation, to −1, perfect correlation in the exact opposite direction (Spearman, 1904). The Kendall rank correlation coefficient (Kendall's *tau* [τ]; Kendall, 1938) is a very closely related statistic that also is used in this context.

expected to occur in measures of reliability for a specific quick-screen psychometric test because reliability, unlike validity (see "Test Validity" section), is a property of the scores obtained from the test as opposed to the test itself and, consequently, is much more sample dependent.

The concept of test reliability is a necessary corequisite, together with test validity, for determining the quality, or usefulness, of all quick-screen psychometric tests for AUDs and SUDs. The two principal measures of reliability involve test-retest reliability and internal test consistency, or the reliability of the items that comprise a test. It also has been noted that the tester and the test-taker, as well as the drug or substance of abuse (e.g., tobacco or heroin),[9] can affect test reliability. These concepts are discussed next.

### Test-Retest Reliability

"Test-retest reliability" is concerned with the temporal stability of a particular test. That is, does the psychometric screening test, when read-ministered in the same manner, at a later date, to the same group of subjects, provide the same results as were originally obtained? Test-retest reliability is determined by: (1) administering a specific psychometric test to a group of subjects (TIME 1); (2) readministering the same test, in the same manner, and to the same group of sub-jects, at a later date (TIME 2); and (3) correlating the scores obtained from testing at both TIME 1 and TIME 2. This correlation (i.e., the Pearson correlation coefficient [r]) between the two sets of scores is commonly known as the reliability, or stability, coefficient. The higher the correlation between the scores obtained for TIME 1 and TIME 2, the higher the test-retest reliability.

However, the time interval between initial testing (TIME 1) and retesting (TIME 2) can be a critical factor in ensuring test reliability. For example, if the time interval is too short, cor-relations may be confounded by the subject's memory of his or her responses when initially tested (i.e., at TIME 1). If the interval is too long, correlations may be confounded by real changes in the characteristic being measured. For example, a subject when retested (TIME 2) may have since started to use the drug or sub-stance of abuse in question and, consequently, report a much higher current use of a drug or substance of abuse than what was reported at initial testing (TIME 1)—when he or she was not using the drug or substance of abuse. In addition, other factors, including maturational and situational factors (e.g., the test-taker being older, hungrier, or more tired at pretest) and testing factors (e.g., effect of previously having taken the test), can confound the interpretation of the test-retest results. Typically, for research purposes, a test-retest time interval of at least 1 week is used in related reliability studies.

### Item Reliability

The reliability of test items, or components, is based on an average of the correlations of all of the individual test items comprising a par-ticular quick-screen psychometric test. Internal consistency, reliability, or inter-item consistency is typically indicated by Cronbach's alpha coefficient[10] or the Kuder-Richardson coefficient (of equivalence—KR20). The calculation of KR20 is appropriate for use with dichotomously scored items (e.g., true or false; yes or no) while the Cronbach alpha is appropriate for use with nondichotomously scored items (e.g., multiple-choice items). Item reliability is a measure of the internal consistency or homogeneity of the test (i.e., a measure of if, and to what extent, all the items of a test measure the same latent variable). As the intercorrelations among the various test items increases, Cronbach's alpha will increase to a maximal statistic value of 1.0.

An important related corollary, based on classical test theory, is that adding additional

---

[9]The drug or substance of abuse can significantly affect the reliability of self-reported use. For example, among adolescents being tested in a youth detention center, reporting the current use of heroin may have a pejorative connotation among staff members whereas admitting to current tobacco use would not.

[10]The generally accepted criterion value for satisfactory item reliability is a Cronbach's alpha coefficient $\geq 0.70$ (Cronbach, 1951).

items of equal reliability to the test will increase the test's reliability. While the addition of these items will increase the overall item reliability of the test, it also may impose several practical clinical limitations. For example, adding additional items may increase testing time, which may result in increased subject fatigue or boredom and, consequently, increase the number of inaccurate or untruthful responses.

## THE TESTER AND THE TEST-TAKER

### The Tester

The value and usefulness of a psychometric test depend not only on its validity and reliability but also on the knowledge and experience, or ability, of the tester. The tester should be able to select the appropriate test for diagnosing the SUD of concern for a particular adolescent. In this regard, testers and interpreters must be aware of the:

1. Basic assumptions, concepts, and principles that govern the test and its use
2. Inherent strengths and limitations of the selected test
3. Testing conditions under which the test should be administered
4. Scoring procedures and interpretation of the test results
5. Inherent ethical considerations and limitations of professional practice as related to their professional licenses as testers or test interpreters
6. Appropriate use of test results

Interrater reliability (also referred to as interrater agreement, consensus, or concordance) is an important related construct. It is the correlation of test scores obtained when the same test is administered to the same subjects (or cohorts) at the same time (i.e., on the same day) by different raters, or testers (e.g., male testers of female subjects versus female testers). Low interrater reliability indicates that either one, or both, of the following are occurring: (1) the test is defective, or lacking in statistical robustness, and requires modification or replacement with a more robust test; or (2) the tester is inadequately trained in testing skills and requires training or retraining.

Interrater reliability also has been used to verify the reliability of self-administered test results when compared to the results obtained by structured interview. Either Pearson's correlation (for a rating scale that uses continuous data) or Spearman's *rho* (for a rating scale that uses ordinal data) can be used to measure the pairwise correlation among testers. A specific statistic developed to measure interrater reliability is kappa—Cohen's *kappa* to compare two raters and Fleiss's *kappa* for any number of raters (Shrout & Fleiss, 1979).

### The Test-Taker

The value and usefulness of a quick-screen psychometric test depend not only on its validity and reliability for detecting the potentially harmful use of drugs and substances of abuse by adolescents but also on the truthfulness of the adolescent, who is being tested (i.e., the test-taker).[11] Thus, when these psychometric tests are administered, testers who are involved directly or indirectly in administering the test and in interpreting its results must obtain answers to the next 17 questions. Careful consideration of these questions and their answers will help to ensure that truthful responses are obtained (i.e., increase the validity of self-report) and, consequently, increase the validity of the test results.

1. Does the adolescent have a sufficient IQ to properly understand and follow the test-taking procedures?
2. Does the adolescent comprehend the items or questions comprising the test?

---

[11] Deliberate conscious deviation from truthful responses in order to meet a personal agenda, such as to avoid incarceration or to continue unwarranted disability payments, is referred to as faking good and faking bad, respectively.

3. Is the adolescent aware of, and does he or she understand, the possible consequences of testing?

4. Is the adolescent sufficiently literate in English to understand and respond truthfully to the questions being asked? If so, then a pencil-and-paper or computerized questionnaire may provide superior results in terms of both compliance and honesty of response than a structured diagnostic interview by a healthcare provider (Knight, Harris, Sherritt, et al., 2007a).

5. Does the adolescent have an adequate reading level for self-administered tests?

6. Does the adolescent have adequate vision for reading instructions and responding to test items?

7. Does the adolescent have adequate hearing for completing tester-administered tests?

8. Was the adolescent referred for psychometric testing primarily because of a general parental concern, a driving while impaired charge, parole sentencing, a threat of expulsion from school, the possible loss of a job, or a child custody proceeding?

9. Is the adolescent aware that self-report data will be corroborated with a clinical interview and other assessment procedures (e.g., interviews with a parent, teacher, or parole officer?)

10. Does the adolescent display characteristics indicative of such mental disorders as conduct disorder/antisocial personality disorder, major depressive disorder, or psychotic disorder?

11. Does the adolescent demonstrate inadequate test-taking behavior (e.g., leaves numerous items blank; answers true to all items)?

12. Is the adolescent currently receiving any pharmacotherapy (e.g., a psychotropic drug for the management of attention-deficit/hyperactivity disorder [A-D/HD], mental depression, insomnia or other sleep disorder, pain disorder, psychotic disorder [e.g., schizophrenia], or seizure disorder) that may affect his or her test performance? (For additional related information, see Pagliaro & Pagliaro, 1999, 2000, 2009.)

13. Is the adolescent currently using a drug or substance of abuse that may affect his or her test performance? (See Chapter 6, *Effects of Drugs and Substances of Abuse on Learning and Memory During Childhood and Adolescence*.)

14. Is the adolescent currently intoxicated or high?

15. Is the adolescent currently in pain or in any other physical or emotional distress?

16. Does the adolescent have any current medical disorder (Type 1 diabetes mellitus) or condition (e.g., recent head injury) that may affect his or her test performance?

17. Is the adolescent accompanied by a parent or other legal guardian?[12]

In addition, building rapport with the test-taker and providing appropriate assurance of confidentiality (i.e., being truthful regarding who will have or who will not have access to self-report information) will help to increase the validity of self-reports regarding sensitive information, including the use of the drugs and substances of abuse (Harrell, 1997; Wish, Hoffman, & Nemes, 1997). In this regard, it has been long recognized (e.g., Williams, Toomey, McGovern, et al., 1995) that adolescents, including young adolescents, should be expected to provide, and can provide, honest responses to sensitive questions about the use of alcohol and other drugs and substances of abuse. Attention to both the

---

[12] Nontruthful reporting on sensitive items, such as the use of drugs and substances of abuse, is most frequently a motivated process deliberately engaged in by the test-taker to: (1) avoid embarrassment in the presence of the interviewer or others; (2) keep personal or family information private; and (3) avoid negative repercussions from a third party (e.g., legal system, parent, teacher or school principal) (McAllister & Makkai, 1991; Tourangeau & Yan, 2007).

previous recommendations and the questions just presented will help to ensure optimal performance of these adolescent test-takers.

## SELECTED QUICK-SCREEN PSYCHOMETRIC TESTS

Several quick-screen psychometric tests are commonly used in an attempt to quickly and accurately detect possible AUDs and other SUDs among adolescents.[13] These tests include

- Alcohol Use Disorders Identification Test (AUDIT)
- Brief Mast (B-MAST)
- CAGE
- Cannabis Abuse Screening Test (CAST)
- Cannabis Use Disorders Identification Test (CUDIT)
- CRAFFT
- Drug Abuse Screening Test (DAST)
- Drug Use Disorders Identification Test (DUDIT)
- Fagerström Test for Nicotine Dependence (FTND)
- Michigan Alcoholism Screening Test (MAST)
- Problem Oriented Screening Instrument for Teenagers (POSIT)
- Rapid Alcohol Problems Screen, Version 4 (RAPS4)
- Rutgers Alcohol Problem Index (RAPI)
- Short Michigan Alcoholism Screening Test (SMAST)
- T-ACE
- TWEAK

This chapter presents an overview of these screening tests with attention to their development and scoring. (Also see Table 7.4.) In order to facilitate their selection and use, attention also is given to their basic test statistics—their sensitivity, specificity, validity, and reliability.

Other related quick-screen psychometric tests have been developed and have been clinically used (e.g., Alcohol Beliefs Scale, Spouse Sobriety Influence Inventory, Teen-Addiction Severity Index [T-ASI]). However, these tests focus more on the identification of factors that may be of assistance in the treatment of individuals who have already been diagnosed with alcoholism—their focus is on the severity of an already confirmed diagnosis. Therefore, these quick-screen psychometric tests are not addressed in this chapter. Similarly, certain quick-screen psychometric tests (e.g., Substance Abuse Questionnaire [SAQ]) that are specifically developed for and primarily limited to diagnosing SUDs among adults are not addressed in this chapter. In addition, quick-screen psychometric tests (e.g., the Substances and Choices Scale [SACS] [Christie, Marsh, Sheridan, et al., 2007]; Revised Mālmo modification of the Michigan Alcoholism Screening Test [Mm-MAST] [Osterling, Berglund, Nilsson, et al., 1993]) that have been used only, or primarily, by the test developer (e.g., the RAFFT [Bastiaens, Francis, & Lewis, 2000; Bastiaens, Riccardi, & Sakhrani, 2002]) or that have been found to be severely limited or weak in regard to statistical testing, are not included in this chapter. Finally, psychometric screening tests that are long and/or difficult to administer or score are likewise not discussed in this chapter. For example, the Adolescent Drinking Index (ADI) recommends a minimum of a bachelor's degree in psychology to score the test results, which must be converted to T-scores and plotted on a profile sheet prior to interpretation.

Although we do not recommend its use (for reasons that we will make explicit in our

---

[13] This chapter focuses on the selection and use of the various quick-screen psychometric tests available for use with adolescents. To date, no comparable statistically appropriate tests have been made available for detecting AUDs and SUDs among children. Thus, clinicians must depend on other assessment methods (e.g., clinical observation and interview) to assist with this formidable task.

**TABLE 7.4    Selected Quick-Screen Psychometric Tests for Detecting the Use of Drugs and Substances of Abuse Among Adolescents**

| Full Test Name | Acronym or Abbreviation | Administration | Number of Items | Average Completion Time (minutes) |
|---|---|---|---|---|
| Alcohol, Smoking and Substance Involvement Screening Test | ASSIST | Structured interview | 71 | 30 |
| Alcohol Use Disorders Identification Test | AUDIT | Self-administered *or* structured interview | 10 | 3 |
| Alcohol Use Disorders Identification Test-Consumption | AUDIT-C | Self-administered *or* structured interview | 3 | 1 |
| Brief Michigan Alcoholism Screening Test | Brief MAST | Self-administered *or* structured interview | 10 | 3 |
| CAGE | CAGE | Self-administered *or* structured interview | 4 | 1 |
| Cannabis Abuse Screening Test | CAST | Self-administered | 6 | 2 |
| Cannabis Use Disorders Identification Test | CUDIT | Self-administered | 10 | 3 |
| CRAFFT | CRAFFT | Self-administered *or* structured interview | 6 | 2 |
| Drug Abuse Screening Test | DAST | Self-administered *or* structured interview | 20 | 5 |
| Drug Abuse Screening Test-Adolescent | DAST-A | Self-administered | 20 | 5 |
| Drug Abuse Screening Test (Short Form) | DAST-10 | Self-administered | 10 | 3 |
| Drug Abuse Screening Test (Revised) | DAST-20 | Self-administered *or* structured interview | 20 | 5 |
| Drug Use Disorders Identification Test | DUDIT | Self-administered | 11 | 3 |
| Fagerström Test for Nicotine Dependence | FTND | Self-administered | 6 | 2 |
| Michigan Alcoholism Screening Test | MAST | Self-administered *or* structured interview | 24 | 5 |
| Michigan Alcoholism Screening Test-Adolescent | MAST-A | Self-administered *or* structured interview | 24 | 5 |
| Michigan Alcoholism Screening Test-Revised | MAST-R | Self-administered | 22 | 5 |
| Problem Oriented Screening Instrument for Teenagers | POSIT | Self-administered | 17 (for substance use/abuse scale) | 5 |
| Rapid Alcohol Problems Screen (Version 4) | RAPS4 | Structured interview | 4 | 2 |
| Rutgers Alcohol Problem Index | RAPI | Self-administered *or* structured interview | 23 | 5 |
| Short Michigan Alcoholism Screening Test (SMAST) | Short MAST | Self-administered | 13 | 3 |
| T-ACE | T-ACE | Self-administered *or* structured interview | 4 | 2 |
| TWEAK | TWEAK | Self-administered *or* structured interview | 5 | 2 |

discussion), we start with the ASSIST for three reasons: (1) it was developed by the World Health Organization (WHO), (2) it is recommended by the National Institute on Drug Abuse (NIDA), and (3) it has been widely used around the world.

## Alcohol, Smoking, and Substance Involvement Screening Test (ASSIST)

The ASSIST was developed for the WHO by an international group of drug and substance use researchers from Australia, Brazil, India,

Thailand, United Kingdom, United States, and Zimbabwe. The test was designed to screen for problem or risky use in 10 domains:

1. Tobacco
2. Alcohol
3. Cannabis
4. Cocaine
5. Amphetamine-like stimulants
6. Sedatives
7. Hallucinogens
8. Inhalants
9. Opioids (i.e., opiate analgesics)
10. Other drugs

Each domain is grouped under one specific multifaceted question. Under the direction of the WHO, the ASSIST was translated into several different languages, including Arabic, Chinese, Farsi, French, German, Hindi, Portuguese, and Spanish (WHO ASSIST, 2002). It includes a brief intervention that has generally been found to be of benefit when used to screen for AUDs and other SUDs in Australia, Brazil, and India. However, when used in the United States, it has not been found to be of benefit (Humeniuk, Dennington, & Ali, 2008).

### Scoring

The ASSIST, in all of its versions, is one of the most complex psychometric screening tests available in regard to both its administration and its scoring. For each of the 10 drug or substance of abuse involvement domains being measured—(1) tobacco; (2) alcohol; (3) cannabis; (4) cocaine; (5) amphetamine; (6) inhalants; (7) sedatives; (8) hallucinogens; (9) opioids; (10) other drugs—7 questions are administered followed by question 8, an additional single-item question concerning injectable drug use. The questions are asked in sequential order (i.e., 1–8) using a structured interview format that encourages interviewers to probe and query responses. Respondents are provided with specific response cards (i.e., Response Card for the drug and substance domains—*substances*;

Response Card for frequency of drug or substance use, *ASSIST Questions 2 to 5*; and Response Card, *ASSIST Questions 6 to 8*) to refer to when making responses. An affirmative response to the single-item prescreen question asked for each drug or substance of abuse domain (i.e., a. "tobacco products" to j. "Other—specify") determines if the tester should proceed with the complete set of questions for that domain (i.e., excluding medical use, "In your life, which of the following substances have you ever used?"). The subsequent domains are assessed or skipped depending on the response to the prescreen question for each of the seven multifaceted questions (e.g., "In the past three months, how often have you used the substances you mentioned [for each of the 10 drug and substance of abuse domains]?").

There are several versions of the ASSIST (e.g., V1.0 through V3.0), including the modified ASSIST (NM ASSIST) that was developed by the NIDA (2010). The NM ASSIST separates prescription stimulant use from methamphetamine use and slightly changes the wording of several of the original ASSIST items, or questions. Although comprehensive in its determination of substance involvement (i.e., low, moderate, or high risk for health and other problems) and type of intervention needed (i.e., no intervention, receive brief intervention, more intensive treatment), the administration of the NM ASSIST by structured interview is time consuming, as is the calculation of scores. Thus, we generally do not recommend the ASSIST or the NM ASSIST as quick-screen psychometric tests. Consequently, we have not included copies of these tests in this chapter.

### Available Test Statistics

**Specificity and Sensitivity**   Reported values for specificity and sensitivity are generally high. For example, Newcombe, Humeniuk, and Ali (2005) reported a specificity of 78% and a sensitivity of 90% for the ASSIST. However, reported values have ranged widely from 50% to 96% depending on several factors. These factors include: (1) the particular drug or substance of abuse being screened; (2) the level of use being screened (e.g., use versus dependence); and (3) the selected discrimination value, or cut-off score, that is used when interpreting the final, summed score (Humeniuk & Ali, 2006).

**Validity and Reliability** The ASSIST has been reported to have satisfactory validity and reliability in Australia, where it is principally used (Hides, Cotton, Berger, et al., 2009; Humeniuk, Ali, Babor, et al., 2008; Newcombe, Humeniuk, & Ali, 2005). For example, criterion-related validity, obtained from correlation with other measures of harmful substance use (e.g., the Addiction Severity Index [ASI]), were moderate (i.e., $r = 0.84$) indicating acceptable validity. Internal test consistency, or item reliability, as indicated by measures of test-retest kappa coefficients, or K-values, ranged from 0.58 to 0.90 for question stems and from 0.61 (sedatives) to 0.78 (opioids) (Ali, Awwad, Babor, et al., 2002; Henry-Edwards, Humeniuk, Ali, et al., 2003). Values for Cronbach's alpha have been reported as 0.85 to 0.95 (WHO ASSIST, 2002). Although the reported values are in an acceptable range, their variance, particularly because they have been derived from Version 2 of the ASSIST, is cause for significant caution.

## Alcohol Use Disorders Identification Test (AUDIT)

The AUDIT is a 10-item quick-screen psychometric test (see Table 7.5) that was specifically designed for international use. It was developed from a six-country WHO collaborative project to detect excessive drinking, or alcohol use disorders (i.e., alcohol abuse or dependence), in primary healthcare settings (Saunders, Aasland, Babor, et al., 1993). The 10-item core questionnaire for adolescents and adults, which requires 7th-grade reading level for completion (Hays, Merz, & Nicholas, 1995), appears to be particularly useful for the early detection of hazardous or harmful

drinking (i.e., risky drinking). It measures the domains of alcohol consumption, alcohol dependence-related drinking behavior, and harmful alcohol use (Babor, Higgins-Biddle, Saunders, et al., 2001; Saunders, Aasland, Babor, et al., 1993). In this regard, it is important to note that the various screening tests used to detect AUDs do not all measure the same construct of alcohol use. See Table 7.6 for related definitions and descriptions of these constructs.

The AUDIT was originally normed using a large representative sample of subjects who accessed services at several primary healthcare facilities. It has since been widely used with diverse populations (e.g., alcohol and other drug and substance users, inpatients, university students) in a wide variety of settings and has continuously been demonstrated to be a valuable and reliable psychometric screening test for detecting AUDs (Fleming, Barry, & MacDonald, 1991; McCusker, Basquille, Khwaja, et al., 2002; Reinert & Allen, 2007; Skipsey, Burleson, & Kranzler, 1997). For example, the AUDIT was found to perform significantly better than either the CAGE or the TWEAK for detecting AUDs for underage drinkers, 12 to 20 years of age, being treated in emergency departments (Kelly, Donovan, Kinnane, et al., 2002). (Also see the AUDIT-C.)

### Scoring

Responses to each item of the AUDIT are scored from 0 to 4, except for items 9 and 10, which are scored 0, 2, or 4. (See Table 7.5 for scoring criteria.) Summing all of the scores provides a possible maximal score of 40. A total score of 2 or more indicates some level of harmful alcohol use. A total score of 8 or higher generally indicates an AUD (i.e., alcohol abuse or dependence) (Conigrave, Saunders, & Reznik, 1995; Mackenzie, Langa, & Brown, 1996; Saunders, Aasland, Babor, et al., 1993). Total scores of 12 or higher provide increased discrimination, or specificity, for predicting

**TABLE 7.5    Alcohol Use Disorders Identification Test (AUDIT)**

| Item/Question | Scoring Criteria [point allocation] |
| --- | --- |
| 1. How often did you have a drink containing alcohol in the past year? | Never, [0]; Monthly or less, [1]; Two to four times a month, [2]; Two to three times a week, [3]; Four or more times a week, [4] |
| 2. How many drinks containing alcohol did you have on a typical day when you were drinking in the past year? | 1 or 2 drinks, [0]; 3 or 4 drinks, [1]; 5 or 6 drinks, [2]; 7 to 9 drinks, [3]; 10 or more drinks, [4] |
| 3. How often did you have 6 or more drinks on one occasion in the past year? | Never, [0]; Monthly or less, [1]; Two to four times a month, [2]; Two to three times a week, [3]; Four or more times a week, [4] |
| 4. How often during the last year have you found that you were not able to stop drinking once you had started? | Never, [0]; Monthly or less, [1]; Two to four times a month, [2]; Two to three times a week, [3]; Four or more times a week, [4] |
| 5. How often during the last year have you failed to do what was normally expected from you because of drinking? | Never, [0]; Monthly or less, [1]; Two to four times a month, [2]; Two to three times a week, [3]; Four or more times a week, [4] |
| 6. How often during the last year have you needed a first drink in the morning to get yourself going after a heavy drinking session? | Never, [0]; Monthly or less, [1]; Two to four times a month, [2]; Two to three times a week, [3]; Four or more times a week, [4] |
| 7. How often during the last year have you had a feeling of guilt or remorse after drinking? | Never, [0]; Monthly or less, [1]; Two to four times a month, [2]; Two to three times a week, [3]; Four or more times a week, [4] |
| 8. How often during the last year have you been injured as a result of your drinking? | Never, [0]; Monthly or less, [1]; Two to four times a month, [2]; Two to three times a week, [3]; Four or more times a week, [4] |
| 9. Have you or someone else been injured as a result of your drinking? | No/Never, [0]; Yes, but not in the last year, [2]; Yes during the last year, [4] |
| 10. Has a relative or friend or doctor or other healthcare worker been concerned about your drinking or suggested you cut down? | No/Never, [0]; Yes, but not in the last year, [2]; Yes, during the last year, [4] |

Modified from: Saunders, Aasland, Babor, et al., 1993.

alcohol-related social problems. However, this increased discrimination is at the cost of reduced test sensitivity (Conigrave, Hall, & Saunders, 1995). Approximately 97% of respondents with a score of 12 or higher have a significant AUD. Of all respondents with a significant AUD, approximately 72% have lower AUDIT scores. (See previous discussion of Types 1 and 2 diagnostic errors.) A lower cut-off score (i.e., 4 or 5) has been suggested by several authors (e.g., Reinert & Allen, 2007) for adolescents and women.

### *Available Test Statistics and Recommendations*

**Specificity and Sensitivity**    Specificity and sensitivity for the AUDIT range from 66% to 100% and approximately 38% to 96%, respectively, for identifying at-risk, hazardous, or harmful drinking behavior (Allen, Litten,

Fertig, et al., 1997; Fiellin, Reid, & O'Connor, 2000; Hill & Chang, 2007; McQuade, Levy, Yanek, et al., 2000). Much of this variability is related to the type of alcohol behavior being screened for (Bradley, Bush, McDonell, et al., 1998). As noted in the discussion of the AUDIT, the various screening tests used to detect AUDs do not all measure the same construct of alcohol use. (See Table 7.6 for related definitions and descriptions of these constructs.) For example, when Saunders and Aasland (1987) first formally tested the AUDIT, they found that harmful drinking had a specificity of 81% and a sensitivity of 87%, while hazardous drinking had a specificity of 98% and a sensitivity of 96%. Similarly, Kriston, Hölzel, Weiser, et al. (2008) found that the mean AUDIT specificity results varied from 0.79 (for AUDs) to 0.88 (for risky/hazardous drinking), and the mean AUDIT

**TABLE 7.6    Clinical Diagnoses and Diagnostic Criteria for Alcohol Use as Defined and Measured by Selected Quick-Screen Psychometric Tests**

| Criterion Behavior: *Type of Drinking and Definition* | Clinical Diagnosis | Diagnostic Criteria |
|---|---|---|
| | Alcohol Use Disorder (AUD) | *Meets criteria for:*<br>• alcohol dependence,<br>• alcohol abuse, or<br>• harmful drinking. |
| | Dependence (Alcoholism) | *At least 3 of the following:*<br>• Tolerance or the need to use increasing amounts of alcohol to achieve desired effects<br>• Alcohol withdrawal with abrupt discontinuation of regular use<br>• Drinking to relieve alcohol withdrawal symptoms<br>• Impaired control (e.g., drinking more or longer than intended or planned)<br>• Preoccupation with obtaining and/or using alcohol<br>• Increased time spent drinking or recovering from drinking episodes<br>• Persistent desire to use alcohol or unsuccessful effort to discontinue or quit alcohol use<br>• Sustains social, occupational, or recreational disability<br>• Alcohol use continues despite adverse consequences associated with its use |
| | Abuse | *At least 1 of the following:*<br>• Fails to fulfill occupational or social obligations (at home, school, or work) due to drinking<br>• Use occurs in physically hazardous situations (e.g., drinking and driving a car or operating other hazardous machinery) or leads to recurrent legal problems<br>• Use continues despite persistent social or interpersonal problems |
| | Harmful drinking | • Clear evidence that alcohol is causing physical or psychological harm<br>• Nature of the harm is clearly identifiable<br>• Alcohol use has persisted at least 1 month or has occurred repeatedly over the past 12-month period<br>• Subject does not meet criteria for alcohol dependence |
| *Men:*<br>• *21 or more* drinks per week[a] *or*<br>• *7 or more* drinks per occasion at least 3 times per week<br>*Women:*<br>• *14 or more* drinks per week[b] *or*<br>• *5 or more* drinks per occasion at least 3 times per week | Hazardous drinking | • Quantity or pattern of use that places patients at risk for adverse consequences |
| *Men:*<br>• *14 or more* drinks per week *or*<br>• *5 or more* drinks per occasion<br>*Women:*<br>• *7 or more* drinks per week *or*<br>• *4 or more* drinks per occasion | Heavy drinking (also referred to as *heavy episodic drinking*) | • Quantity or pattern of use that exceeds a defined threshold<br>• Does not meet criteria for harmful drinking |

*(Continued)*

**TABLE 7.6    Clinical Diagnoses and Diagnostic Criteria for Alcohol Use as Defined and Measured by Selected Quick-Screen Psychometric Tests (Continued)**

| Criterion Behavior: *Type of Drinking and Definition* | Clinical Diagnosis | Diagnostic Criteria |
| --- | --- | --- |
| *Men/Women*: | Risky drinking | • Subject meets the criteria for *either* hazardous or heavy drinking |

[a] Some authors (e.g., Gordon, Maisto, McNeil, et al., 2001) define hazardous drinking for men at a lower rate of consumption (i.e., 16 or more drinks per week).

[b] Some authors (e.g., Gordon, Maisto, McNeil, et al., 2001) define hazardous drinking for women at a lower rate of consumption (i.e., 12 or more drinks per week).

Modified from: American Psychiatric Association, 2000; Bradley, DeBenedetti, Volk, et al., 2007; Carrington Reid, Fiellin, O'Connor, et al., 1999; Hasin, 2003; Kriston, Hölzel, Weiser, et al., 2008; Seale, Boltri, Shellenberger, et al., 2006.

Note: Several terms and definitions of patterns of alcohol use are purported to be measured by the various quick-screen psychometric tests. Developed prior to the publication of the *DSM-IV* and *DSM-5*, these tests do not directly correspond to the drinking behaviors characterized by those diagnostic manuals. Thus, this table presents definitions used in the specific screening tests and their diagnostic criteria. Similarities and differences can be noted.

sensitivity results varied from 0.84 (for AUDs) to 0.81 (for risky/hazardous drinking) among patients in primary care settings.

A German sample of general medical practice patients, using a cut-off score of 5, identified the specificities and sensitivities for selected diagnoses in this way: for a diagnosis of alcohol dependence, specificity 0.88 and sensitivity 0.97; for a diagnosis of AUD, specificity of 0.92 and sensitivity of 0.97; and for a diagnosis of either AUD or at-risk consumption, specificity of 0.91 and sensitivity of 0.97 (Dybek, Bischof, Grothues, et al., 2006).

As expected, the selected cut-off score also significantly affects the observed specificity and sensitivity of the AUDIT (i.e., as the cut-off score of 6 is raised to a cut-off score of 12, the specificity increases but the sensitivity decreases). For example, using a criterion value, or cut-off score, of 8 resulted in a specificity of 94% and a sensitivity of 92% (Saunders, Aasland, Babor, et al., 1993). A cut-off score of 10, for a clinical sample of participants with first-episode psychosis, resulted in a specificity of 91% and a sensitivity of 85% (Cassidy, Schmitz, & Malla, 2008). Although variable, the generally high specificity and sensitivity statistics make the AUDIT a clinically acceptable quick-screen psychometric test for detecting alcohol abuse, AUDs, or hazardous drinking behavior among

adolescents (Cook, Chung, Kelly, et al., 2005; Gómez, Conde, Santana, et al., 2005; Kelly, Donovan, Chung, et al., 2004; Knight, Sherritt, Harris, et al., 2003).

**Validity and Reliability**    The AUDIT has good construct validity. Criterion-related validity is demonstrated by the moderate to high correlations obtained between the AUDIT and, for example, the CAGE, which was 0.78 (Hays, Merz, & Nicholas, 1995) and the MAST, which was 0.88 (Bohn, Babor, & Kranzler, 1995). Concurrent criterion-related validity also has been demonstrated by excellent agreement between scores on the AUDIT and *DSM*-validated diagnoses of AUDs (Fleming, Barry, & MacDonald, 1991; Isaacson, Butler, Zacharek, et al., 1994).

Good test-retest reliability (i.e., 0.88) has been reported for the AUDIT (Daeppen, Yersin, Landry, et al., 2000). The AUDIT also has very good internal consistency (reliability) with Cronbach's alpha coefficients reported in the 0.80 to 0.94 range (Allen, Litten, Fertig, et al., 1997; Barry & Fleming, 1993; Bohn, Babor, & Kranzler, 1995; Kelly, Donovan, Kinnane, et al., 2002; Selin, 2003; Shields & Caruso, 2003). However, the average inter-item correlation among the 10 items comprising the AUDIT was found to be relatively low (i.e., 0.42) (Kelly, Donovan, Kinnane, et al., 2002).

**Other Available Statistics and General Recommendations**   The test appears to be quite robust. For example, comparisons of paper-and-pencil versus computerized administration of the AUDIT reported no significant differences (Chan-Pensley, 1999). In addition, the AUDIT appears to be more sensitive than the B-MAST, CAGE, Mm-MAST, and RAPS (Bradley, Bush, McDonell, et al., 1998; Cherpitel, 1997a, b; Cook, Chung, Kelly, et al., 2005; Mackenzie, Langa, & Brown, 1996; Seppa, Makela, & Sillanaukee, 1995). It also does not appear to be significantly affected by age, gender, or ethnic biases[14] (Adewuya, 2005; Aertgeerts, Buntinx, Ansoms, et al., 2001; Cherpitel, 1997a, b; Clay, 1997; Cook, Chung, Kelly, et al., 2005; Giang, Spak, Dzung, et al., 2005; Medina-Mora, Carreño, & De la Fuente, 1998; Nevitt, Lundak, Codr, et al., 2007; Steinbauer, Cantor, Holzer, et al., 1998). For example, when compared to the CAGE, POSIT, or TWEAK, the AUDIT was found to be an equally or more valid test for detecting excessive drinking or AUDs among adolescents (Chung, Colby, Barnett, et al., 2000; Knight, Sherritt, Harris, et al., 2003). However, some caution is advised when the test is administered to adolescents who are deaf. Some testees, who are deaf, have found the words and phrases in certain test questions difficult to understand because they are not commonly used by people in the deaf culture (Alexander, DiNitto, & Tidblom, 2005).

Shortened versions of the AUDIT (e.g., AUDIT-C, AUDIT-PC, AUDIT-3) generally appear to have lower sensitivity than the full AUDIT (Gómez, Conde, Santana, et al., 2005; McCambridge & Thomas, 2009). In addition, several researchers (e.g., Rist, Glockner-Rist, & Demmel, 2009), have suggested that the shorter versions of the AUDIT do not measure all of the factors associated with AUDs and, therefore, assume that the assessment of alcohol use is equivalent to the assessment of alcohol-induced adverse consequences. We do not generally recommend the use of the shortened versions of the AUDIT, other than the AUDIT-C (see following discussion) because of their: (1) reported lower sensitivity; (2) incomplete measurement of all factors; (3) significantly less available published data on validity and reliability; and (4) minimal savings of testing time for both testers and test-takers when compared to the original AUDIT.

### Alcohol Use Disorders Identification Test-Consumption (AUDIT-C)

The AUDIT-C is a 3-question quick-screen psychometric test that was developed by Bush, Kivlahan, McDonell, et al. (1998) to detect alcohol abuse or heavy drinking.[15] As a shortened version of the standard 10-question AUDIT, it contains only the first 3 questions, which deal explicitly and exclusively with alcohol consumption. (See Table 7.7; also see the AUDIT.)

### *Scoring*

Each response is given a score of 1 to 4 for a possible maximal score of 12. (See Table 7.7 for scoring criteria.) A total score of 4 or higher is considered to be indicative of alcohol abuse or heavy drinking. The AUDIT-C was originally tested and normed using a sample of men who were general medical patients in several Veterans Affairs Medical Centers (Bush, Kivlahan, McDonell, et al., 1998). Subsequently, several studies (e.g., Bradley, DeBenedetti, Volk, et al., 2007; Caviness, Hatgis, Anderson, et al., 2009)

---

[14]Transcultural validity has been established for population samples from Brazil (Lima, Friere, Silva, et al., 2005), Chile (Santis, Garmendia, Acuna, et al., 2009), Finland (Aalto, Alho, Halme, et al., 2009), France (Gache, Michaud, Landry, et al., 2005), India (Carey, Carey, & Chandra, 2003), Italy (Piccinelli, Tessari, Bortolomasi, et al., 1997), Mexico (Medina-Mora, Carreño, & De la Fuente, 1998), Nigeria (Adewuya, 2005), Taiwan (Wu, Huang, Liu, et al., 2008), and Vietnam (Giang, Spak, Dzung, et al., 2005).

[15]"Heavy drinking" was defined as 14 or more drinks per week or 5 or more drinks per drinking occasion. Also see Table 7.6.

**TABLE 7.7   Alcohol Use Disorders Identification Test—Consumption (AUDIT-C)**

| Item/Question | Scoring Criteria [point allocation] |
|---|---|
| 1. How often do you have a drink containing alcohol? | Never, [0]; Monthly or less, [1]; Two to four times a month, [2]; Two to three times a week, [3]; Four or more times a week, [4] |
| 2. How many drinks containing alcohol do you have on a typical day when you are drinking? | 1 or 2, [0]; 3 or 4, [1]; 5 or 6, [2]; 7 to 9, [3]; 10 or more, [4] |
| 3. How often do you have six or more drinks on one occasion? | Never, [0]; Less than monthly, [1]; Monthly, [2]; Weekly, [3]; Daily or almost daily, [4] |

Modified from: Bush, Kivlahan, McDonell, et al., 1998.

confirmed this cut-off score of 4 or higher for men and recommended an optional cut-off score of 3 or higher for women. The scoring of the AUDIT-C is a little more involved than that for other quick-screen psychometric tests. Consequently, the AUDIT-C has been criticized, particularly by clinicians practicing in emergency departments and other busy clinical settings (Kelly, Donovan, Chung, et al., 2009).

### *Available Test Statistics and Recommendations*

Published data have been found regarding the specificity and sensitivity of the AUDIT-C. Gender effects also have been observed and are discussed along with published data regarding the AUDIT-C's validity and reliability.

**Specificity and Sensitivity**   The AUDIT-C was found to have a specificity of 72% and a sensitivity of 86% using a sample of men[16] and a criterion value, or cut-off score, of 4. Bradley, DeBenedetti, Volk, et al. (2007) obtained similar results (i.e., specificity 89% and sensitivity 86%) with the same cut-off score using a similar sample. Bradley, Bush, McDonell, et al. (1998) also reported similar results (i.e., sensitivity of 87%). Using collapsed data from four extant studies involving over 2,500 patients in primary care settings, both men and women, Kriston, Hölzel, Weiser, et al. (2008) determined that the mean specificity of the AUDIT-C varied from 0.68,

when used to detect risky/hazardous drinking, to 0.78, when used to detect AUD. Similarly, they determined that the mean sensitivity of the AUDIT-C varied from 0.97, when used to detect risky/hazardous drinking, to 0.82, when used to detect AUD.

Since its development and initial use, overall, the AUDIT-C appears to have performed slightly better for women than for men in regard to detecting alcohol dependence (Dawson, Grant, Stinson, et al., 2005a, b). Using a sample of women, Bradley, DeBenedetti, Volk, et al. (2007) found a specificity of 91% and a sensitivity of 73% using a cut-off score of 3. Again, with a cut-off score of 3, a specificity of 71% and a high sensitivity of 98% were obtained using a sample of pregnant women (Burns, Gray, & Smith, 2010). Also using a cut-off score of 3, Caviness, Hatgis, Anderson, et al. (2009) reported excellent test statistics for a large sample of women who were incarcerated (i.e., efficacy 91.5%; specificity, 91.5%; sensitivity, 91.6%; positive predictive value, 93%; and negative predictive value, 90%). In addition, the AUDIT-C appears to display greater, although variable, sensitivity in regard to use with North American women of different ethnic backgrounds. For example, in their large cross-sectional validation study using a sample of North American women from their academic family practice clinic, Frank, DeBenedetti, Volk, et al. (2008) reported a significantly higher sensitivity for women of Hispanic descent (i.e., 85%) than for women

---

[16] A cut-off score of 3 was first proposed for men and then changed to 4.

of European descent (70%) or African descent (i.e. 67%).[17]

As with other quick-screen psychometric tests, increasing the criterion value (i.e., cut-off score) results in increased specificity but reduced sensitivity (Aalto, Alho, Halme, et al., 2009; Bradley, Bush, McDonell, et al., 1998; Bush, Kivlahan, McDonell, et al., 1998; Dawson, Grant, & Stinson, 2005a, b). In general, the AUDIT-C performs well for respondents from various continental descents and ethnicities (Frank, DeBenedetti, Volk, et al., 2008). However, sensitivity can vary within this high and acceptable range. For example, Gómez, Conde, Santana, et al. (2005), using a cut-off score of 3 with a large random sample of primary care patients in Spain, reported a specificity of 79.4% and a sensitivity of 100%. Similarly, Tuunanen, Aalto, and Seppä, (2007), using a cut-off score of 6 with a sample of men in Finland, including a significant percentage of binge drinkers, reported a sensitivity of 82.9%. Obviously, as noted by Tuunanen, Aalto, and Seppä (2007), cut-off scores for the AUDIT-C may require adjustment when individuals of different continental descents or ethnicities are screened.

**Validity and Reliability**    The questions of the AUDIT-C have good face validity. In addition, the results of the AUDIT-C correlate well with the results of the full AUDIT (Bush, Kivlahan, McDonell, et al., 1998; Reinert & Allen, 2007). When using a standard cut-off score of 4, the AUDIT-C did not appear to be significantly affected by the method of administration (i.e., electronic delivery by computer, oral interview, self-administered paper-and-pencil test) (Graham, Goss, Xu, et al., 2007). Note that the AUDIT-C was originally tested by sending a hard copy (a paper-and-pencil copy) of the test to sample respondents by mail (Bush,

Kivlahan, McDonell, et al., 1998). Test-retest reliability, after a period of 3 months, ranged from 0.65 to 0.85 (Bradley, McDonell, Bush, et al., 1998).

### Brief MAST (B-MAST)

The B-MAST is a 10-item quick-screen psychometric test derived from the Michigan Alcoholism Screening Test (MAST) by Pokorny, Miller, and Kaplan (1972) to detect alcoholism/alcohol dependence. (Also see the MAST and the Short-MAST.)

### Scoring

Each item, or question, in the B-MAST is assigned a weight of 0 to 5. (See Table 7.8 for scoring criteria.) Items 1 and 2 are scored in reverse. A total score of 6 or higher provides presumptive evidence of alcoholism.

### Available Test Statistics and Recommendations

Limited published data are available for specificity and sensitivity or for validity and reliability.

**Specificity and Sensitivity**    The B-MAST has been found to be significantly less sensitive than the AUDIT, CAGE, or RAPS (Cherpitel, 1997a, b, 1998; Mackenzie, Langa, & Brown, 1996). The sensitivity of the B-MAST in detecting moderate alcohol problems in the general population is low (approximately 30%), presumably because the items deal primarily with severe alcohol problems (Chan, Pristach, & Welte, 1994; Lockhart, Carter, Straffen, et al., 1986). Overall, reported specificity ranges from 80% to 99% and sensitivity ranges from 30% to 78% (Cherpitel, 1997a, b).

**Validity**    The B-MAST has good face validity. In addition, concurrent validity has

---

[17] They also found variable sensitivity among North American men of different ethnic or racial backgrounds, with a sensitivity of 95% for men of European descent, 85% for men of Hispanic descent, and 76% for men of African descent.

TABLE 7.8    Brief MAST (B-MAST)

| Item/Question | Scoring Criteria [point allocation] |
| --- | --- |
| 1. Do you feel you are a normal drinker? | No, [2]; Yes, [0] |
| 2. Do friends or relatives think you are a normal drinker? | No, [2]; Yes, [0] |
| 3. Have you ever attended a meeting of Alcoholics Anonymous (AA)? | No, [0]; Yes, [5] |
| 4. Have you ever lost friends or girlfriends/boyfriends because of your drinking? | No, [0]; Yes, [2] |
| 5. Have you ever gotten into trouble at work because of drinking? | No, [0]; Yes, [2] |
| 6. Have you ever neglected your obligations, your family, or your work for two or more days in a row because you were drinking? | No, [0]; Yes, [2] |
| 7. Have you had delirium tremens (DTs), severe shaking, heard voices, or seen things that weren't there after heavy drinking? | No, [0]; Yes, [2] |
| 8. Have you ever gone to anyone for help about your drinking? | No, [0]; Yes, [5] |
| 9. Have you ever been in a hospital because of your drinking? | No, [0]; Yes, [5] |
| 10. Have you ever been arrested for drunk driving after drinking? | No, [0]; Yes, [2] |

Modified from: Pokorny, Miller, & Kaplan, 1972.

been demonstrated in relation to both the use of the AUDIT and clinical assessment (Connor, Grier, Feeney, et al., 2007).

**Recommendations**    Given the limited availability of published statistics, we generally do not recommend the use of the B-MAST, particularly for adolescents.

## CAGE

The CAGE is a 4-question quick-screen psychometric test (see Table 7.9) that was developed by Ewing in 1968 as part of a clinical study to detect alcoholism (Ewing, 1984). A noted criticism of the CAGE is that it fails to detect heavy drinkers who may lack insight or be in denial (Waterson & Murray-Lyon, 1988). Another concern is its focus on alcoholism and the expectation that, for this reason, it will miss a significant number of people who have harmful or hazardous patterns of alcohol use. Specifically in regard to this latter concern, the AUDIT has demonstrated clinical superiority to the CAGE (McCusker, Basquille, Khwaja, et al., 2002). In addition, the CAGE, overall, performs significantly better for men than for women in regard to detecting alcoholism (Dhalla & Kopec, 2007). A version of the CAGE (i.e., the CAGE-AA) had its item

questions specifically adapted for use with adolescents. However, its psychometric properties, specifically its internal consistency or inter-item reliability, were found to be lacking (Knight, Goodman, Pulerwitz, et al., 2000).

### Scoring

Each affirmative answer is given a score of 1. (See Table 7.9 for scoring criteria.) A total score of 2 or higher is indicative of alcoholism (Buchsbaum, Buchanan, Centor, et al., 1991; Kitchens, 1994; NIAAA, 1995). However, several researchers (e.g., Aertgeerts, Buntinx, & Kester, 2004) have found the CAGE to be of limited screening value at this cut-off score. O'Brien (2008) recommends that a score of 2 or 3 is highly indicative of alcoholism and that a score of 4 is diagnostic of alcoholism.

### Available Test Statistics and Discussion

**Specificity, Sensitivity, and Positive and Negative Predictive Value**    The CAGE generally has demonstrated both a high specificity (77% to 96%) and high sensitivity (61% to 100%) for screening alcoholism (i.e., alcohol abuse and dependence) with a general population of adults (Chan, Pristach, & Welte, 1994; Cherpitel, 1997a, b; do Amaral & Malbergier, 2008; Fiellin, Reid, & O'Connor, 2000;

**TABLE 7.9   CAGE: An Alcoholism Screening Test**

| Item/Question {alternate phrasing} | Scoring Criteria [point allocation] |
| --- | --- |
| 1. Have you ever felt you ought to **CUT** down on your drinking?<br>{Have you ever felt the need to cut down your drinking?} | No, [0]; Yes, [1] |
| 2. Have people **ANNOYED** you by criticizing your drinking?<br>{Have you ever felt annoyed by criticism of your drinking?} | No, [0]; Yes, [1] |
| 3. Have you ever felt bad or **GUILTY** about your drinking?<br>{Have you ever had guilty feelings about drinking?} | No, [0]; Yes, [1] |
| 4. Have you ever had a drink first thing in the morning to steady your<br>nerves or to get rid of a hangover (i.e., as an **EYE-OPENER**)?<br>{Have you ever taken a morning *eye-opener*?} | No, [0]; Yes, [1] |

Modified from: Ewing, 1984; Mayfield, McLeod, & Hall, 1974.

Liskow, Campbell, Nickel, et al., 1995; Maly, 1993; McQuade, Levy, Yanek, et al., 2000). Similar values were reported (i.e., sensitivity, 68%, and specificity, 93%) for a sample of men of American Indian descent (Saremi, Hanson, Williams, et al., 2001). However, the CAGE was found to be relatively insensitive when used with a population of pregnant North American women of European descent (Bradley, Boyd-Wickizer, Powell, et al., 1998). It also was demonstrated to have low sensitivity for North American women of Hispanic descent (Steinbauer, Cantor, Holzer, et al., 1998) and of American Indian descent (i.e., 62%; Saremi, Hanson, Williams, et al., 2001). With adolescent populations, the sensitivity of the CAGE was only 37% (Knight, Sherritt, Harris, et al., 2003). This percentage is much lower than that reported for the AUDIT and the Mm-MAST, both of which also appear to have superior clinical application for this age group (Cook, Chung, Kelly, et al., 2005; Kelly, Donovan, Chung, et al., 2004; Nyström, Peräsalo, & Saläspuro, 1993). However, Knight, Sherritt, Harris, et al. (2003) used a criterion value, or cut-off score, of 1 rather than the recommended cut-off score of 2. Still, several researchers (e.g., Aertgeerts, Buntinx, Bande-Knops, et al., 2000; Chung, Colby, Barnett, et al., 2000; Kelly, Donovan, Kinnane, et al., 2002; O'Hare & Tran, 1997) have reported poor performance of the CAGE with younger subjects. In this context, Dawe, Loxton, Hides, et al. (2002) suggested that quick-screen psychometric tests that focus more on

psychological symptomatology, such as the AUDIT or TWEAK, may be better suited for adolescents and young adults than other tests, such as the CAGE and MAST, which focus more on long-term alcohol related problems.

Aertgeerts, Buntinx, Ansoms, et al. (2001), also using a cut-off score of 1 with a large sample of adults attending general medical practices in Belgium, found a specificity of 81% and a sensitivity of 62% for men. In addition, in this clinical context, the CAGE had a very high negative predictive value (i.e., 93%) but a low positive predictive value (i.e., 34%). However, sensitivity (i.e., 54%) and positive predictive value (i.e., 24%) were significantly lower for women. Similarly, Aertgeerts, Buntinx, Bande-Knops, et al. (2000), using a cut-off score of 1 with a large sample of college freshmen in Belgium, obtained a specificity of 87%, a sensitivity of 42%, a negative predictive value of 90%, and a positive predictive value of 36%. As with other quick-screen psychometric tests, modifying the criterion variable set for the CAGE in order to increase its specificity also decreases its sensitivity (Ewing, 1984)—regardless of what type of alcohol use behavior (e.g., heavy drinking, dependence) is being screened for (Bradley, Bush, McDonell, et al., 1998), as can be seen in Table 7.10.

**Validity and Reliability**   The CAGE has excellent face, or content, validity. However, its strong face validity makes faking quite easy.

TABLE 7.10    Specificity and Sensitivity of the CAGE

| Number of Positive *Yes* Responses per Subject, or Selected Criterion Level | Approximate *Specificity* for the General Population | Approximate *Sensitivity* for the General Population |
|---|---|---|
| 1 | 80% | 98% |
| 2 | 90% | 81% |
| 3 | 99% | 66% |
| 4 | 100% | 37% |

Modified from: Knight, Sherritt, Harris, et al., 2003.

In terms of performance, the CAGE has been found to be comparable to the SMAST (Maisto, Connors, & Allen, 1995). Correlation with the SMAST is 0.70 (Hays, Merz, & Nicholas, 1995) and 0.48 to 0.62 with the AUDIT (Hays, Merz, & Nicholas, 1995; Hodgson, John, Abbasi, et al., 2003). Criterion-related validity as demonstrated by the correlation, or agreement, of the CAGE with *DSM* criteria is high (Liskow, Campbell, Nickel, et al., 1995).

**Discussion**    The CAGE is more quickly administered than the AUDIT or SMAST (i.e., 1 minute versus 3 minutes), and it has an acceptable measure of test-retest reliability of 0.80 to 0.95 (Dhalla & Kopec, 2007; Teitelbaum & Mullen, 2000). However, the internal consistency (reliability) of the CAGE is lower, and its standard error of measurement is larger (Hays, Merz, & Nicholas, 1995). The CAGE has a reported median internal consistency of 0.74 (range of 0.52 to 0.90), and its score reliability appears to vary with the median age of the sample being tested (Shields & Caruso, 2004).

Among adolescents seeking emergency department services, the internal consistency of the CAGE (i.e., Cronbach's alpha) was determined to be 0.66 (Kelly, Donovan, Kinnane, et al., 2002). Although an α of 0.70 or higher is generally desired, an α of 0.66 is an acceptable indicator of internal consistency, particularly for a 4-item test. As with the AUDIT, caution is indicated when the CAGE is used for adolescents who are hearing impaired or deaf, because some of the wording or phrases used in the items have been found to be generally unfamiliar to members of the deaf community (Alexander, DiNitto, & Tidblom, 2005). No significant

differences were found when comparing results for the CAGE when administered by written paper-and-pencil format or by structured interview (Aertgeerts, Buntinx, Fevery, et al., 2000).

### Cannabis Abuse Screening Test (CAST)

The CAST is a 6-item quick-screen psychometric test (see Table 7.11) that was developed by Legleye, Karila, Beck, et al. (2007) to detect cannabis abuse, particularly among adolescents and young adults.

### Scoring

Responses to each item of the CAST are scored 0 or 1 (see Table 7.11 for scoring criteria). The scores are then summed for a possible maximal score of 6. A discriminating, or cut-off, score of 4 is generally considered to be indicative of cannabis abuse (Legleye, Karila, Beck, et al., 2007).

### Available Test Statistics and Recommendations

**Specificity and Sensitivity**    In a general population sample, the specificity and sensitivity for the CAST was reported to be 81.4% and 92.9%, respectively, when using a criterion value, or cut-off score, of 4. In addition, the positive predictive value was 45.8%, and the negative predictive value was 96.5% (Legleye, Karila, Beck, et al., 2007; Piontek, Kraus, & Klempova, 2008).

**Validity and Reliability**    The CAST has good face validity. However, in terms of construct validity, the factor loadings of the CAST

**TABLE 7.11** **Cannabis Abuse Screening Test (CAST)**

| Item/Question | Scoring Criteria [point allocation] |
|---|---|
| 1. Have you ever smoked cannabis before midday? | Never, [0]; rarely, [0]; from time to time, [0]; fairly often, [1]; very often, [1] |
| 2. Have you ever smoked cannabis when you were alone? | Never, [0]; rarely, [0]; from time to time, [0]; fairly often, [1]; very often, [1] |
| 3. Have you ever had memory problems when you smoked cannabis? | Never, [0]; rarely, [0]; from time to time, [0]; fairly often, [1]; very often, [1] |
| 4. Have friends or members of your family ever told you that you ought to reduce your cannabis use? | Never, [0]; rarely, [0]; from time to time, [0]; fairly often, [1]; very often, [1] |
| 5. Have you ever tried to reduce or stop your cannabis use without succeeding? | Never, [0]; rarely, [0]; from time to time, [0]; fairly often, [1]; very often, [1] |
| 6. Have you ever had problems because of your use of cannabis (argument, fight, accident, bad result at school, etc.)? | Never, [0]; rarely, [0]; from time to time, [0]; fairly often, [1]; very often, [1] |

Modified from: Legleye, Karila, Beck, et al., 2007.

items are moderate. In addition, as a measure of convergent validity, it correlates well with the related dimensions of the POSIT when using a cut-off score of 4 (Legleye, Karila, Beck, et al., 2007).

The reliability of the CAST, in terms of internal consistency, is relatively high with a Cronbach's alpha coefficient of 0.81 when used with a general population sample. However, reliability is lower (i.e., 0.74) when used with cannabis users (Legleye, Karila, Beck, et al., 2007).

**Recommendations** Although the overall statistics for the CAST are acceptable, the low positive predictive value (i.e., less than 50%) either indicates that the cut-off score needs to be lowered or that the test items need to be modified (e.g., by the addition of valid and reliable items). We generally do not recommend the use of the CAST because of its low positive predictive value.

**Cannabis Use Disorder Identification Test (CUDIT)**

The CUDIT is a 10-item quick-screen psychometric test (see Table 7.12) based on the AUDIT. Developed by Adamson and Sellman (2003) to detect the cannabis use disorder, its development and testing was predicated on diagnostic criteria obtained from the *DSM-IV*.

*Scoring*

Responses to each item of the CUDIT are given a score of 0 to 4 (see Table 7.12 for scoring criteria). The maximal score possible is 40. A discriminating cut-off score of 8 is generally considered to be equivalent to the *DSM-IV* referenced diagnosis for cannabis dependence (Adamson & Sellman, 2003).[18]

*Available Test Statistics and Recommendations*

**Specificity, Sensitivity, and Positive and Negative Predictive Values** These values were found when using a discrimination, or cut-off, score of 8: specificity, 94.7%; sensitivity, 73.3%, positive predictive value, 84.6%, and negative predictive value, 90.0% (Adamson & Sellman, 2003).

**Validity and Reliability** In terms of construct validity, factor loadings of items were moderate for all items except item 9, injured. A very weak factor loading was obtained for

---

[18] The *DSM-5* does not use the term cannabis dependence.

**TABLE 7.12    Cannabis Use Disorders Identification Test (CUDIT)**

| Item/Question | Scoring Criteria [point allocation] |
|---|---|
| **Over the past 6 months . . .** | |
| 1. How often did you use cannabis? | Never, [0]; monthly or less, [1]; 2 to 4 times a month, [2]; 2 to 3 times a week, [3]; 4 or more times a week, [4] |
| 2. How many hours were you stoned on a typical day when you had been using cannabis? | 1 or 2, [0]; 3 or 4, [1]; 5 or 6, [2]; 7 to 9, [3]; 10 or more, [4] |
| 3. How often were you stoned for 6 or more hours? | Never, [0]; less than monthly, [1]; monthly, [2]; weekly, [3]; daily or almost daily, [4] |
| 4. How often did you find that you were not able to stop using cannabis once you had started? | Never, [0]; less than monthly, [1]; monthly, [2]; weekly, [3]; daily or almost daily, [4] |
| 5. How often did you fail to do what was normally expected from you because of using cannabis? | Never, [0]; less than monthly, [1]; monthly, [2]; weekly, [3]; daily or almost daily, [4] |
| 6. How often did you need to use cannabis in the morning to get yourself going after a heavy session of using cannabis? | Never, [0]; less than monthly, [1]; monthly, [2]; weekly, [3]; daily or almost daily, [4] |
| 7. How often did you have a feeling of guilt or remorse after using cannabis? | Never, [0]; less than monthly, [1]; monthly, [2]; weekly, [3]; daily or almost daily, [4] |
| 8. How often have you had a problem with your memory or concentration after using cannabis? | Never, [0]; less than monthly, [1]; monthly, [2]; weekly, [3]; daily or almost daily, [4] |
| 9. Have you or someone else been injured as a result of your use of cannabis? | No, [0]; Yes, [4] |
| 10. Has a relative, friend, or doctor or other health worker been concerned about your use of cannabis or suggested you cut down? | No, [0]; Yes, [4] |

Modified from: Adamson & Sellman, 2003.

this item, indicating that it probably should not have been included in this quick-screen psychometric test. The reliability of the CUDIT is low to moderate, as indicated by the reported ranges for item total correlation for general and alcohol-dependent population samples. For the general population sample, the reported range was 0.07 to 0.55 (Annaheim, Rehm, & Gmel, 2008). For the alcohol-dependent sample, the reported range was 0.44 to 0.77 (Adamson & Sellman, 2003). Overall, internal consistency for the CUDIT is moderate, as indicated by reported Cronbach's alpha coefficients in the 0.70s range (Adamson & Sellman, 2003; Annaheim, Rehm, & Gmel, 2008). Two items (item 2, *hours stoned*, and item 9, *injured*) have been reported to have lower correlation (i.e., below 0.4) with the total CUDIT score (Annaheim, Rehm, & Gmel, 2008). Thus, the validity and reliability of the CUDIT would be expected to increase if these two items were appropriately modified or deleted.

**Recommendations** Given the noted problems with test items, particularly item 9 (injury), and the relative paucity of psychometric data, we recommend that, until additional valid and reliable supportive data are made available, the CUDIT be used, but that its results be interpreted with due caution.

## CRAFFT

The CRAFFT is a 6-item quick-screen psychometric test (see Table 7.13) that was developed by Knight, Shrier, Bravender, et al. (1999) specifically for adolescent medical patients 14 to 18 years of age. This psychometric test screens for alcohol use, abuse, and dependence. It also can be used to detect these patterns of use for other drugs and substances of abuse. Interestingly, the CRAFFT is the only quick-screen psychometric test that includes a question on drinking (or the use of other drugs and substances of abuse) and driving.

**TABLE 7.13    CRAFFT: An Alcohol and Drug Screening Test**

| | Items/Questions | Scoring Criteria [point allocation] |
|---|---|---|
| C | Have you ever ridden in a **C**ar driven by someone (including yourself) who was *high* or had been using alcohol or drugs? | No, [0]; Yes, [1] |
| R | Do you ever use alcohol or drugs to **R**elax, feel better about yourself, or fit in? | No, [0]; Yes, [1] |
| A | Do you ever use alcohol or drugs while you are by yourself (**A**lone)? | No, [0]; Yes, [1] |
| F | Do you ever **F**orget things you did while using alcohol or drugs? | No, [0]; Yes, [1] |
| F | Do your **F**amily or friends ever tell you that you should cut down on your drinking or drug use? | No, [0]; Yes, [1] |
| T | Have you ever gotten into **T**rouble while you were using alcohol or drugs? | No, [0]; Yes, [1] |

Modified from: Knight, Shrier, Bravender, et al., 1999.

## Scoring

Each affirmative response is given a score of 1 (see Table 7.13 for scoring criteria). A total score of 2 or higher is indicative of problematic patterns of alcohol or other drug and substance use needing treatment, including problem use, abuse, and dependence (Knight, Shrier, Bravender, et al., 1999; Knight, Sherritt, Shrier, et al., 2002).

## Available Test Statistics

**Specificity, Sensitivity, and Positive and Negative Predictive Values**    The optimal psychometrics obtained at the established criterion discrimination, or cut-off score, of 2 are: specificity, 82% to 94%; sensitivity, 76% to 92%; positive predictive value, 67% to 83%; and negative predictive value, 91% to 97% (Knight, Sherritt, Shrier, et al., 2002; Knight, Shrier, Bravender, et al., 1999). Lowering the cut-off score to 1 increased the sensitivity to 100% but decreased the specificity to 58% (Knight, Shrier, Bravender, et al., 1999). In addition, when the CRAFFT was used with adolescents of American Indian descent, these statistics were obtained: a specificity of 76%; a sensitivity of 86%; a positive predictive value of 29% (i.e., unacceptably low); and a negative predictive value of 98% (i.e., excellent) (Cummins, Chan, Burns, et al., 2003).

**Validity and Reliability**    The validity of the CRAFFT does not appear to be significantly affected by the age, gender, continental descent, or ethnicity of respondents. The score obtained from the CRAFFT correlates highly with related diagnostic classifications (i.e., Spearman *rho* = 0.72).

The reliability of the CRAFFT is acceptable. The standardized item α is 0.68 (Knight, Shrier, Bravender, et al., 1999). Although an α of 0.70 or higher is generally desired (see previous discussion in "Item Reliability" section), an α of 0.68 is an acceptable indicator of internal consistency, particularly for a relatively short, 6-item test (Knight, Sherritt, Shrier, et al., 2002). Use of the CRAFFT with a sample of adolescents of American Indian descent yielded an α of 0.81 (Cummins, Chan, Burns, et al., 2003). Test-retest reliability yielded *kappa* values in the range of 0.71 to 0.84 (Levy, Sherritt, Harris, et al., 2004). Test-retest reliability for the CRAFFT is high (i.e., approximately 0.91) (Levy, Sherritt, Harris, et al., 2004).

## Drug Abuse Screening Test (DAST) (Revised)

The DAST (Revised) is a 20-item quick-screen psychometric test (see Table 7.14) that was developed by Skinner (1982) to detect problem use of the drugs and substances of abuse, excluding alcohol. The DAST (Revised)

TABLE 7.14    Drug Abuse Screening Test (DAST) (Revised)

| Item/Question | Scoring Criteria [point allocation] |
|---|---|
| **Over the last 12 months:** | |
| 1. Have you used drugs other than those required for medical reasons? | No, [0]; Yes, [1] |
| 2. Have you abused prescription drugs? | No, [0]; Yes, [1] |
| 3. Do you abuse more than one drug at a time? | No, [0]; Yes, [1] |
| 4. Can you get through the week without using drugs (other than those required for medical reasons)? | No, [1]; Yes, [0] |
| 5. Are you always able to stop using drugs when you want to? | No, [1]; Yes, [0] |
| 6. Have you had blackouts or flashbacks as a result of drug use? | No, [0]; Yes, [1] |
| 7. Do you ever feel bad or guilty about your drug use? | No, [0]; Yes, [1] |
| 8. Does your spouse (or parents) ever complain about your involvement with drugs? [The DAST-A replaces "spouse" with "boyfriend/girlfriend."] | No, [0]; Yes, [1] |
| 9. Has drug abuse ever created problems between you and your spouse or your parents? [The DAST-A replaces "spouse" with "boyfriend/girlfriend."] | No, [0]; Yes, [1] |
| 10. Have you ever lost friends because of your use of drugs? | No, [0]; Yes, [1] |
| 11. Have you ever neglected your family because of your use of drugs? | No, [0]; Yes, [1] |
| 12. Have you ever been in trouble at work (or school, or missed school assignments) because of drug abuse? | No, [0]; Yes, [1] |
| 13. Have you ever lost a job because of drug abuse? [The DAST-A replaces "ever" with "ever been kicked out of school or"] | No, [0]; Yes, [1] |
| 14. Have you gotten into fights when under the influence of drugs? | No, [0]; Yes, [1] |
| 15. Have you engaged in illegal activities in order to obtain drugs? | No, [0]; Yes, [1] |
| 16. Have you ever been arrested for possession of illegal drugs? | No, [0]; Yes, [1] |
| 17. Have you ever experienced withdrawal symptoms (felt sick) when you stopped taking drugs? | No, [0]; Yes, [1] |
| 18. Have you had medical problems as a result of your drug use (e.g., memory loss, hepatitis, convulsions, bleeding, etc.)? | No, [0]; Yes, [1] |
| 19. Have you ever gone to anyone for help for a drug problem? | No, [0]; Yes, [1] |
| 20. Have you ever been involved in a treatment program specifically related to drug use? | No, [0]; Yes, [1] |

Modified from: Skinner, 1982.

was adapted from the original 28-item version of the DAST, which actually was adapted from the MAST. A significant noted difference between the DAST and the MAST is that the DAST items refer to patterns of drug and substance use during the past 12 months while the MAST items refer to patterns of drug and substance use over a lifetime. Similar to the MAST, the DAST appears to perform better for men than for women in regard to detecting problem use of the drugs and substances of abuse. As a self-administered quick-screen psychometric test, the DAST minimally requires a 6th-grade reading level. The revised, shortened 20-item version of the DAST (i.e., 20-item DAST [revised]) has excellent correlation (i.e., $r = 0.99$) with the original 28-item version and also has a more complete set of available test

statistics, thus, it is included in this review. Other versions of the DAST also have been developed and used, including the Drug Abuse Screening Test for Adolescents (DAST-A) and the Drug Use Questionnaire (DAST-10). These and other versions of the DAST are available in several different languages, including English and Finnish.

The DAST-A was developed to detect the use of drugs and substances of abuse among adolescents who were psychiatric inpatients (Martino, Grilo, & Fehon, 2000). Other than some relatively minor wording changes, such as replacing "work" with "school" (see Table 7.14), the DAST-A is exactly the same as the 20-item DAST (revised). The DAST-10 was developed as a 10-item brief version of the original 28-item DAST, and its use has been recommended by the National Institute on Drug Abuse (2010).

### Scoring

Each yes-or-no response on the DAST is assigned 0 or 1 point. (See Table 7.14 for scoring criteria.) The scores are summed for a possible maximal score of 20. A total score of 6 or higher indicates a likely drug or substance use problem (i.e., that *DSM* criteria have been met). The DAST-A is scored exactly like the DAST.

### Available Test Statistics

**Specificity and Sensitivity** The DAST has a high specificity of approximately 81% to 91% (Staley & El-Guebaly, 1990). Reportedly, its sensitivity ranges from 82% to 96% (McCann, Simpson, Ries, et al., 2000; Staley & El-Guebaly, 1990). For a clinical sample of participants with first-episode psychosis, Cassidy, Schmitz, and Malla (2008) obtained a specificity of 73% and a sensitivity of 85% using a criterion value, or cut-off score, of 3.

**Validity and Reliability** The DAST has very good concurrent and discriminant validity and is able to achieve 85% overall accuracy, or efficacy (see Table 7.3), in classifying subjects who are tested according to *DSM* criteria (Gavin, Ross, & Skinner, 1989; Yudko, Lozhkina, & Fouts, 2007). Reportedly, the DAST has high internal consistency, or reliability (i.e., 0.92; El-Bassel, Schilling, Schinke, et al., 1997; McCann, Simpson, Ries, et al., 2000; Staley & El-Guebaly, 1990) and test-retest reliability (i.e., 0.85) (Yudko, Lozhkina, & Fouts, 2007). Skinner (1982) reported a Cronbach's alpha coefficient of 0.92 for the DAST and 0.95 for the 20-item DAST (revised). In fact, all available versions of the DAST have been found to have satisfactory measures of validity and reliability (Yudko, Lozhkina, & Fouts, 2007).

### Drug Use Disorders Identification Test (DUDIT)

The DUDIT is an 11-item self-administered, quick-screen psychometric test (see Table 7.15) developed by Swedish researchers (Berman, Bergman, Palmstierna, et al., 2005). It is used to detect dependence on virtually all of the commonly available drugs and substances of abuse, *excluding* alcohol. The DUDIT is somewhat unique in that a printed list of over 100 generic and brand/trade names, divided into pharmacological categories, is included on the reverse side of the single-page questionnaire to facilitate its self-administration. The DUDIT was originally normed using a large random sample obtained from the Swedish general population. It has since been translated and is available in several different languages, including Danish, Dutch, English, German, Norwegian, Portuguese, and Swedish.[19]

### Scoring

The scoring of the DUDIT is generally more involved than that for most of the other quick-screen psychometric tests. In this regard, it is similar to the AUDIT in terms of both response set and scoring. For items 1 through 9, responses are coded 1, 2, 3, or 4. For items 10 and 11, responses are coded 0, 2, or 4 (see Table 7.15 for scoring criteria). The maximal score possible for the 11-item quick-screen psychometric test is 44. A cut-off score of 6 for men and 2 for women likely indicates a SUD. A score of 25 or higher indicates heavy dependence on drugs or substances of abuse.

### Available Test Statistics and Recommendations

**Specificity and Sensitivity** Among a sample of heavy drug users selected from Swedish inpatient detoxification settings,

---

[19]An extended version, the DUDIT-E, is available (Berman, Palmstierna, Kallmen, et al., 2007). The DUDIT-E contains 54 items and is intended to be used to obtain additional information from individuals who have already been positively screened for drug-related problems. Consequently, the DUDIT-E is not discussed further in this chapter.

TABLE 7.15    Drug Use Disorders Identification Test (DUDIT)

Here are a few questions about drugs. Please answer as correctly and honestly as possible by indicating which answer is right for you.

☐ Man                                    ☐ Woman                              Age_____

| Item or Question | Scoring Criteria [point allocation] |
| --- | --- |
| 1. How often do you use drugs other than alcohol? | Never, [0]; once a month or less often, [1]; 2 to 4 times a month, [2]; 2 to 3 times a week, [3]; 4 times a week or more often, [4] |
| 2. Do you use more than one type of drug on the same occasion? | Never, [0]; once a month or less often, [1]; 2 to 4 times a month, [2]; 2 to 3 times a week, [3]; 4 times a week or more often, [4] |
| 3. How many times do you take drugs on a typical day when you use drugs? | 0, [0]; 1 or 2, [0]; 3 or 4, [1]; 5 or 6, [2]; 7 or more, [4] |
| 4. How often are you influenced heavily by drugs? | Never, [0]; less often than once a month, [1]; every month, [2]; every week, [3]; daily or almost every day, [4] |
| 5. Over the past year, have you felt that your longing for drugs was so strong that you could not resist it? | Never, [0]; less often than once a month, [1]; every month, [2]; every week, [3]; daily or almost every day, [4] |
| 6. Has it happened, over the past year, that you have not been able to stop taking drugs once you started? | Never, [0]; less often than once a month, [1]; every month, [2]; every week, [3]; daily or almost every day, [4] |
| 7. How often over the past year have you taken drugs and then neglected to do something you should have done? | Never, [0]; less often than once a month, [1]; every month, [2]; every week, [3]; daily or almost every day, [4] |
| 8. How often over the past year have you needed to take a drug the morning after heavy drug use the day before? | Never, [0]; less often than once a month, [1]; every month, [2]; every week, [3]; daily or almost every day, [4] |
| 9. How often over the past year have you had guilt feelings or a bad conscience because you used drugs? | Never, [0]; less often than once a month, [1]; every month, [2]; every week, [3]; daily or almost every day, [4] |
| 10. Have you or anyone else been hurt (mentally or physically) because you used drugs? | No, [0]; Yes, but not over the past year, [2]; Yes, over the past year, [4] |
| 11. Has a relative or a friend, doctor or a nurse, or anyone else, been worried about your drug use or said to you that you should stop using drugs? | No, [0]; Yes, but not over the past year, [2]; Yes, over the past year, [4] |

Modified from: Berman, Bergman, Palmstierna, et al., 2005.

prisons, and probation offices, the DUDIT's specificity for predicting drug dependence was 78% when compared to established *DSM-IV* criteria and 88% when compared to established *ICD-10* criteria. Sensitivity for the DUDIT was 90% for both sets of criteria (Berman, Bergman, Palmstierna, et al., 2005).

**Validity and Reliability** The DUDIT has good face validity, and its criterion-related validity, as noted in the previous section, is good when predicting drug dependence based on the *DSM-IV* or *ICD-10* criteria. The DUDIT's reliability also is good, as indicated by its inter-item consistency, which yielded a Cronbach's alpha coefficient of 0.80 (Berman, Bergman, Palmstierna, et al., 2005).

**Recommendations** The DUDIT has good statistical results in relation to its psychometric analysis. However, until additional data are made available concerning its validity, caution is warranted particularly in the context of use with North American adolescents.

## Fagerström Test for Nicotine Dependence (FTND)

The FTND is a 6-item quick-screen psychometric test (see Table 7.16) that was developed by Heatherton, Kozlowski, Frecker, et al. (1991) as an improved version of the original Fagerström Tolerance Questionnnaire (FTQ), developed by Kari Fagerström in 1978. The

**TABLE 7.16    Fagerström Test for Nicotine Dependence (FTND)**

| Item/Question | Scoring Criteria [point allocation] |
|---|---|
| 1. How soon after you wake up do you have your first cigarette? | Within 5 minutes, [3]; 6 to 30 minutes, [2]; 31 to 60 minutes, [1]; after 60 minutes, [0] |
| 2. Do you find it difficult to refrain from smoking in places where it is forbidden such as church, the library, or movie theaters? | Yes, [1]; No, [0] |
| 3. Which cigarette would you hate most to give up? | The first one in the morning, [1]; all others, [0] |
| 4. How many cigarettes do you smoke? (20 cigarettes per pack) | 10 or less, [0]; 11 to 20, [1]; 21 to 30, [2]; 31 or more, [3] |
| 5. Do you smoke more frequently during the first hours after waking than the rest of the day? | Yes, [1]; No, [0] |
| 6. Do you smoke if you are so ill that you are in bed most of the day? | Yes, [1]; No, [0] |

Modified from: Heatherton, Kozlowski, Frecker, et al., 1991.

FTQ was originally developed to determine if nicotine replacement therapy was required for the management of nicotine withdrawal and was found to be a useful test for measuring nicotine dependence.

The FTND, which should be completed only by current, active tobacco smokers, has been translated into several languages and has been tested and used to measure nicotine dependence in many countries, including Brazil, Canada, China, France, Germany, Holland, Japan, Spain, Switzerland, Turkey, and the United States (De Meneses-Gaya, Zuardi, Loureiro, et al., 2009; Etter, Duc, & Perneger, 1999; Huang, Lin, & Wang, 2006; Mikami, Akechi, Kugaya, et al., 1999; Pérez-Ríos, Santiago-Pérez, Alonso, et al., 2009; Pomerleau, Carton, Lutzke, et al., 1994; Richardson & Ratner, 2005; Uysal, Kadakal, Karşidağ, et al., 2004). The FTND also has been tested and used for detecting nicotine dependence among smokers who have posttraumatic stress disorder, schizophrenia, and other mental disorders (e.g., Buckley, Mozley, Holohan, et al., 2005; Weinberger, Reutenaur, Allen, et al., 2007).

Several versions of the FTND have been developed, including the Modified-FTND, a version to which additional possible responses, such as "I have never smoked cigarettes," were added to each question as well as an additional question concerning "inhaling smoke" (Prokhorov, Koehly, Pallonen, et al., 1998); and the FTND-ST (Ebbert, Patten, & Schroeder, 2006), which is used to assess nicotine dependence among users of smokeless tobacco products.[20]

### Scoring

Each of the 6 questions in the FTND is assigned 0 to 3 points depending on the response selected. (See Table 7.16 for scoring criteria.) All of the scores are summed for a possible maximal score of 10. Total scores generally are evaluated as follows: 0 to 2, very low dependence; 3 or 4, low dependence; 5, medium dependence; 6 or 7, high dependence; and 8 to 10, very high dependence.

### Available Test Statistics and Recommendations

**Specificity, Sensitivity, and Positive and Negative Predictive Values** Data are unavailable for adolescent or adult tobacco smokers in North America. A Japanese study (i.e., Mikami, Akechi, Kugaya, et al., 1999)

---

[20] Very poor psychometric statistical performance was reported for both of these versions of the FTND by Ebbert, Patten, and Schroeder (2006) and by Kandel, Schaffran, Griesler, et al. (2005), precluding us from recommending either modified version for clinical use. Thus, copies of these quick-screen tests and further discussion are not included in this chapter.

reported a specificity of 0.80 and a sensitivity of 0.75 when a cut-off score of 5 was used. A Brazilian study (i.e., Menezes-Gaya, Zuardi, Loureiro, et al., 2009) reported a specificity of 0.74 and a sensitivity of 0.80 when a cut-off score of 4 was used. This study also reported a positive predictive value of 0.95 and a negative predictive value of 0.30.

**Validity and Reliability**  Studies of the criterion-related validity of the FTND, in comparison to selected biological markers (e.g., carbon monoxide blood concentrations or saliva cotinine concentrations), among regular tobacco smokers have been performed (e.g., Buckley, Mozley, Holohan, et al., 2005; Burling & Burling, 2003; Huang, Lin, & Wang, 2006). The mean criterion-related validity coefficient was 0.5 (i.e., a moderate but generally unacceptable result). Similarly, measures of concurrent and convergent validity (e.g., when comparing results from the FTND to those obtained using *DSM* criteria) have been disappointing. In this regard, it has been suggested that FTND and *DSM* measure different aspects of nicotine dependence with the FTND providing a stronger measure of physical dependence (Moolchan, Radzius, Epstein, et al., 2002).

The mean of the reported Cronbach's alpha coefficients of item reliability for the FTND is 0.65, range 0.61 to 0.68 (e.g., Etter, 2005; Haddock, Lando, Klesges, et al., 1999; Heatherton, Kozlowski, Frecker, et al., 1991; Okuyemi, Pulvers, Cox, et al., 2007; Pomerleau, Carton, Lutzke, et al., 1994),[21] indicating moderate but generally unacceptable internal consistency for the psychometric test. In this regard, it has been suggested that the deletion of items 2 and 3 (see Table 7.16) may increase the internal consistency of the FTND (de Leon, Diaz,

Becoña, et al., 2003; Etter, Duc, & Perneger, 1999; Uysal, Kadakal, Karşidağ, et al., 2004).

Test-retest reliability was reported as ranging from 0.82 (Weinberger, Reutenauer, Allen, et al., 2007) to 0.92 (Menezes-Gaya, Zuardi, Loureiro, et al., 2009) for tobacco smokers who did not have a dual diagnosis. (See Chapter 8, *Dual Diagnosis Among Adolescents*.) For a sample of U.S. Air Force recruits, average age 19 years, the reported test-retest reliability at 6 weeks was 0.87 (Haddock, Lando, Klesges, et al., 1999). Interrater reliability has been reported as being extremely high (i.e., 0.99) (Menezes-Gaya, Zuardi, Loureiro, et al., 2009).

**Recommendations**  Overall, given the relatively low validity and reliability reported for the FTND as well as the dearth of test statistics for adolescents, we do not generally recommend its use for adolescents.

### Michigan Alcoholism Screening Test (MAST)

The MAST is a 24-item[22] quick-screen psychometric test (see Table 7.17) that was designed by Selzer (1968, 1971) to detect alcoholism among adults while accommodating a lack of candor among respondents. It was normed with samples that were comprised primarily of North American men of European descent, 25 to 44 years of age. An adolescent version, the MAST-A, also has been developed and is used for screening adolescents. With only minor rewording of 3 items, or questions, the MAST-A is essentially the same as the MAST. (See Table 7.17.) The MAST was originally designed to be orally administered to the respondent by a health or social care professional. However, it is frequently used in

---

[21] A Brazilian study (i.e., Menezes-Gaya, Zuardi, Loureiro, et al., 2009) reported a Cronbach's alpha coefficient of 0.83.

[22] Since its initial development, several different versions of the full MAST have become available. These different versions can include from *22* to *25* items. For example, the question "Do you enjoy a drink now and then?" is sometimes included as Question 0. In addition, the question "Do you ever try to limit your drinking to certain times of the day or to certain places?" has been included as the last question and is scored "No, 0; Yes, 1."

**TABLE 7.17    Michigan Alcoholism Screening Test (MAST)**

*Please circle either Yes or No for each item as it applies to you:*

| Scoring Criteria [point allocation] | Item/Question |
|---|---|
| Yes [0]    No [2] | 1. Do you feel you are a normal drinker? |
| Yes [1]    No [0] | 2. Have you ever awakened the morning after some drinking the night before and found that you could not remember a part of the evening before? |
| Yes [1]    No [0] | 3. Does your wife, husband, a parent, or other near relative ever worry or complain about your drinking? |
| Yes [0]    No [2] | 4. Can you stop drinking without a struggle after one or two drinks? |
| Yes [1]    No [0] | 5. Do you ever feel guilty about your drinking? |
| Yes [0]    No [2] | 6. Do friends or relatives think you are a normal drinker? |
| Yes [0]    No [2] | 7. Are you able to stop drinking when you want to? |
| Yes [5]    No [0] | 8. Have you ever attended a meeting of Alcoholics Anonymous (AA)? |
| Yes [1]    No [0] | 9. Have you ever gotten into physical fights when drinking? |
| Yes [2]    No [0] | 10. Has drinking ever created problems between you and your wife, husband, a parent, or other near relative? |
| Yes [2]    No [0] | 11. Has your wife, husband, a parent, or other near relative ever gone to anyone for help about your drinking? |
| Yes [2]    No [0] | 12. Have you ever lost friends or girlfriends/boyfriends because of your drinking? |
| Yes [2]    No [0] | 13. Have you ever gotten into trouble at work because of drinking? [The MAST-A replaces "work" with "school."] |
| Yes [2]    No [0] | 14. Have you ever lost a job because of drinking? |
| Yes [2]    No [0] | 15. Have you ever neglected your obligations, your family, or your work for two or more days in a row because you were drinking? [The MAST-A replaces "work" with "school."] |
| Yes [1]    No [0] | 16. Do you drink before noon fairly often? [The MAST-A does not include "fairly often."] |
| Yes [2]    No [0] | 17. Have you ever been told you have liver trouble? Cirrhosis? |
| Yes [5]    No [0] | 18. After heavy drinking, have you ever had delirium tremens (DTs) or severe shaking, or heard voices, or seen things that weren't really there? |
| Yes [5]    No [0] | 19. Have you ever gone to anyone for help about your drinking? |
| Yes [5]    No [0] | 20. Have you ever been in a hospital because of drinking? |
| Yes [2]    No [0] | 21. Have you ever been a patient in a psychiatric hospital or on a psychiatric ward of a general hospital where drinking was part of the problem that resulted in hospitalization? |
| Yes [2]    No [0] | 22. Have you ever been seen at a psychiatric or mental health clinic, or gone to a doctor, social worker, or clergyman for help with any emotional problem where drinking was part of the problem? |
| Yes [2]    No [0] | 23. Have you ever been arrested for drunken driving while intoxicated or driving under the influence of alcoholic beverages? |
| Yes [2]    No [0] | 24. Have you ever been arrested, even for a few hours, because of other drunken behavior? |

Note: In the original version, a pre-question was included as Question #0, "Do you enjoy a drink now and then?"
Modified from: Selzer, 1968, 1971.

paper-and-pencil format as a self-administered quick-screen psychometric test. The MAST is one of the most widely used quick-screen psychometric tests for detecting alcohol abuse and, for this indication, often is considered to be one of the benchmarks, or standards, to which other quick-screen psychometric tests are compared. However, a noted shortcoming is its inability to distinguish between present and past alcohol problems. Also see the Brief MAST (B-MAST) and the Short MAST (SMAST).

### Scoring

Each item comprising the MAST is assigned a weight of 0 to 5 as specified in the left-hand column of the test. (See Table 7.17 for scoring criteria.) Items 1, 4, 6, and 7 are scored in reverse. The scores are summed for a possible maximal score of 55. Selzer (1971) originally recommended a cut-off score of 5 or higher to identify harmful or hazardous drinking. Ross, Gavin, and Skinner (1990) later recommended a total score of 13 or higher to detect alcoholism. The overall accuracy, or efficacy, of the MAST is 88% (Ross, Gavin, & Skinner, 1990).

### Available Test Statistics

**Specificity and Sensitivity**   Overall, the MAST has good specificity (i.e., up to 95%) and sensitivity (i.e., up to 98%). However, poor results also have been reported, including a specificity of 50% and an overall efficacy of 58% (Zung, 1982). Using a cut-off score of 13, Ross, Gavin, and Skinner (1990) obtained a specificity of 76% and a sensitivity of 91%.

**Validity and Reliability**   The MAST has excellent validity, correctly identifying over 90% of men who have alcoholism. However, a significant variance in measures of criterion-related validity has been reported that appears to be primarily related to the correlation of the diagnostic test or other criterion against which the MAST is validated and the population group that is sampled and tested (Storgaard, Nielsen, & Gluud, 1994). In a sample of patients with psychiatric or mental disorders that was comprised primarily of women, validity estimates were found to be higher than for samples that did not have a higher proportion of women (Teitelbaum & Mullen, 2000). Interestingly, among adolescents, MAST scores demonstrate no gender differences (Nevitt, Lundak, & Galardi, 2006). However, some caution has been advised when the MAST is used for the assessment of Muslim adolescents because it was not developed for this group—a group for whom religion strictly forbids the use of alcohol (Luczak, 2003). Construct validity has been demonstrated by the moderate correlation between the MAST and the AUDIT and the high correlation between the MAST and *DSM* criteria (Conley, 2001).

In regard to reliability, the MAST has been found to have excellent internal consistency

with a reported Cronbach's alpha coefficient of 0.95 (Selzer, Vinokur, & Van Rooijen, 1975). Later studies (e.g., Conley, 2001) found a lower but still strong measure of internal consistency (i.e., 0.86). Its test-retest measures of reliability range from 0.83 to 0.95 for samples of psychiatric patients when test-retest intervals ranged from 1 day to approximately 5 months (Skinner & Sheu, 1982; Zung, 1982).

## Problem Oriented Screening Instrument for Teenagers (POSIT)

The POSIT, a 139-item psychometric screening test, was developed by Elizabeth Rahdert of the NIDA in 1991. It was designed to identify 10 different problem areas of adolescent behavior and health, including mental health, physical health, social skills, and substance use and abuse. The substance use and abuse area is addressed with 17 specific items and has been used as an independent questionnaire. (See Table 7.18.) The POSIT was developed to be self-administered by adolescents and minimally requires a 5th-grade reading level. A computerized version is available.

### Scoring

The entire POSIT is scored using a scoring system available from the NIDA. Empirically derived cut-off scores detect low, medium, or high risk for each of the 10 identified problem areas addressed by the POSIT. For the 17-item substance use and abuse scale, each affirmative response is assigned 1 point for a possible maximal score of 17. (See Table 7.18 for scoring criteria.) A cut-off score of 2 or higher is recommended for the detection of alcohol or drug abuse problems (Latimer, Winters, & Stinchfield, 1997).

### Available Test Statistics

**Specificity and Sensitivity**   Using the recommended cut-off score of 2 or higher, the POSIT substance use and abuse scale was reported to have an efficacy of 84% with a specificity of 79% and a sensitivity of 95%

**TABLE 7.18    Problem Oriented Screening Instrument for Teenagers (POSIT): Substance Use and Abuse Scale**

| Item/Question | Scoring Criteria [point allocation] |
|---|---|
| 1. Do you get into trouble because you use drugs or alcohol at school? | No, [0]; Yes, [1] |
| 2. Have you accidentally hurt yourself or someone else while high on alcohol or drugs? | No, [0]; Yes, [1] |
| 3. Do you miss out on activities because you spend too much money on drugs or alcohol? | No, [0]; Yes, [1] |
| 4. Do you ever feel you are addicted to alcohol or drugs? | No, [0]; Yes, [1] |
| 5. Have you started using more and more drugs or alcohol to get the effect you want? | No, [0]; Yes, [1] |
| 6. Do you ever leave a party because there is no alcohol or drugs? | No, [0]; Yes, [1] |
| 7. Do you have a constant desire for alcohol or drugs? | No, [0]; Yes, [1] |
| 8. Have you had a car accident while high on alcohol or drugs? | No, [0]; Yes, [1] |
| 9. Do you forget things you did while drinking or using drugs? | No, [0]; Yes, [1] |
| 10. During the past month have you driven a car while you were drunk or high? | No, [0]; Yes, [1] |
| 11. Does alcohol or drug use cause your moods to change quickly like from happy to sad or vice versa? | No, [0]; Yes, [1] |
| 12. Do you miss school or arrive late because of your alcohol or drug use? | No, [0]; Yes, [1] |
| 13. Do your family or friends ever tell you that you should cut down on your drinking or drug use? | No, [0]; Yes, [1] |
| 14. Do you have serious arguments with friends or family members because of your drinking or drug use? | No, [0]; Yes, [1] |
| 15. Does your alcohol or drug use ever make you do something you would not normally do like breaking rules, missing curfew, or breaking the law? | No, [0] Yes, [1] |
| 16. Do you have trouble getting along with any of your friends because of your alcohol or drug use? | No, [0]; Yes, [1] |
| 17. Do you ever feel you can't control your alcohol or drug use? | No, [0]; Yes, [1] |

Modified from: Rahdert, 1991.

(Latimer, Winters, & Stinchfield, 1997). Knight, Sherritt, Harris, et al. (2003), using a cut-off score of 1, obtained a mean sensitivity of 84% with a 95% confidence interval of 79% to 90%. Using a sample of adolescent mothers, Scafidi, Field, Prodromidis, et al. (1997) found that the POSIT scales correctly detected 75% of mothers who were drug abusing (i.e., sensitivity) and 84% of mothers who were not drug abusing (i.e., specificity).

**Validity and Reliability**    Criterion-related validity has been found to be moderate to high (Dembo, Schmeidler, Borden, et al., 1996; McLaney, Del Boca, & Babor, 1994). In regard to reliability, Dembo, Schmeidler, Borden, et al. (1996) reported high test-retest reliability among adolescents who were incarcerated on more than one occasion and were tested at the time of initial incarceration and at subsequent times of incarceration, varying from 1 to 33 weeks. Knight, Goodman, Pulerwitz,

et al. (2001) found test-retest reliability, after 1 week, to be greater than 0.70.

**Rapid Alcohol Problems Screen— Version 4 (RAPS4)**

The RAPS4 is a 4-item quick-screen psychometric test (see Table 7.19) that was developed by Cherpitel (2000) to detect alcohol dependence, or alcoholism. As its name implies, it is the fourth revision of the original RAPS, which was developed by Cherpitel in 1995 (Cherpitel, 1995b). The items, or questions, comprising the RAPS4 were taken from other quick-screen psychometric tests that are used for detecting alcoholism or harmful patterns of alcohol use. RAPS4 received its name from the acronyms obtained for each of the four items about drinking that comprise the screening test: *R* for remorse; *A* for amnesia; *P* for performance; and *S* for starter— the need to drink on awakening in the morning (see Table 7.19). A Spanish-language version

TABLE 7.19    Rapid Alcohol Problems Screen—Version 4 (RAPS4)

| Item/Question | Scoring Criteria [point allocation] |
|---|---|
| 1. During the past year, have you had a feeling of guilt or remorse after drinking? (**R**emorse) | No, [0]; Yes, [1] |
| 2. During the past year, has a friend or family member ever told you about things you said or did while you were drinking that you could not remember? (**A**mnesia) | No, [0]; Yes, [1] |
| 3. During the past year, have you failed to do what was normally expected of you because of drinking? (**P**erformance) | No, [0]; Yes, [1] |
| 4. During the past year, do you sometimes take a drink when you first get up in the morning? (**S**tart of the day) | No, [0]; Yes, [1] |

Modified from: Cherpitel, 2000.

also is available (Borges & Cherpitel, 2001; Cherpitel & Borges, 2000).

### Scoring

A positive response to any 1 of the 4 questions on the RAPS4 is considered a positive test for alcohol dependence or alcoholism. (See Table 7.19 for scoring criteria.)

### Available Test Statistics and Recommendations

**Specificity and Sensitivity**    Like the original RAPS, the RAPS4 reportedly performs better than most similar quick-screen psychometric tests in terms of specificity and sensitivity across gender and continental descent, including North Americans of African, European, or Hispanic descent (Cherpitel, 1997b, 1998, 2000, 2002; Cherpitel & Bazargan, 2003).[23] Using a cut-off total score of 1 with a large sample of patients accessing emergency department services, Cherpitel (2000) reported a specificity of 87% and a

sensitivity of 93% for alcohol dependence. However, for harmful drinking or abuse, a significantly lower specificity of 79% and a sensitivity of 55% were found.[24]

**Validity and Reliability**    Published data concerning the validity and reliability of the RAPS4 are not available.

**Recommendations**    We cannot recommend the use of the RAPS4 for adolescents because of its general limited published statistics and total lack of statistical data for North American adolescents.

### Rutgers Alcohol Problem Index (RAPI)

The RAPI is a 23-item[25] self-administered quick-screen psychometric test (see Table 7.20) that was developed by White and Labouvie (1989) to detect problem drinking among adolescents. Factor analysis of the RAPI indicated that it is

---

[23] The RAPS, RAPS4, and RAPS4-QF have been used in several foreign countries (e.g., Argentina; India; Poland). However, their reported test statistics have been disappointing (Cherpitel, Ye, Bond, et al., 2005; Cherpitel, Ye, Moskalewicz, et al., 2005; Cremonte & Cherpitel, 2008; Nayak, Bond, Cherpitel, et al., 2009). Consequently, the use of the RAPS is not supported in this context.

[24] The low sensitivity has been increased significantly to 90% with the addition of 2 quantity–frequency questions: (1) "During the past year, have you consumed five or more drinks on at least one occasion?" and (2) "During the past year, have you consumed alcohol at least once per month?" (Cherpitel, 2002). The modified RAPS4 has been referred to as the RAPS4-QF.

[25] An 18-item version was developed by White and Labouvie (2000) as a replacement for the original 23-item RAPI. The two tests are exactly alike, except for the deletion of items 14, 17, 18, 20, and 22. In addition, the correlation between the two versions is reported to be 0.99. However, very little psychometric data are available for the 18-item version of the RAPI.

TABLE 7.20   Rutgers Alcohol Problem Index (RAPI)

How many times has this happened to you while you were drinking or because of your drinking during the last year?

| Item/Question | Scoring Criteria [point allocation] |
| --- | --- |
| 1. Not able to do your homework or study for a test | None, [0]; 1 to 2 times, [1]; 3 to 5 times, [2]; More than 5 times, [3] |
| 2. Got into fights with other people (friends, relatives, strangers) | None, [0]; 1 to 2 times, [1]; 3 to 5 times, [2]; More than 5 times, [3] |
| 3. Missed out on other things because you spent too much money on alcohol | None, [0]; 1 to 2 times, [1]; 3 to 5 times, [2]; More than 5 times, [3] |
| 4. Went to work or school high or drunk | None, [0]; 1 to 2 times, [1]; 3 to 5 times, [2]; More than 5 times, [3] |
| 5. Caused shame or embarrassment to someone | None, [0]; 1 to 2 times, [1]; 3 to 5 times, [2]; More than 5 times, [3] |
| 6. Neglected your responsibilities | None, [0]; 1 to 2 times, [1]; 3 to 5 times, [2]; More than 5 times, [3] |
| 7. Relatives avoided you | None, [0]; 1 to 2 times, [1]; 3 to 5 times, [2]; More than 5 times, [3] |
| 8. Felt that you needed more alcohol than you used to in order to get the same effect | None, [0]; 1 to 2 times, [1]; 3 to 5 times, [2]; More than 5 times, [3] |
| 9. Tried to control your drinking (tried to drink only at certain times of the day or in certain places, that is, tried to change your pattern of drinking) | None, [0]; 1 to 2 times, [1]; 3 to 5 times, [2]; More than 5 times, [3] |
| 10. Had withdrawal symptoms, that is, felt sick because you stopped or cut down on drinking | None, [0]; 1 to 2 times, [1]; 3 to 5 times, [2]; More than 5 times, [3] |
| 11. Noticed a change in your personality | None, [0]; 1 to 2 times, [1]; 3 to 5 times, [2]; More than 5 times, [3] |
| 12. Felt that you had a problem with alcohol | None, [0]; 1 to 2 times, [1]; 3 to 5 times, [2]; More than 5 times, [3] |
| 13. Missed a day (or part of a day) of school or work | None, [0]; 1 to 2 times, [1]; 3 to 5 times, [2]; More than 5 times, [3] |
| 14. Wanted to stop drinking but couldn't | None, [0]; 1 to 2 times, [1]; 3 to 5 times, [2]; More than 5 times, [3] |
| 15. Suddenly found yourself in a place that you could not remember getting to | None, [0]; 1 to 2 times, [1]; 3 to 5 times, [2]; More than 5 times, [3] |
| 16. Passed out or fainted suddenly | None, [0]; 1 to 2 times, [1]; 3 to 5 times, [2]; More than 5 times, [3] |
| 17. Had a fight, argument or bad feeling with a friend | None, [0]; 1 to 2 times, [1]; 3 to 5 times, [2]; More than 5 times, [3] |
| 18. Had a fight, argument or bad feeling with a family member | None, [0]; 1 to 2 times, [1]; 3 to 5 times, [2]; More than 5 times, [3] |
| 19. Kept drinking when you promised yourself not to | None, [0]; 1 to 2 times, [1]; 3 to 5 times, [2]; More than 5 times, [3] |
| 20. Felt you were going crazy | None, [0]; 1 to 2 times, [1]; 3 to 5 times, [2]; More than 5 times, [3] |
| 21. Had a bad time | None, [0]; 1 to 2 times, [1]; 3 to 5 times, [2]; More than 5 times, [3] |
| 22. Felt physically or psychologically dependent on alcohol | None, [0]; 1 to 2 times, [1]; 3 to 5 times, [2]; More than 5 times, [3] |
| 23. Was told by a friend, neighbor or relative to stop or cut down on drinking | None, [0]; 1 to 2 times, [1]; 3 to 5 times, [2]; More than 5 times, [3] |

Modified from: White & Labouvie, 1989.

composed of three factors: (1) abuse/dependence symptoms; (2) personal consequences of alcohol use; and (3) social consequences of alcohol use (Martens, Neighbors, Dams-O'Connor, et al., 2007). It was normed on a nonclinical sample of adolescent girls and boys ranging in age from 12 to 21 years of age. It requires a 7th-grade reading level.

Several briefer versions of the RAPI have been proposed to reduce gender bias (Earleywine, LaBrie, & Pedersen, 2008) and to facilitate clinical utility (Neal, Corbin, & Fromme, 2006). However, related test statistics are not generally available for these versions of the RAPI.

### Scoring

Each item of the RAPI is scored from 0 to 3 (see Table 7.20 for scoring criteria) and is summed for a possible maximal score of 69. The RAPI was developed for use with normed samples, and, thus, it can be administered with any sample. For example, for the initial clinical sample (age range 14–18 years), the mean scores ranged from 21 to 25, depending on age and gender. Similarly, for a nonclinical sample (age range 15–18 years), mean scores ranged from 4 to 8, depending on age and gender.

### Available Test Statistics and Recommendations

**Specificity and Sensitivity**   A specificity of approximately 75% was obtained for adolescents of American Indian descent (i.e., 76.2%, cut-off score of 21) and for adolescents not of American Indian descent (i.e., 74.6%, cut-off score of 27). Corresponding sensitivities were 80.0% and 53.3%, respectively (Noel, O'Connor, Boudreau, et al., 2010). As in other studies, specificity of the RAPI increased for both groups of adolescents as the cut-off score was increased (i.e., at a cut-off score of 38, specificity increased to 90.5% for adolescents of American Indian descent and to 85.7% for adolescents not of American Indian descent). However, the sensitivity decreased (i.e., at a cut-off score of 38, the sensitivity for adolescents of American Indian

descent decreased to 40.0% and to 46.7% for adolescents not of American Indian descent) (Noel, O'Connor, Boudreau, et al., 2010).

**Validity and Reliability**   The items selected for inclusion in the RAPI were selected from other similar quick-screen psychometric tests with good face validity. Therefore, the RAPI tends to have good face validity as well. Good convergent validity has been established for the RAPI in comparison to the *DSM* criteria for alcohol abuse and dependence (Ginzler, Garrett, Baer, et al., 2007). The internal consistency of the RAPI also is good as demonstrated by a Cronbach's alpha coefficient of 0.88 (Earleywine, La Brie, & Pedersen, 2008) and 0.92 (White & Labouvie, 1989).

## Short Michigan Alcoholism Screening Test (SMAST)

The SMAST, or Short MAST, is a 13-item psychometric screening test (see Table 7.21) that was developed by Selzer, Vinokur, and Van Rooijen (1975) to detect alcoholism (i.e., alcohol abuse/dependence). (Also see the Michigan Alcoholism Screening Test [MAST] and the Brief MAST [B-MAST].)

### Scoring

Each item of the SMAST is scored 0 or 1. Items 1, 4, and 5 are scored in reverse. (See Table 7.21 for scoring criteria.) All scores are summed to provide a possible maximal score of 13. It is recommended that the total scores achieved by respondents be interpreted as: 0 or 1, nonalcoholic; 2, possible alcoholic; and 3 or higher, alcoholic.

### Available Test Statistics and Recommendations

**Specificity and Sensitivity**   The SMAST was used to discriminate between social drinkers (i.e., nonalcoholics) and heavier drinkers (i.e., possible alcoholics and alcoholics) with a sample of traditional Muslim men

**TABLE 7.21    Short Michigan Alcoholism Screening Test (SMAST)**

*Please circle either Yes or No for each item as it applies to you.*

| Scoring Criteria [point allocation] | | Item/Question |
|---|---|---|
| Yes [0] | No [1] | 1. Do you feel you are a normal drinker? |
| Yes [1] | No [0] | 2. Does your wife, husband, a parent, or other near relative ever worry or complain about your drinking? |
| Yes [1] | No [0] | 3. Do you ever feel guilty about your drinking? |
| Yes [0] | No [1] | 4. Do friends or relatives think you are a normal drinker? |
| Yes [0] | No [1] | 5. Are you able to stop drinking when you want to? |
| Yes [1] | No [0] | 6. Have you ever attended a meeting of Alcoholics Anonymous (AA)? |
| Yes [1] | No [0] | 7. Has drinking ever created problems between you and your wife, husband, a parent, or other near relative? |
| Yes [1] | No [0] | 8. Have you ever gotten into trouble at work because of drinking? |
| Yes [1] | No [0] | 9. Have you ever neglected your obligations, your family, or your work for two or more days in a row because you were drinking? |
| Yes [1] | No [0] | 10. Have you ever gone to anyone for help about your drinking? |
| Yes [1] | No [0] | 11. Have you ever been in a hospital because of drinking? |
| Yes [1] | No [0] | 12. Have you ever been arrested for drunken driving while intoxicated or driving under the influence of alcoholic beverages? |
| Yes [1] | No [0] | 13. Have you ever been arrested, even for a few hours, because of drinking? |

Modified from: Selzer, Vinokur, & Van Rooijen, 1975.

living in Kuwait. The SMAST demonstrated a good specificity of 82.5% and an excellent sensitivity of 100% (al-Ansari & Negrete, 1990). In contrast, samples of American southwestern and Plains Indians—both men and women—demonstrated an unacceptable specificity range of 23% to 47% using the recommended cut-off score of 3. However, using the same cut-off score of 3, a very good sensitivity (range, 86% to 95%) was obtained. Using a cut-off score of 2 to detect lifetime alcohol abuse/dependence for samples of primary care patients, mean specificities ranged from 88% to 97% and mean sensitivities ranged from 38% to 82% (Brown & Rounds, 1995; Cleary, Miller, Bush, et al., 1988; Fleming & Barry, 1991).

**Validity and Reliability**    As a quick-screen psychometric test, the SMAST is comparable to the CAGE in regard to detecting alcoholism (Maisto, Connors, & Allen, 1995). Internal reliability has been reported as 0.85 (Barry & Fleming, 1993). However, variability in internal consistency estimates, particularly among women and nonclinical respondents, has been found to adversely affect its overall reliability (Shields, Howell, Potter, et al., 2007).

**Recommendations**    Lack of sufficient data concerning validity, unacceptable variability in reliability, and a dearth of adolescent data prevent us from being able to recommend the clinical use of the SMAST, particularly for adolescents.

### T-ACE

The T-ACE is a 4-item psychometric screening test (see Table 7.22) that was developed by Sokol, Martier, and Ager (1989) to detect alcoholism. Based on the CAGE (see earlier discussion), it was originally used in obstetric settings to detect alcoholism and potential risk for FAS/FASD among pregnant women. Although initially designed to be administered by structured interview, the T-ACE frequently is self-administered. A Brazilian version of the T-ACE has been developed and tested, yielding excellent statistical results (Fabbri, Furtado, & Laprega, 2007; Moraes, Viellas, & Reichenheim, 2005).

### Scoring

Each affirmative response to the items on the T-ACE is given a score of 1. (See Table 7.22 for scoring criteria.) The scores are summed

TABLE 7.22    T-ACE: An Alcoholism Screening Test

| Item/Question | Scoring Criteria [point allocation] |
|---|---|
| 1. Does it take more than it used to for you to get high? (**T**olerance) | No, [0]; Yes, [1] |
| 2. Have you become **A**ngry or **A**nnoyed when others express concern about your alcohol use? | No, [0]; Yes, [1] |
| 3. Have you tried to **C**ut down or quit? | No, [0]; Yes, [1] |
| 4. Have you had an **E**ye-opener? | No, [0]; Yes, [1] |

Modified from: Sokol, Martier, & Ager, 1989.

for a possible maximal score of 4. A total score of 2 or higher is considered to be indicative of alcoholism or risky drinking (see Table 7.6).

### Available Test Statistics and Recommendations

**Specificity and Sensitivity**    The reported specificity of the T-ACE for a cohort of pregnant women was 79% (Russell, 1994; Russell, Martier, Sokol, et al., 1996). Among the male partners of a similar cohort of pregnant women, the T-ACE had a specificity of approximately 50% and a sensitivity of approximately 84% (Chang, McNamara, Orav, et al., 2006). In comparison to a formal structured clinical interview conducted with patients in a psychiatric clinic, the specificity of the T-ACE was found to be 59% and the sensitivity to be 88% (Hill & Chang, 2007). Poor specificity (19% to 34%) was reported with a sample of pregnant women using recommended cut-off scores (Sarkar, Einarson, & Koren, 2010). Increasing the criterion value (i.e., cut-off point) to a score of 3 for a similar sample of North American women of African descent significantly increased the specificity of the T-ACE (Chiodo, Sokol, Delaney-Black, et al., 2010).

In a study of a random sample of 300 participants 18 years of age and older selected from a hospital outpatient clinic, McQuade,

Levy, Yanek, et al. (2000) found that the T-ACE outperformed both the AUDIT and the CAGE. Mean specificity was 91% with a better specificity reported for women (92%) than for men (86%).

The sensitivity of the T-ACE is reportedly higher than that for the CAGE (Russell, 1994), particularly for pregnant North American women of African descent (Bradley, Boyd-Wickizer, Powell, et al., 1998). The T-ACE also has been reported to be more sensitive than obstetric staff assessment for detecting potentially problematic use of alcohol by pregnant women (Chang, Wilkins-Haug, Berman, et al., 1998). The overall sensitivity of the T-ACE with samples of pregnant women ranges from 85% to 100% (Chang, Goetz, Wilkins-Haug, et al., 1999; Russell, Martier, Sokol, et al., 1996; Sarkar, Einarson, & Koren, 2010). For a randomly selected sample of outpatients 18 years of age and older, McQuade, Levy, Yanek, et al. (2000) found the overall sensitivity to be 74%. The sensitivity performance results that were obtained were superior to both the AUDIT (i.e., 68%) and the CAGE (i.e., 68%) and significantly higher for men (i.e., 81%) than for women (i.e., 70%).

**Validity and Reliability**    Published data regarding the validity and reliability of the T-ACE are not available.

**Recommendations**    Test statistics for the T-ACE are limited. In addition, data regarding its use with adolescents, other than that reported by McQuade, Levy, Yanek, et al. (2000) for a random sample of participants 18 years of age and older, are generally lacking. Thus, we generally do not recommend the use of the T-ACE, particularly for adolescents.

### TWEAK

The TWEAK is a 5-item psychometric screening test (see Table 7.23) that was designed by Russell, Martier, Sokol, et al. (1994). It was adapted from the CAGE in order to better detect heavy drinking or alcoholism among

TABLE 7.23    TWEAK: An Alcohol Screening Test

| Item/Question | Scoring Criteria [point allocation] |
|---|---|
| 1. **Tolerance**. How many drinks can you hold?[a] | 5 or more drinks, [2] |
| 2. Have close friends or relatives **W**orried or complained about your drinking in the past year? | No, [0]; Yes, [2] |
| 3. **Eye-opener**. Do you sometimes take a drink in the morning when you first get up? | No, [0]; Yes, [1] |
| 4. **Amnesia**. Has a friend or family member ever told you about things you said or did while you were drinking that you could not remember? | No, [0]; Yes, [1] |
| 5. Do you sometimes feel the need to c(**K**)**ut** down on your drinking? | No, [0]; Yes, [1] |

[a] Version 2, an alternative version of the TWEAK (Chan, Pristach, Welte, et al., 1993), replaces this question and point allocation for scoring with "How many drinks does it take you to get high?" 3 or more drinks, [2].
Modified from: Russell, Martier, Sokol, et al., 1994.

women during pregnancy and was initially tested among pregnant North American women of African descent. Although initially designed to be administered by structured interview, the TWEAK frequently is self-administered. A computerized version also is available.

### Scoring

The TWEAK is composed of 5 questions. (See Table 7.23 for scoring criteria.) Positive responses for questions 1 and 2 are each given a score of 2. Positive responses for questions 3, 4, and 5 are each given a score of 1. The scores are then summed for a possible maximal score of 7. A final total score of 2 or higher for women (McCambridge & Thomas, 2009; Russell, Martier, Sokol et al., 1996) and a final total score of 3 or higher for men (Cherpitel, 1998, 1999) suggests harmful or hazardous alcohol use.

### Available Test Statistics and Recommendations

**Specificity and Sensitivity**    The TWEAK has a reportedly higher specificity and sensitivity than does the CAGE or B-MAST in regard to detecting heavy drinking or alcoholism (Chan, Pristach, Welte, et al., 1993) among pregnant women (Chang, Wilkins-Haug, Berman, et al., 1998; Russell, Martier, Sokol et al., 1996). The TWEAK, although overall more sensitive for men than for women, has been reported to

outperform both the CAGE and the MAST in detecting alcohol abuse and dependence among women (Bradley, Boyd-Wickizer, Powell, et al., 1998; Cherpitel, 1997a). Overall, the TWEAK has demonstrated a specificity of approximately 90% and a sensitivity of approximately 74% (O'Connor & Whaley, 2003; Russell, Martier, Sokol, et al., 1994).

These statistics vary, as noted in the discussion of other quick-screen psychometric tests, with both the population sampled and the cut-off score selected. For example, using a cut-off score of 2 or higher for detecting alcohol problems among women, the TWEAK was found to have a specificity range of 77% to 87% and a sensitivity range of 89% to 91% (Cherpitel, 1995, 1997a; Russell, Martier, Sokol et al., 1996). For adolescents accessing emergency room services, Chung, Colby, Barnett, et al. (2000), using a cut-off score of 1, found the TWEAK to have a specificity of 80% and a sensitivity of 84%. However, overall, the TWEAK generally is considered to be inferior to the AUDIT, particularly when used to detect alcohol problems among women (Bush, Kivlahan, Davis, et al., 2003; Chung, Colby, Barnett, et al., 2000). The TWEAK also appears to be equally sensitive (approximately 90%) when used for North Americans of either African or European descent (Cherpitel, 1997b).

**Validity and Reliability**    Published data regarding the validity of the TWEAK are not available, and the data that are available regarding its reliability are cause for concern. A comparison of the AUDIT, RAPS4, and TWEAK found the TWEAK to have the lowest reliability of the three tests (Cremonte, Ledesma, Cherpitel, et al., 2010). In addition, the internal consistency of the TWEAK is low with a Cronbach's alpha of 0.50, and the average inter-item correlation is very low (i.e., 0.17) (Kelly, Donovan, Kinnane, et al., 2002).

**Recommendations**    Based on the available statistics indicating poor validity and reliability, we generally do not recommend the use of the TWEAK, particularly for adolescents.

## CHAPTER SUMMARY

This chapter has presented 18 common quick-screen psychometric tests that can be used to detect drug and substance use disorders among adolescents along with concerns regarding their clinical use and limitations, including missed diagnosis and misdiagnosis. These psychometric screening tests[26] were presented and discussed with attention to their development, current use, and scoring. In addition, available published statistics, including specificity and sensitivity, positive and negative predictive value, validity, and reliability, were reviewed. Based on these reviews, recommendations were made for the use of the quick-screen psychometric tests for detecting

problematic use of the drugs and substances of abuse among adolescents. While both the clinical interview and assessment remain paramount in diagnosing AUDs and SUDs among adolescents, the appropriate use of the various quick-screen psychometric tests can be of tremendous assistance in facilitating the early detection of these disorders and, consequently, promoting early intervention and appropriate treatment. However, currently, there is no gold standard for detecting AUDs or other SUDs among adolescents. The choice of a specific test will depend primarily on five considerations:

1. The purpose of the quick-screen psychometric test (i.e., to detect problematic patterns of alcohol, cannabis, or other drug and substance use)

2. The performance of the quick-screen psychometric test for correctly detecting what it purports to measure as reflected by its published validity and reliability data

3. The population addressed by the quick-screen psychometric test (e.g., boys versus girls; pregnant adolescent girls and young women versus nonpregnant adolescent girls and young women)

4. The associated statistical data, (e.g., specificity, sensitivity, positive predictive value, and negative predictive value) when available, for the population of interest

5. Expedience and ease of administration and scoring of the selected quick-screen psychometric test

---

[26] Most of these quick-screen psychometric tests were originally developed, clinically tested, and used for adults. However, *minimally*, all of these tests have some demonstrated ability for detecting alcoholism and alcohol dependence, or other drug and substance use (e.g., cannabis use) among late adolescent/young adults, 18 to 20 years of age.

## CHAPTER 8

# *Dual Diagnosis Among Adolescents*

## INTRODUCTION

"Dual diagnosis" is a term that generally refers, quite simply and literally, to the identification of an adolescent (or adult) as having two or more mental disorders at the same time (Pagliaro, 1990). Other closely related terms also have been commonly used, such as: dual addiction—concomitant alcoholism and drug abuse (Kreek & Stimmel, 1984); comorbidity—cases of two diagnosable entities in the realm of substance abuse and mental illness (Belfer, 1993); multiple diagnosis—two or more mental health diagnoses in addition to a substance use diagnosis (e.g., Slesnick & Prestopnik, 2005); and dual disorder—concurrent diagnosis of alcoholism plus a psychiatric diagnosis (Daley, Moss, & Campbell, 1987).

The diversity of these terms and definitions has contributed to much semantic confusion in the published literature and in clinical settings (Fields, 1995). For example, Miller (1994) defined dual diagnosis as the co-occurrence of another disorder (psychiatric or medical) existing independently of an addictive disorder. In another example, Drake, Essock, Shaner, et al. (2001) defined dual diagnosis as the co-occurrence of substance abuse and severe mental illness (i.e., long-term psychiatric disorders). For clarity, the term "dual diagnosis," as used in this reference text, is defined as the occurrence in an adolescent or young adult of one, or more, substance use disorders (SUDs) and one or more other mental disorders (OMDs)[1] that may, or may not, be directly related. (See Figures 8.1 and 8.2.)

As originally recognized over 20 years ago by Keller, Lavori, Beardslee, et al. (1992), the presence of more than one OMD with a SUD is actually more common than once thought. In fact, among the adolescents they studied who had been diagnosed with a SUD, almost three-quarters (74%) had two to four OMDs.

In cases in which a SUD and an OMD are directly related, the SUD most commonly occurs either as an antecedent to, or as a consequence of, the OMD (Lehman, Myers, Corty, et al., 1994; Pagliaro, 1995a).[2] An example of the former is an 18-year-old adolescent boy who, over a few weeks of heavy cannabis use, developed paranoid psychosis.[3] An example

---

[1] In addition, for the sake of parsimony and to further reduce semantic confusion we use the term "other mental disorder" to include all related disorders, diseases, and conditions that typically are *diagnosed* and treated by psychiatrists and psychologists (i.e., all emotional disorders, learning disorders, mental illnesses, psychiatric disorders, and psychological disorders).

[2] Usually the distinction as to whether or not a co-occurring mental disorder is an antecedent to, or a consequent of, a SUD is not particularly relevant in most clinical contexts. However, in cases where the co-occurring mental disorder is an antecedent to the SUD, intervention aimed at ameliorating the co-occurring mental disorder (e.g., major depressive disorder) also will be of significant assistance in ameliorating the related SUD (Deas & Brown, 2006) and vice versa.

[3] He was living at the time in the basement of his parents' home. One evening after heavy cannabis use, he threatened his parents and punched his father, thinking that they were strangers who had invaded the house to kill his parents. In fear, the father subsequently called 911 for assistance. The police arrived in full tactical gear because they knew the adolescent from previous encounters. He did not believe that they were police officers, and a violent struggle ensued as he "tried to protect his family." He was finally handcuffed and placed in leg restraints. However, he continued to violently resist arrest—he was quite strong and muscular, being a body-builder, about 6 feet tall and weighing 200 pounds. He finally succumbed when the

*(continued)*

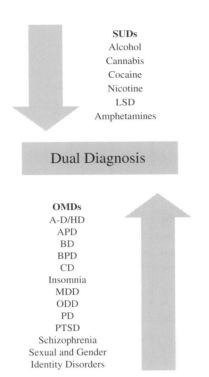

**SUDs**
Alcohol
Cannabis
Cocaine
Nicotine
LSD
Amphetamines

**Dual Diagnosis**

**OMDs**
A-D/HD
APD
BD
BPD
CD
Insomnia
MDD
ODD
PD
PTSD
Schizophrenia
Sexual and Gender
Identity Disorders

**Figure 8.1   Common Substance Use Disorders (SUDs) and Other Mental Disorders (OMDs) That Contribute to Dual Diagnosis Among Adolescents**

of the latter is a young man who began to use cocaine regularly to self-medicate[4] his undiagnosed depression and consequently developed cocaine psychosis.[5] An indirect relationship also may occur. For example, a SUD may be an antecedent to the development of an OMD, as occurs, for example, when an adolescent with latent schizophrenia (a cofactor) uses

lysergic acid diethylamide (LSD), and now has developed active schizophrenia. Figure 8.2 illustrates the many possible relationships that can co-occur between SUDs and OMDs. These relationships often can be further complicated when adolescents and young adults are considered because, as noted by Deas (2006), while adolescents and young adults may be actively developing a SUD and have one or more diagnostic signs and symptoms, they may not yet have developed sufficient signs and symptoms to meet established diagnostic criteria (e.g., *Diagnostic and Statistical Manual of Mental Disorders* [*DSM*] or other diagnostic criteria) to satisfy a formal diagnosis of a SUD.

As previously noted, a significant percentage of adolescents and young adults who present with a primary diagnosis of a SUD or OMD can be expected to have a dual diagnosis.[6] Although several studies and reports have suggested that a dual diagnosis generally can be expected in approximately 10% to 20% of patients who have mental disorders, the authors' clinical experiences and the published literature (e.g., Drake, Essock, Shaner, et al., 2001; Kaminer, Goldberg, & Connor, 2010; Miller, Belkin, & Gibbons, 1994) suggest that the incidence of dual diagnosis is significantly higher (i.e., more than 50% and often closer to 100%) among patients whose primary disorder is a significant SUD (e.g., abusive or compulsive use of a drug or substance of abuse; polyuse of the drugs and substances of abuse; dependence on a drug or substance of abuse) (Pagliaro & Pagliaro, *Clinical Patient Data Files*).

---

[3](*continued*)

paramedics arrived and injected him with an antipsychotic tranquilizer. The adolescent was formally charged, as an adult, with resisting arrest (1 charge) and assault (5 charges) on the five different police officers who were directly involved in his arrest. All charges were dismissed at trial subsequent to our expert forensic testimony (Pagliaro & Pagliaro, *Clinical Patient Data Files*).

[4] Also see later related discussion of self-medication in the "Barriers to Treament" section.

[5] Sadly, the cocaine-induced psychosis that developed from his heavy cocaine use resulted in a tragic motor vehicle crash that killed a young, newly married couple during a high-speed police chase (Pagliaro, Jaglalsingh, & Pagliaro, 1992).

[6] In the authors' clinical practice, which specializes in the treatment of dual-diagnosis patients, it has been noted that the vast majority of the patients themselves generally are unaware that they have a dual diagnosis. Generally, the dual diagnosis has not been diagnosed previously, and the patients are consciously aware only that they are depressed or that they have a drinking problem (i.e., the reason for their referral). They are not aware that they have two, and usually more, mental disorders and that these active disorders generally are highly interrelated (Pagliaro & Pagliaro, *Clinical Patient Data Files*).

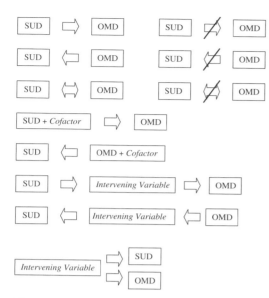

**Figure 8.2   Dual Diagnosis: Possible Relationships Between Substance Use Disorders (SUDs) and Other Mental Disorders (OMDs)**

When compared to adolescents and young adults who have a single SUD *or* mental disorder, adolescents and young adults who have both a SUD and an OMD generally will have: (1) a significantly more severe form of the related disorders; and (2) poorer prognosis in regard to therapeutic outcomes (Bell, 1985; Deas, 2006). In addition, these adolescents and young adults more often will present with other major and significant related health and social care requirements (Galanter, Egelko, Edwards, et al., 1994; Pagliaro & Pagliaro, *Clinical Patient Data Files*), including increased rates of:

- Academic difficulties (e.g., absenteeism, dropping out of or not completing high school; low academic performance) (Also see Chapter 6, *Effects of Drugs and Substances of Abuse on Learning and Memory During Childhood and Adolescence*.)
- Arrest and incarceration
- Difficulty making friends (i.e., poor interpersonal relationships)
- Job loss and unemployment

- Homelessness and reliance on social assistance
- Hospitalization or institutionalization
- Medical disorders (e.g., hepatitis; pregnancy among girls; tuberculosis)
- Noncompliance or poor compliance with prescribed pharmacotherapy and other treatment interventions (e.g., family therapy; group therapy; individual psychotherapy)
- Poor response or no response to treatment interventions
- Recidivism, or relapse
- Suicide, attempted or completed

Also, these adolescents and young adults often display increasingly high-risk behaviors for human immunodeficiency virus (HIV) infection (e.g., unprotected sex with multiple partners; sharing contaminated needles and syringes) (Eisen, Youngman, Grob, et al., 1992; Goldbloom, 1993; Kaminer, Goldberg & Connor, 2010; Niethammer & Frank, 2007). In this regard, the need for the designation of a *tridiagnosis*—a dual diagnosis with the addition of a diagnosis of HIV infection (Pagliaro, 1991)—has become increasingly recognized, particularly in regard to bisexual and gay adolescent boys and young adult men and runaway and homeless adolescents who often live on the streets (Fisher, 1991; Irwin, Edlin, Wong, et al., 1995; Silberstein, Galanter, Marmor, et al., 1994; Slesnick & Prestopnik, 2005). These adolescents have an extremely high incidence of dual diagnosis; reportedly it is between 60% (Slesnick & Prestopnik, 2005) and 90% (Pagliaro & Pagliaro, *Clinical Patient Data Files*; Unger, Kipke, Simon, et al., 1997). (See the later section in this chapter, "Tridiagnosis Among Adolescents: SUDs and OMDs and HIV.")

## DUAL DIAGNOSES AMONG ADOLESCENTS AND YOUNG ADULTS

Adolescents and young adults can present with any number of possible dual diagnoses. In fact, there seems to be an unending number

**TABLE 8.1   Categories of Mental Disorders Most Frequently Associated with Dual Diagnosis Among Adolescents and Young Adults**

| Category | Specific Mental Disorders |
|---|---|
| 1 | Disorders usually first diagnosed in infancy, childhood, or adolescence (e.g., attention-deficit hyperactivity disorder [A-D/HD]; conduct disorder [CD]; oppositional defiant disorder [ODD]) |
| 2 | Anxiety disorders (e.g., panic disorder [PD]; posttraumatic stress disorder [PTSD]) |
| 3 | Mood disorders (e.g., bipolar disorder [BD]; major depressive disorder [MDD]) |
| 4 | Personality disorders (e.g., borderline personality disorder [BPD]) |
| 5 | Psychotic disorders (e.g., schizophrenia) |
| 6 | Sexual or gender identity disorders |
| 7 | Sleep disorders (e.g., insomnia) |

Modified from: Fields, 1995; Gold & Slaby, 1991; Najavits, Weiss, & Shaw, 1997; Pagliaro & Pagliaro, 1996, 2000.

of combinations and permutations of SUDs and OMDs. As noted over two decades ago by Stowell (1991): "Dual diagnosis patients are [generally] heterogeneous as to their psychiatric diagnoses, as well as the various substances they abuse" (p. 98). However, a review of the published literature suggests that the majority of cases of dual diagnosis among adolescents and young adults involve one or more SUDs related to the use of alcohol, amphetamines, cannabis, cocaine, or nicotine and one or more OMDs from seven categories (see Table 8.1), which are discussed in the following sections.

## Dual Diagnosis: SUDs and Mental Disorders Usually First Diagnosed in Infancy, Childhood, or Adolescence

This section discusses dual diagnoses that include a SUD along with another mental disorder that is usually first identified in infancy,

childhood, or adolescence. Of these mental disorders, the ones that are implicated most frequently with a dual diagnosis are A-D/HD, CD, and ODD.[7] Interestingly, all three of these mental disorders involve marked externalizing behaviors and generally are diagnosed prior to the development of a SUD, which usually tends to be diagnosed during late adolescence or early adulthood.

### SUDs and Attention-Deficit/ Hyperactivity Disorder

Worldwide, including the United States, the incidence of A-D/HD is approximately 8%, or 1 in 13 children (Dopheide & Pliszka, 2009; Mayes, Bagwell, & Erkulwater, 2008). Several studies (e.g., Biederman, Wilens, Mick, et al., 1995, 1998; Bukstein, 2008; Clure, Brady, Saladin, et al., 1999; Levin, Evans, & Kleber, 1998; Shrier, Harris, Kurland, et al., 2003; Wilens, 2004) have found that the co-occurrence of SUDs among adolescents and young adults with A-D/HD is several times higher than among matched cohorts or the general population. For example, Wilens and Upadhyaya (2007) reported that adolescents with A-D/HD are twice as likely to smoke tobacco cigarettes. Other researchers (e.g., Modesto-Lowe, Danforth, Neering, et al., 2010) have supported this finding and, further, have found that children with A-D/HD are at significantly increased risk for early tobacco smoking during adolescence.[8] In addition, McClernon and Kollins (2008) suggested that the dual diagnosis involving A-D/HD and tobacco smoking is predicated on a genetic aberration among these adolescents and young adults that affects the regulation of the dopaminergic and nicotinic-acetylcholinergic receptor function. (See related discussion of the mechanism

---

[7] Thus, although mental retardation also is associated with a significant incidence of SUDs among adolescents and young adults (McGillicuddy, 2006; Miller, Belkin, & Gibbons, 1994; Slayter, 2010), the associated dual diagnoses are not as frequently encountered as those involving A-D/HD, CD, or ODD.

[8] This risk can be expected to further increase if the A-D/HD is left untreated—perhaps signifying that tobacco smoking is an attempt to self-medicate the A-D/HD, a condition that usually is medically managed with prescription psychostimulants (e.g., mixed amphetamines [Adderall®]).

of action for nicotine in Chapter 2, *The Psychostimulants*).

A-D/HD among adolescents and young adults also has been implicated in the development of SUDs involving the use of alcohol (i.e., alcohol use disorders [AUDs]). For example, both the incidence of adolescent drunkenness and binge drinking (i.e., consuming 5 or more drinks at one sitting for adolescent boys and young men) are significantly higher for adolescents who have A-D/HD (Molina & Pelham, 2003; Molina, Pelham, Gnagy, et al., 2007). Studies also have found that the association of A-D/HD with a SUD is particularly significant among boys (e.g., Milberger, Biederman, Faraone, et al., 1997), which is not surprising, given the approximately 10-fold overrepresentation of boys over girls with A-D/HD. In these and other cases, the A-D/HD is noted to precede the development of the SUD (Bukstein, 2008).

Marshal and Molina (2006) have suggested that children with A-D/HD and either CD or ODD (i.e., comorbid antisocial behavior—see the next section)[9] are at significant risk for developing a peer-mediated SUD during adolescence. Arias, Gelernter, Chan, et al. (2008) suggested that the impulsivity associated with A-D/HD underlies its correlation with SUDs and their increased severity and associated sequelae (e.g., hospitalizations; suicide attempts).[10] (Also see the discussion of A-D/HD in Chapter 6, *The Effects of Drugs and Substances of Abuse on Learning and Memory During Childhood and Adolescence*) In addition, the significant association between A-D/HD and SUDs has increased concern regarding the diversion and illicit use, particularly among adolescent boys, of the psychostimulants that are medically prescribed to adolescents and young adults for the medical management of

A-D/HD, including the mixed amphetamines (Adderall®) and methylphenidate (Ritalin®) (Bukstein, 2008; Pagliaro & Pagliaro, 2009; Upadhyaya, 2007; Wilens, Adler, Adams, et al., 2008; Wilens & Fusillo, 2007). (Also see related discussion in Chapter 2, *The Psychostimulants*.) Dual diagnosis involving adolescents with A-D/HD also have been related to CD and ODD as well. See the next discussion.

### SUDs and Conduct Disorder

CD appears to be more commonly associated with a SUD among adolescents than are most of the other mental disorders, including MDD (Armstrong & Costello, 2002) (Slesnick & Prestopnik, 2005). A positive parental history of a SUD is significantly correlated with a childhood diagnosis of CD—most likely because of both genetic and environmental factors (e.g., parenting styles; Button, Hewitt, Rhee, et al., 2006; Haber, Jacob, & Heath, 2005; Kramer, Han, Leukefeld, et al., 2009). CD also is significantly more common among boys than girls (Kramer, Han, Leukefeld, et al., 2009; Shrier, Harris, Kurland, et al., 2003).

Quite often, children who are diagnosed with CD also have been diagnosed with A-D/HD prior to the development and diagnosis of a SUD during adolescence or early adulthood (e.g., Burke, Loeber, & Lahey, 2001; Molina, Pelham, Gnagy, et al., 2007). For example, Modesto-Lowe, Danforth, Neering, et al. (2010) found that children with A-D/HD and CD were significantly more likely to develop increasingly harmful patterns of tobacco use during adolescence than were children who did not have A-D/HD and CD or who had only one of these mental disorders. Marshal and Molina (2006) have suggested that a dual diagnosis involving CD may be mediated among adolescents with childhood A-D/HD by the factor of deviant

---

[9] Several studies (e.g., Dopfner, Breuer, Wille, et al., 2008; Lynskey & Fergusson, 1995) have reported an increased risk for both aggressive and antisocial behavior among adolescents with A-D/HD.

[10] Several clinicians and researchers (e.g., Furman, 2005) view A-D/HD as a grouping of neurobehavioral signs and symptoms (e.g., hyperactivity; impulsivity; inattentiveness) that have diverse etiologies and are related to several different neurological or mental conditions rather than as a specific single mental disorder.

peer affiliation (i.e., children and adolescents with A-D/HD and comorbid CD or ODD are at significantly increased risk for developing a peer-mediated SUD during adolescence).

In an earlier study of runaway youth living in youth shelters, Slesnick and Prestopnik (2005) found that a CD-related dual diagnosis usually accompanied two or more SUDs, with 15% of their participants being identified as having 1 SUD, 27% having 2 SUDs, and 38% having 3 SUDs. The number of SUDs that were identified as co-occurring with a diagnosis of CD among the runaway youth who participated in this study quite likely reflects their poly-use of the drugs and substances of abuse. (See Chapter 1, *The Psychodepressants*, Chapter 2, *The Psychostimulants*, and Chapter 3, *The Psychodelics*, for related discussion.)

A diagnosis of CD made during childhood often precedes a diagnosis of a SUD made during adolescence (Brook, Whiteman, Cohen, et al., 1995; White, Xie, Thompson, et al., 2001; Windle, 1990) with the resultant SUD tending to be more severe than usual (Fergusson, Horwood, & Ridder, 2005; Nock, Kazdin, Hiripi, et al., 2006). In these cases, adolescents may receive a subsequent diagnosis of antisocial personality disorder (APD) during late adolescence or early adulthood (Brown, Gleghorn, Schuckit, et al., 1996). (Also see the sections on SUDs and Antisocial Personality Disorder; SUDs and Major Depressive Disorder; SUDs and Oppositional Defiant Disorder.)

### SUDs and Oppositional Defiant Disorder

The combination of a SUD with ODD is another common dual diagnosis identified among adolescents (Armstrong & Costello, 2002). Many of the adolescents in this category also have a diagnosis of comorbid A-D/HD, which, according to Marshal and Molina (2006), may be mediated through deviant peer affiliation. Not surprisingly, a dual diagnosis

involving ODD and a SUD among boys during middle childhood has been highly correlated with delinquent behavior (Loeber, Stouthamer-Loeber, & White, 1999).

### Dual Diagnosis: SUDs and Anxiety Disorders

A dual diagnosis involving an anxiety disorder and a SUD is relatively common among North Americans (Grant, Stinson, Dawson, et al., 2004). This dual diagnosis often is associated with a "history of repetitive childhood physical and/or sexual assault" (p. 807) that tends to be chronic, or long-term. The chronic traumatic nature of this pattern of physical and sexual abuse gives rise to several types of anxiety disorders among adolescents, particularly girls, including PD and PTSD (Clark, Pollock, Bukstein, et al., 1997; Pagliaro & Pagliaro, *Clinical Patient Data Files*; Shrier, Harris, Kurland, et al., 2003). Particular sensitivity should be used for these adolescents in selecting initial therapeutic interventions. In this context, the provision of gender-specific treatment options may significantly decrease an adolescent's anxiety and thus facilitate his or her group involvement and participation in the therapeutic process of recovery. (Also see the section "SUDs and Sexual or Gender Identity Disorders" for further related discussion.) In addition, adequate and appropriate attention must be given to the increased risk for suicide among these adolescents (Makhija, 2007). (For related discussion, see the section "SUDs and Major Depressive Disorder.")

### SUDs and Panic Disorder

Panic disorder, as well as individual panic attacks, can occur among adolescents and young adults in the context of a dual diagnosis (e.g., Goodwin, Lieb, Hoefler, et al., 2004; Wittchen & Essau, 1993).[11] In fact, several different drugs and substances of abuse have

---

[11] We recognize that, according to *DSM* criteria, a panic disorder must not be due to the direct pharmacologic effect of a drug or substance of abuse. However, we do not follow this diagnostic criteria for PD in this chapter.

been associated with PD in the formulation of a dual diagnosis. These drugs and substances of abuse include:

- Alcohol (Hirschfeld, 1996)
- Benzodiazepines (Cowley, 1992; Deacon & Valentiner, 2000)
- Cannabis (Wittchen & Essau, 1993; Wittchen, Frohlich, Behrendt, et al., 2007; Zvolensky, Bernstein, Marshall, et al., 2006; Zvolensky, Lewinsohn, Bernstein, et al., 2008)
- Cocaine (Anthony, Tien, & Petronis, 1989; O'Brien, Wu, & Anthony, 2005; Sareen, Chartier, Paulus, et al., 2006)
- Methylenedioxymethamphetamine (MDMA, ecstasy) (Keyes, Martins, & Hasin, 2008)
- Nicotine (tobacco use) (Breslau & Klein, 1999; Grant, Hasin, Chou, et al., 2004; Zvolensky, Feldner, Leen-Feldner, et al., 2005)
- Opiate-analgesics (Becker, Sullivan, Tetrault, et al., 2008)

As in the case of other dual diagnoses, the relationship between PD and the particular drug or substance of abuse can be varied. (See Figure 8.2.) The major three identified relationships appear to be: (1) panic attacks associated with the acute withdrawal from a particular drug or substance of abuse, including alcohol (Cowley, 1992) and nicotine (Weinberger, Maciejewski, McKee, et al., 2009); (2) PD or panic attacks caused by the use of a particular drug or substance of abuse, such as cannabis (Dannon, Lowengrub, Amiaz, et al., 2004), cocaine (Cox, Norton, Swinson, et al., 1990), or MDMA (Keyes, Martins, & Hasin, 2008); and (3) the use of a drug or substance of abuse for the symptomatic management, or self-medication, of PD or a panic attack,

particularly alcohol (Cox, Norton, Swinson, et al., 1990; Cowley, 1992), the benzodiazepines (Deacon & Valentiner, 2000; Valentiner, Mounts, & Deacon, 2004), and the opiate analgesics (Valentiner, Mounts, & Deacon, 2004). Note that some drugs and substances of abuse (e.g., alcohol) can be related to PD or panic attacks in several different ways. In addition, the PD and the SUD may be independently related to another factor or cofactor, as, for example, medical conditions or procedures, including induced abortion (Coleman, Coyle, Shuping, et al., 2009).

### SUDs and Posttraumatic Stress Disorder

PTSD is another mental disorder that frequently is implicated with a SUD as a dual diagnosis (Eggleston, Calhoun, Svikis, et al., 2009). The most common cause of PTSD among adolescents is childhood trauma generally related to long-term, or chronic, physical and/or sexual abuse (Najavits, Weiss, & Shaw, 1997; Ouimette, Wolfe, & Chrestman, 1996; Triffleman, Marmar, Delucchi, et al., 1995). (See "SUDs and Sexual or Gender Identity Disorders" section for related discussion.) When the perpetrator of the chronic physical or sexual abuse is found to be a parent (or legal guardian), it is also common to find that the parent uses various drugs and substances of abuse, including, primarily, alcohol, cannabis, cocaine, or methamphetamine (Dunlap, Golub, Johnson, et al., 2009; Pagliaro & Pagliaro, *Clinical Patient Data Files*; Wells, 2009).

Another common cause of PTSD among adolescents, which also may have begun during childhood, is bullying at school[12] (Chiodo, Wolfe, Crooks, et al., 2009; Pagliaro & Pagliaro, *Clinical Patient Data Files*; Tharp-Taylor,

---

[12] Whether bullying involves being beaten-up or forced to engage in unwanted sexual acts, children and adolescents often resort to several measures to avoid their contact with bullies. These measures include feigning illness in order to miss school, running away from home, or—in the most extreme situations—both attempting and completing suicide, particularly among students who, prior to bullying, both enjoyed and had done well in school (Pagliaro & Pagliaro, *Clinical Patient Data Files*).

Haviland, & D'Amico, 2009). As found by Eaton, Kann, Kinchen, et al. (2010) in their analysis of nationwide data from the Youth Risk Behavior Surveillance System, 19.9% of the students in their survey had been bullied on school property during the 12 months prior to the survey. They also found that 26% of 9th-grade adolescent girls of European descent had experienced bullying—the overall highest rate of bullying found in the survey.

The mental effects of bullying on victims appear to be the same regardless of whether the bullying consisted predominantly of physical abuse (e.g., getting beaten up; having lunch money stolen everyday), which is more often encountered among boys, or psychosocial abuse (e.g., being called names; being excluded from popular groups or clubs), which is more often encountered among girls. A major form of bullying that commonly occurs among adolescents is cyberbullying. Cyberbullying includes abusive text messaging or posting pictures or video clips depicting fights with the victim or the victim performing personal activities (e.g., dressing or undressing; bathing; performing sexual acts) that were obtained, generally without the victim's knowledge or consent, and widely shared over the Internet via popular social networking Web sites (e.g., Bebo, Facebook, Friendster, MySpace, and YouTube).

Another major cause of PTSD among adolescents that may presage a SUD is the witnessing of major natural disasters (e.g., the BP oil spill in the Gulf of Mexico during 2010; Hurricane Katrina, August 28, 2005) and other terrifying situations (e.g., school shootings; terrorist bombings at popular tourist destinations; youth gang violence that is common on the streets in major North American cities and those along the border states) (Pagliaro & Pagliaro,

*Clinical Patient Data Files*; Wagner, Brief, Vielhauer, et al., 2009; Weems, Taylor, Cannon, et al., 2010).

Adolescents who are diagnosed with PTSD reportedly are 3 to 5 times more likely to develop a SUD than are those who have not been diagnosed with PTSD (Chilcoat & Breslau, 1998; Ouimette & Brown, 2003; Reed, Anthony, & Breslau, 2007). Mechanistically, many agree that the associated use of the drugs and substances of abuse often begins as an attempt to ameliorate or assuage the fear, nightmares, pain, and negative emotions (e.g., feelings of shame related to sexual abuse) associated with PTSD (Khantzian, 1997; Ouimette & Brown, 2003; Pagliaro & Pagliaro, *Clinical Patient Data Files*; Reed, Anthony, & Breslau, 2007).[13] As noted by Brady, Killeen, Brewerton, et al. (2000), this situation lends itself to becoming a vicious cycle because acute withdrawal from the drugs and substances of abuse tends to exacerbate the signs and symptoms that their use was meant to assuage.

## Dual Diagnoses: SUDs and Mood Disorders

Similar to anxiety disorders, mood disorders frequently are involved in dual diagnosis among North Americans (Grant, Stinson, Dawson, et al., 2004). For example, in their study of hospitalized adolescents with an AUD, Clark, Bukstein, Smith, et al. (1995) found that mood disorders occurred more commonly among this group, as did anxiety disorders. This section considers SUDs that commonly co-occur during adolescence with mood disorders, particularly bipolar disorder (BD) and major depressive disorder (MDD).

---

[13] Interestingly, adolescents who are exposed to PTSD-level traumas and do not succumb or otherwise develop criteria for a diagnosis of PTSD do not have an increased risk for the subsequent development of a SUD (Breslau, 2002; Breslau, Davis, & Schultz, 2003; Chilcoat & Breslau, 1998). Perhaps, as reflective of existential philosophy, and first expressed by Ernest Hemmingway (1899–1961) in his classic, *A Farewell to Arms* (1929), these survivors become "stronger at the broken places."

### SUDs and Bipolar Disorder

BD has been found to commonly occur with SUDs as a dual diagnosis among adolescents (Simkin, 2002; Wilens, Biederman, Millstein, et al., 1999).[14] In addition, adolescent-onset BD appears to be associated with a significantly higher risk for the subsequent development of a SUD than does child-onset BD (Wilens, Biederman, Kwon, et al., 2004; Wilens, Biederman, Millstein, et al., 1999). The directionality, or order, of the occurrence of a BD and a SUD remains uncertain (Krishnan, 2005)—in some case reports and studies, the BD precedes the SUD; in others, its follows. (See Figure 8.2.) However, for the vast majority of cases involving adolescents, BD appears to usually precede the development of a SUD (Goldstein & Bukstein, 2010).

A dual diagnosis involving a SUD and BD is of particular concern for adolescents because of its association with "legal and academic difficulties, pregnancy, and suicidality" (Goldstein & Bukstein, 2010, p. 348). Although an anxiety disorder frequently accompanies BD among adolescents, the anxiety disorder often is unrecognized and undiagnosed (Birmaher, Kennah, Brent, et al., 2002; Masi, Toni, Perugi, et al., 2001). BD among adolescents also has been associated with PTSD, which, in turn, also has been associated with SUDs (Steinbuchel, Wilens, Adamson, et al., 2009). (See "SUDs and Anxiety Disorders" section for related discussion.)

### SUDs and Major Depressive Disorder

Of all of the mood disorders, MDD is the most common mental disorder that co-occurs with SUDs (Burke, Burke, & Rae, 1994; Coryell, 1991; Marmorstein, 2010; Rao, 2006; Stowell & Estroff, 1992). This particular dual diagnosis is more common among adolescent girls and young women than it is among adolescent boys and young men (Bukstein, Glancy, & Kaminer, 1992; Clark, Pollock, Bukstein, et al., 1997; Latimer, Stone, Voight, et al., 2002; Shrier, Harris, Kurland, et al., 2003; Whitmore, Mikulich, Thompson, et al., 1997). However, another population group that requires attention is homeless or runaway adolescents with MDD who are particularly at risk for infection with HIV and resultant acquired immune deficiency syndrome (AIDS). Of particular concern, is the observation that these adolescents do not appear to view AIDS as a serious threat or concern. As found by Kaliski, Rubinson, Lawrence, et al. (1990): "If they get AIDS they would die and that would put an end to their worry and struggle" (p. 60). (Also see the "Tridiagnosis Among Adolescents: SUDs and OMDs and HIV" section later in this chapter.)

**Alcohol and Depression**   Genetic factors have been cited as a major contributing factor to the comorbidity between alcoholism and MDD. As noted by Nurnberger, Foroud, Flury, et al. (2002): "This combination of alcoholism and depression tends to run in families" (p. 233). Reporting on data obtained from the National Epidemiologic Survey on Alcoholism and related Conditions, which comprises a sample of over 43,000 U.S. citizens 18 years of age or older, Hasin, Goodwin, Stinson, et al. (2005) found lifetime estimates of MDD to be approximately 13% and 12-month estimates to be approximately 5%. Among adolescents and young adults, MDD has a long association with SUDs, particularly those involving alcohol and the other psychodepressants (see Chapter 1, *The Psychodepressants*) and the psychostimulants cocaine and nicotine (see Chapter 2, *The Psychostimulants*). Of some particular concern is the observation that the reported incidence of MDD has increased significantly from 1980 to 2010.

---

[14] It is estimated that about half of the children and adults who have BD also "have an alcohol abuse problem at some point of their lifetime" (Azorin, Bowden, Garay, et al., 2010, p. 37).

As with other mental disorders, MDD can exist as either an antecedent or consequence of a SUD, particularly one that involves the use of any of the psychodepressants. (See Table 8.2)[15, 16] As noted by Greenbaum, Prange, Friedman, et al. (1991):

> Among the dually diagnosed, controversy exists as to whether substance abuse is a symptom of an underlying mental health problem or, conversely, whether the mental health problem is symptomatic of alcohol or drug use. (p. 582)

Suggested reasons for a consequential association between a SUD and another mental disorder (e.g., depression), include: "physiological symptoms of withdrawal, the apathy of the alcoholic personality, the state of chronic intoxication, and concomitant drug use" (Slaby, 1991, p. 3). In this regard, it is important to note that the principal direct pharmacologic effect of alcohol, and the other sedative-hypnotics, is depression of the CNS (Pagliaro, 1995a; Pagliaro & Pagliaro, 1998, 2009).

Several reasons also have been suggested for an antecedent association. For example, children whose parents have alcoholism have been identified as having a proclivity for developing signs and symptoms of depression. As noted by Perez-Bouchard, Johnson, and Ahrens (1993):

> The dysfunctional family environment that often results from alcoholism or other substance abuse fosters a depressogenic attributional style...that can be a risk factor for future depression. (p. 476)

In addition, among adolescents and young adults who have not yet been diagnosed as being depressed, a tendency to self-medicate with alcohol is commonly observed as an attempt to temporarily diminish the distressing features, including the signs and symptoms of depression (Slaby, 1991): As described by Boyle and Offord (1991): "The risks for drug and alcohol abuse are high among young adults experiencing depression or anxiety who are not undergoing treatment" (p. 699). Or, as identified by Burke, Burke, and Rae (1994): "Age at onset for drug abuse and dependence...appears to peak in the age interval of 15 to 19 if there is a pre-existing mood or anxiety disorder" (p. 454).

In any event, a large prospective study by Crum, Green, Storr, et al. (2008) that followed over 2,300 students from the 1st grade through high school found, for children and adolescents who drank alcohol, that:

> A high level of childhood depressed mood was associated with an earlier onset and increased risk of alcohol intoxication, alcohol-related problems during late childhood and early adolescence, and development of *DSM-IV* alcohol dependence in young adulthood. (p. 702)

The largest study to date aimed at disentangling the relationship between alcohol problems and depressive symptoms among adolescents was conducted by Marmorstein (2009). Participants for this study were drawn from the National Longitudinal Study of Adolescent Health using a sample of over 20,000 adolescents. As reported by Marmorstein:

> The results of this study indicate that alcohol-use-related problems and depressive symptoms have reciprocal, positive effects on each other during the period from early adolescence through early adulthood; however, these effects differ somewhat by gender and age. Overall, higher levels of depressive symptoms were associated with higher initial levels of alcohol problems (particularly among females), as well as faster increases in alcohol problems over time among males. Reciprocally, high levels of alcohol problems were associated with higher initial levels of depressive symptoms (particularly among females). (p. 49)

---

[15] Of the drugs and substances of abuse listed in Table 8.2, alcohol and the other sedative-hypnotics (e.g., benzodiazepines) are the most prominently involved in MDD. Alcohol and the benzodiazepines also happen to be the sedative-hypnotics that are most commonly abused by adolescents. (See Chapter 1, *The Psychodepressants.*)

[16] MDD also can occur together with an AUD as the result of a shared, underlying *cofactor* (Hasin, Stinson, Ogburn, et al., 2007; see Figure 8.2).

**TABLE 8.2  Drugs and Substances of Abuse: Low, Medium, or High Propensity for Inducing Mental Disorders Among[a] Adolescents**

| Mental Disorders | Drugs and Substances of Abuse[a] | | | | | | | |
|---|---|---|---|---|---|---|---|---|
| | ALCOHOL AND OTHER SEDATIVE-HYPNOTICS | OPIATE ANALGESICS | VOLATILE SOLVENTS AND INHALANTS | AMPHETAMINES | CAFFEINE | COCAINE | NICOTINE (TOBACCO) | PSYCHODELICS |
| AMNESTIC[b] | HIGH | | LOW | | | | | LOW |
| ANXIETY | LOW | | | MEDIUM | LOW | MEDIUM | | LOW |
| MOOD | MEDIUM/HIGH | LOW | | | | | | |
| PSYCHOTIC | LOW | | LOW | MEDIUM | | MEDIUM | | HIGH |
| SLEEP | LOW | LOW | LOW | HIGH | MEDIUM | HIGH | LOW | |

[a] Mental disorders other than SUDs.

[b] Also see related discussion in Chapter 6, *Effects of the Drugs and Substances of Abuse on Learning and Memory During Childhood and Adolescence.*

**Alcohol and Suicide**   Regardless of the nature of the association between alcohol use and depression (i.e., as antecedent or consequence), of particular concern is the fact that this combination of an SUD and OMD is all too frequently accompanied by suicide attempts and completed suicide (Grant, Stinson, Dawson, et al., 2004; Makhija, 2007; Makhija & Sher, 2007; Pagliaro, 1995a; Pompili, Serafini, Innamorati, et al., 2010; Runeson & Rich, 1992; Ward, 1992), particularly when AUDs are involved (Carballo, Bird, Giner, et al., 2007; Galaif, Sussman, Newcomb, et al., 2007; Makhija & Sher, 2006; Sher, 2007). As noted by Sher and Zalsman (2005), approximately 2,000 adolescents die annually in the United States as a result of suicide. In a national survey of youth risk behavior, Eaton, Kann, Kinchen, et al. (2010) found that 6.3% of U.S. students had attempted suicide on one or more occasions during the 12 months prior to the survey.

As suggested by Sher, Sperling, Stanley, et al. (2007), suicide attempts and completed suicide are probably due to both the impaired control of aggression and increased impulsivity that is mediated by the use of alcohol. As noted by Berman and Schwartz (1990): "It is generally agreed that there is a progressive increase in depressive mood from abstainer to substance user and a corresponding increase in suicide attempts among adolescents with depression, substance abuse, or both" (p. 310). This observation also is supported by Runeson and Rich (1992), who noted that, "depressive and substance use disorders predominate in the psychopathological backgrounds of suicides of all ages. In five published studies of consecutive suicides by adolescents and young adults, the average reported rates are 41% for major depression and 48% for substance abuse" (p. 197). Accordingly, Quinnett (1995) noted: "The most dangerous combination of risk factors [for suicide] for people of any age is untreated depression combined with substance abuse and addiction" (p. 65).

This observation has been supported by several researchers, including Ganz and Sher (2009), who reported that a concomitant, or comorbid, relationship for alcohol abuse, depression, and suicide could be found in almost three-quarters (i.e., 73%) of adolescents with any of these disorders. As previously noted by Marmorstein (2009) in regard to the relationship between problems related to alcohol use and depressive symptoms, a reciprocal relationship probably also exists in this context involving suicide (i.e., in some cases, signs and symptoms of depression lead to self-medication with alcohol, which together lead to suicide; in other cases, alcohol use leads to depression, which together lead to suicide).

**Cannabis and Depression**   The effects of cannabis on mood (e.g., causing or exacerbating depression) appear to be mediated by the effects of the endocannabinoid system on the neurotransmitters, particularly serotonin (Cannabis damages, 2009). (Also see the "Proposed Mechanism of Psychedelic Action" section for cannabis in Chapter 3, *The Psychodelics.*) Several studies and reports (e.g., Herbal remedy, 2009; Teen "self-medication," 2008) have found that a significant number of adolescents—perhaps up to one-third—use cannabis to self-medicate a variety of disorders, including depression. However, the use of cannabis can exacerbate depression and also can significantly increase suicidal thoughts and suicide attempts. Combination pharmacotherapy (e.g., fluoxetine [Prozac®]) and behavioral therapy have been demonstrated to be an effective intervention for this dual diagnosis (Behavior therapy plus, 2007).

**Cocaine and Depression**   Adolescents and young adults who are depressed and have not yet been diagnosed or otherwise treated for depression often use cocaine as a means to self-medicate their depression (Pagliaro, Jaglalsingh, & Pagliaro, 1992; Weiss, Griffin, & Mirin, 1992).

**Nicotine and Depression**   In their birth cohort longitudinal study, Fergusson, Lynskey, and Horwood (1996) noted that at 16 years of age, adolescents who had depressive disorders were twice as likely to also have nicotine dependence when compared to adolescents who did not have a depressive disorder. Although not yet demonstrated, it is quite likely that adolescents with depressive disorders employ nicotine at least partially as a means of self-medication for the management of their depression. However, as noted by Breslau, Kilbey, and Andreski (1993), other underlying variables may be involved:

> Neuroticism and the correlated psychologic vulnerabilities may commonly predispose to nicotine dependence *and* major depression or anxiety disorders. (p. 941)

In addition, some personality disorders, such as APD, are highly correlated with both the use of drugs and substances of abuse and depression (Coryell, 1991). The presence of these other covariables also helps to explain reported seemingly paradoxical findings, such as "smoking leads to depression" (Steuber & Danner, 2006).

### Problems Involving a Diagnosis of MDD

Unfortunately, because of the nature of the present health care system that tends to compartmentalize mental disorders (e.g., SUDs versus other mental disorders—see the Introduction for an overview of dual diagnosis, including common terms and definitions)—and, consequently, their treatment (for further discussion, see the "Treatment for Adolescents with Dual Diagnosis" section later in this chapter), all too often the concurrent depressive disorders are "misdiagnosed." Consider, for example, the sample of drug-using homicidal adolescents reported by Malmquist (1990):

> Impressive besides the past history connected with drug usage was the finding that only one of the 44 subjects was ever diagnosed as depressed before the acts that led to their being included in this study. The difficulty is partly explained by where they made contact, such as in a court probation system, a chemical dependency referral, a clinic, or a hospital unit. The few times depression was considered, it was viewed as secondary to the primary problem of chemical dependency. A related finding was that 10 of the males and three of the females had previously been through chemical dependency treatment programs. (p. 29)

## Dual Diagnosis: SUDs and Personality Disorders

People who are diagnosed with APD or BPD appear to be at a greater risk for dual diagnosis (Coryell, 1991; Fields, 1995; Norris & Extein, 1991; Slaby, 1991). Both of these personality disorders appear to have their onset during adolescence and include a proclivity for potentially self-damaging impulsive behavior, including bingeing with various drugs and substances of abuse.

### SUDs and Antisocial Personality Disorder—Conduct Disorder

According to *DSM*, APD is not appropriately diagnosed prior to 18 years of age. However, a very closely related and required antecedent to APD is CD. CD is rather commonly encountered among adolescents who have a dual diagnosis and often displays gender differences in regard to both incidence—being identified more commonly among boys than girls—and nature. In this regard, Mezzich, Moss, Tarter, et al. (1994) found that adolescent girls with a dual diagnosis that included CD were more likely than matched adolescent boys to: (1) experiment with nonprescription diet pills; (2) fulfill the criteria for nicotine dependence; (3) begin drinking alcohol at a later date; and (4) have a shorter time interval between the initial use of alcohol and a diagnosis of alcohol abuse or dependence. (Also see next section, "SUDs and Borderline Personality Disorder," and the "SUDs and Schizophrenia" section).

### SUDs and Borderline Personality Disorder

Andrulonis (1991) characterized a gender difference in relation to BPD and the use of the drugs and substances of abuse:

> The borderline female is often on a spectrum of affective disorders, whereas the borderline male more often overlaps with severe conduct disorders, sociopathy, drug addiction and alcoholism, the episodic dyscontrol syndrome,

or the attention deficit hyperactivity disorder with learning disabilities. (p. 23)

Of note is the observation that virtually every disorder or condition identified by Andrulonis in regard to BPD also has been associated with the harmful use of the drugs and substances of abuse (e.g., Boyle & Offord, 1991; Bukstein, Glancy, & Kaminer, 1992; Greenbaum, Prange, Friedman, et al., 1991; Pagliaro & Pagliaro, 2009). From a developmental perspective, Bates and Pandina (1991) identified that adolescent boys who were undergoing substantial personality changes (e.g., a previously extremely passive adolescent who, perhaps in response to long-term excessive bullying [see also earlier section, "SUDs and Post-Traumatic Stress Disorder"], resorts to extremely aggressive behavior) were more likely to experience higher levels of perceived stress in response to disruptive life problems and engage in more intensive use of alcohol and other drugs and substances of abuse than others who were not undergoing these changes.

## Dual Diagnosis: SUDs and Psychotic Disorders—Schizophrenia

Substance use disorders have been noted in several studies among a significant proportion of subjects diagnosed with schizophrenia (e.g., Soyka, Albus, Kathmann, et al., 1993; Thirthalli & Benegal, 2006; van Nimwegen, de Haan, van Beveren, et al., 2005, 2007; Winklbaur, Ebner, Sachs, et al., 2006). In addition, a number of drugs and substances of abuse commonly used by adolescents and young adults can pharmacologically cause, or mimic, psychotic disorders, including schizophrenia. These actions are usually transitory in nature, and they are most often associated with acute intoxication. (See Table 8.2.) For example, the psychostimulants (i.e., amphetamines, cocaine) and the psychodelics (e.g., cannabis; ketamine; LSD; phencyclidine [PCP]) may cause signs and symptoms of psychosis (i.e., delusions, hallucinations, disorganized speech, grossly disorganized or catatonic behavior)

that are virtually indistinguishable from those associated with acute schizophrenia (Pagliaro & Pagliaro, 2009). In fact, the psychodelics commonly have been referred to pharmacologically as psychotomimetics or psychotogens (i.e., drugs that mimic or cause psychosis) (Pagliaro & Pagliaro, 2004). (See related discussion in Chapter 3, *The Psychodelics*.) In addition, as noted by Potvin, Stip, and Roy (2003), several dissociative states (e.g., depersonalization; derealization) also can be caused by the use of alcohol or the opiate analgesics (see related discussion in Chapter 1, *The Psychodepressants*).

### SUDs and Schizophrenia

Schizophrenia, as the prototype psychotic disorder, has been identified as a co-occurring disorder involving several SUDs, including those related to the use of alcohol, amphetamines, caffeine, cannabis, cocaine, and nicotine (Green, Young, & Kavanagh, 2005; Margolese, Malchy, Negrete, et al., 2004; Pagliaro & Pagliaro, 2009; Winklbaur, Ebner, Sachs, et al., 2006). Although schizophrenia usually is first identified among affected people during early adulthood, with a worldwide incidence of approximately 1%, premorbid mental abnormalities (e.g., significant negatively skewed variance in relation to cognition, emotional and neurological maturation, and social competence) and prodromal manifestations (i.e., incipient psychosis) may occur during adolescence (Stowell & Estroff, 1992). In addition to depression and suicide, adolescents and young adults who have schizophrenia may be at a particularly high risk for SUDs and CD—all of which appear to be interrelated.

Among people with schizophrenia, the incidence of comorbid SUDs can be up to 3 times higher than that found for the general population (Green, 2005; Margolese, Malchy, Negrete, et al., 2004; Pagliaro & Pagliaro, 2009; Winklbaur, Ebner, Sachs, et al., 2006). As noted by Green and Brown (2006), the major concerns regarding the co-occurrence of a SUD and schizophrenia include complication of the therapy required for the appropriate management of each condition and poorer short- and long-term outcomes in the management of schizophrenia (e.g., significantly longer durations of hospitalization and a higher incidence of suicide attempts among people who had a dual diagnosis of a SUD and schizophrenia versus those who did not) (Dervaux, Laqueille, Bourdel, et al., 2003; Potvin, Stip, & Roy, 2003; Soyka, Albus, Kathmann, et al., 1993).

In this regard, it appears that many people who have schizophrenia use the drugs and substances of abuse as a means of self-medication in an attempt to decrease associated signs and symptoms, particularly negative symptoms (e.g., apathy, poor social functioning) (Krystal, D'Souza, Gallinat, et al., 2006; Potvin, Stip, & Roy, 2003). Although not universally accepted, this theory helps to explain, at least in part, the high incidence of SUDs diagnosed among people who have schizophrenia. In regard to a dual diagnosis involving a SUD and psychosis among adolescents, cannabis has been the drug or substance of abuse that has received the greatest amount of research attention—probably because it is the most commonly used illicit drug or substance of abuse by this age group.

### Cannabis and Schizophrenia

In their metareview of data published in 58 studies that examined the use of cannabis by participants with psychosis/schizophrenia, Green, Young, and Kavanagh (2005) found several significant summary statistics in regard to use: "current use (23.0%), current misuse (11.3%), 12-month use (29.2%), 12-month misuse (18.8%), lifetime use (42.1%), and lifetime misuse (22.5%)" (p. 306). Cannabis is the drug or substance of abuse that historically has the longest association with schizophrenia (Pagliaro &

Pagliaro, 2004, 2009). Consequently, the majority of data related to dual diagnoses involving SUDs and psychotic disorders involves cannabis. A review of these data revealed six distinct, but not mutually exclusive, relationships between the use of cannabis and the occurrence of psychotic disorders:

1. Among some *non*psychotic users, the use of cannabis can produce transient psychosis (i.e., positive, negative, and cognitive signs and symptoms of schizophrenia) (D'Souza, 2007; D'Souza, Sewell, & Ranganathan, 2009; Linszen & Amelsvoort, 2007; Verdoux & Tournier, 2004). These signs and symptoms are associated with acute cannabis intoxication with high dosages of delta-9-tetrahydrocannabinol (THC) and generally resolve immediately with the administration of an antipsychotic tranquilizer (e.g., haloperidol [Haldol®]) or on their own without intervention in a matter of days following the discontinuation of cannabis use (Pagliaro & Pagliaro, 2009).

2. Among users who have a predisposition to developing schizophrenia (i.e., *pre*-schizophrenic, or genetic vulnerability to developing schizophrenia),[17] the use of cannabis can produce true psychosis (Cannabis could increase, 2007; Daily pot smoking, 2009; Degenhardt & Hall, 2006; Di Forti, Morrison, Butt, et al., 2007; Fernandez-Espejo, Viveros, Nunez, et al., 2009; Hall & Degenhardt, 2008; Hall, Degenhardt & Teeson, 2004; Henquet, Di Forti, Morrison, et al., 2008; Le Bec, Fatseas, Denis, et al., 2009; Muller-Vahl & Emrich, 2008; Tucker, 2009; Verdoux & Tournier, 2004).[18] Risk appears to increase directly in relation

---

[17] This vulnerability can be suggested by a positive family history of schizophrenia and/or prodromal signs and symptoms (e.g., unusual sensory experiences).

[18] The particular relationship between cannabis use and schizophrenia begins with the heavy use of cannabis by adolescents who are genetically vulnerable, followed by the development of schizophrenia during early adulthood (Di Forti, Morrison, Butt, et al., 2007; Rubino & Parolaro, 2008). Adolescents appear to be particularly vulnerable in regard to these deleterious effects because the brain is in the process of completing neuronal maturation begun during the perinatal period (Pagliaro & Pagliaro, 2009; Schneider, 2008). (See related discussion in Chapter 5, *Exposure to the Drugs and Substances of Abuse From Conception Through Childhood*).

to the age of the individual at the time of initiating daily marijuana use and the duration of use (Daily pot smoking, 2009; Long-time cannabis use, 2010). In addition, a gender effect has been suggested—with risk being greater for females than males (Daily pot smoking, 2009).

3. Among users who have untreated, preexisting schizophrenia (i.e., those users who have schizophrenia but as yet have never been diagnosed with schizophrenia or who are currently in remission), the use of cannabis can trigger either a relapse or can exacerbate the latent schizophrenia with the associated resultant signs and symptoms persisting past the period of acute intoxication and, in some cases, indefinitely (D'Souza, 2007; D'Souza, Sewell, & Ranganathan, 2009; Hall, Degenhardt, & Teesson, 2004; van Os, Bak, Hanssen, et al., 2002).

4. Among users who have been diagnosed with schizophrenia and who are receiving treatment (i.e., antipsychotic pharmacotherapy), the use of cannabis is associated with increased rates of noncompliance with, or failure to follow, prescribed antipsychotic pharmacotherapy and consequently increased relapse (Hides, Dawe, Kavanagh, et al., 2006; Zammit, Moore, Lingford-Hughes, et al., 2008).[19]

5. Among some users who have been diagnosed with schizophrenia, the relationship is bidirectional. For example, in their prospective, longitudinal study of 229 patients with a diagnosis of schizophrenia, Foti, Kotov, Guey, et al. (2010) note that: (a) "lifetime rate of cannabis use" was directly associated with earlier onset of psychosis and cannabis use was also associated with an "adverse course of psychotic symptoms in schizophrenia" (p. 987) and (b) adverse psychotic symptoms were associated with an increase in cannabis use.

6. Among users who have active schizophrenia, the use of cannabis is directly related to the degree of personal distress experienced as a result of the psychotic disorder (i.e., the amount of cannabis used and its frequency of use would be reflected by the user's attempts to ameliorate distressing signs and symptoms of schizophrenia—as a form of self-medication) (Henquet, van Os, Kuepper, et al., 2010; Hides, Dawe, Kavanagh, et al. 2006).

These six relationships do not exhaust all possible relationships that can occur between the use of cannabis and schizophrenia. For example, as more is learned about the endogenous cannabinoid, or endocannabinoid, system—including its various components, actions on neurotransmitters and receptors, and genetic mediation—other, as-yet-unidentified factors and cofactors may be discovered that play significant roles in regard to cannabis use and the development of schizophrenia. In addition, as posited by Houston, Murphy, Adamson, et al. (2007), the relationship between cannabis use and schizophrenia may be mediated by one or more additional factors or cofactors. The additional factor identified in their study was childhood sexual abuse. When present, this factor resulted in an interaction effect that significantly increased the correlation between adolescent cannabis use and subsequent development of psychosis (Also see related discussion in the next section).

### Dual Diagnosis: SUDs and Sexual or Gender Identity Disorders

Under the classification of the sexual and gender identity disorders, we have also included physical and sexual abuse of children. Many adolescents (and adults) who have been

---

[19]Although the data presented by Zammit, Moore, Lingford-Hughes, et al. (2008) support this observation, they did not come to the same conclusion.

diagnosed with a SUD together with a gender identity disorder, particularly girls, have been the victims of mental,[20] physical, or sexual abuse during childhood (Castillo Mezzich, Tarter, Giancola, et al., 1997; Dunlap, Golub, & Johnson, 2003; Kendler, Bulik, Silberg, et al., 2000; Langeland & Hartgers, 1998; Miller & Downs, 1995; Nelson, Heath, Madden, et al., 2002). The U.S. Department of Health and Human Services (2006) has estimated that over 1 million children experienced significant abuse in the United States annually and that the related annual number of childhood deaths associated with abuse or neglect is approximately 1,500.

The abuse often is perpetrated by a trusted adult, including a parent or other family member, teacher, or coach. An adolescent girl also may have been victimized by an adult boyfriend. As noted by Bulik, Prescott, and Kendler (2001), child sexual abuse "tends to function more as a nonspecific risk factor that is associated with increased later risk for a range of psychiatric and substance use syndromes" (p. 448). The victims of childhood sexual abuse are often first diagnosed with MDD or PTSD, which is then followed by a diagnosis of a SUD (Cohen, Mannarino, Zhitova, et al., 2003; Hussey, Chang, & Kotch, 2006; Simpson & Miller, 2002). Perhaps not surprisingly, given the nature and extent of associated childhood suffering, related SUDs among adolescents (and adults) tend to be severe and to have a more morbid course, including a poorer long-term prognosis (Pagliaro & Pagliaro, *Clinical Patient Data Files*; Westermeyer, Wahmanholm, & Thuras, 2001). (Also see "SUDs and Major Depressive Disorder" and "SUDs and Posttraumautic Stress Disorder" sections for related discussion.)

Adolescents who have gender identity disorders also are at particular risk for SUDs (Bayatpour, Wells, & Holford, 1992; Gardner & Cabral, 1990; Harrison, Edwall, Hoffman, et al., 1990; Nelson, Heath, Lynskey, et al., 2006). In addition, gay and lesbian youth are at increased risk of SUDs, particularly those involving the use of alcohol (Hughes, 2005; Rosario, Schrimshaw, & Hunter, 2004), and for tridiagnosis (Blake, Ledsky, Lehman, et al., 2001). (See later section, "Tridiagnosis: SUDs, OMDs, and HIV.") Histories of childhood sexual abuse, depression, and family rejection are significant among these adolescents and appear to play a major role in regard to the development of SUDs (Cochran, Mays, Alegria, et al., 2007; Hughes, 2003; Padilla, Crisp, & Rew, 2010; Ryan, Huebner, Diaz, et al., 2009) (see Table 8.3). (Also see "SUDs and Major Depressive Disorders" and "SUDs and Posttraumatic Stress Disorder" sections for related discussion.)

## Dual Diagnosis: SUDs and Sleep Disorders—Insomnia

Both sleep disorders and dual diagnosis commonly occur among adolescents (Gromov & Gromov, 2009; Shibley, Malcolm, & Veatch, 2008). Insomnia has been the primary sleep disorder associated with dual diagnosis among adolescents. However, because of the often concealed nature of the relationship between SUDs and insomnia, significantly less data are available than for the other more common dual diagnoses discussed in this chapter. This concealment is due to several nonexclusive factors, including: (1) the generally low level of attention given to diagnosing sleep disorders among adolescents; (2) the interpretation, or classification, of insomnia as a symptom of another disorder rather than a primary disorder in its own right; and (3) the occurrence of insomnia in association with (in the context of) other categories of mental disorders, particularly anxiety disorders and mood disorders. The underdiagnosis

---

[20] Mental abuse, in this particular context, also includes family rejection of adolescents who are gay or lesbian (Ryan, Huebner, Diaz, et al., 2009). Pederson, Vanhorn, Wilson, et al. (2008), adding "emotional childhood abuse" to this construct, found a significant correlation with later benzodiazepine, cannabis, cocaine, and nicotine use among gay and lesbian adolescents.

**TABLE 8.3 Possible Relationships Among the Use of Drugs and Substances of Abuse, SUDs, and Sexual or Gender Identity Disorders**

1. Sexual or gender identify disorders may be directly related to the pharmacological effect(s) of the drugs and substances of abuse.

2. Stress may independently lead to both sexual or gender identity disorders and the use of drugs or substances of abuse.

3. Drugs and substances of abuse may be used to facilitate sexual behavior or performance.

4. Drugs and substances of abuse may be used to cope or deal with inadequate or undesirable sexual behavior or performance (e.g., to self-medicate sexual and gender identity disorders or feelings related to childhood or adult sexual victimization).

5. Cognitive impairment, including the impairment of higher level cognitive functioning (e.g., reasoning) that is associated with mental disorders (e.g., schizophrenia), may independently lead to substance use and sexual disorders.

6. The use of the drugs and substances of abuse may result from the pattern of socialization required to meet sexual partners (e.g., adolescent boys or girls seeking homosexual or lesbian sex at gay or lesbian bars or clubs).

7. Sexual behavior may be used in order to obtain drugs and substances of abuse or the money necessary to purchase drugs and substances of abuse (e.g., adolescent girls engaging in sex at crack houses in order to obtain crack cocaine).

Modified from: Harrison, Edwall, Hoffman, et al., 1990; Pagliaro, 1995b; Pagliaro & Pagliaro, 2009; Slaby, 1991.

of insomnia among adolescents (Roehrs & Roth, 2008) contributes to both points 2 and 3.[21] In addition, many clinicians do not consider insomnia as a disorder in its own right or recognize that it actually has a high rate of occurrence among adolescents. However, sleep disturbances, including insomnia, are common among adolescents (Ferber, 1996; Johnson, 2006; Kotagal & Pianosi, 2006; Meltzer & Mindell, 2006; Ivanenko & Gururaj, 2009).[22]

In their study of over 1,000 randomly selected adolescents, Johnson, Roth, Schultz, et al. (2006) found that 10.7% reported a lifetime prevalence of insomnia with 88% of these adolescents reporting current symptoms. In addition, the median age of onset was reported to be 11 years of age. Similarly, Roane and Taylor (2008), in their cross-sectional, prospective national study of approximately 4,500 adolescents, found that symptoms of insomnia were reported by 9.4% of the adolescent participants in the study.

"Is insomnia a clinical entity in its own right or is it simply a symptom of an underlying medical or psychological disorder?" (p. 1037). This question, rhetorically asked by Harvey (2001) over a decade ago, still resonates in the clinical community (e.g., Mai & Buysse, 2008). Part of the difficulty in answering this question is due to the significant association of adolescent insomnia with dual diagnosis (Roane & Taylor, 2008).[23]

### SUDs and Insomnia

Child and adolescent insomnia, as well as other sleep disorders, is frequently associated with OMDs, particularly: (1) A-D/HD; (2) anxiety disorders (e.g., PTSD); (3) autism; and (4) MDD (Coulombe, Reid, Boyle, et al., 2010; Ivanenko & Gururaj, 2009; Johnson, Roth, Schultz, et al., 2006; Meltzer & Mindell, 2006; Roane & Taylor, 2008). Etiologically, the relationship can be bidirectional (Shibley, Malcolm, & Veatch, 2008). For example, Johnson, Roth, and Breslau (2006) found that, among adolescents with insomnia and OMDs: "anxiety disorders preceded insomnia 73% of the time," and "insomnia occurred first in 69% of comorbid insomnia and depression cases" (p. 700).

---

[21] It should be noted that insomnia is also commonly underdiagnosed among adults (Edinger & Means, 2005).

[22] In fact, some sleep disorders, such as the delayed sleep phase syndrome, typically have their primary onset during adolescence (i.e., in association with related circadian rhythms and homeostatic changes) (Crowley, Acebo, & Carskadon, 2007; Okawa & Uchiyama, 2007). In this regard, as noted by Kotagal and Pianosi (2006), serum levels of sleep-inducing melatonin increase before the onset of sleep, and this release is shifted to later in the evening during adolescence (i.e., making falling asleep before approximately 10:30 pm generally more difficult).

[23] It should be noted that insomnia, even when related to another mental disorder, is amenable to specific treatment interventions (Pagliaro & Pagliaro, 1999, 2009; Stepanski & Rybarczyk, 2006).

Several relationships have been demonstrated involving insomnia and SUDs. (See Figure 8.2.) For example, insomnia is a common symptom of withdrawal from sedative-hypnotic use. It also can be caused by psychostimulant use (Anders & Eiben, 1997; Orbeta, Overpeck, Ramcharran, et al., 2006; Roehrs & Roth, 2008). (See Table 8.2.) In addition, adolescents may use the drugs and substances of abuse, particularly alcohol, other sedative-hypnotics, or cannabis to self-medicate their insomnia. Insomnia also is associated with several other mental disorders (e.g., A-D/HD, MDD, PTSD) that are likewise highly correlated with SUDs. (See earlier sections in this chapter: "SUDs and Attention-Deficit/Hyperactivity Disorder," "SUDs and Major Depressive Disorder," and "SUDs and Post Traumatic Stress Disorder")

Roane and Taylor (2008) demonstrated the complex, and significant, interrelationship of insomnia in the context of dual diagnosis among adolescents. Using archival data from a nationally based population sample of 4,494 adolescents (12 to 18 years of age) from the National Longitudinal Study of Adolescent Health, they found that, in comparison to adolescents who did not have insomnia, adolescents with insomnia reported:

1. Approximately 50% higher alcohol use (i.e., 32.4% versus 22%)[24]

2. Approximately 50% higher cannabis use (i.e., 18.3% versus 11.5%)

3. Approximately 50% higher incidence of depressive symptoms (i.e., 54.3% versus 31.9%)

4. More than a 100% higher incidence of suicide ideation

5. More than a 300% higher incidence of suicide attempts (i.e., 10.2% versus 2.9%)

## TRIDIAGNOSIS AMONG ADOLESCENTS: SUDS AND OMDS AND HIV

The risk for human immunodeficiency virus (HIV) infection exacerbates the already difficult lives of 1.5 million homeless adolescents in the United States. Homeless youths engage in sexual and substance-abuse behaviors that place them at increased risk of contracting HIV, and they demonstrate other problem behaviors that reduce their coping responses. (Rotheram-Borus, Koopman, & Ehrhardt, et al., 1991, p. 1188)

In a large study of homeless/runaway youth who had "demonstrated all forms of drug abuse," Cohen, MacKenzie, and Yates (1991) found that "they were 6 times more likely to be at risk for HIV infection" (p. 539). Similar findings have been reported in several other studies (e.g., Athey, 1991; Rosenthal, Moore, & Buzwell, 1994). As noted by Kaliski, Rubinson, Lawrence, et al. (1990), the major focus for most homeless/runaway youth is survival— scoring drugs, obtaining food, finding a place to sleep, avoiding being arrested, and avoiding being physically assaulted. Thus, reducing their high-risk behaviors for contracting HIV infection becomes a low priority because it is not seen as an immediate concern.

The nature of the relationship among SUDs, OMDs and HIV infection is clear but can be indirect. (See Figure 8.3.) Several research studies and reports (e.g., Johnson, Aschkenasy, Herbers, et al., 1996; Johnson, McColgan, & Denniston, 1991; Koopman, Rosario, & Rotheram-Borus, 1994; Pagliaro, Pagliaro, Thauberger, et al., 1993) have noted that the use of the drugs and substances of abuse functions as an antecedent risk factor that places adolescents and young adults at significant risk for HIV infection in several specific ways,

---

[24] Of particular interest in this context is the finding that while the consumption of 2 or 3 drinks at bedtime by adolescents initially may promote sleep, this effect generally dissipates within 1 week of continued use and subsequently may result in disturbed sleep (Stein & Friedmann, 2005).

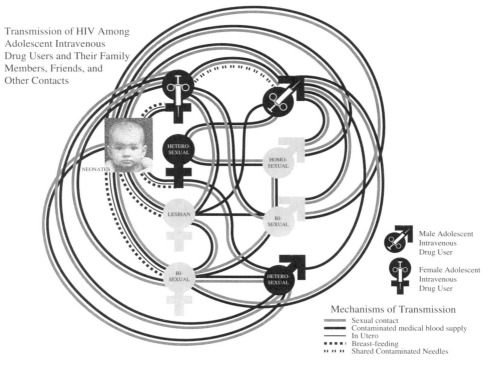

Transmission of HIV Among Adolescent Intravenous Drug Users and Their Family Members, Friends, and Other Contacts

**Figure 8.3   Transmission of HIV Infection Among Infants, Children, Adolescents, and Others**
Reproduced with permission from: A. M. Pagliaro & L. A. Pagliaro (1996), Chapter 6, Dual diagnosis among adolescents (p. 162). In, *Substance use among children and adolescents: Its nature, extent, and effects from conception to adulthood.* New York, NY: John Wiley & Sons.

including: (1) sharing contaminated needles and syringes; (2) decreasing inhibitions and, consequently, increasing the likelihood of engaging in unprotected sex; (3) trading sex for desired drugs or substances of abuse or participating in the sex trade in order to obtain the money needed to buy drugs and substances of abuse; and (4) as a consequence of the last item, having multiple sexual partners and engaging in high-risk, unprotected anal, oral, and vaginal sex.

Bisexual, gay, and lesbian adolescents are at additional risk for HIV because of higher incidence of sex with older sexual partners, including those who may already be HIV positive, and the cultural norms of many bisexual, gay, and lesbian communities, which include using drugs and substances of abuse, particularly alcohol and club drugs (i.e., cocaine, gamma-hydroxybutyrate [GHB], ketamine, and MDMA) as an accepted antecedent to casual,

intimate sexual encounters (Klitzman, Pope, & Hudson, 2000; Pagliaro & Pagliaro, *Clinical Patient Data Files*; Romanelli, Smith, & Pomeroy, 2003; Rosario, Meyer-Bahlburg, Hunter, et al., 1999). (Also see the "SUDs and Sexual or Gender Identity Disorders" section for further related discussion.)

Over the years, several studies have associated risk for SUDs and risky sexual behavior (i.e., risk for HIV infection) with childhood and adolescent sexual abuse (Cohen, Tross, Pavlicova, et al., 2009; Senn, Carey, & Vanable, 2008; Wilson & Widom, 2008). (Also see related discussion in "SUDs and Post-Traumatic Stress Disorder" and "SUDs and Sexual or Gender Identity Disorders" sections.)

Unfortunately, little, if anything, has improved even though we and many others have repeatedly called for greater attention to this critical situation. As noted by Rondinelli,

Ouellet, Strathdee, et al. (2009), commenting on the findings from their large, cross-sectional study of injection drug users 15 to 30 years of age who were sampled from five large cities across the United States, "More than two decades after injection and sexual practices were identified as risk factors for HIV infection, these behaviors remain common among young" injection drug users (p. 167).

This observation and our concerns appear further substantiated by findings from the National Survey and Analysis of the Sexual Health of Adolescents in the United States, conducted by Gavin, MacKay, Brown, et al. (2009) for the Centers for Disease Control and Prevention. In this report, the authors noted:

> Many young people engage in risky sexual behavior.... In 2006, approximately 22,000 adolescents and young adults aged 10 to 24 years in 33 states were living with human immunodeficiency virus/acquired immune deficiency syndrome (HIV/AIDS). (p. 2)

In addition, they found that:

> The annual rate of AIDS diagnoses reported among males aged 15 to 19 years has nearly doubled in the past 10 years from 1.3 cases per 100,000 population in 1997 to 2.5 cases in 2006 (p. 3).

## TREATMENT FOR ADOLESCENTS WITH DUAL DIAGNOSIS

This section presents an overview of the barriers that have been identified regarding the provision of appropriate and efficacious treatment approaches for adolescents who have a dual diagnosis. It also highlights several treatment approaches and programs that have been specifically designed and developed for adolescents.

### Barriers to Treatment

Although the availability of appropriate treatment services for adolescents who have a dual diagnosis has increased significantly during the last two decades, it still remains all too

common for them to be refused admission to a drug abuse treatment center because of their other mental disorder (e.g., clinical depression; schizophrenia) or to be refused admission to a mental health facility because of their problematic use of the drugs and substances of abuse (e.g., compulsive use of alcohol or cocaine) (Ponce & Jo, 1990; Zeitlin, 1999). This "catch-22" situation reflects a general lack of appropriate education and training for health and social care professionals (Belfer, 1993; Carey, Bradizza, Stasiewicz, et al., 1999; Drake, Essock, Shaner, et al., 2001; Renner, 2004), particularly those professionals in mental health and treatment settings for drug and substance abuse. As found by Adger, McDonald, and DeAngelis (1990) in their survey of medical school training:

> At the medical student and residency training levels, only 44% and 40% of programs, respectively, required any formal instruction, and only 27% and 34% respectively, offered an elective for medical students or residents. Although most respondents endorsed the inclusion of both required and elective alcohol and drug education in the curriculum, few programs that did not include it already had a future plan for it. (p. 555)

This situation has not changed significantly in the 20-plus years since that survey was conducted, although some progress has been achieved (e.g., Iannucci, Sanders, & Greenfield, 2009; Polydorou, Gunderson, & Levin, 2008). As noted by Hawkins (2009) in regard to treatment services for adolescents with dual diagnoses:

> In general, current service systems are inadequately prepared to meet this need due to a variety of clinical, administrative, financial, and policy barriers. (p. 197)

Studying the facilitators and barriers to integrated dual disorders treatment, Brunette, Asher, Whitley, et al. (2008) found that the two most prevalent barriers were funding and staffing. However, even when adequate funding was secured and in place, treatment programs continued to have severe staffing problems, particularly a high staff turnover.

In addition, treatment services continue to reflect the widespread and common practice of employing people with histories of SUDs (e.g., recovering alcoholics) as drug counselors for the treatment of adolescents who have a dual diagnosis. Although these people may have an important role to play in the complex treatment of dual diagnosis, they are generally not qualified, either academically or clinically, as primary therapists. For example, as noted by Penick, Nickel, Cantrell, et al. (1990):

> Many of the traditional caregivers in the substance abuse field are, themselves, recovering from chemical dependency; [these individuals generally] tend to know and use only one approach to treatment. If they are recovering themselves, the approach taken is usually the one that "worked" for them. When confronted with failure, substance abuse workers typically have no "fallback" position to draw upon, continuing instead to do "more of the same" rather than shift to a different treatment strategy. (pp. 7–8)

Also, as noted by Huang, Freed, and Espiritu (2006), in primary care settings, which are often the first point of contact with the healthcare system for adolescents with dual diagnosis: "The needs of these youth continue to be under recognized, poorly diagnosed, and inappropriately treated" (p. 453). This sentiment is endorsed by many others (e.g., Gee, Espiritu, & Huang, 2006; Hawkins, 2009; Libby & Riggs, 2005; Rush & Koegl, 2008; Ziedonis, Smelson, Rosenthal, et al., 2005).

Unfortunately, if health and social care providers continue to inadequately meet the therapeutic needs of adolescents who have a dual diagnosis, it can only be expected that these adolescents will continue to manage their disorders themselves—through self-medication with the drugs and substances of abuse—and continue to suffer, unnecessarily, the associated harmful effects (see Table 8.4 for commonly encountered examples).

## Approaches to Treatment

> It is better to cut the shoes to fit the feet rather than the other way around. (Frances and Allen, 1986)

Although obviously not universally adopted or successful, several approaches for treating dual diagnosis were developed over the last 20 years, including: (1) the developmental biopsychosocial disease model (DBDM), proposed by Chatlos (1994) for the specific treatment of adolescents; (2) the dual disorders recovery counseling (DDRC) model proposed by Daley and Salloum (1995), which continues to be endorsed by many clinicians and researchers in the area of dual diagnosis treatment (e.g., Cohen, Mannarino, Zhitova, et al., 2003; Goldsmith & Garlapati, 2004; Wilens & Fusillo, 2007; Zeitlin, 1999); and (3) the holistic model of treatment proposed by Gorski (1995), which also has been adopted by others. Each of these models is briefly described in order to provide readers with some general familiarity with the varied approaches that have been used for the treatment of dual diagnosis. This overview is followed by a brief discussion of a more recent form of treatment that appears to have the potential for increased success: family-based therapies. However, regardless of the approach selected, accurate and comprehensive diagnosis of a SUD and OMD among adolescents is paramount for achieving optimal treatment outcomes. (See also Chapter 9, *Preventing and Treating Child and Adolescent Use of the Drugs and Substances of Abuse*.)

Comprehensive diagnosis necessarily begins with careful attention to the potential for an adolescent to have a concurrent SUD and another mental disorder. In this regard, every adolescent who presents with a potential or actual SUD should be appropriately assessed for any additional mental disorder,

**TABLE 8.4    Adolescent Use of Selected Drugs and Substances of Abuse to Self-Medicate Mental Disorders in the Context of a Dual Diagnosis**

| Dual Diagnosis–Related Mental Disorder | Dual Diagnosis–Related Use of Drug or Substance of Abuse | Comments | References (examples) |
|---|---|---|---|
| Anxiety | Alcohol | Used as a form of self-medication to cope or to reduce high anxiety. This use is associated with a significantly increased risk of suicidal behavior (e.g., suicide attempts). | Alegría, Hasin, Nunes, et al., 2010; Armeli, Todd, Conner, et al., 2008; Bolton, Cox, Clara, et al., 2006; Robinson, Sareen, Cox, et al., 2009. |
| Bipolar disorder | Alcohol | Used as self-medication to ameliorate manic signs and symptoms (e.g., distractability; flight of ideas; irritability). | Bolton, Robinson, & Sareen, 2009. |
| Depression/Major depressive disorder | Alcohol, cannabis, cocaine, nicotine | Alcohol, a psychodepressant, and cannabis, a psychodelic, are used as self-medication in an attempt to forget about whatever is making the adolescent depressed. The psychostimulants cocaine and nicotine are used in an attempt actually to relieve the signs and symptoms of depression and elevate mood, at least temporarily. | Herbal remedy, 2009; Pagliaro, Jaglalsingh, & Pagliaro, 1992; Slaby, 1991. |
| Insomnia | Alcohol, benzodiazepines, cannabis | Used as self-medication to help fall asleep. | Roane & Taylor, 2008; Shibley, Malcolm, & Veatch, 2008. |
| Panic disorder/Panic attacks | Alcohol, benzodiazepines, opiate analgesics | Used as self-medication to symptomatically manage panic disorder or a panic attack. | Cowley, 1992; Cox, Norton, Swinson, et al., 1990; Valentiner, Mounts, & Deacon, 2004. |
| Posttraumatic stress disorder | Alcohol, cannabis, opiate analgesics | Used as self-medication to diminish associated anxieties and fears and to help stop thinking about the precipitating PTSD eliciting event. | Leeies, Pagura, Sareen, et al., 2010; Ouimette, Read, Wade, et al., 2010; Peters, Meshack, Amos, et al., 2010. |
| Psychosis/Schizophrenia | Cannabis | Used primarily to self-medicate negative symptoms (e.g., affect regulation and socialization). | Dekker, Linszen, & De Haan, 2009; Krystal, D'Souza, Gallinat, et al., 2006; Williams & Gandhi, 2008. |

particularly A-D/HD, APD, BP, BPD, CD, MDD, ODD, PD, PTSD, schizophrenia, and sexual or gender identity disorders, and vice versa—every adolescent who presents with a potential or actual mental disorder of A-D/HD, APD, BP, BPD, CD, MDD, ODD, PD, PTSD, schizophrenia, or sexual or gender identity disorders should be assessed for a SUD. (See also Chapter 7, *Detecting Adolescent Use of the Drugs and Substances of Abuse: Selected Quick-Screen Psychometric Tests*.) Once identified, these disorders can be managed either by an appropriately qualified

health or social care provider (e.g., clinical psychologist; family therapist; psychiatrist) or can be cotreated by qualified professionals specializing in the treatment of a specific SUD (e.g., alcohol; cannabis; cocaine) or other specific mental disorders (e.g., A-D/HD; MDD; schizophrenia) (O'Connell, 1990).

Concern, and related recommendations, for the treatment of adolescents with a dual diagnosis often requires multidisciplinary treatment. The need for this type of treatment first was voiced formally in the late 1980s (e.g., Minkoff, 1989; Osher & Kofoed, 1989).

Since that time, the consensus has been that dual diagnoses require simultaneous treatment whenever possible. We now turn to an overview of Chatlos's DBDM.

### Developmental Biopsychosocial Disease Model

Chatlos (1994) specifically addressed the treatment of dual diagnosis among adolescents with his DBDM. Developed for use in community education and prevention settings, it emphasized prevention, intervention, and treatment on a continuum integrating SUDs and OMDs into one process that is opposite of the recovery process. In this context, three factors are seen as central to the development of harmful patterns of adolescent use of the drugs and substances of abuse:

1. Predisposition (e.g., genetic, psychological, and sociocultural factors that lead to an attitude of using drugs and substances of abuse)
2. Initiation (i.e., the availability of drugs and substances of abuse and factors that support their use, including peer influence, perceived harmfulness associated with use, and parental use of the drugs and substances of abuse)
3. Progression (i.e., movement through four states of the mood swing):
   a. Experimentation/learning the mood swing
   b. Regular use/seeking the mood swing
   c. Daily preoccupation/preoccupation with the mood swing
   d. Harmful dependency/using to feel normal

Progression through the mood swing occurs in relation to the interaction of such factors as the strong reinforcement of euphoria associated with the use of the drug or substance of abuse, negative reinforcement associated with withdrawal from use, and the genetic and biochemical effects of the drug or substance of abuse on the adolescent's developing brain—the *enabling* or *maintenance* system. This system includes all people, places, and things surrounding the adolescent that knowingly or unknowingly enable the progression of the use of drugs and substances of abuse and their associated increasing harmful effects.

The mental disorder is the other factor central to the DBDM. According to the model, the mental disorder does not result from the use of a drug or substance of abuse. Rather, it is triggered by a biological or life event. As such, it progresses and is maintained by an enabling system (e.g., a significant family member who has a SUD or OMD or who is physically or emotionally unavailable). Thus, the dual diagnosis is seen as two parallel biopsychosocial processes that are in constant interaction. Treatment is aimed at the source and the temporal sequence along the continuum of the mood swing.

According to the model, the recovery process follows the reverse order of the SUD and OMD process. Initial abstinence requires an intervention into the enabling system and also may involve the admission to an inpatient treatment program. The school and courts may also be involved. A family intervention may be required. Adolescents who enter into treatment and their parents are required to make a commitment to abstinence. Parents also are required to commit to treatment. Following the initial intervention, continued work with the adolescent, family, and school is required to strengthen other parts of the recovery environment, which ultimately transforms the enabling system.

### Dual Disorders Recovery Counseling

According to Daley and Salloum (1995), who considered all patients in their model, dual diagnosis is best approached with integrated treatment using DDRC. Following the establishment of an optimal therapeutic relationship with the adolescent, the therapist extends treatment to specific clinical interventions that involve education, referral, compliance with pharmacotherapy, and self-help programs. Even though the context of treatment often varies depending on an adolescent's unique needs and presenting symptomatology at a particular time (e.g., detoxification; protection from self-injury), it generally focuses on concurrently balancing treatment requirements for each disorder. In this regard, the therapist moves the adolescent, over time, through 6 different phases of treatment—

1. Transition and engagement
2. Stabilization
3. Early recovery
4. Middle recovery
5. Late recovery
6. Maintenance

—while recognizing that each phase has its own possible therapeutic issues, optimal interventions, and criteria for evaluating progress toward recovery. Throughout treatment, the therapist maintains focus on each and every mental disorder identified for a particular adolescent. DDRC views each SUD and other mental disorder as a biopsychological condition that is caused and maintained by a variety of biological, psychological, and social factors and can be used in several treatment contexts (e.g., individual, group, or family treatment; inpatient, residential, partial hospital, outpatient, or aftercare program). "Disorders are seen as *no fault* with a multiplicity of possible relationships between the psychiatric and substance use disorder" (See Figure 8.2) (Daley & Salloum, 1995, p. 16).

### Holistic Model of Treatment

Gorski (1995) considered a more holistic approach to dual recovery emphasizing the need to develop a disorder-specific treatment plan that addressed the unique symptomatology of each presenting disorder along with proper diet, exercise, stress management, communication effectiveness, and balanced living. A problem severity scale was developed and used for identifying and listing both short- and long-term problems.

Gorski (1995) provided effective standard treatment interventions for guiding clinical reasoning about the progressive treatment process that could be adapted to the individual needs of each patient. In regard to managing the symptoms that drive target disorders of chemical dependence and specific related mental and personality disorders, these guidelines integrated components of:

1. Disorder-specific clinical models for symptom management
2. Physical interventions for managing physical problems
3. Cognitive therapy for dealing with irrational thoughts
4. Affective therapy for changing unmanageable feelings
5. Behavioral therapy for changing self-defeating behaviors
6. Social/situational therapy for changing lifestyle factors

Progress reporting identified the target problems and goals for the current treatment episode along with the real results of the treatment.

### Family-Based Therapies

Many other models for the treatment or management of dual diagnosis have been developed and used over the past two decades, but they have not added much to the approaches briefly outlined in this section with the noted exception of family-based therapies. Family-based therapies, including family intervention programs, family systems–based therapies, and family interventions, have at their core the belief that family dysfunction and loss of family support are central to the development and continuation of a dual diagnosis. Since the mid-1990s and continuing to date, this therapeutic approach, which began in the United States and has since spread worldwide, has been widely touted for the treatment of adolescents with a dual diagnosis (e.g., Liddle, 2004; Mueser & Fox, 2002; Richards, Doyle, & Cook, 2009).

Using a variety of therapeutic treatment approaches (e.g., cognitive-behavioral therapy; coping and stress-management techniques; life-skills development; group therapy; parenting skills training), the goals of family-based therapies generally are to: (1) improve communication among family members, including the adolescent who has a dual diagnosis; (2) alter dysfunctional family patterns; and (3) develop the family as a source of healing and support. Building on the theoretical work of Prochaska and DiClemente (1984) (see Chapter 4, *Explaining Child and Adolescent Use of the Drugs and Substances of Abuse*), Slesnick, Bartle-Haring, Erdem, et al. (2009), applied motivational components to their family-based therapeutic interventions in the treatment of runaway adolescents with dual diagnosis. The British National Health Service adopted the version of family-based therapy known as multisystemic therapy (Elliott, 2010) and also formally incorporated motivational interviewing (McCambridge & Strang, 2004) into its treatment program (National Institute on Alcohol Abuse and Alcoholism, 2007). Generally, a team of clinicians works in collaboration, often with a coordinator who manages each case to ensure that a treatment goal is not missed for a particular adolescent and his or her family. The entire family-based therapeutic process is planned and scheduled over a period of 2 to 3 years.

Although family-based therapies currently are quite popular and appear to have significant potential for the treatment of adolescents who have dual diagnoses, it must be noted, as an appropriate caution, that very few rigorous program evaluations of therapeutic outcomes have been carried out and generally, at this time, sufficient empirical support is lacking. However, pending the availability of additional data, we recommend that family-based therapies be used, whenever feasible, as an integral part of comprehensive multidisciplinary and multimodal treatment programs

that include, as appropriate, pharmacotherapy, individual counseling, and school-based teaching and other interventions to help to ensure that each of the adolescent's mental disorders, as specifically related to his or her dual diagnosis, is adequately addressed and treated. (For further related discussion, see Chapter 9, "Family-Based Therapies" section.)

### Individualized Approaches to Treatment

In order to ensure optimal effectiveness, dual diagnosis treatment programs also need to address the unique life experiences and special therapeutic needs of ethnically and culturally diverse groups of North American adolescents, including those who are: (1) of African, Asian, Hispanic, American Indian, or multiple continental descent; (2) bisexual, gay, lesbian, or transgendered; (3) homeless; or (4) residing in inner cities or remote rural areas. As noted by Zweben, Clark, & Smith (1994):

> The patient who has a dual diagnosis is particularly vulnerable to violence, if not from generic mental illness, from a drug-using culture that is conducive to violence. Ethnic dual diagnosis patients may reside in communities where drug-related violence is common. Furthermore, both male and female may have been victims of childhood sexual abuse and violence. Female patients, of course, are at greater risk for violence.... Naturally, a victim of violence with eroded coping skills, a substance abuse problem, and psychiatric problems may not present as an ideal patient.... [Such persons may] either resign themselves to a passive-aggressive demeanor or assume a highly charged aggressive stance. It is critical for the clinician to recognize that a victim of violence, even if presenting as a perpetrator, will be adversely affected by that violence. The African American, Native American, and Hispanic American dual diagnosis patient may be particularly at risk for the violence associated with racial discrimination, including harassment by police, social agencies, and treatment providers. (pp. 115–116)

In order to address the unique life experiences and special therapeutic needs of these and all adolescents who suffer from a dual diagnosis, we developed several guidelines based on our own clinical experience in treating dually diagnosed adolescents. These guidelines are presented in Table 8.5.

Finally, although additional research and demonstrations of clinical efficacy are required, pharmacotherapy for adolescents with dual diagnoses appears to hold significant future potential. For example, topiramate (Topama®) has been used off-label for the treatment of BD among patients with a comorbid diagnosis

**TABLE 8.5  Therapeutic Guidelines Addressing Life Experiences and Special Needs of Adolescents with Dual Diagnoses[a]**

**Therapeutic approaches should always:**

1. Be guided by the individual needs, personality, and cognitive abilities of the adolescent.

2. Provide for a safe and trusting treatment environment.

3. Include integrated and multimodal approaches to treatment, including family-based therapies, with appropriate referrals to other health and social care providers, including integrated outreach services for adolescents who are homeless runaways living on the street or in community youth facilities.

4. Reflect sensitivity and empathy (i.e., a humanist approach).

5. Be active and purposeful (i.e., goal directed toward the successful resolution of *each* identified SUD and OMD).

6. Support abstinence from the use of the drugs and substances of abuse.

7. Provide insight and resolution of psychological conflicts.

8. Build personal self-confidence and self-esteem.

9. Develop and promote healthy defense mechanisms and coping styles.

10. Empower adolescents with a sense of control over their lives and responsibility for their actions and behaviors.

11. Encourage participation in peer self-help programs (as deemed appropriate for the individual adolescent).

12. Ensure follow-up with aftercare (i.e., relapse prevention) services.

[a]Also see related discussion in Chapter 9, *Preventing and Treating Child and Adolescent Use of the Drugs and Substances of Abuse.*

of alcoholism with apparently promising outcomes (Azorin, Bowden, Garay, et al., 2010; Miller & Roache, 2009). Other related pharmacotherapy for the treatment of dual disorders is currently being actively developed and clinically tested.

## CHAPTER SUMMARY

"Dual diagnosis" is defined in this reference text as the co-occurrence within an adolescent or young adult of one or more SUDs and one or more other mental disorders (e.g., CD, MDD). Dual diagnosis frequently is encountered among adolescents and young adults who are seeking treatment for a SUD or another significant mental disorder. Thus, all adolescents and young adults seeking treatment for a SUD should be assessed for other concurrent mental disorders so that appropriate treatment can be planned and implemented.

Although adolescents can present with any number of combinations of SUDs and OMDs, they most frequently present with harmful patterns of alcohol, cannabis, cocaine, or nicotine use in the context of:

- A disorder usually first diagnosed in infancy, childhood, or adolescence (i.e., A-D/HD, CD, ODD)
- A mood disorder (i.e., BD or MDD)
- An anxiety disorder (i.e., PD or PTSD)
- A personality disorder (i.e., BPD)
- A psychotic disorder (e.g., schizophrenia)
- A sexual or gender identity disorder
- A sleep disorder (e.g., insomnia)

Accurate identification of a dual diagnosis among adolescents is essential in regard to planning and providing appropriate treatment, which generally should include an integration of both appropriate pharmacotherapy and psychotherapy.

Examples of the several approaches available for the treatment of adolescents with a dual diagnosis have been briefly presented in this chapter, including the developmental biopsychosocial disease model, dual disorders recovery counseling, the holistic model of treatment, and family-based therapies. The choice of therapies will depend on the unique needs of the adolescent, the clinical training and abilities of the therapist in regard to diagnosis and treatment, and the availability of additional treatment or referral services (e.g., Alateen). Regardless of which treatment modalities are chosen, it is essential to ensure that each and every one of the adolescent's diagnoses is given adequate and appropriate attention. As noted by Daley and Salloum (1995), "A dual focus on treatment reduces the chances that an untreated disorder will increase vulnerability to relapse to another disorder" (p. 16). (Also see Chapter 9, *Preventing and Treating Child and Adolescent Use of the Drugs and Substances of Abuse,* for additional related discussion.)

# CHAPTER 9

## *Preventing and Treating Child and Adolescent Use of the Drugs and Substances of Abuse*

### INTRODUCTION

Exposure to and use of the various drugs and substances of abuse by North American children and adolescents is associated with significant biological, psychological, and sociological harm, as demonstrated in the previous chapters of this text. In this regard, it is obvious that increased attention should be given to preventing, or at least minimizing, the use of the drugs and substances of abuse by children and adolescents and, consequently, their harmful effects, whenever possible. Real benefit also may be achieved with the early and accurate detection of child and adolescent use of the drugs and substances of abuse (see Chapter 7, *Detecting Adolescent Use of the Drugs and Substances of Abuse:* section titled "Selected Quick-Screen Psychometric Tests") and also the identification of children and adolescents who may have a dual diagnosis (see Chapter 8, *Dual Diagnosis Among Adolescents*). Successful treatment outcomes are predicated on the accurate identification and diagnosis of problematic and harmful patterns of using the drugs and substances of abuse. Our analysis and synthesis of the available published literature regarding the various treatment programs that have been developed specifically for children and adolescents across North America indicates that, on average, a significant decrease in the use of the drugs and substances of abuse, although challenging, is achievable and maintainable.

The purpose of this chapter is to present an overview of the treatment programs that are aimed at primary, secondary, and tertiary prevention of child and adolescent use of the drugs and substances of abuse. (See Figure 9.1.) More specifically, this chapter focuses on programs and services that are concerned with:

1. Promoting the continued nonuse of drugs and substances of abuse when use has not yet begun

2. Detecting children and adolescents who have initiated the use of drugs or substances of abuse and encouraging their discontinuation (resumed nonuse) prior to the occurrence of increasingly harmful symptomatology

3. Minimizing the harmful effects associated with the continued use of the drugs and substances of abuse once use has begun, including those effects associated with social and habitual use

4. Helping children and adolescents who have developed patterns of abusive or compulsive use to discontinue (resumed nonuse) or at least minimize (controlled use) the use of the offending drugs and substances of abuse with attention to managing their associated harmful effects

5. Helping children and adolescents to maintain patterns of controlled use or resumed nonuse with attention to preventing the occurrence of relapsed use

As noted in the previous chapters of this text, the use of the drugs and substances of abuse by North American children and adolescents is a long-standing, complex, and pervasive concern.

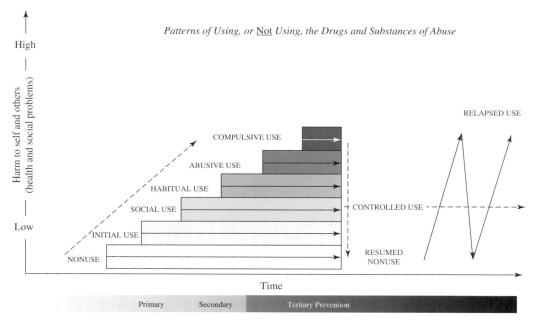

**Figure 9.1    Levels of Prevention in the Context of Increasingly Harmful Patterns of Using Drugs and Substances of Abuse**
Modified from: Pagliaro & Pagliaro (1996).

Therefore, it is patently illogical and naive to expect that a single, overly simplistic prevention approach (e.g., increasing a child's knowledge concerning the dangers associated with the use of the drugs and substances of abuse; increasing an adolescent's self-esteem or decision-making abilities) will always, or even in most cases, be effective. In fact, what is needed in order to achieve optimal efficacious treatment outcomes for children and adolescents is a wide range of primary, secondary, and tertiary services specifically aimed at them and their identified patterns of using the drugs and substances of abuse.

Many different programs and services that focused on preventing the use of the drugs and substances of abuse by North American children and adolescents, or minimizing their harmful effects, were developed and used over the last several decades. However, these programs and services generally have been found to be unsuccessful or largely ineffective[1]—probably because they often ignored, at least to a large degree, the associated underlying biological, psychological, and sociological factors that are involved in determining and affecting the use, or nonuse, of the drugs and substances of abuse by children and adolescents. (Also see Chapter 4, *Explaining Child and Adolescent Use of the Drugs and Substances of Abuse*) The amenability of these factors to primary, secondary, or tertiary prevention techniques are identified in Table 9.1. A quick perusal of this table indicates that virtually all of the factors that have been most commonly associated with the use of the drugs and substances of abuse by children and adolescents are amenable to primary, secondary, or tertiary prevention. However, to be effective, prevention and treatment programs and services must actively and appropriately address these factors.

[1] For example, between 1998 and 2004, the U.S. government spent over $1 billion on the National Youth Anti-Drug Media Campaign. This advertising campaign had three major goals in regard to children and adolescents 9 to 18 years of age: (1) promoting strategies to reject illicit drugs; (2) preventing the initial use of drugs and substances of abuse; and (3) convincing occasional users to discontinue use. Unfortunately, the campaign did not produce the desired results (Hornik & Jacobsohn, 2008–2009).

TABLE 9.1   Child and Adolescent Use of the Drugs and Substances of Abuse: Variables Amenable to Primary, Secondary, or Tertiary Prevention

| Child or Adolescent Dimension Variables | Level of Prevention | | |
|---|---|---|---|
| **Biological Variables** | Primary | Secondary | Tertiary |
| Age | X | ✓ | ✓ |
| Continental descent | X | ✓ | ✓ |
| Gender | X | ✓ | ✓ |
| Genetic predisposition to mental disorders and substance use disorders | X | ✓ | ✓ |
| Physical impairment or disability | X | ✓ | ✓ |
| **Intrapersonal Variables** | | | |
| Antisocial personality disorder | X | ✓ | ✓ |
| Attention-deficit/Hyperactivity disorder | X | ✓ | ✓ |
| Conduct disorder | X | ✓ | ✓ |
| Gender identity crisis/disorder | ✓ | ✓ | ✓ |
| Major depressive disorder | ✓ | ✓ | ✓ |
| Other active mental disorder | | ✓ | ✓ |
| External locus of control | (✓) | ✓ | ✓ |
| Hopelessness | ✓ | ✓ | ✓ |
| Lack of meaning in life | ✓ | ✓ | ✓ |
| Loneliness | ✓ | ✓ | ✓ |
| Low self-esteem | ✓ | ✓ | ✓ |
| Previous use of the drugs and substances of abuse | ✓ | ✓ | ✓ |
| Serious early childhood losses | (✓) | ✓ | ✓ |
| **Interpersonal Variables** | | | |
| Absence of maternal figure or role model | ✓ | ✓ | ✓ |
| Absence of paternal figure or role model | ✓ | ✓ | ✓ |
| Dissatisfaction with family relationships | ✓ | ✓ | ✓ |
| Parent or sibling use of alcohol or other drugs and substances of abuse | (✓) | ✓ | ✓ |
| Parental neglect | ✓ | ✓ | ✓ |
| Peer pressure | (✓) | ✓ | ✓ |
| Physical or sexual abuse | (✓) | ✓ | ✓ |
| Previous inpatient treatment for mental disorders | (✓) | ✓ | ✓ |
| Use of drugs and substances of abuse by close friends or peers | (✓) | ✓ | ✓ |
| **Societal Dimension Variables** | | | |
| Availability of the drugs and substances of abuse | (✓) | ✓ | ✓ |
| Availability and accessibility of social programs and services (treatment) | ✓ | ✓ | ✓ |
| Culture, ethnicity, or continental descent | (✓) | ✓ | ✓ |
| Laws of the land (e.g., legal statutes and sanctions for possession, use, or trafficking) | ✓ | ✓ | ✓ |
| Media messages | ✓ | ✓ | ✓ |

Key: amenable ✓; partially amenable (✓); not amendable X

# PRIMARY, SECONDARY, AND TERTIARY PREVENTION

There are generally three levels of prevention: primary, secondary, and tertiary prevention. Primary prevention is aimed at preventing the initial use of a drug or substance of abuse. For example, it may involve the implementation of drug education programs in primary schools that are aimed at preventing the use of drugs and substances of abuse before it begins. Interdisciplinary action at this level includes preventing the use of drugs and substances of abuse in homes, schools, and public places by way of specialized programs and municipal legislation (e.g., smoke-free restaurants). Programs aimed to decrease the incidence of drinking and driving (e.g., police check stops during holidays) and workplace accidents related to the use of the drugs and substances of abuse at the workplace may be included here.

Secondary prevention involves the early detection of drug and substance use disorders (SUDs) and the provision of immediate therapeutic efforts aimed at: (1) discontinuing the use of the drugs and substances of abuse; (2) reducing the possibility that others in contact with the user will begin to use the drugs and substances of abuse; and (3) limiting any harm associated with the use of the drugs and substances of abuse. Tertiary prevention is aimed at limiting the degree of harm associated with the active use of the drugs and substances of abuse and promoting optimal health and social functioning when harmful effects are irreversible (e.g., human immunodeficiency virus [HIV] infection). Interventions include instruction regarding the management of the associated conditions and diseases with the end goal of maintaining optimal personal functioning and the prevention of further deterioration or loss of function.

Examples of effective approaches to prevention include employee alcohol assistance programs and many harm reduction strategies (Ritter & Cameron, 2006). Harm reduction strategies have formed the basis for several current programs such as needle exchange programs that are aimed at reducing HIV transmission from infected injection drug users to other injection drug users. Another example is the methadone maintenance program that replaces the need to inject heroin several times a day with a once-daily oral dose of methadone. Methadone maintenance programs allow regular long-term heroin users to: lead more productive lives (e.g., care for their children and families, maintain employment); decrease the risk for continued health problems associated with the frequent daily intravenous injection of heroin (e.g., progression of infections to gangrene and the subsequent associated need for limb amputation or septicemia and death); and decrease the harm associated with living on the street (e.g, personal injuries, such as violent beatings) (Pagliaro & Pagliaro, *Clinical Patient Data Files*).

Although researchers have been largely successful in accumulating knowledge regarding the pharmacology, toxicology, abuse potential, and addiction liability of the drugs and substances of abuse for adults, increased attention must be directed specifically toward the prevention and treatment of child and adolescent use of the drugs and substances of abuse (Knudsen, 2009). To this end, two points should be recognized:

1. Certain drugs and substances of abuse (e.g., alcohol; cannabis; tobacco [nicotine]; volatile solvents and inhalants) are particularly attractive to children and adolescents and are used preferentially for many different reasons (e.g., availability and cost; major psychotropic actions; peer pressure; sociocultural norms).

2. Children and adolescents, because of their stages of physical, psychological, and social development, are at particular risk for personal and other related problems associated with their use of the drugs and substances of abuse (e.g., family discord, including, violence and incest; incarceration for such offenses as possession of or dealing illicit drugs and substances of abuse, breaking and entering, and prostitution; infection with sexually transmitted diseases, including gonorrhea, syphilis, and HIV; expulsion from school for drug dealing or possession; morbidity and mortality related to automobile crashes, overdosage death, suicide attempts, and unplanned pregnancy).

What is known for certain is that multimodal prevention and treatment approaches have the greatest potential for success (see Figure 9.2). For example, in addition to psychotherapy, adjunctive pharmacotherapy and participation in Alcoholics Anonymous (AA) or another 12-step program when deemed beneficial, we also encourage our patients to participate in therapeutic storytelling or the use of narratives, art therapy, bibliotherapy, and music therapy as part of their individual or group therapy.

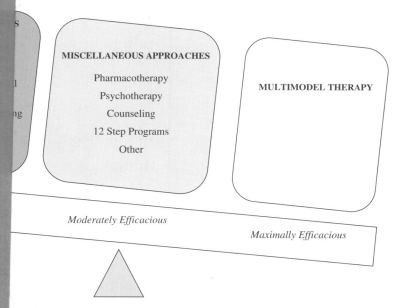

**... ary, Secondary, and Tertiary Prevention Programs and Approaches**

... tten diary entries, ... hared orally. They ... gs, collages, paint- ... that are presented ... esting to note that ... nts later published ... graphies and short ... have found that to ... timodal therapeutic ... both the needs of ... scent and the prop- ... pproaches selected ... ortance of this rec- ... in the discussions

... rms, the best treat- ... lescent use of the ... abuse is primary ... ble effort has been ... o achieve maximal ... d adolescents, the approach must be tailored to meet their individual needs, including those presented by

age, gender (including gender orientation), and continental descent or culture, as well as the specific drugs or substances of abuse that are of immediate concern. In addition, efforts must be made to more widely disseminate available knowledge concerning the use of the drugs and substances of abuse by children and adolescents to parents, teachers, school principals, pediatricians, and others who are concerned about the health and safety of children and adolescents. These concerned adults also need to be able to apply this knowledge effectively in the home, classroom, school, or clinical setting.

It must be recognized that attempts aimed at preventing the use of the drugs and substances of abuse by children and adolescents, although potentially of tremendous benefit, have failed more often than they have succeeded. However, the failures are rarely reported in the published literature and, when they are reported, the "failure" is often hidden, disguised, or minimized by

---

[2] Of course, there must be a good fit, or congruence among the particular child or adolescent being treated, including his or her attributes, needs, and abilities, the selected therapeutic interventions, and the clinician/therapist.

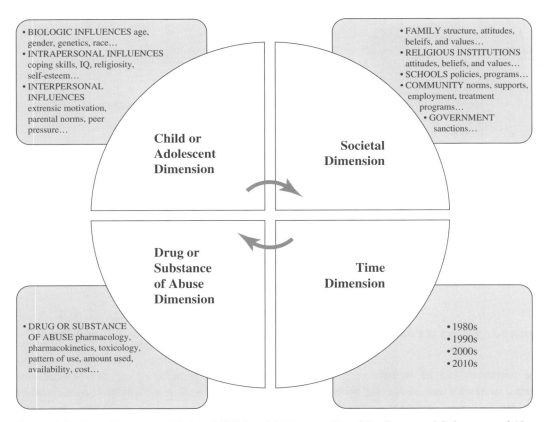

**Figure 9.3    Meta-Interactive Model of Child and Adolescent Use of the Drugs and Substances of Abuse**

misleading and often meaningless phrases. For example, a quick perusal of recently published research studies on our work desk yielded these phrases, among others: "a fairly consistent magnitude of program effects"; "a potentially iatrogenic effect"; "considerable consensus indicates"; "inconclusive"; "more effective than a similar intensity of"; "no main effects"; "positive point-in-time differences"; "positively associated with"; "the vast majority of"; "variation of the heterogeneous effects"; and "correlated with." [3] Although each of these phrases can be used appropriately, in the majority of cases they tend more to obfuscate, rather than to clarify, the research results.

Thus, in order to avoid past mistakes and endlessly reinvent the wheel, the development of efficacious prevention programs and services must address strategies and approaches to treatment that have failed in the past as well as those that have been found to be successful with a particular group of children or adolescents. The Meta-Interactive Model of Child and Adolescent Use of the Drugs and Substances of Abuse (see Figure 9.3) was developed as a comprehensive, integrative model to facilitate this endeavor and is discussed later in this chapter. (Also see the related discussion in Chapter 4, *Explaining Child and Adolescent Use of the Drugs and Substances of Abuse.*)

---

[3] For example, virtually everything can correlate with everything else (i.e., correlations can range from −1 to +1). However, only significant positive correlations are generally of clinical relevance. In addition, even then many clinicians and researchers appear to forget the single most crucial fact—that correlation can, and often does, occur without any relationship to causation.

## Primary Prevention

Primary prevention—preventing children and adolescents from initiating the use of a drug or substance of abuse appears to be the ultimate ideal goal. As such, primary prevention includes: (1) increasing parental and other protective factors associated with child and adolescent nonuse of the drugs and substances of abuse; and (2) reducing childhood and adolescent vulnerabilities to using the drugs and substances of abuse, including their availability; use by parents, friends, or peer groups; and attitudes and values that support their use. Many of the efforts aimed at primary prevention have involved preschool and elementary school programs. However, program inoculations[4] may be required for children and adolescents who have received these programs and who have not, as yet, used a particular drug or substance of abuse.

Other primary prevention programs need to be developed specifically for adolescents who remain drug free but are still at risk for using alcohol, cannabis, cocaine, heroin, methylenedioxymethamphetamine (MDMA, ecstasy), and other drugs and substances of abuse that are commonly used during adolescence and young adulthood. For example, just because a 12-year-old does not drink alcohol does not mean that he or she will not drink alcohol as a 16-year-old. Conversely, alcohol use as a preteen does not preclude the use of primary prevention techniques in relation to preventing future use of tobacco, or other drugs and substances of abuse, such as MDMA.

A review of Table 9.1 indicates that some trait-like variables associated with child or adolescent use of the drugs and substances of abuse (e.g., antisocial personality disorder; external locus of control; genetic predisposition to alcoholism; sensation-seeking

personality) place children and adolescents at particular risk or make them more vulnerable. Primary prevention for these children and adolescents often involves the strengthening of protective factors. Protective factors also may be used effectively with other high-risk or vulnerable children and adolescents who have experienced serious early childhood losses, significant neglect, physical or sexual abuse, or psychiatric inpatient treatment for selected mental disorders that may be related to alcohol and substance use disorders and the development of a dual diagnosis if appropriate preventive treatment is not provided.

Unfortunately, most past attempts at achieving the goals of primary prevention in regard to the use of the drugs and substances of abuse have ended in failure or—at best—in only partial success (Anderson, 2010; Erceg-Hurn, 2008; Grimshaw & Stanton, 2006; Pagliaro & Pagliaro, 1996; Pan & Bai, 2009; Sloboda, Stephens, Stephens, et al., 2009; Thomas & Perera, 2006; Wakefield, Flay, Nichter, et al., 2003). Several reasons for this failure have been suggested, including the lack of appropriate focus and goals, lack of appropriate research-based theory to develop and guide prevention strategies (also see Chapter 4, *Explaining Child and Adolescent Use of the Drugs and Substances of Abuse*), and lack of political commitment or social resolve.

### Lack of Appropriate Focus and Goals

Generally, the purpose of programs and services aimed at preventing the use of drugs and substances of abuse by children and adolescents is to: (1) increase related awareness and understanding among youth, parents, teachers, and communities, and other stakeholders; (2) provide accurate information regarding the nature and extent of the use of

---

[4] In this clinical context, an inoculation is simply defined as planned appropriate therapeutic (e.g., psycho-educational) follow-up intervention. As such, it can be conceptualized as an intervention that can reinforce or strengthen the protection provided by an earlier successful therapeutic intervention, which now may be waning (i.e., losing its protective effectiveness). The therapeutic inoculation can be compared to a booster vaccination. (Also see discussion of the use of therapeutic inoculation in the section, "Social environmental/Learning Model.")

the drugs and substances of abuse and the harm associated with their use; and (3) positively change the related attitudes and values of targeted groups of children and adolescents. However, the focus and priorities of these primarily government-sponsored programs and services are sensitive to public opinion and pressure. Hence, they are often educationally unsound and short-lived (DuPont, 1987; Goodstadt, 1989) (also see the following related discussion regarding the lack of political or social resolve).

Goldstein and Engwall (1992), in their documentary analysis of data from 1970 to 1990, found a decided change in the public's perception of the use of the drugs and substances of abuse by children and adolescents over the several decades studied. They also found changes in the approaches that the government took in regard to primary and secondary prevention. During the 1970s and 1980s, the public did not perceive the use of the drugs and substances of abuse by children and adolescents as a major social problem, and, thus, the approach to primary prevention was soft—although abstinence from use was considered ideal, the promotion of safe or responsible use generally was seen as sufficient.

Programs that encouraged decision making regarding safe and responsible use of the drugs and substances of abuse were funded and developed. These programs included, for example, the Don't Drink and Drive program and the Designated Driver program. However, by the mid-1980s, the public's perception changed, as the use of the drugs and substances of abuse by children and adolescents became the leading social concern in North America. In response, the government hardened its policy. As identified by Goldstein and Engwall (1992), the perspective clearly changed from safe and responsible use to no use or zero tolerance—the slogan "Drug-Free America" supported this message.[5] Subsequently, the first decade of the new millennium witnessed a general return to the more permissive or liberal views of the 1970s in regard to issues related to the use of the drugs and substances of abuse, including the legalization of marijuana and other drugs and substances of abuse and a primary focus on harm reduction.[6]

### Lack of Appropriate Theory to Guide Primary Prevention

The problem has not been too few theories but, conversely, a plethora of theories. Unfortunately, the theories generally have not been clinically tested, and many are philosophically incompatible with the philosophies of the health and social care providers working in particular clinical contexts of practice. (See Chapter 4, *Explaining Child and Adolescent Use of the Drugs and Substances of Abuse*). However, it appears that most previous programs and services designed to prevent child

---

[5] We favor and encourage a more hybrid approach. In terms of primary prevention, we concur that the goal should be abstinence. This position conflicts with the more liberal position of Goldstein and Engwall (1992) and perhaps also with other researchers, who, although in a decided minority, have suggested a positive relationship between a low level of using the drugs and substances of abuse by adolescents and overall psychological adjustment. For example, Shedler and Block (1990), using a sample of 101 18-year-olds, found that "adolescents who had engaged in some degree of experimentation (primarily with marijuana) were the best-adjusted in the sample" (p. 404). This finding appears to be in sharp contrast to the observation by Logan (1991) that "even minimal use of illicit substances may be an indicator of an adolescent's willingness to engage in potentially harmful high-risk behaviors" (p. 27). These contrasting views and results are reflective of the current lack of consensus within the field.

However, for those adolescents for whom abstinence cannot be achieved in keeping with secondary and tertiary models of prevention and health promotion, we encourage safe and responsible use that minimizes the risk of harm to self or others. The levels of harm associated with using the various drugs and substances of abuse that are illustrated in Figure 9.1 are suggested as a guide in this regard.

[6] We have always tended to view harm reduction as a *last resort*. However, in terms of reducing alcohol-related motor vehicle crashes (MVCs) and the transmission of infections associated with the use of contaminated needles and syringes, there exists strong evidence to support its use (e.g., Ritter & Cameron, 2006). See related discussion later in this chapter.

or adolescent use of the drugs and substances of abuse can be classified into one of four models:

1. Information-only model
2. Alternatives model
3. Affective educational/social competency model
4. Social environmental/learning model

The models, listed in chronological order of their predominant use from earliest to latest, continue to be used in various contexts and are briefly discussed in the next sections.

**Information-Only Model**    The information-only model was the first model to be widely used for preventing child and adolescent use of the drugs and substances of abuse. The predominant model of the 1960s and 1970s, it was predicated on two basic assumptions: (1) Youth were ignorant of the harmful effects associated with the use of the drugs and substances of abuse; and (2) if made aware of the harmful effects, youth would refrain from using the drugs and substances of abuse. Unfortunately, both assumptions were generally found to be incorrect. While the model positively affected knowledge acquisition in regard to the drugs and substances of abuse, attitudes and behaviors in regard to their use were, for the most part, not significantly affected (Faggiano, Vigna-Taglianti, Versino, et al., 2008). In some cases, the acquisition of knowledge appeared actually to increase the initial use of the drugs and substances of abuse as children and adolescents became more curious and experimented with them.

In an effort to counteract the piqued curiosity effect and associated youthful experimentation with the drugs and substances of abuse, teacher-led information programs were emphasized. However, as a result of poorly prepared training materials that were also scientifically inaccurate, teachers often found themselves, in most cases unknowingly, exaggerating the harmful effects associated with the use of the drugs and substances of abuse—and utilizing programs (e.g., *Scared Straight*) and techniques that were later found to be largely inaccurate, ineffective, or short-lived.[7] To dissuade use, other programs led teachers to use fear tactics, such as showing a picture of a black, tarry, cancerous lung from a deceased tobacco smoker and then blowing tobacco smoke through a white handkerchief so that children could see for themselves that the solid material in smoke was not removed by cigarette filters or by the lungs. Students who had already experimented with a drug or substance of abuse quickly recognized that their teachers did not know what they were talking about or assumed that the teachers were lying. In this context, misinformation about even one of the harmful consequences associated with the use of a drug or substance of abuse was overgeneralized by students and tended to undermine the teacher's credibility in regard to everything else that was said subsequently in the program, whether it was correct or not.

In response to growing concerns about the lack of efficacy of these programs during the 1970s, the White House Special Action Office for Drug Abuse Prevention called for an end to the use of federally funded drug information material that: used scare tactics; stereotyped "drug users;" and generally provided unfounded, dogmatic statements about the harmful effects associated with the use of a particular drug or substance of abuse (Resnick, 1978). Another major flaw of the information-only model was that its restricted focus discounted or ignored significant variables that were associated with using or not using the drugs and substances

---

[7] For example, teachers frequently claimed that marijuana was highly addictive and caused insanity or that lysergic acid diethylamide (LSD) caused severe birth defects when used during pregnancy—both claims, of which, are false.

of abuse by children and adolescents (e.g., parent, peer, and media influences; individual personality characteristics, including genetic predisposition and sensation-seeking personality characteristics). In an effort to address these inadequacies, information-only programs were replaced by programs that focused on the characteristics of the user, particularly his or her self-esteem.[8]

**Alternatives Model** The alternatives model was used primarily during the late 1970s. This model had seven basic assumptions (Cohen, 1974, pp. 3–4):

1. People take drugs because they want to.
2. People use drugs to feel better or to get high. Individuals experiment with drugs out of curiosity or hope that using drugs can make them feel better.
3. People have been taught by cultural example, media, and others that drugs are an effective way to make them feel better.
4. "Feeling better" encompasses a huge range of mood or consciousness change, including such aspects as oblivion-sleep, emotion shift, energy modification and visions of the divine, and so on.
5. With many mind or mood-altering drugs taken principally for that purpose, individuals may temporarily feel better. However, drugs have substantial short- and long-term disadvantages related to the motive for their use. These include possible physiological damage, psychological deterioration, and cognitive breakdown. Drugs also tend to be temporary, relatively devoid of satisfying translations to the ordinary non-drug state of life, and siphon off energy for long-term constructive growth.
6. Basically, individuals do not stop using drugs until they discover something better.

7. The key to meeting problems of drug abuse is to focus on the *something* better and maximize opportunities for experiencing satisfying nonchemical alternatives. The same key can be used to discourage experimentation or, more likely, keep experimentation from progressing to dependency.

The alternatives model sought to provide alternative activities for children and adolescents that presumably would alleviate their need to use the drugs and substances of abuse. Although most alternative programs focused on physical and recreational activities (e.g., mountain climbing, sky diving, or sports) to keep children and adolescents busy and productive, some focused specifically on building self-confidence, increasing self-esteem, and developing prosocial community values. An example of one of the more comprehensive applications of alternative programs was developed by Cohen (1974; see Table 9.2). Unfortunately, alternative programs did not, in general, prove to be effective in preventing child and adolescent use of the drugs and substances of abuse (Moskowitz, Malvin, Schaeffer, et al., 1983; Schaps, Moskowitz, Malvin et al., 1986; Tobler, 1992).

**Affective Educational/Social Competency Model** The development of the affective educational/social competency model was based, in large part, on Jessor and Jessor's (1977a, b) problem behavior theory. (See Chapter 4, *Explaining Child and Adolescent Use of the Drugs and Substances of Abuse*) As explained by Botvin and Botvin (1992), according to this theory:

> Adolescents engage in problem behaviors such as substance use and premature sexual behavior because these behaviors help the adolescent achieve desired personal goals. To the extent that adolescents perceive these behaviors as functional,

---

[8]The shift in the focus of primary prevention programs was so complete that most of the later programs never even mentioned the drugs and substances of abuse at all. These programs often were based on the humanistic psychology movement of the 1970s and its general notion that if children and adolescents could just be happy with themselves, they would have no reason to use the drugs and substances of abuse.

**TABLE 9.2   Example of a Comprehensive Alternatives Model**

| Level of Experience | Examples of Corresponding Motives | Examples of Possible Alternatives |
|---|---|---|
| Physical | Desire for physical satisfaction; physical relaxation; relief from sickness; desire for more energy; maintenance of physical dependency | Athletics; dance; exercise; hiking; diet; health training; carpentry; gardening or other outdoor work |
| Sensory | Desire to stimulate sight, sound, touch, taste; need for sensual-sexual stimulation; desire to magnify sensorium | Sensory awareness training; sky diving; experiencing sensory beauty of nature (e.g., bird watching, hiking, mountain climbing, sailing) |
| Emotional | Relief from psychological pain; attempt to solve personal perplexities; relief from bad mood; escape from anxiety; desire for emotional insight; liberation of feeling; emotional relaxation | Competent individual counseling; well-run group therapy; instruction in psychology of personal development |
| Interpersonal | To gain peer acceptance; to break through interpersonal barriers; to "communicate," especially nonverbally; defiance of authority figures; cement two-person relationships; relaxation of interpersonal inhibition; solve interpersonal hangups. | Expertly managed sensitivity and encounter groups; well-run group therapy; instruction in social customs; confidence training; social-interpersonal counseling; emphasis on assisting others in distress via education; marriage |
| Social (including sociocultural and environmental) | To promote social change; to find identifiable subculture; to tune out intolerable environmental conditions (e.g., poverty); to change awareness of the "masses" | Social service; community action in positive social change; helping the poor, aged, infirm, young; tutoring disabled people; ecology action |
| Political | To promote political change; to identify with antiestablishment subgroup; to change drug legislation; out of desperation with the social-political order; to gain wealth or affluence or power | Political service; political action; nonpartisan projects such as ecological lobbying; fieldwork with politicians and public officials; running for public office |
| Intellectual | To escape mental boredom; out of intellectual curiosity; to solve cognitive problems; to gain new understanding in the world of ideas; to study better; to research one's own awareness; for science | Intellectual excitement through reading, through discussion, creative games and puzzles; self-hypnosis; training in concentration; synectics—training in intellectual breakthroughs; memory training |
| Creative-Aesthetic | To improve creativity in the arts; to enhance enjoyment of art already produced (e.g., music); to enjoy imaginative mental productions | Nongraded instruction in producing and/or appreciating art, music, drama, crafts, handiwork, cooking, sewing, gardening, writing, singing, etc. |
| Philosophical | To discover meaningful values; to grasp the nature of the universe; to find meaning in life; to help establish personal identity; to organize a belief structure | Discussions, seminars, courses in the meaning of life; study of ethics, morality, the nature of reality; relevant philosophical literature; guided exploration of value systems |
| Spiritual-Mystical | To transcend orthodox religion; to develop spiritual insights; to reach higher levels of consciousness; to have divine visions; to communicate with God; to augment yogic practices; to get a spiritual shortcut; to attain enlightenment; to attain spiritual powers | Exposure to nonchemical methods of spiritual development; study of world religions; introduction to applied mysticism; meditation; yogic techniques |
| Miscellaneous | Adventure, risk, drama, kicks, unexpressed motives; pro-drug general attitudes, etc. | Outward Bound survival training; combinations of alternatives above; pro-natural attitudes; brain-wave training; meaningful employment; etc. |

Source: Cohen (1974, pp. 6–7).

they will be motivated to engage in them. For example, problem behavior may serve as a way of coping with real or anticipated failure, boredom, social anxiety, unhappiness, rejection, social isolation, low self-esteem, and a lack of self-efficacy. These behaviors may also serve as a way of gaining admission to a particular peer group. For adolescents who are not achieving academically, the use of psychoactive substances may provide a way of achieving social status. Adolescents may believe that smoking, drinking, or using drugs will enhance their public image by making them look *cool* or by demonstrating independence from authority figures. Adolescents at the greatest risk of becoming substance users are those who perceive that alternative ways of achieving these same goals are unavailable. (p. 293)

The affective educational/social competency model, which shares many of the assumptions of the alternatives model,[9] was used primarily during the mid-1970s to the mid-1980s. "Social competency" in this context was defined as the ability of students to disagree, refuse, make requests, and initiate conversations. The model was based on two assumptions: (1) Children and adolescents use the drugs and substances of abuse because of low self-esteem and inappropriate social values; and (2) increasing self-esteem among children and adolescents and teaching them values clarification and related problem-solving, decision-making, and communication skills will enable them, of their own volition, to choose *not* to use drugs and substances of abuse.

Thus, as with the alternatives model, programs based on this model did not directly address the use of the drugs and substances of abuse. Instead, these programs focused on

helping children and adolescents to: (1) choose an alternative after carefully considering all other available behaviors and their related consequences; (2) publicly affirm the alternative that was chosen and feel positive about choosing, or prizing, it; and (3) act on their own positive beliefs and choices consistently and regularly (Harmin, Kirschenbaum, & Simon, 1973). The use of values clarification skills was often reinforced by classroom role playing and by each student's maintenance of a private values journal.

Overall, these programs have demonstrated poor outcomes in relation to preventing child and adolescent use of the drugs and substances of abuse, particularly in terms of long-term effects (Botvin, 1986; Del Greco, Breitbach, Rumer, et al. 1986; DuPont, 1987; Hansen, Johnson, Flay, et al., 1988; Murray, Davis-Hearn, Goldman, et al., 1988; Petersen, 1987; Schaps, DiBartalo, Moskowitz, et al., 1981; Stephens, Sloboda, Stephens, et al., 2009).[10] The poor success rate was probably due to several factors. One factor was the inadequate training of teachers in regard to the methods inherent in this model. The high school teachers involved in these programs were generally not specifically trained in promoting self-esteem or teaching values clarification skills. The results of these programs may have been significantly different had the programs been provided by specially trained teachers or school psychologists.

In spite of the strong research evidence that contradicted or discredited the use of information-only and alternatives programs (including programs that combined the two approaches), far too many programs continue to be based on these

---

[9] Some authors actually categorize the alternatives model as a subset, or specialized example, of the affective educational/ social competency model.

[10] Looking back at our own clinical data compiled from a generation of individuals who received unsuccessful treatment as adolescents based primarily on self-esteem models and subsequently were referred to us for treatment, primarily as young adults, it is apparent that for many of those for whom the self-esteem models worked, the results were: (1) increased personal self-esteem; and (2) the direct, but unintended consequence of increased serious use of the drugs and substances of abuse, including successful involvement in drug dealing (e.g., rather than dealing nickel-and-dime bags of marijuana at school, they controlled hundreds of thousands of dollars of cocaine as part of their membership in and rapid advancement up the ranks of criminal youth gangs in their neighborhoods, on their reservations and reserves, or in and around their housing projects in several large cities) (Pagliaro & Pagliaro, *Clinical Patient Data Files*).

approaches (Faggiano, Vigna-Taglianti, Versino, et al., 2008). The critical component of successful programs appears to be their emphasis on teaching and developing direct behavior skills, including refusal skills, communication skills, problem-solving skills, and other direct behavior skills (Bernard, 1988).

In addition, programs that are based on the affective education/social competency model discussed in this section (e.g., Positive Action Program), continue to be actively funded by the National Institute on Drug Abuse (Whitten, 2010), even though their results, in terms of preventing child and adolescent use of the drugs and substances of abuse, are at best mixed. The central idea of the Positive Action Program is "When you do good, you feel good" and the interrelationships among "thoughts," "feelings," and "actions" is reinforced by teachers in grades 1 through 12. The program is based on six specific units, or lesson plans, that address these themes:

- Developing self-concept
- Maintaining a healthy body and mind
- Managing oneself responsibly
- Getting along with others by treating them the way oneself would like to be treated
- Being honest with oneself and others
- Improving oneself continually[11]

These programs attempt to achieve a number of diverse outcomes, including decreasing the rates of child and adolescent use of the drugs and substances of abuse, violent behavior, and voluntary sexual activity. While so doing, they also attempt to increase academic achievement, healthy eating, and school attendance (Snyder,

Vuchinich, Acock, et al., 2010; Whitten, 2010). The many and diverse expectations of these programs inevitably contribute to the poor performance outcomes observed in regard to decreasing the use of the drugs and substances of abuse by children and adolescents.

**Social Environmental/Learning Model**
The social environmental/learning model,[12] largely based on cognitive-social learning theory (Bandura 1977; Evans, Rozelle, Mittlemark, et al., 1978), has been used from the mid-1980s to date with an overall moderate degree of success. The assumptions of the social environmental/learning model are that: (1) social influences (e.g., parents, peers, and media) have a significant effect on child and adolescent use of the drugs and substances of abuse; and (2) children and adolescents can be trained to become aware of and, subsequently, resist social situational pressures (e.g., peer pressure; media messages) to use the drugs and substances of abuse. Using the primary prevention metaphor that children and adolescents can be inoculated against subsequent use of the drugs and substances of abuse, this approach generally has been referred to in the published literature as psychosocial inoculation or social inoculation training (i.e., training that will protect children and adolescents from infection by future social influences to use the drugs and substances of abuse).

Examples of the numerous programs that have been based on this model include: ALERT, D.A.R.E.,[13] Here's Looking at You, Just Say No, Life Skills Training, PALS, and SMART Moves (De Jung, 1987; Dusenbury & Botvin, 1992;

---

[11] In this program and many similar ones, there is no specific unit or focus on the drugs and substances of abuse.

[12] This model also has been referred to as the cognitive/behavioral or social influences model.

[13] The Drug Abuse Resistance Education (D.A.R.E.) program is the largest school-based program in the United States aimed at preventing the use of drugs and substances of abuse by children and adolescents. Over 30 million children and adolescents in grades 6 through 9 have participated in D.A.R.E. programs (D.A.R.E. America, 2007). Unfortunately, most of the comprehensive evaluations of the D.A.R.E. program (e.g., Lynam, Milich, Zimmerman, et al., 1999; Pan & Bai, 2009; Sloboda, Stephens, Stephens, et al., 2009) have found its actual benefit to be questionable or, at best, inconsistent. (See related discussion in section, "School-Based Prevention Programs.") Similar findings, which are not very encouraging, also have been reported for closely related programs, including Lions-Quest Skills for Adolescence (Eisen, Zellman, & Murray, 2003), ALERT (Bell, Ellickson, & Harrison, 1993), and SMART (Hanson, Johnson, Flay, et al., 1988).

Eisen, Zellman, & Murray, 2003; Ellickson & Bell, 1990; Gelb, 1984; Goldstein, Reagles, & Amann, 1990; Kim, 1988; Sweet, 1991; Van Hasselt, Hersen, Null, et al., 1993). Often these programs used student peers as coleaders together with a teacher or school counselor (Klepp, Halper, & Perry, 1986; Mellanby, Rees, & Tripp, 2000; Perry, 1989). In addition to teaching students about the adverse consequences associated with the use of the drugs and substances of abuse, the peer-focused programs generally attempted to integrate these objectives:

- Create a school climate that encourages the development of responsible independence and a positive identity
- Create opportunities for students to learn how to actively and intentionally use their experiences to gain new levels of confidence and competence
- Encourage opportunities for early intervention to deal with adolescent difficulties
- Involve students in identifying and meeting student-perceived needs (*Alberta's peer support program,* 1987, p. 23)

In addition, much of the focus of these programs was directed at socially normed education (e.g., "It's *not* true that everybody does drugs" and "Most people do *not* smoke tobacco") and cognitive-behavioral training (i.e., strategies for resisting the pressure to use drugs and substances of abuse are developed, modeled, and rehearsed).

The student peer facilitators, if appropriately trained and committed to the goals of the program, serve as important role models for other students in the program and contribute significantly to its success (Botvin, Baker, Renick et al., 1984; Gottfredson & Wilson, 2003; Murray, Davis-Hearn, Goldman, et al., 1988). However, as asserted by Tobler (1992), peers do not take the place of well-trained, well-qualified

teachers or counselors and, if not appropriately monitored, may do more harm than good: "A peer leader does not make a peer program" (p. 21). In fact, peer leaders may or may not be able to facilitate the necessary interaction and, in many cases, they benefit more from their active role than do the other group members.[14]

The social environmental/learning model, although not universally successful (e.g., Becker, Agopian, & Yeh, 1992; Hansen & Graham, 1991; Pan & Bai, 2009), has been demonstrated in a number of studies to be effective in preventing or decreasing child or adolescent use of selected drugs and substances of abuse, including alcohol (e.g., Botvin, Baker, Botvin, et al., 1984; Perry, 1989); tobacco (e.g., Biglan, Severson, Ary, et al., 1987; Botvin, Renick, & Baker, 1983; Bühler, A., Schröder & Silbereisen, 2008; Lennox & Cecchini, 2008) and polyuse of the drugs and substances of abuse (e.g., Botvin, Baker, Dusenbury, et al., 1990; Botvin, Baker, Renick, et al., 1984; Botvin & Griffin, 2007; Hansen, Johnson, Flay, et al., 1988; Shope, Copeland, Marcoux, et al., 1996; Skara & Sussman, 2003). The most success demonstrated with this approach to date has been in relation to tobacco smoking. Even in this context, the programs "can be [at best] effective some of the time. However, [even] this conclusion seems somewhat fragile given the considerable differences between [different] studies in the patterns of reported results" (Flay, 1985, p. 473). Thus, it should not be surprising that most studies (e.g., Biglan, Severson, Ary, et al., 1987; Caplan, Weissberg, Grober, et al., 1992; Gorman, 1998; Johnson, Shamblen, Ogilvie, et al., 2009; Malvin, Moskowitz, Schaeffer, et al., 1984; Murray, Davis-Hearn, Goldman, et al., 1988; Shope, Copeland, Kamp, et al., 1998) have failed to demonstrate the long-term effectiveness of these programs in regard to preventing the

---

[14] Commonly, students who are actively involved as peer facilitators or student counselors have noted significant gains in their own self-esteem. In addition, their own leadership and teaching skills are developed or notably improved. While we view these as positive outcomes that should be encouraged, we emphasize that care be taken by group leaders (i.e., the teacher or professional counselor) to help to ensure that these outcomes occur *together* with, and not at the expense of, benefits for the other students in the group.

initial use of the drugs or substances of abuse or reducing their use once use has begun.

None of the four models of prevention has uniformly and consistently demonstrated widespread, long-lasting effectiveness. A clue to their general lack of success may be gleaned by a quick perusal of the variables listed in Table 9.1. For example, a "lack of knowledge about the substances of abuse" is not identified as an important variable, or risk factor, in the model. It is no wonder, then, that the information-only model, which focused on knowledge acquisition alone, had virtually no effect. Similarly, the appearance of "low self-esteem" as an important variable, or risk factor, helps to explain the limited success of the alternatives and the affective educational/social competency models, both of which had self-esteem as a major focus. A similar analysis of future prevention models using the Meta-Interactive Model of Child and Adolescent Use of the Drugs and Substances of Abuse would be expected to predict, a priori, their propensity for success. (See Figure 9.2.)

As governments continue to downsize and reduce spending following the world economic crash of 2008, it appears likely that less and less funding will be available for preventing child and adolescent use of the drugs and substances of abuse. Ineffective or marginally effective programs that waste time and money will have no place in an increasingly stressed school curriculum and budget.[15] With some indication of the prevention strategies that work and the ones that do not, we can begin to develop more effective programs, but many pressing questions remain—questions that echo those passed by Norman and Turner (1993) two decades ago:

1. Do we target high risk youth or the general population? Some researchers contend that the prevention programs currently most widely used may be affecting prevalence of alcohol and other drug use in the general population, but they are failing to reach the 5% to 15% of the adolescent population who are at greatest risk for becoming substance abusers. Although high risk youth are in the minority, they may account for the majority of young adults in the criminal justice system and those involved in drug-related traffic accidents.

2. Do we focus on primary or secondary prevention? Currently the majority of New York State prevention resources are allocated for secondary prevention or counseling those youth who already have problems related to substance use. Some experts believe that if we continue to do secondary prevention we will never have any significant impact on overall substance use and abuse, and that we will be continuing to put Band-Aids® on problems that already exist, as opposed to trying to eliminate the problems through primary prevention strategies.

3. Do we concentrate on First Order or Second Order Change? Most of the prevention efforts of the 1980s and 1990s have been aimed at trying to change the behavior of individuals (second order change). An increasing number of prevention planners believe that the emphasis should be on first order change—that is, addressing the societal problems that are influencing individuals to become substance abusers. Increasing the price of legal substances, banning cigarette and alcohol advertising, and raising the legal drinking age are examples of first order change. (p. 17)

### Lack of Political or Social Resolve

Examples of lack of political or social resolve abound,[16] but are probably clearest in the area of nicotine use in the general form of

---

[15] This concern is not new. In fact, it was widely voiced over two decades ago by Becker, Agopian, and Yeh (1992). Unfortunately, the concern has not been adequately addressed yet.

[16] The lack of resolve also includes the generally chronic underfunding of public sector programs aimed at preventing child and adolescent use of the drugs and substances of abuse over the past three decades—(e.g., McAuliffe, 1990; Meara & Frank, 2005; Minugh, Janke, Lomuto, et al., 2007; Pagliaro & Pagliaro, 1996).

tobacco smoking. As noted in Chapter 2, *The Psychostimulants*, and as recognized by the World Health Organization for over half a century, tobacco smoking has no defined safe level of use and by itself causes more deaths in North America than any other single drug or substance of abuse. However, the use of tobacco—a so-called "soft drug"—remains legal, at least for adults.[17] In addition, tobacco farmers continue to receive government subsidies and export tobacco as a cash crop to countries such as China, where use continues to be on the rise.

In this context, it is not surprising that regulations concerning the distribution and sale of tobacco are generally weak and infrequently enforced, with over 80% of convenience stores and pharmacies sampled found to engage in the illegal sale of tobacco products to minors (Brown & DiFranza, 1992; DiFranza & Brown, 1992; DiFranza, Savageau, & Aisguith, 1996).[18] In fact, legal promotional advertising campaigns designed and produced specifically to encourage the initiation of tobacco smoking among adolescents continue to be widely used across North America (DiFranza, Savageau, & Fletcher, 2009). However, in schools and communities that have developed the necessary political or social resolve, nicotine use by children and adolescents has decreased significantly (DiFranza, 1992; Stead & Lancaster, 2005a). Such successful outcomes demonstrate that proactive community involvement, extended to communities across North America, can be a significant factor in reducing problematic patterns of using drugs and substances of abuse by children and adolescents; such involvement includes, for example, the use of local, state, and federal billboard advertisements and radio and television public service announcements directed at the dangers of drinking and

driving or those associated with methamphetamine (ice, meth) abuse.

One such program, the Vermont Anti-Smoking Campaign, significantly reduced the prevalence of adolescent smoking and did so with a low per-capita cost (Pechmann & Reibling, 2000). Unfortunately, most other programs have not been as successful. For example, formal analysis of the well-funded, multiyear Montana Meth Project found that it had "no discernable impact … on methamphetamine use among Montana's youth" (Anderson, 2010, p. 732). However, most of the successful community programs begin with or involve in-school educationally based prevention strategies, as discussed in the next section.

### School-Based Prevention Programs

A variety of prevention programs have targeted child and adolescent use of the drugs and substances of abuse using several educational approaches (e.g., Botvin & Griffin, 2007; Faggiano, Vigna-Taglianti, Versino, et al., 2008; Fletcher, Bonell, & Hargreaves, 2008; McLaughlin, Holcomb, Jibaja-Rusth, et al., 1993; Moskowitz, Schaps, Schaeffer, et al., 1984; Schaps & Battistich, 1991; Thomas & Perera, 2006). These school-based programs have been developed at local community, city, state or provincial, national, and international levels. However, the implementation of these programs is by no means universal. For example, Ringwalt, Hanley, Vincus, et al. (2008) found, in their analysis of data collected from approximately 1,400 school districts across the United States, that "only 56.5% of the nation's districts with high school grades administered any [drug or] substance use prevention programming in at least one of their constituent high schools" (p. 479).

---

[17] We have steadfastly refrained from using the term "soft" drug in this text or elsewhere because we find it oxymoronic and because it is pharmacologically meaningless and scientifically inaccurate.

[18] The reader need only take an early-morning drive by the nearest convenience store adjacent to a junior high school to see firsthand how easily minors can purchase tobacco cigarettes. Also see the related discussion and current statistics in Chapter 2, *The Psychostimulants*.

Table 9.3 lists several problems, or limitations, that have been identified with school-based prevention programs. These limitations must be recognized and proactively addressed by school boards and concerned community members in order to maximize the potential benefits of school-based programs. If not adequately addressed, school-based prevention programs will continue to have limited success. For example, Ranney, Melvin, Lux, et al. (2006), Dobbins, DeCorby, Manske, et al. (2007), and Müller-Riemenschneider, Bockelbrink, Reinhold, et al. (2008) found, in their respective meta-analyses of school-based tobacco use prevention programs, that, overall, the programs had positive but short-term effects on adolescent smoking behaviors—that is, long-term effectiveness has not been demonstrated. In addition, in their large-scale meta-analysis of randomized controlled trials of school-based programs for preventing child and adolescent smoking, Thomas and Perera (2006) found that only half of their group of best-quality studies yielded results in which the participants in the intervention group smoked less than those in the control group and that many of the studies failed to detect any positive effect for the intervention.

Thus, more often than not, the evaluation of these school-based prevention programs reveals that the intervention worked for some students but not for others (Cuijpers, 2002; Faggiano, Vigna-Taglianti, Versino, et al., 2005; Flay, 1985). For example, Sloboda, Stephens, Stephens, et al. (2009), in their analysis of the universal school-based drug and substance abuse prevention program Take Charge of Your Life, provided to grade 7 and grade 9 students by trained D.A.R.E. police officers, found that the program had a negative effect over the 5 years of their study (i.e., nonusers in grade 7 significantly began using alcohol and tobacco by grade 12)

**TABLE 9.3 School-Based Prevention Programs: Common Major Limitations**

- Target audience is not well defined.
- Program components are not leveled in order to build on each other.
- Program timing does not coincide with age or developmental level of participants.
- Active student involvement is not encouraged.
- Community linkages are weak.
- Program scope is too narrow or too wide.
- Adequate time provisions for implementation and delivery are not made.
- Teachers are underqualified and poorly trained.
- Program design is too simplistic or monolithic.
- Program goals are unrealistic or unachievable.
- Program objectives are unclear or poorly defined.
- Program techniques are faulty.
- Program commitment is lacking in regard to preventing or minimizing the use of drugs and substances of abuse.

while those who used marijuana at baseline decreased use.[19]

Since the late 1990s, state governments, school boards, and other funding agencies attempted to increase the efficacy of school-based programs aimed at preventing the use of the drugs and substances of abuse among children and adolescents by requiring schools to select programming from approved lists of prevention strategies or, when strategies are not listed, to provide evidence of their efficacy (Sloboda, Pyakuryal, Stephens, et al., 2008). During this time, several states also have embedded in law requirements for schools to periodically provide a formal evaluation of the effectiveness of tax-funded school-based programs. For example, "current legislative language requires the California Department of Public Health, California Tobacco Control Program, to evaluate the effectiveness of the school-based *Tobacco Use Prevention Education* (TUPE) program in California every two years" (Park, Dent, Abramsohn, et al., 2010, p. 43). However, these legislative requirements have not resulted in significant improvement in regard to the efficacy of school-based

---

[19] In their review of 20 studies that evaluated the effectiveness of the D.A.R.E. program in the United States, Pan and Bai (2009) found that although some programs worked for some students in preventing or reducing drug and substance use, overall, it was generally not effective. (Also see related discussion in the "Social Environmental/Learning Model" and "Social Skills Training" sections of this chapter.)

prevention programs. For example, both the TUPE and D.A.R.E. programs have produced poor results (Pan & Bai, 2009; Park, Dent, Abramsohn, et al., 2010; also see previous related discussion in this section).

In order to achieve optimal potential success, school-based prevention programs should begin during the early primary school grades and continue through all secondary school grades with attention to the specific needs of the children and adolescents who are receiving these programs and possible social factors that may influence or protect them from using the drugs and substances of abuse (e.g., living in an inner city or small rural community; culture, ethnicity, or continental descent;[20] socioeconomic level; intact, blended, or other family type; community patterns of using drugs and substances of abuse).

The use of appropriate developmental leveling of programs from kindergarten through grade 12 also is essential. This tailoring of programs requires well-defined, realistic goals (e.g., a program that begins in junior high school and attempts to do everything for everyone is quite likely to do little for anyone). These goals should be based on an accurate knowledge of the nature and extent of the use of the drugs and substances of abuse by a particular cohort of students targeted (e.g., a particular school or school district). For example, a

successful comprehensive program developed for students in a rural school district in Omaha, Nebraska, would very likely be ineffective for students in an inner-city school district in New York City, particularly if the program was simply "transplanted."

These data should be collected and then further refined based on a well-designed local needs assessment study followed by a pilot study to test the efficacy of planned interventions. The pilot study can identify areas that require revision before the program is developed and implemented for use at the broader community level or with other comparable cohorts of students in other geographic regions. See Table 9.4 for a prototype of this approach. Although this approach may require much time and costly preparatory work, the alternative, as previously noted—for too many decades, is to provide "ineffective programs [that] waste time and money... [and] occupy space in a stressed curriculum" (Kozlowski, Coambs, Ferrence, et al., 1989, p. 454).[21]

Once the desired goals have been properly identified, effective techniques to achieve these goals should be selected and integrated into the program delivery model (e.g., it has been clearly demonstrated that the information-only and alternative models are almost invariably ineffective; thus, they should not be selected).

---

[20] Several programs have been adapted or specifically created for use with children and adolescents of American Indian or Aboriginal descent. For example, a school-based prevention program was developed and implemented with the Alexis Nakota Sioux Nation (Baydala, Sewlal, Rasmussen, et al., 2009) that "incorporated cultural beliefs, values, language, and visual images" (p. 37) as well as participation of community elders. However, like so many similar programs, it did not demonstrate a significant reduction in regard to the use of the drugs and substances of abuse. (Also see the "Ethnic-Specific Treatment Programs" section later in this chapter.)

[21] For schools that do not have the necessary resources to develop their own tailored curriculum model for preventing the use of the drugs and substances of abuse by their students or would like to begin with a basically sound program that can be modified to best meet their specific needs, we recommend the Learning to Live Drug Free model developed by Flatter and McCormick (1992) for the U.S. Department of Education. As described in the introduction:

> This drug prevention curriculum model provides a framework for prevention education from kindergarten through 12th grade. It provides the basics for starting or expanding drug education; it includes information about drugs, background for teachers on childhood growth and development, sample lesson plans and activities, and suggestions on working with parents and the community. The format is expandable, so that school districts and individual classroom teachers can add or update information—and create their own lessons plans and activities.

> Written primarily for school teachers, administrators, and principals, the curriculum model is also useful for health and social services professionals, parents, business leaders, and other people who want to help prevent drug use among youth. (Flatter & McCormick, 1992, Part 1, p. 1)

**TABLE 9.4   Achieving Schools Without Drugs**

| | |
|---|---|
| Students | • Learn about the effects of drugs and substances of abuse, the reasons why they are harmful, and ways to resist pressures to try them. |
| | • Use an understanding of the dangers posed by the drugs and substances of abuse to help other students avoid them. Encourage other students to resist pressures to use the drugs and substances of abuse and persuade those who use them to seek help. Report students who are selling drugs and substances of abuse to their parents and the school principal. |
| Parents | • Teach standards of right and wrong and demonstrate these standards through personal example, including not using the drugs and substances of abuse and remembering to reinforce this teaching throughout adolescence. |
| | • Be knowledgeable about the drugs and substances of abuse. |
| | • Be aware of the signs and symptoms that may indicate that your child or adolescent is using the drugs or substances of abuse. |
| | • Know what to do when signs or symptoms related to child or adolescent use of the drugs and substances of abuse are observed, and respond promptly. |
| Schools | • Determine the extent and character of student body use of the drugs and substances of abuse and establish a means for monitoring use regularly. |
| | • Establish clear and specific policies and rules regarding the use of the drugs and substances of abuse that include strong corrective actions. |
| | • Enforce established policies and rules against the use of the drugs and substances of abuse fairly and consistently. |
| | • Implement security measures to eliminate drugs and substances of abuse on school premises and at school functions. |
| | • Implement a comprehensive curriculum for preventing the use of drugs and substances of abuse for kindergarten through grade 12. |
| | • Teach that the use of drugs and substances of abuse is wrong and may be harmful. |
| | • Support and strengthen resistance techniques aimed at preventing the use of drugs and substances of abuse. |
| | • Reach out to the community for support and assistance in making the school's antidrug policy and program work. |
| | • Develop collaborative arrangements in which school personnel, parents, school boards, law enforcement officers, treatment organizations, and private groups work together to provide necessary resources. |
| Communities | • Help schools fight student use of the drugs and substances of abuse by providing them with the expertise and financial resources available from community groups and agencies. |
| | • Involve local law enforcement agencies in all aspects of drug and substance abuse prevention, assessment, enforcement, and education. |
| | • Ensure that police and courts have well-established and mutually supportive relationships with the schools. |

Modified from: U.S. Department of Education (1986, 1992).

Quick-fix, uncoordinated programs (e.g., a weekly, 1-hour drug education class) should be replaced with integrated programs throughout the school year, and at all grade levels, that have clearly established community linkages with, for example, parent groups and community agencies.

In this context, several hours per week in lectures, discussions, and community activities can be planned and undertaken—for example, a school-sponsored health walk could be organized, with fees generated from sponsors and donations given to local smoking research, prevention, or treatment programs. Another example of a positive link between schools and their communities is the establishment of drug-free zones around schools. In this approach, school officials and community organizers work together to have local city ordinances passed that make the possession or sale of an illicit drug or substance of abuse within a specified area around a school (e.g., a 2- or 3-block radius) subject to significantly increased penalties in terms of fines and imprisonment. This approach serves as a deterrent to drug dealers and can significantly reduce the availability of illicit drugs and substances of abuse on school grounds. It also decreases the likelihood of students being approached by dealers on the way to school, at recess, in the school parking lot, or on the way home from school.[22, 23]

Finally, the school-based prevention programs will be only as good as the teachers who are involved with the programs. As noted by Tobler (1992) in a review of 153 adolescent drug prevention programs: "Evidence obtained indicates implementation factors, in particular the effect of the leader, may impact the success of the program as much as the type or strategy of the program" (p. 2). Because most teachers have not received adequate preparation in relation to the use of the drugs and substances of abuse during childhood and adolescence—that is, formal courses in the pharmacological, psychological, and sociological factors affecting use—their knowledge and beliefs often are subject to significant bias and error, being influenced predominantly by personal experience, media reporting, or other nonobjective resources.

It is imperative that teachers be provided with formal courses in these areas during their basic education and that they periodically attend continuing education programs taught by experts in the use of drugs and substances of abuse during childhood and adolescence.[24] Such educational strategies have the potential to: (1) help dispel any myths or misconceptions that the teachers may have developed in relation to the use of the drugs and substances of abuse; (2) update teachers regarding changing patterns of use and current prevention or treatment modalities; and (3) alleviate their concerns that students already know more than they do regarding the use of the drugs and substances of abuse. Such programs will more adequately prepare teachers to meet their expanded roles in the educational arena and provide them with a forum to share their experiences and ideas. As noted by Weissberg, Caplan, and Harwood, et al. (1991): "Regardless of a program's quality, its potential for positive effects is diminished when program implementers and [facilitators, including teachers] are poorly trained, have inadequate organizational support for program delivery or lack the necessary skills to provide effective training" (p. 837). Stephens, Sloboda, Grey, et al. (2009) also found that the perceptions that grade 7 and grade 9 students had of their instructors significantly affected their "refusal, communication and decision-making skills, normative beliefs, perceived consequences of use, and substance use" (p. 724).

Perhaps the greatest problem encountered by school-based prevention programs, and the

---

[22] This approach can also be used with other drugs and substances of abuse that may be legal in some areas for adolescents to use. For example, DiFranza (1992, p. 754) suggested these school policies as a model for dealing with tobacco use:

- Students shall *not* be allowed to possess tobacco products on school grounds. Tobacco products brought onto school grounds shall be confiscated.
- Use of tobacco products by students, staff, and visitors shall be prohibited in school buildings, on school property, and at school functions.
- If students possess tobacco products, their parents shall be notified and invited to meet with school personnel concerning the matter.
- Students possessing tobacco products shall be offered treatment for potential nicotine addiction.
- Help with smoking cessation shall be offered to students in school on a regular basis.
- Students possessing tobacco products shall face appropriate disciplinary action.
- All grades, K through 12, shall receive instruction concerning tobacco on an annual basis.

[23] Although rarely accomplished, or even attempted in recent years, we have suggested and continue to support the banning (e.g., by local civic zoning ordinance or bylaw) of the sale of alcohol or tobacco products, or the operation of "head shops," within a specified distance (e.g., a radius of 1 mile) from junior and senior high school property.

[24] Having taught undergraduate students in the Faculty of Education for a number of years, we have noted firsthand the significant knowledge deficits that these future teachers had at the beginning of our courses and the biases they held that usually were based on their own personal experiences with using or observing the use of the various drugs and substances of abuse among parents, siblings, and friends.

most difficult to deal with effectively, is that children and adolescents who may need such programs the most are the most likely to not attend school (Tobler, 1992). As noted earlier in this text, a significant number of children and adolescents cut classes, drop out of school,[25] or become homeless runaways each year in North America. These children and adolescents, who are at significant risk of developing harmful patterns of using the drugs and substances of abuse, generally, would not have access to school-based programs.

## Secondary Prevention

Secondary prevention is concerned with the early detection of child and adolescent use of the drugs and substances of abuse *before* associated harmful effects occur. (See "Selected Quick-Screen Psychometric Tests" in Chapter 7, *Detecting Adolescent Use of the Drugs and Substances of Abuse: Selected Quick-Screen Psychometric Tests.*) It also is concerned with early intervention for children and adolescents who have already begun to use one or more of the drugs and substances of abuse when serious related harmful effects have not yet occurred. For example, secondary prevention strategies may include: (1) programs aimed at convincing high school students, most of whom drink alcohol, not to drink and drive (e.g., Mothers Against Drunk Driving [MADD], Students Against Drunk Driving [SADD]); (2) programs aimed at helping pregnant adolescents, many of whom drink alcohol, not to drink while pregnant; and (3) programs that provide adolescents who are intravenous drug users to use sterile injection equipment to avoid or decrease the risk for being infected with or spreading HIV (e.g., needle exchange programs; safe injection sites).[26]

Secondary prevention techniques could be used with all of the variable risk factors identified in Table 9.1. For example, if it was noted that an adolescent girl was depressed and was using alcohol to self-medicate her depression, perhaps in relation to a gender identity crisis, the provision of or a referral for appropriate counseling, psychotherapy, and other necessary therapy should be made to help her manage her depression and decrease, or cease, her alcohol use (e.g., gender-specific program for lesbian adolescents who have alcoholism). This intervention may help the adolescent girl to resolve her gender identity crisis, resolve the accompanying depression, and consequently prevent the development of increasingly harmful patterns of using the drugs and substances of abuse—patterns that are often seen among lesbian adolescents who are depressed.

Similarly, an older adolescent or young adult living on her own because of family discord associated with her promiscuity and drug-using lifestyle—whose mother recently died in a motor vehicle crash—and is now living back

---

[25] Although high school dropout and completion rates vary from school to school, district to district, city to city, and state to state (Chapman, Laird, & KewalRamani, 2010), approximately 70% of US students, overall, complete high school. Large, inner city schools have been pejoratively labeled as "dropout factories" and, as reported by Koebler (2011), "In New York City and Los Angeles, alone, more than 35,000 students dropped out of school in 2008" (p. 1). The highest rates of school dropout (and, correspondingly the lowest rates of high school completion) have been associated with ethnicity or continental descent. In descending order of school dropout (i.e., lowest high school completion rates) are adolescents of Hispanic descent, American Indian/Alaskan Native descent, African descent, European descent, and Asian descent (Chapman, Laird, & KewalRamani, 2010; Koebler, 2011; Riede, 2011; U.S. Department of Education, 2010.)

[26] To reiterate an important point made several times earlier in this text, we believe that it is our job as authors to provide as comprehensive, unbiased, and factually correct an overview and evaluation of the published data regarding the use of the drugs and substances of abuse by North American children and adolescents as possible. However, we must also recognize our own biases and, when they arise, make them explicit to the reader. This example is one such case. Based on the results of our own research involving adolescent participants, as well as adults, we do not favor the use of needle exchange programs or safe injection sites for adolescents (Pagliaro & Pagliaro, 1992, 1994a; Pagliaro, Pagliaro, Thauberger, et al., 1993). Instead, we recommend that every effort and strategy available be used to assist adolescents to discontinue intravenous drug use.

at home with her alcoholic father (in order to look after him) should be recognized as being at risk for resuming her use of the drugs and substances of abuse and for the development of increasingly harmful patterns of use (e.g., abuse or compulsive use; see Figure 9.1). This adolescent should be assessed regularly for normal grieving and referred to, for example, an adolescent bereavement group for adolescents who have lost loved ones as a result of motor vehicle crashes, monitored for grief resolution, and provided, along with her father, appropriate psychotherapy or counseling, pharmacotherapy, and other required treatment along with appropriate referral to effective self-help programs (e.g., AA), as needed.

## Tertiary Prevention

Tertiary prevention involves minimizing the harm related to a history of regular, long-term use of the drugs and substances of abuse (i.e., abusive and compulsive use) among children and adolescents. (See Chapters 1, 2, and 3; *The Psychodepressants*, *The Psychostimulants*, and *The Psychodelics*, respectively) also see Figure 9.1.) Aspects of tertiary prevention typically involve active medical or psychological treatment that includes residential treatment and rehabilitation with a focus on the achievement of abstinence and relapse prevention (see Table 9.5).

This section provides an overview of the various tertiary prevention treatment approaches that have been specifically developed and used for children and adolescents. Attention also is given to reported outcomes, particularly in regard to success or failure.[27]

Although many such programs exist, they can be conveniently grouped into three major treatment categories:[28] (1) pharmacotherapy; (2) psychotherapy and counseling; and (3) AA and other spiritually based, 12-step programs.

### Pharmacotherapy

Pharmacotherapy has been, and continues to be, the mainstay of the medical management of both acute overdosages involving the various drugs and substances of abuse and their respective withdrawal syndromes. Pharmacotherapy also has been shown to be a useful adjunct to cessation (i.e., drug-assisted abstinence), maintenance (i.e., drug substitution or replacement), and relapse prevention programs. In addition, pharmacotherapy is often a necessary and integral component of the treatment of adolescents who have dual diagnoses. (See Chapter 8, *Dual Diagnosis Among Adolescents.*)

Past advances in regard to the pharmacological treatment of substance use disorders are quite diverse. For example, in regard to the opiate analgesics they include: the use of methadone (Dolophine®) for opiate addiction maintenance (i.e., methadone maintenance) (Fareed, Casarella, Amar, et al., 2010); naltrexone (Revia®) for the treatment of alcohol dependence (Garbutt, 2010); buprenorphine (Buprenex®) as an aid for opiate analgesic detoxification (Flassing, 2010; Kovas, McFarland, McCarty, et al., 2007); and naloxone (Narcan®) for the treatment of opiate analgesic overdosage. Other examples of pharmacological interventions include the use of flumazenil (Anexate®) for the treatment of benzodiazepine overdosage (Seger, 2004) and the use of disulfiram (Antabuse®) for the prevention of resumed drinking among people

---

[27] Several researchers (e.g., Laniado-Laborin, 2010; Ranney, Melvin, Lux, et al., 2006) have noted the need for multiple therapeutic approaches to deal effectively with the varied nature of the problems encountered among children and adolescents with abusive or compulsive use patterns of the drugs and substances of abuse. In this regard, we recommend that the individual approaches to treatment noted in this chapter be considered and applied in the context of the Meta-Interactive Model of Child and Adolescent Use of the Drugs and Substances of Abuse. (See Figure 9.3.)

[28] Other therapeutic modalities exist but either lack empirical evidence of efficacy or are deemed generally inappropriate for use with North American children and adolescents. An example is acupuncture, which has been used primarily with adults for the treatment of various drug and substance use disorders, but with unsubstantiated or extremely variable reports of efficacy (e.g., Cui, Wu, & Luo, 2008; D'Alberto, 2004; Gates, Smith, & Foxcroft, 2006; Margolin, Avants, & Holford, 2002; Margolin, Kleber, Avants, et al., 2002).

**TABLE 9.5   General Guidelines for Managing Children and Adolescents Who Use the Drugs and Substances of Abuse**

**Assessment**

- Conduct a comprehensive assessment prior to planning and initiating treatment[a]
- Maintain an appropriate level of confidentiality for the child or adolescent during all aspects of the assessment and treatment processes.
- Recognize that different types of treatment may be required (i.e., the type of treatment that works best for one child or adolescent may not necessarily work best for another).
- Assess children and adolescents for any accompanying mental disorders (i.e., dual diagnosis) and refer or treat appropriately. (See Chapter 8, *Dual Diagnosis Among Adolescents.*)

**Treatment**

- Be willing to consider available and appropriate treatment approaches and strategies (e.g., AA, cognitive therapy, pharmacotherapy) that may be efficacious for a particular child or adolescent.
- Individualize treatment approaches.
- Remember that reasons for using drugs and substances of abuse may differ from one child or adolescent to another child or adolescent and may also differ for the same child or adolescent over time.
- Be nonjudgmental in approaching treatment.
- Break the denial of problems associated with the use of the drugs and substances of abuse.
- Respect children and adolescents who have problems with the drugs and substances of abuse, including those with dual diagnosis (i.e., SUDS and other mental disorders); do not treat them in condescending ways.
- Provide education in a straightforward, nonbiased way that is appropriately tailored to the cognitive abilities and to the developmental, learning, and social needs of each child and adolescent.
- Work toward realistic and achievable goals that have been mutually agreed on.
- Appropriately address underlying problems (e.g., lack of self-esteem, poor coping skills, previous sexual abuse).
- Involve family, friends, and others, as appropriate, in confrontation, treatment planning, and program implementation.
- Group children and adolescents according to their specific age, continental descent, culture or ethnicity, gender, primary language, socioeconomic level, sexual orientation, or other specific grouping as deemed appropriate and beneficial for the child or adolescent in order to optimize or her treatment and recovery.
- Use community social agencies designed for children and adolescents.
- Provide appropriate child care services for adolescent parents who are in treatment.
- Make referrals to other appropriate health and social care professionals and agencies.
- Develop and use procedures and techniques that help to minimize treatment attrition, or drop-out rates, and to maximize treatment compliance and completion of treatment programs.
- Provide appropriate follow-up, or aftercare, services.
- Remember that success or failure is ultimately the child's or adolescent's responsibility (i.e., do not become codependent or overresponsible).

[a]Also see Chapter 7, *Detecting Adolescent Use of the Drugs and Substances of Abuse: Selected Quick-Screen Psychometric Tests.*

who are abstinent alcoholics (i.e., to prevent relapsed use of alcohol) (Barth & Malcolm, 2010).

Another area of attention has been the active development of dosage formulations and drug delivery systems (i.e., pharmaceutical alterations) that can help to prevent, or to reduce, the harm associated with a particular method of using a drug or substance of abuse. (Also see the discussion of naltrexone injection later in this chapter.) For example, a highly successful approach involved the development of the combination pentazocine/naloxone tablets (Talwin-Nx®) to prevent the illicit intravenous use of pentazocine (Talwin®). As a result of this pharmacological/pharmaceutical strategy,

the illicit intravenous use of pentazocine was almost completely eliminated in the United States, where the oral pentazocine tablets were reformulated to include 0.5 mg of the opiate analgesic antagonist naloxone.

The addition of naloxone to the pentazocine oral tablet formulation prevents illicit intravenous pentazocine use by an interesting mechanism. The naloxone is poorly absorbed from the gastrointestinal (GI) tract following oral ingestion and, thus, as intended, has virtually no effect on the analgesic action of pentazocine when the latter is orally ingested. However, if the Talwin Nx® tablet is crushed, dissolved, and injected intravenously, the naloxone is immediately absorbed, blocking the desired action of the pentazocine at the endogenous central nervous system (CNS) opiate analgesic receptors. Unfortunately, the Talwin Nx® tablet formulation is not available in Canada, where the illicit intravenous use of pentazocine continues, particularly among adolescents and young adults of Aboriginal descent (e.g., First Nations and Inuit Peoples) living in the inner cities, along with its significant harmful effects, including acute overdosage and, with long-term regular use, pulmonary fibrosis (Head, 2001; Shaw, Deering, Jolly, et al., 2010).

Likewise, the transdermal nicotine delivery systems (e.g., Habitrol®, Nicoderm®) and nicotine nasal sprays (Nicotrol NS®) have become important adjuncts to smoking cessation programs and have demonstrated positive effects in relation to decreasing tobacco smoking among adolescents (Maharaj & Ternullo, 2001). On the horizon are a number of promising developments in pharmacology, including several aimed at the pharmacological prevention and treatment of cocaine addiction. As polyuse of the drugs and substances of abuse becomes even more prominent in North America, clinically significant interactions involving the drugs and substances of abuse, and their methods of use, will need to be addressed (Pagliaro & Pagliaro, 1999).

Future developments in the area of pharmacotherapy for the treatment of drug and substance use disorders will involve new strategies, including the use of vaccines. Some preliminary research in this area has involved the development of vaccines for preventing nicotine use (Cerny & Cerny, 2009). The vaccines work by inducing the development of specific antibodies that bind to nicotine once it is absorbed into the bloodstream. The bound nicotine is unable to cross the blood-brain barrier; thus, it is prevented from binding to its receptor sites in the CNS and eliciting its desired actions (Maurer & Bachmann, 2006, 2007). Unable to achieve the desired nicotine effects, smokers will decrease or cease

tobacco cigarette smoking or other nicotine use (e.g., chewing tobacco; applying transdermal nicotine delivery systems). The nicotine vaccines have the potential to reduce tobacco smoking among three principal groups of smokers: (1) current smokers who are trying to quit smoking; (2) former smokers who want to prevent relapse; and (3) adolescent smokers who do not want to become regular, long-term smokers (Vocci & Chiang, 2001).

As previously noted, the major clinical indications for adjunctive pharmacotherapy in regard to actual or potential harmful use of the drugs and substances of abuse include the:

• Treatment and management of acute overdosages involving benzodiazepines and the opiate analgesics
• Treatment and management of specific withdrawal syndromes
• Maintenance of abstinence or prevention of relapsed use
• Addiction maintenance pharmacotherapy (i.e., substituting or replacing a particular drug or substance of abuse with a less harmful one) for opiate analgesics and nicotine (tobacco smoking)
• Treatment and management of dual diagnoses

Each of these areas of adjunctive pharmacotherapy is presented and briefly discussed next.

**Treating and Managing Acute Benzodiazepine and Opiate Analgesic Overdosages**
Specific pharmacological antagonists are available for two groups of the drugs and substances of abuse classified as psychodepressants (i.e., benzodiazepine sedative-hypnotics and opiate analgesics). (See Chapter 1, *The Psychodepressants.*) These antagonists are, respectively, flumazenil (Anexate®, Romazicon®) and naloxone (Narcan®). Both of these antagonists reverse—to a significant degree, if not completely—the acute toxicities and other effects associated with overdosages involving these drugs and substances of abuse.

*Flumazenil (Anexate®) Pharmacotherapy*
Flumazenil (Anexate®) is an essentially pure benzodiazepine receptor antagonist. Flumazenil elicits its antagonistic effects within the CNS by means of competitive inhibition. The onset of action for flumazenil is generally within 2 minutes of intravenous injection with effects lasting for approximately 1 hour. Although flumazenil effectively antagonizes the sedative and hypnotic effects (i.e., conscious sedation or general anesthesia) produced by the benzodiazepines, it is less effective in regard to reversing associated respiratory depression. The use of flumazenil for a person who is physiologically dependent on (i.e., addicted to) the benzodiazepines sometimes may precipitate convulsions (i.e., in association with the onset of the acute benzodiazepine withdrawal syndrome; Flumazenil, 1992; Karavokiros & Tsipis, 1990) (Pagliaro & Pagliaro, 1998, 1999, 2009).

*Naloxone (Narcan®) Pharmacotherapy*
Naloxone (Narcan®) is an essentially pure opiate analgesic antagonist that has virtually no direct observable effects other than its antagonistic effects. These effects are elicited within the CNS by competitive inhibition (i.e., it selectively competes with opiate analgesics for binding sites on endogenous endorphin receptors). By displacing the opiate from its binding sites, naloxone immediately inhibits the pharmacological activity of the opiates, including, in cases of severe overdosage, life-threatening respiratory depression. In addition, when administered to a person who is physiologically dependent on (i.e., addicted to) the opiates, naloxone can precipitate an acute opiate withdrawal syndrome with the usual associated signs and symptoms (e.g., increased blood pressure, nausea, tachycardia, and vomiting). The onset of action for

naloxone is generally within 2 minutes of administration. Effects last for approximately 1 to 2 hours. Consequently, naloxone may need to be periodically readministered in cases of overdosages involving the long-acting opiates (e.g., methadone) (Pagliaro & Pagliaro, 1998, 1999, 2009).

**Treating and Managing Specific Withdrawal Syndromes** Several types of pharmacotherapy have been used, with varying degrees of success, to reduce the unpleasant physiological and psychological signs and symptoms of withdrawal associated with the abrupt discontinuation of the regular, long-term use of various drugs and substances of abuse, including alcohol, cocaine, nicotine, and the opiate analgesics (Taylor & Slaby, 1992).[29]

*Alcohol Withdrawal Syndrome* Acute alcohol withdrawal is often managed quite successfully with a long-acting benzodiazepine—usually chlordiazepoxide (Librium®) or diazepam (Valium®). Benzodiazepine pharmacotherapy for the management of alcohol withdrawal requires a gradual reduction of dosage over a 1- to 2-week period and, when appropriately used, can make the alcohol withdrawal syndrome virtually symptomless (Pagliaro & Pagliaro, 1999). Although less efficacious, clonidine (Catapres®), an alpha-adrenergic agonist that also is clinically used for its antihypertensive effects, has been used as an adjunct for the management of both the alcohol (Alcohol withdrawal syndrome, 2007; Bayard, McIntyre, Hill, et al., 2004; Stanley, Worrall, Lunsford, et al., 2005) and opiate analgesic (e.g., heroin; methadone) withdrawal syndromes (Gold & Dackis, 1984; Gowing, Farrell, Ali, et al., 2002, 2009; Washton & Resnick, 1981). The signs and symptoms of withdrawal are

---

[29] Generally, the signs and symptoms associated with the various withdrawal syndromes are simply the opposite of the normally expected, or desired, pharmacological actions of a particular drug or substance of abuse. For example, the desired actions for the sedative-hypnotics include calmness, muscle relaxation, and sleep. Conversely, the signs and symptoms associated with various sedative-hypnotic withdrawal syndromes include anxiety, muscle tremor (or convulsion), and insomnia.

effectively managed by gradually decreasing the clonidine dosage over a 1- to 2-week period.[30]

*Cocaine Withdrawal Syndrome*   The cocaine withdrawal syndrome (see Chapter 2, *The Psychostimulants*), particularly its associated psychological symptom of craving, has been a significant contributor to the relapsed use of cocaine. Consequently, a number of different drugs, including amantadine (Symmetrel®), antidepressants, antipsychotic tranquilizers, bromocriptine (Parlodel®), carbamazipine (Tegretol®), carbidopa/levodopa (Sinemet®), modafinil (Alertec®, Provigil®), pergolide mesylate (Permax®), topiramate (Topamax®), and valproate (Depakene®, Depakote®) have been used "off-label"[31] for the management of cocaine withdrawal. However, a wide number of studies and reviews have reported the general clinical efficacy associated with these forms of pharmacotherapy for the management of cocaine withdrawal to be poor (e.g., Amato, Minozzi, Pani, et al., 2007; Ballon & Feifel, 2006; de Lima, de Oliveira Soares, Reisser, et al., 2002; de Lima, Farrell, Lima Reisser, et al., 2010; Kumar, 2008; Lima, Lima, Soares, et al., 2002; Lima, Reisser, Soares, et al., 2003; Lima, Reisser, Silva de Lima, et al., 2009; Martinez-Raga, Knecht, & Cepeda, 2008; Reid & Thakkar, 2009; Shinn & Greenfield, 2010; Soares, Lima, Reisser, et al., 2003; Soares, Lima Reisser, Farrell, et al., 2010). Due

to the lack of supportive evidence regarding the efficacy of the pharmacological management of the cocaine withdrawal syndrome, it is not, at this time, recommended for adolescents.

*Nicotine Withdrawal Syndrome*   Another development in the treatment of nicotine withdrawal (i.e., in association with the cessation of tobacco smoking) was the approval of bupropion (Wellbutrin®, Zyban®), an antidepressant (Corelli & Hudmon, 2006). Buproprion pharmacotherapy is continued for 2 to 3 months while monitoring patient response and progress in terms of smoking cessation (Pagliaro & Pagliaro, 1999). (Also see the "Nicotine Replacement Pharmacotherapy" section later in this chapter.)

**Maintaining Abstinence or Preventing Relapse**   Several drugs have been developed to help to ensure continued abstinence among people who have discontinued their regular, long-term abusive or compulsive use of alcohol or opiate analgesics, particularly heroin.[32] Abstinence maintenance pharmacotherapy generally involves either pairing unpleasant effects with the use of a drug or substance of abuse or blocking desired effects when the drug or substance of abuse is used. Thus, abstinence maintenance pharmacotherapy helps to ensure abstinence by means of either an association with aversive stimuli or the blocking of rewarding stimuli.

---

[30] We generally would not recommend pharmacological adjuncts for the management of heroin withdrawal syndrome because it is generally relatively mild and usually can be handled "cold turkey" (i.e., signs and symptoms of the heroin withdrawal syndrome typically resemble those of a bad case of influenza—depending, of course, on both the amount of heroin used daily and the length of time it has been used). However, the methadone withdrawal syndrome may be quite severe with convulsions and other physiological effects that require appropriate treatment under direct medical supervision. Even when not required medically, we strongly recommend that patients undergo methadone withdrawal in an inpatient setting, particularly patients with concomitant histories of long-standing or high-dose use of alcohol or another drug or substance of abuse, in order to provide appropriate psychological support and significantly improve compliance (i.e., ensure that the patient successfully completes the withdrawal process). The average stay for people in detoxification units or centers in these situations is approximately 3 days (Rush & Ekdahl, 1990).

[31] "Off-label" refers to the use of a drug, prescription or nonprescription, for the treatment of a condition or disorder for which it has not received FDA approval (i.e., the drug has received FDA approval for the treatment of a specific condition or disorder, but not the one that is being treated).

[32] Abstinence, in this context, is actually a form of relapse prevention (see the "Relapse Prevention" section later in this chapter).

***Abstinence Maintenance for Alcohol***  The Food and Drug Administration (FDA) has approved three drugs for alcohol abstinence maintenance: (1) acamprosate (Campral®); (2) disulfiram (Antabuse®); and (3) naltrexone (ReVia®) (Garbutt, 2009; Oural, Paris, Sulivan, et al., 2008; Swift, 2007). In addition, topiramate (Topamax®) has been clinically used, "off-label" for this indication and has demonstrated some noted clinical efficacy.

*Acamprosate (Campral®) Pharmacotherapy*
Acamprosate (Campral®) was approved for use by the FDA in 2004 and has since been demonstrated to be safe and effective for the prevention of relapse among abstinent drinkers (Kennedy, Leloux, Kutscher, et al., 2010; Jung & Namkoong, 2006; Rösner, Hackl-Herrwerth, Leucht, et al., 2010). The exact mechanism of action for acamprosate has not been determined (Kiefer & Mann, 2010). The regular, long-term use of alcohol increases the production of N-methyl-D-aspartate (NMDA) receptors. During periods of alcohol withdrawal, these receptors are stimulated by a surge in the release of neurotransmitters, such as glutamate. Acamprosate appears to work by reducing this surge of glutamate (i.e., restoring glutamatergic neurotransmission to normal) (De Witte, Littleton, Parot, et al., 2005; Mason & Heyser, 2010; Swift, 2007).

Available from the manufacturer as a delayed-release oral tablet, acamprosate is ingested daily in 3 divided doses. To increase GI absorption, because of its low oral bioavailability (i.e., approximately 11%), it should be ingested on an empty stomach. A variety of adverse effects have been associated with its use, of which diarrhea is the most commonly reported (Boothby & Doering, 2005; Diehl, Ulmer, Mutschler, et al., 2010). Combination pharmacotherapy for alcohol abstinence maintenance (e.g., acamprosate and naltrexone) as well as adjunctive psychotherapy (e.g., acamprosate and cognitive-behavioral therapy) have been found to increase efficacy significantly (Acamprosate campral, 2005; Boothby & Doering, 2005; Kennedy, Leloux, Kutscher, et al., 2010; Mason, 2001, 2003).

*Disulfiram (Antabuse®) Pharmacotherapy*
Disulfiram (Antabuse®) blocks the metabolism of alcohol at the acetaldehyde stage by means of inhibition of the enzyme acetaldehyde dehydrogenase. Consequently, when alcohol is consumed, even in small quantities, acetaldehyde accumulates in the blood-stream and elicits a number of unpleasant effects, including:

- Blurred vision
- Chest pain
- Confusion
- Copious vomiting
- Dyspnea
- Flushing
- Hyperventilation
- Hypotension
- Nausea
- Respiratory difficulty
- Syncope
- Tachycardia
- Throbbing headache
- Vertigo
- Weakness

The intensity of this reaction, which is known as the disulfiram-alcohol reaction (or more commonly as the Antabuse® reaction or disulfiram flush), is generally proportional to the amount of disulfiram used as a component of the alcohol abstinence maintenance program and to the amount of alcohol consumed at a particular drinking session (Pagliaro & Pagliaro, 1999).

Disulfiram pharmacotherapy is begun following at least 1 day of abstinence from alcohol use in order to avoid precipitating the disulfiram reaction. Subsequently, disulfiram is orally ingested on a daily basis each morning for a period of months to years until abstinence can be maintained without the aid of the drug.[33] Daytime tiredness and night-time sleep disturbances are the most commonly reported adverse effects (Diehl, Ulmer, Mutschler, et al., 2010).

*Naltrexone (ReVia®, Vivitrol®) Pharmacotherapy*   Another FDA-approved form of pharmacotherapy for promoting abstinence in regard to alcohol use is naltrexone (ReVia®, Vivitrol®) pharmacotherapy. Naltrexone, a long-acting oral opiate antagonist, was originally developed and marketed under the brand name Trexan®, for the treatment of abusive and compulsive patterns of opiate analgesic use (i.e., physical dependence, or addiction) (Greenstein, Arndt, McLellan, et al., 1984; Kirchmayer, Davoli, & Verster, 2000; Pagliaro & Pagliaro, 1998, 2009). However, it was discovered by serendipity that it also blocked the disinhibitory euphoria associated with alcohol use.[34] It is usually orally ingested on a daily basis without attention to the timing of meals or the ingestion of food. An injectable form of naltrexone also is available and is considered a major pharmaceutical advancement in regard to naltrexone pharmacotherapy for abstinence maintenance for alcohol (Garbutt, Kranzier, O'Malley, et al., 2005). The naltrexone injection (Vivitrol®; XR-NTX®), an extended-release injectable suspension formulation, is injected intramuscularly by a healthcare provider once a month, which significantly increases compliance with abstinence pharmacotherapy (Lee, Grossman, DiRocco, et al., 2010; Naltrexone injection, 2010; Swift, 2007).

The endogenous opiate system (see Chapter 1, *The Psychodepressants*) plays a significant role in the mediation of the disinhibitory euphoria and other desired effects associated with alcohol use, particularly those associated with the modulation of dopaminergic neurotransmission in the mesolimbic area of the brain (Jung & Namkoong, 2006; Soyka & Rösner, 2010). Consequently, when the receptors are blocked by naltrexone, the associated urge to drink is reduced, thus strengthening the ability to stop drinking. Although additional research is required, it appears that individuals who are carriers of a variant of the mu-opiate receptor gene may be particularly receptive to the efficacious effects of naltrexone pharmacotherapy for promoting abstinence among regular, long-term users of alcohol (Mann & Hermann, 2010).

When used as an adjunct to effective psychotherapy, naltrexone pharmacotherapy has been found to demonstrate significant clinical utility with reports of less craving for alcohol, a lower rate of relapse, and, when drinking, the consumption of fewer drinks per occasion (Naltrexone, 2009; Volpicelli, Clay, Watson, et al., 1995). Nausea is the most common adverse effect associated with the use of naltrexone. However, its long-term safety and efficacy have not been clearly established yet, and the FDA has added a black-box warning to its official monograph stating: "Naltrexone may cause liver damage when taken in large doses" (Naltrexone, 2009, p. 1). In addition, as a potent opiate analgesic antagonist, naltrexone can precipitate the opiate analgesic withdrawal syndrome among regular, long-term users of the opiate analgesics, including those who are being medically managed for chronic pain (e.g., chronic cancer or other malignant pain). Thus, caution must be exercised when naltrexone abstinence maintenance pharmacotherapy

---

[33] Although controlled studies have not demonstrated significant efficacy for disulfiram pharmacotherapy when used alone (i.e., patient compliance has been problematic and clinical results have been inconsistent [Blanc & Daeppen, 2005; Suh, Pettinati, Kampman, et al., 2006]), we have found disulfiram pharmacotherapy to be effective for highly motivated, compliant young adults in their early 20s when used as an initial adjunct to AA or another 12-step program and weekly psychotherapy. Diehl, Ulmer, Mutschler, et al. (2010) have reported similar findings among adults. However, we do not generally recommend disulfiram pharmacotherapy for promoting abstinence from alcohol for adolescents. Both acamprosate and naltrexone are safer to use and more efficacious in this clinical context. (See related discussion in this chapter.)

[34] The CNS depressant effects, including alcohol-related effects on cognition, do not appear to be significantly affected by naltrexone (Naltrexone, 1995). Thus, it is not, and should not be used as a "sobriety pill."

is implemented for these people, who also would require alternative pain relief measures until the effects of naltrexone have dissipated (Pagliaro & Pagliaro, 1999; Volpicelli, Clay, Watson, et al., 1995).

*Topiramate (Topamax®) Pharmacotherapy* Topiramate (Topamax®) is an anticonvulsant that has been used to symptomatically manage various seizure disorders among North American children and adolescents, as well as adults, for over 20 years (Maryanoff, Nortey, Gardocki, et al., 1987). While not FDA approved for alcohol abstinence maintenance, its "off-label" use for this indication has been reported for over a decade (Johnson, Ait-Daoud, Bowden, et al., 2003; Johnson, Rosenthal, Capece, et al., 2007). Several published studies and reviews (e.g., Arbaizar, B., Diersen-Sotos, T., Gómez-Acebo, I et al., 2010; De Souza, 2010; Flórez, Saiz, Garcia-Portilla, et al., 2010; Garbutt, 2009; Johnson & Ait-Daoud, 2010; Johnson, Ait-Daoud, Bowden, et al., 2003; Kenna, Lomastro, Schiesl, et al., 2009) have indicated that, when compared to either placebo or naltrexone abstinence maintenance for alcohol, topiramate abstinence maintenance resulted in:

- Fewer drinks per day
- Fewer drinks per drinking day
- Fewer heavy drinking days
- More days abstinent
- Greater reduction in reports of craving

The mechanism of action for topiramate in regard to abstinence maintenance for alcohol has not yet been determined. However, topiramate appears to modulate dopaminergic neurotransmission in the mesolimbic area of the brain by decreasing the changes in NMDA receptor activity associated with the damage caused by regular, long-term use of alcohol—or heavy drinking. Consequently, dopamine release is inhibited and gamma-aminobutyric acid (GABA) function is enhanced (Johnson, Ait-Daoud, Bowden, et al., 2003; Olmsted & Kockler, 2008).

Topiramate is ingested orally and is rapidly and well absorbed from the GI tract with approximately 70% excreted in unchanged form in the urine. The most common reported adverse effects associated with its use include cognitive impairment (e.g., memory impairment; dizziness), GI distress, paresthesia, psychomotor slowing, and weight loss. These adverse effects may significantly limit its use in regard to abstinence maintenance for alcohol (Arbaizar, Diersen-Sotos, Gómez-Acebo, et al., 2010; Shinn & Greenfield, 2010).

***Abstinence Maintenance for Opiate Analgesics: Naltrexone (Trexan®) Pharmacotherapy*** As noted in the previous section, "Abstinence Maintenance for Alcohol," naltrexone is a long-acting opiate analgesic antagonist. It was originally developed to facilitate abstinence maintenance among abstinent opiate analgesic users (Pagliaro & Pagliaro, 1998). Initially, it was thought that naltrexone would be particularly well-suited for use with health care professionals who had become physically dependent on (addicted to) the opiate analgesics, had been subject to professional disciplinary action because of their physical dependence on opiate analgesics, and wanted to return to full professional practice in work settings that provided ready access to the opiate analgesics. Although generally well-tolerated, and having few associated serious adverse drug effects, oral naltrexone pharmacotherapy did not prove to be particularly efficacious for this indication because of poor patient compliance (Nunes, Rothenberg, Sullivan, et al., 2006; Sullivan, Garawi, Bisaga, et al., 2007). In an effort to improve patient compliance, Nunes, Rothenberg, Sullivan, et al. (2006) added motivational and cognitive-behavioral therapies to the standard regimen of oral naltrexone, but failed to significantly improve patient compliance. In a later review for the Cochrane Database, Minozzi, Amato, Vecchi, et al. (2011) found that "oral naltrexone did not perform better than treatment with [a] placebo" (p. 1).

Sullivan, Garawi, Bisaga, et al. (2007), among others, suggested that improved patient compliance could be achieved by using the recently developed long-acting injectable or implantable formulation of naltrexone. In this regard, Gastfriend (2011) found that the use of the extended-release naltrexone intramuscular injectable formulation (Vivitrol®; XR-NTX®) could significantly improve compliance. Consequently, this formulation of naltrexone has demonstrated significant efficacy in terms of maintaining abstinence among abstinent opiate analgesic users.

### Substitution or Replacement Pharmacotherapy for Opiate Analgesics and Nicotine

Substitution or replacement pharmacotherapy (i.e., drug substitution or drug replacement) is based on the principle of harm reduction—an integral component of tertiary prevention. As such, substitution or replacement pharmacotherapy does not attempt to stop the use of a drug or substance of abuse. Rather, it attempts to change the level of harm associated with its use, including the harm associated with its method of use. In North America, the two major examples of substitution or replacement pharmacotherapy are the substitution of methadone for heroin and the substitution or replacement of tobacco smoking with alternative methods of nicotine use that are less harmful to the pulmonary system. The nicotine substitution products also are used in smoking cessation programs.

*Methadone Substitution or Replacement Pharmacotherapy for Heroin and Other Opiate Analgesics*   Methadone (Dolophine®), a long-acting opiate analgesic, has been used for over 50 years in North America as a legal form of pharmacotherapy for opiate analgesic maintenance, particularly among people who are addicted to heroin and who also have been unable to complete opiate analgesic detoxification successfully. The goal of methadone maintenance pharmacotherapy for the maintenance of opiate addiction is to prevent the occurrence

of the signs and symptoms of the opiate withdrawal syndrome. Thus, it allows people who are addicted to heroin to discontinue their illicit use of heroin while using methadone to ward off the opiate analgesic withdrawal syndrome that would otherwise occur. Opiate analgesic maintenance with methadone also has been associated with a significant reduction in hustling and other undesired behaviors (e.g., breakings and entering) that are commonly used by people to support their heroin addictions.

While prescribed in dosages that do not produce associated euphoria or other desired actions, opiate analgesic maintenance with methadone keeps the "edge off" for these people and thus allows them to maintain parenting, psychotherapy and other therapy, work, and social responsibilities. Although it continues a person's physical and psychological dependence on an opiate analgesic, methadone pharmacotherapy offers five benefits:

1. Elimination of the hazards associated with the intravenous injection of heroin (e.g., HIV infection) because it is orally ingested
2. Decrease in heroin craving
3. Avoidance of both euphoria and excessive sedation
4. Relatively inexpensive and readily available at licensed neighborhood pharmacies
5. Legal availability

(See Chapter 1, *The Psychodepressants*, for additional related discussion.)

Although methadone pharmacotherapy for opiate analgesic maintenance has many benefits, it also has some drawbacks. For example, the withdrawal syndrome associated with methadone use is much more severe than that associated with heroin use. Thus, many people who select to enroll in opiate (methadone) maintenance programs remain in these programs for long periods of time (i.e., several years). People who do not remain in the programs usually return to their original heroin use. In addition, those who are on methadone maintenance have significant risk for using other drugs and substances of abuse, such as alcohol and cocaine—the use of which is not deterred by the use of methadone (Pagliaro & Pagliaro, 1999, 2009). In addition, methadone maintenance has been associated with a disproportionate number of deaths related to opiate analgesic–related poisonings or over-dosages, particularly over the last decade. A large number of these deaths are believed to be iatrogenic and specifically involved the inappropriate use of conversion tables for dosing methadone and initiating methadone maintenance at too high a dosage (i.e., 80 mg/day as opposed to 30 mg/day) (Collins, 2010). Thus, although methadone maintenance programs have been recommended and used successfully for some older adolescent heroin users, we do not recommend these programs for adolescents.

### Nicotine Replacement Pharmacotherapy and Alternative Varenicline (Chantix®) Pharmacotherapy
The widest application of substitution or replacement pharmacotherapy in North America has been the use of nicotine (i.e., nicotine replacement therapy [NRT]) in the forms of chewing gum, inhaler, lozenge, nasal spray, sublingual tablet, and transdermal drug delivery systems, or patches, to manage the nicotine withdrawal syndrome associated with the cessation of tobacco smoking among regular, long-term smokers (Crain & Bhat, 2010; Fant, Buchhalter, Buchman, et al., 2009). Whereas methadone maintenance is just that, maintenance, it is generally expected that nicotine substitutes will be used for short periods of time (e.g., up to 12 weeks). The nicotine substitutes serve as a means to help people to discontinue their regular, long-term nicotine use slowly while experiencing diminished signs and symptoms of the nicotine withdrawal syndrome (Frishman, 2007). While NRT is potentially beneficial, studies over the last two decades have repeatedly demonstrated that the use

of nicotine substitutes is significantly effective only when combined with effective counseling or psychotherapy programs (e.g., Grimshaw & Stanton, 2006). For example, as noted by Covey and Glassman (1991):

> Evidence of the addictive nature of chronic tobacco use suggests that pharmacological interventions, in conjunction with behaviorally oriented therapy, may present the best hope for achieving smoking cessation in refractory smokers. (p. 69)

Or, as noted by Generali (1992):

> Smoking cessation rates associated with nicotine transdermal patch therapy have varied in clinical trials. However, appropriate patient instruction and an extensive behavioral modification program ensure optimal response to transdermal nicotine therapy. (p. 34)

And as noted by Laniado-Laborin (2010):

> The rate of successful smoking cessation at 1 year is 3% to 5% when the patient simply tries to stop, 7% to 16% if the smoker undergoes behavioral intervention, and up to 25% when receiving pharmacologic treatment and behavioral support. (p. 74)

In a study of the use of NRT for North American adolescents, Botello-Harbaum, Schroeder, Collins, et al. (2010) found that adolescents of African descent were significantly less likely to use NRT than were adolescents of European descent. The reason for this significant difference is unknown. Although the majority of adolescents of African descent smoke mentholated cigarettes (see related discussion in Chapter 2, *The Psychostimulants*), this preference did not appear to be directly related to their lower use of NRT (Hyland, Garten, Giovino, et al, 2002).

Varenicline (Chantix®), which is approved by the FDA as a means of first-line pharmacotherapy for facilitating smoking cessation, offers an alternative to the use of NRT (Fant, Buchhalter, Buchman, et al., 2009;

Frishman, 2009). A partial nicotine antagonist, varenicline competitively binds to the nicotinic acetylcholine receptors, particularly the $\alpha_4\beta_2$ subtype. (See related discussion in Chapter 2, *The Psychostimulants.*) Consequently, the ability of nicotine to stimulate the mesolimbic dopamine system is significantly reduced. Varenicline is available as an oral tablet that is ingested 1 or 2 times daily, after meals, for generally 3 to 6 months (U.S. Food and Drug Administration, 2006). The most common adverse reaction associated with varenicline pharmacotherapy is nausea (Garrison & Dugan, 2009; Hays, Croghan, Schroeder, et al., 2010). The FDA requires a black-box warning to the official labeling of Chantix® that includes the statement: "Some people have had changes in behavior, hostility, agitation, depressed mood, and suicidal thoughts" (U.S. Food and Drug Administration, 2009a; Varenicline, 2009, p. 1).

Although associated with nausea and the need for cautious use, varenicline is a suitable pharmacotherapeutic alternative to NRT, particularly for tobacco smokers who have been unsuccessful in achieving smoking cessation with NRT. Several studies (e.g., Gonzales, Rennard, Nides, et al., 2006; Jorenby, Hays, Rigotti, et al., 2006; Nides, Oncken, Gonzales, et al., 2006; Oncken, Gonzales, Nides, et al., 2006; Tonstad, Tønnesen, Hajek, et al., 2006) have demonstrated significant increases in abstinence with the use of varenicline when compared to placebo and/or bupropion pharmacotherapy. For example, Jorenby, Hays, Rigotti, et al. (2006) found that, after 1 year, the rate of continuous abstinence for varenicline was 23% in comparison to 10% for placebo and 15% for bupropion. The efficacy of varenicline can be increased with combination varenicline pharmacotherapy and appropriate cognitive-behavioral psychotherapy (Ebbert, Wyatt, Hays, et al., 2010; Ebbert, Wyatt, Zirakzadeh, et al., 2009; Hays,

Croghan, Schroeder, et al., 2010). (Also see following related discussion in the section, "Psychotherapy and Counseling.")

**Treatment and Management of Dual Diagnoses** Appropriate pharmacotherapy for the symptomatic management of substance use disorders that occur with other mental disorders is a common and integral component of the medical and psychological management of dual diagnoses among adolescents. (See "Psychotherapy and Counseling;" also see Chapter 8, *Dual Diagnosis Among Adolescents*).[35] Conversely, several researchers (e.g., McCarthy, Tomlinson, Anderson, et al., 2005) have noted that failure to treat the co-occurring disorder adequately may significantly contribute to relapsed use of the drug or substance of abuse. (See later related discussion in the section "Relapse Prevention.")

### *Psychotherapy and Counseling*

Whereas children generally respond best to individual psychotherapy and counseling for the management of SUDs and dual diagnoses, both individual and group psychotherapeutic and counseling approaches can be used for adolescents, either on their own or as an adjunct to pharmacotherapy (Azorin, Bowden, Garay, et al., 2010; Miller & Roache, 2009). These approaches include:

- Cognitive therapy
- Peer group therapy
- Family therapy
- Social skills training
- Therapeutic communities
- Short-term residential treatment programs
- Ethnic-specific programs for North American children and adolescents of various continental descents (e.g., Aboriginal, African, Asian, Hispanic)
- Gay- or lesbian-specific adolescent treatment programs

---

[35] Psychotherapy and counseling also are effective and widely used therapies for the symptomatic management of adolescent dual diagnoses (e.g., Di Forti, Morrison, Butt, et al., 2007).

Each of these treatment approaches is briefly discussed in the next sections.[36]

**Cognitive Therapy**    Cognitive therapy is the most commonly used form of psychotherapy for the treatment of adolescents who have developed harmful patterns of using the drugs and substances of abuse. It also is a type of psychotherapy for which related studies have demonstrated empirically established efficacy (e.g., Kaminer, 2002; McHugh, Hearon, & Otto, 2010; Vaughn, 2004; Waldron & Kaminer, 2004). Cognitive therapy, in this context, is based on the assumption that harmful patterns of using the drugs and substances of abuse are indicative of maladaptive coping (i.e., the adolescent has not learned effective ways to cope with his or her problems or to meet certain individual needs that are often developmental needs). Cognitive therapy is therefore directed at the correction or modification of irrational belief systems, maladaptive or deficient coping skills, and faulty thinking patterns or styles.

Training in self-observation, the sharing of thoughts and emotions with the therapist, the systematic analysis of the validity of negative and irrational self-statements, and the gradual substitution of positive logical thinking patterns based on rational belief systems are attempted as part of the cognitive therapy process. Through this process, adolescents gradually are made more aware of their problems, which they may have denied or avoided, and helped to develop the strategies, skills, and abilities they need to deal with them effectively.

The development or strengthening of specific intrapersonal and interpersonal skills, including anger control, leisure time management, problem solving, and resistance training (see Table 9.6 for a more comprehensive

**TABLE 9.6    Intrapersonal and Interpersonal Skills Training Elements**

**Intrapersonal Skills Training Examples**
- Anger management
- Coping skills
- Decision-making skills
- Increasing self-involvement in pleasurable activities
- Managing negative thinking, including managing thoughts about using alcohol or other drugs and substances of abuse
- Planning for emergencies
- Problem solving
- Relaxation training

**Interpersonal Skills Training Examples**
- Assertiveness training
- Communication skills training
  - Communicating in intimate relationships
  - Communicating with children and adolescents
  - Giving and receiving criticism, including criticism about using the drugs and substances of abuse
  - Giving and receiving compliments
  - Initiating conversations
  - Refusing offers to use the drugs and substances of abuse
  - Enhancing social support networks
  - Refusing requests
  - Using body language effectively

Modified from: Kadden (1994).

list) is an integral component of cognitive therapy. Cognitive therapy is often applied in the context of relapse prevention in order to help ensure that the positive gains achieved during early abstinence are maintained. A central component to the achievement of this goal involves teaching children and adolescents how to identify high-risk situations that may lead to patterns of relapsed use and apply previously learned and rehearsed techniques to avoid or deal with them effectively. The Just Say No Campaign is an example of the application of cognitive rehearsal techniques. A relatively simple and popular strategy, its efficacy has been questioned by several researchers and clinicians (e.g., Beck, 1998; Engs & Fors 1988; Fishbein, Hall-Jaimieson, Zimmer, et al, 2002).[37]

---

[36] Although pharmacotherapy and psychotherapy, or counseling, are discussed separately, optimal therapeutic outcomes for adolescents generally involve combination, or multimodal, therapy, as demonstrated by many studies (e.g., Hudman, Corelli, & Prokhorov, 2010; McCaul & Petry, 2003; Swift, 2007).

[37] Interestingly, this particular program has demonstrated particular success when used for children rather than adolescents (Pagliaro & Pagliaro, *Clinical Patient Data Files*).

**Peer Group Therapy**    Peer group psycho-therapy for adolescents also can be extremely effective. As noted by Azima and Richmond (1989):

> There is little doubt that group psychotherapy is the treatment of choice for most adolescents who are in the process of separation from par-ents and who rely strongly on influential peers for identification and direction. The peer group is the natural developmental habitat in which the adolescent manifests his struggle for inde-pendence, a separate identity, and a transitional model of adulthood. The stimulation, activity, and self-disclosure provided by the group cre-ates the therapeutic climate in which adolescents can come to grips with and work through their problems, angers, and frustrations, in an accept-able, meaningful way. (p. xi)

For example, Stead and Lancaster (2005b), in their meta-analysis of group behavioral ther-apy programs for smoking cessation, found that group participants were able to learn behavioral techniques for smoking cessation and provide each other with mutual support. In terms of smoking cessation, they also found that outcomes were superior to those achieved with self-help and similar to those achieved with individual counseling. However, not all psy-chotherapists are equally adept at effectively practicing group psychotherapy. Bratter (1989) observed that:

> Those psychotherapists who can work with addicted adolescents effectively in a group setting possess a quintessential quality that the theologian Paul Tillich has defined as *caritas*, which connotes a non-compromising and non-possessive form of caring. (p. 167)

Additional details of group therapy are dis-cussed in the context of these sections: Family Therapy, Social Skills Training, Therapeutic Communities, and Short-Term Residential Treatment Programs.

**Family Therapy**    The family often plays a significant role in the etiology and mainte-nance of problematic patterns of substance use among children and adolescents, as has been discussed in various chapters of this text. Some general guidelines that can assist family therapists, regardless of their specific theoreti-cal orientations, are presented in Table 9.7. As noted by Bukstein and Van Hasselt (1993), "Intervention with substance-abusing adoles-cents that fails to proactively involve the fam-ily in treatment is unlikely to yield significant short- or long-term improvements" (p. 465).[38] Cognizant of this association, family therapy attempts to correct the dysfunctional behavior of family members, both individually and as a group (Friedman & Granick, 1990; Joanning, Thomas, Newfield, et al., 1991; Kaufman, 1990; Szapocznik & Williams, 2000). Lewis, Piercy, Sprenkle, et al. (1990, p. 88) described the Purdue Brief Family Therapy Model, a "mixed" family therapy model, noting its seven major goals, which we believe are appli-cable to many types of family therapy:

1. To decrease a family's resistance to treatment
2. To redefine substance use as a family problem
3. To reestablish appropriate parental influence
4. To interrupt dysfunctional family sequences of behavior
5. To assess the interpersonal function of the substance use
6. To implement change strategies consistent with the family's interpersonal functioning
7. To provide assertion training skills for child and adolescent family members to resist peer pressures to engage in substance use

---

[38] In addition, several studies have validated the efficacy of family therapy for the treatment of both children and adoles-cents with fetal alcohol spectrum disorder (e.g., Peadon, Rhys-Jones, Bower, et al., 2009; also see related discussion in Chapter 1, *The Psychodepressants*) and adolescent mothers who use the drugs and substances of abuse and neglect or physically abuse their children (e.g., Donohue, 2004; also see related discussion in Chapter 5, *Exposure to the Drugs and Substances of Abuse From Conception Through Childhood*).

**TABLE 9.7   General Guidelines for Family Therapists**

- Respect the hierarchal structure of the family, if appropriate. If not, try to help the family reestablish a functional hierarchy.
- Listen to what is being said and not said, asking relevant questions for both.
- Do not interrupt a family member while he or she is speaking to ask for clarification. Wait until the family member has finished.
- Observe nonverbal behavior closely, as a basis for understanding family relationships and for possible intervention.
- Give equal attention to each family member.
- Do not attempt to minimize problems to the family. Be honest and open.
- Empathize with the stated family issues.
- Be nonjudgmental so that the family feels free to discuss problems without fear of censure.
- Establish open communication patterns early in therapy.
- Be aware of your own biases (and countertransference tendencies).
- Be flexible enough to shift your approach if you find that it is not working.
- Do not give advice, only suggestions as they fit the therapeutic plan.
- Do not allow oneself to be triangulated or manipulated. *You* are the therapist.
- Evaluate each individual in terms of depression, guilt, self-esteem, etc.
- When you sense the family feels it has failed, attempt to bring up past successful experiences as reinforcement.
- Become a role model to the family.
- Allow the family to see you as a person who can make mistakes and own up to these mistakes. Allow them to see you as a person with feelings.
- Try to have a purpose and reason for all of your actions or lack of action.
- Do not copy another therapist's style. Be yourself. Act in a manner that is comfortable for you and fits your personality.
- Your role is to provide options for the family to select and pursue. You plant a seed for positive growth that will enable the therapeutic process to bring about a change.

Modified from: Frankel (1990).

Family therapy[39] (see Table 9.8) attempts to correct the dysfunctional behavior of family members, both individually and as a group (Kosten, Hogan, Jalali, et al., 1986). Behavioral and strategic-structural family therapies are the most commonly used, except for mixed therapies. These systemic approaches are briefly discussed in the context of their application to the treatment of harmful patterns of adolescent use of the drugs and substances of abuse.

***Behavioral Family Therapy***   Behavioral family therapy for children and adolescents who display harmful patterns of using the drugs and substances of abuse and their families consists predominantly of those techniques that were: (1) developed and validated by empirical study with children and adolescents who were identified as delinquent; and (2) applied in child welfare and criminal justice contexts (e.g., Alexander, Waldon, Newberry, et al., 1990; Bry, Conboy, & Bisgay, 1986; Donohue, Azrin, Allen, et al., 2009; Rueger & Liberman, 1984). These techniques typically include contingency and behavioral contracting and training.

Contingency or behavioral contracting involves identifying, operationally defining, and agreeing to a set of desired child or adolescent target behaviors, such as completing household chores (e.g., taking out the garbage; cleaning one's room; getting homework done well and on time) and complying with time schedules (e.g., specified times for coming home after school or returning from an evening date). Consequences (e.g., punishments, such as grounding, or restricting the adolescent to the home premises) for breaking these contracts and rewards (reinforcements, such as an allowance, access to his or her cell phone, or permission to drive the family car) for complying

---

[39] When the concept of circular or reciprocal causality is applied, this approach is commonly referred to as a systemic (i.e., family systems–oriented) approach or model (Lewis, Piercy, Sprenkle, et al., 1990). This approach or model should not be confused with systemic family therapy, a particular model of family therapy that uses a cybernetic process. Systemic intervention or treatment differs from psychological and pharmacological approaches because of the inherent focus of these intervention strategies. The focus of the latter is on the child or adolescent as an individual, whereas the focus of the former is on the entire family as a group that includes a member(s) (i.e., the adolescent) who displays harmful patterns of using the drugs and substances of abuse. In this regard, the adolescent member is often identified as the "thermostat" of family health and functioning. Thus, therapists attempt (optimally) to assess and treat all the members of the family, including nuclear and extended family members, or significant others, as a group.

**TABLE 9.8   Types of Family Therapy and Major Focus or Components**

| Type of Family Therapy | Major Focus or Components |
| --- | --- |
| Behavioral | Assertiveness training<br>Contingency contracting<br>Parent management training<br>Problem-solving skills training |
| Contextual (Functional) | Integration of behavioral, cognitive, emotional, and spiritual aspects of family |
| Strategic-Structural | Restructure maladaptive patterns |
| Systemic | Address behavioral limit-setting and intergenerational conflicts |
| Mixed | A combination of various family therapy components |

Note: While this categorization has been selected to facilitate organization and discussion, it is recognized that other, perhaps more comprehensive or detailed categorizations of types of family therapy also are available.

with them are explicitly defined and used to positively modify the adolescent's behavior. "Contingency management approaches to drug abuse derive from the operant behavioral psychology of B. F. Skinner" and are based on "the belief that behavior is learned and reinforced by interaction with environmental contingencies" (Bigelow & Silverman, 1999, p. 16). As noted by Higgins and Petry (1999):

Contingency management interventions almost always involve one or more of the following generic contingencies to motivate increases and decreases in the frequency of a therapeutically desirable and undesirable behavior: (a) positive reinforcement involves delivery of a desired consequence (e.g., a voucher exchangeable for retail items), contingent on the individual meeting a therapeutic goal (e.g., negative urinalysis test results); (b) negative reinforcement involves removing an aversive or confining circumstance (e.g., living at home under parent or legal guardian supervision with a judicial requirement for ankle bracelet monitoring), contingent on meeting a target therapeutic goal (e.g., attending counseling sessions); (c) positive punishment involves delivery of a punishing consequence (e.g., a professional reprimand), contingent on evidence of

undesirable behavior (e.g., positive urinalysis test results); and (d) negative punishment involves removal of a positive condition (e.g., the monetary value of a voucher to be earned is reduced), contingent on evidence of the occurrence of an undesirable behavior (e.g., missing a scheduled counseling session). (p.122)

Contingency management techniques have been applied quite often in such contexts as closed youth detention and treatment facilities and other settings amenable to the use of a token economy system (Peirce, Petry, Stitzer, et al., 2006). In these contexts, seven core issues need to be adequately identified and addressed in order to maximize the potential for success:

1. The target behavior, which must be both observable and measureable

2. The target population (e.g., adolescents who: are users of a particular drug or substance of abuse, have a dual diagnosis, or have a high recidivism rate)

3. The type of reinforcer or incentive (e.g., youth detention center privileges; on-site prize distribution; token economy vouchers)

4. The amount or value of the incentive (i.e., generally, the greater the incentive, the greater the response)

5. The frequency of incentive distribution (i.e., generally, the response will be greater if the incentive is presented soon after the target behavior is achieved or demonstrated)

6. The timing of the distribution of the incentive (i.e., generally the more rapidly the incentive is distributed in relation to the target behavior, the more effective it will be)

7. The duration of the reinforcement intervention (i.e., the longer the duration, the greater the success—it appears that a minimal duration of 6 months generally is required for individuals to internalize the desired behavior) (Petry, 2000, p. 9)

The training component of behavioral family therapy often is directed toward assertiveness training, parent management training, and problem-solving skills training. Assertiveness training assists children and adolescents to learn and rehearse techniques that can help them to resist peer pressure to use the drugs and substances of abuse. Parent management training helps parents to improve their communication with their children, establish common goals, and reestablish their appropriate influence within the family structure. Parent training focuses on altering inappropriate parental behavior(s) and teaching parents, using role playing and practice, new skills for managing positive and negative behaviors noted in their children or adolescents (Wells, 1988; Wells & Forehand, 1981). Problem-solving skills training is aimed at assisting all family members to learn to become less dogmatic and more accepting of applying alternative strategies for solving family problems. The problem-solving approach has four principal components: (1) defining the problem;[40] (2) generating a number of alternative solutions for the defined problem;[41] (3) evaluating the positive and negative aspects of each solution; and (4) selecting the best available (practical and "do-able") solution for that particular family unit (Robin & Foster, 1988).

Stormshak and Dishion (2009) describe the family checkup intervention, which integrates aspects of behavioral family therapy into schools (i.e., establishing a family resource center in schools). Twenty years of related research have demonstrated its efficacy in reducing the long-term risk for adolescent use of the drugs and substances of abuse. However, caregiver participation and adolescent results are extremely variable.

### Strategic-Structural Family Therapy

Strategic-structural family therapy, or simply structural family therapy, attempts to "restructure" maladaptive family boundaries that separate family members from each other in destructive ways (Szapocznik & Williams, 2000). For example, a mother and son may form a close, protective alliance that excludes the father from the knowledge that his son is a homosexual and that he also uses several drugs and substances of abuse in harmful ways as a result of his frequent participation at both local and distant circuit parties. In reaction to this exclusion, the father may feel alienated from his once-close family and become increasingly indifferent to his wife and distant and unsupportive of, or openly hostile toward, his son. In another example, a young adolescent mother may be involved in a constant, bitter conflict with her fiancé over her methamphetamine use and involve their young children in the conflict by making them take her side. In this situation, the mother also may physically or verbally abuse one of her children, using him or her as a scapegoat for the displacement of her own anger, frustration, and sense of blame (i.e., responsibility for the situation).

The general strategies incorporated with strategic-structural family therapy include reframing, validation, and facilitated communication. Reframing, a method also used in cognitive psychotherapy, simply is the process of conceptualizing a problem in a new and different way. The purpose of reframing is generally to: (1) place a problem in proper (generally smaller) perspective; and (2) to lessen the negative views that the family members have regarding their perceived notion of the cause of the problem. For example, a mother may identify her daughter's alcohol use as an act of defiance. The therapist may reframe the adolescent daughter's alcohol use as an expression of insecurity, low self-esteem, or a need to establish autonomy. This reframing of the reasons related to the daughter's alcohol use may facilitate shifting the treatment approach

---

[40] This component of the problem-solving approach is conceptually equivalent to what has been referred to in a scientific or medical context as the generation of multiple working hypotheses.

[41] This component of the problem-solving approach is often referred to as brainstorming.

from one of punishment to one of understanding and support.

The term "validation" refers to the process by which the therapist, in acting as a role model for family members, acknowledges and expresses an understanding of each family member's concerns, feelings, and desires. This approach encourages each family member to listen to, or hear out, the concerns, feelings, and desires of other family members before reacting to them or judging them.

In order to facilitate communication among family members, various techniques are taught and used during family therapy sessions. For example, individual family members may be taught to use the expression "I feel" as opposed to "you feel." This communication technique helps to avoid casting blame based on "mindreading" and allows other family members to clarify their own feelings. It also allows family members to state for themselves what they feel as opposed to responding to what a family member thinks they feel. As such, the "I feel" communications tend to engender more empathetic responses than do "you feel" communications, which tend to elicit decidedly more defensive responses.

***Multidimensional Family Therapy and Other Family Therapy*** Based on self-report responses at posttreatment, multidimensional family therapy—directed by professional family therapists in community clinics—appears to be efficacious in regard to decreasing alcohol, cannabis, and other drug use among minority ethnic youth (Liddle, Dakof, Parker, et al., 2001; Liddle, Rowe, Dakof, et al., 2004). Multisystemic therapy (MST) also appears to have therapeutic benefit—based on the analysis of hair and urine samples posttreatment and at a 4-year follow-up assessment—when

used to decrease cannabis use among juvenile offenders of various ethnic minorities (Henggeler, Clingempeel, Brondino, et al., 2002; Henggeler, Melton, Brondino, et al., 1997; Henggeler, Melton, & Smith, 1992). However, this form of family therapy did not reduce cocaine use in this group of participants. MST is directed by professional therapists in home and community clinic settings.

**Social Skills Training**   Social skills training attempts to help children and adolescents who have insufficient social skills to interact more effectively with their friends, peers, teachers, parents, and employers.[42] Social skills training involves detailed, focused training sessions that deal with common child and adolescent problems related to their poor social skills and thus include:

- Nonverbal expression
- Refusing unreasonable requests
- Making difficult requests
- Expressing and receiving positive emotions
- Replying appropriately to criticism
- Initiating social conversations (Oei & Jackson, 1980)

The training approach also has been applied successfully in juvenile closed-custody correctional settings (Pagliaro & Pagliaro, *Clinical Patient Data Files*).[43]

Based on the observation that many children and adolescents, who engage in harmful patterns of using the drugs and substances of abuse, have interpersonal, family, school, and vocational problems that appear to be related to deficits in social skills, individual and group training programs generally rely on therapist role modeling, role playing, and homework assignments.   Proper use of these techniques

---

[42] Social skills training also has been demonstrated to be of potential benefit for the treatment of children with fetal alcohol spectrum disorder (Peadon, Rhys-Jones, Bower, et al., 2009). Also see related discussion of FASD in Chapter 1, *The Psychodepressants*).

[43] The targeted behavior among youth for these social skills, school-based programs has not been limited to reducing the use of the drugs and substances of abuse but also has included reducing problems with bullying and violence (Mytton, DiGuiseppi, Gough, et al., 2006; Vreeman & Carroll, 2007).

can help children and adolescents to deal with anger and frustration, reduce high levels of social anxiety, communicate with others more effectively, become more assertive, and avoid being pressured by peers to do things that they do not really want to do (Van Hasselt, Hersen, & Milliones, 1978; Van Hasselt, Null, Kempton, et al., 1993).

**Therapeutic Communities** Therapeutic communities (TCs) are based on the assumption that harmful patterns of using the drugs and substances of abuse are primarily symptomatic of psychosocial maladaptation to society, often as a result of incompetence in dealing with stress or social privation and alienation. Reflective of the growing egalitarian, antiestablishment movements of the 1960s, TCs were developed to operate more democratically and less rigidly than were the more traditional and authoritarian mental health and psychiatric residential facilities at the time. Residents were viewed as active and equal coparticipants with staff in dealing with their own and each other's issues in regard to the use of the drugs and substances of abuse (i.e., providing self-help and mutual self-help, respectively) (Hanson, 2002). As noted by O'Brien and Biase (1984), the three major goals of TC programs are:

1. To eliminate the user's drug-taking behavior
2. To assist the user in learning to respond to distress (personal and environmental) in a more healthy manner
3. To assist users to readjust and return to the outside community as a functioning, independent person (p. 16)

These goals are achieved by providing residential care for adolescents who have abusive or compulsive patterns of using the drugs and substances of abuse. The residential care usually is provided for 3 to 12 months and gives adolescents the opportunity, often mandated in the context of the juvenile criminal justice system, to live with others who have similar problems in a highly structured homelike environment (Jainchill, Hawke, De Leon, et al., 2000). The TC provides a setting where everyone shares in the work and responsibility to see that community problems are minimized. Ideally, during their residential treatment, adolescents will be able to increasingly learn skills and assume responsibilities, which they can transfer to the larger community upon their completion of the program.

TC also requires that regular meetings be held throughout the day in informal settings (e.g., sitting around the kitchen table). These meetings serve to facilitate the operation of the TC (e.g., division of work; provision of feedback on the quality of residents' work performance) and provide a format for decision-making processes. A significant amount of therapy also occurs informally throughout the day, during which residents learn to take responsibility for; and perform; their tasks while interacting with the other residents. Recreational and leisure activities also provide a means for socializing and learning to interact more positively with others.

Most TCs practice a form of egalitarianism. For example, in regard to deciding how to handle a resident who is having difficulty getting along with other residents or in dealing with setting a program policy, all residents have an equal opportunity to share input and have an equal vote with the staff members.[44] All TCs

---

[44] The primary clinical and custodial staff members employed by TCs generally are paraprofessionals who have successfully rehabilitated themselves from previous abusive or compulsive use of various drugs and substances of abuse with the assistance of a TC program. Ancillary staff members include professionals from various disciplines (e.g., law; medicine; psychology) who are generally used on a contractual basis (De Leon, 1985). Although this staffing pattern is beginning to change with the use of more certified addictions counselors and social workers, the utilization of clinical psychologists and other university-educated social and healthcare professionals generally remains low in these programs (Dye, Ducharme, Johnson, et al., 2009).

require total abstinence from the use of alcohol, cocaine, heroin, lysergic acid diethylamide (LSD), and marijuana but may allow caffeine (i.e., coffee) and nicotine (i.e., tobacco) use.

Although TC programs have been widely used across North America for the last 50-plus years, research studies demonstrating their superior efficacy over other treatment approaches are lacking. As noted by Smith, Gates, and Foxcroft (2006) in their review of randomized controlled studies of the use of TC programs for the Cochrane Database, "There is little evidence that TCs offer significant benefits in comparison with other residential treatment, or that one type of TC is better than another" (p. 1). However, some modifications to traditional TCs (e.g., outpatient TCs; short-term residential TCs) have demonstrated significant reductions in efficacy outcomes (Dye, Ducharme, Johnson, et al., 2009).

Adolescents who complete TC programs have been found to show a success rate of more than 75%. However, most adolescents (i.e., approximately 75%) do not complete the entire course of treatment provided by a TC. For these adolescents, "outcome results indicate that reduction of illicit drug use, crime, and unemployment is commensurate to the length of time of participation in a therapeutic community" (Coombs, 1981, p. 199) and to not associating with deviant peers posttreatment (e.g., Jainchill, Hawke, DeLeon, et al., 2000). In an effort to increase adolescents' participation and attendance in TCs, several authors (e.g., Hanson, 2002; Jainchill, 1997; Jainchill, Hawke, & Messina, 2005; Melnick, De Leon, Hawke, et al., 1997) have suggested specific changes to make the TCs more responsive to adolescent needs. These changes include:

- Reducing the waiting time between initial contact with the program and entry into the program
- The employment of more staff members who are older adolescents or young adults
- The development and use of gender specific therapy groups and culturally- and ethically-specific therapy groups

- The use of on-site school teachers
- The inclusion of mothering or parenting issues
- The incorporation of child care programs
- The integration of visiting family therapy

**Short-Term Residential Treatment Programs** Short-term (in comparison to TCs) residential treatment programs (e.g., Hazelden) began to develop during the early 1970s in response to several identified needs. These needs included: a growing need for services, particularly for adolescents who had problems related to cocaine use; a desire among patients for treatment services other than those where they may be "institutionalized" for months; and limitations placed by third-party insurance carriers for the reimbursement of fees paid for provided treatment services (i.e., often with a 30-day limit). See Table 9.9 for an overview of the program objectives and elements comprising a "typical" short-term residential treatment program.

**Ethnic-Specific Treatment Programs** As noted previously in this text, North American children and adolescents of African descent generally have significantly lower rates of using the drugs and substances of abuse than do those of other continental descents. In addition, as noted by O'Malley, Johnston, Bachman, et al. (2006), schools

**TABLE 9.9 Typical Short-Term Residential Treatment Program Objectives and Key Elements**

**Program Objectives**

1. Maintain sobriety.
2. Learn about substance abuse and the process of recovery.
3. Recognize the effects of substance abuse on self and others (i.e., family, friends, coworkers).
4. Develop strategies to maintain sobriety.
5. Share thoughts and feelings with others (i.e., during group therapy sessions).
6. Utilize the basics of the AA program.

**Key Program Elements**

1. Personal inventory and plan
2. Daily schedule of program activities
3. Educational component
4. Group therapy sessions
5. Provision of safe and supportive environment

Modified from: Laundergan & Williams (1993).

that have predominantly students of African descent typically have lower rates of use of the drugs and substances of abuse at all grades. However, perhaps surprisingly, given the support for ethnic minority programs by the federal government (e.g., McBride, Terry-McElrath, VanderWaal, et al., 2008) over the last four decades, there is a paucity of data to support ethnic-specific treatment programs.

For example, Huey and Polo (2008), from their review of evidence-based psychosocial treatments for North American youth of African, Alaskan Native, American Indian, Asian, Hispanic, or "other" continental descent, reported that "no well-established treatments were identified" (p. 262). Part of the reason for this paucity of related data appears to be the underrepresentation of minority youth in treatment studies concerned with patterns of adolescent use of the drugs and substances of abuse treatment, which, in turn, is at least partially due to the significantly higher than expected drop-out rates of North American youth of African descent for these studies (Magruder, Ouyang, Miller, et al., 2009). Interventions that provided evidence for possible or probable efficacious tertiary prevention among ethnic minority youth who used drugs and substances of abuse all involved a central component involving family therapy. (See the earlier "Family Therapy" section for related discussion.)

**Bisexual, Gay, and Lesbian Treatment Programs**    As noted by several researchers (e.g., Corliss, Rosario, Wypij, et al., 2010)

and reported in previous chapters of this text, bisexual, gay, or lesbian adolescents are significantly more likely to display harmful patterns of using the various drugs and substances of abuse than are their heterosexual peers. Consequently, research studies and findings concerning efficacious treatment approaches aimed at better meeting the needs of bisexual, gay, and lesbian adolescents is urgently needed. Unfortunately, such research is not available. Until it becomes available, other treatment programs that have demonstrated success with heterosexual adolescents should be used.[45]

### Alcoholics Anonymous

Alcoholics Anonymous was started in 1935 in Akron, Ohio, by Bill W. (a stockbroker) and Bob S. (a physician), who were its first two members. AA has since spread across North America and now holds meetings worldwide. Particularly in North America, AA has become the most frequently used form of alcohol treatment with over 1 million recovering members (Laudet, 2008). According to several researchers and therapists (e.g., Room & Greenfield, 1993; Weisner, Greenfield, & Room, 1995), the popularity of AA is due in large part to its American themes of individualism, equality, and spirituality, which are embodied in the 12 steps.[46] (See Table 9.10.) As noted by Kurtz (1988, 1993), the organizational structure of AA also supports these themes in that there is no central authority or hierarchy,

---

[45] In this regard, we have, when possible—and with good results—used group therapy approaches for small groups of bisexual, gay, or lesbian adolescents in order to focus therapy more specifically on the drugs and substances of abuse that are commonly used by these adolescents and the lifestyle issues that contribute to their use (e.g., to cope with the common stresses associated with being bisexual, gay, or lesbian; to better socialize with others at parties and clubs). Although we do not practice family therapy, when deemed beneficial, we do make referrals to qualified family therapists who specialize in providing family therapy for bisexual, gay, or lesbian adolescents.

[46] The same themes that account for much of the success attributed to AA also make it an inappropriate treatment approach for some adolescents. The spiritual characteristics of AA are reflected by the wording of the 12 steps and also in both the generally accepted motto, "Let go and let God," and the Serenity Prayer, which is often used to conclude group meetings:

God grant me the serenity to accept the things I cannot change, the courage to change the things I can, and the wisdom to know the difference. Reinhold Niebuhr (1892–1971)

Our clinical experience indicates that regardless of gender, ethnicity, or sexual orientation, most adolescents who have alcoholism and other problems related to using the drugs and substances of abuse generally can derive significant benefit from AA as a component of their psychotherapy. However, we also have found over the last two decades that an increasing number of adolescents who identify themselves as either atheist or agnostic generally reject AA as a component of their therapy because they find its tenets philosophically incompatible with their own personal views of the world (i.e., lack of belief in God) (Pagliaro & Pagliaro, Clinical Patient Data Files).

**TABLE 9.10   The 12 Steps of Alcoholics Anonymous**

1. We admitted that we were powerless over alcohol, that our lives had become unmanageable.
2. We came to believe that a Power greater than ourselves could restore us to sanity.
3. We made a decision to turn our will and our lives over to the care of God as we understood Him.
4. We made a searching and fearless moral inventory of ourselves.
5. We admitted to God, to ourselves, and to another human being the exact nature of our wrongs.
6. We were entirely ready to have God remove all these defects of character.
7. We humbly asked Him to remove our shortcomings.
8. We made a list of all persons we had harmed, and became willing to make amends to them all.
9. We made direct amends to such people wherever possible, except when to do so would injure them or others.
10. We continued to take personal inventory, and when we were wrong promptly admitted it.
11. We sought through prayer and meditation to improve our conscious contact with God as we understood Him, praying only for knowledge of His will for us and the power to carry that out.
12. Having had a spiritual awakening as a result of these steps, we tried to carry this message to alcoholics and to practice these principles in all our affairs.

Source: *Alcoholics Anonymous—Big Book*, 2002.

the only officer in AA groups is a secretary, and members avoid the use of last names.

AA is regarded as neither a medical nor a psychological approach for the treatment of alcoholism (Borkman, 2008). As such, the organization maintains that alcoholism is a disease without cure and that treatment is social[47] or spiritual (McGee, 2000). As noted by Vaillant (2005): "The suggested mechanism of action of AA is that it employs four factors widely shown to be effective in relapse prevention in addictions: (1) external supervision; (2) substitute dependency; (3) new caring relationships; and (4) increased spirituality" (p. 431). AA relies on a rather informal form of group therapy and social support (i.e., frequent meetings with other fellow recovering members who maintain total abstinence from alcohol use) and a buddy system (i.e., the use of sponsors who have remained sober for a period of time by working the 12 steps and who can thus show newcomers the way to sobriety). As part of the group therapy, members hear from other members that they are not alone and that they share common, painful experiences in relation to their alcohol use. In addition, in conjunction with Step 1, members learn to overcome their strong denial of their own drinking problem. The confrontation of denial is both clearly and directly reflected in the members' introductions of themselves at AA group meetings: "Hello, my name is ____, and I'm an alcoholic."

Members are encouraged to work through and practice the 12 steps on a daily basis and, because the AA model purports that there is no cure for alcoholism[48], maintain lifelong abstinence by continued membership in the "fellowship" (i.e., AA) and regularly attend meetings. For many alcoholics, AA provides both the social support necessary to maintain abstinence and an effective surrogate for their previously patterned drinking time or "familiar bar scene" (i.e., AA meetings serve as a place to go on evenings, weekends, and holidays for socialization with friends who, in addition to other benefits, provide understanding and help to alleviate social isolation and loneliness).[49]

[47] In this regard, AA has often been labeled a social form of treatment.

[48] This AA belief would be consonant with what we describe as compulsive use. (See Figure 9.1 and Chapters 1, 2, and 3, respectively, *The Psychodepressants*, *The Psychostimulants*, and *The Psychedelics*, for additional details.) In this regard, we would concur with the AA philosophy that, once the compulsive level of use has been achieved, treatment, in order to have optimal opportunity for success, must include a lifetime of total abstinence.

[49] The number of AA meetings that a current member attends generally ranges from 1 daily to 1 weekly. The number of meetings attended on a regular basis is dictated, in large part, by factors such as the amount of time that a member has been sober (e.g., 1 day versus 1 year), the personality of the member (e.g., avoidant, dependent, or compulsive), and accessibility (e.g., is the scheduled meeting nearby?; does the member require and have available transportation?; is the style of the meeting compatible with the member's needs?). However, in some cases an individual member will develop a cultlike relationship with AA (i.e., will become obsessive and compulsive regarding AA doctrine; will limit social interaction to AA meetings and members; will increasingly become estranged from other social groups, such as family and colleagues) (Pagliaro & Pagliaro, *Clinical Patient Data Files*). These situations, although encountered relatively infrequently, should be monitored for and dealt with as part of the patient's program of psychotherapy.

The overall effectiveness of AA is difficult to ascertain for a number of reasons:

- AA maintains no formal records.
- Very few scientific studies have been conducted to formally measure its success.
- Available data are primarily observational.
- Sufficient theory to explain the inherent mechanisms of AA is lacking.
- Research is not an AA mandate.
- The amount of time that members remain active in AA is extremely variable.
- Drop-out rates are high (Alford, Koehler, & Leonard, 1991; Fingarette, 1988; Kelly & Myers, 2007; Miller & McCrady, 1993).

Obviously, the approach used by AA will not be suitable for all adolescents, and we would not recommend it as the sole approach to therapy. However, for patients who are willing to attend the meetings, we have found AA to be an effective and useful adjunct to individual psychotherapy, as have others (e.g., Ferri, Amato, & Davoli, 2006; Sussman, 2010) and can highly recommend it in this context.[50, 51] In addition, the efficacy of AA programs appears to be substantiated de facto by the large number of members who speak positively about it and the use of the AA approach by similar groups (e.g., Cocaine Anonymous [CA], Crystal Meth Anonymous [CMA], Gamblers Anonymous [GA], and Narcotics Anonymous (NA]). It also has been extended to other 12-step self-help groups[52] for families with parents or other family members, respectively, who use the drugs and substances of abuse in harmful ways (e.g., Al-Ateen; Al-Anon; Families of Alcoholics [FA]; Laudet, 2008). In addition, AA has consistently been rated highly by health and social care professionals (e.g., Chang, Astrachan, & Bryant, 1994).

### Relapse Prevention

The rate of relapse, or recidivism, following "successful" treatment of harmful patterns of drug and substance use among children and adolescents is quite high (Chung & Maisto, 2006). (See Figure 9.4.) Although much research has examined treatment factors, such as the involvement of family in treatment, provision of special services, staff characteristics, and time in treatment, these factors cannot account for the majority of variance in posttreatment return to problematic patterns of substance use. Obviously, much more research is required in this area. Factors implicated as causative or contributory to relapse include cognitive factors (*stinking-thinking*), increased craving, interpersonal problems, lack of coping abilities, and negative affective states (McKay, 1999). In addition, it has been noted that a "complicated and dynamic interplay of distal and proximal factors" plays a major role in the relapse process (McKay, Franklin, Patapis, et al., 2006, p. 109).

Our own clinical experience and the currently available research data suggests that the use of these three recommendations would at least minimize the potential for relapsed use:

---

[50] Although adolescents have been reported to attend adolescent AA meetings, mixed adolescent-adult meetings, and primarily adult AA meetings (Kelly, Myers, & Brown, 2002), we recommend that adolescent boys and girls only attend AA meetings that are comprised of other adolescent members (e.g., those AA programs that meet in youth correctional treatment centers). Due to their age and the possible psychopathology related to their use of the drugs and substances of abuse (e.g., active SUDs; dual diagnosis), adolescents comprise a population group that is particularly vulnerable. Thus, attention to this consideration is required when identifying appropriate AA groups for adolescents. In addition, consideration should be given to gender-specific (e.g., all male) or sexual orientation-specific (e.g., lesbian) groups.

[51] As with most forms of psychotherapy or counseling, efficacy of AA for adolescents is highly correlated with frequency of attendance (Kelly, Dow, Yeterian, et al., 2010; Kelly, Meyers, & Brown, 2002) and duration of attendance (Chi, Kaskutas, Sterling, et al., 2009).

[52] Also referred to as 12-step facilitation (TSF) programs.

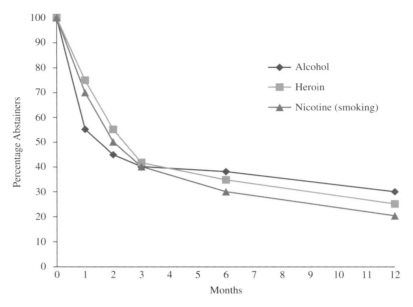

**Figure 9.4　Typical Relapse Rates Following Successful Treatment for Compulsive Use of the Drugs and Substances of Abuse**
Source: Preventing and treating substance use among children and adolescents, Chapter 10 in *Substance use among children and adolescents: Its nature, extent, and effects from conception to adulthood* (p. 265), by A. M. Pagliaro and L. A. Pagliaro, 1996, New York, NY: Wiley. Reprinted with permission.

1. Individualize treatment to the specific needs and characteristics of the child or adolescent (i.e., "cut the shoe to fit the foot").[53]

2. Employ specific indicators or performance goals to objectively evaluate the success of treatment outcomes and, subsequently, the degree of relapse or efficacy of relapse prevention. (See Table 9.11.)

3. Periodically, as individually indicated, prophylactically reassess children and adolescents and proactively intervene to prevent relapse.

Some of this periodic monitoring is addressed, for example, in aftercare programs and in continued attendance at AA meetings, both of which have been positively correlated with significantly higher rates, or duration, of posttreatment abstinence (Chi, Kaskutas, Sterling, et al., 2009; Johnson & Herringer, 1993; Kennedy & Minami, 1993; McBride,

1991; Pagliaro & Pagliaro, *Clinical Patient Data Files*). We suggest, particularly for children and adolescents who have engaged in abusive or compulsive patterns of using the drugs or substances of abuse, that the propensity for relapsed use and returning to compulsive use should be considered a lifelong concern (i.e., we do not subscribe to, nor do we endorse, the often-noted belief among both parents and some clinicians or therapists that the harmful use of the drugs and substances of abuse is just a phase or something children and adolescents will grow out of [i.e., that they will, as a matter of course, "mature out"]).

Whenever possible, once children and adolescents are abstinent, we gradually decrease the frequency and length of their psychotherapy sessions (e.g., from biweekly, to weekly, to every other week, to monthly, to every other month, to telephone contact every 6 months). This strategy helps to maintain a

---

[53] The use of patient-treatment matching has been known and used for over two decades (e.g., Kaminer & Frances, 1991; Mattson, 1994; Project MATCH, 1993). However, usually due to economic and/or time constraints, patient-treatment matching remains the exception to the rule.

**TABLE 9.11    Performance Criteria for the Evaluation of Treatment Success and Relapse Prevention**

- Interviewer's clinical evaluation of improvement
- School/job/home and social adjustment (e.g., regular attendance and improved performance)
- Self-reported reduction in, or discontinuation of, the use of the drugs and substances of abuse
- Reduction in sociopathy (e.g., reduced delinquent behavior)
- Intrapersonal adjustment (e.g., with family, friends, and classmates or peers)
- Social involvement (e.g., membership in Scouts or Guides, in school choir or orchestra, on school or other organized sport teams)
- Abstinence

Modified from: Foster, Horn, & Wanberg (197, p. 1079).

communication linkage and help line for each patient. This strategy also demonstrates continued concern and provides an opportunity for the early detection of problems by the therapist and for patients to request needed assistance before problems get out of control. In our practice, this strategy has resulted in a long-term (i.e., as long as we can maintain patient contact, generally in excess of 5 years) relapse rate of less than 20% (Pagliaro & Pagliaro, *Clinical Patient Data Files*).

## META-INTERACTIVE MODEL OF CHILD AND ADOLESCENT USE OF THE DRUGS AND SUBSTANCES OF ABUSE

The Meta-Interactive Model of Child and Adolescent Use of the Drugs and Substances of Abuse (Figure 9.3) can serve as a particularly helpful model for considering primary, secondary, and tertiary prevention in regard to specific characteristics (e.g., age and developmental level) associated with various patterns of child and adolescent use of the drugs and substances of abuse. The model consists of four interacting dimensions: (1) child or adolescent dimension; (2) drug or substance of abuse dimension; (3) societal dimension; and (4) time dimension. The

milieu associated with child and adolescent use of the drugs and substances of abuse is uniquely characterized for each individual as the complete set of interacting variables from each of the four dimensions at a particular point in time. The model helps to account for the multidimensional etiology and context of child and adolescent use of the drugs and substances of abuse and serves as a useful heuristic device, providing an orderly and logical approach for understanding these complex phenomena.

The model can help to plan specific, individual treatment strategies by identifying the presenting antecedent or consequential variables in each dimension that appear to contribute to use, are amenable to change, and require attention. For example, if specific stresses and maladaptive coping mechanisms are identified among the psychological variables in the child or adolescent dimension, techniques for stress reduction and the development of better coping abilities would be an integral component of the treatment plan. If a lack of family support is identified as a major contributing factor to drug and substance use among the social variables in the child or adolescent dimension, intervention might include attempts to increase family support (i.e., family therapy might be considered). If a lack of adequate healthcare resources (e.g., specifically designed programs aimed at providing appropriate services to children and adolescents, including appropriately trained and qualified staff) is identified as a major factor contributing to the use of the drugs and substances of abuse in the societal dimension, intervention may include attempts to increase social assistance (i.e., develop and provide specific social programs for children and adolescents) and the training of clinical child and adolescent psychiatrists and psychologists, counselors, family therapists, pediatricians, social workers, and other health and social care professionals in regard to the specific approaches needed for delivering optimal treatment for children and adolescents who have SUDs.

Evaluation of treatment is one of the most crucial yet perhaps the most frequently overlooked steps in the treatment process. It is useless to prescribe treatment, or for a child or adolescent to rigorously follow a plan of treatment, if the treatment is ineffective. Evaluation can be readily performed by using the model to compare specific variables of interest before treatment (i.e., baseline assessment), during treatment (i.e., formative evaluation), and at a predetermined interval(s) after treatment is completed (i.e., summative evaluation). Although program evaluators and researchers are often particularly interested in the summative evaluation in terms of program success and recidivism rates, others (e.g., counselors, therapists) may be more interested in the formative evaluation because an ineffective treatment plan can be modified midstream in order to optimize therapy for an individual child or adolescent.

For example, if unemployment is a social variable in the child or adolescent dimension that is identified, for a particular adolescent, as a major contributory factor to his or her use of a drug or substance of abuse and, if sufficient attention is not given to appropriate educational (e.g., general equivalency diploma programs; tutoring for math or reading deficits), job training (e.g., schoolwork programs, vocational educational programs), and employment strategies (e.g., resume development, subsidized job work programs for youth), the prognosis is bleak—in spite of other treatment interventions.

The model also is useful because it can reveal factors that may, for a particular child or adolescent, contribute to relapsed use if not addressed. Such factors may include inadequate coping abilities when the youth is faced with significant stressors, such as the death of a parent, a diagnosis of cancer, an encounter with a bully at school, or a police arrest. In addition, the model can be useful as a framework for helping children and adolescents better understand the factors affecting their own use of the drugs and substances of abuse and, thus, enable them to become active participants in their own treatment planning and implementation.

**TABLE 9.12    Components for an Optimal Adolescent-Oriented Treatment Program**

- Academic assistance
- Adolescent support groups
- Alcohol/substance use education
- Child care
- Components to build self-esteem
- Dual diagnosis treatment
- Employment/vocational counseling
- Family therapy
- Financial counseling
- Follow-up (aftercare)
- Group therapy
- HIV counseling and testing
- Housing assistance (transitional housing)
- Individual therapy
- Legal services
- Life-skills programs
- Medical care
- Mothering and parenting courses
- Nutritional counseling
- Outreach and in-home services
- Relapse prevention programs
- Stress management programs
- Transportation
- Violence and sexual abuse services

Finally, it should be noted and made explicit that in order to achieve optimal use of the model it should be applied in the context of a drug and substance abuse treatment program that incorporates many of the desired components discussed in this chapter. See for example, Table 9.12.

## CHAPTER SUMMARY

This chapter presented an overview of the many treatment programs and approaches aimed at the primary, secondary, and tertiary prevention of child and adolescent use of the drugs and substances of abuse. Targeting youth, parents, teachers, communities, and other stakeholders, these programs and approaches generally focus on increasing awareness and understanding of the use of drugs and substances of abuse by children and adolescents. They also provide accurate information about the drugs and substances of abuse and their harmful effects. Finally, these programs and approaches attempt to positively change the related attitudes and values of targeted groups of children and adolescents. As such, they reflect four general models: (1) the information-only model; (2) the alternatives model; (3) the affective educational/social competency model; and (4) the social environmental/learning model. However, formal research evaluation of the actual efficacy of these models in regard to preventing child and adolescent use of the drugs and substances of abuse has found that none has uniformly demonstrated widespread, long-lasting effectiveness.

Tertiary prevention programs and approaches also were presented and discussed, including available pharmacological advances aimed at reducing the use of selected drugs and substances of abuse and their associated harm. Future developments also were highlighted, including, for example, vaccines for preventing nicotine use. Attention, too, was given to pharmacotherapy for managing overdosages and specific withdrawal syndromes (e.g., alcohol, cocaine, and nicotine withdrawal). Substitution, or replacement, pharmacotherapy for therapeutically maintaining the use of specific drugs and substances of abuse also was presented (e.g., methadone substitution pharmacotherapy for maintaining opiate analgesic use and nicotine replacement pharmacotherapy for tobacco smoking cessation).

Finally, the chapter concluded with a brief review of psychotherapy and counseling approaches that have proven beneficial for the treatment of adolescents who use drugs and substances of abuse in harmful ways, including: cognitive therapy; peer group therapy; various types of family therapy—behavioral family therapy, strategic-structural family therapy; and social skills training. Therapeutic communities; short-term residential treatment programs, ethnic-specific treatment programs; bisexual, gay- and, lesbian-oriented treatment programs; AA, and other relapse prevention programs also were discussed.

Much effort has been directed toward finding effective programs and techniques aimed at preventing and treating harmful patterns of using the drugs and substances

of abuse among children and adolescents. However, to date, only marginal success has been achieved in these areas, as demonstrated by: (1) the increasing numbers of children and adolescents who initiate alcohol use, tobacco smoking, and other use of the drugs and substances of abuse (2) the numbers of children and adolescents who continue to use drugs and substances of abuse regardless of being aware of the harm associated with their use; and (3) the extremely high recidivism rates that accompany virtually all current treatment programs and approaches.

While multimodal therapy appears to provide the best results, the theme that is consistently and repeatedly found in the research literature is that children and adolescents who develop increasingly harmful patterns of using the drugs and substances of abuse respond differently to different treatment approaches (i.e., what works best for one child or adolescent may not work best or, in some cases, at all, for another child or adolescent). Thus, instead of attempting to find and use the single "best" program, it is recommended that health and social care professionals become familiar with the various types and approaches to prevention and treatment and then select the one(s) that is (are) best suited to the specific needs of the child or adolescent for whom they are planning treatment. In this regard, the Meta-Interactive Model of Child and Adolescent Use of the Drugs and Substances of Abuse can serve as a particularly useful heuristic device for the primary, secondary, and tertiary prevention of child and adolescent use of the drugs and substances of abuse. With the use of this model to identify related variables that require attention, and with knowledge of successful and unsuccessful programs, we can begin to develop more effective prevention and treatment programs for children and adolescents—both those who have not yet begun use of a drug or substance of abuse and those who have already begun to use and are developing increasingly harmful patterns of use.

# Abbreviations Used in the Text

**A**

| | |
|---|---|
| AA | Alcoholics Anonymous |
| A-D/HD | attention-deficit/hyperactivity disorder |
| ADR | adverse drug reaction |
| AEEI | Alcohol Education Evaluation Instrument |
| AEs | alcohol expectancies |
| AIDS | acquired immune deficiency syndrome |
| AMA | American Medical Association |
| APA | American Psychological Association |
| APD | antisocial personality disorder |
| ARBD | alcohol-related birth defect |
| ARND | alcohol-related neurodevelopmental disorder |
| ASAM | American Society of Addictions Medicine |
| ASSIST | Alcohol, Smoking, and Substance Involvement Screening Test |
| AUDs | alcohol use disorders |
| AUDIT | Alcohol Use Disorders Identification Test |
| AUDIT-C | Alcohol Use Disorders Identification Test-Consumption |

**B**

| | |
|---|---|
| BAC | blood alcohol concentration |
| BD | bipolar disorder |
| B-MAST | Brief MAST |
| BPD | borderline personality disorder |
| BSFT | brief strategic family therapy |
| BZD | benzodiazepine |

**C**

| | |
|---|---|
| CA | Cocaine Anonymous |
| CAP | Cognitive Affective Pharmacogenic |
| CAST | Cannabis Abuse Screening Test |

| | |
|---|---|
| CBT | cognitive-behavioral therapy |
| CD | conduct disorder |
| CDC | Centers for Disease Control |
| CEWG | Community Epidemiology Work Group |
| CMA | Crystal Meth Anonymous |
| CNS | central nervous system |
| COPD | chronic obstructive pulmonary disease |
| CRF | corticotropin-releasing factor |
| CSA | catecholamine system activity (theory) |
| CTZ | chemoreceptor trigger zone |
| CUDIT | Cannabis Use Disorders Identification Test |

**D**

| | |
|---|---|
| D | dopamine |
| D.A.R.E. | Drug Abuse Resistance Education |
| DAT | dopamine transmitter |
| DAST | Drug Abuse Screening Test |
| DAWN | Drug Abuse Warning Network |
| DBDM | Developmental Biopsychosocial Disease Model |
| DDRC | Dual Disorders Recovery Counseling |
| DEA | Drug Enforcement Agency |
| DSM | *Diagnostic and Statistical Manual of Mental Disorders* |
| DTs | delirium tremens |
| DUDIT | Drug Use Disorders Identification Test |
| DUI | driving under the influence (of alcohol) |
| DWI | driving while impaired/intoxicated |

**E**

| | |
|---|---|
| ED | emergency department |
| ETS | environmental tobacco smoke |

**F**

| | |
|---|---|
| FA | families of alcoholics |
| FACES | Family Adaptability and Cohesion Evaluation Scale |
| FAE | fetal alcohol effects |
| FAEE | fatty acid ethyl esters |

| | |
|---|---|
| FAS | fetal alcohol syndrome |
| FASD | fetal alcohol spectrum disorder |
| FDA | Food and Drug Administration |
| fMRI | functional magnetic resonance imaging |
| FTND | Fagerström Test for Nicotine Dependence |

**G**

| | |
|---|---|
| GABA | gamma-aminobutyric acid |
| GBL | gamma-butyrolactone |
| GC/MS | gas chromatography/mass spectrometry |
| GGT | gamma-glutamyl transpeptidase |
| GHB | gamma-hydroxybutyrate |
| GI | gastrointestinal |

**H**

| | |
|---|---|
| HIV | human immunodificiency virus |
| HPA | hypothalamic-pituitary-adrenal |
| 5-HT | 5-hydroxytryptamine (serotonin) |

**I**

| | |
|---|---|
| ICD | International Classification of Diseases |
| IDU | injection drug user |
| IGR | intrauterine growth retardation |
| IQ | intelligence quotient |
| IVDU | intravenous drug user |

**L**

| | |
|---|---|
| $LD_{50}$ | lethal dose for 50% of the population; median lethal dose |
| LC/MS | liquid chromatography/mass spectrometry |
| LPP | life process program (theory) |
| LSA | lysergic acid amide |
| LSD | lysergic acid diethylamide |

**M**

| | |
|---|---|
| MADD | Mothers Against Drunk Driving |
| MAO | monoamine oxidase |
| MAST | Michigan Alcoholism Screening Test |

| MDA | methylenedioxyamphetamine |
| MDD | major depressive disorder |
| MDFT | multidimensional family therapy |
| MDMA | methylenedioxymethamphetamine |
| MRI | magnetic resonance imaging |
| MST | multisystemic therapy |

**N**

| NA | Narcotics Anonymous |
| nAChR | nicotinic acetylcholine receptor |
| n.d. | no date |
| NIAAA | National Institute on Alcohol Abuse and Alcoholism |
| NIDA | National Institute on Drug Abuse |
| NMDA | N-methyl-D-aspartate |
| NSDUH | National Survey on Drug Use and Health |

**O**

| ODD | oppositional defiant disorder |
| OMDs | other mental disorders |
| OR | odds ratio |

**P**

| PATS | Partnership for a Drug-Free America Survey |
| PCP | phencyclidine |
| PD | panic disorder |
| PET | positron emission tomography |
| pH | hydrogen ion concentration |
| PNS | peripheral nervous system |
| POSIT | Problem Oriented Screening Instrument for Teenagers |
| PTSD | post-traumatic stress disorder |

**R**

| RAPI | Rutgers Alcohol Problem Index |
| RAPS | Rapid Alcohol Problem Screen |

**S**

| | |
|---|---|
| SAD | somatosensory affectional deprivation (theory) |
| SADD | Students Against Drunk Driving |
| SBIRT | screening, brief intervention, and referral to treatment |
| SES | socioeconomic status |
| SFRS | Structural Family Rating System |
| SGA | small for gestational age |
| SIDS | sudden infant death syndrome |
| SMAST | Short Michigan Alcoholism Screening Test |
| SUDs | substance use disorders |

**T**

| | |
|---|---|
| TC | therapeutic community |
| THC | tetrahydrocannabinol |
| TSF | Twelve-Step Facilitation |
| TSNA | tobacco-specific nitrosamine |
| TUPE | Tobacco Use Prevention Education |

**U**

| | |
|---|---|
| U.S. | United States |
| USDEA | United States Drug Enforcement Administration |

**W**

| | |
|---|---|
| WHO | World Health Organization |

# References[1,2]

## A

Aalto, M., Alho, H., Halme, J. T., et al. (2009). AUDIT and its abbreviated versions in detecting heavy and binge drinking in a general population survey. *Drug and Alcohol Dependence, 103*(1–2), 25–29.

Abdel-Latif, M. E., Pinner, J., Clews, S., et al. (2006) Effects of breast milk on the severity and outcome of neonatal abstinence syndrome among infants of drug-dependent mothers. *Pediatrics, 117,* e1163–e1169.

Abel, E. L. (1995). An update on incidence of FAS: FAS is not an equal opportunity birth defect. *Neurotoxicology and Teratology, 17*(4), 437–443.

Abel, E. L., Martier, S., Kruger, M., et al. (1993). *Ratings of fetal alcohol syndrome facial features by medical providers and biomedical scientists. Alcoholism, Clinical & Experimental Research, 17,* 717–721.

Abel, E. L., & Sokol, R. J. (1987). Incidence of fetal alcohol syndrome and economic impact of FAS-related anomalies. *Drug and Alcohol Dependence, 19,* 51–70.

Abel, E. L., & Sokol, R. J. (1991). A revised conservative estimate of the incidence of FAS and economic impact. *Alcoholism, Clinical and Experimental Research, 15,* 514–524.

Abraham, H. D., & Aldridge, A. M. (1993). Adverse consequences of lysergic acid diethylamide. *Addiction, 88*(10), 1327–1334.

Acamprosate campral for alcoholism. (2005). *Medical Letter on Drugs and Therapeutics, 47*(1199), 1–3.

Accortt, N. A., Waterbor, J. W., Beall, C., et al. (2002). Chronic disease mortality in a cohort of smokeless tobacco users. *American Journal of Epidemiology, 156*(8), 730–737.

Ackerman, J. P., Riggins, T., & Black, M. M. (2010). A review of the effects of prenatal cocaine exposure among school-aged children. *Pediatrics, 125*(3), 554–565.

Adamson, S. J., & Sellman, J. D. (2003). A prototype screening instrument for cannabis use disorder: The Cannabis Use Disorders Identification Test (CUDIT) in an alcohol-dependent clinical sample. *Drug and Alcohol Review, 22*(3), 309–315.

Addiction Research Foundation/World Health Organization. (1981). Report of an ARF/WHO Scientific Meeting on the Adverse Health and Behavioral Consequences of Cannabis Use. Toronto, Canada: Addiction Research Foundation.

Addis, A., Dolovich, L. R., Einarson, T. R., et al. (2000). Motherisk update: Can we use anxiolytics during pregnancy without anxiety? *Canadian Family Physician, 46,* 549–551.

Adewuya, A. O. (2005). Validation of the Alcohol Use Disorders Identification Test (AUDIT) as a screening tool for alcohol-related problems among Nigerian university students. *Alcohol and Alcoholism, 40*(6), 575–577.

Adgent, M. A. (2006). Environmental tobacco smoke and sudden infant death syndrome: A review. *Birth Defects Research Part B. Developmental & Reproductive Toxicology, 77*(1), 69–85.

Adger, H., McDonald, E. M., & DeAngelis, C. (1990). Substance abuse education in pediatrics. *Pediatrics, 88,* 555–560.

Adolescent cigarette smoking holds at lowest recorded levels. (2010). *NIDA Notes, 23*(2), 19.

Adrian, M. (2003). How can sociological theory help our understanding of addictions? *Substance Use & Misuse, 38*(10), 1385–1423.

Aertgeerts, B., Buntinx, F., Ansoms, et al. (2001). Screening properties of questionnaires and laboratory tests for the detection of alcohol abuse or dependence in a general practice population. *British Journal of General Practice, 51,* 206–217.

Aertgeerts, B., Buntinx, F., Bande-Knops, J., et al. (2000). The value of CAGE, CUGE, and AUDIT in screening for alcohol abuse and dependence among college freshmen. *Alcoholism, Clinical and Experimental Research, 24*(1), 53–57.

---

[1]During the preparation of this text, several times the number of references found in this list were obtained and analyzed. However, *only* those references that have been actually cited at least once in the body of the text of the various individual chapters have been included in this list. Unfortunately, text page constraints prevent listing all the uncited references and providing an annotation of why they were not cited, the major reasons being: (1) did not provide any additional unique data; (2) were not well researched or written; (3) were based exclusively on animal studies; (4) provided usage statistics from outside of North America; and/or (5) were redundant with the already cited references.

[2]The reference citation, "Pagliaro & Pagliaro, *Clinical Patient Data Files,*" refers to unpublished data collected by the authors, in the formal course of their professional academic roles as clinician scientists, from their patients, research subjects, and students, from the 1970s to date.

Aertgeerts, B., Buntinx, F., Fevery, J., et al. (2000). Is there a difference between CAGE interviews and written CAGE questionnaires? *Alcoholism, Clinical and Experimental Research, 24*(5), 733–736.

Aetgeerts, B., Buntinx, F., & Kester, A. (2004). The value of the CAGE in screening for alcohol abuse and alcohol dependence in general clinical populations: A diagnostic meta-analysis. *Journal of Clinical Epidemiology, 57*(1), 30–39.

Ahijevych, K., & Garrett, B. E. (2004). Menthol pharmacology and its potential impact on cigarette smoking behavior. *Nicotine & Tobacco Research, 6*(Suppl. 1), S17–S28.

Akers, R. L. (1977). *Deviant behavior: A social learning approach* (2nd ed.). Belmont, CA: Wadsworth.

Akers, R. L., Krohn, M. D., Lanza-Kaduce, L., et al. (1979). Social learning and deviant behavior: A specific test of a general theory. *American Sociological Review, 44,* 636–655.

al-Ansari, E. A., & Negrete, J. C. (1990). Screening for alcoholism among alcohol users in a traditional Arab Muslim society. *Acta Psychiatrica Scandinavica, 81*(3), 284–288.

Alberta's peer support program. (1987). *Health Promotion, 26,* 23.

Alcoholics Anonymous—Big Book (2002). *Alcoholics Anonymous: The big book* (4th ed., revised). Hazelden, MN: Hazelden Information & Educational Services.

Alcohol implicated in rising toll of fatal car crashes involving young women drivers. (2010, February 12). *ScienceDaily,* pp. 1–2. Retrieved from http://www.sciencedaily.com/releases/2010/02/100217224233.htm

Alcohol Use USA. (2010, January 6). Retrieved from http://www.alcohol-and-drug-guide.com/alcohol-use-usa.html

Alcohol withdrawal syndrome: How to predict, prevent, diagnose and treat it. (2007). *Prescrire International, 16*(87), 24–31.

Alegría, A. A., Hasin, D. S., Nunes, E. V., et al. (2010). Comorbidity of generalized anxiety disorder and substance use disorders: Results from the National Epidemiologic Survey on Alcohol and Related Conditions. *The Journal of Clinical Psychiatry, 71*(9), 1187–1195.

Alexander, J., Waldon, H. B., Newberry, A. M., et al. (1990). The functional family therapy model. In A. S. Friedman & S. Granick (Eds.), *Family therapy for adolescent drug abuse* (pp. 183–199). New York, NY: Lexington.

Alexander, T., DiNitto, D. M., & Tidblom, I. (2005). Screening for alcohol and other drug use problems among the deaf. *Alcoholism Treatment Quarterly, 23*(1), 63–78.

Alford, G. S., Koehler, R. A., & Leonard, J. (1991). Alcoholics Anonymous-Narcotics Anonymous model

inpatient treatment of chemically dependent adolescents: A 2-year outcome study. *Journal of Studies on Alcohol, 52*(2), 118–126.

Allen, J. P., Litten, R. Z., Fertig, J. B., et al. (1997). A review of research on the Alcohol Use Disorders Identification Test (AUDIT). *Alcoholism, Clinical and Experimental Research, 21*(4), 613–619.

Allen, J. S., & Drabman, R. S. (1991). Attributions of children with learning disabilities who are treated with psychostimulants. *Learning Disability Quarterly, 14,* 1991.

Ali, R., Awwad, E., Barbor, T., et al. (2002). The Alcohol, Smoking and Substance Involvement Screening Test (ASSIST): Development, reliability and feasibility. *Addiction, 97*(9), 1183–1194.

Ali, S. R., Krugar, M., & Houghton, J. (2002). Upper airway obstruction and acute lung injury associated with cocaine abuse. *International Journal of Clinical Practice, 56*(6), 484–485.

Allen, B., Jr., & Unger, J. B. (2007). Sociocultural correlates of menthol cigarette smoking among adult African Americans in Los Angeles. *Nicotine & Tobacco Research, 9*(4), 447–451.

Allen, J. P., Litten, R. Z., Fertig, J. B., et al. (1997). A review of research on the Alcohol Use Disorders Identification Test (AUDIT). *Alcoholism, Clinical and Experimental Research, 21*(4), 613–619.

Allen, S. S., Bade, T., Hatsukami, et al. (2008). Craving, withdrawal, and smoking urges on days immediately prior to smoking relapse. *Nicotine & Tobacco Research, 10*(1), 35–45.

Al Mamun, A., O'Callaghan, F., Alati, R., et al. (2006). Does maternal smoking during pregnancy predict the smoking patterns of young adult offspring? A birth cohort study. *Tobacco Control, 15,* 452–457.

Alterman, A. I. (1987). Patterns of familial alcoholism, alcoholism severity, and psychopathology. *The Journal of Nervous & Mental Disease, 176,* 167–175.

Alterman, A., & Tarter, R. (1986). An examination of selected typologies: Hyperactivity, familial, and antisocial alcoholism. *Recent Developments in Alcoholism, 4,* 169–189.

Aluli, N. E., Reyes, P. W., Brady, S. K., et al. (2010). All-cause and CVD mortality in Native Hawaiians. *Diabetes Research and Clinical Practice, 89*(1), 65–71.

Alves, C., & Lima, R. V. (2009). Dietary supplement use by adolescents [in Portuguese]. *Jornal de Pediatria, 85*(4), 287–294.

Amato, L., Minozzi, S., Pani, P. P., et al. (2007). Antipsychotic medications for cocaine dependence. *Cochrane Database of Systematic Reviews, 18*(3), CD006306. Retrieved from http://www.ncbi.nlm.nih.gov/pubmed/17636840

Ameri, A. (1999). The effects of cannabinoids on the brain. *Progress in Neurobiology, 58*(4), 315–348.

American Academy of Clinical Toxicology, & European Association of Poisons Centres and Clinical

Toxicologists. (1999). Position statement and practice guidelines on the use of multi-dose activated charcoal in the treatment of acute poisoning. *Journal of Toxicology, Clinical Toxicology, 37*(6), 731–751.

American Academy of Pediatrics. (2001). Alcohol use and abuse: A pediatric concern. *Pediatrics, 108*(1), 185–189.

American Academy of Pediatrics, Committee on Drugs. (2001). The transfer of drugs and other chemicals into human milk. *Pediatrics, 108*(3), 776–789.

American Academy of Pediatrics, Committee on Substance Abuse and Committee on Children with Disabilities. (1993). *Pediatrics, 91*, 1004–1006.

American Association of Poison Control Centers. (2011, January 3). Quick facts on poison exposures in the United States. Retrieved from http://www.1-800-222-1222.info/stats/home.asp

American Educational Research Association, Psychological Association, & National Council on Measurement in Education. (1999). *Standards for educational and psychological testing.* Washington, DC: Author.

American Psychiatric Association. (2000). *Diagnostic and statistical manual of mental disorders* (4th ed., text revision). Washington, DC: Author.

American Psychiatric Association (2011). Substance-related disorders. Retrieved from http://www.dsm5.org/ProposedRevisions/Pages/Substance-RelatedDisorders.aspx

Anachebe, N. F. (2006). Racial and ethnic disparities in infant and maternal mortality. *Ethnicity & Disease, 16*(2, Suppl. 3), S71–S76.

Anders, T. F., & Eiben, L. A. (1997). Pediatric sleep disorders: A review of the past 10 years. *Journal of the American Academy of Child & Adolescent Psychiatry, 36*(1), 9–20.

Anderson, B., Storfer-Isser, A., Taylor, H. G., et al. (2009, March 30). Associations of executive function with sleepiness and sleep duration in adolescents. *Pediatrics, 123*(4), e701–e707.

Anderson, C. E., & Loomis, G. A. (2003). Recognition and prevention of inhalant abuse. *American Family Physician, 68*(5), 869–874.

Anderson, D. M. (2010). Does information matter? The effect of the Meth Project on meth use among youths. *Journal of Health Economics, 29*(5), 732–742.

Anderson, H. R., & Cook, D. G. (1997). Passive smoking and sudden infant death syndrome: Review of the epidemiological evidence. *Thorax, 52*(11), 1003–1009.

Anderson, M. (2010). Benzodiazepines for prolonged seizures. *Archives of Disease in Childhood. Education and Practice Edition, 95*(6), 183–189.

Anderson, P. (2009, August 6). Nonprescription opioid use prevalent among older teens. *Medscape Medical News,* pp. 1–2. Retrieved from http://www.medscape.com/viewarticle/707082_print

Anderson, P., de Bruijn, A., Angus, K., et al. (2009). Impact of alcohol advertising and media exposure on adolescent alcohol use: A systematic review of longitudinal studies. *Alcohol and Alcoholism, 44*(3), 229–243.

Andrews, W. N. (1972). Amotivational syndrome. *Canadian Medical Association Journal, 107*(4), 279.

Andrulonis, P. A. (1991). Disruptive behavior in boys and the borderline personality disorder in men. *Annals of Clinical Psychiatry, 3*, 23–26.

Anderson, P. O., Sauberan, J., Lane, J. R., et al. (2007). Hydrocodone excretion into breastmilk: The first two reported cases. *Breastfeeding Medicine, 2*, 10–14.

Anglin, M. D., Burke, C., Perrochet, B., et al. (2000). History of the methamphetamine problem. *Journal of Psychoactive Drugs, 32*(2), 137–141.

Anglin, D., Spears, K. L., & Hutson, H. R. (1997). Flunitrazepam and its involvement in date or acquaintance rape. *Academic Emergency Medicine, 4*, 323–326.

Annaheim, B., Rehm, J., & Gmel, G. (2008). How to screen for problematic cannabis use in population surveys? An evaluation of the Cannabis Use Disorders Identification Test (CUDIT) in a Swiss sample of adolescents and young adults. *European Addiction Research, 14*(4), 190–197.

Anthony, J. C., Tien, A. Y., & Petronis, K. R. (1989). Epidemiologic evidence on cocaine use and panic attacks. *American Journal of Epidemiology, 129*(3), 543–549.

Apgar, V. (1953). A proposal for a new method of evaluation of the newborn infant. *Current Research in Anesthesia and Analgesia, 32*(4), 260–267.

Appelboam, A., & Oades, P. J. (2006). Coma due to cannabis toxicity in an infant. *European Journal of Emergency Medicine, 13*(3), 177–179.

Araki, H., Suemaru, K., & Gomita, Y. (2002). Neuronal nicotinic receptor and psychiatric disorders: Functional and behavioral effects of nicotine. *Japanese Journal of Pharmacology, 88*(2), 133–138.

Arbaizar, B., Diersen-Sotos, T., Gómez-Acebo, I., et al. (2010). Topiramate in the treatment of alcohol dependence: A meta-analysis [in Spanish]. *Actas Españolas de Psiquiatria, 38*(1), 8–12.

Arendt, M., Rosenberg, R., Foldager, L., et al. (2007). Withdrawal symptoms do not predict relapse among subjects treated for cannabis dependence. *The American Journal of Addictions, 16*(6), 461–467.

Arias, A. J., Gelernter, J., Chan, G., et al. (2008). Correlates of co-occurring ADHD in drug-dependent subjects: Prevalence and features of substance dependence and psychiatric disorders. *Addictive Behaviors, 33*(9), 1199–1207.

Armeli, S., Todd, M., Conner, T. S., et al. (2008). Drinking to cope with negative moods and the immediacy of drinking within the weekly cycle among college students. *Journal of Studies on Alcohol, 69*(2), 313–322.

Armstrong, T. D., & Costello, E. J. (2002). Community studies on adolescent substance use, abuse, or dependence and psychiatric comorbidity. *Journal of Consulting and Clinical Psychology, 70*(6), 1224–1239.

Arnett, J. J. (1994). Sensation seeking: A new conceptualization and a new scale. *Personality and Individual Differences, 16*, 289–296.

Arnett, J. J. (1998). Learning to stand alone: The contemporary American transition to adulthood in cultural and historical context. *Human Development, 41*, 295–315.

Arnett, J. J. (2000). Emerging adulthood: A theory of development from the late teens through the twenties. *American Psychologist, 55*, 469–480.

Arnett, J. J. (2004). *Emerging adulthood: The winding road from the late teens through the twenties*. New York, NY: Oxford University Press.

Arnett, J. J. (2005, Spring). The developmental context of substance use in emerging adulthood. *Journal of Drug Issues*, 235–254.

Arnold, G. L., Kirby, R. S., Langendoerfer, S., et al. (1994). Toluene embryopathy: Clinical delineation and developmental follow-up. *Pediatrics, 93*(2), 216–220.

Aronow, R., Paul, S. D., & Woolley, P. V. (1972). Childhood poisoning: An unfortunate consequence of methadone availability. *JAMA, The Journal of the American Medical Association, 219*(3), 321–324.

Arria, A., Derauf, C., Lagasse, L., et al. (2006). Methamphetamine and other substance use during pregnancy: Preliminary estimates from the infant development, environment, and lifestyle (IDEAL) study. *Maternal and Child Health Journal, 10*, 293–302.

Asante, K. O., & Nelms-Maztke, J. (1985). Report on the survey of children with chronic handicaps and fetal alcohol syndrome in the Yukon and Northwest British Columbia. Whitehorse, BC: Council for Yukon Indians.

Ashton, C. H. (2001). Pharmacology and effects of cannabis: A brief review. *The British Journal of Psychiatry, 178*, 101–106.

Aspy, C. B., Mold, J. W., Thompson, D. M., et al. (2008). Integrating screening and interventions for unhealthy behaviors into primary care practices. *American Journal of Preventive Medicine, 53*(5, Suppl.), S373–S380.

Associated Press. (2009, August 14). Police say mother poisoned baby's milk. Boston Globe. Retrieved from http://www.boston.com/news/nation/articles/2009/08/14/police_say_mother_poisoned_baby...

Associated Press. (2011, April 25). Regulator will treat E-Cigarettes like tobacco. *The New York Times*, pp. 1–3. Available: http://www.nytimes.com/2011/04/26/business/26tobacco.html?_r...

Astley, S. J. (2004). *Diagnostic guide for fetal alcohol spectrum disorders: The 4-Digit Diagnostic Code* (3rd ed.). Seattle, WA: University of Washington Publication Services.

Astley, S. J. (2010). Profile of the first 1,400 patients receiving diagnostic evaluations for fetal alcohol spectrum disorder at the Washington State Fetal Alcohol Syndrome Diagnostic & Prevention Network. *Canadian Journal of Clinical Pharmacology, 17*(1), e132–e164.

Astley, S. J., & Clarren, S. K. (1996). A case definition and photographic screening tool for the facial phenotype of fetal alcohol syndrome. *The Journal of Pediatrics, 129*(1), 33–41.

Astley, S. J., & Clarren, S. K. (2000). Diagnosing the full spectrum of fetal alcohol-exposed individuals: Introducing the 4-Digit Diagnostic Code. *Alcohol and Alcoholism, 35*(4), 400–410.

Astorino, T. A., & Roberson, D. W. (2010). Efficacy of acute caffeine ingestion for short-term high-intensity exercise performance: A systematic review. *Journal of Strength and Conditioning Research, 24*(1), 257–265.

Athey, J. L. (1991). HIV infection and homeless adolescents. *Child Welfare, 70*(5), 517–528.

Attention, memory deficits still apparent in FAS adolescents. (1994). *Brown University Digest of Addiction Theory and Appplication, 13*(8), 6.

Austin, M.-P., Ross, C., Murray, R. E., et al. (1992). Cognitive function in major depression. *Journal of Affective Disorders, 25*, 21–30.

Ausubel, D. P. (1958). *Drug addiction: Physiological, psychological, and sociological aspects*. New York, NY: Random House.

Ausubel, D. P. (1968). *Educational psychology: A cognitive view*. New York, NY: Holt, Rinehart and Winston.

Azima, F. J., & Richmond, L. H. (Eds.). (1989). *Adolescent group psychotherapy*. Madison, CT: International Universities Press.

Azorin, J. M., Bowden, C. L., Garay, R. P., et al. (2010). Possible new ways in the pharmacological treatment of bipolar disorder and comorbid alcoholism. *Neuropsychiatric Disease and Treatment, 6*, 47–46.

**B**

Babor, T. F., Higgins-Biddle, J. C., Saunders, J. B., et al. (2001). *AUDIT: The Alcohol Use Disorders Identification Test: Guidelines for use in primary care* (2nd ed.). Geneva, Switzerland: World Health Organization.

Babor, T. F., McRee, B. G., Kassebaum, P. A., et al. (2007). Screening, Brief Intervention, and Referral to Treatment (SBIRT): Toward a public health approach to the management of substance abuse. *Substance Abuse, 28*(3), 7–30.

Bachs, L., & Morland, H. (2001). Acute cardiovascular fatalities following cannabis use. *Forensic Science International, 124*(2–3), 200–203.

Bada, H. S., Das, A., Bauer, C. R., et al. (2007). Impact of prenatal cocaine exposure on child behavior problems through school age. *Pediatrics, 119*, e348–e359.

Baer, J. S. (1991). Implications for early intervention from a biopsychosocial perspective on addiction. *Behaviour Change, 8*(2), 51–59.

Bailey, J. E., Campagna, E., & Dart, R. C. (2008). The underrecognized toll of prescription opioid abuse on young children. *Annals of Emergency Medicine, 20*(10), 1–6.

Baisch, M. J., Fox, R. A., & Goldberg, B. D. (1989). Breastfeeding attitudes and practices among adolescents. *The Journal of Adolescent Health Care, 10*(1), 41–45.

Baldridge, E. B., & Bessen, H. A. (1990). Phencyclidine. *Emergency Medicine Clinics of North America, 8*(3), 541–550.

Balfour, D. J., Wright, A. E., Benwell, M. E., et al. (2000). The putative role of extra-synaptic mesolimbic dopamine in the neurobiology of nicotine dependence. *Behavioural Brain Research, 113*(1–2) 73–83.

Ballon, J. S., & Feifel, D. (2006). A systematic review of modafinil: Potential clinical users and mechanisms of action. *The Journal of Clinical Psychiatry, 67*(4), 554–566.

Banakar, M. K., Kudlur, N. S., & George, S. (2009). Fetal alcohol spectrum disorder (FASD). *Indian Journal of Pediatrics, 76*(11), 1173–1175.

Bandstra, E. S., & Burkett, G. (1991). Maternal-fetal and neonatal effects of in utero cocaine exposure. *Seminars in Perinatology, 15*(4), 288–301.

Bandstra, E. S., Morrow, C. E., Mansoor, E., et al. (2010). Prenatal drug exposure: Infant and toddler outcomes. *Journal of Addictive Diseases, 29*(2), 245–258.

Bandura, A. (1977). *Social learning theory.* New York, NY: General Learning.

Barbaresi, W. J., Katusic, S. K., Colligan, R. C., et al. (2002). How common is attention-deficit/hyperactivity disorder? Incidence in a population-based birth cohort in Rochester, Minn. *Archives of Pediatric and Adolescent Medicine, 156*(3), 217–224.

Barbaresi, W. J., Katusic, S. K., Colligan, R. C., et al. (2007). Long-term school outcomes for children with attention-deficit/hyperactivity disorder: A population-based perspective. *Journal of Developmental and Behavioral Pediatrics, 28*(4), 265–273.

Barbee, J. G. (1993). Memory, benzodiazepines, and anxiety: Integration of theoretical and clinical perspectives. *The Journal of Clinical Psychiatry, 54*(supplement), 86–97.

Barclay, L. (2009, April 29). Inhalant use disorders among delinquent adolescents: A survey of inhalant use disorders among delinquent youth: Prevalence, clinical features, and latent structure of *DSM-IV* Diagnostic criteria. *Medscape Psychiatry & Mental Health Viewpoints*, pp. 1–2. Retrieved from http://www.medscape.com/viewarticle/701993_print

Barkley, R. A., Fischer, M., Smallish, L., et al. (2003). Does the treatment of attention-deficit/hyperactivity disorder with stimulants contribute to drug use/abuse? A 13-year prospective study. *Pediatrics, 111*, 97–109.

Barlow, A., Mullany, B. C., Neault, N., et al. (2010). Examining correlates of methamphetamine and other drug use in pregnant American Indian adolescents. *American Indian and Alaska Native Mental Health Research, 17*(1), 1–24.

Barnes, G. E. (1979). Solvent abuse: A review. *The International Journal of the Addictions, 14*, 1–26.

Barnes, G. M. (1984). Evaluation of alcohol education: A reassessment using socialization theory. *Journal of Drug Education, 14*(2), 133–150.

Barnes, G. M., & Welte, J. W. (1986). Patterns and predictors of alcohol use among 7–12th grade students in New York State. *Journal of Studies on Alcohol, 47*(1), 53–62.

Barnwell, S. S., Earleywine, M., & Wilcox, R. (2006). Cannabis, motivation, and life satisfaction in an internet sample. *Substance Abuse Treatment, Prevention, and Policy, 1*, 2

Barr, H. L., Langs, R. J., Holt, R. R., et al. (1972). *LSD: Personality and experience.* New York, NY: Wiley.

Barry, K. L., & Fleming, M. F. (1993). The Alcohol Use Disorders Identification Test (AUDIT) and the SMAST-13: Predictive validity in a rural primary care sample. *Alcohol and Alcoholism, 28*(1), 33–42.

Barth, K. S., & Malcolm, R. J. (2010). Disulfiram: An old therapeutic with new applications. *CNS Neurological Disorders—Drug Targets, 9*(1), 5–12.

Bartu, A., Dusci, L. J., & Ilett, K. F. (2010). Transfer of methylamphetamine and amphetamine into breast milk following recreational use of methylamphetamine. *British Journal of Clinical Pharmacology, 67*(4), 455–459.

Basavarajaiah, S., Shah, A., & Sharma, S. (2007). Sudden cardiac death in young athletes. *Heart, 93*, 287–289.

Baskerville, J. R., Tichenor, G. A., & Rosen, P. B. (2001). Toluene induced hypokalemia: Case report and literature review. *Emergency Medicine Journal, 18*(6), 514–516.

Bass, M. (1970). Sudden sniffing death. *JAMA, The Journal of the American Medical Association, 212*(12), 2077–2079.

Bastiaens, L., Francis, G., & Lewis, K. (2000). The RAFFT as a screening tool for adolescent substance use disorders. *The American Journal on Addictions, 9*(1), 10–16.

Bastiaens, L., Riccardi, K., & Sakhrani, D. (2002). The RAFFT as a screening tool for adult substance use disorders. *The American Journal of Drug and Alcohol Abuse, 28*(4), 681–691.

Basu, D., Jhirwal, O. P., Singh, J., et al. (2004). Inhalant abuse by adolescents: A new challenge for Indian physicians. *Indian Journal of Medical Sciences, 58*(6), 245–249.

Bateman, D. A., & Chiriboga, C. A. (2000). Dose-response effect of cocaine on newborn head circumference. *Pediatrics, 106*(3), e33.

Bateman, D. A., & Heagarty, M. C. (1989). Passive free-base cocaine ("crack") inhalation by infants and toddlers. *American Journal of Diseases of Children, 143*(1), 25–27.

Bates, M. E., & Pandina, R. J. (1991). Personality stability and adolescent substance use behaviors. *Alcoholism, Clinical and Experimental Research, 15*, 471–477.

Bateson, A. N., (2002). Basic pharmacologic mechanisms involved in benzodiazepine tolerance and withdrawal. *Current Pharmaceutical Design, 8*(1), 5–21.

Battjes, R. J. (1984). Symbolic interaction theory: A perspective on drug abuse and its treatment. *The International Journal of the Addictions, 18*, 675–688.

Bauer, C. R., Langer, J. C., Shankaran, S., et al. (2005). Acute neonatal effects of cocaine exposure during pregnancy. *Archives of Pediatrics and Adolescent Medicine, 159*(9), 824–834.

Bauman, J. L., & DiDomenico, R. J. (2002). Cocaine-induced channelopathies: Emerging evidence on the multiple mechanisms of sudden death. *Journal of Cardiovascular Pharmacology and Therapeutics, 7*(3), 195–202.

Bauman, J. L., Grawe, J. J., Winecoff, A. P., et al. (1994). Cocaine-related sudden cardiac death: A hypothesis correlating basic science and clinical observations. *Journal of Clinical Pharmacology, 34*(9), 902–911.

Baumrind, D., & Moselle, K. A. (1985). A developmental perspective on adolescent drug abuse. *Advances in Alcohol and Substance Abuse, 4*, 41–67.

Bayard, M., McIntyre, J., Hill, K. R., et al. (2004). Alcohol withdrawal syndrome. *American Family Physician, 69*(6), 1443–1450.

Bayatpour, M., Wells, R. D., & Holford, S. (1992). Physical and sexual abuse as predictors of substance use and suicide among pregnant teenagers. *The Journal of Adolescent Health, 13*, 128–132.

Baydala, L. T., Sewlal, B., Rasmussen, C., et al. (2009). A culturally adapted drug and alcohol abuse prevention program for aboriginal children and youth. *Progress in Community Health Partnerships, 3*(1), 37–46.

Bays, J. (1992). The care of alcohol- and drug-affected infants. *Pediatric Annals, 21*(8), 485–495.

Beattie, R. (2005, July 30). Putting the crack baby myth to bed: Researchers fail to link cocaine use and neonatal outcomes. National Review of Medicine, 2(13). Retrieved from http://www.nationalreviewofmedicine.com/issue/2005/07 30/2 feature04 13.html

Beauvais, F., Jumper-Thurman, P., & Burnside, M. (2008). The changing patterns of drug use among American Indian students over the past 30 years. *American Indian and Alaska Native Mental Health Research, 15*(2), 15–24.

Beauvais, F., Wayman, J. C., Jumper-Thurman, P., et al. (2002). Inhalant abuse among American Indian, Mexican American, and non-Latino white adolescents. *The American Journal of Drug and Alcohol Abuse, 28*(1), 171–187.

Beck, A. T. (1967). *Depression: Clinical, experimental and theoretical aspects.* New York, NY: Harper & Row.

Beck, J. E. (1998). 100 years of "just say no" versus "just say know": Reevaluating drug education goals for the coming century. *Evaluation Review, 22*(1), 15–45.

Becker, H. K., Agopian, M. W., & Yeh, S. (1992). Impact evaluation of Drug Abuse Resistance Education (DARE). *Journal of Drug Education, 22*(4), 283–291.

Becker, H. S. (1967). History, culture and subjective experience: An exploration of the social bases of drug-induced experiences. *Journal of Health and Social Behavior, 8*, 163–176.

Becker, K., El-Faddagh, M., Schmidt, M., et al. (2008). Interaction of dopamine transporter genotype with prenatal smoke exposure on ADHD symptoms. *The Journal of Pediatrics, 152*, 263–269.

Becker, M., Warr-Leeper, G. A., & Leeper, H. A. (1990). Fetal alcohol syndrome: A description of oral motor, articulatory, short-term memory, grammatical, and semantic abilities. *Journal of Communicative Disorders, 23*, 97–124.

Becker, W. C., Sullivan, L. E., Tetrault, J. M., et al. (2008). Non-medical use, abuse and dependence on prescription opioids among U.S. adults: Psychiatric, medical and substance use correlates. *Drug and Alcohol Dependence, 94*(1–3), 38–47.

Becker-Mattes, A., Mattes, J. A., Abikoff, H., et al. (1985). State-dependent learning in hyperactive children receiving methylphenidate. *The American Journal of Psychiatry, 142*(4), 455–459.

Behavior therapy plus medication may help teens with depression and substance use disorders (2007, November 7). *ScienceDaily*, pp. 1–2. Retrieved from http://www.sciencedaily.com/releases/2007/11/071105 164448.htm

Beirness, D. J., & Beasley, E. E. (2010). A roadside survey of alcohol and drug use among drivers in British Columbia. *Traffic Injury Prevention, 11*(3), 215–221.

Beirness, D. J., & Porath-Waller, A. J. (2009). *Clearing the smoke on cannabis: Cannabis use and driving* (pp. 1–7). Ottawa, ON: Canadian Centre on Substance Abuse.

Bejerot, N. (1972). *Addiction: An artificially induced drive.* Springfield, IL: Thomas.

Belafsky, H. A., Breslow, S., Hirsch, L. M., et al. (1969). Meprobamate during pregnancy. *Obstetrics & Gynecology, 34*(3), 378–386.

Belfer, M. L. (1993). Substance abuse with psychiatric illness in children and adolescents: Definitions and terminology. *American Journal of Orthopsychiatry, 63*(1), 70–79.

Bell, R. M., Ellickson, P. L., & Harrison, E. R. (1993). Do drug prevention effects persist into high school? How Project ALERT did with ninth graders. *Preventive Medicine, 22*(4), 463–483.

Bennett, D. S., Bendersky, M., & Lewis, M. (2008). Children's cognitive ability from 4 to 9 years old as a function of prenatal cocaine exposure, environmental risk, and maternal verbal intelligence. *Developmental Psychology, 44*(4), 919–928.

Bennett, M. E., Walters, S. T., Miller, J. H., et al. (2000). Relationship of early inhalant use to substance use in college students. *Journal of Substance Abuse, 12*(3), 227–240.

Benowitz, N. L. (1999). Nicotine addiction. *Primary Care, 26*(3), 611–631.

Benowitz, N. L., Herrera, B., & Jacob, P. (2004). Mentholated cigarette smoking inhibits nicotine metabolism. *The Journal of Pharmacology and Experimental Therapeutics, 310*(3), 1208–1215.

Benzodiazepine use in British Columbia: Is it consistent with recommendations? (2005). *Canadian Family Physician, 51*(4), 514–515.

Berger, S., Utech, L., & Hazinski, M. F. (2004). Sudden death in children and adolescents. *Pediatric Clinics of North America, 51*, 1653–1677.

Bergman, U., Rosa, F. W., Baum, C., et al. (1992). Effects of exposure to benzodiazepine during fetal life. *Lancet, 340*, 694–696.

Berman, A. H., Bergman, H., Palmstierna, T., et al. (2003). *DUDIT: The Drug Use Disorders Identification Test Manual* (Version 1.0, translated by Anne H. Berman). Stockholm, Sweden: Karolinska Institutet.

Berman, A. H., Bergman, H., Palmstierna, T., et al. (2005). Evaluation of the Drug Use Disorders Identification Test (DUDIT) in criminal justice and detoxification settings and in a Swedish population sample. *European Addiction Research, 11*(1), 22–31.

Berman, A. H., Palmstierna, T., Kallmen, H., et al. (2002). *The DUDIT-E study.* Stockholm, Sweden: Karolinska Institutet. Retrieved from http://www.emedda.europa.eu/html.cfm/index61869EN.html

Berman, A. H., Palmstierna, T., Kallmen, H., et al. (2007). The self-report Drug Use Disorders Identification Test-Extended (DUDIT-E): Reliability, validity, and motivational index. *Journal of Substance Abuse Treatment, 32*, 357–369.

Berman, A. L., & Schwartz, R. H. (1990). Suicide attempts among adolescent drug users. *American Journal of Diseases of Children, 144*, 310–314.

Berman, M. E., & Coccaro, E. F. (1998). Neurobiologic correlates of violence: Relevance to criminal responsibility. *Behavioral Sciences and the Law, 16*(3), 303–318.

Berman, S., O'Neill, J., Fears, S., et al. (2008). Abuse of amphetamines and structural abnormalities in the brain. *Annals of the New York Academy of Sciences, 1141*, 195–220.

Bernard, B. (1988, January). Peer programs: The lodestone to prevention. *Prevention Forum,* 6–12.

Bernstein, G. A., Carroll, M. E., Crosby, R. D., et al. (1994). Caffeine effects on learning, performance, and anxiety in normal school-age children. *The Journal of the American Academy of Child and Adolescent Psychiatry, 33*(3), 407–415.

Bernstein, G. A., Carroll, M. E., Dean, N. W., et al. (1998). Caffeine withdrawal in normal school-age children. *The Journal of the American Academy of Child and Adolescent Psychiatry, 37*(8), 858–865.

Bernstein, G. A., Carroll, M. E., Thuras, P. D., et al. (2002). Caffeine dependence in teenagers. *Drug and Alcohol Dependence, 66*(1), 1–6.

Bernstein, K. T., Bucciarelli, A., Piper, T. M., et al. (2007). Cocaine- and opiate-related fatal overdose in New York City, 1990–2000. *BioMed Central Public Health, 7*, 31.

Berry, J., van Gorp, W. G., Herzberg, D. S., et al. (1993). Neuropsychological deficits in abstinent cocaine abusers: Preliminary findings after two weeks of abstinence. *Drug and Alcohol Dependence, 32*(3), 231–237.

Bertrand, J. (2009). Interventions for children with fetal alcohol spectrum disoders (FASDs): Overview of findings for five innovative research projects. *Research in Developmental Disabilities, 30*(5), 986–1006.

Bertucci, V., & Krafchik, B. R. (1994). Diagnosis: Fetal alcohol syndrome. *Pediatric Dermatology, 11*, 180.

Bianchi, V., Ivaldi, A., Raspagni, A., et al. (2010). Use of carbohydrate-deficient transferrin (CDT) and a combination of GGT and CDT (GGT-CDT) to assess heavy alcohol consumption in traffic medicine. *Alcohol and Alcoholism, 45*(3), 247–251.

Biederman, J., Newcorn, J., & Sprich, S. (1991). Comorbidity of attention deficit hyperactivity disorder with conduct, depressive, anxiety, and other disorders. *The American Journal of Psychiatry, 148*, 564–577.

Biederman, J., Wilen, T., Mick., E., et al. (1995). Psychoactive substance use disorders in adults with attention deficit hyperactivity disorder (ADHD): Effects of ADHD and psychiatric comorbidity. *The American Journal of Psychiatry, 152*(11), 1652–1658.

Biederman, J., Wilens, T. E., Mick, E., et al. (1998). Does attention-deficit hyperactivity disorder impact the developmental course of drug and alcohol abuse and dependence? *Biological Psychiatry, 44*(4), 269–273.

Bigelow, G. E., & Silverman, K. (1999). Theoretical and empirical foundations of contingency management treatments for drug abuse. In G. E. Bigelow, K. Silverman, & S. T. Higgins (Eds.), *Motivating behavior change among illicit-drug abusers: Research on contingency management interventions* (pp. 15–31). Washington, DC: American Psychological Association.

Biglan, A., Severson, H., Ary, D., et al. (1987). Do smoking prevention programs really work? Attrition and the internal and external validity of an evaluation of a refusal skills training program. *Journal of Behavioral Medicine, 10*(2), 159–171.

Birmaher, B., Kennah, A., Brent, D., et al. (2002). Is bipolar disorder specifically associated with panic disorder in youths? *The Journal of Clinical Psychiatry, 63*, 414–419.

Black, R. F. (1996). Transmission of HIV-1 in the breast-feeding process. *Journal of the American Dietetic Association, 96*(3), 267–274.

Blackburn, C. M., Bonas, S., Spencer, N. J., et al. (2004). Parental smoking and passive smoking in infants: Fathers matter too. *Health Education Research, 20*(2), 185–194.

Blaho, K., Merigian, K., Winbery, S., et al. (1997). Clinical pharmacology of lysergic acid diethylamide: Case reports and review of the treatment of intoxication. *American Journal of Therapeutics, 4*(5–6), 211–221.

Blake, S. M., Ledsky, R., Lehman, T., et al. (2001). Preventing sexual risk behaviors among gay, lesbian, and bisexual adolescents: The benefits of gay-sensitive HIV instruction in schools. *American Journal of Public Health, 91*(6), 940–946.

Blakely, R. D., & Bauman, A. L. (2000). Biogenic amine transporters: Regulation in flux. *Current Opinion in Neurobiology, 10*(3), 328–336.

Blanc, M., & Daeppen, J. B. (2005). Does disulfiram still have a role in alcoholism treatment? [in French]. *Revue Medicale Suisse, 1*(26), 1728–1730, 1732–1733.

Blatman, S. (1974). Narcotic poisoning of children (1) through accidental ingestion of methadone and (2) in utero. *Pediatrics, 54*(3), 329–332.

Blick, S. K., & Keating, G. M. (2007). Lisdexamfetamine. *Paediatric Drugs, 9*(2), 129–135.

Block, R. I., & Ghoneim, M. M. (1993). Effects of chronic marijuana use on human cognition. *Psychopharmacology (Berlin), 110*(1–2), 219–228.

Blum, R. W. (1987). Adolescent substance abuse: Diagnostic and treatment issues. *Pediatric Clinics of North America, 34*, 523–537.

Bohn, D. K. (2003). Lifetime physical and sexual abuse, substance abuse, depression, and suicide attempts among Native American women. *Issues in Mental Health Nursing, 24*, 233–252.

Bohn, M. J., Babor, T. F., & Kranzler, H. R. (1995). The Alcohol Use Disorders Identification Test (AUDIT): Validation of a screening instrument for use in medical settings. *Journal of Studies on Alcohol, 56*(4), 423–432.

Bolton, J., Cox, B., Clara, I., et al. (2006). Use of alcohol and drugs to self-medicate anxiety disorders in a nationally representative sample. *The Journal of Nervous and Mental Disease, 194*(11), 818–825.

Bolton, J. M., Robinson, J., & Sareen, J. (2009). Self-medication of mood disorders with alcohol and drugs in the National Epidemiologic Survey on Alcohol and Related Conditions. *Journal of Affective Disorders, 115*(3), 367–375.

Bombard, J. M., Rock, V. J., Pederson, L. L., et al. (2008). Monitoring polytobacco use among adolescents: Do cigarette smokers use other forms of tobacco? *Nicotine & Tobacco Research, 10*(11), 1581–1589.

Booth, W., & O'Connor, A-M. (2010, November 28). Mexican cartels emerge as top source for U.S. meth. *Washington Post*. Retrieved from http://www.washingtonpost.com/wp-dyn/content/article/2010/11/23/AR2010112303703_...

Boothby, L. A., & Doering, P. L. (2005). Acamprosate for the treatment of alcohol dependence. *Clinical Therapeutics, 27*(6), 695–714.

Borgen, L. A., Okerholm, R. A., Lai, A., et al. (2004). The pharmacokinetics of sodium oxybate oral solution following acute and chronic administration to narcoleptic patients. *Journal of Clinical Pharmacology, 44*, 253–257.

Borges, A., & Cherpitel, C. J. (2001). Selection of screening items for alcohol abuse and alcohol dependence among Mexicans and Mexican Americans in the emergency department. *Journal of Studies on Alcohol, 62*, 277–285.

Borges, G., Cherpitel, C., Orozco, R., et al. (2006). Multicentre study of acute alcohol use and non-fatal injuries: Data from the WHO collaborative study on alcohol and injuries. *Bulletin of the World Health Organization, 84*(6), 453–460.

Borkman, T. (2008). The twelve-step recovery model of AA: A voluntary mutual help association. *Recent Developments in Alcoholism, 18*, 9–35.

Boros, C. A., Parsons, D. W., Zoanetti, G. D., et al. (1996). Cannabis cookies: A cause of coma. *Journal of Paediatrics and Child Health, 32*(2), 194–195.

Botello-Harbaum, M., Schroeder, J. R., Collins, C. C., et al. (2010). Nicotine replacement therapy use among adolescent smokers seeking cessation treatment. *Ethnicity & Disease, 20*(2), 180–184.

Botvin, G. J. (1986). Substance abuse prevention research: Recent developments and future directions. *The Journal of School Health, 56*, 370.

Botvin, G. J., Baker, E., Botvin, E. M., et al. (1984). Prevention of alcohol misuse through the development of personal and social competence: A pilot study. *Journal of Studies on Alcohol, 45*(6), 550–552.

Botvin, G. J., Baker, E., Dusenbury, L., et al. (1990). Preventing adolescent drug abuse through a multimodal cognitive-behavioral approach: Results of a 3-year study. *Journal of Consulting and Clinical Psychology, 58*(4), 437–446.

Botvin, G. J., Baker, E., Renick, N. L., et al. (1984). A cognitive-behavioral approach to substance abuse prevention. *Addictive Behaviors, 9*(2), 137–147.

Botvin, G. J., & Botvin, E. M. (1992). Adolescent tobacco, alcohol, and drug abuse: Prevention strategies, empirical findings, and assessment issues. *Developmental and Behavioral Pediatrics, 13*, 290–301.

Botvin, G. J., & Griffin, K. W. (2007). School-based programmes to prevent alcohol, tobacco and other drug use. *International Review of Psychiatry, 19*(6), 607–615.

Botvin, G. J., Renick, N. L., & Baker, E. (1983). The effects of scheduling format and booster sessions on a broad-spectrum psychosocial approach to smoking prevention. *Journal of Behavioral Medicine, 6*(4), 359–379.

Bowes, W. A., Jr. (1980). The effect of medications on the lactating mother and her infant. *Clinical Obstetrics and Gynecology, 23*(4), 1073–1080.

Bowman, K. G. (2007). When breastfeeding may be a threat to adolescent mothers. *Issues in Mental Health Nursing, 28*(1), 89–99.

Boyd, C. J., McCabe, S. E., & d'Arcy, H. (2003). Ecstasy use among college undergraduates: Gender, race and sexual identity. *Journal of Substance Abuse Treatment, 24*(3), 209–215.

Boyle, M. H., & Offord, D. R. (1991). Psychiatric disorder and substance use in adolescence. *Canadian Journal of Psychiatry, 36*, 699–705.

Bracken, M.B., Triche, E.W., Belanger, K., et al. (2003). Association of maternal caffeine consumption with decrements in fetal growth. *American Journal of Epidemiology, 157*(5), 456–466.

Brackney, M., Baumbach, J., Ewers, C., et al. (2009). Agranulocytosis associated with cocaine use—Four states, March 2008–November 2009. *MMWR, Morbidity and Mortality Weekly Report, 58*(49), 1381–1385. Retrieved from http://www.cdc.gov/mmwr/preview/mmwrhtml/mm5849a3.htm

Bradford Baldridge, E., & Bessen, H. A. (1990). Phencyclidine. *Emergency Medicine Clinics of North America, 8*(3), 541–550.

Bradley, K. A. (1992). Screening and diagnosis of alcoholism in the primary care setting. *Western Journal of Medicine, 156*(2), 166–171.

Bradley, K. A., Boyd-Wickizer, J., Powell, S. H., et al. (1998). Alcohol screening questionnaires in women: A critical review. *JAMA, The Journal of the American Medical Association, 280*(2), 166–171.

Bradley, K. A., Bush, K. R., McDonell, M. B, et al. (1998). Screening for problem drinking: Comparison of CAGE and AUDIT. *Journal of General Internal Medicine, 13*(6), 379–389.

Bradley, K. A., DeBenedetti, A. F., Volk, R. J., et al. (2007). AUDIT-C as a brief screen for alcohol misuse in primary care. *Alcoholism, Clinical and Experimental Research, 31*(7), 1208–1217.

Bradley, K. A., McDonell, M. B., Bush, K., et al. (1998). The AUDIT alcohol consumption questions: Reliability, validity, and responsiveness to change in older male primary care patients. *Alcoholism, Clinical and Experimental Research, 22*(8), 1842–1849.

Brady, K. T., Killeen, T. K., Brewerton, T., et al. (2000). Comorbidity of psychiatric disorders and posttraumatic stress disorder. *The Journal of Clinical Psychiatry, 61*(Suppl. 7), 22–32.

Bramstedt, K. A. (2007). Caffeine use by children: The quest for enhancement. *Substance Use & Misuse, 42*(8), 1237–1251.

Bratter, T.E. (1989). Group psychotherapy with alcohol and drug addicted adolescents: Special clinical concerns and challenges. In F. J. Azima & L. H. Richmond (Eds.), *Adolescent group psychoterhapy* (pp. 163–189). Madison, CT: International Universities Press.

Brault, M., Dussault, C., Bouchard, J., et al. (2004). The contribution of alcohol and other drugs among fatally injured drivers in Quebec: Final results. In *Proceedings of the 17th International Conference on Alcohol, Drugs and Traffic Safety* (CD ROM).

Brecher, E. M. (1972). *Licit and illicit drugs.* Mt. Vernon, NY: Consumers Union.

Breitling, L. P., Twardella, D., Hoffmann, M. M., et al. (2010). Prospective association of dopamine-related polymorphisms with smoking cessation in general care. *Pharmacogenomics, 11*(4), 527–536.

Breivogel, C. S., & Childers, S. R. (1998). The functional neuroanatomy of brain cannabinoid receptors. *Neurobiology of Disease, 5*(6 Part B), 417–431.

Brenneman, G., Rhoades, E., & Chilton, L. (2006). Forty years in partnership: The American Academy of Pediatrics and the Indian Health Service. *Pediatrics, 118*(4), e1257–e1263.

Brent, R. L. (2004). Environmental causes of human congenital malformations: The pediatrician's role in dealing with these complex clinical problems caused by a multiplicity of environmental and genetic factors. *Pediatrics, 113*(Suppl. 4), 957–968.

Breslau, N. (2002). Epidemiologic studies of trauma, posttraumatic stress disorder, and other psychiatric disorders. *Canadian Journal of Psychiatry, 47*(10), 923–929.

Breslau, N., Davis, G. C., & Schultz, L. R. (2003). Posttraumatic stress disorder and the incidence of nicotine, alcohol, and other drug disorders in persons who have experienced trauma. *Archives of General Psychiatry, 60*(3), 289–294.

Breslau, N., Kilbey, M. M., & Andreski, P. (1993). Vulnerability to psychopathology in nicotine-dependent smokers: An epidemiologic study of young adults. *The American Journal of Psychiatry, 150*, 941–946.

Breslau, N., & Klein, D. F. (1999). Smoking and panic attacks: An epidemiologic investigation. *Archives of General Psychiatry, 56*(12), 1141–1147.

Brice, C. F., & Smith, A. P. (2002). Effects of caffeine on mood performance: A study of realistic consumption. *Psychopharmacology (Berlin), 164*(2), 188–192.

Brill, H., & Hirose, T. (1969). The rise and fall of a methamphetamine epidemic: Japan 1945–1955. *Seminars in Psychiatry, 1*(2), 179–194.

Brody, A. L., Mandelkern, M. A., London, E. D., et al. (2002). Brain metabolic changes during cigarette craving. *Archives of General Psychiatry, 59*(12), 1162–1172.

Brook, J. S., Brook, D. W., Scovell Gordon, A. S., et al. (1990). The psychosocial etiology of adolescent drug use: A family interactional approach. *Genetic, Social & General Psychology Monographs, 116*(2), 111–267.

Brook, J. S., Lukoff, I. F., & Whiteman, M. (1977a). Correlates of adolescent marijuana use as related to age, sex and ethnicity. *Yale Journal of Biology and Medicine, 50*, 383–390.

Brook, J. S., Lukoff, I. F., & Whiteman, M. (1977b). Peer, family, and personality domains as related to adolescents' drug behavior. *Psychological Reports, 41*, 1095–1102.

Brook, J. S., Lukoff, I. F., & Whiteman, M. (1978). Family socialization and adolescent personality and their association with adolescent use of marijuana. *The Journal of Genetic Psychology, 133*, 261–271.

Brook, J. S., Lukoff, I. F., & Whiteman, M. (1980). Initiation into adolescent marijuana use. *The Journal of Genetic Psychology, 137*, 133–142.

Brook, J. S., Nomura, C., & Cohen, P. (1989a). A network of influences on adolescent drug involvement: Neighborhood, school, peer, and family. *Genetic, Social, & General Psychology Monographs, 115*(1), 123–145.

Brook, J. S., Nomura, C., & Cohen, P. (1989b). Prenatal, perinatal, and early childhood risk factors and drug involvement in adolescence. *Genetic, Social, & General Psychology Monographs, 115*(2), 221–241.

Brook, J. S., Pahl, K., & Ning, Y. (2006). Peer and parental influences on longitudinal trajectories of smoking among African Americans and Puerto Ricans. *Nicotine & Tobacco Research, 8*(5), 639–651.

Brook, J. S., Whiteman, M., Cohen, P., et al. (1995). Longitudinally predicting late adolescent and young adult drug use: Childhood and adolescent precursors. *Journal of the American Academy of Child & Adolescent Psychiatry*, 334, 1230–1238.

Brook, J. S., Whiteman, M., & Gordon, A. S. (1985). Father absence, perceived family characteristic and stage of drug use in adolescence. *British Journal of Developmental Psychology, 2*, 87–94.

Brook, J. S., Whiteman, M., Gordon, A. S., et al. (1986). Dynamics of childhood and adolescent personality traits and adolescent drug use. *Developmental Psychology, 22*, 403–414.

Brook, J. S., Zhang, C., Finch, S. H., et al. (2010). Adolescent pathways to adult smoking: Ethnic identity, peer substance use, and antisocial behavior. *The American Journal on Addictions, 19*(2), 178–186.

Brouette, T., & Anton, R. (2001). Clinical review of inhalants. *The American Journal on Addictions, 10*(1), 79–94.

Broughton, B. (2010, April 22). Preteen marijuana use linked to comorbid substance abuse and psychological disorders. *Medscape Medical News*. Retrieved from http://www.medscape.com/viewarticle/720652_print

Brouhard, B. H. (1994). Cocaine ingestion and abnormalities of the urinary tract. *Clinical Pediatrics, 33*, 157–158.

Brown, J., Brown, M., & Bowes, J. B. (1983). Effects of lorazepam on rate of forgetting, on retrieval from semantic memory and on manual dexterity. *Neuropsychologia, 21*, 501–512.

Brown, J., McColm, R., Aindow, J., et al. (2009). Nursing assessment and management of alcohol-related brain damage in young people. *Nursing Times, 105*(41), 20–23.

Brown, J., McKone, E., & Ward, J. (2010). Deficits of long-term memory in ecstasy users are related to cognitive complexity of the task. *Psychopharmacology (Berlin), 209*(1), 51–67.

Brown, L. J., & DiFranza, J. R. (1992). Pharmacy promotion of tobacco use among children in Massachusetts. *American Pharmacy, NS32*(5), 45–48.

Brown, R. L., & Rounds, L. A. (1995). Conjoint screening questionnaires for alcohol and other drug abuse: Criterion validity in a primary care practice. *Wisconsin Medical Journal, 94*, 135–140.

Brown, R. T., Coles, C. D., Smith, I. E., et al. (1991). Effects of prenatal alcohol exposure at school age. II. Attention and behavior. *Neurotoxicology and Teratology, 13*, 369–376.

Brown, S. (1988). *Treating adult children of alcoholics: A developmental perspective*. New York, NY: Wiley.

Brown, S., & Lewis, V. (1995). The alcoholic family: A developmental model of recovery. In S. Brown & I. D. Yalom (Eds.), *Treating alcoholism* (pp. 279–315). San Francisco, CA: Jossey-Bass.

Brown, S. A., Gleghorn, A., Schuckit, M. A., et al. (1996). Conduct disorder among adolescent alcohol and drug abusers. *Journal of Studies on Alcohol, 57*(3), 314–324.

Browne, M. L. (2006). Maternal exposure to caffeine and risk of congenital anomalies: A systematic review. *Epidemiology, 17*(3), 324–331.

Browne, M. L., Bell, E. M., Druschel, C. M., et al. (2007). Maternal caffeine consumption and risk of cardiovascular malformations. *Birth Defects Research. Part A, Clinical and Molecular Teratology, 79*(7), 533–543.

Browne, M. L., Hoyt, A. T., Feldkamp, M. L., et al. (2011). Maternal caffeine intake and risk of selected birth defects in the National Birth Defects Prevention Study. *Birth Defects Research, Part A, Clinical and Molecular Teratology, 91*(2), 93–101.

Bruehl, A. M., Lende, D. H., Schwartz, M., et al. (2006). Craving and control: Methamphetamine users' narratives. *Journal of Psychoactive Drugs* (Suppl. 3), 385–392.

Brunette, M. F., Asher, D., Whitley, R., et al. (2008). Implementation of integrated dual disorders treatment: A qualitative analysis of facilitators and barriers. *Psychiatric Services, 59*(9), 989–995.

Bry, B. H., Conboy, C., & Bisgay, K. (1986). Decreasing adolescent drug use and school failure: Long-term effects of targeted family problem-solving training. *Child and Family Behavior Therapy, 8*, 43–59.

Bryant Ludden, A., & Wolfson, A. R. (2010). Understanding adolescent caffeine use: Connecting use patterns with expectancies, reasons, and sleep. *Health Education & Behavior, 37*(3), 330–342.

Bubar, M. J., McMahon, L. R., De Deurwaerdere, P., et al. (2003). Selective serotonin reuptake inhibitors enhance cocaine-induced locomotor activity and dopamine release in the nucleus accumbens. *Neuropharmacology, 44*(3), 342–353.

Buchsbaum, D. (1994). Effectiveness of treatment in general medicine patients with drinking problems. *Alcohol Health & Research World, 18*, 140–145.

Buchsbaum, D., Buchanan, R., Centor, R, et al. (1991). Screening for alcohol abuse using CAGE scores and likelihood ratios. *Annals of Internal Medicine, 15*, 774–777.

Buckley, T. C., Mozley, S. L., Holohan, D. R., et al. (2005). A psychometric evaluation of the Fagerström Test for Nicotine Dependence in PTSD smokers. *Addictive Behaviors, 30*(5), 1029–1033.

Budney, A. J., & Hughes, J. R. (2006). The cannabis withdrawal syndrome. *Current Opinion in Psychiatry, 19*(3), 233–238.

Bühler, A., Schröder, E., Silbereisen, R. K. (2008). The role of life skills promotion in substance abuse prevention: A mediation analysis. *Health Education Research, 23*(4), 621–632.

Buisson, B., & Bertrand, D. (2002). Nicotine addiction: The possible role of functional upregulation. *Trends in Pharmacological Sciences, 23*(3), 130–136.

Buka, S. L., Shenassa, E. D., & Niaura, R. (2003). Elevated risk of tobacco dependence among offspring of mothers who smoked during pregnancy: A 30-year prospective study. *The American Journal of Psychiatry, 160*(11), 1978–1984.

Bukowski, J. A. (2001). Review of the epidemiological evidence relating toluene to reproductive outcomes. *Regulatory Toxicology and Pharmacology, 33*(2), 147–156.

Bukstein, O. (2008). Substance abuse in patients with attention-deficit/hyperactivity disorder. *Medscape Journal of Medicine, 10*(1), 24.

Bukstein, O., Glancy, L. J., & Kaminer, Y. (1992). Patterns of affective comorbidity in a clinical population of dually diagnosed adolescent substance abusers. *The Journal of the American Academy of Child and Adolescent Psychiatry, 31*, 1041–1045.

Bukstein, O., & Van Hasselt, V. B. (1993). Alcohol and drug abuse. In A. S. Bellack & M. Hersen (Eds.), *Handbook of behavior therapy in the psychiatric setting* (pp. 453–475). New York, NY: Plenum.

Bulik, C. M., Prescott, C. A., & Kendler, K. S. (2001). Features of childhood sexual abuse and the development of psychiatric and substance use disorders. *The British Journal of Psychiatry, 179*, 444–449.

Bullen, C., McRobbie, H., Thornley, S., et al. (2010). Effect of an electronic nicotine delivery device (e cigarette) on desire to smoke and withdrawal, user preferences and nicotine delivery: Randomized cross-over trial. *Tobacco Control, 19*(2), 98–103.

Burd, L. & Hofer, R. (2008). Biomarkers for detection of prenatal alcohol exposure: A critical review of fatty acid ethyl esters in meconium. *Birth Defects Research, Part A: Clinical and Molecular Teratology, 82*(7), 487–493.

Burge, M., Hunsaker, J. C., & Davis, G. J. (2009). Death of a toddler due to ingestion of sulfuric acid at a clandestine home methamphetamine laboratory. *Forensic Science and Medical Pathology, 5*(4), 298–301.

Burke, J. D., Burke, K. C., & Rae, D. S. (1994). Increased rates of drug abuse and dependence after onset of mood or anxiety disorders in adolescence. *Hospital & Community Psychiatry, 45*, 451–455.

Burke, J. D., Loeber R., & Lahey, B. B. (2001). Which aspects of ADHD are associated with tobacco use in early adolescence? *Journal of Child Psychology and Psychiatry and Allied Disciplines, 42*, 493–502.

Burke, L. M. (2008). Caffeine and sports performance. *Applied Physiology, Nutrition, and Metabolism, 33*(6), 1319–1334.

Burling, A. S., & Burling, T. A. (2003). Comparison of self-report measures of nicotine dependence among male drug/alcohol-dependent cigarette smokers. *Nicotine & Tobacco Research, 5*(5), 625–633.

Burns, E., Gray, R., & Smith, L. A. (2010). Brief screening questionnaires to identify problem drinking during pregnancy: A systematic review. *Addiction, 105*(4), 601–614.

Burns, R. S., & Lerner, S. E. (1978). Phencyclidine deaths. *Journal of the American College of Emergency Physicians, 7*(4), 135–141.

Burns, R. S., Lerner, S. E., Corrado, R., et al. (1975). Phencyclidine—States of acute intoxication and fatalities. *Western Journal of Medicine, 123*(5), 345–349.

Burns, T. M., Shneker, B. F., & Juel, V. C. (2001). Gasoline sniffing multifocal neuropathy. *Pediatric Neurology, 25*(5), 419–421.

Bush, K. R., Kivlahan, D. R., Davis, T. M., et al. (2003). The TWEAK is weak for alcohol screening among female Veterans Affairs outpatients. *Alcoholism, Clinical and Experimental Research, 27*(12), 1971–1978.

Bush, K. R., Kivlahan, D. R., McDonell, M. B. et al. (1998). The AUDIT alcohol consumption questions (AUDIT-C): An effective brief screening test for problem drinking. Ambulatory Care Quality Improvement Project (ACQUIP). Alcohol Use Disorders Identification Test. *Archives of Internal Medicine, 158*(16), 1789–1795.

Bush, P. G., Mayhew, T. M., Abramovich, D. R., et al. (2000a). A quantitative study on the effects of maternal smoking on placental morphology and cadmium concentration. *Placenta 2000, 21*, 247–256.

Bush, P. G., Mayhew, T. M., Abramovich, D. R., et al. (2000b). Maternal cigarette smoking and oxygen diffusion across the placenta. *Placenta 2000, 21*, 824–833.

Button, T. M., Hewitt, J. K., Rhee, S. H., et al. (2006). Examination of the causes of covariation between conduct disorder symptoms and vulnerability to drug dependence. *Twin Research and Human Genetics: The Official Journal of the International Society for Twin Studies, 9*(1), 38–45.

Buxton, J. A., & Dove, N. A. (2008). The burden and management of crystal meth use. *CMAJ, Canadian Medical Association Journal, 178*(12), 1537–1539.

# C

Caballo, J. J., Bird, H., Giner, L., et al. (2007). Pathological personality traits and suicidal ideation among older adolescents and young adults with alcohol misuse: A pilot case-control study in a primary care setting. *International Journal of Adolescent Medicine and Health, 19*(1), 79–89.

Cahill, H. W. (2007). Challenges in adopting evidence-based school drug education programmes. *Drug and Alcohol Review, 26*(6), 673–679.

Calamaro, C. J., Mason, T. B., & Ratcliffe, S. J. (2009). Adolescents living the 24/7 lifestyle: Effects of caffeine and technology on sleep duration and daytime functioning. *Pediatrics, 123*(6), e1005–e1010.

Calhoun, B. C., & Watson, P. T. (1991). The cost of materal cocaine abuse: I. Perinatal cost. *Obstetrics and Gynecology, 78*(5 part 1), 731–734.

Cambridge, J., & Thomas, B. A. (2009). Short forms of the AUDIT in a Web-based study of young drinkers. *Drug and Alcohol Review, 28*(1), 18–24.

Campbell, D. T., & Fiske, D. W. (1959). Convergent and discriminant validation by the multitrait-multimethod matrix. *Psychology Bulletin, 56*, 81–105.

Cannabis almost doubles risk of fatal crashes. (2005, December 5). *ScienceDaily*, pp. 1. Retrieved from http://www.sciencedaily.com/releases/2005/12/051205 115540.htm

Cannabis could increase risks of psychotic illness by 40 percent. (2007, August 1). *ScienceDaily*, pp. 1–2. Retrieved from http://www.sciencedaily.com/releases/ 2007/07/070731125526.htm

Cannabis damages young brains more than originally thought, study finds. (2009, December 20). *ScienceDaily*, p. 1. Retrieved from http://www .sciencedaily.com/releases/2009/12/091217115834.htm

Caplan, M., Weissberg, R. P., Grober, J. S., et al. (1992). Social competence promotion with inner-city and suburban young adolescents: Effects on social adjustment and alcohol use. *Journal of Consulting and Clinical Psychology, 60*(1), 56–63.

Caprara, D. L., Klein, J., & Koren, G. (2006). Diagnosis of fetal alcohol spectrum disorder (FASD): Fatty acid ethyl esters and neonatal hair analysis. *Annali dell'Istituto Superiore di Sanità, 42*(1), 39–45.

Caputo, F., & Bernardi, M. (2010). Medications acting on the GABA system in the treatment of alcoholic patients. *Current Pharmaceutical Design, 16*(19), 2118–2125.

Caraballo, R. S., Novak, S. P., & Asman, K. (2009). Linking quantity and frequency profiles of cigarette smoking to the presence of nicotine dependence symptoms among adolescent smokers: Findings from the 2004 National Youth Tobacco Survey. *Nicotine & Tobacco Research, 11*(1), 49–57.

Car crashes: Fatigue, slippery roads, and inexperience more critical than thought. (2007, November 2). *ScienceDaily*, pp. 1–2. Retrieved from http://www.sciencedaily.com/ releases/2007/10/071031090812.htm

Carey, K. B., Bradizza, C. M., Stasiewicz, P. R., et al. (1999). The case for enhanced addictions training in graduate programs. *Behavior Therapist, 22*, 27–31.

Carey, K. B., Carey, M. P., Chandra, P. S., et al. (2003). Psychometric evaluation of the Alcohol Use Disorders Identification Test and Short Drug Abuse Screening Test with psychiatric patients in India. *The Journal of Clinical Psychiatry, 64*(7), 767–774.

Carmo, J. T., & Pueyo, A. A. (2002). A adaptação ao português do Fagerström test for nicotine dependence (FTND) para avaliar a dependência e tolerância à nicotina em fumantes brasileiros [in Portuguese]. *Revista Brasileira de Medicina, 59*(1–2), 73–80.

Carpenter, M. J., & Gray, K. M. (2010). A pilot randomized study of smokeless tobacco use among smokers not interested in quitting: Changes in smoking behavior and readiness to quit. *Nicotine & Tobacco Research, 12*(2), 136–143.

Carrington Reid, M., Fiellin, D. A., & O'Connor, P. G. (1999). Hazardous and harmful alcohol consumption in primary care. *Archives of Internal Medicine, 159*, 1681–1689.

Carroll, L. (1866). *Alice's adventures in wonderland.* London, UK: Macmillan.

Carroll, M. E. (1990). PCP and hallucinogens. In C. K. Erickson, M. A. Javors, W. W. Morgan, et al. (Eds.), *Addiction potential of abused drugs and drug classes* (pp. 167–190). New York, NY: Wiley.

Carter, L. P., Griffiths, R. R., & Mintzer, M. Z. (2009). Cognitive, psychomotor, and subjective effects of sodium oxybate and triazolam in health volunteers. *Psychopharmacology (Berlin), 206*(1), 141–154.

Carter, L. P., Koek, W., & France, C. P. (2009). Behavioral analysis of GHB: Receptor mechanisms. *Pharmacology & Therapeutics, 121*(1), 100–114.

Carter, L. P., Pardi, D., Gorsline, J., et al. (2009). Illicit gamma-hydroxybutyrate (GHB) and pharmaceutical sodium oxybate (Xyrem): Differences in characteristics and misuse. *Drug and Alcohol Dependence, 104*(1–2), 1–10.

Carter, L. P., Richards, B. D., Mintzer, M. Z., et al. (2006). Relative abuse liability of GHB in humans: A comparison of psychomotor, subjective, and cognitive effects of supratherapeutic doses of triazolam, pentobarbital, and GHB. *Neuropsychopharmacology, 31*(11), 2537–2551.

Carter, S., Paterson, J., Gao, W., et al. (2008). Maternal smoking during pregnancy and behaviour problems in a birth cohort of 2-year-old Pacific children in New Zealand. *Early Human Development, 84*, 59–66.

Caruso, K., & Bensel, R. (1993). Fetal alcohol syndrome and fetal alcohol effects: The University of Minnesota experience. *Minnesota Medicine, 76*, 25–29.

Cassels, C. (2010a, February 10). APA releases proposed draft of the DSM-5. *Medscape Medical News*, pp. 1–4. Retrieved from http://www.medscape.com/viewarticle/ 716807?sssdmh=dml.588982&src=nldne&uac=14454 4HX

Cassels, C. (2010b, December 15). Daily marijuana use in teens highest since the 1970: Increase may reflect 'softening' of attitudes among young people that marijuana is not harmful. *Medscape Medical News*. Retrieved from http://www.medscape.com/viewarticle/734288_print

Cassidy, C. M., Schmitz, N., & Malla, A. (2008). Validation of the alcohol use disorders identificaion test and the drug abuse screening test in first episode psychosis. *Canadian Journal of Psychiatry, 53*(1), 26–33.

Castellanos, F. X., & Rapoport, J. L. (2002). Effects of caffeine on development and behavior in infancy and childhood: A review of the published literature. *Food Chemistry and Toxicology, 40*(9), 1235–1242.

Castillo Mezzich, A., Tarter, R. E., Giancola, P. R., et al. (1997). Substance use and risky sexual behavior in female adolescents. *Drug and Alcohol Dependence, 44*(2–3), 157–166.

Caviness, C. M., Hatgis, C., Anderson, B. J., et al. (2009). Three brief alcohol screens for detecting hazardous drinking in incarcerated women. *Journal of Studies on Alcohol and Drugs, 70*(1), 50–54.

Center for Health & Justice at TASC. (2005, January 11). *Substance use disorders and primary care*, pp. 1–3. Retrieved from www.centerforhealthandjustice.org/externalpublications.html

Centers for Disease Control and Prevention. (1996). Accessibility to minors of cigarettes from vending machines—Broward County, Florida, 1996. *MMWR, Morbidity and Mortality Weekly Report, 45*(47), 1036–1038.

Centers for Disease Control and Prevention. (1997, February 14). Ingestion of cigarettes and cigarette butts by children. Rhode Island, January 1994–July 1996. *MMWR, Morbidity and Mortality Weekly Report, 46*(6), 125–128.

Centers for Disease Control and Prevention. (2002). Prevalence of selected maternal behaviors and experiences, pregnancy risk assessment monitoring system. *MMWR, Morbidity and Mortality Weekly Report, 51*(SS2), 1–26.

Centers for Disease Control and Prevention. (2004a, December 24). Alcohol consumption among women who are pregnant or who might become pregnant—United States, 2002. *MMWR, Morbidity and Mortality Weekly Report, 53*(50), 1178–1181.

Centers for Disease Control and Prevention (2004b, September 24). Alcohol-attributable deaths and years of potential life lost—United States, 2001. *MMWR, Morbidity and Mortality Weekly Report, 53*(37), 866–870.

Centers for Disease Control and Prevention. (2006). Improved national prevalence estimates for 18 selected major birth defects—United States, 1999–2001. *MMWR, Morbidity and Mortality Weekly Report, 54*, 1301–1305.

Centers for Disease Control and Prevention. (2008a). Disparities in secondhand smoke exposure—United States, 1988–1994 and 1999–2004. *MMWR, Morbidity and Mortality Weekly Report, 57*(27), 744–747.

Centers for Disease Control and Prevention. (2008b, August 6). Any tobacco use in 13 states—Behavioral risk factor surveillance system, 2008. *MMWR, Morbidity and Mortality Weekly Report, 59*(30), 946–950.

Centers for Disease Control and Prevention. (2009, December 22). Teen births. Retrieved from http://www.cdc.gov/nchs/fastats/teenbrth.htm

Centers for Disease Control and Prevention. (2010a). Ecstasy overdoses at a New Year's Eve rave—Los Angeles, California, 2010. *MMWR, Morbidity and Mortality Weekly Report, 59*(22), 677–681.

Centers for Disease Control and Prevention. (2010b, March 18). Poisoning in the United States: Fact sheet. Retrieved from http://www.cdc.gov/HomeandRecreationalSafety/Poisoning/poisoning-factsheet.htm

Centers for Disease Control and Prevention. (2010c, October 22). Drivers aged 16 or 17 years involved in fatal crashes—United States, 2004–2008. *MMWR, Morbidity and Mortality Weekly Report, 59*(41), 1329–1334.

Centers for Disease Control and Prevention. (2010d, October 8)). Vital signs: Binge drinking among high school students and adults—United States, 2009. *MMWR, Morbidity and Mortality Weekly Report, 59*(39), 1274–1279.

Cerny, E. H., & Cerny, T. (2009). Vaccines against nicotine. *Human Vaccines, 5*(4), 200–205.

Chae, S.-M., & Covington, C. Y. (2009). Biobehavioral outcomes in adolescents and young adults prenatally exposed to cocaine: Evidence from animal models. *Biological Research for Nursing, 10*(4), 318–330.

Chan, A. W., Pristach, E. A., & Welte, J. W. (1994). Detection by the CAGE of alcoholism or heavy drinking in primary care outpatients and the general population. *Journal of Substance Abuse, 6*(2), 123–135.

Chan, A. W., Pristach, E. A., Welte, J. W., et al. (1993). Use of the TWEAK test in screening for alcoholism/heavy drinking in three populations. *Alcoholism, Clinical and Experimental Research, 17*(6), 1188–1192.

Chan, D., Klein, J., Karaskov, T., et al. (2004). Fetal exposure to alcohol as evidenced by fatty acid ethyl esters in meconium in the absence of maternal drinking history in pregnancy. *Therapeutic Drug Monitoring, 26*(5), 474–481.

Chaney, N. E., Franke, J., Wadlington, W. B. (1988). Cocaine convulsions in a breast-feeding baby. *The Journal of Pediatrics, 112*, 134–135.

Chang, G., Goetz, M. A., Wilkins-Huang, L., et al. (1999). Identifying prenatal alcohol use: Screening instruments versus clinical predictors. *The American Journal on Addictions, 8*(2), 87–93.

Chang, G., McNamara, T., Orav, E. J., et al. (2006). Identifying risk drinking in expectant fathers. *Birth: Issues in Perinatal Care, 33*(2), 110–116.

Chang, G., Wilkins-Haug, L., Berman, S., et al. (1998). Alcohol use and pregnancy: Improving identification. *Obstetrics & Gynecology, 91*(6), 892–898.

Chang, L., Alicata, D., Ernst, T., et al. (2007). Structural and metabolic brain changes in the striatum associated with methamphetamine abuse. *Addiction, 102* (Suppl. 1), 16–32.

Chang, L., Smith, L. M., LoPresti, C., et al. (2004). Smaller subcortical volumes and cognitive deficits in children with prenatal methamphetamine exposure. *Psychiatry Research, 132*(2), 95–106.

Chang, Y. J., Lai, M. W., Kong, M. S., et al. (2005). Accidental ingestion of ecstasy in a toddler. *Journal of the Formosan Medical Association, 104*(12), 946–947.

Chan-Pensley, E. (1999). Alcohol-Use Disorders Identification Test: A comparison between paper and pencil and computerized versions. *Alcohol and Alcoholism, 34*(6), 882–885.

Chapman, C., Laird, J., & KewalRamani, A. (2010). *Trends in high school dropout and completion rates in the United States: 1972–2008. Compendium Report* (NCES 2011–012). Washington, DC: National Center for Education Statistics, Institute of Education Sciences, U.S. Department of Education.

Chasnoff, I. J. (1992). Cocaine, pregnancy, and the growing child. *Current Problems in Pediatrics, 22*(7), 302–321.

Chasnoff, I. J., Burns, W. J., Hatcher, R. P., et al. (1983). Phencyclidine: Effects on the fetus and neonate. *Developmental Pharmacology and Therapeutics, 6*(6), 404–408.

Chassin, L., McLaughlin Mann, L., & Sher, K. J. (1988). Self-awareness theory, family history of alcoholism, and adolescent alcohol involvement. *Journal of Abnormal Psychology, 97*(2), 206–217.

Chatlos, J. C. (1994). Dual diagnosis in adolescent populations. In N. S. Miller (Ed.), *Treating coexisting psychiatric and addictive disorders: A practical guide* (pp. 85–110). Center City, MN: Hazelden.

Chavez, G. F., Cordero, J. F., & Becerra, J. E. (1988). Leading major congenital malformations among minority groups in the United States, 1981, 1986. *MMWR, Morbidity and Mortality Weekly Report, 47*(Supplement 3), 17–24.

Chavez, G. F., Mulinare, J., & Cordero, J. F. (1989). Maternal cocaine use during pregnancy as a risk factor for congenital urogenital anomalies. *JAMA, The Journal of the American Medical Association, 262*(6), 795–798.

Chavkin, W. (2001). Cocaine and pregnancy—Time to look at the evidence. *JAMA, The Journal of the American Medical Association, 285*(12), 1626–1628.

Chawla, J., & Suleman, A. (2008). Neurologic effects of caffeine. *eMedicine Neurology*, pp. 1–11. Retrieved from http://emedicine.medscape.com/article/1182710-print

Chein, I., Gerard, D. L., Lee, R. S., et al. (1964). *The road to H: Narcotics, delinquency, and social policy*. New York, NY: Basic Books.

Chen, K., & Kandel, D. B. (1995). The natural history of drug use from adolescence to the mid-thirties in a general population sample. *American Journal of Public Health, 85*(1), 41–47.

Cherpitel, C. J. (1995a). Analysis of cut points for screening instruments for alcohol problems in the emergency room. *Journal of Studies on Alcohol, 56*(6), 695–700.

Cherpitel, C. J. (1995b). Screening for alcohol problems in the emergency room: A rapid alcohol problems screen. *Drug and Alcohol Dependence, 40*, 133–137.

Cherpitel, C. J. (1997a). Brief screening instruments for alcoholism. *Alcohol Health & Research World, 21*(4), 348–351.

Cherpitel, C. J. (1997b). Comparison of screening instruments for alcohol problems between black and white emergency room patients from two regions of the country. *Alcoholism, Clinical and Experimental Research, 21*(8), 1391–1397.

Cherpitel, C. J. (1998). Differences in performance of screening instruments for problem drinking among blacks, whites and Hispanics in an emergency room population. *Journal of Studies on Alcohol, 59*(4), 420–426.

Cherpitel, C. J. (1999). Screening for alcohol problems in the U.S. general population: A comparison of the CAGE and TWEAK by gender, ethnicity, and services utilization. *Journal of Studies on Alcohol, 60*, 705–711.

Cherpitel, C. J. (2000). A brief screening instrument for problem drinking in the emergency room: The RAPS4. Rapid Alcohol Problems Screen. *Journal of Studies on Alcohol, 61*(3), 447–449.

Cherpitel, C. J. (2002). Screening for alcohol problems in the U.S. general population: Comparison of the CAGE, The RAPS 4, and RAPS4-QF by gender, ethnicity, and service utilization. Rapid Alcohol Problems Screen. *Alcoholism, Clinical and Experimental Research, 26*(11), 1686–1691.

Cherpitel, C. J., & Bazargan, S. (2003). Screening for alcohol problems: Comparison of the AUDIT, RAPS4 and RAPS4-QF among African American and Hispanic patients in an inner city emergency department. *Drug and Alcohol Dependence, 71*(3), 275–280.

Cherpitel, C. J., & Borges, A. (2000). Performance of screening instruments for alcohol problems in the ER: A comparison of Mexican-Americans and Mexicans in Mexico. *The American Journal of Drug and Alcohol Abuse, 26*, 683–702.

Cherpitel, C. J., Ye, Y., Bond, J., et al. (2005). Cross-national performance of the RAPS4/RAPS4-QF for tolerance and heavy drinking: Data from 13 countries. *Journal of Studies on Alcoholism, 66*(3), 428–432.

Cherpitel, C. J., Ye, Y., Moskalewicz, J., et al. (2005). Screening for alcohol problems in two emergency service samples in Poland: Comparison of the RAPS4, CAGE, and AUDIT. *Drug and Alcohol Dependence, 80*(2), 201–207.

Chesley, S., Lumpkin, M., Schatzki, A., et al. (1991). Prenatal exposure to benzodiazepine – I. *Neuropharmacology, 30*(1), 53–58.

Chevaleyre, V., Takahashi, K. A., & Castillo, P. E. (2006). Endocannabinoid-mediated synaptic plasticity in the CNS. *Annual Review of Neuroscience, 29*, 37–76.

Chi, F. W., Kaskutas, L. A., Sterling, S., et al. (2009). Twelve-step affiliation and 3-year substance use outcomes among adolescents: Social support and religious service attendance as potential mediators. *Addiction, 104*(6), 927–939.

Chilcoat, H. D., & Breslau, N. (1998). Posttraumatic stress disorder and drug disorders: Testing causal pathways. *Archives of General Psychiatry, 55*(10), 913–917.

Chiodo, D., Wolfe, D. A., Crooks, C., et al. (2009). Impact of sexual harassment victimization by peers on subsequent adolescent victimization and adjustment: A longitudinal study. *The Journal of Adolescent Health, 45*(3), 246–252.

Chiodo, L. M., Sokol, R. J., Delaney-Black, V., et al. (2010, January 4). Validity of the T-ACE in pregnancy in predicting child outcome and risk drinking. *Alcohol,* p. 1. Retrieved from http://www.ncbi.nlm.nih.gov/pubmed/20053522

Chiriboga, C. A. (2003). Fetal alcohol and drug effects. *Neurologist, 9*(6), 267–279.

Choi, B. C. K., & Pak, A. W. P. (2005, January). A catalog of biases in questionnaires. *Preventing Chronic Disease: Public Health Research, Practice, and Policy, 2*(1), 1–13. Retrieved from http://www.cdc.gov/pcd/issues/2005/jan/04_0050.htm

Chriqui, J. F., Ribisl, K. M., Wallace, R. M., et al. (2008). A comprehensive review of state laws governing Internet and other delivery sales of cigarettes in the United States. *Nicotine & Tobacco Research, 10*(2), 253–265.

Christian, M. S., & Brent, R. L. (2001). Teratogen update: Evaluation of the reproductive and developmental risks of caffeine. *Teratology, 64*(1), 51–78.

Christie, G., Marsh, R., Sheridan, J., et al. (2007). The substances and choices scale (SACS)—The development and testing of a new alcohol and other drug screening and outcome measurement instrument for young people. *Addiction, 102*(9), 1390–1398.

Chudley, A. E., Conry, J., Cook, J. L., et al. (2005). Fetal alcohol spectrum disorder: Canadian guidelines for diagnosis. *CMAJ, Canadian Medical Association Journal, 172*(5 Suppl.), S1–S21.

Chung, T., Colby, S. M., Barnett, N. P., et al. (2000). Screening adolescents for problem drinking: Performance of brief screens against *DSM-IV* alcohol diagnoses. *Journal of Studies on Alcohol, 61*(4), 579–587.

Chung, T., & Maisto, S. A. (2006). Relapse to alcohol and other drug use in treated adolescents: Review and reconsideration of relapse as a change point in clinical course. *Clinical Psychology Review, 26*(2), 149–161.

Church, M. W. (1993). Does cocaine cause birth defects? *Neurotoxicology and Teratology, 15*, 289.

Chyka, P. A., Seger, D., Krenzelok, E. P., et al. (2005). Position paper: Single-dose activated charcoal. *Clinical Toxicology, 43*(2), 61–87.

Clark, D. B., Pollock, N., Bukstein, O. G., et al. (1997). Gender and comorbid psychopathology in adolescents with alcohol dependence. *Journal of the American Academy of Child & Adolescent Psychiatry, 36*(9), 1195–1203.

Clarren, S. K., & Smith, D. W. (1978). Medical progress: The fetal alcohol syndrome. *The New England Journal of Medicine, 298*, 1063–1067.

Clay, S. W. (1997). Comparison of AUDIT and CAGE questionnaires in screening for alcohol use disorders in elderly primary care outpatients. *The Journal of the American Osteopathic Association, 97*(10), 588–592.

Cleary, P. D., Miller, M., Bush, B. T., et al. (1988). Prevalence and recognition of alcohol abuse in a primary care population. *The American Journal of Medicine, 85*, 466–471.

Cloninger, C. R. (1987). Neurogenetic adaptive mechanisms in alchoholism. *Science, 236*, 410–416.

Cloward, R. A., & Ohlin, L. E. (1960). *Delinquency and opportunity.* New York, NY: Free Press.

Clure, C., Brady, K. T., Saladin, M. E., et al. (1999). Attention-deficit/hyperactivity disorder and substance use: Symptom pattern and drug choice. *The American Journal of Drug and Alcohol Abuse, 25*(3), 441–448.

Cocaine facts & figures. (2010, January 11). Office of National Drug Control Policy, pp. 1–9. Retrieved from http://www.whitehousedrugpolicy.gov/drugfact/cocaine/cocaine_ff.html

Cocaine use USA. (2010, January 6). *Alcohol-and-Drug-Guide.com,* pp. 1–2. Retrieved from http://www.alcohol-and-drug-guide.com/cocaine-use-usa.html

Cochran, S. D., Mays, V. M., Alegria, M., et al. (2007). Mental health and substance use disorders among Latino and Asian American lesbian, gay, and bisexual adults. *Journal of Consulting and Clinical Psychology, 75*(5), 785–794.

Coghlan, A. J., Gold, S. R., Dohrenwend, E. F., et al. (1973). A psychobehavioral residential drug abuse program: A new adventure in adolescent psychiatry. *The International Journal of the Addictions, 8*, 767–777.

Cohen, A. Y. (1974). *The journey beyond trips: Alternatives to drugs.* Edmonton, AB: Alberta Alcohol and Drug Abuse Commission.

Cohen, E., MacKenzie, R. G., & Yates, G. L. (1991). HEADSS, a psychosocial risk assessment instrument: Implications for designing effective intervention programs for runaway youth. *The Journal of Adolescent Health, 12*, 539–544.

Cohen, J. A., Mannarino, A. P., Zhitova, A. C., et al. (2003). Treating child abuse-related posttraumatic stress and comorbid substance abuse in adolescents. *Child Abuse & Neglect, 27*(12), 1345–1365.

Cohen, L. R., Tross, S., Pavlicova, M., et al. (2009). Substance use, childhood sexual abuse, and sexual risk behavior among women in methadone treatment. *The American Journal of Drug and Alcohol Abuse, 35*(5), 305–310.

Cohen, R. S. (2009). Fentanyl transdermal analgesia during pregnancy and lactation. *Journal of Human Lactation, 25*, 359–361.

Cohen, S. (1967). *The beyond within: The LSD story.* New York, NY: Atheneum.

Cohen, S. (1981). Adolescence and drug abuse: Biomedical consequences. In D. J. Lettieri & J. P. Ludford (Eds.), *Drug abuse and the American adolescent* (NIDA Research Monograph No. 38, pp. 104–112). Rockville, MD: U.S. Department of Health and Human Services, National Institute on Drug Abuse.

Cokkinides, V., Bandi, P., McMahon, C., et al. (2009). Tobacco control in the United States—Recent progress and opportunities. *CA: A Cancer Journal for Clinicians, 59*(6), 352–365.

Colby, S. M., Tiffany, S. T., Shiffman, S., et al. (2000). Are adolescent smokers dependent on nicotine? A review of the evidence. *Drug and Alcohol Dependence, 59*(Suppl. 1), S83–S95.

Coleman, P. K., Coyle, C. T., Shuping, M., et al. (2009). Induced abortion and anxiety, mood, and substance abuse disorders: Isolating the effects of abortion in the national comorbidity study. *Journal of Psychiatric Research, 43*(8), 770–776.

Coleman, S. B. (1978). Sib group therapy: A prevention program for siblings from drug-addicted families. *The International Journal of the Addictions, 13*(1), 115–127.

Coleman, S. B. (1979a). Cross-cultural approaches to addict families. *Journal of Drug Education, 9*(4), 293–299.

Coleman, S. B. (1979b). Siblings in session. In E. Kaufman & P. Kaufman (Eds.), *Family therapy of drug and alcohol abuse* (pp. 131–143). New York, NY: Gardner.

Coleman, S. B. (1980). Incomplete mourning and addict/family transactions: A theory for understanding heroin abuse. In D. J. Lettieri, M. Sayer, & H. Wallenstein Pearson (Eds.), *Theories on drug abuse: Selected contemporary perspectives* (NIDA Research Monograph No. 30, pp. 83–89). Rockville, MD: U.S. Department of Health and Human Services, National Institute on Drug Abuse.

Coleman, S. B. (1985). The surreptitious power of the sibling cohort: An echo of sin and death. In S. B. Coleman (Ed.), *Failures in family therapy* (pp. 27–72). New York, NY: Guilford Press.

Coleman, S. B., & Davis, D. I. (1978). Family therapy and drug abuse: A national survey. *Family Process, 17*, 21–29.

Coleman, S. B., & Stanton, M. D. (1978a). An index for measuring agency involvement in family therapy. *Family Process, 17*(4), 479–483.

Coleman, S. B., & Stanton, M. D. (1978b). The role of death in the addict family. *Journal of Marriage and Family Counseling, 4*(1), 79–90.

Coles, C. D. (1993). Saying "goodbye" to the "crack baby." *Neurotoxicology and Teratology, 15*, 290–292.

Coles, C. D., Brown, R. T., Smith, I. E., et al. (1991). Effects of prenatal alcohol exposure at school age. I. Physical and cognitive development. *Neurotoxicology and Teratology, 13*, 357–367.

Collier, S. A., Browne, M. L., Rasmussen, S. A., et al. (2009). Maternal caffeine intake during pregnancy and orofacial clefts. *Birth Defects Research. Part A, Clinical and Molecular Teratology, 85*(10), 842–849.

Collins, A. C. (1990). An analysis of the addiction liability of nicotine. In C. K. Erikson, M. A. Javors, W. W. Morgan, et al. (Eds.), *Addiction potential of abused drugs and drug classes* (pp. 83–101). New York, NY: Wiley.

Collins, R. L., Ellickson, P. L., McCaffrey, D., et al. (2007). Early adolescent exposure to alcohol advertising and its relationship to underage drinking. *The Journal of Adolescent Health, 40*(6), 527–534.

Collins, T. R. (2010, February 8). Deaths from methadone overdose disproportionate to number of prescriptions. *Medscape Medical News.* Retrieved from http://www.medscape.com/viewarticle/716603_print

Colombel, F. (2007). Memory bias and depression: A critical commentary [in French]. *Encephale, 33*(pt. 1), 242–248.

Comings, D. E. (1990). *Tourette syndrome and human behavior.* Duarte, CA: Hope Press.

Committee on Substance Abuse. (2010). Alcohol use by youth and adolescents: A pediatric concern. *Pediatrics, 125*, 1078–1087.

Cone-Wesson, B. (2005). Prenatal alcohol and cocaine exposure: Influences on cognition, speech, language, and hearing. *Journal of Communication Disorders, 38*(4), 279–302.

Conigrave, K. M., Hall, W. D., & Saunders, J. B. (1995). The AUDIT questionnaire: Choosing a cut-off score. Alcohol Use Disorder Identification Test. *Addiction, 90*(10), 1349–1356.

Conigrave, K. M., Saunders, J. B., & Reznik, R. B. (1995). Predictive capacity of the AUDIT questionnaire for alcohol-related harm. *Addiction, 90*, 1479–1485.

Conley, T. B. (2001). Construct validity of the MAST and AUDIT with multiple offender drunk drivers. *Journal of Substance Abuse Treatment, 20*(4), 287–295.

Connolly, G. N., Richter, P., Aleguas, A., et al. (2010). Unintentional child poisonings through ingestion of conventional and novel tobacco products. *Pediatrics, 125*(5), 896–899.

Connor, J. P., Grier, M., Feeney, G. F., et al. (2007). The validity of the Brief Michigan Alcohol Screening Test (bMast) as a problem drinking severity measure. *Journal of Studies on Alcohol and Drugs, 68*(5), 771–779.

Connors, G. J., & Volk, R. J. (2004, August). Self-report screening for alcohol problems among adults. Bethesda, MD: National Institute on Alcohol Abuse and Alcoholism.

Cook, R. L., Chung, T., Kelly, T. M., et al. (2005). Alcohol screening in young persons attending a sexually transmitted disease clinic: Comparison of AUDIT, CRAFT, and CAGE instruments. *Journal of General Internal Medicine, 20*(1), 1–6.

Coombs, R. H. (1981). Back on the streets: Therapeutic communities' impact upon drug users. *American Journal on Drug and Alcohol Abuse, 8*, 185–201.

Cooper, A. J., & Egleston, C. V. (1997). Accidental ingestion of ecstasy by a toddler: Unusual cause for convulsion in a febrile child. *Journal of Accident and Emergency Medicine, 14*(3), 183–184.

Cooper, J. R., Bloom, F. E., & Roth, R. H. (1978/1991), *The biochemical basis of neuropharmacology.* New York, NY: Oxford University Press.

Cooper, Z. D., & Haney, M. (2009). Actions of delta-9-tetrahydrocannabinol in cannabis: Relation to use, abuse, dependence. *International Review of Psychiatry, 21*(2), 104–112.

Corbett, J. A., Trimble, M. R., & Nichol, T. C. (1978/1985). Behavioral and cognitive impairments in children with epilepsy: The long-term effects of anticonvulsant drugs. *Journal of the American Academy of Child Psychiatry, 24*, 17–23.

Corelli, R. L., & Hudmon, K. S. (2006). Pharmacologic interventions for smoking cessation. *Critical Care Nursing Clinics of North America, 18*(1), 39–51, xii.

Corliss, H. L., Rosario, M., Wypij, D., et al. (2010). Sexual orientation and drug use in a longitudinal cohort study of U.S. adolescents. *Addictive Behaviors, 35*(5), 517–521.

Cornelius, J. R., Chung, T., Martin, C., et al. (2008). Cannabis withdrawal is common among treatment-seeking adolescents with cannabis dependence and major depression, and is associated with rapid relapse to dependence. *Addictive Behaviors, 33*(11), 1500–1505.

Cornelius, M. D., & Day, N. L. (2009). Developmental consequences of prenatal tobacco exposure. *Current Opinion in Neurology, 22*(2), 121–125.

Cornelius, M. D., Goldschmidt, L., De Genna, N., et al. (2007). Smoking during teenage pregnancies: Effects on behavioral problems in offspring. *Nicotine & Tobacco Research, 9* (7), 739–750.

Cornelius, M. D., Leech, S. L., Goldschmidt, L., et al. (2000). Prenatal tobacco exposure: Is it a risk factor for early tobacco experimentation? *Nicotine & Tobacco Research, 2*(1), 45–52.

Cornelius, M. D., Leech, S. L., Goldschmidt, L., et al. (2005). Is prenatal tobacco exposure a risk factor for early adolescent smoking? A follow-up study. *Neurotoxicology and Teratology, 27*(4), 667–676.

Cornelius, M. D., Richardson, G. A., Day, N. L., et al. (1994). A comparison of prenatal drinking in two recent samples of adolescents and adults. *Journal of Studies on Alcohol, 55*, 412–419.

Cornelius, M. D., Ryan, C. M., Day, N. L., et al. (2001). Prenatal tobacco effects on neuropsychological outcomes among preadolescents. *Journal of Developmental & Behavioral Pediatrics, 22*, 217–225.

Coryell, W. (1991). Genetics and dual diagnosis. In M. S. Gold & A. E. Slaby (Eds.), *Dual diagnosis in substance abuse* (pp. 29–41). New York, NY: Dekker.

Coulombe, J. A., Reid, G. J., Boyle, M. H., et al. (2010, April 25). Sleep problems, tiredness, and psychological symptoms among healthy adolescents. *Journal of Pediatric Psychology, 35*(7), 790–799.

Couper, F. J., Chopra, K., & Pierre-Louis, M. L. (2005). Fatal methadone intoxication in an infant. *Forensic Science International, 153*(1), 71–73.

Courtney, K. E., & Polich, J. (2009). Binge drinking in young adults: Data, definitions, and determinants. *Psychological Bulletin, 135*(1), 142–156.

Couturier, E. G., Laman, D. M., van Duijn, M. A., et al. (1997). Influence of caffeine and caffeine withdrawal on headache and cerebral blood flow velocities. *Cephalalgia, 17*(3), 188–190.

Covey, L. S., & Glassman, A. H. (1991). New approaches to smoking cessation. *Physician Assistant, 15*, 69–70, 73–74, 77.

Cowley, D. S. (1992). Alcohol abuse, substance abuse, and panic disorder. *The American Journal of Medicine, 92*(1A), 41S–48S.

Cox, B. J., Norton, G. R., Swinson, R. P., et al. (1990). Substance abuse and panic-related anxiety: A critical review. *Behavioral Research and Therapy, 28*(5), 385–393.

Cox, R. G., Zhang, L., Johnson, W. B., et al. (2007). Academic performance and substance use: Findings from a state survey of public high school students. *TheJournal of School Health 2007, 77*(3), 109–115.

Cox, S., Posner, S. F., Kourtis, A. P., et al. (2008). Hospitalizations with amphetamine abuse among pregnant women. *Obstetrics & Gynecology, 111*(2, pt. 1), 341–347.

Cox, W. M. (1987). Personality theory and research. In H. T. Blane & K. E. Leonard (Eds.), *Psychological theories of drinking and alcoholism* (pp. 55–89). New York, NY: Guilford Press.

Craig, R. D. (1985). State-dependent learning produced by diazepam ingestion in human subjects. *Dissertation Abstracts International, 46*(5-B), 1679.

Crain, D., & Bhat, A. (2010). Current treatment options in smoking cessation. *Hospital Practice (Minneapolis), 38*(1), 53–61.

Cremonte, M., & Cherpitel, C. J. (2008). Performance of screening instruments for alcohol use disorders in emergency department patients in Argentina. *Substance Use & Misuse, 43*(1), 125–138.

Cremonte, M., Ledesma, R. D., Cherpitel, C. J., et al. (2010). Psychometric properties of alcohol screening tests in the emergency department in Argentina, Mexico and the United States. *Addictive Behaviors, 35*(9), 818–825.

Crocetti, M. (2008). Inhalants. *Pediatrics in Review, 29*(1), 33–34.

Crome, I. B., Bloor, R., & Thom, B. (2006). Screening for illicit drug use in psychiatric hospitals: Whose job is it? *Advances in Psychiatric treatment, 12*, 375–383.

Cromie, W. J. (1998, March 12). Researchers see how cocaine affects the brain. *Harvard Gazette*, 1–4. Retrieved from http://www.news.harvard.edu/gazette/1998/03.12/ResearchersSeeH.html

Cronbach, L. J. (1951). Coefficient alpha and the internal structure of tests. *Psychometrika, 16*(3), 297–334.

Cronbach, L. J., & Meehl, P. E. (1955). Construct validity in psychological tests. *Psychological Bulletin, 52*, 281–302.

Crowley, J., & Courtney, R. (2003). The relationship between drug use, impaired driving and traffic accidents. *Illicit Drugs in Road Traffic Symposium.* Retrieved from http://www.pomidou.coe.int/.../English/route/route_en187.html

Crowley, S. J., Acebo, C., & Carskadon, M. A. (2007). Sleep, circadian rhythms, and delayed phase in adolescence. *Sleep Medicine, 8*(6), 602–612.

Cruickshank, C. C., & Dyer, K. R. (2009). A review of the clinical pharmacology of methamphetamine. *Addiction, 104*(7), 1085–1099.

Crum, R. M., Green, K. M., Storr, C. L., et al. (2008). Depressed mood in childhood and subsequent alcohol use through adolescence and young adulthood. *Archives of General Psychiatry, 65*(6), 702–712.

Cui, C. L., Wu, L. Z., & Luo, F. (2008). Acupuncture for the treatment of drug addiction. *Neurochemical Research, 33*(10), 2013–2022.

Cuijpers, P. (2002). Effective ingredients of school-based drug prevention programs. A systematic review. *Addictive Behaviors, 27*(6), 1009–1023.

Cummins, L. H., Chan, K. K., Burns, K. M., et al. (2003). Validity of the CRAFFT in American-Indian and Alaska Native adolescents: Screening for drug and alcohol risk. *Journal of Studies on Alcohol, 64*, 727–732.

Curran, H. V., Gardiner, J. M., Java, R. I., et al. (1993). Effects of lorazepam upon recollective experience in recognition memory. *Psychopharmacology (Berlin), 110*, 374–378.

Curtis, E. K. (2006). Meth mouth: A review of methamphetamine abuse and its oral manifestations. *General Dentistry, 54*(2), 125–129.

## D

Dackis, C. A., & Gold, M. S. (1990). Addictiveness of central stimulants. In C. K. Erikson, M. A. Javors, W. W. Morgan, et al. (Eds.), *Addiction potential of abused drugs and drug classes* (pp. 9–26). New York, NY: Wiley.

Dackis, C. A., & O'Brien, C. P. (2001). Cocaine dependence: A disease of the brain's reward centers. *Journal of Substance Abuse Treatment, 21*(3), 111–117.

Daeppen, J. B., Yersin, B., Landry, U., et al., (2000). Reliability and validity of the Alcohol Use Disorders Identification Test (AUDIT) imbedded within a general health risk screening questionnaire: Results of a survey in 332 primary care patients. *Alcoholism, Clinical and Experimental Research, 24*(5), 659–665.

Dahlstrom, A., Ebersjo, C., & Lundell, B. (2008). Nicotine in breast milk influences heart rate variability in the infant. *Acta Paediatrica, 97*(8), 1075–1079.

Daily pot smoking may hasten onset of psychosis. (2009, December 21). *ScienceDaily*, pp. 1–2. Retrieved from http://www.sciencedaily.com/releases/2009/12/091220 144936.htm

D'Alberto, A. (2004). Auricular acupuncture in the treatment of cocaine/crack abuse: A review of the efficacy, the use of the National Acupuncture Detoxification Association protocol, and the selection of sham points. *Journal of Alternative & Complementary Medicine, 10*(6), 985–1000.

Daley, D. C., Moss, H., & Campbell, F. (1987). *Dual disorders: Counseling clients with chemical dependency and mental illness.* Center City, MN: Hazelden.

Daley, D. C., & Salloum, I. M. (1995, October). Focusing on dual disorders. *Professional Counselor, 15–16*, 24–26.

Dani, J. A., & De Biasi, M. (2001). Cellular mechanisms of nicotine addiction. *Pharmacology, Biochemistry, and Behavior, 70*(4), 439–446.

Dani, J. A., Ji, D., & Zhou, F.M. (2001). Synaptic plasticity and nicotine addiction. *Neuron, 31*(3), 349–352.

Danion, J. M., Peretti, S., Grange, D., et al. (1992). Effects of chlorpromazine and lorazepam on explicit memory, repetition priming and cognitive skill learning in healthy volunteers. *Psychopharmacology (Berlin), 108*(3), 345–351.

Dannon, P. N., Lowengrub, K., Amiaz, R., et al. (2004). Comorbid cannabis use and panic disorder: Short term and long term follow-up study. *Human Psychopharmacology, 19*(2), 97–101.

D.A.R.E. America. (2007). *D.A.R.E. America Annual Report.* Inglewood, CA: Author.

Darwish, M., Martin, P. T., Cevallos, W. H., et al. (1999). Rapid disappearance of zaleplon from breast milk after oral administration to lactating women. *Journal of Clinical Pharmacology, 39*(7), 670–674.

Dascombe, B. J., Karunaratna, M., Cartoon, J., et al. (2010). Nutritional supplementation habits and perceptions of elite athletes within a state-based sporting institute. *Journal of Science in Medicine and Sport, 13*(2), 274–280.

David, S. P., Munafo, M. R., Murphy, M. F., et al. (2008). Genetic variation in the dopamine D4 receptor (DRD4) gene and smoking cessation: Follow-up of a randomized trial of transdermal nicotine patch. *The Pharmacogenomics Journal, 8*(2), 122–128.

Davis, J. K., & Green, J. M. (2009). Caffeine and anaerobic performance: Ergogenic value and mechanisms of action. *Sports Medicine, 39*(10), 813–832.

Dawe, S., Loxton, N. J., Hides, L., et al. (2002). *Review of diagnostic and screening for alcohol and other drug use and other psychiatric disorders.* Canberra, Australia: Commonwealth Department of Health and Aged Care.

Dawe, S., Seinen, A., & Kavanagh, D. (2000). An examination of the utility of the AUDIT in people with schizophrenia. *Journal of Studies on Alcohol, 61*(5), 744–750.

Dawson, D. A., Grant, B. F., & Stinson, F. S. (2005a). Effectiveness of the derived Alcohol Use Disorders Identification Test (AUDIT-C) in screening for alcohol use disorders and risk drinking in the US general population. *Alcoholism, Clinical and Experimental Research, 29*(5), 844–854.

Dawson, D. A., Grant, B. F., & Stinson, F. S. (2005b). The AUDIT-C: Screening for alcohol use disorders and risk drinking in the presence of other psychiatric disorders. *Comprehensive Psychiatry, 46*(6), 405–416.

DEA, Drug Information. (2006). *Heroin* (pp. 1–3). U.S. Drug Enforcement Administration. Retrieved from http://www.justice.gov/dea/concern/heroin.html

Deacon, B. J., & Valentiner, D. P. (2000). Substance use and non-clinical panic attacks in a young adult population. *Journal of Substance Abuse, 11*(1), 7–15.

Deas, D. (2006). Adolescent substance abuse and psychiatric comorbidities. *The Journal of Clinical Psychiatry, 67*(Suppl. 7), 18–23.

Deas, D., & Brown, E. S. (2006). Adolescent substance abuse and psychiatric comorbidities. *The Journal of Clinical Psychiatry, 67*(7), e02.

Degenhardt, L., Chiu, W. T., Conway, K., et al. (2009). Does the "gateway" matter? Associations between the order of drug use initiation and the development of drug dependence in the National Comorbidity Study Replication. *Psychological Medicine, 39*(1), 157–167.

Degenhardt, L., & Hall, W. (2006). Is cannabis use a contributory cause of psychosis? *Canadian Journal of Psychiatry, 51*(9), 556–565.

De Jung, W. (1987). A short-term evaluation of Project DARE Drug Abuse Resistance Education: Preliminary indications of effectiveness. *Journal of Drug Education, 17*, 279–294.

Dekker, N., Linszen, D. H., & De Haan, L. (2009). Reasons for cannabis use and effects of cannabis use as reported by patients with psychotic disorders. *Psychopathology, 42*(6), 350–360.

Delaney-Black, V., Chiodo, L. M., Hannigan, J. H., et al. (2010). Just say "I don't": Lack of concordance between teen report and biological measures of drug use. *Pediatrics, 126*(5), 887–893.

Delaney-Black, V., Chiodo, L. M., Hannigan, J. H., et al. (2011). Prenatal and postnatal cocaine exposure predict teen cocaine use. *Neurotoxicology and Teratology, 33*(1), 110–119.

De La Rosa, M. (2002). Acculturation and Latino adolescents' substance use: A research agenda for the future. *Substance Use & Misuse, 37*(4), 429–456.

De Leon, G. (1985). The therapeutic community: Status and evolution. *The International Journal of the Addictions, 20*, 823–844.

de Leon, J., Diaz, F. J., Becoña, E., et al. (2003). Exploring brief measures of nicotine dependence for epidemiological surveys. *Addictive Behaviors, 28*, 1481–1486.

Del Greco, L., Breitbach, L., Rumer, S., et al. (1986). Four-year results of a youth smoking prevention program using assertiveness training. *Adolescence, 21*, 631–640.

de Lima, M. S., de Oliveira Soares, B. G., Reisser, A. A., et al. (2002). Pharmacological treatment of cocaine dependence: A systematic review. *Addiction, 97*(8), 931–949.

de Lima, M., Farrell, M., Lima Reisser, A. A., et al. (2010, February 17). WITHDRAWN: Antidepressants for cocaine dependence. *Cochrane Database of Systematic Reviews, 2*, CD002950.

Dell, C. A. (2005, November 7–9). *What the data tells us about youth volatile solvent abuse (VSA) in Canada* (PowerPoint presentation). Inhalant Abuse among Children and Adolescents Conference: Consultation on Building an International Research Agenda, Rockville, MD.

Della Grotta, S., Lagasse, L. L., Arria, A. M., et al. (2010). Patterns of methamphetamine use during pregnancy: Results from the Infant Development, Environment, and Lifestyle (IDEAL) Study. *Maternal & Child Health Journal, 14*(4), 519–527.

Dembo, R. (1979). Substance abuse prevention programming and research: A partnership in need of improvement. *Journal of Drug Education, 9*, 189–208.

Dembo, R., Farrow, D., Schmeidler, J., et al. (1979). Testing a causal model of environmental influences on the early drug involvement of inner city junior high school youths. *The American Journal of Drug and Alcohol Abuse, 6*(3), 313–336.

Dembo, R., Pilaro, L., Burgos, W., et al. (1979). Self-concept and drug involvement among urban junior high school youths. *The International Journal of the Addictions, 14*, 1125–1144.

Dembo, R., Schmeidler, J., Borden, P., et al. (1996). Examination of the reliability of the Problem Oriented Screening Instrument for Teenagers (POSIT) among arrested youths entering a juvenile assessment center. *Substance Use & Misuse, 31*(7), 785–824.

Dembo, R., & Shern, D. (1982). Relative deviance and the process of drug involvement among inner-city youths. *The International Journal of the Addictions, 17*, 1373–1399.

De Meneses-Gaya, I. C., Zuardi, A. W., Loureiro, S. R., et al. (2009). Psychometric properties of the Fagerström Test for Nicotine Dependence. *Jornal Brasileiro de Pneumologia, 35*(1), 78–82.

Denny, E. B., & Hunt, R. R. (1992). Affective valence and memory in depression: Dissociation of recall and fragment completion. *Journal of Abnormal Psychology, 101*, 575–580.

Department of Health and Human Services. (2010, March 19). Regulations restricting the sale and distribution of cigarettes and smokeless tobacco to protect children and adolescents. *Federal Register, 75*(53), 13225–13232.

Derauf, C., LaGasse, L. L., Smith, L. M., et al. (2007). Demographic and psychosocial characteristics of mothers using methamphetmaine during pregnancy: Preliminary results of the infant development, environment, and lifestyle study (IDEAL). *The American Journal of Drug and Alcohol Abuse, 33*(2), 281–289.

Dervaux, A., Laqueille, X., Bourdel, M. C., et al. (2003). Cannabis and schizophrenia: Demographic and clinical correlates [in French]. *Encephale, 29*(1), 11–17.

Des Jarlais, D. C., Arasteh, K., Perlis, T., et al. (2007). The transition from injection to non-injection drug use: Long-term outcomes among heroin and cocaine users in New York City. *Addiction, 102*(5), 778–785.

de Sola Llopis, S., Miguelez-Pan, M., Pena-Casanova, J., et al. (2008). Cognitive performance in recreational ecstasy polydrug users: A two-year follow-up study. *Journal of Psychopharmacology, 22*(5), 498–510.

De Souza, A. (2010). The role of topiramate and other anticonvulsants in the treatment of alcohol dependence: A clinical review. *CNS Neurological Disorders—Drug Targets, 9*(1), 45–49.

De Witte, P., Littleton, J., Parot, P., et al. (2005). Neuroprotective and abstinence-promoting effects of acamprosate: Elucidating the mechanism of action. *CNS Drugs, 19*(6), 517–537.

Dews, P. B., O'Brien, C. P., & Bergman, J. (2002). Caffeine: Behavioral effects of withdrawal and related issues. *Food Chemistry and Toxicology, 40*(9), 1257–1261.

Dezateux, C., & Stocks, J. (1997). Lung development and early origins of childhood respiratory illness. *British Medical Bulletin, 53*, 40–57.

Dhalla, S., & Kopec, J. A. (2007). The CAGE questionnaire for alcohol misuse: A review of reliability and validity studies. *Clinical and Investigative Medicine, 30*(1), 33–41.

Diabetes mellitus and heart disease risk factors in Hawaiians. (1994). The Native Hawaiian Health Research Project, RCMI Program. *Hawaii Medical Journal, 53*(12), 340–343, 364.

Di Chiara, G. (2000). Role of dopamine in the behavioural actions of nicotine related to addiction. *European Journal of Pharmacology, 393*(1–3), 295–314.

Dickmann, P. J., Mooney, M. E., Allen, S. S., et al. (2009). Nicotine withdrawal and craving in adolescents: Effects of sex and hormonal contraceptive use. *Addictive Behavior, 34*(6–7), 620–623.

Didato, G., & Nobili, L. (2009). Treatment of narcolepsy. *Expert Review of Neurotherapeutics, 9*(6), 897–910.

Diehl, A., Ulmer, L., Mutschler, J., et al. (2010). Why is disulfiram superior to acamprosate in the routine clinical setting? A retrospective long-term study in 353 alcohol-dependent patients. *Alcohol and Alcholism, 45*(3), 271–277.

Di Forti, M., Morrison, P. D., Butt, A., et al. (2007). Cannabis use and psychiatric and cognitive disorders: The chicken or the egg? *Current Opinion in Psychiatry, 20*(3), 228–234.

DiFranza, J. R. (1992). Preventing teenage tobacco addiction. *Journal of Family Practice, 34*, 753–756.

DiFranza, J. R., & Brown, L. J. (1992). The Tobacco Institute's "It's the Law" campaign: Has it halted illegal sales of tobacco to children? *American Journal of Public Health, 82*(9), 1271–1273.

DiFranza, J. R., & Lew, R. A. (1995). Effect of maternal cigarette smoking on pregnancy complications and sudden infant death syndrome. *Journal of Family Practice, 40*, 385–394.

DiFranza, J. R., Savageau, J. A., & Aisguith, B. F. (1996). Youth access to tobacco: The effects of age, gender, vending machine locks, and "It's the Law" programs. *American Journal of Public Health, 86*(2), 221–224.

DiFranza, J. R., Savageau, J. A., & Fletcher, K. E. (2009). Enforcement of underage sales laws as a predictor of daily smoking among adolescents: A national study. *BioMed Central Public Health, 9*, 107.

DiFranza, J. R., Savageau, J. A., Fletcher, K., et al. (2007). Symptoms of tobacco dependence after brief intermittent use: The development and assessment of nicotine dependence in youth-2 study. *Archives of Pediatric and Adolescent Medicine, 161*, 704–710.

Di Marzo, V., Melck, D., Bisogno, T., et al. (1998). Endocannabinoids: Endogenous cannabinoid receptor ligands with neuromodulatory action. *Trends in Neurosciences, 21*(12), 521–528.

Dinse, H. (1997). Ecstasy (MMDA) intoxication. An overview [in German]. *Der Anaesthesist, 46*(8), 697–703.

Dinsmoor, M. J., Irons, S. J., & Christmas, J. T. (1994). Preterm rupture of the membranes associated with recent cocaine use. *American Journal of Obstetrics and Gynecology, 171*(2), 305–308.

do Amaral, R. A., & Malbergier, A. (2008). Effectiveness of the CAGE questionnaire, gamma-glutamyltransferase and mean corpuscular volume of red blood cells as markers for alcohol-related problems in the workplace. *Addictive Behaviors, 33*(6), 772–781.

Dobbins, M., DeCorby, K., Manske, S., et al. (2007). Effective practices for school-based tobacco use prevention. *Preventive Medicine, 46*(4), 289–297.

Domino, E. F. (2002). Conflicting evidence for the dopamine release theory of nicotine/tobacco dependence. *Japanese Journal of Psychopharmacology, 22*(5), 181–184.

D'Onofrio, G., McCausland, J. B., Tarabar, A. F., et al. (2006). Illy: Clinical and public health implications of a street drug. *Substance Abuse, 27*(4), 45–51.

Donohue, B. (2004). Coexisting child neglect and drug abuse in young mothers: Specific recommendations for treatment based on a review of the outcome literature. *Behavior Modification, 28*(2), 206–233.

Donohue, B., Azrin, N., Allen, D. N., et al. (2009). Family behavior therapy for substance abuse and other associated problems: A review of its intervention components and applicability. *Behavior Modification, 33*(5), 495–519.

Donovan, J. E. (2007). Really underage drinkers: The epidemiology of children's alcohol use in the United States. *Prevention Science, 8*(3), 192–205.

Donovan, J. E. (2009). Estimated blood alcohol concentrations for child and adolescent drinking and their implications for screening instruments. *Pediatrics, 123*(6), e975–e981.

Donovan, J. E., & Jessor, R. (1984). *The structure of problem behavior in adolescence and young adulthood* (Research Report No. 10, Young Adult Follow-Up Study). Boulder, CO: University of Colorado, Institute of Behavioral Studies.

Dopfner, M., Breuer, D., Wille, N., et al. (2008). How often do children meet *ICD-10/DSM-IV* criteria of attention deficit-/hyperactivity disorder and hyperkinetic disorder? Parent-based prevalence rates in a national sample—Results of the BELLA study. *European Child & Adolescent Psychiatry, 17*(Suppl. 1), 59–70.

Dopheide, J. A., & Pliszka, S. R. (2009). Attention-deficit-hyperactivity disorder: An update. *Pharmacotherapy, 29*(6), 656–679.

Dorsch, K. D., & Bell, A. (2005). Dietary supplement use in adolescents. *Current Opinion in Pediatrics, 17*(5), 653–657.

Doubeni, C. A., Li, W., Fouayzi, H., et al. (2008). Perceived accessibility as a predictor of youth smoking. *Annals of Family Medicine, 6*(4), 323–330.

Doubeni, C. A., Li, W., Fouayzi, H., et al. (2009). Perceived accessibility of cigarettes among youth: A prospective cohort study. *American Journal of Preventive Medicine, 36*(3), 239–242.

Doubeni, C. A., Reed, G., & DiFranza, J. R. (2010). Early course of nicotine dependence in adolescent smokers. *Pediatrics, 125*(6), 1127–1133.

Dow-Edwards, D. (1993). The puzzle of cocaine's effects following maternal use during pregnancy: Still unsolved. *Neurotoxicology and Teratology, 15*, 295–296.

Drabble, L., Midanik, L.T., & Trocki, K. (2005). Reports of alcohol consumption and alcohol-related problems among homosexual, bisexual and heterosexual respondents: Results from the 2000 National Alcohol Survey. *Journal of Studies on Alcohol, 66*(1), 111–120.

Drake, R. E., Essock, S. M., Shaner, A., et al. (2001). Implementing dual diagnosis services for clients with severe mental illness. *Psychiatric Services, 52*(4), 469–476.

Driscoll, C. D., Streissguth, A. P., & Riley, E. P. (1990). Prenatal alcohol exposure: Comparability of effects in humans and animal models. *Neurotoxicology and Teratology, 12*(3), 231–237.

Drug trafficking in the United States (n.d.). Retrieved from http://www.usdoj.gov/dea/pubs/intel/01020/index.html

Dryden, C., Young, D., Hepburn, M., et al. (2009). Maternal methadone use in pregnancy: Factors associated with the development of neonatal abstinence syndrome and implications for healthcare resources. *British Journal of Obstetrics and Gynaecology, 116*(5), 665–671.

D'Souza, D. C. (2007). Cannabinoids and psychosis. *International Review of Neurobiology, 78*, 289–326.

D'Souza, D. C., Sewell, R. A., & Ranganathan, M. (2009). Cannabis and psychosis/schizophrenia: Human studies. *European Archives of Psychiatry and Clinical Neuroscience, 259*(7), 413–431.

Duffy, A., & Milin, R. (1996). Case study: Withdrawal syndrome in adolescent chronic cannabis users. *Journal of the American Academy of Child & Adolescent Psychiatry, 35*(12), 1618–1621.

Duffy, M. R., & Swart, M. (2006). Severe ecstasy poisoning in a toddler. *Anaesthesia, 61*(5), 498–501.

Duimstra, C., Johnson, D., Kutsch, C., et al. (1993). A fetal alcohol syndrome surveillance pilot project in American Indian communities in the Northern Plains. *Public Health Reports, 108*, 225–229.

Dunlap, E., Golub, A., & Johnson, B. D. (2003). Girls' sexual development in the inner city: From compelled childhood sexual contact to sex-for-things exchanges. *Journal of Child Sexual Abuse, 12*(2), 73–96.

Dunlap, E., Golub, A., Johnson, B. D., et al. (2009). Normalization of violence: Experiences of childhood abuse by inner-city crack users. *Journal of Ethnicity in Substance Abuse, 8*(1), 15–34.

Dunn, D. T., Newell, M. L., Ades, A. E., et al. (1992). Risk of human immunodeficiency virus type 1 transmission through breastfeeding. *Lancet, 340*(8819), 585–588.

DuPont, R. L. (1987). Prevention of adolescent chemical dependency. *Pediatric Clinics of North America, 34*, 495–505.

DuPont, R. L., & Saylor, K. E. (1992). Depressant substances in adolescent medicine. *Pediatrics in Review, 13*(10), 381–386.

Duran, B., Malcoe, L. H., Skipper, B., et al. (2004). Child maltreatment prevalence and mental disorders outcomes among American Indian women in primary care. *Child Abuse & Neglect, 28*, 131–145.

Dusenbury, L., & Botvin, G. J. (1992). Substance abuse prevention: Competence enhancement and the development of positive life options *Journal of Addictive Diseases, 11*, 29–45.

Dybek, I., Bischof, G., Grothues, J., et al. (2006). The reliability and validity of the Alcohol Use Disorders Identification Test (AUDIT) in a German general practice population sample. *Journal of Studies on Alcohol, 67*(3), 473–481.

Dybing, E., & Sanner, T. (1999). Passive smoking, sudden infant death syndrome (SIDS) and childhood infections. *Human & Experimental Toxicology, 18*(4), 202–205.

Dye, M. H., Ducharme, L. J., Johnson, J. A., et al. (2009). Modified therapeutic communities and adherence to traditional elements. *Journal of Psychoactive Drugs, 41*(3), 275–283.

Dyer, J. E., Roth, B., & Hyma, B. A. (2001). Gamma-hydroxybutyrate withdrawal syndrome. *Annals of Emergency Medicine, 37*(2), 147–153.

Dyer, O. (2007). Codeine linked to breastfeeding danger. *National Review of Medicine, 4*(11), 1–2. Retrieved from http://www.nationalreviewofmedicine.com/issue/2007/06_15/4_patients_practice04_11.html

# E

Earleywine, M., LaBrie, J. W., & Pedersen, E. R. (2008). A brief Rutgers Alcohol Problem Index with less potential for bias. *Addictive Behaviors, 33*(9), 1249–1253.

Early exposure to tobacco smoke causes asthma and allergy. (2008, July 24). *ScienceDaily*, pp. 1–2. Retrieved from http://www.sciencedaily.com/releases/2008/07/080723170835.htm

Eaton, D. K., Kann, L., Kinchen, S., et al. (2010). Youth risk behavior surveillance—United States, 2009. *Morbidity and Mortality Weekly Report, Surveillance Summaries, 2010, 59*(5), 1–142.

Eberhard, S., Nordström, G., Höglund, P., et al. (2009). Secondary prevention of hazardous alcohol consumption in psychiatric out-patients: A randomized controlled study. *Social Psychiatry and Psychiatric Epidemiology, 44*(12), 1013–1021.

Ebbert, J. O., Wyatt, K. D., Hays, J. T., et al. (2010). Varenicline for smoking cessation: Efficacy, safety, and treatment recommendations. *Patient Preference and Adherence, 4*, 355–362.

Ebbert, J. O., Wyatt, K. D., Zirakzadeh, A., et al. (2009). Clinical utility of varenicline for smokers with medical and psychiatric comorbidity. *International Journal of Chronic Obstructive Pulmonary Disease, 4*, 421–430.

Ebbert, J. O., Patten, C. A., & Schroeder, D. R. (2006). The Fagerström Test for Nicotine Dependence-Smokeless Tobacco (FTND-ST). *Addictive Behaviors, 31*(9), 1716–1721.

Edinger, J. D., & Means, M. K. (2005). Chapter 59, Overview of insomnia: Definitions, epidemiology, differential diagnosis, and assessment (pp. 702–713). In M. H. Kryger, T. Roth, & W. C. Dement (Eds.), *Principles and practice of sleep medicine* (4th ed.). Philadelphia, PA: Elsevier/Saunders.

Edwards, J. E., Rudy, A. C., Wermeling, D. P., et al. (2003). Hydromorphone transfer into breast milk after intranasal administration. *Pharmacotherapy, 23*, 153–158.

Edwards, K. E., & Wenstone, R. (2000). Successful resuscitation from recurrent ventricular fibrillation secondary to butane inhalation. *British Journal of Anaesthesia, 84*(6), 803–805.

Egeland, G. M., Perham-Hester, K. A., Gessner, B. D., et al. (1998). Fetal alcohol syndrome in Alaska, 1977–1992: An administrative prevalence derived from multiple data sources. *American Journal of Public Health, 88*(5), 781–786.

Eggert, L. L., Seyl, C. D., & Nicholas, L. J. (1990). Effects of a school-based prevention program for potential high school dropouts and drug abusers. *The International Journal of the Addictions, 25*, 773–801.

Eggleston, A. M., Calhoun, P. S., Svikis, D. S., et al. (2009). Suicidality, aggression, and other treatment considerations among pregnant, substance-dependent women with posttraumatic stress disorder. *Comprehensive Psychiatry, 50*(5), 415–423.

Eifinger, F., Roth, B., Kroner, L. et al. (2008). Severe ecstasy poisoning in an 8-month-old infant. *European Journal of Pediatrics, 167*(9), 1067–1070.

Eisen, M., Zellman, G. L., & Murray, D. M. (2003). Evaluating the Lions-Quest "Skills for Adolescence" drug education program. Second-year behavior outcomes. (2003). *Addictive Behaviors, 28*(5), 883–897.

Eisen, S. V., Youngman, D. J., Grob., M. C., et al. (1992). Alcohol, drugs, and psychiatric disorders: A current view of hospitalized adolescents. *Journal of Adolescent Research, 7*, 250–265.

Eiserman, J. M., Diamond, S., & Schensul, J. J. (2005). "Rollin' on E": A qualitative analysis of ecstasy use among inner city adolescents and young adults. *Journal of Ethnicity in Substance Abuse, 4*(2), 9–38.

El-Bassel, N., Schilling, R. F., Schinke, S., et al. (1997). Assessing the utility of the Drug Abuse Screening Test in the workplace. *Research on Social Work Practice, 7*, 99–114.

Eliason, M. J., & Williams, J. K. (1990). Fetal alcohol syndrome and the neonate. *The Journal of Perinatal & Neonatal Nursing, 3*(4), 64–72.

Ellickson, P. L., & Bell, R. M. (1990). Drug prevention in junior high: A multi-site longitudinal test. *Science, 247*, 1299–1305.

Elliott, D. S., & Ageton, R. A. (1976). *The relationship between drug use and crime among adolescents. Drug use and crime: Report of panel on drug use and criminal behavior.* Research Triangle Park, NC: Research Triangle Institute.

Elliott, D. S., Huizinga, D., & Ageton, S. S. (1985). *Explaining delinquency and drug use.* Newbury Park, CA: Sage.

Elliott, J. (2010, August 1). Keeping my son out of trouble. *BBC News Health*, pp. 1–3. Retrieved from http://www.bbc.co.uk/news/health-10786202

Ellison, K. (2009, November 22). Medical marijuana: No longer just for adults. *The New York Times.* Retrieved from http://www.nytimes.com/2009/11/22/health/22sfmedical.html?pagewanted=print

Ellsworth, M. A., Stevens, T. P., & D'Angio, C. T. (2010). Infant race affects application of clinical guidelines when screening for drugs of abuse in newborns. *Pediatrics, 125*(6), e1379–e1385.

El Menyar, A. A. (2006). Drug-induced myocardial infarction secondary to coronary artery spasm in teenagers and young adults. *Journal of Postgraduate Medicine, 52*(1), 51–56.

El Menyar, A. A., El-Tawil, M., & Al Suwaidi, J. (2005). A teenager with angiographically normal epicardial coronary arteries and acute myocardial infarction after butane inhalation. *European Journal of Emergency Medicine, 12*(3), 137–141.

Elwood, W. N. (1998). *TCADA Research Brief: "Fry"—A study of adolescents' use of embalming fluid with marijuana and tobacco.* Austin, TX: Texas Commission on Alcohol and Drug Abuse.

Emergency Nurses Association. (2004). Emergency Nurses Position Statement (2004). Approved by the ENA Board of Directors July 2004. Statistical citations available at: www.ena.org/about/position/AlcoholScreening.asp

England, L., Brenner, R., Bhaskar, B., et al. (2003). Breastfeeding practices in a cohort of innercity women: The role of contraindications. *BioMed Central Public Health, 3*, 28.

England, L. J., Levine, R. J., Mills, J. L., et al. (2003). Adverse pregnancy outcomes in snuff users. *American Journal of Obstetrics and Gynecology, 189*(4), 939–943.

English, J. P., Willius, M. D., & Berkson, J. (1940). Tobacco and coronary disease. *JAMA, The Journal of the American Medical Association, 115*(16), 1327–1329.

Engs, R. C., & Fors, S. W. (1988). Drug abuse hysteria: The challenge of keeping perspective. *The Journal of School Health, 58*(1), 26–28.

Environmental Protection Agency. (2003). Fact sheet: National survey on environmental management of asthma and children's exposure to environmental tobacco smoke. Retrieved from www.epa.gov/iag

Epstein, J. A., & Botvin, G. J. (2008). Media resistance skills and drug skill refusal techniques: What is their relationship with alcohol use among innercity adolescents? *Addictive Behaviors, 33*(4), 528–537.

Epstein, J. A., Botvin, G. J., & Diaz, T. (2001). Linguistic acculturation associated with higher marijuana and polydrug use among Hispanic adolescents. *Substance Use & Misuse, 36*(4), 477–499.

Epstein, J. A., Zhou, X. K., Bang, H., et al. (2007). Do competence skills moderate the impact of social influences to drink and perceived social benefits of drinking on alcohol use among inner-city adolescents? *Prevention Science, 8*(1), 65–73.

Erceg-Hurn, D. M. (2008). Drugs, money, and graphic ads: A critical review of the Montana Meth Project. *Prevention Science, 9*(4), 256–263.

Eskenazi, B., & Castorina, R. (1999). Association of prenatal maternal or postnatal child environmental tobacco smoke exposure and neurodevelopmental and behavioral problems in children. *Environmental Health Perspectives, 107*, 991–1000.

Etter, J. F. (2005). A comparison of the content-, construct- and predictive validity of the cigarette dependence scale and the Fagerstrom test for nicotine dependence. *Drug and Alcohol Dependence, 77*(3), 259–268.

Etter, J. F., Duc, T. V., & Perneger, T. V. (1999). Validity of the Fagerstrom test for nicotine dependence and of the Heaviness of Smoking Index among relatively light smokers. *Addiction, 94*(2), 269–281.

Eustace, L. W., Kang, D. H., & Coombs, D. (2003). Fetal alcohol syndrome: A growing concern for health care professionals. *Journal of Obstetric, Gynecologic, & Neonatal Nursing, 32*(2), 215–221.

Evans, D. E. (2009). Nicotine self-medication of cognitive-attentional processing. *Addiction Biology, 14*(1), 32–42.

Evans, R., Rozelle, R., Mittlemark, M., et al. (1978). Deterring the onset of smoking in children: Knowledge of immediate physiological effects and coping with peer pressure, media pressure, and parent modeling. *Journal of Applied Social Psychology, 8*, 126–135.

Evans, S. M., & Griffiths, R. R. (1992). Caffeine tolerance and choice in humans. *Psychopharmacology (Berlin), 108*(1–2), 51–59.

Evans, S. M., & Griffiths, R. R. (1999). Caffeine withdrawal: A parametric analysis of caffeine dosing conditions. *The Journal of Pharmacology and Experimental Therapeutics, 289*(1), 285–294.

Ewing, J. A. (1984). Detecting alcoholism: The CAGE questionnaire. *JAMA, The Journal of the American Medical Association, 252*(14), 1905–1907.

## F

Fabbri, C. E., Furtado, E. F., & Laprega, M. R. (2007). Alcohol consumption in pregnancy: Performance of the Brazilian version of the questionnaire T-ACE [in Portuguese]. *Revista Saúde Pública, 41*(6), 979–984.

Fagan, P., Brook, J. S., Rubenstone, E., et al. (2009). Longitudinal precursors of young adult light smoking among African Americans and Puerto Ricans. *Nicotine & Tobacco Research, 11*(2), 139–147.

Fagerström, K.-O. (1978). Measuring degree of physical dependence to tobacco smoking with reference to individualization of treatment. *Addictive Behaviors, 3*(3–4), 235–241.

Faggiano, F., Vigna-Taglianti, F. D., Versino, E., et al. (2005, April 18). School-based prevention for illicit drugs' use. *Cochrane Database of Systematic Reviews, 2*, CD003020.

Faggiano, F., Vigna-Taglianti, F. D., Versino, E., et al. (2008). School-based prevention for illicit drug use: A systematic review. *Preventive Medicine, 46*(5): 385–396.

Fagnano, M., Conn, K. M., & Halterman, J. S. (2008). Environmental tobacco smoke and behaviors of inner-city children with asthma. *Ambulatory Pediatrics, 8*(5), 288–293.

Fairbairn, W. H. D. (1952). *Psychoanalytic studies of the personality.* London, UK: Routledge & Kegan Paul.

Fang, C. C., & Lai, T. I. (2006). Ecstasy poisoning in a toddler (comment). *Journal of the Formosan Medical Association, 105*(10), 866.

Fant, R. V., Buchhalter, A. R., Buchman, A. C., et al. (2009). Pharmacotherapy for tobacco dependence. *Handbook of Experimental Pharmacology*, (192),487–510.

Faraone, S. V., Sergeant, J., Gillberg, C., et al. (2003). The worldwide prevalence of ADHD: Is it an American condition? *World Psychiatry, 2*(2), 104–113.

Fareed, A., Casarella, J., Amar, R., et al. (2010). Methadone maintenance dosing guideline for opioid dependence, a literature review. *Journal of Addictive Diseases, 29*(1), 1–14.

Farooq, M. U., Bhatt, A., & Patel, M. (2009). Neurotoxic and cardiotoxic effects of cocaine and ethanol. *Journal of Medical Toxicology, 5*(3), 134–138.

Farst, K., Duncan, J. M., Moss, M., et al. (2007). Methamphetamine exposure presenting as caustic ingestions in children. *Annals of Emergency Medicine, 49*(3), 341–343.

Fasouliotis, S. J., & Schenker, J. G. (2000). Maternal-fetal conflict. *European Journal of Obstetrics & Gynecololgy and Reproductive Biology, 89*(1), 101–107.

Fauman, B. J., & Fauman, M. A. (1982). Phencyclidine abuse and crime: A psychiatric perspective. *Bulletin of the American Academy of Psychiatry & the Law, 10*(3), 171–176.

FDA Public Health Advisory. (2007). Use of codeine by some breastfeeding mothers may lead to life-threatening side effects in nursing babies. Retrieved from http://www.fda.gov/cder/drug/advisory/codeine.htm

Feldman, K. W., & Mazor, S. (2007). Ecstasy ingestion causing heatstroke-like, multiorgan injury in a toddler. *Pediatric Emergency Care, 23*(10), 725–726.

Feldman, R. S., & Quenzer, L. F. (1984). *Fundamentals of neuropsychopharmacology*. Sunderland, MA: Sinauer.

Female auto crash rates increase alarmingly; airbags can be dangerous for tall and small people. (2007, May 17). *ScienceDaily*, pp. 1–2. Retrieved from http://www.sciencedaily.com/releases/2007/05/070516071550.htm

Ferber, R. (1996). Childhood sleep disorders. *Neurologic Clinics, 14*(3), 493–511.

Fergusson, D. M., Boden, J. M., & Horwood, L. J. (2006). Cannabis use and other illicit drug use: Testing the cannabis gateway hypothesis. *Addiction, 101*(4), 556–569.

Fergusson, D. M., & Horwood, L. J. (2001). Cannabis use and traffic accidents in a birth cohort of young adults. *Accident; Analysis and Prevention, 33*(6), 703–711.

Fergusson, D. M., Horwood, L. J., & Beautrais, A. L. (2003). Cannabis and educational achievement. *Addiction, 98*(12), 1681–1692.

Fergusson, D. M., Horwood, L. J., & Ridder, E. M. (2005). Show me the child at seven: The consequences of conduct problems in childhood for psychosocial functioning in adulthood. *Journal of Child Psychology and Psychiatry, 46*(8), 837–849.

Fergusson, D. M., Lynskey, M. T., & Horwood, L. J. (1996). Comorbidity between depressive disorders and nicotine dependence in a cohort of 16-year-olds. *Archives of General Psychiatry, 53*(11), 1043–1047.

Fernandez-Espejo, E., Viveros, M. P., Nunez, L., et al. (2009). Role of cannabis and endocannabinoids in the genesis of schizophrenia. *Psychopharmacology (Berlin), 206*(4), 531–549.

Ferrara, S. D., Zotti, S., Tedeschi, L., et al. (1992). Pharmacokinetics of gamma-hydroxybutyric acid in alcohol-dependent patients after single and repeated oral doses. *British Journal of Clinical Pharmacology, 34*, 231–235.

Ferreira, S. E., de Mello, M. T., Pompéia, S., et al. (2006). Effects of energy drink ingestion on alcohol intoxication. *Alcoholism,Clinical and Experimental Research, 30*(4), 598–605.

Ferreira, S. E., de Mello, M. T., Rossi, M. V., et al. (2004). Does an energy drink modify the effects of alcohol in a maximal effort test? *Alcoholism,Clinical and Experimental Research, 28*(9), 1408–1412.

Ferri, M., Amato, L., & Davoli, M. (2006, July 19). Alcoholics Anonymous and other 12-step programmes for alcohol dependence. *Cochrane Database of Systematic Reviews*, 3, CD005032.

Fesinmeyer, M. D. (2006, July 14). Smokeless tobacco, Swedish snus, and pancreatic cancer (poster). Washington, DC: The 13th World Conference on Tobacco OR Health. Retrieved from http://2006.confex.com/uicc/wctoh/techprogram/P4821.HTM

Festinger, L. (1957). *A theory of cognitive dissonance*. Stanford, CA: Row Peterson.

Fields, R. (1995). Dual diagnosis: Definition, population, treatment. *Professional Counselor, 10*(2), 16.

Fiellin, D. A., Reid, M. C., & O'Connor, P. G. (2000). Screening for alcohol problems in primary care: A systematic review. *Archives of Internal Medicine, 160*(13), 1977–1989.

Filley, C. M., Halliday, W., Kleinschmidt-DeMasters, B. K. (2004). The effects of toluene on the central nervous system. *Journal of Neuropathology & Experimental Neurology, 63*(1), 1–12.

Finch, B. K., Vega, W. A., & Kolody, B. (2001). Substance use during pregnancy in the state of California, USA. *Social Science & Medicine, 52*, 571–583.

Findlay, J. W., DeAngelis, R. L., Kearney, M. F., et al. (1981). Analgesic drugs in breast milk and plasma. *Clinical Pharmacology & Therapeutics, 29*(5), 625–633.

Finestone, H. (1957). Cats, kicks, and color. *Social Problems, 5*, 3–13.

Fingarette, H. (1988). *Heavy drinking: The myth of alcoholism as a disease*. Berkeley, CA: University of California.

Finn, P. R., & Pihl, R. O. (1987). Men at high risk for alcoholism: The effect of alcohol on cardiovascular response to unavoidable shock. *Journal of Abnormal Psychology, 96*, 230–236.

Finn, P. R., & Pihl, R. O. (1988). Risk for alcoholism: A comparison between two different groups of sons of alcoholics on cardiovascular reactivity and sensitivity to alcohol. *Alcoholism, Clinical & Experimental Research, 12*, 742–747.

Fischer, B., Rehm, J., & Hall, W. (2009). Cannabis use in Canada: The need for a 'public health' approach. *Canadian Journal of Public Health, 100*(2), 101–103.

Fishbein, M., Hall-Jamieson, K., Zimmer, E., et al. (2002). Avoiding the boomerang: Testing the relative effectiveness of antidrug public service announcements before a national campaign. *American Journal of Public Health, 92*(2), 238–245.

Fisher, D. G. (Ed.). (1991). *AIDS and alcohol/drug abuse: Psychosocial research*. New York, NY: Harrington Park.

Flagler, E., Baylis, F., & Rodgers, S. (1997). Bioethics for clinicians: 12. Ethical dilemmas that arise in the care of pregnant women: Rethinking "maternal-fetal conflicts." *CMAJ, Canadian Medical Association Journal, 156*(12), 1729–1732.

Flassing, J. (2010). Buprenorphine: A more accessible treatment for opioid dependence. *Journal of the American Academy of Physician Assistants, 23*(9), 40–43.

Flatter, C. H., & McCormick, K. (1992). *Learning to live drug free: A curriculum model for prevention* (ED/OESE92-36R). Washington, DC: U.S. Department of Education.

Flay, B. R. (1985). Psychological approaches to smoking prevention: A review of findings. *Health Psychology, 4*(5), 449–488.

Fleming, M. F., & Barry, K. L. (1991). A three-sample test of a masked alcohol screening questionnaire. *Alcohol and Alcoholism, 26*, 81–91.

Fleming, M. F., Barry, K. L., & MacDonald, R. (1991). The Alcohol Use Disorders Identification Test (AUDIT) in a college sample. *The International Journal of the Addictions, 26*, 1173–1185.

Fletcher, A., Bonell, C., & Hargreaves, J. (2008). School effects on young people's drug use: A systematic review of intervention and observational studies. *The Journal of Adolescent Health, 42*(3), 209–220.

Florescu, A., Ferrence, R., Einarson, R. T., et al. (2007). Reference values for hair cotinine as a biomarker of active and passive smoking in women of reproductive age, pregnant women, children, and neonates: Systematic review and meta-analysis. *Therapeutic Drug Monitoring, 29*(4), 437–446.

Flórez, G., Saiz, P. A., Garcia-Portilla, P., et al. (2010). Topiramate for the treatment of alcohol dependence: Comparison with naltrexone. *European Addiction Research, 17*(1), 29–36.

Flumazenil. (1992). *The Medical Letter on Drugs and Therapeutics, 34*, 66–68.

Food Standards Agency. (2008, November 3). Food Standards Agency publishes new caffeine advice for pregnant women (pp. 1–2). Retrieved from http://www.food.gov.uk/news/pressreleases/2008/nov/cafffeineadvice

Forrester, M. B. (2006a). Alprazolam abuse in Texas, 1998–2004. *Journal of Toxicology and Environmental Health, Part A: Current Issues, 69*(3–4), 237–243.

Forrester, M. B. (2006b). Flunitrazepam abuse and malicious use in Texas, 1998–2003. *Substance Use & Misuse, 41*(3), 297–306.

Foster, F. M., Horn, J. L., & Wanberg, K. W. (1972). Dimensions of treatment outcome. *Quarterly Journal of Studies on Alcohol, 33*, 1079–1098.

Foti, D. J., Kotov, R., Guey, L. T., et al. (2010). Cannabis use and the course of schizophrenia: 10-year follow-up after first hospitalization. *The American Journal of Psychiatry, 167*, 987–993.

Fox, C., & Forbing, S. (1991). Overlapping symptoms of substance abuse and learning handicaps: Implications for educators. *Journal of Learning Disabilities, 24*, 24–31.

Fox, H. C., Jackson, E. D., & Sinha, R. (2009). Elevated cortisol and learning and memory deficits in cocaine dependent individuals: Relationship to relapse outcomes. *Psychoneuroendocrinology, 34*(8), 1198–1207.

Fox, H. C., Parrott, A. C., & Turner, J. J. (2001). Ecstasy use: Cognitive deficits related to dosage rather than self-reported problematic use of the drug. *Journal of Psychopharmacology, 15*(4), 273–281.

Frances, R. J., & Allen, M. H. (1986). The interaction of substance-use disorders with nonpsychotic psychiatric disorders. In R. Michels & J. O. Cavenar (Eds.), *Psychiatry* (Volume 1). New York, NY: Basic Books.

Frank, D. A., Augustyn, M., Knight, W. G., et al. (2001). Growth, development, and behavior in early childhood following prenatal cocaine exposure: A systemic review. *JAMA, The Journal of the American Medical Association, 285*(12), 1613–1625.

Frank, D., DeBenedetti, A. F., Volk, R. J., et al. (2008). Effectiveness of the AUDIT-C as a screening test for alcohol misuse in three race/ethnic groups. *Journal of General Internal Medicine, 23*(6), 781–787.

Frank, D. A., Jacobs, R. R., Beeghly, M., et al. (2002). Level of prenatal cocaine exposure and scores on the Bayley Scales of Infant Development: Modifying effects of caregiver, early intervention, and birth weight. *Pediatrics, 110*(6), 1143–1152.

Frank, D. A., & Zuckerman, B. S. (1993). Children exposed to cocaine prenatally: Pieces of the puzzle. *Neurotoxicology and Teratology, 15*, 298–300.

Frankel, L. (1990). Structural family therapy for adolescent substance abusers and their families. In A. S. Friedman & S. Granick (Eds.), *Family therapy for adolescent drug abuse* (pp. 47–61). New York, NY: Lexington.

Franklin, C. (1992). Family and individual patterns in a group of middle-class dropout youths. *Social Work, 37*, 338–344.

Frary, C. D., Johnson, R. K., & Wang, M. Q. (2005). Food sources and intakes of caffeine in the diets of persons in the United States. *Journal of the American Dietetic Association, 105*(1), 110–113.

Frederick, C. J. (1972). Drug abuse as self-destructive behavior. *Drug Therapy, 2*, 49–68.

Frederick, C. J. (1973). Drug abuse: A self-destructive enigma. *Maryland State Medical Journal, 22,* 19–21.

Frederick, C. J., & Resnik, H. L. (1971). How suicidal behaviors are learned. *American Journal of Psychotherapy, 25,* 37–55.

Frederick, C. J., Resnik, H. L., & Wittlin, B. J. (1973). Self-destructive aspects of hard core addiction. *Archives of General Psychiatry, 28*(4), 579–585.

Freese, T. E., Obert, J., Dickow, A., et al. (2000). Methamphetamine abuse: Issues for special populations. *Journal of Psychoactive Drugs, 32*(2), 177–182.

Fregosi, R. F., & Pilarski, J. Q. (2008). Prenatal nicotine exposure and development of nicotinic and fast amino acid-mediated neurotransmission in the control of breathing. *Respiratory Physiology & Neurobiology, 164*(1–2), 80–86.

Freud, S. (1930/1989). *Civilization and its discontents.* New York, NY: Norton.

Fried, P. A., & Smith, A. M. (2001). A literature review of the consequences of prenatal marihuana exposure. An emerging theme of a deficiency in aspects of executive function. *Neurotoxicology and Teratology, 23*(1), 1–11.

Fried, P. A., & Watkinson, B. (1990). 36- and 48-month neurobehavioral follow-up of children prenatally exposed to marijuana, cigarettes, and alcohol. *Journal of Developmental and Behavioral Pediatrics, 11*(2), 49–58.

Friedman, A. S., Bransfield, S., & Kreisher, C. (1994). Eary teenage substance use as a predictor of educational-vocational failure. *The American Journal on Addictions, 3,* 325–336.

Friedman, A. S., & Granick, S. (Eds.). (1990). *Family therapy for adolescent drug abuse.* New York, NY: Lexington.

Frishman, W. H. (2007). Smoking cessation pharmacotherapy—Nicotine and non-nicotine preparations. *Preventive Cardiology, 10*(2 Suppl. 1), 10–22.

Frishman, W. H. (2009). Smoking cessation pharmacology. *Therapeutic Advances in Cardiovascular Disease, 3*(4), 287–308.

Fuller, D. E., Hornfeldt, C. S., Kelloway, J. S., et al. (2004). The Xyrem risk management program. *Drug Safety, 27*(5), 293–306.

Furman, L. (2005). What is attention-deficit hyperactivity disorder (ADHD)? *Journal of Child Neurology, 20,* 994–1002.

# G

Gache, P., Michaud, P., Landry, U., et al. (2005). The Alcohol Use Disorders Identification Test (AUDIT) as a screening tool for excessive drinking in primary care: Reliability and validity of a French version. *Alcoholism, Clinical and Experimental Research, 29*(11), 2001–2007.

Gahlinger, P. M. (2004). Club drugs: MDMA, gamma-hydroxybutyrate (GHB), rohypnol, and ketamine. *American Family Physician, 69*(11), 2619–2627.

Galaif, E. R., Sussman, S., Newcomb, M. D., et al. (2007). Suicidality, depression, and alcohol use among adolescents: A review of empirical findings. *International Journal of Adolescent Medicine and Health, 19*(1), 27–35.

Galanter, M., Egelko, S., Edwards, H., et al. (1994). A treatment system for combined psychiatric and addictive illness. *Addiction, 89,* 1227–1235.

Gallant, D. M., & Head-Dunham, R. (1991). Alcohol and drug abuse prevention in adolescents. *Alcoholism, Clinical and Experimental Research, 15*(2), 308.

Galloway, G. P., Frederick, S. L., Staggers, F. E. Jr, et al. (1997). Gamma-hydroxybutyrate: An emerging drug of abuse that causes physical dependence. *Addiction, 92*(1), 89–96.

Gandey, A. (2010, November 19). Propoxyphene withdrawn from US market. *Medscape Medical News.* Retrieved from http://www.medscape.com/viewarticle/732887_print

Ganz, D., & Sher, L. (2009). Suicical behavior in adolescents with comorbid depression and alcohol abuse. *Minerva Pediatrica, 61*(3), 333–347.

Garbutt, J. C. (2009). The state of pharmacotherapy for the treatment of alcohol dependence. *Journal of Substance Abuse Treatment, 36*(1), S15–S23.

Garbutt, J. C. (2010). Efficacy and tolerability of naltrexone in the management of alcohol dependence. *Current Pharmaceutical Design, 16*(19), 2091–2097.

Garbutt, J. C., Kranzier, H. R., O'Malley, S. S., et al. (2005). Efficacy and tolerability of long-acting injectable naltrexone for alcohol dependence: A randomized controlled trial. *JAMA, The Journal of the American Medical Association, 293,* 1617–1625.

Garcia, S. A. (1993). Maternal drug abuse: Laws and ethics as agents of just balances and therapeutic interventions. *International Journal of the Addictions, 28,* 1311–1339.

Garcia-Algar, O., Vall, O., Alameda, F., et al. (2005). Prenatal exposure to arecoline (areca nut alkaloid) and birth outcomes. *Archives of Disease in Childhood. Fetal and Neonatal Edition, 90,* F276–F277.

Garcia-Bournissen, F., Nesterenko, M., Karaskov, T., et al. (2009). Passive environmental exposure to cocaine in Canadian children. *Paediatric Drugs, 11*(1), 30–32.

Gardner, J. J., & Cabral, D. A. (1990). Sexually abused adolescents: A distinct group among sexually abused children presenting to a children's hospital. *Journal of Paediatrics and Child Health, 26,* 22–24.

Gareri, J., Klein, J., & Koren, G. (2006). Drugs of abuse testing in meconium. *Clinica Chimica Acta, 366,* (1–2), 101–111.

Gareri, J., Lynn, H., Handley, M., et al. (2008). Prevalence of fetal ethanol exposure in a regional population-based sample by meconium analysis of fatty acid ethyl esters. *Therapeutic Drug Monitoring, 30*(2), 239–245.

Garey, R. E. (1979). PCP (phencyclidine): An update. *Journal of Psychedelic Drugs, 11*(4), 265–275.

Garofalo, R., Mustanski, B. S., McKirnan, D. J., et al. (2007). Methamphetamine and young men who have sex with men: Understanding patterns and correlates of use and the asosociation with HIV-related sexual risk. *Archives of Pediatric & Adolescent Medicine, 161*(6), 591–596.

Garrison, G., & Mueller, P. (1998). Clinical features and outcomes after unintentional gamma hydroxybutyrate (GHB) overdose. *Journal of Toxicology, Clinical Toxicology, 36*, 503–504.

Garrison, G. D., & Dugan, S. E. (2009). Varenicline: A first-line treatment option for smoking cessation. *Clinical Therapeutics, 31*(3), 463–491.

Garry, A., Rigourd, V., Amirouche, A., et al. (2009). Cannabis and breastfeeding. *Journal of Toxicology.* Retrieved from http://www.ncbi.nlm.nih.gov/pubmed/20130780

Gastfriend, D. R. (2011). Intramuscular extended-release naltrexone: Current evidence. *Annals of the New York Academy of Sciences, 1216*, 144–166.

Gates, S., Smith, L. A., & Foxcroft, D. R. (2006, January 25). Auricular acupuncture for cocaine dependence. *Cochrane Database of Systematic Reviews, 1*, CD005192.

Gatof, D., & Albert, R.K. (2002). Bilateral thumb burns leading to the diagnosis of crack lung. *Chest, 121*(1), 289–291.

Gavin, D. R., Ross, H. E., & Skinner, H. A. (1989). Diagnostic validity of the Drug Abuse Screening Test in the assessment of *DSM-III* drug disorders. *British Journal of Addiction, 84*(3), 301–307.

Gavin, L., MacKay, A. P., Brown, K., et al. (2009, July 17). Sexual and reproductive health of persons aged 10–24 years—United States, 2002–2007. *Morbidity and Mortality Weekly Report, Surveillance Summaries, 58*(SS06), 1–58.

Gaz, D., & Sher, L. (2009). Suicidal behavior in adolescents with comorbid depression and alcohol abuse. *Minerva Pediatrica, 61*(3), 333–347.

Gee, R. L., Espiritu, R. C., & Huang, L. N. (2006). Adolescents with co-occurring mental health and substance use disorders in primary care. *Adolescent Medicine Clinics, 17*(2), 427–452.

Gehrman, C. A., & Hovell, M. F. (2003). Protecting children from environmental tobacco smoke (ETS) exposure: A critical review. *Nicotine & Tobacco Research, 5*(3), 289–301.

Gelb, L. N. (1984). *Just say no.* Washington, DC: US Government Printing Office.

Generali, J. A. (1992). Nicotine transdermal patches. *Facts and Comparisons Drug Newsletter, 11*, 33–34.

Gerald, L. B., Gerald, J. K., Gibson, L., et al. (2009). Changes in environmental tobacco smoke exposure and asthma morbidity among urban school children. *Chest, 135*(4), 911–916.

Gettman, J. (1995, March). Highwitness news: Marijuana and the human brain. *High Times*, 26–29.

Gettman, J. (2006). Special report: Marijuana production in the United States (2006). *The Bulletin of Cannabis Reform*, 2. Retrieved from http://www.drugscience.org/Archive/bcr2/bcr2_index.html

Ghoneim, M. M., Block, R. I., Ping, S. T., et al. (1993). The interactions of midazolam and flumazenil on human memory and cognition. *Anesthesiology, 79*(6), 1183–1192.

Ghoneim, M. M, Hinrichs, J. V., & Mewaldt, S. P. (1984). Dose response analysis of the behavioral effects of diazepam: Learning and memory. *Psychopharmacology (Berlin), 82*, 291–295.

Giang, K. B., Spak, F., Dzung, T. V., et al. (2005). The use of AUDIT to assess level of alcohol problems in rural Vietnam. *Alcohol and Alcoholism, 40*(6), 578–583.

Giedd, J. N. (2004). Structural magnetic resonance imaging of the adolescent brain. *Annals of the New York Academy of Sciences, 1021*, 77–85.

Giedd, J. N., Blumenthal, J., Jeffries, N. O., et al. (1999). Brain development during childhood and adolescence: A longitudinal MRI study. *Nature Neuroscience, 2*(10), 861–863.

Gieron-Korthals, M. A., Helal, A., & Martinez, C. R. (1994). Expanding spectrum of cocaine induced central nervous system malformations. *Brain & Development, 16*, 253–256.

Gilchrist, L. D., Hussey, J. M., Gillmore, M. R., et al. (1996). Drug use among adolescent mothers: Prepregnancy to 18 months postpartum. *The Journal of Adolescent Health, 19*(5), 337–344.

Gill, J. R., Hayes, J. A., deSouza, I. S., et al. (2002). Ecstasy (MDMA) deaths in New York City: A case series and review of the literature. *Journal of Forensic Sciences, 47*(1), 121–126.

Gillen, R. W., Kranzler, H. R., Bauer, L. O., et al. (1998). Neuropsychologic findings in cocaine-dependent outpatients. *Progress in Neuro-Psychopharmacology & Biological Psychiatry, 22*(7), 1061–1076.

Gilliland, F. D., Berhane, K., Islam, T., et al. (2003). Environmental tobacco smoke and absenteeism related to respiratory illness in schoolchildren. *American Journal of Epidemiology, 157*(10), 861–869.

Gingras, J. L., Weese-Mayer, D. E., Hume, R. F., et al. (1992). Cocaine and development: Mechanisms of fetal toxicity and neonatal consequences of prenatal cocaine exposure. *Early Human Development, 31*(1), 1–24.

Ginsberg, K. A., Blacker, C. M., Abel, E. I., et al. (1991). Fetal alcohol exposure and adverse pregnancy outcomes. *Contributions to Gynecology and Obstetrics, 18*, 115–129.

Ginzler, J. A., Cochran, B. N., Domenech-Rodriguez, M., et al. (2003). Sequential progression of substance use among homeless youth: An empirical investigation of the gateway hypothesis. *Substance Use & Misuse, 38*(3–6), 725–758.

Ginzler, J. A., Garrett, S. B., Baer, J. S., et al. (2007). Measurement of negative consequences of substance use in street youth: An expanded use of the Rutgers Alcohol Problem Index. *Addictive Behaviors, 32*(7), 1519–1525.

Girard, F., Le Tacon, S., Maria, M., et al. (2008). Ventricular fibrillation following deodorant spray inhalation [in French]. *Annales Françaises Anesthésie et Réanimation, 27*(1), 83–85.

Glasmacher, A., Hahn, C., Hoffmann, F., et al. (2006). A systematic review of phase-II trials of thalidomide monotherapy in patients with relapsed or refractory multiple myeloma. *British Journal of Haematology, 132*(5), 584–593.

Glatstein, M. M., Finkelstein, Y., & Scolnik, D. (2009). Accidental methadone ingestion in an infant: Case report and review of the literature. *Pediatric Emergency Care, 25*(2), 109–111.

Glatstein, M. M., Garcia-Bournissen, F., Finkelstein, Y., et al. (2008). Methadone exposure during lactation. *Canadian Family Physician, 54*(12), 1689–1690.

Glueck, S., & Glueck, E. (1950). *Unravelling juvenile delinquency*. New York, NY: Commonwealth Fund.

Glueck, S., & Glueck, E. (1968). *Delinquents and non-delinquents in perspective*. Cambridge, MA: Harvard University.

Gold, M. S., & Dackis, C. A. (1984). New insights and treatments: Opiate withdrawal and cocaine addiction. *Clinical Therapeutics, 7*(1), 6–21.

Gold, M. S., & Slaby, A. E. (1991). *Dual diagnosis in substance abuse*. New York, NY: Dekker.

Gold, S. R. (1980). The CAP control theory of drug abuse. In D. J. Lettieri, M. Sayer, & H. Wallenstein Pearson (Eds.), *Theories on drug abuse: Selected contemporary perspectives* (NIDA Research Monograph No. 30, pp. 8–11). Rockville, MD: U.S. Department of Health and Human Services, National Institute on Drug Abuse.

Gold, S. R., & Coghlan, A. J. (1975–1976). Locus of control and self-esteem among adolescent drug abusers: Effects of residential treatment. *Drug Forum, 5*(2), 185–191.

Goldberg, L. (1968). Drug abuse in Sweden. *Bulletin on Narcotics, 20*, 1–12.

Goldbloom, D. S. (1993). Alcohol misuse and eating disorders: Aspects of an association. *Alcohol & Alcoholism, 28*, 375–381.

Golden, G. S. (1991). Role of attention deficit hyperactivity disorder in learning disabilities. *Seminars in Neurology, 11*(1), 35–41.

Goldsmith, R. J., & Garlapati, V. (2004). Behavioral interventions for dual-diagnosis patients. *Psychiatric Clinics of North America, 27*(4), 709–725.

Goldstein, A. P., Reagles, K. W., & Amann, L. L. (1990). *Refusal skills: Preventing drug use in adolescents*. Champaign, IL: Research Press.

Goldstein, B. I., & Bukstein, O. G. (2010). Comorbid substance use disorders among youth with bipolar disorder: Opportunities for early identification and prevention. *The Journal of Clinical Psychiatry, 71*(3), 348–358.

Goldstein, M. B., & Engwall, D. B. (1992). The politics of prevention: Changing definitions of substance use/abuse. *Journal of Health & Social Policy, 3*(3), 69–83.

Golka, K., & Wiese, A. (2004). Carbohydrate-deficient transferrin (CDT)—A biomarker for long-term alcohol consumption. *Journal of Toxicology and Environmental Health, Part B: Critical Reviews, 7*(4), 319–337.

Golub, A., & Johnson, B. D. (1994). The shifting importance of alcohol and marijuana as gateway substances among serious drug users. *Journal of Studies on Alcohol, 55*(5), 607–614.

Golub, A., Johnson, B.D., Sifaneck, S. J., et al. (2001). Is the U.S. experiencing an incipient epidemic of hallucinogen use? *Substance Use & Misuse, 36*(12), 1699–1729.

Gómez, A., Conde, A., Santana, J. M., et al. (2005). Diagnostic usefulness of brief versions of Alcohol Use Disorders Identification Test (AUDIT) for detecting hazardous drinkers in primary care settings. *Journal of Studies on Alcohol, 66*(2), 305–308.

Gonzales, D., Rennard, S. I., Nides, M., et al. (2006). Varenicline, an alpha4beta2 nicotinic acetylcholine receptor partial agonist, vs. sustained-release bupropion and placebo for smoking cessation: A randomized controlled trial. *JAMA, The Journal of the American Medical Association, 296*(1), 47–55.

Gonzales, R., Mooney, L., & Rawson, R. A. (2010). The methamphetamine problem in the United States. *Annual Review of Public Health, 31*, 385–398.

Gonzalez-Maeso, J., & Sealfon, S.C. (2009). Psychedelics and schizophrenia. *Trends in Neurosciences, 32*(4), 225–232.

Good, M. M., Solt, I., Acuna, J. G., et al. (2010). Methamphetamine use during pregnancy: Maternal and neonatal implications. *Obstetrics & Gynecology, 116*(2, pt. 1), 330–334.

Goodlett, C. R., Horn, K. H., & Zhou, F. C. (2005). Alcohol teratogenesis: Mechanisms of damage and strategies for intervention. *Experimental Biology and Medicine, 230*, 394–406.

Goodman, D. R., James, R. C., & Harbison, R. D. (1982). Placental toxicology. *Food and Chemical Toxicology, 20*(1), 123–128.

Goodstadt, M. S. (1989). Substance abuse curricula vs. school drug policies. *The Journal of School Health, 59*, 246–250.

Goodwin, R. D., Lieb, R., Hoefler, M., et al. (2004). Panic attack as a risk factor for severe psychopathology. *The American Journal of Psychiatry, 161*(12), 2207–2214.

Gordon, A. J., Maisto, S. A., McNeil, M., et al. (2001). Three questions can detect hazardous drinkers. *Journal of Family Practice, 50*(4), 313–320.

Gore, T. (1991). A portrait of at-risk children. *Journal of Health Care for the Poor and Underserved, 2*(1), 95–105.

Gorenstein, C., Bernik, M. A., & Pompeia, S. (1994). Differential acute psychomotor and cognitive effects of diazepam on long-term benzodiazepine users. *International Clinical Psychopharmacology, 9*, 143–153.

Gorman, D. M. (1988). The irrelevance of evidence in the development of school-based drug prevention policy, 1986–1996. *Evaluation Review, 22*(1), 118–146.

Gorski, T. T. (1995, August). Brief therapy for dual recovery: II. Treatment planning and step-by-step interventions. *Professional Counselor, 27*, 52–53.

Gorsuch, R. L. (1980). Interactive models of nonmedical drug use. In D. J. Lettieri, M. Sayer, & H. Wallenstein Pearson (Eds.), *Theories on drug abuse: Selected contemporary perspectives* (NIDA Research Monograph No. 30, pp. 18–23). Rockville, MD: U.S. Department of Health and Human Services, National Institute on Drug Abuse.

Gorsuch, R. L., & Butler, M. C. (1976a). Initial drug abuse: A review of predisposing social psychological factors. *Psychological Bulletin, 83*(1), 120–137.

Gorsuch, R. L., & Butler, M. C. (1976b). Toward developmental models of non-medical drug use. In S. B. Sells (Ed.), *The effectiveness of drug abuse treatment* (Vol. 3, pp. 29–76). Cambridge, MA: Ballinger.

Gottfredson, D. C., & Wilson, D. B. (2003). Characteristics of effective school-based substance abuse prevention. *Prevention Science, 4*(1), 27–38.

Gouzoulis-Mayfrank, E., & Daumann, J. (2006). Neurotoxicity of methylenedioxyamphetamines (MDMA; ecstasy) in humans: How strong is the evidence for persistent brain damage? *Addiction, 101*(3), 348–361.

Gouzoulis-Mayfrank, E., & Daumann, J. (2009). Neurotoxicity of drugs of abuse—The case of methylenedioxyamphetamines (MDMA, ecstasy), and amphetamines. *Dialogues in Clinical Neuroscience, 11*(3), 305–317.

Gouzoulis-Mayfrank, E., Daumann, J., Tuchtenhagen, F., et al. (2000). Impaired cognitive performance in drug free users of recreational ecstasy (MDMA). *Journal of Neurology, Neurosurgery, and Psychiatry, 68*(6), 719–725.

Gouzoulis-Mayfrank, E., Fischermann, T., Rezk, M., et al. (2005). Memory performance in polyvalent MDMA (ecstasy) users who continue or discontinue MDMA use. *Drug and Alcohol Dependence, 78*(3), 317–323.

Gowing, L. R., Farrell, M., Ali, R. L., et al. (2002). Alpha2-adrenergic agonists in opioid withdrawal. *Addiction, 97*(1), 49–58.

Gowing, L. R., Farrell, M., Ali, R. L., et al. (2009, April 15). Alpha2-adrenergic agonists for the management of opioid withdrawal. *Cochrane Databases of Systematic Reviews, 2*, CD002024.

Graham, A., Goss, C., Xu, S., et al. (2007). Effect of using different modes to administer the AUDIT-C on identification of hazardous drinking and acquiescence to trial participation among injured patients. *Alcohol & Alcoholism, 42*(5), 423–429.

Graham, K. (1988). Reasons for consumption and heavy caffeine use: Generalization of a model based on alcohol research. *Addictive Behaviors, 13*, 209–214.

Graham, T. E. (2001). Caffeine and exercise: Metabolism, endurance and performance. *Sports Medicine, 31*(11), 785–807.

Grant, B. F., Hasin, D. S., Chou, S. P., et al. (2004). Nicotine dependence and psychiatric disorders in the United States. *Archives of General Psychiatry, 61*(11), 1107–1115.

Grant, B. F., Stinson, F. S., Dawson, D. A., et al. (2004). Prevalence and co-occurrence of substance use disorders and independent mood and anxiety disorders: Results from the National Epidemiologic Survey on Alcohol and Related Conditions. *Archives of General Psychiatry, 61*(8), 807–816.

Grant, P., Bell, K., Stewart, D., et al. (2010). Evidence of methamphetamine exposure in children removed from clandestine methamphetamine laboratories. *Pediatric Emergency Care, 26*(1), 10–14.

Gray, N. J. (2008). Health information on the Internet—A double-edged sword? *The Journal of Adolescent Health, 42*(5), 432–433.

Greaves, G. (1974). Toward an existential theory of drug dependence. *The Journal of Nervous and Mental Disease, 159*, 263–274.

Greaves, G. (1980). An existential theory of drug dependence. In D. J. Lettieri, M. Sayer, & H. Wallenstein Pearson (Eds.), *Theories on drug abuse: Selected contemporary perspectives* (NIDA Research Monograph No. 30, pp. 24–28). Rockville, MD: U.S. Department of Health and Human Services, National Institute on Drug Abuse.

Green, A. I. (2005). Schizophrenia and comorbid substance use disorder: Effects of antipsychotics. *The Journal of Clinical Psychiatry, 66*(Suppl. 6), 21–26.

Green, A. I., & Brown, E. S. (2006). Comorbid schizophrenia and substance abuse. *The Journal of Clinical Psychiatry, 67*(9), e08.

Green, B., Young, R., & Kavanagh, D. (2005). Cannabis use and misuse prevalence among people with psychosis. *The British Journal of Psychiatry, 187*, 306–313.

Green, C. R., Mihic, A. M., Nikkel, S. M., et al. (2009). Executive function deficits in children with fetal alcohol spectrum disorders (FASD) measured using Cambridge Neuropsychological Tests Automated Battery (CANTAB). *Journal of Child Psychology and Psychiatry, 50*(6), 688–697.

Greenbaum, P. E., Prange, M. E., Friedman, R. M., et al. (1991). Substance abuse prevalence and comorbidity with other psychiatric disorders among adolescents with severe emotional disturbances. *The Journal of the American Academy of Child and Adolescent Psychiatry, 30*, 575–583.

Greenberg, J. A., Owen, D. R., & Geliebter, A. (2010). Decaffeinated coffee and glucose metabolism in young men. *Diabetes Care, 33*(2), 278–280.

Greenstein, R. A., Arndt, I. C., McLellan, A. T., et al. (1984). Naltrexone: A clinical perspective. *The Journal of Clinical Psychiatry, 45*(9, pt. 2), 25–28.

Griffiths, R. R., & Chausmer, A. L. (2000). Caffeine as a model drug of dependence: Recent developments in understanding caffeine withdrawal, the caffeine dependence syndrome, and caffeine negative reinforcement. *Nihon Shinkei Seishin Yakurigaku Zasshi, 20*(5), 223–231.

Grimm, D., Pauly, E., Poschl, J., et al. (2005). Buprenorphine and norbuprenorphine concentrations in human breast milk samples determined by liquid chromatography-tandem mass spectrometry. *Therapeutic Drug Monitoring, 27,* 526–530.

Grimshaw, G. M., & Stanton, A. (2006, October 18). Tobacco cessation interventions for young people. *Cochrane Database of Systematic Reviews*, 4, CD003289.

Gromov, I., & Gromov, D. (2009). Sleep and substance use and abuse in adolescents. *Child & Adolescent Psychiatric Clinics of North America, 18*(4), 929–946.

Gross, A., & Klys, M. (2002). Suicide by propane-butane inhalation: A case report and literature review [in Polish]. *Archiwum Medycyny Sadowej Kryminologii, 52*(1), 37–42.

Gross, S. R., Barrett, S. P., Shestowsky, J. S., et al. (2002). Ecstasy and drug consumption patterns: A Canadian rave population study. *Canadian Journal of Psychiatry, 47*(6), 546–551.

Grov, C., Kelly, B. C., & Parsons, J. T. (2009). Polydrug use among club-going young adults recruited through time-space sampling. *Substance Use & Misuse, 44*(6), 848–864.

Groves, W. E. (1974). Patterns of college student drug use and life-styles. In E. Josephson & E. Carroll (Eds.), *Drug use: Epidemiological and sociological approaches*. New York, NY: Winston-Wiley.

Grucza, R. A., Norberg, K. E., & Bierut, L. J. (2009). Binge drinking among youth and young adults in the United States: 1979–2006. *Journal of the American Academy of Child & Adolescent Psychiatry, 48*(7), 692–702.

Grunbaum, J. A., Kann, L., Kinchen, S. A., et al. (2002). Youth risk behavior surveillance—United States, 2001. *The Journal of School Health, 72*(8), 313–328.

Guerri, C., Pascual, M. (2010). Mechanisms involved in the neurotoxic, cognitive, and neurobehavioral effects of alcohol consumption during adolescence. *Alcohol, 44*(1), 15–26.

Guidotti, T. L. (1989). Critique of available studies on the toxicology of kretek smoke and its constituents by routes of entry involving the respiratory tract. *Archives of Toxicology, 63*(1), 7–12.

Gupta, M., Bailey, S., & Lovato, L. M. (2009). Bottoms up: Methamphetamine toxicity from an unusual route. *The Western Journal of Emergency Medicine, 10*(1), 58–60.

Gupton, A., Thompson, L., Arnason, R. C., et al. (1995). Pregnant women and smoking. *Canadian Nurse, 91*(7), 26–30.

Gustafson, E. M. (2005). History and overview of school-based health centers in the US. *Nursing Clinics of North America, 40*(4), 595–606.

Gwin Mitchell, S., Kelly, S. M., Brown, B. S., et al. (2009). Uses of diverted methadone and buprenorphine by opioid-addicted individuals in Baltimore, Maryland. *TheAmerican Journal on Addictions, 18*(5), 346–355.

# H

Haber, J. R., Jacob, T., & Heath, A. C. (2005). Paternal alcoholism and offspring conduct disorder: Evidence for the "common genes" hypothesis. *Twin Research and Human Genetics: The Official Journal of the International Society for Twin Studies, 8*(2), 120–131.

Habis, A., Tall, L., Smith, J., et al. (2007). Pediatric emergency medicine physicians' current practices and beliefs regarding mental health screening. *Pediatric Emergency Care, 23*(6), 387–393.

Haddad, J., & Messer, J. (1994). Fetal alcohol syndrome: Report of three siblings. *Neuropediatrics, 25,* 109–111.

Haddock, C. K., Lando, H., Klesges, R. C., et al. (1999). A study of the psychometric and predictive properties of the Fagerström Test for Nicotine Dependence in a population of young smokers. *Nicotine & Tobacco Research, 1*(1), 59–66.

Hall, W. (2009). The adverse health effects of cannabis use: What are they, and what are their implications for policy? *International Journal of Drug Policy, 20*(6), 458–466.

Hall, W., & Degenhardt, L. (2000). Cannabis use and psychosis: A review of clinical and epidemiological evidence. *Australian and New Zealand Journal of Psychiatry, 34*(1), 26–34.

Hall, W., & Degenhardt, L. (2008). Cannabis use and the risk of developing a psychotic disorder. *World Psychiatry, 7*(2), 68–71.

Hall, W., Degenhardt, L., & Teesson, M. (2004). Cannabis use and psychotic disorders: An update. *Drug and Alcohol Review, 23*(4), 433–443.

Hall, W. D., & Lynskey, M. (2005). Is cannabis a gateway drug? Testing hypotheses about the relationship between cannabis use and the use of other illicit drugs. *Drug and Alcohol Review, 24*(1), 39–48.

Hamilton, R., McGlone, L., MacKinnon, J. R., et al. (2010). Ophthalmic, clinical and visual electrophysiological findings in children born to mothers prescribed substitute methadone in pregnancy. *British Journal of Ophthalmology, 94*(6), 696–700.

Hammond, S. K. (2009). Global patterns of nicotine and tobacco consumption. *Handbook of Experimental Pharmacology*, (192), 3–28.

Handen, B. L., Breaux, A. M., Gosling, A., et al. (1990). Efficacy of methylphenidate among mentally retarded children with attention deficit hyperactivity disorder. *Pediatrics, 86*(6), 922–930.

Haney, M. (2005). The marijuana withdrawal syndrome: Diagnosis and treatment. *Current Psychiatry Reports, 7*(5), 360–366.

Hannig, V. L., & Phillips, J. A., (1991). Maternal cocaine abuse and fetal anomalies: Evidence for teratogenic effects of cocaine. *Southern Medical Journal, 84,* 498–499.

Hannigan, J. H., & Bowen, S. E. (2010). Reproductive toxicology and teratology of abused toluene. *Systems Biology in Reproductive Medicine, 56*(2), 184–200.

Hannon, P. R., Willis, S. K., Bishop-Townsend, V., et al. (2000). African-American and Latina adolescent mothers' infant feeding decisions and breastfeeding practices: A qualitative study. *The Journal of Adolescent Health, 26*(6), 399–407.

Hansen, W. B., & Graham, J. W. (1991). Preventing alcohol, marijuana, and cigarette use among adolescents: Peer pressure resistance training versus establishing conservative norms. *Preventive Medicine, 20,* 414–430.

Hansen, W. B., Johnson, C. A., Flay, B. R., et al. (1988). Affective and social influences approaches to the prevention of multiple substance abuse among seventh grade students: Results from project SMART. *Preventive Medicine, 17*(2), 135–154.

Hanson, B. (1985). *Life with heroin: Voices from the inner city.* Lanham, MD: Lexington Books.

Hanson, G. R. (2002). *Therapeutic community.* National Institute on Drug Abuse Research Report Series. Rockville, MD: National Institute on Drug Abuse.

Hanson, J. W., Jones, K. L., & Smith, D. W. (1976). Fetal alcohol syndrome. Experience with 41 patients. *Journal of the American Medical Association, 235,* 1458–1460.

Hanson, K. L., & Luciana, M. (2010). Neurocognitive impairments in MDMA and other drug users: MDMA alone may not be a cognitive risk factor. *Journal of Clinical and Experimental Neuropsychology, 32*(4), 337–349.

Harding, W. M., Zinberg, N. E., Stelmack, S. M., et al. (1980). Formerly-addicted-now-controlled opiate users. *The International Journal of the Addictions, 15,* 47–60.

Harmin, M., Kirschenbaum, H., & Simon, S. B. (1973). *Clarifying values through subject matter: Applications for the classroom.* Minneapolis, MN: Winston Press.

Harnack, L. Stang, J., & Story, M. (1999). Soft drink consumption among US children and adolescents: Nutritional consequences. *Journal of the American Dietetic Association, 99,* 436–441.

Harrell, A. V. (1997). The validity of self-reported drug use data: The accuracy of responses on confidential self-administered answered sheets. *NIDA Research Monograph, 167,* 37–58.

Harris, L. H., & Paltrow, L. (2003). The status of pregnant women and fetuses in US criminal law. *JAMA, The Journal of the American Medical Association, 289,* 1697–1699.

Harris, S. R., Osborn, J. A., Weinberg, J., et al. (1993). Effects of prenatal alcohol exposure on neuromotor and cognitive development during early childhood: A series of case reports. *Physical Therapy, 73,* 608–617.

Harrison, L. D., Backenheimer, M., & Inciardi, J. A. (1995). Cannabis use in the United States: Implications for policy (pp. 237–247). In P. Cohen & A. Sas (Eds.), *Cannabisbeleid in Duitsland, Frankrijk en de Verenigde*

*Staten.* Amsterdam, Netherlands: Universiteit van Amsterdam.

Harrison, P. A., Edwall, G. E., Hoffman, N. G., et al. (1990). Correlates of sexual abuse amongst boys in treatment for chemical dependency. *Journal of Adolescent Chemical Dependency, 1*(1), 53–67.

Hart, C. L., Gunderson, E. W., Perez, A., et al. (2008). Acute physiological and behavioral effects of intranasal methamphetamine in humans. *Neuropsychopharmacology, 33*(8), 1847–1855.

Hartley, D. F., Elsabagh, S., & File, S. E. (2004). Binge drinking and sex: Effects on mood and cognitive function in healthy young volunteers. *Pharmacology, Biochemistry and Behavior, 78,* 611–619.

Harvey, A. G. (2001). Insomnia: Symptom or diagnosis. *Clinical Psychology Review, 21*(7), 1037–1059.

Hasin, D. (2003). Classification of alcohol use disorders. *Alcohol Research & Health, 27*(1), 5–17.

Hasin, D. S., Goodwin, R. D., Stinson, F. S., et al. (2005). Epidemiology of major depressive disorder: Results from the National Epidemiologic Survey on Alcoholism and Related Conditions. *Archives of General Psychiatry, 62,* 1097–1106.

Hasin, D. S., Keyes, K. M., Alderson, D., et al. (2008). Cannabis withdrawal in the United States: Results from NESARC. *The Journal of Clinical Psychiatry, 69*(9), 1354–1363.

Hasin, D. S., Stinson, F. S., Ogburn, E., et al. (2007). Prevalence, correlates, disability, and comorbidity of *DSM-IV* alcohol abuse and dependence in the United States: Results from the National Epidemiologic Survey on Alcohol and Related Conditions. *Archives of General Psychiatry, 64*(7), 830–842.

Hatsukami, D. K., Stead, L. F., & Gupta, P. C. (2008). Tobacco addiction. *Lancet, 371*(9629), 2027–2038.

Hauer, P. (2010). Systemic affects of methamphetamine use. *South Dakota Medicine, 63*(8), 285–287.

Havlik, D. M., & Nolte, K. B. (2000). Fatal "crack" cocaine ingestion in an infant. *American Journal of Forensic Medicine and Pathology, 21*(3), 245–248.

Hawkins, E. H. (2009). A tale of two systems: Co-occurring mental health and substance abuse disorders treatment for adolescents. *Annual Review of Psychology, 60,* 197–227.

Hawkins, J. D., Lishner, D. M., Catalano, R. F., et al. (1985). Childhood predictors of adolescent substance abuse: Toward an empirically grounded theory. *Journal of Children in a Contemporary Society, 18,* 11–48.

Haycock, P. C. (2009). Fetal alcohol spectrum disorders: The epigenetic perspective. *Biology of Reproduction, 81*(4), 607–617.

Hays, J. T., Croghan, I. T., Schroeder, D. R., et al. (2010, October 12). Varenicline for tobacco dependence treatment in recovering alcohol-dependent smokers: An open-label pilot study. *Journal of Substance Abuse Treatment, 40*(1), 102–107.

Hays, J. T., & Spickard, W. A., Jr. (1987). Alcoholism: Early diagnosis and intervention. *Journal of General Internal Medicine, 2*(6), 420–427.

Hays, R. D., Merz, J. F., & Nicholas, R. (1995). Response burden, reliability, and validity of the CAGE, Short MAST, and AUDIT alcohol screening measures. *Behavioral Research Methods, Instruments, & Computers, 27*, 277–280.

Head, D. (2001). Alcohol and drugs: A perspective from corrections in the Province of Saskatchewan. *FORUM on Corrections Research, 13*(3), 1–4.

Health Canada. (2010a, March 19). Food and nutrition: Caffeine in food. Retrieved from http://www.hc-sc.gc.ca/fn-an/securit/addut/caf/food-caf-aliments-eng.php

Health Canada. (2010b, June 30). Health concerns: Canadian alcohol and drug use monitoring survey—Summary of results of 2009. Retrieved from http://www.hc-sc.gc.ca/hc-ps/drugs-drogues/stat/_2009/summary-sommaire-eng.php

Health Canada. (2011, February 1). Drugs and health products: Medical use of marijuana. Retrieved from http://www.hc-sc.gc.ca/dhp-mps/marijuana/index-eng.php

Heatherley, S. V., Hancock, K. M., & Rogers, P. J. (2006). Psychostimulant and other effects of caffeine in 9- to 11-year-old children. *Journal of Child Psychology and Psychiatry, 47*(2), 135–142.

Heatherton, T. F., Kozlowski, L. T., Frecker, R. C., et al. (1991). The Fagerström Test for Nicotine Dependence: A revision of the Fagerström Tolerance Questionnaire. *British Journal of Addiction, 86*(9), 1119–1127.

Heavy alcohol use suggests a change in normal cognitive development in adolescents. (2010, October 20). *ScienceDaily*, pp. 1–2. Retrieved from http://www.sciencedaily.com/releases/2010/10/101019162151.htm

Hebb, D. O. (1949). *The organization of behavior.* New York, NY: Wiley.

Heck, K. E., Braveman, P., Cubbin, C., et al. (2006). Socioeconomic status and breastfeeding initiation among California mothers. *Public Health Reports, 121*(1), 51–59.

Hedlund, J. L., & Vieweg, B. W. (1984). The Michigan Alcoholism Screening Test (MAST): A comprehensive review. *Journal of Operational Psychiatry, 15*, 55–64.

Heeschen, C., Weis, M., Aicher, A., et al. (2002). A novel angiogenic pathway mediated by non-neuronal nicotinic acetylcholine receptors. *The Journal of Clinical Investigation, 110*(4), 527–536.

Heffelfinger, A. K., Craft, S., White, D. A., et al. (2002). Visual attention in preschool children prenatally exposed to cocaine: Implications for behavioral regulation. *Journal of the International Neuropsychological Society, 8*, 12–21.

Heffernan, T. M. (2008). The impact of excessive alcohol use on prospective memory: A brief review. *Current Drug Abuse Reviews, 1*(1), 36–41.

Heffernan, T. M., Clark, R., Bartholomew, J., et al. (2010). Does binge drinking in teenagers affect their everyday prospective memory? *Drug and Alcohol Dependence, 109*(1–3), 73–78.

Heidemann, S. M., & Goetting, M. G. (1990). Passive inhalation of cocaine by infants. *Henry Ford Hospital Medical Journal, 38*(4), 252–254.

Heil, S. H., & Subramanian, M. G. (1998). Alcohol and the hormonal control of lactation. *Alcohol Health & Research World, 22*(3), 178–184.

Helmus, T. C., Downey, K. K., Wang, L. M., et al. (2001). The relationship between self-reported cocaine withdrawal symptoms and history of depression. *Addictive Behaviors, 26*(3), 461–467.

Hemmingway, E. (1929). *A farewell to arms.* New York, NY: Charles Scribner's Sons.

Hemminki, K., & Vineis, P. (1985). Extrapolation of the evidence on teratogenicity of chemicals between humans and experimental animals: Chemicals other than drugs. *Teratogenesis, Carcinogenesis, and Mutagenesis, 5*, 251–318.

Hendin, H. (1973a). College students and LSD: Who and why? *The Journal of Nervous and Mental Disease, 156*, 249–258.

Hendin, H. (1973b). Marijuana abuse among college students. *The Journal of Nervous and Mental Disease, 156*, 259–270.

Hendin, H. (1974a). Amphetamine abuse among college students. *The Journal of Nervous and Mental Disease, 158*, 256–267.

Hendin, H. (1974b). Beyond alienation: The end of the psychedelic road. *The American Journal of Drug and Alcohol Abuse, 1*, 11–23.

Hendin, H. (1974c). Students on heroin. *The Journal of Nervous and Mental Disease, 158*, 240–255.

Hendin, H. (1975). *The age of sensation.* New York, NY: Norton.

Hendin, H. (1980). Psychosocial theory of drug abuse: A psychodynamic approach. In D. J. Lettieri, M. Sayer, & H. Wallenstein Pearson (Eds.), *Theories on drug abuse: Selected contemporary perspectives* (NIDA Research Monograph No. 30, pp. 195–200). Rockville, MD: U.S. Department of Health and Human Services, National Institute on Drug Abuse.

Hendin, H., & Haas, A. P. (1985). The adaptive significance of chronic marijuana use for adolescents and adults. *Advances in Alcohol and Substance Abuse, 5*, 99–115.

Hendin, H., Pollinger, A., Ulman, et al. (1981). *Adolescent marijuana abusers and their families* (NIDA Research Monograph No. 40). Rockville, MD: U.S. Department of Health and Human Services, National Institute on Drug Abuse.

Hendrick, B. (2010, December 14). 30 million Americans admit they drive drunk. *WebMD Health News*. Retrieved from http://www.medscape.com/viewarticle/734215_print

Heng, C. K., Badner, V. M., & Schlop, L. A. (2008). Meth mouth. *New York State Dental Journal, 74*(5), 50–51.

Henggeler, S. W., Clingempeel, W. G., Brondino, M. J., et al. (2002). Four-year follow-up of multisystemic therapy with substance-abusing and substance-dependent juvenile offenders. *The Journal of the American Academy of Child and Adolescent Psychiatry, 41*, 868–874.

Henggeler, S. W., Melton, G. B., & Brondino, M. J., et al. (1997). Multisystemic therapy with violent and chronic juvenile offenders and their families: The role of treatment fidelity in successful dissemination. *Journal of Consulting and Clinical Psychology, 65*, 821–833.

Henggeler, S. W., Melton, G. B., & Smith, L. A. (1992). Family preservation using multisystemic therapy: An effective alternative to incarcerating serious juvenile offenders. *Journal of Consulting and Clinical Psychology, 60*, 953–961.

Henggeler, S. W., Pickrel, S. G., & Brondino, M. J. (1999). Multisystemic treatment of substance abusing and dependent delinquents: Outcomes, treatment fidelity, and transportability. *Mental Health Services Research, 1*, 171–184.

Heninger, M., & Hanzlick, R. (2008). Nonnatural deaths of adolescents and teenagers: Fulton county, Georgia, 1985–2004. *The American Journal of Forensic Medicine and Pathology, 29*(3), 208–213.

Henningfield, J. E., Shiffman, S., Ferguson, S. G., et al. (2009). Tobacco dependence and withdrawal: Science base, challenges and opportunities for pharmacotherapy. *Pharmacology and Therapeutics, 123*(1), 1–16.

Henningfield, J. E., & Zeller, M. (2006). Nicotine psychopharmacology research contributions to United States and global tobacco regulation: A look back and a look forward. *Psychopharmacology (Berlin), 184*, 286–291.

Henquet, C., DiForti, M., Morrison, P., et al. (2008). Gene-environment interplay between cannabis and psychosis. *Schizophrenia Bulletin, 34*(6), 1111–1121.

Henquet, C., van Os, J., Kuepper, R., et al. (2010). Psychosis reactivity to cannabis use in daily life: An experience sampling study. *The British Journal of Psychiatry, 196*, 447–453.

Henry-Edwards, S., Humeniuk, R., Ali, R., et al. (2003). *The Alcohol, Smoking and Substance Involvement Screening Test (ASSIST): Guidelines for use in primary care (Draft Version 1.1 for field testing)*. Geneva, Switzerland: World Health Organization.

Herbal remedy: Teens often use cannabis for relief, not recreation, study finds. (2009, April 24). *ScienceDaily*, pp. 1–2. Retrieved from http://www.sciencedaily.com/releases/2009/04/090422191724.htm

Heroin use USA. (2010, January 6). Alcohol-and-drug-guide.com, pp. 1–2. Retrieved from http://www.alcohol-and-drug-guide.com/heroin-use-usa.html

Hersey, J. C., Ng, S. W., Nonnemaker, J. M., et al. (2006). Are menthol cigarettes a starter product for youth? *Nicotine & Tobacco Research, 8*(3), 403–413.

Hersh, J. H. (1989). Toluene embryopathy: Two new cases. *Journal of Medical Genetics, 26*(5), 333–337.

Hersh, J. H., Podruch, P. E., Rogers, G., et al. (1985). Toluene embryopathy. *The Journal of Pediatrics, 106*(6), 922–927.

Hertzman, M., & Bendit, E. A. (1975). Alcoholism and destructive behavior. In A. R. Roberts (Ed.), *Self-destructive behavior* (pp. 164–187). Springfield, IL: Thomas.

Hicks, M., Tough, S. C., Premji, S., et al. (2009). Alcohol and drug screening of newborns: Would women consent? *Journal of Obstetrics & Gynaecology Canada, 31*(4), 331–339.

Hides, L., Cotton, S. M., Berger, G., et al. (2009). The reliability and validity of the Alcohol, Smoking and Substance Involvement Screening Test (ASSIST) in first-episode psychosis. *Addictive Behaviors, 34*(10), 821–825.

Hides, L., Dawe, S., Kavanagh, D. J., et al. (2006). Psychotic symptom and cannabis relapse in recent-onset psychosis. *The British Journal of Psychiatry, 189*, 137–143.

Higdon, J. V., & Frei, B. (2006). Coffee and health: A review of recent human research. *Critical Reviews in Food Science and Nutrition, 46*(2), 101–123.

Higgins, P. G., Clough, D. H., Frank, B., et al. (1995). Changes in health behaviors made by pregnant substances users. *The International Journal of the Addictions, 30*(10), 1323–1333.

Higgins, S. T., & Petry, N. M. (1999). Contingency management. Incentives for sobriety. *Alcohol Research & Health, 23*(2), 122–127.

Hill, H. E. (1962). The social deviant and initial addiction to narcotics and alcohol. *Quarterly Journal of Studies on Alcohol, 23*, 562–582.

Hill, K. P., & Chang, G. (2007). Brief screening instruments for risky drinking in the outpatient psychiatry clinic. *The American Journal on Addictions, 16*(3), 222–226.

Hill, R. M., Hegemier, S., & Tennyson, L. M. (1989). The fetal alcohol syndrome: A multihandicaped child. *Neurotoxicology, 10*, 585–596.

Hindmarch, I., Sherwood, N., & Kerr, J. S. (1993). Amnestic effects of triazolam and other hypnotics. *Progress in Neuro-Psychopharmacology & Biological Psychiatry, 17*, 407–413.

Hingson, R. W., Heeren, T., Winter, M., et al. (2005). Magnitude of alcohol-related mortality and morbidity among U.S. college students ages 18–24: Changes from 1998 to 2001. *Annual Review of Public Health, 26*, 259–279.

Hingson, R. W., Heeren, T., Zakocs, R. C., et al. (2002). Magnitude of alcohol-related mortality and morbidity among U.S. college students ages 18–24. *Journal of Studies on Alcohol, 63*(2), 136–144.

Hingson, R. W., Zha, W., & Weitzman, E. R. (2009, July). Magnitude of and trends in alcohol-related mortality and morbidity among U.S. college students ages 18–24, 1998–2005. *Journal of Studies on Alcohol and Drugs* (Suppl. 16), 12–20.

Hirschfeld, R. M. (1996). Panic disorder: Diagnosis, epidemiology, and clinical course. *The Journal of Clinical Psychiatry, 57*(Suppl. 10), 3–8.

Hirschman, E. C. (1992). Cocaine as innovation: A social-symbolic account. *Advances in Consumer Research, 19*, 129–139.

Hochhauser, M. (1978a). Adolescent drug abuse and the development of behavior. *International Journal of Addictions, 13*(6), 1013–1019.

Hochhauser, M. (1978b). Chonobiological factors in drug abuse. In A. J. Schecter (Ed.), *Drug dependence and alcoholism: Vol. 2. Social and behavioral issues* (pp. 855–864). New York, NY: Plenum Press.

Hochhauser, M. (1978c). Drugs as agents of control. *Journal of Psychedelic Drugs, 10*(1), 65–69.

Hochhauser, M. (1980). A chronobiological control theory. In D. J. Lettieri, M. Sayer, & H. Wallenstein Pearson (Eds.), *Theories on drug abuse: Selected contemporary perspectives* (NIDA Research Monograph No. 30, pp. 262–268). Rockville, MD: U.S. Department of Health and Human Services, National Institute on Drug Abuse.

Hodgson, R. J., John, B., Abbasi, T., et al. (2003). Fast screening for alcohol misuse. *Addictive Behaviors, 28*(8), 1453–1463.

Hofhuis, W., de Jongste, J. C., & Merkus, P. J. (2003). Adverse health effects of prenatal and postnatal tobacco smoke exposure on children. *Archives of Disease in Childhood, 88*, 1086–1090.

Hofmann, A. (1970). Notes and documents concerning the discovery of LSD. *Agents and Actions, 1*(3), 148–150.

Hofmann, A. (1979). How LSD originated. *Journal of Psychedelic Drugs, 11*(1–2), 53–60.

Hofmann, A. (1980). *LSD—My problem child.* New York, NY: McGraw-Hill.

Hogervorst, E., Bandelow, S., Schmitt, J., et al. (2008). Caffeine improves physical and cognitive performance during exhaustive exercise. *Medicine & Science in Sports & Exercise, 40*(10), 1841–1851.

Hollister, L. E. (1986). Health aspects of cannabis. *Pharmacological Reviews, 38*, 1–20.

Hong, R., Matsuyama, E., & Nur, K. (1991). Cardiomyopathy associated with the smoking of crystal methamphetamine. *JAMA, The Journal of the American Medical Association, 265*(9), 1152–1154.

Hope, J. (2008, May 23). Cocaine overdose hospital admissions rise 400 per cent in just four years. *Mail Online*, pp. 1–4. Retrieved from http://www.dailymail.co.uk/news/article-1021485/Cocaine-overdose-hospital-admissions-rise-400-cent-j...

Hopfer, C., Mendelson, B., Van Leeuwen, J. M., et al. (2006). Club drug use among youths in treatment for substance abuse. *The American Journal on Addictions, 15*(1), 94–99.

Hopkins, R. B., Paradis, J., Roshankar, T., et al. (2008). Universal or targeted screening for fetal alcohol exposure: A cost-effectiveness analysis. *Journal of Studies on Alcohol and Drugs, 69*(4), 510–519.

Horne, R. S., Ferens, D., Watts, A. M., et al. (2002). Effects of maternal tobacco smoking, sleeping position, and sleep state on arousal in healthy term infants. *Archives of Disease in Childhood–Fetal and Neonatal Edition, 87*(2), F100–F105.

Hornik, R., & Jacobsohn, L. (2008, December–2009, January). The best laid plans: Disappointments of the National Youth Anti-Drug Media Campaign. *Leonard Davis Institute Issue Brief, 14*(2), 1–4.

Horowitz, A., Galanter, M., Dermatis, H., et al. (2008). Use of and attitudes toward club drugs by medical students. *Journal of Addictive Diseases, 27*(4), 35–42.

Hoshi, R., Mullins, K., Boundy, C., et al. (2007). Neurocognitive function in current and ex-users of ecstasy in comparison to both matched polydrug-using controls and drug-naïve controls. *Psychopharmacology (Berlin), 194*(3), 371–379.

Houston, J. E., Murphy, J., Adamson, G., et al. (2007). Childhood sexual abuse, early cannabis use, and psychosis: Testing an interaction model based on the National Comorbidity Survey. *Schizophrenia Bulletin, 34*(3), 580–585.

Howlett, A. C., Breivogel, C. S., Childers, S. R., et al. (2004). Cannabinoid physiology and pharmacology: 30 years of progress. *Neuropharmacology, 47*, 345–358.

Howard, M. O., Balster, R. L., Cottler, L. B., et al. (2008). Inhalant use among incarcerated adolescents in the United States: Prevalence, characteristics, and correlates of use. *Drug and Alcohol Dependence, 93*(3), 197–209.

Howard, M. O., & Perron, B. E. (2009). A survey of inhalant use disorders among delinquent youth: Prevalence, clinical features, and latent structure of *DSM-IV* diagnostic criteria. *BioMed Central Psychiatry, 9*, 8.

Hoyme, H. E. (1990). Teratogenically induced fetal anomalies. *Clinics in Perinatology, 17*(3), 547–567.

Hoyme, H. E., May, P. A., Kalberg, W. O., et al. (2005). A practical clinical approach to diagnosis of fetal alcohol spectrum disorders: Clarification of the 1996 institute of medicine criteria. *Pediatrics, 115*(1), 39–47.

Hser, Y. I. (1997). Self-reported drug use: Result of selected empirical investigations of validity. *NIDA Research Monograph, 167*, 320–343.

Hu, G., & Baker, S. P. (2008). Reducing black/white disparity: Changes in injury mortality in the 15–24 year age group, United States, 1999–2005. *Injury Prevention, 14*(3), 205–208.

Hu, X. T. (2007). Cocaine withdrawal and neuro-adaptations in ion channel function. *Molecular Neurobiology, 35*(1), 95–112.

Huang, C. L., Lin, H. H., & Wang, H. H. (2006). Psychometric evaluation of the Chinese version of the Fagerstrom Tolerance Questionnaire as a measure of cigarette dependence. *Journal of Advanced Nursing, 55*(5), 596–603.

Huang, C. L., Lin, H. H., & Wang, H. H. (2006). The psychometric properties of the Chinese version of the Fagerstrom Test for Nicotine Dependnece. *Addictive Behaviors, 31*(12), 2324–2327.

Huang, L. N., Freed, R., & Espiritu, R. C. (2006). Co-occurring disorders of adolescent in primary care: Closing the gaps. *Adolescent Medicine Clinics, 17*(2), 453–467.

Huba, G. J., & Bentler, P. M. (1979). Phencyclidine use in high school: Tests of models. *Journal of Drug Education, 9*, 285–291.

Huba, G. J., & Bentler, P. M. (1980). The role of peer and adult models for drug taking at different stages in adolescence. *Journal of Youth and Adolescence, 9,* 465–499.

Huba, G. J., Wingard, J. A., & Bentler, P. M. (1979a). Adolescent drug use and intentions to use drugs in the future: A concurrent analysis. *Journal of Drug Education, 9*(2), 145–151.

Huba, G. J., Wingard, J. A., & Bentler, P. M. (1979b). Beginning adolescent drug use and peer and adult interaction patterns. *Journal of Consulting and Clinical Psychology, 47*(2), 265–276.

Huba, G. J., Wingard, J. A., & Bentler, P. M. (1980a). Application of a theory of drug use to prevention programs. *Journal of Drug Education, 10*(1), 25–38.

Huba, G. J., Wingard, J. A., & Bentler, P. M. (1980b). Framework for an interactive theory of drug use. In D. J. Lettieri, M. Sayer, & H. Wallenstein Pearson (Eds.), *Theories on drug abuse: Selected contemporary perspectives* (NIDA Research Monograph No. 30, pp. 95–101). Rockville, MD: U.S. Department of Health and Human Services, National Institute on Drug Abuse.

Huba, G. J., Wingard, J. A., & Bentler, P. M. (1980c). Longitudinal analysis of the role of peer support, adult models, and peer subcultures in beginning adolescent substance use: An application of setwise canonical correlation methods. *Multivariate Behavioral Research, 15,* 259–279.

Huba, G. J., Wingard, J. A., & Bentler, P. M. (1981a). A comparison of two latent variable causal models of adolescent drug use. *Journal of Personality and Social Psychology, 40*(1), 180–193.

Huba, G. J., Wingard, J. A., & Bentler, P. M. (1981b). Intentions to use drugs among adolescents: A longitudinal analysis. *The International Journal of the Addictions, 16,* 331–339.

Hudman, K. S., Corelli, R. L., & Prokhorov, A. V. (2010). Current approaches to pharmacotherapy for smoking cessation. *Therapeutic Advances in Respiratory Disease, 4*(1), 35–47.

Huey, S. J., Jr., & Polo, A. J. (2008). Evidence-based psychosocial treatments for ethnic minority youth. *Journal of Clinical Child & Adolescent Psychology, 37*(1), 262–301.

Hughes, T. L. (2003). Lesbians' drinking patterns: Beyond the data. *Substance Use & Misuse, 38*(11–13), 1739–1758.

Hughes, T. L. (2005). Alcohol use and alcohol-related problems among lesbians and gay men. *Annual Review of Nursing Research, 23,* 283–325.

Hughes, T. L., & Wilsnack, S.C. (1997). Use of alcohol among lesbians: Research and clinical implications. *American Journal of Orthopsychiatry, 67*(1), 20–36.

Huizinga, D., & Elliott, D. S. (1981). *A longitudinal study of drug use and delinquency in a national sample of youth: An assessment of causal order* (Project Report No. 16, National Youth Survey). Boulder, CO: University of Colorado, Behavioral Research Institute.

Hull, J. G. (1981). A self-awareness model of the causes and effects of alcohol consumption. *Journal of Abnormal Psychology, 90*(6), 586–600.

Hull, J. G., Levenson, R. W., Young, R. D., et al. (1983). Self-awareness-reducing effects of alcohol consumption. *Journal of Personality and Social Psychology, 44*(3), 461–473.

Hull, J. G., & Levy, A. S. (1979). The organizational functions of the self: An alternative to the Duval and Wicklund model of self-awareness. *Journal of Personality and Social Psychology, 37*(5), 756–768.

Hull, J. G., & Young, R. D. (1983a). The self-awareness-reducing effects of alcohol: Evidence and implications. In J. Suls & A. G. Greenwald (Eds.), *Psychological perspectives on the self* (Vol. 2, pp. 159–190). Hillsdale, NJ: Erlbaum.

Hull, J. G., & Young, R. D. (1983b). Self-consciousness, self-esteem, and success-failure as determinants of alcohol consumption in male social drinkers. *Journal of Personality and Social Psychology, 44,* 1097–1109.

Hume, R. F., Gingras, J. L., Martin, L. S., et al. (1994). Ultrasound diagnosis of fetal anomalies associated with in utero cocaine exposure: Further support for cocaine-induced vascular disruption teratogenesis. *Fetal Diagnosis and Therapy, 9,* 239–245.

Humeniuk, R., & Ali, R. (2006). Validation of the Alcohol, Smoking and Substance Involvement Screening Test (ASSIST) and Pilot Brief Intervention: A technical report of Phase II findings of the WHO ASSIST Project. Geneva, Switzerland: World Health Organization.

Humeniuk, R., Ali, R., Babor, T. F., et al. (2008). Validation of the Alcohol, Smoking and Substance Involvement Screening Test (ASSIST). *Addiction, 103*(6), 1039–1047.

Humeniuk, R., Dennington, V., & Ali, R. (2008). *The effectiveness of a brief intervention for illicit drugs linked to the Alcohol, Smoking and Substance Involvement Screening Test (ASSIST) in primary health care settings: A technical report of Phase III findings of the WHO Assist Randomized Controlled Trial.* Geneva, Switzerland: World Health Organization.

Hurt, C. B., Torrone, E., Green, K., et al. (2010). Methamphetamine use among newly diagnosed HIV-positive young men in North Carolina, United States, from 2000 to 2005. *Public Library of Science One, 5*(6), e11314. Retrieved from http://www.ncbi.nlm.nih.gov/pubmed/20593025

Hussey, J. M., Chang, J. J., & Kotch, K. B. (2006). Child maltreatment in the United States: Prevalence, risk factors, and adolescent health consequences. *Pediatrics, 118*(3), 933–942.

Hutchings, D. E. (1993). The puzzle of cocaine's effects following maternal use during pregnancy: Are there reconcilable differences? *Neurotoxicology and Teratology, 15,* 281–286.

Huxley, A. (1960). *The doors of perception: Heaven & hell.* London, UK: Chatto & Windus.

Hyde, R.F., Paxton, R., Carr, T.E., et al. (1982). Nicotine chewing-gum. *British Medical Journal* (Clinical Research Edition), *285*(6344), 811–812.

Hyde, Z., Comfort, J., McManus, A., et al. (2009, September). Alcohol, tobacco and illicit drug use amongst same-sex attracted women: Results from the Western Australian Lesbian and Bisexual Women's Health and Well-Being Survey. *BioMed Central Public Health, 9*, 317.

Hyland, A., Garten, S., Giovino, G. A., et al. (2002). Mentholated cigarettes and smoking cessation: Findings from COMMIT (Community Intervention Trial for Smoking Cessation). *Tobacco Control, 11*(2), 135–139.

Hyman, S. E. (2005). Addiction: A disease of learning and memory. *The American Journal of Psychiatry, 162*(8), 1414–1422.

## I

Iannucci, R., Sanders, K., & Greenfield, S. F. (2009). A 4-year curriculum on substance use disorders for psychiatry residents. *Academic Psychiatry, 33*(1), 60–66.

Ikonomidou, C., Bittigau, P., Koch, C., et al. (2001). Neurotransmitters and apoptosis in the developing brain. *Biochemical Pharmacology, 62*(4), 401–405.

Ilett, K. F., Hale, T. W., Page-Sharp, M., et al. (2003). Use of nicotine patches in breast-feeding mothers: Transfer of nicotine and cotinine into human milk. *Clinical Pharmacology and Therapeutics, 74*, 516–524.

Ilett, K. F., Paech, M. J., Page-Sharp, M., et al. (2008). Use of a sparse sampling study design to assess transfer of tramadol and its O-desmethyl metabolite into transitional breast milk. *British Journal of Clinical Pharmacology, 65*(5), 661–666.

Impact on lungs of one cannabis joint equal to up to five cigarettes. (2007, August 2). *ScienceDaily*, pp. 1–2. Retrieved from http://www.sciencedaily.com/releases/2007/07/070731085550.htm

Indlekofer, F., Piechatzek, M., Daamen, M., et al. (2009). Reduced memory and attention performance in a population-based sample of young adults with a moderate lifetime of cannabis, ecstasy and alcohol. *Journal of Psychopharmacology, 23*(5), 495–509.

Infante-Rivard, C., Fernandez, A., Gauthier, R., et al. (1993). Fetal loss associated with caffeine intake before and during pregnancy. *JAMA, The Journal of the American Medical Association, 270*, 2940–2943.

Ingram, R. E., & Holle, C. (1992). Cognitive science of depression. In D. J. Stein & J. E. Young (Eds.), *Cognitive science and clinical disorders* (pp. 187–209). New York, NY: Harcourt Brace Jovanovich.

Intelligence brief: Huffing—The abuse of inhalants. (2001, November). Retrieved from http://www.usdoj.gov/ndic/pubs/708/708t.htm

Involvement by young drivers in fatal alcohol-related motor-vehicle crashes—United States, 1982–2001. (2002, December 6). *Morbidity and Mortality Weekly Report, Surveillance Summaries, 51*(48), 1089–1091.

Irwin, K. L., Edlin, B. R., Wong, L., et al. (1995). Urban rape survivors: Characteristics and prevalence of human immunodeficiency virus and other sexually transmitted infections. *Obstetrics & Gynecology, 85*, 330–336.

Isaacson, J. H., Butler, R., Zacharek, M., et al. (1994). Screening with the Alcohol Use Disorders Identification Test (AUDIT) in an inner city population. *Journal of General Internal Medicine, 9*, 550–553.

Ivanenko, A., & Gururaj, B. R. (2009). Classification and epidemiology of sleep disorders. *Child and Adolescent Psychiatric Clinics of North America, 18*(4), 839–848.

Izquierdo, I., & Medina, J. H. (1991). GAGAA receptor modulation of memory: The role of endogenous benzodiazepines. *Trends in Pharmacological Sciences, 12*(7), 260–265.

## J

Jackowski, C., Römhild, W., Aebi, B., et al. (2005). Autoerotic accident by inhalation of propane-butane gas mixture. *American Journal of Forensic Medicine and Pathology, 26*(4), 355–359.

Jacob, M. S., Carlen, P. L., Marshman, J. A., et al. (1981). Phencyclidine ingestion: Drug abuse and psychosis. *The International Journal of the Addictions, 16*(4), 749–758.

Jacobson, M. F., Goldman, A. S., & Syme, R. H. (1981). Coffee and birth defects. *Lancet, 1*, 1415–1416.

Jacqz-Aigrain, E., Serreau, R., Boissinot, C., et al. (2007). Excretion of ketoprofen and nalbuphine in human milk during treatment of maternal pain after delivery. *Drug Monitor, 29*, 815–818.

Jainchill, N. (1997). Therapeutic communities for adolescents: The same and not the same. In G. De Leon (Ed.), *Community as method: Therapeutic communities for special populations and special settings* (pp. 162–178). Westport, CT: Praeger.

Jainchill, N., Hawke, J., De Leon, G., et al. (2000). Adolescents in therapeutic communities: One-year posttreatment outcomes. *Journal of Psychoactive Drugs, 32*(1), 81–94.

Jainchill, N., Hawke, J., & Messina, M. (2005). Post-treatment outcomes among adjudicated adolescent males and females in modified therapeutic community treatment. *Substance Use & Misuse, 40*(7), 975–996.

Jansson, L. M., Choo, R. E., Harrow, C., et al. (2007). Concentrations of methadone in breast milk and plasma in the immediate perinatal period. *Journal of Human Lactation, 23*, 184–190.

Jansson, L. M., Dipietro, J. & Elko, A. (2005). Fetal response to maternal methadone administration. *American Journal of Obstetrics & Gynecology, 193*(3, pt. 1), 611–617.

Jansson, L. M., Velez, M. Harrow, C. (2004). Methadone maintenance and lactation: A review of the literature and current management guidelines. *Journal of Human Lactation, 20*(1), 62–71.

Jaszyna-Gasior, M., Schroeder, J. R., Thorner, E. D., et al. (2009). Age at menarche and weight concerns in relation to smoking trajectory and dependence among adolescent girls enrolled in a smoking cessation trial. *Addictive Behaviors, 34*(1), 92–95.

Jessor, R. (1985). Bridging etiology and prevention in drug abuse research. In C. LaRue Jones & R. J. Battjes (Eds.), *Etiology of drug abuse: Implications for prevention* (NIDA Research Monograph No. 56, A RAUS Review Report, pp. 257–268). Rockville, MD: U.S. Department of Health and Human Services, National Institute on Drug Abuse.

Jessor, R., Carman, R., & Grossman, P. H. (1968). Expectations of need satisfaction and drinking patterns of college students. *Quarterly Journal of Studies on Alcohol, 29*, 101–116.

Jessor, R., Collins, M. I., & Jessor, S. L. (1972). On becoming a drinker: Social-psychological aspects of an adolescent transition. In F. A. Seixas (Ed.), *Nature and nurture in alcoholism* (pp. 199–213). New York, NY: Academy of Sciences.

Jessor, R., Graves, T. D., Hanson, R. C., et al. (1968). *Society, personality and deviant behavior: A study of a tri-ethnic community.* New York, NY: Holt, Rinehart and Winston.

Jessor, R., & Jessor, S. L. (1973). A social psychology of marijuana use. *Journal of Personality and Social Psychology, 26*, 1–15.

Jessor, R., & Jessor, S. L. (1975). Adolescent development and onset of drinking: A longitudinal study. *Journal of Studies on Alcohol, 36*(1), 27–51.

Jessor, R., & Jessor, S. L. (1977a). A multivariate appraisal of problem-behavior theory. In R. Jessor & S. Jessor (Eds.), *Problem behavior and psychosocial development: A longitudinal study of youth* (pp. 127–142). New York, NY: Academic Press.

Jessor, R., & Jessor, S. L. (1977b). *Problem behavior and psychosocial development: A longitudinal study of youth.* New York, NY: Academic Press.

Jessor, R., & Jessor, S. L. (1978). *Theory testing in longitudinal research on marijuana use.* In D. B. Kandel (Ed.), Longitudinal research on drug use (pp. 41–71). New York, NY: Wiley.

Jeynes, W. H. (2002). The relationship between the consumption of various drugs by adolescents and their academic achievement. *The American Journal of Drug and Alcohol Abuse, 28*(1), 15–35.

Jo, Y. H., Talmage, D. A., & Role, L. W. (2002). Nicotinic receptor-mediated effects on appetite and food intake. *Journal of Neurobiology, 53*(4), 618–632.

Joanning, H., Thomas, F., Newfield, N., et al. (1991). Organizing a coordinated family treatment model for the inpatient and outpatient treatment of adolescent drug abuse. *Journal of Family Psychotherapy, 1*, 29–47.

Johansen, A. M., Wilcox, A. J., Lie, R. T., et al. (2009). Maternal consumption of coffee and caffeine-containing beverages and oral clefts: A population-based case-control study in Norway. *American Journal of Epidemiology, 169*(10), 1216–1222.

Johns, A. (2001). Psychiatric effects of cannabis. *The British Journal of Psychiatry, 178*, 116–122.

Johnson, N. (2001). Tobacco use and oral cancer: A global perspective. *Journal of Dental Education, 65*(4), 328–339.

Johnson, A. L., Morrow, C. E., Accornero, V. H., et al. (2002). Maternal cocaine use: Estimated effects on mother-child play interactions in the preschool period. *Journal of Developmental and Behavioral Pediatrics, 23*(4), 191–202.

Johnson, B. A., & Ait-Daoud, N. (2010). Topiramate in the new generation of drugs: Efficacy in the treatment of alcoholic patients. *Current Pharmaceutical Design, 16*(19), 2103–2112.

Johnson, B. A., Ait-Daoud, N., Bowden, C. L., et al. (2003). Oral topiramate for treatment of alcohol dependence: A randomized controlled trial. *Lancet, 361*(9370), 1677–1685.

Johnson, B. A., Rosenthal, N., Capece, J. A., et al. (2007). Topiramate for treating alcohol dependence: A randomized controlled trial. *JAMA, The Journal of the American Medical Association, 298*(14), 1641–1651.

Johnson, B. D. (1973). *Marijuana users and drug subcultures.* New York, NY: Wiley.

Johnson, B. D. (1980). Toward a theory of drug subcultures. In D. J. Lettieri, M. Sayer, & H. Wallenstein Pearson (Eds.), *Theories on drug abuse: Selected contemporary perspectives* (NIDA Research Monograph No. 30, pp. 110–119). Rockville, MD: U.S. Department of Health and Human Services, National Institute on Drug Abuse.

Johnson, D. (2011). Cigarette warning labels to be introduced. *Long Island Press*, pp. 1-6. Retrieved from http://www.longislandpress.com/2011/06/21/cigarette-warning-labels-to-be-introduced/

Johnson, E., & Herringer, L. G. (1993). A note on the utilization of common support activities and relapse following substance abuse treatment. *The Journal of Psychology, 127*, 73–77.

Johnson, E. M., McColgan, B. R., & Denniston, R. W. (1991). *Preventing HIV infection among youth* (DHHS Publication No. ADM 91–1774). Rockville, MD: U.S. Department of Health and Human Services.

Johnson, E. O. (2006). Epidemiology of insomnia: From adolescence to old age. *Sleep Medicine Clinics, 1*(3), 305–317.

Johnson, E. O., Roth, T., & Breslau, N. (2006). The association of insomnia with anxiety disorders and depression: Exploration of the direction of risk. *Journal of Psychiatric Research, 40*(8), 700–708.

Johnson, E. O., Roth, T., Schultz, L., et al. (2006). Epidemiology of *DSM-IV* insomnia in adolescence: Lifetime prevalence, chronicity, and an emergent gender difference. *Pediatrics, 117*(2), e247–e256.

Johnson, K. W., Shamblen, S. R., Ogilvie, K. A., et al. (2009). Preventing youths' use of inhalants and other harmful legal products in frontier Alaskan communities: A randomized trial. *Prevention Science, 10*(4), 298–312.Johnson, N. (2001). Tobacco use and oral cancer: A global perspective. *Journal of Dental Education, 65*(4), 328–339.

Johnson, T. P., Aschkenasy, J. R., Herbers, M. R., et al. (1996). Self-reported risk factors for AIDS among homeless youth. *AIDS Education and Prevention, 8*(4), 308–322.

Johnston, L. D., O'Malley, P. M., Bachman, J. G., et al. (2008). *Monitoring the Future national results on adolescent drug use. Overview of key findings, 2007.* Bethesda, MD: National Institute on Drug Abuse.

Johnston, L. D., O'Malley, P. M, Bachman, J. G., et al. (2010a). *Monitoring the Future national results on adolescent drug use: Overview of key findings, 2009.* Bethesda, MD: National Institute on Drug Abuse.

Johnston, L. D., O'Malley, P. M., Bachman, J. G., et al. (2010b, December 14). Marijuana use is rising; ecstasy use is beginning to rise; and alcohol use is declining among U.S. teens. Ann Arbor, MI: Michigan News Service. Retrieved from http://www.monitoringthefuture.org

Johnston, P., Rhodes, W., & Carrigan, K. (2000, December). *Estimation of heroin availability 1995–1998.* Washington, DC: Office of National Drug Control Policy.

Jones, H. E., Kaltenbach, K., Heil, S. H., et al. (2010). Neonatal abstinence syndrome after methadone or buprenorphine exposure. *The New England Journal of Medicine, 363,* 2320–2331.

Jones, K. L. (1991). Developmental pathogenesis of defects associated with prenatal cocaine exposure: Fetal vascular disruption. *Clinics in Perinatology, 18,* 139–146.

Jones, K. L., & Smith, D. W. (1973). Recognition of the fetal alcohol syndrome in early infancy. *Lancet, 2,* 999–1001.

Jones, K. L., & Smith, D. W. (1975). The fetal alcohol syndrome. *Teratology, 12*(1), 1–10.

Jorenby, D. E., Hays, J. T., Rigotti, N. A., et al. (2006). Efficacy of varenicline, an alpha4beta2 nicotinic acetylcholine receptor partial agonist, vs. placebo or sustained-release bupropion for smoking cessation: A randomized controlled trial. *JAMA, The Journal of the American Medical Association, 296*(1), 56–63.

Jorgensen, K. M. (1992). The drug-exposed infant. *Critical Care Nursing Clinics of North America, 4,* 481–485.

Juliano, L. M., & Griffiths, R. R. (2004). A critical review of caffeine withdrawal: Empirical validation of symptoms and signs, incidence, severity, and associated features. *Psychopharmacology (Berlin), 176*(1), 1–29.

Jung, Y. C., & Namkoong, K. (2006). Pharmacotherapy for alcohol dependence: Anticraving medications for relapse prevention. *Yonsei Medical Journal, 47*(2), 167–178.

**K**

Kadden, R. M. (1994). Cognitive-behviporal approaches to alcoholism treatment. *Alcohol Health & Research World, 18,* 279–286.

Kaemingk, K. L., Mulvaney, S., & Halverson, P. T. (2003). Learning following prenatal alcohol exposure: Performance on verbal and visual multitrial tasks. *Archives of Clinical Neuropsychology, 18*(1), 33–47.

Kaestle, C. E. (2009). How girls and boys get tobacco: Adults and other sources. *Journal of Adolescent Health, 45*(2), 208–210.

Kahn, A., Sawaguchi, T., Sawguchi, A., et al. (2002). Sudden infant death: From epidemiology to physiology. *Forensic Science International, 130*(Suppl.), S8–S20.

Kalant, H. (2004). Adverse effects of cannabis on health: An update of the literature since 1996. *Progress in Neuro-psychopharmacology & Biological Psychiatry, 28*(5), 849–863.

Kaliski, E. M., Rubinson, L., Lawrence, L., et al. (1990). AIDS, runaways, and self-efficacy. *Family & Community Health, 12,* 60–67, 71.

Kam, P. C., & Yoong, F. F. (1998). Gamma-hydroxybutyric acid: An emerging recreational drug. *Anaesthesia, 53*(12), 1195–1198.

Kaminer, Y. (2002). Adolescent substance abuse treatment: Evidence-based practice in outpatient services. *Current Psychiatry Reports, 4*(5), 397–401.

Kaminer, Y. (2010). Problematic use of energy drinks by adolescents. *Child & Adolescent Psychiatric Clinics of North America, 19*(3), 643–650.

Kaminer, Y., & Frances, R. J. (1991). Inpatient treatment of adolescents with psychiatric and substance abuse disorders. *Hospital & Community Psychiatry, 42,* 894–896.

Kaminer, Y., Goldberg, P., & Connor, D. F. (2010). Psychotropic medications and substances of abuse interactions in youth. *Substance Abuse, 31*(1), 53–57.

Kandel, D. (1975). Stages in adolescent involvement in drug use. *Science, 190,* 912–914.

Kandel, D., Schaffran, C., Griesler, P., et al. (2005). On the measurement of nicotine dependence in adolescence: Comparisons of the mFTQ and a *DSM-IV*-based scale. *Journal of Pediatric Psychology, 30*(4), 319–332.

Kandel, D. B. (1980a). Developmental stages in adolescent drug development. In D. J. Lettieri, M. Sayer, & H. Wallenstein Pearson (Eds.), *Theories on drug abuse: Selected contemporary perspectives* (NIDA Research Monograph No. 30, pp. 120–127). Rockville, MD: U.S. Department of Health and Human Services, National Institute on Drug Abuse.

Kandel, D. B. (1980b). Drug and drinking behavior among youth. *Annual Review of Sociology, 6,* 235–285.

Kandel, D. B. (1986). Process of peer influences in adolescence. In R. K. Silberiesen, K. Eyferth, & G. Rudinger (Eds.), *Development as action in context: Problem behavior and normal youth development* (pp. 203–227). Berlin, Germany: Springer.

Kandel, D. B., & Andrews, K. (1987). Processes of adolescent socialization by parents and peers. *The International Journal of the Addictions, 22*, 319–342.

Kandel, D. B., Davies, M., Karus, D., et al. (1986). The consequences in young adulthood of adolescent drug involvement. An overview. *Archives of General Psychiatry, 43*(8), 746–754.

Kandel, D. B., & Faust, R. (1975). Sequence and stages in patterns of adolescent drug use. *Archives of General Psychiatry, 32*, 923–932.

Kandel, D. B., Kessler, R. C., & Margulies, R. Z. (1978a). Antecedents of adolescent initiation into stages of drug use: A developmental analysis. *Journal of Youth and Adolescence, 7*(1), 13–40.

Kandel, D. B., Kessler, R. C., & Margulies, R. Z. (1978b). Antecedents of adolescent initiation into stages of drug use: A developmental analysis. In D. B. Kandel (Ed.), *Longitudinal research on drug use: Empirical findings and methodological issues* (pp. 73–99). New York, NY: Wiley.

Kandel, D. B., Treiman, D., Faust, R., et al. (1976). Adolescent involvement in legal and illegal drug use: A multiple classification analysis. *Social Forces, 55*(2), 439–458.

Kandel, D. B., Wu, P., & Davies, M. (1994). Maternal smoking during pregnancy and smoking by adolescent daughters. *American Journal of Public Health, 84*(9), 1407–1413.

Kandel, D. B., Yamaguchi, K., & Chen, K. (1992). Stages of progression in drug involvement from adolescence to adulthood: Further evidence for the gateway theory. *Journal of Studies on Alcohol, 53*(5), 447–457.

Kandel, D. B., Yamaguchi, K., & Klein, L. C. (2006). Testing the gateway hypothesis. *Addiction, 101*(4), 474–476.

Kaplan, H. B. (1975a). Increase in self-rejection as an antecedent of deviant responses. *Journal of Youth and Adolescence, 4*, 438–458.

Kaplan, H. B. (1975b). *Self-attitudes and deviant behavior.* Pacific Palisades, CA: Goodyear.

Kaplan, H. B. (1980a). *Deviant behavior in defense of self.* New York, NY: Academic Press.

Kaplan, H. B. (1980b). Self-esteem and self-derogation theory of drug abuse. In D. J. Lettieri, M. Sayer, & H. Wallenstein Pearson (Eds.), *Theories on drug abuse: Selected contemporary perspectives* (NIDA Research Monograph No. 30, pp. 128–131). Rockville, MD: U.S. Department of Health and Human Services, National Institute on Drug Abuse.

Kaplan, H. B., Martin, S. S., & Robbins, C. (1984). Pathways to adolescent drug use: Self-derogation, peer influence, weakening of social controls, and early substance use. *Journal of Health and Social Behavior, 25*, 270–289.

Kapur, R. P., Cheng, M. S., & Shephard, T. H. (1991). Brain hemorrhages in cocaine-exposed human fetuses. *Teratology, 44*, 11–18.

Karavokiros, K. A., & Tsipis, G. B. (1990). Flumazenil: A benzodiazepine antagonist. *Drug Intelligence and Clinical Pharmacy, Annals of Pharmacotherapy, 24*, 976–981.

Karch, D. L., Dahlberg, L. L., & Patel, N. (2010, May 14). Surveillance for violent deaths – National Violent Death Reporting System, 16 states, 2007. *Morbidity and Mortality Weekly Report, Surveillance Summaries, 59*(4), 1–50.

Karch, S. B. (2005). Cocaine cardiovascular toxicity. *Southern Medical Journal, 98*(8), 794–799.

Karp, R. J., Qazi, Q., Hittleman, J., et al. (1993). Fetal alcohol syndrome. In R. J. Karp (Ed.), *Malnourished children in the United States: Caught in the cycle of poverty* (pp. 101–108). New York, NY: Springer.

Kaufman, E. (1990). Adolescent substance abusers and family therapy. In A. S. Friedman & S. Granick (Eds.), *Family therapy for adolescent drug abuse* (pp. 47–61). New York, NY: Lexington.

Kaufman, K. R., Petrucha, R. A., Pitts, F. N., et al. (1983). PCP in amniotic fluid and breast milk: Case report. *The Journal of Clinical Psychiatry, 44*(7), 269–270.

Kawashima, K., & Fujii, T. (2003). The lymphocytic cholinergic system and its biological function. *Life Sciences, 72*(18–19), 2101–2109.

Kaye, S., McKetin, R., Duflou, J., et al. (2007). Methamphetamine and cardiovascular pathology: A review of the evidence. *Addiction, 102*(8), 1204–1211.

Keegan, J. Parva, M., Finnegan, M., et al. (2010). Addiction in pregnancy. *Journal of Addictive Diseases, 29*(2), 175–191.

Keiger, C. J., Case, L. D., Kendal-Reed, M., et al. (2003). Nicotinic cholinergic receptor expression in the human nasal mucosa. *Annals of Otology, Rhinology, and Laryngology, 112*(1), 77–84.

Keisler, B. D., Armsey, T. D. (2006). Caffeine as an ergogenic aid. *Current Sports Medicine Reports, 5*(4), 215–219.

Kelder, S. H., Prokhorov, A., Barroso, C. S., et al. (2003). Smoking differences among African American, Hispanic, and White middle school students in an urban setting. *Addictive Behaviors, 28*(3), 513–522.

Kelemen, W. L., & Fulton, E. K. (2008). Cigarette abstinence impairs memory and metacognition despite administration of 2 mg nicotine gum. *Experimental and Clinical Psychopharmacology, 16*(6), 521–531.

Kellar, K. J., Davila-Garcia, M. I., & Xiao, Y. (1999). Pharmacology of neuronal nicotinic acetylcholine receptors: Effects of acute and chronic nicotine. *Nicotine & Tobacco Research, 1*(Suppl. 2), 117–120.

Keller, M. B., Lavori, P. W., Beardslee, W., et al. (1992). Clinical course and outcome of substance abuse disorders in adolescents. *Journal of Substance Abuse Treatment, 9*, 9–14.

Kelly, B. C., & Parsons, J. T. (2008). Predictors and comparisons of polydrug and non-polydrug cocaine use in club subcultures. *The American Journal of Drug and Alcohol Abuse, 34*(6), 774–781.

Kelly, B. C., Parsons, J. T., & Wells, B. E. (2006). Patterns and prevalence of club drug use among club-going young adults. *Journal of Urban Health, 83*, 884–895.

Kelly, J. F., Dow, S. J., Yeterian, J. D., et al. (2010). Can 12-step group participation strengthen and extend the benefits of adolescent addiction treatment? A prospective analysis. *Drug and Alcohol Dependence, 110*(1–2), 117–125.

Kelly, J. F., & Myers, M. G. (2007). Adolescents' participation in Alcoholics Anonymous and Narcotics Anonymous: Review, implications and future directions. *Journal of Psychoactive Drugs, 39*(3), 259–269.

Kelly, J. F., Myers, M. G., & Brown, S. A. (2002). Do adolescents affiliate with 12-step groups? A multivariate process model of effects. *Journal of Studies on Alcohol, 63*(3), 293–304.

Kelly, T. M., Donovan, J. E., Chung, T., et al. (2004). Alcohol use disorders among emergency department-treated older adolescents: A new brief screen (RUFT-Cut) using the AUDIT, CAGE, CRAFFT, and RAPS-QF. *Alcoholism, Clinical and Experimental Research, 28*(5), 746–753.

Kelly, T. M., Donovan, J. E., Chung, T., et al. (2009). Brief screens for detecting alcohol use disorder among 18–20 year old young adults in emergency departments: Comparing AUDIT-C, RAPS4-QF, FAST, RUFT-Cut, and *DSM-IV* 2-Item Scale. *Addictive Behaviors, 34*(8), 668–674.

Kelly, T. M., Donovan, J. E., Kinnane, J. M., et al. (2002). A comparison of alcohol screening instruments among under-aged drinkers treated in emergency departments. *Alcohol & Alcoholism, 37*(5), 444–450.

Kendall, M. (1938). A new measure of rank correlation. *Biometrika, 30*(1–2), 81–89.

Kendall, R., & Jablensky, A. (2003). Distinguishing between validity and utility of psychiatric diagnoses. *The American Journal of Psychiatry, 160*(1), 4–12.

Kendler, K. S., Bulik, C. M., Silberg, J., et al. (2000). Childhood sexual abuse and adult psychiatric and substance use disorders in women: An epidemiological and co-twin control analysis. *Archives of General Psychiatry, 57*(10), 953–959.

Kenna, G. A., Lomastro, T. L., Schiesl, A., et al. (2009). Review of topiramate: An antiepileptic for the treatment of alcohol dependence. *Current Drug Abuse Reviews, 2*(2), 135–142.

Kennedy, B. P., & Minami, M. (1993). The Beech Hill Hospital/Outward Bound Adolescent Chemical Dependency Treatment Program. *Journal of Substance Abuse Treatment, 10*, 395–406.

Kennedy, K. I., Fortney, J. A., Bonhomme, M. G., et al. (1990). Do the benefits of breastfeeding outweigh the risk of postnatal transmission of HIV via breastmilk? *Tropical Doctor, 20*(1), 25–29.

Kennedy, W. K., Leloux, M., Kutscher, E. C., et al. (2010). Acamprosate. *Expert Opinion on Drug Metabolism & Toxicology, 6*(3), 363–380.

Kenny, P. J., & Markou, A. (2001). Neurobiology of the nicotine withdrawal syndrome. *Pharmacology, Biochemistry, and Behavior, 70*(4), 531–549.

Kernberg, O. (1967). Borderline personality organization. *Journal of the American Psychoanalytic Association, 15*(3), 641–685.

Kernberg, O. F. (1975). *Borderline condiitons and pathological narcissism.* New York, NY: Jason Aronson.

Keyes, K. M., Martins, S. S., & Hasin, D. S. (2008). Past 12-month and lifetime comorbidity and poly-drug use of ecstasy users among young adults in the United States: Results from the National Epidemioloic Survey on Alcohol and Related Conditions. *Drug and Alcohol Dependence, 97*(1–2), 139–149.

Khalsa, J. H., Genser, S., Francis, H., et al. (2002). Clinical consequences of marijuana. *Journal of Clinical Pharmacology, 42*(11, Suppl.), 7S–10S.

Khantzian, E. J. (1974). Opiate addiction: A critique of theory and some implications for treatment. *American Journal of Psychotherapy, 28*(1), 59–70.

Khantzian, E. J. (1980). An ego/self theory of substance dependence: A contemporary psychonanalytic perspective. In D. J. Lettieri, M. Sayer, & H. Wallenstein Pearson (Eds.), *Theories on drug abuse: Selected contemporary perspectives* (NIDA Research Monograph No. 30, pp. 29–33). Rockville, MD: U.S. Department of Health and Human Services, National Institute on Drug Abuse.

Khantzian, E. J. (1985). The self-medication hypothesis of addictive disorders: Focus on heroin and cocaine dependence. *The American Journal of Psychiatry, 142*(11), 1259–1264.

Khantzian, E. J. (1997). The self-medication hypothesis of substance use disorders: A reconsideration and recent applications. *Harvard Review of Psychiatry, 4*, 231–244.

Khantzian, E. J. (2004). Book review [*Trauma and substance abuse: Causes, consequences, and treatment of comorbid disorders.* P. Ouimette & P. J. Brown (Eds.)]. *The American Journal of Psychiatry, 161* (3), 587–588.

Khantzian, E. J., Mack, J. E., Schatzberg, A. F. (1974). Heroin use as an attempt to cope: Clinical considerations. *The American Journal of Psychiatry, 131*(2), 160–164.

Kharasch, S. J., Glotzer, D., Vinci, R., et al. (1991). Unsuspected cocaine exposure in young children. *American Journal of Diseases of Children, 145*(2), 204–206.

Kiefer, F, & Mann, K. (2010). Acamprosate: How, where, and for whom does it work? Mechanism of action, treatment targets, and individualized therapy. *Current Pharmaceutical Design, 16*(19), 2098–2102.

Kim, R. J., & Jackson, D. S. (2008). A comparison of adolescent methamphetamine and other substance users in Hjawai'i. *Hawaii Medical Journal, 67*(11), 294–300, 302.

Kim, S. (1988). A short and long-term evaluation of Here's Looking at You alcohol education program. *Journal of Drug Education, 18*, 171–184.

Kim, S., Hoffman, I. R., Pike, M. A., et al. (1984). An outcome evaluation instrument for alcohol education, prevention, and intervention programs. *Journal of Drug Education, 14*(4), 331–346.

Kim, S., & Newman, S. H. (1982). Synthetic-dynamic theory of drug abuse: A revisit with empirical data. *The International Journal of the Addictions, 17*, 913–923.

Kimura, R., Ushiyama, N., Fujii, T., et al. (2003). Nicotine-induced Ca2+ signaling and down-regulation of nicotinic acetylcholine receptor subunit expression in the CEM human leukemic T-cell line. *Life Sciences, 72*(18-19), 2155–2158.

King, G., Alicata, D., Cloak, C., et al. (2010). Neuropsychological deficits in adolescent methamphetamine abusers. *Psychopharmacology (Berlin), 212*(2), 243–249.

King, G. R., Pinto, G., Konen, J., et al. (2002). The effects of continuous 5-HT(3) receptor antagonist administration on the subsequent behavioral response to cocaine. *European Journal of Pharmacology, 449*(3), 253–259.

Kintz, P., Villain, M., Dumestre-Toulet, V., et al. (2005). Methadone as a chemical weapon: Two fatal cases involving babies. *Therapeutic Drug Monitoring, 27*(6), 741–743.

Kirchmayer, U., Davoli, M., & Verster, A. (2000). Naltrexone maintenance treatment for opioid dependence. *Cochrane Database of Systematic Reviews, 2,* CD001333.

Kirshner, L. (2011). D. C. Circuit rules FDA cannot block e-cigarette imports—Sottera, Inc. v FDA. *American Journal of Law & Medicine, 37*(1), 194–198.

Kitchens, J. M. (1994). Does this patient have an alcohol problem? *JAMA, Journal of the American Medical Association, 272,* 1782–1787.

Klasser, G. D., & Epstein, J. (2005). Methamphetamine and its impact on dental care. *Journal of the Canadian Dental Association, 71*(10), 759–762.

Klein, J., Karaskov, T., & Korent, G. (1999). Fatty acid ethyl esters: A novel biologic marker for heavy in utero ethanol exposure: A case report. *Therapeutic Drug Monitoring, 21*(6), 644–646.

Klein, J., & Koren, G. (1999). Hair analysis—a biological marker for passive smoking in pregnancy and childhood. *Human & Experimental Toxicology, 18*(4), 279–282.

Klein, M., & Kramer, F. (2004). Rave drugs: Pharmacological considerations. *Journal of the American Association of Nurse Anesthetists, 72*(1), 61–67.

Klein, T. W., Lane, B., Newton, C. A., et al. (2000). The cannabinoid system and cytokine network. *Proceedings of the Society for Experimental Biology and Medicine, 225*(1), 1–8.

Klein-Schwartz, W., & Oderda, G. M. (2002). Pediatric poisoning. In L. Pagliaro & A. M. Pagliaro (Eds.), *Problems in Pediatric Drug Therapy* (4th ed.) (pp. 245–282). Washington, DC: American Pharmaceutical Association.

Klepp, K. I., Halper, A., & Perry, C. L. (1986). The efficacy of peer leaders in drug abuse prevention. *The Journal of School Health, 56*(9), 407–411.

Klerman, L. (2004). Protecting children: Reducing their environmental tobacco smoke exposure. *Nicotine & Tobacco Research, 6*(Suppl. 2), S239–S253.

Klitzman, R. L., Pope, H. G., Jr., & Hudson, J. I. (2000). MDMA ("ecstasy") abuse and high-risk sexual behaviors among 169 gay and bisexual men. *The American Journal of Psychiatry, 157*(7), 1162–1164.

Klupp, N., Risser, D., Stichenwirth, M., et al. (2000). Fatal methadone poisoning of a child [in German]. *Wiener Klinische Wochenschrift, 112*(8), 365–367.

Knapp, K., & Lenz, W. (1963). Embryopathy due to thalidomide [in Spanish]. *Espanola de Pediatria, 19,* 39–45.

Knight, C. A., Knight, I., & Mitchell, D. C. (2006). Beverage caffeine intakes in young children in Canada and the US. *Canadian Journal of Dietetic Practice and Research, 67*(2), 96–99.

Knight, J. R., Goodman, E., Pulerwitz, T., et al. (2000). Reliabilities of short substance abuse screening tests among adolescent medical patients. *Pediatrics, 104*(4, pt. 2), 948–953.

Knight, J. R., Goodman, E., Pulerwitz, T., et al. (2001). Reliability of the Problem Oriented Screening Instrument for Teenagers (POSIT) in adolescent medical practice. *The Journal of Adolescent Health, 29*(2), 125–130.

Knight, J. R., Harris, S. K., Sherritt, L., et al. (2007a). Adolescents' preference for substance abuse screening in primary care practice. *Substance Abuse, 28*(4), 107–117.

Knight, J. R., Harris, S. K., Sherritt, L., et al., (2007b). Prevalence of positive substance abuse screen results among adolescent primary care patients. *Archives of Pediatrics & Adolescent Medicine, 161*(11), 1035–1041.

Knight, J. R., Sherritt, L., Harris, S. K., et al. (2003). Validity of brief alcohol screening tests among adolescents: A comparison of the AUDIT, POSIT, CAGE, AND CRAFFT. *Alcoholism, Clinical and Experimental Research, 27*(1), 67–73.

Knight, J. R., Sherritt, L., Shrier, L. A., et al. (2002). Validity of the CRAFFT Substance Abuse Screening Test among adolescent clinic patients. *Archives of Pediatrics and Adolescent Medicine, 156,* 607–614.

Knight, J. R., Shrier, L., Bravender, T., et al. (1999). A new brief screen for adolescent substance abuse. *Archives of Pediatrics and Adolescent Medicine, 153*(6), 591–596.

Knight, J. R., Wechsler, H., Kuo, M., et al. (2002). Alcohol abuse and dependence among U.S. college students. *Journal of Studies on Alcohol, 63*(3), 263–270.

Knopman, D. (1991). Unaware learning versus preserved learning in pharmacologic amnesia: Similarities and differences. *Journal of Experimental Psychology: Learning, Memory, & Cognition, 17,* 1017–1029.

Knudsen, H. K. (2009). Adolescent-only substance abuse treatment: Availability and adoption of components of quality. *Journal of Substance Abuse Treatment, 36*(2), 195–204.

Knudsen, K., Jonsson, U., & Abrahamsson, J. (2010). Twenty-three deaths with gamma-hydroxybutyrate overdose in western Sweden between 2000 and 2007. *Acta Anesthesiologica Scandinavica, 54*(8), 987–992.

Knupfer, G. (1991). Abstaining for foetal health: The fiction that even light drinking is dangerous. *British Journal of Addiction, 86,* 1063–1073.

Kodituwakku, P. W. (2009). Neurocognitive profile in children with fetal alcohol spectrum disorders. *Developmental Disabilities Research Reviews, 15*(3), 218–224.

Koebler, J. (2011). National high school graduation rates improve. *US News & World Report*. Retrieved from http://www.usnews.com/education/blogs/high-school-notes/2011/06/13/national-high-schoo...

Koesters, S. C., Rogers, P. D., & Rajasingham, C. R. (2002). MDMA ("ecstasy") and other "club drugs." The new epidemic. *Pediatric Clinics of North America, 49*(2), 415–433.

Kohen, D. (2005). Psychotropic medication and breastfeeding. *Advances in Psychiatric Treatment, 11*, 371–379.

Kolecki, P. (1998). Inadvertent methamphetamine poisoning in pediatric patients. *Pediatric Emergency Care, 14*(6), 385–387.

Kollins, S. H. (2008). A qualitative review of issues arising in the use of psychostimulant medications in patients with ADHD and co-morbid substance use disorders. *Current Medical Research and Opinion, 24*(5), 1345–1357.

Konkol, R. J. (1994). Is there a cocaine baby syndrome? *Journal of Child Neurology, 9*, 225–226.

Koob, G. F. (2008). A role for brain stress systems in addiction. *Neuron, 59*, 11–34.

Koob, G. F. (2009). Review: Brain stress systems in the amygdala and addiction. *Brain Research, 1293*, 61–75.

Koob, G. F., & Simon, E. J. (2009). The neurobiology of addiction: Where we have been and where we are going. *Journal of Drug Issues, 39*(1), 115–132.

Koopman, C., Rosario, M., & Rotheram-Borus, M. J. (1994). Alcohol and drug use and sexual behaviors placing runaways at risk for HIV infection. *Addictive Behaviors, 19*(1), 95–103.

Kopelman, M. D. (1991). Frontal dysfunction and memory deficits in the alcoholic Korsakoff syndrome and Alzheimer-type dementia. *Brain, 114*, 117–137.

Koren, G. (1991). Drinking and pregnancy. *CMAJ, Canadian Medical Association Journal, 145*(12), 1552,1554.

Koren, G. (1993). Cocaine and the human fetus: The concept of teratophilia. *Neurotoxicology and Teratology, 15*, 301–304.

Koren, G., Fantus, E., & Nulman, I. (2010). Managing fetal alcohol spectrum disorder in the public school system: A needs assessment pilot. *Canadian Journal of Clinical Pharmacology, 17*(1), e79–e89.

Koren, G., Gladstone, D., Robeson, C., et al. (1992). The perception of teratogenic risk of cocaine. *Teratology, 46*(6), 567–571.

Koss, M. P., Yuan, N. P., Dightman, D., et al. (2003). Adverse childhood exposure and alcohol dependence among seven Native American tribes. *American Journal of Preventive Medicine, 25*, 238–244.

Kosten, T. R., Hogan, I., Jalali, B., et al. (1986). The effect of multiple family therapy on addict family functioning: A pilot study. *Advances in Alcohol & Substance Abuse, 5*(3), 51–62.

Kotagal, S., & Pianosi, P. (2006). Sleep disorders in children and adolescents. *British Medical Journal, 332*, 828.

Kovas, A. E., McFarland, B. H., McCarty, D. J., et al. (2007). Buprenorphine for acute heroin detoxification: Diffusion of research into practice. *Journal of Substance Abuse Treatment, 32*(2), 199–206.

Kozer, E., & Koren, G. (2001). Effects of prenatal exposure to marijuana. *Canadian Family Physician, 47*, 263–264.

Kozlowski, L. T., Coambs, R. B., Ferrence, R. G., et al. (1989). Preventing smoking and other drug use: Let the buyers beware and the interventions be apt. *Canadian Journal of Public Health, 80*, 452–456.

Kramer, T. L., Han, X., Leukefeld, C., et al. (2009). Childhood conduct problems and other early risk factors in rural adult stimulant users. *The Journal of Rural Health, 25*(1), 50–57.

Kreek, M. J., & Stimmel, B. (Eds.) (1984). *Dual addiction: Pharmacological issues in the treatment of concomitant alcoholism and drug abuse*. New York, NY: Haworth.

Kreslake, J. M., Wayne, G. F., & Connolly, G. N. (2008). The menthol smoker: Tobacco industry research on consumer sensory perception of menthol cigarettes and its role in smoking behavior. *Nicotine & Tobacco Research, 10*(4), 705–715.

Krishnan, K. R. (2005). Psychiatric and medical comorbidities of bipolar disorder. *Psychosomatic Medicine, 67*(1), 1–8.

Kriston, L., Hölzel, L., Weiser, A.-K., et al. (2008). Meta-analysis: Are 3 questions enough to detect unhealthy alcohol use? *Annals of Internal Medicine, 149*(12), 879–888.

Krystal, J. H., D'Souza, D., C., Gallinat, J., et al. (2006). The vulnerability to alcohol and substance abuse in individuals diagnosed with schizophrenia. *Neurotoxicity Research, 10*(3–4), 235–252.

Kuczkowski, K. M. (2009). Caffeine in pregnancy. *Archives of Gynecology and Obstetrics, 280*(5), 695–698.

Kuhar, M. M., & Pilotte, N. S. (1996). Neurochemical changes in cocaine withdrawal. *Trends in Pharmacological Sciences, 17*(7), 260–264.

Kulaga, V., Pragst, F., Fulga, N., et al. (2009). Hair analysis of fatty acid ethyl esters in the detection of excessive drinking in the context of fetal alcohol spectrum disorders. *Therapeutic Drug Monitoring, 31*(2), 261–266.

Kulig, J. W. (2005). Tobacco, alcohol, and other drugs: The role of the pediatrician in prevention, identification, and management of substance abuse. *Pediatrics, 115*(3), 816–821.

Kumar, R. (2008). Approved and investigational uses of modafinil: An evidence-based review. *Drugs, 68*(13), 1803–1839.

Kunins, H. V., Belllin, BE., Chazotte, C., et al. (2007). The effect of race on provider decisions to test for illicit drug use in the peripartum setting. *Journal of Womens Health, 16*(2), 245–255.

Kuper, H., Adami, H. O., & Boffetta, P. (2002). Tobacco use, cancer causation and public health impact. *Journal of Internal Medicine, 252*(6), 455–466.

Kuper, H., Boffetta, P., & Adami, H. O. (2002). Tobacco use and cancer causation: Association by tumour type. *Journal of Internal Medicine, 252*(3), 206–224.

Kurtz, E. (1988). AA: The story. San Francisco, CA: Harper & Row.

Kurtz, E. (1993). Research on Alcoholics Anonymous: The historical context. In B. S. McCrady & W. R. Miller (Eds.), *Research on Alcoholics Anonymous* (pp. 13–26). New Brunswick, NJ: Rutgers Center of Alcohol Studies.

Kurzthaler, I., Hummer, M., Miller, C., et al. (1999). Effect of cannabis use on cognitive functions and driving ability. *The Journal of Clinical Psychiatry, 60*(6), 395–399.

# L

Labouvie, E. W. (1986). Alcohol and marijuana use in relation to adolescent stress. *The International Journal of the Addictions, 21*, 333–345.

Labouvie, E. W. (1987). Relation of personality to adolescent alcohol and drug use: A coping perspective. *Pediatrician, 14*(1–2), 19–24.

Labouvie, E. W., Pandina, R. J., Raskin White, H., et al. (1990). Risk factors of adolescent drug use: An affect-based interpretation. *Journal of Substance Abuse, 2*(3), 265–285.

Laegreid, L., Olegard, R., Conradi, N., et al. (1990). Congenital malformations and maternal consumption of benzodiazepines: A case-controlled study. *Developmental Medicine & Child Neurology, 32*, 432–441.

Lambers, D., & Clark, K. (1996). The maternal and fetal physiologic effects of nicotine. *Seminars in Perinatalogy, 20*, 115–126.

Lampinen, T. M., McGhee, D., & Martin, I. (2006). Increased risk of "club" drug use among gay and bisexual high school students in British Columbia. *The Journal of Adolescent Health, 38*(4), 458–461.

Lamy, S., & Thibaut, F. (2010). Psychoactive substance use during pregnancy: A review [in French]. *Encephale, 36*(1), 33–38.

Landry, M. J. (1992). An overview of cocaethylene, an alcohol-derived, psychoactive, cocaine metabolite. *Journal of Psychoactive Drugs, 24*(3), 273–276.

Langeland, W., & Hartgers, C. (1998). Child sexual and physical abuse and alcoholism: A review. *Journal of Studies on Alcohol, 59*(3), 336–348.

Langhorne, J. E., & Loney, J. (1979). A four-fold model for subgrouping the hyperkinetic/MBD syndrome. *Child Psychiatry & Human Development, 9*, 153–159.

Langley, K., Holmans, P., Van den Bree, M., et al. (2007). Effects of low birthweight, maternal smoking during pregnancy and social class on the phenotypic manifestations of Attention Deficit Hyperactivity Disorder and associated antisocial behaviour: Investigation in a clinical sample. *BioMed Central Psychiatry, 7*, e26.

Laniado-Laborin, R. (2010). Smoking cessation intervention: An evidence-based approach. *Postgraduate Medicine, 122*(2), 74–82.

Lanier, D., & Ko, S. (2008). Screening in primary care settings for illicit drug use: Assessment of screening instruments A supplemental evidence update for the U.S. Preventive Services Task Force. Evidence synthesis No. 58, Part 2. Agency Healthcare Research and Quality (AHRQ) Publication No. 08–05108-EF-2. Rockville, MD: U.S. Department of Health and Human Services.

Lankenau, S. E., Bloom, J. J., & Shin, C. (2010). Longitudinal trajectories of ketamine use among young injection drug users. *The International Journal on Drug Policy, 21*(4), 306–314.

Lankenau, S. E., & Clatts, M. C. (2004). Drug injection practices among high-risk youths: The first shot of ketamine. *Journal of Urban Health, 81*(2), 232–248.

Lankenau, S. E., & Sanders, B. (2007). Patterns of ketamine use among young injection drug users. *Journal of Psychoactive Drugs, 39*(1), 21–29.

Lankenau, S. E., Sanders, B., Bloom, J. J., et al. (2007). First injection of ketamine among young injection drug users (IDUs) in three U.S. Cities. *Drug and Alcohol Dependence, 87*(2–3), 183–193.

Lapus, R. M. (2007). Activated charcoal for pediatric poisonings: The universal antidote? *Current Opinion in Pediatrics, 19*(2), 216–222.

Lason, W. (2001). Neurochemical and pharmacological aspects of cocaine-induced seizures. *Polish Journal of Pharmacology, 53*(1), 57–60.

Late, M. (2007). Screening detects alcohol, drug abuse problems: New codes for health providers released to improve reimbursement. *Nations Health, 37*(10), pp. 1–2. Retrieved from http://www.medscape.com/viewarticle/568692

Latimer, W. W., Stone, A. L., Voight, A., et al. (2002). Gender differences in psychiatric comorbidity among adolescents with substance use disorders. *Experimental and Clinical Psychopharmacology, 10*(3), 310–315.

Latimer, W. W., Winters, K. C., & Stinchfield, R. D. (1997). Screening for drug abuse among adolescents in clinical and correctional settings using the Problem-Oriented Screening Instrument for Teenagers. *The American Journal of Drug and Alcohol Abuse, 23*(1), 79–98.

Laudet, A. B. (2008). The impact of alcoholics anonymous on other substance abuse-related twelve-step programs. *Recent Developments in Alcoholism, 18*, 71–89.

Laundergan, J. C., & Williams, T. (1993). The Hazelden Residential Family Program: A combined systems and disease model approach. In T. J. O'Farrell (Ed.), *Treating alcohol problems: Marital and family interventions*. New York, NY: Guilford.

Laws, K. R., & Kokkalis, J. (2007). Ecstasy (MDMA) and memory function: A meta-analytic update. *Human Psychopharmacology, 22*(6), 381–388.

Le Bec, P. Y., Fatseas, M., Denis, C., et al. (2009). Cannabis and psychosis: Search of a causal link through a critical and systematic review [in French]. *Encephale, 35*(4), 377–385.

Lee, J. D., Grossman, E., DiRocco, D., et al. (2010). Extended-release naltrexone for treatment of alcohol dependence in primary care. *Journal of Substance Abuse Treatment, 39*(1), 14–21.

Lee, S. J., & Levounis, P. (2008). Gamma hydroxybutyrate: An ethnographic study of recreational use and abuse. *Journal of Psychoactive Drugs, 40*(3), 245–253.

Leeies, M., Pagura, J., Sareen, J., et al. (2010). The use of alcohol and drugs to self-medicate symptoms of post-traumatic stress disorder. *Depression and Anxiety, 27*(8), 731–736.

Legleye, S., Karila, L., Beck, F., et al. (2007). Validation of the CAST, a general population Cannabis Abuse Screening Test. *Journal of Substance Use, 12*(4), 233–242.

Lehman, A. F., Myers, C. P., Corty, E., et al. (1994). Prevalence and patterns of "dual diagnosis" among psychiatric inpatients. *Comprehensive Psychiatry, 35*, 106–112.

Leiderman, D. B., Balish, M., & Bromfield, E. B. (1991). Effect of valproate on human cerebral glucose metabolism. *Epilepsia, 32*, 417–422.

Leigh, G., & Skinner, H. A. (1988). Physiological assessment. In D. M. Donovan & G. A. Marlatt (Eds.), *Assessment of addictive behaviours: A reference book for the caring professions* (pp. 112–136). London, UK: Hutchinson.

Lemoine, P., Harousseau, H., Borteyru, J. P., et al. (1968). Children of alcoholic parents: Abnormalities observed in 127 cases. *Ouest-médicine, 8*, 476–482.

Lennox, R. D., & Cecchini, M. A. (2008, March 19). The NARCONON drug education curriculum for high school students: A non-randomized, controlled prevention trial. *Substance Abuse Treatment, Prevention, and Policy, 3*, 8.

Lenz, W. (1962). How can the physician prevent dangers for the offspring? [in German]. *Die Medizinische Welt, 48*, 2554–2558.

Leonard, S., & Bertrand, D. (2001). Neuronal nicotinic receptors: From structure to function. *Nicotine & Tobacco Research, 3*(3), 203–223.

Leone, M. A., Vigna-Taglianti, F., Avanzi, G., et al. (2010, February 17). Gamma-hydroxybutyrate (GHB) for treatment of alcohol withdrawl and prevention of relapses. *Cochrane Database of Systematic Reviews, 2*, CD006266.

Lerman, C., Jepson, C., Wileyto, E. P., et al. (2010). Genetic variation in nicotine metabolism predicts the efficacy of extended-duration transdermal nicotine therapy. *Clinical Pharmacology & Therapeutics, 87*(5), 553–557.

Lesar, S. (1992). Prenatal cocaine exposure: The challenge to education. *Infant-Toddler Intervention. The Transdisciplinary Journal, 2*(1), 37–52.

Lessov-Schlaggar, C. N., Hops, H., Brigham, J., et al. (2008). Adolescent smoking trajectories and nicotine dependence. *Nicotine & Tobacco Research, 10*(2), 341–351.

Lester, B. M., Bagner, D. M., Liu, J., et al. (2009). Infant neurobehavioral dysregulation: Behavior problems in children with prenatal substance exposure. *Pediatrics, 124*(5), 1355–1362.

Lester, B. M., El Sohly, M., Wright, L.L., et al. (2001). The maternal lifestyle study: Drug use by meconium toxicology and maternal self-report. *Pediatrics, 107*(2), 309–317.

Lester, B. M., & LaGasse, L. (2010). Children of addicted women. *Journal of Addictive Diseases, 29*(2), 259–276.

Leung, K. S., & Cottler, L. B. (2008). Ecstasy and other club drugs: A review of recent epidemiologic studies. *Current Opinion in Psychiatry, 21*(3), 234–241.

Levenson, R. W., Oyama, O. N., & Meek, P. S. (1987). Greater reinforcement from alcohol for those at risk: Parental risk, personality risk, and sex. *Journal of Abnormal Psychology, 96*, 242–253.

Levin, E. D. (2002). Nicotinic receptor subtypes and cognitive function. *Journal of Neurobiology, 53*(4), 633–640.

Levin, F. R., Evans, S. M., & Kleber, H. D. (1998). Prevalence of adult attention-deficit hyperactivity disorder among cocaine abusers seeking treatment. *Drug and Alcohol Dependence, 52*(1), 15–25.

Levy, D. T., Miller, T. R., & Cox, K. C. (1999, October). *Costs of underage drinking: Updated edition.* Washington, DC: U.S. Department of Justice, Office of Justice Programs, Office of Juvenile Justice and Delinquency Prevention.

Levy, D. T., Mumford, E. A., Cummings, M. K., et al. (2004). The relative risks of a low-nitrosamine smokeless tobacco product compared with smoking cigarettes: Estimates of a panel of experts. *Cancer Epidemiology, Biomarkers & Prevention, 13*, 2035–2042.

Levy, S., Sherritt, L., Harris, S. K., et al. (2004). Test-retest reliability of adolescents' self-report of substance use. *Alcoholism, Clinical and Experimental Research, 28*(8), 1236–1241.

Levy, S., Vaughan, B. L., & Knight, J. R. (2002). Office-based intervention for adolescent substance abuse. *Pediatric Clinics of North America, 49*(2), 329–343.

Lewin, K. (1951). *Field theory in social science:: Selected theoretical papers.* New York, NY: Harper and Brothers.

Lewis, D., Moore, C., Morrissey, P., et al. (1997). Determination of drug exposure using hair: Application to child protective cases. *Forensic Science International, 84*(1–3), 123–128.

Lewis, R. A., Piercy, F. P., Sprenkle, D. H., et al. (1990). Family-based interventions for helping drug-abusing adolescents. *Journal of Adolescent Research, 5*(1), 82–95.

Libby, A. M., Orton, H. D., Novins, D. K., et al. (2004). Childhood physical and sexual abuse and subsequent alcohol and drug use disorders in two American-Indian tribes. *Journal of Studies on Alcohol, 65*(1), 74–83.

Libby, A. M., & Riggs, P. D. (2005). Integrated substance use and mental health treatment for adolescents: Aligning organizational and financial incentives. *Journal of Child and Adolescent Psychopharmacology, 15*(5), 826–834.

Liddle, H. A. (2004). Family-based therapies for adolescent alcohol and drug use: Research contributions and future research needs. *Addiction, 99*(Suppl. 2), 76–92.

Liddle, H. A., Dakof, G. A., Parker, K., et al. (2001). Multidimensional family therapy for adolescent drug abuse: Results of a randomized clinical trial. *The American Journal of Drug and Alcohol Abuse, 27*, 651–687.

Liddle, H. A., Rowe, C. L., Dakof, G. A., et al. (2004). Early intervention for adolescent substance abuse: Pretreatment to posttreatment outcomes of a randomized clinical trial comparing multidimensional family therapy and peer group treatment. *Journal of Psychoactive Drugs, 36*, 49–63.

Lima, A. R., Lima, M. S., Soares, B. G., et al. (2002). Carbamazepine for cocaine dependence. *Cochrane Database of Systematic Reviews, 2*, CD002023.

Lima, C. T., Friere, A. C. C., Silva, A. P. B., et al. (2005). Concurrent and construct validity of the AUDIT in an urban Brazilian sample. *Alcohol and Alcoholism, 40*(6), 584–589.

Lima, M. S., Reisser, A. A., Silva de Lima, M., et al. (2009, January 21). WITHDRAWN:Carbamazepine for cocaine dependence. *Cochrane Database of Systematic Reviews, 1*, CD002023.

Lima, M. S., Reisser, A. A., Soares, B. G., et al. (2003). Antidepressants for cocaine dependence. *Cochrane Database of Systematic Reviews, 2*, CD002950.

Lin, Z., & Uhl, G. R. (2002). Dopamine transporter mutants with cocaine resistance and normal dopamine uptake provide targets for cocaine antagonism. *Molecular Pharmacology, 61*(4), 885–891.

Linares, T. J., Singer, L. T., Kirchner, H. L., et al. (2006). Mental health outcomes of cocaine-exposed children at 6 years of age. *Journal of Pediatric Psychology, 31*(1), 85–97.

Lindemalm, S., Nydert, P., Svensson, J. O., et al. (2009). Transfer of buprenorphine into breast milk and calculation of infant drug dose. *Journal of Human Lactation, 25*, 199–205.

Lindermann, R. (1991). Congenital renal tubular dysfunction associated with maternal sniffing of organic solvents. *Acta Paediatrica Scandinavica, 80*(8–9), 882–884.

Lindesmith, A. R. (1947). *Opiate addiction.* Bloomington, IN: Principia.

Linszen, D., & van Amelsvoort, T. (2007). Cannabis and psychosis: An update on course and biological plausible mechanisms. *Current Opinion in Psychiatry, 20*(2), 116–120.

Lippi, G., Plebani, M., & Cervellin, G. (2010). Cocaine in acute myocardial infarction. *Advances in Clinical Chemistry, 51*, 53–70.

Liskow, B., Campbell, J. Nickel, E. J., et al. (1995). Validity of the CAGE questionnaire in screening for alcohol dependence in a walk-in (triage) clinic. *Journal of Studies on Alcohol, 56*(3), 277–281.

Litovitz, T. L., Felberg, L., Soloway, R. A., et al. (1995). 1994 annula report of the American Association of Poison Control Centers Toxic Exposure Surveillance System. *The American Journal of Emergency Medicine, 13*(5), 551–597.

Little, B. B., Snell, L. M., & Rosenfeld, C. R. (1990). Failure to recognize fetal alcohol syndrome in newborn infants. *American Journal of Diseases of Children, 144*, 1142–1146.

Llewellyn, A., & Stowe, Z. N. (1998). Psychotropic medications in lactation. *The Journal of Clinical Psychiatry, 59*(Suppl. 2), 41–52.

Lockhart, S. P., Carter, Y. H., Straffen, A. M., et al. (1986). Detecting alcohol consumption as a cause of emergency general medical admissions. *Journal of Research on Socialized Medicine, 79*(3), 132–136.

Loeber, R., Stouthamer-Loeber, M., & White, H. R. (1999). Developmental aspects of delinquency and internalizing problems and their association with persistent juvenile substance use between ages 7 and 18. *Journal of Clinical Child Psychology, 28*(3), 322–332.

Logan, B. N. (1991). Adolescent substance abuse prevention: An overview of the literature. *Community Health, 13*, 25–36.

Loke, W. H., Hinrichs, J. V., & Ghoneim, M. M. (1985). Caffeine and diazepam: Separate and combined effects on mood, memory, and psychomotor performance. *Psychopharmacology (Berlin), 87*, 344–350.

Loney, J. (1980). The Iowa theory of substance abuse among hyperactive adolescents. In D. J. Lettieri, M. Sayer, & H. Wallenstein Pearson (Eds.), *Theories on drug abuse: Selected contemporary perspectives* (NIDA Research Monograph No. 30, pp. 132–136). Rockville, MD: U.S. Department of Health and Human Services, National Institute on Drug Abuse.

Loney, J., Langhorne, J. E., & Paternite, C. E. (1978). An empirical basis for subgrouping the hyperkinetic/minimal brain dysfunction syndrome. *Journal of Abnormal Psychology, 87*, 431–441.

Long-term cannabis users may have structural brain abnormalities. (2008, June 3). *ScienceDaily*, p. 1. Retrieved from http://www.sciencedaily.com/releases/2008/06/080602160845.htm

Long-time cannabis use associated with psychosis. (2010, March 2). *ScienceDaily*, p. 1. Retrieved from http://www.sciencedaily.com/releases/2010/03/100301165726.htm

López-Moreno, J. A., Gonzalez-Cuevas, G., Moreno, G., et al. (2008). The pharmacology of the endocannabinoid system: Functional and structural interactions with other neurotransmitter systems and their repercussions in behavioral addiction. *Addiction Biology, 13*(2), 160–187.

Lorenc, J. D. (2003). Inhalant abuse in the pediatric population: A persistent challenge. *Current Opinion in Pediatrics, 15*(2), 204–209.

Lu, L. H., Johnson, A., O'Hare, E. D, et al. (2009). Effects of prenatal methamphetamine exposure on verbal memory revealed with functional magnetic resonance imaging. *Journal of Developmental & Behavioral Pediatrics, 30*(3), 185–192.

Lu, M. C., & Halfon, N. (2003). Racial and ethnic disparities in birth outcomes: A life-course perspective. *Maternal and Child Health Journal, 7*(1), 13–30.

Luczak, S. E. (2003). Construct of alcohol problems: Invariance across religions. *Dissertation Abstracts International: Section B, 63*(9), 4377.

Ludlow, F. H. (1857). *The hasheesh eater: Being passages from the life of a Pythagorean*. New York, NY: S. G. Rains.

Lukoff, I. F. (1972). *Social and ethnic patterns of reported heroin use and contiguity with drug users*. New York, NY: Addiction Research and Treatment Corporation Evaluation Team.

Lukoff, I. F. (1974). Issues in the evaluation of heroin treatment. In E. Josephson & E. E. Carroll (Eds.), *Drug use: Epidemiological and sociological approaches* (pp. 129–157). New York, NY: Wiley.

Lukoff, I. F. (1977). Consequences of use: Heroin and other narcotics. In J. D. Rittenhouse (Ed.), *The epidemiology of heroin and other narcotics* (NIDA Research Monograph No. 16, pp. 195–227). Rockville, MD: U.S. Department of Health and Human Services, National Institute on Drug Abuse.

Lukoff, I. F. (1980). Toward a sociology of drug use. In D. J. Lettieri, M. Sayer, & H. Wallenstein Pearson (Eds.), *Theories on drug abuse: Selected contemporary perspectives* (NIDA Research Monograph No. 30, pp. 201–211). Rockville, MD: U.S. Department of Health and Human Services, National Institute on Drug Abuse.

Lundqvist, T. (2005). Cognitive consequences of cannabis use: Comparison with abuse of stimulants and heroin with regard to attention, memory and executive functions. *Pharmacology, Biochemistry, and Behavior, 81*(2), 319–330.

Lustbader, A. S., Mayes, L. C., McGee, B. A., et al. (1998). Incidence of passive exposure to crack/cocaine and clinical findings in infants seen in an outpatient service. *Pediatrics, 102*(1), e5.

Lutfiyya, M. N., Shah, K. K., Johnson, M., et al. (2008). Adolescent daily cigarette smoking: Is rural residency a risk factor? *Rural and Remote Health, 8*(1), 875.

Lynam, D. R., Milich, R., Zimmerman, R., et al. (1999). Project DARE: No effects at 10-year follow-up. *Journal of Consulting and Clinical Psychology, 67*(4), 590–593.

Lynskey, M., & Hall, W. (2000). The effects of adolescent cannabis use on educational attainment: A review. *Addiction, 95*(11), 1621–1630.

Lynskey, M. T., & Fergusson, D. M. (1995). Childhood conduct problems, attention deficit behaviors, and adolescent alcohol, tobacco, and illicit drug use. *Journal of Abnormal Child Psychology, 23*, 281–302.

## M

Maccarrone, M., & Finazzi-Agro, A. (2002). Endocannabinoids and their actions. *Vitamins and Hormones, 65*, 225–255.

Mace, W. (1992). A right brain model of substance abuse. *Family Dynamics of Addiction Quarterly, 2*(1), 60–68.

MacKenzie, D., Langa, A., & Brown, T. M. (1996). Identifying hazardous or harmful alcohol use in medical admissions: A comparison of audit, cage and brief mast. *Alcohol and Alcoholism, 31*(6), 591–599.

Macnab, A., Anderson, E., & Susak, L. (1989). Ingestion of cannabis: A cause of coma in children. *Pediatric Emergency Care, 5*(4), 238–239.

Madadi, P., Koren, G., Cairns, J., et al. (2007). Safety of codeine during breastfeeding: Fatal morphine poisoning in the breastfed neonate of a mother prescribed codeine. *Canadian Family Physician, 53*, 33–35.

Madadi, P., Ross, C., Hayden, M., et al. (2009). Pharmacogenetics of neonatal opioid toxicity following maternal use of codeine during breast feeding: A case-control study. *Clinical Pharmacology & Therapeutics, 85*(1), 31–35.

Maddahian, E., Newcomb, M. D., & Bentler, P. M. (1988). Adolescent drug use and intention to use drugs: Concurrent and longitudinal analyses of four ethnic groups. *Addictive Behaviors, 13*(2), 191–195.

Madea, B., & Mußhoff, F. (2009). Knock-out drugs: Their prevalence, modes of action, and means of detection. *Deutsches rzteblatt International, 106*(20), 341–347.

Madras, B. K., Compton, W. M., Ävula, D., et al. (2009). Screening, brief interventions, referral to treatment (SBIRT) for illicit drug and alcohol use at multiple healthcare sites: Comparison at intake and 6 months later. *Drug and Alcohol Dependence, 99*(1–3), 280–295.

Magruder, K. M., Ouyang, B., Miller, S., et al. (2009). Retention of under-represented minorities in drug abuse treatment studies. *Clinical Trials, 6*(3), 252–260.

Maharaj, K., & Ternullo, S. (2001). Using nicotine replacement therapy in treating nicotine addiction in adolescents. *The Journal of School Nursing, 17*(5), 278–282.

Mahowald, M. B. (1992). Maternal-fetal conflict: Positions and principles. *Clinical Obstetrics & Gynecology, 35*(4), 729–737.

Mai, E., & Buysse, D. J. (2008). Insomnia: Prevalence, impact, pathogenesis, differential diagnosis, and evaluation. *Sleep Medicine Clinics, 3*(2), 167–174.

Maisto, S. A., Connors, G. J., & Allen, J. P. (1995). Contrasting self-report screens for alcohol problems: A review. *Alcoholism, Clinical and Experimental Research, 19*(6), 1510–1516.

Makhija, N. J. (2007). Childhood abuse and adolescent suicidality: A direct link and an indirect link through alcohol and substance misuse. *International Journal of Adolescent Medicine and Health, 19*(1), 45–51.

Makhija, N. J., & Sher, L. (2007). Preventing suicide in adolescents with alcohol use disorders. *International Journal of Adolescent Medicine and Health, 19*(1), 53–59.

Malcolm, R.J. (2003). GABA systems, benzodiazepines, and substance dependence. *The Journal of Clinical Psychiatry, 64*(3 Suppl.), 36–40.

Maldonado, R., & Rodriguez de Fonseca, F. (2002). Cannabinoid addiction: Behavioral models and neural correlates. *The Journal of Neuroscience, 22*(9), 3326–3331.

Maldonado-Devincci, A. M., Badanich, K. A., & Kirstein, C. L. (2010). Alcohol during adolescence selectively alters immediate and long-term behavior and neurochemistry. *Alcohol, 44*(1), 57–66.

Malinauskas, B. M., Aeby, V. G., Overton, R. F., et al. (2007). A survey of energy drink consumption patterns among college students. *Nutrition Journal, 6*, 35.

Mallick, J. L., Kirby, K. C., Martin, F., et al. (1993). A comparison of the amnesic effects of lorazepam in alcoholics and non-alcoholics. *Psychopharmacology (Berlin), 110*, 181–186.

Malmquist, C. P. (1990). Depression in homicidal adolescents. *Bulletin of the American Academy of Psychiatry and Law, 18*(1), 23–36.

Malson, J. L., Sims, K., Murty, R., et al. (2001). Comparison of the nicotine content of tobacco used in bidis and conventional cigarettes. *Tobacco Control, 10*(2), 181–183.

Malvin, J. H., Moskowitz, J. M., Schaeffer, G. A., et al. (1984). Teacher training in affective education for the primary prevention of adolescent drug abuse. *The American Journal of Drug and Alcohol Abuse, 10*(2), 223–235.

Maly, R. C. (1993). Early recognition of chemical dependence. *Primary Care, 20*(1), 33–50.

Manji, S., Pie, J., Loomes, C., et al. (2009). A review of the verbal and visual memory impairments in children with foetal alcohol spectrum disorders. *Developmental Neurorehabilitation, 12*(4), 239–247.

Mann, K., & Hermann, D. (2010). Individualised treatment in alcohol-dependent patients. *European Archives of Psychiatry & Clinical Neuroscience, 260*(Suppl. 2), S116–S120.

Manos, M. J., Tom-Revzon, C., Bukstein, O. G., et al. (2007). Changes and challenges: Managing ADHD in a fast-paced world. *Journal of Managed Care Pharmacy, 13*(9 Suppl. B), S2–S13.

Manschreck, T. C., Schneyer, M. L., Weisstein, C. C., et al. (1990). Freebase cocaine and memory. *Comprehensive Psychiatry, 31*(4), 369–375.

Mansvelder, H. D., & McGehee, D. S. (2002). Cellular and synaptic mechanisms of nicotine addiction. *Journal of Neurobiology, 53*(4), 606–617.

Maraj, S., Figueredo, V. M., & Lynn Morris, D. (2010). Cocaine and the heart. *Clinical Cardiology, 33*(5), 264–269.

Marceaux, J. C., Dilks, L. S., & Hixson, S. (2008). Neuropsychological effects of formaldehyde use. *Journal of Psychoactive Drugs, 40*(2), 207–210.

Marcell, A. V., Halpern-Felsher, B., Coriell, M., et al. (2002). Physicians' attitudes and beliefs concerning alcohol abuse prevention in adolescents. *American Journal of Preventive Medicine, 22*(1), 49–55.

Marcellus, L. (2007). Is meconium screening appropriate for universal use? Science and ethics say no. *Advances in Neonatal Care, 7*(4), 207–214.

Marcos, A. C., & Johnson, R. E. (1988). Cultural patterns and causal processes in adolescent drug use: The case of Greeks versus Americans. *The International Journal of the Addictions, 23*, 545–572.

Marczinski, C. A., & Fillmore, M. T. (2006). Clubgoers and their trendy cocktails: Implications of mixing caffeine into alcohol on information processing and subjective reports of intoxication. *Experimental and Clinical Psychopharmacology, 14*(4), 450–458.

Margolese, H. C., Malchy, L., Negrete, J. C., et al. (2004). Drug and alcohol use among patients with schizophrenia and related psychoses: Levels and consequences. *Schizophrenia Research, 67*(2–3), 157–166.

Margolin, A., Avants, S. K., & Holford, T. R. (2002). Interpreting conflicting findings from clinical trials of auricular acupuncture for cocaine addiction: Does treatment context influence outcome? *Journal of Alternative and Complementary Medicine, 8*(2), 111–121.

Margolin, A., Kleber, H. D., Avants, S. K., et al. (2002). Acupuncture for the treatment of cocaine addiction: A randomized controlled trial. *JAMA, The Journal of the American Medical Association, 287*(1), 55–63.

Marijuana smoke contains higher levels of certain toxins than tobacco smoke. (2007, December 18). *Science Daily*, p. 1. Retrieved from http://www.sciencedaily.com/releases/2007/12/071217110328.htm

Marijuana smokers face rapid lung destruction—As much as 20 years ahead of tobacco smokers. (2008, January 27). *ScienceDaily*, pp. 1–2. Retrieved from http://www.sciencedaily.com/releases/2008/01/080123104017.htm

Marin, S. J., Keith, L., Merrell, M., et al. (2009). Evaluation of a new ELISA kit for the detection of benzodiazepines in meconium. *Journal of Analytical Toxicology, 33*(3), 177–181.

Marmorstein, N. R. (2009). Longitudinal associations between alcohol problems and depressive symptoms: Early adolescence through early adulthood. *Alcoholism, Clinical & Experimental Research, 33*(1), 49–59.

Marmorstein, N. R. (2010). Longitudinal associations between depressive symptoms and alcohol problems: The influence of comorbid delinquent behavior. *Addictive Behaviors, 35*(6), 564–571.

Maron, B. J. (2003). Sudden death in young athletes. *The New England Journal of Medicine, 349*, 1064–1075.

Marra, E. F. (1967). *Intoxicant drugs*. Buffalo State University of New York.

Marshal, M. P., & Molina, B. S. G. (2006). Antisocial behaviors moderate the deviant peer pathway to substance use in children with ADHD. *Journal of Clinical Child & Adolescent Psychology, 35*(2), 216–226.

Marshall, L., Schooley, M., Ryan, H., et al. (2006, May 19). Youth tobacco surveillance—United States, 2001–2002. *Morbidity and Mortality Weekly Report, Surveillance Summaries, 55*(3), 1–56.

Marsolek, M. R., White, N. C., & Litovitz, T. L. (2010). Inhalant abuse: Monitoring trends by using poison control data, 1993–2008. *Pediatrics, 125*(5), 906–913.

Martens, M. P., Neighbors, C., Dams-O'Connor, K., et al. (2007). The factor structure of a dichotomously scored Rutgers Alcohol Problem Index. *Journal of Studies on Alcohol and Drugs, 68*(4), 597–606.

Martin, B. R., Mechoulam, R., & Razdan, R.K. (1999). Discovery and characterization of endogenous cannabinoids. *Life Sciences, 65*(6–7), 573–595.

Martin, J. A., Hamilton, B. E., Sutton, P. D., et al. (2009, January 7). Births: Final data for 2006. *National Vital Statistics Reports, 57*(7), 1–16.

Martin, M. L., & Khoury, M. J. (1992). Cocaine and single ventricle: A population study. *Teratology, 46*(3), 267–270.

Martin, M. L., Khoury, M. J., Cordero, J. F., et al. (1992). Trends in rates of multiple vascular disruption defects, Atlanta, 1968–1989: Is there evidence of a cocaine teratogenic epidemic? *Teratology, 45*(6) 647–653.

Martinez, A., Larrabee, K., Monga, M. (1996). Cocaine is associated with intrauterine fetal death in women with suspected preterm labor. *American Journal of Perinatology, 13*(3), 163–166.

Martinez-Raga, J., Knecht, C., & Cepeda, S. (2008). Modafinil: A useful medication for cocaine addiction? Review of the evidence from neuropharmacological, experimental and clinical studies. *Current Drug Abuse Reviews, 1*(2), 213–221.

Martino, S., Grilo, C. M., & Fehon, D. C. (2000). Development of the Drug Abuse Screening Test for Adolescents (DAST-A). *Addictive Behaviors, 25*(1), 57–70.

Martins, S. S., & Alexandre, P. K. (2008). The association of ecstasy use and academic achievement among adolescents in two U.S. national surveys. *Addictive Behaviors, 34*(1), 9–16.

Martins, S. S., Storr, C. L., Alexandre, P. K., et al. (2009). Adolescent ecstasy and other drug use in the National Survey of parents and youth: The role of sensation-seeking, parental monitoring and peer's drug use. *Addictive Behaviors, 33*(7), 919–933.

Maryanoff, B., Nortey, O., Gardocki, J., et al. (1987). Anticonvulsant O-alkyl sulfamates. 2,3:4,5-Bis-O-(1-methylethylidene)-beta-D-fructopyranose sulfamate and related compounds. *Journal of Medicinal Chemistry, 30*(5), 880–887.

Masi, G., Toni, C., Perugi, G., et al. (2001). Anxiety disorders in children and adolescents with bipolar disorder: A neglected comorbidity. *Canadian Journal of Psychiatry, 46*, 797–802.

Mason, B. J. (2001). Treatment of alcohol-dependent outpatients with acamprosate: A clinical review. *The Journal of Clinical Psychiatry, 62* (Suppl. 20), 42–48.

Mason, B. J. (2003). Acamprosate. *Recent Developments in Alcoholism, 16*, 203–215.

Mason, B. J., & Heyser, C. J. (2010). The neurobiology, clinical efficacy and safety of acamprosate in the treatment of alcohol dependence. *Expert Opinion on Drug Safety, 9*(1), 177–188.

Mason, M. J. (1995). A preliminary language validity analysis of the Problem Oriented Screening Instrument for Teenagers (POSIT). *Journal of Child and Adolescent Substance Abuse, 4*(3), 61–68.

Mason, P. E., & Kerns, W. P.. (2002). Gamma hydroxybutyric acid (GHB) intoxication. *Academic Emergency Medicine, 9*(7), 730–739.

Mason, W. A., Hitchings, J. E., & Spoth, R. L. (2009). Longitudinal relations among negative affect, substance use and peer deviance during the transition from middle to late adolescence. *Substance Use & Misuse, 44*(8), 1142–1159.

Massey, C. C., & Shulman, J. D. (2006). Acute ethanol toxicity from ingesting mouthwash in children younger than age 6, 1989–2003. *Pediatric Dentistry, 28*(5), 405–409.

Matheson, I., Sande, H. A., & Gaillot, J. (1990). The excretion of zopiclone into breast milk. *British Journal of Clinical Pharmacology, 30*, 267–271.

Mathias, R. (1995). NIDA survey provides first national data on drug use during pregnancy. *NIDA Notes, 10*, 6–7.

Matson, M. E. (1994). Patient-treatment matching: Rationale and results. *Alcohol, Health & Reseach World, 18*, 287–295.

Matteucci, M. J., Auten, J. D., Crowley, B., et al. (2007). Methamphetamine exposures in young children. *Pediatric Emergency Care, 23*(9), 638–640.

Mattson, S. N., & Roebuck, T. M. (2002). Acquisition and retention of verbal and nonverbal information in children with heavy prenatal alcohol exposure. *Alcoholism,Clinical and Experimental Research, 26*(6), 875–882.

Mau, M. K., Asao, K., Efird, J., et al. (2009). Risk factors associated with methamphetamine use and heart failure among Native Hawaiians and other Pacific Island peoples. *Vascular Health and Risk Management, 5*, 45–52.

Maurer, P., & Bachmann, M. F. (2006). Therapeutic vaccines for nicotine dependence. *Current Opinion in Molecular Therapeutics, 8*(1), 11–16.

Maurer, P., & Bachmann, M. F. (2007). Vaccination against nicotine: An emerging therapy for tobacco dependence. *Expert Opinion on Investigational Drugs, 16*(11), 1775–1783.

Maxwell, J. C. (2001). Deaths related to the inhalation of volatile substances in Texas: 1988–1998. *The American Journal of Drug and Alcohol Abuse, 27*(4), 689–697.

May, P. A. (1991). Fetal alcohol effects among North American Indians: Evidence and implications for society. *Alcohol Health and Research World, 15*(3), 239–248.

May, P. A., & Gossage, J. P. (2001). Estimating the prevalence of fetal alcohol syndrome. A summary. *Alcohol Research & Health, 25*(3), 159–167.

May, P. A., Gossage, J. P., Kalberg, J. P., et al. (2009). Prevalence and epidemiologic characteristics of FASD from various research methods with an emphasis on recent in-school studies. *Developmental Disabilities Research and Review, 15*(3), 176–192.

May, P. A., Gossage, J. P., Smith, M., et al. (2010). Population differences in dysmorphic features among children with fetal alcohol spectrum disorders. *Journal of Developmental and Behavioral Pediatrics, 31*(4), 304–316.

May, P. A., Hymbaugh, K. J., Aase, J. M., et al. (1983). Epidemiology of fetal alcohol syndrome among American Indians of the southwest. *Social Biology, 30*(4), 374–387.

May, P. A., McCloskey, J., & Gossage, J. P. (2000). Fetal alcohol syndrome among American Indians: Epidemiology, issues, and research. NIAAA Research Monographs, National Institute on Alcohol Abuse and Alcoholism. Issues in Fetal Alcohol Syndrome Prevention. 10th Special Report to the U.S. Congress on Alcohol and Health. U.S. Department of Health and Human Services, National Institutes of Health, pp. 323–338.

Mayes, L. C. (2002). A behavioral teratogenic model of the impact of prenatal cocaine exposure on arousal regulatory systems. *Neurotoxicology and Teratology, 24*(3), 385–395.

Mayes, R., Bagwell, C., & Erkulwater, J. (2008). ADHD and the rise in stimulant use among children. *Harvard Review of Psychiatry, 16*(3), 151–166.

Mayfield, D., McLeod, G., & Hall, P. (1974). The CAGE questionnaire: Validation of a new alcoholism screening instrument. *The American Journal of Psychiatry, 131*(10), 1121–1123.

Mayo-Smith, M. F. (1997). Pharmacological management of alcohol withdrawal. A meta-analysis and evidence-based practice guideline. *JAMA, The Journal of the American Medical Association, 278*, 144–151.

Mbulo, L. (2008). Changes in exposure to second-hand smoke among youth in Nebraska, 2002–2006. *Preventing Chronic Disease, 5*(3), A84.

McAllister, I., & Makkai, T. (1991). Correcting for the underreporting of drug use in opinion surveys. *The International Journal of the Addictions, 26*(9), 945–961.

McAuliffe, W. E. (1990). Health care policy issues in the drug abuser treatment field. *Journal of Health Politics, Policy, and Law, 15*(2), 357–385.

McBride, D. C., Terry-McElrath, Y. M., VanderWaal, C. J., et al. (2008). US Public Health Agency involvement in youth-focused illicit drug policy, planning, and prevention at the local level, 1999–2003. *American Journal of Public Health, 98*(2), 270–277.

McBride, J. L. (1991). Abstinence among members of Alcoholics Anonymous. *Alcoholism Treatment Quarterly, 8*, 113–121.

McBride, W. G. (1961). Thalidomide and congenital abnormalities. *Lancet, 2*, 1358.

McCabe, S. E., Boyd, C., Hughes, T. L., et al. (2003). Sexual identity and substance use among undergraduate students. *Substance Abuse, 24*(2), 77–91.

McCambridge, J., & Strang, J. (2004). The efficacy of single-session motivational interviewing in reducing drug consumption and perceptions of drug-related risk and harm among young people: Results from a multi-site cluster randomized trial. *Addiction, 99*(1), 39–52.

McCambridge, J., & Thomas, B. A. (2009). Short forms of the AUDIT in a web-based study of young drinkers. *Drug and Alcohol Review, 28*(1), 18–24.

McCann, B. (1992, March). Alcoholism ages brain by up to 20 years. *Journal, 2*.

McCann, B. S., Simpson, T. L., Ries, R., et al. (2000). Reliability and validity of screening instruments for drug and alcohol abuse in adults seeking valuation for attention-deficit hyperactivity disorder. *The American Journal on Addictions, 9*, 1–9.

McCann, U. D., Mertl, M., Eligulashvili, V., et al. (1999). Cognitive performance in (+/–) 3,4-methylenedioxymethamphetamine (MDMA, "ecstasy") users: A controlled study. *Psychopharmacology (Berlin), 143*(4), 417–425.

McCarron, M. M., Schulze, B. W., Thompson, G. A., et al. (1981). Acute phencyclidine intoxication: Clinical patterns, complications, and treatment. *Annals of Emergency Medicine, 10*(6), 290–297.

McCarthy, D. M., Tomlinson, K. L., Anderson, K. G., et al. (2005). Relapse in alcohol - and drug-disordered adolescents with comorbid psychopathology: Changes in psychiatric symptoms. *Psychology of Addictive Behaviors, 19*(1), 28–34.

McCarthy, J. J., & Posey, B. L. (2000). Methadone levels in human milk. *Journal of Human Lactation, 16*(2), 115–120.

McCaul, M. E., & Petry, N. M. (2003). The role of psychosocial treatments in pharmacotherapy for alcoholism. *The American Journal on Addictions, 12*(Suppl. 1), S41–S52.

McClave-Regan, A. K., & Berkowitz, J. (2010). Smokers who are also using smokeless tobacco products in the US: A national assessment of characteristics, behaviours, and beliefs of "dual users." *Tobacco Control, 20*(3), 239–242.

McClernon, F. J., & Kollins, S. H. (2008). ADHD and smoking: From genes to brain to behavior. *Annals of the New York Academy of Sciences, 1141*, 131–147.

McCord, W., & McCord, J. (1960). *Origins of alcoholism.* Stanford, CA: Stanford University Press.

McCormack, T. (1999). Fetal syndromes and the charter: The Winnipeg glue-sniffing case. *Canadian Journal of Law and Society, 14*(2), 77–99.

McCullough, M. (2010, January 19). Corzine signs law to legalize medical marijuana. *Philadelphia Daily News.* Retrieved from http://articl.wn.com/view/2010/01/19/Corzine_signs_law_to_legalive _medical_marijuana/

McCusker, M. T., Basquille, J., Khwaja, M., et al. (2002). Hazardous and harmful drinking: A comparison of the AUDIT and CAGE screening questionnaires. *Quarterly Journal of Medicine, 95*, 591–595.

McDonald, R. M., & Towberman, D. B. (1993). Psychosocial correlates of adolescent drug involvement. *Adolescence, 28*(112), 925–936.

McDonough, M., Kennedy, N., Glasper, A., et al. (2004). Clinical features and management of gamma-hydroxybutyrate (GHB) withdrawal: A review. *Drug and Alcohol Dependence, 75*(1), 3–9.

McGarvey, E. L., Clavet, G. J., Mason, W., et al. (1999). Adolescent inhalant abuse: Environments of use. *The American Journal of Drug and Alcohol Abuse, 25*(4), 731–741.

McGeary, J. (2009). The DRD4 exon 3 VNTR polymorphism and addiction-related phenotypes: A review. *Pharmacology, Biochemistry, and Behavior, 93*(3), 222–229.

McGee, E. M. (2000). Alcoholics Anonymous and nursing: Lessons in holism and spiritual care. *Journal of Holistic Nursing, 18*(1), 11–26.

McGillicuddy, N. B. (2006). A review of substance use research among those with mental retardation. *Mental Retardation and Developmental Disability Research Reviews, 12*(1), 41–47.

McGinnis, J. M., & Foege, W. H. (1993). Actual causes of death in the United States. *JAMA, The Journal of the American Medical Association, 270,* 2207–2212.

McGlone, L., Mactier, H., Hamilton, R., et al. (2008). Visual evoked potentials in infants exposed to methadone in utero. *Archives of Disease in Childhood, 93*(9), 784–786.

McGlone, L., Mactier, H., & Weaver, L. T. (2009). Drug misuse in pregnancy: Losing sight of the baby? *Archives of Disease in Childhood, 94*(9), 708–712.

McGregor, C., Srisurapanont, M., Jittiwutikarn, J., et al. (2005). The nature, time course and severity of methamphetamine withdrawal. *Addiction, 100*(9), 1320–1329.

McHugh, R. K., Hearon, B. A., & Otto, M. W. (2010). Cognitive behavioral therapy for substance use disorders. *Psychiatric Clinics of North America, 33*(3), 511–525.

McKay, J. R. (1999). Studies of factors in relapse to alcohol, drug and nicotine use: A critical review of methodologies and findings. *Journal of Studies on Alcohol, 60*(4), 566–576.

McKay, J. R., Franklin, T. R., Patapis, N., et al. (2006). Conceptual, methodological, and analytical issues in the study of relapse. *Clinical Psychology Review, 26*(2), 109–127.

McKenzie, J. D. (1969). *Trends in marijuana use.* College Park, MD: University of Maryland Counseling Center.

McKinnon, S. A., O'Rourke, K. M., Thompson, S. E., et al. (2004). Alcohol use and abuse by adolescents: The impact of living in a border community. *The Journal of Adolescent Health, 34*(1), 88–93.

McLaney, M. A., Del Boca, F., & Babor, T. (1994). A validation study of the problem-oriented screening instrument for teenagers (POSIT). *Journal of Mental Health, 3*(3), 363–376.

McLaughlin, R. J., Holcomb, J. D., Jibaja-Rusth, M. L., et al. (1993). Teacher ratings of student risk for substance use as a function of specialized training. *Journal of Drug Education, 23*(1), 83–95.

McQuade, W. H., Levy, S. M., Yanek, L. R., et al. (2000). Detecting symptoms of alcohol abuse in primary care settings. *Archives of Family Medicine, 9,* 814–821.

Meara, E., & Frank, R. G. (2005). Spending on substance abuse treatment: How much is enough? *Addiction, 100*(9), 1240–1248.

Medina-Mora, E., Carreño, S., & De la Fuente, J. R. (1998). Experience with the Alcohol Use Disorders Identification Test (AUDIT) in Mexico. *Recent Developments in Alcoholism, 14,* 383–396.

Medina-Mora, M. E., & Real, T. (2008). Epidemiology of inhalant use. *Current Opinion in Psychiatry, 21*(3), 247–251.

Melian, A. M., Burillo-Putze, G., Campo, C. G., et al. (2004). Accidental ecstasy poisoning in a toddler. *Pediatric Emergency Care, 20*(8), 534–535.

Mellanby, A. R., Rees, J. B., & Tripp, J. H. (2000). Peer-led and adult-led school health education: A critical review of available comparative research. *Health Education Research, 15*(5), 533–545.

Mellin, G. W., & Katzenstein, M. (1962). The saga of thalidomide. Neuropathy to embryopathy, with case reports of congenital anomalies. *The New England Journal of Medicine, 267,* 1184–1192.

Melnick, G., De Leon, G., Hawke, J., et al. (1997). Motivation and readiness for therapeutic community treatment among adolescents and adult substance abusers. *The American Journal of Drug and Alcohol Abuse, 23*(4), 485–506.

Meltzer, L. J., & Mindell, J. A. (2006). Sleep and sleep disorders in children and adolescents. *Psychiatric Clinics of North America, 29*(4), 1059–1076.

Menezes-Gaya, C., Zuardi, A. W., & Loureiro, S. R. (2009). Is the Fagerström Test for Nicotine Dependence a good instrument to assess tobacco use in patients with schizophrenia? [letter]. *Revista Brasileira de Psiquiatria, 31*(3), 281–292.

Mennella, J. (2001). Alcohol's effect on lactation. *Alcohol Research & Health, 25*(3), 230–234.

Menninger, K. A. (1938). *Man against himself.* New York, NY: Harcourt Brace.

Meny, R. G., Naumburg, E. G., Alger, L. S., et al. (1993). Codeine and the breastfed neonate. *Journal of Human Lactation, 9,* 237–240.

Mercer, G. W., Hundleby, J. D., & Carpenter, R. A. (1978). Adolescent drug use and attitudes toward family. *Canadian Journal of Behavioural Science, 10*(1), 79–90.

Mercer, G. W., & Kohn, P. M. (1980). Child-rearing factors, authoritarianism, drug use attitudes, and adolescent drug use: A model. *The Journal of Genetic Psychology, 136,* 159–171.

Mercer, G. W., & Smart, R. G. (1974). The epidemiology of psychoactive and hallucinogenic drug use. In

R. J. Gibbons, Y. Israel, H. Kalant, et al. (Eds.), *Research advances in alcohol and drug problems* (Vol. 1, pp. 303–307). New York, NY: Wiley.

Merewood, A., Brooks, D., Bauchner, H., et al. (2006). Maternal birthplace and breastfeeding initiation among term and preterm infants: A statewide assessment for Massachusetts. *Pediatrics, 118*(4), e1048-e1054.

Merrell, C., & Tymms, P. B. (2001). Inattention, hyperactivity and impulsiveness: Their impact on academic achievement and progress. *British Journal of Educational Psychology, 71*(pt. 1), 43–56.

Mersy, D. J. (2003). Recognition of alcohol and substance abuse. *American Family Physician, 67*(7), 1529–1532.

Merton, R. K. (1957). *Social theory and social structure* (rev. ed.). New York, NY: Free Press.

Messick, S. (1995). Validity of psychological assessment: Validation of inferences from persons' responses and performances as scientific inquiry into score meaning. *American Psychologist, 50*, 741–749.

Mezzich, A. C., Moss, H., Tarter, R. E., et al. (1994). Gender differences in the pattern and progression of substance use in conduct-disordered adolescents. *The American Journal on Addictions, 3*, 289–295.

Michaud, D. S., Giovannucci, E., Willett, W. C., et al. (2001). Coffee and alcohol consumption and the risk of pancreatic cancer in two prospective United States cohorts. *Cancer Epidemiology, Biomarkers & Prevention, 10*(5), 429–437.

Michels, K. B., Holmberg, L., Bergkvist, L., et al. (2002). Coffee, tea, and caffeine consumption and breast cancer incidence in a cohort of Swedish women. *Annals of Epidemiology, 12*(1), 21–26.

Mikami, I., Akechi, T., Kugaya, A., et al. (1999). Screening for nicotine dependence among smoking-related cancer patients. *Japanese Journal of Cancer Research, 90*(10), 1071–1075.

Milberger, S., Biederman, J., Faraone, S. V., et al. (1996). Is maternal smoking during pregnancy a risk factor for attention deficit hyperactivity disorder in children? *The American Journal of Psychiatry, 153*, 1138–1142.

Milberger, S., Biederman, J., Faraone, S. V., et al. (1997). Associations between ADHD and psychoactive substance use disorders. Findings from a longitudinal study of high-risk siblings of ADHD children. *The American Journal of Addictions, 6*(4), 318–329.

Miller, B. A., & Downs, W. R. (1995). Violent victimization among women with alcohol problems. *Recent Developments in Alcoholism, 12*, 81–101.

Miller, G. A. (1956). The magical number seven, plus or minus two: Some limits on our capacity for processing information. *Psychological Review, 63*, 81–97.

Miller, J., & Roache, J. (2009). Benefits of topiramate treatment in a dual-diagnosis patient. *Psychosomatics, 50*(4), 426–427.

Miller, J. W., Naimi, T. S., Brewer, R. D., et al. (2007). Binge drinking and associated health risk behaviors among high school students. *Pediatrics, 119*(1), 76–85.

Miller, K. E. (2008). Energy drinks, race, and problem behaviors among college students. *The Journal of Adolescent Health, 43*(5), 490–497.

Miller, L., Davies, M., & Greenwald, S. (2000). Religiosity and substance use and abuse among adolescents in the National Comorbidity Survey. *Journal of the American Academy of Child & Adolescent Psychiatry, 39*(9), 1190–1197.

Miller, N. S. (1994). The interactions between coexisting disorders. In N. S. Miller (Ed.), *Treating coexisting psychiatric and addictive disorders: A practical guide* (pp. 7–21). Center City, MN: Hazelden.

Miller, N. S., Belkin, B. M., & Gibbons, R. (1994). Clinical diagnosis of substance use disorders in private psychiatric populations. *Journal of Substance Abuse Treatment, 11*(4), 387–392.

Miller, T. R., Levy, D. T., Spicer, R. S., et al. (2006). Societal costs of underage drinking. *Journal of Studies on Alcohol, 67*, 519–528.

Miller, W. R., & McCrady, B. S. (1993). The importance of research on Alcoholics Anonymous. In B. S. McCrady & W. R. Miller (Eds.), *Research on Alcoholics Anonymous* (pp. 3–11). New Brunswick, NJ: Rutgers Center of Alcohol Studies.

Millsaps, C. L., Azrin, R. L., & Mittenberg, W. (1994). Neuropsychological effects of chronic cannabis use on the memory and intelligence of adolescents. *Journal of Child & Adolescent Substance Abuse, 3*(1), 47–55.

Mimiaga, M. J., Reisner, S. L., Fontaine, Y. M., et al. (2010). Walking the line: Stimulant use during sex and HIV risk behavior among black urban MSM. *Drug and Alcohol Dependence, 110*(1–2), 30–37.

Minino, A. (2010, May). Mortality among teenagers aged 12–19 years: United States, 1999–2006. *National Center for Health Statistics Data Brief, 37*, 1–8.

Minkoff, K. (1989). An integrated treatment model for dual diagnosis of psychosis and addiction. *Hospital & Community Psychiatry, 40*, 1031–1036.

Minozzi, S., Amato, L., Vecchi, S., et al. (2011, April 13). Oral naltrexone maintenance treatment for opioid dependence. *Cochrane Database of Systematic Reviews, 4*(CD001333). Retrieved from http://www.ncbi.nih.gov/pubmed/21491383

Mintzer, M. Z., & Griffiths, R. R. (1999). Triazolam and zolpidem: Effects on human memory and attentional processes. *Psychopharmacology (Berlin), 144*(1), 8–19.

Minuchin, S. (1974). *Families and family therapy.* Cambridge, MA: Harvard University Press.

Minugh, P. A., Janke, S. L., Lomuto, N. A., et al. (2007). Adolescent substance abuse treatment resource allocation in rural and frontier conditions: The impact of including organizational readiness to change. *The Journal of Rural Health, 23*(Suppl.), 84–88.

Mirchandani, H. G., Mirchandani, I. H., Hellman, F., et al. (1991). Passive inhalation of free-base cocaine ("crack") smoke by infants. *Archives of Pathology & Laboratory Medicine, 115*(5), 494–498.

Mitchell, E. A., Ford, R. P., Stewart, A. W., et al. (1993). Smoking and the sudden infant death syndrome. *Pediatrics, 91*(5), 893–896.

Mitchell, E. A., & Milerad, J. (2006). Smoking and the sudden infant death syndrome. *Reviews on Environmental Health, 21*(2), 81–103.

Mittenberg, W., & Motta, S. (1993). Effects of chronic cocaine abuse on memory and learning. *Archives of Clinical Neuropsychology, 8,* 477–483.

Modesto-Lowe, V., Danforth, J. S., Neering, C., et al. (2010). Can we prevent smoking in children with ADHD: A review of the literature. *Connecticut Medicine, 74*(4), 229–236.

Modesto-Lowe, V., & Petry, N. M. (2001). Recognizing and managing "illy" intoxication. *Psychiatric Services, 52*(12), 1660.

Moffitt, K. H., Singer, J. A., Nelligan, D. W., et al. (1994). Depression and memory narrative type. *Journal of Abnormal Psychology, 103,* 581–583.

Mohaupt, S. M., & Sharma, K. K. (1998). Forensic implications and medical-legal dilemmas of maternal versus fetal rights. *Journal of Forensic Sciences, 43*(5), 985–992.

Molina, B. S., & Pelham, W. E. (2003). Childhood predictors of adolescent substance use in a longitudinal study of children with ADHD. *Journal of Abnormal Psychology, 112,* 497–507.

Molina, B. S., Pelham, W. E., Gnagy, E. M., et al. (2007). Attention-deficit/hyperactivity disorder risk for heavy drinking and alcohol use disorder is age specific. *Alcoholism, Clinical & Experimental Research, 31*(4), 643–654.

Molina, D. K., & Hardgrove, V. M. (2011). Fatal cocaine interactions: A review of cocaine-related deaths in Bexar County, Texas. *The American Journal of Forensic Medicine and Pathology, 32*(1), 71–77.

Montgomery, D., Plate, C., Alder, S. C., et al. (2006). Testing for fetal exposure to illicit drugs using umbilical cord tissue vs meconium. *Journal of Perinatology, 26*(1), 11–14.

Montoya, A. G., Sorrentino, R., Lukas, S. E., et al. (2002). Long-term neuropsychiatric consequences of "ecstasy" (MDMA): A review. *Harvard Review of Psychiatry, 10*(4), 212–220.

Moolchan, E. T., Radzius, A., Epstein, D. H., et al. (2002). The Fagerstrom Test for Nicotine Dependence and the Diagnostic Interview Schedule: Do they diagnose the same smokers? *Addictive Behaviors, 27*(1), 101–113.

Moore, C., Negrusz, A., & Lewis, D. (1998). Determination of drugs of abuse in meconium. *Journal of Chromatography B: Biomedical Sciences and Applications, 713*(1), 137–146.

Moraes, C. L., Viellas, E. F., & Reichenheim, M. E. (2005). Assessing alcohol misuse during pregnancy: Evaluating psychometric properties of the CAGE, T-ACE and TWEAK in a Brazilian setting. *Journal of Studies on Alcohol, 66*(2), 165–173.

Moran Sanchez, I., Navarro-Mateu, F., Robles Sanchez, F., et al. (2008). Evaluation of the validity of AD/HD diagnoses in referrals from paediatrics to the child psychiatry clinic [in Spanish]. *Atencion Primaria, 40*(1), 29–33.

Moreira, F. A., & Lutz, B. (2008). The endocannabinoid system: Emotion, learning, and addiction. *Addiction Biology, 13*(2), 196–212.

Moretti, M. E. (2009). Psychotropic drugs in lactation. *Canadian Journal of Clinical Pharmacology, 16*(1), e49–e57.

Morgan, M. J. (1999). Memory deficits associated with recreational use of "ecstasy" (MDMA). *Psychopharmacology (Berlin), 141*(1), 30–36.

Morris, B. J., Cochran, S. M., & Pratt, J. A. (2005). PCP: From pharmacology to modeling schizophrenia. *Current Opinion in Pharmacology, 5*(1), 101–106.

Morrow, C. E., Vogel, A. L., Anthony, J. C., et al. (2004). Expressive and receptive language functioning in preschool children with prenatal cocaine exposure. *Journal of Pediatric Psychology, 29,* 543–554.

Moskowitz, J. M., Malvin, J., Schaeffer, G. A., et al. (1983). Evaluation of a junior high school primary prevention program. *Addictive Behaviors, 8*(4), 393–401.

Moskowitz, J. M., Schaps, E., Schaeffer, G. A., et al. (1984). Evaluation of a substance abuse prevention program for junior high school students. *The International Journal of the Addictions, 19*(4), 419–430.

Mueser, K. T., & Fox, L. (2002). A family intervention program for dual disorders. *Community Mental Health Journal, 38*(3), 253–270.

Muilenburg, J. L., & Johnson, W. D. (2006). Inhalant use and risky behavior correlates in a sample of rural middle school students. *Substance Abuse, 27*(4), 21–25.

Muilenburg, J. L., & Legge, J. S., Jr. (2008). African American adolescents and menthol cigarettes: Smoking behavior among secondary school students. *The Journal of Adolescent Health, 43*(6), 570–575.

Muisener, P. P. (1994). *Understanding and treating adolescent substance abuse.* Thousand Oaks, CA: Sage.

Müller-Riemenschneider, F., Bockelbrink, A., Reinhold, T., et al. (2008). Long-term effectiveness of behavioural interventions to prevent smoking among children and youth. *Tobacco Control, 17*(5), 301–302.

Muller-Vahl, K. R., & Emrich, H. M. (2008). Cannabis and schizophrenia: Towards a cannabinoid hypothesis of schizophrenia. *Expert Review of Neurotherapeutics, 8*(7), 1037–1048.

Mullins, K. J. (2010). U.S. drug czar targets Native American meth labs in ad campaign. *Digital Journal.* Retrieved from http://www.digitaljournal.com/article/291318

Murphy, P. N., Wareing, M., Fisk, J. E., et al. (2009). Executive working memory deficits in abstinent ecstasy/MDMA users: A critical review. *Neuropsychobiology, 60*(3–4), 159–175.

Murray, D. M., Davis-Hearn, M., Goldman, A., et al. (1988). Four- and five-year follow-up results from four seventh-grade smoking prevention strategies. *Journal of Behavioral Medicine, 11*(4), 395–405.

Murray, J. B. (2002). Phencyclidine (PCP): A dangerous drug, but useful in schizophrenia research. *The Journal of Psychology, 136*(3), 319–327.

Murray, R. M. (1977). Screening and early detection instruments for disabilities related to alcohol consumption. In G. Edwards, M. Keller, J. Moser, et al. (Eds), *Alcohol-related disabilities* (pp. 89–105, WHO Offset Publication No. 32). Geneva, Switzerland: World Health Organization.

Musshoff, F., Padosch, S. A., Kroener, L. A., et al. (2006). Accidental autoerotic death by volatile substance abuse or nonsexually motivated accidents? *The American Journal of Forensic Medicine and Pathology, 27*(2), 188–192.

Musty, R. E., & Kaback, L. (1995). Relationship between motivation and depression in chronic marijuana users. *Life Sciences, 56*(23–24), 2151–2158.

Mvula, M. M., Miller, J. M. Jr., & Ragan, F. A. (1999). Relationship of phencyclidine and pregnancy outcome. *The Journal of Reproductive Medicine, 44*(12), 1021–1024.

Myers, C. S., Taylor, R. C., Moolchan, E. T., et al. (2008). Dose-related enhancement of mood and cognition in smokers administered nicotine nasal spray. *Neuropsychopharmacology, 33*(3), 588–598.

Mytton, J., DiGuiseppi, C., Gough, D., et al. (2006, July 19). School-based secondary prevention programmes for preventing violence. *Cochrane Database of Systematic Reviews*, 3, CD004606.

# N

Nagata, C., Mizoue, T., Tanaka, K., et al. (2006). Tobacco smoking and breast cancer risk: An evaluation based on a systematic review of epidemiological evidence among the Japanese population. *Japanese Journal of Clinical Oncology, 36*(6), 387–394.

Nahas, G. G., Zeidenberg, P., & Lefebure, C. (1975). Kif in Morocco. *The International Journal of the Addictions, 10*(6), 977–993.

Najavits, L. M., Weiss, R. D., & Shaw, S. R. (1997). The link between substance abuse and posttraumatic stress disorder in women. A research review. *The American Journal on Addictions, 6*(4), 273–283.

Naltrexone. (2009, February 1). *MedlinePlus*, pp. 1–4. Retrieved from http://www.nlm.nih.gov/medlineplus/druginfo/meds/a685041.html

Naltrexone injection. (2010, May 1). *MedlinePlus*, pp. 1–4. Retrieved from http://www.nlm.nih.gov/medlineplus/druginfo/meds/a609007.html

Nanson, J. L., & Hiscock, M. (1990). Attention deficits in children exposed to alcohol prenatally. *Alcoholism, Clinical & Experimental Research, 14*, 656–661.

Nash, J. E., & Persaud, T. V. (1988). Embryopathic risks of cigarette smoking. *Experimental Pathology, 33*, 65–73.

Natakusumah, A., Irwanto, Piercy, F., et al. (1992). Cohesion and adaptability in families of adolescent drug abusers in the United States and Indonesia. *Journal of Comparative Family Studies, 23*(3), 389–411.

National Capital Poison Center. (2011, January 3). Poisonings: The local picture (2009). *Poisoning Statistics*, pp. 1–4. Retrieved from http://www.poison.org/stats/

National Center on Addictions and Substance Abuse at Columbia University (CASA). (2000, May 10). Missed opportunity: The CASA National Survey of Primary Care Physicians and Patients [press release]. Retrieved from www.casacolumbia.org/absolutenm/PressReleases.asp?articleid=125&zoneid=49

National Drug Intelligence Center. (2001, May). Heroin. *California Central District Drug Threat Assessment*, pp. 1–8. Retrieved from http://www.justice.gov/ndic/pubs0/668/heroin.htm

National Institute for Health and Clinical Excellence. (2007, March). Community-based interventions to reduce substance misuse among vulnerable and disadvantaged children and young people. Retrieved from www.nice.org.uk

National Institute on Alcohol Abuse and Alcoholism. (1995). *The physician's guide to helping patients with alcohol problems*. Washington DC: Government Printing Office (Publication NIH 95–3769).

National Institute on Alcohol Abuse and Alcoholism. (2004). NIAAA Council approves definition of binge drinking. *NIAAA Newsletter, 3*, 3.

National Institute on Alcohol Abuse and Alcoholism. (2007, January). Alcohol and tobacco. *Alcohol Alert, 71*, 1–6.

National Institute on Drug Abuse. (2009, November 9). *Cocaine* (pp. 1–2). Retrieved from http://www.drugabuse.gov/drugpages/cocaine.html

National Institute on Drug Abuse. (2010, May 19). Drug Use Questionnaire [DAST–10]. *Diagnosis & Treatment of Drug Abuse in Family Practice*, pp. 1–2. Retrieved from http://archives.drugabuse.gov/diagnosis-treatment/DAST-10.html

National Institutes of Health Consensus Development Conference Statement: Diagnosis and treatment of attention-deficit/hyperactivity disorder (ADHD). (2000). *Journal of the American Academy of Child & Adolescent Psychiatry, 39*(2), 182–193.

Nau, H. (1986). Species differences in pharmacokinetics and drug teratogenesis. *Environmental Health Perspectives, 70*, 113–129.

Nawrot, P., Jordan, J., Eastwood, J., et al. (2003). Effects of caffeine on human health. *Food Additives & Contaminants, 20*(1), 1–30.

Nayak, M. B., Bond, J. C., Cherpitel, C. J., et al. (2009). Detecting alcohol-related problems in developing countries: A comparison of 2 screening measures in India. *Alcoholism, Clinical and Experimental Research, 33*(12), 2057–2066.

Neal, D. J., Corbin, W. R., & Fromme, K. (2006). Measurement of alcohol-related consequences among high school and college students: Application of item response models to the Rutgers Alcohol Problem Index. *Psychological Assessment, 18*(4), 402–414.

Nehlig, A., Daval, J. L., & Debry, G. (1992). Caffeine and the central nervous system: Mechanisms of action, biochemical, metabolic and psychostimulant effects. *Brain Research and Brain Research Reviews, 17*(2), 139–170. Retrieved from http://www.ncbi.nlm.nih.gov/pubmed/1356551

Nelson, E. C., Heath, A. C., Lynskey, M. T., et al. (2006). Childhood sexual abuse and risks for licit and illicit drug-related outcomes: A twin study. *Psychological Medicine, 36*(10), 1473–1483.

Nelson, E. C., Heath, A. C., Madden, P. A., et al. (2002). Association between self-reported childhood sexual abuse and adverse psychosocial outcomes: Results from a twin study. *Archives of General Psychiatry, 59*(2), 139–145.

Nestor, L., Roberts, G., Garavan, H., et al. (2008). Deficits in learning and memory: Parhippocampal hyperactivity and frontocortical hypoactivity in cannabis users. *NeuroImage, 40*(3), 1328–1339.

Neuman, R. Lobos, E., Reich, W., et al. (2007). Prenatal smoking exposure and dopaminergic genotypes interact to cause a severe ADHD subtype. *Biological Psychiatry, 61*, 1320–1328.

Neumark, Y. D., Delva, J., & Anthony, J. (1998). The epidemiology of adolescent inhalant drug involvement. *Archives of Pediatrics & Adolescent Medicine, 152*, 781–786.

Neuspiel, D. R. (1992). Cocaine-associated abnormalities may not be causally related [letter]. *American Journal of Diseases of Children, 146*, 278.

Neuspiel, D. R. (1993). Cocaine and the fetus: Mythology of severe risk. *Neurotoxicology and Teratology, 15*, 305–306.

Nevitt, J. R., Lundak, J., & Codr, J., et al. (2007). An analysis of audit scores of adolescent offenders in two Midwestern counties. *Psychological Reports, 100* (3, pt. 1), 700–706.

Nevitt, J. R., Lundak, J., & Galardi, G. (2006). Profile of adolescent alcohol offenders in two rural midwestern counties. *Psychological Reports, 98*(2), 379–384.

Newcomb, M. D., & Bentler, P. M. (1988). *Consequences of adolescent drug use: Impact on the lives of young adults.* Newbury Park, CA: Sage.

Newcomb, M. D., Maddahian, E., & Bentler, P. M. (1986). Risk factors for drug use among adolescents: Concurrent and longitudinal analyses. *American Journal of Public Health, 76*, 525–531.

Newcombe, D. A., Humeniuk, R. E., & Ali, R. (2005). Validation of the World Health Organization Alcohol Smoking and Substance Involvement Screening Test (ASSIST): Report of results from the Australian site. *Drug and Alcohol Review, 24*(3), 217–226.

Newell, M. L. (1991). The natural history of vertically acquired HIV infection. The European Collaborative Study. *Journal of Perinatal Medicine, 19*(Suppl. 1), 257–262.

Newlin, D. B., & Thomson, J. B. (1990). Alcohol challenge with sons of alcoholics: A critical review and analysis. *Psychological Bulletin, 108*, 383–402.

Newport, F. (2009a, January 28). State of the states: Importance of religion. *Gallup*, pp. 1–3. Retrieved from http://www.gallup.com/poll/114022/State-States-Importance-Religion.aspx

Newport, F. (2009b, March 23). Despite recession, no uptick in Americans' religiosity. *Gallup*, pp. 1–3. Retrieved from http://www.gallup.com/poll/117040/Despite-Recession-No-Upstick-Americans-Regiosity...

Nichols, D. E. (2004). Hallucinogens. *Pharmacology & Therapeutics, 101*(2), 131–181.

NIDA. (2008, August). Club drugs (GHB, ketamine, and Rohypnol). *NIDA InfoFacts*, pp. 1–3.

Nides, M., Oncken, C., Gonzales, D., et al. (2006). Smoking cessation with varenicline, a selective alpha-4 beta-2 nicotinic receptor partial agonist: Results from a 7-week, randomized, placebo- and bupropion-controlled trial with 1-year follow-up. *Archives of Internal Medicine, 166*, 1561–1568.

Niethammer, O., & Frank, R. (2007). Prevalence of use, abuse and dependence on legal and illegal psychotropic substances in an adolescent inpatient psychiatric population. *European Child & Adolescent Psychiatry, 16*(4), 254–259.

Ninan, P.T. (2001). Pharmacokinetically induced benzodiazepine withdrawal. *Psychopharmacology Bulletin, 35*(4), 94–100.

Nischal, K. K. (2010). Maternal drug abuse and ocular morbidity: More than meets the eye? (Editorial). *British Journal of Ophthalmology, 94*, 671.

Nitsun, M., Szokol, J. W., Saleh, H. J., et al. (2006). Pharmacokinetics of midazolam, propofol, and fentanyl transfer to human breast milk. *Clinical Pharmacology & Therapeutics, 79*(6), 549–557.

Nnadi, C. U., Mimiko, O. A., McCurtis, H. L., et al. (2005). Neuropsychiatric effects of cocaine use disorders. *Journal of the National Medical Association, 97*(11), 1504–1515.

Nocerino, E., Amato, M., & Izzo, A.A. (2000). Cannabis and cannabinoid receptors. *Fitoterapia, 71* (Suppl. 1), S6–S12.

Nock, M. K., Kazdin, A. E., Hiripi, E., et al. (2006). Prevalence, subtypes, and correlates of *DSM-IV* conduct disorder in the National Comorbidity Survey Replication. *Psychological Medicine, 36*, 699–710.

Noel, M., O'Connor, R. M., Boudreau, B., et al. (2010). The Rutgers Alcohol Problem Index (RAPI): A comparison of cut-points in First Nations Mi'kmaq and non-Aboriginal adolescents in rural Nova Scotia. *International Journal of Mental Health and Addiction, 8*, 336–350.

Nogueira, L., Kalivas, P. W., & Lavin, A. (2006). Long-term neuroadaptations produced by withdrawal from repeated cocaine treatment: Role of dopaminergic receptors in modulating cortical excitability. *The Journal of Neuroscience , 26*(47), 12308–12313.

Nordeng, H., Zahlsen, K., & Spigset, O. (2001). Transfer of carisoprodol to breast milk. *Therapeutic Drug Monitoring, 23*, 298–300.

Norem-Hebeisen, A. A., & Lucas, M. S. (1977). A developmental model for primary prevention of chemical abuse. *Journal of Drug Education, 7*(2), 141–148.

Norman, E., & Turner, S. (1993). Adolescent substance abuse prevention programs: Theories, models, and research in the encouraging 80s. *The Journal of Primary Prevention, 13*, 3–20.

NORML (2011). State by state laws. Retrieved from htttp://norml.org/index.cfm?Group_ID=4516

Norris, C. R., & Extein, I. L. (1991). Diagnosing dual diagnosis patients. In M. S. Gold & A. E. Slaby (Eds.), *Dual diagnosis in substance abuse* (pp. 159–184). New York, NY: Dekker.

Norris, K. C., Thornhill-Joynes, M., Robinson, C., et al. (2001). Cocaine use, hypertension, and end-stage renal disease. *American Journal of Kidney Diseases, 38*(3), 523–528.

Novins, D. K., Beals, J., & Mitchell, C. M. (2001). Sequences of substance use among American Indian adolescents. *Journal of the American Academy of Child & Adolescent Psychiatry, 40*(10), 1168–1174.

Nucci, P., & Brancato, R. (1994). Ocular effects of prenatal cocaine exposure. *Ophthalmology, 101*, 1321.

Nulsen, C. E., Fox, A. M., & Hammond, G. R. (2010). Differential effects of ecstasy on short-term and working memory: A meta-analysis. *Neuropsychology Review, 20*(1), 21–32.

Nunes, E. V., Rothenberg, J. L., Sullivan, M. A., et al. (2006). Behavioral therapy to augment oral naltrexone for opioid dependence: A ceiling on effectiveness? *The American Journal of Drug and Alcohol Abuse, 32*(4), 503–517.

Nunnally, J., & Bernstein, I. (1994). *Psychometric theory* (3rd ed.). New York, NY: McGraw-Hill.

Nurnberger, J. I., Jr., Foroud, T., Flury, L., et al. (2002). Is there a genetic relationship between alcoholism and depression? *Alcohol Research & Health, 26*(3), 233–240.

Nyström, M., Peräsalo, J., & Saläspuro, M. (1993). Screening for heavy drinking and alcohol-related problems in young university students: The CAGE, the Mm-MAST and the trauma score questionnaires. *Journal of Studies on Alcoholism, 54*(5), 528–533.

# O

O'Brien, C. P., (2008). The CAGE Questionnaire for detection of alcoholism: A remarkably useful but simple tool. *JAMA, The Journal of the American Medical Association, 300*(17), 2054–2056.

O'Brien, D. (2005, August 24). *Manitoba's sniff crisis has given birth to a tragic trend . . . Babies smell like gas. Winnipeg Free Press*, pp. A1–A2.

O'Brien, M. C., McCoy, T. P., Rhodes, S. D., et al. (2008). Caffeinated cocktails: Energy drink consumption, high-risk drinking, and alcohol-related consequences among college students. *Academic Emergency Medicine, 15*(5), 453–460.

O'Brien, M. P. (2008, June). *Epidemiologic trends in drug abuse, Proceedings of the Community Epidemiology Work Group (Volume 1): Highlights and Executive Summary*. Bethesda, MD: National Institute on Drug Abuse, U.S. Department of Health and Human Services, National Institutes of Health.

O'Brien, M. S., Wu, L. T., & Anthony, J. C. (2005). Cocaine use and the occurrence of panic attacks in the community: A case-crossover approach. *Substance Use & Misuse, 40*(3), 285–297.

O'Brien, W., & Biase, D. V. (1984). The therapeutic community: A current perspective. *Journal of Psychoactive Drugs, 16*, 9–21.

O'Callaghan, F. V., O'Callaghan, M., Najman, J. M., et al. (2006). Prediction of adolescent smoking from family and social risk factors at 5 years, and maternal smoking in pregnancy and at 5 and 14 years. *Addiction, 101*(2), 282–290.

Ochoa, K. C., Hahn, J. A., Seal, K. H., et al. (2001). Overdosing among young injection drug users in San Francisco. *Addictive Behaviors, 26*(3), 453–460.

O'Connell, D. F. (Ed.) (1990). *Managing the dually diagnosed patient: Current issues and clinical approaches*. New York, NY: Haworth.

O'Connell, J. M., Novins, D. K., Beals, J., et al. (2007). Childhood characteristics associated with stage of substance use of American Indians: Family background, traumatic experiences, and childhood behaviors. *Addictive Behaviors, 32*(12), 3142–3152.

O'Connell, T., Kaye, L., & Plosay, J. J. (2000). Gamma-hydroxybutyrate (GHB): A newer drug of abuse. *American Family Physician, 62*, 2478–2483.

O'Connor, A., & Schweber, N. (2009, November 7). Driver said to have used marijuana regularly. *New York Times*. Retrieved from http://www.nytimes.com/2009/11/07/nyregion/07taconic.html?pagewanted=print

O'Connor, M. J., & Whaley, S. E. (2003). Alcohol use in pregnant low-income women. *Journal of Studies on Alcohol, 64*(6), 773–783.

Oddy, W. H., & O'Sullivan, T. A. (2009). Energy drinks for children and adolescents. *British Medical Journal, 339*, b5268.

Oei, T., & Jackson, P. (1980). Long-term effects of group and individual social skills training with alcoholics. *Addictive Behavior, 5*, 129–136.

Oetting, E. R., & Beauvais, F. (1987). Common elements in youth drug abuse: Peer clusters and other psychosocial factors. *Journal of Drug Issues, 17*, 133–151.

Oetting, E. R., & Beauvais, F. (1990–1991). Orthogonal cultural identification theory: The cultural identification of minority adolescents. *The International Journal of the Addictions, 25*, 655–685.

Office of National Drug Control Policy. (2010, January 6). *Heroin facts & figures* (pp. 1–8). Retrieved from http://www.whitehousedrugpolicy .gov/DrugFact/heroin/heroin_ff.html

Offidani, C., Pomini, F., Caruso, A., et al. (1995). Cocaine during pregnancy: A critical review of the literature. *Minerva Ginecologica, 47*(9), 381–390.

O'Hare, T. (2005). Comparing the AUDIT and 3 drinking indices as predictors of personal and social drinking problems in freshman first offenders. *Journal of Alcohol and Drug Education, 49*(3), 37–61.

O'Hare, T., & Tran, T. V. (1997). Predicting problem drinking in college students: Gender differences and the CAGE questionnaire. *Addictive Behaviors, 22*(1), 13–21.

Okawa, M., & Uchiyama, M. (2007). Circadian rhythm sleep disorders: Characteristics and entrainment pathology in delayed sleep phase and non-24-h sleep-wake syndrome. *Sleep Medicine Reviews, 11*(6), 485–496.

Okuyemi, K. S., Pulvers, K. M., Cox, L. S., et al. (2007). Nicotine dependence among African American light smokers: A comparison of three scales. *Addictive Behaviors, 32*(10), 1989–2002.

Olmsted, C. L., & Kockler, D. R. (2008). Topiramate for alcohol dependence. *Annals of Pharmacotherapy, 42*(10), 1475–1480.

Olney, J. W., Wozniak, D. F., Jevtovic-Todorovic, V., et al. (2002). Drug-induced apoptotic neurodegeneration in the developing brain. *Brain Pathology, 12*(4), 488–498.

Olsen, J., Overvad, K., & Frische, G. (1991). Coffee consumption, birthweight, and reproductive failures. *Epidemiology, 2*, 370–374.

Olson, C. H. (1994). The effects of prenatal alcohol exposure on child development. *Infants and Young Children, 6*(3), 10–25.

Olson, D. H. (1980). *Clinical rating scales for the circumplex model of marital and family systems: Family social science.* St. Paul, MN: University of Minnesota Press.

Olson, D. H. (1986). Circumplex model VII: Validation studies and FACES III. *Family Process, 25*(3), 337–352.

Olson, D. H., Russell, C., & Sprenkle, D. (1979). Circumplex model of marital and family systems II: Empirical studies and clinical interventions. In J. Vincent (Ed.), *Advances in family intervention, assessment and theory* (pp. 128–179). Greenwich, CT: JAI Press.

Olson, D. H., Russell, C., & Sprenkle, D. (1980). Marital and family therapy: A decade review. *Journal of Marriage and the Family, 42*, 973–993.

Olson, D. H., Russell, C., & Sprenkle, D. (1983). Circumplex model of marital and family systems VI: Theoretical update. *Family Process, 22*(1), 69–83.

Olson, D. H., Sprenkle, D., & Russell, C. (1979). Circumplex model of marital and family systems I: Cohesion and adaptability dimensions, family types, and clinical applications. *Family Process, 18*, 3–28.

Olson, H. C., Sampson, P. D., Barr, H., et al. (1992). Prenatal exposure to alcohol and school problems in late childhood: A longitudinal prospective study. *Development and Psychopathology, 4*, 341–359.

Olson, K. R. (2010). Activated charcoal for acute poisoning: One toxicologist's journey. *Journal of Medical Toxicology, 6*, 190–198.

O'Malley, P. M., & Johnston, L. D. (2002, March). Epidemiology of alcohol and other drug use among American college students. *Journal of Studies on Alcohol,* Suppl. 14, 23–39.

O'Malley, P. M., Johnston, L. D., Bachman, J. G., et al. (2006). How substance use differs among American secondary schools. *Prevention Science, 7*(4), 409–420.

O'Mara, N.B., & Nahata, M.C. (2002). Drugs excreted in human breast milk. In L. A. Pagliaro & A. M. Pagliaro (Eds.), *Problems in pediatric drug therapy* (4th ed., pp. 201–243). Washington, DC: American Pharmaceutical Association.

Oncken, C., Gonzales, D., Nides, M., et al. (2006). Efficacy and safety of the novel selective nicotinic acetylcholine receptor partial agonist, varenicline, for smoking cessation. *Archives of Internal Medicine, 166*, 1571–1577.

Orbeta, R. L., Overpeck, M. D., Ramcharran, D., et al. (2006). High caffeine intake in adolescents: Associations with difficulty sleeping and feeling tired in the morning. *The Journal of Adolescent Health, 38*(4), 451–453.

Orford, J. (1985). *Excessive appetites: A psychological view of addictions.* New York, NY: Wiley.

Osher, F. C., & Kofoed, L. L. (1989). Treatment of patients with psychiatric and psychoactive substance use disorders. *Hospital & Community Psychiatry, 40*, 1025–1030.

Osmond, H. (1957, March 14). A review of the clinical effects of psychotomimetic agents. *Annals of the New York Academy of Sciences, 66*, 418–434.

Osterling, A., Berglund, M., Nilsson, L. H., et al. (1993). Sex differences in response style to two self-report screening tests on alcoholism. *Scandinavian Journal of Social Medicine, 21*(2), 83–89.

Oteri, A., Salvo, F., Caputi, A. P., et al. (2007). Intake of energy drinks in association with alcoholic beverages in a cohort of students of the School of Medicine of the University of Messina. *Alcoholism, Clinical and Experimental Research, 31*(10), 1677–1680.

Ouimette, P., & Brown, P. J. (2003). *Trauma and substance abuse: Causes, consequences, and treatment of comorbid disorders.* Washington, DC: American Psychological Association.

Ouimette, P., Read, J. P., Wade, M., et al. (2010). Modeling associations between posttraumatic stress disorder and substance use. *Addictive Behaviors, 35*(1), 64–67.

Ouimette, P. C., Wolfe, J., & Chrestman, K. R. (1996). Characteristics of posttraumatic stress disorder-alcohol abuse comorbidity in women. *Journal of Substance Abuse, 8*(3), 335–346.

Oural, L., Paris, M. V., Sullivan, O., et al. (2008). Pharmacological review of alcoholic dependence treatment [in Spanish]. *Vertex: Revista Argentina de Psiquiatría, 19*(77), 512–521.

Ozsungur, S., Brenner, D., & El-Sohemy, A. (2009). Fourteen well-described caffeine withdrawal symptoms factor into three clusters. *Psychopharmacology (Berlin), 201*(4), 541–548.

# P

Padilla, Y. C., Crisp, C., & Rew, D. L. (2010). Parental acceptance and illegal drug use among gay, lesbian, and bisexual adolescents: Results from a national survey. *Social Work, 55*(3), 265–275.

Pagliaro, A. M. (1990). Death of the medical model of addictions. *Proceedings of the Western Pharmacology Society, 33*, 286.

Pagliaro, A. M. (1991). The contributions of psychologic theories to the understanding of abusable psychotropic abuse phenomenon. *Canadian Psychology, 32*, 334.

Pagliaro, A. M. (1992). Producing knowledge of substance abusology: Assessment, choice, and evaluation of psychological theories of substance abuse [abstract]. *Canadian Psychology, 33*, 398.

Pagliaro, A. M. (1994). The nature of scientific knowledge production. Evidence from the transdisciplinary science of substance abusology [abstract]. *Canadian Psychology, 35*(2a), 40–43.

Pagliaro, A. M. (1997). Explaining substance use among women [abstract]. *Canadian Psychology, 38*(2a), 34.

Pagliaro, A. M. (1998). Drug-induced automatism: Theory and pharmacologic mechanisms [abstract]. *Canadian Psychology, 39*(2a), 88.

Pagliaro, A. M. (2002). Abusable psychotropic use among children and adolescents. In L. A. Pagliaro & A. M. Pagliaro (Eds.), *Problems in pediatric drug therapy* (4th ed., pp. 347–385). Washington, DC: American Pharmaceutical Association.

Pagliaro, A. M., Lang, R. A., & Pagliaro, L. A. (1998). Symposium: Drug-induced automatism—Implications for forensic psychologists [abstract]. *Canadian Psychology, 39*(2a), 88.

Pagliaro, A. M., & Pagliaro, L. A. (1992). Sentenced to death? HIV infection and AIDS in prisons—Current and future concerns. *Canadian Journal of Criminology, 34*, 201–214.

Pagliaro, A. M., & Pagliaro, L. A. (1994a). Just punishment? HIV and AIDS in correctional facilities. *Forum on Corrections Research, 6*(3), 40–43.

Pagliaro, A. M., & Pagliaro, L. A. (1995). Abusable psychotropic use among children and adolescents. In L. A.

Pagliaro & A. M. Pagliaro (Eds.), *Problems in pediatric drug therapy* (3rd ed., pp. 507–540). Hamilton, IL: Drug Intelligence.

Pagliaro, A. M., & Pagliaro, L. A. (1996). *Substance use among children and adolescents.* New York, NY: Wiley.

Pagliaro, A. M., & Pagliaro, L. A. (1999). The phenomenon of drug and substance abuse among the elderly—the Mega-Interactive Model of Substance Abuse among the Elderly (MIMSAE): Part II. *Journal of Pharmacy Technology, 10*, 22–33.

Pagliaro, A. M., & Pagliaro, L. A. (2000). *Substance use among women: A reference and resource guide.* Philadelphia, PA: Brunner/Mazel.

Pagliaro, A. M., & Pagliaro, L. A. (2003). Addictionologists' perspective on catastrophic injury. In K. Anchor (Ed.), *The handbook of catastrophic injury* (pp. 213–227). Nashville, TN: American Board of Disability Analysts.

Pagliaro, A. M., Pagliaro, L. A., Thauberger, P.C., et al. (1993). Knowledge, behaviours, and risk perception of intravenous drug users in relation to HIV infection and AIDS: The PIARG projects. *Advances in Medical Psychotherapy, 6*, 1–28.

Pagliaro, L. A. (1983). Up in smoke? A brief review of marijuana toxicity. *Kerygma*, (41), 1–4.

Pagliaro, L. A. (1987). Some problems encountered with urine screening. *AADAC Developments, 7*, 5.

Pagliaro, L. A. (1988, June). Marijuana and hashish: What are the risks? *Let's Talk, 13*, 12–14.

Pagliaro, L. A. (1991). The deja vu experience [letter]. *The American Journal of Psychiatry, 148*, 1418.

Pagliaro, L. A. (1992). The straight dope: Focus on learning – interpreting the interpretations. *Psynopsis, 14*(2), 8.

Pagliaro, L. A. (1993a). Issues in substance abuse for Canadian teachers. In L. L. Stewin & S. J. McCann (Eds.) *Contemporary educational issues: The Canadian mosaic* (2nd ed.). Toronto, ON: Copp Clark Pitman.

Pagliaro, L. A. (1993b). The straight dope: "Strawberry fields forever." The return of LSD. *Psynopsis, 15*(2), 18.

Pagliaro, L. A. (1995a). Adolescent depression and suicide. *Canadian Journal of School Psychology, 11*, 191–201.

Pagliaro, L. A. (1995b). Psychopharmacology updates: Marijuana reconsidered. *Psymposium, 5*(2), 12–13.

Pagliaro, L. A. (1996, Summer). The straight dope: Timothy has passed—On the use of psychedelics. *Psynopsis, 9*.

Pagliaro, L. A., Jaglalsingh, L., & Pagliaro, A. M. (1992). Cocaine use and depression. *CMAJ, Canadian Medical Association Journal, 147*, 1636.

Pagliaro, L. A., & Pagliaro, A. M. (Eds.) (1983). *Pharmacologic aspects of aging.* St. Louis, MO: C. V. Mosby.

Pagliaro, L. A., & Pagliaro, A. M. (Eds.) (1987). *Problems in pediatric drug therapy* (2nd ed.). Hamiliton, IL: Drug Intelligence.

Pagliaro, L. A., & Pagliaro, A. M. (1992). The phenomenon of drug and substance abuse among the elderly, part 1: An overview. *Journal of Pharmacy Technology, 8*, 65–73.

Pagliaro, L. A., & Pagliaro, A. M. (1993). The phenomenon of abusable psychotropic use among North American youth. *Journal of Clinical Pharmacology, 33*(8), 676–690.

Pagliaro, L. A., & Pagliaro, A. M. (1995). Drugs as human teratogens. In L. A. Pagliaro & A. M. Pagliaro (Eds.), *Problems in pediatric drug therapy* (3rd ed., pp. 103–243). Hamilton, IL: Drug Intelligence.

Pagliaro, L. A., & Pagliaro, A. M. (1998). *The pharmacological basis of psychotherapeutics: An introduction for psychologists.* Philadelphia, PA: Brunner/Mazel.

Pagliaro, L. A., & Pagliaro, A. M. (1999). *PPDR: The psychologists' psychotropic drug reference.* Philadelphia, PA: Brunner/Mazel.

Pagliaro, L. A., & Pagliaro, A. M. (2002). Drugs as human teratogens and fetotoxins. In L. A. Pagliaro & A. M. Pagliaro (Eds.), *Problems in pediatric drug therapy* (4th ed., pp. 87–200). Washington, DC: American Pharmaceutical Association.

Pagliaro, L. A., & Pagliaro, A. M. (2004). *Pagliaros' comprehensive guide to drugs and substances of abuse.* Washington, DC: American Pharmacists Association.

Pagliaro, L. A., & Pagliaro, A. M. (2009). *Pagliaros' comprehensive guide to drugs and substances of abuse* (2nd ed.). Washington, DC: American Pharmacists Association.

Pan, W., & Bai, H. (2009). A multivariate approach to a meta-analytic review of the effectiveness of the D.A.R.E. program. *International Journal of Environmental Research and Public Health, 6*(1), 267–277.

Pandina, R. J., & Johnson, V. (1989). Familial drinking history as a predictor of alcohol and drug consumption among adolescent children. *Journal of Studies on Alcohol, 50*(3), 245–253.

Pandina, R. J., & Johnson, V. (1990). Serious alcohol and drug problems among adolescents with a family history of alcoholism. *Journal of Studies on Alcohol, 51*(3), 278–282.

Pandina, R. J., Labouvie, E. W., & Raskin White, H. (1984). Potential contributions of the life span developmental approach to the study of adolescent alcohol and drug use: The Rutgers Health and Human Development Project, a working model. *Journal of Drug Issues, 14*(2), 253–268.

Pandina, R. J., & Raskin White, H. (1981). Patterns of alcohol and drug use of adolescent students and adolescents in treatment. *Journal of Studies on Alcohol, 42*(5), 441–456.

Pandina, R. J., & Schuele, J. A. (1983). Psychosocial correlates of alcohol and drug use of adolescents in treatment. *Journal of Studies on Alcohol, 44*(6), 950–973.

Parascandola, M. (2001). Cigarettes and the US Public Health Service in the 1950s. *American Journal of Public Health, 91*(2), 196–205.

Park, H. Y., Dent, C., Abramsohn, E., et al. (2010). Evaluation of California's in-school tobacco use prevention education (TUPE) activities using a nested school-longitudinal design, 2003–2004 and 2005–2006. *Tobacco Control, 19*(Suppl. 1), i43–i50.

Parkin, A. J., Dunn, J. C., Lee, C., et al. (1993). Neuropsychological sequelae of Wernicke's encephalopathy in a 20-year-old woman: Selective impairment of a frontal memory system. *Brain and Cognition, 21*, 1–19.

Parrott, A. C. (2006). MDMA in humans: Factors which affect the neuropsychobiological profiles of recreational ecstasy users, the integrative role of bioenergetic stress. *Journal of Psychopharmacology, 20*(2), 147–163.

Parrott, A. C., Lees, A., Garnham, N. J., et al. (1998). Cognitive performance in recreational users of MDMA of "ecstasy": Evidence for memory deficits. *Journal of Psychopharmacology, 12*(1), 79–83.

Parsons, J. T., Grov, C. & Kelly, B. C. (2009). Club drug use and dependence among young adults recruited through time-space sampling. *Public Health Reports, 124*(2), 246–254.

Parsons, J. T., Halkitis, N., & Bimbi, D. (2006). Club drug use among young adults frequenting dance clubs and other social venues in New York City. *Journal of Child & Adolescent Substance Abuse, 15*, 1–14.

Parsons, J. T., Kelly, B. C., & Weiser, J. D. (2007). Initiation into methamphetamine use for young gay and bisexual men. *Drug and Alcohol Dependence, 90*(2–3), 135–144.

Parsons, J. T., Kelly, B. C., & Wells, B. E. (2006). Differences in club drug use between heterosexual and lesbian/bisexual females. *Addictive Behaviors, 31*(12), 2344–2349.

Partnership for a Drug-Free America. (2006, May 16). The Partnership Attitude Tracking Study (PATS): Teens in grades 7 through 12, 2005. New York, NY: Author.

Partnership for a Drug-Free America and Metlife Foundation. (2010, March 2). *2009 Parents and Teens Attitude Tracking Study Report* (pp. 3–26). New York, NY: Author.

Passie, T., Halpern, J. H., Stichtenoth, D. O., et al. (2008). The pharmacology of lysergic acid diethylamide: A review. *CNS Neuroscience and Therapeutics, 14*(4), 295–314.

Patel, M. M., Belson, M. G., Longwater, A. B., et al. (2005). Methylenedioxymethamphetamine (ecstasy)-related hyperthermia. *The Journal of Emergency Medicine, 29*(4), 451–454.

Pattenden, S., Antova, T., Neuberger, M., et al. (2006). Parental smoking and children's respiratory health: Independent effects of prenatal and postnatal exposure. *Tobacco Control, 15*(4), 294–301.

Paulson, M. J., Coombs, R. H., & Richardson, M. A. (1990). School performance, academic aspirations, and drug use among children and adolescents. *Journal of Drug Education, 20*, 289–303.

Pavlov, I. P. (1927). *Conditioned reflexes: An investigation of the physiological activity of the cerebral cortex* [translated and edited by G. V. Anrep]. London, UK: Oxford University Press.

Peadon, E., Rhys-Jones, B., Bower, C., et al. (2009). Systematic review of interventions for children with Fetal Alcohol Spectrum Disorders. *BioMed Central Pediatrics, 9*, 35.

Pearson, M. A., Hoyme, H. E., Seaver, L. H., et al. (1994). Toluene embryopathy: Delineation of the phenotype and comparison with fetal alcohol syndrome. *Pediatrics, 93*(2), 211–215.

Pechmann, C., & Reibling, E. T. (2000). Anti-smoking advertising campaigns targeting youth: Case studies from USA and Canada. *Tobacco Control, 9*(Suppl. 2), 1118–1131.

Pederson, C. L., Vanhorn, D. R., Wilson, J. F., et al. (2008). Childhood abuse related to nicotine, illicit and prescription drug use by women: Pilot study. *Psychological Reports, 103*(2), 459–466.

Peele, S., Brodsky, A., & Arnold, M. (1991). *The truth about addiction and recovery: The Life Process Program for outgrowing destructive habits.* New York, NY: Simon & Schuster.

Pegues, D. A., Engelgau, M.M., & Woernle, C. H. (1994). Prevalence of illicit drugs detected in the urine of women of childbearing age in Alabama public health clinics. *Public Health Reports, 109*(4), 530–538.

Penick, E. C., Nickel, E. J., Cantrell, P. F., et al. (1990). The emerging concept of dual diagnosis: An overview and implications. In D. F. O'Connell (Ed.), *Managing the dually diagnosed patient: Current issues and clinical approaches* (pp. 1–54). New York, NY: Haworth.

Pennings, E. J., Leccese, A. P., & Wolff, F. A. (2002). Effects of concurrent use of alcohol and cocaine. *Addiction, 97*(7), 773–783.

Pentney, A.R. (2001). An exploration of the history and controversies surrounding MDMA and MDA. *Journal of Psychoactive Drugs, 33*(3), 213–221.

Perez, A., Scribano, P. V., & Perry, H. (2004). An intentional opiate intoxication of an infant: When medical toxicology and child maltreatment services merge. *Pediatric Emergency Care, 20*(11), 769–772.

Perez, E., Chu, J., & Bania, T. (2006). Seven days of gamma-hydroxybyrate (GHB) use produces severe withdrawal. *Annals of Emergency Medicine, 48*(2), 219–220.

Perez-Bouchard, L., Johnson, J. L., & Ahrens, A. H. (1993). Attributional style in children of substance abusers. *The American Journal of Drug and Alcohol Abuse, 19*, 475–489.

Perez-Reyes, M., & Wall, M. E. (1982). Presence of delta9-tetrahydrocannabinol in human milk. *The New England Journal of Medicine, 307*(13), 819–820.

Pérez-Ríos, M., Santiago-Pérez, M. I., Alonso, B., et al. (2009). Fagerstrom test for nicotine dependence vs heavy smoking index in a general population survey. *BioMed Central Public Health, 9*, 493.

Perkins, K.A., Gerlach, D., Broge, M., et al. (2001). Dissociation of nicotine tolerance from tobacco dependence in humans. *The Journal of Pharmacology and Experimental Therapeutics, 296*(3), 849–856.

Perron, B. E., & Howard, M. O. (2008). Perceived risk of harm and intentions of future inhalant use among adolescent inhalant users. *Drug and Alcohol Dependence, 97*(1–2), 185–189.

Perron, B. E., & Howard, M. O. (2009). Adolescent inhalant use, abuse and dependence. *Addiction, 104*(7), 1185–1192.

Perry, C. L. (1989). Prevention of alcohol use and abuse in adolescence: Teacher- vs. peer-led intervention. *Crisis—The J ournal of Crisis Intervention and Suicide Prevention, 10*(1), 52–61.

Pertwee, R. G. (2000). Cannabinoid receptor ligands: Clinical and neuropharmacological considerations, relevant to future drug discovery and development. *Expert Opinion on Investigative Drugs, 9*(7), 1553–1571.

Peters, R. J., Jr., Kelder, S. H., Meshack, A., et al. (2005). Beliefs and social norms about cigarettes or marijuana sticks laced with embalming fluid and phencyclidine (PCP): Why youth use "fry." *Substance Use & Misuse, 40*(4), 563–571.

Peters, R. J., Jr., Meshack, A., Amos, C., et al. (2010). The association of drug use and post-traumatic stress reactions due to Hurricane Ike among Fifth Ward Houstonian youth. *Journal of Ethnicity in Substance Abuse, 9*(2), 143–151.

Peters, R. J., Jr., Meshack, A. F., Kelder, S. H., et al. (2007). Alprazolam (Xanax) use among southern youth: Beliefs and social norms concerning dangerous rides on "handlebars." *Journal of Drug Education, 37*(4), 417–428.

Peters, R. J., Jr., Tortolero, S. R., Addy, R. C., et al. (2003). Drug use among Texas alternative school students: Findings from Houston's Safer Choices 2 Program. *Journal of Psychoactive Drugs, 35*(3), 383–387.

Petersen, R. C., (1987). *Drug abuse and drug abuse research. The second triennial report to Congress.* Rockville, MD: U.S. Department of Health and Human Services, National Institute on Drug Abuse.

Petry, N. M. (2000). A comprehensive guide to the application of contingency management procedures in clinical settings. *Drug and Alcohol Dependence, 58*(1–2), 9–25.

Philipp, B. L., Merewood, A., & O'Brien, S. (2003). Methadone and breastfeeding: New horizons. *Pediatrics, 111*(6 part 1), 1429–1430.

Phillips, K., Luk, A., Soor, G. S., et al. (2009). Cocaine cardiotoxicity: A review of the pathophysiology, pathology, and treatment options. *American Journal of Cardiovascular Drugs, 9*(3), 177–196.

Piaget, J., & Inhelder, B. (1969). *The psychology of the child.* London, UK: Routledge and Kegan Paul.

Piccinelli, M., Tessari, E., Bortolomasi, M., et al. (1997). Efficacy of the alcohol use disorders identification test as a screening tool for hazardous alcohol intake and related disorders in primary care: A validity study. *British Medical Journal, 314*(7078), 420–424.

Picciotto, M. R., & Corrigall, W. A. (2002). Neuronal systems underlying behaviors related to nicotine addiction: Neural circuits and molecular genetics. *The Journal of Neuroscience, 22*(9), 3338–3341.

Peirce, J. M., Petry, N. M., Stitzer, M. L., et al. (2006). Effects of lower-cost incentives on stimulant abstinence in methadone maintenance treatment: A national drug abuse treatment clinical trials network study. *Archives of General Psychiatry, 63*(2), 201–208.

Pierre, N., Emans, S. J., Obeidallah, D. A., et al. (1999). Choice of feeding method of adolescent mothers: Does ego development play a role? *Journal of Pediatric and Adolescent Gynecology, 12*(2), 83–89.

Pilgrim, J. L., Gerostamoulos, D., & Drummer, O. H. (2010). Deaths involving serotonergic drugs. *Forensic Science International, 198*(1–3), 110–117.

Piomelli, D. (2003). The molecular logic of endocannabinoid signalling. *Nature Reviews Neuroscience, 4*, 873–884.

Piontek, D., Kraus, L., & Klempova, D. (2008). Short scales to assess cannabis-related problems: A review of psychometric properties. *Substance Abuse Treatment, Prevention, and Policy, 3*, 25–35.

Piper, B. J. (2007). A developmental comparison of the neurobehavioral effects of ecstasy (MDMA). *Neurotoxicology & Teratology, 29*(2), 288–300.

Plessinger, M. A., & Woods, J. R. (1991). The cardiovascular effects of cocaine use in pregnancy. *Reproductive Toxicology, 5*, 99–113.

Pokorny, A. D., Miller, B. A., & Kaplan, H. B. (1972). The Brief MAST: A shortened version of the Michigan Alcoholism Screening Test. *The American Journal of Psychiatry, 129*(3), 342–345.

Pollak, C. P., & Bright, D. (2003). Caffeine consumption and weekly sleep patterns in US seventh-, eighth-, and ninth-graders. *Pediatrics, 111*(1), 42–46.

Polster, M. R., McCarthy, R. A., O'Sullivan, G., et al. (1993). Midazolam-induced amnesia: Implications for the implicit/explicit memory distinction. *Brain & Cognition, 22*, 244–265.

Polydorou, S., Gunderson, E. W., & Levin, R. F. (2008). Training physicians to treat substance use disorders. *Current Psychiatry Reports, 10*(5), 399–404.

Polzin, G. M., Stanfill, S. B., Brown, C. R., et al. (2007). Determination of eugenol, anethole, and coumarin in the mainstream cigarette smoke of Indonesian clove cigarettes. *Food and Chemical Toxicology, 45*(10), 1948–1953.

Pomerleau, C. S., Carton, S. M., Lutzke, M. L., et al. (1994). Reliability of the Fagerstrom Tolerance Questionnaire and the Fagerstrom Test for Nicotine Dependence. *Addictive Behaviors, 19*(1), 33–39.

Pompili, M., Serafini, G., Innamorati, M., et al. (2010). Suicidal behavior and alcohol abuse. *International Journal of Environmental Research and Public Health, 7*(4), 1392–1431.

Ponce, D. E., & Jo, H. S. (1990). Substance abuse and psychiatric disorders: The dilemma of increasing incidence of dual diagnosis in residential treatment centers. *Residential Treatment for Children and Youth, 8*(2), 5–15.

Pope, H. G., Gruber, A. J., Hudson, J. I., et al. (2001). Neuropsychological performance in long-term cannabis users. *Archives of General Psychiatry, 58*(10), 909–915.

Pope, H. G., Gruber, A. J., Hudson, J. I., et al. (2002). Cognitive measures in long-term cannabis users. *Journal of Clinical Pharmacology, 42*(11 supplement), 41S–47S.

Popovic, B., Bhattacharya, P., & Sivaswamy, L. (2009). Lisdexamfetamine: A prodrug for the treatment of attention-deficit/hyperactivity disorder. *American Journal of Health-System Pharmacy, 66*(22), 2005–2012.

Porkka-Heiskanen, T. (1999). Adenosine in sleep and wakefulness. *Annals of Medicine, 31*(2), 125–129.

Porkka-Heiskanen, T. (2011). Methylxanthines and sleep. *Handbook of Experimental Pharmacology*, (200), 331–348.

Potvin, S., Stip, E., & Roy, J. Y. (2003). Schizophrenia and addiction: An evaluation of the self-medication hypothesis [in French]. *Encephale, 29*(3, pt. 1), 193–203.

Practice parameter for the assessment and treatment of children and adolescents with substance use disorders. (2005). *The Journal of the American Academy of Child and Adolescent Psychiatry, 44*(6), 609–621.

Prescott, J. W. (1980). Somatosensory affectional deprivation (SAD) theory of drug and alcohol use. *NIDA Research Monograph, 30*, 286–296.

Presley, C. A., Meilman, P. W., & Leichliter, J. S. (2002). College factors that influence drinking. *Journal of Studies on Alcohol* (Suppl. 14), S82–S90.

Preuss, U. W., Watzke, A. B., Zimmermann, J., et al. (2010). Cannabis withdrawal severity and short-term course among cannabis-dependent adolescent and young adult inpatients. *Drug and Alcohol Dependence, 106*(2–3), 133–141.

Prochaska, J. O., & DiClemente, C. C. (1984). *The transtheoretical approach: Crossing the traditional boundaries of therapy.* Malabar, FL: Krieger.

Project Match (Matching Alcoholism Treatment to Client Heterogeneity): Rationale and methods for a multisite clinical trial matching patients to alcoholism treatment. (1993). *Alcoholism, Clinical & Experimental Research, 17*, 1130–1145.

Prokhorov, A. V., Koehly, L. M., Pallonen, U. E., et al. (1998). Adolescent nicotine dependence measured by the Modified Fagerström Tolerance Questionnaire at two time points. *Journal of Child & Adolescent Substance Abuse, 7*(4), 35–47.

Pugatch, D., Strong, L. L., Has, P., et al. (2001). Heroin use in adolescents and young adults admitted for drug detoxification. *Journal of Substance Abuse, 13*(3), 337–346.

## Q

Quednow, B. B., Jessen, F., Kuhn, K. U., et al. (2006). Memory deficits in abstinent MDMA (ecstasy) users: Neuropsychological evidence of frontal dysfunction. *Journal of Psychopharmacology, 20*(3), 373–384.

Query, W. T., & Megran, J. (1984). Influence of depression and alcoholism on learning, recall, and recognition. *Journal of Clinical Psychology, 40*, 1097–1100.

Quinnett, P. G. (1995). *Suicide: The forever decision. For those thinking about suicide, and for those who know, love, or counsel them.* New York, NY: Crossroad Publishing.

Quinton, M. S., & Yamamoto, B. K. (2006). Causes and consequences of methamphetamine and MDMA toxicity. *The AAPS Journal, 8*(2), E337–E447.

## R

Racine, A., Joyce, T., & Anderson, R. (1993). The association between prenatal care and birth weight among women exposed to cocaine in New York City. *JAMA, The Journal of the American Medical Association, 270*, 1581–1586.

Rado, S. (1933). The psychoanalysis of pharmacothymia. *The Psychoanalytic Quarterly, 2*, 1–23.

Rahdert, E. (1991). *Problem Oriented Screening Instrument for Teenagers (POSIT).* Bethesda, MD: NIDA.

Rainey, J. M., Jr., & Crowder, M. K. (1975). Prolonged psychosis attributed to phencyclidine: Report of three cases. *The American Journal of Psychiatry, 132*(10), 1076–1078.

Rajkumar, S. V. (2004). Thalidomide: Tragic past and promising future. *Mayo Clinic Proceedings, 79*(7), 899–903.

Ramaekers, J. G., Berghaus, G., van Laar, M., et al. (2004). Dose related risk of motor vehicle crashes after cannabis use. *Drug and Alcohol Dependence, 73*(2), 109–119.

Ramaekers, J. G., Robbe, H. W., & O'Hanlon, J. F. (2000). Marijuana, alcohol and actual driving performance. *Human Psychopharmacology, 15*, 551–558.

Ramo, D. E., Grov, C., Delucchi, K., et al. (2010). Typology of club drug use among young adults recruited using time-space sampling. *Drug and Alcohol Dependence, 107*(2–3), 119–127.

Randall, T. (1992). Infants, children test positive for cocaine after exposure to second-hand crack smoke. *JAMA, The Journal of the American Medical Association , 267*(8), 1044–1045.

Ranheim, T., & Halvorsen, B. (2005). Coffee consumption and human health—Beneficial or detrimental?—Mechanisms for effects of coffee consumption on different risk factors for cardiovascular disease and type 2 diabetes mellitus. *Molecular Nutrition & Food Research, 49*(3), 274–284.

Ranney, L., Melvin, C., Lux, L., et al. (2006, June). Tobacco use: Prevention, cessation, and control. *Evidence Report—Technology Assessment*, (140), 1–120.

Rao, P., Quandt, S.A., & Arcury, T.A. (2002). Hispanic farmworker interpretations of green tobacco sickness. *The Journal of Rural Health, 18*(4), 503–511.

Rao, U. (2006). Links between depression and substance abuse in adolescents: Neurobiological mechanisms. *American Journal of Preventive Medicine, 31*(6 Suppl. 1), 161–174.

Rasmussen, C. (2005). Executive functioning and working memory in fetal alcohol spectrum disorder. *Alcoholism, Clinical & Experimental Research, 29*(8), 1359–1367.

Rasmussen, C., & Bisanz, J. (2009). Executive functioning in children with fetal alcohol spectrum disorders: Profiles and age-related differences. *Child Neuropsychology, 15*(3), 201–215.

Rasmussen, C., Pei, J., Manji, S., et al. (2009). Memory strategy development in children with foetal alcohol spectrum disorders. *Developmental Neurorehabilitation, 12*(4), 207–214.

Raveis, V. H., & Kandel, D. B. (1987). Changes in drug behavior from the middle to the late twenties: Initiation, persistence, and cessation of use. *American Journal of Public Health, 77*(5), 607–611.

Raymon, L. P., & Isenschmid, D. S. (2009). The possible role of levamisole in illicit cocaine preparations (letter). *Journal of Analytical Toxicology, 33*(9), 620–622.

Reed, P. L., Anthony, J. C., & Breslau, N. (2007). Incidence of drug problems in young adults exposed to trauma and posttraumatic stress disorder: Do early life experiences and predispositions matter? *Archives of General Psychiatry, 64*(12), 1435–1442.

Refuerzo, J. S., Sokol, R. J., Blackwell, S. C., et al. (2002). Cocaine use and preterm premature rupture of membranes: Improvement in neonatal outcome. *American Journal of Obstetrics & Gynecology, 186*(6), 1150–1154.

Reid, M. S., & Thakkar, V. (2009). Valproate treatment and cocaine cue reactivity in cocaine dependent individuals. *Drug and Alcohol Dependence, 102*(1–3), 144–150.

Reinert, D. F., & Allen, J. P. (2007). The alcohol use disorders identification test: An update of research findings. *Alcoholism, Clinical and Experimental Research, 31*(2), 185–199.

Reissig, C. J., Strain, E. C., & Griffiths, R. R. (2009). Caffeinated energy drinks A growing problem. *Drug and Alcohol Dependence, 99*(1–3), 1–10.

Remafedi, G., Jurek, A. M., & Oakes, J. M. (2008). Sexual identity and tobacco use in a venue-based sample of adolescents and young adults. *American Journal of Preventive Medicine, 35*(6 Suppl.), S463–S470.

Remkes, T. (1993). Saying no – Completely. *Canadian Nurse, 89*(6), 25–28.

Renner, J. A., Jr. (2004). How to train residents to identify and treat dual diagnosis patients. *Biological Psychiatry, 56*(10), 810–816.

Researchers find factors that encourage cannabis use among university students. (2007, December 19). *ScienceDaily*, pp. 1–2. Retrieved from http://www.sciencedaily.com/releases/2007/12/071218113506.htm

Resnick, H. S. (1978). *It starts with people: Experiences in drug abuse prevention* (NIDA Publication No. 79–590). Washington, DC: U.S. Department of Health, Education, and Welfare.

Reus, V. I., Weingartner, H., & Post, R. M. (1979). Clinical implications of state-dependent learning. *The American Journal of Psychiatry, 136*(7), 927–935.

Reuters. (2011, June 21). U.S. unveils graphic cigarette warning labels. *National Post*, pp. 1–5. Available: http://news.nationalpost.com/2011/06/21/u-s-unveils-graphic-cigarette-warning-labels/

Ricca, V., Castellini, G., Mannucci, E., et al. (2009). Amphetamine derivatives and obesity. *Appetite, 52*(2), 405–409.

Richards, M., Doyle, M., & Cook, P. (2009). A literature review of family interventions for dual diagnosis: Implications for forensic mental health services [abridged]. *Advances in Dual Diagnosis, 2*(4), 5–11.

Richardson, C. C., & Ratner, P. A. (2005). A confirmatory factor analysis of the Fagerstrom Test for Nicotine Dependence. *Addictive Behaviors, 30*(4), 697–709.

Richardson, G. A., Goldschmidt, L., Leech, S., et al. (2010, January-February). Prenatal cocaine exposure: Effects on mother- and teacher-rated behavior problems and growth in school-age children. *Neurotoxicology and Teratolology, 32*, 69–77.

Richardson, G. A., Goldschmidt, L., & Wilford, J. (2009). Continued effects of prenatal cocaine use: Preschool development. *Neurotoxicology and Teratology, 31*(6), 325–333.

Richardson, G. A., Ryan, C., Willford, J., et al. (2002). Prenatal alcohol and marijuana exposure: Effects on neuropsychological outcomes at 10 years. *Neurotoxicology and Teratology, 24*(3), 309–320.

Richardson, H. L., Walker, A. M., & Horne, R. S. C. (2009). Maternal smoking impairs arousal patterns in sleeping. *Sleep, 32*(4), 515–521.

Richardson, J. L., Dwyer, K., McGuigan, K., et al. (1989). Substance use among eight-grade students who take care of themselves after school. *Pediatrics, 84*(3), 556–566.

Richman, P. B., & Nashed, A. H. (1999). The etiology of cardiac arrest in children and young adults: Special considerations for ED management. *The American Journal of Emergency Medicine, 17*(3), 264–270.

Richter, P., Hodge, K., Stanfill, S., et al. (2008). Surveillance of moist snuff: Total nicotine, moisture, pH, un-ionized nicotine, and tobacco-specific nitrosamines. *Nicotine & Tobacco Research, 10*(11), 1645–1652.

Riede, P. (2011, June 14). High school graduation rates improve slightly, but gaps remain. *The Post Standard*. Retrieved from http://blog.syracuse.com/news/print.html?entry=/2011/06/high_school_graduation_rates_i.h...

Rigourd, V., Amirouche, A., Tasseau, A., et al. (2008). Retrospective diagnosis of an adverse drug reaction in a breastfed neonate: Liquid chromatography–tandem mass spectrometry quantification of dextropropoxyphene and norpropoxyphene in newborn and maternal hair. *Journal of Analytical Toxicology, 32*, 787–789.

Riley, E. P., & McGee, C. L. (2005). Fetal alcohol spectrum disorders: An overview with emphasis on changes in brain and behavior. *Experimental Biology and Medicine, 230*(6), 357–365.

Ringwalt, C., Hanley, S., Vincus, A. A., et al. (2008). The prevalence of effective substance use prevention curricula in the nation's high schools. *The Journal of Primary Prevention, 29*(6), 479–488.

Rist, F., Glockner-Rist, A., & Demmel, R. (2009). The Alcohol Use Disorders Identification Test revisited: Establishing its structure using nonlinear factor analysis and identifying subgroups of respondents using latent class factor analysis. *Drug and Alcohol Dependence, 100*(1–2), 71–82.

Ritter, A., & Cameron, J. (2006). A review of the efficacy and effectiveness of harm reduction strategies for alcohol, tobacco and illicit drugs. *Drug and Alcohol Review, 25*(6), 611–624.

Rivers, K. O., & Hedrick, D. L. (1992). Language and behavioral concerns for drug-exposed infants and toddlers. *Transdisciplinary Journal, 2*(1), 63–73.

Rizk, B., Atterbury, J. L., & Groome, L. J. (1996). Reproductive risks of cocaine. *Human Reproduction Update, 2*(1), 43–55.

Roane, B. M., & Taylor, D. J. (2008). Adolescent insomnia as a risk factor for early adult depression and substance abuse. *Sleep, 31*(10), 1351–1356.

Roberts, G. M., Nestor, L., & Garavan, H. (2009). Learning and memory deficits in ecstasy users and their neural correlates during a face-learning task. *Brain Research, 1292*, 71–81.

Robin, A. L., & Foster, S. L. (1988). *Negotiating parent adolescent conflict: A behavioral-family systems approach*. New York, NY: Guilford.

Robin, R. W., Saremi, A., Albaugh, B., et al. (2004). Validity of the SMAST in two American Indian tribal populations. *Substance Use & Misuse, 39*(4), 601–624.

Robins, L. N. (1966). *Deviant children grown up: A sociological and psychiatric study of sociopathic personality*. Baltimore, MD: Williams & Wilkins.

Robins, L. N. (1973). *A follow-up of Vietnam drug users* (Interim Final Report, Special Action Office Monograph, Series A, No. 2). Washington, DC: U.S. Government Printing Office.

Robins, L. N. (1974). *The Vietnam drug user returns* (Final Report, Special Action Office Monograph, Series A, No. 2). Washington, DC: U.S. Government Printing Office.

Robins, L. N. (1975). Alcoholism and labeling theory. In W. R. Gove (Ed.), *The labeling of deviance* (pp. 21–33). New York, NY: Wiley.

Robins, L. N. (1977). Surveys of target populations. In L. G. Richards & L. B. Blevens (Eds.), *The epidemiology of drug abuse: Current issues* (NIDA Research Monograph No. 10, pp. 39–48). Rockville, MD: U.S. Department of Health and Human Services, National Institute on Drug Abuse.

Robins, L. N. (1978a). The interaction of setting and predisposition in explaining novel behavior: Drug initiations before, in, and after Vietnam. In D. B. Kandel (Ed.), *Longitudinal research on drug use: Empirical findings and methodological issues* (pp. 179–196). New York, NY: Wiley.

Robins, L. N. (1978b). Sturdy childhood predictors of adult antisocial behavior: Replications from longitudinal studies. *Psychological Medicine, 8,* 611–622.

Robins, L. N. (1980). The natural history of drug abuse. In D. J. Lettieri, M. Sayer, & H. Wallenstein Pearson (Eds.), *Theories on drug abuse: Selected contemporary perspectives* (NIDA Research Monograph No. 30, pp. 215–224). Rockville, MD: U.S. Department of Health and Human Services, National Institute on Drug Abuse.

Robins, L. N., Davis, D. H., & Wish, E. (1977). Detecting predictors of rare events: Demographic, family, and personal deviance as predictors of stages in the progression toward narcotic addictions. In J. S. Strauss, H. M. Babigian, & M. Roff (Eds.), *The origins and course of psychopathology: Methods of longitudinal research* (pp. 379–406). New York, NY: Plenum Press.

Robins, L. N., Helzer, J. E., & Davis, D. H. (1975). Narcotic use in Southeast Asia and afterward: An interview study of 898 Vietnam returnees. *Archives of General Psychiatry, 23,* 955–961.

Robins, L. N., Hesselbrock, M. Wish, E., et al. (1978). Polydrug and alcohol use by veterans and nonveterans. In D. A. Smith, S. M. Anderson, M. Buxton, et al. (Eds.), *A multicultural view of drug abuse: Proceedings of the National Drug Abuse Conference, 1977* (pp. 74–90). Cambridge, MA: Schenkman.

Robins, L. N., & Murphy, G. E. (1967). Drug use in a normal population of young Negro men. *American Journal of Public Health, 57*(9), 1580–1596.

Robinson, G. C., Conry, J. L., & Conry, R. F. (1987). Clinical profile and prevalence of fetal alcohol syndrome in an isolated community in British Columbia. *CMAJ, Canadian Medical Association Journal, 137*(3), 203–207.

Robinson, J., Sareen, J., Cox, B. J., et al. (2009). Self-medication of anxiety disorders with alcohol and drugs: Results from a nationally representative sample. *Journal of Anxiety Disorders, 23*(1), 38–45.

Robles, G. I., Singh-Franco, D., & Ghin, H. L. (2008). A review of the efficacy of smoking-cessation pharmacotherapies in nonwhite populations. *Clinical Therapeutics, 30*(5), 800–812.

Rodu, B., & Cole, P. (2002). Smokeless tobacco use and cancer of the upper respiratory tract. *Oral Surgery, Oral Medicine, Oral Pathology, Oral Radiology, and Endodontics, 93*(5), 511–515.

Rodu, B., & Cole, P. (2010). Evidence against a gateway from smokeless tobacco use to smoking. *Nicotine & Tobacco Research, 12*(5), 530–534.

Roehrs, T., Merlotti, L., Zorick, F., et al. (1994). Sedative, memory, and performance effects of hypnotics. *Psychopharmacology (Berlin), 116*(2), 130–134.

Roehrs, T., & Roth, T. (2008). Caffeine: Sleep and daytime sleepiness. *Sleep Medicine Reviews, 12*(2), 153–162.

Roeseler, A., & Burns, D. (2010). The quarter that changed the world. *Tobacco Control, 19*(Suppl. 1), i3–i15.

Rogers, C. R. (1969). *Freedom to learn.* Columbus, OH: Merrill.

Rogers, G., Elston, J., Garside, R., et al. (2009, January). The harmful health effects of recreational ecstasy: A systematic review of observational evidence. *Health Technology Assessment, 13*(6), 1–354.

Rogers, J. M. (2009). Tobacco and pregnancy. *Reproductive Toxicology, 28*(2), 152–160.

Rokeach, M. (1970). *Beliefs, attitudes, and values: A theory of organization and change.* San Francisco, CA: Jossey-Bass.

Romanelli, R., Smith, K. M., & Pomeroy, C. (2003). Use of club drugs by HIV-seropositive and HIV-seronegative gay and bisexual men. *Topics in HIV Medicine, 11*(1), 25–32.

Rondinelli, A. J., Ouellet, L. J., Strathdee, S. A., et al. (2009). Young adult injection drug users in the United States continue to practice HIV risk behaviors. *Drug and Alcohol Dependence, 104*(1–2), 167–174.

Room, R., & Greenfield, T. (1993). Alcoholics Anonymous, other 12-step movements and psychotherapy in the US population, 1990. *Addiction, 88,* 555–562.

Rosario, M., Meyer-Bahlburg, H. F., Hunter, J., et al. (1999). Sexual risk behaviors of gay, lesbian, and bisexual youth in New York City: Prevalence and correlates. *AIDS Education and Prevention, 11*(6), 476–496.

Rosario, M., Schrimshaw, E. W., & Hunter, J. (2004). Predictors of substance use over time among gay, lesbian, and bisexual youths: An examination of three hypotheses. *Addictive Behaviors, 29*(8), 1623–1631.

Rose, J. S., & Dierker, L. C. (2010). *DSM-IV* nicotine dependence symptom characteristics for recent-onset smokers. *Nicotine & Tobacco Research, 12*(3), 278–286.

Rose, J. S., Dierker, L. C., & Donny, E. (2010). Nicotine dependence symptoms among recent onset adolescent smokers. *Drug and Alcohol Dependence, 106*(2–3), 126–132.

Rosenberg, M. H., Deerfield, L. J., & Baruch, E. M. (2003). Two cases of severe gamma-hydroxybutyrate withdrawal delirium on a psychiatric unit: Recommendations for management. *The American Journal of Drug and Alcohol Abuse, 29*(2), 487–496.

Rosenberg, N. M., Meert, K. L., Knazik, S. R., et al. (1991). Occult cocaine exposure in children. *American Journal of Diseases of Children, 145*(12), 1430–1432.

Rosenthal, D., Moore, S., & Buzwell, S. (1994). Homeless youths: Sexual and drug-related behavior, sexual beliefs and HIV/AIDS risk. *AIDS Care, 6*(1), 83–94.

Rosett, H. L. (1980). A clinical perspective of the fetal alcohol syndrome. *Alcoholism, Clinical and Experimental Research, 4*, 119–122.

Rosett, H. L., Weiner, L., Lee, A., et al. (1983). Patterns of alcohol consumption and fetal development. *Journal of the American College of Obstetricians and Gynecologists, 61*, 539–546.

Rosman, A. S., & Lieber, C. S. (1990). Biochemical markers of alcohol consumption. *Alcohol Health & Research World, 14*, 210–218.

Rösner, S. Hackl-Herrwerth, A., Leucht, S., et al. (2010, September 8). Acamprosate for alcohol dependence. *Cochrane Database of Systematic Reviews, 9*, CD004332.

Ross, G. R. (1994). *Treating adolescent substance abuse: Understanding the fundamental elements.* Needham, Heights, MA: Allyn & Bacon.

Ross, H. E., Gavin, D. R., & Skinner, H. A. (1990). Diagnostic validity of the MAST and the alcohol dependence scale in the assessment of *DSM-III* alcohol disorders. *Journal of Studies on Alcoholism, 51*(6), 506–513.

Rossenberg, L., Mitchell, A. A., Shapiro, S., et al. (1982). Selected birth defects in relation to caffeine-containing beverages. *JAMA, The Journal of the American Medical Association, 247*, 1429–1432.

Rotheram-Borus, M. J., Koopman, C., & Ehrhardt, A. A. (1991). Homeless youths and HIV infection. *American Psychologist, 46*(11), 1188–1197.

Rotter, J. B. (1954). *Social learning and clinical psychology.* Englewood Cliffs, NJ: Prentice-Hall.

Rotter, J. B., Chance, J. E., & Phares, E. J. (1972). *Applications of a social learning theory of personality.* New York, NY: Holt, Rinehart and Winston.

Rubin, R. (2008, January 20). New studies, different outcomes on caffeine, pregnancy. *USA Today*, pp. 1–3. Retrieved from http://www.usatoday.com/news/health/2008–01–20–caffeine_N.htm

Rubino, T., & Parolaro, D. (2008). Long lasting consequences of cannabis exposure in adolescence. *Molecular and Cellular Endocrinology, 286*(1–2 Suppl. 1), S108–S113.

Rubinstein, M. L., Benowitz, N. L., Auerback, G. M., et al. (2009). Withdrawal in adolescent light smokers following 24-hour abstinence. *Nicotine & Tobacco Research, 11*(2), 185–189.

Rucklidge, J. J. (2008). Gender differences in ADHD: Implications for psychosocial treatments. *Expert Review of Neurotherapeutics, 8*(4), 643–655.

Rueger, D. B., & Liberman, R. P. (1984). Behavioral family therapy for delinquent and substance-abusing adolescents. *Journal of Drug Issues, 14*, 403–418.

Ruha, A. M., & Yarema, M. C. (2006). Pharmacologic treatment of acute pediatric methamphetamine toxicity. *Pediatric Emergency Care, 22*(12), 782–785.

Runeson, B. S., & Rich, C. L. (1992). Diagnostic comorbidity of mental disorders among young suicides. *International Review of Psychiatry, 4*, 197–203.

Rush, B., & Ekdahl, A. (1990). Recent trends in the development of alcohol and drug treatment services in Ontario. *Journal of Studies on Alcohol, 51*(6), 514–522.

Rush, B., & Koegl, C. J. (2008). Prevalence and profile of people with co-occurring mental and substance use disorders within a comprehensive mental health system. *Canadian Journal of Psychiatry, 53*(12), 810–821.

Rush, C. R., Higgins, S. T., Bickel, W. K., et al. (1993). Acute behavioral effects of lorazepam and caffeine, alone and in combination, in humans. *Behavioural Pharmacology, 5*, 245–254.

Russell, M. (1994). New assessment tools for risk drinking during pregnancy: T-ACE, TWEAK, and others. *Alcohol Health & Research World, 18*(1), 55–61.

Russell, M., Martier, S. S., Sokol, R. J., et al. (1994). Screening for pregnancy risk-drinking. *Alcoholism, Clinical and Experimental Research, 18*(5), 1156–1161.

Russell, M., Martier, S. S., Sokol, R. J., et al. (1996). Detecting risk drinking during pregnancy: A comparison of four screening questionnaires. *American Journal of Public Health, 86*(10), 1435–1439.

Ryan, C., Huebner, D., Diaz, R. M., et al. (2009). Family rejection as a predictor of negative health outcomes in white and Latino lesbian, gay, and bisexual young adults. *Pediatrics, 123*(1), 346–352.

## S

Saad, L. (2008, December 23). Americans believe religion is losing clout. *Gallup*, pp. 1–6. Retrieved from http://www.gallup.com/poll/113533/Americans-Believe-Religion-Losing-Clout.aspx

Sadava, S. W. (1984). Concurrent multiple drug use: Review and implications. *Journal of Drug Issues, 4*, 623–636.

Sadava, S. W. (1987). Interactional theory. In H. T. Blane & K. E. Leonard (Eds.), *Psychological theories of drinking and alcoholism* (pp. 90–130). New York, NY: Guilford Press.

Sadava, S. W., Thistle, R., & Forsyth, R. (1978). Stress, escapism and patterns of alcohol and drug use. *Journal of Studies on Alcohol, 39*(5), 725–736.

Safra, M. J., & Oakley, G. P. (1975). Association between cleft lip with or without cleft palate and prenatal exposure to diazepam. *Lancet, 2*, 478–480.

Saito, T., & Murakami, S. (1998). Tobacco dependence. *Japanese Journal of Alcohol Studies and Drug Dependence, 33*(5), 549–556.

Sakai, J. T., Hall, S. K., Mikulich-Gilbertson, S. K., et al. (2004). Inhalant use, abuse, and dependence among adolescent patients: Commonly comorbid problems. *Journal of the American Academy of Child & Adolescent Psychiatry, 43*(9), 1080–1088.

Salaspuro, M. (1999). Carbohydrate-deficient transferrin as compared to other markers of alcoholism: A systematic review. *Alcohol, 19*(3), 261–271.

Salazar-Martinez, E., Willett, W. C., Ascherio, A., et al. (2004). Coffee consumption and risk for type 2 diabetes mellitus. *Annals of Internal Medicine, 140*(1), 1–8.

Salisbury, A. L., Ponder, K. L., Padbury, J. F., et al. (2009). Fetal effects of psychoactive drugs. *Clinics in Perinatology, 36*(3), 595–619.

Sampson, P. D., Streissguth, A. P., Bookstein, F. L., et al. (1997). Incidence of fetal alcohol syndrome and prevalence of alcohol-related neurodevelopmental disorder. *Teratology, 56*(5), 317–326.

Sampson, P. D., Streissguth, A. P., Bookstein, F. L., et al. (2000). On categorizations in analyses of alcohol teratogenesis. *Environmental Health Perspectives, 3*, 421–428.

Sanchis, A., Rosique, D., & Catala, J. (1991). Adverse effects of maternal lorazepam on neonates. *DICP, Annals of Pharmacotherapy, 25*, 1137–1138.

Sanders, C. E., Field, T. M., & Diego, M. A. (2001). Adolescents' academic expectations and achievement. *Adolescence, 36*(144), 795–802.

Sanders, M. J., & Bursch, B. (2002). Forensic assessment of illness falsification, Munchausen by proxy, and factitious disorder, NOS. *Child Maltreatment, 7*(2), 112–124.

San Francisco Health Department (2010). Medical cannabis dispensary inspection. Retrieved from http://www.sfdph.org/dph/files/EHSdocs/MedCannabis/publichearing.pp

Santis, R., Garmendia, M. L., Acuna, G., et al. (2009). The Alcohol Use Disorders Identification Test (AUDIT) as a screening instrument for adolescents. *Drug and Alcohol Dependence, 103*(3), 155–158.

Sapundzhiev, N., & Werner, J. A. (2003). Nasal snuff: Historical review and health related aspects. *The Journal of Laryngology and Otology, 117*(9), 686–691.

Sarche, M., & Spicer, P. (2008). Poverty and health disparities for American Indian and Alaska Native children: Current knowledge and future prospects. *Annals of the New York Academy of Sciences, 1136*, 126–136.

Sareen, J., Chartier, M., Paulus, M. P., et al. (2006). Illicit drug use and anxiety disorders: Findings from two community surveys. *Psychiatry Research, 142*(1), 11–17.

Saremi, A., Hanson, R. L., Williams, D. E., et al. (2001). Validity of the CAGE questionnaire in an American Indian population. *Journal of Studies on Alcoholism, 62*(3), 294–300.

Sarkar, M., Einarson, T., & Koren, G. (2010). Comparing the effectiveness of TWEAK and T-ACE in determining problem drinkers in pregnancy. *Alcohol & Alcoholism, 45*(4), 356–360.

Sastry, B. V. (1991). Placental toxicology: Tobacco smoke, abused drugs, multiple chemical interactions, and placental function. *Reproduction, Fertility and Development, 3*(4), 355–372.

Satcher, D. (2001). *2001 Surgeon General report: Women and smoking.* Department of Health and Human Services, Centers for Disease Control and Prevention, National Center for Chronic Disease Prevention and Health Promotion, Office on Smoking and Health. Retrieved from http://www.cdc.gov/tobacco/sgr_forwomen.htm

Satel, S. (2006). Is caffeine addictive?—A review of the literature. *The American Journal of Drug and Alcohol Abuse, 32*(4), 493–502.

Saunders, J. B., & Aasland, O. G., (1987). *World Health Organization Collaborative Project on the identification and treatment of persons with harmful alcohol consumption: Report on Phase I: Development of a screening instrument.* Geneva, Switzerland: World Health Organization .

Saunders, J. B., Aasland, O. G., & Babor, T. F., et al. (1993). Development of the Alcohol Use Disorders Identification Test (AUDIT): WHO Collaborative Project on Early Detection of Persons with Harmful Alcohol Consumption—II. *Addiction, 88*(6), 791–804.

Sauvageau, A., & Racette, S. (2006). Autoerotic deaths in the literature from 1954 to 2004: A review. *Journal of Forensic Sciences, 51*(1), 140–146.

Savage, J., Brodsky, N. L., Malmud, E., et al. (2005). Attentional functioning and impulse control in cocaine-exposed and control children at age ten years. *Journal of Developmental & Behavioral Pediatrics, 26*, 42–47.

Saxen, I., & Saxen, L. (1975). Association between maternal intake of diazepam and oral clefts. *Lancet, 2*, 498.

Saylor, B., Fair, M., Deike-Sims, S., et al. (2007). The use of harmful legal products among pre-adolescent Alaskan students. *International Journal of Circumpolar Health, 66*(5), 425–436.

Scafidi, F. A., Field, T., Prodromidis, M., et al. (1997). Psychosocial stressors of drug-abusing disadvantaged adolescent mothers. *Adolescence, 32*(125), 93–100.

Scanlon, J. W. (1991). The neuroteratology of cocaine: Background, theory, and clinical implications. *Reproductive Toxicology, 5*(2), 89–98.

Schaps, E., & Battistich, V. (1991). Promoting health development through school-based prevention: New approaches. In E. N. Goplerud (Ed.), *Preventing adolescent drug use: From theory to practice* (pp. 127–181). Rockville, MD: U.S. Department of Health and Human Services, Office for Substance Abuse Prevention.

Schaps, E., DiBartalo, R. D., Moskowitz, J., et al. (1981). A review of 127 drug abuse prevention program evaluations. *Journal of Drug Issues, 11*, 17–43.

Schaps, E., Moskowitz, J., Malvin, J. H., et al. (1986). Evaluation of seven school-based prevention programs: A final report on the Napa Project. *The International Journal of the Addictions, 21*, 1081–1112.

Scharf, M. B., Lai, A. A., Branigan, B., et al. (1998). Pharmacokinetics of gammahydroxybutyrate (GHB) in narcoleptic patients. *Sleep 1998, 21*, 507–514.

Scheffler, R. M., Brown, T. T., Fulton, B. D., et al. (2009). Positive association between attention-deficit/hyperactivity disorder medication use and academic achievement during elementary school. *Pediatrics, 123*(5), 1273–1279.

Scheier, L. M., & Botvin, B. J. (1995). Effects of early adolescent drug use on cognitive efficacy in early-late adolescence: A developmental structural model. *Journal of Substance Abuse, 7*(4), 379–404.

Schensul, J. J., Diamond, S., Disch, W., et al. (2005). The diffusion of ecstasy through urban youth networks. *Journal of Ethnicity in Substance Abuse, 4*(2), 39–71.

Schepis, T. S., Adinoff, B., & Rao, U. (2008). Neurobiological processes in adolescent addictive disorders. *The American Journal on Addictions, 17*(1), 6–23.

Schifano, F. (2004). A bitter pill. Overview of ecstasy (MDMA, MDA) related fatalities. *Psychopharmacology (Berlin), 173*(3–4), 242–248.

Schmidt, R. J., Romitti, P. A., Burns, T. L., et al. (2009). Maternal caffeine consumption and risk of neural tube defects. *Birth Defects Research Part A: Clinical and Molecular Teratology, 85*(11), 879–889.

Schmidt, S. (2010, August 11). Health Canada eyes tighter rules for alcoholic energy drinks. *Postmedia News*, pp. 1–7. Retrieved from http://www.canada.com/health/Health+Canada+eyes+tighter+rules+alcoholic+energy+drin...

Schneider, M. (2008). Puberty as a highly vulnerable developmental period for the consequences of cannabis exposure. *Addiction Biology, 13*(2), 253–263.

Schubiner, H. (2005). Substance abuse in patients with attention-deficit hyperactivity disorder: Therapeutic implications. *CNS Drugs, 19*(8), 643–655.

Schuckit, M. A. (1980a). A theory of alcohol and drug abuse: A genetic approach. In D. J. Lettieri, M. Sayer, & H. Wallenstein Pearson (Eds.), *Theories on drug abuse: Selected contemporary perspectives* (NIDA Research Monograph No. 30, pp. 297–302). Rockville, MD: U.S. Department of Health and Human Services, National Institute on Drug Abuse.

Schuckit, M. A. (1980b). Alcoholism and genetics: Possible biological mediators. *Biological Psychiatry, 15*(3), 437–447.

Schuckit, M. A., Goodwin, D. A., & Winokur, G. (1972). A study of alcoholism in half siblings. *The American Journal of Psychiatry, 128*, 1132–1136.

Schuman-Olivier, Z., Albanese, M., Nelson, S. E., et al. (2010). Self-treatment: Illicit buprenorphine use by opioid-dependent treatment seekers. *Journal of Substance Abuse Treatment, 39*(1), 41–50.

Schwartz, R. H., Milteer, R., & LeBeau, M. A. (2000). Drug-facilitated sexual assault ('date rape'). *Southern Medical Journal, 93*(6), 558–561.

Schwarz, E. B., Postlethwaite, D. A., Hung, Y-Y., et al. (2007). Documentation of contraception and pregnancy when prescribing potentially teratogenic medications for reproductive-age women. *Annals of Internal Medicine, 147*(6), 370–376.

Schweer, L. H. (2009). Pediatric SBIRT: Understanding the magnitude of the problem. *Journal of Trauma Nursing, 16*(3), 142–147.

Schydlower, M., & Perrin, J. (1993). Prevention of fetal alcohol syndrome [letter]. *Pediatrics, 92*, 739.

Seale, J. P., Boltri, J. M., Shellenberger, S., et al. (2006). Primary validation of a single screening question for drinkers. *Journal of Studies on Alcohol, 67*, 778–784.

Searight, R. (2009). Realistic approaches to counseling in the office setting. *American Family Physician, 79*(4), 277–284.

Sebelius, K. (2011, June 21). New graphic warning labels designed to reduce the deadly effects of smoking. *The White House Blog*, pp. 1–2. Available: http://www.whitehouse.gov/blog/2011/06/21/new-graphic-warning-labels-designed-reduce...

Segal, B. (1974). Locus of control and drug and alcohol use in college students. *Journal of Alcohol & Drug Education, 19*(3), 1–5.

Segal, B. (1978). Sensation seeking and drug use. In D. J. Lettieri (Ed.), *Drugs and suicide: When other coping strategies fail* (pp. 149–166). Beverly Hills, CA: Sage.

Segal, B. (1983). Drugs and youth: A review of the problem. *The International Journal of the Addictions, 18*, 429–433.

Segal, B. (1985). Confirmatory analyses of reasons for experiencing psychoactive drugs during adolescence. *The International Journal of the Addictions, 20*(11–12), 1649–1662.

Segal, B., Huba, G. J., & Singer, J. L. (1980). Reasons for drug and alcohol use by college students. *The International Journal of the Addictions, 15*, 489–498.

Seger, D. L. (2004). Flumazenil—Treatment or toxin. *Journal of Toxicology—Clinical Toxicology, 42*(2), 209–216.

Selin, K. H. (2003). Test-retest reliability of the Alcohol Use Disorder Identification Test in a general population sample. *Alcoholism, Clinical and Experimental Research, 27*(9), 1428–1435.

Selzer, M. L. (1968). Michigan Alcoholism Screening Test (MAST): Preliminary report. *University of Michigan Medical Center Journal, 34*(3), 143–145.

Selzer, M. L. (1971). The Michigan Alcoholism Screening Test: The quest for a new diagnostic instrument. *The American Journal of Psychiatry, 127*(12), 1653–1658.

Selzer, M. L., Vinokur, A., & van Rooijen, L. (1975). A self-administered short Michigan Alcoholism Screening Test (SMAST). *Journal of Studies on Alcohol, 36*(1), 117–126.

Senn, T. E., Carey, M. P., & Vanable, P. A. (2008). Childhood and adolescent sexual abuse and subsequent sexual risk behavior: Evidence from controlled studies, methodological critique, and suggestions for research. *Clinical Psychological Review, 28*(5), 711–735.

Seppa, K., Makela, R., & Sillanaukee, P. (1995). Effectiveness of the Alcohol Use Disorders Identification Test in occupational health settings. *Alcoholism, Clinical and Experimental Research, 19*(4), 999–1003.

Serwach, J. (2009, December 14). Smoking continues gradual decline among U.S. teens, smokeless tobacco threatens a comeback. Retrieved from http://www.ns.umich.edu/htdocs/releases/story.php?id=7455

Sewell, R. A., & Petrakis, I. L. (2011). Does gamma-hydroxybutyrate (GHB) have a role in the treatment of alcoholism? *Alcohol and Alcoholism, 56*(1), 1–2.

Sewell, R. A., Poling, J., & Sofuoglu, M. (2009). The effect of cannabis compared with alcohol on driving. *The American Journal on Addictions, 18*(3), 185–193.

Sexton, R. L., Carlson, R. G., Leukefeld, C. G., et al. (2006). Methamphetamine use and adverse consequences in the rural southern United States: An ethnographic overview. *Journal of Psychoactive Drugs,* (Suppl. 3), 393–404.

Sexton, R. L., Carlson, R. G., Leukefeld, C. G., et al. (2009). An ethnographic exploration of self-reported violence among rual methamphetamine users. *Journal of Ethnicity in Substance Abuse, 8*(1), 35–53.

Shaffer, H. J. (1987). The epistemology of "addictive disease": The Lincoln-Douglas debate. *Journal of Substance Abuse Treatment, 4,* 103–113.

Shaffer, H. J., & Eber, G. B. (2002). Temporal progression of cocaine dependence symptoms in the US National Comorbidity Survey. *Addiction, 97*(5), 543–554.

Shankaran, S., Lester, B. M., Das, A., et al. (2007). Impact of maternal substance use during pregnancy on childhood outcome. *Seminars in Fetal and Neonatal Medicine, 12*(2), 143–150.

Shaw, S. Y., Deering, K. N., Jolly, A. M., et al. (2010). Increased risk for hepatitis C associated with solvent use among Canadian Aboriginal injection drug users. *Harm Reduction Journal, 7*(16), 1–8.

Shaywitz, B. A., & Shaywitz, S. E. (1991). Comorbidity: A critical issue in attention deficit disorder. *Journal of Child Neurology, 6*(Supplement), S13–S22.

Shedler, J., & Block, J. (1990). Adolescent drug use and psychological health: A longitudinal inquiry. *American Psychologist, 45,* 612–630.

Sheinbaum, K. A., & Badell, A. (1992). Physiatric management of two neonates with limb deficiencies and prenatal cocaine exposure. *Archives of Physical Medicine and Rehabilitation, 73*(4), 385–388.

Shepherd, G., & Ferslew, B. C. (2009). Homicidal poisoning deaths in the United States 1999–2005. *Clinical Toxicology, 47*(4), 342–347.

Sheppard, M. A., Snowden, C. B., Baker, S. P., et al. (2008). Estimating alcohol and drug involvement in hospitalized adolescents with assault injuries. *The Journal of Adolescent Health, 43*(2), 165–171.

Sher, K. J. (1987). Stress response dampening. In H. T. Blane & K. E. Leonard (Eds.), *Psychological theories of drinking and alcoholism* (pp. 227–271). New York, NY: Guilford Press.

Sher, K. J., & Levenson, R. W. (1982). Risk for alcoholism and individual differences in the stress-response-dampening effect of alcohol. *Journal of Abnormal Psychology, 91*(5), 350–367.

Sher, L. (2006). Alcohol and suicide: Neurobiological and clinical aspects. *Scientific World Journal, 6,* 700–706.

Sher, L., Sperling, D., Stanley, B. H., et al. (2007). Triggers for suicidal behavior in depressed older adolescents and young adults: Do alcohol use disorders make a difference? *International Journal of Adolescent Medicine and Health, 19*(1), 91–98.

Sher, L., & Zalsman, G. (2005). Alcohol and adolescent suicide. *International Journal of Adolescent Medicine and Health, 17*(3), 197–203.

Shetty, K., & Brown, J. (2009). Oral cancer risk factors among Mexican American Hispanic adolescents in South Texas. *Journal of Dentistry for Children, 76*(2), 142–148.

Shetty, V., Mooney, L. J., Zigler, C. M., et al. (2010). The relationship between methamphetamine use and increased dental disease. *Journal of the American Dental Association, 141*(3), 307–318.

Shibley, H. L., Malcolm, R. J., & Veatch, L. M. (2008). Adolescents with insomnia and substance abuse: Consequences and comorbidities. *Journal of Psychiatric Practice, 14*(3), 146–153.

Shields, A. L., & Caruso, J. C. (2003). Reliability generalization of the Alcohol Use Disorders Identification Test. *Educational and Psychological Measurement, 63*(3), 404–413.

Shields, A. L., & Caruso, J. C. (2004). A reliability induction and reliability generalization study of the CAGE questionnaire. *Educational and Psychological Measurement, 64*(2), 254–270.

Shields, A. L., Howell, R. T., Potter, J. S., et al. (2007). The Michigan Alcoholism Screening Test and its shortened form: A meta-analytic inquiry into score reliability. *Substance Use & Misuse, 42*(11), 1783–1800.

Shinn, A. K., & Greenfield, S. F. (2010). Topiramate in the treatment of substance-related disorders: A critical review of the literature. *The Journal of Clinical Psychiatry, 71*(5), 634–648.

Shirley, D. G., Walter, S. J., & Noormohamed, F. H. (2002). Natriuretic effect of caffeine: Assessment of segmental sodium reabsorption in humans. *Clinical Science, 103*(5), 461–466.

Shoemaker, F. W. (1993). Prevention of fetal alcohol syndrome [letter]. *Pediatrics, 92,* 738–739.

Shontz, F. C. (1993). A personological integration of chemical dependence and physical disability. In A. W. Heinemann (Ed.), *Substance abuse and physical disability* (pp. 21–39). Binghamton, NY: Haworth Press.

Shontz, F. C., & Spotts, J. V. (1986). Who are the drug users? *Drugs & Society, 1*(1), 51–74.

Shope, J. T., Copeland, L. A., Kamp, M. E., et al. (1998). Twelfth grade follow-up of the effectiveness of a middle school-based substance abuse prevention program. *Journal of Drug Education, 28*(3), 185–197.

Shope, J. T., Copeland, L. A., Marcoux, B. C., et al. (1996). Effectiveness of a school-based substance abuse prevention program. *Journal of Drug Education, 26*(4), 323–337.

Shoptaw, S. J., Kao, U., Heinzerling, K., et al. (2009). Treatment for amphetamine withdrawal. *Cochrane Database of Systematic Reviews, 2,* CD003021.

Shrier, L. A., Harris, S. K., Kurland, M., et al. (2003). Substance use problems and associated psychiatric symptoms among adolescents in primary care. *Pediatrics, 111*(6, pt. 1), e699–e705.

Shrout, P., & Fleiss, J. L. (1979). Intraclass correlation: Uses in assessing rater reliability. *Psychological Bulletin, 86*(2), 420–428.

Shulgin, A., & Shulgin, A. (1991). *PiHKAL: A chemical love story.* Berkeley, CA: Transform Press.

Shulgin, A. T. (1964). Psychotomimetic amphetamines: Methoxy 3,4–dialkoxyamphetamines. *Experientia, 20*(7), 366–367.

Shulgin, A. T. (1966). The six trimethoxyphenylisopropylamines (trimethoxyamphetamines). *Journal of Medicinal Chemistry, 9*(3), 445–446.

Shulgin, A. T. (1973). Stereospecific requirements for hallucinogenesis. *Journal of Pharmacy and Pharmacology, 25*(3), 271–272.

Shulgin, A. T. (1975). Drugs of abuse in the future. *Clinical Toxicology, 8*(4), 405–456.

Shulgin, A. T. (1979). Chemistry of phenethylamines related to mescaline. *Journal of Psychedelic Drugs, 11*(1–2), 41–52.

Shulgin, A. T. (1981). Profiles of psychedelic drugs: 10. DOB. *Journal of Psychoactive Drugs, 13*(1), 99.

Shulgin, A. T. (1986). The background and chemistry of MDMA. *Journal of Psychoactive Drugs, 18*(4), 291–304.

Shulman, J. D., & Wells, L. M. (1997). Acute ethanol toxicity from ingesting mouthwash in children younger than 6 years of age. *Pediatric Dentistry, 19*(6), 404–408.

Shytle, R. D., Silver, A. A., Lukas, R. J., et al. (2002). Nicotinic acetylcholine receptors as targets for antidepressants. *Molecular Psychiatry, 7*(6), 525–535.

Sidlo, J., Valuch, J., Ocko, P., et al. (2009). Fatal methadone intoxication in an 11-month-old male infant. *Soudni Lekarstvi, 54*(2), 23–25.

Sidney, S. (2002). Cardiovascular consequences of marijuana use. *Journal of Clinical Pharmacology, 42*(11, Suppl.), 64S–70S.

Siegel, E., & Wason, S. (1990). Sudden death caused by inhalation of butane and propane. *The New England Journal of Medicine, 323*(23), 1638.

Siegel, J. T., Alvaro, E. M., Patel, N., et al. (2009). "... you would probably want to do it. Cause that's what made them popular": Exploring perceptions of inhalant utility among young adolescent nonusers and occasional users. *Substance Use & Misuse, 44*(5), 597–615.

Siegel, R. K. (1978). Phencyclidine, criminal behavior, and the defense of diminished capacity. *NIDA Research Monograph No. 21, Phencylidine (PCP) abuse: An appraisal* (pp. 272–288). Bethesda, MD: National Institute on Drug Abuse.

Sigmon, S. C., Herning, R. I., Better, W., et al. (2009). Caffeine withdrawal, acute effects, tolerance, and absence of net beneficial effects of chronic administration: Cerebral blood flow velocity, quantitative EEG,
and subjective effects. *Psychopharmacology (Berlin), 204*(4), 573–585.

Silberstein, C., Galanter, M., Marmor, M., et al. (1994). HIV-1 among inner city dually diagnosed inpatients. *The American Journal of Drug and Alcohol Abuse, 20,* 101–113.

Simkin, D. R. (2002). Adolescent substance use disorders and comorbidity. *Pediatric Clinics of North America, 49*(2), 463–477.

Simon, S. L., Dean, A. C., Cordova, X., et al. (2010). Methamphetamine dependence and neuropsychological functioning: Evaluating change during early adolescence. *Journal of Studies on Alcohol and Drugs, 71*(3), 335–344.

Simpson, T. L., & Miller, W. R. (2002). Concomitance between childhood sexual and physical abuse and substance use problems. A review. *Clinical Psychology Review, 22*(1), 27–77.

Sindelar, H. A., Barnett, N. P., & Spirito, A. (2004). Adolescent alcohol use and injury. A summary and critical review of the literature. *Minerva Pediatrica, 56*(3), 291–309.

Singer, L. T., Arendt, R., Minnes, S., et al. (2000). Neurobehavioral outcomes of cocaine-exposed infants. *Neurotoxicology and Teratology, 22,* 653–666.

Singer, L. T., Linares, T. J., Ntiri, S., et al. (2004). Psychosocial profiles of older adolescent MDMA users. *Drug and Alcohol Dependence, 74*(3), 245–252.

Singer, L. T., Minnes, S., Short, E., et al. (2004). Cognitive outcomes of preschool children with prenatal cocaine exposure. *JAMA, The Journal of the American Medical Association, 291*(20), 2448–2456.

Singer, M., Clair, S., Schensul, J., et al. (2005). Dust in the wind: The growing use of embalming fluid among youth in Hartford, CT. *Substance Use & Misuse, 40*(8), 1035–1050.

Singh, G. K., Kogan, M. D., & Dee, D. L. (2007). Nativity/immigrant status, race/ethnicity, and socioeconomic determinants of breastfeeding initiation and duration in the United States, 2003. *Peditrics, 119*(Supplement 1), S38–S46.

Single, E. W. (1988). The availability theory of alcohol-related problems. In C. D. Chaudron & D. A. Wilkinson (Eds.), *Theories on alcoholism* (pp. 325–351). Toronto, ON: Addiction Research Foundation.

Singleton, R., Holve, S., Groom, A., et al. (2009). Impact of immunizations on the disease burden of American Indian and Alaska Native children. *Archives of Pediatrics & Adolescent Medicine, 163*(5), 446–453.

Sinha, R. (2008). Chronic stress, drug use, and vulnerability to addiction. *Annals of the New York Academy of Sciences, 1141,* 105–130.

Siqueira, L. M., & Crandall, L. A. (2006). Inhalant use in Florida youth. *Substance Abuse, 27*(4), 27–35.

Sisselman, S. G., Mofenson, H. C., & Caraccio, T. R. (1996). Childhood poisonings from ingestion of cigarettes. *Lancet, 347*(8995), 200–201.

Skara, S., & Sussman, S. (2003). A review of 25 long-term adolescent tobacco and other drug use prevention program evaluations. *Preventive Medicine, 37*(5), 451–474.

Skinner, B. F. (1931). The concept of the reflex in the description of behavior. *The Journal of General Psychology, 5*, 427–458.

Skinner, H. A. (1982). The Drug Abuse Screening Test. *Addictive Behaviors, 7*(4), 363–371.

Skinner, H. A., & Sheu, W. J. (1982). Reliability of alcohol use indices: The Lifetime Drinking History and the MAST. *Journal of Studies on Alcohol, 43*, 1157–1170.

Skipsey, K., Burleson, J. A., & Kranzler, H. R. (1997). Utility of the AUDIT for the identification of hazardous or harmful drinking in drug-dependent patients. *Drug and Alcohol Dependence, 45*, 157–163.

Slaby, A. A. (1991). Dual diagnosis: Fact or fiction? In M. S. Gold & A. E. Slaby (Eds.), *Dual diagnosis in substance abuse* (pp. 3–28). New York, NY: Dekker.

Slattery, M. L., West, D. W., Robison, L. M., et al. (1990). Tobacco, alcohol, coffee, and caffeine as risk factors for colon cancer in a low-risk population. *Epidemiology, 1*(2), 141–145.

Slaughter, L. (2000). Involvement of drugs in sexual assault. *The Journal of Reproductive Medicine, 45*, 425–430.

Slayter, E. M. (2010). Disparities in access to substance abuse treatment among people with intellectual disabilities and serious mental illness. *Health & Social Work, 35*(1), 49–59.

Slesnick, N., Bartle-Haring, S., Erdem, G., et al. (2009). Troubled parents, motivated adolescents: Predicting motivation to change substance use among runaways. *Addictive Behaviors, 34*(8), 675–684.

Slesnick, N., & Prestopnik, J. (2005). Dual and multiple diagnosis among substance using runaway youth. *The American Journal of Drug and Alcohol Abuse, 31*(1), 179–201.

Sloboda, Z., Pyakuryal, A., Stephens, P. C., et al. (2008). Reports of substance abuse prevention programming available in schools. *Prevention Science, 9*(4), 276–287.

Sloboda, Z., Stephens, R. C., Stephens, P. C., et al. (2009). The Adolescent Substance Abuse Prevention Study: A randomized field trial of a universal substance abuse prevention program. *Drug and Alcohol Dependence, 102*(1–3), 1–10.

Slutsker, L. (1992). Risks associated with cocaine use during pregnancy. *Obstetrics & Gynecology, 79*, 778–789.

Smart, L. S., Chibucos, T. R., & Didier, L. A. (1990). Adolescent substance use and perceived family functioning. *Journal of Family Issues, 11*(2), 208–227.

Smart, R. G., Adlaf, E. M., Porterfield, K. M., et al. (1990). *Drugs, youth and the street.* Toronto, ON: Addiction Research Foundation.

Smiley, A. (1999). Marijuana not a factor in driving accidents. *news@UofT*. Retrieved from http://www.newsandevents.utoronto.ca/bin19990329a.asp

Smith, C., Faris, R., Lundquist Denton, M., et al. (2003). Mapping American adolescent subjective religiosity and attitudes of alienation toward religion: A research report. *Sociology of Religion, 64*(1), 111–133.

Smith, G. H. (1993). Intervention strategies for children vulnerable for school failure due to exposure to drugs and alcohol. *The International Journal of the Addictions, 28*, 1435–1470.

Smith, G. M. (1977). *Correlates of personality and drug use—1.* (RAUS Cluster Review No. 3). Rockville, MD: U.S. Department of Health and Human Services, National Institute on Drug Abuse.

Smith, G. M. (1980). Perceived effects of substance use: A general theory. In D. J. Lettieri, M. Sayer, & H. Wallenstein Pearson (Eds.), *Theories on drug abuse: Selected contemporary perspectives* (NIDA Research Monograph No. 30, pp. 50–58). Rockville, MD: U.S. Department of Health and Human Services, National Institute on Drug Abuse.

Smith, G. M., & Fogg, C. P. (1977). Psychological antecedents of teenage drug use. In R. G. Simmons (Ed.), *Research in community and mental health: An annual compilation of research* (Vol. 1, pp. 87–102). Greenwich, CT: JAI Press.

Smith, G. M., & Fogg, C. P. (1978). Psychological predictors of early use, late use, and nonuse of marihuana among teenage students. In D. B. Kandel (Ed.), *Longitudinal research on drug use: Empirical findings and methodological issues* (pp. 101–113). New York, NY: Wiley.

Smith, G. M., & Fogg, C. P. (1979). Psychological antecedents of teen-age drug use. *Research in Community and Mental Health, 1*, 87–102.

Smith, J. D., Tracy, J. I., & Murray, M. J. (1993). Depression and category learning. *Journal of Experimental Psychology, 122*, 331–346.

Smith, K. M., Larive, L. L., & Romanelli, F. (2002). Club drugs: Methylenedioxymethamphetamine, flunitrazepam, ketamine hydrochloride, and gamma-hydroxybutyrate. *American Journal of Health-System Pharmacy: AJHP, 59*(11), 1067–1076.

Smith, L. A., Gates, S., & Foxcroft, D. (2006, January 25). Therapeutic communities for substance related disorder. *Cochrane Database of Systematic Reviews, 1*, CD005338.

Smith, L. M., LaGasse, L. L., Derauf, C., et al. (2006). The Infant Development, Environment, and Lifestyle Study: Effects of prenatal methamphetamine exposure, polydrug exposure, and poverty on intrauterine growth. *Pediatrics, 118*(3), 1149–1156.

Smith, R. A., & Glynn, T. J. (2000). Epidemiology of lung cancer. *Radiologic Clinics of North America, 38*(3), 453–470.

Smitherman, C. H. (1994). The lasting impact of fetal alcohol syndrome and fetal alcohol effect on children and adolescents. *Journal of Pediatric Health Care, 8*, 121–126.

Smolinske, S. C., Spoerke, D. G., Spiller, S. K., et al. (1988). Cigarette and nicotine chewing gum toxicity in children. *Human Toxicology, 7*(1), 27–31.

Snodgrass, S. R. (1994). Cocaine babies: A result of multiple teratogenic influences. *Journal of Child Neurology, 9*(3), 227–233.

Snyder, C. A., Wood, R. W., Graefe, J. F., et al. (1988). "Crack smoke" is a respirable aerosol of cocaine base. *Pharmacology, Biochemistry, and Behavior, 29*(1), 93–95.

Snyder, F., Vuchinich, S., Acock, A., et al. (2010). Impact of the Positive Action program on school-level indicators of academic achievement, absenteeism, and disciplinary outcomes: A matched-pair, cluster randomized, controlled trial. *Journal of Research on Educational Effectiveness, 3*(1), 26–55.

Soares, B. G., Lima, M. S., Reisser, A. A., et al. (2003). Dopamine agonists for cocaine dependence. *Cochrane Database of Systematic Reviews, 2*, CD003352.

Soares, B., Lima Reisser, A. A., Farrell, M., et al. (2010, February 17). WITHDRAWN: Dopamine agonists for cocaine dependence. *Cochrane Database of Systematic Reviews, 2*, CD003352.

Sokol, R. J., & Clarren, S. K. (1989). Guidelines for use of terminology describing the impact of prenatal alcohol on the offspring. *Alcoholism, Clinical and Experimental Research, 13*(4), 597–598.

Sokol, R. J., Martier, S. S., & Ager, J. W. (1989). The T-ACE questions: Practical prenatal detection of risk-drinking. *American Journal of Obstetrics and Gynecology, 160*(4), 863–868.

Soldz, S., & Dorsey, E. (2005). Youth, attitudes and beliefs toward alternative tobacco products: Cigars, bidis, and kreteks. *Health Education and Behavior, 32*(4), 549–566.

Soldz, S., Huyser, D. J., & Dorsey, E. (2003). Characteristics of users of cigars, bidis, and kreteks and the relationship to cigarette use. *Preventive Medicine, 37*(3), 250–258.

Solowij, N., & Battisti, R. (2008). The chronic effects of cannabis on memory in humans: A review. *Current Drug Abuse Reviews, 1*(1), 81–98.

Solowij, N., & Michie, P. T. (2007). Cannabis and cognitive dysfunction: Parallels with endophenotypes of schizophrenia. *Journal of Psychiatry & Neuroscience, 32*(1), 30–52.

Solowij, N., Michie, P. T., & Fox, A. M. (1991). Effects of long-term cannabis use on selective attention: An event-related potential study. *Pharmacology, Biochemistry & Behavior, 40*, 683–688.

Solowij, N., Stephens, R. S., Roffman, R. A., et al. (2002). Cognitive functioning of long-term heavy cannabis users seeking treatment. *JAMA, The Journal of the American Medical Association, 287*(9), 1123–1131.

Sood, B., Delaney-Black, V., Covington, C., et al. (2001). Prenatal alcohol exposure and childhood behavior at age 6 to 7 years: I. Dose-response effect. *Pediatrics, 108*(2), E34.

Sorg, B. A., & Newlin, D. B. (2002). Sensitization as a mechanism for multiple chemical sensitivity: Relationship to evolutionary theory. *Scandinavian Journal of Psychology, 43*, 161–167.

Sowell, E. R., Leow, A. D., Bookheimer, S. Y., et al. (2010). Differentiating prenatal exposure to methamphetamine and alcohol versus alcohol and not methamphetamine using tensor-based brain morphometry and discriminant analysis. *The Journal of Neuroscience, 30*(11), 3876–3885.

Sowell, E. R., Thompson, P. M., Holmes, C. J., et al. (1999). In vivo evidence for post-adolescent brain maturation in frontal and striatal regions. *Nature Neuroscience, 2*(10), 859–861.

Soyka, M., Albus, M., Kathmann, N., et al. (1993). Prevalence of alcohol and drug abuse in schizophrenic inpatients. *European Archives of Psychiatry and Clinical Neuroscience, 242*(6), 362–372.

Soyka, M., & Rösner, S. (2010). Nalmefene for treatment of alcohol dependence. *Expert Opinion on Investigational Drugs, 19*(11), 1451–1459.

Spadari, M., Glaizal, M., Tichadou, L., et al. (2009). Accidental cannabis poisoning in children: Experience of the Marseille poison center [in French]. *La Presse Médicale, 38*(11), 1563–1567.

Spagnolo, A. (1993). Teratogenesis of alcohol. *Annali dell'Instituto Superiore di Sanita, 29*(1), 89–96.

Spear, H. J. (2006). Breastfeeding behaviors and experiences of adolescent mothers. *MCN: The American Journal of Maternal/Child Nursing, 31*(2), 106–113.

Spear, L. P. (1993). Missing pieces of the puzzle complicate conclusions about cocaine's neurobehavioral toxicity in clinical populations: Importance of animal models. *Neurotoxicology and Teratology, 15*, 307–309.

Spearman, C. (1904). The proof and measurement of association between two things. *American Journal of Psychology, 15*, 72–101.

Spiller, H. A. (2004). Epidemiology of volatile substance abuse (VSA) cases reported to US poison centers. *The American Journal of Drug and Alcohol Abuse, 30*(1), 155–165.

Spindler, G. (1952). Personality and peyotism in Menomini Indian acculturation. *Psychiatry, 15*, 151–159.

Spirito, A., Rasile, D. A., Vinnick, L. A., et al. (1997). Relationship between substance use and self-reported injuries among adolescents. *The Journal of Adolescent Health, 21*, 221–224.

Spohr, H. L., & Steinhausen, H. C. (1984). The course of alcoholic embryopathy [in German]. *Monatsschrift Kinderheilkunde, 132*, 844–849.

Spohr, H. L., Willms, J., & Steinhausen, H. C. (1993). Prenatal alcohol exposure and long-term developmental consequences. *Lancet, 34*, 907–910.

Spohr, H. L., Willms, J., & Steinhausen, H. C. (2007). Fetal alcohol spectrum disorders in young adulthood. *The Journal of Pediatrics, 150*(2), 175–179.

Sporer, K. A. (1999). Acute heroin overdose. *Annals of Internal Medicine, 130*(7), 584–590.

Spotts, J. V., & Shontz, F. C. (1980a). *Cocaine users: A representative case approach.* New York, NY: Free Press.

Spotts, J. V., & Shontz, F. C. (1980b). A life theme theory of chronic drug abuse. In D. J. Lettieri, M. Sayer, & H. Wallenstein Pearson (Eds.), *Theories on drug abuse: Selected contemporary perspectives* (NIDA Research Monograph No. 30, pp. 59–70). Rockville, MD: U.S. Department of Health and Human Services, National Institute on Drug Abuse.

Spotts, J. V., & Shontz, F. C. (1982). Ego development, dragon fights, and chronic drug abusers. *The International Journal of the Addictions, 17*, 945–976.

Spotts, J. V., & Shontz, F. C. (1984a). Correlates of sensation seeking in heavy, chronic drug users. *Perceptual Motor Skills, 58*, 427–435.

Spotts, J. V., & Shontz, F. C. (1984b). Drugs and personality: Extroversion-introversion. *Journal of Clinical Psychology, 40*, 624–628.

Spotts, J. V., & Shontz, F. C. (1984c). Drug induced ego states: 1. Cocaine: Phenomenology and implications. *The International Journal of the Addictions, 19*, 119–151.

Spotts, J. V., & Shontz, F. C. (1984d). The phenomenological structure of drug induced ego states: 2. Barbiturates and sedative-hypnotics: Phenomenology and implications. *The International Journal of the Addictions, 19*, 295–326.

Spotts, J. V., & Shontz, F. C. (1985). A theory of adolescent substance abuse. In J. S. Brook, D. J. Lettieri, D. W. Brook, et al. (Eds.), *Alcohol and substance abuse in adolescence* (pp. 117–138). New York, NY: Haworth Press.

Square, D. (1997). Fetal alcohol syndrome epidemic on Manitoba reserve. *CMAJ, Canadian Medical Association Journal, 157*(1), 59–60.

Stafford, J. R., Rosen, T. S., Zaider, M., et al. (1994). Prenatal cocaine exposure and the development of the human eye. *Ophthalmology, 101*, 301–308.

Stagg Elliott, V. (2007). More teens test positive for drugs, alcohol at sick care visits. Amednews.com, pp. 1–3. Retrieved from http://www.ama-assn.org/amednews/2007/11/26/hlsc1126.htm

Staley, D., & El-Guebaly, N. (1990). Psychometric properties of the Drug Abuse Screening Test in a psychiatric patient population. *Addictive Behaviors, 15*, 257–264.

Staller, J., & Faraone, S. V. (2006). Attention-deficit hyperactivity disorder in girls: Epidemiology and management. *CNS Drugs, 20*(2), 107–123.

Stanfill, S. B., Brown, C. R., Yan, X. J., et al. (2006). Quantification of flavor-related compounds in the unburned contents of bidi and clove cigarettes. *Journal of Agricultural and Food Chemistry, 54*(22), 8580–8588.

Stanley, K. M., Worrall, C. L., Lunsford, S. L., et al. (2005). Experience with an adult alcohol withdrawal syndrome practice guideline in internal medicine patients. *Pharmacotherapy, 25*(8), 1073–1083.

Stanton, M. D. (1977). The addict as savior: Heroin, death, and the family. *Family Process, 16*(2), 191–197.

Stanton, M. D. (1978a). Family therapy for the drug user: Conceptual and practical considerations. *Drug Forum, 6*, 203–205.

Stanton, M. D. (1978b). Some outcome results and aspects of structural family therapy with drug addicts. In D. A. Smith, S. M. Anderson, M. Buxton, et al. (Eds.), *A multicultural view of drug abuse: Proceedings of the National Drug Abuse Conference, 1977* (pp. 378–388). Cambridge, MA: Schenkman.

Stanton, M. D. (1978c). The family and drug misuse: A bibliography. *TheAmerican Journal of Drug and Alcohol Abuse, 5*(2), 151–170.

Stanton, M. D., & Coleman, S. B. (1980). The participatory aspects of indirect self-destructive behavior: The addict family as a model. In M. L. Farberow (Ed.), *The many faces of suicide: Indirect self-destructive behavior* (pp. 187–203). New York, NY: McGraw-Hill.

Stanton, M. D., & Todd, T. C. (1982a). *The family therapy of drug abuse and addiction.* New York, NY: Guilford Press.

Stanton, M. D., & Todd, T. C. (1982b). The therapy model. In M. D. Stanton & T. C. Todd (Eds.), The family therapy of drug abuse and addiction (pp. 109–153). New York, NY: Guilford Press.

Stanton, M. D., Todd, T. C., Heard, D. B., et al. (1978). Heroin addiction as a family phenomenon: A new conceptual model. *The American Journal of Drug and Alcohol Abuse, 5*(2), 125–150.

Statistics Canada. (2008, April 2). 2006 census: Ethnic origin, visible minorities, place of work and mode of transportation. *The Daily*, pp. 1–5. Retrieved from http://www.statcan.gc.ca/daily-quotidien/080402/dq080402a-eng.htm

Stead, L. F., & Lancaster, T. (2005a, January 25). Interventions for preventing tobacco sales to minors. *Cochrane Database of Systematic Reviews, 1*, CD001497.

Stead, L. F., & Lancaster, T. (2005b, April 18). Group behavior therapy programmes for smoking cessation. *Cochrane Database of Systematic Reviews, 2*, CD001007.

Stein, M. D., & Friedmann, P. D. (2005). Disturbed sleep and its relationship to alcohol use. *Substance Abuse, 26*(1), 1–13.

Steinbauer, J. R., Cantor, S. B., Holzer, C. E., et al. (1998). Ethnic and sex bias in primary care screening tests for alcohol use disorders. *Annals of Internal Medicine, 129*(5), 353–362.

Steinbuchel, P. H., Wilens, T. E., Adamson, J. J., et al. (2009). Posttraumatic stress disorder and substance use disorder in adolescent bipolar disorder. *Bipolar Disorder, 11*(2), 198–204.

Steinglass, P. (1975). The simulated drinking gang: An experimental model for the study of a systems approach to alcoholism. I. Description of the model. *The Journal of Nervous and Mental Disease, 161*, 100–109.

Steinglass, P. (1979). Family therapy with alcoholics: A review. In E. Kaufman & P. Kaufman (Eds.), *Family therapy of drug and alcohol abuse* (pp. 147–186). New York, NY: Gardner Press.

Steinglass, P. (1980). A life history model of the alcoholic family. *Family Process, 19*, 211–225.

Steinglass, P., Bennett, L. A., Wolin, S. J., et al. (1987). *The alcoholic family*. New York, NY: Basic Books.

Steinglass, P., Davis, D. I., & Berenson, D. (1977). Observations of conjointly hospitalized "alcoholic couples" during sobriety and intoxication: Implications for theory and therapy. *Family Process, 16*, 1–16.

Steinglass, P., Weiner, S., & Mendelson, J. H. (1971a). A systems approach to alcoholism: A model and its clinical application. *Archives of General Psychiatry, 24*(5), 401–408.

Steinglass, P., Weiner, S., & Mendelson, J. H. (1971b). Interactional issues as determinants of alcoholism. *The American Journal of Psychiatry, 128*(3), 275–280.

Stepanski, E. J., & Rybarczyk, B. (2006). Emerging research on the treatment and etiology of secondary or comorbid insomnia. *Sleep Medicine Reviews, 10*, 7–18.

Stephens, P. C., Sloboda, Z., Grey, S., et al. (2009). Is the receptivity of substance abuse prevention programming affected by students' perceptions of the instructor? *Health Education & Behavior, 36*(4), 724–745.

Stephens, P. C., Sloboda, Z., Stephens, R. C., et al. (2009). Universal school-based substance abuse prevention programs: Modeling targeted mediators and outcomes for adolescent cigarette, alcohol and marijuana use. *Drug and Alcohol Dependence, 102*(1–3), 19–29.

Stephens, R. S., Pelham, W. E., & Skinner, R. (1984). State-dependent and main effects of methylphenidate and pemoline on paired-associate learning and spelling in hyperactive children. *Journal of Consulting & Clinical Psychology, 52*(1), 104–113.

Stephens-Hernandez, A. B., Livingston, J. N., Dacons-Brock, K., et al. (2007). Drama-based education to motivate participation in substance abuse prevention. *Substance Abuse Treatment, Prevention, and Policy, 2*, 11.

Steuber, T. L., & Danner, F. (2006). Adolescent smoking and depression: Which comes first? *Addictive Behaviors, 31*(1), 133–136.

Stewart, S. H., Sherry, S. B., Comeau, M. N., et al. (2011). Hopelessness and excessive drinking among Aboriginal adolescents: The mediating roles of depressive symptoms and drinking to cope. *Depression Research and Treatment*. Retrieved from http://www.ncbi.nlm.nih.gov/pubmed/21197100

Stick, S. M., Burton, P. R., Gurrin, L., et al. (1996). Effects of maternal smoking during pregnancy and a family history of asthma on respiratory function in newborn infants. *Lancet, 348*, 1060–1064.

Stijnenbosch, P. J., Zuketto, C., Beijaert, P. J., et al. (2010). GHB withdrawal delirium [in Dutch]. *Nederlands Tijdschrift voor Geneeskunde, 154*, A 1086.

Stillwell, M. E. (2002). Drug-facilitated sexual assault involving gamma-hydroxybutyric acid. *Journal of Forensic Sciences, 47*(5), 1133–1134.

Stirling, J., Jr. (2007). Beyond Munchausen syndrome by proxy: Identification and treatment of child abuse in a medical setting. *Pediatrics, 119*(5), 1026–1030.

Stone, K. C., LaGasse, L. L., Lester, B. M., et al. (2010). Sleep problems in children with prenatal substance exposure: The maternal lifestyle study. *Archives of Pediatrics & Adolescent Medicine, 164*(5), 452–456.

Storgaard, H., Nielsen, S. D., & Gluud, C. (1994). The validity of the Michigan Alcoholism Screening Test (MAST). *Alcohol and Alcoholism, 29*(5), 493–502.

Stormshak, E. A., & Dishion, T. J. (2009). A school-based, family-centered intervention to prevent substance use: The family check-up. *The American Journal of Drug and Alcohol Abuse, 35*(4), 227–232.

Storr, C. L., Westergaard, R., & Anthony, J. C. (2005). Early onset inhalant use and risk for opiate initiation by young adulthood. *Drug and Alcohol Dependence, 78*(3), 253–261.

Stowell, R. J. (1991). Dual diagnosis issues. *Psychiatric Annals, 21*, 98–104.

Stowell, R. J., & Estroff, T. W. (1992). Psychiatric disorders in substance-abusing adolescent inpatients: A pilot study. *The Journal of the American Academy of Child and Adolescent Psychiatry, 31*, 1036–1040.

Stratton, K., Howe, C., & Battaglia, F. C. (1996). *Fetal alcohol syndrome: Diagnosis, epidemiology, prevention and treatment*. Washington, DC: Institute of Medicine and National Academy.

Strauss, A. A., Modaniou, H. D., & Bosu, S. K. (1981). Neonatal manifestations of maternal phencyclidine (PCP) abuse. *Pediatrics, 68*(4), 550–552.

Streissguth, A. P., Barr, H. M., & Sampson, P. D. (1990). Moderate prenatal alcohol exposure: Effects on child IQ and learning problems at age 7½ years. *Alcoholism,Clinical and Experimental Research, 14*(5), 662–629.

Streissguth, A. P., Barr, H. M., Sampson, P. D., et al. (1994). Maternal drinking during pregnancy: Attention and short-term memory in 14-year-old offspring—A longitudinal prospective study. *Alcoholism, Clinical and Experimental Research, 18*, 202–218.

Streissguth, A. P., Bookstein, F. L., Sampson, P. D., et al. (1989). Neurobehavioral effects of prenatal alcohol: Part III. PLS analyses of neuropsychologic tests. *Neurotoxicology and Teratology, 11*(5), 493–507.

Streissguth, A. P., Randels, S. P., & Smith, D. F. (1992). Fetal alcohol syndrome [Reply to letter to the editor].

*The Journal of the American Academy of Child and Adolescent Psychiatry, 31*, 563–564.

Strote, J., Lee, J.E., & Wechsler, H. (2002). Increasing MDMA use among college students: Results of a national survey. *The Journal of Adolescent Health, 30*(1), 64–72.

Substance Abuse and Mental Health Administration. (2006). *Results from the 2005 National Survey on Drug Use and Health: National findings*. Office of Applied Studies, NSDUH Series H-30, DHHS, Publication No. SMA 06–4194. Rockville, MD: Author.

Substance Abuse and Mental Health Services Administration. (2010, March 18). *The TEDS report: Pregnant teen admissions to substance abuse treatment: 1992 and 2007*. Rockville, MD: Office of Applied Studies.

Substance abuse: Frequent alcohol consumption among women of childbearing age. (1994). *Weekly Epidemiology Record, 69*, 180–182.

Suchman, E. A. (1968). The "hang-loose" ethic and the spirit of drug use. *Journal of Health and Social Behavior, 9*, 146–155.

Sugie, H., Sasaki, C., Hashimoto, C., et al. (2004). Three cases of sudden death due to butane or propane gas inhalation: Analysis of tissues for gas components. *Forensic Science International, 143*(2–3), 211–214.

Suh, J. J., Pettinati, H. M., Kampman, K. M., et al. (2006). The status of disulfiram: A half of a century later. *Journal of Clinical Psychopharmacology, 26*(3), 290–302.

Sullivan, M. A., Garawi, F., Bisaga, A., et al. (2007). Management of relapse in naltrexone maintenance for heroin dependence. *Drug and Alcohol Dependence, 91*(2–3), 289–292.

Sussman, S. (2010). A review of Alcoholics Anonymous/Narcotics Anonymous programs for teens. *Evaluation & the Health Professions, 33*(1), 26–55.

Sussman, S., Pentz, M. A., Spruijt-Metz, D., et al. (2006). Misuse of "study drugs": Prevalence, consequences, and implications for policy. *Substance Abuse Treatment, Prevention, and Policy, 9*(1), 15.

Swanson, J. M., Cantwell, D., Lerner, M., et al. (1991). Effects of stimulant medication on learning in children with ADHD. *Journal of Learning Disabilities, 24*(4), 219–230.

Sweet, R. W. (1991). *OJJDP and boys and girls clubs of America: Public housing and high-risk youth* (NCJ No. 128412). Washington, DC: U.S. Department of Justice.

Swetlow, K. (2003, June). Children at clandestine methamphetamine labs: Helping meth's youngest victims. *Office for Victims of Crime Bulletin* (pp. 1–12). Washington, DC: U.S. Department of Justice.

Swift, R. (2007). Emerging approaches to managing alcohol dependence. *American Journal of Health-System Pharmacy, 64*(5, Suppl. 3), S12–S22.

Szapocznik, J., Kurtines, W., Santisteban, D. A., et al. (1990). Interplay of advances between theory, research, and application in treatment interventions aimed at behavior problem children and adolescents. *Journal of Consulting and Clinical Psychology, 58*, 696–703.

Szapocznik, J., & Williams, R. A. (2000). Brief Strategic Family Therapy: Twenty-five years of interplay among theory, research and practice in adolescent behavior problems and drug abuse. *Clinical Child and Family Psychological Review, 3*(2), 117–134.

## T

Tabor, B. L., Smith-Wallace, T., & Yonekura, M. L. (1990). Perinatal outcome associated with PCP versus cocaine use. *The American Journal of Drug and Alcohol Abuse, 16*, 337–348.

Tanaka, K., Tsuji, I., Wakai, K., et al. (2006). Cigarette smoking and liver cancer risk: An evaluation based on a systematic review of epidemiologic evidence among Japanese. *Japanese Journal of Clinical Oncology, 36*(7), 445–456.

Tarabar, A. F., & Nelson, L. S. (2004). The gamma-hydroxybutyrate withdrawal syndrome. *Toxicology Reviews, 23*(1), 45–49.

Tarter, R. E. (1983). The causes of alcoholism: A biopsychological analysis. In E. Gottheil, K. A. Druley, T. E. Skoloda, et al. (Eds.), *Etiologic aspects of alcohol and drug abuse* (pp. 173–201). Springfield, IL: Thomas.

Tarter, R. E. (1990). Evaluation and treatment of adolescent substance abuse: A decision tree method. *The American Journal of Drug and Alcohol Abuse, 16*(1–2), 1–46.

Tarter, R. E., Alterman, A. I., & Edwards, K. L. (1985). Vulnerability to alcoholism in men: A behavior-genetic perspective. *Journal of Studies on Alcohol, 46*(4), 329–356.

Tarter, R. E., Alterman, A. I., & Edwards, K. L. (1988). Neurobehavioral theory of alcoholism etiology. In C. D. Chaudron & D. A. Wilkinson (Eds.), *Theories on alcoholism* (pp. 73–102). Toronto, ON: Addiction Research Foundation.

Tarter, R. E., & Edwards, K. L. (1988). Psychological factors associated with the risk for alcoholism. *Alcoholism, Clinical & Experimental Research, 12*, 4761–480.

Tarter, R. E., Kabene, M., Escallier, E. A., et al. (1990). Temperament deviation and risk for alcoholism. *Alcoholism, Clinical & Experimental Research, 14*, 380–382.

Tarter, R. E., Laird, S. B., Kabene, M., et al. (1990). Drug abuse severity in adolescents is associated with magnitude of deviation in temperament traits. *British Journal of Addiction, 85*, 1501–1504.

Tarter, R. E., & Mezzich, A. C. (1992). Ontogeny of substance abuse: Perspectives and findings. In M. Glantz & R. Pickens (Eds.), *Vulnerability to drug abuse* (pp. 149–177). Washington, DC: American Psychological Association.

Tata, P. R., Rollings, J., Collins, M., et al. (1994). Lack of cognitive recovery following withdrawal from long-term benzodiazepine use. *Psychological Medicine, 24*, 203–213.

Tavani, A., Gallus, S., Dal Maso, L., et al. (2001). Coffee and alcohol intake and risk of ovarian cancer: An Italian case-control study. *Nutrition and Cancer, 39*(1), 29–34.

Tavani, A., & La Vecchia, C. (2004). Coffee, decaffeinated coffee, tea and cancer of the colon and rectum: A review of epidemiological studies, 1990–2003. *Cancer Causes & Control, 15*(8), 743–757.

Taylor, D. R., Fergusson, D. M., Milne, B. J., et al. (2002). A longitudinal study of the effects of tobacco and cannabis exposure on lung function in young adults. *Addiction, 97*(8), 1055–1061.

Taylor, W. A., & Slaby, A. E. (1992). Acute treatment of alcohol and cocaine emergencies. In M. Galanter (Ed.), *Recent developments in alcoholism: Vol. 10. Alcohol and cocaine: Similarities and differences* (pp. 179–191). New York, NY: Plenum.

Teen "self-medication" for depression leads to more serious mental illness, new report reveals. (2008, May 10). *ScienceDaily*, pp. 1–2. Retrieved from http://www.sciencedaily.com/releases/2008/05/080509105348.htm

Teitelbaum, L., & Mullen, B. (2000). The validity of the MAST in psychiatric settings: A meta-analytic integration. Michigan Alcoholism Screening Test. *Journal of Studies on Alcoholism, 61*(2), 254–261.

Teixeira, F., Hojyo, M. T., Arenas, R., et al. (1994). Thalidomide: Can it continue to be used? *Lancet, 344*(8916), 196–197.

Temple, J. L. (2009). Caffeine use in children: What we know, what we have left to learn, and why we should worry. *Neuroscience & Biobehavioral Reviews, 33*(6), 793–806.

Tenenbein, M. (1984). Continuous naloxone infusion for opiate poisoning in infancy. *The Journal of Pediatrics, 105*(4), 645–648.

Terry, L. (1964). *1964 Surgeon General report: Reducing the health consequences of smoking.* Department of Health and Human Services, Centers for Disease Control and Prevention, National Center for Chronic Disease Prevention and Health Promotion, Office on Smoking and Health. Retrieved from http://www.cdc.gov/tobacco/sgr/sgr_1964.htm

Tharp-Taylor, S., Haviland, A., & D'Amico, E. J. (2009). Victimization from mental and physical bullying and substance use in early adolescence. *Addictive Behaviors, 34*(6–7), 561–567.

Thirthalli, J., & Benegal, V. (2006). Psychosis among substance users. *Current Opinion in Psychiatry, 19*(3), 239–245.

Thomas, R., & Perera, R. (2006, July 19). School-based programmes for preventing smoking. *Cochrane Database of Systematic Reviews, 3*, CD001293.

Thun, M. J., Henley, S. J., & Calle, E. E. (2002). Tobacco use and cancer: An epidemiologic perspective for geneticists. *Oncogene, 21*(48), 7307–7325.

Timberlake, D. S., & Huh, J. (2009). Demographic profiles of smokeless tobacco users in the U.S. *American Journal of Preventive Medicine, 37*(1), 29–34.

Timmermann, G. (2008). A study of teratogenic and fetotoxic effects of large doses of meprobamate used for a suicide attempt by 42 pregnant women. *Toxicology and Industrial Health, 24*(1–2), 97–107.

Tobler, N. S. (1992). Drug prevention programs can work: Research findings. *Journal of Addictive Diseases, 11*, 1–28.

Toklas, A. B. (1954). *The Alice B. Toklas cookbook.* New York, NY: HarperCollins.

Tong, E. K., England, L., & Glantz, S. A. (2005). Changing conclusions on secondhand smoke in a sudden infant death syndrome review funded by the tobacco industry. *Pediatrics, 115*(3 Suppl.), e356–e366.

Tonkin, R. S. (1987). Adolescent risk-taking behavior. *The Journal of Adolescent Health Care, 8*, 213–220.

Tonstad, S., Tønnesen, P., Hajek, P., et al. (2006). Effect of maintenance therapy with varenicline on smoking cessation: A randomized controlled trial. *JAMA, The Journal of the American Medical Association, 296*(1), 64–71.

Tourangeau, R., & Yan, T. (2007). Sensitive questions in surveys. *Psychological Bulletin, 133*(5), 859–883.

Trezza, V., Cuomo, V., & Vanderschuren, L. J. (2008). Cannabis and the developing brain: Insights from behavior. *European Journal of Pharmacology, 585*(2–3), 441–452.

Triffleman, E. G., Marmar, C. R., Delucchi, K. L., et al. (1995). Childhood trauma and posttraumatic stress disorder in substance abuse inpatients. *The Journal of Nervous and Mental Disease, 183*(3), 172–176.

Trimble, M. R., & Thompson, P. J. (1983). Anticonvulsant drugs, cognitive function, and behavior. *Epilepsia, 24*(Supplement 1), S55–S63.

Trtchounian, A., Williams, M., & Talbot, P. (2010). Conventional and electronic cigarettes (e-cigarettes) have different smoking characteristics. *Nicotine & Tobacco Research, 12*(9), 905–912.

Tsai, J., Floyd, R. L., Green, P. P., et al. (2007). Patterns and average volume of alcohol use among women of childbearing age. *Maternal and Child Health Journal, 11*(5), 437–445.

Tucker, P. (2009). Substance misuse and early psychosis. *Australasian Psychiatry, 17*(4), 291–294.

Tunving. K. (1987). Psychiatric aspects of cannabis use in adolescents and young adults. *Pediatrician, 14*, 1–2.

Tuunanen, M, Aalto, M., & Seppä, K. (2007). Binge drinking and its detection among middle-aged men using AUDIT, AUDIT-C and AUDIT-3. *Drug and Alcohol Review, 26*(3), 295–299.

**U**

Uhl, G. R., Hall, F. S., & Sora, I. (2002). Cocaine, reward, movement and monoamine transporters. *Molecular Psychiatry, 7*(1), 21–26.

Unger, J. B., Allen, B., Jr., Leonard, E., et al. (2010). Menthol and non-menthol cigarette use among black smokers in Southern California. *Nicotine & Tobacco Research, 12*(4), 398–407.

Unger, J. B., Kipke, M. D., Simon, T. R., et al. (1997). Homeless youths and young adults in Los Angeles: Prevalence of mental health problems and the relationship between mental health and substance abuse disorders. *American Journal of Community Psychology, 25*(3), 371–394.

Unger, J. B., Ritt-Olson, A., Wagner, K. D., et al. (2009). Parent-child acculturation patterns and substance use among Hispanic adolescents: A longitudinal analysis. *The Journal of Primary Prevention, 30*(3–4), 293–313.

United Press International. (2010, November 28). Mexico cornering the U.S. meth market. *UPI.com.* Retrieved from http://www.upi.com/Top_News/World-News/2010/11/28/Mexico-cornering-the-US-meth...

Unrug-Neervoort, A., van Luijtelaar, G., & Coenen, A. (1992). Cognition and vigilance: Differential effects of diazepam and buspirone on memory and psychomotor performance. *Neuropsychology, 26,* 146–150.

Upadhyaya, H. P. (2007). Managing attention-deficit/hyperactivity disorder in the presence of substance use disorder. *The Journal of Clinical Psychiatry, 68* (Suppl. 11), 23–30.

U.S. Department of Education. (1986). *Schools without drugs* (ED 270 715). Washington, DC: Author.

U.S. Department of Education. (1992). *Success stories from drug-free schools: A guide for educators, parents, and policymakers* (ED/OESE 92-47R). Washington, DC: Author.

U.S. Department of Education, National Center for Education Statistics. (2010). *The condition of education 2010* (NCES 2010–028). Washington, DC: Author.

U.S. Department of Health and Human Services (2001, December 19). *Monitoring the Future survey release: Smoking among teenagers decreases sharply and increase in ecstasy use slows.* Atlanta, GA: Centers for Disease Control and Prevention, National Center for Chronic Disease Prevention and Health Promotion.

U.S. Department of Health and Human Services. (2006). The health consequences of involuntary exposure to tobacco smoke: A report of the Surgeon General. Atlanta, GA: Author, Centers for Disease Control and Prevention. Retrieved from http://www.cdc.gov/tobacco/data_statistics/sgr/sgr_2006/index.htm

U.S. Department of Health and Human Services, Administration on Children, Youth and Families (2006). *Child maltreatment 2004.* Washington, DC: U.S. Government Printing Office.

U.S. Department of Health, Education and Welfare. (1964). *Smoking and health: Report of the Advisory Committee to the Surgeon General of the Public Health Services.* Washington, DC: Author.

U.S. Food and Drug Administration. (2006, May 11). FDA approves novel medication for smoking cessation [press release].

U.S. Food and Drug Administration. (2009a, July 1). Public health advisory: FDA requires new boxed warnings for the smoking cessation drugs Chantix and Zyban.

Retrieved from http://www.fda.gov/Drugs/DrugSafety/PostmarketDrugSafetyInformationforPatientsandP...

U.S. Food and Drug Administration (2009b). Tobacco products: Flavored tobacco. Retrieved from http://www.fda.gov/TobaccoProducts/ProtectingKidsfromTobacco/FlavoredTobacco/defa...

U.S. Food and Drug Administration (2010a). Tobacco products: Protecting kids from tobacco. Retrieved from http://www.fda.gov/TobgaccoProducts/ProtectingKidsfromTobacco/default.htm

U.S. Food and Drug Administration (2010b). Tobacco products: Regulations restricting the sale and distribution of cigarettes and smokeless tobacco. Retrieved from http://www.fda.gov/TobaccoProducts/ProtectingKidsfromTobacco/RegsRestrictingSale/d...

U.S. Preventive Services Task Force. (2004). Screening and behavioral counseling interventions in primary care to reduce alcohol misuse: Recommendation statement. *Annals of Internal Medicine, 140,* 554–556.

Use of Swedish "snus" is linked to a doubled risk of pancreatic cancer. (2007, May 11). *Science Daily.* Retrieved from http://www.sciencedaily.com/releases/2007/05/070510095314.htm

Uysal, M. A., Kadakal, F., Karşidağ, C., et al. (2004). Fagerstrom test for nicotine dependence: Reliability in a Turkish sample and factor analysis. *Tuberk Toraks, 52*(2), 115–521.

## V

Vaillant, G. E. (1983a). *The natural history of alcoholism.* Cambridge, MA: Harvard University Press.

Vaillant, G. E. (1983b). Natural history of male alcoholism. *Archives of General Psychiatry, 39,* 127–133.

Vaillant, G. E. (1983c). Natural history of male alcoholism: 5. Is alcoholism the cart of the sociopathy? *British Journal of Addiction, 78,* 317–326.

Vaillant, G. E. (1992). Prospective evidence for the effects of environment upon alcoholism. In S. Saitoh, P. Steinglass, & M. A. Schuckit (Eds.), *Alcoholism and the family: The Fourth International Symposium of the Psychiatric Research Institute of Tokyo* (pp. 71–83). New York, NY: Brunner/Mazel.

Vaillant, G. E. (1995). *The natural history of alcoholism revisited.* Cambridge, MA: Harvard University Press.

Vaillant, G. E. (2005). Alcoholics Anonymous: Cult or cure? *Australian and New Zealand Journal of Psychiatry, 39*(6), 431–436.

Valentiner, D. P., Mounts, N. S., & Deacon, B. J. (2004). Panic attacks, depression and anxiety symptoms, and substance use behaviors during late adolescence. *Journal of Anxiety Disorders, 18*(5), 573–585.

van Dam, R. M. (2008). Coffee consumption and risk of type 2 diabetes, cardiovascular disease, and cancer. *Applied Physiology, Nutrition, and Metabolism, 33*(6), 1269–1283.

van Dam, R. M., & Hu, F. B. (2005). Coffee consumption and risk of type 2 diabetes: A systematic review. *JAMA, The Journal of the American Medical Association, 294*(1), 97–104.

van Dam, R. M., Willett, W. C., Manson, J. E., et al. (2006). Coffee, caffeine, and risk of type 2 diabetes: A prospective cohort study in younger and middle-aged U.S. women. *Diabetes Care, 29*(2), 398–403.

van den Anker, J. N., & Sauer, P. J. (1992). Effect of cocaine use on the fetus. *The New England Journal of Medicine, 327*(19), 1394.

VanderWaal, C. J., McBride, D. C., Terry-McElrath, Y. M., et al. (2006). The role of public health agencies in providing access to adolescent drug treatment services. *The Journal of Adolescent Health, 39*(6), 916–924.

Vandrey, R., Budney, A. J., Kamon, J. L., et al. (2005). Cannabis withdrawal in adolescent treatment seekers. *Drug and Alcohol Dependence, 78*(2), 205–210.

Van Dyke, D. C., & Fox, A. A. (1990). Fetal drug exposure and its possible implications for learning in the preschool and school-aged population. *Journal of Learning Disabilities, 23*, 160–163.

Van Hasselt, V. B., Hersen, M., & Milliones, J. (1978). Social skills training for alcoholics and drug addicts: A review. *Addictive Behaviors, 3*, 221–233.

Van Hasselt, V. B., Hersen, M., Null, J. A., et al. (1993). Drug abuse prevention for high-risk African American children and their families: A review and model program. *Addictive Behaviors, 18*, 213–234.

Van Hasselt, V. B., Null, J. A., Kempton, T., et al. (1993). Social skills and depression in adolescent substance abusers. *Addictive Behaviors, 18*, 9–18.

Van Hook, S., Harris, S. K., Brooks, T., et al. (2007). The "six T's": Barriers to screening teens for substance abuse in primary care. *The Journal of Adolescent Health, 40*(5), 456–461.

Van Leeuwen, J. M., Hopfer, C., Hooks, S., et al. (2004). A snapshot of substance abuse among homeless and runaway youth in Denver, Colorado. *Journal of Community Health, 29*(3), 217–229.

van Nimwegen, L., de Haan, L., van Beveren, N., et al. (2005). Adolescence, schizophrenia and drug abuse: A window of vulnerability. *Acta Psychiatrica Scandinavica, 427* (Suppl.), 35–42.

van Nimwegen, L., de Haan, L., van Beveren, N., et al. (2007). Adolescence, schizophrenia and drug abuse: Interactive vulnerability. A hypothesis [in Dutch]. *Tijdschrift voor Psychiatrie, 49*(3), 169–178.

van Noorden, M. S., Kamal, R., de Jong, C. A., et al. (2010). Gamma-hydroxybutyric acid (GHB) dependence and the GHB withdrawal symdrome: Diagnosis and treatment [in Dutch]. *Nederlands Tijdschrift voor Geneeskunde, 154*, A1286.

van Noorden, M. S., van Dongen, L. C., Zitman, F. G., et al. (2009). Gamma-hydroxybutyrate withdrawal syndrome: Dangerous but not well-known. *General Hospital Psychiatry, 31*(4), 394–396.

van Os, J., Bak, M., Hanssen, M., et al. (2002). Cannabis use and psychosis: A longitudinal population-based study. *American Journal of Epidemiology, 156*, 319–327.

Varela, M., Nogue, S., Oros, M., et al. (2004). Gamma hydroxybutyrate use for sexual assault. *Emergency Medicine Journal, 21*(2), 255–256.

Varenicline. (2009, October 1). *MedlinePlus*, pp. 1–4. Retrieved from http://www.nlm.nih.gov/medlineplus/druginfo/meds/a606024.html

Vargas, P. A., Brenner, B., Clark, S., et al. (2007). Exposure to environmental tobacco smoke among children presenting to the emergency department with acute asthma: A multicenter study. *Pediatric Pulmonology, 42*(7), 646–655.

Vaughn, M. G. (2004). Adolescent substance abuse treatment: A synthesis of controlled evaluations. *Research on Social Work Practice, 14*(5), 325–335.

Verdoux, H., & Tournier, M. (2004). Cannabis use and risk of psychosis: An etiological link? *Epidemiologia Psichiatria Sociale, 13*(2), 113–119.

Vetulani, J. (2001). Drug addiction. Part II. Neurobiology of addiction. *Polish Journal of Pharmacology, 53*(4), 303–317.

Vickers, M. (1969). Gammahydroxybutyric acid. *International Anesthesiology Clinics, 7*, 75–89.

Vidailhet, P., Danion, J. M., Kauffmann-Muller, F., et al. (1994). Lorazepam and diazepam effects on memory acquisition in priming tasks. *Psychopharmacology (Berlin), 115*(3), 397–406.

Vilela, R. J., Langford, C., McCullagh, L., et al. (2002). Cocaine-induced oronasal fistulas with external nasal erosion but without palate involvement. *Ear, Nose, & Throat Journal, 81*(8), 562–563.

Vocci, F. J., & Chiang, C. N. (2001). Vaccines against nicotine: How effective are they likely to be in preventing smoking? *CNS Drugs, 15*(7), 505–514.

Volkan, K. (1994). *Dancing among the Maenads: The psychology of compulsive drug use*. San Francisco, CA: Lang.

Volkow, N. D. (2009). Letter from the director: Inhalant abuse. *NIDA Research Report Series*, pp. 1–2. Retrieved from http://www.nida.nih.gov/ResearchReports/Inhalants/Inhalants.html

Volkow, N. D., Chang, L., Wang, G.-J., et al. (2001). Low level of brain dopamine D2 receptors in methamphetamine abusers: Association with metabolism in the orbitofrontal cortex. *The American Journal of Psychiatry, 158*(12), 2015–2021.

Volkow, N. D., Fowler, J. S., & Wang, G.-J. (2002). Role of dopamine in drug reinforcement and addiction in humans: Results from imaging studies. *Behavioral Pharmacology, 13*, 355–366.

Volkow, N. D., Fowler, J. S., & Wang, G.-J. (2003). The addicted human brain: Insights from imaging studies. *The Journal of Clinical Investigation, 111*(10), 1444–1451.

Volkow, N. D., Rosen, B., & Farde, L. (1997). Imaging the living human brain: Magnetic resonance imaging and positron emission tomography. *Proceedings of the National Academy of Sciences, 94*, 2787–2788.

Volkow, N. D., Wang, G.-J., Fowler, J. S., et al. (1997). Decreased striatal dopaminergic responsiveness in detoxified cocaine-dependent subjects. *Nature, 386*(6627), 830–833.

Volkow, N. D., Wang, G.-J., Fowler, J. S., et al. (1999). Reinforcing effects of psychostimulants in humans are associated with increases in brain dopamine and occupancy of D(2) receptors. *The Journal of Pharmacology and Experimental Therapeutics, 291*(1), 409–415.

Volkow, N. D., Wang, G.-J., Fowler, J. S., et al. (2000). Cocaine abusers show a blunted response to alcohol intoxication in limbic brain regions. *Life Sciences, 66*(12), PL161–PL167.

Volpicelli, J. R., Clay, K. L., Watson, N. T., et al. (1995). Naltrexone in the treatment of alcoholism: Predicting response to naltrexone. *The Journal of Clinical Psychiatry, 56*(Suppl. 7), 39–44.

Vreeman, R. C., & Carroll, A. E. (2007). A systematic review of school-based interventions to prevent bullying. *Archives of Pediatrics & Adolescent Medicine, 161*(1), 78–88.

# W

Wachsman, L., Schuetz, S., Chan, L. S., et al. (1989). What happens to babies exposed to phencyclidine (PCP) in utero? *The American Journal of Drug and Alcohol Abuse, 15*(1), 31–39.

Wagner, K. D., Brief, D. J., Vielhauer, M. J., et al. (2009). The potential for PTSD, substance use, and HIV risk behavior among adolescents exposed to Hurricane Katrina. *Substance Use & Misuse, 44*(12), 1749–1767.

Wagner, K. D., Ritt-Olson, A., Soto, D. W., et al. (2008). The role of acculturation, parenting, and family in Hispanic/Latino adolescent substance use: Findings from a qualitative analysis. *Journal of Ethnicity in Substance Abuse, 7*(3), 304–327.

Wakefield, M., Flay, B., Nichter, M., et al. (2003). Effects of anti-smoking advertising on youth smoking: A review. *Journal of Health Communication, 8*(3), 229–247.

Wakschlag, L. S., & Hans, S. L. (2002). Maternal smoking during pregnancy and conduct problems in high–risk youth: A developmental framework. *Development and Psychopathology, 14*(2), 351–369.

Wakschlag, L. S., Pickett, K. E., Cook, E., et al. (2002). Maternal smoking during pregnancy and severe antisocial behavior in offspring: A review. *American Journal of Public Health, 92*, 966–974.

Waldo, C. R., McFarland, W., Katz, M. H., et al. (2000). Very young gay and bisexual men are at risk for HIV infection: The San Francisco Bay Area Young Men's Survey II. *Journal of Acquired Immune Deficiency Syndromes, 24*(2), 168–174.

Waldron, H. B., & Kaminer, Y. (2004). On the learning curve: The emerging evidence supporting cognitive-behavioral therapies for adolescent substance abuse. *Addiction, 99*(Suppl. 2), 93–105.

Wallace, P. (1991). Prevalence of fetal alcohol syndrome largely unknown. *Iowa Medicine, 81*(9), 381.

Walpole, I., Zubrick, S., Pontre, J., et al. (1991). Low to moderate maternal alcohol use before and during pregnancy, and neurobehavioural outcome in the newborn infant. *Developmental Medicine and Child Neurology, 33*, 875–883.

Walsh, G. W., & Mann, R. E. (1999). On the high road: Driving under the influence of cannabis in Ontario. *Canadian Journal of Public Health, 90*(4), 260–263.

Walsh, S. L., Stoops, W. W., Moody, D. E., et al. (2009). Repeated dosing with oral cocaine in humans: Assessment of direct effect, withdrawal, and pharmacokinetics. *Experimental and Clinical Psychopharmacology, 17*(4), 205–216.

Wang, M. (2010, April 12). Perinatal drug abuse and neonatal drug withdrawal. *Emedicine.* Retrieved from http://emedicine.medscape.com/article/978492-overview

Wang, P., Molina, C. P., Maldonado, J. E., et al. (2010). In utero drugs of abuse exposure testing for newborn twins. *Journal of Clinical Pathology, 63*(3), 259–261.

Wang, R. Y. (1999). pH-dependent cocaine-induced cardiotoxicity. *The American Journal of Emergency Medicine, 17*(4), 364–369.

Wang, Y. G., Swick, T. J., Carter, L. P., et al. (2009). Safety overview of postmarketing and clinical experience of sodium oxybate (Xyrem): Abuse, misuse, dependence, and diversion. *Journal of Clinical Sleep Medicine, 5*(4), 365–371.

Ward, A. J. (1992). Adolescent suicide and other self-destructive behaviors: Adolescent attitude survey data and interpretation. *Residential Treatment for Children and Youth, 9*(3), 49–64.

Warner, K. E., & Mackay, J. (2006). The global tobacco disease pandemic: Nature, causes, and cures. *Global Public Health, 1*(1), 65–86.

Warren, K. R., & Li, T. K. (2005). Genetic polymorphisms: Impact on the risk of fetal alcohol spectrum disorders. *Birth Defects Research Part A: Clinical and Molecular Teratology, 73*(4), 195–203.

Washton, A. M., & Resnick, R. B. (1981). Clonidine in opiate withdrawal: Review and appraisal of clinical findings. *Pharmacotherapy, 1*(2), 140–146.

Waterson, E. J., & Murray-Lyon, I. M. (1988). Are the CAGE questions outdated? *British Journal of Addiction, 83*, 113–115.

Watson, J., Deary, I., & Kerr, D. (2002). Central and peripheral effects of sustained caffeine use: Tolerance is incomplete. *British Journal of Clinical Pharmacology, 54*(4), 400–406.

Watson, J. B. (1913). Psychology as the behaviorist views it. *Psychological Review, 20*, 158–177.

Wechsler, H., Davenport, A., Dowdall, G., et al. (1994). Health and behavioral consequences of binge drinking in college: A national survey of students at 140 campuses. *JAMA, The Journal of the American Medical Association, 272*, 1672–1677.

Wechsler, H., Kuo, M., Lee, H., et al. (2000). Environmental correlates of underage alcohol use and related problems of college students. *American Journal of Preventive Medicine, 19*(1), 24–29.

Weems, C. F., Taylor, L. K., Cannon, M. F., et al. (2010). Post traumatic stress, context, and the lingering effects of the Hurricane Katrina disaster among ethnic minority youth. *Journal of Abnormal Child Psychology, 38*(1), 49–56.

Weil, A. T. (1972). *The natural mind: A new way of looking at drugs and the higher consciousness.* Boston, MA: Houghton Mifflin.

Weinberger, A. H., Desai, R. A., & McKee, S. A. (2010). Nicotine withdrawal in U.S. smokers with current mood, anxiety, alcohol use, and substance use disorders. *Drug and Alcohol Dependence, 108*(1–2), 7–12.

Weinberger, A. H., Maciejewski, P. K., McKee, S. A., et al. (2009). Gender differences in associations between lifetime alcohol, depression, panic disorder, and post-traumatic stress disorder and tobacco withdrawal. *The American Journal of Addictions, 18*(2), 140–147.

Weinberger, A. H., Reutenauer, E. L., Allen, T. M., et al. (2007). Reliability of the Fagerström Test for Nicotine Dependence, Minnesota Nicotine Withdrawal Scale, and Tiffany Questionnaire for Smoking Urges in smokers with and without schizophrenia. *Drug and Alcohol Dependence, 86*(2–3), 278–282.

Weingartner, H. J., Hommer, D., Lister, R. G., et al. (1992). Selective effects of triazolam on memory. *Psychopharmacology (Berlin), 106*, 341–345.

Weingartner, H. J., Putnam, F., George, D. T., et al. (1995). Drug state-dependent autobiographical knowledge. *Experimental and Clinical Psychopharmacology, 3*(3), 304–307.

Weisner, C., Greenfield, T., & Room, R. (1995). Trends in the treatment of alcohol problems in the US general population, 1979 through 1990. *American Journal of Public Health, 85*, 55–60.

Weiss, G., Kruger, E., Danielson, U., et al. (1975). Effect of long-term treatment of hyperactive children with methylphenidate. *CMAJ, Canadian Medical Association Journal, 112*, 159–165.

Weiss, R. D., Griffin, M. L., & Mirin, S. M. (1992). Drug abuse as self-medication for depression: An empirical study. *The American Journal of Drug and Alcohol Abuse, 18*, 121–129.

Weissberg, R. P., Caplan, M., & Harwood, R. L. (1991). Promoting competent young people in competence-enhancing environments: A systems-based perspective on primary prevention. *Journal of Consulting and Clinical Psychology, 59*(6), 830–841.

Weissenborn, R., & Duka, T. (2003). Acute alcohol effects on cognitive function in social drinkers: Their relationship to drinking habits. *Psychopharmacology (Berlin), 165*(3), 306–312.

Weitzman, M., Gortmaker, S., & Sobol, M. A. (1992). Maternal smoking and behavior problems of children. *Pediatrics, 90*(3), 342–349.

Wellman, R. J., Sugarman, D. B., DiFranza, J. R., et al. (2006). The extent to which tobacco marketing and tobacco use in films contribute to children's use of tobacco: A meta-analysis. *Archives of Pediatric & Adolescent Medicine, 160*(12), 1285–1296.

Wells, K. (2009). Substance abuse and child maltreatment. *Pediatric Clinics of North America, 56*(2), 345–362.

Wells, K. C. (1988). Family therapy. In J. L. Matson (Ed.), *Handbook of treatment approaches in childhood psychopathology* (pp. 45–61). New York, NY: Plenum.

Wells, K. C., & Forehand, R. (1981). Childhood behavior problems in the home. In S. M. Turner, K. S. Calhoun, & H. E. Adams (Eds.), *Handbook of clinical behavior therapy.* New York, NY: Wiley.

Werley, M. S., Coggins, C. R., & Lee, P. N. (2007). Possible effects on smokers of cigarette mentholation: A review of the evidence relating to key research questions. *Regulatory Toxicology and Pharmacology, 47*(2), 189–203.

Westermeyer, J., Wahmanholm, K., & Thuras, P. (2001). Effects of childhood physical abuse on course and severity of substance abuse. *The American Journal on Addictions, 10*(2), 101–110.

Westover, A. N., McBride, S., & Haley, R. W. (2007). Stroke in young adults who abuse amphetamines or cocaine: A population-based study of hospitalized patients. *Archives of General Psychiatry, 64*(4), 495–502.

What's a cancer drug doing in cocaine? (2009, December 18). *Wall Street Journal*, p. 1. Retrieved from http://blogs.wsj.com/health/2009/12/18/whats-a-cancer-drug-doing-in-cocaine/tab/print/

Wheeler, S. F. (1993). Substance abuse during pregnancy. *Primary Care, 20*, 191–207.

White, H. R., & Labouvie, E. W. (1989). Toward the assessment of adolescent problem drinking. *Journal of Studies on Alcohol, 50*(1), 30–37.

White, H. R., & Labouvie, E. W. (2000). Longitudinal trends in problem drinking as measured by the Rutgers Alcohol Problem Index [abstract]. *Alcoholism, Clinical and Experimental Research, 24*(5, Suppl. 1), 76A.

White, H. R., Xie, M., Thompson, W., et al. (2001). Psychopathology as a predictor of adolescent drug use trajectories. *Psychology of Addictive Behaviors, 15*, 210–218.

Whitmore, E. A., Mikulich, S. K., Thompson, L. L., et al. (1997). Influences on adolescent substance dependence: Conduct disorder, depression, attention deficit hyperactivity disorder, and gender. *Drug and Alcohol Dependence, 47*(2), 87–97.

Whitten, L. (2009). Studies link family of genes to nicotine addiction. *National Institute on Drug Abuse: NIDA Notes, 22*(6), 1, 10–14.

Whitten, L. (2010). School-wide program reduces problem behaviors and improves academic outcomes. *NIDA Notes, 23*(2), 8–9.

Wigle, D. T., Arbuckle, T. E., Turner, M. C., et al. (2008). Epidemiologic evidence of relationships between reproductive and child health outcomes and environmental chemical contaminants. *Journal of Toxicology & Environmental Health Part B: Critical Review, 11*(5–6), 373–517.

Wikstrom, A. K., Cnattingius, S., Galanti, M. R., et al. (2010). Effect of Swedish snuff (snus) on preterm birth. *BJOG: An International Journal of Obstetrics and Gynaecology, 117*(8), 1005–1010.

Wikstrom, A. K., Stephansson, O., & Cnattingius, S. (2010). Tobacco use during pregnancy and preeclampsia risk: Effects of cigarette smoking and snuff. *Hypertension, 55*(5), 1254–1259.

Wijetunga, M., Seto, T., Lindsay, J., et al. (2003). Crystal methamphetamine-associated cardiomyopathy: Tip of the iceberg? *Journal of Toxicology and Clinical Toxicology, 41*(7), 981–986.

Wikler, A. (1953). *Opiate addiction.* Springfield, IL: Thomas.

Wilens, T. E. (2004). Attention-deficit/hyperactivity disorder and the substance use disorders: The nature of the relationship, subtypes at risk, and treatment issues. *Psychiatric Clinics of North America, 27*(2), 283–301.

Wilens, T. E., Adler, L. A., Adams, J., et al. (2008). Misuse and diversion of stimulants prescribed for ADHD: A systematic review of the literature. *Journal of the American Academy of Child & Adolescent Psychiatry, 47*(1), 21–31.

Wilens, T. E., Biederman, J., Kwon, A., et al. (2004). Risk of substance use disorders in adolescents with bipolar disorder. *Journal of the American Academy of Child & Adolescent Psychiatry, 43*(11), 1380–1386.

Wilens, T. E., Biederman, J., Millstein, R. B., et al. (1999). Risk for substance use disorders in youths with child- and adolescent-onset bipolar disorder. *Journal of the American Academy of Child & Adolescent Psychiatry, 38*(6), 680–685.

Wilens, T. E., & Fusillo, S. (2007). When ADHD and substance use disorders intersect: Relationship and treatment implications. *Current Psychiatry Reports, 9*(5), 408–414.

Wilens, T. E., & Upadhyaya, H. P. (2007). Impact of substance use disorder on ADHD and its treatment. *The Journal of Clinical Psychiatry, 68*(8), e20.

Wilkins-Haug, L. (1997). Teratogen update: Toluene. *Teratology, 55*(2), 145–151.

Wilkins-Haug, L., & Gabow, P. A. (1991). Toluene abuse during pregnancy: Obstetric complications and perinatal outcomes. *Obstetrics & Gynecology, 77*, 504–509.

Willford, J. A., Richardson, G. A., Leech, S. L., et al. (2004). Verbal and visuospatial learning and memory function in children with moderate prenatal alcohol exposure. *Alcoholism, Clinical & Experimental Research, 28*(3), 497–507.

Williams, C. L., Toomey, T. L., McGovern, P., et al. (1995). Development, reliability, and validity of self-report alcohol-use measures with young adolescents. *Journal of Child & Adolescent Substance Abuse, 4*(3), 17–40.

Williams, D. R., & Cole, S. J. (1998). Ventricular fibrillation following butane gas inhalation. *Resuscitation, 37*(1), 43–45.

Williams, J. F., & Storck, M. (2007). Inhalant abuse. *Pediatrics, 119*(5), 1009–1017.

Williams, J. M., & Gandhi, K. K. (2008). Use of caffeine and nicotine in people with schizophrenia. *Current Drug Abuse Reviews, 1*(2), 155–161.

Willmann, S., Edginton, A. N., Coboeken, K., et al. (2007). Risk to the breast-fed neonate from codeine treatment to the mother: A quantitative mechanistic modeling study. *Clinical Pharmacology & Therapeutics, 86*, 634–643.

Willows, N. D., Veugelers, P., Raine, K., et al. (2009). Prevalence and sociodemographic risk factors related to household food security in Aboriginal peoples in Canada. *Public Health Nutrition, 12*(8), 1150–1156.

Wilsnack, S. C., & Wilsnack, R. W. (1979). Sex roles and adolescent drinking. In H. T. Blane & M. E. Chafetz (Eds.), *Youth, alcohol, and social policy* (pp. 183–224). New York, NY: Plenum Press.

Wilson, C. R., Harris, S. K., Sherritt, L., et al. (2008). Parental alcohol screening in pediatric practices. *Pediatrics, 122*(5), e1022–e1029.

Wilson, H. W., & Widom, D. S. (2008). An examination of risky sexual behavior and HIV in victims of child abuse and neglect: A 30-year follow-up. *Health Psychology, 27*(2), 149–158.

Windle, M. A. (1990). A longitudinal study of antisocial behaviors in early adolescence as predictors of late adolescent substance use: Gender and ethnic group differences. *Journal of Abnormal Psychology, 99*(1), 86–91.

Winecker, R. E., Goldberger, B. A., Tebbett, I. R., et al. (2001). Detection of cocaine and its metabolites in breast milk. *Journal of Forensic Sciences, 46*, 1221–1223.

Wingard, J. A., Huba, G. H., & Bentler, P. M. (1979a). *A longitudinal analysis of personality structure and adolescent substance use.* Los Angeles, CA: UCLA/NIDA Center for Adolescent Drug Abuse Etiologies.

Wingard, J. A., Huba, G. H., & Bentler, P. M. (1979b). The relationship of personality structures to patterns of adolescent drug use. *Multivariate Behavioral Research, 14*, 131–143.

Wingert, W. E., Feldman, M. S., Kim, M. H., et al. (1994). A comparison of meconium, maternal urine and neonatal urine for detection of maternal drug use during pregnancy. *Journal of Forensic Sciences, 39*(1), 150–158.

Winick, C. (1959–1960). The use of drugs by jazz musicians. *Social Problems, 7*(3), 240–253.

Winick, C. (1961a). How high the moon—Jazz and drugs. *Antioch Review, 21*, 53–68.

Winick, C. (1961b). Physician narcotic addicts. *Social Problems, 9*(2), 174–186.

Winick, C. (1962a). Maturing out of narcotic addiction. *U.S. Bulletin on Narcotics, 14*, 1–7.

Winick, C. (1962b). The taste of music. *Jazz Monthly, 9*, 8–11.

Winick, C. (1964). The life cycle of the narcotic addict and of addiction. *U.N. Bulletin on Narcotics, 16*, 1–11.

Winick, C. (1968). *The new people*. New York, NY: Pegasus Press.

Winick, C. (1973). Some reasons for the increases in drug dependence among middle-class youths. In H. Silverstein (Ed.), *Sociology of youth* (pp. 433–440). New York, NY: Macmillan.

Winick, C. (1974a). Drug dependence among nurses. In C. Winick (Ed.), *Sociological aspects of drug dependence* (pp. 155–165). Cleveland, OH: CRC.

Winick, C. (1974b). Note on a theory of the genesis of drug dependence among adolescents. *Addictive Diseases, 1*, 5–6.

Winick, C. (1974c). A sociologic theory of the genesis of drug dependence. In C. Winick (Ed.), *Sociological aspects of drug dependence* (pp. 3–13). Cleveland, OH: CRC.

Winick, C. (1980). A theory of drug dependence based on role, access to, and attitudes toward drugs. In D. J. Lettieri, M. Sayer, & H. Wallenstein Pearson (Eds.), *Theories on drug abuse: Selected contemporary perspectives* (NIDA Research Monograph No. 30, pp. 225–235). Rockville, MD: U.S. Department of Health and Human Services, National Institute on Drug Abuse.

Winklbaur, B., Ebner, N., Sachs, G., et al. (2006). Substance abuse in patients with schizophrenia. *Dialogues in Clinical Neuroscience, 8*(1), 37–43.

Winslow, B. T., Voorhees, K. I., & Pehl, K. A. (2007). Methamphetamine abuse. *American Family Physician, 76*(8), 1169–1174.

Winters, K. C., (2004, August). Assessment of alcohol and other drug use behaviors among adolescents. National Institute on Alcohol Abuse and Alcoholism Publications, pp. 1–19. Retrieved from http://pubs.niaaa.nih.gov/publications/assesing%20alcohol/behaviors.htm

Winters, K. C., & Kaminer, Y. (2008). Screening and assessing adolescent substance use disorders in clinical populations. *The Journal of the American Academy of Child and Adolescent Psychiatry, 47*(7), 740–744.

Wish, E., Hoffman, J., & Nemes, S. (1997). The validity of self-reports of drug use at treatment admission and at followup: Comparisons with urinalysis and hair assay. *NIDA Research Monograph, 167*, 200–226.

Wister, A. V., & Avison, W. R. (1982). "Friendly persuasion": A social network analysis of sex differences in marijuana use. *International Journal of Addiction, 17*(3), 523–541.

Witlin, A. G., & Sibai, B. M. (2001). Perinatal and maternal outcome following abruption placentae. *Hypertension in Pregnancy, 20*(2), 195–203.

Wittchen, H. U., & Essau, C. A. (1993). Epidemiology of panic disorder: Progress and unresolved issues. *Journal of Psychiatric Research, 27*(Suppl. 1), 47–68.

Wittchen, H. U., Frolich, C., Behrendt, S., et al. (2007). Cannabis use and cannabis use disorders and their relationship to mental disorders: A 10-year prospective-longitudinal community study in adolescents. *Drug and Alcohol Dependence, 88*(Suppl. 1), S60–S70.

Wojnar-Horton, R. E., Kristensen, J. H., Yapp, P., et al. (1997). Methadone distribution and excretion into breast milk of clients in a methadone maintenance programme. *British Journal of Clinical Pharmacology, 44*(6), 543–547.

Wojtowicz, J. M., Yarema, M. S., & Wax, P. M. (2008). Withdrawal from gamma-hydroxybutyrate, 1,4-butanediol and gamma-butyrolactone: A case report and systematic review. *CJEM, Canadian Journal of Emergency Medical Care, 10*(1), 69–74.

Wolsko, C., Mohatt, G. V., Lardon, C., et al. (2009). Smoking, chewing, and cultural identity: Prevalence and correlates of tobacco use among the Yup'ik—The Center for Alaska Native Health Research (CANHR) study. *Cultural Diversity & Ethnic Minority Psychology, 15*(2), 165–172.

Woolf, A., Burkhart, K., Caraccio, T., et al. (1997). Childhood poisoning involving transdermal nicotine patches. *Pediatrics, 99*(5), E4.

World Health Organization. (2010). *Tobacco Facts.* p. 1. Retrieved from http://www.who.int/tobacco/mpower/tobacco_facts/en/index.html

World Health Organization ASSIST Working Group. (2002). The Alcohol, Smoking and Substance Involvement Screening Test (ASSIST): Development, reliability and feasibility. *Addiction, 97*(9), 1183–1194.

World Health Organization. (2009). *WHO report on the global tobacco epidemic, 2009: Implementing smoke-free environments*. Geneva, Switzerland: Author.

World-wide cocaine cut mystery. (2010, January 4), pp. 1–3. Retrieved from http:/www.mindhacks.com/blog/2010/01worldwide_cocaine_c.html

Wu, L. T. (2005). *Inhalant use in the United States: Correlates and consequences* [PowerPoint presentation]. Inhalant Abuse Among Children and Adolescents: Building an International Research Agenda Conference, November 7–9. Retrieved from http://209.128.81.248/view/7e8d-OEG5Y/Inhalant_Use_in_the_Unived_States_Correlates_and_Consequences_flash_ppt_presentation

Wu, L. T., & Howard, M. O. (2007). Is inhalant use a risk factor for heroin and injection drug use among adolescents in the United States? *Addictive Behaviors, 32*(2), 265–281.

Wu, L. T., Pilowsky, D. J., & Schlenger, W. E. (2004). Inhalant abuse and dependence among adolescents in the United States. *The Journal of the American Academy of Child and Adolescent Psychiatry, 43*(10), 1206–1214.

Wu, L. T., Ringwalt, C. L., Weiss, R. D., et al. (2009). Hallucinogen-related disorders in a national sample of adolescents: The influence of ecstasy/MDMA use. *Drug and Alcohol Dependence, 104*(1–2), 156–166.

Wu, L. T., Schlenger, W. E., & Galvin, D. M. (2006). Concurrent use of methamphetamine, MDMA, LSD, ketamine, GHB, and flunitrazepam among American youths. *Drug and Alcohol Dependence, 84*(1), 102–113.

Wu, P., Liu, X., & Fan, B. (2010). Factors associated with initiation of ecstasy use among US adolescents: Findings from a national survey. *Drug and Alcohol Dependence, 106*(2–3), 193–198.

Wu, S. I., Huang, H. C., Liu, S. I., et al. (2008). Validation and comparison of alcohol-screening instruments for identifying hazardous drinking in hospitalized patients in Taiwan. *Alcohol and Alcoholism, 43*(5), 577–582.

Wurmser, L. (1994). Preface. In K. Volkan, *Dancing among the Maenads: The psychology of compulsive drug use* (pp. xiii–xxii). San Francisco, CA: Lang.


# Y

Yaba, new form of meth, now appearing in U.S. (2003, March 16). *DEA—U.S. Drug Enforcement Administration Newsletter Update.* Retrieved from http://www.usdoj.gov/dea/ongoing/yaba012903.html

Yamaguchi, K., & Kandel, D. B. (1984). Patterns of drug use from adolescence to young adulthood: III. Predictors of progression. *American Journal of Public Health, 74*, 673–681.

Yamaguchi, K., & Kandel, D. B. (1985a). Dynamic relationships between premarital cohabitation and illicit drug use: An event history analysis of role socialization. *American Sociological Review, 50*, 530–546.

Yamaguchi, K., & Kandel, D. B. (1985b). On the resolution of role incompatibility: A life event history analysis of family roles and marijuana use. *American Journal of Sociology, 90*, 1284–1325.

Yamamoto, B. K., Moszczynska, A., & Gudelsky, G. A. (2010). Amphetamine toxicities: Classical and emerging mechanisms. *Annals of the New York Academy of Sciences, 1187*, 101–121.

Yeo, K. K., Wijetunga, M., Ito, H., et al. (2007). The association of methamphetamin use and cardiomyopathy in young patients. *The American Journal of Medicine, 120*(2), 165–171.

Yewell, J., Haydon, R., Archer, S., et al. (2002). Complications of intranasal prescription narcotic abuse. *Annals of Otology, Rhinology, and Laryngology, 111*(2), 174–177.

Yinger, J. M. (1965). *Toward a field theory of behavior: Personality and social structure.* New York, NY: McGraw-Hill.

*Youth Smoking Survey 2004–2005.* Ottawa, ON: Health Canada. Retrieved from www.hc-sc.gc.ca

Youth tobacco surveillance—United States, 2000. (2001). Office on Smoking and Health, National Center for Chronic Disease Prevention and Health Promotion (pp. 1–88). American Legacy Foundation, Washington, DC, and CDC Foundation, Atlanta, Georgia. Retrieved from http://www.cdc.gov/mmwr/preview/mmwrhtml/ss5004a1.htm

Yu, M. (2010, December 23). Tobacco use among American Indian or Alaska Native middle- and high-school students in the United States. *Nicotine and Tobacco Research.* Retrieved from http://www.ncbi.nlm.nih.gov/pubmed/21183589

Yudko, E., Lozhkina, O., & Fouts, A. (2007). A comprehensive review of the psychometric properties of the Drug Abuse Screening Test. *Journal of Substance Abuse Treatment, 32*(2), 189–198.


# Z

Zammit, S., Moore, T. H. M., Lingford-Hughes, A., et al. (2008). Effects of cannabis use on outcomes of psychotic disorders: Systematic review. *The British Journal of Psychiatry, 193*, 357–363.

Zeitlin, H. (1999). Psychiatric comorbidity with substance misuse in children and teenagers. *Drug and Alcohol Dependence, 55*(3), 225–234.

Zepf, F. D., Holtmann, M., Duketis, E., et al. (2009). Withdrawal syndrome after abuse of GHB (gamma-hydroxybutyrate) and its physiological precursors—Its relevance for child and adolescent psychiatrists [in German]. *Zeitschrift fur Kinder- und Jugendpsychiatrie, 37*(5), 413–420.

Zevin, S., & Benowitz, N. L. (1999). Drug interactions with tobacco smoking. An update. *Clinical Pharmacokinetics, 36*(6), 425–438.

Zhu, N. Y., LeGatt, D. F., & Turner, A. R. (2009). Agranulocytosis after consumption of cocaine adulterated with levamisole (letter). *Annals of Internal Medicine, 150*(4), 287–289.

Zickler, P. (2003). Nicotine's multiple effects on the brain's reward system drive addiction. *NIDA Notes, 17*(6), 1, 6.

Ziedonis, D. M., Smelson, D., Rosenthal, R. N., et al. (2005). Improving the care of individuals with schizophrenia and substance use disorders: Consensus recommendations. *Journal of Psychiatric Practice, 11*(5), 315–339.

Zimmerman, E. F. (1991). Substance abuse in pregnancy: Teratogenesis. *Pediatric Annals, 20*(10), 541–544, 546–547.

Zinberg, N. E. (1971, December 5). GIs and OJS in Vietnam. *New York Times Magazine*, pp. 37, 112, 114, 116, 118, 120, 122–124.

Zinberg, N. E. (1972a). Heroin use in Vietnam and the United States: A contrast and a critique. *Archives of General Psychiatry, 26*, 486–488.

Zinberg, N. E. (1972b). Rehabilitation of heroin users in Vietnam. *Contemporary Drug Problems, 1*, 263–294.

Zinberg, N. E. (1974a). *"High" states: A beginning study* (Drug Abuse Council Publication No. SS–3). Washington, DC: Drug Abuse Council.

Zinberg, N. E. (1974b). The search for rational approaches to heroin use. In P. G. Bourne (Ed.), *Addiction: A comprehensive treatise* (pp. 149–174). New York, NY: Academic Press.

Zinberg, N. E. (1975). Addiction and ego function. *The Psychoanalytic Study of the Child, 30*, 567–588.

Zinberg, N. E. (1979). Nonaddictive opiate use. In R. L. DuPont, A. Goldstein, & J. O'Donnell (Eds.), *Handbook on drug abuse* (pp. 303–313). Rockville, MD: U.S. Department of Health and Human Services, National Institute on Drug Abuse.

Zinberg, N. E. (1980). The social setting as a control mechanism in intoxicant use. In D. J. Lettieri, M. Sayer, & H. Wallenstein Pearson (Eds.), *Theories on drug abuse: Selected contemporary perspectives* (NIDA Research Monograph No. 30, pp. 236–244). Rockville, MD: U.S. Department of Health and Human Services, National Institute on Drug Abuse.

Zinberg, N. E., & DeLong, J. V. (1974). Research and the drug issue. *Contemporary Drug Problems, 3*, 71–100.

Zinberg, N. E., & Fraser, K. M. (1979). The role of the social setting in the prevention and treatment of alcoholism. In J. H. Mendelson & N. K. Mello (Eds.), *The diagnosis and treatment of alcoholism* (pp. 457–483). New York, NY: McGraw-Hill.

Zinberg, N. E., & Harding, W. M. (1979). Control over intoxicant use: A theoretical and practical overview. *Journal of Drug Issues, 9*, 121–143.

Zinberg, N. E., Harding, W. M., Stelmack, S. M., et al. (1978). Patterns of heroin use. *Annals of the New York Academy of Sciences, 311*, 10–24.

Zinberg, N. E., Harding, W. M., & Winkeller, M. (1977). A study of social regulatory mechanisms in controlled illicit drug users. *Journal of Drug Issues, 7*(2), 117–133.

Zinberg, N. E., & Jacobson, R. C. (1976). The natural history of "chipping." *The American Journal of Psychiatry, 133*(1), 37–40.

Zinberg, N. E., Jacobson, R. C., & Harding, W. M. (1975). Social sanctions and rituals as a basis of drug abuse prevention. *The American Journal of Drug and Alcohol Abuse, 2*(2), 165–182.

Zinberg, N. E., & Robertson, J. A. (1972). *Drugs and the public* (pp. 58–86). New York, NY: Simon & Schuster.

Zoja, L. (1989). *Drugs, addiction and initiation: The modern search for ritual.* Trans. M. E. Romano & R. Mercurio. Boston, MA: Sigo.

Zubek, J. P. (Ed.). (1969). *Sensory deprivation: Fifteen years of research.* New York, NY: Meredith Press.

Zucker, R. A. (1976). Parental influences on the drinking patterns of their children. In M. Greenblatt & M. A. Schuckit (Eds.), *Alcoholism problems in women and children* (pp. 211–238). New York, NY: Grune & Stratton.

Zucker, R. A. (1979). Developmental aspects of drinking through the young adult years. In H. T. Blane & M. E. Chafetz (Eds.), *Youth, alcohol, and social policy* (pp. 91–146). New York, NY: Plenum Press.

Zucker, R. A., & Devoe, C. I. (1975). Life history characteristics associated with problem drinking and antisocial behavior in adolescent girls: A comparison with male findings. In R. D. Wirt, G. Winokur, & M. Roff (Eds.), *Life history research in psychopathology* (Vol. 4, pp. 109–134). Minneapolis, MN: University of Minnesota Press.

Zucker, R. A., & Lisansky Gomberg, E. S. (1986). Etiology of alcoholism reconsidered: The case for a biopsychosocial process. *American Psychologist, 41*, 783–793.

Zucker, R. A., Noll, R. B., Draznin, T. H., et al. (1984, April). *The ecology of alcoholic families: Conceptual framework for the Michigan State University longitudinal study.* Presented at the National Council on Alcoholism, National Alcoholism Forum, Detroit, MI.

Zuckerman, M. (1969). Theoretical formulations 1. In J. P. Zubek (Ed.), *Sensory deprivation: Fifteen years of research* (pp. 407–449). New York, NY: Appleton-Century-Crofts.

Zuckerman, M. (1979). *Sensation seeking: Beyond the optimal level of arousal.* Hillsdale, NJ: Erlbaum.

Zuckerman, M. (1983a). A biological theory of sensation seeking. In M. Zuckerman (Ed.), *Biological bases of sensation seeking, impulsivity, and anxiety* (pp. 37–76). Hillsdale, NJ: Erlbaum.

Zuckerman, M. (1983b). Sensation seeking: The initial motive for drug abuse. In E. Gottheil, K. A., Druley, T. E., Skoloda, et al. (Eds.), *Etiologic aspects of alcohol & drug abuse* (pp. 202–220). Springfield, IL: Thomas.

Zuckerman, M. (1983c). A summing up with special sensitivity to the signals of reward in future research. In M. Zuckerman (Ed.), *Biological bases of sensation seeking, impulsivity, and anxiety* (pp. 249–260). Hillsdale, NJ: Erlbaum.

Zuckerman, M. (1984). Sensation seeking: A comparative approach to a human trait. *Behavioral and Brain Sciences, 7*, 413–471.

Zuckerman, M. (1987). Is sensation seeking a predisposing trait for alcoholism? In E. Gottheil, K. A. Druley, S. Pashko, et al. (Eds.), *Stress and addiction* (pp. 283–301). New York, NY: Brunner/Mazel.

Zuckerman, M., Kolin, E. A., Price, L., et al. (1964). Development of a sensation-seeking scale. *Journal of Consulting Psychology, 28*, 477–482.

Zuckerman, M., & Link, K. (1968). Construct validity for the sensation-seeking scale. *Journal of Consulting and Clinical Psychology, 32*(4), 420–426.

Zuckerman, M., & Neeb, M. (1979). Sensation seeking and psychopathology. *Psychiatry Research, 1*(3), 255–264.

Zuckerman, M., Persky, H., & Link, K. (1967). Relation of mood and hypnotizability: An illustration of the state versus trait distinction. *Journal of Consulting Psychology, 31*, 464–470.

Zuckerman, M., Schultz, D. P., & Hopkins, T. R. (1967). Sensation seeking and volunteering for sensory deprivation and hypnosis experiments. *Journal of Consulting Psychology, 31*(4), 358–363.

Zung, B. J. (1980). Factor structure of the Michigan Alcoholism Screening Test in a psychiatric outpatient population. *Journal of Clinical Psychology, 36*(2), 1024–1030.

Zung, B. J. (1982). Evaluation of the Michigan Alcoholism Screening Test (MAST) in assessing lifetime and recent problems. *Journal of Clinical Psychology, 38*(2), 425–439.

Zung, B. J., & Charalampous, K. D. (1975). Item analysis of the Michigan Alcoholism Screening Test. *Journal of Studies on Alcohol, 36*, 127–132.

Zvolensky, M. J., Bernstein, A., Marshall, E. C., et al. (2006). Panic attacks, panic disorder, and agoraphobia: Associations with substance use, abuse, and dependence. *Current Psychiatry Reports, 8*(4), 279–285.

Zvolensky, M. J., Feldner, M. T., Leen-Feldner, E. W., et al. (2005). Smoking and panic attacks, panic disorder, and agoraphobia: A review of the empirical literature. *Clinical Psychology Review, 25*(6), 761–789.

Zvolensky, M. J., Lewinsohn, P., Bernstein, A., et al. (2008). Prospective associations between cannabis use, abuse, and dependence and panic attacks and disorder. *Journal of Psychiatric Research, 42*(12), 1017–1023.

Zvosec, D. L., Smith, S. W., & Hall, B. J. (2009). Three deaths associated with use of Xyrem. *Sleep Medicine, 10*(4), 490–493.

Zweben, J. E., Clark, H. W., & Smith, D. E. (1994). Traumatic experiences and substance abuse: Mapping the territory. *Journal of Psychoactive Drugs, 26*(4), 327–344.

# Index[1,2]

## A

---

[1]This index contains all the major subject entries for the data included in this text. In order to facilitate its use, the following notations have been added in addition to page entries: (1) "fig" for figure; (2) "fign" for figure endnote; (3) "fn" for text footnote; (4) "t" for table; and (5) "tn" for table endnote. Street names for drugs and drug-related slang terms are denoted by quotation marks.

[2]Some of the brand/trade names (denoted by ®), which are included in this index, are no longer licitly manufactured in North America (i.e., have been discontinued by the manufacturer because they have been replaced by a generic version or may have been officially withdrawn from use by FDA regulation). However, they remain available from other countries, or from illicit producers within North America, and are fairly easily obtained by means of purchase over the Internet. Therefore, we have included these drug names in this text and index.

---

[3]This is a good example of the dangers associated with using slang terms and street names. Because their meanings are neither formalized nor standardized and can vary from user group to user group, from geographic location to geographic location, and from time to time, miscommunication can easily result. In order to be able to fully communicate, in the context of clinical practice, with drug and substance users, familiarity with, and use of, these terms (i.e., the argot of the "addict") are required. However, given the obvious "dangers", we strongly suggest that clinicians verify with their patients, as we routinely do, that the names or terms used mean the "same thing" to both the user and the clinician.

# About the Authors

*Louis A. Pagliaro* is currently professor emeritus, University of Alberta, and codirector of the Substance Abusology and Clinical Pharmacology Research Group. He was formerly a professor in the Department of Educational Psychology as well as on the Faculty of Pharmacy and Pharmaceutical Sciences at the University of Alberta, where he taught and supervised undergraduate and graduate students in the areas of drug and substance abuse and the biological basis of clinical psychology for over 30 years. He is a registered psychologist and previous president of the College of Alberta Psychologists. His area of specialty clinical practice is the treatment of people across the life span who have substance use disorders, including dual disorders. He also consults widely as a forensic psychologist in the area of psychotropic drug use, including the drugs and substances of abuse.

*Ann Marie Pagliaro* is currently professor emeritus, University of Alberta, and codirector of the Substance Abusology and Clinical Pharmacology Research Group. She was formerly a professor in the Faculty of Nursing at the University of Alberta, where she taught and supervised undergraduate and graduate students in the area of drug and substance abuse for over 30 years. Her primary area of undergraduate and graduate supervision and teaching was health promotion with a specialty focus on the prevention and treatment of substance use disorders across the life span with particular attention to children and adolescents. Her specialty area of research continues to be theory development and evaluation in regard to increasing the understanding of why people use the various drugs and substances of abuse.

The Pagliaros, full-time members of the academic staff at the University of Alberta from 1977 to 2008, taught thousands of students, published over 300 professional scientific articles, and consulted extensively for numerous governmental and professional organizations locally, nationally, including the White House Office of Drug Abuse, and internationally. Six of their previous textbooks have focused explicitly on children and adolescents. Their most recent textbook, *Pagliaros' Comprehensive Guide to Drugs and Substances of Abuse* (2nd ed.), was published in 2009. This is the 17th professional book and reference text that they have coauthored.